The Papacy
An Encyclopedia

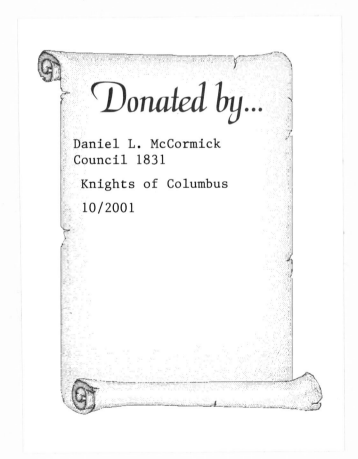

CONSULTANT, ENGLISH LANGUAGE EDITION
John W. O'Malley, *Weston Jesuit School of Theology*

EDITORIAL BOARD
Philippe Boutry   Olivier Guyotgeannin   Philippe Levillain
François-Charles Uginet   Jean-Louis Voisin

TRANSLATORS
Deborah Blaz   Bernard Daly   Mark Georgiev
Vera Gianinni   Margaret Harris   Lysa Hochroth
Gilda Roberts   David Streight

TRANSLATION REVIEW
Alfred Desautels, S.J.   Marie-Hélène Gold
Sebastian Dungan   Huguette McDonnell
Gerard Messier, A.A.   Hélène Potter
Marie-Claude Thompson   Joan Weber

SPECIAL THANKS TO
John Baldovin, S.J.   Uta-Renate Blumenthal
Andrew Blume   John E. Lynch, C.S.P.
John P. McIntyre, S.J.   Thomas Massaro, S.J.
Chris Matthews   Robert Pichette   Lynda Robitaille
Francis A. Sullivan, S.J.   Michel Thériault

Published with the assistance of the Centre national du livre in France
and the Goodbooks Foundation

The Papacy
An Encyclopedia

VOLUME 3

Quietism—Zouaves, Pontifical

Philippe Levillain, *Université de Paris X*
GENERAL EDITOR

Routledge
New York   London

Published in 2002 by
Routledge
29 West 35th Street
New York, NY 10001

Published in Great Britain by
Routledge
11 New Fetter Lane
London EC4P 4EE

Originally published as *Dictionnaire historique de la papauté*,
© Librairie Arthème Fayard, 1994

10   9   8   7   6   5   4   3   2   1

Library of Congress Cataloging-in-Publication Data

Dictionnaire historique de la papauté. English
    The papacy: an encyclopedia / Philippe Levillain, general editor; John W. O'Malley, English language edition editor.
      p. cm.
    Includes bibliographical references and index.
    ISBN 0-415-92228-3 (set)
    ISBN 0-415-92229-1 (volume 1)
    ISBN 0-415-92230-5 (volume 2)
    ISBN 0-415-93752-3 (volume 3)
    1. Papacy—Dictionaries. I. Levillain, Philippe, 1940– II. O'Malley, John W. III Title.

BX955.2 .D53 2002
282'.092'2—dc21
[B]

    2001041859

Printed on acid-free, 250-year-life paper
Manufactured in the United States of America

Contents

Volume 1
Entries A to Z   *vii*
Preface and Acknowledgments   *xv*
Introduction to the French Edition   *xvii*
Abbreviations   *xxvii*
Contributors   *xxix*
The Encyclopedia: A–F   1–614

Volume 2
Entries A to Z   *vii*
The Encyclopedia: G–P   615–1266

Volume 3
Entries A to Z   *vii*
The Encyclopedia: Q–Z   1267–1647
Appendices:
    Chronological List of Popes   1649
    Martyred Popes   1656
    Popes Who Are Saints   1657
Index   1659

Entries A to Z

Volume 1

Abbreviator
Academies, Pontifical
Acts of Peter
"Ad Limina" Visits
Adeodatus I
Adeodatus II
Administration, Papal
Administrative Offices, Roman
Africa and the Papacy
Agapitus I
Agapitus II
Agatho
[Albert] (Adalbert)
Alexander I
Alexander II
Alexander III
Alexander IV
Alexander V
Alexander VI
Alexander VII
Alexander VIII
Alexandria
Allocution by the Pope to the Roman Rota
Allocution, Consistorial
Almoner, Apostolic
Altar, Papal
Alum of Tolfa/ Tolfa Alum
Americanism
Anacletus I
[Anacletus II]
Anastasius I
Anastasius II
Anastasius III
Anastasius IV
[Anastasius Bibliothecarius]
Anathema
Angels
Angelus
Angevins
Anglicanism
Anicetus
Animals
Annates
Annona
Annuario Pontificiµo
Anterus
Antichrist
Antioch
Antipope
Apartments, Papal
Apocrisarius

Apologetic
Apostasy
Apostolic Camera
Apostolic Constitutions
Appeal to the Pope
Appointment of Bishops
Appointment of Bishops, History
Approbations, Papal
Arbitration, Papal
Archaeology, Christian
Architecture, Papal
Armies, Papal
Arms, Papal
Artists, Foreign, in Rome
Assassination Attempts Against the Pope
Assumption of the Virgin Mary
Asylum, Right of
Audience
Auditor, Rota
Automobiles, Papal
Avignon, Papacy of
Banking and the Papacy
Banners
Baptistry
Barbarians
Barber, Pope's
Basilicas, Major
Basilicas, Minor
Beatification
Bells
Benedict I
Benedict II
Benedict III
Benedict IV
Benedict V
Benedict VI
Benedict VII
Benedict VIII
Benedict IX
[Benedict X]
Benedict XI
Benedict XII
[Benedict XIII]
Benedict XIII
[Benedict XIV]
Benedict XIV
Benedict XV
Benedictions, Papal
Benefaction
Benefices, Vacant
Biretta, Cardinal's

ENTRIES

Bishop of Rome
Blessed or Holy Hat and Sword
Bollatica
Boniface I
Boniface II
Boniface III
Boniface IV
Boniface V
Boniface VI
[Boniface VII]
Boniface VIII
Boniface IX
Breviary, Roman
Brief
Bull
Byzantine Popes, 534–715
Byzantium and the Papacy
Caius
Calendar
Calendar, Gregorian
Callistus I
Callistus II
[Callistus III]
Callistus III
Camerlengo
Canon
Canon Law
Canonical Collections
Canonization
Canossa (Fortress)
Cardinal
Cardinal "In Petto"
Cardinal Nephew
Cardinal Protector
Career
Carnival
Carthage
Cartography
Castel Sant'angelo
Castrati of the Papal Chapel
Catacombs
Catacombs, Saints' Bodies in the
Catechism, Roman
Catechism, Roman (1992)
Catherine of Siena
Caudatary
Causes of Canonization
Celestine I
Celestine (II)
Celestine II
Celestine III
Celestine IV
Celestine V
Censure, Canonical
Ceremonial, Papal

The Chair of St. Peter
Chamberlain
Chancellors and Vice Chancellors
Chancery, Papal
Chapel, Papal
Chaplain, Papal
Chef, Pope's
Chinea
Christian Democracy
[Christopher]
Church-State Conflict (Sarcerdotium / Imperium 1125–
    1356)
Churches, National, in Rome
Churches of the Orient (Antiquity and Middle Ages)
Cinema, Popes and
Citizenship, Vatican
Civiltà Cattolica
Clement I
Clement II
[Clement III]
Clement III
Clement IV
Clement V
Clement VI
[Clement VII]
Clement VII
Clement VIII
Clement IX
Clement X
Clement XI
Clement XII
Clement XIII
Clement XIV
Code of Canon Law (1917)
Code of Canon Law (1983)
Code of Canons of the Eastern Churches
Coins, Papal
Collectors
Colleges of Rome
Collegiality
Colosseum
Commissions, Papal
Committees, Papal
Common and Small Services
Conciliar Movement
Conclave
Conclavist
Concordat
Conference of Bishops
Congregation, Plenary (Congregatio Plenaria)
Congregations, Roman
Conon
Consistorial Advocate
Consistory
[Constantine]

Constantine
Constantine I
Constitution, Apostolic
Constitution, Dogmatic
Cornelius
Coronation, Imperial
Coronation, Papal
Councils, Ecumenical
Councils, Particular or Local
Councils, Pontifical
Court, Papal
Cross, Processional, Papal
Crusades
Cults, Eastern
Curia
Cursor, Apostolic
Custom
Damasus I
Damasus II
Dante
Datary, Apostolic
Deacons
Death of the Pope, Middle Ages
Decorations
Decretals
Decretum of Gratian
Deposition of a Pope
The Deputy
Devotion to the Pope
Diaconia
Dicastery
Dictatus Papae
Diocese of Rome
Dioceses "In Partibus"
Dioceses, Suburbicarian
Dionysius
Dioscorus
Diplomatic Corps Accredited to the Holy See
Dispensation
Dominicans
Donation of Constantine
Donus
Easter-Date Controversies
Ecumenism
Eleutherius
Encyclical
Enlightenment
Eugene I
Eugene II
Eugene III
Eugene IV
Eulalius
Europe
Eusebius
Eutychian

Evangelization
Evaristus
Ex Cathedra
Exarchate of Ravenna
Excavations in St. Peter's
Exclusion
Exemption
Expectative Grace
Fabian
Fabric of St. Peter
Family, Papal, Middle Ages
Fathers of the Church, Greek
Fathers of the Church, Latin
Feasts of Papal Rome
Felix I
[Felix II]
Felix III
Felix IV
[Felix V]
Ferula
Finances, Papal
First French Empire and the Papacy
Fisherman's Ring (Anulus Piscatoris)
Flabellum
Floreria
Forgeries
Formosus
Franciscans
Franks
Freemasonry
French Revolution and the Papacy

Volume 2
Gallicanism
Games, Roman Empire
Garb, Ecclesiastical, within the Vatican
Gelasius I
Gelasius II
Gendarmes, Pontifical
Gentlemen of His Holiness
Ghibellines
Gospel of Peter
Gospels, the, and Papal Authority
Great Schism of the West (1378–1417)
Greeks in Italy
Gregory I
Gregory II
Gregory III
Gregory IV
Gregory V
[Gregory VI]
Gregory VI
Gregory VII
[Gregory VIII]
Gregory VIII

ENTRIES

Gregory IX
Gregory X
Gregory XI
Gregory XII
Gregory XIII
Gregory XIV
Gregory XV
Gregory XVI
Guelphs
Habemus Papam
Hadrian I
Hadrian II
Hadrian III
Hadrian IV
Hadrian V
Hadrian VI
Helsinki Conference
Heraldry
Heresies
Hilarus
Hippolytus
Holy Childhood, Pontifical Society of the
Holy Office, Congregation of the
Holy Places
Holy Roman Empire
Holy See or Apostolic See
Holy Sepulcher of Jerusalem
Holy Year
Honorius I
[Honorius II]
Honorius II
Honorius III
Honorius IV
Hormisdas
Household, Papal
Humor
Hyginus
Hymn, Papal
Image of Rome in Literature
Imprimatur
Incardination
Index
Index, Congregation of the
Indulgences
Infallibility
Innocent I
Innocent II
[Innocent III]
Innocent III
Innocent IV
Innocent V
Innocent VI
Innocent VII
Innocent VIII
Innocent IX

Innocent X
Innocent XI
Innocent XII
Innocent XIII
Inquisition
Interdict
Investiture Controversy
Jansenism
Jesuits
Joan
[John]
John I
John II
John III
John IV
John V
John VI
John VII
John VIII
John IX
John X
John XI
John XII
John XIII
John XIV
John XV
[John XVI]
John XVII
John XVIII
John XIX
John XX
John XXI
John XXII
[John XXIII]
John XXIII
John Paul I
John Paul II
Josephism
Judaism
Judges Delegate
Julian the Apostate
Julius I
Julius II
Julius III
Jurisdictionalism
Keys
Kulturkampf
Laity, Middle Ages
Lando
Lateran IV Council (1215)
Lateran V Council (1512–7)
Lateran Councils
Lateran Pacts
Latinity
[Lawrence]

Legate
Leo I
Leo II
Leo III
Leo IV
Leo V
Leo VI
Leo VII
Leo VIII
Leo IX
Leo X
Leo XI
Leo XII
Leo XIII
Lepanto (1571)
Letters to the Pope
Liber Censuum
Liber Pontificalis
Liberalism
Liberius
Linus
Liturgical Chant, Roman
Liturgy
Lombards
Lucius
Lucius II
Lucius III
Magisterium
Marcellinus
Marcellus I
Marcellus II
Marinus I, also Martin II
Marinus II, also Martin III
Mark
Martin I
Martin IV
Martin V
Marxism and the Papacy
Mass, Papal: Liturgical Objects
Master of the Sacred Palace
Medallions, Papal
Media, Communication, and the Vatican
Milan
Military Orders
Military Ordinariates
Miltiades (or Melchiades)
Minutante
Missal, Tridentine
Missionary Union, Pontifical
Missions
Modernism
Modernity
Monasticism
Monumentality and Roman Urbanism (1848–1922)
Mosaics

Movimento Cattolico
Museums, Vatican
National Cleric
Navy, Papal
Nepotism
Nicholas I
Nicholas II
Nicholas III
Nicholas IV
[Nicholas V]
Nicholas V
Nicolaism
Nobility, Roman
Noble Guard
Normans of Southern Italy and Sicily
Notary, Apostolic
Novatian
Novemdiales
Nunciature
Nuncio
Obelisks of Rome
Observatory, Vatican
Offenses Against the Pope
Oldest Daughter of the Church
Onomastics, Pontifical
Opus Dei
Orders, Pontifical
Ordinations, Anglican
Organizations, International, the Holy See and
Osservatore Romano
Ostpolitik
Oxford Movement
Painting
Palace, Apostolic
Palatine
Palatine Guard
Pantheon
Papal States
Papism
[Paschal]
Paschal I
Paschal II
[Paschal III]
Passport, Vatican
Patrimony of St. Peter
Patronage, Papal
Paul (St. Paul the Apostle)
Paul I
Paul II
Paul III
Paul IV
Paul V
Paul VI
Pavilion
Pelagius I

Pelagius II
Penalties, Ecclesiastical
Penitentiary, Apostolic
Persecutions
Peter (St. Peter the Apostle)
Petitions
[Philip]
Photography
Pilgrimage
Pius I
Pius II
Pius III
Pius IV
Pius V
Pius VI
Pius VII
Pius VIII
Pius IX
Pius X
Pius XI
Pius XII
Plague and the Papacy
Pontian
Poor Relief
Pope
Portantina Papale
Possesso
Postage Stamps
Prefect of the City
Prefecture of the Papal Household
Prejudices
Prelatures
Press Office of the Holy See
Primacy, Papal
Private Lives, Popes'
Privileges, Pauline and Petrine
Profession of Faith and Oath of Fidelity
Propaganda Fide, Congregation of
Propagation of the Faith
Prophecies, Modern
Prophecies of Malachy
Protonotary
Province, Ecclesiastical
Provisions, Papal

Volume 3

Quietism
Quirinal (Pontifical Palace of Montecavallo)
Railway Station, Vatican
Ravenna
Reform, Catholic
Reform, Gregorian
Reformation (1517–65)
Regalia
Region, Ecclesiastical

Registers, Papal
Renaissance Humanism and the Papacy
Reserved Cases and Causes
Residences, Papal
Resignations, Papal
Rioni
Roman Confraternities
Roman Empire
Roman Republic (1798–9)
Roman Republic of 1849
Romanus
Rome
Rosary
Rose, Golden
Rota, Tribunal of the
Sabinian
Sack of Rome
Sacred College
Sacred College, Plenary Meeting of the
St. John Lateran, Basilica of
St. Mary Major, Basilica of
St. Paul's Outside the Walls, Basilica of
St. Peter the Apostle, Society of
St. Peter's Basilica
Saints, Veneration of
Saracens
Schism
Scriptor
Secret, Pontifical
Secretariat of Briefs
Secretariat of Briefs to Princes
Secretariat of State
Secretariats of the Roman Curia
Sedia Gestatoria
See, Vacant and Impeded
Seminaries
Senate, Roman, and the Papacy
Sergius I
Sergius II
Sergius III
Sergius IV
Severinus
Sickness of the Pope, Middle Ages
Silverius
Silvester I
Silvester II
Silvester III
[Silvester IV]
Simony
Simplicius
Siricius
Sisinnius
Sistine Chapel
Sixtus I
Sixtus II

Sixtus III
Sixtus IV
Sixtus V
Slavery
Social Communications
Social Documents
Social Teaching
Societies, Pontifical Mission
Soter
Spoil
Stations, Roman
Stephen (Popes)
Stephen I
Stephen (II)
Stephen II (III)
Stephen III (IV)
Stephen IV (V)
Stephen V (VI)
Stephen VI (VII)
Stephen VII (VIII)
Stephen VIII (IX)
Stephen IX (X)
Subcinctorium
Subsidiarity
Substitute of the Secretariat of State
Suburbicarian Italy
Superintendent of the Ecclesiastical State
Suspension
Swaddling Clothes, Consecrated
Swiss Guard
Syllabus of Errors
Symmachus
Synod of Bishops
Tax / Tithe, Crusade
Telephone
Telesphorus
Theocracy, Papal, Middle Ages
[Theoderic]
[Theodore]
Theodore I
Theodore II
Third Rome (Moscow)
Tiara
Titles, Cardinals'
Titles, Papal
Tombs of the Popes
Travelers' Views of Rome and the Vatican
Travels of John Paul II
Travels of Paul VI

Travels of Popes, 536–1809
Trent, Council of
Tribunals, Apostolic
Turks
Ultramontanism
Uniates
Unity, Italian
Universities, Catholic
Universities, Medieval
Urban I
Urban II
Urban III
Urban IV
Urban V
Urban VI
Urban VII
Urban VIII
[Ursinus]
Valentine
Vatican I (Ecumenical Council of)
Vatican II (Ecumenical Council of)
Vatican City State
Vatican Gardens
Vatican Labor Union
Vatican Library
Vatican Radio
Vatican Secret Archives
Vatican Television
Vaticanist
Vestments, Pope's Liturgical
Veto
Vicariate, Apostolic
Victor I
Victor II
Victor III
[Victor IV]
[Victor IV (V)]
Vigilius
Vitalian
Viterbo
Wars of Italy, French (16th century)
World War I
World War II
Worms, Concordat of (1122)
Zacharias
Zephyrinus
Zosimus
Zouaves, Pontifical

Q

QUIETISM. Quietism has to be defined on the basis of the condemnations the papacy issued against the so-called Quietists in the 1680s. The term, construed from the Latin *quies*, meaning rest, was used to describe the men and women who were accused of practicing, in improper, exaggerated fashion, the "prayer of quiet" during which the soul abandons reflection, love, and will to give itself up totally to divine love.

The affair began on 18 July 1685, when the Roman papal guard arrested a fifty-eight-year-old Spanish priest, Miguel Molinos, who had come to Rome in 1663 to promote the process of BEATIFICATION of one of his illustrious compatriots from Valencia, Francesco Jeronimo Simo (d. 1612). His task as postulator left him with the leisure to act as spiritual director to certain Romans and to sum up his experiences in a book published in Spanish, in Rome, in 1675, under the title *Guía espiritual*. The book, which was translated into Italian in 1677 and then into French in 1688, was an immediate success but provoked a prolonged argument with the JESUITS, who rushed to the defense of traditional meditation as against the "new contemplatives," whom they considered dangerous. With Molinos enjoying the protection of bishops and cardinals, his Jesuit rivals suffered censure and condemnation in 1681 and 1682.

Molinos's victory was short-lived, however. The affair took on a completely different significance when Louis XIV expressed doubts about the orthodoxy of those in the entourage of INNOCENT XI, his old enemy. The pope, it seemed, was not about to protect Molinos, who was suspected of the new heresy known as quietism. On the point of revoking the Edict of Nantes to prove to all Europe that he was worthy of his title of Most Christian King, Louis XIV might well have found a means of embarrassing the pope.

For Innocent XI, there was now no way of escaping the inquiry into the theories of Molinos that many were insisting on, in particular the archbishop of Naples, Carac-ciolo, who in 1682 made himself heard and in November 1685 arranged for the Spanish INQUISITION to condemn the *Guía*. The papal trial, led by the HOLY OFFICE, lasted two years, which the accused spent shut up in the papal jails, and at the end of which he "confessed." He was thereupon condemned to life in prison, on 3 September 1687, together with his secretary, while sixty-eight propositions "recognized" by him as faithfully reflecting his thought were condemned in the bull *Coelestis Pastor* of 19 November 1687—the official birth certificate of "the last heresy."

Molinos's supporters at the CURIA, among them Cardinal Petrucci, were forced to make a public retraction. The hunt for the Quietists was on. Between 1687 and 1690, the Roman Inquisitors placed on the INDEX a series of spiritual works deemed heretical. Most of the authors were French, such as Benoît de Canfeld, Jean de Bernières, and François Malaval—a way of indicating to Louis XIV that he might have kept a sharper eye on his kingdom's spiritual publications.

The affair might have rested there, but it sprang into life again with a series of arrests ordered by Louis XIV in Parisian ultramontane milieus he suspected of quietism—that new heresy which Rome had just defined under pressure from him, the king! Among those imprisoned were Father François de La Combe, a Barnabite from Savoy, who was sent to the Bastille on 3 October 1687, and his friend Jeanne Bouvier de La Motte, the widow Guyon. Mme Guyon had spent the preceding years in Savoy and Piedmont and from January to September 1688 was sent to the convent of the Visitation in Paris. In November 1687, the bishop of Geneva censured her *Moyen court pour faire oraison* (1685) as well as de La Combe's *Lettre d'un serviteur de Dieu* (1686), both of which were placed on the Index, in 1688 and 1689 respectively.

With that, order seemed restored. Father de La Combe, who had been moved from one prison to another and forced to confess to unavowable crimes, gradually went mad. Mme Guyon, freed thanks to her friendships at court, became one of the familiars of Mme de Maintenon and her house at Saint-Cyr, and even won the active and devoted support of the Abbé de Fénelon, who was promoted as tutor to the duke of Burgundy, the heir presumptive of Louis XIV.

But the affair flared up again in 1693, when some of Mme Guyon's writings were seized, at Saint-Cyr, by the bishop of Chartres on a canonical visit. To justify herself in the face of the serious accusations of quietism once more brought against her, Mme Guyon launched a lengthy theological and spiritual debate on the "prayer of quiet" and pure love that opposed her defender Fénelon to Bossuet, the champion of orthodoxy, who quickly proved a formidable adversary. In 1697, Fénelon therefore requested that the matter be brought to Rome. There, Pope INNOCENT XII could pass judgment on the orthodoxy of his *Explication des Maximes des saints*, in which he defended Mme Guyon's positions on pure love, a spiritual doctrine according to which the individual should love God without seeking any reward, even giving up eternal salvation out of total love of God. On 12 March 1699, under pressure from Louis XIV, the Roman trial resulted in condemnation of the book by the brief *Cum alias*, to which Fénelon, since 1698 an exile in his diocese of Cambrai, submitted. The brief confirmed the censure pronounced in 1694 by Archbishop Harlay of Paris against Mme Guyon's writings. She herself was imprisoned in the Bastille from 1698 to 1703, and died in exile at Blois in 1717.

What were the Quietists accused of? First, according to the sixty-eight propositions of the bull *Coelestis Pastor*, of putting forth erroneous theories on "the prayer of quiet." These supposedly tended toward pantheism, on the one hand, because they recommended the annihilation of the soul in God, and toward moral indifference, on the other, because they proclaimed a condition of sinlessness supposedly attained by the soul when it reached the state of repose and answered prayer. Second, owing to this conclusion as to impeccability, the Quietists were accused of "abominable" practices between spiritual directors and the women in their care (carnal "violences" of diabolical origin that could not be resisted). Historians and theologians of our day are agreed that the propositions of the bulls and briefs covering the first accusation have no foundation in the works of the so-called Quietists. Likewise, the accusations as to their morals were founded on untrue denunciations and baseless falsifications, whether they concerned Molinos (d. 1696), who lived and died devoutly, Father de La Combe, whom his "confessions" drove mad, or Mme Guyon, whose reputation Bossuet never managed to tarnish.

Rather, the bases of the accusations brought against the Quietists are to be sought in the accusers in Rome, who at the time were expressing their own fears and fantasies. The accusations of pantheism and moral indifference derive directly from the Inquisition's trials of the Beghards and Beguines and the Brethren of the Free Spirit in the 14th century, and, more recently, from those of the 16th-century Spanish *alumbrados* as well as of the Pelagini of Brescia in 1657. The accusations of loose morals derive from the same sources, but also exemplify the veritable sexual obsession of large numbers of religiously minded persons of the period, an obsession that was expressed in terms of diabolism. Other troublesome elements of 17th-century religious life emerge in the propositions condemned in 1687: the excessive importance attached to mortification, liturgical festivals, confession, and the degree of control exercised by superiors and bishops. Similarly, the privileged relations between nuns and their directors, which could be of no import or, at times, instances of an innocent love, always gave superiors cause for concern. The most important result of the condemnation of the Quietists was that for several centuries mysticism was held suspect in Catholicism, and religious life in the 18th century suffered an impoverishment.

Christian Renoux

Bibliography

Armogathe, J. R. *Le Quiétisme*, Paris, 1973.

Canosa, R., and Colonnello, I. *L'ultima eresia. Quietisti e Inquisizione in Sicilia tra Seicento e Settecento*, Palermo, 1986.

Cognet, L. *Crépuscule des mystiques, Bossuet-Fénelon*, Tournai, 1958, rev. 1991; "Mme Guyon," *DS*, 6 (1967), 1306–36.

Coslet, D. G. *Madame Jeanne Guyon: Child of Another Era*, Fort Washington, Penn., 1984.

de Guibert, J. *Documenta ecclesiastica christianae perfectionis studium spectantia*, Rome, 1931.

Dudon, P. *Le Quiétiste espagnol Michel Molinos,* Paris, 1921.

Fénelon, *Correspondance*, ed. J. Orcibal and J. Le Brun, Paris, 1972–92, 15 vols.

Fiorani, L. "Monache e monasteri romani nell'età del quietismo," *Ricerche per la storia religiosa di Roma*, I (1977), 63–112.

Fiorani, L. "Per la storia dell'antiquiestismo romano," *L'uomo e la storia. Studi Petrocchi*, Roma, 1983, 1, 299–343.

Gondal, M. L. *Madame Guyon: un nouveau visage* (1648–1717), Paris, 1989.

Guyon, J. *Jeanne Guyon: An Autobiography*, New Kensington, Penn., 1997.

Knox, R. A. *Enthusiasm*, Oxford, 1950, pp. 231–318.

Le Brun, J. *La Spiritualité de Bossuet*, Paris, 1972.

Le Brun, J. "Quiétisme en France," *DS*, 12 (1986), 2805–42.

Orcibal, J. "Fénelon et la cour romaine (1700–1715)," *MAH*, 1940, 235–348.

Orcibal, J. *Le Procès des Maximes des saints devant le Saint-Office*, Rome, 1968.

Pacho, E. "Molinos," *DS*, 10 (1980), 1486–1514.

Pacho, E. "Quiétisme en Italie et en Espagne," *DS*, 12 (1986), 2756–805.

Petrocchi, M. *Il quietismo italiano del Seicento*, Rome, 1948.

Pourrat, P. "Quiétisme," *DTC*, 13 (1936), 1537–81.

Signorotto, G. *Inquisitori e mistici nel Seicento italiano. L'eresia di Santa Pelagia*, Bologna, 1989.

Tellechea-Idagoa, I., ed. *Molinosiana*, Madrid, 1987.

Zovato, P. *La polemica Bossuet-Fénelon, introduzione critico-bibliografica*, Padua, 1968.

QUIRINAL (PONTIFICAL PALACE OF MONTE-CAVALLO).

Two colossal ancient statues stand erect among the ruins on the Quirinal Hill. The Dioscuri—Castor and Pollux—rein in their galloping steeds, apparent survivors amid the annihilation surrounding them. These mythical statues (*Opus Fidiae, Opus Praxiteles*), which adorned the square from the Quattrocento, until recent times gave their name to the site and the palace that would one day be built upon it: Montecavallo (hill of the horse).

The Quirinal Hill was known to be blessed with "good air," besides affording an outstanding view of the city. Seeking to escape the insalubrious summers at the Vatican, from the 16th to the 18th century several popes— GREGORY XIII, SIXTUS V, PAUL V, URBAN VIII, ALEXANDER VII, CLEMENT XII and, finally, BENEDICT XIV—had laid out on the site an ensemble of structures and gardens that was to rank as one of the finest of the papal residences. The site had been coveted since the early 16th century and divided into a number of properties, the largest of which belonged to a Neapolitan family, the Carafa, and in 1540 was leased to a member of the Farnese family, Orazio. He was succeeded in 1550 by Cardinal Ippolito d'Este, who, though still a lessee, gave his name to the *vigna*, or summer residence, for more than forty years. The son of Duke Alfonso and Lucrezia Borgia and the tyrannical protector of Ariosto, the cardinal was the creator of the famous villa at Tivoli, whose architecture he had entrusted to Pirro Ligorio. It may have been this architect who was employed at the Quirinal in the *vigna*, which was constantly enlarged to provide a vast area for the gardens. Among the most beautiful in Rome, they boasted a maze and a large array of antique statuary, amid topiary created by Girolamo da Carpi, according to Vasari's account.

The d'Este period ended with the death in 1586 of Ippolito's nephew, Cardinal Luigi, who was his legal heir. In 1587, the Carafa, who still owned the site, sold the greater part of their holding to Pope Sixtus V, who thus designated the palace as papal property. However, before that date, a palace had been erected in the d'Este gardens that was designed as a papal summer residence. Pope Gregory XIII had obtained permission from Luigi d'Este to build a *palazzina* at one end of the hill, toward Trevi, having stayed at Montecavallo several times at the cardinal's invitation. This was the first nucleus of the buildings that make up the palace we see today. Built in 1583, the structure was situated at the extreme left of the present-day palace and was considered the masterpiece of the Bolognese architect Ottaviano Mascherino (1524–1606). In the facade giving onto the courtyard, which is fairly well preserved, the architect proposed a harmonious arrangement with a double loggia, in the style of Peruzzi's design at the Farnesina. His plan was to extend this *palazzina* up to the Strada Pia, by surrounding or demolishing an existing structure belonging to the d'Este that stood at an angle to the street. In the next stage, the two-story building was topped with a tower (1584), a *belvedere-altana*, which "doveva procurare un colpo d'occhio non solo sulla città ma fino al mare." The other highlight of this new palace was the oval spiral staircase, which was executed in a restricted space to give an effect even more strongly accentuated than that of the examples preceding it, such as Bramante's at the Vatican and Vignola's at Caprarola. The staircase was punctuated by twin "Tuscan" columns. The whole of this Mascherino project is documented by priceless architect's drawings preserved at the Accademia di San Luca in Rome, which explain the progression of the plan toward the Strada Pia. Sadly, nothing remains of the decoration of the *palazzina*, the chapel with its frescoes by Cavaliere d'Arpino, or the wall paintings of Giovanni and Cherubino Alberti (1553–1615, 1558–1601) in one of the courtyards, to name a few examples.

Sixtus V was an exceptional pope as regards city planning and the construction he undertook in Rome during his short, five-year reign, a period in which the city took on a new face and adopted a fresh scale. Also, virtually from the moment he became its owner, the pope conceived grandiose plans for his new domain at the Quirinal. Replacing Mascherino with the architect Domenico Fontana (1543–1607), a Lombard, he entrusted him with designing the piazza in front of the palace. Fontana leveled it, moved the group of the Dioscuri by turning them into the axis of the Strada Pia, gave them new plinths, and saw to their restoration; at the center of the group, a little fountain was also created, at the pope's behest. As for the palace, the previous architect's plan was followed but developed further (the wing of Gregory XIII's palace was extended to the square, at an angle to the street).

Before the reign of Paul V, of capital importance for this survey, a series of brief pontificates (URBAN VII, GREGORY XIV, INNOCENT IX) ended with that of

CLEMENT VIII, who devoted his attention to the gardens. These were laid out in the Italian style, with squares regularly marked by edgings of box, and adorned with numerous antique statues from the d'Este collection. Below Gregory XIII's palace, the broad slope leading to Trevi was employed to house the famous *Fontana dell'organo* (organ fountain) and Parnassus grotto, decorated with polychrome stucco in the spirit of the Frascati ornamental gardens. Paul V's reign coincided with the age of the Church Triumphant, when the Counter Reformation, rigorously enforced, caused the entire city to be covered with sumptuous monuments, as art played its role in edifying the masses.

At the Quirinal, immediately after his election, Paul V decided to call a halt to the work of his predecessors and give the structure a larger scale. The first task was to finish what had been begun, that is, one entire wing had to be built, toward the garden, to enclose the great palace *cortile*. Work proceeded on this from 1605 to 1610. Flaminio Ponzio, another Lombard (ca. 1560–1613), worked to reuse the architectural motifs of the previous architects. The idea was that the new wing should provide sufficient space for papal ceremonies, particularly consistories. For that reason, at the center of the wing a raised hall was constructed, lit by seven windows and lending an aura of great solemnity to that part of the building. Later (1611–12), it was decorated with frescoes by Orazio Gentileschi and Agostino Tassi (since disappeared). Again, it was Flaminio Ponzio who built Paul V's private chapel in the same wing, adjacent to the great halls. This still intact jewel was adorned by the greatest painter then in Rome, Guido Reni (1575–1642), with the assistance of his fellow artists Albani, Antonio Carracci, and Lanfranco (who painted the *Annunciation* above the altar, the *Birth of the Virgin*, and the *Madonna of the Needlework*, which count among his masterpieces).

To provide access to this new section of the palace, Ponzio erected a monumental two-flight staircase, a solemn entrance that terminates this first part of Paul V's great building works at the Quirinal, and that allows for a masterly play of light through the arcades opening onto the garden. All of Ponzio's design has the same spirit of restrained elegance, grand classicism, and severe ostentation proper to early 17th-century Rome that one finds in the Pauline chapel of St. Mary Major and the facade of St. Peter's.

This masterpiece was to be Flaminio Ponzio's last work at the Quirinal. The second phase of Paul V's building plans for the palace was entrusted to a newcomer, after a long, seven-year delay. This phase saw the planning and execution of a considerable enlargement of the palace, not merely additions to existing parts of the building. (In view of the popes' more and more frequent stays in the palace, some called it a "second Vatican.") The job of totally rebuilding, on a vast, monumental scale, the

corner palace on the Strada Pia and Fontana's square was given by Paul V to Carlo Maderno (1556–1629), a northerner who had completed the majestic facade of St. Peter's. From 1614, work was begun on his plans for a palatine chapel and adjacent ceremonial hall, modeled on the Sistine Chapel and *Sala Regia* at the Vatican. The square acquired a main gateway flanked with columns and topped at a later stage with Bernini's Benediction loggia. The new spaces, two-storied and austerely elegant, terminated, so to speak, the previous century's achievements at the palace. They would provide a setting for one of the greatest painted decorations of the period and indeed of later times. First of all, Paul V's ambitious plan for the new chapel (which bears his name, *Cappella Paolina*) was only partly realized. Bare, whitewashed walls provide the backdrop for a barrel vault richly ornamented with stuccoes inspired by antiquity and embossed with gold, the work of Martino Ferrabosco. But the adjacent *Sala Regia* would concentrate the interest and effort of artists of the first rank, who conceived a celebrated overall design. The first artist, Agostino Tassi (1566–1644), was a *quadraturista*, and to him we owe the general idea of the upper part of the decoration. This shows Eastern spectators and ambassadors, leaning on their elbows or over the balustrades or arcaded loggias as they watch, curious, the grand ceremonies taking place below. The spaces between these scenes are taken up by images from the Old Testament flanked by the Virtues or by the heraldic emblems of the Borghese, apportioned symmetrically. Indeed, the original plan called for the entire wall area, not only the upper section, to be decorated with a frieze. A drawing by the painter Giovanni Lanfranco is adapted to Tassi's scheme and designed for the lower sections: it unfolds a complex ensemble of bas-reliefs, cartouches, twin columns, and false tapestries that provide a particularly ample effect. The fresco decoration in 1616 and 1617, which was finally limited to the upper section for unknown reasons, again called for the work of several hands. Lanfranco was responsible for the two ends of the hall and for certain ambassadorial scenes. Among the most successful, they, early baroque, herald seventy years beforehand the themes developed by Le Brun and his school in the Staircase of the Ambassadors at Versailles. The final touch of the decoration of the *Sala Regia* was added in 1619, when the twin doors of the chapel were surmounted with Taddeo Landini's great bas-relief, the 16th-century *Christ Washing the Feet of the Apostles,* transferred from one of the chapels of St. Peter's.

Urban VIII limited his efforts to timely embellishments (the Benediction loggia, and an enlargement of the square). After him, the story of the external architecture of the palace concerns only the section along the Strada Pia. This is the extremely long, narrow wing giving onto the garden known as the *Manica lunga,* or long sleeve, designed to house the pope's family, of which Alexander VII would build the first section, as far as S. Andrea al Quirinale. But Alexander is associated above all with the last great decoration undertaken in the palace, from 1655 to 1657, in a hitherto neglected wing. This was the wing built to Fontana's designs toward the end of the pontificate of Sixtus V and lit by thirteen windows on the Piazza di Montecavallo. The painter entrusted with this task was one at the peak of his art, the leader of a school.

The great Pietro da Cortona had, just the year before, finished the complex decoration of the Innocent X gallery at the Pamphili Palace on the Piazza Navona, having previously painted the Barberini salon and Medici apartments at the Pitti Palace. The painter had aged by this time and would limit his activity to supervising the work and selecting the sixteen artists to paint frescoes on subjects from the Old and New Testaments. Of these, two grand compositions, which were assigned to Mola and Maratta (*Joseph Recognized by His Brethren* and the *Nativity*), were to close off the ensemble, at either end of the gallery. One wonders if Pietro da Cortona was reserving for himself the decoration of the gallery vault. If so, this would have provided a unity, lost forever when this great space was divided up into three large salons by lateral walls.

In any event, the area was complex and difficult—a long, narrow hall with many windows along the sides. One of Cortona's drawings has been found, and gives a sense of the method he devised to enliven these long sides and make the walls "vanish" through the use of trompe l'oeil architecture—twinned columns that provide a view of illusionist *prospettive*, enlarging the space and emphasizing the alternately arranged frescoes, oval-shaped and rectangular *quadri riportati* set in bold cartouches and frames. Here, too, the entire wall—not only the frieze, part of which has been preserved—was to be broadly structured from top to bottom in rhythmic units that were narrow or wide, sumptuous, and had a relief effect, the whole providing an air of solemn monumentality.

After Alexander VII, Popes INNOCENT XIII and Clement XII continued the work on the so-called *Manica lunga* wing, with Clement XII entrusting the completion of it in 1730 to a new architect, the Florentine Ferdinando Fuga (1699–1781). He would relieve the horizontal monotony of the structure with a surprise, the *Palazzina del Segretaria delle cifre*, a small building richer in detail and outline in which he had a chance to express himself more fully. This he also achieved, at the same date, when he completed the building on the square designed to house the papal stables and part of the guard and which had been begun by A. Specchi in 1722.

Yet the most characteristic mark of the 18th century, after the grandiose structures glorifying the popes of the Church Triumphant, was an almost symbolic one: a little architectural jewel that would be built in the gardens, to provide refreshment in the hot summers and to allow advantage to be taken of the winter vegetation, by the most Voltairean of popes, the brilliant, cultivated Benedict XIV. The *Stanza all' inglese*, or *caffeaus*, a pavilion typical of those in many royal parks in Europe at that time, was built by Fuga from 1741 in a simple, refined style of architecture, far removed from the rococo in its neo-Renaissance lines. Fuga designed it around a closed portico that formed an atrium and gave onto two salons richly ornamented in gold stucco that served as a frame for canvases by Masucci, Batoni, Van Bloemen, and Costanzi. The rooms culminated in two masterpieces of the Roman Settecento representing the *vedute* of the Quirinal Square and Benedict XIV's visit to St. Mary Major. Both canvases are the painter's homage to the architect, Fuga, and to the pope himself, who promoted the new Palace of the Consulta on the Quirinal Square as well as the new facade of St. Mary Major.

Accordingly, until the arrival of the tumultuous turn of the century, the palace was to live its state life without major changes. An interesting question in this connection is how the interior of the apostolic palace appeared to 18th-century visitors and writers of memoirs. All are agreed in finding the apartments simple, even at times ill-kept. The reception apartments were unique in being hung with red damask ornamented with gold braid (the *Sala Regia* was the only room to have, beneath the frescoes, a decoration of blue leather with silver flowers and arabesques). Elsewhere, the furnishings, consisting of consoles, antechamber seats in wood painted to resemble stone, and religious paintings, all suggested a prelate's lodging (a famous Titian hung over the altar in the Pauline chapel). Before 1870, few tapestries were hung in the principal rooms except for some rather mediocre productions from the papal workshop of the Ospizio di San Michele. In the early 19th century, these were joined by gifts to the palace, such as the Gobelins after Jouvenet and Restout on religious themes (scenes from the New Testament) that Napoleon gave to PIUS VII in 1805.

As for objets d'art, most of the popes chose to live in the least beautiful rooms in the palace, which were furnished very simply (e.g., INNOCENT X, Innocent XI, BENEDICT XIII). Benedict XIV, in contrast, was extremely proud of his famous collection of large Chinese porcelain vases ("Non vi è principe che ne abbia altrettanto," he was fond of saying). The collection remained in the palace after 1870 and can still be seen today. With their baroque pedestals of carved, gilded wood bearing arms, the vases exemplify the taste for chinoiserie so prevalent in the 18th century and which spread even to a pope. As a whole, the Quirinal typifies the solemn furnishing of the great Roman palaces, no doubt well suited to austere apostolic simplicity but hardly to the taste of the occupying French officials charged with establishing an imperial palace between 1811 and 1814: "This palace was designed for the sovereign of a small state who is always alone and usually a monk, and its small apartments have nothing in the way of conveniences," observed the architect of the time.

The French interlude need not detain us, Pope Pius VII having left his residence from 1809 to 1814. However, it should be noted that the alterations to the palace were accepted by the popes on their return more or less as they found them (the popes used the new rooms Napoleon had created: the so-called Ministers' Salon, Grand Cabinet, or Topographical Cabinet; and for Marie-Louise, three large salons created in what had been Alexander VII's gallery; new doors with their precious frames, fireplaces, and marble flooring). Pius VII and his successors even went so far as to tolerate the great paintings intended to exalt the new Caesar, the result of scholarly commissions headed by Denon and Canova. (Pius VII is said to have observed, "If these paintings are too risqué, we will call them Madonnas!")

But this pope, so buffeted by history, revealed himself more characteristically in another context. This was when he inaugurated at the Quirinal the reactionary pseudo-Raphaelesque pietism so prized at the beginning of the new century, when Italian culture, as G. Briganti has pointed out, would show increasing signs of exhaustion. Typical of this period is the monochrome decoration of the Pauline chapel (1818) in a trompe l'oeil architecture of pilasters and niches framing the apostles and the evangelists—so discordant with Maderno's architecture and the gilded stuccoes of the ceiling. Under Pius IX, the same style would be taken up again with the commissioning of large paintings by Purists and Nazarenes for the reception apartments (Overbeck; T. Minardi, *La Propagation du christianisme*, 1864).

More successful was the final arrangement of the group of the Dioscuri, on the square. During the French period, R. Stern, who in 1814 was named architect of the sacred palaces (and would take charge of the great enterprise of the Chiaramonti Museum at the Vatican, his masterpiece),

set up in front of the statues the great antique granite basin from the Forum Boarium. The last noteworthy change, before the ending of the popes' temporal power, to a site that Stendhal praised as one of the finest in Rome, was that ordered by Pius IX in 1866 and entrusted to the architect Vespignani. Sadly, he destroyed the baroque spatial character of the square, mutilating, for good measure, the beautiful stable building by removing the horses' ramp as well as the portico of the building of the Swiss Guards.

But it was the breaching of the Porta Pia in September 1870 that sounded the knell of the old palace as a papal residence. A new page of history was about to be turned with the deliberations of the Council of Ministers on 26 October 1870, declaring the Quirinal Palace the royal palace of a united Italy.

Pierre Arizzoli-Clementel

Bibliography

Briganti, G. *Il Palazzo del Quirinale*, Rome, 1962.

de Feo, V. *La Piazza del Quirinale, storia, archittetura, urbanistica*, Rome, 1973.

d'Onofrio, C. *Le Fontane di Roma*, 1957.

Il Palazzo del Quirinale, il mondo artistico a Roma nel periodo napoleonico, Rome, 1989.

Lötz, W. "Vignole et Giacomo della Porta," *Le Palais Farnèse*, I, 1, Rome, 1981.

Pacifici, V. *Hippolito d'Este, cardinal di Ferrara*, 1920.

Schleier, E. "Les projects de Lanfranco pour le décor de la Sala Regia au Quirinal et pour la loge des Bénédictions à Saint-Pierre," *Revue de l'Art*, 1970, 7.

Spagnesi, G. F. *La Piazza del Quirinale e le antiche scuderie papali*, Rome, 1970.

Vasari, G. *Le Vite . . .*, ed. Milanesi, 1880, VI, 477ff.

Wasserman, J. "The Quirinal Palace in Rome," *The Art Bulletin*, XLV, 3 (1963).

Wiribal, N. "Contributi alle ricerche sul cortonisimo in Roma. I. Pittori della galleria d'Alessandro VII nel palazzo del Quirinale," *Bollettino d'Arte*, 1960.

R

RAILWAY STATION, VATICAN. In reality, almost totally dependent on the outside for its (albeit small) population's provisions, the Vatican City State is the perfect example of a patrimonial state (U. Toschi). The State's communications with the outside are forced, by reason of the city's isolation, to pass through Italian territory by means that are regulated by the Roman government. A short stretch of railway—a few hundred meters, finished in 1932—connects Vatican City with the Rome-Viterbo railway line. The Vatican City station is the monumental, neoclassical *stazione d'onore di San Pietro*. In its center there is a portico flanked by two impressive columns, upon which sits a shield bearing the Vatican City's coat of arms. Access to the station, which is located near the Cortile del Belvedere (number 42), is through a wide esplanade, either via the stairway descending from the Apostolic Tribunal and Piazza Santa Marta, or by Viale dell'Osservatorio, which runs along the Governorate and joins Viale dello Seminario Etiopico (which leads to Radio-Vatican's buildings) in the square in front of the station.

Today, transportation for either travelers or personal goods takes place more often via automobile or truck, since the railway is used almost exclusively for the nearly daily transport of equipment and merchandise. Tariff agreements, which also cover postal and telegraphic services, have been worked out with the Italian government. The Holy See has affirmed its right to construct an airport and to manage its own planes, although the entire air space above Vatican City has been decreed off limits to air traffic.

Philippe Levillain

Bibliography

Gessi, L. *La Città del Vaticano*, IV, Rome, 1935.

Toschi, U. "The Vatican City State from the Standpoint of Political Geography," *Geographical Review*, 21, 1931, 529–38.

RAVENNA. At the beginning of the 5th century, the Roman emperor of the West established his residence in Ravenna, in Italy about 100 kilometers northeast of Florence, which thus became a highly important political center. This role continued under the German kings Odoacre and Theodoric, then was confirmed after the reconquest of Ravenna in 540 by the Byzantine general Belisarius. Henceforth, the city would be the seat of the exarch, the supreme head of the army and administration in Byzantine Italy. Next to the exarch, the chief Eastern dignitary was the bishop of Ravenna, who in the 5th century was endowed with metropolitan powers.

This exalted rank encouraged the prelates to strengthen their authority in ecclesiastical matters. The first one to bear the title of archbishop was Bishop Maximian (546–54), whose prestige was emphasized in the mosaic in the church of San Vitale, which depicts him directly in front of Emperor Justinian. Thus, the bishop soon came to be seen as the second-ranking person in the EXARCHATE OF RAVENNA, enjoying powers all the greater in that his church possessed a vast fortune in landholdings. Not surprisingly, in the 7th century the archbishops of Ravenna balked at being dependent on Rome, especially as regards their nomination and the conferring of the *pallium*. This desire for emancipation, together with the prelates' political stature, explains why Emperor Constans II in 666 granted the archbishop the privilege of autocephaly. Not subject to Rome, the archbishop would be consecrated by three suffragan bishops and would receive the *pallium* from the emperor's hands.

The privilege of autocephaly, first acquired by Archbishop Maurus, came to an end in 680, when Archbishop Theodore submitted to the pope; yet anti-Roman feeling persisted in Ravenna. After the sack of Ravenna by the Lombard Aistulf in 751, Pope STEPHEN II appealed to Pepin, king of the Franks, who promised to "restore" the annexed territories to the Roman republic. Following Pepin's anti-Lombard campaigns of 755–6, the pope received the cities of the Exarchate (that is, of the *provincia Ravennantium*) and the Pentapolis, and he sent his agents to Ravenna. Here they exercised civil and military rule in his name, provoking the resistance of Archbishop Sergius. The latter, having been threatened by Stephen II, finally obtained from PAUL I the authority to act *veluti exarchus* (in the capacity of an exarch), but through papal delegation. On Sergius's death, his successors, in particular archbishops Leo (770/1–777/8), George (837–46), John (850–78), and Romanus (878–88), reaffirmed their independence of and hostility to the papacy. Moreover, these anti-Roman sentiments were shared by a whole group; they found expression in the *Liber pontificalis*, which Angellus of Ravenna began to compile around 830, to the glory of his church and on the model of the Roman LIBER PONTIFICALIS.

The 10th century was marked by the long reign of Archbishop Peter (927–71). Under his episcopate, Otto I had himself crowned emperor in 962, promising the pope to restore the Exarchate and the Pentapolis. In fact, the pope's eminent authority became recognized only very gradually. Otto I had a palace built in Ravenna, and the archbishops became the agents of the Ottonian emperors, then of the Salians, who endowed them with a large number of counties. Notable examples of these are archbishops Gerbert d'Aurillac (998–99), Arnald, brother of the emperor Henry II (1013–19), and especially Wibert (1073–1100), whom Henry IV made the antipope CLEMENT III. In the 12th century, papal influence once again made itself felt under Gautier's episcopacy (1118–44). After an eclipse, it reappeared with Archbishop Gerard (1170–90), while the communal movement slowly eroded the exceptional power of the Ravenna prelates.

Jean-Pierre Brunterch

Bibliography

Brown, T. S. "The Church of Ravenna and the Imperial Administration of the Seventh Century," *English Historical Review*, 94 (1979) pp. 1–28.

Diehl, C. *Études sur l'administration byzantine dans l'exarchat de Ravenne (568–751)*, Paris, 1888 (BEFAR, 53).

Guillou, A. *Régionalisme et indépendance dans l'Empire byzantin au VIIᵉ siècle, l'exemple de l'Exarchat et de la Pentapole d'Italie*, Rome, 1969 (Istituto storico italiano per il Medio Evo, Studi storici, 75–6).

Heidrich, I. *Ravenna unter Erzbischof Wibert (1073–1100): Untersuchungen zur Stellung des Erzbischofs und Gegenpapstes Clemens III. in seiner Metropole*, Sigmaringen, 1984 (Vorträge und Forschungen herausgegeben vom Konstanzer Arbeitskreis für mittelalterliche Geschichte, 32).

Simonini, A. *La chiesa ravennate, splendore e tramonto di una metropoli*, s.l.n.d., Ravenna, 1964; *Autocefalia ed Esarcato in Italia*, Ravenna, 1969.

Storia di Ravenna, 3 vols., Ravenna, 1991–3.

REFORM, CATHOLIC. Faced with cultural changes that alter its message, the Church has always found itself swept by currents spreading abroad the ideal of reform. But there is a big step between the ideal and its effective realization. The term Catholic Reform is used to describe the internal change in the Catholic Church in the 16th century. As Hubert Jedin points out, this change is far more extensive than the Counter Reformation alone even if the latter concept conveys the combative characteristic, in part, of post-Tridentine Catholicism. Yet there should be no mistaking the fact that, although the struggle against the REFORMATION accelerated and focused the internal reform of Catholicism, it did not give rise to it, since this internal reform predates the Protestant rupture. From the Church of the late Middle Ages to the Church of the baroque, change was profound but continuous.

Reforms in the Medieval Church. According to the saying, *Ecclesia semper reformanda*, if the Church is always to be reformed, the goals are not always the same. The reforming ideal that gave rise to Catholic reformation was born at the council of Vienne in 1311, with the notion of *reformatio in capite et in membris*: a reform of the papacy and of the various organisms of the Church. A century earlier, the LATERAN IV COUNCIL (1215) had launched a far-reaching pastoral reform by linking the salvation of every Christian to confession and obligatory communion in his or her parish every year at Easter. This desire for reform corresponds to a transformation of medieval culture that began with the earliest decline of scholasticism and the first problems of the new urban economy.

The expression *reformatio in capite et in membris* represented an ideal that from then on was present at the very heart of the Christian Church and was gradually spread abroad through the preaching of the mendicant friars. The ideal was expressed as a desire to return to the time of the apostles to live a life of true brotherhood. The conflict between religious and secular clergies encouraged a maturing of the pastoral ideal that began in the Carolingian era and that exalted the care of souls by defining the rights, obligations, and dignity of the one exercising it. The *reformatio* was also the concern of the papacy that had its seat in AVIGNON, a city located on the trade route used by the great population centers and in touch with all the vital forces of medieval Europe. Reform developed an increasingly efficient administration and both launched and curbed the new developments arising from Christian dynamism. Thus, it inspired the Franciscan Spirituals, those champions of total poverty (1316–17), and marginalized a large component of popular religion by condemning divination and magic (1320–6).

A real effort to oblige parish priests to administer confession properly and to provide their flocks with proper instruction began to be felt. To this end, pastoral visits were encouraged, and synodal statutes were disseminated and even translated, to be read to the congregation. Besides the diocesan rituale (book of rites), priests charged with the care of souls soon (between 1380 and 1550) had at their disposal technical literature such as the *Manuale* of the Aragonese Guy de Montrocher or Jean Gerson's *Opus tripartitum*. But problems of diffusion were insurmountable, because of the disparate training of priests and the inertia due to the benefice system.

The upheavals of the Black Death and the GREAT SCHISM (1378–1417) checked and drained any effective realization of clerical reform. Reform at that time became a leitmotiv, an ideal, an obligatory criticism of ecclesial structures, and was no longer a program for action, even less an episcopal policy. Owing to the struggle among the popes and then between pope and council, the dissipation of power in the Church hindered any general or centralized solution and failed to encourage any power of imaginative invention on the part of the bishops.

Nonetheless, religious life had great dynamism, being nurtured by preaching, PILGRIMAGES, plays, and images. The obsessional cult of the Passion is often best remembered, and certainly the veneration of the Five Wounds, the Seven Last Words, and, in the 16th century, the Way of the Cross reflects this sensibility; yet new devotions also became popular. The feast of Corpus Christi, established by CLEMENT V in 1314 and included in the Roman MISSAL in the second half of that century, became in the 15th century a high point of the liturgical year, eclipsing the Ascension and Pentecost. Relics and the Blessed Sacrament were carried together in processions that more and more became grandiose mass events: the court of heaven had its visible manifestation in the local Church.

The development of the cult of the Real Presence can also be seen in the 15th century in the widespread use of the tabernacle, in lighting effects, and in the solemnization of the carrying of the Viaticum. The elaboration of the Eucharist was not merely an outgrowth of the new rituals; it corresponded to a perception of the mass that was developed gradually in the medieval period and that reached maturity with the growth of veneration of the suffering Christ. For the 15th-century Christian, the mass was the renewal of Christ's salvific sacrifice. To behold it in a broken but glorious body was coherent with the cult of saints' relics and the cross. In wills, requests for anniversary masses reached a high point between 1480 and 1520. The cult of the Virgin changed form. Pietàs, associated with the cult of the Passion, multiplied, but so did Annunciations. In the 15th century, the ANGELUS became widespread, and soon was prayed three times a day, so that the *Ave Maria* was as often recited as the *Patenoster*. Joan of Arc and her girlhood friends wove crowns of roses for Mary, and members of the confraternities of the Virgin wore crowns and garlands of flowers for funerals, masses, and feasts. The Dominican Tertiaries now combined recital of episodes from the lives of the Virgin and Christ with the weaving of roses into rosaries. Meditation on the mysteries of the ROSARY, spread by the Dominican Alain de La Roche (1485), would become standard only in the 16th century.

What these devotions had in common was formation of the interior life through the intermediary of a cult that appealed to the emotions. The Devotio Moderna, a movement for association of the Christian with Christ in a first stage leading to the marriage of the soul and God, which arose in the preceding century in monastic milieus, spread among the laity. While the educated read their Books of Hours, the illiterate, listening to the chanting of the customary prayers, had access to the new devotion. Behind the profusion of rituals, beyond the mechanical practice of devotion, and stimulated by development of the examination of conscience, a growing elite of "virtuosos of the religious" experienced personal, interior dialogue with Christ and his saints. Alert to the suggestions of the conscience, they looked to the Church to conform to its vocation as a gathering place for a holy people under the leadership of exemplary pastors. The return of peace made possible a restoration of the institution and elaboration of a policy of reforms, promoted by both the Church and the state; Saxony (1485) and France (1485, 1493), for example, tried to carry out reform through the state.

Continuous Reform and the Counter Reformation (1490–1563). Having failed to begin *in capite*, with the papacy, reform began *in membris* and in a highly dispersed fashion. The religious orders, which were more or less centralized and relatively homogeneous, were the first to seek the "apostolic life" laid down in the original rule. Monastic orders, adversely affected by economic crisis, had experienced a lasting decrease in recruitment. But movements for reform were not slow in coming. For example, the Congregation of St. Justina of Padua welcomed both humanism and the Devotio Moderna. The German congregations of Melk and Bursfeld and the Spanish congregation of Valladolid followed suit, as the action of Garcia de Cisneros at Monserrat, for one, exemplifies. From the end of the Hundred Years' War, the Cluniacs strove for reform, under the leadership of Abbots Jean de Bourbon and then Jacques d'Amboise (1481), as did those of Marmoutier and Chezal-Benoît and the recluses of Fontevrault. Many Parisian humanists entered monastic orders at the time, for example Guy Jouenneaux at Chezal-Benoît (1492) and Jean Raulin at Cluny (1497). There they initiated reform. The mendicants brought about reform even more swiftly. We need mention only the Dominicans Antonius of Florence and

Savonarola, Francis of Paola, the Franciscan founder of the Minims, and the Carmelite Laurent Bureau. The canons regularly underwent a similarly important reform, the best-known being those of the Congregation of Windelsheim in the Netherlands, ardent propagators of the Devotio Moderna. Reforms, now urgent because of the common eschatological nature of the aspiration to salvation, were undertaken in an atmosphere of sometimes unsustainable tension. Violence was not rare; it may have hindered the reforms of the Cluniacs and Franciscans. But the quest for reform was just as widespread among the laity. Numerous foundations are owed to them, for instance Battista Vernazza and the Oratory of Divine Love in Genoa (1497), Jerome Emiliani and the Somaschi, Antonio Maria Zaccaria and the Barnabites, and, later, Ignatius of Loyola and the JESUITS.

The reform of the diocesan clergy was more complex. In this time of "abuses," several very great bishops stand out, whose activities remain to be studied. The Tridentine model Gian Matteo Giberti, bishop of Verona (1495–1543), is not an isolated case. To stay with France, François d'Estaing in Rodez (1460–1529) and Guillaume Briçonnet in Lodève and then Meaux (1470–1534), originally humanists of Paris, who moved in intellectual Gallican circles, attempted a reform of their dioceses, visiting and supervising in person priests entrusted with the care of souls, and organizing preaching, particularly in the years 1517–20. The episcopal ideal, reaffirmed throughout the 15th century, reached a maturity that Gasparo Contarini, originally a layman and later cardinal from Venice, illustrated in 1526 with the publication of his *De officio episcopi*. All these men shared the idea that reform must come about first of all through reform of the clergy, whose pastoral responsibility, extolled for generations by preachers, was now being called for in pamphlets and other popular literature.

Henceforth, the pastor was likened to Christ himself; he was the good shepherd, responsible beyond his own salvation for the salvation of his flock. He must be educated to preach and give counsel; he must have a settled residence in order to set an example of morality; he was the salt of the earth, set apart to lead the community of believers. The realization of this ideal came up against major economic and institutional difficulties. If the reforms were not always brought to their conclusion for want of administrative power and political continuity, the attempts at application gave the clerical body a clear vision of the goal to be aimed for and the precise problems to be surmounted. The essence of these ideas would be found in the decisions of the council of TRENT.

Reform on the part of the bishops was real but discontinuous, tied as it was to the will and conscience of a few personalities, to their financial and administrative capacity, and to their physical and political strength. Through the system of capitular elections, still widely in force,

episcopal sees were reserved for dynasties capable of long-term action. Based on a balancing of local forces, the system did not always encourage dynamic politics. Reform of the clergy accordingly became lost in the thicket of local interests.

This reform, which was on the verge of success, was solely clerical. The idea of lay autonomy was alien to it, and soon even considered heretical. It is clear that the idea did not embrace all the aspirations of the body of Christians, especially when, in its attempt to control, it clashed with the increasingly competent manner in which the lay elites were running the parishes. These difficulties perhaps explain why the Church was unable to embark on a dynamic reform, but the main obstacle is surely to be sought in the papacy. It was not that Rome was hostile to reform, as several fruitless attempts at curial reform under the 15th-century popes show. The papacy of the early 16th century (JULIUS II, LEO X, CLEMENT VII) was absorbed in temporal matters and paralyzed by the threat of the rising superiority of the council. For it, reform was merely a secondary objective.

Clement VII (1523–34), by not deciding to hold a council, left the initiative of Church reform to Lutheranism. PAUL III (1534–49), elected by those who wanted a council and reforms, finally summoned to the SACRED COLLEGE a few of the most eminent supporters of reform: Contarini, Pole, Carafa, Sadoleto, Cervini, and Morone. It was Contarini who presided over the famous commission that produced the *Consilium de emendanda Ecclesia* (1537), which in a limited way guided papal action until the end of the century.

For political reasons, the opening of the council would be delayed until 1545, but the approval of the Theatines, Barnabites, and Jesuits together with the creation of the HOLY OFFICE was evidence of a fresh pontifical determination to coordinate aspirations toward reform. The council, convened to rebuild Church unity, ended with the acknowledgment of a division. A large portion of the conciliar decrees was taken up with a point-by-point refutation of the Protestant Reformation, yet the concern of the council was also, indissociably, to ensure that the aspirations and experiments prior to the Reformation were applied. The realization of the continuous reform of Catholicism was the work of the council and the papacy. What had been undertaken with dynamism but in discontinuous fashion, locally and humbly, deep in the ecclesial body, was now put forward and promoted, in a spirit all the more unanimous in view of the apparent urgency.

The council of Trent aimed to treat dogmas and discipline with equal attention. While the Protestant Reformation largely served as a guide to the positions the council adopted on matters of dogma, because the council fathers debated the catalogs of errors the response of the council was not a simple one. Above all, there was disquiet over what the faith and the practices of the eternal Church would become. The decrees of the council of Trent were the fruit of debates and reconciliation between the intransigents, who called for a clear response to HERESY, and the humanists, who sought to proclaim the faith in terms of the culture of their time. The result was the elaboration of dogmatic definitions perfectly suited to the debates and vocabulary of the period.

Particularly characteristic were the decrees on the sources of Revelation, on justification, and on the sacraments. Scripture was the basis of Christianity, but its accurate interpretation belonged solely to the Church. Justification was a work of collaboration between humankind and God. The sacraments were efficacious visible signs. The reply to Protestant critics came first, but the definitions of the Eucharist went much further than simple polemics. If the defense of the Real Presence and the use of the term transubstantiation were well in line with medieval evolution, its definition as food for souls and antidote for daily sins, through the permanent reiteration of sacrifice, was the impetus to frequent communion. Despite juridical and philosophical pressures, marriage was reaffirmed as a sacrament of full partnership which "conjoined" baptized Christians perfectly, though this conjunction was not ensured either by the contract or by natural necessity alone. The disciplinary decrees concerning the residence of bishops and parish priests grew directly out of the previous debates. Because the decrees were the result of a maturing of reforms throughout the whole Church, and, even more, because there was a coordinated diffusion, they gradually had an impact.

The Principles of Reform of the Catholic Church (1564–1660). The council's great strength was that it was applied by bishops who had attended the debates and was immediately promoted by the popes. Pope PIUS IV on 26 January 1564 not only sanctioned the decrees as a group, but also created a congregation to oversee their execution. His nephew Charles Borromeo organized the practical application by means of the local synods of 1565 and 1569, establishing a canonical procedure. With the rapid publication of the Roman CATECHISM (1566) and new liturgical books (the BREVIARY, 1568; the missal, 1570; the rituale, 1614) and the imposition of uniformity on all dioceses that did not have a liturgy more than two hundred years old, as well as the strengthening of the permanent nunciatures, the papacy undertook to enforce the decrees of the council.

The reform of the Curia by SIXTUS V (1588) is proof of this desire for efficiency. At the same time, the transformation of Rome and the return of the popes to a proper way of life, changed, profoundly and lastingly, the image of the pope and his actions. The pope's definitive domination over the council in the exercise of power in the Church consecrated this evolution. Yet this domination

was not inevitable. Episcopal collegiality was also ensured by the strengthening of the bishops' power throughout the conciliar debates. The decrees would never have been applied if the provincial synods, soon destined to wither away, had not acted forcefully and quickly.

In fact, though several states directly or tacitly refused to accept the council as state law (e.g., France), the dogmatic and disciplinary decrees were generally accepted locally and put into practice. It was some time, however, before the results of the council really made themselves felt at the parish level.

Whereas bishops and parish priests abided by the requirement of residence, the catechism was not regularly preached until around 1630, and the Forty Hours' Devotion, though developed by the Barnabites in 1530, became customary only after 1630. The SEMINARIES undertook a uniform formation of priests only in the late 17th century. Architecture arrived at a new kind of interior space within the churches in order to provide a setting for the celebration of the Eucharist, to coordinate it with the salutary increase in the number of masses and with preaching, and to introduce the faithful, as they prayed, into the divine world, made close and familiar by the raising of domes and the use of splendid decoration. This baroque art developed in Italy from 1580, but its canons were not drawn up until the period 1630–60. In spite of the aspirations of the faithful and the unfailing determination of the bishops, the quality of the popes and the devotion of the new orders, and the goad of Protestantism, it took over a century to reform Catholicism according to the canons of the council of Trent.

Nicole Lemaitre

Bibliography

Alberigo, G. "Réforme en tant que critère de l'histoire de l'église," *RHEF*, 76 (1981), 72–83.

Bireley, R. *The Refashioning of Catholicism, 1450–1700*, Washington, D.C., 1999.

Bossy, J. *Christianity and the West, 1400–1700*, Oxford, 1985.

Bossy, J. *The English Catholic Community, 1570–1850*, New York, 1976.

Delumeau, J. *Le Catholicisme entre Luther e Voltaire*, Paris, 1979 (*Nouvelle Clio*, 30 BIS).

Donnelly, J. P., and Maher, M. W., eds. *Confraternities and Catholic Reform in Italy, France, and Spain*, Kirksville, Mo., 1999.

Église et vie religieuse en France, 1450–1530. Colloque de Tours, RHEF, 77, 1991.

Evennett, H. O. *The Spirit of the Counter Reformation*, Cambridge, 1968.

Histoire de la France religieuse, ed. J. Le Goff and R. Rémond, 2, Paris, 1988.

Hsia, R. P. *The World of Catholic Renewal, 1540–1770*, Cambridge, 1998.

Il concilio di Trento nella vita spirituale e culturale del Mezzogiorno. Atti del convegno di Maratea, G. de Rosa, A. Cestaro, ed., Potenza, 1988.

La Réforme des réguliers en France de la fin du XVe siècle à la fin des Guerres de religion, Colloque de Fontevrault, RHEF, 65, 1979.

Les Débuts de la réforme catholique dans les pays de langue française 1560–1620. Colloque de Nancy, RHEF, 75, 1989.

Olin, J. C. *Catholic Reform: From Cardinal Ximenes to the Council of Trent, 1495–1563*, New York, 1990.

O'Malley, J. W., ed. *Catholicism in Early Modern History: A Guide to Research*, St. Louis, 1988.

O'Malley, J. W. *Trent and All That: Renaming Catholicism in the Early Modern Era*, Cambridge, Mass., 2000.

Ramsey, A. W. *Liturgy, Politics, and Salvation: The Catholic League in Paris and the Nature of Catholic Reform, 1540–1630*, Rochester, N.Y., 1999.

Rapp, F. *L'Église et la vie religieuse en occident à la fin du Moyen Âge*, Paris, 1999 (*Nouvelle Clio*, 25).

Scarisbrick, J. J. *The Reformation and the English People*, Oxford, 1984.

Strutture ecclesiastiche in Italia e in Germania prima della Riforma, P. Prodi, P. Johanek (ed.), Bologna, 1984.

Venard, M. "Réforme, Réformation, Préréforme, Contre-Réforme . . . Étude de vocabulaire chez les historiens français de langue française," *Historiographie de la Réforme*, ed. P. Joutard, Paris, 1977, 352–65.

REFORM, GREGORIAN.

The so-called Gregorian reform—named after its most illustrious protagonist, Pope GREGORY VII (1073–85)—has been described as "the greatest fact of the religious history of the Middle Ages" (A. Fliche). It may be useful to take a look at the debates concerning it, in order to gain a better understanding of the place of this reform in present-day historiography.

Gregorian Reform: A Historian's Debate.

The French medievalist Augustin Fliche deserves the credit for giving the first detailed picture of the Gregorian reform. Drawing on 19th-century scholarship, Fliche conceived of the Gregorian movement as the reform-minded papacy's response to a situation of political, social, and moral crisis that reached its peak in the 10th century. The collapse of state structures with the last Carolingians, the rise of "feudal anarchy," the crisis in Rome when the papacy fell prey to local aristocratic factions, the deep-seated moral crisis of a clergy corrupted by the commerce in high positions and sacraments (SIMONY), and the incontinence of priests (NICOLAISM)—against this backdrop, the Grego-

rian reform appeared as the triumph of principles centered on the idea of *libertas Ecclesiae* and made workable thanks to the Church's pyramidal structure.

For Fliche, the goal of Gregory VII's reform was the building up of a bureaucratic centralism in Rome and the parallel elaboration of a theocratic ideology. "The liberation of the Church being impossible without a perfect unity of action," he writes, "the papacy, which had been crushed by imperial caesaropapism and the tyranny of the Roman nobility, had to consider freeing itself and setting up, on a solid basis, its authority over the Christian world. The exalting of the Apostolic See together with an ecclesiastical centralization subordinating all the local Churches to Rome, and the exalting of a theocratic doctrine that obliged kings to conform their government and policies to the moral and religious directives of the Holy See—in the final analysis, that is the most salient feature of the Gregorian reform, the one that conditions and explains all the others." However dated Fliche's argument may seem today, it had the merit of stressing the revolutionary nature of the rupture that the reform sanctioned between *Sacerdotium* and *Imperium*. Moreover, Fliche aptly divided the various phases of the reform into the three acts of a drama:

1) A "pre-Gregorian or "caesaropapist" act, marking a strong initial phase when reform was instituted through concerted action on the part of Emperor Henry III and the first reforming popes, of German origin, from CLEMENT II (1046–7) to LEO IX (1048–54).

2) A Gregorian act properly speaking, characterized by a gradual affirmation of Roman primacy under NICHOLAS II (1059–61) and ALEXANDER II (1061–73) and by Gregory VII's "theocratic" radicalism.

3) A "post-Gregorian" act in which, beginning with the reigns of URBAN II (1088–99) and PASCHAL II (1099–1118), means of practical application were set in place that allowed both the papacy and the empire to establish bases of coexistence, through the concordat of WORMS (1122). This coexistence marks both the chronological ending of the reform and the substantial victory of its principles.

After Fliche, a second major historiographical stage was reached in 1936 with the appearance of the work of Gerd Tellenbach. Rejecting the ideas of "10th-century crisis" and "feudal anarchy," Tellenbach showed convincingly that, far from fitting into such a context, Gregorian ideology instead made a decisive break with a different "world order" of Carolingian-Ottonian origin, which still showed signs of life in Henry III's plans for reform. For Tellenbach, this imperial ideology was founded on the idea of an essential unity between Church and State and on a unified consciousness of political power.

If, in such a system, the temporal and the spiritual were conceived as differing from each other and as situated at different levels of political practice, there was nonetheless no conflict or structural element of rivalry between the two. Until the middle of the 11th century, it seems, the Church had no ambition to dominate universal society, or any temptation to absorb natural law—that is, the law of the State—into a supernatural justice defined as the law of the Church. Instead, within the empire, that is, the sole totalitarian political reality, there can simply be discerned a Church defined in organic fashion as the Church of the Empire (*Reichskirche*). Unconcerned with aspiring to an essential *libertas*, this Church of the Empire claimed and was effectively granted only franchises—*libertates*—understood in a restrictive sense as a group of concrete autonomies of a political, juridical, and economic nature.

It was in the name of this unitary ideal that Henry III instigated the first phase of his reform. Also, it is by analyzing Henry III's measures toward reform that Tellenbach restored contemporary MONASTICISM to its rightful place. In the reforms originating in Cluny, Tellenbach perceived the source—at once monastic, ascetic, and aristocratic—from which the emperor drew the themes of reform that were the order of the day in the years 1040–50. This reform, which emphasized the struggle against nicolaism and especially simony, at first had no quarrel with the bases of the traditional imperial *Weltordnung*. The ideological break came, according to Tellenbach, with Gregory VII himself. Only then was a new ideology set in place, one that was coherent and activist, founded on the affirmation of Roman primacy and the Church's aspiration to exercise a supreme, all-competent power.

This idea of rupture itself implied a new ecclesiology based no longer on the granting of *libertates* but on an uncompromising claim of *libertas Ecclesiae* and *justitia*, that is, recognition of the Church as the source of all law. Among the Gregorians' various ideological positions, Tellenbach makes much of the most radical themes: the repeated affirmation of the revolutionary nature of the Gospel message and of Rome's ecclesial mission, together with the refusal of any compromise with the temporal powers. While Tellenbach's thesis clearly marks great progress in our understanding of the Gregorian reform, it is nonetheless true that for him as for Fliche the Gregorian era was still essentially a confrontation in high places between the empire and the papacy.

Gregorian studies burgeoned against this historiographical background beginning in 1947, with the rich series of *Studi Gregoriani* and the research arising from them. The most original contributions of this blossoming of studies may be listed under five headings, as follows:

1) Closer awareness of social history had an obvious effect on our problem. Scholars have sought to trace in the Gregorian reform not only the expression of an ideology imposed from above by a clerical elite but also the response to a desire for reform emanating from below.

2) Together with concern for in-depth study of the social terrain of reform, there has been interest in the study of regional areas. In France, Italy, and Germany especially, diocesan monographs have multiplied.

3) Equally apparent is the desire to illuminate the role of the monastic milieus, and not just that of Cluny, in the reform movement. The importance of the eremetic movements in particular has been evaluated more fully.

4) The need arose for a better understanding of the sources and the canonical problems linked to the reform. Attention was given to questions of textual tradition and of the structure and purpose of the canonical collections connected with the reform. This came about after a long period which, with certain exceptions like Paul Fournier, favored narrative sources and the literature of controversy over juridical and speculative sources.

5) A pressing need was seen to link the history of the ecclesial institution built up by the reform to the general history of the forms and power structures within Christendom in the 11th and 12th centuries. Far from appearing a reaction to a mythical "feudal anarchy," the Gregorian reform more and more revealed itself as the intelligent adaptation of the Church as *institutio* to a well-structured feudal society, which it aimed to dominate from within.

Accordingly, it is possible to measure the richness and variety of the thematic developments that historiography has been introducing into the study of this subject during the past twenty years. If the expression "Gregorian reform" is still in current usage, it is obvious that the contribution of Gregory VII and his entourage has continually been reduced in favor of a wider conception of the vast movement of renewal that guided the Church in the 11th century and the first quarter of the 12th century.

The Stages of the Reform: Symptoms (1014–46). Clear signs presaging reform are already evident in the first half of the 11th century. At the provincial synods of Rome and Ravenna (1014), and in particular at the great synod of Pavia in 1022, presided over by Pope BENEDICT VIII and Emperor Henry II, emphasis was placed on the struggle against simoniacal ordinations, the moral quality of the clergy, and the necessary link between a well-regulated priestly life and the administering of the sacraments. In close agreement with the principles affirmed at these synods were the great canonical collections of the period, for example the *Decretum* of Burchard of Worms, which was compiled around 1012 and distributed widely over the next ten years. On several essential matters, the laws therein expressed views that seem to foreshadow those of the Gregorians: a declaration of war for clerical celibacy and against simony, the exaltation of the role of bishops, and valorization of the priestly office as sacramental mediator. The reform of cathedral chapters such as those of Bamberg and Hildesheim that was undertaken during the reign of Henry II gives a measure of the results inspired by these ideals. At the same time, the hagiographical literature, along with *vitae* such as those of Bernward of Hildesheim, Burchard of Worms, and Ulric of Augsburg, produced the first ideal type of the reforming bishop—one who was eager to bring back his diocesan clergy to the norms of canonical life, that is, to a communal life founded on the apostolic model, and who was imbued with ascetic values of monastic origin that would serve well in a pastoral setting. In Italy, Ravenna became an important center of reform under Archbishop Gebhard of Eichstätt (1027–44). His suffragan John, bishop of Cesena, proposed to his cathedral chapter in 1042 a program of priestly living based on the imitation of the apostles and personal poverty.

This link between the beginnings of the reform and the first rise of the canonical movement is attested to elsewhere: at Fano in the Marches, at S. Lorenzo of Oulx in Piedmont, at S. Frediano in Lucca, at St-Ruf in Avignon, etc. At the very heart of the empire, reforming bishops like Wazo of Liège (1042–8) reacted against the abuses inherent in the system of the Church of the Empire. Without calling into question the loyalty due to the emperor in temporal matters (*de secularibus*), Wazo insisted on the obedience due to the pope *in spiritualibus*, thereby adumbrating a theme rich in promise for the future.

Papal Reform Before Gregory VII (1046–73). These first aspirations to reform, in the years 1010–40, were thus real but still diffuse and uncoordinated. A decisive step was taken in 1046 by Emperor Henry III. Imbued with a sense of the sacredness of the imperial office, as well as sincerely inspired by the principles of reform drawn up in the monasteries, particularly Cluny and Gorze, Henry III was determined to free the papacy from its involvement in struggles over local influence by setting on the papal throne a series of German popes: Clement II (1046–7), DAMASUS II (1047–8), and, especially, Leo IX (1048–54), whose pontificate marks a major stage on the road to reform. Under his rule, the schism of Michael Cerularius (1054) not only signified a definitive break with the CHURCHES OF THE ORIENT but also prepared the ground for the papacy's concentration on claiming for the Roman Church supremacy over all the local Churches. Though Leo IX did not come into open conflict with the emperor, he committed the papacy to a path of clear insistence on *libertas Ecclesiae*. Under the leadership of persistent theoreticians such as Cardinal Humbert of Silva Candida and Peter Damian, the struggle against lay investiture and simony was waged to good effect. At the synod of Vercelli (1050), the papacy settled the problem of the validity of the sacraments and ordinations conferred by simoniacal bishops, following the moderate line put forward by Peter Damian in his *Liber gratissimus* (1051). Clerical communal life was held up

as a concrete model for priests, and emphasis was placed on the personal poverty of canons, in the spirit of the Rule of St. Augustine.

Leo IX's successors, Nicholas II (1059–61) and Alexander II (1061–73), followed up these new measures as they waged their own campaigns. The central element of the reform mechanism set in place at the Lateran synod of 1059 resulted, with the decree *In nomine Domini*, in the restriction of free papal election to the college of cardinal bishops, but access to election was extended to cardinal priests and cardinal deacons shortly afterward. The consequences of this decree can hardly be overestimated. By breaking completely with the tradition of the Church of the Empire, the new procedure for papal elections had as its aim to guarantee *libertas Ecclesiae* at the very summit of the Church, while the emperor received a right of approval and ratification. Another result of the 1059 decree was that the Sacred College was granted an exclusive prerogative and therefore an eminent canonical standing. The college accordingly became the central nucleus of the Roman CURIA. It should also be kept in mind that the decree on papal election was integrated into a wider policy of reform designed to affirm the Church's essential function as sacramental mediator.

The Gregorian Period (1073–85). The sometimes dramatic story of the INVESTITURE CONTROVERSY will not be retold here. At that time, the confrontation between *Regnum* and *Sacerdotium* impelled Gregory VII to break definitively with a tradition whereby the emperor appeared as the legitimate sacramental head of an imperial Church. Gregory's theocratic claim pitted against this old order the ideal of a Roman Church, founded by divine right on apostolic primacy and in which the emperor, defined as "the head of the laity" (*caput laicorum*), had as his particular duty to counter the heresy of simony and the inveterate sickness of *fornicatio clericorum*. In this context, the famous episode of CANOSSA (1077) appears not so much a deliberate attempt to humiliate Henry IV as a means of affirming the superiority of the Church over the imperial office.

Moreover, one ought not exaggerate the significance of the most important decisions made during Gregory VII's pontificate, particularly at the reform synods of 1074 and 1078. None of the themes developed there was really new. As at the great synod of 1059, the struggle against simony and nicolaism as well as the need to promote the communal life of the clergy remained the order of the day. With his passion and intransigence, on all these points the pope was more a continuer than an innovator. On the other hand, the entourage of Gregory VII should be given credit for a clearer, more coherent canonical formulation of the principles expressed by all the popes since Leo IX. Under Gregory VII, the most important canonical collections were compiled or published, with the result that canon law became an essential element in the consolidation of the achievements of the preceding decades. At the same time, the violent confrontation between *Regnum* and *Sacerdotium* found expression in a flourishing literature of controversy between Gregorians and imperials, which played its part in clarifying the stakes of the debate and to which its publishers gave the generic term *libelli de lite*. At stake was the constitution, under the primacy of the Holy See, of a strongly hierarchized ecclesial institution, whose function of sacramental mediation had to be guaranteed by the moral and cultural quality of the clergy, who dispensed grace free of all corrupting interference from the laity.

Toward Appeasement: The Consolidation of Gregorian Principles (1085–1124).

Under Gregory VII's successors, from VICTOR III (1086–7) to CALLISTUS II (1119–24), the reform passed through various stages, from a period of abrupt confrontation to one of compromise, based on a calmer appreciation of the possibilities for applying Gregorian ideals. Ivo of Chartres merits consideration. Drawing all the consequences of the principle of the separation of the spiritual and temporal powers of bishops outlined a half-century before by Wazo of Liège, the canonist Ivo of Chartres set forth the terms of a compromise based on the compatibility between two types of investiture, the one ecclesiastical and the other secular. The first type was defined as relating to the bishops' spiritual prerogatives, the second to their powers of temporal government and management of ecclesiastical goods. Under Pope Urban II (1088–99), who came from Cluny, Philip I of France and his nobles renounced the practice of the lay investiture of major benefices with crozier and ring (*anulo et baculo*), without, however, relinquishing their right of approval of the newly elected pope and of investiture *pro temporalibus*. A few years later, in 1105, Paschal II (1099–1118) signed a similar agreement with the king of England, Henry I. In Germany and Italy, where, because of the original structure of the Church of the Empire, the episcopate was more closely integrated in politics, the working out of a compromise was more laborious. A first accord, which Henry V won from Paschal II after the imperial coronation, was rejected by the Lateran council of March 1112 as contrary to canonical tradition and Gregorian principles. The succession of Countess Matilda in 1115 revived a conflict that culminated in the emperor's excommunication. After Paschal II died in 1118, Henry V set the antipope GREGORY VIII (1118–21) against the newly elected GELASIUS II (1118–19). Only after the death of Gelasius II would his canonical successor, Callistus II, resolve the schism and enter into renewed negotiations with the emperor, which resulted on 23 September 1122 in the concordat of Worms.

Based on two parallel declarations, one from the pope and the other from the emperor, and not on a formal convention, the 1122 agreement finally laid down the bases of coexistence between the two powers. The emperor's excommunication was lifted. He renounced investiture with ring and crozier and pledged to respect free episcopal elections and ordinations, as well as to restore its possessions and regalia to the Church of Rome. He promised Callistus peace and the aid that was his due. For his part, the pope recognized the emperor's right to invest newly elected bishops with the scepter, the symbol of the benefits and political functions (regalia) associated with episcopal duties. Doubtless the concordat left behind shadowy areas and uncertainties. The pope, in particular, gave the emperor only a vague right of oversight of episcopal elections. Despite its imperfections and the ambiguities inherent in certain concepts such as regalia, the Worms accord had the merit of extending to the imperial lands the application of the Chartres principle of double investiture, which had been tested in France and England. The ecumenical council that met at the Lateran in 1123 and 1139 reaffirmed the victory of a solution safeguarding the core of the Gregorian claim to *libertas Ecclesiae*.

The Fundamental Achievements of the Gregorian Reform.

The history of the stages through which the reform passed makes it possible to restore its significance and its chronological density. But that is insufficient in view of the richness of this movement, which profoundly changed the Church's institutional frameworks, doctrinal points of reference, and spiritual horizons. An attempt at a balance sheet follows.

The primary and most visible achievement of the Gregorian reform is associated with its successful struggle for the moral renewal of the clergy and against simony, nicolaism, and lay investiture. In one conciliar decision after another and under the pen of the greatest theoreticians of the reform, simony was pursued not only as a vice (*pravitas*) that had its roots in lay investiture and corrupted all religious values through venality, but as a heresy (*simoniaca haeresis*). It was accordingly condemned as an error in a matter of faith, one denying the free gift of God (Humbert of Silva Candida's finding) or, even worse, like a new Arianism, aimed at separating the Holy Spirit and the Son from the Father (Peter Damian and Geoffrey of Vendôme). Simony entered the mid-12th century in Gratian's *Decretum*, as in the common doctrine of the 13th-century canonists and theologians from Raymond of Peñafort to Thomas Aquinas, having the status of a heresy.

In the first "pre-Gregorian" provincial councils, such as those of Bourges (1031), Rouen (1063), and Lisieux (1064), and especially in the series of great general councils convened by the reform popes beginning with

Leo IX (Rome 1050, Rome 1074, Melfi 1089, Clermont 1095, Reims 1119), the canons chosen to combat clerical marriage and concubinage were combined with those opposing simony. Certainly, the Gregorian reform merely reaffirmed the ancient discipline of the Latin Church on clerical celibacy. And yet the context favoring reform in the 11th century gave the struggle against nicolaism a new range and one that revealed the complexity of the factors involved in it. In fact, insistence on the strict moral integrity of the clergy was not simply one of the aims of the reform that the papacy and the Gregorian episcopate tried to impose from on high on the whole clerical world. On this point, pontifical and episcopal action joined forces with popular aspirations that found vehement expression in the mid-11th century, in the Milanese Patarenes, for example, or in the words of particularly virulent itinerant preachers like St. Dominic of Sora (1031), a great denouncer of priests who were married or living in concubinage.

Sensitive to the repercussions of this theme among the laity, Gregory VII even incited the faithful to go on liturgical "strike" by recommending that they desert churches in which incontinent priests exercised their ministry. It is also important not to separate this struggle for the observance of clerical celibacy from another struggle, one waged just as energetically by the reformers, for the laity's observance of conjugal discipline. In both areas, the real objective had to do more with ecclesiology than morality. The goal was to institute an ordering of the *societas christiana* in which, following a renovated Augustinian conception, alongside the monks (*virgines*) enclosed in the separate life that was the essence of their state, it was the duty of the priests (*pastores continentes*) to provide a framework for a Christian people that was itself defined as an *ordo conjugatorum* through its sacramental participation in the institution of marriage.

On the other hand, one should take into account the economic background and the reality of material interests at issue here. For the reformers, to struggle for clerical celibacy was also to struggle for keeping patrimonies intact and, in particular, for maintaining the endowments of rural parishes that were threatened with dispersion as priests' families proliferated. To further the canonical order and clerical communal life was also to offer the diocesan clergy a concrete framework for a well-regulated priestly life, which was both attractive on the spiritual level and likely to ensure a better application of the norms of continence and personal poverty prescribed for it. The encounter between, on the one hand, the efforts in favor of clerical communal life made by many reforming bishops beginning in the 1040s and, on the other, the coherence of a priestly model devised by the papacy after the Lateran synod (1059) illustrates Rome's capacity to coordinate and centralize experiences originating in the domain of episcopal reform.

This link between ideal goals and practical means of reform can be seen even more clearly in what can be considered another fundamental achievement of the Gregorian reform: the constitution of an ecclesial hierarchy based on apostolic primacy and served by a centralized and increasingly efficient Roman bureaucracy. Anxious at first to ensure for itself appropriate means of action, the papacy made the ancient PATRIMONY OF ST. PETER the nucleus of a veritable pontifical state, with sizable lands and fortresses over which flew the *vexillum sancti Petri*, and provided with military, financial, and administrative capabilities. In the logic of this state structure, the papacy acquired the central institutions it needed to be able to carry out the functions of an instrument of government. As the old Patrimony of St. Peter gradually grew into a papal state, over the years 1050–1120, a parallel development took place. The old building of the Lateran *palatium* became the *Curia romana*, a term that entered current usage from the reign of Urban II (1088–99) and was used to describe the papal bureaucracy's complex of central offices. Its original nucleus was the college of cardinals, firmly based on its exclusive privilege of electing the new pope, thanks to the decree of 1059. In the era of Humbert of Silva Candida and Peter Damian the milieu of the Gregorian reform, imbued with the ideal of *Renovatio*, envisaged the Sacred College as a new Senate, embodying the takeover of the Rome of the Caesars by the Rome of St. Peter.

In the last quarter of the 11th century, the Roman Curia, which was actually contemporary with the *curia regis* with which the great Western monarchies were equipped at the time, expanded to include specialized services that had their equivalents in France, England, and, of course, the *curia imperatoris*. The papal CHANCERY, which grew from a college of *notarii* and *scriniarii* headed by a *bibliothecarius*, usually of bishop's rank, began to be organized from the 11th century as a service specializing in the expedition of papal documents. But the decisive moves were taken from 1088, when Pope Urban II appointed as chancellor of the Roman Church the cardinal deacon John of Gaeta, the future Gelasius II. This was the period when the great papal privileges were given their standard form. For example, standardization of papal documents was imposed with the adoption of a uniform script, the so-called curial minuscule, and the definitive adoption of the leaden BULL. The revival in curial prose of the rhythmic *clausulae* and the *cursus leoninus* is indicative of the cultural orientations of a bureaucracy that was itself enamored with *renovatio* in the paleo-Christian style.

Along with the Chancery, a CHAPEL—the *capella papalis*—was organized, largely on the model of the imperial chapel. Begun in the period from Nicholas II to Gregory VII, it took on more precise form under Urban II and Paschal II, and became a real center of liturgical renewal. At the beginning of Gregory VII's reign, in particular, in 1075, the custom of the Papal CORONATION was instituted, which from the 12th century had been linked with a stational liturgy and thereby anchored in the Roman area. In the same period, the ideological importance of the crowning of the pope was affirmed using the symbolism of the state: the TIARA worn by the pope, both miter and crown, was exalted as the sign of the dual sovereignty of Peter's successor, *mitra pro sacerdotio, corona pro regno*.

Last, again during the pontificate of Urban II, the Roman Curia followed the Cluniac model and acquired a service that specialized in the economic management of the Church's temporal power, the APOSTOLIC CAMERA. A former Cluniac monk was appointed *camerarius domini papae* in 1105. Though the actual words *Camera apostolica* are not attested before Urban II, the new institution marked the end of a policy that had been in force since the mid-11th century. Well before he became pope, Gregory VII himself, in his capacity as archdeacon of the Roman Church (1059), had tried to ensure and extend the collection of taxes owed to the Holy See from all those who sought to be under the protection of St. Peter and invoked the benefit of *libertas romana*. Indeed, one of the characteristics of the Gregorian idea seems to have been to establish a system of regular collections and provide an economic basis for a policy of reform that was as mindful of its means as it was uncompromising in its ideals. One can imagine how, in the controversial literature that grew out of the reform, Gregory VII's cupidity, sometimes related to the purported Jewish origins attributed to him by his detractors, became one of the themes of the imperial propaganda.

To administer this sprawling bureaucracy, the cardinals took on a managerial role, at the head of the various dicasteries. Other institutions, emerging from the reform or reactivated by it, ensured the working of the new governmental structure. The institution of papal LEGATES gave the papacy an efficient instrument for liaison and the transmission of reform initiatives. The development of the procedure of APPEAL to the Holy See, in the case of contested episcopal elections for instance, followed the same course. Likewise the obligation imposed on archbishops from the middle of the 11th century to come in person to Rome to receive the *pallium*, the insignia of their office. From the 12th century, the swearing of an oath of obedience to the pope and the obligation of bishops to make periodic "AD LIMINA" VISITS served to strengthen these methods of controlling the local Churches.

Similarly, it is owing to the Gregorian reform that CANON LAW was drawn up to serve the apostolic primate—a law that could not be confused with civil law and that derived its principles and norms solely from the sovereign authority of the Church. Building on the mate-

rial provided by the Fathers of the Church, the decisions of former councils, and the Pseudo-Isidorean corpus, the reformers produced, in a few decades (1060 to ca. 1110), a complete series of canonical collections fairly closely linked to the influence of the papacy. Worthy of mention are the collection under LXXIV headings (*Diversorum sententiae patrum*), described by Paul Fournier as "the first manual of canon law of the 11th-century reform," and long erroneously attributed to Cardinal Humbert; the so-called Britannica collection (ca. 1090), compiled, like its predecessors, in Rome; and the *Polycarpus* of Cardinal Gregory of S. Crisogono (1104–13). Outside Italy, a similar profusion of works was produced, with the collection in XVII books, the *Liber Tarraconensis*, that in VII books, and that in XIII books. At the end of the 11th century, this activity climaxed in the three collections attributed to Ivo of Chartres: the *Decretum*, the *Panormia*, and the *Tripartita*. The great work of synthesis accomplished around 1140 by the *Decretum* of Gratian marks a culminating point as well as the limits of definitive reception of the canonists' activity, carried out since the 1060s and correctly called a "great turning point in the history of law" by Paul Fournier.

It should be added that the proliferation of canonical collections contemporary with the Gregorian reform should not be separated here from the more important fact of the relative stability of their contents. This was ensured by frequent use of the same sources from one collection to another. The stability can be quantified by noting, for instance, that more than two-thirds of the earliest "Gregorian" collection, that under LXXIV headings, was integrated into Gratian's Decretum after passing by way of extensive borrowings into more than thirty extant collections, both unpublished and published. Accordingly, it is the manner in which a collection is built up and the arrangement of the collected materials, rather than the materials themselves, that in the end give each collection its originality and reveal, instead of a juridical monolithism, the trends peculiar to the group from which it came. Moreover, whatever prudence is called for in describing these canonical collections as "Gregorian," the coherence of the themes of reform bequeathed to the thinking of the Church in the second half of the 11th century by the canonists' anthologizing work should not be underestimated. Apostolic primacy and papal supremacy in jurisdictional matters; the rights and duties of bishops; the norms of living demanded of the general clergy; sacramental legislation and, in particular, the rules relating to marriage—these are the strong points around which was organized a juridical thinking that reflected, in the end fairly faithfully, the major preoccupations of the reform.

Beyond certain thematic choices exercised here and there, the elaboration of a law of the autonomous Church strengthened the status of the papacy as a sovereign, supranational authority, dominating the entire *societas christiana* and, essentially, superior to all secular authority. The total concept that thus emerges from the theoretical work of the jurists and theologians of the reform is that of a *respublica christiana*, a *christianitas* that is above all political entities and founded on a divine right to dominate them. These extreme views belonging to an unyielding spiritual monism characterize the properly Gregorian phase of the 11th-century ecclesiastical reform. In these views, Gerd Tellenbach has situated the decisive moment of rupture with the old unitary order of the Carolingian-Ottonian world, still present in Henry III's plans for reform. After Gregory VII, once the time had passed for the violent confrontations that arose from the affirmation of these theocratic ideas, the Church worked with shrewd reformers like Ivo of Chartres to find concordatory formulas. From the time of Gratian's reign, these formulas would be used to reestablish canonical teaching, on a dualist basis, in matters regarding the relations between Church and State.

Such solutions of balance—or compromise—were a far cry from the rupture caused by the Gregorian reform between *Regnum* and *Sacerdotium*. A particular achievement of Gregory VII was to set *Sacerdotium* on the path toward claiming all the rights and prerogatives of sovereignty. In so doing, he made the Church responsible for a historical project that exceeded the possibilities of individual *regna*. With Gregory VII, the pope claimed to be *princeps et verus imperator*. Beyond the vicissitudes of the Investiture Controversy, the Gregorian phase of the reform, defined as its critical phase when it opposed pope and emperor in a rivalry for supreme power, made it possible for an ultimately uniform ideology of sovereignty to be built up over the long term. As Ernst H. Kantorowicz has pertinently noted, "Up to the end of the Middle Ages, the hierarchical apparatus which the Roman Church erected from the middle of the 11th century [. . .] showed a tendency to become the perfect prototype of an absolute, rational monarchy set up on a mystical basis, whereas, at the same time, the State increasingly tended to become a quasi-Church and, in other respects, a mystical monarchy set up on a rational basis." Kantorowicz has therein shed light on the ideological progress and techniques of a manipulation of political concepts owing to which, from the time of the Gregorian reform, the "mysteries of the Church" (*arcana Ecclesiae*), spiritual in nature, were transferred to the state so as to produce "mysteries of the State," the new, secular *arcana imperii* that are at the root of modern absolutism.

The Gregorian Reform and Art. Recent research has brought to light the importance of the Gregorian reform from the standpoint of the history of art, in particular of iconography.

In Rome itself, it is hardly surprising to find traces of an artistic activity designed to perpetuate the memory of the papal triumph in the wake of the Investiture Controversy. Thus, in an audience hall at the Lateran Palace, Callistus II had the reforming popes shown trampling underfoot the antipopes put forward by the emperors. Here, for the first time, the popes were represented frontally sitting enthroned, wearing the *pallium* and tiara, kicking the antipopes as they lay on the ground in the ancient iconographic posture of the vanquished. Furthermore, Callistus II had himself depicted on his throne, with Emperor Henry V at his side and along with the pope holding a long roll of parchment showing the concordat of Worms. Next door, in the chapel of St. Nicholas, was a fresco of the Virgin and Child, in the style of a former icon venerated in Rome. On either side of the group is the series of reforming popes, from Alexander II to Callistus II, together with popes from the earliest days of the Church (PETER, SILVESTER, ANACLETUS, LEO THE GREAT, and Gregory the Great). Thus, images clearly referring to recent events were displayed alongside iconographic reference to the model offered by the first popes. In a more subtle way, the desire to return to the values of the *Ecclesia primitiva* also inspired, in other paintings and mosaics, the return to an iconography and forms suggested by antiquity. One example is the apsidal mosaic in S. Clemente in Rome. In this way, the Gregorian ideal of *Renovatio Ecclesiae* found a place in Rome in an artistic movement characterized by a renaissance of antique and paleo-Christian art.

Outside Rome, it is more difficult to identify what, in the great vogue of Roman art, is incontestably owing to the direct inspiration of the Gregorian reform. One of the surest trails can be followed by studying the actions of certain protagonists of reform and their role as associates of the movement. For instance, Nicholas II, while still only bishop of Florence, had the church of S. Lorenzo built in the paleo-Christian style. Likewise, Desiderius, abbot of Monte Cassino and the future Pope Victor III, had the basilica of the great abbey rebuilt and decorated in imitation of the paleo-Christian basilicas of Rome. It is appropriate, too, to study works emanating from significant sources: Rome, Monte Cassino, exempt abbeys such as Cluny and its daughter institutions, or the Trinity of Vendôme under the abbacy of the cardinal abbot Geoffrey, and so on. It is evident, then, that the reforming prelates attached considerable importance to art as an expression of their ideal and as a way of edifying the faithful. In the early years of the reform, they set artists to copying antique and paleo-Christian forms as a way of re-creating the framework of the *Ecclesiae primitivae forma*, both in the architectural domain and in that of carved or painted decoration as at Cluny or Berzé-la-Ville. They also encouraged artists to work on more complex iconographic subjects: the personification of *Ecclesia*, pontifical iconography, the representation of Sts. Peter and Paul, the *Traditio legis*, and Christological and, especially, Eucharistic subjects, etc. A determining role in the iconographic flowering of the 11th to 12th centuries and in what is customarily termed the "12th-century renaissance" can unquestionably be assigned to the Gregorian reform.

Pierre Toubert

Bibliography

Alberigo, G. *Cardinalato e Collegialità. Studi sull'ecclesiologia tra l'XI e il XIV secolo*, Florence, 1969.

Blumenthal, U. *The Investiture Controversy: Church and Monarchy from the Ninth to the Twelfth Century*, Philadephia, 1988.

Blumenthal, U. *Papal Reform and Canon Law in the Eleventh and Twelfth Centuries*, Brookfield, Vt., 1998.

Capitani, O. *Tradizione ed interpretazione: dialettiche ecclesiologiche del sec. XI*, Rome, 1990.

Cowdrey, H. E. J. *The Age of Abbot Desiderius: Montecassino, the Papacy, and the Normans in the Eleventh and Early Twelfth Centuries*, Oxford, 1983.

Cowdrey, H. E. J. *The Cluniacs and the Gregorian Reform*, Oxford, 1970.

Cowdrey, H. E. J. *Pope Gregory VII, 1073–1085*, Oxford, 1998.

Cushing, K. G. *Papacy and Law in the Gregorian Revolution: The Canonistic Work of Anselm of Lucca*, Oxford, 1998.

Das Papstwahldekret von 1059. Überlieferung und Textgestalt, ed. D. Jasper, Sigmaringen, 1986 ("*Beitr. z. Gesch. u. Quellenk. des MA*," 12).

Diversorum patrum sententie sive Collectio in LXXIV titulos digesta, ed. J. T. Gilchrist, Vatican City, 1973 ("*Monumenta Iuris Canonici. Series B: Corpus Collectionum*" I).

The epistolae vagantes of Pope Gregory VII, ed. and trans. H. E. J. Cowdrey, Oxford, 1972.

Fliche, A. *La Réforme grégorienne*, Louvain-Paris, 3 vols., 1924–37 ("Spicilegium sacrum Lovaniense," *Études et documents*, 6, 9, 16).

Investiturstreit und Reichsverfassung, ed. J. Fleckenstein, Sigmaringen, 1973 ("Vortr. u. Forsch.," 17).

Jordan, K. *Die Entstehung der römischen Kurie. Ein Versuch mit Nachtrag*, Darmstadt, 1962.

Kitzinger, E. "The Gregorian Reform and the Visual Arts: A Problem of Method," *TRHS*, 5, XXII (1972), 87–102.

Ladner, G. B. *Images and Ideas in the Middle Ages*, Rome, 1983, 2 vols. ("Storia e Letteratura," 155–6).

MGH, Die Briefe der deutschen Kaiserzeit, IV., 1–3: *Die Briefe des Petrus Damiani*, ed. K. Reindel, Munich, 1983–9.

MGH, Epist. sel., 2. *Das Register Gregors VII. (Gregorii VII Registrum)*, ed. E. Caspar, Berlin, 1920–3, 2 vols.

MGH, SS, Libelli de lite imperatorum et pontificum saeculis XI. et XII. conscripti, ed. E. Dümmler et al., Hannover, 1891–7, repr. anast., 1956–7.

Miccoli, G. *Chiesa Gregoriana. Ricerche sulla Riforma del secolo XI*, Florence, 1966.

Mirbt, C. *Die Publizistik im Zeitalter Gregors VII.*, Leipzig, 1894.

Robinson, I. S. *Authority and Resistance in the Investiture Contest*, New York, 1978.

Studi Gregoriani per la storia di Gregorio VII e della Riforma gregoriana, ed. G. B. Borino, Rome, I–XIII (1947–89).

Tellenbach, G. *Libertas, Kirche und Weltordnung im Zeitalter des Investiturstreites*, Stuttgart, 1936, Eng. trans. R. F. Bennett, Oxford, 1939.

Toubert, P. *Un art dirigé, Réforme grégorienne et iconographie*, Paris, 1990.

Toubert, P. "Église et État au XIe siècle: la signification du moment grégorien pour la genèse de l'État moderne," *État et Église dans la genèse de l'État moderne*, Madrid, 1986, 9–22.

Ullmann, W. *The Growth of Papal Government in the Middle Ages*, London, 3rd ed., 1970.

Violante, C. *Studi sulla Christianità medievale*, Milan, 1972.

Werner, E. *Pauperes Christi. Studien zu sozial-religiösen Bewegungen im Zeitalter des Reformpapsttums*, Leipzig, 1956.

REFORMATION (1517–65). Martin Luther's profuse and extremely varied writings devote a substantial amount of space to polemical representations of the papacy—some have said that the reformer's whole life (1483–1546) was a war with Rome. However, adherence to this one view runs the considerable danger of reducing the Reformation merely to its ecclesiological dimension. To concentrate on this half-century of religious crisis is also to risk neglecting the centuries-long duration of the "age of reform" (from the 13th to the first decades of the 17th century), as well as its complexity, for this period saw the establishment of the anthropological, political, and cultural concepts on which modern Europe is based. It is a mistake to forget that the Reformation is only a particular episode of that long, complex evolution. Here, the length of this period as well as its political implications will be kept in mind, but the cycle of the eight pontificates of this half-century is what is of special interest as marking the progress of the movement for reform. These pontificates range from the period of polemical debate, with LEO X (1513–21), through the period of rupture, with HADRIAN VI (1522–3) and CLEMENT VII (1523–34), up to that of the forming of denominations, which began with PAUL III (1534–49) and was well established by the time of the death of PIUS V (1559–65).

From Polemics to Rupture. According to the collective Protestant memory, long reinforced by official historiography, the Reformation began on 31 October 1517. That was the day on which, in the Saxon city of Wittenberg, Dr. Martin Luther, an Augustinian Hermit and professor of theology, posted ninety-five theses essentially condemning INDULGENCES. Here, Luther noted that indulgences never guaranteed salvation or sanctification and that God alone could pardon the penitent sinner. Originally conceived for a university debate, Luther's Latin theses were rapidly translated, printed, and disseminated throughout Germany, and reached a huge audience that was immediately fired with admiration for the Wittenberg theologian. The fact is that, beyond Luther's criticism of the practice of indulgences, certainly radical in its formulation but in no way previously unheard of, the theses had an implicitly "political" content, since they justified the territorial states' refusal of all external interference, notably in the matter of levying taxes. The theses also had a "national" dynamic, echoing the "complaints of the German nation" concerning the pecuniary demands of the Roman Curia.

While the swift reaction on the part of the local and Roman authorities seems to show that they were aware of what was at stake, clearly no one in authority understood the strength of conviction behind a message the immediate thrust of which was in no way rupture with Rome—not Albert of Brandenburg, archbishop of Mainz, to whom Luther sent the text of his theses in vain; nor the Dominican Johann Tetzel, entrusted with preaching indulgences, who invoked the authority of the Church; nor even Johann Eck, professor at the University of Ingolstadt, who also emphasized the problem of authority in the Church and hence for the papacy, and drew Luther into a territory from which he would never emerge; nor, in Rome, Silvester Prierias, who in June 1518 wrote a *Dialogue on the Bold Affirmations of Luther Relative to the Power of the Pope*, to which Luther replied by opposing the infallibility of Sacred Scripture to papal INFALLIBILITY; nor even Cardinal Cajetan, the pontifical legate, who met Luther in Augsburg in October 1518. And yet, if he was already questioning the authority dispensed by the pope, Luther at that time was far from breaking with the Roman Church. For example, the day after the Augsburg meeting he wrote a pamphlet entitled *From the Ill-Informed Pope to the Better-Informed Pope*. The moderate tone, however, was not long in deteriorating. In a debate organized in Leipzig (June–July 1519), under pressure from Eck, Luther declared that the Church had no need of an earthly leader since Christ was its head, and the rock on which it was founded was faith in Christ, not in the successor of Peter. The primacy of the Church of Rome was not an article of faith, nor were the general councils infallible.

The four great reforming writings of 1520 allow us to trace the outlines of Luther's conception of the papacy. In June, in his *On the Papacy of Rome*, Luther affirmed that papal power is neither absolute nor granted by divine right and declared that the pope himself is also subject to the authority of Sacred Scripture. In August, in his *Manifesto to the German Nobility*, he attacked the three bulwarks of the "Romanists": the medieval thesis of the superiority of clerical power to secular power, the pope's claim to possess a binding interpretation of Scripture, and his power alone to convene and confirm a council. Against these claims, Luther set the principles of universal priesthood, of the intelligibility of Scripture, and of the ecclesial responsibility of the nobility. In his *Prelude to the Babylonian Captivity of the Church*, Luther affirmed that the sacraments had become a means of subjection as administered by priests. He reduced them to two, baptism and the Eucharist, and denounced the doctrines of transubstantiation, of Eucharistic sacrifice, and of communion under one species. Finally, in his *Treatise on Christian Freedom* (October 1520), together with a letter dedicated to Leo X, Luther set forth his own doctrine, based on the opposition between the spiritual freedom and the servitude of the Christian: "The Christian is a free man, master of all things and subject to no man. The Christian is an obedient servant, he is subject to all." After the election of Charles V as emperor (June 1519), the Roman Curia completed the delayed procedure for dealing with the elector of Saxony. The bull *Exsurge Domine* of 15 June 1520, published in Germany on 17 June with the help of Johann Eck and known in Wittenberg by 3 October, censured forty-one of Luther's theses. The bull was publicly burnt in Wittenberg, along with many scholastic works and works of canon law, on 10 December of that year. On 3 January 1521, with the bull *Decet romanum pontificem*, Luther and his supporters were excommunicated. The break was made.

The Shattering of the Christian World and the Consolidation of the States (1521–35). On 18 May 1521, the diet of Worms ratified the excommunication. Luther was placed under the ban of the Holy Roman Empire—which he took lightly, being protected by the elector of Saxony—and the theological confrontation became the stuff of politics. Lutheran ideas began to spread, first among the urban populations, to the point that some have called the Reformation an "urban happening." This was the case in Saxony and Thuringia—in Wittenberg, of course, but also Zwickau and Erfurt—and especially in the free imperial cities of Upper Germany, Nuremberg, Augsburg, Schwäbisch Hall, and, above all, Strasbourg. The same happened in Switzerland, particularly Zurich, where on 29 January 1523, the municipal council itself organized the first of several debates. On this occasion, Zwingli (1484–1531) wrote sixty-seven theses teaching that faith is born through the direct inspiration of the Spirit, without the mediation of the Word. Thus the Reformation was officially introduced. In 1525, the mass was suppressed and replaced by a highly austere service. A sort of imperial papacy was instituted, as evidenced by matrimonial regulations. The movement also won ground in Bern (1528), Saint Gall (1528), and Basel (1529). Despite the resistance of the central rural cantons, which in 1526 organized a debate in pro-Catholic Baden, the Reformation continued to spread until the Protestants suffered a military defeat at Cappel (October 1531). The defeat fixed, for several centuries to come, the confessional boundary in Switzerland. These urban reformations sometimes took a radical form, ranging from iconoclastic practices, as at Wittenberg and Zurich, through the establishment of Anabaptist communities—in Zurich and Strasbourg—and even that of a new Jerusalem, as at Münster in Westphalia (1534–5), to the detriment of nascent or established orthodox groups.

The clarion call of reform also found an answering echo in certain social groups whose identity was being threatened or was still in formation. These were the clergy, who provided the first battalions of preachers; the order of Knights of the Empire, who, hurt by the rise of the territorial states, took up arms in 1522–3; and the peasant communities, eager to defend their liberties, who rose up in 1524–6 and were severely put down by the princely armies, having been disavowed by Luther. The Reformation thus would offer the territorial states a way of showing their independence from the emperor, and at the same time would bring their populations—who were "visited" and "taught"—to order and obedience. This politicization of the religious crisis was soon to make of Luther's supporters a force with which the emperor, then warring with France and the Ottoman Empire, had to come to terms. This was the situation in 1526, at the diet of Speyer. Charles V, at war with Francis I, was forced to accommodate the Lutherans, especially since the defeat at Mohacs by the Turks had revived the specter of the infidel. Three years later, in 1529, at the second diet of Speyer, the emperor's measures caused several princes and cities to "protest" his hostility toward the Reformation. The diet of Augsburg, which took place the following year, provided the opportunity, at the emperor's request, for a first "confession of faith" on the part of the reformers. This was drawn up in non-polemical fashion by Melanchthon, though it failed to find favor with the Catholic theologians, who hastily came up with a *Confutatio*. The Protestant camp even formed a military organization (the Schmalkaldic League, 1531), with which the emperor was forced to negotiate on 23 July 1532 (the treaty of Nuremberg). Certain states joined the Protestant camp at the time: Mecklenburg (1533), Pomerania and Württemberg (1534), Brandenburg and the duchy of Saxony (1539).

Beyond the empire, in the northern European lands, which were far from Rome and poorly integrated into an excessively Latin Christendom, the ideas of reform would also help raise national consciousness. In Denmark, the Reformation took root thanks to the preaching of Hans Tausen and the support of King Frederick I (1523–33), whose son, Christian III (1534–59), ensured the victory of the movement. An ecclesiastical ordinance, drawn up by Johann Bugenhagen (1485–1558), gave the Church a Lutheran constitution that resembled an imperial papism (1537). By contrast, in Norway and Iceland, both under the Danish crown, the Reformation was brought in by force and Catholic resistance took on a national coloration. In Sweden, on the other hand, the new ideas were spread abroad by the brothers Olaf and Lawrence Petersen. Here, too, the movement took up the "national" cause. At the diet of Västerås, King Gustav I Vasa decreed the free preaching of the Gospel (1527). Yet the Reformation was implanted slowly, with the adaptation to the new ideas taking more than a century. Last, Lutheran ideas spread in the Baltic countries and in Finland. In the east, though the city of Riga espoused the Reformation in 1523, the grand master of the Teutonic Knights, Albert of Brandenburg, secularized his order's lands and, by bringing in the Reformation, formed them into the duchy of Prussia. Lutheran ideas were also welcomed in the rest of Europe, particularly in England, France, Spain, and Italy, though they did not give rise to a mass movement there, at least during the first two decades of the Reformation.

The papacy was helpless to stem the tide. Hadrian VI's desires for reform—he sent the nuncio Chieregati to the diet of Nuremberg (1522–3) to make public acknowledgment of the sins of the Church—disturbed the supporters of the old order but failed to convince those of the evangelical movement. Clement VII's attitude was quite different. He favored political action—at the risk of drawing the papacy into bloody conflicts (the sack of Rome by the imperial troops in 1527)—and refused to hold a council, finally managing to discredit the papacy in the eyes of the people, who looked for conduct more appropriate in a spiritual leader. Accordingly, it is not to be wondered at that the image of the papacy continually declined in Protestant thinking, to the point of being confused with that of the ANTICHRIST. Evoked for the first time in one of Luther's letters, dated 18 December 1518, this theme was developed in his text against the bull of excommunication (*Adversus execrabilem Antichristi bullam*). To Luther, the pope spoke against Christ and instead of Christ. The proof, according to him, was the Roman Church's affirmation of the sacrificial nature of the mass. The pope is often paralleled with the Turks. These represent the secular Antichrist, and the pope is the spiritual Antichrist. He claims for himself the interpretation of Holy Scripture and does not allow Scripture to be his judge. He imposes new laws and places them on the same level as the Word of God. Finally, he attacks justification by faith in imposing on Christians the obligation to obey him if they wish to be saved.

Alongside these theological writings, in Latin and meant to be read by professionals, there appeared writings in the vernacular, frequently accompanied by satirical engravings, which were meant to be read by the people. One example is the *Passional Christi und Antichristi*, published in Wittenberg in 1521, with engravings by Cranach. Here, the papacy was presented as the reign of the Antichrist, announcing the end of a world turned upside down. Two years later, the engravings accompanying a new pamphlet drawn up by Luther and Melanchthon showed the pope, in irreverent fashion, in the form of a donkey or a calf.

The Beginnings of Orthodoxies and Denominationalism. Although it did not register in the behavior of the Roman people, the election of Paul III marked a turning point in the history of the papacy. It indicated not so much the end of the Renaissance as the beginnings of a new legitimation based on emphasis on religious authority. The turning point was marked by the establishment of a papal state similar to the other territorial states (with the development and rationalization of the administration, the rise of diplomatic and military potential, and heavier taxation), the strengthening of the power residing in the family (nepotism), and a growing investment in things cultural (books, the arts, festivities). Yet there was no stemming the progress of an extremely variform Reformation. Charles V was confronted with the failure of a religious policy founded on constraint and the hope of a council. That hope was negated by the splitting up of faiths, the political tensions among states (especially France and the Holy Roman Empire), and the ill will of the papacy. Accordingly, the emperor attempted in the 1540s to find a theological, and German, solution.

This was the great period of theologians' colloquies—without Luther—in Haguenau, Worms, and Regensburg (1540–1), where, in the presence of the legate Contarini, agreement seems to have been reached on the thorny problem of justification. In the wake of these efforts, which proved fruitless, the emperor once again was tempted to take the initiative, seeing the weakening of the Protestant camp (the neutralization of Philip of Hesse on account of his bigamy, and the defection of Maurice of Saxony). His arms prevailed at Mühlberg (24 April 1547), allowing him at the diet of Augsburg in 1548 to put forward a compromise, the Interim, which satisfied no one. With the treaty of Passau (1552), which was concluded with the Protestant camp, once again commanded by Maurice of Saxony, the Interim was suspended. In 1555, the diet of Augsburg sanctioned the religious division of the empire into Catholics on the one hand and

supporters of the Augsburg Confession on the other, and consecrated the authority of temporal power in the territories.

In 1536, the same year that John Calvin (1509–64) published his *Institutes of the Christian Religion* and settled in Geneva, that city had officially adopted the Reformation. Calvin, exiled in 1538 for the intransigence of his thinking, returned to Geneva after three years of exile in Strasbourg. Although he still faced resistance from various sections of the population, he imposed his will, making the city a Church-city, a "Protestant Rome." Like Luther's movement, Calvinism spread throughout Europe, at first in France, where it followed the Lutheran tidal wave. Toward 1561, after the failure of the Colloquy of Poissy and on the eve of the wars of religion, France had more than 670 reformed churches including perhaps close to a quarter of the population, in spite of Henry II's repressive measures. In 1559, the first national synod of French reformed Churches was held, which drew up a *Discipline* and accepted a *confession de foi*. In 1571, this became known as the Confession of La Rochelle.

Calvinism also touched Germany, in particular the Palatinate of the elector Frederick III (the catechism of Heidelberg, 1563) and the Rhineland, where refugees from the Low Countries gathered. In Scotland, Calvin's ideas took root, in a more democratic formulation owed to John Knox (ca. 1505–72), and gave birth to the Presbyterian Church.

Calvinism, with its rigorous stress on predestination, quickly became the dominant religion in the Netherlands. Here, it expressed the aspirations of a people eager to defend its traditional liberties against the "absolutist" claims of the king of Spain, Philip II, the champion of Catholic renewal. At the eastern frontier of Europe, the movement also spread to Poland, where it found an echo among the nobility, who were numerous, cultivated, and politically ambitious, and to Hungary and Bohemia, where it gave the nobility a weapon with which to stand up to the reinforcement of Habsburg power.

But without any doubt it was in England that the reform movement would best express "national" aspirations. Moreover, it at once took on an anti-Roman cast, traditional in that country, while the theological options, long indecisive, were relegated to the background. An additional factor was the domestic difficulties that in 1527 impelled Henry VIII (1509–47) to shake off papal tutelage in order to secure the annulment of his marriage to Catherine of Aragon. His claim was dismissed in 1530, and a year later the king had Parliament endow him with the title of Supreme Head of the Church of England, while the ecclesiastical tribunal of Canterbury invalidated his marriage to Catherine (1533). The king's secret marriage to Anne Boleyn was then made public.

When Clement VII declared the tribunal's two decisions null and void and threatened Henry VIII with excommunication, the king replied with the vote, in Parliament, of the Act of Supremacy (1534). In 1536, while the monasteries were being suppressed, a confession of faith in the Ten Articles indicated a rapprochement with Lutheran thinking, confirmed by the royal injunctions of 1536 to 1538, which provoked uprisings in the population (the pro-Catholic Pilgrimage of Grace). In 1538, Paul III excommunicated the king and freed his subjects from their oath of loyalty. The Six Articles of 1539 reflected a retreat to a formulation closer to Catholicism. The King's Book of 1543 is even resolutely anti-Protestant. Thus "Anglicanism" represented an institutional separation from Rome, a kind of GALLICANISM, with no clear break with traditional doctrine.

A new stage was reached with Edward VI (1547–53). At first, the Six Articles were repealed, the situation of Catholics was alleviated, the law against heretics was abolished, and a Prayer Book preserving most of the traditional liturgy was published in 1549, though it met strong resistance in the western part of the country. In 1552, a second Prayer Book appeared, which owed much to the theology of Martin Bucer (1491–1551). A new confession of faith in Forty-Two Articles was next promulgated (1553). Mary Tudor's reign (1553–8) represents a major break, not so much because of its immediate but short-lived antireform measures (recatholicization, at times "bloody," of the kingdom, and her marriage in 1554 to Philip II of Spain) as because of its long-term effects on the English collective memory (tenacious antipapism and anti-Spanish sentiment). Elizabeth's reign (1558–1603) consolidated the Anglican reform for all time. Renouncing the title of Supreme Head of the Church of England, she became its "Governor" (1559). The 1552 Prayer Book and the Act of Supremacy were reestablished by Parliament (1559), and the anti-Catholic legislation of 1534 was once again enforced. In 1563, the bishops defined the Thirty-Nine Articles, which replaced the Forty-Two Articles and constitute the official confession of faith to this day. Anglicanism was definitively established. Still close in its practices to a Catholicism that was nevertheless totally marginalized on English soil, and of Protestant inspiration from its conception, it did not wholly satisfy the spiritual aspirations of those who soon sought in Puritanism, and later in the Nonconformist Churches, more substantial nourishment.

The papacy took upon itself the Reformation it had been unable to check. Under Paul III, it now threw itself into a movement for religious reform. Even more than the reform of the Curia, which was once again entrusted to a cardinals' commission but had to confront the practice of plurality and the power of nepotism and patronage, the long-delayed decision to hold a council shows the depth of the change (2 June 1536, the bull of convocation of the council in Mantua). True, the first anticipated result—the extirpation of HERESY—came up against the refusal of the Protestants to attend a council that had been convened precisely in order to condemn them. At the request of the elector Johann Frederick of Saxony, Luther then drew up the Articles of Schmalkalden reaffirming the Protestant positions: the pope "is not *jure divino*, that is to say, by virtue of the Word of God, the head of the whole of Christianity, for that belongs to one alone, namely Jesus Christ, but only the bishop or the pastor of the Church of Rome and of those who, voluntarily or out of obedience to a human institution (that is, to a temporal institution), have attached themselves to him, not so as to be subject to him as to a master, but to be at his side like brothers." Luther's attitude remained constant even when, after the peace of Crécy between Charles V and Francis I (September 1544), it was at last possible to hold the council of TRENT. At that time, a year before his death, Luther published one of the harshest attacks on the papacy, *Against the Papacy in Rome, an Institution of the Devil* (*Wider das Papstum zur Rom vom Teufel gestiftet*). It includes nine engravings (ten in certain editions). Assiduously chosen by Luther, they depict the diabolical origin of the papacy. The pope is once again represented in the form of a donkey in order to convey the monstrous character of the papacy, which is accused of sexual dissoluteness, hermaphroditism, and sodomy. One of the engravings shows the pope astride a sow, an image of the council forever promised and deferred, and now useless because "filthy," as the caption explains. It is the ultimate illustration of visceral antipapist feeling, which for several centuries would be one of the components of Lutheran orthodoxy.

From 1545 to 1547, that is, in the preliminary stages, the council concentrated on the problems posed by Luther: Revelation, original sin, justification, the sacraments, the priesthood. During the pontificate of JULIUS III (1550–5), in the second stage, in which a delegation of German Protestants took part to no avail from 1551 to 1552, the council dealt with the Eucharist, confession, and the sacrament of the sick. Finally, after a long gap corresponding to the pontificates of MARCELLUS II (1555) and PAUL IV (1555–9), in its third and last stage the council took up the sacrament of holy orders, purgatory, indulgences, and the cult of the saints. The time for counterattack had come. This relied on a growing control of the people (the INDEX of prohibited books in 1559 and 1565, and reinforcement of the INQUISITION where political power and public opinion tolerated it), on a redefinition of orthodoxy (the Tridentine profession of faith in 1564, the CATECHISM in 1565), a standardization and romanization of liturgical practices, and a genuine investment in reform (from the founding of the Society of Jesus in 1540 to the development of new collective or individual forms of devotion). Choosing as its first arena the Latin part of the old Christendom, which had remained intact throughout, the counterattack next moved to the empire, following the ancient marks of the limes, and then launched into the reconquest of surrounding territories such as Poland (1564).

Martin Luther's criticisms—the words of a theologian, quickly disseminated and amplified thanks to printing and translation into the vernacular languages—spread like wildfire throughout the Germanic world and even to the limits of the Christian world, becoming an ever more powerful force to reckon with in the political, social, and cultural spheres.

As for the ecclesiastical authorities, conscious as they were of the interests that were calling into question even the development of the political side of a papacy about to spread its wings, like most of the European states they misjudged the magnetic attractiveness of the Reformation message. This message had broken away from the ecclesial sphere and caused the Christian world to burst apart, reactivating the old fault line that divided the Latin from the Anglo-Saxon, legitimizing "national" affirmations, and giving rise to new social and cultural identities. Long on the defensive, the papacy finally emerged renewed from a conflict that forced it to rethink the development of its spiritual side. It was a protracted, slow process that ended only in the 19th century. Yet it did not call a halt to the shattering of a Christian world henceforward based on a plurality of confessions, a multiplicity of nations, and a diversity of cultural models.

Gérald Chaix

Bibliography

Bast, R. J., and Gow, A. C., eds. *Continuity and Change: The Harvest of Late Medieval and Reformation History: Essays Presented to Heiko A. Oberman on His 70th Birthday*, Leiden and Boston, 2000.

Bäumer, M. *Martin Luther und der Papst*, Münster, 1970 (*Katholisches Leben und Kirchenreform im Zeitalter der Glaubensspaltung*, 30).

Bizer, E. *Luther und der Papst*, Munich, 1958 (*Theol. Existenz heute*, 69).

Bossy, J. *Christianity in the West, 1400–1700*, Oxford, 1985.

Brady, T. A. Jr., *Turnings Swiss: Cities and Empire, 1450–1550*, Cambridge, 1985 (*Cambridge Studies in Early Modern History*).

Chaunu, P. *Églises, culture et Société (1517–1620). Essai sur Réforme et Contre-réforme*, Paris, 1981.

Chaunu, P. *Le Temps des Réformes*, Paris, 1975.

Constant, G. *La réforme en Angleterre. Le schisme anglican. Henri VIII*, Paris, 1930.

Delumeau, J. *Catholicism Between Luther and Voltaire*, Philadelphia, 1977; *Naissance et affirmation de la Réforme*, 4th ed., Paris, 1981.

Dickens, A. G. *The English Reformation*, 2nd ed., London, 1967.

Elton, G. R., ed. *The Reformation 1520–1559*, Cambridge, 1990.

Evans, G. R. *Problems of Authority in the Reformation Debates*, Cambridge, 1992.

Greengrass, M. *The Longman Companion to the European Reformation c. 1500–1618*, London and New York, 1998.

Johnston, A. *The Protestant Reformation in Europe*, London and New York, 1991.

Kingdon, R. M. *Church and Society in Reformation Europe*, London, 1985.

Léonard, E. C. *Histoire générale du protestantisme*, 1, Paris, 1961.

Lienhard, M. *Martin Luther. Un temps une vie un message*, Paris, Geneva, 1983.

Lindberg, C. *The European Reformations*, Oxford, 1996.

McClung Hallmann, B. *Italian Cardinals, Reform, and the Church as Property*, Berkeley–Los Angeles–London, 1985 (*Publications of the UCLA Center for Medieval and Renaissance Studies*, 22).

Oberman, H. A. *The Dawn of the Reformation: Essays in Late Medieval and Early Reformation Thought*, Grand Rapids, 1992.

Oberman, H. A. *The Impact of the Reformation*, Grand Rapids, Mich., 1994.

Ozment, S. *Protestants: The Birth of a Revolution*, New York, 1993.

Pettegree, A., ed. *The Early Reformation in Europe*, Cambridge and New York, 1992.

Prodi, P. *Il Sovrano pontifice—un corpo e due anima: la Monarchia papale nella prima et à moderna*, Bologna, 1982, Eng. trans., Cambridge, 1987.

Scribner, B. *For the Sake of Simple Folk: Popular Propaganda for the German Reformation*, Cambridge, 1981; "Demons, Defecation, and Monsters: Popular Propaganda for the German Reformation," *History Today*, 1982 (repr. in *Popular Culture and Popular Movements in Reformation Germany*, London, 1987, 277–99).

Stauffer, R. *La Réforme*, Paris, 1970.

Venard, M. *Histoire de la France réligieuse*, vol. 1: XVI–XVIIIe siècle, Paris, 1988, 222–63.

Vogler, B. *Le Monde germanique et helvétique à l'époque des réformes, 1517–1618*, 2 vols., Paris, 1981 (*Regards sur l'histoire*, 40–1).

REGALIA. The term regalia first appeared in the 13th century to denote a type of intervention on the part of the king of France in the life of the Church in his kingdom—his right to administer the revenues of a diocese when the see was vacant (later called a "temporal regalia"). From that, though in a more limited number of cases, derived his right to appoint bishops to benefices without the care of souls, essentially canonries (called in the 17th century the "spiritual regalia").

That definition must immediately be qualified on several counts. Until the 15th century, the regalia could also be applied to certain large abbeys. In addition, the regalia is not, etymologically, a "royal right" but rather the right to exercise, directly and temporarily, the "royal rights" (regalia) considered as delegated to a prelate and his Church. Because of this, all the great territorial rulers were able to dispose of it, the reserving of the regalia to the king of France alone being one of the many aspects of the growth of monarchical power. Thus, in 1180, the Capetian king could (in theory) exercise the right over twenty-six episcopal sees. At the same time, however, the Plantagenet king managed to confer it on twenty-eight bishops holding sees in the French kingdom. Yet by the 14th century the duke of Brittany was, apart from the king, the only prince of the realm who succeeded in exercising it. Finally, and most important, the regal rights could be based only on custom, found juridical justification only at a very late stage, and was claimed as a universal royal right only in the modern era, when in fact its financial return was relatively meager. After constituting a particular and, at times, important part of the royal receipts, the revenues from the regalia were definitively turned over to the Sainte-Chapelle by Charles IX, even though thereafter the money could be used for the prompt financing of various expenses.

Originally, the regalia was the undifferentiated component of the complex of rights the prince could exercise over the ecclesiastical, and in particular the episcopal, patrimony. It was closely tied to the notion that the patrimony went back to an appropriation of goods seized in the public domain (the fisc), then to the right of guardianship exercised by the king over the Churches of the kingdom. The regalia does not really appear until the 12th century, with the development of the written administration, but also with the settling of the INVESTITURE CONTROVERSY. A similarity, on the feudal model, then came about between the endowment of the temporal patrimony on the newly elected prelate (in exchange for his oath of loyalty) and the reinforced right of the prince to ensure the bail (that is, protection as well as actual administration) of the temporal during the vacancy.

In the 12th and 13th centuries, the right of regalia was at the same time better codified, applied more systematically, and clearly distinguished from the right of SPOILS (the institutionalized pillage of the Church's chattels on the death of a bishop), which was often given up in exchange for recognition of the regalia. Applying it, however, was invariably a matter of relative strength. The Capetians always exercised it readily and often, and almost always in the royal domain, on a particularly shifting map. Under Louis VII and Philip Augustus, whereas juridical thinking was beginning to slow the growth of royal power, the sovereign could also relinquish the exercise of his regalian right either in exchange for substantial financial compensation (Arras, Auxerre under Philip Au-

gustus) or as a benevolent measure that was all the less costly in that it applied to sees where royal influence was barely beginning to make itself felt (southwest France).

On the other hand, when the regalia was fully exercised, it seemed to weigh heavily. Evidence of this is in the justifying accounts produced by the royal administrators (custodes regalium), some of which have been preserved and are rich in detail. Another example is the complaints brought to the papacy, in the name of the inalienability of the ecclesiastical patrimony. The regalia was never attacked for its own sake, nor did the 13th-century papacy ever condemn anything but its excessive promptness, when it could raise its voice in addressing so precious an ally (INNOCENT III in 1206–7, GREGORY IX in 1239, NICHOLAS III in 1278, HONORIUS IV in 1285). In 1274, the council of Lyon II forbade any new extension of the regalia. There could be no clearer recognition of its customary legitimacy.

After the brief episode of the quarrel between Philip the Fair and BONIFACE VIII, the AVIGNON papacy adapted itself well to the regalia, especially since it shared the areas of intervention with the king. The latter normally exercised the regalia over thirty-one dioceses (list compiled in the Chamber of Accounts, which now controlled the administration of the royal "domain"). The pope meanwhile took equivalent action in the dioceses of the Midi, whose revenues were called "vacant" (fructus intercalares, fructus medii temporis). In both cases, it was not always a question of good business for finances, royal or papal, which had to pay expenses with revenues raised on the spot at the price of heavy management costs. The accusation, often raised, that the appointment or investiture was delayed so that it could be profited from longer is thus only half based on fact. From the 15th century, the decline in papal fiscality was equaled by the growing influence of the rulers on the affairs of the Gallican clergy ("regalism").

In the modern era, medieval practices continued to be followed (withdrawal of the regalia after the one elected had sworn the oath, abandonment of the regalia against redemption, recognition of customary rights, such as those of the sees of Autun and Lyon, to ensure for themselves and reciprocally the regalia of the vacant seat). But theory became systematized. Royal absolutism took up the last customary exemptions (Angers in 1524, Breton dioceses in 1598), before affirming the extension of royal right to the whole of the kingdom, in 1607 and, later, 1673. This happened on the occasion of the resistance of the two Jansenist bishops of Alet and Pamiers and the last struggle with the papacy, under INNOCENT XI (royal edict of January 1682, prepared and ratified in the Assembly of the Clergy). The regalia disappeared of its own accord with the Civil Constitution of the Clergy, even if, in 1813, Napoleon I still laid an ephemeral claim to it.

Olivier Guyotjeannin

Bibliography

Gaudemet, J. "Régale," *DDC*, 7 (1965), 493–532.

REGION, ECCLESIASTICAL. The ecclesiastical region is a uniting of neighboring ecclesiastical provinces (CODE OF CANON LAW of 1983, c. 433 § 1). The region originated in the VATICAN II council and has no antecedents, either in the canonical tradition or in the Code of 1917. In canonical statutes, the term itself is practically unknown in its current meaning, save for the 18 "conciliar regions" in which the Italian dioceses are grouped (Congregation of Bishops and Regulars, instruction, 24 August 1889). In the first plans of the Vatican II council—where the region was related to plenary councils (Code of 1917, c. 281) and described as a "conciliar region"—it was a division grouping together various ecclesiastical PROVINCES over which the plenary council exercised its power.

After pointing out that "where it seems advantageous, ecclesiastical provinces should be organized into ecclesiastical regions, [whose] organization is to be determined by law," the council fathers invited the conference of bishops to study the question of "fixing the boundaries of such provinces or establishing such regions, according to the norms already laid down for the fixing of diocesan boundaries" and to "submit their plans and proposals to the Apostolic See" (decree *Christus Dominus*, no. 40, 30 and 41).

The first schemas of the revision of the Code of 1983 made the creation of the region obligatory. It was conceived as the combining of all the ecclesiastical provinces of one and the same nation, under the authority of the conference of bishops (for better coordination of relations with the civil powers). It was also given juridical personality *ipso jure*, since the conferences of bishops were beginning to exercise juridical power.

The relation between territory and authority was set up, in these schemas, as follows: An ecclesiastical region would be erected on the national level. It would be headed by a conference of regional bishops, and the regional council would hold regular meetings in the region. In countries having a large number of dioceses, each region could be divided into several districts, grouping together several neighboring ecclesiastical provinces. The ecclesiastical provinces are maintained with a conference of provincial bishops at their head. They can also from time to time hold provincial councils.

R. Castillo Lara, secretary of the commission for the revision of the Code, pointed out that this draft was contrary to the decisions of the council, which did not envisage the obligatory creation of a structure between the ecclesiastical provinces and the supreme authority of the Church. This intermediate structure appeared useless, since the bishops' conferences already filled that role.

Furthermore, it would be dangerous to establish ecclesiastical regions of a sort that would be identified with a country and would automatically have juridical personality, since that would risk encouraging instances of nationalism within the Church.

As a result, the region may be created "if there is a perceived use for it." It was up to the bishops' conference to propose and to the Holy See to proceed to erect it (c. 433 § 1). The Apostolic See may grant the region juridical personality through its own power of government (c. 433 § 2). The region therefore is not, in the Code, a jurisdictional entity placed above the dioceses. The regions vary widely among themselves, depending on whether or not they receive juridical personality; or on whether or not the assembly of bishops of the region is given a power of government; or on whether or not a conference of bishops has been formally constituted in the region, and whether or not it is dependent on another national bishops' conference.

In addition, the norm in force does not contain the idea of a region grouping together dioceses or ecclesiastical provinces that is dependent on the same conference of bishops. There might be groupings of adjacent provinces that belong to areas having numerous particular Churches.

The aim of gathering ecclesiastical provinces into ecclesiastical regions is essentially pastoral: to foster cooperation and common action in the geographical domain corresponding to the particular Churches that belong to it (c. 434). However, the Code contains no disposition that would make the deliberations of the bishops' assembly of the region binding for the bishops that are part of it. This assembly provided for by the Code of 1983 is distinct from the conference of bishops.

The only possible obligation would be that deriving from the *affectus collegialis*, binding the bishops one to another. Moreover, the same canon states expressly that the powers granted by the Code to the bishops' conference "are not within the competence of that assembly," except in the case of special concession by the Apostolic See. An auxiliary bishop may not preside over the conferences of bishops of the ecclesiastical region (Pontifical Commission for the Authentic Interpretation of the Code of Canon Law, reply, 19 January 1988).

The ecclesiastical region is distinct from the so-called conciliar region, which is a combination of several neighboring dioceses, established according to various criteria. In Italy, the regions were designed for the meeting of plenary councils, the annual meetings of bishops, and the study of causes of nullity of marriage. After the Code of 1917, the Consistorial Congregation and the Congregation of the Council considerably modified the way the conciliar regions worked (decree, 15 February 1919). The regional tribunals for matrimonial affairs were also reorganized (*motu proprio Qua cura*, 31 December 1938). After the council, the regional conferences of bishops were reorganized (Regulation of Conferences of Bishops of Ecclesiastical Regions, June 1967).

In France, the assembly of cardinals and archbishops created nine apostolic regions: the Parisian region (now Île-de-France), North, West, Center, Southwest, Midi, Provence-Mediterranean, East-Central, and East (October 1961).

Dominique Le Tourneau

Bibliography

Arrieta, J. I. "Instrumentos supradiocesanos para el gobierno de la Iglesia particular," *Ius Canonicum*, 24 (1984), 607–43; "Provincia y región eclesiástica," *Le nouveau Code de droit canonique. Actes du Vo Congrès international de droit canonique, Ottawa, 1984*, Ottawa, 1986, 607–25.

Bonet, M. "La région ecclésiastique après Vatican II," *L'Année canonique*, XII (1969), 55–63.

Goergen, J. "Die Region," *Österreichisches Archiv für Kirchenrecht*, 30 (1979), 82–131.

Mathorel, F. "La région apostolique française," *L'Année Canonique*, XXIX (1985–6), 281–304.

REGISTERS, PAPAL. By "papal registers" are meant the books into which the CHANCERY entered copies of each letter it sent out. The registers illustrate the workings of the Church's central administration and the way in which its power gradually became centralized. They also provide a picture of the mores of the relevant period as well as the relations of the Church with the civil powers.

It is generally agreed that papal registers were in existence in the 4th century. There is testimony concerning various eras—for example, fourteen papyrus scrolls in the Vatican Archives corresponding to the fourteen years of the pontificate of GREGORY I that were still preserved in the 9th century but are known only today through later compilations. The "register" of JOHN VIII is a partial copy from a later date. The "register" of GREGORY VII, the originality of which is doubtful, is clearly extremely selective. ANACLETUS II and ALEXANDER III also have registers, but it is not until INNOCENT III that the papacy begins systematically to preserve registers on parchment, though these are still highly selective.

There are various sorts of papal registers:

—The Vatican registers. This is the oldest and most important series. Numbering 2,042, they essentially contain apostolic letters. The volumes are arranged according to the succession of the Roman pontiffs and classified in chronological order for each pontificate. They begin with the pontificate of Innocent III, in 1198. However, the series is incomplete. From the 13th century, they are presented, with a few lacunae, in a single series that goes up to 1597, during the pontificate of CLEMENT VIII (1592–1605). These are the Vatican registers, properly speaking.

—The Avignon registers. So called because they were long held in Avignon. Beginning with the pontificate of JOHN XXII (1316–34), they end in 1415 with that of GREGORY XII (1406–15) and number 349 volumes in all. These are the originals of the corresponding Vatican registers. They include *litterae communes* of the Chancery and *litterae secretae* of the Camera. They also contain documents of certain antipopes.

—The Lateran registers. Long deposited in the Lateran Palace, these consist of 2,467 volumes, beginning with the pontificate of BONIFACE IX, in 1389, and ending in 1897, with that of LEO XIII (1878–1903). They concern only Church administration, and do not cover political relations with sovereigns. They are a continuation of the *litterae communes* of the Avignon registers. A substantial portion was lost when the Vatican papers were moved to Paris on Napoleon's orders.

—The registers of PETITIONS: these consist of 7,365 volumes, for the period 1342–1899.

—The registers *della Secretaria Camerae*: a total of 222 volumes, from 1470–1796.

—The registers *della segretaria dei Brevi*: these cover the period from 1566 to 1846, and number 5,660 volumes.

—The registers of the *Brevia Lateranensia*: a collection of 852 volumes, for the period 1490 to 1800.

—The registers of the *Brevia seu epistolae ad principes*: a collection of 292 volumes, for the period 1560 to 1836.

Dominique Le Tourneau

Bibliography

Battelli, G. "Registri pontifici," *EC*, X, Vatican City, 1953, 656–60 (bibliography).

Mollat, G. "Registres pontificaux," *DDC*, VII, Paris, 1965, 536–8.

Rabikauskas, P. *Diplomatica pontifica*, Rome, 4th ed., 1980.

RENAISSANCE HUMANISM AND THE PAPACY. Renaissance humanism was a cultural and scholarly program of studies in the humanities, especially grammar, rhetoric, history, poetry, and moral philosophy, based on their standard ancient writers in Latin and, to a lesser extent, in Greek. Humanists produced many writings dealing with the ancient world, then applied moral principles and social and civic lessons derived from the past to contemporary issues. They also took a critical and historical approach toward all received knowledge, especially that from the Middle Ages. Humanism in its core was neither religious or antireligious, and did not support or reject particular forms of government. It was an educational, cultural, and scholarly program marked by a keen curiosity to understand and evaluate, and a willingness to criticize all human endeavor.

During the Renaissance (1400–1600) the papacy's relationship with humanism and humanists evolved. Many popes and prelates gave humanism and humanists considerable encouragement and support. In the 15th century, the humanists living and working in Rome adapted humanism to circumstances and ideas unique to the papacy and Rome, but they also pursued their own scholarly agendas. From the middle of the 16th century, popes directed humanists toward scholarly activities that would serve the religious aims of Catholicism.

The papacy played no significant role in the early stages of the humanist movement because it was preoccupied with the GREAT SCHISM and other threats to its authority in the early 15th century. NICHOLAS V (1447–55), the first pope to support humanistic learning, began the Vatican Library (*Biblioteca Apostolica Vaticana*) and collected 800 Latin and 353 Greek manuscripts for it. He also brought humanists to Rome to translate or retranslate Greek classical and patristic texts into Latin, believing that this would make accessible to western Christians a large body of Greek material, aiding in the renewal of the Catholic clergy. Nicholas V brought George of Trebizond (1395–1472/3), Lorenzo Valla (1407–57), and other leading humanists to Rome and funded their scholarship or helped them obtain positions in the *Curia Romana* and elsewhere in the city.

These brilliant humanists did not always hold views in accord with those of the papacy. For example, while serving the King of Naples before he came to Rome, Valla published two works highly critical of the papacy and the clergy. The first was his famous *De falso credita et ementita Constantini donatione declamatio* [On the falsely believed and fictitious DONATION OF CONSTANTINE, 1440] which demonstrated that the text in which Emperor Constantine I (d. 337) reputedly had bequeathed his empire to Pope SILVESTER I (314–35) and his successors was an 8th-century forgery. Valla's criticism of the text undermined the papacy's claim to its temporal state and the right to intervene in the affairs of secular governments. His other work (also 1440) rejected the claim that the clerical state gave clergymen a greater possibility of obtaining salvation than laymen. Despite these differences popes and cardinals often overlooked such attacks and hired humanists anyway, because they were original and brilliant scholars. Of course, they did not attack the papacy while in its employ, and they usually participated in some enterprise desired by popes or cardinals. Indeed, after coming to Rome in 1450 Valla initiated modern textual criticism of the Bible with an analysis of the text of the New Testament and produced other studies touching religious issues.

Cardinal Bessarion (1403 or 1408–72), a Greek prelate and humanist who sought unity between the Latin and Greek churches, settled in Rome in 1440. He translated Greek works into Latin and was a firm supporter of Plato's philosophy. As he supported other scholars who did the same, his household became a center for humanistic and scholarly activity.

The immediate successors of Nicholas V did little for humanism. PIUS II (1458–64) was an eminent and prolific humanistic author before becoming pope, but as pope he focused his attention on other causes. Pope PAUL II (1464–71) suppressed the Roman Academy, a group of humanists who met for dinner and literary and historical discussions. Paul II believed the rumor that several members of the academy were irreligious pagans and homosexuals, and that they plotted to overthrow the papal government. He arrested and had several of them tortured, but there was no plot, the academy humanists were not irreligious pagans, and no homosexual activities took place at the meetings. All charges were dropped and the humanists released from prison and restored to their positions within a few months. The Roman Academy came back to life after Paul II's death, and Roman humanism and humanists suffered no permanent damage.

Humanism in Rome again moved forward under the enthusiastic patron SIXTUS IV (1471–84). A traditional Scholastic theologian previously untouched by the new learning, Sixtus IV recognized the importance of supporting humanists as a way to boost papal prestige in the diplomatic and political struggles with Italian civil rulers, who were doing the same. Just as important, Sixtus IV strengthened the Vatican Library, opened its doors to more readers, and appointed the humanist Bartolomo Sacchi (called "il Platina," 1421–81) its first official librarian in 1475. The Vatican Library owes its real beginning as perhaps the world's premier library for the humanities and religious studies to Sixtus IV.

While some popes supported them and others did not, humanists steadily acquired positions in Rome and expanded their activities and influence. Many found employment at good salaries in the *Curia Romana*, possibly the largest bureaucracy in Italy. The *Curia Romana* worked in Latin, the language in which the humanists were so skilled. They were even more valued as the *Curia Romana* switched from medieval to classical Latin. By the second decade of the 16th century, the *Curia Romana* offered nearly 2,000 positions for which humanists were qualified although, of course, they did not fill all of them.

Others found employment as secretaries, advisors, and pedagogues in the households of popes and prelates, especially the twenty or so cardinals who lived in Rome. The papal household grew to a maximum of 2,000 members under LEO X (1513–21), and cardinals had average households of 120, with some considerably larger. The

University of Rome, while never as distinguished as the universities of Bologna and Padua, offered more professorships to distinguished humanists than other universities. It had six to ten humanists in the 1470s, 1480s, and 1490s, and twenty in 1514. Some popes who wanted humanists in Rome to undertake particular scholarly tasks, or to have them on hand in order to compose Latin poems and deliver orations for papal functions, arranged for them to hold university professorships. Positions in the *Curia Romana*, or in the household of the pope or a cardinal or as a university professor, provided income and security while leaving ample time to study and write.

Very few humanists were Romans. Instead, they came as individuals seeking employment or in the entourage of prelates. Some left after a few years, but the majority remained. Because its practitioners were transients, Roman humanism lacked an ideology expressing the values of a particular city, state, or region, as humanism often did for Italian republics and princedoms and northern monarchies. Instead, Roman humanists pursued typical scholarly activities but in ways that emphasized ancient Rome and the papacy.

Roman humanists stressed the importance of classical Latin, and adopted Ciceronian Latin as its perfect expression, but Ciceronianism meant more than style and vocabulary. By writing exclusively in Ciceronian Latin, Roman humanists believed that they could recreate the cultural ideals of ancient Rome in their own time. They sought to revive Cicero's concept of *humanitas*, the knowledge of how to live as a cultivated and morally upright member of society.

The humanists combined their great admiration for ancient Rome with praise for the papacy. They praised and studied ancient Roman culture and civilization and saw the 15th-century papacy as the defender of classical culture. They linked the greatness of ancient Rome to the papacy. Just as ancient Rome had governed the ancient world and had set cultural standards for it, so the modern papacy would lead Renaissance Europe spiritually and would set its cultural principles. Because Roman humanists integrated classical culture and Catholic Christianity, it made perfect sense to them to praise the papacy in Ciceronian Latin and to refer to God as "Jupiter" and the pope as "*Julius Caesar.*"

The union of ancient and papal Rome produced certain emphases in humanists' writings. They wrote theological works, not in traditional medieval Scholastic terminology, but in Ciceronian Latin and from a humanistic rhetorical perspective. Since they saw the fathers of the first centuries of Christianity as an extension of the culture of classical antiquity, they translated Christian patristic writings from Greek into Latin and produced editions of the Latin fathers.

The best expression of the humanistic identification of ancient culture with service to the Renaissance papacy and church was the treatise *De cardinalatu* (1510) by the humanist Paolo Cortesi (1465–1510). Just as Niccolò Machiavelli portrayed the successful prince, and Baldassare Castiglione the perfect courtier, so Cortesi portrayed the humanist cardinal as an ideal Renaissance type. The humanist cardinal should be trained in humanistic studies and should let humanistic knowledge and ideals guide his decisions, especially when serving the pope. In so doing he would advance both classical learning and the interests of the church. Indeed, they were natural partners, in Cortesi's view.

INNOCENT VIII (1484–92), ALEXANDER VI (1492–1503), and PIUS III (1503) did little for or against humanism. By contrast, JULIUS II (1503–13) had numerous humanists in his government and entourage. By this time humanism was accepted as a central feature of the Renaissance papacy. It continued to dominate the cultural life of Rome under the humanistically educated LEO X (1513–21), even though he sometimes supported mediocrities and his profligate spending sowed the seeds of future problems. The two eminent Ciceronian humanists, Pietro Bembo from Venice (1470–cardinal in 1539, d. 1547) and Jacopo Sadoleto from Ferrara (1477–cardinal in 1536, d. 1547) were prominent figures in the papal secretariat.

Popes also supported humanists who lived far from Rome. When these men sent copies of their works ornamented with lavish dedications to popes, the latter normally responded with tangible expressions of gratitude—money, a gift, occasionally a pension. Northern European humanists such as Desiderius Erasmus (c. 1466–1536) confidently expected that popes would lend support in scholarly disputes, and they sometimes did. But Erasmus also savagely attacked papal and clerical abuses, including simony, nepotism, concubinage, and militarism. His criticism of the papacy reached a climax in his *Julius Exclusus* [Julius Excluded from Heaven, written 1513, published 1518], a scathing but very funny satire. It described how St. Peter barred from heaven the armor-clad and bloodstained soldier-pope Julius II because of his many wars and extravagant worldliness. Erasmus also criticized Roman humanists for their alleged paganism and excessive reliance on Ciceronian Latin in his *Ciceronianus* (The Ciceronian, 1528).

Even though the level of support varied from pope to pope, humanism had become so well established that papal Rome was the most important center for humanistic studies in Europe in the 50 years from the beginning of the pontificate of Sixtus IV through the end of that of Leo X. The combination of strong patronage, a large number of major humanists working in Rome, and the writings they produced, made it so.

Then times changed. Roman humanists heartily detested the Dutch pope, ADRIAN VI (1522–3) because he did not spend as freely as his predecessor. CLEMENT VII

(1523–34) was too preoccupied with the military and diplomatic problems of Italy and the Lutheran religious rebellion in northern Europe, to pay much attention to humanism. Then disaster struck: the undisciplined troops of Emperor Charles V sacked Rome in May 1527. Some humanists were killed and many fled during the months of murder, pillage, and desecration that followed. The imperial army did not leave the devastated city until February 1528, and the pope did not return until October. The great age of Renaissance humanism in papal Rome had ended.

As the papacy slowly adjusted to the new age of the Catholic Reformation, it viewed humanism differently. The papacy would no longer support a wide variety of individuals and projects, but only those viewed as important to the mission of the church. The papacy would also prohibit and expurgate works by humanists infected by Protestantism or judged to be overly critical of Catholic practices and clerical abuses.

The transition began with PAUL III (1534–49). While well educated in humanistic studies and a strong supporter of individual humanists, including the Venetian Gasparo Contarini (1483–1542) whom he raised to cardinal, Paul III also summoned the council of TRENT and established the Roman Inquisition in 1542. PAUL IV (1555–9) was too preoccupied with fighting heresy and Spain to pay attention to humanism.

PIUS IV (1559–65) began a new era in the relationship between the papacy and humanism. Well educated in humanistic studies, he could recite long classical Latin passages from memory. More important, Pius IV began a program of papal support for the editing and printing of major patristic and medieval Catholic authors, plus basic liturgical works, prepared according to the highest standards of humanistic historical and philological criticism. He brought Paolo Manuzio (1512–70) to Rome, a talented humanist and an important publisher of classical texts. Pius IV gave Manuzio a considerable sum to establish his press in Rome, which would print the new editions. Thanks to papal subsidies, Manuzio published the works of the Church fathers Gregory of Nyssa, Cyprian, Jerome, and Theodoret, plus the decrees of the Council of Trent, the Tridentine Catechism, and revised Breviary, between 1561 and 1570. Pius IV also supported the humanist Guglielmo Sirleto (1514–85), the Vatican librarian, whom he raised to cardinal in 1565. But Pius IV also issued the Tridentine *Index of Prohibited Books* in 1564, which banned some of Erasmus' works. Indeed, a handful of the same scholars who edited early Christian authors also expurgated humanistic books, such as Erasmus' *Adages*, a collection of proverbs drawn from classical works garnished with the author's commentary attacking contemporary abuses.

Although PIUS V (1566–72) was not particularly sympathetic to humanism, the papal program of Catholic scholarly renewal carried on by scholars with humanistic skills, continued. GREGORY XIII (1572–85) was the most important pope in the program of Catholic scholarship. He supported the preparation of the first edition of the *Martyrologium Romanum* [Roman Martyrology, 1584], a historical account of early Christian martyrs. He asked Carlo Sigonio (c. 1522–84), professor of humanistic studies at the University of Bologna in the papal state, to write a history of the Catholic Church in the late Roman Empire and the early Middle Ages. However, when Sigonio concluded, as had Lorenzo Valla a century earlier, that the Donation of Constantine was fictitious and that papal temporal and spiritual power was not a seamless historical progression but had developed in starts and stops, papal censors forced him to make changes. The discovery of a major catacomb in 1578 led to a flurry of Christian archeological studies carried on by humanist scholars often supported by the papacy and lasting to the end of the century and beyond. By contrast, 15th-century Roman humanists had practically ignored the catacombs because of their obsession with classical archeology.

SIXTUS V (1585–90) and CLEMENT VIII (1592–05) did not support humanistic studies as strongly as their predecessors, but they did see preparation of the revised *Vulgate*, the traditional Latin text of the Bible (a project that had engaged many scholars for years), to completion and publication in 1592. They also supported Cesare Baronio (1538–1607) and his *Annales ecclesiastici* [Annals of the Church, 12 vols., begun in the 1570s, published 1598–1607], a history of the Catholic Church to 1198, with many documents. In 1592 Clement VIII brought the distinguished Platonist Francesco Patrizi (1529–97) to Rome to teach Platonic philosophy at the university. Patrizi's strong anti-Aristotelianism provoked much opposition from Roman Scholastic theologians who relied on Aristotle for the philosophical framework of their theology. Under pressure from the CONGREGATION OF THE INDEX, Patrizi had to make changes to his major Platonic work. Platonism did not prosper in Rome.

In general, popes from PIUS IV onward only supported humanistic scholarly projects, and the humanists who prepared them, when directly related to the history and theology of Catholicism or when documenting Catholic and papal claims in scholarly battles with Protestants. The more eclectic and secular Roman humanism of the period 1450 to 1527 was gone. The Collegio Romano (founded in 1551 and staffed by the Jesuits) became the most important center for teaching humanistic studies, as well as theology and mathematics, in Rome. But humanistic studies at the Collegio Romano served the Jesuit theological program which followed St. Thomas Aquinas. The University of Rome had reopened in 1535, but it was a smaller institution than before and cared little for humanistic studies. Nevertheless, Marc-Antoine Muret (1521–85), one of the most distinguished humanists in Italy, taught there from 1563 until his death. He produced commentaries on Cicero, Horace, Tacitus, and other authors, and pursued a humanistic approach to Roman civil law.

From the pontificate of Nicholas V through the end of the 16th century the papacy and humanism had one of the most mutually supportive and productive relationships ever seen among church, government, and scholars.

Paul F. Grendler

Bibliography

Barberi, F. *Paolo Manuzio e la Stamperia del Popolo Romano (1561–1570) con documenti inediti.* Rome, 1942; rpt. Rome, 1985.

Bignami Odier, J. *La Bibliothèque Vaticane de Sixte IV à Pie XI. Recherches sur l'histoire des collections de manuscripts avec la collaboration de José Ruysschaert,* Vatican City, 1973.

Coluccia, G. L. *Niccolò V umanista. Papa e riformatore: renovatio politica e morale,* Venice, 1998.

D'Amico, J. F. *Renaissance Humanism in Papal Rome. Humanists and Churchmen on the Eve of the Reformation,* Baltimore and London, 1983.

D'Amico, J. F. *Roman and German Humanism, 1450–1550,* Edited by Paul F. Grendler, Aldershot, Eng., 1993.

Fois, M. *Il pensiero cristiano di Lorenzo Valla nel quadro storico-culturale del suo ambiente.* Rome, 1969.

Grafton, A., ed. *Rome Reborn: The Vatican Library and Renaissance Culture,* Washington, D. C., and Vatican City, 1993.

Lebowsky, L. "Bessarione," in *Dizionario biografico degli italiani,* vol. 9, Rome, 1967, pp. 686–696.

Lee, E. *Sixtus IV and Men of Letters,* Rome, 1978.

Miglio, M. *Storiografia pontificia del Quattrocento,* Bologna, 1975.

Monfasani, J. *George of Trebizond. A Biography and a Study of his Rhetoric and Logic,* Leiden, 1976.

O'Malley, J. W. *Praise and Blame in Renaissance Rome. Rhetoric, Doctrine, and Reform in the Sacred Orators of the Papal Court, c. 1450–1521,* Durham, N.C., 1979.

O'Malley, J. W. *Rome and the Renaissance: Studies in Culture and Religion,* London, 1981.

Pastor, 1–24.

Stinger, C. *The Renaissance in Rome.* Bloomington, IN, 1985.

Weiss, R. *The Renaissance Discovery of Classical Antiquity,* Oxford, 1969.

REPRESENTATIONS, DIPLOMATIC. See Nuncio.

RESERVED CASES AND CAUSES.

Definitions. To reserve is the act by which a superior, by virtue of his power of jurisdiction, assumes the exclusive right to treat certain questions, though in practice he may surrender most such cases to a lesser authority. The Roman pontiff possesses full and supreme powers of jurisdiction that he can exercise freely throughout the structure of the Church. He can therefore reserve to his personal judgment certain of the most important causes. This custom has existed from the very first centuries of the Church; St. Cyprian and St. Irenaeus make reference to it, and the council of Arles (314) appealed to the pope to determine the date of Easter in the universal Church.

These reserved causes were called *causae majores* (matters of special gravity) by Innocent I in 404 (*Epist. II, ad Victric. Rotomag.*). The 1917 CODE OF CANON LAW defines them as "matters of special gravity which are reserved, by their nature or by positive right, to the Roman pontiff alone" (c. 220). The distinction between "nature" and "right" is discussed below.

Causes reserved by their nature can be absolute, as in the definition of dogma or the proclamation of a saint, which entails the infallibility of the pope; others can be delegated by the pope; and still others are reserved to the pope only when he deems it opportune to treat them personally or through the Roman CURIA. The bishop is not a simple vicar of the pope: by episcopal ordination, he receives a real power of government, besides those of teaching and sanctification. However, this power can be restricted for the use of the Church or for the good of the faithful in causes which the Roman pontiff's right or decree reserves to the supreme authority of the Church or to some other authority (1983 Code of Canon Law, c. 381 § 1). This corresponds to the canonical tradition and to the disposition of VATICAN II: the diocesan bishop has the faculty of dispensation from the general law "unless a special reserve has been done by the supreme authority of the Church" (decree *Christus Dominus*, no. 8).

Causes reserved in virtue of positive right are more numerous. They normally figure in the Code of Canon Law and fall under five categories: (1) doctrinal causes, such as defense of the faith and morals, dogmatic definition, and proclamation of the blessed and of saints; (2) legislative causes, such as the conclusion of CONCORDATS, the enactment of universal laws, and the power of exemption therefrom; (3) administrative causes, such as the erection of dioceses and other jurisdictional entities of the Church, the nomination of bishops and other prelates, and the creation of Catholic UNIVERSITIES and faculties; (4) judicial causes, such as judgments of heads of state and high ecclesiastic dignitaries, or decisions on certain matrimonial causes; and (5) judiciary causes, such as the lifting of censures reserved to the Holy See.

Reserve of Benefices. Benefices occupy a large place in ancient Church law. Clement IV (1265–8) legitimized an ancient custom by establishing a general and absolute reserve of all benefices that became vacant at the Roman

Curia (decretal *Licet ecclesiarum*, 27 August 1265, *In Sexto*, I, III, tit. II, c. 1). Little by little the Roman pontiffs enlarged the area of reserves, to the point that on the death of Urban V (1370), the papal right to grant benefices was almost total.

The councils of Paris (1396, 1398) demanded the return to common law, and civil governments also protested against this. A royal edict (27 July 1398) abolished papal reservations, withdrawing benefices from the authority of Benedict XII. When Martin V wished to reestablish them (*Rules of the Chancery*, 12 November 1417), he was forced to enter into concordats with the nations represented at the council of Constance (15 April 1418). The council of Basel abolished, with a few exceptions, the reserves not listed in the *Corpus iuris canonici*, dispositions found in the Pragmatic Sanction of Bourges (7 July 1438) and later in the concordat of Bologna with France (1516). Similar dispositions figure in the concordat of WORMS with Germany (1448). These reserves are explained by a concern to end the simoniacal granting of ecclesiastical offices, to remove these offices from the influence of feudal lords, and to encourage a policy of cooperation with the civil authorities.

Reserved Cases. This is a limitation or restriction of jurisdiction that directly affects the confessor, whose jurisdiction was withdrawn in regard to specific sins. The expression "reserved cases" also covers reserved sins and, by extension, reserved censures. The reserve may pertain to these in various combinations: (1) to the sin itself without censure (for example, the sin of a priest who unduly absolved partisans of the French Nationalist and Royalist Group, since, by express order of the Roman pontiff, the penitentiary had declared a special reserve in this sense on 16 November 1928); (2) the sin with censure, the lifting of the censure being within the competence of the superior; (3) a censure that inhibits the receipt of the sacraments and is therefore indirectly linked to the sin; or (4) a censure that does not inhibit the receipt of the sacraments, in which case the sin could be absolved by the confessor, the censure being still effective. The reserve has a twofold purpose: disciplinary, because it aims at ending abuses and safeguarding the common good; and therapeutic, because it distances the faithful from sin by making their absolution more difficult. In the case of censures, the reserve is also an augmentation of the punishment.

From the time of the Decian PERSECUTION, bishops instituted penitentiaries for the confession of apostates (Socrates, *Histoire ecclésiastique*, V, c. XIX). When public penance fell into desuetude, the bishops continued to reserve to themselves the absolution of the most horrible crimes, particularly public ones (second council of Limoges, 1031). Episcopal reserves are therefore a vestige of the former discipline, which reserved reconciliation of penitents to the bishop. The need of bishops to appeal to the pope in the most complicated cases—in particular, by sending homicide cases to Rome so that they could be absolved by the Roman pontiff—gave rise around the 9th century, to papal reserves (Benedict XIV, *De synodo dioecesano*, 1, V, c. IV, n.3). Certain penitents themselves took the road to Rome in the hope of obtaining an easier pardon before the pope was made aware of the censure imposed on them (council of Seligenstadt, c. 18, 1023; council of Limoges, 1031).

The first papal reserve, strictly speaking, goes back to the council of Clermont (c. 10, 1130), which reserved to the pope the absolution of someone who had struck a cleric, a regulation reiterated at the council of Reims (c. 13, 1131), adopted by the second Lateran council (c. 15, 1139) and repeated by Gratian (*Decretum*, caus. XVIII, q. IV, c. 28). A London council (1143) reserved to the pope absolution of those using violence against churches, cemeteries, and clerics. Attacked by Protestants, the council of TRENT reaffirmed the right of reserve of the Roman pontiff and of bishops, a right included in the power of the KEYS (sess. XIV, cap. 7 et c. 11). Sixtus V was the first to reserve to himself a sin to the exclusion of a censure, for a case of SIMONY in the promotion of sacred orders (bull *Sanctum et salutare*, 5 January 1589), which Clement VIII confirmed (bull *Romanum Pontificem*, 28 February 1596). Benedict XIV reserved to himself the sin of someone who falsely accuses a confessor of the crime of solicitation (bull *Sacramentum paenitentiae*, 1 June 1741). Pius IX reorganized the discipline of the reserve and drew up an authoritative list of reserved censures (constitution *Apostolicae Sedis*, 12 October 1869). The Congregation of the HOLY OFFICE modified the conditions of the reserve by ordinaries (instruction of 16 July 1916), a disposition again found in the 1917 Code of Canon Law (c. 893–900).

The code distinguishes sins reserved on account of the sin itself (*ratione sui*) and sins reserved by reason of the censure attached to the sin (*ratione censurae*). Certain sins were reserved *ratione sui* to the local ordinary or to the superior of an exempt religious clerical institution, or to the abbot *sui juris*. The false denunciation of the crime of solicitation in relation to an innocent priest was the only sin reserved *ratione sui* to the Holy See. Added later was the special reserve on the absolution of members of the French Nationalist and Royalist Group. The censures reserved to the Holy See were *simpliciter*, or *speciali modo*, or rather *specialissimo modo*.

The 1983 Code of Canon Law no longer speaks of reserved sins, the reserve having been suppressed at the request of the Apostolic Penitentiary (*Communicationes* 7 [1983], p. 259). The reservation of sins *ratione censurae* has disappeared, since the prohibition of celebrating or receiving the sacraments, which the reserved censures include, concerns only legality, not validity. Similarly, the reserve *ratione sui* has disappeared, given that the previous regulations have not been restated.

Present Legislation. Various kinds of causes fall under the exclusive competence of the Roman pontiff, particularly the right to judge heads of state, cardinals, and papal legates in criminal causes and other causes that he claims for himself (c. 1405 § 1). It falls under the competence of the Roman pontiff to release a petitioner from apostolic chastity (c. 291); to convoke and preside over ecumenical councils and to ratify and promulgate their deliberations (c. 338 and 341); to convoke, preside, conclude, transfer, and dissolve the synod of bishops; to ratify the election of its members, to designate others, and to fix its agenda (c. 344 and 347); to create cardinals (c. 351); to erect particular Churches (c. 373) and to confirm their particular rituals (c. 372 § 2); to nominate bishops or confirm those legitimately elected (c. 377 § 1); to accept or refuse the resignation of a diocesan bishop from his post (c. 401 § 1); to constitute, suppress, or modify ecclesiastical provinces (c. 431 § 3); to establish, suppress, or modify episcopal conferences (c. 449 § 1); to exempt institutes of consecrated life from the authority of the local ordinary (c. 591); to direct and coordinate missionary work (c. 782 § 1); to approve or determine the elements required for the validity of sacraments (c. 841); to concede the power to grant indulgences (c. 995 § 2); to determine the diriment impediments to marriage (c. 1075 § 1); to add a diriment impediment clause to the prohibition of marriage (c. 1077 § 2); to dissolve for just cause an unconsummated marriage between baptized persons or of a baptized partner with an unbaptized partner (c. 1142); to grant special blessings (c. 1169 § 2); to grant dispensations from private vows (c. 1196); to fix the order of sacred time for the universal Church (c. 1244 § 1 and 1246 § 2); to judge certain persons (c. 1405 § 1 and 1406 § 2); and to grant a dispensation in the case of an unconsummated marriage (c. 1698 § 2).

A certain number of censures are reserved to the Apostolic See in the following instances: sacrilege against the Eucharist (c. 1367); physical violence against the person of the pope (c. 1370) or his assassination (c. 1397); absolution of an accomplice in a sin against the sixth commandment (c. 1378 § 1); episcopal consecration without papal approval (c. 1382); and direct violation of the secrecy of the confessional by the confessor (c. 1388 § 1). Other causes reserved to the Apostolic See include the following: the court of the Roman ROTA judges bishops in contentious causes, the primate abbot or abbot superior of a monastic congregation, the moderator of a religious institution of pontifical right, and dioceses and other ecclesiastic persons, physical or juridical, having the Roman pontiff for superior (c. 1405 § 3); the supreme court of the Apostolic Signatura judges, in judiciary matters, breach of contract, requests for return of status, and other appeals against sentences of the Roman Rota concerning the status of persons, exemptions from suspicion against the judges of the Rota, conflicts of competence between courts, and, in contentious administrative matters, appeals against special administrative acts, administrative conflicts that the pope entrusts to it, administration litigation that the dicasteries defer to it, and conflicts of competence between the DICASTERIES (c. 1445).

In respect to offenses reserved to the congregation of PROPAGANDA FIDE, criminal action is not extinguished by prescription after three years (c. 1362 § 1, 1⁰). This congregation ensures that publications of the faithful respect the faith and morals, and that any published errors are refuted; it judges offenses against the faith and more serious offenses against morals in the celebration of the sacraments. Matters relating to the privilege of the faith are its responsibility (apostolic constitution *Pastor bonus*, 28 June 1988, art. 51–3).

The Apostolic See must intervene to conclude concordats with civil authorities (c. 3); promulgate laws for the universal Church (c. 8 § 1); authorize the erection of an interdiocesan seminary (c. 237 § 20); readmit persons to clerical status (c. 293); create personal prelatures (c. 294) and establish their status (c. 295 § 1); nominate auxiliary bishops endowed with special faculties (c. 403 § 2) and the coadjutor bishop with right of succession (c. 403 § 3); revoke a diocesan administrator (c. 403 § 2); institute ecclesiastical regions (c. 433); ratify the acts of a special council (c. 446); ratify the statutes of episcopal conferences (c. 451); determine the matters for which episcopal conferences may promulgate general decrees (c. 455 § 1); ratify decrees made by the conference of bishops (c. 456); pronounce on the international initiatives and actions of episcopal conferences (c. 459 § 2); merge and unite institutes of consecrated life (c. 582); close an institute of consecrated life and rule on the disposal of its material goods (c. 584); close the principal house of an institute (c. 616 § 4); close an autonomous monastery of cloistered nuns (c. 616 § 4); grant an indult of exclaustration (c. 686); approve statutes of conferences of major superiors and create them as juridical persons (c. 709); encourage and direct the ecumenical movement (c. 755 § 1); erect or approve ecclesiastical universities and faculties (c. 816 and 817); organize the schedule and discipline of the sacred liturgy and approve liturgical books (c. 833 § 1 and 2); grant indulgences and the power to grant them (c. 995); grant radical sanation (retroactive validation of a marriage that was invalid because of a cardinal impediment) (c. 1165); establish new sacramentals (c. 1167 § 1); authorize the removal and transfer of sacred relics and specially venerated images (c. 1190 § 2 and 3); grant the power to exempt from private vows (c. 1196, 30); authorize the disposal of ecclesiastical property (c. 1292 § 2) the value of which exceeds the limit established by the episcopal conference of the region or of precious objects, with important material, artistic, or historic value (Congregation of the Council, 12 July 1919); reduce the fees for masses (c. 1308 § 1 and 1310 § 3); and hear and determine the non-consummation of marriage (c. 1698 and 1699 § 2).

The dispensations reserved to the Holy See include the following: from laws (c. 87); indults allowing one who has professed perpetual vows to leave a religious institute of pontifical right (c. 691 § 2) with the dispensation of vows and obligations arising from profession (c. 692) or to leave a secular institute of pontifical right (c. 727 § 1); allowing a bishop to proceed to episcopal ordination without the participation of other bishops (c. 1014); to dispense from more than a year of the age required for presbyterial and diaconate ordination (c. 1031 § 4); from irregularities in cases of ordination (c. 1047 § 1–3); from the impediment to marriage on leaving holy orders, from perpetual public vows of chastity made in a religious institute of pontifical right, or from a crime under c. 1090 (c. 1078 § 2); and from promissory oaths (c. 1203).

Dominique Le Tourneau

Bibliography

Bridge, A. "Reserve. Cas reserves," *DTC*, XIII (1937), 2441–61.

"Censures (peines)" *DDC*, III, (1942), 170–233.

Du Parquier, G. "Reserve des benefices ecclesiastiques," *DDC*, VII (1965), 604–55.

Farugga, N. *De Casuum conscientiae reservatione juxta codicem juris canonici*, Turin, 2e ed., 1922.

Gentile, A. "Riserva e casi riservati" *EC*, X, 1953, 965–9.

Mollat, G. "Reserves," *DDC*, VII, (1965), 635–40.

Steiger, J. "Causes majeures," *DTC*, II (1910), 2039–42.

RESIDENCES, PAPAL. The first official papal residence, from the 4th century, was the Lateran, still today the cathedral and seat of the bishop of Rome. Toward the middle of the 8th century, the old episcopal palace underwent radical changes. ZACHARIAS (741–52), the first of a long line of builder-popes, invested his entire fortune in the reconstruction of the *patriarchium*, which he had found in a state of dilapidation at the time of his election. No doubt it was owing to the sorry state of the buildings that one of this pope's predecessors, JOHN VII (705–7), had even attempted to move the Lateran residence to the Palatine.

Zacharias had several of the palace rooms decorated with frescoes. Next to the portico, he built a *triclinium*, or dining room, and a large fortified tower that could be used for accommodation. Another dining room was added on the upper floor. Pope Zacharias was also responsible for the vast portico in front of the facade of the palace and from which a great staircase led to the upper story of the residence.

HADRIAN I (772–95) carried on Zacharias' efforts in determined fashion. To the monumental ensemble, he added a second residential tower, which was decorated in its turn. Hadrian also had the portico restored, and ordered the construction of "several other buildings," about which his biographer in the LIBER PONTIFICALIS gives no information.

The action of his immediate successor, LEO III (795–816), was decisive. To him, the palace owes, among other things, two reception halls, the *triclinium majus*, and a vast hall later known as the "Sala del Concilio," modeled after the imperial palace in BYZANTIUM. Leo restored the long corridor on the top floor of the palace as well as the solarium, built by Hadrian. To the areas reserved for the liturgy, he added an oratory in honor of St. Michael.

GREGORY IV (827–44) built another *triclinium*, a *habitaculum*, and three bedchambers, and also restored the baths and storage areas. He was the last of the great builder-popes of the Carolingian era.

Within a hundred years, the Lateran Palace had been transformed into a sumptuous residence, worthy of the Carolingian renaissance. The palace was given imperial status. Even all the secular objects were meant to "surpass [those of] all other palaces." Significantly, these changes were realized by popes who had carried out a policy of autonomy vis-à-vis Byzantium. The changes were contemporary with the False DONATION, which had identified the Lateran as the former palace of CONSTANTINE, who was supposed to have given it to Pope SILVESTER I (314–35) along with all the other insignia of his power. It is certainly no accident that, by the beginning of the 8th century, the palace, hitherto called *patriarchum*, was given the imperial name *palatium*.

Throughout the early Middle Ages, the area of the Lateran, then on the city outskirts, remained relatively isolated. It even needed protection. In the 9th century, the old titular church of the Ss. Quattro Coronati was replaced by a fortified church with an entrance tower that strategically commanded the Via Major. During the INVESTITURE CONTROVERSY, the fortifications were intensified. On the Coelian Hill, the buildings of the monastery of Ss. Giovanni e Paolo, erected between 1099 and 1118, occupied a fairly important defensive position. In the mid-12th century, these were even added to, and the mighty tower was raised to its present imposing height.

The papacy's preoccupation with establishing a defensive sector around the Lateran lasted at least until the 13th century. A town had grown up consisting of hundreds of houses, several of which served to house the Lateran canons, members of the papal court, and leading Roman families, as well as craftsmen and merchants. There were also a number of hospitals, for visitors and pilgrims, in one of which St. Francis of Assisi stayed in

1209–10. The largest of these, the Ospedale di S. Giovanni, which was built at the beginning of the 13th century, was situated on the west side of the square. Roads led from either side of the hospital, which still stands today, to the catacombs of St. Sebastian, the church of S. Stefano Rotondo, the Ss. Quattro Coronati, and S. Clemente. The area of the square in front of the palace and basilica of the Lateran evidently had been closed off, from ancient times, toward the north where stood the 1st-century Claudian aqueduct, which supplied water to the public baths near the palace (attested to by the 8th century) as well as to other places. Nevertheless, this complex of buildings never succeeded in rivaling the "Borgo" that had grown up around St. Peter's.

In the 11th century, when the papal program of reform was under way, the Lateran became an essential pivot of papal politics as the papacy sought to reinforce its authority at the heart of the Christian world. After the Concordat of WORMS (1122), the palace and its chapels were restored and decorated with frescoes. From 1063 to 1198, the basilica became the official papal burial place. Again at the end of the 13th century, the popes set up a systematic program to restore and embellish the Lateran and to develop housing in the area. Thus, for centuries the Lateran was the true administrative and political center of the Christian community in Rome, as well as the heart of the central government of the Church. However, the development of this pole, spatially opposite that of St. Peter's, led to a sort of rivalry, which began in the 4th century and continued to dominate the city's religious history and urban evolution for hundreds of years, with each of the basilicas putting forward claims to primacy. This protracted competition, which at times grew intensely polemical (12th century), more or less came to an end in the 13th century, when the popes chose the Vatican Hill as their place of residence.

The first attempt to build a papal residence at the Vatican was made in preparation for Charlemagne's visit in 799–800. Pope Leo III built a magnificent *triclinium*, with an apsis in mosaic, together with baths. The use of this *palatium Caroli* was still attested to in the 12th century. The building was a kind of imitation Lateran Palace. A quarter of a century later, Pope Gregory IV added, for his own use, a guest house "so as to be able to rest there after matins and the mass."

Only occasionally did these houses serve as papal residences in early medieval times. Between 847 and 853, Leo IV enclosed the Vatican Hill and the area up to the bridge over Tiber with walls and gates, substantial portions of which still exist today, and declared the "Borgo" a city with its own laws, the Civitas Leonina. The Lateran church continued to be the cathedral of Rome, and the Lateran Palace, the official residence of the popes. From the time of the creation of the Leonine City, and for three hundred years, no pope seems to have established resi-

dence in the "Borgo," if we except the fact that GREGORY VII took refuge in Castel Sant'Angelo when he was expelled from the Lateran in 1084. It was not until the end of the 12th century that a second attempt was made to establish a papal presence in St. Peter's. This time it was no longer a question of a "replica in miniature of the Lateran" (R. Krautheimer). The plan marked a turning point, and St. Peter's in fact began to be chosen as the true alternative residence to the Lateran.

Built to the south of the basilica before 1151 by EUGENE III, the new palace had first been conceived as a place of temporary refuge for the pope, who so many times had been forced to flee the Lateran during the periods of Roman revolt. Peace, of a kind, had been established in the second half of the 12th century, with the result that more and more often the popes took up residence—though only for brief periods—on the Vatican Hill. HADRIAN IV (1154–9) spent close to a year and a half in the Leonine City, and CELESTINE III (1191–8) made the Vatican his principal residence.

INNOCENT III (1198–1216) took action in a decisive manner, on two levels. First, he restored and enlarged the palace of Eugene III, south of the basilica. He restored the state areas (*aula* and loggia) and built a chaplaincy and a new chapel. The pope also had walls built around the whole palace and towers placed on the gates. Inside the palace enclosure, he purchased a house in which to lodge his physician. Next, he ordered the construction of administrative buildings to the north of St. Peter's basilica, on the sides of the Mons Scaccorum. This housed four offices of the Curia: the bread pantry, the butler's office, the kitchen, and the farriery. Extension to the north of the basilica was continued throughout the 13th century. During the Avignon period, the old pope's palace to the south of St. Peter's was gradually turned into pilgrims' lodgings.

In the 15th century, the old palace gave up its original purpose for all time. In 1446, EUGENE IV had a women's hospital built there. North of the basilica, Innocent III had constructed only administrative buildings. One of his successors, Pope INNOCENT IV (1243–54), further emphasized the tendency of the papacy to make the Vatican Hill the place of papal residence. He had built, "beside St. Peter's, a palace, a very fine tower with chambers, and bought vineyards there." This building, the first papal palace to the north of the basilica, was in fact a tower-cum-manor house, capable of serving as both residence and fortress. It may be that Innocent IV was driven to make this decision by the state into which the former palace of Eugene III and Innocent III, south of the basilica, had fallen, and also, perhaps, by the insalubrious climate of the area. In any event, Innocent IV's decision, which according to his biographer was taken on the pope's return from an important general council in Lyon (1253), marks an undeniable turning point.

Innocent IV does not seem to have resided there (his itinerary attests to a very short stay in St. Peter's between the end of May and the beginning of June 1254). But certainly the palace corresponded to a new concept of its function, one more suited to the demands of court life. Over the long term, Innocent IV's choice was fundamental. As far as the papal residence at St. Peter's is concerned, he in fact sanctioned the relocation once and for all from the south to the north of the basilica, where the apostolic palace still stands today. The choice of St. Peter's was supported, too, by considerations of an ecclesiological nature. The church of St. Peter's became the *mater ecclesiarum*, a title that the Lateran had long been privileged to hold.

Around 1280, another change took place. The papacy had returned after a fairly long period of residence in cities to the north of Latium, in particular VITERBO. The Roman Pope NICHOLAS III, whose Orsini family for decades had had connections with St. Peter's basilica besides holding Castel Sant'Angelo since the mid-1200s, transformed Innocent IV's tower-cum-manor house into a "luxurious papal residence" (R. Krautheimer). According to some chroniclers, the pope even arranged for the planting of "a garden of great dimensions [with] trees of every kind." The geographical map of Paulinus of Venice shows that these gardens (on the site of the present-day Cortile della Pigna and Belvedere) included a large park for exotic ANIMALS.

It is also significant that two of Nicholas III's immediate successors chose to reside for a lengthy period outside the Lateran. Pope HONORIUS IV (1285–7) took up quarters (1286–7) in the palace that he had commissioned for himself and his family (Savelli) on the Aventine. The first Franciscan pope, NICHOLAS IV (1288–92), restored the palace next to ST. MARY MAJOR and often stayed there (1287, 1298, 1290, 1292), and he died in that palace on 4 April 1292.

Between 1198 and 1304, the Roman Curia was absent from Rome for approximately two-thirds of the pontificates of the period. If certain lengthy papal vacancies are also taken into account, the papal COURT of the 13th century resided for only some forty years in the Eternal City. Six popes of the period, among them all the French popes (URBAN IV, CLEMENT IV, MARTIN IV), never went to Rome. Their entire pontificates were spent in the PAPAL STATES, with the exception of that of CELESTINE V (1294), who remained for almost the duration in the kingdom of Sicily, of which he had been a subject before being elected pope. His successor, Pope BONIFACE VIII (1294–1303), never left the boundaries of the Papal States, and spent approximately half his pontificate outside Rome, especially in Anagni, his natal city.

Although subjected to constant wandering (more than two hundred moves in one century), the papal court enjoyed long periods of stability, in Lyon (1245–51, 1273–75) and in the cities of the Papal States. Between 1198 and 1304, the Curia spent some forty years in Viterbo, Anagni, Orvieto, Perugia, Tivoli, and Ferentino. Over the same period, the popes left Rome on more than fifty occasions for some location in the Papal States. When circumstances favored it, these moves followed a relatively regular seasonal rhythm. The departure dates were generally between April and June; the return dates, between October and November. In the earliest years of the 13th century, during the pontificate of Innocent III, who innovated here as elsewhere, a regular alternation on the part of the Roman Curia can be recognized. It would spend the winter in the Lateran and the summer in some city in the Papal States. This alternation became traditional under Popes HONORIUS III and GREGORY IX and was also observed in systematic fashion by Boniface VIII. The regular move makes it possible to assign a date to the *De mirabilibus Urbis Romae* of "Magister Gregorius," who speaks of the Lateran as the pope's *palatium hiemale*. The curial itineraries of the 13th century show that from 1226 no pope spent an entire summer in Rome.

Such regular alternation presupposes impressive logistical organization. The relocation of the Roman Curia in the 13th century involved several hundred persons: the members of the pope's *familia* (some two hundred), the cardinals and their suites, the procurators, the *mercatores Curiae*, the Chancery *scriptores*, the bishops paying their "AD LIMINA" VISITS, the prelates who had come to the Curia to solve judicial problems, the pilgrims, and so on. Responsibility for organizing the move fell to the APOSTOLIC CAMERA, which could draw up agreements with the cities. The agreements that have come down to us (as for the city of Viterbo, 1266) show that the communes were to promise free hospitality to the great dignitaries of the Curia. They also were required to fix limits for rents, the value of which could quadruple the moment the pope arrived, with the Curia, in one of these cities of Latium. The communes had to guarantee safety on the roads, reimbursement for victims of violence or robbery, and the maintenance of a stable currency. For as long as the Curia was in transit, on the road to or from the city, the commune was required to keep close watch over its paths and roadways, throughout the district. In particular, the pope's baggage, which was sent on to arrive before he did, was to be given the most careful protection against attack, by day or night. The rate of the different currencies was fixed in advance. Safety for the duration of the stay was to be ensured either by police measures or by the exercise of papal justice, or by the exclusion of any local privilege granted to the members of the Curia. The *podestas* and consuls should see to it that the marshal of law was prevented from the free exercise of his office and customary jurisdiction over all the curialists and persons of their suite. As long as the Curia's stay lasted, no curialist could obtain the right of the city. The flax basins should be taken away and moved to the rush bed.

In the 13th century, the towns to the north and south of Rome were well aware of the economic importance entailed by the presence of such a complex court, one, moreover, that would attract visitors of all kinds (ambassadors, pilgrims, penitents, etc.). As early as 1251, Matthew Paris pointed out that Perugia gave Innocent IV an honorable reception because the advantages his arrival would procure were well known. In 1268–70 and in 1304, local authorities (Viterbo, Perugia) put pressure on the cardinals to end an excessively long vacancy of the Apostolic See. The death of a pope and the prolonged absence of a successor inevitably caused severe economic hardship to the cities that welcomed the Roman Curia.

The reason for so much moving about was first and foremost, especially in the first half of the 13th century, the inability of the popes to dominate the city of Rome politically. Next was the conflict with Frederick II, which forced several popes (Gregory IX, Innocent IV) to flee the Eternal City. Yet many of the papal court's relocations were linked to the exercise of feudal power. For example, in 1208 Innocent III made an extended tour of the Campagna and Maritime territories to strengthen feudal ties in a province that shared a frontier with the kingdom of Sicily.

A 13th-century pope could also be a feudal lord by rights belonging to him personally. The mobility of the Roman Curia, therefore, was sometimes linked to the territorial interests of the pope and his family. Boniface VIII did not hesitate to take advantage of the moves of the court in order to visit castles and forts belonging to the Caetani. This was well noted by the Aragonese ambassadors in 1299.

Besides motives of a political nature, with which historiography has concerned itself in the past, there were reasons of health. The dates of these regular moves as well as the sources themselves attest, clearly and precisely, to the emergence of new requirements associated with the *cura corporis*, from the very beginning of the 13th century—once again, from the pontificate of Innocent III. Before the 13th century, allusions by chroniclers and papal biographers to the need for leaving Rome during the summer are rare. In his *Life* of Pope PAUL I (756–67), ANASTASIUS BIBLIOTHECARIUS stressed the fact that the pope died in the summertime (28 June), at the monastery of ST. PAUL'S OUTSIDE THE WALLS, where he had fled to escape the extreme heat. To justify the move made by GREGORY VI (1045–6) to Palestrina, Leo of Ostia warned that "the summer in Rome is contrary to the human body." In the *Life* of St. Anselm (d. 1109), the English historian Eadmer (d. after 1128) relates that Pope URBAN II (1088–99) allowed the saint to escape the hot Roman summer and take refuge in the monastery of the Holy Savior in Telese, to write *Cur Deus homo*.

In the second half of the 12th century, the appearances of the papal court in the cities of Latium suddenly became more frequent. Eugene III (1145–53) is said to have built a palace in Segni; Hadrian IV died in Anagni on 1 September 1159; ALEXANDER III (1159–81) sojourned at Tusculum; and LUCIUS III (1181–5) was elected at Velletri. However, it is not until the pontificate of Innocent III (1198–1216) that the references become more frequent and systematic, notably in the official biographies of that pope and of Gregory IX (1227–41) and Innocent IV (1243–54), which repeatedly emphasize the popes' regular moves and often stress reasons of hygiene and health. Malaria became endemic in Rome from the end of the 6th century. What was new, in the 13th century, was the desire and ability to carry out the regular alternations of place of an already extremely complex court.

In most of these cities of Latium, the popes built castles and palaces over the course of the 13th century. Only a few are still standing today (Anagni, Viterbo), and they can be studied in detail. In Anagni, two popes built residential palaces for themselves. That of Gregory IX was erected on lands that had belonged to his father. Today, the building forms part of the monastery of Charity. Its construction was to have been completed by the first quarter of the 13th century. In 1227, in fact, the pope presented it to his nephew Mattia de Papa, meanwhile reserving his right to live in it. It is in this palace, in 1233, that Gregory IX welcomed Frederick II and his entourage. Here, in 1254, Innocent IV received the ambassadors of the kingdom of Sicily. The palace became the property of the Caetani in 1297, when Gregory IX's heirs sold it to the nephew of Pope Boniface VIII, the marquess Pietro Caetani.

Boniface VIII's own palace, which for long was confused with the one bought by Pietro Caetani, was meant to be the largest and most impressive structure in Anagni. The building probably dates to the last quarter of the 13th century. Cardinal Benedetto Caetani seems to have lived there from 1283. The remains of the palace make up the foundations of the present Traietto Palace. The palace appears to have declined from 1303, just after the notorious attempt to seize the pope, led by Nogaret. In 1526, the Dominican Leandro Alberti da Bologna described Anagni as "the ruins of the palace of Boniface VIII." By 1749, only a few walls remained, and by 1764, the building seems to be completely destroyed.

In Perugia, the city statutes stipulated that the pope had the right to reside in the palace of the commune, in apartments usually inhabited by the *podestas*.

Between 1260 and 1280, the papal court resided in Viterbo almost without interruption. The city offered many thermal baths. In his *Perspectiva*, a veritable medieval encyclopedia of optic science written by Witelo during his stay at the papal court (ca. 1275 to ca. 1277), the author recounts how he studied the refraction of light beneath a waterfall next to some thermal springs (*Scopolo*) that he habitually visited with the curialists. As early as 1255, the Viterbo chroniclers made much of the authorities' plans to erect a new palace "so that the pope might come to Viterbo." When Pope ALEXANDER IV established his residence there, in 1257, it was decided to turn the bishop's palace into a papal residence. The alterations were completed in 1266, and the city *podesta*, Raniero Gatti, had an inscription affixed to the new papal palace. In 1267, Pope JOHN XXI died in Viterbo, having been badly injured in the collapse of a room he had had built in the papal palace.

The mobility of the Roman Curia had important ecclesiological consequences. The traditional identity between Rome and the papal seat was fundamentally changed, the shift being clearly perceptible by the beginning of the 13th century. When the abbot of Andres came to Viterbo in 1207 to visit the pope, he exclaimed, "I arrived in Viterbo and there I found Rome" ("Viterbium tandem deveni et ibidem Romam inveni"). Later, Innocent IV's biographer described Lyon, the city the pope had chosen as the provisional seat of the Curia, as an *altera Roma*. Under ALEXANDER III, "ad limina" visits were made exclusively to the Apostolic See (Rome). Toward the end of the 12th century, Huguccio (1188–91) believed that *limina* now meant the place of residence of the Roman Curia.

A half-century later, Innocent IV introduced in his commentary to the *Decretals* (1246–51) a new formulation, by drawing an even closer connection between "ad limina" visits and the pope's person: the "ad limina" visit is made "ubi papa est." By suggesting an even more precise formulation, "ubi papa, ibi Roma," Hostiensis (d. 1270) helped coin the definitive canonical dictum that, thanks to the influence of Baldus, became fixed in the formula "ubi est papa, ibi est Roma." This was a development of capital importance, one influenced by Roman law, according to which "Rome is where the emperor is," a maxim to which Frederick II himself had recourse to justify his absence from the kingdom of Germania. In short, it was no longer the city of Rome that served as the symbolic link between the bishops and the pope, but the pope's very person. That is why Hostiensis affirmed, "Non locus sanctificat hominem, sed homo locum."

Thus, the popes of the 13th century tried out a plan involving a double move, leaving the Lateran for the Vatican Hill (and, in subsidiary fashion, for St. Mary Major and the Aventine) and alternating their place of residence, which allowed them to spend the winter in Rome and the summer in one or another of the pleasant little towns of Latium. The abandoning of the centuries-old fixed residence in the Lateran and the relative loosening—at the residential level—of the traditional ties

with Rome foreshadowed the decision of Pope CLEMENT V (1304–16) not to return to Italy after his election as pope but instead to establish residence in France, at first temporarily and then (1308–9) once and for all in the city of Avignon. After the protracted "Avignon exile" (1308–78), the popes returned to the options of their 13th-century predecessors. The Vatican, now restored and enlarged to suit the tastes of the Italian Quattrocento, would be the palace where the papacy, Roman once more, would have its official residence—and would have it to this day. From now on, in fact, the papal residence (Vatican) and the official seat of the bishop of Rome (the Lateran) were separated forever.

Agostino Paravicini Bagliani

Bibliography

Dykmans, M. "Les transferts de la Curie Romaine du XIIIe au XVe siècle," *Archivio della Società romana di storia patria*, 103 (1980), 91–116.

Ehrle, F. *Der vatikanische Palast in seiner Entwicklung bis zur Mitte des 15. Jahrhunderts*, Vatican City, 1935.

Frascarelli, F. "La Curia papale a Perugia nel Duecento," *Annali della Facoltà di lettere e filosofia. Università. degli Studi di Perugia*, 16–17 (1978–80), 41–99.

Hampe, K. "Eine Schilderung des Sommeraufenthaltes der römischen Kurie unter Innozenz III. in Subiaco 1202," *Historische Vierteljahrsschrift*, 8 (1905), 509–35.

Herklotz, I. "Der Campus Lateranensis im Mittelalter," *Römisches Jahrbuch für Kunstgeschichte*, 22 (1985), 3–42.

Herklotz, I. "Der mittelalterliche Fassadenportikus der Lateranbasilika und seine Mosaiken. Kunst und Propaganda am Ende des 12. Jahrhunderts," *Römisches Jahrbuch für Kunstgeschichte*, 25 (1989), 27–95.

Herklotz, I. *'Sepulcra' e 'Monumenta' del medioevo*, Rome, 1985.

Krautheimer, R. *Rome: Profile of a City*, 312–1308, Princeton, 1980.

Krautheimer, R. *St. Peter's and Medieval Rome*, Rome, 1985.

Lauer, P. *Le Palais de Latran*, Paris, 1911.

Le Vatican et la Rome chrétienne, Vatican City, 1935.

Maccarone, M. "Ubi est papa, ibi est Roma," in *Aus Kirche und Reich . . . Festschrift für Friedrich Kempf*, Sigmaringen, 1983, 370–82.

Panza, A., and Ferretti, R. "Anagni nel XIII. secolo. Iniziative edilizie e politica pontificia," *Storia della città* (1978), 33–76.

Paravicini Bagliani, A. "La mobilità della Curia romana nel secolo XIII. Riflessi locali," *Società e istituzioni dell'Italia communale: L'essempio di Perugia (secoli XII–XIV)*, Perugia, 1988, 155–278.

Paravicini Bagliani, A. *Medicina e scienze della natura alla corte dei papi del Duecento*, Spoleto, 1991.

Schmidt, T. *Libri rationum Camerae Bonifatii papae VIII (Archivum Secretum Vaticanum, collect. 446 necnon Intr. et ex. 5)*, Vatican City, 1984.

Silvestrelli, M. R. "L'edilizia pubblica del Comune di Perugia: dal 'palatium comunis' al 'palatium novum populi,'" *Società e istituzioni dell'Italia communale: L'essempio di Perugia (secoli XII–XIV)*, Perugia, 1988, 494 ff.

Steinke, K. B. *Die mittelalterlichen Vatikanpaläste und ihre Kapellen. Baugeschichtliche Untersuchung anhand der schriftlichen Quellen*, Vatican Apostolic Library, 1984.

See also PALACE, APOSTOLIC; QUIRINAL.

RESIGNATIONS, PAPAL.

The popes of the early Christian period and the high Middle Ages were able to resign, though we do not know precisely the conditions for resignation, if in fact these were laid out. Yet the question of the pope's resigning his office did not arise until CELESTINE V abdicated in 1294 and the legitimacy of his successor, BONIFACE VIII, was systematically questioned. These resignations presented jurists with a new problem, on which ruling was made with reservations and later was evoked amid polemics.

Three years after voting for Boniface VIII, the cardinals of the Colonna expressed doubts as to the validity of the resignation of Celestine V. The principal arguments of the opponents of the new pope (who would thereby become an ANTIPOPE) were highly diverse: papal authority, the highest on earth and conferred by God alone, can be taken away only by God; the marriage uniting the pope to the Church is indissoluble; resignation cannot be permitted because of the dangers it would entail for government of the Church.

The replies (Giles of Rome, *De renuntiatione papae*, 1297; John of Paris, *De potestate regia et papali*, 1313) were no less copious. They explored the question of DEPOSITION, the distinction between papal power and the person of the pope, and the modalities of the proclamation of resignation (which does not have to be approved: *papa a nemine judicatur*, as had been stated already in the DICTATUS PAPAE, an element insistently taken up in the CODE OF CANON LAW of 1917, canon 221, and in that of 1983, canon 332 § 2: *ad validitatem requiritur ut renuntiatio libere fiat et rite manifestetur, non vero ut a quopiam acceptetur*).

List of Papal Resignations.

—MARTIN I, 954–5. The pope, taken prisoner by the *basileus* and deported to Chersonese in the Crimea, is said to have approved or at any rate not condemned the election, in his lifetime, of another pope, EUGENE I, carried out in order to forestall an imperial candidate. This at least tacit agreement was said to be a preliminary step toward resignation.

—BENEDICT V, 964. Deposed on 23 June by Emperor Otto I, the pope refused to defend himself and accepted the sentence. This was equivalent to a half-resignation, if one is to believe his (pro-imperial) contemporary Liutprand of Cremona, according to whom the pope himself removed his vestments and papal insignia.

—JOHN XVIII, 1009. When he died in June or July 1009, the pope seems to have been merely a monk of St. Paul's outside the Walls. The sources are too meager for us to know whether, toward the end of his pontificate, this pope, urged by the actual head of Rome, Crescentius, and still somewhat active, chose to resign of his own volition or was forced into doing so.

—SILVESTER III, 1045. Expelled from Rome by his rival BENEDICT IX on 10 March 1045, thereafter he had charge only of his diocese of Sabina, which proves that he resigned (he was formally deposed at the synod of Sutri on 20 December 1046).

—Benedict IX, 1045. He resigned his office on 1 May 1045 in favor of GREGORY VI (who was subsequently deposed, on 24 December 1046).

—Celestine V, 1294. First formal abdication, 13 December 1294. Its canonical legitimacy, promoted by his successor, the future Boniface VIII, who believed there were precedents, was the subject of debate (see the entries on both these popes) and was expressed in a highly symbolic ceremony (including a reading of the act of abdication and a stripping off of the papal insignia by the pope in full conclave).

—GREGORY XII, 1415. Deposed by the council of Pisa at the same time as BENEDICT XIII (5 June 1409), he resigned on 4 July 1415 at the council of Constance. He was made cardinal bishop of Oporto and legate before his death in 1417.

Olivier Guyotjeannin

Bibliography

Eastman, J. R. *Papal Abdication in Later Medieval Thought*, Lewiston, N.Y., 1996.

Granfield, P. "Papal resignation," *The Jurist*, Washington, 38 (1978), 118–31.

RIONI.

Administrative divisions of the city of Rome whose name, attested to in this form for the first time at the beginning of the 14th century, is an Italianization of the Latin word *regiones*. Medieval and modern Rome had thirteen and fourteen *rioni*: Rione I Monti, II Trevi, III Colonna, IV Campo Marzio, V Ponte, VI Parione, VII Regola, VIII Sant'Eustachio, IX Pigna, X Campitelli, XI

Sant'Angelo, XII Ripa, XIII Trastevere, and XIV Borgo (included in 1586).

The origin of the *rioni* goes back to the 11th and 12th centuries. As Rome expanded during that period, the need was felt for a new administrative division of the city. The new method of division bore no direct relation to the previous system of regional division—14 Augustan regions, 7 ecclesiastical divisions created in the 3rd century, and 12 Byzantine regions, the existence of which is still hypothetical—and was adapted to the configuration of the inhabited space and the districts created by renewed urbanization after the year 1000.

In the second half of the 11th century appear the first references to regions whose names were later given to the *rioni*: *regio* Sancti Angeli (1059), Campitelli and Sancti Eustachii (1061), Ponte (1073), Pinea (1079), etc. Soon after the establishment of the commune (1143), a short-lived agreement was drawn up, in 1149, between the senators and Pope EUGENE III (1145–53), which for the first time referred to an administrative division of the city into *contradae*. The pact was in fact sworn by the people on the basis of four representatives by way of *contrada*. Again, it was on the basis of these divisions that the Romans swore the peace of 1188 between pope and commune. Pope CLEMENT III (1187–91) appointed ten men "for each *contrada* of all the *regiones* of the city," half of which took the oath. As subdivisions of the *regiones*, in the second half of the 12th century the *contradae* made up the agreed upon administrative divisions, though there is no mention of their number or size.

Only the *contradae* were given a name, the *regiones* being designated by the names of the constituent *contradae*, either two or three depending on the case. (For example, the three *contradae* Montium, Biberatice, and Colyssei thus constituted what would be the *rione* Monti.) In the 13th century, the importance of the *contrada* in Roman political life seems to have lessened as against that of the *regio*, which then became the accepted topographical unit. In the autumn of 1203, when the Senate came up for reelection, twelve *mediani* were appointed to choose the fifty-six senators: very likely these were the representatives of the 12 regions. As a result of a treatise compiled in the 1220s which grouped together several chapters of the *Mirabilia*, a short historical account was drawn up of the city divisions, from antiquity. It listed the Roman divisions and included 12 principal regions subdivided into 26 subsidiary areas, including Trastevere, the Tiber island, and the Leonine City. Probably by the middle of the 13th century, and certainly by the beginning of the next, these 12 regions had become 13, with the integration of Trastevere. By 1305, in fact, the merchants' statutes were confirmed by the captain of the people and the council of the thirteen *anziani*, "that is to say, one per urban region."

A few years later, around 1313, the census of the Roman churches known as the "Turin catalog" began with a listing of the 13 regions "known, in a debased, vulgar tongue, as *rioni*" and which, with the exception of 2, match those of the 1220s listing. Finally, in the last decades of the 14th century, the custom grew of calling each *regio* after the name of the first *contrada* that constituted it, as is still done today. For instance, the *regio Montium et Biberaticae* was named *regio Montium*, the *regio Trivii et viae Latae*, *regio Trivii*, and so on. As for the Leonine City, it did not become the 14th *rione* until 1586, after being incorporated for a time in the *rione* Ponte. Thus, in the Middle Ages the administration of the Roman commune was based on the distribution of the population into 13 divisions. The *rioni* representatives, varying in number from one period to the next but usually consisting of one or two per region, sat on the grand council of the commune. Elections to all offices were ensured by electoral colleges chosen according to the topographical base of the *rioni*. Before the creation of the commune in 1143, perhaps even in the 10th century, the city militia consisted of twelve corps called *regiones*. In 1118, the troops, combined under the authority of the prefect and the heads of the leading families in order to free Pope GELASIUS II (1118–19), who had been abducted by Cencio Frangipane, included the "12 regions of the city of Rome, the Trasteverines, and the inhabitants of the island." The twelve standard-bearers of the militia corps took part in the corteges of the papal processions.

In the 14th century, the communal army was still led into combat by the *caporioni*, with the banners of the *rione* waving before them: "lo rione delli Monti vao denanti" (Anonimo Romano, *Cronica*, Milan, 1979, III, 93–4). An elementary territorial division on which the administrative system was based, the *rione* also constituted a community with a strong personality. Together, the adult men of the quarter made up the *rione* council (the *universitas*), which boasted its own staff: a provost (*antepositus*), a treasurer (*camerarius*), and, certainly, a notary. Like every individual in good standing, the *rione* could have possessions and rights. For instance, the treasurer of the *regio* Arenula in 1367 sold the fishing rights enjoyed by the region from time immemorial to one section of the coast. The charitable and devotional fraternities that sprang up in the 14th century were integrated into the existing topographical framework and, like the Confraternity of the Holy Savior *ad Sanctam Sanctorum*, copied their structures from the *rioni* system, thus exemplifying the latter's perfect adaptation to urban life.

Étienne Hubert

Bibliography

Duchesne, L. "Les circonscriptions de Rome au Moyen Age," *Revue des questions historiques*, 24 (1878),

217–25, "Les régions de Rome au Moyen Age," 10 (1890), 126–49, repr. in *Scripta Minora, Études de topographie romaine et de géographie ecclésiastique*, Rome, 1973 (*Collection de l'école française de Rome*, 13), 91–114.

Halphen, L. *Études sur l'administration de Rome au Moyen Age (751–1252)*, Paris, 1907 (Bibliothèque de l'École pratique des hautes études, sciences historiques et philologiques, 166), 7–15.

Hubert, É. *Espace urbain et habitat à Rome du Xe siècle à la fin du XIIIe siècle*, Rome, 1990 (*Collection de l'École française de Rome*, 135; *Nuovi Studi Storici*, 7), 70–96.

Re, C. "Le regioni di Roma nel Medio Evo," *Studi e documenti di storia e diritto*, 10 (1889), 349–81.

RISORGIMENTO. See **Unity, Italian**.

RITUAL. See **Liturgy**.

ROMAN CONFRATERNITIES. The presence of lay confraternities and associations has been an essential component of Roman history. They united broad segments of the Roman population, both native and foreign, for spiritual, charitable, cultic, and missionary purposes. From the 13th through the end of the 19th centuries, these brotherhoods tried both to express a religious conscience and to constitute a spontaneous and systematic force to combat the permanent or periodic ills of Roman society. During their heyday, between the 15th and 18th centuries, more than 150 new societies emerged in the City while groups of existing confraternities that shared the same goals and spiritual privileges merged with each other.

The confraternities always generated enormous interest; the chronicles of travelers and pilgrims express their astonishment at the magnificent monuments of Rome and at the large number of its people in the service of piety and one's fellow man. Ecclesiastical writers of the 16th and 17th centuries like the English priest Gregory Martin or the Italian Camillo Fanucci linked the active solidarity of the lay groups to the aspiration of Christian and papal Rome to "lead the Churches in charity." But it was only more recently that scholarly interest turned to their historical prevalence and significance. A number of extended studies were produced in the 19th century, particularly by foreign scholars interested in finding the institutional forms that allowed national groups to flourish in the multicultural community that was Rome. After a relative lull, interest revived again in the latter half of the 20th century, with an emphasis now on the interaction of confraternities with marginal groups (e.g., prisoners, women, Jews, prostitutes, the poor), on the rich cultural patronage provided by the brotherhoods, and on the role they played in

advancing Catholic reform. While there is as yet no comprehensive survey of Roman confraternities, it is possible to sketch some of the themes that characterize their central role in the civic and religious community.

Historical Survey. The question of when confraternal activity first began in Rome is a complicated one. While the nucleus of the Raccomandati della Virgine came together in the 1260s, it would be artificial to set an exact date. There were earlier groups, like the Romana fraternitas, an influential society that included clergy but whose functions remain unclear. National groups also existed at an earlier time.

Symbolic kinship ties were part of the common currency of social groups, particularly for those who had few natural kin at hand, as was the case for many in Rome. The lay Order of Santo Spirito, founded by the Frenchman Guy de Montpellier, had been in existence for a few years when INNOCENT III entrusted it with the Roman hospital of S. Spirito in Sassia in 1204. It operated independently, much like a confraternity, until 1446, when EUGENE IV ordered it to take the rule of the Third Order of St. Augustine, so as better to regulate the relationship between its male and female members, and between them and the poor, sick, and orphaned whom they served.

If the peculiar situation of Rome gave rise to such groups, it also made them more mutable, with members, regulations, activities, and worship in frequent flux. Some, like the San Salvatore and Sancta Sanctorum, gained social and municipal prominence by the later 13th and 14th centuries, and it is this prominence that legitimates the assertion that confraternal activity took on new importance by the later middle ages. A wide range of Romans was drawn to the confraternities in this period: research on some confraternities of the 14th and 15th centuries has revealed a substantial presence by merchants and farmers, who certainly constituted some of the most dynamic components of economic life in the 14th century. This is especially evident in the groups of Santa Maria in Portico, Santa Maria delle Grazie, and Santa Maria della Consolazione. In all cases, social status is a factor that varies from one confraternity to another. While the congregation of the Nobili welcomed the most prestigious aristocracy inside its doors, the most marginalised of the poor, along with the blind, the lame, and the crippled, turned to the Visitation. As A. Martini showed, some confraternities arose within guilds and professional corporations, with conflicts sometimes developing between the material and economic interests of the corporation and the more strictly spiritual interests of the confraternity.

Women took part in the religious and charitable activities of many Roman confraternities in this period but were barred from administration. Like men, they were normally nominated and screened, and they needed to pass a vote by the membership before they could join in weekly or monthly devotions, participate in periodic processions or feasts, or draw on charity. Some groups enrolled the wives of members without this review, and in fact most female members were the wives, widows, sisters, or daughters of male members. They governed themselves as a distinct group within the confraternity and sometimes organized public charity (e.g., providing dowries, running hospitals, visiting the sick) on a major scale. Up to the 15th century, confraternal religious devotion for men and women emphasized daily prayers, penitential observances, and frequent confession and communion. From then on, the confraternities played a greater role in the city's public religious life through processions, liturgical celebrations, and performance of devotional and didactic plays called *sacre rappresentazioni*. Given contemporary values, this greater public role resulted in a greater marginalization of women in confraternal corporate life.

In the second half of the 15th century and the beginning of the 16th, the three forces of a restored papacy, the humanist movement, and devotional reform combined to bring new prominence to Rome as a universal city, and create new roles for confraternities within it. A. Esposito has shown that confraternities played two almost contradictory roles. On one hand, traditionally powerful families whose official roles were being diminished as the popes took power away from the civic government sought in charitable confraternities a vehicle for continuing influence and authority. In this way, control of confraternal wealth and power compensated for the loss or reduction of civic status. At the same time, confraternities were also among those agencies the popes employed in order to wean the Romans from those same traditional civic institutions that challenged, or at least operated independently of, the papacy. Papal patronage could increase a confraternity's spiritual and financial assets, and an influx of members employed in the papal bureaucracy brought with it subtle ties of dependence or allegiance. Entry into confraternities brought these often foreign bureaucrats access to Rome's indigenous power structures, while also making them open to the influence of local families and institutions. Papal fiat could also vault a confraternity from relative obscurity to significant responsibility as the administrator of a hospital, or the overseer of poor relief. The experience of S. Spirito in Sassia in the 13th century would be repeated by S. Trinità dei Pellegrini in 1575, when Gregory XIII authorized it to establish the city's first workhouse and endowed it with powers and revenues to undertake the task. The number of paupers it welcomed and fed rose from more than 60,000 in 1550 to 170,000 in 1576. Confraternal membership soared to 3,000, and Romans generally contributed massively to its economic needs, with alms collected in pub-

lic places bringing in between 66% and 77% of total revenues. Yet what was easily granted could as easily be taken away. Sixtus V transferred the Trinità's consolidated responsibilities and resources to another confraternally run poorhouse called the Ospedale dei Mendicanti in 1587, and Clement VIII decentralized poor relief among a host of confraternities when he came to the papal throne in 1592. In short, the confraternities became thoroughly wrapped up in the local politics of governing Rome as these politics were complicated by the expansion of Rome's bureaucratic reach into a reconsolidated Papal State in the 15th century, and out into a reformed church in the 16th and 17th.

Yet the Church universal built on the Church local, and nowhere do we see this more clearly than in the history of a confraternity like the Gonfalone during this period. This was an amalgam of four groups, the oldest (Raccomondati della Virgine) with roots in the flagellant movement of the 1260s. In 1486 they merged under a banner (or *gonfalone*) that depicted the Madonna della Misericordia. S. Pagano has prepared an inventory of the Gonfalone's archive, and several illuminating studies by A. Esposito, B. Wisch, and N. Newbigin have shown how Rome's "two poles," the civic and the papal, came together in this prominent brotherhood. It was, as Wisch has written, a central part of the "ritual fabric" of Rome. From 1490 to 1539, it staged a large and splendid Easter Passion Play in the Coliseum. The play itself became the best known in Italy (28 editions published between 1456 and 1866), and in performance it merged Florentine dramatic forms with a Roman dramatic setting. The Gonfalone confraternity emerged as the virtual lay patron of Holy Week festivities in Rome, yet recurring violence against the Jewish community in the wake of the plays led Pope Paul III to suppress them in 1539. With some help from Paul IV in 1556, the Gonfalone developed nocturnal public flagellant processions on Maundy Thursday in place of the Passion Play. These in turn formed the core of a new identity for the confraternity, and also the focus for a public demonstration of piety that brought hundreds of *confratelli* from dozens of companies into the darkened streets bearing candles and whips, moving from their local churches to converge on St. Peter's.

The brothers of the Gonfalone adapted their devotions and rituals at a time of spiritual upheaval. Charitable initiatives multiplied as never before, as confraternities sought to help those, like prisoners, prostitutes, and the poor, who were pushed to the margins of society. V. Paglia and J. Weisz have studied the origins, ritual, and artwork of groups dedicated to helping prisoners. In 1488, a group of Florentines established S. Giovanni Decollato to help comfort or convert criminals in their last hours before execution, and to ensure a proper burial for them. Michelangelo and Vasari would both eventually join this group of expatriate Florentines, though it is unlikely that they were among those black-robed fratelli who sat with prisoners in their cells, walked with them to the scaffold, held devotional pictures before their eyes, or whispered prayers in their ears in order to calm them through the prolonged rituals of a public execution. Prisoners left in jails like the notorious Tor di Nona could, from 1575, gain food, bedding, medicine, and spiritual comfort from members of the Pietà dei Carcerati, established in 1575 by the French Jesuit Jean Tellier. These were later joined in prison work by S. Girolamo della Carità.

Like many of the new religious orders founded in the spiritual ferment of the time, the Jesuits found in the confraternities an ideal means of underwriting their educational and charitable work with marginal groups, and of extending their ideals to large numbers of pious laity generally. In 1542, Ignatius Loyola established three groups to support charitable shelters for the support and conversion of the vulnerable poor: the Compagnia della Grazia to maintain the Casa di S. Marta, sheltering former prostitutes and battered wives; the Compagnia di S. Caterina to support a conservatory for the daughters of prostitutes and other vulnerable girls who might be drawn into the profession; and the Confraternita di S. Giuseppe to run a catechumen house sheltering Jews who had recently converted to Christianity and who, as a result, were thrown out of their communities. Out of these Roman experiments, Loyola developed the model that, in the modified form of the later Marian congregations, was to be exported to Jesuit provinces around the world. Based on this model, Jesuits instituted confraternities of wealthy and influential patrons to administer, fund, and politically promote providing shelter to marginalized social groups for their immediate benefit and with the longer-term goal of their conversion. While these confraternities and congregations eventually grew to include merchants, professionals, and artisans, they were always segregated by social class. In this way, they marked a broader social and spiritual shift of the period known as "ennobling." The idealistic egalitarianism of medieval confraternities had been implemented with all-enveloping capes and hoods that obscured individual identity and fostered collective devotional exercises. This was always more a rhetorical ideal than an actual reality, and even 15th-century groups like the Raccomandati di S. Salvatore (which administered the extensive properties of the Lateran hospital) and SS. Annunziata alla Minerva had closed their ranks to all but the highborn and prominent. The new confraternities of the Tridentine period dispensed with egalitarian rhetoric and openly accommodated the social hierarchies of the early modern period in order to promote broader social and charitable goals.

Sixteenth-century reform was about more than charity. Protestants were not the only ones who found laxity, indi-

rection, mismanagement, and corruption within the Church. These reforms would require the active supervision of a bishop, so the council of Trent, in Session 22 (1562), gave bishops the authority to visit confraternities, checking their statutes, books, and activities and ordering improvements where necessary. This was a serious departure from the relative autonomy of previous centuries, and Roman confraternities, no less than others elsewhere in Italy, protested, resisted, and evaded this rule. In 1604, Clement VIII issued the bull *Quaecumque*, which confirmed the authority of the bishops in critical areas ranging from statutes to management of testamentary legacies.

Quaecumque formalized a movement that had already been at work for decades, through which Roman confraternities fashioned ties of patronage with sodalities across Europe and around the world. This took at least four forms. First, the "archconfraternity" gathered subordinate confraternities within the hierarchy. The pope would endow a particular Roman confraternity with a rich treasury of indulgences, and then authorize it to share these by affiliating with existing confraternities in other cities and towns. The affiliates paid a fee for this privilege (for beyond access to spiritual merits, they often gained status locally through their Roman connection), and agreed to adopt the rules of their Roman archconfraternity. In this way, S. Spirito in Sassia gained 170 affiliations in the course of the 16th century alone, while S. Trinità received 100, and SS. Crocifisso 30. Over the longer term, Santa Maria dell'Orazione e Morte spread beyond Italy into other European states and reached even Asia and America, becoming eventually a community of around 5,000 groups scattered throughout the world.

Second, in a slight variation on this, charitable confraternities of long standing generated offshoots from those who wished to imitate their work. Members of the Order of Santo Spirito established hospitals throughout France and Spain, in the Americas, and even in Palestine; by the late 16th century, more than 500 hospitals worldwide were linked to this Roman institution.

Third, as seen above, new religious orders, particularly the Jesuits, made Rome the laboratory for experiments with confraternal forms that they then exported to the provinces. Others worthy of mention include Gaetano Thiene, founder of the Theatines, the Dominican Tommaso Stella, Filippo Neri, Bonsignore Cacciaguerra, and Camillo De Lellis.

Fourth, new devotional currents that had arisen elsewhere were brought to Rome for ratification, support, and reexport. The three most significant in terms of numbers were those of the Rosary, the Holy Sacrament, and Christian Doctrine. The first Rosary confraternity was established in Germany by Jacob Sprenger in 1475 and recruited thousands of members across Europe. Holy Sacrament confraternities were established by the end of the fifteenth century to promote eucharistic piety. Rome's first one was founded by Tommaso Stella at Santa Maria sopra Minerva in 1539. In twenty years, it branched out into the parishes and surpassed 4,000 members (in a population of 80,000 inhabitants). The first Christian Doctrine confraternity had been established in northern Italy in 1536 to teach reading, writing, arithmetic, and catechism in a Sunday school format. It reached Rome by 1560, and by 1609, 370 lay women and 270 lay men, drawn from all social classes, taught poor Roman children as members of these groups; a further 460 were nonteaching supporters. Together, these volunteers brought education to literally thousands of Roman children. Each of these three movements generated dozens of local confraternities gathering thousands of local members, often in parochially organized brotherhoods. Numbers aside, another "foreign" devotion that had great impact locally was the Company of the Oratory of Divine Love, originating in Genoa in 1496, but a powerful example of charity and a gathering for the moderate "spirituali" through the first half of the 16th century. In hospitals like Rome's San Giacomo degli Incurabili, its members pioneered medical care for victims of venereal disease. A very elitist society, frequented by intellectuals and important clergymen (among them Marcantonio Flaminio), the Oratory was one of those numerous cells that, by the practice of a more internal spirituality and active charity toward the poor, would seek and demonstrate a path of religious renewal in the 16th century.

Building international confraternal networks centered in Rome seems characteristic of Tridentine reform, but the development predated the Council. Taken together however, these networks increased, at the lay level, the emotive and administrative connections binding believers in places as far-flung as Munich, Manila, and Montreal to a central hub in Rome. And Trent had an undeniable influence in stimulating local confraternal piety. By the early 17th century, when Rome had 110,000 inhabitants, it could count 107 confraternities, of which 60 had been created in the years following the Council.

Rome's Jewish community also found confraternities to be an effective vehicle for organizing its charitable and religious life and for socializing its younger members. The traditional *gemilut hasadim* gathered legacies to support widows and the poor, and to subsidize dowries. A separate brotherhood may have paid fines, debts, and the costs of incarceration for Jews who found themselves in Roman prisons. After imposition of the ghetto by Paul IV in 1555, the community was drawn more closely into itself, and devotional confraternities fostered the sense of a holy community within the ghetto walls, both through regular prayers and the spread of messianic Kabbalistic doctrines.

Confraternities declined in the 18th century as the elites began moving away from the collective devotion and charitable causes that they espoused. Brotherhoods formed around new popular devotions, most notably the Sacred Heart, but the end of the century was marked by serious political challenges. Napoleon occupied Rome in 1798, but his Jacobean Roman republic was replaced by the direct of annexation of Rome to the French empire in 1809. These years saw the suppression of numerous confraternities and the expropriation of their properties and resources. The return of the pope in 1814 did little to alter the process of fragmentation, and reorganization of the old network of the confraternities that continued until the city emerged as the capital of a united Kingdom of Italy in 1870. A new lay city and a new secular state were born of the Risorgimento. The characteristic problems of modern urbanism, such as increased immigration from the countryside and the destruction of the traditional social fabric of the city multiplied. As seen above, the state passed numerous laws reforming the operations and expropriating the assets of the confraternities. Despite a period of adaptation, most had difficulty surviving, and the era of the confraternities as significant participants in Roman spiritual, charitable, and artistic activity was effectively over.

Traditional Approaches and Historical Debates. Among the earliest significant studies of confraternities was that of Cardinal C. L. Morichini, on charitable institutions in 19th-century papal Rome. The work appeared in 1870, just as the Papal States disappeared in the face of Italian unification. Some confraternities succumbed with them and the rest encountered enormous difficulties in surviving. Morichini was a great specialist in these institutions, and his passionate defense of the confraternities attempted to show how beneficial they had been for the life of the city, and particularly for the underprivileged social classes.

Morichini offered historical analyses and comparative surveys on the practical activities of the societies of his time, and took an approach clearly favorable to the institutional Catholic Church and to Rome itself. He believed that charitable activities expressed the solidarity of religious groups with those whom they served, and he focused on a range of services provided to various classes of the poor: health and shelter for the sick, pilgrims, orphans, the aged, the destitute, and single girls; primary education and Sunday schools for the working classes; and charity in the prison environment. Among his examples here were the confraternity of the Trinità dei Pellegrini (the institution founded in 1548 by Filippo Neri to offer health care and hospitality to the huge masses of pilgrims), the Dodici Apostoli, the congregation of the Divina Pietà, and the groups of Dottrina Cristiana, which sustained an impressive catechetical movement, not only in Rome, but in Italy and beyond. As for Roman prisoners, whose tragic condition he was more immediately aware of, Morichini discussed at length the work done by specific institutions, such as the confraternities of San Girolamo della Carità, of San Giovanni Decollato, and of the Pietà dei Carcerati. His approach, particularly critical of 19th-century Roman government, was that "religion must be the first means of reform in the prisons," and confraternities could be the vehicle for that reform.

A few years later, Leon Lallemand, a lawyer and official of the General Administration of Public Assistance, wrote a comprehensive study of charity in the Christian world. A volume on Rome opened this panoramic work. Lallemand gave considerable attention to the confraternities and their activities in poor relief, and in both his particulars and his stance as an apologist for the brotherhoods, he depends heavily on Morichini. Both saw the brotherhoods as expressing a religious and social solidarity that the modern world still had need of, a view in the spirit of LEO XIII's 1891 encyclical *Rerum Novarum*. Lallemand's findings were at times nostalgic and even polemical, with the state expropriation of religious patrimonies suggesting to him "the image of a besieged city." Both he and Morichini identified with the Church in its increasingly bitter fight with the new Italian state, and this intense political and religious engagement informs their histories.

They were not alone. The struggle between Church and State in post-Risorgimento Italy stimulated an abundant and heterogeneous literature, little of it particularly analytical or objective. Laws passed by the Italian parliament from 1862 onward drastically changed the structure of the confraternities, and reformed the operation and organization of charitable bodies throughout the new nation. The position of the Roman confraternities was regulated by a series of laws promulgated from 1870 to 1890 that effectively transferred their assets over to charitable bodies managed by the commune of Rome. This resulted in the rapid disappearance of a large number of these institutions, some already worn out, others still in full flower and well represented in the social life of the city, such as the Holy Sacrament and Christian Doctrine confraternities.

The debate over confraternities became the lightning rod for broader concerns, and propaganda, libel, and inflammatory polemics flowed freely as both sides aimed to win over public opinion. In response to the likes of Morichini and Lallemand, Querino Querini, a lawyer, wrote a major work on Roman benevolence from antiquity to the present time. Not a historian by profession, Querini ventured into somewhat fanciful arguments on benevolence in the ancient civilizations of Asia, Greece, and Egypt. His long and ambitious study was more interesting when detailing the economic aspects of charitable societies, and presented a great quantity of data on the effectiveness of patrimonies and on the remaining activities. Like the Catholic approaches considered above, liberal and secularist approaches also emphasized the charitable and benevolent activities of confraternities. While both sides recognized the importance of the subject, both were equally compromised by their enthusiastic participation in the heated political and religious debates of the time.

These debates were of less concern to non-Italians, and during these same years and into the early 20th century, scholars from other parts of Europe directed their attention to the confraternities that had gathered the various "foreign" communities of Rome, whether from beyond the Alps or just from other cities in the Italian peninsula, like Siena or Bergamo. Some made an effort to base their studies on archival documents. On the whole, studies on the national foreign confraternities were superior to those on Italian expatriate communities. German, French, and Belgian scholars made particularly noteworthy contributions. The Germanic communities were discussed in the works of A. De Waal on the Campo Santo Teutonico and J. Schmidlin on the national church of Santa Maria dell'Anima. Schmidlin's book is an exemplary and pioneering work. He reconstructs the history of the church of Santa Maria dell'Anima and of the national society at its head, with emphasis on its internal operations, the development of the statutes, the vitality of the association, and the social condition of its members. This society, purportedly born out of a fusion of Nordic communities present at Rome from the time of Charlemagne, was constituted around a hospice intended to welcome poor pilgrims of German origin and donated by the papal soldier Hans Peters d'Utrecht. In 1386, the latter put at the disposition of the pilgrims three houses contiguous to his property in the Parione district. It was the first nucleus of a community that would take a more defined shape in the 15th century.

Other historians made similar contributions, including M. Vaes on the Belgians and Flemish of the 16th and 17th centuries, J. Bonnard on the Lorrains, A. Castan on the Burgundians of Franche-Comte, and B. Pocquet Du Haut-Jusse on the Bretons. Spanish, Illyrian, and English institutions were also studied at a later time. On the whole, these are very vivid, brief accounts of active communities seeking satisfactory integration into the city, usually through ecclesiastical offices and jobs in the Curia. Upon establishment, each had a particular identity, linked in some way to the region of origin and to the roles that the members played in Roman civil and ecclesiastic society. One example was the French confraternity of the Conception of the Virgin, of St. Denis and of St. Louis, an influential community of prelates and ecclesiastics endowed with benefices, of notaries, agents, and employees. From the second half of the 15th century, people of this kind came from across Europe, drawn to Rome by the development of the papal state and the new possibilities that it opened up.

20th-Century Historiography. Research on confraternities has continued to follow the three paths traced by 19th-century historians, examining their charitable work, their religious missionary role, and their role in gathering national communities. In addition, art, theater, and ritual have received far greater attention. Fewer monographs have emerged, but there has been a flowering of conferences, articles, and essay collections.

In particular, a stream of studies that appeared between 1930 and 1950 linked the history of the confraternities more closely to that of the Church. These presented the expansion of pious associations as an important aspect of the more extended process of reform and reconquest that Catholicism experienced in the 15th and 16th centuries. From the 1960s onwards, the study of confraternities generally, and of Roman confraternities in particular, gained in sophistication for a number of reasons. One was the work of certain specialists, such as G. G. Meersseman, the historian of Dominican confraternities. Another was the emergence of specialized institutes in the 1970s, such as Perugia's Centro di documentazione sul movimento dei disciplinati, which sponsored conferences and publications. A third was the holding of specialized conferences that stimulated research by large numbers of specialists and generated important essay collections. Most noteworthy for the history of Roman confraternities were two conferences held in 1978 and 1982, whose published proceedings demonstrated the advances in the scope and scholarly depth of postwar scholarship. They traced the entire history of the confraternities from the Middle Ages to the 19th century, shedding new light on some old problems, such as charitable activities and national confraternities, and giving new attention to artistic patronage and to religious texts used by the brotherhoods. Among the signal contributions of the latter collection is a painstakingly assembled directory of confraternal archives in various public and private places in the City, including the historical archives of the Vicariate, of the Vatican, and of the State. A register of approximately 140 collections of documents provides a comprehensive inventory, as well as historical notes. It expands on a parallel census of the Roman confraternities in their churches published in 1963 by M. Maroni Lumbroso in collaboration with A. Martini. The earlier document reviewed the vast network of former and still-existing confraternities and provided a quick historical overview of each of them, dealing as well with the history of churches, the oratories, and the evolution of statutes.

To conclude this brief review of the themes and problems of the history of Roman confraternities, it must be recognized that few other phenomena so profoundly marked the life of the City. Rome's religious, social, economic, and art history cannot avoid reference to the confraternities for a number of reasons: their wide diffusion; their large memberships of both men and women, Chris-

tians and Jews, Romans and "foreigners"; their dynamic relationship with papal and civic government; their expression of religious vitality and their critical role in the great reforms in the 13th, 15th, and 16th centuries; their hospitals for the needy of all classes; their charitable care of their members and of Romans generally; and their contribution to the art, architecture, music, and drama of the city. Confraternities echoed and influenced, shared and shaped the history of Rome.

Luigi Fiorani
Nicholas Terpstra

Bibliography

Black, C. *Italian Confraternities in the Sixteenth Century*, Cambridge, 1989.

Bonnard, J. *Histoire de l'eglise de Saint-Nicolas in Agone de la confraternité des Lorrains la Rome*, Rome-Paris, 1932.

Castan, A. *La Confrérie, l'église et l'hôpital de Saint-Claude des Bourguignons de la Franche-Comteé à Rome*, Paris-Besançon, 1881.

De Waal, A. *La schola francorum fondata da Carlo Magno e l'ospizio teutonico del Campo Santo nel secolo xv.* (Rome: 1897).

Esposito, A. *Un altra Roma*, Rome, 1995.

Fanucci, C. *Trattato di tutte le opere pie dell'alma citta di Roma*, Rome, 1601.

Fernandez Alonso, J. "Santiago delos Españoles y la archicofradia de la Santisima Resurreccion de Roma hasta 1754," *Anthologia annua*, 8 (1960), 279–329.

Fiorani, L. "Dicussioni e ricerche sulle confraternite romane negli ultimi cento anni," *Ricerche per la storia religiosa di Roma*, 6 (1985), 11–105.

Lallemand, L. *Histoire de la charité à Rome*, Paris, 1878.

Lazzerini, A., ed. *Arciconfraternite e confraternite. La società christiana a Roma e in Italia dalla riforma ai nostri giorni*, CD-ROM, Rome, Opera Madonna del Divino Amore Seconda, 1998.

Maroni Lumbroso, M., and Martini, A. *Le confraternite romane nelle loro chiese* (Rome: 1963). *Le confraternite romane; esperienza religiosa società committenza artistica* (Colloquio della Fondazione Caetani, Rome, 1982), and a special issue on confraternities of the journal *Ricerche per la storia religiosa di Roma*, 5 (1984).

Martin, G. *Roma Sancta*, 1581; repr., Rome, 1969.

Martini, A. *Arti mestieri e fede nella Roma dei Papi*, Bologna, 1965.

Mazjeric, G. *Istituto de San Girolamo degli Illirici (1453–1953)*, Rome, 1953.

Morichini, C. L. *Degl'istituti di carità per l'assistenza e l'educazione dei poveri e dei prigionieri*, Rome, 1870.

O'Regan, N. *Institutional Patronage in Post-Tridentine Rome: Music at the SS. Trinità dei Pellegrini, 1550–1650*, London, 1995.

Pagano, S. *L'archivio dell'arciconfraternità del Gonfalone; cenni storici e inventario (Collectanea Archivi Vaticani, 26)*, Vatican City, 1990.

Paglia, V. *La pietà dei Carcerati. Confraternite e società a Roma nei secoli XVI-XVIII*, Rome, 1980.

Paglia, V. *La morte confortata. Riti della paura e mentalità religiosa a Roma nell'età moderna*, Rome, 1982.

Pas Chini, P. "Le compagnie de Divino Amore nella beneficenza publica nei primi decenni del Cinquecento," *Tre ricerche sulla storia della chiesa nel Cinquecento*, Rome, 1945, 3–88.

Pocquet du Haut-Jussé, B. "La compagnie de saint Yves des Bretons," *Mélanges d'archeólogie et d'histoire*, 37 (1918–19): 201–83.

Querini, Q. *La beneficenza romana dagli antichi tempi fino ad oggi, studio storico critico*, Rome, 1892.

Schmidlin, J. *Geschichte der deutschen Nationalkirche in Rom. Santa Maria dell'Anima.* (Fribourg in Br.: 1906).

Serra, A. *Problemi dei beni ecclesiastici nella società preindustriale; le confraternite di Roma moderna*, Rome, 1983.

Stow, K. ed. *The Jews in Rome*, 2 vols., Leiden, 1995.

Terpstra, N., ed. *The Politics of Ritual Kinship*, Cambridge, 2000: A. Esposito. "Men and Women in Roman confraternities in the fifteenth and sixteenth centuries: roles, functions, expectations" and L. Lazar, "The first Jesuit confraternities and marginalized groups in sixteenth century Rome."

Vaes, M. "Les fondations hospitalières à Rome du VXe au XVIIe siècle," *Bulletin de l'Institut historique belge*, 1 (1919): 161–371.

Weisz, J. *Pittura e Misericordia: The Oratory of S. Giovanni Decollato in Rome*, Ann Arbor, 1984.

Wisch, B., and D. C. Ahl, eds. *Confraternities and the Visual Arts in Renaissance Italy*, Cambridge, 2000, notably the articles by E. Howe, "Appropriating Space: Woman's Place in Confraternal Life at Santo Spirito in Sassia, Rome," N. Newbigin, "The Decorum of the Passion: The Plays of the Confraternity of the Gonfalone in the Roman Collosseum, 1490–1539," and B. Wisch, "New Themes for New Rituals: The *Crucifixion Altarpiece* by Roviale Spagnuolo for the oratory of the Gonfalone in Rome."

ROMAN EMPIRE.

Up to Constantine. Originating in the victory of Actium (2 September 31 B.C.), which put an end to the crisis of the Roman Republic and to the civil wars that had bloodied Rome and Italy since the Gracchi, the imperial regime conceived by Caesar was organized by his great-nephew and heir, Octavius, who was given the name Augustus on 16 January 27 B.C. Creation of the empire continued throughout his reign (29 B.C. to 14 A.D.), the princedom of Augustus in fact being a monarchy hidden behind a republican veil: the old institutions were maintained, but more or less emptied of their powers, which in reality were concentrated in the hands of the prince. It was he who held the *imperium* (supreme power originating in military power), the *potestas* (civil power absorbing the powers of consul and tribune, united for the first time in the hands of one man), and the *auctoritas* (of the same root as *augur* and *augustus*, representing the added authority that is a gift of the gods, a sort of charism). Augustus says it himself in his *Res gestae divi Augusti*, 34: "I have had no more power than the others who were my colleagues in the magistrature, but I have prevailed over all of them by virtue of my *auctoritas*." Thirteen times a consul, invested with particular powers whenever the need arose or during the frequent periods of crisis, honored with twenty imperial salutes on the occasion of his generals' victories, which were won by the delegating of his *imperium*, in the year 12 B.C. he finally received the title of sovereign pontiff (which made him the head of the official religion of Rome), and in the year 2 the title of father of the homeland, conferred on him unanimously by the people and the SENATE.

Having succeeded in restoring civil peace, reestablishing order, and giving the people of Rome prosperity and confidence in the future, Augustus was able to establish a regime that lasted five centuries in the West and that would be prolonged well beyond that in the Byzantine Empire in the East. Founded on a solid army and a structured administration, the princedom of Augustus also based itself on a cult of the sovereign: during his lifetime, the emperor was honored in his function—his *Genius* and his *Numen* were worshiped; after his death, his apotheosis placed him among the gods, and he became *divus* and was given divine honors. To enforce the unity of the empire, a whole consisting of territories and peoples of diverse cultures, one cult, with its priests and liturgy, was organized little by little, at the provincial level around altars and temples dedicated to Rome and to Augustus, and at the municipal level by the *flamines* and *sevires* of Augustus. Participation in this popular cult was rapidly held to be inseparable from political power and proof of loyalty to the emperor. By refusing to sacrifice, the Christians left themselves open to being marginalized, accused of "hatred for the human race," and held responsible for breaking the *pax deorum* and therefore for all the ills of humanity. Whence the persecutions.

The Julio-Claudian emperors (Tiberius, Caligula, Claudius, and Nero) all took Augustus as their model, with each orienting the regime according to his personal tendencies. The first literary allusion to the Christians appeared under Claudius: "He expelled from Rome the Jews, who agitated constantly, spurred on by Chrestus"

(Suetonius, *Cl.* 25, 11)—a witness to the propaganda of the apostles and of the disciples in Jewish circles and to the disturbances provoked in the synagogues. The burning of Rome in 64 under Nero gave rise to the first PERSECUTION, which was not an official act but a pointed manifestation of the general hostility.

After the civil war, which, upon the death of Nero, set the partisans of Galba, of Otho, and of Vitellius against one another (68–9), the dynasty of the Flavians (Titus and Domitian, 69–96) gained the ascendancy with Vespasian. Following the Julio-Claudians, who had been Roman patricians, there came to power the class of the Italian municipal leaders (Vespasian was from Rieti), who through their merits rose to senatorial rank. After the disorders of the pronunciamentos of 68–9, this "bourgeois" dynasty reestablished peace, restored order in the administration and the finances, reorganized the provinces, and reinforced the frontier defenses. To consolidate the unity of the provinces, the imperial cult was given new impetus. The authoritarianism of Domitian placed him in difficulty with the Senate and led to bloody persecutions. The Christians were among the persecuted. The fact remains that the beneficial measures of the Flavian emperors paved the way for the apogee of the century of the Antonines, but also that their taste for regulation opened the path to autocracy, if not to outright bureaucratic control.

In 96, the brief reign of Nerva (96–8) began the period regarded as the apogee of the Roman Empire. Until 192 (the death of Commodus), the imperial throne was occupied by a succession of princes of Italian families that had emigrated to the provinces: Trajan and Hadrian originally came from Italica in Baetica, and Antoninus Pius was a descendant of a family of Nîmes; only Marcus Aurelius was Italian, but his preceptors and counselors were from the provinces. The 2nd century was the age of the economic, social, and cultural blossoming of the provinces.

The warrior emperor Trajan (98–117) was successful in his conquest of Dacia (present-day Romania), the only province situated on the left bank of the Danube, then of Arabia, and finally of Armenia and Mesopotamia, which were won from the Parthians. In Rome, he initiated the sumptuous Forum which still carries his name. In Italy, he was the savior of small agricultural enterprises and of the families of poor citizens, who were helped by his alimentary institutions. It is easy to understand why the Senate bestowed on him the title *optimus princeps*. When asked by Pliny the Younger, governor of the province of Pontus Bithynia, what attitude to adopt toward Christians who had been denounced as such to the provincial authorities, he issued the following statute law: no anonymous denunciations; for Christians denounced by informers and avowing themselves Christians, the death penalty; for those who denied the charge, acquittal. This statute law was applied throughout the 2nd century. It did not encourage persecution.

Hadrian, his successor (117–38), was a resolute pacifist. He spent a good part of his reign making journeys of inspection throughout his empire, founding new cities, promoting the preservation of old cities (many colonies were named after him), and undertaking massive works of urbanization, notably in Athens, which became the center of the *Panhellenion* under the protection of Zeus Olympios, with whom Hadrian himself was identified as he inspected the troops, as he was in Lambese in Numidia in July 128. To ensure peace, he reinforced the border defenses of the *limes*. But he was drawn into a new war with the Jews, the most ferocious since the fall of Jerusalem under Titus in 71. His plan to establish on the ruins of Jerusalem a Roman colony called Aelia Capitolina (placed, obviously, under the patronage of Jupiter Capitolinus), aggravated by his prohibition of the ritual of circumcision, provoked a fierce revolt in 132. One Roman legion was destroyed, and the war went on until 135. The reconquered Jerusalem became, under the name Aelia Capitolina, the capital of the consular province of Syria-Palestine. Legislation favoring small and medium-sized farms contributed to an expansion of agriculture and rural life in the provinces. In Rome, where he did not like to stay—he ordered the building of the imperial palace of Tibur, wrongly called Hadrian's Villa of Tivoli—he nevertheless undertook great works of construction, in particular the Pantheon, built by Agrippa, the friend and son-in-law of Augustus, which was completely transformed, as well as the Temple of Venus in the Roman Forum, and the mausoleum that bears his name on the banks of the Tiber (the present CASTEL SANT'ANGELO).

As much as Hadrian loved to travel, his successor, Antoninus Pius (138–61) loved to stay at home. His primary interest lay in administration, and he gave increasing importance to the prince's Council and to the jurisconsults who made it up; he allowed high-ranking functionaries the time to prove their ability, and he ensured good finances by means of wise savings. To the Jews, he restored the right to circumcise their sons. Upon the death of Empress Faustina, he had a great temple built in her honor in the Forum. Upon his own death, it became the Temple of Antoninus and Faustina.

With Marcus Aurelius, a philosopher emperor came to power, a man of duty, and also a prince of bad luck (161–80). A believer in Stoicism who had found the time to write an anthology of *Meditations*, he was forced, in spite of his preference for reflection above all else, to spend the greater part of his reign on the battlefield. He was faced with three major problems. First of all, the invasions. In the East, an attack by the Parthian king Vologese III in Armenia and Syria, bringing severe losses for the Romans, obliged him to send his coregent, Lucius Verus, who, surrounded by brilliant generals, saved the situation. But the army came back decimated by an epidemic of the PLAGUE, contracted in Armenia. Having spread throughout the Mediterranean region, the epidemic caused at least a million deaths; Lucius Verus succumbed to it, and in 180 Marcus Aurelius himself fell victim. The Parthian war had another consequence: the usurpation of Avidius Cassius, one of the generals of the Syrian campaign, who proclaimed himself Augustus. In itself, this was not serious: Avidius Cassius was killed by his own troops. But it was the first warning of a series of ambitious acts that would weaken the state a few decades later. During this period, there were other invasions on the Danube, and later on the Rhine: the Quades, the Marcomans, and the Iazyges crossed the Danube and lay siege to Aquileia. For the first time since the era of Marius, Italy was threatened directly, and there was panic in Rome. The *limes* of the Rhine was not spared, as some Chattes tribes made their presence felt there; the excavations of Argentoratum (Strasbourg) revealed traces of destruction in the civilian quarters outside the wall that could be dated to the years 165 to 175. And the Black Door in Besançon must have been erected to celebrate the victories won over the Germans. In order to repel the invasions, Marcus Aurelius had to undertake massive recruitment, create new legions, and strengthen the authority of the generals: the army became the priority, something that paved the way for a military empire.

Marcus Aurelius had another serious problem: that of the Christians, who had become a problem owing to the spread of Christianity and the accumulation of grievances against them in public opinion (cf. the *True Discourse* of Celsus). The affair of the martyrs of Lyon and Vienne (177) gave the emperor occasion to confirm the statute law established by Trajan. *Raison d'état* must always triumph.

Upon his death (180), Marcus Aurelius was succeeded by his son Commodus, whose authoritarian excesses and measures against the upper classes were responsible for his being called "worse than Caligula, worse than Nero." But there were no persecutions against the Christians.

His assassination gave rise to a huge crisis, from 193 to 197, the most severe since the year of the four emperors (68–9). The provincial armies—with Pescennius Niger in Syria, Septimius Severus in Pannonia, and Clodius Albinus in Brittany—were set in competition, confronted by one emperor chosen by the Senate, Pertinax, and another, Didius Julianus, chosen by the praetorium. The unity of the empire was threatened.

Victorious over his competitors, Septimius Severus became emperor in 197, and then admitted his two sons Caracalla and Geta to a share of his power. Originally from Leptis Magna, in Tripolitania, he was the first provincial emperor. His wife, Julia Domna, was from Syria, born to a great family of Emesus. The Severian dynasty (197–235) marked the triumph of the provinces, particularly those of North Africa and Syria. The African and Syrian clans dominated life in the empire.

On the political plane, this period was marked by a singular strengthening of imperial authority and central bureaucracy, led by the procurators of equestrian rank to the detriment of the Senate (with some exaggeration, historians see in it an affirmation of the *dominium* as against the earlier *principatus*); certainly, more and more as a matter of course the emperor was called *dominus noster*. Since he owed his throne to the army and the barbarian threat loomed large, there was also an important strengthening of the army and its prerogatives. Authoritarian and militarist, the empire of Severus became interventionist in the economic field and demanding in the financial one. This made him unpopular with the ruling social classes, but gained him favor with the disinherited. He set out on some new paths.

Two innovations are worth noting. With the edict of Caracalla (*Constitutio Antoniniana*) of 212, every free man in the empire became a Roman citizen; from then on, there were only citizens and slaves. On the religious plane, there was on the one hand a growing irritation with the Christians, who were accused of sacrilege and lack of respect for the Roman religion and were held responsible for every evil, and on the other a growing intransigence on the part of the apologists for Christianity, of whom the best example is Tertullian (*Apology, To the Nations*). In 202, Septimius Severus prohibited proselytizing by Jews and Christians, and the number of martyrs grew: in Alexandria, in Carthage, and in Lyon, where St. Irenaeus died.

The death of Alexander Severus in 235 on the Rhenish front opened a new phase in the history of the empire with a massive half-century-long crisis (235–85), which, thanks to Diocletian and his successors, issued in an almost complete recasting of the state and a thorough reorganization of the imperial administration.

Set in motion by Marcus Aurelius and partly averted under the Severians, the crisis of the 3rd century had been of unprecedented gravity because it had affected all areas. There was a kind of military anarchy: forty-four emperors and usurpers between Maximin of Thrace and Carinus, some of whom reigned only a few months and over only a segment of the empire. Some, like Valerian and Gallienus (253–68) or Aurelian (270–5), who tried to rectify the situation, were killed. The armies had become masters of the political game. Still, unity was safeguarded in spite of attempts to constitute a Gallic empire (Postumus and Tetricus) and a kingdom of Palmyrus (Odeinath and Zenobia) in the East.

The economic crisis was no less severe: the dilapidation of the state budget, the devaluation of the official currency, inflation partly due to military expenditures, insecurity, and armed robbery ruined the agriculture of some provinces and hampered trade; in order to repopulate empty areas, it was necessary to settle BARBARIANS inside the borders of the empire; those barbarians increasingly served in the army, which began to become barbarized. The reduction of the population contributed to the crisis. Naturally, a social crisis followed: the upper classes were affected by the militarization of the public sector, and the lower classes by the general economic difficulties.

In addition, a moral crisis ensued on account of the invasions and the general anarchy, as well as the religious controversies. For the first time, in 250, Emperor Decius gave the anti-Christian persecution a universal and systematic character. In 257, an edict forbade the Christian cult and, under penalty of death, obliged bishops, priests, and deacons to offer sacrifice to the gods of Rome (the martyrdom of St. Cyprian in Carthage and of Pope SIXTUS II in Rome).

With Diocletian, a soldier of fortune from Illyria, began what is called the Late Empire (to avoid the pejorative "Low Empire"), marked by a recasting of the imperial regime (285–305). Allying a political preoccupation (consolidating the central power) with a military preoccupation (guarding the frontiers), he associated with his absolute status a second Augustus, and then two Caesars, and founded the "tetrarchy"—rule by two pairs made up of an Augustus and a Caesar for twenty years; then came the *Vicennalia*, with the retirement of the two Augustuses and the succession to power of the two Caesars, who called themselves Caesars. They divided the empire: Diocletian and Galerius established themselves at Nicomedia and at Sirmium, Maximian and Constantius Chlorus at Milan and at Trier; but so that unity would be safeguarded, Diocletian was *Augustus maximus* and in the supreme position. In a parallel way, there came a strengthening of imperial absolutism (with a court etiquette and "sacred" councils) and the birth of a new administration (vicars at the head of dioceses, new governors heading provinces that had been split in two, with an Italy divided into districts). The military was reorganized (with *limitanei* at the borders, *comitatenses* inside the empire). Monetary and fiscal reform, accompanied by economic measures (the edict on maximum prices), was not sufficient to bring back prosperity. As far as the Christians are concerned, the edicts of Diocletian and of Galerius (302–4) ushered in the cruelest of all the persecutions, which lasted until 312. In reaction, the "Peace of the Church" followed.

Marcel Le Glay

Bibliography

Albertini, *L'Empire romain*, Paris, 1929, 4th enlarged ed., 1970 (Peuples et Civilisations, IV).

Le Gall, J., and Le Glay, M. *L'Empire romain*, I, *Le Haut-Empire de la bataille d'Actium (31 av. J. C.) à l'assassinat de Sévère Alexandre (235 ap. J. C.)*, Paris, 1987.

From Constantine to Charlemagne. With the defeat of the usurper Maxentius at the battle of the Milvian Bridge in 312, Constantine was hailed as "liberator of the city" and established as Augustus of the western Roman empire. Attributing his military success to divine assistance from the god of the Christians, Constantine forged a policy of religious toleration to which his eastern counterpart Licinius subscribed in the agreement known as the "Edict" of Milan (313). Property confiscated from Christians in the recent persecutions of Diocletian and Galerius was to be returned and restitution made for whatever had been destroyed; all were free to worship whatever deities they chose, because such worship was conducive to the concord of the empire. Whether one regards the experience at the Milvian bridge as Constantine's "conversion" or reserves that designation for his deathbed baptism in 337, the events of 312–13 mark the beginning of Roman imperial interest in and ultimately identification with the Christian church. The process thus set in motion was to lead to both imperial favor and interference in ecclesiastical affairs as church and empire began to improvise a relationship that would require repeated renegotiation in subsequent centuries.

Confronted with theological controversy raging in the eastern regions of the church about the divinity of the Son (*Logos*, Word), Constantine summoned bishops throughout the empire to assemble at Nicaea in order to end the dispute and restore concord. In rejecting Arianism the Council of Nicaea also established a mechanism for doctrinal decision-making that, for the first time, was meant to apply to all the churches. Called and financed by the emperor, the council set a precedent that held sway into the Middle Ages in the West and throughout the Byzantine empire. Emergent patterns of dependence and discord, fraternity and friction between church and empire proved long-lived as well.

In 324 Constantine became sole ruler of a united empire, having defeated his pagan colleague Licinius at the battle of Chrysopolis on the thin pretext of his having violated the principles of the Milan agreement by threatening to renew persecution of Christians. Turning his attention to the East, Constantine ordered the rebuilding of the ancient city of Byzantium on the Bosphorus and moved his court to Nicomedia as he awaited completion of the project and dedication of the new eastern imperial capital of Constantinople in 330. Imperial and ecclesiastical politics continued to intertwine as Constantine grew more intent on public harmony than doctrinal correctness in face of Arian persistence after Nicaea. At the same time bishops near the imperial court became adept at sensing shifts in the political atmosphere and shaping their policies accordingly.

On the death of Constantine (337) his empire was divided among his three surviving sons, with Constantius II achieving sole rule in 350. Constantius faced external threats on the empire's frontiers with Persia as well as along the Rhine and Danube. Confronted by continuing ecclesiastical conflict Constantius tilted his religious policy strongly toward Arianism, and the majority of eastern bishops followed suit in a series of councils in the late 350s. With no heirs of his own, Constantius elevated his cousin Julian to Caesar (355) and sent him to Gaul, where his military and administrative success alarmed Constantius sufficiently to order him to the Persian frontier instead. Unwillingly acclaimed Augustus by his troops in 360, Julian edged toward open revolt when Constantius refused him recognition; civil war was avoided only by the unexpected death of Constantius en route to engage Julian, who acceded to the imperial purple in 361.

Although raised Christian and installed in the minor order of lector, Julian had come to despise the religion of his murderous cousins and turned instead to the old gods, attempting to promote a pagan restoration during his brief reign as emperor (361–3). He even revived for himself the title of Pontifex Maximus that dated back to the reign of Augustus. As much to antagonize Christians as to gain favor among Jews, Julian proposed to rebuild the Temple in Jerusalem and restore sacrifices there; the project was halted by a minor earthquake, which later Christians took as a sign of divine displeasure and license for a wave of anti-Judaism in the following generation. Julian perished in an ill-conceived campaign on the Persian frontier, bringing Constantine's line to an end. He was briefly succeeded by Jovian (363–4), a Christian, who was followed by Valentinian I (364–5) in the West and his brother Valens (364–8) in the East.

For the remainder of the century two issues dominated the imperial agenda: defense of the empire's frontiers and establishment of a modus vivendi with the church. These issues were especially critical in the West, where migrations and military incursions by so-called "barbarians" threatened the Rhine-Danube frontier, and resistance to Christianity remained strong among the old Roman aristocracy. The Roman bishop Damasus (366–84) did much to make Christianity palatable to upper-class Romans, with initial success among aristocratic women and, later, their husbands and sons. Emperors from the house of Valentinian and the newly established Theodosian line ruled nearly to the end of the century, shaping patterns of relationship between church and empire that would endure into the late middle ages and beyond.

Even as the army attempted to defend Rome's frontiers, an increasingly large proportion of its leadership came from the same Germanic peoples it sought to exclude from the empire. Valentinian I undertook campaigns in Britain and along the upper Rhine and Danube, where he died in 375 and was succeeded by his son Gratian (375–83), whom he had already appointed Augustus in 367. Valens waged war against the Visigoths along the lower Danube, then marched on Antioch and attempted to regain Armenia. Valens was killed in 378 and his army destroyed at Adrianople in a poorly planned battle with the Goths who had been flooding into the empire since 376. Gratian put a young Spanish general, Theodosius, in charge of the Gothic war and elevated him to eastern Augustus in 379. The Ostrogoths were driven back, becoming subjects of the Huns, while Theodosius negotiated a treaty with the Visigoths in 382, allowing them to remain within the empire in exchange for military service. In 383 Gratian was killed in Gaul by the usurper Maximus, who in turn was killed by Theodosius in 387 after attempting to take Italy. Geopolitical pressures increased in subsequent decades, bringing about the gradual disintegration of the western empire even as Christianity was officially embracing the heritage of Rome as its own.

In the West, bishop Ambrose of Milan (373–97) achieved a complex ascendency over Roman emperors in matters where spiritual and imperial power and politics converged. Two dramatic encounters with the eastern emperor Theodosius I (379–95) are particularly telling. After defeating the usurper Maximus, Theodosius remained in Milan, acting for all practical purposes as sole emperor. Theodosius ran afoul of Ambrose in 388 by ordering the bishop of Callinicum (on the Euphrates) to finance the rebuilding of a synagogue that had been destroyed by a Christian mob. Arguing in a private letter to the emperor and then in a public sermon that it would be unjust and unfaithful for the church to benefit Jews in any way, and dangerous to Theodosius' political and religious well-being as well, Ambrose refused to continue with the eucharist until Theodosius rescinded his order. Theodosius relented. He gave way again in 390 and did public penance after Ambrose excommunicated him for ordering the slaughter of thousands in Thessalonica in retribution for the murder of an army commander there.

Theodosius drastically limited the scope of paganism, tolerating and sometimes authorizing the destruction of temples. He issued a series of edicts that culminated in the outlawing of pagan cult and the closing of all temples in 391. He likewise imposed strict penalties against heretics, raising the stakes from exile and confiscation of property to capital punishment. Following Constantine's precedent, Theodosius convened the Council of Constantinople in 381 to settle doctrinal controversies about the divinity of the Holy Spirit and other issues stemming from the Council of Nicaea. With his legislation against pagans and heretics, restrictions on Jews, and robust support of orthodoxy, Theodosius can rightly be said to have established Christianity as the religion of the empire.

The 5th century saw the disintegration of the Roman empire in the West as Goths, Vandals, and Huns overran its frontiers. The growing isolation of the West combined with political retrenchment in the East to magnify long-standing cultural differences between the two parts of the empire. Later political and ecclesiastical divisions have roots in this unsettled time, as does the evolution of the papacy as a western institution.

Theodosius I was succeeded by his young sons Arcadius (395–408) in the East and Honorius (395–423) in the West, neither of them particularly capable rulers. Consequently, the Vandal general Stilicho, who had commanded imperial troops under Theodosius, effectively ruled as regent in the West. Rebuffed in his attempts to extend his reach to Constantinople, Stilicho occupied himself with attempts to recover Illyricum (which had been ceded to the East) for the western empire. In the process he held the Gothic invaders in check during the early 400s, but ultimately did not succeed in either endeavor and in 408 he was summarily executed.

Alaric and his Visigoths sacked Rome in 410, stirring murmurs of alarm and setting off a wave of withdrawal among the moneyed populace to properties they thought more secure. Augustine's theological reflection on history and providence in his monumental *City of God* was prompted in some measure by pagan charges of Christianity's responsibility for this hitherto unimaginable event. The Vandals, who had reached Gaul and Spain by 406, crossed the Straits of Gibralter to enter North Africa in 429, laying siege to Hippo as Augustine was dying in 430, and taking Carthage in 439. Frankish tribes moved into northern Gaul, Burgundians into the east; Angles, Saxons, and Jutes continued their migrations into Britain. For a time the Huns provided mercenaries to the Roman army and helped keep other tribes at bay, but peace treaties and annual subsidies to the Huns did not prevent their forays into the Balkans in the 440s. Turned back from Gaul in 451, Attila (d. 453) and his troops reached Rome in 452 without any resistance from the military. A delegation led by the Roman bishop Leo I ("the Great," 440–61) is said to have persuaded Attila to spare the city. Leo was less successful in 455 when Vandals plundered the city but refrained from widespread slaughter and destruction.

From 455–76, the army raised and deposed western emperors at will. In 476 the Visigothic general Odovacer was declared king of Italy by his troops and the figurehead western emperor, Romulus Augustus, was deposed. Although the eastern emperor Zeno (474–91) still ruled in Constantinople, for all practical purposes the empire had ceased to exist in the West. This new political arrangement was solidified when the Ostrogoth Theodoric invaded Italy at Zeno's urging, took RAVENNA in 493, killed Odovacer, and in 497 was recognized by the emperor Anastasius (491–518) as king in Italy; he ruled until 526, nominally as representative of the emperor. By the end of the fifth century, Ostrogoths ruled much of Italy, Visigoths controlled Spain and its provinces, Vandals most of Roman Africa, and Franks

under Clovis (481–511) held a large part of Gaul. Clovis led the Franks to Christianity when he converted in 496; nearly a century later Recared I (586–601) of Spain accepted catholic Christianity in 587 (the Visigoths had been Arian, or heterodox, Christians since the mid-4th century), thus laying the foundations for what would become western Christendom.

In the East, Theodosius II (408–50) succeeded his father Arcadius, who had proclaimed him Augustus on his birth in 402. Theodosius achieved little in his own right, but was subject to the influence of his regent, the competition of his sister and his wife, and the designs of imperial officials. The most notable achievements of his reign were building the Theodosian Wall around Constantinople (413), issuing the Theodosian Code (426) that collected the edicts of Christian emperors and clarified the use of legal precedents, and concluding a long peace with the Persians (422). Lacking a male heir, Theodosius was succeeded by Marcian (450–7), a retired soldier, who entered into a pro forma marriage with Pulcheria. It was Pulcheria, with support from Pope Leo I of Rome and Flavian, Patriarch of Constantinople, who engineered the reversal of the "robber council" of Ephesus (449) by calling the Council of Chalcedon in 451, which established a standard of Christological orthodoxy that was enthusiastically received in the West but met with opposition from some groups of eastern Christians (monophysites) who refused to accept its authority.

Complex political maneuvering after Marcian's death resulted in the elevation of Leo I (457–74) as emperor. Despite frequent military engagements with Vandals and Ostrogoths seeking to expand eastward, Leo, Zeno, and Anastasius managed to preserve the eastern empire and leave it relatively prosperous at the same time as Germanic kingdoms were taking root in the West. Justin I (518–27), who emerged as emperor out of the intrigue following Anastasius' death, is perhaps most important for naming his nephew Justinian as his successor.

Justinian (527–65) simultaneously advanced the ideal of empire and weakened its reality, his impulsive policies mitigated somewhat by the political astuteness of his wife Theodora (died 548). In pursuit of a reunited empire Justinian sent his general, Belisarius, into Africa to evict the Vandals (533), after which he proceeded to Sicily (535), Rome (538), and Ravenna to unseat the Goths (540). By the end of the 540s, however, the Goths had recovered almost all of Italy, only to be displaced once again by Justinian's forces. An exarchate was established in Ravenna for the emperor's representative. Despite Justinian's public benefactions, his "recovery" of Italy met with a mixed reception, and ruinous taxation devastated the Italian cities and countryside. Pressure from the Persians distracted the emperor from his western efforts, as did his failure to resolve the continuing theological controversy with the monophysites. The bubonic PLAGUE reached Constantinople in 543 and spread westward, seriously reducing the population and cutting the army's manpower. It is difficult to evaluate the effectiveness of Justinian's reconquest, which was undone a scant three years after his death by the Lombard invasion of Italy in 568.

In the legal arena, Justinian's achievements were more enduring. The *Code of Justinian* (529) collected and categorized imperial decrees from Constantine onward, the *Digest* (533) excerpted opinions of jurists, and the *Institutes* (533) served as a manual for students. These works preserved the Roman legal heritage in an accessible and useful format that later served as a foundation for legal developments in medieval Europe.

For the remainder of the sixth century and much of the seventh, the eastern empire was pressured by the Lombards, Avars, Slavs, and Persians. Successive emperors staved off these threats until Maurice (582–602) reached a peace with the Persian Chosroes II in 591. Maurice was murdered by rebellious troops led by the centurion Phocas, who ruled as emperor until he himself was overthrown in 610. Heraclius was then named emperor (610–42). Through repeated campaigns Heraclius subdued the Persians and began reconstructing his empire, having lost territories in Greece and the Balkans to the Slavs. His attempts to resolve the religious conflict between orthodox and monophysite Christians (and thereby also improve relations with the western church) were unsuccessful, provoking controversy with several bishops of Rome. Later emperors were no more successful either religiously or militarily.

The rise of Islam in the 620s had introduced a new factor into the complex politics of the eastern empire and its neighbors, ultimately altering relations with the West as well. The first Islamic forces attacked the Byzantine frontier in Palestine in 630, with Mohammed planning another expedition before he died in 632. By 636 Heraclius had lost Syria at the battle of the Yarmuk; a decade later Roman Mesopotamia was lost; Jerusalem fell in 638. Persia became an Arab possession in 637 and was renamed Iraq. Egypt became a province of the caliphate in 642. Constantinople withstood a major siege in 674–7 and again in 717–18, halting the Moslem advance on the eastern frontier and securing the city for the Byzantines until the crusaders captured it in 1204. The slow conquest of North Africa began in 642 and was only completed at the end of the century. Visigothic Spain fell in 711. Muslim progress into western Europe was only halted near Tours in 732 by the Frankish armies of Charles Martel (mayor of the palace, 719–41).

What remained of the Roman empire continued in the Greek-speaking East—Turkey, Greece, a small area of the Balkans, the exarchate in Ravenna, and parts of southern Italy and Sicily. From the late 4th century onward in the West, the Church and its institutions had gradually filled the power vacuum created by the transfer of the imperial capital to Constantinople and the political disruptions caused by waves of Germanic invasions and migrations. At the end of the 6th century, the Roman Church under Pope GREGORY I the Great (590–604) was repairing the aqueducts and city walls, distributing food to the needy, and paying the army for the defense of the city. The relative powerlessness of the exarchate in dealing with the Lombards led Gregory to conclude a separate peace with them in 598, bypassing the emperor Maurice in Constantinople.

Of the new kingdoms that began to take form in the West, those of the Franks and the Lombards were to prove the most significant. Clovis' conquests of other Germanic tribes had brought the kingdom of Francia into being among the Franks and the Gallo-Romans. Despite the divisions and consolidations that accompanied each succeeding Frankish king's partition of his territory among his sons, and the growing ineffectiveness of the "fainthearted kings," Francia became the dominant political reality in western Europe. The Italian peninsula was occupied by Lombards in the north and in the semi-independent duchies of Benevento and Spoleto, while the vast landholdings of the Roman Church in central Italy marked the vestiges of the western empire. It was only a matter of time before these forces would collide.

In Merovingian Gaul, the mayors of the palace had ruled the kingdom for some time when Pepin III, "the Short" (mayor, 741–51), wrote a disingenuous letter (c. 750) to Pope ZACHARIAS (741–52) inquiring whether it was right for one to hold the title of king while another carried out the actual work of ruling. Zachary affirmed that it was better for power and title to coincide and he ordered "by apostolic authority" that Pepin should become king. Childeric III (743–51), the last of the Merovingian kings, was deposed, tonsured, and sent to a monastery. Pepin was elected king of the Franks (751–68) at an assembly at Soissons, and anointed by the missionary bishop Boniface representing the Pope. With these actions, the last pretenses of empire in the West vanished. The symbiotic but uneasy relationship between bishops of Rome and Frankish kings—soon to be emperors themselves—had begun.

In a matter of years Pope STEPHEN II (752–57) found himself in need of Pepin's aid against the Lombard king Aistulf (749–56). Stephen journeyed to Francia in 754 as a supplicant to Pepin, who received him deferentially and pledged his assistance. In turn Stephen anointed Pepin and his sons Charles and Carloman, confirming their kingship of the Franks and conferring on them the title of "Patrician of the Romans." Pepin discharged his debt to St. Peter by "returning" Pavia, Ravenna, and other captured territories to the papacy. The *Donation of Pepin* provided the first formal basis for papal claims to temporal sovereignty in this region. About this time and most likely arising from Roman sources, the spurious *Donation of Constantine* appeared, which traced such claims back to Constantine's purported gift of Rome and its territories to Bishop Silvester (314–35) as the emperor departed for his newly renamed capital in Constantinople.

Pepin's kingdom was divided between his sons Carloman (d. 771) and Charles (768–814), who became King of the Franks on Carloman's death. Charlemagne expanded his kingdom through the conquest of the Saxons and other Germanic groups. After capturing Pavia in 774, he began to refer to himself as "King of the Franks and Lombards and Patrician of the Romans," virtually annexing northern Italy to Francia. As much out of piety as politics he followed his father's lead in protecting papal interests in Italy. Under Popes HADRIAN I (772–95) and LEO III (795–816), the papacy became so dependent on this Frankish alliance that Leo owed his life to envoys who rescued him from a hostile Roman faction in 799. In gratitude and perhaps also an attempt to restore the balance of power, Leo crowned Charlemagne emperor at mass on Christmas Day in 800. Whether out of humility, as his biographer Einhard suggests, or resentment at its political implications, Charlemagne was distressed enough by this act to declare that he would never have attended church had he known the Pope's plans. The dramatic events of 799 and 800 mark an ambiguous restoration of empire in the West, no longer Roman but Frankish. The questions implicit in the interactions of Leo III and Charlemagne would play themselves out in subsequent centuries as western Christendom repeatedly sought to define the relationship between papacy and empire.

Francine Cardman

Bibliography

Barker, J. *Justinian and the Later Roman Empire*, Madison, 1966.

Brown, P. *The Rise of Western Christendom: Triumph and Diversity, AD 200–1000*, Cambridge, Mass., and Oxford, 1996.

Cameron, A. *The Later Roman Empire*, Cambridge, Mass., 1993.

Cameron, A. *The Mediterranean World in Late Antiquity, AD 395–600*, London, 1993.

Fletcher, R. *The Barbarian Conversion: From Paganism to Christianity*, Berkeley, Calif., 1997.

Herrin, J. *The Formation of Christendom*, Princeton, 1987.

Jones, A. H. M. *The Decline of the Ancient World*, London, 1966.

Wallace-Hadrill, J. M. *The Barbarian West 400–1000*, 3rd rev. ed., Oxford, 1985.

Williams, S., and Friell, G. *Theodosius: The Empire at Bay*, New Haven, Conn., 1994.

ROMAN REPUBLIC (1798–9). Proclaimed on 15 February 1798 following the action of the French forces, the Roman Republic represented a significant turning point in the history of the Papal States. This is owing not so much to its duration (just over a year, until 29 September 1799) as to its political, religious, cultural, and civil consequences.

Research by certain scholars—L. Sciout, A. Dufourcq, V. E. Giuntella, M. Battaglini, and A. Cretoni—makes it possible to discern the principal political phases marking the creation, declaration, and fall of the Revolutionary government of Rome. At first, the agreements signed by the Directory and the papal government (the armistice of Boulogne, 21 June 1796; the treaty of Tolentino, 19 February 1797) seemed to make French occupation of the capital only remotely likely, if not impossible. But after the assassination of General Léonard Duphot (27 December 1797), it became obvious that Paris's intentions had radically changed. The French government cunningly presented the crime as willfully perpetrated by Rome and therefore calling for revenge. The ambassador Joseph Bonaparte was recalled to Paris, and diplomatic relations with the PAPAL STATES were suspended. An expeditionary force was drawn up, under the command of General Alexandre Berthier, to march on Rome and avenge the crime. The affair ended abruptly in victory, thanks in particular to the feeble resistance mounted to the invaders. A few days after the surrender by the garrison of the fortress of CASTEL SANT' ANGELO (10 February 1798), the Republic was proclaimed in the Campo Vaccino (the ancient Roman forum), where a grandiose, highly symbolic ceremony was held that included a reading of the *Acte du peuple souverain*.

The new administration was based on the division of land. According to the law of 2 Germinal VI (23 March 1798), the territory was split into eight departments: Cimino, with its chief town Viterbo; Circeo, with Anagni; Clitunne, with Spoleto; Metauro, with Ancona; Musone, with Macerata; Tevere, with Rome; Trasimeno, with Perugia; and Tronto, with Fermo. The institutions of the new state were regulated by an appropriate constitution, inspired (though with a few modifications) by that of year III in France, as was the case with the other Revolutionary territories.

The fact that the Constitution had been imposed (it was neither voted on nor agreed to after public parliamentary debates), together with the ensuing, sometimes conflictual, action of the Directory commissioners (Daunou, Monge, and Florent) and the generals heading the French forces in Rome (Berthier, Masséna, Gouvion-Saint-Cyr, MacDonald, and Championnet) has been a leading subject of debate for those seeking a sense of Roman political life in 1798–9. This political life was, in large measure, conditioned by the presence of the occupiers, from both a political and an economic viewpoint. The actions of the executive (Consulate), the two legislative chambers (SENATE and Tribunate), the judiciary (Tribunal of First Instance), and the financial agencies (Prefecture) were in fact always under the direct control of the French civilian and military authorities. Thanks to the broad powers granted them by articles 368 and 369 of the Constitution, those authorities intervened in local legislation on several occasions, directly enacting legal measures without the approval of parliament.

This interference, as well as the technical unpreparedness of many local administrators, the exaggerated separation of the two chambers, and the disagreements among various organs of government, sometimes had a paralyzing effect on the system, so much so that in July 1799 General Garnier entrusted the management of affairs of state to a provisional government Committee.

Adding to the difficulties faced by the institutional authority was an extremely serious economic crisis, inherited to a large extent from the papal regime and aggravated in part by the contingencies of war. An attempt was made to stem problems arising from an excess of paper money by selling lands that had formerly belonged to Church institutions (henceforward declared the property of the state), and by imposing taxes on the more affluent citizens and raising levies (by whatever means). The economic crisis, exacerbated by a poor harvest and the exodus of farmers discouraged by having failed to obtain the payments promised by the state, helped in large measure to shatter the social consensus the Republic had enjoyed at first.

The effects of this collapse of the alliance with the masses were felt more keenly in the countryside than in the capital. Rome experienced only one organized counterrevolutionary uprising (the revolt of 25 February 1798 in Trastevere), but on the outskirts of the state the anti-French insurrections were many and bloody (the departments of Trasimeno and Circeo). The reasons for the discrepancy may be sought in the greater amount of social control exercised in Rome by the police forces and the non-mobile National Guard as compared with the rural areas. Yet the different conditions in town and country should also be borne in mind. If the problem of public opinion regarding the Republic is assessed over a lengthy period, the discrepancy between the rural and the urban communities stands out dramatically. In fact, the Revolution was unable to keep its promises to free the countryside, announced in the first months of 1798. It failed to end the traditionally subordinate role of the provinces vis-à-vis the capital, and Rome retained its privileges, continuing to take the lead both in matters of provisioning and in other sectors of public life. Social relations remained unchanged, the division of lands (agrarian law) was not put into effect, the military committed robberies and acts of violence, and heavy taxation was imposed, as

was conscription. All these, along with considerations of a religious nature, had a negative influence on popular opinion with regard to the Republic.

Furthermore, the image of the French as atheists and infidels, spread abroad by counterrevolutionary propaganda, accentuated hostility to the new institutions. In the months before the troops reached the frontiers of the Papal States, there were many cases of collective visions in an anti-Republican context (miracles of weeping Virgins), and the authorities' attempts to suppress roadside holy images as a way of preventing counterrevolutionary assemblies were of little use. The occupiers and patriots in the government did not adopt any measures apt to offend popular religious feeling, and the Constitution preferred to keep silent on the relations between State and Church. Nevertheless, the resolutions against ecclesiastical hierarchies (from the forced withdrawal from Rome of PIUS VI to the suppression of many monasteries) and the requirement of the oath of loyalty to the Republic (large numbers of French priests had emigrated to Rome following the promulgation of the Civil Constitution of the Clergy in 1791) had the effect, in part, of alienating the people from the recently constituted state.

The rupture was even more dramatic after the crisis of the first Neapolitan occupation of Rome (27 November to 15 December 1798). The Bourbon troops caused widespread destruction, hopes were raised by those nostalgic for the Ancien Régime, and the regular distribution of food became more and more problematic. All this caused a series of difficulties that the Republican authorities, returned to power, found hard to resolve, and attempts to reorganize services during this delicate political period were fruitless.

A failed consensus, the difficult contingencies of war, a financial crisis and unprecedented inflation, a political class that was ill prepared, a sometimes stifling occupying presence—such were the negative factors characterizing the short life of the Roman Republic. And yet the period 1798–9 plays a major role in the history of the Papal States, both from the point of view of political and institutional structures and from the human point of view. Most important, for the first time the state government was administered by laymen, no longer by churchmen. Research by Casini and Giuntella has helped uncover the character of the leading Roman elites who joined the Republic. From a geographical point of view, many non-Romans took part in the government (Antonio Brizi, Francesco Benedetti, Pietro Reppi, Federico Zaccaleoni, Agostino Bassi, Filippo Brunetti, the Corona brothers). Even men from other Italian states held important political and cultural posts (Urbano Lampredi, Faustino Gagliuffi, Vincenzio Russo, Giuseppe Marj).

On the social level, there was a striking participation of jurists (Carlo Luigi Constantini, Francesco Riganti, Nicola Corona, Marsilio Cipriani, Filippo Brunetto, Filippo Maria Renazzi), physicians (Camillo Corona, Liborio Angelucci), aristocrats (Pio Bonelli, Francesco Sforza Cesarini, Francesco Santacroce, Luigi Pallavicini, Marcantonio, Francesco, and Camillo Borghese) and priests (notably from the Piarist order: Faustino Gagliuffi, Scipione Breislak, Urbano Lampredi). As for the voice of the people, historians have generally considered it negligible. Yet the analysis of legal dossiers produced in the wake of the collapse of the Republican government (Archivio di Stato, file Giunta di Stato) reveals that many more members of the public took part than might have been thought possible—even if prosopographic research alone can describe such popular participation.

The importance of these representations in the government and the introduction of *homines novi* into positions of leadership helped change the political life of the country. During the years 1798–9, as in the other Jacobin republics, political journalism made its appearance. Daily newspapers and periodicals (more or less tied to the government) interpreted events and molded a revolutionary public opinion (*Monitore di Roma*, *Il banditore della verità*, *Gazzetta di Roma*). Moreover, from the outset revolutionary clubs and societies were founded, aimed at grouping together patriots, making room for political criticism, instructing the people on the principles of the Constitution, and drawing up plans for transforming society (the Society of the Emulators of Brutus, the Constitutional Club, the Society of Agriculture, Commerce, and the Arts). All the traditional social centers, cultivated or not, organized or informal (salons, academies, fraternities, cafés, inns, hostelries), were influenced by the new political evolution.

To sum up, the revolution of institutions helped to overthrow and alter political, social, cultural, and communal life in the provinces and the capital. In particular, it accelerated the process of transformation and modernization of the state apparatus and the city services, bringing Rome, to a certain extent, in line with other European capitals. These developments, far from being thought of as imports from abroad and alien to the nation's needs (an opinion held for years by a moderate or conservative nationalist historiography), can be seen as responses to precise requests from the most enlightened local milieus. It is no accident that as soon as the Republic fell after the victory of the coalition forces (29 September 1799), many Republican innovations remained in place (from freedom of trade to regular night illumination, or the numbering of houses) or were readopted over the following decades (for instance, the abolition of torture as a penalty, and the opening of the ghetto and the assimilation of Jews into the rest of society). Furthermore, other experiments of those two years were felt as an invitation to take a fresh look at hitherto obsolete mechanisms, institutions, and systems of government (the restructuring of the territorial administration, the creation of a new penal code, the introduction of norms regulating public employment).

Thus, an overall judgment of the Roman Republic cannot be limited to considerations of a chronological nature, limited to a brief period. Besides giving a new role to Rome and the state as a whole in the international context of the age, the Republic helped transform local life, morality, and customs and to form a common substratum between the capital and the other Italian capital cities. These changes, together with a system of political apprenticeship practiced within institutions that were similar in structure, and with the development of close ties among patriotic groups from the various republics, were to have a decisive effect on the Risorgimento of the 19th century.

Marina Formica

Bibliography

Archival sources: The most important source is one in the Archivio di Stato in Rome entitled *Repubblica romana del 1798–1799*. This source should be complemented by the proceedings of the Committee of State (1799–1800) and the papers to be found in less homogeneous sources (e.g., the *Miscellanea di carte politiche e riservate*). Equally important are the documents in the Archives nationales de France (for a preliminary overview: B. Peroni, *Fonti per la storia d'Italia dal 1798 al 1815 nell'Archivio nazionale di Parigi*, Rome, 1936), the Archives du ministère des Affaires étrangères, Paris, and especially the Archives de la guerre, Vincennes.

Assemblee della Repubblica romana (1798–99), published by V. E. Giuntella (I: Bologna, 1954; II: Bologna, 1977).

Battaglini, M. *Le istituzioni di Roma giacobina*, Milan, 1971.

Bibliografia della Repubblica romana, published by V. E. Giuntella, Rome, 1957.

Caffiero, M. "Simboli e cerimoniali a Roma tra rivoluzione e restaurazione," *Spazi sacri e luoghi della santità*, published by S. Boesch Gajano and L. Scaraffia, Turin, 1990 (republished in M. Caffiero, *La nuova era. Miti e profezie dell'Italia in Rivoluzione*, Genoa, 1991).

Casini, T. "Il parlamento della Repubblica romana del 1798–99," *Rassegna storica del Risorgimento*, 1916.

Collezione di carte pubbliche, proclami, editti, ragionamenti ed altre produzioni tendenti a consolidare la rigenerata Repubblica romana, Rome, 1798–9, 5 vols.

Correspondance des directeurs de l'Académie de France à Rome. Nouvelle série II: Directorat de Suvée 1795–1807, published by G. Brunel and I. Julia, Rome, 1984.

Cretoni, A. *Roma giacobina*, Rome, 1971.

De Felice, R. *La vendita dei Beni nazionali nella Repubblica romana del 1798–99*, Rome, 1960.

Dufourcq, A. *Le Régime jacobin en Italie. Étude sur la République romaine 1798–99*, Paris, 1900.

Formica, M. "Potere e popolo. Alcuni interrogativi sulla Repubblica romana giacobina," *Studi romani*, 3–4, 1989; "'Vox populi, vox dei'? Tentativi di formazione dell'opinione pubblica a Roma (1798–1799)," *Dimensioni e problemi della ricerca storica*, 2, 1989.

Formica, M. "Forme di sociabilità politica nella Repubblica romana del 1798," *Dimensioni e problemi della ricerca storica*, 1, 1991.

Giuntella, V. E. "La giocobina Repubblica romana," *Archivio della società romana di storia patria*, 1950; "Le classi sociali della Roma giacobina," *Rassegna storica del Risorgimento*, 1951; *Bibliografia storica*.

Minciotti Tsoukas, C. *I "torbidi del Trasimeno"* (1798). *Analisi di una rivolta*, Milan, 1988.

Miniero, A. "Il Monitore di Roma. Un giornale giacobino?" *Rassegna storica del Risorgimento*, 71, 1984.

Sala, G. A. "Diario romano 1798–99," *Scritti di Giuseppe Antonio Sala pubblicati sugli autografi da Giuseppe Cugnoni*, Rome, 1882–88, 4 vols. (republished by V. E. Giuntella, Rome, 1980).

Sciout, L. "Le Directoire et la République romaine," *Revue des questions historiques*, 1886, XXXIX.

ROMAN REPUBLIC OF 1849. On 8 February 1849, the Constituent Assembly met in the Chancery Palace in Rome, having been elected the previous 21 January by some 250,000 voters of the Papal State. Of the 142 deputies present, 120 adopted the following text, proposed by the Bolognese deputy Quirico Filopanti:

"Art. 1: The papacy has fallen in fact and in law from the temporal government of the Roman state. Art. 2: The Roman pontiff will retain all the guarantees necessary for the independence and the exercise of his spiritual power. Art. 3: The form of government of the Roman state will be pure democracy, and it will adopt the glorious name of Roman Republic. Art. 4: The Roman Republic will have relations with the rest of Italy conformable to membership in a single nation."

On 5 February, at the first session of the Assembly, the old consistorial lawyer Carlo Armellini, who had defected from the ecclesiastical state to the Republic, solemnly harangued the deputies: "Our people, the first in Italy to have rewon its liberty, has summoned you to the Capitol to inaugurate a new era for the motherland, to shake off yokes domestic and foreign, and to rebuild a nation purified of the burden of the old tyranny and the constitutional lies of yesterday. . . . We shall inaugurate your immortal works under the auspices of these two holy words: Italy and the People."

Immortal the Roman Republic was not to be. Barely five months later, on 3 July 1849, French troops under General Oudinot laid siege to Rome, ending the Republican government and reestablishing the authority of Pope PIUS IX. The Roman Republic of 1849 takes its place in the history of the national democratic movement that spread throughout Europe, beginning in 1846, from Rome to Palermo, from Naples to Venice and Milan, from Paris to Vienna and Budapest—at once "the springtime of nations" and a Romantic-era revolution that a military and political reaction would terminate violently in 1848 and 1849.

Yet the Roman Republic also has certain distinctive characteristics. It questioned, radically, the temporal dimension of papal power; it was bound up with the traditions of secularity and democracy; and, under the authority of the most eminent figures of the national movement for the revival (Risorgimento) of a still profoundly disunited Italy—Giuseppe Mazzini, Giuseppe Garibaldi—it laid down innovative political models. It finally perished, not without glory, under the weight of foreign military intervention. As a reminder of that glory, Garibaldi's statue on the Janiculum Hill still proudly dominates the Eternal City.

The liberal illusions of the first months of Pius IX's pontificate, together with the irresistible current impelling the inhabitants of the Papal States to reject en bloc the structures of the "government of priests," belong largely to the earliest history of the Roman Republic. As soon as he acceded to the pontificate (16 June 1846), Pius IX gathered around him a state congregation that was to draw up the most pressing reforms, made necessary by three decades of almost complete institutional paralysis. A relatively broad amnesty of the political prisoners of the preceding regime (17 July 1846) met with huge popular enthusiasm. Censorship of the press was eased (15 March 1847); a Council of Ministers was established for the first time (18 June 1847), and then reorganized to comply with modern criteria (29 December 1847); and laymen were gradually appointed to head the chief state administrations. Rome was given a Civil Guard (5 July 1847). A twenty-four-member consultative Council, or *Consulta di Stato*, the members of which were appointed by the pope at the suggestion of the provincial and communal council, was constituted, made up of moderate liberals and reformers. Finally, the pope agreed to a constitution, or *Statuto* (14 March 1848), that turned the Sacred College of Cardinals into a Senate and provided for the election of two councils (duly approved by the pope), a High Council (*Alto Consiglio*) and a Council of State (*Consiglio di Stato*), the members of which were officially appointed on 13 May. For the first time in the history of the ecclesiastical state, semirepresentative institutions were set up, taking the place of the moderate absolutism that hitherto had been the political form of the papal government.

At this same time, the question of Italian UNITY took a decisive new turn (the collapse of a Customs Union, negotiated by Msgr. Corboli Bussi; the revolts in Milan and Venice against the Austrian occupation; the outbreak of war between Piedmont and Austria). A crisis was provoked by the hesitation of Pius IX. He refused to accept the idea of the Papal State's participation in a war, as contrary to the universal mission of the Supreme Head of the Church according to the allocution of 29 April 1848. Yet, in a letter of 3 April, he had asked the emperor of Austria to come up with a solution that would conform to the principles of nationalism. All this vacillation reinforced hostility against him as an "enemy of the motherland" (*nemico della patria*) and launched Rome and the State into a political crisis, aggravated by social and economic problems as well as by popular agitation, from which emerged the strong personality of Angelo Brunetti, known as Ciceruacchio.

During 1848, the more radical ministry of Terenzio Mamiani (who was called to the Ministry of the Interior on 4 May) accentuated the crisis of confidence involving the pope, his ministers, and public opinion. The liberal economist Pellegrino Rossi, the former ambassador of Louis-Philippe to Rome, who was appointed on 16 September to end the crisis and restore the authority of the papal government, was assassinated on the steps of the Chancery Palace on 15 November. Nine days later, on 24 November 1848, Pius IX secretly left Rome, where his safety was no longer assured, to take refuge in Gaeta, in the states of Ferdinand II of Naples.

It would be ten more weeks before the legitimacy of the supreme pontiff was fully referred to the elected representatives of the Roman Republic. On 25 November, the president of the Council of Ministers, the auditor of the ROTA Emanuele Muzzarelli, announced that "the ministry, united with the chamber of the people's representatives and the senator of Rome, will take any further measures that circumstances may make necessary." A provisional Junta (*Provvisoria e Supreme Giunta di Stato*), presided over by the senator of Rome, Prince Tommaso Corsini, was formed on 11 December by a solemn act of the new body, which the cardinal secretary of state, Giacomo Antonelli, immediately disavowed in the pope's name.

A provisional ministry was formed on 23 December, under the presidency of Muzzarelli, with Armellini at the Ministry of the Interior. It was he who, on 29 December, convened a National Constituent Assembly elected throughout the former Papal States (now the Stato Romano) by universal male vote (on the basis of 21 years of age for a voter, and 25 for eligibility). The provisional Junta was dissolved on 3 January, following the dismissal of the senator of Rome, Corsini. The election results were proclaimed in Rome on 28 January, and the Roman Republic came into being on 10 February 1849 after the collapse of the pope's temporal government. Pius IX issued a solemn protest to the European powers on 14 February, which was read—and hooted down—at the bar of the National Assembly on 19 Feburary. All bridges were now forever broken between the new regime and the papacy, which saw its only salvation in foreign intervention.

The history of the Roman Republic is too brief to enable the historian to take the measure of its achievements. On the institutional level, the regime's regular functioning was quickly called into question on account of the worsening internal and external problems. An executive Committee was set up on 11 February leading to the proclamation of the Constitution. It consisted of three members, the two Roman lawyers Carlo Armellini and Mattia Montecchi and the Neapolitan revolutionary lawyer Aurelio Saliceti. The first ministry was created on 14 February, under the presidency of Muzzarelli, with a young revolutionary nobleman from Forli, Aurelio Saffi, at the Interior, Pietro Sterbini at Public Works, and Pompeo Di Campello at War. This ministry put forward the first measures characteristic of the new political and juridical order: the abolition of episcopal jurisdiction over universities and teaching colleges, except for seminaries (25 February); the solemn abolition of the tribunal of the Holy Office (28 February), on the proposition of Prince Carlo Bonaparte; the abolition of all the privileges of the Church's temporal jurisdiction (3 March); the suppression of the prior censorship of newspapers (5 March); the transformation of the Civil Guard into the National Guard (18 March).

Elected on 24 March at the Assembly, the Genoese Giuseppe Mazzini, the charismatic revolutionary head of Young Italy, who had returned after a long exile in London, rapidly acquired a decisive influence on the conduct of Republican politics. After the announcement of the resumption of hostilities between Piedmont and Austria (12 March), a prelude to the military fall of Piedmont at Novara (23 March), and the abdication of King Charles-Albert, the executive Committee yielded to a Triumvirate of public safety with dictatorial powers (29 March 1849), consisting of Giuseppe Mazzini, Aurelio Saffi, and Carlo Armellini. The latter energetically led the defense of the Republic and, encouraged by Mazzini, took some measures that were more reforming than truly revolutionary: the lodging of poor families in the palace of the Holy Office (4 April); the suppression of the Farm of Salt (15 April); a law (theoretical and unapplied) on the distribution of Church lands to peasants (15 April); and the suppression of the Distribution of Indirect Rights in the legations (9 May).

A plan for a democratic constitution was finally presented for discussion at the Assembly on 27 April. It was preceded by a preamble of eight fundamental principles (among them, "Sovereignty resides in the people through eternal law"; "The democratic regime has for its principles equality, liberty, and fraternity"; "The Republic considers all peoples as brothers; it respects all nationalities; it fights for Italy"; "The exercise of civil and political rights is independent of religious beliefs"; "The head of the Catholic Church will receive from the Republic all the guarantees necessary for the independent exercise of spiritual power"). The Assembly conferred legislative power on a single assembly of Representatives, elected every three years by universal male suffrage. Executive power was given to three consuls elected every three years by the Assembly by a two-thirds majority. Also established were a Council of State, a Council of Ministers, and a National Guard.

The Roman Republic was at the same time the occasion of an intense process of politicization. For the first time since the short-lived Roman Republic of 1798, general elections and then local elections introduced mechanisms for forming public opinion and defining political strategies within a civic culture that was doubly weakened, both by the outmoded absolutism of the papal government and by the habit of secrecy and conspiracy that had prevailed for a half-century among opponents of the regime. If popular participation in debates and discussions was limited, newspapers and posters mushroomed, and new types of political association appeared in the cities and small towns, in the shape of clubs and "speaking places" (F. Rizzi), that transformed networks of clienteles into "parties," landowners into "notables," and administrators into "government agents."

At the same time, under the divergent influences of the federalists (Cernuschi) and the unitarians (Mazzini), the limited horizons of municipal and local life opened up to plans and hopes for Italian unity. In this regard, the 1849 Roman Republic marks an important step in the consolidation of the ideas of the Risorgimento as a political culture and national program, as well as in the crystallization of the role of Rome as the future capital of a united Italy.

Nevertheless, the short existence of the Republic was overshadowed by the economic and social problems in which the new regime became inextricably entangled. The financial and monetary crisis arose from the extraordinarily high public debt, a legacy of the papal regime (forty-six million crowns in the form of devalued treasury bonds in the hands of individuals and foreign banks, mainly French and English). Aggravating it was the crisis in agriculture and industry, the collapse of commerce, and the flight of capital, as well as a policy of national workshops adopted to combat unemployment (the financing by the state of the reconstruction of the basilica of St. Paul's outside the Walls) a policy of expedients that did not succeed in arresting the rapid deterioriation of the Roman currency. The recognition of the state's public debt as a "national" and "inviolable" obligation (14 February) hardly restored confidence. The nationalization of ecclesiastical possessions (21 February) met with hostility on the part of the Church and Catholic milieus and anxiety on the part of peasant and urban clients of the convents and hospitals. The possessions of religious bodies and property in mortmain, a list of which was officially printed on 19 May, were declared up for sale from 4 March. Yet they found few buyers owing to the regime's uncertain future and the impracticability of the new state's prompt granting of its new goods to individuals.

On 21 February, the Banca Romana began to issue bills with a speculative price based on the future results of the sale of ecclesiastical possessions, and in a decree dated 28 February the state refused to accept payment of duty in treasury bonds or banknotes. The Republic voted in a law on forced borrowing (25 February). The shortage of currency, especially in small denominations, resulted in the introduction of the copper coins dubbed *moneta erosa* (eroded money), authorized by a decree of 3 March, and low-value bonds guaranteed by the local municipalities. In the final months, Mazzini took more radical steps: the requisition of individuals' hoards of gold and silver (19 April); the imposition of a forced loan of thirty-thousand crowns to the Santa Casa of Loreto (27 May); and a massive issue of low-value treasury bonds (14 June). These final measures gave rise to galloping inflation and the growing discredit of the regime among the landed classes, while anarchy, both monetary and, soon, political, gradually threatened the unity of the Roman states. Rome would be almost isolated by the other provinces of the Republic in the face of French military intervention.

This intervention had been called for by Catholic opinion throughout Europe from the time of Pius IX's flight to Gaeta. In the spring of 1849, it got under way. In Paris, the Constituent Assembly, still dominated by the moderates, on 17 April decreed the dispatch of a French army of intervention to Civitavecchia. The Assembly was determined to set the head of the universal Church once more on his throne, indifferent to the democratic and national aspirations of the pope's subjects, and perturbed by the internal development of the regime, weakened as it was by the growing number of local powers. On the other hand, the Assembly was also subject to the influence of those representing financial interests invested in the former Papal State, and hostile to Austria's newly preponderant influence in northern Italy. On 21 April, twelve thousand men left Marseille under the command of General Oudinot, who had been given ambiguous instructions. On 25 April, they landed at Civitavecchia. On 28 April, General Oudinot detected plotting against the Republic and marched on Rome to abet it. There, his advance guards were repulsed on 30 April.

The French elections, fixed for 15 May, which halted Oudinot's progress, brought a one-month respite to the Republican government, which mobilized opinion in favor of massive resistance to a certain future attack. Meanwhile, a mission to Rome led by Lesseps, under the direction of Drouyn de Lhuys, the minister of foreign affairs, tried to negotiate a settlement. But the triumphant winner in the French elections was the conservative Catholic party. On 1 June, General Oudinot communicated to the Republican authorities that he had received orders to seize "the fortress," meaning Rome. Meanwhile, in Paris, an uprising, during which the boulevards rang with cries of "Long live the Roman Republic!" failed. This impelled the president of the Council, Odilon Barrot, and the president of the Republic, Louis-Napoleon Bonaparte (who, as a former *carbonaro*, had been compromised in the Roman revolt of 1831), to have done with the democratic movement both inside and outside the French frontiers.

The final phase of the Roman Republic was dominated by resistance to the twenty-six-day siege (4–30 June 1849) laid by the French forces. Rome, though on the whole passive, stood firm, despite repeated bombardments, and Mazzini confessed himself powerless to prevent large numbers of soldiers and officers of the National Guard from deserting. It was the volunteers, under the command of Garibaldi and Manara, who led the main fighting under the city walls, while General Oudinot, through a series of tactical maneuvers, gradually tightened his vise. The military operations, brief but violent, were concentrated on the Janiculum, where, during the night of 30 June, after some violent fighting at the Villa Spada, the last resistance of the Roman Republic was broken.

That very day, in Paris, the National Assembly, which had solemnly adopted on 1 July a stillborn democratic Constitution, deliberated whether to bring the armed struggle to an end. On 3 July, General Oudinot's troops penetrated the silent, mostly hostile city. Thus began an occupation that would last, under a variety of forms, until 1870.

The deputies dispersed on 4 July, and the Assembly closed its business, but not before it issued a final protest: "In the name of God and the Roman people, which has freely elected its representatives by universal suffrage, in conformity also with article 5 of the French Constitution, the Roman Constituent Assembly protests, before Italy, before France, and before the civilized world, against the violent invasion of its seat carried out by the French armies at six o'clock on the evening of 4 July 1849."

After setting up a provisional government, on 21 July General Oudinot published a proclamation of Pius IX, dated from Gaeta on 17 July, "to his dearly beloved subjects": "God has raised his arm and has commanded the tempestuous waves of anarchy and impiety to cease. It is he who has led the Catholic armies so that they might uphold the rights of a trampled humanity and an embattled faith, as well as those of the Holy See and of Our Sover-

eignty. May he be praised eternally, he who, in the midst of his wrath, forgets not pity."

On 31 July, a new triumvirate (*Commissione governativa di Stato*) made up of cardinals Della Genga Sermattei, nephew of LEO XII, Vannicelli Casoni, and Altieri received the powers necessary to bring about the final restoration of the temporal government of the popes. Pius IX, who had been living in exile in Gaeta and then in Portici, returned to Rome only on 12 April 1850, accompanied by the cardinal secretary of state Antonelli. Henceforth, both men would be braced in defense of an ecclesiastical state, which they considered the guarantee of the freedom of the Church and the Apostolic See. Twenty years before the definitive collapse of a theocratic structure that had come into being fifteen centuries earlier in the wake of the disappearance of the Western Roman Empire, the Roman Republic of 1849 constituted, in both its greatness and its limitations, a decisive calling into question of the principle of the temporal sovereignty of the papacy. At the same time, it provided a fertile field of experiment for Italy's national and democratic movement, the Risorgimento.

Philippe Boutry

Bibliography

Beghelli, G. *La Repubblica Romana del 1849*, Lodi, 1874.

Demarco, D. *Pio IX e la Rivoluzione Romana del 1848. Saggio di storia economico sociale*, Modena, 1947.

Demarco, D. *Una rivoluzione sociale. La Repubblica Romana del 1849 (16 novembre 1848 – 3 luglio 1849)*, Naples, 1944.

Farini, L. C. *Lo Stato Romano dall'anno 1815 all'anno 1850*, Turin, 1850–3, 4 vols.

Gatta, B. "Le elezioni del 1849," *Archivio della Società romana di storia patria*, LXXII, 1949, 3–27.

Ghisalberti, A.-M. *Roma da Mazzini a Pio IX. Ricerche sulla restaurazione papale del 1849-1850*, Milan, 1958.

Giovagnoli, R. *Pellegrino Rossi e la Rivoluzione Romana*, Rome, 1898–1911, 3 vols.

Leovinson, E. *G. Garibaldi e la sua legione nello Stato Romano*, Rome, 1904–7, 3 vols.

Leti, G. *Le Rivoluzione e la Repubblica Romana*, Milan, 1913.

Rizzi, F. *La coccarda e le compane. Comunità rurali e Repubblica Romana nel Lazio (1848–1849)*, Milan, 1988.

Rodelli, L. *La Repubblica Romana del 1849 con appendice di documenti*, Pisa, 1955.

Rusconi, C. *La Répubblica Romana del 1849*, Capolago, 1852.

Spada, G. *Storia della Rivoluzione di Roma e della Restaurazione del Governo Pontificio dal 10; giugno 1846 al 15 luglio 1849*, Florence, 1868–9, 3 vols.

ROMANUS. *(b. Gallese, ?). Elected pope at the end of July or beginning of August 897, deposed in November 897.*

Like Pope MARINUS I, Romanus came from Gallese (near Cività Castellana). The son of one Constantine (not identified), he was appointed archpriest of S. Pietro in Vincoli and in late July or early August 897 was elected pope. The two documents drawn up during his pontificate for the sees of Elne and Gerona, to which should be added documents for Grado and Metz, now lost, give no indication of any particular political leanings or a clear position vis-à-vis the Formosan controversy. According to a 15-century catalog of the popes, Romanus spoke out against the anti-Formosans, particularly against Pope STEPHEN VI. That is doubtful, however, if the fact that Romanus may have been deposed in late November 897 by supporters of the Formosan party is taken into account. According to a notice in the codex Parisinus lat. 5140 dating from the 11th century (but which may refer to Stephen VI), he became a monk. This is perhaps what explains the raising to true papal dignity of a person such as THEODORE II, capable of acting more energetically in favor of Formosus. Nothing is known about the death or burial place of Romanus.

Klaus Herbers

Bibliography

JL I, 441; II, 705.

LP, 2, 230.

Morera, J. "Los papiros de la catedral de Gerona. Apendice: Bula del Papa Formose, Bula del Papa Roman," *Miscelanea J. Morera*, Barcelona, 1967, 105–18.

Scholz, S. *Transmigration und Translation. Studien zum Bistumeswechsel der Bischöffe von der Spätantike bis zum hohen Mittelalter*, Cologne-Weimar-Vienna, 1992 (*Kölner Historische Abhandlungen* 37), 225.

Zimmermann, H. *Papstabsetzungen des Mittelalters*, Graz-Vienna-Cologne, 1968, 59.

Zimmermann, H. *Papsturkunden 896–1046*, 2/988, 9–12.

ROME.

Middle Ages: City and Populations. The sources for studying the urban history of medieval Rome are essentially of two kinds. Up to the 9th or 10th century, they are virtually limited to the papal biographies of the LIBER PONTIFICALIS, which give only indirect information on the city. For the 10th to 14th centuries, one can consult the cartularies of the Roman churches and monasteries, as well as rare family archives. The latter contain countless notarized contracts of the sale and rental of property holdings, with the earliest specimens dating back to the 10th century. In addition, there is a rich series of notaries' minute books. Two irreplaceable documentary collections have been almost entirely lost: the communal archives, which disappeared in the sack of 1527, and urban chronicles, with the notable exception of the anonymous *Life of Cola di Rienzo*.

In the chronological arc formed on the upward curve by the Gothic wars and on the downward curve by the Avignon popes' return to Rome, the available sources make it possible to distinguish two medieval periods. The first extends roughly from the 6th century to the mid-11th and is characterized by the gradual fragmentation of inhabited areas inside the Aurelian wall; the second, covering the period from the 11th century to the 14th, is distinguished by the concentration of the inhabitated area close to the banks of the Tiber and the resulting abandonment to farm and waste land of most of approximately 1,500 hectares.

Fourth-century Rome still shone, but its luster was the afterglow of the past. Abandoned by the emperors, who preferred Constantine's new Rome on the Bosporus, it still housed the million inhabitants who had formed the population of the *urbs* since Augustus' reign. This was not to last long, however. Alaric's sack of 410, after a siege lasting nearly two years, and that of Genseric's Vandals in 455, caused the collapse of a city that lacked forces to defend and, especially, to revive it. In the middle of the 5th century, Rome's population amounted to 500,000 at very most.

Although this radical decrease naturally affected the city's density, it does not appear to have changed its geography, at least up to the cusp of the 5th to 6th centuries. This is revealed by studies of the topographical placement of Christian buildings that were in use at the end of the 5th century, since these indicate the way the population was distributed (Vieillard, Reekmans). It becomes clear that the area inhabited at that time was approximately that of imperial Rome. The official, monumental center made up of the Forum-Palatine-Capitol group and the Campo Marzio, like the boundaries of the great villas of the aristocracy, had been untouched by the Christianization of the city, no doubt because these areas were sparsely inhabited. Titular churches and sanctuaries were distributed as follows: on the Quirinal and the Esquiline, with a major concentration around the basilica of Pope LIBERIUS (352–66), rebuilt by SIXTUS III (432–40) (ST. MARY MAJOR); from the Constantinian basilica of the Lateran to the Coliseum, and also on the Coelian Hill; near the baths of Caracalla at the beginning of the Appian Way; at the foot of the PALATINE and toward the Circus Maximus, close to the lively quarter of the Velabrum; on the Aventine, near the port of Rome; in the inhabited areas surrounding the Campo Marzio; and, finally, in the densely populated Trastevere.

In this panorama, the Gothic wars of the first half of the 6th century mark a turning point. Between 536 and 552, sieges and conquests pitted Goths against Byzantines. In 537–8, Rome was besieged by Vitiges, who slashed the aqueducts. In 546, it was besieged by Totila, then by Belisarius in 547. It was conquered by Totila in 549–50 and finally captured by Narses in 552. These disasters accelerated a decline that had begun in the 5th century and left the city exhausted. From the mid-6th century to the 8th, Rome experienced one of the darkest periods of its history. The city's population plummeted, according to customary estimates, to a few tens of thousands of inhabitants, and these were decimated by epidemics (e.g., the plague of 590).

The outline of the urban habitat is hard to define. Doubtless the old quarters of the city continued to be inhabited in scattered fashion. However, what was new was the growth of housing in the monumental center. Evidence of this is the siting of Christian churches, from the beginning of the 6th century, in the Forum (SS. Cosma e Damiano, Sta. Maria Antiqua, and later St. Hadrian in the Curia) and in the Campo Marzio, where for the first time a pagan temple, the PANTHEON, was converted into a church, St. Mary and All the Martyrs, by Pope BONIFACE IV (608–15). The appearance of cemeteries even inside the Forum and Campo Marzio is further evidence of this geographical shift of the inhabited area, which is usually attributed to the destruction of the aqueducts.

In the second half of the 8th century and in the century following, a considerable revival of building—public, religious, and secular—characterized the Carolingian period and seems to have checked the decline of Rome. From GREGORY the Great (590–604) to PAUL I (757–67), the *Liber pontificalis* cites barely 80 references to papal orders for the construction and restoration of Christian monuments. In contrast, the popes from HADRIAN I (772–95) to JOHN VIII (872–82) undertook more than 180 similar works. The biography of LEO III (795–816) lists the gifts the pope made in 806 or 807 to all the churches, sanctuaries, monasteries, and oratories of Rome, which then numbered 117. Moreover, the list is not comprehensive, omitting most of the cemeterial churches and a few urban ones. The *Liber pontificalis* also mentions repairs that Hadrian I caused to be carried out on four aqueducts that had been almost unusable (Aqua Claudia, Aqua Iovia, Aqua Traiana, and Aqua Virgo), with his successors GREGORY IV (827–44), SERGIUS II (844–7), and NICHOLAS I (858–67) continuing the work.

For the preceding period, the size of the population and its distribution in the Roman area are still matters for conjecture, despite the relatively abundant documentation, enriched by the first pilgrims' guide, compiled around 800 and known as the *Einsiedeln Itinerary*. The topographical implanting of deaconries, centers of social welfare—of which there were 18 from the end of the 8th century—and churches remains the guiding index. In the 9th century, the monumental center probably continued to be filled at an even faster rate. By now, the Forum contained nearly 15 churches and oratories. In the Campo Marzio,

more than 20 churches and monasteries went up in the area enclosed by the Tiber, the Quirinal to the east, and the Capitol to the south. And yet there does not seem to have been a simultaneous abandonment of the hills: the Quirinal, Esquiline, Coelian, and Aventine, for instance, continued to be inhabited, if thinly, up to the 13th–14th centuries.

Symbolic of the period, the Vatican region underwent a remarkable boom with the growth of pilgrims' scholae in the 8th and 9th centuries and Charlemagne's creation of a residence near ST. PETER's. After being sacked in 846 by the SARACENS, who pillaged the basilica, the area was surrounded by a wall which Pope LEO IV (847–55) built from 848–52 on the initiative and with the financial help of Emperor Lothar. Thereafter, under the name Civitas Leoniana, it became the city's new religious and political pole. Yet the rise in construction and public works does not seem to have been based on any real urban growth, nor did it promote such an increase. No doubt we must instead see such developments as the material result of Rome's conquering stance as the religious capital of the West (Delogu).

Even less is known of the period from the late 9th century to the beginning of the 11th. From the last decades of the 9th century, the entries in the *Liber pontificalis* regarding the popes' building activities are few and far between, while notarized documents—which from the 11th century become the best source for urban history—are still very fragmentary. Yet one can trace the shape of the inhabited area, characterized at the time by a landscape of isolated settlements and scattered housing. The Tiber plain had not yet begun to attract the mass of the population, a large part of which lived in small dispersed centers, veritable hamlets inside the wall, as well as in isolated houses. In the 10th and 11th centuries, certain dwellings were the object of a transaction of which the deed has been preserved. This shows that over a quarter of them were scattered on the hills and close to the walls. The Quirinal, Esquiline, and Coelian hills were still partly inhabited, while the Aventine was once the site of the paternal home of Prince Alberic, who founded a monastery there, and Otto III's political aspirations encouraged him to build his palace on the Palatine.

In the Forum and in the Campo Marzio and, on the other side of the river, in the Leonine City and Trastevere, where the heart of the population was beginning to be concentrated, houses were still very much dispersed. Churches and monasteries of recent foundation acted as poles of attraction for the population (S. Maria Nova in the Forum, S. Ciriaco in the Via Lata, S. Lorenzo in Lucina, and S. Silvestro in Capite in the Campo Marzio, SS. Cosma e Damiano in Mica Aurea in Trastevere). Here nuclei of settlements grew up, still isolated from one another—the embryos of future city quarters.

The documentation changes in character from the 10th and 11th centuries. Cartularies of churches and monasteries provide a large quantity of notarized deeds concerned specifically with housing. The sale and rental of houses as well as deeds parceling out land provide direct information on the urban expansion that changed the Roman landscape from around the year 1000. At that time, a general economic and demographic increase took place from which Rome was not exempt.

The phenomenon of increasing dispersal and fragmentation that had defined the preceding period ceased from the first half of the 11th century, giving way to an opposite trend. Henceforward, development was characterized by the concentration of dwellings near the Tiber, a vector of growth, and a contrasting opening up of space inside the Aurelian wall so as to create two distinct areas, one inhabited and the other not, the first urban and the second rural—and clearly perceived as such by the Romans.

The trend that had begun in the 1010s slowed between the mid-11th century and the first quarter of the 12th as the capital of Christianity reeled from the blows of the Gregorian reform, the Investiture Controversy, and the concordat of Worms. The most violent episode in this period was the SACK of the city in 1084 by Robert Guiscard and his Norman followers. The Normans had come to the aid of GREGORY VII, who was being besieged by Emperor Henry IV. Henry himself was responsible for the destruction of part of the Septizodium of Septimius Severus. If Rome did not entirely go up in flames, as a certain romantic historiographer claimed who relied on sources hostile to the reforming pope, the areas around S. Lorenzo in Lucina and along the Via Maior linking the Lateran to the Coliseum, together with San Clemente and the church of the Quattro Santi Coronati, still suffered severe damage.

In the years 1120–30, growth resumed with renewed vigor, reaching a peak around 1280, when it again lost steam. It would not be repeated until the Renaissance. Far from being spontaneous, urban expansion was controlled in large measure by the ecclesiastical establishments; some of the most dynamic of these became veritable real estate promoters. Monasteries and churches granted building land at conditions advantageous for the buyers, trying to attract the newly immigrant population in order to ensure better management of their patrimony. In so doing, they also achieved their primary goal, an increase in their congregations. The best documented parcelings are those to the north of the city, which radically transformed the landscape. Here, three monasteries—S. Ciriaco in the Via Lata by the first half of the 11th century, S. Maria in Campo Marzio and S. Silvestro in Capite in the 12th and 13th centuries—were chiefly responsible for the whole or partial urbanization of the RIONI of Trevi, Colonna, and Campo Marzio. In other sections of the city, certain monastic establishments did not lag far behind. Thus SS. Andrea e Gregorio in Clivo Scauri, on the Coelian hill, undertook in the 11th century to populate the area known as Orrea between the Tiber and Aventine, and, in the 13th century, the southern corner of the Palatine. Another example is that of SS. Cosma e Damiano in Mica Aurea (today S. Cosimato), which in the second half of the 12th century strove to attract people to the relatively uninhabited Trastevere. The result of these real estate operations was the establishment of new neighborhoods laid out in regular urban fashion and with a modest, homogeneous social makeup. These contrasted with the older urbanized center at the bend of the Tiber, where the towers and palaces of nobles and barons stood side by side with the humbler dwellings of their clients and family members.

The commune, born in 1143 in a context of demographic and economic boom, does not appear to have played a significant part in the urban expansion—unless the disappearance of its archives is responsible for that impression. Besides the repair of walls and certain bridges, the creation in the early 13th century of the office of the *magistri aedificiorum Urbis*, which was responsible for regulating matters relating to buildings and roads, is evidence of the interest the Senate took in urban problems. Their attention also extended to the monuments of Antiquity, the "glory of the Roman people," which the communal magistrates strove to preserve "so that they may endure as long as the world" (senatorial judgment concerning Trajan's Column dated 27 March 1162). On the other hand, the Senate does not seem to have undertaken the public works program that turned most Italian cities of that period into permanent building sites. The only important public construction was that carried out in autumn 1348, in the wake of the Black Death, of the monumental votive staircase leading up to the church of S. Maria d'Aracoeli.

Rome was not spared from the catastrophes and epidemics that swept the second half of the 14th century. The periodic return of the plague every 15 or 20 years—1348, 1363, 1383, 1400—battered a population that may (the indices are lacking) have numbered about 30,000 souls. On 9 and 10 September 1349, the city suffered an earthquake that, most notably, caused part of the Coliseum to crumble and the top of the tower of the Conti to collapse. Certain districts were abandoned at that time, or would have been but for special measures. In the 14th century, the area around S. Maria in Pallara was thus abandoned, causing the Palatine to be definitely deserted; in 1386, the conservators enacted special statutes granting exemption from taxes and many other privileges to the inhabitants of the Via Maggiore, linking St. John Lateran and the Coliseum, in order to halt the depopulation of the area.

Nevertheless, the sources we possess concerning this practice—notarized deeds and inventories of inherited estates—do not give a picture of a city brought down low by disaster. Before the return of the papacy, extensive immigration from Latium and more distant regions seems to have tempered the effects of demographic catastrophes. The Avignon exile did not, in fact, drain the vital forces of the city. In the urban history of Rome, the 14th century is one of economic and social affirmation of a dominant class of *homines novi*, landowners, agricultural entrepreneurs, and merchants, of whom the "popular" regime of the *felice società* of the Balestrieri, the Pavesati, and the government of the Banderesi from 1358 to 1398 were the political expression (Maire-Vigueur).

With the return of the papacy in 1377 and the GREAT SCHISM (1378–1417), Rome henceforth emerged from the Middle Ages.

Étienne Hubert

Bibliography

Bertolini, O. *Roma di fronte a Bisanzio e ai Longobardi*, Bologna, 1941 (*Storia di Roma*, 9).

Brezzi, P. *Roma e l'Impero Medioevale*, 774–1252, Bologna, 1947 (*Storia di Roma*, 10).

Castagnoli, F., Cecchelli, C., Giovanni, G., and Zocca, M. *Topografia e urbanistica di Roma*, Bologna, 1958 (*Storia di Roma*, 22).

Delogu, P. "The Rebirth of Rome in the 8th and 9th Centuries," *The Rebirth of Towns in the West, A.D. 700–1050*, ed. R. Hodges and B. Hobley, CBA Research Report 68 (1988), 32–42.

Duchesne, L. Scripta Minora. *Études de topographie romaine et de géographie ecclésiastique*, Rome, 1973 (Collection de l'École Française de Rome, 13); *Roma e l'età carolingia, Atti della giornate di studio* (1976), Rome, 1976.

Dupré-Theseider, E. *Roma dal Comune di Popolo alla Signoria Pontificia* (1252–1377), Bologna, 1952 (*Storia di Roma*, 11).

Hubert, É. *Espace urbain et habitat à Rome du Xe siècle à la fin du XIIIe siècle*, Rome, 1990 (*Collection de l'École française de Rome*, 135; *Nuovi studi storici*, 7).

Hubert, É. "Patrimoines immobiliers et habitat à Rome au Moyen Age: la *Regio Columnae* du XIe siècle à la fin du XIIIe siècle," *MEFRM*, 101 (1989), 133–75.

Insolera, I. *Roma: Imagini e realtà dal x al xx secolo*, Bari, 1980 (*Le città nella storia d'Italia*).

Krautheimer, R. *Rome: Profile of a City, 312–1308*, Princeton, 1980.

Maire-Vigueur, J. C. "Classe dominante et classes dirigeantes à Rome à la fin du Moyen Age," *Storia della Città*, 1 (1976), 4–26.

Reekmans, L. "L'implantation monumentale chrétienne dans le paysage urbain de Rome de 300–850," *Actes du XIe congrès international d'archéologie chrétienne* (1986), Rome, 1989 (Collection de l'École Française de Rome, 123; *Studi di antichità cristiana*, 41), 2, 861–915.

Roma anno 1300, Atti della IV settimana di studi di storia dell'arte medievale dell'Università di Roma "La Sapienza" (1980), Roma, 1983.

Viellard, R. *Recherches sur les origines de la Rome chrétienne: Essai d'urbanisme chrétien, Mâcon*, 1941, 2nd ed., Rome, 1959.

Ward-Perkins, B. *From Classical Antiquity to the Middle Ages: Urban Public Buildings in Northern and Central Italy, A.D. 300–850*, Oxford, 1984.

See also BYZANTIUM AND THE PAPACY.

Middle Ages: Government. At the end of the 6th century, after 13 centuries of history and greatly weakened by the bloody war between the Byzantines and Goths (535–53), the Roman SENATE died a natural death. For a long time there had been a steady transference in Rome of public functions from the State to the Church. After the Byzantine reconquest, the city administration still retained part of its services. It was still headed by the *prefectus urbis*, who in theory had the same duties as before, but the management of public services was now gradually being turned over to the pope. During the papacy of GREGORY the Great, food provisioning, though under the control of the city government, was already almost entirely the responsibility of the bishop of Rome, as was another major branch of municipal administration, the maintenance of the city ramparts. Thirty years later, under the pontificate of HONORIUS I (625–38), the service managing the upkeep of aqueducts also came under papal authority. The Senate disappeared, as did the city prefecture, in fact if not by fiat, the last mention of a *prefectus urbis* dates from 599, and, aside from a reference in 772, the prefecture reappears regularly only in 965. As regular services under the prefect were interrupted toward the end of the 6th century, the popes began to carry out certain duties of the temporal government in Rome in the place of the constituted lay authorities.

The institution of the duchy of Rome—a territorial jurisdiction centered in Rome that was headed by a general, or *dux*, who enjoyed military and civil powers—took place after 582 within the framework of a general political and administrative reorganization of the territories of Byzantine Italy. The duchy was aimed at confronting the LOMBARDS. At this time, the *prefectus urbis* became gradually less important, although he retained his authority in the judicial domain and in that of urban policing and public order. From the second half of the 7th century, he was apparently replaced by the *dux* heading the civil and military administration of the city and its surrounding area, and the government of Rome passed into the hands of the *dux* as well as the pope, who now counted as an important force in the civil life of the city. The duumvirate of pope and duke was strengthened as a result of the Lombard invasion carried out by King Liutprand against the Roman duchy in 739, when Lombard forces invaded the duchy and camped at the gates of Rome, pillaging the surrounding territory. The Roman people were forced to seek help from other quarters than the emperor. In an attempt to defend the city and its outlying region, GREGORY III (731–41) and Duke Stephen created a new political body, the *Ecclesia Santa Dei et ejus peculiaris populus*. This led, in practice, to the formation of an autonomous Roman duchy under the protection of St. Peter and the Church; it would become the nucleus of the future PAPAL STATES.

The popes' temporal power thus gradually increased, as did their lands. The Papal States began actually to take shape a few years later, when Gregory III's successors, popes ZACHARIAS (741–52) and STEPHEN II (752–57), established the first alliances with the FRANKS and thus laid the foundations for a restoration of the Western Empire. At this time, with the end of Byzantine rule over northern and central Italy (RAVENNA was seized by the Lombards in 751), the Byzantine duchies in Italy became autonomous, while the pope replaced the duke and the imperial government in the administration of the duchy of Rome, exercising his sovereignty and becoming to all intents and purposes a temporal overlord.

In the second half of the 8th century, this new situation had an effect on the administration of the city. Henceforth, the pope took the place of the duke and was head of the *res publica Romanorum*, whose center was Rome. Thus the spiritual lord of the city was now the supreme local authority. He enjoyed the support of an efficient bureaucratic organization made up of the *judices de clero*, who were entrusted with managing the affairs of the Church and the city of Rome. The principal officers of the ecclesiastical bureaucracy and its actual administrators were as follows: the *primicerius notarorium*, who until the 10th century was the head of the CHANCERY and who was charged with directing the most delicate political affairs; the *secundicerius*, his deputy; the *arcarius*, who headed the financial administration; the *sacellarius*, who during the 12th century, together with the *arcarius*, was replaced by the chamberlain, a single functionary who managed the papal treasury; the *protoscriniarius*, head of the *scrinium* and the secretaries of the chancery; the *primus defensor*, doubtless a Church attorney, and the *nomenclator*, charged with defending widows, orphans, and prisoners.

Having thus set itself up as a political force, no longer only spiritual, all the Roman Church needed was a formal acknowledgment of its sovereign rights and its new independence vis-à-vis all temporal powers which it had acquired by inheriting the authority of the Byzantine functionaries in the duchy of Rome. From 781, on more than one occasion, the Church received this recognition from Charlemagne.

Toward the mid-8th century, Roman documents again begin to speak of a "Senate." Alongside the increasingly powerful ecclesiastical aristocracy of the *proceres Ecclesiae* and the *judices de clero*, there emerged a new Roman aristocratic class, that of the *optimates* and *judices de militia*, whose members—a civil aristocracy that had disappeared in the continual warring with the Lombards—began to assume the title of *nobiles senatores*. In other words, the birth of the temporal realm of the popes was accompanied by a first *renovatio senatus*.

One of the problems of the history of Rome, and certainly one of the most controversial and difficult to resolve, is whether or not the Senate persisted during the period between the late 6th century and the *renovatio senatus*, properly speaking, of 1143–4. According to recent studies, the Senate referred to in the second half of the 8th century no longer had anything to do with the old assembly. The term had been unearthed by a small, homogeneous local aristocratic group. Thus, the argument in favor of the continuity of the Roman Senate in medieval times appears untenable. On the other hand, it seems clear that after the rupture of the 7th century, the name and prestige of the Senate had regained currency in Rome, and it was the new military aristocracy that took over the old title of senator. From then on, up to the middle of the 11th century, the Roman aristocracy (although with other social connotations) tried in various ways to gain control of the *patriarchium* of the Lateran—now no longer only the seat of Church government but the center of gravity of all Roman political life. During the painful phase of the conflict with Byzantium and under the Lombard threat, the two Roman aristocratic classes, ecclesiastic and military, had formed an alliance to provide the Holy See with unconditional support; once the new political organism was formed, the military aristocracy saw its political ambitions satisfied. However, relations between the pope and the two aristocracies subsequently deteriorated. Members of the military aristocracy, systematically excluded from the Roman government which henceforth was monopolized by the *proceres Ecclesiae*, tried to regain control of the levers of power by force after the death of PAUL I (767). For a few years, Rome was torn by internal factions intent on gaining control of the Holy See. The dissension was briefly laid to rest with the election of HADRIAN I (771–95). Nevertheless, the problem persisted, since the Roman lay aristocracy, impelled not only by concrete interests but also by the memory of ancient usage, continued to claim the right to govern the city. It opted to join forces with the ecclesiastical aristocracy and penetrated the highest reaches of power, finally becoming a breeding ground for the recruitment of cardinal clergy and the training of managers of the new body of state.

According to Pierre Toubert, there existed, at the beginning of the 10th century, no Senate in the strict sense of term: an assembly with a distinct role. Nonetheless, the leading Roman class continued to call itself *senatus* or *ordo senatorius*, thus proving, at least, that it had a strong sense of itself as a group. This elite, unified social class, of uncertain ancestry, based its power on a double foundation: an economic one, clearly, but also another that was bureaucratic, inasmuch as the members of the Roman aristocracy henceforth were entrusted with the most important offices of the pontifical *palatium*. It was from this senatorial group that those members were chosen who, in the pope's name, administered justice, supervised the urban and rural militias, and managed the patrimony of the Church. At the beginning of the 10th century, there was no longer any opposition between lay aristocracy and ecclesiastical bureaucracy but rather a single restricted social group, the *ordo senatorius*, which enjoyed undisputed control of all the levers of power.

The political vicissitudes of 10th-century Rome are closely tied to the *primates romani* and the triumph of local forces. During the first 20 years of the century, the Roman state was dominated by the figure of the patrician Theophylact. The fact that he took over the reins of power as a representative of the Roman aristocracy as a whole, which in turn gave him unanimous support, lent his leadership peculiar stability, without opposition in any form. This also allowed him to set up a dynastic rule. His family's power continued after his death (around 924) until the middle of the century, first with his daughter Marozia (924–32), then with his grandson Alberic (932–54). Thus, for the first time it became possible to subordinate papal dignity to an exclusively Roman political force represented by a local family line. Theophylact was determined, moreover, to reorganize the economy of the PATRIMONY and to restore social order and peace, in particular by confronting the serious problems of Saracen raids and highway robbery. Aside from their destabilizing effect, these threatened the movement of pilgrims, goods, and money. The immediate interests of the Church of Rome and the lay aristocracy thus coincided perfectly with Theophylact's actions.

The coming to power of Alberic, Theophylact's grandson, created an entirely new situation in Rome. In 932, he put an end to the dictatorship of his mother, Marozia. His mother, who had married Hugh of Provence in her third marriage, abandoned the family political line and presented a serious threat to Roman autonomy. To the urban nobility and the Romans, she appeared too closely linked to the Burgundian intruders who had followed her husband. Such were the causes of the so-called general uprising of citizens. The links between Alberic and the Romans at the time of the revolt of 932 are unclear. According to the chronicler Liutprand of Cremona, Alberic was regularly elected *dominus* by the Roman peo-

ple, while Benedict of S. Andrea of Monte Soracte refers more convincingly to sworn agreements that were concluded before the uprising. What is certain is that Alberic, who emerged from the revolt victorious, must have aggravated the citizens' resentment.

Alberic held on to power in virtually undisputed fashion for more than 20 years, enjoying total supremacy. He succeeded in strengthening his autocratic power by completely replacing the pope in the temporal government of Rome and its environs, gaining the support of a small group of members of the Palatine aristocracy and bureaucracy, and at the same time acting through the intermediary of suburbican bishops. His exclusive personal authority, which was backed by powerful landholdings and consequently by his own militias and functionaries, did not encourage him to take on a particular post within the framework of Roman administration. He preserved the forms of government as they existed, at the same time imposing his influence on them. All the urban magistratures continued to function, but under his control.

The successive popes who occupied the throne of St. Peter over the 20 years of the reign of the *princeps* wielded no effective power. In Rome at that time, two outstanding divisions of power coexisted: one religious, represented by the pope, and the other civil, exercised with force and authority by Alberic. Nonetheless, shortly before his death, he appeared to realize that the government of Rome could be entrusted only to the pontiffs. To guarantee his family a dominant position, he made the Romans swear to elect his son Octavian as pope.

Roman political life in the second half of the 10th century, except for the end of Alberic's regime, exhibited two new trends. On the one hand, there was the growth of imperial power, which, with the restoration of empire in the person of Otto I, weighed heavily on the Romans; on the other, the obvious movement from principate to oligarchy in Rome's domestic politics. Alberic's death and the baneful period of the papacy of his son Octavian (JOHN VII) ended definitively the leading position that Theophylact's family had maintained for 50 years. Thereafter, several families squabbled over power in Rome.

At the very end of the 10th century, the Roman aristocracy managed once more to seize the reins of power, aided by the high curial clergy. The principal representatives of this aristocracy at the time were the Crescenzi. Without in any way cherishing hopes of placing a family member on the papal throne, the Crescenzi used every means at their disposal to exercise their power, in particular by manipulating pontifical elections and intervening directly in the temporal administration of the Church. The year 985 is said to mark the beginning of the patriciate of Giovanni, a son of Crescenzio de Theodora. The pope having made him *patricius*—a lay representative of the pope—for some years, he instituted a mode of accommodation between the pope and the NOBILITY. In Contrast, his brother Crescenzio II set up a veritable dictatorship. During the last years of the 10th century, all the city's bureaucratic services were under his tight control, leaving the pope without any say in the government.

The Crescenzi dominance ended with the intervention of Otto III (998), but it was repeated a few years later in the decade 1002–12. The death of Otto III and the failure of his impossible imperial plan had demonstrated clearly to the Romans that it was time to give the city a political system similar to the one in force during the first half of the 10th century, before the arrival of the Saxons. Once more Rome withdrew into itself, and once more it was governed by a patriciate chosen from among the most distinguished local lineage of the day, the Crescenzi. The Roman aristocracy again wielded effective power in the city, supported by the patrician Giovanni (1002–12), son of Crescenzio II. According to the governmental formula adopted by his predecessors, Giovanni was the political governor of Rome. He administered justice, aided by his relatives whom he entrusted with the main municipal posts, while the popes remained free to fulfill their apostolate.

Giovanni died in 1012. The Crescenzi were replaced by a rising new family, the Tuscolani. The Roman political scene changed radically, and the dualism between ecclesiastical authority and aristocratic power that had been established at the beginning of the 10th century came to an end. The Tuscolani, who long enjoyed a monopoly in Rome's political leadership, were able to restore the heritage of the *princeps*. Understanding that the only power capable of imposing its authority on Rome was that of the pope, they tried mainly to control the papacy. Thus, instead of appointing a *princeps* or *patricius* with full political powers alongside a pope entrusted solely with spiritual duties, they preferred to hand over the government of Rome to a pope chosen from the family and to assume the principal city positions.

In this way, for 30 years the Tuscolani held papal office (popes BENEDICT VIII, 1013–24, JOHN XIX, 1024–33, and BENEDICT IX, 1033–45, were all related to the counts of Tuscolum) and enjoyed uncontested power in Rome. They succeeded in shrewdly juggling the interests of the papacy and those of the local aristocracy until this balance collapsed as a result of a complex of circumstances. Chief among these were the mediocrity of Benedict IX, the fear of the oligarchs faced with the clear affirmation of a dynastic principle, and the restoration of imperial authority in the person of Henry III, who was far more committed than his predecessors to Church reform. Thus, on the eve of the Gregorian REFORM, the extravagant power of the Tuscolani dynasty, which had been founded on the monopoly of pontifical dignity, was broken, yet its actions had important repercussions. Abandoning the dual system of government and the criterion of sharing power

in order to concentrate on a strengthened pontifical dignity, the Tuscolani exercised the gradual assertion of papal power and prepared the way for the *Reformpapsttum*, giving rise to the process that led to the decree of 1059 on pontifical election.

In the mid-11th century, the political framework of Rome and Latium changed radically with the advent of reform. It was at this time that the new procedure was established that regulated papal elections: the right to name and elect the candidate was reserved for cardinals, that is, bishops of suburbicarian dioceses and titular heads of Roman churches. From the reign of GREGORY VII (1073–85), the pope set himself up as sovereign ruler of a unified state. Thus, the Holy See abandoned the patrimonial concept of his domains and adopted that of the state. To confront problems raised by this power, a profound transformation of the organs of government took place. For example, from the second half of the 11th century we see the disappearance of the *palatium* and the old papal bureaucracy and the increased power of the Roman CURIA. The administrative duties of the seven Palatine judges were gradually reduced, as was the number of the principal officers of the pontifical bureaucracy, until they disappeared for good in the second half of the 12th century. By contrast, the college of cardinals took on greater and greater importance and authority. This electoral body of the papacy became the pivot of the new pontifical administration and, from the first quarter of the 12th century, appears as an effective central organ of government.

The decisive change in the Holy See's political system occurred from the second half of the 11th century. The Holy See freed itself from the weighty influence that the old Roman oligarchy had long exercised over it. At the same time, within the framework of the civil organization new social forces and new leading families (Pierleoni, Frangipane, Normanni, Sant-Eustachio) made their entrance on the Roman political scene. For several more decades, the antireform sentiments of the old aristocracy survived, although they had been the main target of the reform movement. Often, these aristocrats used the destabilizing weapon of the coronation of ANTIPOPES to rebel against central authority; but over the first quarter of the 12th century, these families, who had begun to emerge by the end of the preceding century, gradually gained greater financial and political power. In short, the time had come to create a new city order. The war with Tivoli (1142–3) and the Romans' grumblings following the talks the pope had initiated with the defeated city provoked an unforeseen and violent uprising and encouraged the Romans to renovate the Roman Senate.

Much has been said and written about whether this revolt was democratic in nature, and about the makeup of the *populus romanus*, about which nothing is known save that it took an active part in the rebellion. What is certain is that it is very risky to see in the *renovatio senatus* of 1143 the sign of a corporate political consciousness. That is too reminiscent of the history of the northern Italian communes. In Rome, the communal life of the artisans and small merchants had not yet attained that solid structure which in other communes found expression in political action. Instead, the protagonists of the revolt belonged to the class of *cives possidentes*, the petty nobility and bourgeoisie who had fought in the Tivoli war and objected to the pope's decision to deal with their old enemy.

The revolt of 1143 and the proclamation of the Senate were not immediately followed by a definition of that body's tasks and sphere of activity. It is even highly probable that the papal prefecture continued to function, all the while preserving its prerogatives and tasks. It was not for several months that a definition of the new organ of government was determined. A patrician, Giordano Pierleoni, was elected who had supreme power in the city; and in autumn 1144, the Senate embarked on its official life as an annually elected assembly. The next year (15 February 1145), the Senate asked the new pontiff to recognize and legalize its position. The blank refusal it met with only hardened the senators' position. The urban prefecture was abolished and all rights entrusted to the commune. Toward the end of the year, the two sides reached agreement. The patriciate was abolished and the prefecture set up once again.

The Senate won papal recognition, but the investiture of its members was the prerogative of the pope. Nonetheless, EUGENE III's departure from Rome immediately after the short-lived peace and his travels to Lombardy and France meant that, in the years immediately after 1145, the post of prefecture lacked all authority, and the Senate wielded practically total administrative power in the city.

Despite its name, which evoked the ancient Capitoline assemblage and its seat, the Capitol, the revived Senate corresponded to the legislative councils of the other Italian communes and, like them, had duties of a political, legislative, financial, and judicial nature. Its members (originally about 50, then more) were elected by a parliament and held office for a year, from 1 November.

Eugene III's return to Italy in 1148 and the ensuing war with the Romans (beginning in spring 1149) led the two sides to draw up a new agreement (November 1149). The senators agreed to make important concessions to the pope (oath of loyalty, total restitution of regalian rights and monies taken from ecclesiastical institutions, repair of fortifications and dismantling of defenses outside the city), proving that Rome's claims to autonomy were by that time considerably weakened. Over the next 20 years, the Roman commune found itself in a difficult position. The serious differences between Emperor Frederick I Barbarossa and popes HADRIAN IV and ALEXANDER III, the popes' long absence from Rome because of the 1159

SCHISM, and the emperor's extremely rigid attitude toward the commune—to which he refused to grant autonomy—generally encouraged rapprochement with the popes. Only for very brief periods was there alliance with the empire, provoked exclusively by the change in relations between the Roman commune and the pope, and the emperor's influence in Rome gradually declined from 1167.

As a result of an agreement made with Alexander III (Anagni pact of November 1176), Frederick I gave back to the pope the urban prefecture he had obtained 10 years earlier from the Romans and definitively gave up all interference in Rome's internal administration. The dispute with the emperor thus settled, Alexander III again preoccupied himself with Rome and its relations with the commune. The latter, weakened because of the alliance between the two greater powers, quickly lost its autonomy. In the first months of 1178, a new agreement was reached whereby it was decided that the senators should swear loyalty to the pope and restore the regalian rights that the commune had long ago usurped from the pope. Still, disputes between the city and the pontiff persisted, and in the years following Alexander III's death (1181), the resumption of the relentless struggle with the empire, the popes' absence from Rome, and the succession of three popes in a mere seven years to the seat of St. Peter (LUCIUS III, URBAN III, and GREGORY VIII, 1181–88) greatly weakened the Holy See's local position.

Only the election of CLEMENT III, a pope of Roman birth, changed the situation. On 31 March 1188, an agreement of great historical importance was reached between the pope and the commune. Clement III managed to regain practically all that the papacy had lost over the past 40 years. With his supremacy once again imposed, the senators recognized him as their lord and requested that he endow them with powers of investiture. They promised to restore to him all regalian rights, the Senate, and the city, and to defend Rome. One of the consequences of the agreement was an increase in the number of senators and the entrance of a large number of members of the highest classes (such as the Cenci, Boboni, Parenzi, Malabranca, and Astalli). Numerous representatives of noble Roman families with close ties to the pope entered the administration and took on important posts, thus obviously enabling Clement III to control the commune more easily.

At this time there occurred an instance in which a single man seized control of the Senate. According to recent research, this man, Benedetto Carushomo, was neither a *homo novus* nor a people's representative hoisted by it to power. On the contrary, he seems to have belonged to the senatorial class. As a result, his seizure of power originated in the Senate itself, although it is highly likely that the "people" supported him. The change in institutions that came in with Benedetto was of short duration

(1191–3), and, after his dismissal and incarceration, the Senate once again exercised collective control. Nevertheless, the experiment had immediate repercussions. In a few years' time, the imposition of such a dictator was again attempted on several occasions. In time, an alternation of one or two senators became the norm. Still, the pope quickly reestablished his control over them.

INNOCENT III played an active part in this restoration. In the course of his long pontificate (1198–1216), he strove to give Rome and the PATRIMONY a solid administrative and governmental framework that lasted throughout the 13th century. Innocent III restored the post of prefect, whose duties were, however, much curtailed to the benefit of the commune. He did away with the municipal officers of the districts, to which he dispatched his own functionaries. He modified the system of senatorial election, reserving to himself the right of nomination to the highest city magistrature. This affirmation of ecclesiastical jurisdiction over the Patrimony soon rekindled the antagonism of the Romans. In the first years of Innocent III's papacy, the Roman commune resumed its activity, provoking various incidents encouraged by ever-eager aspirations to civil autonomy as well as by the growing importance of rivalries between the noble families, who tried to seize commanding positions in the city and Curia. Once again, the turmoil ended with the reinstatement of ecclesiastical supremacy over Roman life, whereupon Innocent III was once more able to direct his attention to the Patrimony. Yet, at his death, the Romans' discontent resurged in a fresh agitation aimed at abolishing the system he had set in place. In 1225, the choice of Parenzo as senator was a clear sign of rejection of the temporal supremacy of the Curia. It demonstrated the desire of the civil forces to claim communal rights.

In May 1234, Rome experienced yet another revolt, the most serious of all those arising from clashes with the pope over the past hundred years. The commune—encouraged by Senator Luca Savelli, the boldest defender of civil autonomy in the 13th century—wanted to exercise direct power over vast domains that were directly under the pope's jurisdiction. Further, it requested a restoration of the free election of the Senate and the rights to mint coinage and to collect salt taxes. GREGORY IX retaliated by excommunicating the commune's officers and declaring war. Victorious, he signed an accord with the Romans in the spring of 1235. Nonetheless, although all the lands seized during the uprising were restored to the pope, some of the commune's old privileges were recognized, such as the free election of senators and the rights to mint coins and to demand salt taxes.

Meanwhile, deteriorating relations between the pontiff and Frederick II had impelled the emperor to instigate the creation in Rome of a party devoted to him. From 1236 to 1241, Frederick II wielded great influence in Rome. His supporters fomented antagonistic relations with the parti-sans of the pope, and the resultant strife forced Gregory IX to flee the city on several occasions. The fierce rivalry between the two Roman parties and the support that each found in the city is also shown by the fact that, in 1238, two senators were elected, representing the two leading trends: Giovanni Poli, pro-imperial, and Oddone di Giordano Colonna, who favored the pope. Then, as had happened in the past, relations between the Romans and the pontiff fluctuated, but papal domination was still preferable to imperial absolutism.

Furthermore, there were a host of moral and practical reasons linking the Romans to the Church, in particular the fact that, in the absence of the papal court, the many advantages that ensued from its presence were lacking. Parallel with what had happened or was shortly to happen in many other cities in communal Italy, the evolution of Rome's political and institutional history at the beginning of the second half of the 13th century was characterized by the affirmation of the *popolo*, which asserted itself in the summer of 1252 after an uprising about which little is known. Obliged to choose the supreme city magistrate, the people opted for radical reform by turning to a non-Roman, one of those professional *podestàs* who went from town to town offering their services. The request for this service was addressed to a friendly city, Bologna, whose communal government appointed Brancaleone degli Andalò, member of a well-known family of professional *podestàs*. As a condition of his acceptance, he stipulated that he be appointed senator for three years.

From the beginning (August 1252), Brancaleone exhibited energy and firmness by hanging several members of the most powerful noble Roman families who had been accused of murder and up to that time left unpunished. Amid vicissitudes, and by following a policy essentially of balance and mediation with regard to the pope and the pretender to the imperial crown, he tried to organize the Roman commune in line with the great Italian people's communes. With some success, he reorganized the political structure of the Roman commune in a more "democratic" direction. He created the post of people's captain and gave broad powers to the council of *boni homines*, who represented the 13 urban *rioni*. In 1255, he set up the government of corporations. At the same time, he carried out a policy of expanding the territorial district subject to Rome. His open hostility toward the aristocracy, as well as discontent among the people, did not prevent his mandate from being renewed. Nonetheless, in November 1255 he was taken prisoner in the midst of a fresh uprising. Although victorious over their powerful rival, the great barons did not modify the institutions he had put in force, and the post of senator was once again entrusted to a professional magistrate, Emanuele de Madio from Brescia. The people's captain was also a non-Roman, but his identity is not known.

Senator Emanuele de Madio began by pursuing the path opened by Brancaleone. He ended by coming to an open understanding with the families of the great aristocracy, thus unleashing the violent and victorious popular uprising of April 1256. Brancaleone was set free, but Emanuele de Madio kept his post. The experience of the 1256 uprising made him more prudent in his dealing with the people, yet in May of the same year, this did not prevent another insurrection from deposing him and reelecting Brancaleone. Giving up mediation and declaring himself pro-imperial, Brancaleone then resumed his effective, intransigent policy. He found in popular acclaim the support he needed for it. Clearly opposed to the nobility, this policy prevailed through the two years of his second mandate up to his death (summer 1258), its most characteristic symbol being the destruction of a large number of nobles' towers.

At Brancaleone's death, the city once again was governed by two Roman senators (late 1258). Thereafter, up to the election of Charles of Anjou (1263), these men came from the nobility favored by the pope (they were often his relatives), who, once elected, often ended up vigorously defending the interests of the commune, at times to the disadvantage of the Curia. The election of Charles of Anjou as senator and the commitments he made on accepting the post represented a decisive stage in the history of papal power in Rome. At the end of his first mandate (May 1266), a new phase of popular government began which led to the election of a captain of the Roman people, Angelo Capocci. Supporting him was a council made up of 26 *boni homines* from various regions as well as the consuls of the corporations and *arti*, and a new senator in the person of Henry of Castille (summer 1267). Resuming Brancaleone's political program of popular accommodation, Henry quickly opposed the interests of the Church, interfering with jurisdictional prerogatives.

The elimination of Conradin of Swabia and Henry of Castille, after the intervention of Charles of Anjou, allowed Charles to wrest the title of senator (1266) from the pontiff for a second time. This time, it was established that the mandate should last for 10 years. The post was clearly an important though controlled overlordship, since it was based on precise agreements. However, for the papacy it was necessary that Charles's domination over the city not exceed the established limits. This would avoid the abuse of the sovereign's power, which would certainly have been strengthened with a long-lasting dictatorship, to the disadvantage of the papal authority.

The election to the papal throne of NICHOLAS III Orsini (1277), a member of one of the leading noble Roman families, made it possible to scale down the vast power that Charles of Anjou had acquired in Rome. To reinforce the pope's power, Charles had to be gradually eliminated

from the city and central Italy, meanwhile preventing his mandate from being prolonged. Scarcely a few months after his coronation, Nicholas promulgated an extremely important bull, *Fundamenta militantis ecclesiae* (18 July 1278), which has been described as a "Magna Carta of the relations between the pontiff and the Roman people from this moment on." It asserted the sovereign pontiff's entire claim on Rome and the negation of all power originating in the people. By taking precise, strict measures regarding future senatorial elections, over which papal control was becoming ever tighter, and by putting a firm stop to non-Roman candidatures, Nicholas III inaugurated the seigniorial period of the history of the Roman commune. In September of that same year, he himself was elected senator. Thus the king-senator was succeeded by a pope-senator who inherited from his predecessor a classic framework of absolute power, in which all offices were henceforth combined in the senator's hands and the rights of the people virtually extinguished.

Nevertheless, by the reign of MARTIN IV, Nicholas III's charter was partly forgotten, and in 1281 the pontiff entrusted the senatorial regency to Charles of Anjou. Made senator for the third time, the king of Sicily was now at the pinnacle of his power. But Charles's return was not welcomed by the Romans. Less than three years later, a new popular revolt broke out in Rome (January 1284). Once again a people's captain was acclaimed, this time in the person of Giovanni di Cencio Malabranca. The pope found himself forced to make important concessions, among them the essential one of the return of the administration of Roman finances to Romans through the new post of communal treasurer. With Martin IV's successors—save for the very brief interval of a non-Roman senator appointed under CELESTINE V—the custom begun by Nicholas III of making the pontiffs senators for life was perpetuated. The pontiffs, in their turn, appointed two vicars chosen from among members of the highest Roman nobility.

In June 1305, the election of a French pope, CLEMENT V, once again created a peculiar situation in Rome. For several decades now, the popes (in certain cases Romans by birth, like Nicholas III, HONORIUS IV, and BONIFACE VIII) had been more and more closely linked to the city, where they resided in stable fashion and of which the Romans more and more regarded them as sovereigns. After the death of BENEDICT XI and even before the college of cardinals had decided on his successor, a new popular upheaval occurred in Rome. A people's captain and a senator were elected, both non-Romans (Giovanni da Ignano, a Bolognese, and Paganino di Mosca della Torre, a Milanese). As happened in other cities that enjoyed popular government, the leaders were entrusted respectively with guaranteeing the people's interests vis-à-vis the highly placed and with representing the commune outside Rome and administering justice. It may have been their regime that saw the promulgation of the *Leges populi romani et senatus consulta super iustitia Columnensium contra iniquitates Bonifacianas*, through which the Senate rendered justice to the Colonnas and demanded that they be equitably recompensed. This new popular experiment lasted barely a year, after which the system returned to one of government by two senators of noble origin whom the pope recognized as his representatives.

Over the following years, this regime, based on the collaboration of the leading families of the Roman nobility, alternated with other brief experiments in popular government that were ended each time by predictable seigniorial reactions—first with Louise of Savoy (1310–12), because of Henry VII's demotion—then with Jacopo del fu Giovanni di Arlotto degli Stefaneschi (October 1312–February 1313). Agitation in Rome again compelled the pope to turn to a loyal ruler, a non-Roman, with the result that, at the end of 1313, Robert of Anjou was named senator. Besides presenting himself as a sure defender of the GUELPHS, he considered himself always and solely a vicar of the senator-pope, whom he held in total devotion. He governed the city for 14 years without taking up residence in it, ruling through the intermediary of vicars picked mainly from among the members of the highest Roman nobility. The last days of the Angevin mandate once again saw the government of Rome move in a popular direction (June 1327). A new body was created to be responsive to the people, made up of 52 members (4 per *rione*), to which was soon added the people's captain. Thus, once again, a democratic regime was restored; it immediately took anti-nobility measures and welcomed and crowned Ludwig of Bavaria (17 January 1328).

The consequences of this brief popular, pro-imperial interlude were profound. When Ludwig of Bavaria left Rome, where his position had become untenable (beginning of August), once again two senators were elected in the pope's name, yet the Romans did not succeed in securing the pardon of JOHN XXII until February 1330. In the meantime, Robert of Anjou had resumed his post as senator-vicar for the pope, which he retained up to the term of 1336, usually entrusting his duties to two Roman nobles. It was under him that the Romans, perhaps tired of experiments in independence and sensing the advantage of direct papal control over the city, conferred on the pope other magistratures that they had hitherto kept for themselves (controller of offices, captain, and rector), virtually decreeing Rome's definitive subjection and the end of communal autonomy.

Nonetheless, for another few years Rome continued to be profoundly shaken by internal struggles, most often provoked by violent quarrels between the aristocratic families. The people were discontented and anxious, but also divided. Toward the end of 1337, the pope attempted to ease the tension by appointing two non-Roman senators, Giovanni di Cante de' Gabrielli and Bosone di Novello, both of Gubbio, but they failed to reduce the tension. In late 1339, another popular insurrection occurred; also short-lived, it was an attempt to apply the constitutional system of the *popolo* of Florence. New corporations were set up, as well as a college of 13 priors (one for each *rione*) under the direction of a gonfaloniere of justice, who was placed at the head of the government of the city. Changes of regime succeeded at a rapid pace. There was a constant search for a system that would make it possible to preserve an inner balance that was continually threatened by the anarchy of the nobles and the lack of effective government. As early as January 1340, two new senators were elected. In March, these were replaced by two other senators, who were thrown out in their turn by a violent uprising in May, followed by the election of two more senators in September. Thus, up to 1347, the pontiff continued to entrust the four posts conferred on him by the Romans (senator, captain, controller, and defender) to members of the noble families, with the result that a government of nobles was installed in Rome. Another brief interruption of popular government ensued in late 1342, when, taking advantage of the absence of the two senators sent on embassy to the pontiff, the 13 *boni viri* seized power entirely and sent their own ambassador to Avignon to explain to the pope the objectives of the popular party. At the head of this embassy was Cola di Rienzo, who would not return to Rome until July or August 1344.

Throughout the three years following his return to Rome, Cola busied himself skillfully in setting forth his political plan for all to see. He strove to raise the consciousness of a whole stratum of the population that suffered only disadvantages from the feudal government of the great nobles: landlords and employers of the great agricultural enterprises (*bobacterii* or *cavalerotti*), merchants, artisans, and traders. He proposed that the communal institutions be reformed in a popular, anti-aristocratic direction. The social contract that he succeeded in obtaining was very broad, and on 20 May 1347, he carried out a coup d'état. A popular assembly meeting at the Capitol granted him full powers, decreeing that he would exercise them in concert with the pontifical vicar. Both were named rectors of the city. Shortly afterward, Cola took the title of tribune. His political program consisted of 15 measures that were approved by the assembly on 20 May. These were concrete measures, aimed above all at abolishing the overreaching power of the nobles by dismantling their military apparatus, erasing their factions and clienteles, reorganizing the communal militia, and recovering the communal patrimony which the nobles had long since usurped.

During the first months, Cola the tribune succeeded in winning the consensus of the Roman population in its bitter struggle against feudalism. Although Cola's efforts at first met with CLEMENT VI's approval, very soon (even before word reached Avignon of the coronation ceremonies that had taken place in August) Avignon's hostility toward his policy was plain. The measures against the nobles and the administrative reorganization of the new regime could not but displease the conservative powers. War with the nobles flared up without delay. At the beginning of October, the nobles started a series of raids which proceeded to devastate the Roman Campagna. On 20 November, a decisive confrontation took place with a veritable massacre of nobles outside the Porta San Lorenzo. However, the commune's military victory was fruitless, for Cola went into a phase of apathy and inaction. His supporters were discouraged, while the nobles were able to regain the upper hand in part and to put an end to his regime. Two judgments of late 1347 and February 1348 excommunicated Cola and annulled his measures. Imprisoned in the Castel Sant'Angelo, he managed to escape in autumn 1348.

Before Cola returned to Rome (after sojourns in the Abruzzi and Prague and imprisonment in Avignon for more than a year), a government was restored in Rome that was founded on the same political and social bases as those of the first tribunate (14 September 1353). One of the leaders of the popular party, Francesco Baroncelli, was named tribune. In the beginning of 1354, he was succeeded by Guido dei Patrizi, whose position was immediately recognized by the cardinal-legate Gil de Albornoz, who appointed him senator. However, when Guido dei Patrizi showed himself unable to stand up to the Colonna coalition, Cola, who had accompanied Albornoz to war, succeeded in having the legate name him senator. Nevertheless, he was henceforth in the service of the pope, and he apparently gave up for good all plans of communal reform. With his role reduced to the rank of a simple pontifical functionary, Cola lost all credibility among his first supporters and soon found himself isolated. Thus, it was not difficult for a rebel movement instigated by the nobles most hostile to him to capture him and put him to death (8 October 1354).

Cola's death brought about the unexpected return of calm to the city. After a brief provisional government by the Thirteen, once again two senators were appointed (first half of 1355). Over the following years, and after a brief replacement (from September 1357 to November 1358), Cardinal Albornoz completed a plan of reform designed to give Rome a new interior political organization by placing it in a centralized system making the Papal States a veritable monarchy governed from the top. Nicholas III's measure requiring Roman citizenship of the senators was abrogated, but the senators' authority and autonomy were henceforth much reduced. In March 1358, there appeared a new provisional magistrature which, unlike the preceding ones, became stable and was then approved and made into law by the cardinal-legate on his return to power (possibly at the beginning of 1359). The magistrature consisted of seven *reformatores reipublicae* or governors, all of them rigorously chosen from among the Roman citizenry; they formed part of the private or restricted council in the place of the *boni homines*, becoming the true central engine and executive organ of the commune. Albornoz's reforms led to the creation and organization of the "Felice Società dei Balestrieri e Pavesati," a military body also endowed with political functions (to safeguard the popular regime, with aims that were obviously anti-nobility). Consisting of two troops of 1,500 Roman citizens who played a part in policing and keeping order, the militia was commanded by two political chiefs, the bannerets, who had under their command two provosts each, probably the actual military chiefs.

Over these years, the city gained a new statutory structure that bore the mark, in its formulation, of the popular regime then in force in Rome. The nobles were completely excluded from government, and it was stipulated that their misdemeanors would be punished more severely than those of the people. The senator himself, who was to be chosen from a locality within 40 miles from Rome, could not be allied to any noble to the third degree. In June 1363, URBAN V, who favored the city's new regime, granted the seven reformers permission to exercise control over an outgoing senator. Thus the Romans regained one of the privileges they had lost a few years earlier. The relative autonomy they had recently won ended with the return to Rome of GREGORY XI (January 1377). The signing of a pact allowed him to reform the "Felice Società" as he saw fit, and he was granted the seigniory of Rome. His successor, URBAN VI, went further: he sought to limit the tenure of the communal posts as he saw fit, whereas it usually lasted six months. He also wanted to nominate not only the senator but also, in certain cases, the conservators, bannerets, marshal, and other Capitoline officers, thus making his control felt. Events after his death allowed the Roman commune again to acquire a certain authority in contrast to the rapid decline of the pope's, but this trend did not last long. Even the agreements with the newly elected BONIFACE IX, giving the commune full powers over the city, were short-lived. A series of rebellions forced the pope to leave Rome and, to secure his return, the citizens had to accept very harsh conditions (Assisi pact of 8 August 1393) which again granted the pope the privilege of nominating the senator, among other powers.

It has been said that in July 1398 the free commune of Rome vanished forever. After yet another revolt of the *populares*, led by one of three conservators in charge, a merchant named Pietro Mattuzzi, and the subsequent overthrow of his government by the opposing party of the nobles (23 August 1395), the latter remained in power for nearly three years. But in late June 1398, Mattuzzi attempted another coup d'état against the regime of the nobles at the side of the condottiere Paolo Orsini. Nevertheless, this move only served the interests of the pope, who profited from the situation to deprive the two parties of all authority and then to eliminate them, thus managing to become uncontested ruler of Rome. The troubles that followed Mattuzzi's expedition in fact forced the nobles in the government to return the reins of the city to the pope, thus accomplishing a *resignatio pleni dominii* (5 July 1398) that decreed the end of the medieval commune and laid the groundwork for Rome to become the papal residence in the Renaissance and the modern era. Another attempted revolt of the nobles (August 1398) was repressed bloodily, whereupon their influence yielded to the absolute authority of the pope, while all public life passed under the direct control of the pontifical administration.

Cristina Carbonetti
Marco Venditelli

Bibliography

Arnaldi, G. "Alberico di Roma," *DBI*, 1 (1960), 647–56.

Arnaldi, G. "Le origini del Patrimonio di San Pietro," *Storia d'Italia*, ed. G. Galasso, 7/2, Turin, 1987, 1–151.

Arnaldi, G. "Mito e realtà del secolo x romano e papale," *Settimane di studio el Centro Italiano di Studi sull'Alto Medioevo*, 38 (1990), Spoleto, 1991, 27–53.

Arnaldi, G. "Rinascita, fine, reincarnazione e successive metamorfosi del senato romano (secoli v–xii)," *ASR*, 105 (1982), 5–56.

Bartolini, F. "Per la Storia del Senato Romano nel secoli XII e XIII," *Bullettino dell'Istituto Storico Italiano par il Medioevo e Archivio Muratoriano*, 60 (1946), 1–108.

Bertolini, O. *Roma di fronte a Bisanzio e ai Longobardi*, Bologna, 1941 (*Storia di Roma*, 9).

Brentano, R. *Rome before Avignon: A Social History of Thirteenth-Century Rome*, London, 1974.

Brezzi, P. *Roma e l'Impero medioevale (774–1252)*, Bologna, 1947 (*Storia di Roma*, 10).

de Boüard, A. *Le Régime politique et les institutions de Rome au Moyen Age, 1251–1347*, Paris, 1920 (*BEFAR*, 118).

Dupré-Theseider, E. *Roma dal comune di popolo alla signoria pontificia 77*, Bologna, 1952 (*Storia di Roma*, 11).

Esch, A. *Bonifaz IX. und der Kirchenstatt*, Tübingen, 1969.

Esch, A. "La fine del libero comune di Roma nel giudizio dei mercanti fiorentini: Lettere romane degli anni 1396–1398 nell'Archivio Datini," *Bullettino dell'Istituto Storico Italiano per il Medioevo e Archivio Muratoriano*, 86 (1976–7), 235–77.

Falco, G. *La Santa Romana Repubblica*, 2nd ed., Naples, 1954.

Fedele, P. "L'era del Senato," *ASR*, 35 (1912), 583–611.

Frugoni, A. "Sulla Renovatio Senatus del 1143 e l'Ordo Equestris," *Bullettino dell'Istituto Storico Italiano e Archivio Muratoriano*, 62 (1950), 161–74.

Gregorovius, F. *Storia della città di Roma nel Medio Evo dal secolo v al xvi*, Ital. ed., 9 vols., Venice, 1872–6.

Halphen, L. *L'Administration de Rome au Moyen Age (751–1252)*, Paris, 1907.

Maire Vigueur, J. C. "Classe dominante et classes dirigeantes à Rome à la fin du Moyen Age," *Storia della città*, 1 (1976), 4–26.

Maire Vigueur, J. C. "Cola di Rienzo," *DBI*, 26 (1982), 662–75.

Mansell, R. "Il senato romano ed Eugenio III," *Bullettino dell'Archivio paleografico italiano*, 2–3 (1956–7), 127–34.

Miglio, M. "Gruppi sociali ed azione politica nella Roma di Cola di Rienzo," *Studi Romani*, 23 (1975), 442–57.

Moscati, L. *Alla origini del comune romano: Economia, società, istituzioni*, Naples, 1980 (*Quaderni di Clio*, 1).

Moscati, L. "Benedetto Carushomo summus senator a Roma," *Miscellanea in Onore di Ruggero Moscati*, Naples, 1985, 73–87.

Moscati, L. "Una cum sexaginta senatoribus," *Clio*, 20/4 (1984), 52–545.

Natale, A. "La felice Società dei Balestrieri e dei Pavesati a Roma e il governo dei Banderesi dal 1358 al 1408," *ASR*, 62 (1939), 1–176.

Noble, T. F. X. *The Republic of St. Peter: The Birth of the Papal State, 680–825*, Philadelphia, 1984.

Paschini, P. *Roma nel Rinascimento*, Bologna, 1940 (*Storia di Roma*, 9).

Re, C. *Statuti della città di Roma*, Rome, 1880.

Rodocanachi, E. *Les Institutions communales de Rome sous la papauté*, Paris, 1901.

Toubert, P. "Il Patrimonio di San Pietro, fino alla metà del secolo XI," *Storia d'Italia*, ed. G. Galasso, VII/2, Turin, 1987, 153–228.

Toubert, P. *Les Structures du Latium médiéval: Le Latium méridional et la Sabine du IXe à la fin du XIIe siècle*, 2 vols., Rome, 1973 (*BEFAR*, 221).

Waley, D. "Lo Stato papale dal periodo feudale a Martino V," *Storia d'Italia*, ed. G. Galasso, VII/2, Turin, 1987, 229–320.

Waley, D. *The Papal State in the Thirteenth Century*, London-New York, 1961.

See also PAPAL STATES.

Modern Era. After the long hiatus of Avignon and the crisis of the GREAT SCHISM—a period of 108 years—the second Rome was born with NICHOLAS V (1447–55), who set out to rebuild the crumbling ST. PETER'S BASIL-

ICA and create VATICAN CITY. Both projects would not be completed until the 17th century. Around 1500, Rome already numbered 25,000 or 30,000 inhabitants and SIXTUS IV, INNOCENT VII and ALEXANDER VI were summoning to Rome the best artists of the day. Under JULIUS II (1503–13) and LEO X (1513–21), the period when Bramante, Raphael, and Michelangelo were working in Rome, the city eclipsed Florence as the artistic and cultural capital of Italy. Rome became the beacon of Renaissance cities. This primacy would continue in the Baroque era until around 1660. When Charles V's troops laid waste to a Rome during the SACK of 1527, the rise in the city's population was not permanently affected, however: in 1600, Rome counted at least 100,000 inhabitants (the census not including Jews), compared with 55,000 in 1526 (before the sack) and 45,000 in 1555.

Throughout the 16th century, a truly new city arose along the banks of the Tiber. At least 54 churches were erected or completely rebuilt in that century, among them St. Peter's, the largest in the world. Sixty palaces were erected. Twenty surviving aristocratic villas date to the Cinquecento, several being genuine palaces. New housing was put up for recent immigrants. More than 30 new streets were laid, those opened by SIXTUS V (1585–90) alone extending more than 20 kilometers, especially in the upper part of the city, which the pope was striving to repopulate, far from the flooding Tiber. Three ancient aqueducts were restored between 1565 and 1612, measuring 108 kilometers in all. At the end of the 16th century, Rome each day received by aqueduct 86,319 cubic meters of drinking water, supplemented in 1612 by the 94,187 cubic meters of the Acqua Paola. From the renovation of the Acqua Vergine (1572) until the end of the century, at least 35 public fountains were offered to the Romans. No other city in Europe could boast such figures around 1600.

Despite the grandiose nature of Julius II's projects and the brilliant works of the Renaissance, the new Rome's greatest rise took place in the second half of the 16th century. Public admiration focuses on the Sistine frescoes and Raphael's Loggia, the charm and elegance of San Pietro in Montorio and the Farnesina, the refined simplicity of the palace of the Chancery, and the monumental amplitude of the Farnese palace; yet, quantitatively speaking, it was from 1560 onward that the city of popes acquired its new face. This was the time of the Catholic REFORM—long known as the COUNTER REFORMATION—when the popes wanted to give grandeur and dignity to their capital and to emphasize their authority, both under attack by the Protestants. They restored the HOLY YEARS and laid out squares and streets so that pilgrims visiting the most venerable "seven churches" of Rome could walk in procession down straight, noble avenues as they made their way to the basilicas with their majestic façades, often fronted with an OBELISK. Nicholas V, as a prince of the Renaissance, had declared: "If I had money, I would

spend it entirely on books [he created the VATICAN LIBRARY] and buildings." But as pope of the Catholic renewal, Sixtus V wrote in 1590, in a text that can be taken as his testament in matters of construction: "Unshakable seat and venerable throne of the blessed Peter, prince of apostles, domicile of the Christian religion, mother and common fatherland of all the faithful, safe haven for all the nations from all over the world who flock to her, Rome has need not only of divine protection and sacred, spiritual strength. She must also have the beauty rendered by material comfort and decoration." During the 1600 Holy Year, nearly 600,000 pilgrims converged on the eternal city.

Inevitably, one wonders where and how the popes, cardinals, and Roman aristocracy found the funds to pay for so much construction and city planning. At a time when money flowed from the Americas to Italy by way of Spain and Genoa, the popes and nobles did much borrowing, while bonds on pontifical debt—*luoghi di monti*—found ready buyers. Logically, the popes had to impose ever heavier taxes in the Papal States in order to pay the yearly interest on their loans. But there came a time in the 17th century when debts far outweighed revenues. The result was partial bankruptcies, while great families that were financially drained, such as the Colonna and Orsini, yielded pride of place to newcomers, usually the families of the popes' successive CARDINAL NEPHEWS.

The dome of St. Peter's, designed by Michelangelo and executed (with some modifications) by Giacomo della Porta, was completed in 1593. It was 145 meters high, surpassing by 31 meters that of Sta. Maria del Fiore in Florence. Thereafter, domes multiplied in Rome. In the urban landscape they ensured continuity between the Renaissance and the Baroque age, within which we note an initial period of austerity. The art of the Catholic Reform began, in fact, in an atmosphere of sober solemnity, as is evidenced by the exterior of the Gesù. This was the period when Catholicism was caught up in its efforts of reconquest. Further examples are the Collegio Romano, a veritable barracks (1578) conceived by Ammanati, and the palaces that the Lombard Domenico Fontana built at the Vatican and the Lateran for Sixtus V are imposing, monotonous edifices. In this period of struggle, religious music—for example, that of Ingeneri (d. 1592), Palestrina (d. 1594) and Nanini (d. 1607), strove to be liturgical and spare, stressing line rather than color.

One difference between the religious art of this new Rome and that of the preceding periods is that it follows precise rules far more than in the past. In a climate of controversy, art became apologetic and functional. From now on, it lost part of the freedom and fantasy it had earlier enjoyed. "It is hard to imagine," writes E. Mâle regarding the frescoes in the Pauline chapel at ST. MARY

MAJOR (begun in 1611), "that Cavaliere d'Arpino, Guido Reni, Baglione and Cigoli chose their subjects themselves. However well educated they may have been, it is still difficult to believe that they knew the history of St. Gregory Thaumaturgus, of Heraclius and of the iconoclastic emperors. Clearly, they had to represent heroes of whom they were ignorant the day before." Along with this aesthetic stricture went a strong dose of prohibition. The nude, henceforth admitted in mythological representations—for example, at the Farnese palace—was no longer allowed in churches, and, more generally, sacred and profane art went their separate ways.

The FABRIC OF ST. PETER's turned down Caravaggio's *Madonna of the Palafrenieri* because, said Bellori, the Virgin was represented in "a vulgar manner" and "the infant Jesus is naked." The clergy of Sta. Maria della Scala, in Trastevere, similarly refused another work by Caravaggio, the *Death of the Virgin*, because Mary's belly was swollen like that of a drowned person, and her legs were bare. The rejections reflect the negative aspect of a self-conscious artistic policy.

St. Charles Borromeo (d. 1584), the nephew of PIUS IV, in his *Instructiones fabricae et suppellectilis ecclesiae*, requested that the house of God be given a majestic façade decorated with statues and a layout that allowed for processions inside the edifice and the deployment of a noble LITURGY. In a concern for effective pedagogy, rood screens were forbidden because they separated the congregation from the celebrant; the choir was shortened, and the altar raised, and the church was made smaller and reduced to a central nave, with little oratories to encourage mental prayer tucked into the side walls. To help the people follow the service, instead of many-colored stained glass the churches had large white or yellow windows that let in the light. Because choral music was developing and a larger number of musical instruments were allowed in the sanctuary—the first "oratorio" was given in Rome in 1600—even though the emphasis was more and more on preaching, houses of worship turned into lecture and concert halls with carefully conceived acoustics. The urge to teach also explains the monumental appearance of pulpits and altarpieces. The desire to enhance the importance of the sacraments led to the building of confessionals—a 16th-century innovation— and balustrades that served as communion tables. These were the major, peculiarly Roman trends driving Catholic religious art after the council of TRENT.

The urge toward pedagogy and control in the artistic domain is inseparable from an evolution toward centralization which manifested itself both in the Papal States and in the government of the Catholic Church. At the end of the 16th century, the papacy's temporal domain was governed by an administration that was relatively well developed for the time, despite interventions between spiritual and temporal affairs that seem strange to us

today. Under the pope's immediate authority there was now a de facto first minister, the CARDINAL NEPHEW or, when there was none, the secretary of state, whose activity relegated that of the CONSISTORIES to the background. The third figure of the hierarchy (or the second, when a cardinal nephew was present) was the cardinal CAMERLENGO, on whom the whole administration of the Church's temporal domain converged. This domain was split up into legations headed by cardinals, sometimes personalities who had proved embarrassing for the central power. Rome arranged for its own staff to fill their absences, in particular appointing treasurers responsible for collecting direct taxes.

Most important, from the reign of Sixtus V, all the high functionaries of the state were ecclesiastics of revocable rank and therefore more amenable than laymen to taking orders from a theocratic government—hence the many contemporary references to the "ecclesiastical state." At the end of the 16th century, the Roman nobility complained bitterly about this "tyranny of priests." The fact is that the authority of envoys from Rome was gradually replacing the old feudal power at the local level. Likewise, the autonomy of cities was becoming blurred, especially that of Rome, where communal finances were a mere memory. The city was overseen by the tenant of the CASTEL SANT'ANGELO, who was appointed by the pope, while the chief of criminal police was the governor, who was at the same time vice-camerlengo. A similar system held true in Bologna. A French traveler passing through in 1574 noted, "All that remains of the Republic is the name and certain ceremonies."

Along with a greater docility of the local administration went a growing specialization of the central offices, thanks in the main to the CONGREGATIONS of cardinals, virtual specialized governmental committees that became permanent in the 16th century and proliferated from the reigns of GREGORY XIII and SIXTUS V. They met once a week. Some of them concerned themselves with religious questions on an international scale, such as the Congregation of the Holy Office of INQUISITION, the first of which was created under PAUL III in 1542, and that of the INDEX, which dates to 1571, an initiative of PIUS V. But other congregations saw their responsibilities limited to the temporal domain of the Church—for instance, the congregations of the ANNONA or food provisioning, of roads and bridges, the wartime fleet (necessary because of the Turkish threat), the University of Rome, the congregation "for the reduction of taxes," the so-called *consulta* (a kind of general administrative tribunal), or the congregation of "good government," created in 1592 to propose reforms in favor of the governed and soon also called on to verify the finances of the communes. The chief author and organizer of these congregations was Sixtus V. He brought the total to 15 and made them into a coherent whole, completed over the following centuries. Regarding the Papal State, it is likely that the French government in Henry IV's time had no such specialized central bureaus at its disposal.

In the papal territories, where anarchy reigned up to the 16th century, the consolidation of the state did not proceed without resistance or incidents of violence. In 1532, the papal forces secretly entered Ancona, a sort of maritime republic that was largely autonomous. The people were disarmed and soon watched over by a strong fortress. The city of Macerata was chosen as capital of the Marches, although the role should have gone to Ancona. In 1540, during the "salt war," occurred the defeat of Perugia and the Baglioni, longtime lords of the city. The Umbrian capital was in its turn controlled by a fortress. In 1542, Paul III's soldiers conquered Ascanio Colonna, who had also rebelled against the pope because of the salt tax. Paliano, the stronghold of the Colonna, could now do no harm. In 1585 Count Pepoli, the most respected nobleman in Bologna, was condemned to death and executed for failing to hand over a bandit who had sought refuge in his palace. On the death of Alfonso II d'Este (1597), Ferrara returned to the pontifical state. From then on it would be governed by legates.

This policy of recovery continued in the 17th century. In 1631 the little duchy of Urbino was reunited painlessly, the reigning family, the Della Rovere, having died out by that time. In contrast, the question of the duchy of Castro (1640–9) created a commotion and provoked an intra-Italian war. In reality, it arose from a clash between Rome's desire for centralization, the illusions of URBAN VIII—who believed he had a good army—the arrogance and debts of Odoardo Farnese, the cupidity of the Barberini nephews, the fears and hopes of the French and Spanish governments, and finally the conflicting intrigues of the French and Spaniards. Odoardo Farnese, duke of Parma and Piacenza, also held the small duchy of Castro, a fief that had been given to his ancestors by the great benefactor of the family, Paul III. For a long time the Farnese had enormous debts, and on the Roman marketplace they had issued loans guaranteed by the resources of the duchy of Castro. But Odoardo did not pay the interest due on his borrowings, and the creditors took their complaint to Urban VIII.

Urged by his nephews, Urban VIII decided to teach a lesson to a vassal who was arrogant and contemptuous. In 1641, 15,000 men seized Castro. His nephews also prodded the pope to take military action against Parma and Piacenza. The result was anxiety in Italy and the formation of a league, encouraged by France, among Venice, Modena, Florence, and Parma. Confused military operations ensued (1642–4). At first the papal troops swept into the Romagna. This was followed by panic in Rome, where the walls were hurriedly put up that today surround the Janiculum. Next came delaying tactics on the part of Farnese, whose soldiers deserted during the winter. Finally,

operations resumed in the spring of 1643 as the allies split up, each rival being in turn victor and vanquished. Peace came in 1644, when Urban VIII handed back Castro. But five years later, Odoardo's successor was suspected of arranging the murder of the new bishop of Castro, appointed by Rome against his wishes. Once again papal troops attacked Castro, which resisted and then surrendered. The city was razed. On the ruins, a column was put up with the inscription: "Here was Castro."

These inglorious deeds should not distract us from the Catholic "Renaissance" that Rome unleashed on the world in the wake of the council of Trent. The capital of Catholicism remained an astonishing city, especially in view of its mission to spread abroad the message of the one who had proclaimed, "Blessed are the poor in spirit." Ironically, neither poverty nor work appeared to be honored in the period of religious renewal. Nevertheless, Rome was no longer the licentious, pagan city against which Savonarola and Luther had hurled their anathemas. PIUS V (1566–72), an authoritarian ascetic who is said to have wanted to sell off the nude Classical statues and drive the courtesans out of his capital, at least made an effort to change the city's moral climate. Still, he did not succeed in making Rome one vast convent. Once this demanding pope had died, and when, after the death of Sixtus V (1590), the heroic period of Catholic Reform came to an end, the city once again could smile and come to life. From then on, it tempered piety with humor, majesty with nonchalance, and ceremonial pomp with the grace of art. At least it had a dignified countenance that was enhanced by the nobility of its architectural setting and the frequency of the spectacular canonization ceremonies (28 in the 17th century).

The strengthened authority of the papacy gave all its weight to as precise as possible an application of the decisions of the council of Trent. In a revealing gesture, as soon as he was elected in 1565, Pius V sent conciliar texts to the archbishops of Goa, Mexico, Guatemala, Honduras, and Venezuela. Synods were then held in many parts so that the spirit of the council might seep into the daily life of Catholics. But, most important, many took place in the years following the council.

One of the most important of the council's decisions concerned SEMINARIES. Some 20 of these opened in Italy between 1564 and 1584, 26 in Spain between 1565 and 1616, and 8 in the Low Countries before 1620; in France and the empire, their creation was delayed by the wars of religion. To encourage Catholicism's reconquest of countries that had gone over to Protestantism or had been quarreled over by Rome and the Reformation, seminaries were created "in exile." One example in Rome is the German College (1552), to which was added a Hungarian College (1578). From that date there was an English seminary in Rome and several others in the Low Countries. In the empire, where diocesan seminaries for a long time were few in number, the Jesuits urged the creation of "pontifical" seminaries under the governance of the Holy See: in Vienna (1574), Dillingen (1576), Graz (1578), Olomouc (1578), Braunsberg (1578), Fulda (1584) and Ingolstadt (1600). These establishments developed into academies or universities patterned after the Collegio Romano created by St. Ignatius in 1556, which from 1585 became the brilliant Gregorian University, named after Gregory XIII, who encouraged its rise.

The first, heroic period of the Catholic Renaissance, which may be said to end around 1630, was characterized in particular by the militant action of new or revived religious orders. On the death of Ignatius Loyola in 1556, the Society of Jesus already consisted of a thousand members and administered about a hundred foundations. A century later, more than 15,000 Jesuits and 550 foundations were recorded. The Capuchins, a branch of the Franciscan order, separated in 1528 and experienced initial difficulties, but by 1643 they numbered 21,000, distributed among 1,379 houses. Jesuits and Capuchins throughout the world constituted the progressive wing of Catholic Reform—contributing, however, to the growth of a climate of sharp intolerance.

No less brilliant was the success of certain women's orders. In 1562, St. Teresa of Jesus, already a great mystic and eager to return to the austerity of the primitive rule of her order, established in Avila the first monastery of reformed Carmelites. By 1648, Spain had about a hundred Carmelite convents of strict observance, Italy had 92, and France 55. Unlike the cloistered Carmelites, the orders of the Ursulines, Visitandines, and Daughters of Charity established new congregations which offered the female apostolate unprecedented scope. The Daughters of Charity managed hospitals, created small centers of good works in both towns and the countryside, and increased the number of primary schools. They ran about a hundred houses in 1660, 250 in 1711, and 426 in the mid-18th century, including 51 "little schools" in Paris.

The growing number of seminaries and the rise of religious congregations should be placed within a far wider context: that of the global expansion of Catholicism, which heretofore had never spread out over such vast territories. Rome became a world capital. The new religious conquest was comparable to that of apostolic times, no longer on the scale of a Mediterranean empire but on that of the whole world. In the 16th and 17th centuries, there was a feeling in the Roman Church that the losses suffered in the Protestant secessions were largely compensated for by gains beyond the seas. Having been on the defensive against the Turks, who were checked at LEPANTO (1571) and then in Vienna (1683), the Catholic Church went on the spiritual offensive in the pagan world that opened out before it. The Congregation for the PROPAGATION OF THE FAITH, definitively set up in 1622, strove to coordinate missionary activities on a global scale and, in the overseas dependencies of Spain and Portugal, to undo the damage wrought by the so-called "patronage" system, which gave undue power to the kings over the Church in their territories.

Concerning Africa and Asia, a few salient facts should be recalled. In 1597, an episcopal seat was created in the Congo. Goa became a bishopric in 1534, and Francis Xavier tirelessly traveled throughout India and Southeast Asia from 1542 to 1552. He died on an island off the Chinese coast, but not before having introduced Christianity to Japan. At the end of the 16th century and during the 17th, India continued to be traversed by Catholic missionaries such as the Italian Roberto de Nobili and the Portuguese John de Britto. At the end of the 17th century, Christians in India and Ceylon numbered around 800,000. In Japan in the last decade of the 16th century, they totaled 300,000. At the same time, the Jesuit Matteo Ricci was striving to introduce Christianity into China. Around 1700, there were some 200,000 Catholics in the Celestial Empire and 117 missionaries, often of a high intellectual level, who ministered to 114 residences and 244 churches and oratories. Finally, in the 16th century a Catholic nation was born in the Philippines, while in the next century a Church arose in Indochina.

The results in Asia were encouraging, but limited. In contrast, a veritable religious epic took place in the Americas, though there should be no disguising the sometimes brutal nature of the process of conversion. EVANGELIZATION here began with a Franciscan mission that left Europe in 1500 for the Antilles. In Mexico, it followed immediately in the wake of Cortés' expedition (1519). Mexico and its dependencies were scarcely occupied when the southward movement to Peru began from Panama (1532), after which came the annexation of an empire even vaster than the first. In South America, the process of conversion was slower than in Mexico. Nevertheless, by 1575 a regular ecclesiastical organization already covered the immense Spanish domain in the Americas, built around the two archbishoprics of Mexico City and Lima. In Brazil, the history of Christianity does not begin until the establishment, in 1549, of a catechesis center for Indians in São Paulo. In 1640, Portuguese America had but one bishopric, in Bahía. Yet it was here that the Society of Jesus attempted to protect the Indians from slave hunters by setting up the *reducciones*, or Indian villages governed by Jesuits, that were to arouse the hostility of the Iberian rulers in the 18th century.

In 1790, Mexico and South America between them had 7 archbishoprics, 36 bishoprics, more than 70,000 churches, and at least 850 monasteries. But north of the Río Grande it was a different story: only 2 episcopal seats—one, in Quebec, having been in existence since

1674, and the other, in Baltimore, established in 1789—an unmistakably modest achievement in North America. Still, Great Britain, which emerged victorious over France, had had to allow the French Canadians in 1774 "the free practice of the faith of the Church of Rome," and later a Catholic community began to take shape in the new United States. This account is obviously but a bare summary, but it does suggest the historic evidence of a global expansion of Catholicism, especially in the 16th and 17th centuries. Never before had Rome extended its spiritual authority over such vast areas. In 1596, with the "Union" of Brest-Litovsk, it even managed to bring back under its protection part of the Orthodox of Ukraine and Belorussia (the "Uniates").

It is easy to understand how such successes, reinforced by Henry IV's return to Catholicism (1593) and the Protestant defeat at White Mountain (1620), gradually helped relax the atmosphere in Rome, despite the occasional return of tension signaled by the execution of the pantheist Giordano Bruno (1600), the condemnation of Galileo (1633), and the pontificate of the virtuous, austere INNOCENT XI (1676–89). When Catholicism regained its self-assurance from 1610 to 1620, the formal severity of Roman art, as evidenced in the second half of the 16th century, little by little gave way to movement, fantasy, color, and emotion. Façades became lighter thanks to a contrasting play of light and shadow; they bulged or curved inward. Pietro da Cortona's church of SS. Luca e Martina at the Forum (1635) is the first example of a convex façade.

Bernini would create no grander work than S. Andrea al Quirinale (1658–70), where a curvilinear pronaos rises up from a porticoed façade. Yet the most persuasive and successful examples of this architecture in Rome are the admirable S. Ivo alla Sapienza (1642–50) and the elegant undulations of S. Carlo alle Quattro Fontane (1638–67), both by Borromini. As the exteriors lost their rigidity, the interiors of palaces and churches were now covered with polychrome marble and facings of stucco and, thanks to cunning trompe-l'oeil, opened up to luminous skies where the architecture seems to dissolve. Illusion looms large in this period, with artificially expanded spaces and unrealistic decoration; a triumph in this area is the *Glory of St. Ignatius* (1685), which the elder Pozzo painted on the dome of the church of St. Ignatius in Rome, and in which the sky positively pervades the building. It is not coincidental that, in 1632, the Barberini palace acquired a theater capable of seating three thousand people, and that Bernini designed models for curtains for the operatic stage.

It is precisely in terms of a theatrical aesthetic that we should approach certain major works of Bernini: the baldachin in St. Peter's, the Triton Fountain at the Barberini palace, the amazing Fountain of the Four Rivers in the Piazza Navona, which became a grand courtyard leading to INNOCENT X's palace, and St. Peter's square itself. Maderna (d. 1629), who completed the new St. Peter's by changing into a Latin cross the Greek cross planned by Bramante and Michelangelo and erected the long, severe façade (112 meters wide and 44 meters high), envisaged a narrow square in front of the basilica, not too deep and rigid in form. Bernini in 1656–7 abandoned this plan, which precluded all effects of surprise, and designed an ellipse measuring 260 by 60 meters which created the illusion of a space greater than it was in reality. The square was to appear like an inner courtyard, which would surprise the visitor arriving by the narrow streets of the Borgo.

Rome is firmly in first place in the prize-list of Italian artistic creation in the 17th century. True, the urban population showed only a gradual increase (around 135,000 inhabitants in 1690). The pace of construction wound down. Fewer new streets and dwellings were put up than in the preceding century, fewer ancient aqueducts repaired. But the city gained in beauty what it lost in dynamism. In no other part of the Italian peninsula did Baroque city planning find happier formulas. Later, Charles de Brosses, speaking of the two symmetrical churches built on the Piazza del Popolo in the 17th century by Rainaldi, said: "I do not think there is anywhere in the world a city whose entrance by land creates such a favorable feeling of anticipation."

With Bernini, Rome up to 1670 was the workplace of not only the greatest architect but also the greatest sculptor of the age. His tombs of URBAN VIII (1642–7) and ALEXANDER VII (after 1671) in St. Peter's in Rome have an impressive eloquence. But at the very beginning of his career, when he was only 21 years old, he had sculpted *Daphne Pursued by Apollo and Changed into a Laurel Bush* (1619), a dazzling work in which it is hard to tell what to admire most: the naturalness of the movement or the virtuosity that transforms marble into flesh, wood, fabric, tresses, and foliage. The artist's boldness and ardor and his skill in stagecraft again impress in the *Transverbation of St. Teresa* (1644–51). It is no surprise that in his day the artist won fame comparable to that of Michelangelo or Rubens.

Since Rome at that time was the artistic capital of Europe, various pictorial styles coexisted or succeeded one another. It was here that Caravaggio painted his masterpieces, giving rise after his death (1610) to the so-called Luminist style of painting. In the Farnese palace between 1595 and 1603, the Carracci, closing the door on Mannerist caprice, opened the way for the great Baroque interiors. The skilled profusion of stucco and paintings in this palace would serve as a model for hundreds of galleries in the palaces and castles of the 17th century. At the same time, the cult of Raphael, which had been kept very much alive in Rome, and the sense of monumental composition led Carracci's Bolognese disciples to a classical form of art which enjoyed the preference of the Roman Accademia di S. Luca. Guido Reni and Guercino are the best representatives of this art, which features harmonious nudes, clear groupings, and elegant mythological scenes. Nevertheless, it is not to them that we owe the most "classical" works of 17th-century Rome, but to two French artists who chose to live there: Nicolas Poussin (1594–1665) and Claude Gellée, known as le Lorrain (1600–82?). At the time, they were venerated in Italy as the artists who were the closest to Antiquity. Through Raphael's teaching, their timeless, serene painting meets the Platonic ideal of beauty. The fame of the artists and of the papal city makes it easy to understand Colbert's foundation in 1666 of the French Academy in Rome, patterned after that of S. Luca. Rome's prestige also explains why the daughter of Gustavus Adolphus, Christina of Sweden, a Catholic convert, came to end her days there. Her tomb is in St. Peter's.

By contrast, the 18th century, in Rome and in the whole Catholic world, was one of breathless change. The capital of Catholicism, profiting from its rapid progress, saw another small increase in its population, reaching 162,000 inhabitants in 1780. Never did so many pilgrims flock to it as in 1750. The Grand Tour brought the European elite to Rome, including President de Brosses, Goethe, and Fragonard. Brilliant architectural triumphs, notably the Trevi fountain and the staircase of the Trinità del Monte, lent added seduction to the city. But the Baroque aesthetic now found itself in competition with Neoclassicism. The excavations on the PALATINE began in 1720, those of Hadrian's villa at Tivoli in 1724. A German scholar who had converted to Catholicism, J.-J. Winckelmann (d. 1768), was named prefect of antiquities of Rome, then librarian of the Vatican. His *History of Ancient Art* (1764) defined the canons of the beautiful in total opposition to the exuberance of the Baroque and the frivolity of the Rococo. Piranese (1720–78), a Venetian who had moved to Rome, reinforced this theory with his collections of engravings, meanwhile helping to spread the Egyptian style. Another Venetian-born artist, Canova, produced his first masterpieces in Rome. His *Apollo Crowned with Laurels* and the two tombs of CLEMENT XIII and CLEMENT XIV signify the acceptance of an ample, serene aesthetic at the opposite pole from Baroque exuberance. At the same time, from 1777 the Vatican opened its galleries of ancient art, decorated in the Pompeian style, and Valadier suggested redesigning the Piazza del Popolo and the Pincio according to a Neoclassical esthetic—a goal he would realize in the years 1813–20. But by then Rome was tending to become a conservatory of forms, virtually a museum.

The fact is that it did not face up to the host of difficulties that assailed it, some local, others international. The result was an accumulation of misfortunes, errors, and disrupting change. With the Austrian War of Succession (1740–8), Italy once again echoed with the tramp of armies, a reminder of its harsh experience between 1494 and 1559. The imperial troops and those of the Bourbons of Naples clashed violently near Velletri, and the Roman Campagna was devastated. Severe drought followed in 1763–4. More serious perhaps, malaria spread its ravages through the capital. At the end of the 17th century, INNOCENT XI had compressed the expenses of the pontifical state, reduced the public debt, and broken with the tradition of nepotism. BENEDICT XIV (1740–58), the pope who won Voltaire's praise, tried to imitate him. But aside from this exception, the 18th-century popes were stodgy, ineffective in fighting administrative inertia, and once again prone to nepotism. On the eve of the FRENCH REVOLUTION, the Church's temporal domain struck foreigners as a backward, ill-governed territory, at the same time that efforts at modernization had been realized in Lombardy, Tuscany, Parma, and the Two Sicilies.

On both the religious and the international levels, the papacy also gave an impression of powerlessness in the 18th century. In vain did the bull *Unigenitus* (1713) once more condemn JANSENISM: the current of opposition in Rome that it had crystalized persisted in France and elsewhere, as witness the synod of Pistoia in 1786, inspired by Bishop Ricci. The Jansenist journal *Les Nouvelles ecclésiastiques*, an intelligent though bitter publication, appeared regularly from 1728 to 1803, albeit clandestinely, one subscriber being Pietro Leopoldo, grand duke of Tuscany. In the same context of opposition to papal power, in 1723 the Church of Utrecht came into being, separate from Rome. In 1763, a book entitled *De statu Ecclesiae* appeared under the signature of Febronius, bishop coadjutor of Trier, which supported the freedom of the national Churches faced with the despotism of the Curia—whence the term "Febronianism." In France, neither of the two condemnations of FREEMASONRY (1738 and 1751) was published, nor were they seriously pursued in the Papal States.

The Jansenist troubles prevented Rome from devoting its calm attention to the highly consequential debate over "Chinese rites." Taking into account the tragic annihilation of Japanese Christianity in the persecutions of the 1630s, the papacy should have adopted an extremely prudent attitude in the matter of Chinese customs. Indeed, the Jesuits were eager to de-Westernize Christianity and adopt from Asian civilizations everything that was not incompatible with the Gospel. By contrast, the Dominicans, Franciscans, and apostolic vicars from foreign missions followed St. Augustine in exalting the power of grace, refused any compromises, and called for complete conversions, even if these were rare. The conflict over "Chinese rites" lasted a hundred years. It was ended in 1749 by BENEDICT XIV, who denied, purely and simply, all "permissions" authorizing Chinese Catholics to carry on their ancestral practices.

This rigidity was in reality a sign of weakness. One can see the extent of this weakness, as evidenced in the 18th century, by considering Rome's overall attitude toward the Jesuits, whose suffering extended from China to the Americas. In 1759, the marquis de Pombal suppressed the Society of Jesus in the Portuguese territories: 80 fathers were executed, several hundred imprisoned, and a thousand deported. Three years later, the complaint of the Marseilles ship-owners against Father Lavalette (of Martinique) and the province of the French Jesuits allowed parliament to confiscate all the possessions the Society of Jesus held in France. In 1764, Louis XV, against his own deep-seated feelings, dissolved the order in that country. The same measures were taken in 1767 by Charles III in Spain and in the Spanish colonies, where the Jesuits were accused of inciting the Guaraní of Paraguay to revolt. Five thousand Jesuits were arrested. This marked the end of the famous "reductions." In the final stage, CLEMENT XIV in 1773 abolished the order and had its superior general imprisoned in the Castel Sant'Angelo, where he died. It was in this context that, in 1783, Joseph II with a stroke of the pen closed all the monasteries of contemplative orders in Austria and the Low Countries, and that in 1789 the archbishop of Mainz turned that city's Dominican monastery into a home for aged priests. The Civil Constitution of the Clergy was not far off. Close at hand, too, in 1798 were the occupation of Rome by troops of the Directory and the transformation, even though short-lived, of the States of the Church into the "Roman Republic."

This event, unimaginable 10 years earlier, did not constitute a historical terminus. The papacy recovered its capital city, and the 19th century was, from the Catholic viewpoint, one of great missionary activity. Still, 1798 marked the time when the history of the "second Rome" ended in all respects. New vistas opened up that differed widely from those of the past. The popes and the splendid city from which they governed a religion and a state were extremely well adapted to the thinking, the hierarchies, and the structure of the *ancien régime*. Were they as well prepared to position themselves in convincing fashion in the post-revolutionary world?

Jean Delumeau

Bibliography

Delumeau, J. *Vie économique et sociale de Rome dans la seconde moitié du XVIᵉ siècle*, Paris, 1957.

ROME, CONTEMPORARY ERA. See Monumentality and Roman Urbanism.

ROME, DIOCESE OF. See Diocese of Rome.

ROME GHETTO. See Judaism.

ROSARY. A prayer that is both vocal and mental, the rosary is a form of devotion the practice of which consists essentially in reciting the Lord's Prayer and ten Hail Marys, while meditating on one episode in the life of Christ. Fifteen "mysteries" are proposed for meditation, grouped in three series of five: joyful, sorrowful, and glorious.

The history of the rosary begins with the development of Marian piety in the East in forms that were acclamatory and repetitive. The custom became fairly widespread in the West after the translation into Latin, in the 9th century, of the ancient Greek hymn *Akathistos*. In the meantime, the laity, out of ignorance of Latin or simply of writing, was being increasingly excluded from the singing of the psalms, which for centuries had formed the backbone of Christian worship; accordingly, the *Pater noster* came to be included under the heading of the psalter and its recitation chosen or prescribed as a substitute. Whether, in the 12th century, the angel's salutation was added to the *Pater noster* or replaced it, occasional references to a Psalter of Mary (three sets of fifty Hail Marys) for laymen or laywomen who could not use the Psalter of David for their prayer can be found.

It was mainly in the lands of the Rhine, the Moselle, and the Scheldt that this type of prayer first arose during the 13th century. In the beguinages and Cistercian monasteries, the repetition of the Hail Mary was not intended to be simply verbal but implied mental contemplation and an emotional response to the Virgin's joys and sorrows, the Savior's five wounds, and so on. In the Rhineland and Flanders, from the 14th century on, the final word of the salutation—Jesus—was often followed by a short phrase, for example, "Jesus, who pardoned the good thief." In the 15th century, some Carthusians—notably at Trier with Adolf of Essen (d. 1439) and later Dominic of Prussia (d. 1460)—soon became specialists in little phrases of this nature. They gave the name "rosaries" to the collections they compiled (like the "rosaries" made elsewhere of philosophical or juridical texts), then to the devotion itself, which they spread abroad through their networks as a method of conversion and a mode of spiritual life. What was called "rosary" here continued to be known in other areas as the Psalter of Mary, the chaplet or little hat, in which the string of *Aves* addressed to the Virgin evokes the crowns of flowers that gallants would offer young girls.

The Breton Dominican Alain de La Roche (d. 1475), who preached a devotion that he attributed erroneously to St. Dominic, inaugurated a new stage in its propagation by founding, in Douai in 1470, a Confraternity of the Psalter of the Virgin Mary. Its members were enjoined to recite the psalter each day, a practice that bound them together in a vast spiritual solidarity. The same advantages were offered by the Confraternity of the Rosary, which another Dominican, Joachim Sprenger (d. 1495), established in 1475 in his monastery in Cologne. Presented as the fulfillment of a vow made upon the freeing of a besieged stronghold, the initiative at once attracted the adherence of the German emperor, Frederick III, as well as the granting of indulgences by a pontifical legate and soon by Pope SIXTUS IV himself (20 May 1478). Thus, the history of these confraternities was characterized from the beginning by a policy of social prestige and ecclesiastical approval that would last for at least two centuries. Their expansion, very rapid in Germany, at once followed in Italy. Integrating these groups immediately into its preaching mission, the Dominican order gradually acquired a monopoly that was definitively sanctioned by Pope PIUS V in 1569.

The destruction of the Turkish fleet at LEPANTO, on 7 October 1571, by a coalition of the Christian naval forces, marks a date in the history of this devotion. Various circumstances helped spread the conviction of the powerful intervention of Mary of the Rosary, invoked that same day in the confraternities. In 1572, Pius V instituted the liturgical celebration of Our Lady of Victory.

An abundant iconography bears witness not only to the proliferation of the confraternities but, even more, to the fundamental importance acquired by recitation of the rosary or chaplet in the pious exercises of individual Christians. In the 18th century, the rosary would be at the heart of the popular missions preached by St. Louis-Marie Grignion de Montfort. In the 19th century, the Association of the Living Rosary, founded in 1826 by Pauline Jaricot, would play a leading role in the spread of the devotion, until the town of Lourdes became a kind of world capital of the rosary. Pope LEO XIII addressed to the universal Church his many encyclicals and exhortations on this topic, in line with his other paraliturgical initiatives. Among the papal interventions of the 20th century, the most penetrating pages are perhaps those of PAUL VI, in his apostolic exhortation *Marialis cultus* of 2 February 1974 (*AAS*, vol. 66, pp. 152–62).

André Duval

Bibliography

Acta sanctae Sedis necnon magistrorum et capitulorum generalium S. Ordinis Praedicatorum pro Societate Rosarii, 4 vols., Lyon, 1891.
Duval, A. "Rosaire," *DS*, 13 (1988), 937–80.
Klinkhammer, K. J. *Adolf von Essen und seine Werke. Der Rosenkranz in der geschitlichen Situation seiner Entstehung und in seinem bleibenden Anliegen*, Frankfurt-am-Main, 1972 (*Frankfurter theologische Studien*, 13).
Meersseman, G. G. *Der Hymnos akathistos im Abendland*, Freiburg, 1958–60 (*Spicilegium Friburgense*, 2–3).
Meersseman, G. G. *Ordo fraternitatis. Confraternite e pietà dei laici nel medioevo*, Rome, 1977 (*Italia sacra*, 24, 25, 26).
Van Den Oudendijk Pieterse, F. H. A. *Dürers Rosenkranzfest en de Ikonographie der duitse Rosenkranzgroepen ven de XVe en het Begin des XVIe Eeuw*, Amsterdam-Antwerp, 1939.
Winston, A. "Tracing the Origins of the Rosary: German Vernacular Texts," *Soeculum*, 68 (July, 1993) pp. 619–36.

ROSE, GOLDEN. A sacred ornament representing a rose or rosebush that is made of wrought gold and blessed each year by the pope. The pope presented it as a favor to eminent individuals, notably kings and queens, to leading centers of Catholic worship or pilgrimage, and to civic communities as a public honor.

In its earliest form, the ornament was a stem supporting a single flower, with a cusp hidden at the center of the petals in which balm and musk were placed to perfume it. The VATICAN LIBRARY (Barb. lat. 3030, 94r) has an 18th-century representation of a Golden Rose presented by INNOCENT IV (1243–54) to the chapter of St-Just in Lyon.

At the beginning of the 14th century, the design tended to become more elaborate. It incorporated thorny, entwined stems with leaves and clusters of buds around the central flower. Precious stones were added to enhance the appearance of the ornament and increase its value. Later, the complete Golden Rose was presented in a vase and on a pedestal, both of which were usually silvered and richly decorated with bas-reliefs, and showed the arms of the supreme pontiff.

The most renowned Italian goldsmiths were chosen to craft these ornaments, whose value varied depending on the generosity and economic standing of the donor. In the Golden Rose sent by CLEMENT IX to Queen Marie-Thérèse of France in 1668, the gold alone weighed almost 9 pounds/4 kilograms. Many of these historically and symbolically valuable objects were melted down so that the precious metal could be recovered for monetary purposes. Only a few rare specimens of the Golden Rose have survived. One is in the Musée de Cluny in Paris, another in the Palazzo Comunale of Siena, and two at the Schatzkammer of the Hofburg in Vienna; examples can also be found in the treasury of the cathedral of Benevento and the Sacred Museum of the Vatican Library.

The Church has always enjoyed the prerogative of attributing spiritual significance to material objects. The practice allowed the pope to exhort beneficiaries to cultivate virtues corresponding to their duties and status. Though it is impossible to establish the chronology of the origins of the Golden Rose, these are nevertheless acknowledged to go back to early medieval times. The first certain reference to the ornament is given in a bull dated

1049 in which LEO IX (1049–54) exempts the convent of the Holy Cross in Woffenheim in Alsace from the jurisdiction of the local bishops on the condition that the abbess each year send a rose in pure gold, or its equivalent, to the Apostolic See. The rose had to weigh 2 ounces/57 grams and be delivered one week before the Fourth Sunday of Lent. Judging from the letter, it is clear that the custom whereby the pope went in procession with the rose had by that time been established in Rome.

The earliest mention of the gift of a rose by the pope is in the chronicle of St. Martin of Tours. When URBAN II (1088–99) was traveling in France after preaching the First CRUSADE, he offered it to Count Foulques of Anjou, who declared that in memory of the gift he and his heirs would henceforth carry it each year in the Palm Sunday procession.

However great the artistic and monetary value of the rose, for the pope that was of secondary importance compared with the spiritual message the ornament was designed to send, as the letter accompanying the gift invariably indicated. In one sense, it represented Christ himself and was an assurance of eternal felicity, a source of joy and happiness. Of all the flowers in nature, the rose is considered the most beautiful and the most fragrant. Hence, the hope that the divine perfume of the symbolic rose would impregnate the spirit of the one who received it and grant him or her generosity of heart.

This spiritual significance was conferred on the Golden Rose by a ritual blessing bestowed by the pope. It was done at a ceremony that took place before the liturgy of the Sunday known as Laetare, because of the antiphon *Laetare Jerusalem* in the Introit, but which was also known as the Sunday of the Rose on account of the blessing preceding the celebration of the papal mass. The benediction took place in the *aula dei paramenti*, the balm and musk being added at the end of the prayer. The cardinals were convened, and the pope decided with them who should receive the rose that year. Generally, the recipient was not at the papal court, and the gift had to be entrusted to a royal ambassador in residence or a papal legate whose special task it was to hand over the Golden Rose according to a precise protocol.

Charles Burns

Bibliography

Burns, C. *Golden Rose and Blessed Sword: Papal Gifts to Scottish Monarchs*, Glasgow, 1970; "Papal Gifts and Honours for the Earlier Tudors," *MHP* 50 (1983), 173–97.

Cartari, C. *La Rosa d'Oro Pontificia*, Rome, 1681.

Cornides, E. *Rose und Schwert im päpstlichen Zeremoniell*, Vienna, 1967.

Müntz, E. "Les Roses d'Or pontificales," *Revue de l'Art chrétien* 44 (1901), 1–11.

ROTA, TRIBUNAL OF THE. As with many institutions, it is difficult to pinpoint the exact origins of this tribunal. Most probably it developed gradually over the second half of the 12th and especially the first part of the 13th century.

Previously, and apparently from earliest times, the pope reserved for himself the right to judge in person disputes of a judicial nature sent to Rome from Churches in various parts of the world. Little by little, the judicial activity of the Holy See became such that it caused severe problems with the consistory of cardinals, at that time the only body to examine cases on which the pope had reserved the right to pronounce final sentence.

That is why, in the 12th century, Bernard of Clairvaux did not hesitate to call the consistory of cardinals "judices orbis," as a consultive body to the pope ("De Consideratione" IV). Yet at the same time he reproached his former disciple, Pope EUGENE III (1145–53), for wasting time in pronouncing judgments. He advised him to entrust to others what he was accustomed to dealing with on his own. Nevertheless, under Eugene III's immediate successors, the cardinals were still supposed to examine cases on which the pope himself pronounced judgment.

INNOCENT III (1198–1216) found himself forced to resolve this problem, owing to the accumulation of cases sent to Rome for a variety of reasons: the rebirth of Roman law, the development of CANON LAW from Gratian's time, the growth of reform on the part of the Holy See within the framework of institutions, especially the consistory, and, finally, an increasingly centralized Church government.

It is true that Innocent III had at his disposal a complete qualified staff among the members of his entourage. Indeed, his predecessor, URBAN II (1088–99), included in his court *cappellani papae* as well as *subdiaconi sanctae Romanae Ecclesiae* who had the necessary juridical abilities to deal with these matters. Moreover, it is not unlikely that some of these men were already entrusted with the pronouncement of certain sentences. But it is not until the pontificate of Innocent III that they were regularly called on to handle such matters, though the cardinals were not excluded from exercising the responsibility. At this time, the pope kept the major cases for himself. A report would be addressed to him concerning the case in general, and after consulting the cardinals in consistory, he would pronounce sentence on his own.

Only toward the end of his pontificate (1212) did Innocent III authorize the *cappellani* who had examined the case to pronounce sentence themselves, while retaining the obligation to secure the opinion of the cardinals. Over the years, the latter apparently little by little lost interest in playing this minor role, which is why they were replaced by "jurisperiti." At this time, too, the pope reserved for himself the right to confirm the sentence brought in his name.

In the mid-13th century, the nascent organization began to crystallize. In 1246 appeared the title "auditor generalis causarum sacri Palatii," and in 1274 the collegial character of the institution became clear. Owing to a shortage of qualified cardinals and jurists, the *auditores* became accustomed to exchanging advice among their colleagues. Some judicial judgments can be found at this time that refer to the practice: ". . . cum aliis palatii apostolici coauditoribus generalibus collatione sive relatione fideli . . ." The tribunal was thus constituted as such, though the number of its members was not yet fixed. Under CLEMENT IV (1265–8) it numbered 7, under NICHOLAS IV (1288–92), 5, under BONIFACE VIII (1294–1303), 14, under JOHN XXII (1314–34), 8, and under BENEDICT XII (1334–42), 21.

It may be useful to recall here that France invariably had an "auditor" within this institution, from its earliest days. From Pierre de Colmieu, around 1230, to our own day, an uninterrupted line of fifty-eight French "auditors," whose names form an extant list, ensured the presence of that country at the heart of the tribunal.

It is from this period that the term "Rota," as designating the apostolic tribunal, can be dated. The reason for the name is still a matter of controversy, despite general agreement that it goes back to the Avignon period of the papacy. For some, the name comes from the wheeled desk in the Hall of Deliberations, carrying the register of cases and acts of procedure, which thus could be placed directly before each of the deliberants (printing not yet having been invented). For others, the term referred to the meeting hall itself, which was in the form of a rotunda. Others claim it is of Roman origin, since the name rota was given to the marble or porphyry table in the Vatican basilica, around which the pope and the cardinals assembled with their counselors whenever major cases were being tried. Whatever the origin, papal documents began to use the term "tribunal of the Rota" only around 1423.

Moreover, during the 15th and 16th centuries, the importance of this institution underwent continual growth. The fame of the apostolic tribunal at this time derived not only from the extent of its responsibilities (in religious matters, it covered the whole world, in the civil realm, all the papal territories) but also from the expertise of its members. They gave decisions that carried authority similar to that of "common opinions" owing to the number of auditors called upon to uphold them. As a result, there arose the problem of the value of the juridical positions that could be taken against them. Thus, emphasis was laid on the role played by the Rota's decisions in the determination of the *jus commune* of the Church. True, to establish this jurisprudence, the auditors were chiefly inspired by the reasons for the settlement of the litigation rather than by systematic reference to "authorities"; but they also relied on *aequitas canonica* (defined by Hostiensis as "justitia dulcore misericordiae temperata"), which allowed them to give their judgments or solutions better adapted to the needs of their age.

With this in mind, a collection began to be made of the *conclusiones* and *decisiones* of the tribunal of the Rota, and, with the advent of printing in the 16th century, volumes containing its decisions appeared in great numbers. The practice continued almost without interruption over the following centuries. And following PIUS X's reorganization of the Roman Curia (29 June 1908), the official collection of the *S. Romanae Rotae Decisiones seu Sententiae* (Rome, 1909–86) continues to play the same role in the administration of justice in the Church.

The 16th and 17th centuries saw a dimming of the luster of the tribunal of the Rota. This was influenced by three factors, linked to the vicissitudes of history.

Within the Church, Sixtus V had reorganized the Curia with the constitution IMMENSA in 1588. This constitution brought about the birth and development of the ROMAN CONGREGATIONS, which determined their own matters of concern and were presided over by a cardinal. From the tribunal of the Rota, they took over a certain number of lawsuits that traditionally fell under its competence. Moreover, the administrative procedure of these congregations, characterized by flexibility, speed, and financial economy, had grown through infringement on the judicial domain actually reserved for the Rota.

The general history of that period shows a lessening of the influence of the Church owing to the progress of Protestantism and the development of royal absolutism in the various states of the civilized world, which brought about a correlative and manifest reduction in the number of suits passed to the tribunal of the Holy See.

As regards historical circumstances and their influence on the decisions of the Rota, one particular case concerning France is worthy of note, from the beginning of the 19th century. In the "civil" matters passed on to them from the Papal States, the auditors were required, while observing the characteristics of the *aequitas canonica* traditionally appropriate to their judgments, to follow the laws that obtained in the city. This occurred during the occupation of the Papal States by the armies of Napoleon I (1809–15). The emperor had proclaimed the annexation of Rome to France and thus imposed the French Civil Code by force of arms. But after 1815, when the pontificate of PIUS VII (1800–23) was restored, the Rota judges were required to continue applying the Code beyond the period of French occupation, because of the rule *tempus regit actum*, whereby a judge cannot apply the present norm to litigation begun before it came into force. The reasoning of the auditors of the Rota rested on a triple argument, in which can be recognized the characteristics of traditional jurisprudence:

1) Although the invader did not enjoy legitimate sovereignty, he exercised certain prerogatives and had the

right to enact laws to administer the city. The subjects were bound to obey these laws, provided they were not contrary to natural or divine law, or ecclesiastical laws.

2) The invader's acts are null in the eyes of the law but not as regards fact, and it is true that a certain number of measures taken by him remain in place (the argument of opportunity based on the necessary stability of the social order and the security of juridical relations).

3) In the edict of Pius VII proclaiming the return to the old law and the abolition of French legislation, there was no retroactive clause calling into question the juridical acts and deeds that had been concluded or had arisen during the Napoleonic occupation; from that, it must be concluded that the supreme pontiff intended to confirm and leave as they were the juridical situations in the state.

The doctrine of the Rota here is clear and faithful to its own tradition. It relies at one and the same time on practical considerations and on theoretical arguments allowing it to adapt to the troubled circumstances of the time.

Throughout the rest of the 19th century, the activity of the Roman Rota suffered a veritable eclipse. Indeed, with the *Regolamento legislativo giudiziario*, Pope GREGORY XVI (1831–46) virtually put an end to the existence of the apostolic tribunal as it had existed hitherto. Now, while remaining a "tribunal extraordinary" for cases from elsewhere, its role was reduced to that of an "ordinary tribunal of appeal" for ecclesiastical or civil suits brought to it by Rome or the Papal States. That is to say, in the latter case its activity ceased with the abolition of the pontifical state. The royal decree of 27 October 1870 ended it, and, further, the so-called Law of Guarantees of 30 November 1870 refused to recognize its judiciary sentences, admitting only the administrative acts of the Holy See. Nonetheless, the tribunal of the Rota continued to exist with sharply reduced activity regarding certain cases of a spiritual order, even though in 1895 Pope LEO XIII (1878–1903) entrusted the Rota with the task of setting forth a deliberative vote of the College for the causes of beatification.

Although during the 19th century the Rota suffered a loss of influence in the universal Church, in the next century the supreme pontiffs once again assigned it its place, thanks to three apostolic constitutions that brought about the reorganization of the Curia. The first, promulgated by Pope Pius X on 29 June 1908 (constitution *Sapienti consilio*), provided for the establishment of judicial power in the universal Church by making a clear distinction between it and the administrative power of the congregations, a principle whose application it was required to oversee, both in the constitution itself and in the *lex propria* annexed to it. Both these documents established the composition, framework, and limits of the tribunal's jurisdiction, while at the same time determining the fundamental norms of the procedure to be observed therein. Both clearly established that the Roman Rota is an apos-

tolic tribunal of appeal, which judged, in the second or even third instance, sentences pronounced before the lower tribunals (at the time, diocesan and metropolitan "officialities"; more recently, regional ecclesiastical tribunals of first and second instance)—namely, all cases involving a marriage nullity, to say nothing, of course, of contentious cases brought against ecclesiastical personnel, or moral ecclesiastical persons; the latter are rarer, at this time, than are the former kinds of cases.

A few years later, the Code of Canon Law promulgated by Pope BENEDICT XV (apostolic constitution *Providentissima Mater Ecclesia*) collected and confirmed all the provisions previously taken by Pius X in juridical matters, and promulgated them as laws of the universal Church. Further, the new Code determined the rules to be observed in contentious or penal procedures.

Although the Rota's task was to be a tribunal of appeal in the Church, it should be noted that in certain cases it can function as a tribunal of first instance, that is, in contentious suits brought against residential bishops, against dioceses, or against any other moral ecclesiastical person directly subject to the Holy See. Also, naturally, the Rota functions as an apostolic tribunal of first instance by special delegation when the pope, either directly or through the intermediary of the Apostolic Signatura, assigns it a case to deal with in the first degree. Later, on 1 September 1934, Pope PIUS XI approved the new *Normae Sacrae Romanae Rotae Tribunalis*. This document, with its 185 articles, made it possible to bring into line with the Code of Canon Law and the judiciary experience thereafter, all the official documents previously promulgated since the reform of Pope Pius X. The results of this new reorganization were that the tribunal of the Rota is the only office of the Curia not presided over by a cardinal, and that it is made up of an undetermined number of prelate "auditors," from a variety of nations, who form a college presided over as *primus inter pares* by the eldest in function, the dean. The latter must represent the college of prelate auditors and assume the administration of the tribunal, assisted by the two eldest auditors after him, the *seniores auditorum*.

1) The tribunal of the Rota judges in collegial fashion in plenary session *videntibus omnibus* through the express arrangement of the supreme pontiff, or when it must retry a case already submitted to its judgment that has been remitted to it in its entirety by the Apostolic Signatura.

2) For all other cases, the Rota judges by means of chambers of three judges, called a *ternus*, who are established in order of protocol. Each *ternus* is presided over by the eldest of the auditors in function, the dean, who usually also assumes in the *ternus* the duties of reporter or *Ponens*; he writes and signs the sentence, his assessors being the cosignatories.

A second, more recent constitution, promulgated by Pope PAUL VI on 15 August 1967 (apostolic constitution *Regimini Ecclesiae universae*), was aimed at adapting to the decisions of the VATICAN II council the various offices existing in the Curia and setting up the new curial institutions created by the council's decisions. This document devotes space to the tribunal of the Rota. It confirms in their entirety the Rota's previous duties on the judiciary level, and extends them, albeit not specifically, to all matrimonial cases, even those that hitherto came under the Congregation for the Doctrine of the Faith, leaving untouched the duty to defer to that congregation questions specifically concerned with doctrine.

Here one should stress the role played in the post-conciliar Church by the Rota's judiciary activity over the last decades: on the one hand, by the number of cases handed to it; on the other, especially, by the interest of its jurisprudence in matrimonial questions, which has taken into account progress in the human sciences and the reliable data provided by these in order to appreciate the determination of the "human element" in religious and sacramental matters. Recent sentences, which are regularly published in the *Decisiones*, have built up a corpus of canonical doctrine that has been sufficiently tested to become the source of several "canons" of legislation on marriage (alliance, sacrament, and institution), promulgated in the new Code of Canon Law of 25 January 1983 by Pope JOHN PAUL II (apostolic constitution *Sacra disciplinae leges*).

Last, in a third constitution relating to the Curia, Pope John Paul II used the apostolic constitution *Pastor bonus* of 28 June 1988 to adapt the structures of the Roman Curia to the demands of the new Code of Canon Law promulgated by him five years earlier.

This apostolic constitution deals specifically with the tribunal of the Roman Rota in five articles (art. 126–30) that, in the few modifications which they make to the preceding ones, take into account the centuries of experience briefly sketched above. For the first time, the function of the Rota within the universal Church is outlined in a legislative text. It is to safeguard rights within the Church, foster unity of jurisprudence, and by virtue of its own decisions come to the assistance of the lower tribunals (art. 126); the prelates of this tribunal lose the age-old title of "auditor." From now on, they will be known as "judges," so that their title is adapted to the reality of their function, since an auditor, by definition, was originally never other than an instructing judge. Moreover, this role is restored to him in all the Church tribunals by the new Code of Canon Law (c.1580–2).

The constitution adds two qualities to those required in the "judges." In addition to the titles and diplomas hitherto required, it stipulates that the judges must be persons of proven doctrine and experience; and they can be recruited from various parts of the world (cf. art. 127). A final new requirement concerns the dean of the college of judges. Heretofore, he had attained this position *ipso jure* by virtue of the seniority of his appointment in the judicial function; henceforth, he is to be chosen by the supreme pontiff from within the college of judges and appointed *ad certum tempus*. With this change, the supreme legislator seems to indicate that seniority is not necessarily a guarantee of the qualities required in one destined to fill a position of this importance (art. 127).

The very nature of the matters proposed to the Church lawgivers over the centuries allows us to define the activity of its tribunals as Pope JOHN XXIII formulated it: "One thing alone constitutes the motive guiding the Church's spiritual action in the century: the salvation of souls, *salus animarum*. This is the spirit that must animate the action of the tribunal of the Church; it is a ministry of truth because it reaches out to the salvation of the soul of whoever has recourse to these tribunals" (allocution to the tribunal of the Rota, 13 December 1961).

Bernard de Lanversin

Bibliography

del Rè, N. *La Curia Romana*, Rome, 1970.

La Curia Romana nelle Const. Ap "Pastor bonus," Rome, 1990.

Lefebvre, C. *Rote Romaine, DDC*, under VII, 39–40, Paris, 1960–1.

Mamberti, D. *Étude sur les décisions rotales de 1814, 1916*, Rome, 1985.

SABINIAN. *(b. Blera in Tuscany, ? d.—Rome, 22 February 606). Consecrated pope on 13 September 604. Buried at St. Peter's in Rome.*

His life is known to us only through a brief note in the *LIBER PONTIFICALIS*, some letters of Gregory the Great, his epitaph, and a legend related two centuries after his death by John the Deacon.

Nothing is known of the social position of his father Bonus, or of anything of Sabinian's life until his ordination as deacon of the Church of Rome, before 592. Sent by Gregory the Great as *apocrisarius*, or pope's representative, to Constantinople in July 493, he formed ties with the court, the patriarch, and many others who corresponded with Gregory. He returned to Rome in the spring of 597, leaving no trace in the sources until his consecration.

The choice of a deacon is evidence of the power of the diocesan clergy, who were reacting against the rule of Gregory, a nobleman and a monk. According to the *Liber pontificalis*, Sabinian "gave ecclesiastical duties to the clergy" and thus began to restore to the diocesan clergy the positions previously granted to religious priests by his predecessor, having himself attained the diaconate by climbing every rung of the ecclesiastical ladder.

We know nothing of his other religious activities except his ordination of twenty-six bishops and his improvements to the lighting in ST. PETER'S. On the other hand, he offers a good example of the entrusting of civil positions by the emperor to the bishops. After famine struck Rome in 605, Sabinian "opened the Church's granaries and sold 30 barrels of wheat [2 quintals] for 1 sou." This action is often taken to signify nothing more than a sale of public wheat at the average market price, which the civil services of the *annona* had regularly realized in former times and which the popes had continued. Nevertheless, John the Deacon relates a legend whereby Gregory the Great appeared to his successor and exhorted him to be charitable before killing him with a blow to the head on account of his stubbornness. The *Liber pontificalis* adds that the procession carrying his remains had to make its way to St. Peter's via a detour outside the city walls; clearly, the authorities feared trouble. So great a hatred presupposes that he had made a harmful decision. In fact, the pope sold wheat that had hitherto been distributed, thus abolishing, either on his own or on the emperor's orders, the free ANNONA—a public benefit, not a charitable distribution to the poor—from which the Romans had benefited since the days of the republic and which his predecessor had continued to ensure. Although identical measures were taken at this time throughout the empire, Sabinian's action won him a lasting evil reputation among the people.

Jean Durliat

Bibliography

JW, 1, 220.
LP, 1, 315.
Durliat, J. *De la ville antique à la ville byzantine*, Rome, 1990, 141–3.
John the Deacon, *Vie de Grégoire le Grand, PL* 75, 58.
Schneider, 16 = Icur, 4157.

See also BYZANTIUM AND THE PAPACY.

SACERDOTIUM / IMPERIUM. See **Church-State Conflict.**

SACK OF ROME. For all its notoriety, the sack of Rome in 1527 is but one example of the many outrages committed in great cities, from the capture of Jerusalem by the Romans to that of Constantinople by the Turks. In Rome alone, at least seven other instances can be cited. In 410, Alaric's Visigoths pillaged Rome, Pope INNO-

CENT I having fled the city. After their meeting with Pope LEO I in 455 Genseric's Vandals systematically took control of the city, though avoiding both fire and massacre. In 638, on the death of HONORIUS I, the Byzantine troops of the *cartulary* Maurice and the exarch Isaac seized the Lateran palace, where SEVERINUS was waiting to be consecrated. The sequestering of the papal treasury—which, for the emperor's representatives, was a pledge for the soldiers' pay—is presented by Western sources as an act of pillage. Emperor Constans II, received by the pope in 663, carried out a peaceful sack of the city by stripping the bronze from a number of ancient monuments (among them the roof of the Pantheon, which by then had been converted into the church of Sta. Maria ad Martyres). In 756, troops of the Lombard king Aistoff laid siege to Rome and looted the ecclesiastical properties in the surrounding area. They spared St. Peter's, but, according to a pontifical letter, they pillaged many churches and papal patrimonies. The best-documented damage was the seizure by the Lombards of many relics. The SARACENS in 846 pillaged St. Paul's Outside the Walls and St. Peter's. Finally, the Normans under Robert Guiscard penetrated the city to free GREGORY VII, besieged in the Castel Sant'Angelo. However, in the face of heavy resistance by many inhabitants, they soon abandoned the city to pillage, particularly on the Coelian Hill.

The most dramatic of all the sacks of Rome occurred in 1527 at a time of general crisis, after the plague of 1523 and before the great flood of 1530, when the tensions of the pontifical city burst into the open and the absence of any national sentiment in the peninsula was plain. At the fifth Lateran council, steps had been taken to curb the cardinals' ostentation, to restrain apocalyptic prophecies, and to prevent the distribution of pamphlets which, at the instigation of Luther and Erasmus, attacked the mixture of profane and sacred that prevailed in Rome in the sphere of papal authority. The problems of the pontificate of CLEMENT VII echoed the crisis of the 1510s, with one difference: now, the threat of external domination no longer came from France, but from the Empire. Among the causes of the disaster were the instability of the Curia and the anarchic behavior of the Romans, who no longer supported the pope. Already in 1526, the Colonna family, in collusion with imperial agents, even attacked and devastated the Vatican.

As A. Chastel has written, "This catastrophic event split Roman life in two, as it were, destroying traditions and customs, at a time when the struggle against the Reformation was profoundly changing people's thinking. Every domain—diplomatic, religious, political, cultural, urban, and artistic—suffered one or more serious consequences from the events of 1527 and the years after it." This seems all the more tragic in that, in the communal consciousness, the capital of Christianity enjoyed a providential immunity. Now a veritable attack was being made on the permanence of the Church. Yet in the Vatican Palace itself, the predominance of the papacy over the secular rulers had been reaffirmed in monumental fashion in the Stanze, particularly the Sala di Costantino (completed in 1524), where the Sacred College held its official meetings. The frescoes were a reminder to all of the claim that Constantine had offered Rome to the pope, thus marking the superiority of his bishop over any emperor. The anti-Roman attack called into question both Rome, portrayed by its opponents as a city of corruption and home of the Devil, and the pontiff's temporal power, particularly as portrayed in Luther's German Bible (published in 1522) and its illustrations by Cranach. The dominant themes of Roman thinking were turned inside out by the Lutherans. Against the dogma of the city's providential role and the divine institution of papal authority, they set the implacable representation of Rome as Babylon and the pope as Antichrist. Luther was excommunicated, and from then on, any allusion to the pope north of the Alps was tinged with hostility and insolence.

The people's minds at this time were consumed by the idea of imminent catastrophe, by omens and prophetic visions of all kinds. This eschatological trend, which became accentuated around 1525, was a manifestation of a general anxiety. It encouraged a state of collective excitation, the chief obsessions being the end of the world and the destruction of Rome and the pope. On every side, it was prophesied that Rome would be seized, but those most directly affected refused to believe it. Varchi writes, "The point had been reached when not only monks in the pulpit but even ordinary Romans went into the squares proclaiming, with loud threats and shouts, the ruin of Italy and the end of the world." For the Lutherans, the symbolic havoc in the city became an indispensable means toward the renewal of Christian faith. Thus, the accelerating riots, crime, panic, and execration finally led to tragedy.

The conflict began after the promulgation of the brief of 2 June 1526, iterating the inviolable rights of the sovereign pontiff. In response, the "memoir of Granada" declared that the pope's language was un-Christian and should be rebuked by the emperor and condemned by the council. On 22 May 1526, the official formation of the Holy League at Cognac, after François I's return from captivity, had led to rupture. In the league army were grouped, on one side, the Venetian contingents, and on the other, the French under Lautrec. The only general capable of leading these forces was Giovanni delle Bande Nere, a Medici, but he died on 22 November 1526.

Charles de Bourbon, constable of France, aided by Alfonso d'Este, led the imperial army, which mustered 10,000 Lutheran *Landsknechte* under the command of Frundsberg—at that time, a new type of soldiery. The prince of Orange led the cavalry, which consisted of

5,000 to 6,000 Spaniards, the *tercieros*, and of Italians whose brutality on campaign exceeded that of the French. But the army had neither artillery nor an organized commissariat, and its various groups lacked any common binding strategy. Charles de Bourbon could hold his men only by promising them the booty of Rome.

On 25 March 1527, CLEMENT VII sought an agreement with the viceroy Lannoy, whose visit in torrential rain everyone took as a bad omen. Feeling confident, the pope thereupon disbanded the papal militias. Disregarding the agreement, Charles de Bourbon regrouped his troops in northern Italy and marched down on Rome, sparing Florence and Bologna. They advanced along the Tiber, while the league forces followed some distance away without intervening—Lautrec would not cross the Susa Pass until the beginning of August.

On Sunday, 5 May, the imperial forces reached Rome after a series of fortunate events. They invested the city easily under cover of fog. The Spanish took up their position on the Piazza Navona, the Landsknechte on the Campo dei Fiori, and the Italians in front of the Castel Sant'Angelo. There was not even a siege. But Charles de Bourbon died during the second wave of the assault (his funeral was held in the Sistine Chapel), and he was succeeded by Philibert de Chalon. The imperials' task was all the easier because the Romans were not prepared to react in support of a pope who was unpopular because of his taxation and adverse propaganda.

Clement VII and 13 cardinals were then held hostage in the Castel Sant'Angelo. From 6 June, the pope started negotiating with all sides. The capitulation provided for a fine of 400,000 ducats, and the pontiff pardoned the conquerors in advance. He would lift "all censures, excommunications, penalties and interdicts which [the captains and soldiers] may have incurred for acts previously committed against His Holiness and the Apostolic See."

Rome, the great center of banking and commerce, then suffered a ferocious sack, at once systematic and chaotic in the absence of command. Ransoms were demanded under threat and violence. There was a huge transfer of gold, jewels, and other riches. The pillagers resold everything they had stolen on the market, whereupon the looting began anew. It is hard to tell how much treasure was lost. The greater part of the Church's gold and silver objects were melted down. As a contemporary observed, "All the saints' relics which they [the imperials] found, they have turned into playthings." Nevertheless, many relics were recovered as early as the following year. Another grave loss came from the destruction of archives and libraries. The wealth of the Roman libraries was one of the great achievements of pontifical Rome. Thus, this disappearance of the sources of knowledge distressed the humanists most of all. The commentators are unanimous: houses were destroyed, churches looted, and ecclesiastical documents reduced to ashes. According to

Melanchthon, all these crimes—"pillagings, overthrow of the imperial city, profanation of the temples, looting of libraries, assassination of priests, rape of virgins and matrons, etc."—were acts of pure madness, inspired by a hostility to culture. As a final scourge, malaria flared up in Rome over the summer.

The emperor Charles V did not learn of the sack for some time and did not dare to depose the pope. It was a delicate matter to claim that a vanquished, humiliated sovereign pontiff was harmful to order. Baldassare Castiglione himself, then posted to Spain, while denying none of the corruptions of modern Rome, declared that this attack on the *caput mundi* could neither justify nor excuse such a sacrilege. He claimed Rome had a unique significance against which no Christian people should raise a hand. Rome, made sacred by the Church and by history, should never suffer nameless abominations.

On 28 November 1527, Clement VII fled the Castel Sant'Angelo and took up residence in Orvieto, one of the safer cities of the Papal States, pending the definitive evacuation of Rome in February 1528. He did not return to Rome until October 1528, and only gradually would the city be reoccupied by its people.

When the troops left in February 1528, they numbered 5,000 Germans, 4,000 Spaniards, and 2,500 Italians, or just half of the manpower of 1527. The rest had died of malaria or left to seek other adventures. It was a time when "bells were no longer rung, no church was open, no one said Mass . . . No one knew how to describe it, or what to compare it to, save the destruction of Jerusalem. . . . All this had not happened by chance but as a result of divine justice" (A. Chastel).

The event appeared to the Erasmians as a well-deserved punishment, and to others as a warning of Providence. J. Burckhardt wrote in 1894: "One noteworthy outcome would emerge from the devastation of Rome, namely a renewal that was both spiritual and temporal." The sack was a marked watershed; the Roman climate of the years around 1525 owed its brilliance to an exceptional convergence of talents. It also signaled the beginning of the COUNTER REFORMATION, which would give the Eternal City back its dynamism and allow it to rebuild with new prospects. By making clearer the need for the council of Trent and the movement for Catholic reform, the sack of Rome swung the Church and Italy from the High Renaissance into the Baroque age. In fact, the imperials' sack of Rome hit a city that was swarming with artists, most of whom belonged to the school of Raphael. Their dispersal in the wake of the catastrophe has been described as a "diaspora." The Curia was preoccupied with the repair and restoration of Rome and the Church; with the building of the new St. Peter's in particular, one of the most acutely resented profanations was finally made good.

Oliver Guyotjeannin
Sylvia Chambadal

Bibliography

Burckhardt, J. *The Civilization of the Renaissance in Italy*, 15th ed., New York, 1958.

Chamberlain, E. A. *The Sack of Rome*, London, 1979.

Chastel, A. *The Sack of Rome, 1527*, trans. Beth Archer, Princeton, N.J., 1983.

Hook, J. *The Sack of Rome, 1527*, London, 1972.

Lenzi, M. *Il Sacco di Rome del 1527*, Rome, 1978.

SACRED COLLEGE. The term "Sacred College" denotes the whole group of cardinal-bishops, priests, and deacons, the highest dignitaries of the Roman Church after the pope, who enjoy the privileges of electing the sovereign pontiff, collegially and in conclave, and of administering the current affairs of the Church during a vacancy of the Apostolic See. They also assist the pope in the administration of the Church in the congregations and dicasteries of the Curia, and may be called on to advise either as individuals or collegially.

From its Origins to the Reform of Sixtus V. Although CARDINALS, priests, and later deacons and bishops appeared beginning in the 8th century, the origins of the Sacred College go back to the beginning of the 12th century at the earliest, the date when cardinal-deacons effectively joined the group of cardinals. The bull *In nomine Domini* (1059) of Pope NICHOLAS II, giving the cardinal-bishops the privilege of pontifical election, and the extension of this privilege to the other cardinals at the time of the schism by Guibert of Ravenna in 1084, laid the foundations of the Sacred College, which could not fully exercise its right until the election of INNOCENT II (1130).

Eclipsing the Roman SYNOD, the CONSISTORY, which was first held under URBAN II (1088–99), was (after the papal election), the place where the Sacred College could give fullest expression to its power. From the mid-13th century, the cardinals met at the Curia (still quite itinerant). Some of them took on particular administrative duties (e.g., vice chancellor, grand penitentiary, apostolic chamberlain) and were rewarded with sizable incomes. In 1289, Pope NICHOLAS IV, in the bull *Coelestis altitudo*, granted them half the regular revenues of the Church. This was added to the share already paid since the 12th century (which became half after 1295) of the "common services" paid for by the bishops and abbots appointed by the pope. From 1334, BENEDICT XII added to this the returns from "AD LIMINA" VISITS. Administration accomplished by the chamber of the Sacred College, headed by the cardinal chamberlain, or camerlengo, of the Sacred College (not to be confused with the cardinal chamberlain, later CAMERLENGO, of the Roman Church), who was designated each year jointly by the pope and the cardinals and assisted by a clerk and servants. The sums spent collegially were redistributed only among those present in the Curia, excluding the legates, who as compensation were granted the right of lodging (procurations) wherever they traveled.

Clear oligarchical trends became apparent from the 13th century: very weak manpower (at times down to six cardinals); a tendency to prolong the vacancy of the Apostolic See; and later, especially from the time of the Avignon papacy, NEPOTISM. The highest privilege, the election of the pope, which was confirmed and regulated by ALEXANDER III at the third Lateran council in 1179 (reaffirmation of equality between the three orders; a minimum of a two-thirds vote required for election), was completed by the installation of the CONCLAVE by GREGORY X in 1274; one of the principal goals was to restrict the length of the election as well as external influence. The establishment of the papacy in Avignon from 1309 to 1376 brought about a temporary predominance of the French over the Italians, as well as a peak in claims on the part of the Sacred College. At the conclave of 1352, it sought for the first time to impose on the pope its control over its own number (a maximum of 20), the recruitment of its members, any possible measures against them, and the confirmation of its revenues. This first "capitulation" of the conclavists was abolished by the newly elected INNOCENT VI, who could not tolerate such an attack on the principle of the pope's PLENITUDO POTESTATIS.

Under the Avignon popes, the consistory was also the Sacred College's tribunal, where the cardinals defended their opinions, often with force, vis-à-vis the pope, including the matter of the creation of cardinals. On the doctrinal and ecclesiological planes, a confrontation arose between the champions and adversaries of apostolic filiation and the divine origin of the Sacred College, even though the cardinalate had no sacramental foundation—a doctrine opposed to that of the perfection of the episcopate and tending to grant the cardinals part of the *plenitudo potestatis*. The GREAT SCHISM of the West (1378–1417) dealt a severe blow to the Sacred College. It was split in two, then in three (1409), deprived of a great part of its revenues, and, above all, accused of having desired the schism and being unable to end it. Some suggested its abolition, but it managed to hold its ground, to defend its electoral privilege (save at the time of the election of MARTIN V in 1417), and to come together again at the heart of a unitary college.

Its decline was accentuated as the popes of the 15th and 16th centuries reaffirmed their absolute power, increasing the college's membership from around 20 to 75, establishing NEPOTISM as a principle, and playing the dissenting factions against each other. The Italians once again took the lead, especially from the reign of PAUL II (1464–71), and hopes for internationalizing the college had no more than a limited effect. The consistory began to be set aside with the creation of the first Roman CON-GREGATIONS (in 1542, PAUL III created that of the Holy Office or INQUISITION; in 1564, PIUS IV that of the COUNCIL, at the end of the council of Trent; in 1571, PIUS V that of the INDEX).

From the Reform of Sixtus V to the End of the 19th Century. The reform of the Roman Curia by SIXTUS V (1585–90) dealt another blow to the cardinals' powers. In 1586, he fixed their number at a maximum of 70 (6 bishops, 50 priests, 14 deacons; these figures were in use up to John XXIII), and excluded from access to the Sacred College any relative of a living cardinal. In 1587, he reorganized the cardinals' titles and created new ones. But most important, in 1588 he used the bull *Immensa Dei* to create 12 new congregations (6 for ecclesiastical affairs and 6 for the administration of the Papal States). He reserved for himself the presidency of the congregation of the Inquisition and placed a cardinal prefect at the head of the 14 others. The last congregation, that of the PROPAGANDA FIDE, was added in 1622. At the same time, the consistory was not to meet except for certain solemn manifestations. From this time, the preeminence of the cardinals took on a more personal character. They acted as the pope's individual collaborators, their collegial power being in evidence only when there was a vacancy of the Apostolic See.

Until the promulgation of the CODE OF CANON LAW in 1917, the Sacred College saw no major modification save in the evolution of its composition. Despite the popes' promises and the wishes of the councils, the pronounced Italian dominance began to diminish only under PIUS IX (1846–78): 72% of the cardinals were Italian during 1565–1605, 82% during 1605–55, 80% during 1655–1799, 78% during 1800–46, and 58% under Pius IX. Second and third in proportion were the French (around 8%) and Spanish (around 5%). The inclusion of the North American continent did not take place until 1875 (with John McClosky). From the doctrinal point of view, the reaffirmation of the dogma of papal INFALLIBILITY by Pius IX at Vatican I (1869–70) caused all traces of collegiality between the pope and the Sacred College to disappear.

The Sacred College in the 20th Century. PIUS X's reform of the Curia in 1908 and, above all, the promulgation by BENEDICT XV of the new Code of Canon Law (*Codex juris canonici*, canons 230–41) in 1917 wrote into the texts the evolution of the place and role of the cardinals in the universal Church. The essential privilege of the Sacred College is the election of the pope. If the Apostolic See becomes vacant, the college must content itself with managing current affairs, preparing for the funeral of the deceased pontiff, and undertaking the election of his successor. The college enjoys a sovereignty that is transitory, limited, and collective. Executive power is exercised in its name by the three house heads (dean of bishops, likewise dean of the Sacred College; prior of priests; prior of deacons) and the cardinal camerlengo of the Sacred College. It does not have the right of exercising jurisdiction or pontifical power, except in the case of imminent danger (as at the elections of PIUS VII and Pius IX), and therefore cannot create new cardinals, confer the insignia on already created cardinals, nominate or confirm bishops, or confer benefices. In normal times, each cardinal assists the pope with his counsel when requested. The cardinals of the Curia also head congregations and dicasteries ("ministries" of the pontifical state). Moreover, they take on liturgical functions, especially at the pope's coronation or consecration (the prior of deacons announces *urbi et orbi* the election and crowning of the new pope).

After 1917, the Sacred College did not undergo important modification until after the Second World War. Although begun at the end of the 19th century, internationalization, in the strong sense of the term, was effective only from JOHN XXIII's papacy (1958–63). This was the pope who, on 10 March 1961, decreed that the bishoprics of several sees in the vicinity of Rome, would henceforth be no more than a title for the cardinal-bishops, who would lose their particular administration, the better to devote themselves to that of the universal Church. He decided on 15 April 1962 that all the cardinals, no matter what their "order" within the Sacred College, should be promoted to the episcopacy, thus setting all the cardinals on the same basis of equality. Similarly, he was the first pope to exceed, in his appointments to the cardinalate, the figure of 70 cardinals fixed by Sixtus V.

John's successor, PAUL VI (1963–78), continued the policy of openness, especially toward the Eastern churches. He offered the red hat to several Eastern patriarchs, a dignity that some of them rejected because they deemed it inferior to their patriarchate, whence the *motu proprio* of 11 February 1965, *Ad purporatorum patrum*, likening any patriarch raised to the cardinalate to a cardinal-bishop and giving him neither the title of suburbicarian bishop nor the title of Church of Rome.

Nevertheless, Paul VI emphasized the regulation of the cardinals' powers. On 1 October 1970, the decree *Ingravescentem aetatem* limited the right to vote at the conclave to those who had not reached the age of 80. Then, without setting a limit to the membership of the Sacred College, he fixed at 120 the maximum number of voters, in the 1975 constitution *Romano pontifice eligendo*. This document also deals with the functions of the Sacred College as well as certain Curial services *sede vacante*.

In spite of the generalization of episcopal consecration for all the cardinals, the opposition between cardinals' college and episcopal college had not diminished. The second Vatican council (1962–65) and Paul VI's institution in 1965 of the SYNOD OF BISHOPS relaunched the debate. It was even proposed to substitute the second for the first in the elective function. In 1967 and 1969, by contrast, the pope stressed their complementarity: the synod reflects episcopal collegiality, while the college of cardinals embodies the prerogative of the pope's personal government, each instance playing in fact no more than a consultative role.

Canon law now in force rests chiefly on canons 349–59 of the new code of Canon Law promulgated by JOHN PAUL II in 1983. The code does not set any limit to the number of cardinals, save for the 120 enjoying privilege of election (among those under 80). At the cardinals' promotion of June 1988, for instance, they numbered 161 in all (some, such as Father Henri de Lubac, were created even though they were over age 80). One innovation was that the cardinals were asked to hand the pope the resignation of their curial functions when they reached age 75 (canon 354).

The cardinals make up a college divided into three orders: suburbicarian bishops, called "cardinals of the Holy Roman Church," along with the patriarchs of the Eastern Churches, called "cardinals of the Holy Church"; priests receiving a cardinal's title in Rome, most of whom head dioceses outside Rome; and deacons, titularies of a Roman deaconry who reside at the Curia. The college is entrusted with the task of electing the pope and aiding him, whether collegially in the consistories, or individually in the various dicasteries for the daily administration of the Church. Although the pope's freedom to choose the cardinals is reaffirmed (canon 351), it is traditional to designate the holders of the most important bishoprics and the leading functionaries of the Curia. The executive organ of the Sacred College is made up of the dean (the bishop of Ostia) and the sub-dean, both chosen from among the cardinal-bishops, appointed by the pope, and assisted by a secretariat.

From the beginning of his pontificate, John Paul II has on several occasions convened all the cardinals in plenary assembly in Rome: in 1979, to examine the reorganization of the Curia and questions relating to culture, science, and art; in 1982, to study the new code in preparation and the economic problems of the Holy See; and in 1985, on the reorganization of the government of the Church, especially the Curia and the dicasteries. Finally, with the constitution *Pastor bonus* of 28 June 1988, the pope promoted a great reform of the Roman Curia, creating a Council of Cardinals to study organizational problems and the economy of the Holy See; this was composed of 15 cardinals appointed for 5 years from among bishops from different parts of the world. The aim of this reform was, in the spirit of ecclesial communion promoted by VATICAN II, to put the Curia and the dicasteries more effectively at the service of the universal Church and the local Churches.

Pierre Jugie

Bibliography

Bertone, T. "Il servizio del cardinalto al ministero del successore di Pietro," *Salesianum*, 48 (1986), 109–21.

Broderick, J. F. "The Sacred College of Cardinals: Size and Geographical Composition (1099–1986)," *AHP*, 25 (1987), 7–71.

Gatz, E. "Kardinal—Kardinalskollegium," *Theologische Realenziklopädie*, 17 (1988), 628–35.

Grégoire, R. "Il sacro collegio cardinalizio dall'elezione di Sisto IV all'elezione di Giulio II (1471–1513)," *Atti e memorie della società savonese di storia patria*, new series, 24 (1988), 209–32.

Kittler, G. *The Papal Princes: A History of the Sacred College of Cardinals*, New York, 1960.

Lecler, J. "Le cardinalat de l'Église romaine: Son évolution dans l'histoire," *Études* (journal of the Company of Jesus), 330 (1969), 871–83.

Molien, A. "Collège (Sacri)," *DDC*, 3 (1942), 990–1000.

Pfaff, V. "Die Kardinäle unter Papst Coelestin III. (1191–1198), III. Teil," *ZRGKA*, 75 (1989), 401–7.

Rossi, A. [cardinal, dean of the Sacred College], *Il collegio cardinalizio*, Vatican City, 1990 (popular work).

Van Lierde, P. and Giraud, A. *Le Sénat de l'Église: Le Sacré Collège*, Paris, 1963.

Vigotti, G. *Papi, cardinali, arcivescovi e vescovi milanesi*, Milan, 1987.

Weber, C. *Kardinäle und Prälaten in den letzten Jahrzehnten des Kirchenstaates*, Tübingen, 1978.

SACRED COLLEGE, PLENARY MEETING OF THE.

Responding to a wish expressed during the two conclaves of 1978, JOHN PAUL II held a meeting of the entire membership of the SACRED COLLEGE in the Synod Hall (above the Paul VI *aula*) from 5 to 9 November 1979. The pope's first intention in doing so was to soothe the hostile feelings aroused in the Sacred College by a reform introduced by PAUL VI (1963–75). According to this reform, cardinals over eighty years of age would be excluded from participating in papal elections (though they would still be eligible for election). The aim was to dissuade the conclave from electing a person whose age would likely entail too short (or too long) a pontificate.

That 1979 meeting was followed by three more, held in 1982, 1985, and 1991, the first two in the autumn and the third in the spring. After reflection, the cardinals expressed their opinions concerning reports sent them prior to the meeting. The pope gave an opening speech and presided over the first session, and the secretary of state took over thereafter.

The plenary meetings of the Sacred College have a merely consultative role. The Code of Canon Law of 1983 does not repeat the expression in the Code of 1917 that describes the assembly of cardinals "of the Holy Roman Church," as the "Senate of the Roman pontiff."

But article 23 of the apostolic constitution *Pastor bonus* (28 June 1988) states; "More serious business of a general character can be usefully dealt with, if the supreme pontiff so decides, by the cardinals assembled in plenary consistory according to proper law."

The plenary meetings of the Sacred College permitted John Paul II, up until 1985, to create a climate of collegial confidence in the enforcing of reforms such as that of the Roman Curia (apostolic constitution *Pastor bonus*, 28 June 1988) or in the reflection on the question of the state of the finances of the Holy See. The meetings also extended to the tackling of immense problems, such as the place of the Church in contemporary culture, pastoral care of families, and bioethics. Thus, they testify to the attention paid by the Holy See to burning questions on which public opinion expects immediate answers. They serve as channels of communication with the other bishops as well as the faithful. And they allow collegiality to function as a mode of concerted deliberation that alleviates permanent responsibility of the Holy See. As John Paul II put it at the 1991 meeting, "If your function and your merit are above all to ensure the succession to the Roman see of Peter, at the same time it surely also falls to you to be close to the one who is the successor of Peter in his tasks and his preoccupations."

Philippe Levillain

Bibliography

Molien, A. "Sacré Collège," *DDC* III, 991.

Rossi, A. *Il collegio cardinalice*, Vatican City, 1990, 45ff.

d'Onorio, J. B. *Le Pape et le gouvernement central de'Eglise*, Paris, 1992, 430–2.

SACRED PALACE. See **Palace, Apostolic.**

ST. JOHN LATERAN, BASILICA OF.

Middle Ages. In medieval Rome, the basilica of the Lateran was one of the places most evocative of memories of ancient Rome and of Christ himself. Around this sanctuary—which, owing to the false Donation of Constantine, was not only the cathedral of Rome but also the head of all Christian Churches (*omnium Urbis et Orbis ecclesiarum mater et caput*)—a pilgrim could at the same time touch relics of the Lord and traces of the Roman Empire. Here, where the pope and his government resided, this remarkable conjunction also symbolized the paired keys given to Peter's successor.

Close to the basilica, the visitor could admire the equestrian statue of Marcus Aurelius, then believed to represent Constantine, as well as the palladium of Rome, the she-wolf; these works were moved to the capitol in 1538 and 1471, respectively. On columns were exhibited the head and hand, holding the globe, from a colossal statue of Constantine, as well as the *Boy with a Thorn*. The visitor might also read the tablet of the Lex Vespasiani. The significance of these wonders, which were described in all the medieval Roman guidebooks, is complex. The statues of Constantine recalled his alleged transfer to the Church of imperial sovereignty. The same was symbolized, in a way, by the inscription of the Law of Vespasian, whereby the Senate and the Roman people entrusted to Constantine the imperial *potestas*. Constantine's globe illustrated the universality of this dominion. Moreover, these objects took on legendary importance in people's eyes. The fragments of Constantine's statue were popularly seen as the remains of the giant Samson, while the *Boy with a Thorn* was considered an idol, both laughable and frightening. For the educated clergy of the Curia, these works bore witness to the long-gone splendor of antiquity.

Within the complex of buildings were the precious relics of the Passion of Christ. For example, the Lateran cloister contained a well-known relic of the Woman of Samaria (in fact, it dates from the Carolingian period), together with the slab of porphyry on which the soldiers played dice as they cast lots for Christ's garment, and a column bearing a bronze cock, a reminder of St. Peter's denial. The most important object was the table of the Mensura Christi from the main apse of the council hall, supported by four columns and said to be the same height as the Savior. The Scala Sancta, believed to be the stairway leading to Pilate's judgment hall in Jerusalem and to have been brought to Rome by St. Helena, came from the Patriarchum, the old Lateran palace. When Sixtus V had this palace built to Domenico Fontana's design, he preserved the staircase that the Savior trod at his Passion, moving it to where it could provide access to the St. Lawrence chapel. Thus, when the faithful climbed it on their knees, it was both to honor the relics contained in that oratory and to follow, in a way, the Stations of the Cross. In the St. Lawrence chapel itself, which is known as the Sancta Sanctorum because of the number and importance of the relics kept there, it is the miraculous painting of the Pantocrator that stands out. According to tradition, this outstanding work was begun by St. Luke but could be completed only with the help of the angels.

This accumulation of works from antiquity and testimonies of Christianity justified the peculiar fervor enjoyed by the cathedral of Rome (it was only from Gregory I's reign that it was dedicated to St. John) and reflected on its bishop, the Roman pontiff. Thus, little by little, the Lateran came to be conflated in Christian consciousness with the universal Church, as is illustrated by Innocent III's dream in which he saw St. Francis supporting the swaying basilica.

The building itself was restored under popes Sergius I (687–701) and Hadrian I (772–95) and later rebuilt several times: in the 10th century under Sergius III

(904–11), then, after the fire of 1308 by CLEMENT V; and after another fire in 1361, under URBAN V and GREGORY XI, by the Sienese architect Giovanni Stefano. More repair work was done under MARTIN V (1417–31) and EUGENE IV (1431–47), not to mention Borromini's complete refurbishing. Before the façade was reconstructed in the 17th century, it was fronted by a quadriportico, like many of the great Constantinian basilicas. Later it was given a simple portico, built between 1159 and 1191 by Nicolò d'Angeli; however, the two Roman campaniles flanking the side façades are still extant. It was by the side façade on the north arm of the transept that the medieval pilgrim entered the basilica, since this gave access to the large square in front of the Lateran palace; this façade was rebuilt in 1370–78, in a very severe style. As far as the medieval period is concerned, the interest of the Lateran lies not so much in its architecture as in the many works of art accumulated over the period.

The first example from the medieval era is to be found not in the basilica proper, but alongside the baptistry founded by Constantine. Around this, several annexes were put up in the Paleo-Christian period, which JOHN IV (640–42) enhanced with a chapel dedicated to the Dalmatian martyrs. This pope, who came from the Balkans, was particularly sensitive to the suffering of Christians in those lands, which had been ravaged by the Slavs, and he sent an emissary to ransom his captive compatriots and rescue the relics of the martyrs of Split. The chapel built to house the relics thus has a mosaic in the apse showing Peter and Paul, the two Sts. John, St. Venantius, and nine other Dalmatian martyrs, depicted around the Virgin Protector (perhaps to symbolize the Roman Church helping the persecuted). Excavations in the Christian cemetery of Split have revealed funerary inscriptions and empty sarcophaguses that precisely match the saints of the St. Venantius chapel. The sanctuary also contains a mosaic of the Pantocrator, shown half-length, very like the one in St. Vitale in Ravenna.

Under CELESTINE III and on the orders of his cardinal-chamberlain, Cencius, bronze doors were made for the baptistry and cloister of the chapel of St. John the Evangelist. They were cast around 1196 by Umberto and Pietro da Piacenza (their name was later erased by some Sienese workmen and disguised as that of their own city). In the 12th and 13th centuries, the change from the decorative tradition of the Cosmati, or cosmatesque, mosaic-workers to the more personal art of Gothic craftsmen took place as a gradual, ambiguous evolution. A niche decorated with mosaics and a bas-relief represents a bishop holding a model of the ciborium from the altar of St. Mary Magdalene (the second most important in the basilica, it supposedly contained the body of the saint). Only a few fragments of the altar built by Deodato di Cosma at the end of the 13th century still survive in the cloister—evidence, together with the mosaic, of this lost work.

The best examples of the talents of the Roman marble-workers, however, are to be found in the basilica cloister, created in the first third of the 13th century by the Vassalletto dynasty. Here the fluted, twisted columns, the rich Corinthian capitals, the many-colored inlaid work, and the exuberance of the vegetation of the spandrels make for a veritable walk in heaven rather than an austere cloistered space. Again, when the Sancta Sanctorum was rebuilt in 1277, it was another cosmatesque master, Arnolfo di Cambio, who executed what was probably his first Roman work. The monument of Cardinal Riccardo Annibaldi, a pontifical notary (1276), may have been commissioned by Charles of Anjou. The tomb, which has been much retouched and broken up—the elements of it that remain are a frieze on a mosaic background and the recumbent figure, while the association with the monument of the statues of Sts. Peter and Paul and a kneeling pope has occasioned much debate—is similar to the tomb Arnolfo would execute for Cardinal de Braye at Orvieto (ca. 1282). But cosmatesque art would still find expression at the beginning of the 15th century, in the sanctuary paving executed under Martin V.

In the apse, which was rebuilt under Leo XIII, the mosaic has been reconstituted rather than restored. Only the lower section gives an authentic vision of the work that Jacopo Torriti and Jacopo de Camerino undertook at the command of NICHOLAS IV (1288–92), whose papal throne is actually in the basilica cloister. This pope had commissioned the Paleo-Christian apse, to which he added a transept. The image of Christ that was in the upper part of the apse was particularly venerated: indeed, its creation was considered miraculous. Just as Constantine was imagined to have proclaimed Christianity from the top of the tribunal of the Lateran, so the Lateran was symbolically likened to Mount Sinai, where Moses, having received the revelation of the Law, proclaimed the covenant of God with the Jewish people. From this it was deduced that the half-length image of the Savior, probably dating from Early Christian times, miraculously reproduced the appearance of the Almighty on Mount Sinai. It was, therefore, probably not touched when Nicholas IV commissioned the building of the apse. In the central section, intercessors pray for humanity around the Cross, which is surmounted by a column. They consist of the customary two members of the *deisis*, Mary and John the Baptist, together with two Franciscan saints, Il Poverello himself and Anthony of Padua, who are placed significantly in front of the four apostles, Peter, John the Evangelist, Paul, and Andrew. Even though they are shorter in stature than the other saints, their favored place reminds us that Nicholas IV was the first Franciscan pope. The innovation was so bold that BONIFACE VIII is said to have ordered the figure of St. Anthony, at least, to be destroyed, but the iconoclastic workmen allegedly fell backward at the first blow of the hammer.

In the lower section, the themes are taken from the earliest days of Christianity. The four rivers of Paradise, springing from the hill on which the Cross stands, refresh deer and sheep, while in the decorative band at the bottom, cupids, dolphins, fish, and beasts disport themselves in the water and recall antique models (one even wonders if there are not some physical traces of the paleo-Christian work). The viewer thus has the impression that Torriti must have greatly respected the early mosaic, at least in his composition, short of introducing a few extra figures. Among these are the pope himself, who is placed humbly at the feet of the Virgin, and the two little Franciscans, placed among the nine saints who occupy the lower part between the windows, and who certainly represent Jacopo da Camerino (identified by an inscription) and Torriti himself (whose figure should be linked with the artist's signature, a little above it).

In the reign of Boniface VIII, the so-called Benediction loggia was erected, on the occasion of the 1300 jubilee. It was adorned with frescoes at the time of building, or a little later. After the loggia was destroyed in 1585–6, only a fragment of these remained. Badly damaged and much restored, this fragment is now housed inside the basilica (however, a drawing at the Ambrosian Library in Milan shows the original composition as a whole). The painting, which may date back to 1300 or later, has long been believed to be a commemorative one showing Boniface VIII proclaiming the jubilee from the loggia. It has also been suggested that it shows the newly elected pope (chosen 23 January 1295) taking possession of the Lateran, in which case the work may date from around 1297. In this view, the figure on the extreme right would be that of the "departing" pontiff, CELESTINE V, recalling the legitimacy of Boniface VIII's election amid the struggle with the great Roman families. Many see the hand of Giotto or his studio in this work.

The surviving works of Giovanni Stefano, mentioned above, are essentially the ciborium of the high altar (sadly, much restored in 1851), which was inaugurated in 1370, thanks to donations made by Charles V of France, and designed to preserve the heads of the two apostles, rediscovered in 1368; and a wooden altar said to be that of the first popes. The basilica also included frescoes, destroyed in 1646, which were begun by Gentile da Fabriano in 1427–8 and continued by Pisanello in 1431–2 (one fragment, the *Head of King David*, which may be the work of Gentile da Fabriano, is in the Palazzo Venezia in Rome). The bronze tomb of Martin V (1417–31) is beneath the main altar. With its realistic, robust, almost incisive rendering, its provenance is much disputed between Donatello and Michelozzo—or, according to Vasari, another Florentine, Simone Ghini, who had worked with Filareto on the door of St. Peter's. According to these views, the date of the tomb may be between ca. 1433 and 1445. Only the upper part remains of the monument of the renowned humanist Lorenzo Valla, who was buried in the cloister in 1457. Another tomb, that of the cardinal of Portugal, Antonio Martinez Chiaves (d. 1447), which was executed around 1460, is the archaizing masterpiece of Isaia of Pisa and his school, unfortunately reworked by Borromini. Surrounding the recumbent figure were the three theological virtues and the four cardinal virtues, as well as an Annunciation.

Pierre-Yves Le Pogam

Bibliography

Cecchelli, C. "Il tesoro di San Giovanni in Laterano," *Federico II e l'arte del Duecento in Italia, Atti della III settimana di studi di Storia dell'arte medioevale dell'Università di Roma,* Rome, 1978, *Galatina,* 1990, II, 153–8.

de Nicola, G. "Il tesoro di San Giovanni in Laterano," *Bollettino d'arte,* 1909.

Egger, H. "Kardinal Antonio Martinez de Chaves und sein Grabmal in San Giovanni in Laterano," *Miscellanea Francesco Ehrle,* Rome, 1924, 415–31.

Grandi, C. "Giotto recuperato a San Giovanni in Laterano," *Scritti in onore di Lionello Venturi,* Rome, 1956.

Josi, E. *Il chiostro lateranense: Cenno storico e illustrazione,* Vatican City, 1970.

Kühlenthal, M. "Zwei Grabmäler des Frühen Quattocento in Rom: Kardinal Martinez de Chiavez und Papst Eugen IV," *Römisches Jahrbuch für Kunstgeschichte,* 16 (1976), 17–56.

Ladner, G. B. "Statue Bonifaz VIII. in der Lateranbasilika und die Entstehung der dreifach gekrönten Tiara," *Römische Quartalschrift für christliche Altertumskunde und für Kirchengeschichte,* 1934, 35–69.

Lauer, P. *Le Palais du Latran: Étude historique et archéologique,* Paris, 1911.

Maddalo, S. "Bonifacio VIII e Jacopo Stefaneschi. Ipotesi di lettura dell'affresco della loggia lateranense," *Studi Romani,* 31, 1983, 129–51.

Malmstrom, R. E. "The Building of the Nave Piers at San Giovanni in Laterano after the Fire of 1361," *Rivista di archeologia cristiana,* 1967, 155–64.

Martinucci, F. *Intorno alle riparazioni eseguite all'altare papale lateranense e suo tabernacolo,* Rome, 1854.

Mitchell, C. "The Lateran Fresco of Bonifacio VIII," *Journal of the Warburg and Courtauld Institutes,* 1951, 1–6.

Monferini, A. "Il ciborio lateranense e Giovanni di Stefano," *Commentari,* 1962, 182–212.

Ortolani, S. *San Giovanni in Laterano,* Rome, n.d. [1925] (Le chiese di Roma illustrate, 13).

Sartorio, G. A. "Il Ciborio di Adeodato in San Giovannil in Laterano," *L'Amatore d'Arte,* 1921, 3–4.

Schiavo, A. *Il Laterano, Palazzo e Battistero,* Rome, 1969.

Tomei, A. and Battistelli, C., "La storia dei monumenti Annibaldi in San Giovanni in Laterano, Analisi documentaria," *Arte medievale,* 1983, 203–14.

Valentini, A. *La patriarcale Basilica lateranense,* 2 vols., Rome, 1845–55.

16th to 20th Centuries. The study of the church in this complex is inseparably linked to that of the entire Lateran. Abandoned by the popes in the 14th century (on his return from Avignon in 1377, GREGORY XI settled into the Vatican), the Lateran experienced a period of such decline that, in the mid-16th century, PAUL III did not hesitate to suggest to the canons of the chapter that the old papal residence be pulled down for materials to repair the church (*Per poterne cavare una grandissima quantità di tegole e travi per la riparazione della chiesa*). In a concrete sign of this lack of interest, the statue of Marcus Aurelius, formerly on the square of St. John's, was moved in 1538 to that of the capitol.

The Lateran began to regain its old importance, however, when Cardinal Felice Peretti was raised to the pontificate in 1585 under the name SIXTUS V. The new pope made it one of the cardinal points of his city planning, which implied redefining the space on both the symbolic and the functional level. Domenico Fontana (1543–1607), to whom the work of building was entrusted, enthusiastically praised the scope of the undertaking: "The Church of St. John Lateran being the chief of all the churches in the world, Pope Sixtus V, our lord, has taken it into consideration. He wanted to build, at the same time as the loggia of benedictions and next to it, an apostolic palace of grand dimensions. . . . The square of the Lateran has been embellished by our lord."

The main aim was to give pilgrims easy access to the basilica. For this reason, the west façade was emphasized, since it could be seen by people coming from Rome (*in vista del popolo che viene da Roma*). Thus, from 1585 to 1589, the architect built the Benediction loggia, which consists of five travertine arcades on two levels and today constitutes a secondary entrance to the church; it is surmounted by two bell towers dating from the 13th century. Over the previous medieval patriarchium he erected a new palace, a reinterpretation of the model for the Farnese palace. He isolated the Scala Sancta, as well as the Sancta Sanctorum, whose simple façade echoes the scheme of the Benediction loggia (the five lower arcades were closed between 1854 and 1856). In 1588, to define the axis of the square, he had an enormous Egyptian obelisk dating from the 15th century B.C. moved from the Circus Maximus, where it had been discovered; the obelisk had once stood before the temple of Amun in Thebes. On Easter 1587, the pontiff was able to give the traditional blessing from the new loggia (which did not yet have the Mannerist frescoes it later acquired).

Around the end of the 16th century and the beginning of the 17th, the whole Late Mannerist restoration of the decoration of the transept began (1597–1601), the architectural changes being given to Giacomo della Porta. Cavaliere d'Arpino gathered around him the foremost artists of the day (Cesare Nebbie, Paris Nogari, Giovanni Baglione, G.-B. Ricci, and others) to paint the story of Constantine and the origins of the basilica. The same artists worked on the palace, the Scala Sancta, and the Benediction loggia. Surviving records of payments show that supervision was entrusted to Giovanni Guerra and Cesare Nebbia.

17th Century: Innocent X and Borromini. INNOCENT X (1644–55) commissioned Francesco Borromini to refurbish the basilica. From a fresco in the church of S. Martino ai Monti as well as the artist's own drawings, we can tell what the original building looked like and how radical were the architect's changes. In less than five years (1647–50), the interior of the basilica was transformed and made ready to welcome the pilgrims of the 1650 Holy Year. The main nave gives an impression of austerity. There is not much color: some whites and grays, interrupted by the dark green of the columns. The composition is punctuated by colossal pillars containing recesses framed by columns of green marble taken from the ancient basilica. In the early 18th century, statues of the 12 apostles were placed in the recesses, the work of Camillo Rusconi, Lorenzo Ottoni, Giuseppe Mazzochi, Pierre Legros, Pierre Monnot, and others. Around 1718, the same artists executed oval medallions depicting the prophets, which were set in the upper frieze. In the middle section are high-reliefs in stucco of scenes from the Old and New Testaments, the work of Alessandro Algardi (1595–1654) and his collaborators, Antonio Raggi (1624–86), and Gian Antonio de Rossi (1616–95). The general effect is somewhat cold and disappointing, perhaps because it was the result of a compromise. Borromini had planned for a dome to rest on the columns, but he was forced to keep the carved-wood ceiling—actually a very fine work—executed in the 16th century by F. Boulanger and Vico di Raffaele, with decorations by Daniele da Volterra and Luzio Luzi.

In a sense, the artist's genius found its best expression in the lower, white side aisles where Borromini's traditional decorative repertoire of garlands, angels, and so on is given full play. Moreover, the artist hit on the idea—there is nothing like it in Roman Baroque—of not destroying the "memories" of the Lateran's glorious past but showing them mounted, as it were, in the new setting by making free reuse of the various fragments. In this way, the 17th-century concave and convex curves serve as frames for early tombs, in particular those of cardinals Paolo Mellini (d. 1527), Casati Di Giussano (d. 1290).

Statues by Isaia da Pisa for the funerary monument of Cardinal Antonio Martinez de Chiaves (d. 1447) now adorned the tomb of Cardinal Acquaviva. Borromini also used the cosmatesque paving created under MARTIN V (1417–31), representing the dove of the Pamphili. The great 17th- and 18th-century frescoes on the wall in the rear of the side chapels were designed to be seen in perspective from the central nave.

In 1657, Borromini also worked on the baptistry, where one can see a cornice with the arms of Pope ALEXANDER VII. The baptistry had been considerably reworked under URBAN VIII (1612–44) and decorated by Andrea Sacchi, but the originals were moved to the nearby palace.

18th Century: Façade of Alessandro Galilei. From the end of the 17th century, there was discussion of a new façade for St. John Lateran. On the side of the basilica facing St. John's gate and the city walls, the brick façade that had been restored by ALEXANDER III in the late 12th century was still in place. Borromini's drawings had not been found, and this, according to Pozzo père, gave the architects the opportunity to make new plans (*diede occasione agli architetti di far nuove idee*). Pozzo actually came up with several himself, but they never saw the light of day. Thus, it is no surprise that when, in 1732, Pope CLEMENT XII proposed a competition for a new façade, the most renowned architects took part: Luigi Vanvitelli, Nicola Salvi, G. Battista Galli, known as Il Bibbiena, Filippo Raguzzini, and so on. The judges were just as well known, while the jury included all the establishment artists of the day: Antoine Derizet, Pier Paolo Ghezzi, Paolo Pannini, Sebastiano Conra, and others.

The competition took place amid a debate between the partisans of the late baroque and artists who championed earlier architectural styles. The winner, the Florentine Alessandro Galilei, had spent time in England, where he came to appreciate Palladio's influence on architecture. Galilei designed a façade that was monumental, imposing, and symmetrical. In it, he went back to the Tuscan tradition and Fontana's experiments with the Benediction loggia and the Scala Sancta. Pilasters and columns are supported on a high stylobate decorated with the keys of St. Peter and the arms of Clement XII; they are arranged around a portico and a central loggia that ends in a tympanum with the image of the Savior. A grand balustrade crowns the building and the 15 colossal statues, over 7 meters high. The figure of Christ giving the blessing, surrounded by St. John the Apostle, St. John the Baptist, and the Evangelists and Doctors of the Church, seems to be suspended picturesquely in the sky. The portico is also the work of Galilei; the rich bronze panels of the middle door came from the Curia. On the right is the holy door, with inscriptions recalling the last four jubilee years. In

the left-hand nave, the hand of Galilei is visible in the Corsini chapel. Elegant and classical, with white-and-gold allegorical statues and reliefs, it houses the tomb of Clement XII. Also in the 18th century (1743), Ferdinando Fuga built the strange building containing the mosaic that once decorated the Triclinium Leonianum, the popes' dining room in the patriarchium, which was torn down in 1733.

19th Century: Restorations of Leo XIII. Between 1878 and 1881, the choir and apse were made over by Francesco Vespignani following the drawings of his father, Virgilio. Unfortunately, these changes entailed the destruction of the ambulatory of NICHOLAS IV (1288–92). The mosaic by Jacopo Torriti and Jacopo da Camerino was clumsily moved and, even though the iconographical arrangement was preserved, its careless restoration no longer bears any relation to the early mosaic. In all, the changes were not very successful. Yet Francesco Grandi (1831–91), who executed the frescoes in the choir, wanted to give posterity a reminder of the restoration by painting the architect Vespignani presenting his plan to LEO XIII. The ungraceful building linking the basilica to the baptistry externally was also erected in this period.

Since the 14th century, no pope has resided at the Lateran. But St. John's remains the principal church of Rome, the "Mother and head of all the churches of the city of the world," as is repeated twice in the inscription on Galilei's facade (*Sacros. Lateran. Eccles. / omnium urbis et orbis / Ecclesiarum mater / et caput*"). This is the cathedral of the pope, and he is here bishop of Rome. JOHN XXIII underlined this quality of a local church when, in 1962, he decided to set up in the Lateran palace the Vicariate, the seat of the diocesan administration. The plan was put into effect a few years later by PAUL VI. At that time, he moved to the Vatican the Museo Gregoriano Profano (founded in 1844 by GREGORY XV), the Museo Pio Cristiano (founded in 1854 by PIUS IX), and the Museo Missionario-Etnologico (founded by PIUS XI in 1926). The Museo Storico Vaticano (founded in 1987) remains at the Lateran.

Extraterritorial and yet the church of Rome, the Lateran is associated with Rome's grandest hours. It was at the palace of the Lateran, in the Sala de la Conciliazione, that on 11 February 1929, cardinal Gasparri signed the famous Lateran agreements that put an end to the conflict between the papacy and the Italian state. The pope was no longer a voluntary prisoner, and Catholics could once again take part in political life. The Vatican State was born. Relations were set up between the civil and religious powers. The grandiose processions of former days have gone, but when the pope solemnly takes "possession" of his basilica, he follows the same route as in medieval times. He stops at the foot of the capitol, where the mayor comes down to greet him in the first contact between two of the principal authorities of the city. These contacts are extremely close. It is at St. John Lateran that Paul VI wanted to hold the service in memory of Italian premier Aldo Moro, murdered by the Red Brigades. And when, on 26 July 1993, a bomb exploded and caused huge damage to Fontana's Benediction loggia and the façade of the palace next to it, the crime was immediately taken as a challenge to both Italy and the papacy, in this place that is the very symbol of Rome.

In a curious way, France too is linked to the history of the Lateran. To celebrate the restoration of ties between France and the Holy See, Henry IV presented the Lateran with the gift of the abbey of Clairac (in the department of Lot-et-Garonne), together with its revenues. Beneath Fontana's portico, the bronze statue of the king, sculpted by Nicolas Cordier of Lorraine, was offered by the chapter in 1606 as a token of its gratitude to the king. Each year, on 13 December, the feast day of St. Lucy and the anniversary of the birth of Henry IV, the chapter of the Lateran celebrates a mass for France. The ambassador to the Holy See attends in the canons' stall as the representative of the president of the republic. He is incensed and receives liturgical honors. In spite of several interruptions, the tradition has been preserved up to the present.

Noëlle de La Blanchardière

Bibliography

Fiel, P. *Le Chapitre du Latran et la France*, Rome, Paris, 1935.

Lauer, P. *Le Palais du Latran: Étude historique et archéologique*, Paris, 1911.

"L'urbanistica nell'età di Sisto V," *Storia della città*, 40, Milan, 1987.

Portoghesi, P. *Borromini: Architettura come linguaggio*, Rome, 1967.

ST. MARY MAJOR, BASILICA OF.

Antiquity. Situated at the top of the Esquiline Hill, St. Mary Major (Italian, Maggiore) is the fourth of the patriarchal basilicas of Rome (after St. John Lateran, St. Peter's of the Vatican, and St. Paul's Outside the Walls). Today it is seen as a masterpiece of the Roman Baroque, but the building still preserves important elements of the Paleo-Christian edifice, transformed or masked by later restorations. Beginning in the pontificate of LEO XII (1823–9), several campaigns of excavation and restoration have made it possible to reconstruct the former church (architecture and mosaic decoration), whose history is also relatively well documented in texts.

In the 6th century, the *LIBER PONTIFICALIS* credits Pope LIBERIUS with the construction of a basilica bearing his name near "Livia's market" (*macellum Liviae*). Uncov-

ered in the Forum Esquilinum, the market had been restored in the 4th century under the reigns of emperors Valentinian, Valens, and Gratian, and was still in use in the 5th century. It may well have been traces of this market that were found in the area of the present-day apse of St. Mary Major; this would confirm the topographical indication given in the papal chronicle.

The existence of the basilica and its designation as the *basilica Liberii* are attested from the second half of the 4th century by the *Liber precum*, a pamphlet written by the supporters of Ursinus. This relates how, in 366, DAMASUS' troops attacked the *basilica Liberiana* and regrouped inside it, Damasus having invested the episcopal basilica (St. John Lateran). It is likely that this *basilica Liberiana* is to be identified with the *basilica Sicininum* cited by Ammianus Marcellinus, whose Roman *defensor ecclesiae* called for its restitution to the emperor in 367, during the troubles surrounding Damasus' election. This is actually the first testimony to the activity of the *defensor ecclesiae*. The designation *basilica Sicininum*, which is of topographical origin, may imply that Liberius had turned an ancient civil basilica on the Sicininum into a church. The indication given in the *Gesta Liberii*, which attribute to the bishop only the building of an "apse" in the fifth Augustan region, may provide confirmation of this hypothesis.

The part the basilica played in the fight for the pontifical succession is evidence of its importance, even if merely symbolic. (The importance of places of worship as a sign or instrument of a candidate's legitimacy was illustrated in Milan, 20 years later, in the conflict between Ambrose and Auxentius II, and in Rome itself a century later during the struggle between Eulalius and Boniface.) No material trace of the basilica from this era has been found, however. The entry of SIXTUS III in the *Liber pontificalis* establishes direct continuity between Liberius's construction and the basilica of St. Mary, pointing out that the latter was "formerly known as the basilica of Liberius" and that it is situated "near Livia's market." But it is only this early tradition that sets up continuity between the two buildings, there being no archeological indication to confirm or deny it. In the hypothesis of continuity, the disappearance of the Liberian structure might be explained by a reconstruction *ex novo* on the same site. But damage resulting from the Ursinian conflicts could also have caused its destruction, and the two monuments were not necessarily superimposed exactly.

It is certain, however, that the building the *Liber pontificalis* attributes to Sixtus III today forms the nucleus of St. Mary Major. Both the inscription that can still be read on the triumphal arch ("*Syxtus episcopus plebidei*") and that on the reverse of the façade, which is preserved in early collections ("*Virgo Maria tibi xystus nova tecta dicavi . . .*"), confirm the dedication to the Virgin—probably on 5 August 434, according to the notice in the *Hieronymian Martyrology*. But it can be assumed, for various reasons, that construction began before Sixtus's pontificate, during the first third of the 5th century, under the pontificate of INNOCENT I, BONIFACE I, or CELESTINE I.

The Esquiline quarter to the northwest, though thickly populated in the 5th century (it was the site of the Domus Magna of Junius Bassus, which around 470 passed to the Gothic general Valila), must have lacked any important religious building, particularly if one assumes the destruction of the Liberian basilica. Here houses of worship multiplied, especially with the transformation into a church of the basilica of Junius Bassus around 480 (Sant' Andrea in Catabarbara) and, at the same time, the start of the building of Santa Bibiana a little farther east; this was followed, at the turn of the 6th century, by the reconstruction of San Martino ai Monti on the site of an ancient *titulus*. Nonetheless, St. Mary Major was not one of the local mission churches, but rather a building designed first and foremost for the episcopal liturgy—the third (since Liberius), after St. John Lateran to the south of the city (since Sylvester) and St. Peter's to the west (since Liberius). In the 5th century, the first Christmas mass was celebrated here. Thus, the church became part of a program to organize sacred space and the liturgical year. The papal chronicle lists the rich donations of liturgical objects that accompanied the construction (altar, patens, a scyphus of gold and silver, vases, chalices, censers, etc.) and complemented the gesture of episcopal largesse toward the Roman community ("Sixtus to the people of God"). Along with these gifts, no doubt, were monies that probably came from collections and donations, and at this period reflected imperial endowments as well.

Moreover, beyond the role of this new building in the episcopal mission, one can see in the dedication to the Theotokos a sign of the bishop of Rome's interest in the Christological and Marian debate that took place in the 5th century. (It seems far-fetched, however, to posit a direct link between the building of the church of St. Mary Major and the council of Ephesus, held in 431.)

The basilica, which was of huge proportions (length without the apse, 73.50 meters; width, 35 meters; diameter of the apse, 7 meters), was of a type common at the time. It had a broad central nave ending in a semicircular apse (discovered 0.63 meters below present ground level, in the extension of the triumphal arch, the foundation area of which has the same appearance as that of the 5th-century basilica walls) and, originally, two side naves; there was no transept. The original façade was no doubt situated like the present one and does not appear to have been fronted by an atrium. The naves are separated by two rows of columns of Proconnesos marble (except for six of cipolin marble, reworked in the 18th century). These columns, which have Ionic capitals, are linked not by an architrave properly speaking, but rather by arches sealed with masonry, a method also used in the contemporary Lateran baptistry. Above them, the walls of the central nave were punctuated by grooved pilasters surmounted by Corinthian capitals, separated from the basic structure by a frieze with a foliage design. The pilasters created compartments, the lower part of which was occupied by aediculae of stucco topped with pediments that were alternately triangular and semicircular, while the upper part consisted of high windows. All these features—the church's proportions (the ratio of 1 to 4 between length and width is the same as that of St. Sabine, also from the 5th century, while the 4th-century buildings had a ratio of 1 to 3), the architectural decoration with its borrowings of elements from 2nd-century Roman architecture (Ionic capitals, wall modeling), and the peculiar technique of the platband surmounting the columns—exemplify an architectural style that can be placed just after the "Classical renaissance" of the Theodosian era.

But it is the mosaic decoration that attracts attention above all else. This is the earliest preserved example of a grand basilican program (it was followed by those of St. Peter's, St. Paul's Outside the Walls, and perhaps the Lateran, for all of which Pope Leo's intervention seems to have been decisive). The decoration also completes the image of the new papal largesse, especially evident from the 5th century onward. Today, what remains is the decoration of the triumphal arch and that of the upper part of the central nave, divided among the tabernacles under the windows. The disappearance of the decoration of the apse, and perhaps that of the other side of the façade, makes it difficult to give an overall interpretation of the iconographic program. As things stand today, it is easier to interpret the two groups individually—that of the nave and that of the arch of the apse—even if it is not possible to combine them under a single typological reading.

The scenes on the north wall, which are all taken from Genesis, tell the story of Abraham and Jacob; those on the south wall illustrate the lives of Moses (Exodus, Numbers, Deuteronomy, complemented by Acts 7, 22) and Joshua. In the choice of these images of the history of Israel, which portray the Jewish people as the Roman people and borrow from the vocabulary of contemporary imperial art (especially the crossing of the Red Sea, with the allusion to the battle of the Milvian Bridge, and the offering of Melchizedek), it is possible to see not only an illustration of the history of Salvation, with events from the time of promises, which has its place in every church, but also an identification of sacred history and Roman history, a constant of the theology of history since Constantine's victory. The iconography of the triumphal arch has also given rise to a variety of interpretations. Some try to explain it only in the light of the proclamation of Ephesus, which proclaimed the Virgin Mary as the Mother of God. It may instead express the ideology of the new Christian Rome—the Church of Rome—"head of the world thanks to the sacred seat of the most blessed Peter, who dominates more widely by divine religion than by terrestrial power" (Sermon 82 in honor of Peter and Paul), as LEO I expressed it a few years later.

It may also be viewed as a reflection of the liturgical calendar that was established in the 5th century. Rather than reading horizontally, it might be better first to read the scenes following the half arc. On the left (north), where Peter and Jerusalem are depicted, is the commemoration of the birth corresponding to the feast of Christmas, showing the figures of the Church, together with the circumcision (Annunciation to Mary and Joseph, Adoration of the Magi with the association of Mary and the synagogue, Massacre of the Innocents). On the right (south), where Paul and Bethlehem are shown, is the commemoration of the presentation to the Gentiles, celebrated at Epiphany (presentation to the Temple, Joseph's dream, Jesus' meeting with Aphrodisius, the Magi meeting Herod). But the figures of Peter and Paul also illustrate, in their placement to either side with the empty throne occupying the keystone of the arch, the specifically Roman theme of the joint reign of the two apostles and the ecclesial unity so constantly defended by the Apostolic See since the pontificate of Damasus. This reading by half-arc might also be combined with a horizontal one—the program of the triumphal arch thus fulfilling that of the nave, with the story of the birth of the Messiah (the time of grace).

Finally, one should note the many questions that the mosaics of St. Mary Major have raised regarding the genesis of Christian art. In fact, the mosaics in the nave constitute one of the leading arguments in support of the thesis of a manuscript origin of Biblical iconography, given certain peculiarities of choice of scenes, composition, and iconographical details. It may transpire that the models for these mosaics were Roman biblical manuscripts, which are presumed to have existed from the 5th century.

Françoise Monfrin

Bibliography

ICUR, 2, 435, 111; 2, 71, 42.

Brodsky, N. A. "L'iconographie oublié de l'arc éphésien de Sainte-Marie-Majeure . . . Rome," *Byzantion*, 31, 1961, 1–90.

Deckers, J. G. *Der alttestamentliche Zyklus von S. Maria Maggiore in Rom* (Habelt Disserationsdrucke, Reihe klassicher Archäologie, 8), Bonn, 1976.

Duchesne, L. *LP*, I, 207–10 and 232–7.

Karpp, H. *Die Mosaiken in Santa Maria Maggiore zu Rom*, Baden-Baden, 1966.

Krautheimer, R. *Corpus basilicarum christianarum Romae*, III, Vatican City (1967), 1–60 (with bibliography).

Krautheimer, R. *Rome: Profile of a City, 312–1308*, Princeton, N.J., 2000.

Liber precum, coll. Avellana, ed. Guerther, 1, 6, 3; 6, 2, 49.

Pietri, C. "Le origini," *Imago Mariae: Tesori d'arte della civiltà cristiana*, catalog of the Roman Exhibition, Palazzo de Venezia, 20 June–2 October 1988, 1–6.

Pietri, C. *Roma Christiana*, esp. 25–8, 1583, 1587–90 (with bibliography).

Middle Ages. It was in medieval times that the Marian aspect of this basilica gained overriding importance, as evident both in its new name and in the works of art that were installed there. First known simply as the basilica of Liberius and later as that of SIXTUS III, throughout the early Middle Ages the church was known as Beata Maria ad Praesepe (St. Mary of the Crib). From the 6th century on, the basilica contained at least one representation of the "grotto" at Bethlehem, offering the faithful for their veneration an image of the place of the Savior's incarnation. It might also be argued that, since no Nativity scene was represented in the 5th-century mosaics, there must have been a grotto in the basilica at that time. This exact replica of the early Christian sanctuary in Palestine even included a reproduction of the tomb of St. Jerome, who wished to be buried in the grotto. Quite naturally, from there it was but a short step to the belief that this was the very grotto itself, transported miraculously like the Holy House of Loreto, along with relics of the crib and of St. Jerome.

Other cribs were set up elsewhere—such as those installed by JOHN VII (705–7) in St. Peter's and by GREGORY IV (827–44) in St. Mary's in Trastevere—but none was as famous as that of St. Mary Major. The original crib, which may have dated back to Sixtus III, disappeared at an indeterminate point and was rebuilt under INNOCENT III by Marchione l'Aretino. Around that time, it was placed toward the middle of the right-hand nave, not far from its present position. At the end of the 13th century (perhaps around 1291), as Vasari writes, Arnolfo di Cambio was entrusted with its decoration. This included a prophet and sibyl on the bend of the entrance arch, along with St. Joseph, the Magi, and the ox and ass in the passage surrounding the altar. As for the Virgin and Child, in the 16th century they were replaced by a new group, of lower quality, attributed to Vasoldo. That the work was commissioned by NICHOLAS IV, the first Franciscan pope, is easy to explain: for him, its importance would lie not only in Roman tradition but also in an episode from the life of St. Francis in which Il Poverello recreated the scene of the Nativity. Arnolfo created a masterpiece—although this is not apparent from the monument's present state—one which, with its almost trompe-l'oeil effect, was superbly in keeping with the devotional and emotional atmosphere of the site. Under SIXTUS V, the grotto was moved to a spot beneath the altar of the new chapel of the Holy Sacrament, but today the relics of the crib are in the confession chapel, below the high altar.

Another venerable reminder of the mother of the Savior is the icon of the Virgin known as Salus Populi Romani, found above the altar in the Pauline chapel. It has been there since 1613, having previously adorned a Gothic tabernacle in the central nave. Attributed by legend to St. Luke, the mosaic is said to have arrived miraculously from Constantinople in the iconoclastic period, following the same route as the *Acheiropoiete* icon of Christ in St. John Lateran. A procession of the icon of the Virgin was instituted by STEPHEN II (752–7) and then LEO IV (847–55). This took place during the night of 14–15 August and was extremely popular in Rome, arousing such high spirits that Sixtus V had to forbid it to prevent debauchery. The painting was covered with silver in Innocent III's reign and the face itself veiled with a painted cloth, like the icon in the Lateran. These adornments were removed under PIUS X, making it possible to recognize the icon as one modeled after the Hodigitria in St. Sophia, but its original date and place of execution are debated (Rome or the East, 9th or 13th century).

Thus, the image that offers the most beautiful representation of the Virgin—and today the most famous one—is the mosaic in the apse. As at St. John Lateran—and this work was also by Torriti—Nicholas IV had it restored when he was rebuilding the entire apse and adding a narrow transept. Early influences are not as readily felt here as at St. John, in spite of the same aquatic scenes from antiquity and the foliage and pavilion of the Paleo-Christian period. More modern than the St. John painting, this composition stresses the coronation of the Virgin, an iconographic innovation deriving from French art. Whereas in St. Mary's in Trastevere, a half-century earlier, Christ held the Virgin in an affectionate gesture but occupied the central place, from now on the Son, who is crowning her, and his Mother are shown symmetrically. The royal couple of the Song of Songs is adored by angels and saints, arranged in more canonical order than at St. John Lateran. St. John the Baptist and the three principal apostles here take precedence over St. Francis and St. Anthony of Padua. The pope, however, keeps his privileged place immediately at the feet of St. Peter, with Jacopo Colonna, the titular cardinal of the basilica, facing him.

In the lower part, five scenes from the life of the Virgin and two episodes relating to St. Jerome and St. Mathias (whose relics were believed to be in the basilica) complete the main painting. The order of episodes is disturbed only by the scene of the Dormition in the middle of the sequence, where particular stress is laid on the dogma of the Assumption in relation to the Coronation above. Torriti, who is identified by an inscription, perhaps depicted himself at the foot of the Virgin's bed in the Dormition scene, along with another Franciscan and a layman, probably his assistants. Work on the mosaics, which may have been commissioned by Nicholas IV, continued three or four years after the pope's death (1292). Around this time, frescoes were executed in the left arm of the transept which have been compared to the work of Pietro Cavallini, Giotto, and the Master of Isaac; they show saints and prophets within large medallions.

The designation St. Mary Major did not appear until the mid-9th century, but would persist until today. From the 10th or 11th century, another Marian legend arose from which the basilica acquired the name Our Lady of the Snows. During the night of 4 or 5 August, at the hottest season of the year, Pope Liberius and a Roman patrician, John, are said to have had a vision of the Virgin, who commanded them to build a basilica in the part of the city where the snow fell. The next day, after comparing what each had seen, they found a site covered with snow that marked the plan of the new church.

This legend (the date of 5 August may be explained by the date of consecration of Sixtus III's basilica) was illustrated on the façade of the basilica in a double series of mosaics, which probably were separated in the past. In the upper section, Christ is surrounded by the Tetramorph (as described in Revelation 4:7): four angels, and eight saints. Beneath his feet is an inscription including the name Filippo Rusuti, who would later pursue his career in Assisi and France, where his name is to be found in various archival documents dating from the beginning of the 14th century. This section may date to the papacy of Nicholas IV.

In the lower section, the legend is told in four paintings: Liberius's vision, that of the patrician John, John telling his story to the pope, and Christ and the Virgin sending down the snow. Commissioned by cardinals Jacopo and Pietro Colonna, whose portraits are no longer visible, these mosaics were probably not executed until after 1306, when the Colonna regained political power in Rome. As a result, the four panels are often attributed to other artists, including Gaddo Gaddi, for reasons of style and following Vasari's caveat. The dating has a certain importance, since these picturesque scenes also contain examples of exceedingly advanced architectural perspective. In early times, the mosaics were protected by the portico put up in the reign of EUGENE III (1145–53). Later, with the construction of the new 18th-century façade, they were hidden inside the loggia, remaining intact. However, part of the mosaics were destroyed during repair work, while the rest were badly restored under BENEDICT XIV.

In the 15th century, the legend of the snow cropped up in other works of art. A triptych, now split up, was commissioned from Masaccio and Masolino for the high altar. The central panel illustrates the miracle of the snow, while the other side shows the Assumption of the Virgin (Naples, National Gallery of Capodimonte). The side panels, which show St. John the Baptist, St. John the Evangelist, St. Jerome, and St. Martin, are at the National Gallery in London and the Johnson Collection in Philadelphia. The presence of this last saint, whose features are those of MARTIN V, recalls the underlying meaning of the painting. Like Pope Liberius of the legend, Martin V was at that time reestablishing Christian Rome after the disruptions of the schism. It might therefore be presumed that the painting was commissioned in 1423, at the time of the jubilee celebrating this Christian restoration. That implies that Masaccio may have traveled to Rome around that time, but this hypothesis would in turn justify the echoes of Paleo-Christian painting in the frescoes of the Brancacci chapel. (For instance, the Tribute of St. Peter would be easier to understand if Masaccio had seen St. Paul's Outside the Walls.)

Fifty years later, under SIXTUS IV (1471–84), the miracle of the snow was again the subject of an important work. The French cardinal Guillaume d'Estouteville, archpriest of the basilica from 1455 to 1483, carried out the pope's wishes by seeing to the construction of a new high altar. The decoration was given to Mino del Reame, an artist about whom little is known and whose existence has even been disputed. The decoration was split up when the ciborium was replaced by Fuga's baldachin. However, four bas-reliefs from the decoration remain, set into the lower part of the passageway of the apse. They are devoted to the life of the Virgin (Nativity, Adoration of the Magi, Assumption with the donor, and the miracle of the snow). Also extant is a representation of the Virgin in the grand sacristy, signed *Opus Mini*. This same cardinal was then building the church of St. Augustine in Rome and at the same time overseeing the building of the choir of Mont-Saint-Michel, in flamboyant Gothic style.

Few of the works of art in the basilica are not connected to the Virgin, but mention should be made of the art of the cosmatesque craftsmen. Like many other Roman churches, St. Mary Major boasts a pavement of this type. Executed under Eugene III (1145–53), it was donated by the Roman noblemen Scoto and Giovanni Paparone, who are represented on horseback, armed with breastplate and sword. The monument of Gonsalvo Rodriguez, archbishop of Toledo and cardinal of Albano (d. 1299), bears witness to the long continuation of the art of these Roman workers in marble. Signed by Giovanni di Maestro Cosma, *civis romanus*, who was known as a sculptor, mosaicist, and architect, it is adorned with orna-mental motifs in the cosmatesque style. At the center of the mosaic is the figure of the cardinal, kneeling before the Virgin and Child and flanked by St. Mathias and St. Jerome (who bear inscriptions pointing out the spot in the basilica where their relics are preserved, that of Jerome, naturally, saying *Recumbo praesepis ad antrum*). But the tomb that forms the lower part of the monument, with its recumbent figure on a catafalque between two angels holding a curtain, is fairly close in style to the contemporary tombs executed by Arnolfo di Cambio—a sign of the eclecticism of the cosmatesque artists.

In the same decorative style is the upper story of the 11th-century campanile, with its ornamentation of red brick and earthenware, which had just been completed on GREGORY XI's return from Avignon (1377). Finally, there exist some very fragmentary remains of the frescoes done by Piero della Francesca or his workshop for the St. Michael chapel (in particular, St. Luke and his ox).

Pierre-Yves Le Pogam

Bibliography

Alexander, S. S. "Carolingian Restoration of the Mosaics of Santa Maria Maggiore in Rome," *Gesta*, 16 (1977), 13–22.

Berliner, R. "Arnoldo di Cambios Praesepe," *Beiträge für Georg*.

Biasiotti, G. "La basilica di Santa Maria Maggiore prima della innovazioni del secolo XVI," *MAH*, 1915, 15–40.

Biasiotti, G. "La riproduzione della Grotta della Natività di Bethleem nella basilica di Santa Maria Maggiore in Roma," *Dissertazioni della Pontificia accademia romana di archeologia*, 1921, Rome, II, 95–110.

Cecchelli, C. *I Mosaici della Basilica di Santa Maria Maggiore*, Turin, 1956.

Gradner, J. "Pope Nicholas IV and the Decoration of Santa Maria Maggiore," *Zeitschrift für Kunstgeschichte*, 36 (1973), 1–50.

Lavagnino, E. and Moschini, V. *Santa Maria Maggiore*, Rome, n.d. [1924] (Le chiese di Roma illustrate, 7).

Martinelli, A. *Santa Maria Maggiore nell'Esquilino*, Rome, 1975.

Taccone Galucci, D. *Monografia della patriarcale Basilica di Santa Maria Maggiore*, Rome, 1911.

From the 16th Century. During the Renaissance, Cardinal Guillaume d'Estouteville caused the side naves of the basilica to be arched over and a coffered ceiling to be hung over the central nave. Attributed to Giuliano da Sangallo, it bears the coat of arms of ALEXANDER VI. In the 17th and 18th centuries, the basilica became a leading building site of the Counter Reformation, with two funerary chapels commissioned by popes SIX-TUS V and PAUL V, and then of the Baroque era, with the creation of a new façade and apse. Nevertheless, the addition of the two great chapels did not alter the edifice, which retained its hypostyle basilican structure with three naves.

In spite of his brief papacy, Sixtus V (1585–90) left his artistic mark on Rome, which lost its medieval character at that time. He enhanced the basilica by giving it a star-shaped forecourt and built the chapel that bears his name (to the right of the choir). The pope's official architect, Domenico Fontana (1543–1607), who worked for him from 1574, was commissioned to build this chapel in 1586. It was designed to house the oratory of the Crib, which Fontana placed beneath the altar (here the pope celebrated the first Christmas Mass, when this was not done at the high altar); the reliquary of wood from the Crib, donated by Philip III and Margarita of Spain in 1606, was later stolen during the French occupation of 1798. Sixtus V's chapel was built on the plan of a Greek cross and adorned with a cupola decorated with frescoes in the Mannerist style. Like the painted decoration, the carved ornamentation responded to the "pragmatic" style favored by the council of TRENT. However, it is unsatisfactory on the aesthetic level because in this particular period, the available artists were apt to be second-rate and produced few works of quality.

The chapel is an example of the use of many-colored marble, often taken from buildings of antiquity. This shows an obvious taste for ostentation, but the effects in this chapel are discordant, to say the least. On either side of the chapel are the monumental tombs of PIUS V and Sixtus V (executed in his lifetime), whose composition in reredos form was conceived to exalt the majesty of the pontificate. Sixtus V had the remains of Pius V moved from St. Peter's to St. Mary Major so that they could be housed in a monumental tomb; he also started the process of canonization of his predecessor, which was completed in 1712.

Not long afterward, another building project was undertaken, this time by Paul V. He commissioned a chapel that was built by Flaminio Ponzio from 1605 to 1611. Like the preceding one, it was designed on a Greek cross plan and surmounted by a high dome. The decoration of colored marble combined with gilding creates an effect of splendor. Along the side walls are the monumental tombs of popes CLEMENT VIII and Paul V; even though the sculptures seem more fluid, there are weaknesses in the narrative reliefs, which are divided up into separate paintings. The whole is set in the scheme of a triumphal arch, so massive and ornate that the sculpted decoration seems reduced to the size of figurines. Compared with their models in Sixtus V's chapel, these tombs evidence a growing interest in the accumulation of decorative detail. Despite the apparent uniformity of the decoration, one

notes discrepancies of style and quality, a clumsy integration of the sculpture into the architectural composition, and in particular a lack of basic structure, all typical of Late Mannerism.

Among the artists who took part in this enterprise, which was directed by Cavaliere d'Arpino, were Nicolas Cordier, Ippolito Buzio, Camillo Mariani, Pietro Bernini, Stefano Maderno, and Silla da Viggiu, who was responsible for the statues of the two pontiffs. Cavaliere d'Arpino executed the pictorial decoration of the pendentives of the dome and the lunette window above the altar. The Florentine artist Ludovico Cardi, known as Il Cigoli, painted the dome, following an iconographic design faithfully in line with the Counter Reformation's affirmation of the cult of the Virgin. The design is interesting in its attempt to unify space, but not as innovative as it appears. The frescoes in the lunettes are the work of Guido Reni.

The enterprise is typical of official commissions of the early 17th century, in that all these artists—Mannerists, those of the transition period and modernists—worked side by side under the eclectic academism of Cavaliere d'Arpino. Here Bernini got his start as a sculptor, working alongside his father, and it was here that he attracted the attention of the cardinal's nephew, Scipione Borghese, one of the most generous art patrons of the period and adviser to the pope in the choice of artists. It was he who promoted Guido Reni, the painter of the large isolated figures of saints. The icon of the Virgin was placed in this chapel in 1613, surrounded by a halo of angels. Here her aid was particularly sought in times of crisis, for instance, Pius V commanded that celebrations of thanksgiving be increased after the battle of LEPANTO, and INNOCENT XI ordered a *Te Deum* sung when the Turks were defeated before Vienna in 1683 and, later, in 1716 after Prince Eugene's victory at Peterwardein.

A grand project got under way in 1676, when Carlo Rainaldi designed a huge structure to link the chapels of Sixtus V and Paul V. Following up a failed design by Bernini of 1669, Rainaldi built the apse on the Piazza dell'Esquilino, surmounting it with the twin cupolas of the two chapels.

At the beginning of the 18th century, CLEMENT XI instigated important works of restoration in order to strengthen the basilica's structure. The pope insisted that the new ornamentation harmonize visually with the old. Above all, he wanted the mosaics of the façade preserved—a prudent move that reflected the growing interest in things medieval. In 1707, Cardinal Porto Carrero offered 3,000 scudi for the entrance grilles of the basilica. These were designed by Carlo Fontana and installed over the following years.

The façade was cleaned and restored by the Florentine architect Ferdinando Fuga (1699–1781), a leading figure in Roman architecture of the first half of the 18th century, whose style was influenced both by Borromini and by the rise of Neoclassicism. At St. Mary Major, from 1743–1750, Fuga executed an elegant, dramatic design. Against the original façade of the basilica he set a loggia for benedictions and three wide arcades that allowed the mosaics to be viewed. He used a double row of superimposed columns, producing a subtle play of light and shadow, surmounted by an arch or portions of entablature to form a continuous framework against which to set aediculae. Despite a dryness of architectural detail, the whole produces a fine theatrical effect. The porch was connected to the adjoining palaces by a concave wall offset at the second story. This was a characteristic feature of the 18th century, when the city was considered as a unified whole and the buildings related one to another. Fuga's style resembles the Late Baroque, although it lacks that style's spontaneity and animation. The structured appearance of this façade is even more obvious when one compares it with that of St. John Lateran.

Between 1741 and 1750 BENEDICT XIV ordered the restoration of the interior of the basilica. Fuga salvaged the old columns, paring down the thickest ones and shortening those that were too tall. In so doing, he remade all the pedestals and capitals in the Ionic style, giving the colonnade its present harmonious proportions. Finally, along the walls of the side aisles he placed Ionic pilasters opposite each column. Thanks to these many efforts of renovation, the basilica has preserved its Paleo-Christian structure, while presenting, on the exterior, Baroque façades that are fertile fields for scenographic research.

Sylvie Chambadal

Bibliography

Johns, C. M. S. "Clement XI and Santa Maria Maggiore in the Early Eighteenth Century," *Journal of the Society of Architectural Historians*, 45 (1986), 283–96.

Martinelli, A. *Santa Maria Maggiore sull' Esquilino*, Rome, 1975.

Ostrow, S. F, and Johns, C. M. S. Johns, "Illuminations of S. Maria Maggiore in the Early Sesttecento," *Burlington Magazine*, 1990, 528–34.

Taccon-Gallucci, D. *Monografia della Patriarcale Basilica di Santa Maria Maggiore*, Rome, 1911.

ST. PAUL THE APOSTLE. See **Paul.**

ST. PAUL'S OUTSIDE THE WALLS, BASILICA OF. **Middle Ages.** A disastrous fire in 1823 spared only the ciborium, the confession, part of the transept, the apse, the triumphal arch, and the Roman campanile (the last, however, was replaced during the subsequent reconstruction). These are, therefore, the elements about which most is now known, but the works lost in the destruction are documented in drawings and descriptions. From the façade to the apse, the basilica was constantly enriched during medieval times.

The first preserved document is a manuscript executed around 870 in France, in the Carolingian illumination workshop of Rheims. This is the famous Bible of St. Paul's, whose presence is attested in the basilica from the 11th century. It is probable that it was a gift from Charles the Bald when he was crowned emperor of Rome (875), together with the ivory chair that would become the Cathedra Petri in ST. PETER'S BASILICA. This is a monumental manuscript; its illustrations follow the tradition of Bibles produced in Tours in the mid-9th century, but it exemplifies a fusion of the characteristics of Rheims illumination with innovations of the court of Charles the Bald.

The basilica door was commissioned by Hildebrand, abbot of St. Paul's, in 1070, when he was restoring his community to its original discipline. Before he became abbot, he had been a monk there, and later administrator; he was to become Pope GREGORY VII. Hildebrand caused the door to be replaced with the help of Pantaleone, a leading merchant of Amalfi, who had it cast in Constantinople by a certain Staurachios of Chio, who signed his work. Even if Hildebrand specified the iconographic program, certain details as well as its style place the work firmly in the Byzantine tradition. Burned, blackened, and badly damaged by the fire, the door was restored under PAUL VI so that now visitors can admire it from the inside, on the other side of the façade. Beginning in the papacy of JOHN XXII, the façade was ornamented with mosaics which today are displayed on the other side of the triumphal arch. Attributed to Pietro Cavallini, they depict Christ in benediction between Sts. Luke, Mark, Peter, and Paul. The nave was similarly adorned with mosaic panels, some of which are believed to date to the 5th century; the rest were probably redone by Cavallini around 1277–80, during the pontificate of NICHOLAS III, and possibly in a second program before 1287 (New Testament scenes).

The mosaic of the apse was executed by Venetian artisans who were summoned successively by INNOCENT III, HONORIUS III, and GREGORY IX. Honorius, who asked the doge Pietro Ziani to send him mosaicists (1218), had himself represented at the feet of the blessing Christ. The Savior is shown amid Sts. Paul, Peter, Luke, and Andrew (note that in his own basilica, St. Paul, who is placed at Christ's right hand, logically takes precedence over St. Peter). In the lower band, a jeweled cross surmounts an altar and is surrounded by two angels, the apostles, the Holy Innocents, and the kneeling figures of the abbot Giovanni Gaetani (1212–16) and the sacristan Adinolfo. Few original elements remain in this mosaic, which has been heavily restored; among them should be noted the head of St. Peter, now enclosed in the basilica sacristy.

The Pashal candelabra, executed by Niccoló di Angelo and Pietro Vassalletto in the late 12th century to early 13th, is adorned with acanthus leaves and fantastic animals at the base, while the rest of the candelabra depicts scenes from the Passion, the Resurrection, and the Ascension. The cloister, which bears the signature of one Master Pietro (*magister Petrus fecit hoc opus*), usually identified as Vassalletto, was begun under the abbatiate of Pietro da Capua between 1103 and 1208. After two interruptions, it was completed in 1235. Its double columns represent a whole repertoire of ornamental forms—twisted or straight, grooved or decorated with mosaics. Above them runs a string course with a famous inscription on three of its sides, and on the fourth, various carvings (Adam and Eve, a wolf teaching a goat). A 13th-century wooden statue of St. Paul that was half-burned in the fire of 1823 was considered in the Middle Ages to be an authentic portrait of the apostle and thus the subject of great veneration.

The ciborium of the high altar was commissioned by the abbot Bartolomeo in 1285. According to the inscription (*Hoc opus fecit Arnolphus cum socio Petro*), this is a work by Arnolfo di Cambio, whose assistant was identified in the past as Pietro Cavallini. Even though this attribution is often rejected by modern scholars, it is possible to identify the respective contributions of the two artists and their studio. The baldachin floats on a light architectural structure employing several elements of the late Gothic style. These seem to be inspired, in particular, by the art that could have been seen in all its glory in the Sainte-Chapelle in Paris, a few decades earlier. This would, therefore, be one of the first uses in Rome of the French Gothic vocabulary, but fused with contributions from the cosmatesque tradition. In the corners are statues of Sts. Peter, Paul, Luke, and Benedict (the latter because the basilica was served by Benedictine monks); the spandrels contain bas-reliefs representing Adam and Eve, Abel and Cain, Constantine and Theodosia, and the offering of the ciborium itself to St. Paul.

In the chapel in the left arm of the transept is a crucifix formerly attributed, by general agreement, to Pietro Cavallini (based on Vasari's evidence), but today considered by some to be a Sienese work from the late 13th century or the first half of the 14th (perhaps from Maitani's entourage). This crucifix with its dramatic realism—the feet are damaged and the hands mutilated, and it has been much restored—would have appealed to St. Bridget of Sweden, the "prophetess of the North" (d. 1373), who used to pray in the sanctuary. Another crucifix often attributed to Cavallini is in Bernini's chapel in St. Peter's. The cloister also contains a marble statue of BONIFACE IX being enthroned (1389–1404). The attribution and dating of this work are the subject of fierce debate, in particular because its original site is uncertain.

Pierre-Yves Le Pogam

Bibliography

Barbier de Montault, X. *Description de la Basilique de Saint-Paul-hors-les-murs . . . Rome*, Rome, 1886.

Cecchelli, C. *San Paolo fuori le mura (Roma nobilis)*, Rome, 1953; *San Paolo fuori le Mura a Roma*, ed. and with intro. by C. Pietrangeli, Rome, 1989 (Chiese monumentali d'Italia).

d'Amato, C. "L'arredamento liturgico e il tesoro della Basilica di San Paolo," *Benedictina*, 1975, 373–89.

de Bruyne, L. *L'antica serie di ritrati papali della Basilica di San Paolo fuori le mura*, Rome, 1934.

Eleen, L. "The Frescoes from the Life of St. Paul in San Paolo fuori le mura in Rome: Early Christian or Medieval?" *The Roman Tradition in Wall Decoration, RACAR, Revue d'art canadien*, 12 (1985), 251–9.

Jullian, R. "Le candélabre pascal de Saint-Paul-hors-les-Murs," *Mélanges d'archéologie et d'histoire publiés par l'École française de Rome*, 45, 1928.

Lavagnino, E. *San Paolo sulla via Ostiense*, Rome, 1924; *La basilica di San Paolo sulla via Ostiense*, Rome, 1933.

Lavagnino, E. "Il crocefisso della Basilica di San Paolo," *Rivista del R. Istituto di Archeologia e Storia dell'Arte*, 1941, 217–27.

Nicolai, N. M. *Della Basilica di San Paolo*, Rome, 1815.

Pesarini, S. "La Basilica di San Paolo sulla Via Ostiense prima della innovazioni del secolo XVI," *Studi Romani*, 1013, 384–427.

Schuster, I. *La basilica e il monasterio di San Paolo fuori le Mura*, Turin, 1934.

White, J. "Cavillini and the Lost Frescoes in San Paolo," *Studies in Late Medieval Italian Art*, London, 1984, 76–95.

16th to 20th Centuries. During the night of 15 to 16 July 1823, an enormous fire destroyed the basilica. The intense emotion that this aroused reflected the antiquity and liturgical and religious importance of the building, an obligatory stop for pilgrims. In his *Promenades romaines*, Stendhal relates how he saw the site immediately after the catastrophe: "I visited St. Paul's the day after the fire. I found a severe beauty and an imprint of disaster of which, in the arts, only Mozart's music can give an idea. Everything bespoke the horror and chaos of this lamentable event; the church was encumbered with smoldering black beams that were half burnt; great fragments of columns that had been split from top to bottom threatened to collapse at the least rumble. The Romans who filled the church were in consternation." PIUS VII died at dawn on 20 August without having learned of the disaster.

The church on the eve of its destruction was not fundamentally different from the monument of the Paleo-Christian and medieval eras. In the 17th century, the chapel of the Holy Sacrament (today dedicated to St.

Lawrence) had been built after the drawings of Carlo Maderno (1615). It was adorned with frescoes and paintings by Lanfranco in 1624–45. This series, centered on the Eucharist, remained in place for only a few years; today, the canvases are dispersed among various museums. In the 18th century, BENEDICT XIII (1724–30) ordered the rebuilding of the exterior portico of the basilica, which had collapsed on 1 May 1724. BENEDICT XIV (1740–58) concentrated on the interior decoration. He had the mosaics of the apse and the frescoes of the central nave restored, entrusting the painter Salvatore Monosilo with the task of continuing the series of papal portraits begun in the 5th century by Pope LEO I (440–61). These were, in short, not radical transformations, but rather works of embellishment and restoration.

The fire changed everything. The devastation was immense. Luigi Rossini's engravings show the scope of the disaster: the only parts left standing were the apse, the triumphal arch, the outer walls of the side naves, the façade, and the campanile. Restoration might have been attempted, but at that date people thought of only one solution—reconstruction. In the name of reconstruction, some things were sacrificed that had been spared the flames, such as the campanile, which was demolished and replaced with the curious bell tower erected by Luigi Poletti between 1840 and 1860. Arguments arose not over whether to rebuild, but over what criteria to adopt. Should they put up an entirely new structure, a showcase of contemporary architecture? Or—as the scholars recommended, backed by the Academy of St. Luke and specialists like Carlo Fea, superintendent of antiquities—should they opt for a reconstruction identical to the old, in a quasi-archeological scheme?

In the end, the conservative view prevailed. Giuseppe Valadier, who had put forward a revolutionary design based on a Greek cross plan that bore no relation to the form of the old basilica, was eliminated. LEO XIII, in a brief of 1825 in which he appealed to the generosity of the whole world, explained that no innovation would be carried out in the architectural forms and proportions *niuna innovazione dovrà dunque introdursi nelle forme e proporzioni architettoniche.* Responsibility for the work was given to Pasquale Belli, an architect of no great originality, who was succeeded by Luigi Poletti (1792–1869) and Virginio Vespignani (1808–82).

Chateaubriand, in his *Mémoires d'Outre-Tombe,* tells how, when he was ambassador, he went to St. Paul's to watch the men at work, and, leaning "on some charred block of porphyry," meditated on "the history of Christianity in the West." The building site was the most important in 19th-century papal Rome. Work went on until 1928, the date of completion of the quadriportico, or even until 1930 (baptistry of A. Foschini). In 1840, however, GREGORY XVI was able to consecrate the confession altar, surmounted with Arnolfo's restored ciborium. On 10 December 1854 PIUS IX solemnly inaugurated the new basilica before a crowd of cardinals and bishops who had flocked to Rome for the proclamation of the dogma of the Immaculate Conception. Their names are inscribed on six marble plaques mounted on the wall of the apse.

The site had once been an insalubrious marshland and was now a faceless working-class section of the city. Thus, the reconstructed basilica arose seemingly apart from the city itself—indeed "outside the walls." The plan, in the form of a Latin cross, is readily perceptible from the outside. On the Tiber side, the principal façade is fronted by an immense quadriportico (70 meters on each side), executed by Guglielmo Calderini between 1890 and 1928. This bears no relation to the original atrium, which is known from Lafréry's engraving (1575), or to the narthex that replaced it in the 18th century, but it does correspond to the image that was held at the time of Paleo-Christian basilicas. The statues and mosaics are pure 19th century; Giuseppe Obici's statue of St. Paul conforms to the aesthetic ideal of celebratory sculpture of the time. The mosaics consist of three bands: at the bottom, the prophets, Isaiah and Jeremiah, Ezekiel and Daniel; in the middle, the Lamb of God, on a hill from which four rivers flow to refresh the flock of believers; at the top, Christ blessing, flanked by St. Peter and St. Paul. The central bronze door was conceived by Antonio Maraini in 1929 based on an iconographic program of Cardinal Ildefonso Schuster, then abbot of St. Paul's. It depicts the apostles Peter and Paul preaching. On the right is the jubilee door, on the other side of which was placed the restored mosaic, the masterpiece of Staurachios of Chio. The so-called Gregorian portico opens onto the north part of the transept; it was so named because it was executed by L. Poletti during the pontificate of Gregory XVI (1831–46). The long wall alongside the Via Ostiense, which is quite bare of decoration, perhaps explains why Louis Veuillot wrote, cruelly and partly unjustly, in 1862: "What do we see before our eyes, a granary, a factory, a train station?"

The interior is divided into five naves and, with its forest of columns, gives an impression of vastness. Yet in spite of the gleaming marbles, this academic interpretation of the Paleo-Christian style is very cold, and the various decorations fail to enliven it. In the upper part are 36 frescoes that took about 20 artists only three years to complete (1857–60); they show scenes from the life of St. Paul, according to the Acts of the Apostles. Most notable are the contributions by Francesco Podesti and Pietro Gagliardini, two of the best fresco painters of the period; Carlo Gavardini esteemed for the quality of his colors; and Francesco Coghetti and Francesco Grandi, for their dramatic conception of the scenes. These artists, whose work is in the tradition of Filippo Agricola, Vincenzo Camuccini, and Tommaso Minardi—who are also represented in the basilica—reacted against the excesses of Baroque decoration by adopting a painstaking, balanced execution and a somewhat formal composition. They were also mainly responsible for the mosaic medallions of the popes, from St. Peter to JOHN PAUL II, which are arranged around the ambulatory of the basilica and echo the fresco portraits of the old church. (The 41 medallions that escaped the fire are in the little monastery museum.) The alabaster windows, installed in 1928, admit a dim light.

In the middle of the edifice, over the papal altar and the confession, is the ciborium of Arnolfo di Cambio. This is the heart of the basilica. On either side of the apse, whose great mosaic has been heavily restored, are four chapels. The chapel of the Holy Sacrament (formerly called the chapel of the Crucifix, because of the 15th-century wooden figure of Christ) contains a statue of St. Bridget of Sweden by Maderno, recalling the saint's habit of praying in the sanctuary. A mosaic of the Virgin from the first quarter of the 13th century, made in Byzantium, is the much venerated image before which, in 1541, Ignatius of Loyola and his first companions solemnly pronounced their vows as they inaugurated the Society of Jesus. The St. Lawrence chapel retains Maderno's structure; those of St. Benedict and St. Stephen were built by Poletti. In the north transept is Camuccini's fine painting of the conversion of St. Paul, which is matched, in the south transept, by a mosaic copy of the *Assumption of the Virgin* by Giulio Tomano and Francesco Penni, based on a drawing by Raphael. Paintings by Minardi, Agricola, and Camuccini, as well as sculptures by Salvatore Revelli, A.-M. Laboureur, E. Maccagnani and others, adorn the basilica in accordance with the standards of the time and make it a gallery of 19th-century art—without, however, managing to fill this great empty space.

Adjoining the basilica is the monastery. The first evidences of a monastic community near St. Paul's date to 604; this was a women's order, which was soon matched by a community of monks. In the 9th century, in an imitation of LEO IV's Leonine City, which he built to protect St. Peter's, JOHN VII (872–82) saw to the defenses of St. Paul's by building a fortified wall of 13 towers. The district inside he named Giovannipoli, or Castrum San Pauli; all traces of it vanished during the 16th century. This was not an idle precaution: in 846, a Saracen fleet sailed up the Tiber, after seizing Ostia and Porto, and sacked both basilicas. In the 10th century, the monastery passed into the hands of the Benedictines of Cluny, then in the 15th century to the congregation of Monte Cassino, to which the monks belong to this day. They are entrusted with the service of the church; thus, St. Paul's is the only major "monastic" basilica, albeit under papal administration.

In the past, the abbey had considerable possessions, with fiefs scattered throughout the Roman Campagna and Latium. It thus exerted an intellectual influence that has not entirely disappeared. In 1678, a college of philosophy

and theology, the Collegio Teologico Anselmiano, was founded in the convent; it has now been moved to the Aventine. St. Paul's also saw the birth of two flourishing congregations, that of Solesmes (its founder, Prosper Guéranger, made his monastic profession at St. Paul's in 1836) and that of Bueren in Germany. Cardinal Schuster, archbishop of Milan, who in April 1945 served as intermediary between Mussolini and the Committee for the Liberation of Northern Italy, was abbot of St. Paul's. *Benedictina*, the journal of monastic history, is published there. Other cultural treasures include a picture gallery (with, especially, works by Antoniazzo Romano and Gaspare Traversi) a lapidary museum which holds 2,700 inscriptions from the Roman, Paleo-Christian, and medieval periods, and the library, containing the famous Bible of Charles the Bald.

The basilica has been associated with some of the finest moments of the Church. It was at St. Paul's that, on 25 January 1959, JOHN XXIII announced the three great projects of his pontificate: the Roman synod, the publication of a new Code of Canon Law, and, most important, the calling of a council, Vatican II. It was also here, at the end of Vatican II, that PAUL VI convened the council Fathers on 4 December 1965 for an ecumenical prayer. In general, however, the basilica does not represent as important a religious pole for Rome as do St. Peter's, St. John Lateran, and St. Mary Major.

Noëlle de La Blanchardiére

Bibliography

San Paolo fuori le mura a Roma, a cura di Carlo Pietrangeli, Florence, 1988 (includes complete bibliography).

Schuster, I. *La basilica e il monastero di S. Paolo fuori le mura*, Turin, 1934.

ST. PETER THE APOSTLE. See Peter.

ST. PETER THE APOSTLE, SOCIETY OF. The Society was founded in Caen, Normandy, in 1889 by Stéphanie Bigard and her daughter Jeanne, to alert the Christian community to the problem of the formation and support of indigenous clergy in the mission churches, after the apostolic vicar of Nagasaki wrote to them describing the need to educate local clergy (1 June 1889). The Society of St. Peter the Apostle also sought to encourage the faithful to give spiritual and material aid to candidates to the priesthood, since the Congregation for the PROPAGATION OF THE FAITH and the missionary bishops were unable to bear the financial burden of creating seminaries and educating local clergy.

The HOLY SEE recognized the society in 1890, entrusting it with the building of the pontifical seminary of

Kandy, Sri Lanka. Three years later, LEO XIII recommended it again (apostolic letter *Ad Extrema Orientis oras*, 24 June 1892). On 12 July 1895, he sent it his first BENEDICTIONS. The bishop of Sées (dep. Orne, France) approved the society, and on 13 October 1895 the regular council was instituted. The Congregation for the Propagation of the Faith in its turn encouraged the initiative (10 September 1896).

Unable to obtain civil corporate status for their foundation, the Bigards turned to the Catholic government of Fribourg, in Switzerland, which welcomed them and on 6 September 1902 approved the St. Peter Institute, granting it civil corporate status the following 18 October.

After Mme Bigard, the mother, died in 1903, the society was entrusted to Mme Chapot de Neuville, Mother Mary of the Passion, the founder and general superior of the missionary Franciscan Sisters of Mary. She in turn handed it over to Cardinal van Rossum, prefect of the Congregation for the Propagation of the Faith. In 1919, the latter appointed Canon Bossens, the under-secretary of the congregation as director general of the Society of St. Peter the Apostle.

The Holy See approved its statutes on 18 April 1920, *ad triennium* in the preliminary stages; the society then became subordinate to the Congregation for the Propagation of the Faith. On 3 May 1922, it received the official title of Pontifical Society, and thereafter it spread rapidly in most dioceses of EUROPE and North America.

Later, its office was moved for good from Fribourg to Rome (*motu proprio Vix ad Summus pontificatus*, 24 June 1929). Coordination with the pontifical missionary work of the Congregation for the Propagation of the Faith was provided for, and their respective statutes approved at the same time (*motu proprio Decessor noster*, 24 June 1929).

More recently, the Society of St. Peter the Apostle has also taken steps to assist in preparation of the men and women candidates for the religious life.

Funds obtained by the establishment of scholarships, the payment of pensions, subscriptions, and other gifts have allowed for the building and development of numerous small and large diocesan seminaries. In this way, the society has made a significant contribution to the rise of local clergies.

Dominique Le Tourneau

ST. PETER'S BASILICA.

Antiquity. The Constantinian basilica was built in the Vatican district, an area on the right bank of the Tiber, bounded to the north by the Vatican hills and to the east by the river, and served by three principal roads—the Aurelian, Cornelian, and Triumphal ways. Marshy and insalubrious, the area was always somewhat on the margin of urban development. Julius Caesar's plan to set up a new Campus Martius there by diverting the Tiber was not put into effect, and the area was mainly occupied by large estates.

Some of these estates belonged to the imperial family (the gardens of Agrippina and Nero), which had erected various buildings designed for spectacles. One of these was the Circus of Nero or Caligula, at the foot of the Vatican hill, which was probably abandoned by the second half of the 2nd century; its north side corresponds to the left-hand nave of the present basilica. Its obelisk, imported from Heliopolis in Egypt, now stands in the middle of St. Peter's square. There were also one or two naumachias (areas for mock naval battles) to the west of Hadrian's mausoleum. At least one temple is known to have been built in the area, the Phrygianum (a temple to Cybele, no doubt from the 2nd century). About 20 taurobolic altars (for sacrificing bulls) have been preserved, evidence that the temple was in active use between 295 and 300, until the edicts decreeing the closing of pagan temples. No trace however, has been found of the "temple of Apollo" said to have been the site of the Constantinian basilica, according to the *LIBER PONTIFICALIS* (I, 176).

The southern part of the area (that enclosed between the circus to the south and the naumachia and Phrygianum to the north) was used as a necropolis from the Augustan era on. In the 1st century A.D., burials seem to have been rather modern, using mainly ditches *alla capuccina*. From the 2nd century on, more luxurious mausoleums became increasingly plentiful; these had stucco decoration, either painted or done in mosaic.

The erection of Hadrian's mausoleum and the Aelius bridge probably encouraged the growth of this necropolis in the 3rd century. Some of the great surface mausoleums were preserved up to the 16th century, in some cases owing to their having been turned into churches. One example is Santa Maria alle Febere, a great circular mausoleum from the 2nd century; another is the mausoleum from Caracalla's time that SYMMACHUS dedicated to St. Andrew. From inscriptions and the decoration of certain mausoleums around St. Peter's, we know that Christians also used this necropolis (there are a few cases of the reuse of pagan mausoleums, e.g., that of the Iulii), perhaps in the 3rd century but certainly in the 4th.

The entry on Pope SILVESTER I in the *Liber pontificalis* credits Constantine with the construction of the basilica and the inclusion of the memoria of the apostle (*Liber pontificalis*, I, 176–8). The attribution is confirmed by other literary, epigraphic, and archaeological sources. Three inscriptions preserved in ancient sylloges recall the emperor's action: the inscription on the triumphal arch (*Quod duce te mundus surrexit in astra triumphans/Hanc Constantinus victor tibi condidit aulam*) (ICUR, NS, 2, 4092 = Diehl 1752); inscription in the apse (*Iustitiae sedi, fidei domus, aula pudoris/Haec est quam cernis, pietas quam possidet omnis/Quae patris et fili virtutibus inclyta gaudet/Auctoremque suum genitoris laudibus aequat*) (ICUR NS, 2, 4094 = Diehl 1753); inscription in the apse (*Constantini . . . expiata . . . hostili incursione*) (ICUR, NS, 2, 4095).

However, these testimonies do not make it possible to establish a sure date for the beginning and completion of the work of building, which no doubt was far from finished at the emperor's death. The title *victor*, the mention of the "father and son," and the allusion to an imperial victory allow us to give the inscriptions a date later than, respectively, 323 (the date when this title appeared in imperial acclamations), 324 (Constantine's victory over Lucinius), and 340–350–361 (Constantine II the Younger, Constans, Constantius II). Consequently, they provide a first terminus post quem for the completion of the building. Moreover, the date 324 is fully confirmed by the location of the lands that made up the basilican patrimony. Since these are all in the eastern part of the Empire (Egypt, Syria, the Euphrates), Constantine cannot have been able to take possession of them until after his victory over Licinius. Nevertheless, the building work could have been begun at an earlier date.

On the other hand, on 28 March 349, in a law addressed to the praetorium prefect Limenius, Constans recalled the punishments provided for all attacks on the sepulchers, to take effect retroactively from 333 (CTh IX, 17, 2 = CJ IX, 19, 3). The building of the church entailed the destruction of a large number of tombs. Some scholars, therefore, have hypothesized that the date of 333 might have been calculated by Constans in order to speed up the Vatican building operation and to prevent the construction of the basilica from falling victim to the law. According to this hypothesis, work would have begun before 333. Thus, the chronological bracket of 324–33 has been arrived at for the commencement of construction.

There is also the question of the inscription on the golden cross given by the emperor and transcribed by the *Liber pontificalis* (I, 176), with its reference to "Helena augusta." This can only be linked to the establishment of the apostolic memoria, not the basilica itself. The inscription has to be dated between 325 and 330 (the probable dates of attribution of the title *augusta* to Helena and of her death).

The date of completion for the greater part of construction can also be determined approximately. For the commemoration of Peter, the year 354 calendar provided only for a ceremony *in catacumbas*, which shows that the Vatican basilica was not yet in use. However, it must have been in use in 356, when Constantius caused money to be placed on the apostle's tomb in an attempt to appease Liberius (Athanasius, *Hist. Arianorum*, 37). Finally, Marcellina, sister of Bishop Ambrose of Milan, professed herself a virgin on Christmas Eve "beside the apostle Peter" (*De Virgin.* 3, 1). Bearing in mind Ambrose's biography, we can determine an approximate date—between 358, Liberius's return from exile, and 360, the probable date of Ambrose's departure from Rome—for the attestation of the first liturgical ceremony known to have taken place in the basilica, and thus its official opening for worship. We can therefore give as the *termini post quem* for the start of the construction of St. Peter's the date of 333, that of 354 for the completion of the greater part of the work, and 356–60 for the date of the first use of the church.

Thus, this building project took place in the second part of Constantine's reign, and his successor was able to bring it to completion. (The many graffiti of the Constantinian era and the burial sites in the apse area also tend to confirm that the part of the church devoted to the apostolic memoria was long accessible to pilgrims before the final work of installation prevented direct access: note especially the graffiti on wall G, next to the heart of the memoria, among which it is impossible to decipher Peter's name, despite the assertions of some archaeologists.) The relative modesty of the Constantinian endowments, compared to those accompanying the foundation of St. John Lateran (the revenue from lands and the gifts of precious metal to the cathedral were three times as high) or that of the Labican basilica, also argue for a construction date in the second half of his reign. At that time, the imperial endowment resources were doubtless limited by the generosity of the early years, and they also went in preference to civic programs in the Holy Land (the donation of St. Peter's thus is analogous to that of ST. PAUL'S OUTSIDE THE WALLS.

The Basilica. The construction of the new basilica in the 16th century brought about the destruction of all the superstructures of the Constantinian building, which had over the centuries known scarcely any profound change, but a large number of ancient views and recent excavations make it possible to recapture the essence of the 4th-century edifice. Among the views—drawings, surveys, and paintings—note particularly Tiberio Alfarono's plan and description from the end of the 16th century, as well as the drawings of Dosio and Tasselli in the early 17th century. Notable among the excavations were those carried out between 1940 and 1970 around the confession, when foundations and sections of the walls in elevation were found in the apse, transept, and nave.

The site from which St. Peter's would rise was a funerary area of uneven terrain (it had a gentle east–west slope and a declivity of 11 meters from north to south) and marshy soil. The singular choice of an area so little suited to construction—quite apart from the juridical problems presented by its new attribution—called for major drainage operations (still necessary at the end of the 4th century, in Damasus' reign) and earthworks, the tombs being reused as foundation caissons. The only explanation for the choice is clearly the preexistence of a structure that was worthy of being respected and enhanced.

The basilica had the peculiarity of being oriented to the west. It consisted of five naves, with a central nave flanked by two narrower lateral naves (around 26 meters long by 10 meters wide). These were lined with four rows of 22 marble columns each, surmounted by Corinthian capitals. The colonnade separating the central nave from the adjacent ones was surmounted by an architrave, while the columns between the two lateral naves were linked by a blind arcade. The central nave (height, 38 meters), lit directly by high windows set above the framework of the lateral naves (height, 32 and 22 meters, respectively), was overhung by a ceiling of gilded coffers (cf. Prudentius, *Peristephanon*, XII) beneath the saddleback roof.

The five 87-meter-long naves abutted against a huge transept nearly 100 meters long (north to south) and doubtless the same height as the central nave—a true independent transversal nave, with the "tau cross" form characteristic of St. Peter's. The north and south ends of this transept (extending beyond the naves) were separated by a triple blind arcade set in the continuation of the nave's side walls. (Some have suggested that these exedrae had a roof that was independent and lower than that of the rest of the transept.) To the east, the transept was clearly separated from the naves by four series of triple blind arcades linking the pillars terminating the colonnades. A semicircular apse opened up at the west end of the transept, in the axis of the central nave. Twelve meters deep and around 18 meters wide, it was probably the only vaulted part of the basilica. The east façade of the church was—whether from the beginning or only in a second period, but still in the 4th century, we do not know—preceded by a great rectangular atrium, in the center of which was a fountain that was topped with a large pine cone and, over that, a ciborium. The building techniques used for the basilica—a bond of brick that apparently had no stucco cladding, and foundations of *opus caementicum* and *opus listatum*—are comparable in every respect with those of other Constantinian structures.

Thus, in its general outline, St. Peter's fits in perfectly with the general development of the architecture of basilicals and baths of the Low Empire (cf., in Rome, the Curia, the Basilica Iulia, or the Temple of Venus and Rome; in Trier, the Aula Palatina). But insofar as this was the first known reliquary edifice in the West—the relic being that of the founder of the Church—it frequently served as an original model (e.g., in the Carolingian period) for Western religious architecture, even though it showed only relatively minor differences from St. John Lateran and St. Paul's Outside the Walls, for example.

The Apostolic Memoria. The relic that determined the construction of the basilica was in the middle of the opening of the apse. There can be no doubt that this relic was a special structure in the Vatican necropolis. Yet great prudence is called for in the matter of the precise identification of the structure—whether a tomb or simply a commemorative monument—and, in offering hypotheses as to its original state.

The basilica was erected over a narrow street edged to the north and south with tombs and funerary chambers, all of which were razed during the construction. One structure was spared and partially preserved in the Constantinian basilica, but its original form, changes, and overall chronology remain extremely obscure. Without going into detail, it may be noted that, based mainly on hypotheses of restoration, the structure was made up of a fragment of a retaining wall of the necropolis. Called the "red wall" because of its coating, it dates back to the second half of the 2nd century. It was preserved at a height of 2.45 meters above the original floor. Resting against it is a little aedicula, which may be contemporary, directly over a small underground cavity. Usually this monument is supposed to be a superimposition of two recesses, the lower one having an entablature with a marked projection (the hypothesis of a mensa seems far from convincing).

This structure very likely formed the nucleus of the Constantinian memoria and is the one identified with the apostolic Vatican "trophy," mentioned at the beginning of the 3rd century by the Roman cleric Gaius (Eusebius, *Ecc. Hist.*, II, 25, 7). The reference calls for two comments. First, the use of the word *tropaion* is one of the arguments in favor of the idea that the Vatican structure was conceived as a commemorative monument, not as Peter's tomb. Second, it is significant that the apostle's trophy should be mentioned precisely in this period, in the context of the polemic with the montanist Proclus. Excavations carried out in the area of the Confession, together with evidence from certain illustrated documents and ancient descriptions, have helped archaeologists to envision what the memoria looked like. However, this evidence should be used with extreme caution, since the documents and descriptions all postdate the Constantinian arrangement, which had been altered in the interim (note in particular, *LP*, 1, 176). The casket of Pola ivory, now in the Archaeological Museum in Venice, dates at the earliest to the beginning of the 5th century. In any case, the Constantinian memoria has been envisioned as a parallelepipedal block covered with plaques of marble (roughly 3 × 2 × 2 meters), protected by chancel gates inserted between columns of twisted marble that support a baldachin. The original trophy must have been visible, if not accessible, through an opening made in the masonry covering in Constantine's time.

Later Development. The changes and additions that Constantine's basilica underwent are closely linked to the various measures the Church took in its organization of Roman religious life. The insertion of the confession was, naturally, a main object of concern for the bishops of Rome. Two centuries after Constantine (during the pontificates of PELAGIUS II and GREGORY I), the principal change was the design of a crypt aimed at channeling and facilitating the movement of pilgrims. With the floor of the presbyterium raised 1.45 meters, the memoria could now be reached by a circular corridor and an axial corridor, both situated around 0.6 meters below the Constantinian level. (This crypt must have closely resembled that of St. Pancrazio, built during the pontificate of HONORIUS I, around 630.) A fixed altar was probably installed over the memoria (possibly the altar found below that of CALLISTUS II), and the original columns were moved. Henceforth they would support an architrave occupying the whole width of the apse (see the description of the crypt and pilgrims' manifestations of devotion in Gregory of Tours, *De Gloria martyrum*, I, 28, *PL* 71, 728 ff.).

The raids of the Goths clearly caused destruction. The testimony of Orosius (*Hist. adv. paganos, 7, 39*), recalling the protection owed to the relics of Peter and Paul, is contradicted by those of Jerome, (*Epist.* 127, 13 and 130, 5) and Augustine (*Civ. Dei*, 1, 16). Furthermore, St. Peter's benefited from SIXTUS III's policy of restoration and embellishment (*Liber pontificalis*, I, 235). The confession of Peter was decorated with silver, and probably also with a work in silver-gilt representing the apostolic college. The apse vault, over the confession, was also decorated, then restored on several occasions, but few elements remain to make it possible to restore its iconography. In the 370s, there may have been a representation connected with the theme so dear to the Church of Rome, a *Traditio legis*.

As a martyr's church, St. Peter's obviously attracted a large number of burials. A certain number of mausoleums came to be grafted onto the Constantinian monument: for instance, the mausoleum of the Anicii (390–410), situated just behind the apse, and particularly the great circular mausoleum connected by a double-apsed narthex to the south arm of the transept, which at the beginning of the 5th century received the bodies of Honorius and his two wives, Maria and Thermantia. Furthermore, from the reign of LEO the Great, St. Peter's was the site of most of the pontifical sepulchers (Simplicius, Gelasius, Anastasius II, and their successors, without interruption).

The influx of pilgrims brought about an increase in lodging places and charitable centers, as well as some work on the approaches to the basilica. At the end of the 4th century, DAMASUS initiated some changes (access, drainage, and installation of a cantharus: cf. Prudentius, *Peristephanon*, 12, 35 and *Vita Liberii*). Later, SIMPLICIUS I, SYMMACHUS, and JOHN I began major alterations in the atrium, which we know was used for ecclesiastical gatherings by the end of the 4th century. (Paulinus of Nola, *Epist.* 13, 11, *CSEL*, 30, 93, notes that Pammachius replaced the traditional funerary banquet of the ninth day of obsequies for his wife with agapes to benefit the poor.) New galleries and access stairways were built, a fountain was set up below the atrium, and buildings were provided for the poor.

Besides episcopal undertakings, the basilica benefited from the enthusiasm of pilgrims, expressed in more or less sizable gifts that are often recognized only by references in the accompanying inscriptions: decorative elements (paintings, mosaics, votive crowns), liturgical objects, and so on.

Originally designed to commemorate Peter and to organize the saint's veneration, the basilica quite early seems to have served the episcopal liturgy. A religious rivalry between the center and periphery of Rome soon sprang up, to be resolved only when the episcopal palace was moved to the Vatican (significantly, it was for St. Peter's that Liberius intended a series of episcopal portraits: cf. *Liber pontificalis*). The Church soon played its part in the organization of the stational liturgy. It was at St. Peter's that, from Liberius's time at the latest, the first festival of the liturgical year, Christmas, was celebrated, whereas Easter was celebrated at the Lateran. In Leo's reign, the basilica also was the place where the Ascension was commemorated, and part of the ceremonies of Pentecost as well.

From Damasus' papacy the basilica had a baptistry, situated at the northern end of the transept. It was decorated with mosaics given by a pious woman named Anastasia (*Epigrammata Damasiana*, 3, Ferrua, 92). Thus, in a way St. Peter's became the double of the cathedral of St. John Lateran (by the 5th century, as regards the preparation for Easter). The sources tell of particular ceremonies that apparently took place in the basilica: priestly ordinations in December, profession of vows of virginity in Liberius's reign, and reconciliation of penitents on Thursdays.

Throughout the 4th and 5th centuries—from the time of the dramatic episode concerning Liberius—several important events in the religious life of Rome took place in St. Peter's. Choosing to be close to St. Peter's remains meant, in a way, providing a physical display of the continuity of the apostolic tradition on which the primacy of the see was based, taking part in its material presence. This happened at the council of Rome of 386 (Siricius), the synod of 431 (Celestine), and especially 433, when, in the context of negotiations for the Henoticon, Sixtus III convened the episcopal assembly "around the blessed apostle Peter" in order to make a solemn proclamation of the unity and new-found peace of the Church (coll. Veron. 30–31; Schwartz, 107–9). Thus was born a tradition that linked to St. Peter's the synod celebrating the anniversary of the pontifical election, and it played a part in making the basilica that had risen over the relic of the prince of apostles a shrine of Roman ecclesiology.

Françoise Monfrin

Bibliography

Apollonj-Ghetti, B. M., Ferrua, A., Josi, E., and Kirschbaum, E. *Esplorazioni sotto la confessione di San Pietro in Vaticano negli anni 1940–1949*, Rome (1951).

Carcopino, J. "Pierre (fouilles de Saint-)," *Dictionnaire de la Bible*, Suppl. 7 (1966), 51–69; 519–22.

Krautheimer, R. *Corpus basilicarum christianarum Romae*, 5, Vatican (1977), 165–286.

Marrou, H. I. "Vatican (fouilles du)," *DACL*, 15 (1952), 3310–46.

Pesch, R. *Simon-Petrus (Päpste und Papstum*, 15, Stuttgart (1980).

Pietri, C. "Graffito," *Realenzyklopädie für Antike und Christentum*, 12 (1983), 638–67.

Seston, W. "Hypothèse sur la date de la basilique constantinienne de Saint-Pierre de Rome," *Cahiers archéologiques*, 2 (1947), 153–9.

Walsh, J. E. *Le Tombeau de saint Pierre*, Paris, 1984.

Middle Ages. St. Peter's basilica once possessed fabulous treasures, worthy of the precious relics that the pilgrims came to venerate—the tomb of St. Peter and the image of Christ known as the "Veronica"—and certainly comparable to those of the Sancta Sanctorum. But the SACKS OF ROME, particularly that of 1527, and the pillaging of Napoleon's armies reduced them virtually to nothing. Nonetheless, among the rare objects antedating the 19th century and certainly coming from St. Peter's is the celebrated Crux Vaticana, which was offered, probably as an ex-voto, by the Byzantine emperor Justin II (563–78). This is a reliquary of silver-gilt adorned with precious stones, some of which Empress Sophia paid for with her jewels.

In the Middle Ages, the apostle's confession was surmounted by a baldachin. Gregory the Great, the first pope to celebrate Mass there, raised the floor of the area of the apse about 1.45 meters, so that the aedicula would be high enough to serve as an altar. At the same time, a crypt was created to give pilgrims easy access. If it does indeed date from this time, this is one of the earliest examples of such a crypt. Its type—a ring-shaped passage following the contour of the apse, with a corridor leading back to the confession—would serve as a model for many Roman crypts to come, especially in the 11th century, when martyrs' bodies were moved from the catacombs to the churches within the walls.

The basilica façade from the time of LEO I had been decorated with mosaics depicting the Savior, surrounded by the Tetramorph and worshipped by the 24 old men. Under SERGIUS I, the image of the Savior was replaced by that of the Lamb, probably to counter the decisions of the 692 Trullan council forbidding this iconographic equivalence. In any event, the decoration was largely redone under GREGORY IX and later under NICHOLAS III. At the beginning of the 8th century, a Greek-born pope, JOHN VII, built a crib oratory patterned after that of St. Mary Major. This masterpiece of Byzantine art, with its gold background against which delicate forms and colors create an almost otherworldly setting, has survived only in fragments. Among them are the Adoration of the Magi in St. Mary's in Cosmedin, and the portrait of the pontiff, a frail scholarly figure holding the model of his oratory, in the Vatican Grottoes. The bell tower of old St. Peter's was the most ancient in Rome, having been erected by STEPHEN II in 754. We know it from 16th-century drawings, but there is no evidence these depict the prototype of the other Roman bell towers, since it must have been restored many times from the 8th century on.

In the Carolingian period, one monument would come to symbolize in a special way the profound links between the papacy and the Frankish monarchy. The catacombs of Domitilla contained the remains of a young girl of early Christian times, a certain Petronilla. In the 4th century, a legend grew up that the unknown child was a saint, even a martyr. In the 6th century, she was believed to be St. Peter's daughter (through a particular interpretation of the beautiful inscription, *Aureliae Petronillae filiae dulcissimae*), and her sarcophagus became an object of pilgrimage. When Pope Stephen II came to crown Pepin the Short at Saint-Denis, he named Petronilla the patron of the king of the Franks, probably to symbolize what was henceforth to be the filial nature of the relations between him and the Roman Church. In this way, France became the "eldest daughter of the Church." In 757, Stephen's successor, PAUL I, moved the relics of Petronilla to one of the two mausoleums built for Theodosius's family; the other was dedicated to St. Andrew, who was believed to be Peter's brother. The chapel was decorated with frescoes that told the history of Constantine, whom the Frankish king emulated. Later, under LEO III, it was even more richly adorned. After St. Peter's was sacked by the Saracens in August 846, LEO IV restored the chapel, but more soberly. It was for this chapel that a French cardinal, Jean Bilhères of Lagraulas, commissioned Michelangelo's Pietà, which was moved to the basilica when the mausoleum was destroyed in 1544.

Another remarkable Carolingian monument has been preserved, but because it was encased in its Baroque reliquary, its age and significance were discovered only very recently (1971). Known as the "chair of St. Peter," it was in fact the royal throne of Charles the Bald, which he probably presented to Pope JOHN VIII when he was crowned emperor on 25 December 875. It was basically a wooden structure, the upper back part of which was covered with enamelwork and precious stones (now gone). The rest was overlain with small plates of ivory, attributed by scholars to the Palatine school of Charles the Bald, and more precisely to a workshop in eastern France that flourished between 860 and 866. Of particular interest is the head-and-shoulders portrait of the emperor himself, on the crosspiece of the chairback. On its front, the chair includes another series of ivory plates that were not part of the original design (they show six monsters and the 12 labors of Hercules), carved with a delicacy that verges on the precious; their date has been widely disputed. A velvet covering was added in 1481 by order of SIXTUS IV, for the chair served as the pope's seat. It was also used to represent the throne of Peter in the eponymous ceremonies on 22 February, a custom that gradually gave rise to the popular belief that it was the apostle's very seat. In the mid-17th century, this notion was confirmed by the Church, and ALEXANDER VII commissioned Bernini to create a monumental casket for the precious relic.

What remain of the works ordered by the great Pope INNOCENT III are a few fragments of the apse mosaic, commissioned from Venetian or Sicilian workers (reflecting the pope's protection of young Frederick II) or at least artists sensitive to the Byzantine influence, as at St. Paul's. The composition included Christ surrounded by the apostles Peter and Paul and, in the lower band, the mystic Lamb between Innocent III (preserved, together with a phoenix, in the Conti chapel at Poli in Latium) and the Church of Rome (now in the Barracco Museum in Rome). The facade of the Niche of the Pallia is still protected by a bronze grille, a gift of Innocent III. The grille preserved an enamel gate which the pope had ordered from Limousin workshops in the second decade of the 13th century. This is attested by the style of the fragments that have come down to us: the Savior and five apostles, today in the Museo Sacro, which have long been linked with this commission. More recently, scholars have realized that the "tympanum" of Limousin enamels that came from Santa Maria in Vulturella and are now in the museum of the Palazzo Venezia might have come from the same workshop. The front of the tympanum shows the mystic Lamb surrounded by the Tetramorph and prophets, and, most interesting, the back (which is only engraved) depicts a pope presiding over a council. This surely represents, not in portrait form but as an image of an ecclesiological program, Innocent III surrounded by the fathers of LATERAN IV. Together with the figure of Savior above it, it doubtless formed the door of the Niche of the Pallia, where the custom of placing metropolitans' insignia the night before they were consecrated by the pope recalled the unity of the Church in obedience to Peter's successor.

The reign of BONIFACE VIII and, in a general way, the turn of the 13th and 14th centuries represented a particularly lavish period for St. Peter's, reaching a climax in 1300 with the first jubilee. In both sculpture and painting, this pope, eager for prestige and justification, employed the greatest artists of his time. He commissioned his own tomb from Arnolfo di Cambio, as well as the small chapel in which it would be housed, while the votive panel in mosaic was entrusted to Jacopo Torriti as early as Boniface's election in 1294. The tomb may have been completed in 1296, by 1300 at the latest. This symbol of ostentation would provoke Guillaume of Nogaret's accusation of idolatry during the conflict between Boniface and Philip the Fair, under the pretext that the pope had had himself represented on the monument. The chapel disappeared in 1605. Its crown evoked the French Gothic style, as did that of the ciborium of St. Paul. The pope's sarcophagus, however, survives in the Vatican Grottoes, while debate continues over whether various fragments—such as the bust of the pope in blessing (Pontifical Apartments) or two angels raising curtains (Vatican Grottoes)—should be attributed to Arnolfo or in fact belong to the monument. The recumbent figure of Boniface VIII, even if not a faithful likeness of the pope's features, perfectly conveys the violent, even tragic character of his papacy, in the cold, solemn display of the corpse on its catafalque.

The bronze statue of St. Peter that is venerated in the basilica should in all probability be linked to the same artists. It is extremely archaic in character; one explanation for this is the possible existence of a Paleo-Christian model (as is the case with the marble statue once placed in the portico and now in the Vatican Grottoes). For this reason, critics were for a long time reluctant to pinpoint its date of execution. From the 16th century, the statue was even believed to be a reworked statue of Jupiter, and after that a work of late antiquity; however, a technical examination of the work has vindicated those who, at the end of the 19th century, placed the casting in the 1300s, even in the school of Arnolfo di Cambio. In fact, the statue may well be the work of Arnolfo himself, possibly connected with the 1300 jubilee, for which Boniface VIII may have commissioned the statue, turning to the sculptor who designed his tomb. At times covered with pontifical ornaments (the custom goes back to 1736, usually for 29 June and other solemn occasions), the statue has to be seen stripped of this panoply for the viewer to appreciate Arnolfo's work. The figure combines the calm majesty of the sinner who welcomes and pardons and the almost terrifying image of a passionately forceful judge. He rests solidly on his right leg, which expresses the stability of the Roman see, and relaxes the other, which is extended more freely. With his right hand, he freely dispenses blessings, while the left hand firmly clutches the keys of the kingdom. In short, the apostle offers the worshipper the double aspect of an implacable idol and a benevolent father—an image that might also in turn embody the pope, his vicar.

At the end of the 13th century or the beginning of the 14th, Cardinal Stefaneschi, (Boniface VIII died in 1303) nephew of Boniface VIII and a renowned Parisian doctor in canon law, commissioned for the basilica porch (more precisely, the back of the entrance portico) a representation of Christ saving St. Peter as he walks on the waters of Lake Tiberias, while the other apostles tremble with fear or cower in the bottom of their boat (Matthew 14:22–33)—whence the popular name "Navicella" given to this famous mosaic. Cardinal Stefaneschi had himself represented in a corner of the scene. The parallel with the papacy, constantly buffeted by the events of the century but always supported by Christ's hand, was meant to teach the faithful even as the scale and intensity of the mosaic impressed the pilgrims.

Pilgrims were said to have followed a custom of turning around once they were inside the atrium in order to worship the sun. In order to end this pernicious custom, Cardinal Stefaneschi had commissioned a virtual billboard; the copy of the Navicella measures less than 9.50 by 13.50 meters, whereas the original must have been around one-third greater in area. The date of the work and Giotto's part in it are all the more subject to debate because, in 1610, the mosaic was removed and entirely redone. The only remaining original features are the main lines of the composition and two fragments (two busts of angels in medallions), one preserved in Boville Ernica and the other in the Vatican Grottoes. The fragments, even if not from the master's hand, testify to the ability of his studio to use the mosaic technique, traditional in Rome, as well as that of fresco; in addition, they reflect a style in which the transcendence of Byzantine art was deeply imbued with a wholly human gentleness. The precise dates that have been put forward by scholars since the 17th century—ranging from 1298 to 1320—are quite without foundation; probable dates are the year of the jubilee, 1300, or, based on stylistic analysis and on an archival document, around 1310. Moreover, the iconography inspired by Stefaneschi—which shows the ship of the Church gravely shaken—would correspond better to this period than to the time of Boniface VIII's triumph.

Giotto's role in St. Peter's is equally controversial in another work, also commissioned by Stefaneschi. This is a polyptych that Giotto was asked to produce between 1300 and 1333 (most likely toward the end of that period). It was originally intended for the high altar in the sanctuary, the predella of which is still at St. Peter's, in the canons' chapter, while the middle section is in the Vatican Pinacoteca. The central panel, showing Christ in benediction with the cardinal at his feet, is certainly the work of the master, with its illusionist portrayal of the throne, impeccably rendered in perspective. The side panels and predella, although betraying the hand of specific pupils, perfectly fit the overall composition. On the other side of the central panel, the figure of St. Peter enthroned is flanked by Cardinal Stefaneschi, shown offering the model of the altarpiece, and a hermit with miter and halo, identified by some as CELESTINE V, who was canonized in 1313.

After the return from Avignon and the end of the Great Schism, artistic activity at once picked up again in Rome under MARTIN V, who at St. John Lateran engaged both Masaccio and Gentile da Fabriano. Almost nothing remains of their works, but the same eclecticism is to be found in the next papacy. EUGENE IV, who had commissioned a golden miter from Ghiberti, entrusted one of his aides, Antonio Averlino, known as Filarete, with the creation of the bronze door of St. Peter's (1439–45). Trained in Florence, Filarete would become familiar with ancient classicism during his stay in Rome. This was an opportunity for him to place the martyr-apostles in an ancient setting worthy of an archaeologist, while pagan mythology served to decorate the sumptuous foliage around the bas-reliefs with lively motifs. The design was completed, at the pope's request, by the representation of recent events—the crowning of Sigismund by Eugene IV (1433) and the acts of the Council of Florence, which ended in 1439. The show of pomp, originally reinforced by gilding, and the desire for a display of erudition at the service of papal prestige, cannot disguise the lack of iconographic or stylistic unity.

At the same time, Donatello was entrusted with the creation of the tabernacle intended for the papal chapel of the Holy Sacrament, which today is in St. Peter's in the Benefactors' chapel (1432–3). At the other extreme from Filarete's scholarly, composed art, Donatello's work (he was assisted by Michelozzo in the lower part) conveys without any care for elegance the dramatic cry of the disheveled holy women at the Entombment. Eugene IV's own funerary monument, which was executed by Isaia da Pisa between 1447 and 1453, is today at the church of the Holy Savior in Lauro. The tomb of NICHOLAS V, whose verse epitaph is attributed to Eneas Silvius Piccolomini, the future PIUS II, has been split up. That of PAUL II, probably executed between 1474 and 1478 by Giovanni Dalmata, Mino da Fiesole, and their workshop, has met the same fate; most of the elements are in the Vatican Grottoes, except for two friezes, which are in the Louvre.

The ciborium known as that of Sixtus IV intrigues historians as regards both attribution and restoration. Probably begun under Pius II and completed under Sixtus IV, this monument surmounted the confession altar, which dated to the time of CALLISTUS II (1119–24), and was dismantled in 1590. Based on the surviving elements (four large bas-reliefs and eight small ones), it is possible to propose a reasonable solution. The bas-reliefs formed the four sides of the entablature, with the eight small ones making up the right angles, two by two; the entablature was supported by four columns. This type of ciborium, with a cubical upper section, is found in the other major basilicas (except for St. Paul's), which might be explained by a desire for ostentation and a wish to protect relics in better conditions than those provided by the confessions. Although protection against theft was not always ensured (in 1438, the precious stones of the primary reliquaries of the apostles were stolen from St. John Lateran), exposing them high up facilitated their veneration by the faithful and made possible the realization of an iconographic program that all could see. In the case of Sixtus IV's ciborium, the wish to instruct the faithful was combined with gusto of execution, together with such strong archaizing influences (whole sections of the Trajan column were reproduced) that some have described the work as a pastiche. Its attribution is still an open question, although it is possible to distinguish two principal hands or workshops in the execution.

Around 1490–3, the tomb of Sixtus IV was commissioned from Antonio Pollaiolo by the deceased pope's nephew, Giulano della Rovere, the future JULIUS II. Today in the Vatican Grottoes, the bronze monument represents the pontiff lying down, surrounded by figures of the virtues and the liberal arts. The nervous agitation of the drapery and the vibrant contours of the face express vividly the righteous force of this humanist pope. The same artist was engaged for the tomb of INNOCENT VIII, which he executed in 1498, probably with the help of his brother Piero. Today, this is the oldest funerary monument in the basilica, but it was reworked during the building of the new St. Peter's: the figure of the pope, with his right arm raised in benediction, used to be below the sarcophagus where the gisant lay. The spearhead, which Innocent VIII holds in his left hand, commemorates Longinus's lance, which the Ottoman sultan Bajazet II had presented to the pontiff. Here, too, energy is Pollaiolo's keyword, but Innocent's monument, in which the bronze is partly gilded, is perhaps not as moving as the figure of Sixtus IV, where the material has the somberness of jade.

Pierre-Yves Le Pogam

Bibliography

Barbier de Montault, X. *Les Souterrains et le trésor de Saint-Pierre . . . Rome ou description des objets d'art et d'archéologie qu'ils renferment*, Rome, 1866.

Burger, F. "Die Statuen vom Ciborium Sixtus IV. in den Grotten des Vatikans," *Zeitschrift für bildenden Kunst*, 1904, 225–30.

Burger, F. "Neuaufgefundene Skulptur und Arkitektur Fragmente vom Grabmal Paulus II," *Jahrbuch der königlichen Preussischen Kunstsammlungen*, 1906, 29–141.

Burger, F. "Das Konfessionstabernakel Sixtus IV und sein Meister," *Jahrbuch der königlichen Preussischen Kunstsammlungen*, 1907, 95–116, 150–67.

Calvesi, M. *Les Trésors du Vatican*, Geneva, 1962.

Carloni, R. "Un problema di attribuzione risolto: La statua marmorea di San Pietro in Vaticano," *Roma anno 1300*, 1983, 633–42.

D'Arrigo, M. "Alcune osservazioni sullo stato originario della tomba di Bonifacio VIII," *Federico II e l'arte del Duecento in Italia, Atti della III settimana di studi di Storia dell'arte medioevale dell'Università di Roma*, Rome, 1978, Galatina, 1980, I, 373–8.

de Nicola, G. "Il sepolcro di Paolo," *Bollettino d'arte*, 1908, 388 ff.

De Waal, A. "Gli antichi tesori sacri della Basilica Vaticana," *Dissertazioni della Pontificia accademia romana di Archeologia*, Rome, 1894.

Donati, L. "L'attività in Roma di Giovanni Dalmata di Trau: La tomba di Paolo II," *Archivio storico per la Dalmazia*, 1931, 523–34, 1932, 55–66.

Galassi Paluzzi, C. *San Pietro in Vaticano*, 3 vols., Rome, 1963–5 (Le chiese di Rome illustrate, 74–8 bis).

Galassi Paluzzi, C. *La basilica di San Pietro*, Bologna, 1975 (Roma Christiana, 17).

Gardner, J. "The Stefaneschi Altarpiece: A Reconsideration," *Journal of the Warburg and Courtauld Institutes*, 1974, 57–103.

Gauthier, M. M. "La clôture émaillée de la confession de Saint-Pierre au Vatican lors du concile de Latran IV, 1215," *Synthronon: Art et archéologie de la fin de l'Antiquité et du Moyen* Age. Paris, 1968, 237–46.

Giordani, P. "Studi sulla scultura romana del Quattrocento: I bassorilievi del tabernacolo di Sisto IV," *L'Arte*, 1907, 263–75.

Kheel, C. "Giotto's Navicella Byzantinised," *Art Bulletin*, 68, no. 3, 1986, 484–5.

Körte, W. "Die 'Navicella' des Giotto," *Festschrift Wilhelm Pinder*, Leipzig, 1938, 223–63.

La cattedra lignea di San Pietro in Vaticano, Rome, 1971.

Lipinsky, A. *Il tesoro di San Pietro, Guida inventario*, Vatican City, 1950.

Maccarone, M. "Il sepolcro di Bonifacio VIII nella Basilica Vaticana," *Roma anno 1300*, Rome, 1983, 753–71.

Muñoz, A. "Reliquie artistiche della vecchia basilica vaticana a Boville Ernica," *Bollettino d'arte*, 1911, 161–82.

Müntz, E. and Frothingham, A. L. "Il tesoro della basilica di San Pietro in Vaticano dal XIII secolo al XV secolo," *ASR*, 1883, 1–137.

Orlando, F. *Il Tesoro di San Pietro*, Milan, 1958.

Paeseler, W. "Giottos Navicella und ihre Spätantikes Vorbild," *Römisches Jahrbuch für Kungstgeschichte*, 1941, 49–162.

Piccininni, R. "Sui cicli affrescati nel portico dell'antica Basilica Vaticana," *Federico II e l'arte del Duecento in Italia, Atti della III settimana di studi di Storia dell'arte medievale dell'Università di Roma*, Rome, 1978, Galatina, 1980, II, 33–40.

Salmi, M. "Il problema della statua bronzea di San Pietro nella Basilica Vaticana," *Bollettino d'arte*, 1960, 22–9.

Smith, J. and Barnes, A. *Saint Peter in Rome*, Rome, 1975.

Spencer, J. R. "Filarete's Bronze Doors at St. Peter's: A Cooperative Project with Complications of Chronology and Technique," W. S. Sheard and J. T. Paoletti, ed., *Collaboration in Italian Renaissance Art*, New Haven and London, 1978, 33–57.

Tronzo, W. "The Prestige of Saint Peter's: Observations on the Function of Monumental Narrative Cycles in Italy," H. L. Kessler and M. S. Simpson, ed., *Pictorial Narrative in Antiquity and the Middle Ages*, Washington and Baltimore, 1984 = Studies in History of Art, 16, 1985, Symposium Series, IV, 93–112.

Venturi, L. "La data dell'attività romana di Giotto," *L'Arte*, 1918, 229–35.

Venturi, L. "La 'Navicella' di Giotto," *L'Arte*, 1922.

Vitali, F. *Federico II e l'arte del Duecento in Italia, Atti della III settimata di studi di Storia dell'arte medievale dell'Università di Roma*, Rome, 1978, Galatina, 1980, II, 159–72.

Vitizthum, G. "Zu Giottos Navicella," *Italienische Studien Paul Schubring zum 60. Geburtstag gewidmet*, Leipzig, 1929, 144–55.

von Tschudi, H. "Das Konfessionstabernakel Sixtus IV. in St. Peter in Rom," *Jahrbuch der königlichen Preussischen Kunstsammlungen*, 1887, 11–24.

Modern and Contemporary Era. The basilica of St. Peter's gained ever greater importance after the return of the popes from Avignon and the end of the GREAT SCHISM. The papacy's age-old link to the city—from the time of the first bishop of Rome, St. Peter—was proudly affirmed, and this led to the enlargement of the basilica built over his tomb. Moreover, because the popes had gradually abandoned the Lateran palace for that of the Vatican, St. John Lateran—the real cathedral of Rome—found itself replaced de facto by the basilica where the presumed chair of St. Peter was preserved. Finally, in the 16th century, the symbolic power of the basilica had to be reinforced in order to counter the Protestants, who were insisting on the collegial mission of the apostles to the detriment of the authority of Peter's successors.

The first reconstruction plans date back to NICHOLAS V (1447–55), but real work on the new church began only under JULIUS II (1503–13), who ordered that half the Constantinian basilica be pulled down. The rebuilding of St. Peter's spread over more than a century, while the work of embellishment continued up to the 20th century. This was the papacy's most important building project, for which funds had to be raised from a wide variety of sources. The FABRIC OF ST. PETER'S received the exclusive right to promulgate indulgences, which had serious consequences for the Church. John Tetzel's preaching in Germany in 1516–17, aimed at gathering funds for the new St. Peter's, led Luther to nail on the door of Wittenberg cathedral his famous 95 theses against the traffic in indulgences, the starting point of the REFORMATION.

History of Rebuilding. After much discussion, Julius II (1503–13) summoned the architect Donato Bramante (1444–1514), and work began on 18 April 1506. Bramante had conceived a church in the shape of a Greek cross surmounted by a dome. He wanted, he said, to "perch the Pantheon on top of Maxentius's basilica," and planned a much larger building than the one that was eventually elected. By the death of Julius II, followed shortly by Bramante's, the four semicircular arches that supported the dome had been built, as well as the choir and the apse. LEO X (1513–21) in 1514 called on Raphael (1483–1520), who was aided by Giuliano da Sangallo and Fra Giocondo. Between 1520 and 1546, the architect with overall responsibility for the project was Antonio da Sangallo the Younger (1483–1546), with Baldasare Peruzzi acting as his second-in-command. Finally, in 1546, PAUL III (1534–49) summoned Michelangelo (1475–1564).

Many of the plans each architect drew up are available to us. All agreed on the need for a dome, but some preferred buildings designed on a centered plan, usually in the shape of a Greek cross and inspired by the martyria, which were closer to Renaissance ideals and allowed for an ambulatory around St. Peter's tomb. Others, by contrast, suggested plans in the shape of a Latin cross, with a longer nave; they believed that it was important to keep alive the memory of Constantine's basilica and to make it possible for more of the faithful to attend the pontifical Mass celebrated over the tomb. In addition, a Doric structure was built as a provisional measure to protect the high altar and confession and was not destroyed until 1591.

Michelangelo set his stamp on the work, returning to the centered design originally proposed by Bramante. He wanted a square church, anchored by apses to the north, south, and east, and to the west by a colonnade inspired by that of the PANTHEON. The interior clearly revealed a Greek-cross plan with four immense chapels linking the four naves. The first two to be built were the chapel of the Column and that of the Kings of France, or St. Michael's chapel; the Gregorian chapel was built and decorated under GREGORY XIII (1572–85), and the Clementine chapel under CLEMENT VIII (1592–1605). Construction was already well under way when Michelangelo died, and his successors—essentially, Giacomo Vignola (1507–73) and Giacomo della Porta (1540–1602)—were ordered by the popes to follow the models he had left behind. The last stone of the dome was laid in SIXTUS V's reign (1585–90), on 14 May 1590.

Also under Sixtus V, at the cost of huge expense and effort, Domenico Fontana in 1586 erected an obelisk from Nero's Circus. Other obelisks had been set up in front of St. Mary Major and St. John Lateran, but the greatest was kept in reserve for St. Peter's. As the work progressed, the popes set about commissioning altarpieces for the basilica. Cesare Nebbia, Girolamo Muziano, Nicolo Pomarancio, Lodovico Cigoli, and others produced scenes from St. Peter's life during the papacies of Gregory XIII, Sixtus V, and especially Clement VIII. It was this last pope who ordered mosaics for the pendentives (based on Nebbia's drawings) and for the dome, which was decorated according to the cartoons of Cavaliere d'Arpino.

Nevertheless, the church was radically altered by PAUL V (1605–21), who in the early 17th century ordered Carlo Maderno (1556–1629), the new basilican architect, to lengthen the nave by three bays, thus establishing a definitive plan in the shape of a Latin cross. The prolongation of the nave had awkward consequences. The dome was now farther away from the façade and could hardly be seen by a visitor standing at the foot of the basilica. Paul V, eager to see his name on the new church, then commissioned Carlo Maderno to design a façade, which was completed in 1614. It has been severely criticized: too wide for its height and clearly showing two stories (that of the entrance and that of the Benediction loggia), with an attic story above, the façade suggested a palace rather than a church. There was a plan to balance the design with two bell towers surmounting the two outer bays, but these were never built. The whole façade exuded an immense sense of order, reinforced by the columns around the door. Soon, statues of Christ and the apostles topped the attic story. Below the Benediction loggia was a bas-relief by Alessandro Bonvicino showing the handing over of the keys.

With the completion of the edifice, it remained to enhance it with decoration worthy of its architecture. This task fell to the popes of the 17th and 18th centuries. GREGORY XV (1621–23) commissioned some major paintings for the 1625 jubilee year. But URBAN VIII (1623–44), who had consecrated the new basilica on 18 November 1626—13 centuries after the first consecration by Pope Sylvester—was the one to whom St. Peter's owes its present character.

Not until 1629 did Urban VIII engage Bernini as basilica architect, although in 1624 he had asked him to redesign the crossing of the transept. From then until his death, there were few moments when Bernini (1598–1680) was not busy with either the ornamentation of the church or the reworking of its architecture. The basilica owes its character largely to his efforts. First of all was the question of the alteration of the crossing, below the dome and over St. Peter's tomb. In the Middle Ages, the altar was surmounted by a baldachin, and it was

this that led Bernini to conceive the gigantic baldachin of bronze, resting on serpentine columns that were inspired both by the Constantinian basilica and, in particular, by the columns of the temple of Solomon. The baldachin is 29 meters high. The shape of the columns and the volutes that top them help give the monument its exceptional energy. The ancient bronze adornments of the Pantheon were sacrificed to provide material for the baldachin. Everywhere, on the columns and bronze draperies, are the Barberini bees. Bernini also hollowed out large recesses in the pillars supporting the dome and had four statues created, corresponding to the most precious relics in the basilica. The holy spear is evoked by the statue of St. Longinus, the work of Bernini himself; the head of St. Andrew by the statue of that saint, executed by François Duquesnoy; for the Sudarium, Francesco Mochi carved a statue of St. Veronica; and, finally, the fragments of the true Cross are evoked by a statue of St. Helena, the work of Andrea Bolgi.

Other major monuments in the basilica were entrusted to Bernini. He designed the pope's tomb in the choir, balancing it with that of Paul III, which he moved from the Gregorian chapel, removing two of the Virtues that adorned it. He was responsible, from 1630, for erecting the monument to Countess Matilda of Tuscany (second pillar on the right). He also provided drawings for the decoration of the nave and began to build the campaniles called for by Maderno.

A large part of St. Peter's most famous paintings were also executed under Urban VIII. These include the *Martyrdom of St. Sebastian* by Domenico Domenichino and *Christ Walking upon the Waters* by Giovanni Lanfranco, both commissioned in 1625; and the *Martyrdom of St. Erasmus* by Poussin and the *Martyrdom of St. Processo and St. Martiniano* by Valentino, commissioned in 1629.

Bernini's long dominance over the building of St. Peter's was briefly called into question after the death of Urban VIII. INNOCENT X (1644–55), in a reaction against his predecessor, submitted Bernini's plans to a committee of architects, ordered the demolition of the first campanile Bernini had put up on the façade, and concerned himself chiefly with St. John Lateran. He caused the cathedral of Rome to be completely reworked by Borromini for the 1650 Jubilee. Neverthless, at St. Peter's the work of decorating the nave went on; beyond the choir, the Barberini bees yielded place to the Pamphili dove.

The last great works that give the basilica its character were realized in the reign of ALEXANDER VII (1655–67). At this time, Bernini once more found himself overseeing the building at St. Peter's. What still had to be done was to place in the center of the apse a monument worthy of the basilica. The choice fell on the Carolingian chair, at that time held to be that of St. Peter himself. Between 1657 and 1666, Bernini oversaw the construction of the enormous bronze throne that serves as its reliquary, supported by statues of the four Fathers of the Church—St. Athanasius, St. Ambrose, St. John Chrysostom, and St. Augustine. On the back of the chair is a bas-relief representing Christ telling Peter, *Pasce oves meas*; over the chair, two cherubs hold aloft the pontifical arms. Over the whole, Bernini carved a glory of gilded bronze surrounding a window in which the dove of the Holy Spirit glows in the golden light that permeates the basilica.

The completion of the interior decoration was done in tandem with the exterior building program. Once again, it was Bernini who was charged with the task of designing a new square in front of the basilica. The colonnade was erected to mask the uneven buildings surrounding the square, to amplify Maderno's façade (which was deemed unworthy of the rest of the basilica), and finally to allow the largest possible crowds to see the pope when he gave his blessing *urbi et orbi* from the loggia of St. Peter's or from his palace apartment. In designing the square, Bernini had to take into account the obelisk set up in 1586. The solution was an elliptical square. The colonnades form a portico through which carriages could pass. They are connected to the basilica by two arms; that on the right leads to the Scala Regia. A third arm, designed to close off the square, was never built.

Also under Alexander VII, Bernini was responsible for creating a monumental approach to the Vatican palace from St. Peter's square. He came up with the Scala Regia. At the spot where one left the stairway and turned to join the atrium of the basilica, he placed another distinguished work, his statue of Constantine (1662–70), thereby creating a theatrical effect for visitors before they even entered the nave.

Virtually all that was left to Alexander VII's successors was to complete a program of decoration that was well under control. CLEMENT X (1670–76) once again called on Bernini to build and decorate the chapel of the Holy Sacrament. The colonnade was to be adorned with 140 statues of saints, executed from Bernini's drawings. The sculptures were not finished until the reign of CLEMENT XI (1700–21). It was during his papacy, too, that the long series of statues of the founders of orders was begun, designed to fill the niches of the choir, transept, and nave. Left to the initiative of the religious orders, these were not completed until the 20th century.

In the beginning of the 18th century, it was decided systematically to copy all the paintings in mosaic work, even if that meant commissioning new ones to replace those that no longer appealed to contemporary taste. New monuments were erected during the 18th century, especially under CLEMENT XII (1730–40) and BENEDICT XIV (1740–58): pontifical tombs, monuments to commemorate rulers who had died in Rome, the Charlemagne of Cornacchini (1735) (as a pendant in the atrium of Bernini's Constantine), and monumental statues of the Virtues.

The popes of the 19th and 20th centuries were satisfied with marginal additions to the basilica. The architect Giuseppe Valadier completed the façade under PIUS VII. In lieu of ending it with campaniles, as Maderno and Bernini had planned to do, he set two clocks over the last bays. To maintain the decorative tradition of the basilica, Rome's best sculptors were commissioned to create new papal tombs. To the shock of the Roman artists, a Danish Protestant sculptor, Albert Thorvaldsen, was asked to work on the tomb of PIUS II. Only the monument of PIUS XII and that of JOHN XXIII clash with the decorative scheme carried out since the 17th century.

The only major alteration of the 20th century followed the signing of the LATERAN ACCORDS. At that time, the basilica's statute was laid down. The square and the basilica belonged to the Vatican City State, their safety being guaranteed by the Italian state (which explains why the police were able to intervene during the attempted assassination of JOHN PAUL II in 1981). Improved access to Rome was provided by the Via della Conciliazione, after many houses in the Borgo were pulled down. The street was intended to symbolize the new agreement between a unitary Rome and the Holy See. The effect of St. Peter's square was now utterly changed. The colonnade was the place where a great artery ended, no longer a square that came into view at the last moment of approach.

Symbolism. Despite the centuries of building and the many popes who wanted to set their mark on the basilica, one is still struck by the overall unity of the monument, the new symbol of the Catholic Church. Taken as a whole, basilica and square have an extraordinary coherence.

St. Peter's basilica is the most immense church in Christendom, the popes having continually taken pains to see that no Catholic church was built that would surpass it in size. St. Peter's supremacy over Rome has remained a constant preoccupation of the Holy See, even after the loss of the popes' temporal power. In 1927, PIUS XI received assurance that the cupola of the Roman synagogue would not be gilded and thus would not risk eclipsing that of St. Peter's. At the end of the 1980s, John Paul II objected to a plan to build a mosque in Rome that would have been larger than the basilica.

Nonetheless, owing to the perfect proportions of the architecture and the decision to place only colossal statues in the church, the gigantic scale of the edifice is not at first obvious. Attempts were therefore made to make it so. For example, guides never failed to point out that the baldachin (29 meters) was the same height at the Farnese palace, or that the fonts at the entrance to the central nave were supported by children (sculpted between 1722 and 1725) taller than any visitor. Further, although the dome had a diameter (42 meters) slightly less than that of the Pantheon, it was the highest of all the domes on Catholic churches (132.5 meters). To stress the exceptional length of the nave (186 meters), the dimensions of some of the largest churches in Christianity were indicated in gilded bronze lettering on the paving, from St. Paul's in London (158 meters) to St. Sophia in Istanbul (110 meters).

Just as the superiority of St. Peter's over other Christian churches had to represent the supremacy of the successor of the prince of the apostles, so the strength and splendor of the basilica must bear witness to the perpetuity and magnificence of the Catholic Church. The implicit model remained the temple of Solomon, interpreted as a symbol of the Church: in 1596, the Spanish Jesuit J. B. Villalpando had provided a carefully researched reconstruction of it. Only the most durable materials were used for St. Peter's, chiefly marble and bronze. Paintings, regarded as too fragile, were copied in mosaic from the end of the 17th century. Works predating the reconstruction of the basilica were gradually replaced. The tomb of SIXTUS IV, which remained in the basilica until the mid-18th century, was moved to the Vatican Grottoes. All that was left from the medieval period was Arnolfo Di Cambio's statue of St. Peter—perhaps because tradition had it that it was cast with the bronze of the statue of Jupiter at the Capitol—as well as Michelangelo's Pietà, and Giotto's Navicella, restored in 1610. The new church also retained Pollaiolo's tomb of INNOCENT VIII (1498).

Whereas the works of art commissioned up to the mid-17th century were intended to stress, in their subject matter, the supremacy of the Catholic Church, Bernini's works helped make St. Peter's a place that was admired as much for its artistic perfection as for the holiness of the relics it contained. Thus, the 18th-century popes insisted that their basilica contain only art of the first order. They did not hesitate to substitute pontifical tombs for altars or paintings that provided a precise iconographic cycle of the life of St. Peter. Many paintings executed at the end of the 16th century were not copied in mosaic, the latter popes preferring to replace them with works by great living artists or even with recognized masterpieces moved from other churches in Rome. For instance, Cavaliere d'Arpino's St. Michael was replaced by a mosaic copy of Guido Reni's painting of the saint for Sta. Maria della Concezione. Similarly, Domenico Passignano's *Crucifixion of St. Peter* was not copied; instead, the mosaic followed that of Guido Reni, at that time in S. Paolo alle Tre Fontane.

Certain major works of art were moved to more conspicuous sites. In 1794, under Benedict XIV, Michelangelo's Pietà, which had long been housed in the chapel of the Column to the left of the apse, was placed in the first chapel on the right. The symbolism of the basilica underwent a true evolution, which we can understand by studying the old guides. Over the years, it is not so much the message of the images that was stressed as their plastic qualities. St. Peter's became a symbol of the Church owing to its artistic perfection. Thus, the 1977 attack on the Pietà—which has since been protected behind glass—was aimed at the masterpiece preserved in St. Peter's, not at the image of the dead Christ.

Nothing was left to chance in the working out of the message to be conveyed by the statues, paintings, and other works of art—a summary of the dogma of the Church that upheld the power of the popes. The basilica set up a panorama of humanity's providential history. The domes of the side naves show prophets and sibyls and scenes from the Old Testament that prefigure the work of Salvation. The main dome is devoted to Christ and the apostles, and the pendentives to the evangelists. The whole church is bathed in the golden light that breathes from the apse, with its painting of the dove of the Holy Spirit.

The greatest emphasis, however, is on St. Peter and his mission. The two major monuments of the church provide august settings for the relics of the first bishop of Rome—his tomb, surmounted with the baldachin, and his chair, borne heavenward by four Fathers of the Church. Christ's founding words, on which Catholic ecclesiology rests, are inscribed in Greek and Latin in letters over 1.4 meters high, around the cupola as well as above the cornice. The power of the keys is conveyed by the passage *Tu es Petrus . . .* (Matt. 16, 18–19), and the universal mission by *Pasce oves meas* (John 21, 16–17). These texts are repeated by various images spread around the church. On the façade, a bas-relief by Alessandro Bonvicino (1614) represents the handing over of the keys, which is also the subject of a lost painting by Pomarancio, formerly placed near the choir, and another by Muziano, in the Benefactors' sacristy. Over the middle door of the atrium is a bas-relief designed by Bernini that shows Christ entrusting his sheep to St. Peter, a theme again taken up on the Cathedra Petri. Opposite this bas-relief is the copy of Giotto's Navicella representing Christ supporting St. Peter (Matt. 14, 28) while the other apostles tremble with fear; the same theme is echoed in a painting by Lanfranco, situated between the right transept and the choir.

The episodes of the life of St. Peter and his miracles figure in a large number of the mosaics decorating the basilica. For example, in the baptistry chapel, alongside the customary Baptism of Christ (after Carlo Maratta) is *St. Peter Baptizing Saints Processo and Martiniano* (after Passeri) and *St. Peter Baptizing the Centurion Cornelius* (after A. Procaccini).

Relics from St. Peter's family, preserved in the basilica, were given places of honor. The head of his brother, St. Andrew—returned to the church of Patras by PAUL VI in 1964—was formerly placed on the same level as three distinguished relics of Christ: the true Cross, the Veronica, and the Holy Lance. Above the body of St. Petronilla, supposed to be St. Peter's daughter, is a mosaic based on one of the largest paintings executed for the basilica (the work of Guercino, today at the Pinacoteca on the Capitol); it shows the burial of a young girl.

Quite naturally, Peter's successors have their place in the basilica. For the most part, they are represented in bas-relief on the pillars of the nave. But it is chiefly the popes' funerary monuments that help affirm the continuity of the Church. For a long time, the basilica served as a necropolis, but since there was little room for the tombs of the popes of the Middle Ages, many of them were moved to the Grottoes, and some to other churches (Pius II and PIUS III to Sant'Andrea della Valle, CALLISTUS III and ALEXANDER VI to Sta. Maria di Monserato). Only the monument of Innocent VIII (1484–92) by Antonio Pollaiolo was retained in the basilica, even though its various elements were reassembled between 1619 and 1621, creating an appearance different from the initial conception. It may be that this tomb, which was too small for the new basilica, was kept because the pope is holding the holy lance, which he had received from Bajazet II and which was one of the most precious relics preserved in St. Peter's. In the 16th and 17th centuries, as long as the basilica remained unfinished, the placement of the tombs was provisional. That of Julius II, initially planned for St. Peter's, was finally set up in S. Pietro in Vincoli; that of Paul III, originally in the Gregorian chapel, was moved to the choir. Even when the building was finished, certain popes preferred to be buried in the churches of their order (CLEMENT XIV at the Santissimi Apostoli, BENEDICT XIII at Sta. Maria sopra Minerva), in former basilicas which they had restored (PIUS IX at S. Lorenzo Fuori le Mura, Clement XII and LEO XIII at St. John Lateran, etc.), or else in churches founded by their families (Gregory XV at Sant'Ignazio, Innocent X at Sant'Agnese in Agona).

Nevertheless, many popes are buried in St. Peter's. Most of them were given monuments, either commissioned by themselves or, more usually, erected by their families or by the cardinals they had appointed. Monuments were sometimes set up long after the pontiff's death, and it could happen that the body was not buried within the monument but under a marble slab or in the Vatican Grottoes. Bernini, in his restoration of the tomb of Paul III and execution of that of Urban VIII, provided the type of composition that was adopted in the majority of cases. The pope's statue is surrounded by allegorical figures representing his principal virtues, while bas-reliefs show the salient actions of his pontificate. In the tomb of Alexander VII, which is perched over a door, he demonstrated an ingenious method of getting out of a decidedly unfavorable situation. In the 17th and 18th centuries, artists built tombs to these models, including some for popes who were long dead (that of Gregory XIII, who

died in 1585, was remade between 1715 and 1721, at cardinal Buoncompagni's expense).

The following popes have statues in the basilica: Innocent VIII, Paul III, Gregory XIII, GREGORY XIV, LEO XI, Urban VIII, Alexander VII, Clement X, INNOCENT XI, ALEXANDER VIII, INNOCENT XII, Benedict XIV, CLEMENT XIII, Pius VII, LEO XII, PIUS VIII, GREGORY XVI, PIUS X, BENEDICT XV, PIUS XI, Pius XII, and John XXIII. Those commemorated with a simple slab are LEO II, LEO III, and LEO IV. Finally, in the Vatican Grottoes are the tombs, either complete or in fragments, of DAMASUS, BONIFACE II, BONIFACE IV, GREGORY V, HADRIAN IV, NICHOLAS III, BONIFACE VIII, BENEDICT XII, URBAN VI, INNOCENT VII, Nicholas V, Callistus III, PAUL II, Sixtus IV, JULIUS III, MARCELLUS II, INNOCENT IX, INNOCENT XIII, PIUS VI, BENEDICT XV, Pius XI, Pius XII, John XXIII, PAUL VI, and JOHN PAUL I.

The tombs of Peter's successors around the apostle's tomb emphasize the continuity of the Roman Church. Other monuments are there to recall the temporal power of the popes, as well as the subordination of kings to the power of the Church. In the atrium, face-to-face, are the statues of two founders of Christian empires who were considered subjects of the pope: Bernini's Constantine and Conacchini's Charlemagne. In the basilica proper, the most noteworthy monuments of this kind are a bas-relief by Alessandro Algardi representing Leo the Great arresting Attila, and another, by Bernini, exalting Countess Matilda of Tuscany. The carving is meant both to celebrate the woman who had defended the Holy See from imperial threats and to honor one who, by bequeathing all her possessions to the pope, had made possible the extension of the Papal States in Roman Tuscany. She is shown holding up the tiara while, beneath her statue, a bas-relief depicts Emperor Henry IV kneeling before GREGORY VII at Canossa.

Together with those popes buried in the Grottoes are many cardinals and a few sovereigns: Otto II, Charlotte of Savoie-Lusignan, Christina of Sweden, the English pretender James III Stuart, and both his sons. In the basilica are monuments commemorating sovereigns who converted to Catholicism and renounced their temporal kingdoms for the heavenly kingdom, taking refuge in Rome: Queen Christina of Sweden (monument built to designs by Carlo Fontana, 1696–1702); the last of the Stuarts, Queen Marie-Clementine Sobieski (built in 1739 by Filippo Bracci); and James Stuart and his sons (sculpted by Antonio Canova).

The Church militant is also represented in the apse, the transept, and the nave by monumental statues of the founders of the main religious orders. The niches, which are on two levels, were filled with statues left to the initiative of each order and set in place as they were completed. The earliest statues are close to the choir: St. Dominic (1706), St. Francis (1725), Elias, founder of the

Carmelites (1727), and St. Benedict (1735); the most recent ones are in the nave, in raised recesses. The role of the laity is also emphasized. From the beginning of the 16th century, the popes strove to remodel the city of Rome in order to give pilgrims freer access to St. Peter's, a policy that came to fruition with the creation of the Via della Conciliazione. In front of the basilica, pilgrims are embraced by the arms of the colonnade, and surmounted by statues of saints when they come to receive the papal blessing. Finally, in both the atrium and the nave, allegorical statues remind them of the Christian virtues—the three theological and the four cardinal virtues. The basilica of St. Peter's functions at the same time as one of the most holy places of pilgrimage and as a demonstration of the superiority of the Catholic religion.

Christian Michel

Bibliography

Batattaglia, R. *La cattedra Berniniana di San Pietro*, Rome, 1943.

Borsi, U. *Bernini Architetto*, Milan, 1980.

de Tolnay, C. *Michelangelo V: The Final Period*, Princeton, 1960.

Enggass, R. *Early Eighteenth-Century Sculpture in Rome*, State College, Penn., 1976.

Francia, E. *San Pietro: da Bramante a Raffaello*, Rome, 1975.

Galassi Paluzzi, C. *San Pietro in Vaticano*, Rome, 1965, 3 vols.

Hibbard, H. *Carlo Maderno and Roman Architecture 1580–1650*, London, 1991.

Krautheimer, R. *The Rome of Alexander VII, 1655–1667*, Princeton, N.J., 1985.

Lavin, I. *Bernini and the Crossing of Saint Peter's*, New York, 1968.

Lavin, I. *Bernini and the Unity of the Visual Arts*, New York and London, 1980.

Montagu, J. *Roman Baroque Sculpture*, New Haven 1989.

Montini, R. *Le tombe dei Papi*, Rome, 1957.

Pietrangeli, C. ed., *La basilica di San Pietro*, Florence, 1989.

Rice, L. *The Altars and Altarpieces of New St. Peter's: Outfitting the Basilica*, New York, 1997.

Thelen, H. *Zur Entstehungsgeschichte der Hochaltararchitektur von St Peter in Rom*, Berlin, 1967.

Titi, F. *Studio di Pittura, scoltura et architettura nelle chiese di Roma*, 1674–1763. Contarti and S. Romano, ed., Florence, 1987.

Venuti, R. *Descrizione topografica e istorica di Roma moderna*, Rome, 1764, reed. 1977.

Villapando, J. B. *In Ezechielem explanationes et apparatus urbis ac templi Hierosolymitani, commentariis et imaginibus illustratus*, Rome, 1596–1624.

Wolff-Metternich, F. *Die Entstehung der Peterskirche zu Rom im 16. Jahrhundert*, Vienna and Munich, 1972.

SAINTS, VENERATION OF. In Christian antiquity, the veneration of saints was first and foremost a particular form of funerary worship, in this case applied to martyrs. The sole difference was that the family of the deceased was enlarged to embrace the entire Christian community. In Rome, as in the rest of the Empire, peace within the Church also marked the beginning of far-reaching changes. Worship was legal and took on more visible, official forms, thanks to imperial patronage and intervention by the pope. It is sometimes difficult to distinguish the papal initiatives from among the actions taken by the priests, but it may be affirmed that from the 4th century, all actions taken by the Roman clergy had at least the prior approval of the bishop. Once this principle was established, it became possible to discern the real policies behind the papal interventions. The cult of the saints promoted the christianization of the city of Rome and strengthened the geographical and temporal influence of the Church. Roman regulations on the manifestations of worship showed a caution unequaled in the rest of the Christian world. This reinforced the bishop's control, allowing him to place the veneration of saints at the service of a pastoral based on a very Roman and very developed sense of the unity of the church.

The Veneration of Saints and the Christianization of Rome. The popes were involved in efforts for the maintenance and upkeep of martyrs' tombs and the construction of cultural buildings, and in this way demonstrated their involvement in the cult of the saints. Even before peace had come to the Church, people displayed their pious devotion at the tombs of those who had died defending their faith. The anniversary of the death of a martyr was celebrated—doubtless later in Rome than in the east—with a *refrigeruim*, which differed from the traditional banquets only in the prevailing mood of the devotees. There were pious visits by the first pilgrims, who left their graffiti on the sanctuary at the via Appia in memory of their passage there. We know little about the role played by the bishops of Rome in encouraging these practices, and the later accounts of the lives of the saints provide no reliable information on this subject. However, after 313, the bishop of Rome accepted the benefits of imperial patronage and, therefore, took a more active part in construction efforts. We will not attempt to describe here the numerous instances of papal intervention that may be found in the entries on each of the popes of the period, or in those on the Paleo-Christian buildings of Rome.

At first, the imperial family took the initiative of donating great funeral basilicas to the city of Rome. The basilica of the Apostles on Via Appia, and the basilica ad *catacumbas*, where the faithful meet to venerate the memory of Peter and Paul, were built by the imperial family. So were the modern *martyrium* on Via Tiburtina, a large basilica near Lawrence's tomb, (which was also reconditioned) on the Via Nomentana, and the Agnes Basilica near Constance's mausoleum. Finally, there was the St. Peter's *martyrium* built on the spot where, according to tradition, his tomb had been situated.

During this early period, the buildings ordered by the popes were rather modest. Mark (336) built a basilica in the Bassilla cemetery, on the Solaria Vecchia, and JULIUS I (337–52) had a basilica constructed *ad Callistum* on via Aurelia, as well as a *martyrium* in the Valentine cemetery on via Flaminia.

For the next 50 years the roles of the imperial family and those of the bishops of Rome were reversed, as far as the construction of public buildings was concerned. The imperial family did have a basilica built on honor of St. Paul, in place of the small martyrium on the Ostiense. However, it was thanks to the efforts of successive popes that "the cult of martyrs was given monumental surroundings for the meetings of the faithful, near the tombs of the saints whose anniversaries were recorded on the calendar." (*Roma christiana*, pg. 514). DAMASUS I (366–84) was very active in ordering new construction in the cemeteries. His eulogium of the martyrs established the list of saints whom the public could worship, and his liturgical arrangement facilitated access to the tombs and the meetings of the faithful. He constructed the first underground basilica in the Valentine cemetery in honor of the martyr Hermes, and on the via Tiburtina; the *memoria* of Hippolytus, the antipope who was reconciled with the Church before dying a martyr. He invented (in the archaeological sense of the word) the tomb of the two martyrs, Protus and Hyacinth, and confirmed that of Eutychius. Damasus is known to have been responsible for many innovations and constructions, and among these he built five or six *ad corpus* basilicas and was involved in the construction of eleven other buildings. SIRICIUS, his successor, carried on his work, although the activities of successive popes mainly consisted of maintaining and decorating the structures built by their predecessors.

The sites and structures for the cult of the martyrs were located outside of the city. During the second half of the 5th, and in the 6th centuries, the veneration of saints also took place within the city, through the consecration of *tituli* and the importation of relics (see *infra*). In the suburban cemeteries, the bishop of Rome merely protected whatever existed there. In view of the prevailing hard times, they could do little else. There were four earthquakes in the city of Rome between the times of Siricius and SYMMACHUS (498–514). The city withstood three assaults, followed by sacking. Between the years 590 and 604, from the papacy of HORMISDAS to that of GREGORY I,

there were four sieges and at least one serious flood. In the midst of these trying times, Symmachus, VIGILIUS (537–55), and PELAGIUS II (579–90) were the most enterprising popes, whereas the cemeteries were rather abandoned under the papacy of JOHN II (561–74). John the Deacon, in writing about the material situation of the church in the 6th century, is quite accurate when he states: "while Pope Gregory constructed few new basilicas in his lifetime, he was conscientious in repairing the existing ones every year." Apart from the emergence of geographical design (with the initial efforts being made by the imperial family in the 4th century) and the construction efforts of successive popes in the second half of the century (then the maintenance and repair), there were other efforts made by the bishops of Rome. For example, the network of basilicas begun by the imperial families was completed, thus realizing the "plan of a systematic conquest for pilgrimage and prayer" (*Roma christiana*, p. 557). This geographical conquest, completed during the pontificate of Siricius, was further complemented with the march of time.

As new churches and basilicas were built to fill the existing gaps in the number of sacred buildings, the progressive development of a calendar for the veneration of saints also filled the gaps in the times for liturgy, thus making it possible to commemorate the anniversaries of martyrs throughout the year. Two points of reference are available to us today: the *depositio martyrum*, which was included in the calendar dating from 354, but which was written in 336, and the *Hieronymian Martyrology*, developed in the 5th century in Northern Italy, which gives us a good idea of Roman practices of the times, since it states the exact sites where the feast days of specific saints were celebrated. These calendars were developed as a result of a private initiative, but the public worship of the martyrs was official. From the 4th to the 5th centuries, the feast days were more numerous, but not because there were new martyrs. The list of martyrs had been closed when the persecutions ended, and while champions of orthodoxy such as Athanasius were venerated in the east, no such practices were observed in Rome.

The names of the deceased bishops were included in the canon of the mass after those of the martyrs, but there was, at that time, no difference between the liturgical practice and the veneration of the martyrs.

It is true that new names appeared at the end of the 5th century, but these were "imported martyrs," not new saints. It was not until the 6th century that there was public cult of saints who had not been martyrs, and who were venerated in the churches devoted to them, like St. Martin. In the calendars of the 4th and 5th centuries, the number of saints days was increased. In this way, the feasts of martyrs were observed throughout the liturgical year and filled periods during which there were no established feast days. Neither the *depositio martyrum* nor the martyrology make mention of many feast days between February and mid-April, which is the period devoted to Lent and Easter. The summer months, however, offer a real festival of saints days from June to September. The calendar thus fills the empty periods of episcopal liturgy and indicates a number of activities taking place in the large cemeteries; it represents the simultaneous conquest of time and space.

In line with the efforts toward christianization, there were also feast days which happened to coincide with pagan festivals. The feast of Saint Sebastian on 20 January was already being celebrated in 336. It fell on the day of the *ludi Palatini*. The feasts of Gordian on 10 May, and of Achileus and Nereus on 12 May, which were observed by Damasus, also correspond to a period of pagan games. The feast of Felicity and her seven sons was another celebration introduced by Damasus. It had the double advantage of distracting the faithful from the *ludi Apollinaris* on 10 July and being observed in several cemeteries at the same time, because the martyrs were not all buried together in the same place. It therefore offered several places where Christians could meet simultaneously. There is no doubt that the veneration of saints was an effective tool for conversion.

Roman Discipline. The regulation of the rituals of worship was intended to make them more ecclesial and to control an excessive piety reminiscent of pagan worship. In regulating the cult of saints, Rome was not adopting a policy that differed radically from that of other churches; it merely applied it more rigorously and systematically.

The 4th century was marked by the efforts of the church to exercise some control over the cult of martyrs. As it had been in Milan at the time of Ambrose, the practice of the *refrigerium*, which tended sometimes to degenerate into drinking bouts, was banned by the pope at the end of the 4th century, perhaps during Damasus' episcopate. This ban was not respected, since we know that at the end of the 4th century, people met to celebrate it in St. Peter's. However, archaeological and epigraphic sources confirm that the funeral banquets gradually ceased to be observed. The graffiti make no further mention of them after 373, and the gravediggers no longer built *mensae* where the faithful could place their offerings. The new liturgical arrangements after 375 show that more and more often, a mass was celebrated on the feast of the *depositio*.

The Church was even stricter in ensuring that the bodies of the martyrs were protected. Apart from the obvious desire to have a larger number of the faithful gain access to the saints (enlargement of tombs, addition of stairs, spaces where pilgrims could circulate) there were also efforts made to avoid too much direct contact with the bodies of the martyrs. A wall or enclosure was erected to avoid excessive proximity. The structure had small windows, (*fenestellae*), to allow the faithful to see. Perhaps from the 4th century, and definitely from the end of the 5th century, pieces of cloth were passed through these windows to be sanctified through contact with the body of the martyr. One may note by the way that while the objective sought was the protection of the saint, the effect was that soon the saint's body was considered sacred; the consequences of this are seen beginning in the 6th century.

The Roman discipline on relics was very strict. The bishop of Rome prohibited all translatory movement of the bodies and, even more categorically, any division of them. There are accounts that are of a much later date, but both refer to "a very old custom." In 519, Pope Hormisdas refused to allow the emperor to have relics of St. Lawrence. At the end of the 6th century, Pope Gregory refused a request from the empress for "the head of Saint Paul, or any other part of this body." The sincerity of this strict policy cannot be doubted, and it is in stark contrast to an earlier policy prevailing in the east. In 356 Constantinople imported the body of St. Timothy, and the following year that of the apostle Andrew. This was perhaps an indication of the rivalry existing between the two capitals that manifested itself in many ways. In this particular domain, Rome unquestionably dominated Constantinople, which possessed no relics of martyrs.

The refusal to divide the bodies of the saints did not, however, prevent the distribution of relics. Hormisdas sent the emperor a fragment of the grill of Saint Lawrence, and Gregory gave the empress silver keys containing shavings from the chains of St. Peter. The symbolism of these gifts was powerful. Queen Theodelina, who had received the same present as the empress, sent a priest to Rome to seek relics to put in the sanctuary she was building in Monza. He returned with vials of oil that had burned on the tombs, a list of which provides us with a precious inventory of the martyrs venerated in Rome at the beginning of the 7th century. More ordinary pilgrims had to be content with *brandea*, simple pieces of cloth that had touched the saint's tomb. Thus Rome, in its stringent approach to the veneration of saints not only differed from the churches of the east, but also from some western churches. The bishops of Milan, Bologna, and Brescia exchanged the relics of those saints created during Ambrose's episcopate. After the translations, the body of Saint Chrysogonus of Aquilea was venerated in two places at once, beginning in the 5th century.

There is one other domain where the discipline prevailing in Rome was not imitated by any other church. For the entire period under study, Rome refused to include the reading of the acts of the martyrs in the liturgy, a practice permitted or tolerated in Africa since the Council of Hippo in 397. Elsewhere in Italy the situation was rather ambiguous. The poems of Paulinus of Nola in honor of Felix were read during the celebration of the *natalis* of the saint, but we are not sure at what point. When Gregory was getting ready to write the *Dialogues*, he could find no trace of any book containing the passion of the saints in the Roman lectionaries. The *Gelasian Decree*, a text falsely attributed to that pope, but reflecting the Roman practices of his day, explicitly prohibited the reading of the Passion during the celebration of mass, and included among the banned books, two of the more fanciful passions, those of George and Saints Cyricus and Julitta. It is noteworthy that in both these cases not only did the Church of Rome not have others following its example, but rather, under Gregory's pontificate, chose to align itself with the more flexible practices of other churches.

The Cult of Saints in the Service of the Roman Pastoral. The strict control maintained by the bishop over the veneration of saints would lead one to believe that it served Roman pastoral initiative. However, a closer inquiry reveals that after having been the instrument for the conversion to Christianity, the bishop was instrumental in developing the sense of the universality and unity of the Church and affirming the strength of the episcopacy.

Hence, a special brief mention must be made of the veneration of the apostles. It is far too important an element of Roman ecclesiology to be dealt with under this heading, and there are entries that deal specifically with the subject (see articles on Peter and Paul). As Paulinus of Nola (353–431) stated, the presence in Rome of the bodies of the apostles ensured for the city a status once conferred upon it by the Empire and by its arms. All churches shared the sentiments of this Italian bishop. The large number of bodies of martyrs in Rome was a great source of prestige, and from the 4th century acted as a powerful magnet for pilgrims. Despite the large number of martyrs, Rome added more new saints to its calendar, and one must look more closely at the reason for this, as it reflects profound changes in the cult of saints and expresses a firm intention on the part of the Church.

The addition of new saints was made possible only by the transformation of the rituals of the veneration of saints. From funereal rituals which could only be practiced on the actual tomb; the practice became rather more abstract and dependent on liturgical words and gestures. There is no doubt that the reading aloud of the names of the saints in the canon of mass helped take the ritual of worship away from the cemeteries and into the churches. Meanwhile, the idea that the virtues of the saints were preserved intact in the relics was also becoming more widespread. From the 4th century, the churches in the towns, which until then had merely been meeting places for the faithful, bearing the names of their founders, began to be dedicated to various saints. The relics took the place of the bodies of the saints, and each church became a sort of *memoria martyrum*, and, with the introduction of saints who had not been martyrs, a *memoria sanctorum*. Damasus I built a church that he dedicated to Lawrence (San Lorenzo in Damaso), and perhaps a basilica built in honor of CLEMENT I, who was already considered a martyr (San Clemente). Siricius (384–99) and INNOCENT I (401–417) built on the Esquiline a chapel dedicated to Hippolytus, martyr and antipope who had been restored to the unity of the church. SIXTUS III (432–40) dedicated the basilica of Liberinus (today St. Mary Major) to the Virgin Mary, and to "the apostles" he dedicated a church that had already been built. It was later known as Saint-Peter-in-Chains (Saint-Pierre-aux-Liens), although it is not known whether the chain relics present in the church were already venerated before it was consecrated. Furthermore, the notes of the priests present at the Roman Council of 499 only make mention of a "*titulus san Matthei.*" Churches without titulus were also constructed within the city. SIMPLICIUS (468–483) built a basilica on the Celio (San Stefano Rotondo), dedicated to Saint Stephen and another to Saint Andrew, beside the St. Mary Major church. One may note that up until then, only the saints of the New Testament and Roman saints (one deacon and two popes) had been venerated in Rome. That situation was changed, however, when Symmachus (498–514) built a church dedicated to the Sicilian saint Agatha and introduced the cult to Saints Cosmas and Damian by dedicating to them a chapel close to St. Mary Major. FELIX III (526–30) also dedicated a church to them, built within an unused public building on the forum, which was granted to the Church by Theodoricus.

The notes of the priest at the Rome Council in 595 show that by then the metamorphosis was complete. All titular churches were consecrated to the honor of a saint. One may well use the word *metamorphosis* because the old churches, which formerly bore the names of their founders, were given either a new name or that of the saint whose relics they contained. Sometimes the founders of the churches were themselves canonized and had the same names as the martyrs to whom the churches were subsequently dedicated. For example, the *titulus Pammachi* (the name of the friend of Saint Jerome) was called the Church of Saints John and Paul (more likely Roman martyrs than the apostles, or the baptist). The *titulus Vestinae* became Saint-Vitale, (a Bologna martyr venerated at Ravenna), the Cecilia of the church bearing that name was not the generous matron who donated a part of an *insula* to the Christian community, but rather the gracious Roman martyr, the chaste wife of Valerian. "*Chrysogonus*" no longer referred to the name of the founder of the Trastevere church but to the martyr of Aquilea. The cult of the saints had become such an integral part of the manifestation of faith that no holy mystery was celebrated without the saints being associated with it.

We have seen that this change also ushered in the worship of "foreign" martyrs in Rome. The acceptance into Rome of the great saints of Christendom was prompted by a deliberately ecumenical approach.

By worshipping the great Eastern saints or St. Martin, "the apostle of the Gauls," the Roman church wished rather to affirm the universality of the Church than to appropriate the saints. Indeed, this latter tendency could sometimes be observed in other places, where relics imported from somewhere else would give rise to a local martyr, and here the example of St. Euphemia at Aquilea comes to mind.

Sometimes the introduction of the cult to a new saint was the result of a very specific policy: Saint Andrew, the patron of Constantinople, had a large church built in his honor when relations between the two capitals were renewed after 518. During the schism, Gelasius had chosen to consecrate a church to the memory of St. Euphemia. The martyr of Chalcedon was the protector of the great council of 451 whose authority GELASIUS I claimed was flouted when Constantinople refused to condemn Acacius. When FELIX IV dedicated the church at the forum to Cosmas and Damian, Emperor Justinian built a vast basilica in their honor at St. Cyr. Was this an indication of hagiographic custom or simply pious competition between the emperor and the pope who enjoyed the protection of Theodoric, king of the Goths?

The veneration of the Italian saints was an expression of the close relationship between their towns of origin and Rome. There were Sicilian and Campanese saints. A church had already been built by Symmachus in honor of Agatha of Catania when, in 593, Pope Gregory placed her relics in the church built for the Arians under Ricimer. This church had perhaps already been consecrated to them from the end of the 5th century. Gelasius dedicated an oratory to Nicander of Capua, as did Symmachus to Sossius of Missina. Both were regions where the papal tradition was strongly entrenched. There were also martyrs from Milan (from 404 Nabor and Nazarius, and later Gervose and Protase, from Ravenna (Apollinaris), and indirectly, from Aquilea, with Chrysogonus—from the three metropolitan bishoprics of Italy. The veneration of saints always helped the faithful to become more aware of the unity of the Church, whether it was a question of affirming the authority of Rome, or the close links between the Church of Rome and its sister churches.

The Pope and the Veneration of Saints. The popes had a more direct impact on the veneration of saints, first because of their personal devotion, and second because they themselves were the objects of veneration.

It is not our intention here to describe in detail the veneration of saints by the popes of antiquity. However, we can provide some examples, of which the most exten-

sively documented is their choice of burial sites. In the relatively short time between the end of the persecution and the papacy of LEO I, the popes chose their own final resting places, and their choices were influenced more of often than not by their desire to be buried close to a saint. SYLVESTER I, who died in 335, wished to be buried beside the saints: did he choose the Priscilla cemetery because of his predecessors MARCELLINUS I and MARCELUS I, who had been martyrs, or was it because of Felix and Phillip, the two sons of Felicity? Whatever the reason may be, his example was followed by LIBERIUS in 356 and Vigilius in 555. By that time, Vigilius himself was considered a saint beside whom it was a privilege to be buried. This was confirmed by an itinerary for pilgrims dating from the 7th century. In 352, Julius was buried in the Calepode Cemetery "beside a very holy tomb, so that he too could receive the tribute of the faithful." The "very holy tomb" was that of his predecessor, Callistus. ZOSIMUS (418), Sixtus III (440), and HILARUS (468) all left instructions to be buried near the body of St. Lawrence, close to the Via Tiburtiana Basilica. The edifices constructed by them during their lifetimes reflect the ultimate expression of their personal piety: Sixtus III had the confessional decorated and founded another church in honor of St. Lawrence. Hilarus built an entire complex near the basilica, possibly for the use of pilgrims, and constructed a monastery in which the saint could be venerated on a permanent basis, and which could also be consistently maintained. Boniface decorated Felicity's tomb and was buried in 422 in an oratory close by. It is generally felt that Boniface's devotion may be explained by the fact that during the schism that marked the beginning of his papacy, he was forced to live for some time in a cemetery. Special circumstances in the life of a pope also contributed to his veneration of one particular saint. For example, while Hilarus was a deacon under Pope Leo and also when he was his legate during the terrible "Latrocinium of Ephesus," (August 449), he took refuge in the *martyrium* of St. John. Once he became pope, he built three chapels around the baptistery of the Lateran, one of which is dedicated to John the Evangelist and another to John the Baptist. An inscription recalls that Hilarus received the saint's protection.

Pope Leo I, and all of the popes after Simplicius (with the exception of Vigilius) were buried at St. Peter's. It is still an example of the veneration of the saint, but it is also an unequivocal sign of the primacy of Rome. This manifestation confirmed an ancient tendency of papal liturgy, which consisted in honoring, in particular, those martyrs who had been members of the clergy and especially bishops. In fact, during that period the popes were the objects of veneration, even though they were not martyrs. Like those of other cities, the bishops of Rome were listed in the *memento* of the dead, after the martyrs. The calendar of 354 has kept the *depositio episcoporum* beside the *depositio martyrum*. LUCIUS I, who died in 254, heads the first list, which is the most ancient record of popes. However, for a long period during which the cult of saints was restricted exclusively to martyrs, the popes had to be content with this liturgical tribute. When saints who were not martyrs (the confessors) first appeared in the martyrology, deceased popes became saints in their own right. Habitually their *depositio* was commemorated on the anniversary of their death. In the crypt of the popes, where nine bishops of Rome are buried, only martyrs were specially venerated until the time of Damasus: Callistus himself, and to a lesser degree Cornelius and Pontian. But the devotion gradually spread to include all the popes. For example, in the 7th century the basilica of Priscilla, where Pope Sylvester was buried, was renamed the basilica of St. Sylvester. On the other hand, the author of the itinerary overlooks (could it be deliberate?) the fact that Liberius (d. 356), and Vigilius (d. 555) were also buried there. The complexity of the theological and political debates in which these two popes were involved earned for them veritable *damnatio memoriae*.

But the veneration of popes was not peculiar to Rome. In the 5th and 6th centuries, in the period following the persecution, all churches (at least those in the west) were careful to sanctify their own history. Over the years, only the greatest popes (such as a Leo or a Gregory) received veneration, which could be compared to that accorded to martyrs and other confessors. The personal devotion of particular popes to specific saints had little effect on the overall respect with which saints were regarded in Rome. Indeed, it is Rome's sensitivity to its saints and the concept of sainthood that imbue it with a sense of unity. For example, it was Lawrence's stature as a great Roman saint that made him so venerated by the popes. His greatness as a saint was not attributed to him because of the veneration of the popes. In Rome, as elsewhere, and perhaps in a more controlled way, the cult of saints in antiquity became inseparable from the expression of faith. It is not a deviation of popular piety or the influence of paganism; it is rather an element of Christian pastoral sensitivity.

Claire Sotinel

Bibliography

Acta Sanctorum, published by the Bollandist Fathers, 3rd edition, Paris, 1863.

Amore, A. *I martiri di Roma*, Rome, 1975.

Brown, P. *The Cult of Saints: Its Rise and Function in Latin Christianity*, Chicago, 1981.

De Gaiffier, B. "La lecture des actes des martyrs dans la prière liturgique," *Anallecta Bollandiana*, 72 (1954) 138–42.

Delahaye, H. *Sanctus, essai sur le culte des saints dans l'Antiquité* (Subsidia hagiographica, 17), Brussels, 1927.

DeRossi, *Inscriptiones Christianae Urbis Romae septimo saeculo antiquiores*, Rome, 1861–88.

Liber Sacramentiorum Romae aecclesiae ordinis anni circuli, éd. C. Mohlberg, Rome, 1960.

Mandouze, A. (dir), *Histoire des saints et de la sainteté chrétienne, 3: Des évêques et des moines reconnus par le peuple*, 314–604, Paris, 1987.

Pietri, C. *Roma Christiana* (*BEFAR*, 234), Rome, 1976; "Donateurs et pieux établissements d'après le légendier romain, dans *Hagiographie, cultures et sociétés, IVᵉ–XIIᵉ s.*, Rome, Études Augustiniennes, 1981; "L'évolution du culte des saints aux premiers siècles chrétiens: du témoin à l'intercesseur," *Les Fonctions des saints dans le monde occidental* (IIIᵉ–XIII 1ᵉ siècle), Rome, 1991, 15–36.

Sejorne, P. "Saints (culte des)," *DTC* 14, Paris, 1939.

SARACENS. The word "Saracens" is of Greek origin, and Ptolemy used it to designate the inhabitants of the northern Sinai Peninsula. In Byzantium, it gradually came to denote the Arabs as a group, and after that, Islamized communities. The Fathers of the Church were familiar with the word, but in the 9th century other terms were still being employed concurrently, among them Agareni, Ismaeliti, and Mauri. Thereafter, Saraceni rapidly won out. Several etymologies have been suggested, that of "son of Sarah" suggesting a remote Semitic connection.

This was the preferred term of the pontifical chancery, a generic term that for a long time was a synonym for "Turk" or "infidels." In the Romance languages, its meaning was extended to include idolaters and Gypsies, and, in modern argot, the workers in a publishing house that has been placed on the Index. As an adjective, it could signify "Middle Eastern" (e.g., of fabrics), "pagan" ("Saracen law" being a metaphor for the overly scholarly "paganism"), "cruel" or "rogue."

The papacy suffered at the hands of the Saracens much later than did the Eastern Empire or Visigoth Spain. At the begining of the 9th century, Rome and central Italy, like the other parts of a barely stabilized Frankish Empire, experienced sudden attacks by highly mobile invaders. It would be a serious mistake to view the chaotic events of the 9th to early 11th centuries as the clash of two empires or the prefiguring of the crusades. Except for Sicily, which was methodically conquered from 827, the "Saracens" of Italy were bands of adventurers, often brought in as mercenaries, who worked together with the numerous "brigands," socially displaced Christians.

Like the Normans, the Saracens first raided from the sea. From Sardinia, they sacked Centumcellae in 813. Corsica, and to a greater degree Sicily, provided them with more bases. In 846, a flotilla drew up alongside the beach at Ostia, sailed up the Tiber, and pillaged the areas of Rome outside the Aurelian wall, including the basilicas of St. Peter's and St. Paul's Outside the Walls. The response was swift and effective. After Gregory IV built, unsuccessfully, a fortress at Ostia (Gregoriopolis), Leo IV fortified the Leonine City in Rome and in 854 rebuilt and fortified Centumcellae on the present site of Civitavecchia (Leopolis). John VIII fortified St. Paul's Outside the Walls and acquired a navy. In 849, another raid was checked by the fleets of Naples and Amalfi off Ostia.

The danger was more serious in southern Italy, whose political dismemberment would later ensure the Normans' success. Here the Saracens settled in. In 838, they occupied Brindisi and Taranto; from there, the autonomous Byzantine duchy of Naples called on their help against the Lombards of Benevento. In 841, they destroyed Capua and settled in Bari for some 30 years. The emperor's son, Louis II, came down to fight them, aided by the Byzantines. The results were mixed. Pope John VIII pursued the struggle, with the agreement and in the place of the new emperor, Charles the Bald. He succeeded in drawing the bishop of Naples away from the Saracen camp. Naples, Gaeta, and Amalfi paid them tribute. Various Saracen bands set up camp as far as Sabina and the mouth of the Garigliano.

The great abbeys were sacked: San Vicenzo of the Volturno in 881, Monte Cassino in 883, Farfa in 897. Pressure came to a head in the years 880–910, threatening Roman pilgrimages and devastating the great estates. The papacy reacted with the aid of the Roman barons, the Byzantine fleet, and the cities of the Campagna, brought together by John X. In August 915, the raiders' lair at Garigliano was attacked and destroyed and the area around it mopped up. The danger moved toward northern Italy and Provence and pulled back to the extreme south of Italy.

In the 11th century, the papacy supported various operations in which "reconquest" contested with piracy. In 1016, Benedict VIII personally took part in the naval battle of Luni, which allowed the forces of Pisa and Genoa to win Sardinia. Papal consent may have been given in 1087 to the short-lived sack of Mahdia (Tunisia) and certainly, in 1092, to the Pisan seizure of Corsica. In 1113–14, Paschal II gave the Cross to the participants in a raid, organized by Pisa, against the Balearics. Now crusade was in the air.

From then on, the papacy had to act on another front. It had to continually renew the basically ineffective prohibition against Christian trade with Islam: wood, arms, textiles, horses, slaves (Slavs, who were also Christians— one cannot always be particular), as well as spices, precious textiles, and gold. Letters registered by the papal chancery under Innocent IV (1243–54), demonstrate how the pope lifted the excommunication incurred on these grounds by the inhabitants of the March of Ancona (Registres, no. 73) and the diocese of Tarragona (no. 3731), and gave out authorizations for trading to the inhabitants of the diocese of Cuenca (no. 3303), Mallorca (no. 3731), and the Latin Empire of Constantinople (nos. 6586 and 6831).

Religious and intellectual relations had to be approached with similar subtlety. Any attempt at missionary activity was vain, but a better acquaintance with Islam was soon acquired. The Qur'an was translated on the initiative of the abbot of Cluny in 1141–3. Ignorance was rife, and on both sides. Yet for all the Christians who continued to believe that Muhammad worshiped Venus and Apollo and that the "Mohammedans" were pagans or heretics, there were many intellectuals of the 13th century who proclaimed their admiration for Arab science.

The real contacts were through Spain rather than Rome, yet the papal court was in a good position to become acquainted with Islam. Anasthasius Bibliothecarius in the 9th century was still receiving Byzantine works of uneven reliability. Nonetheless, Gregory VII wrote in 1076 to Prince Al-Nasir on the consecration of a bishop in the Algerian port of Bougie: "We owe this charity, you and I, to each other even more than we owe it to other peoples, since we recognize and confess, in a different way it is true, one God whom we praise and worship each day as the creator of the ages and master of this world." Words written for the occasion, certainly, but which nevertheless reflect the clear-eyed consciousness of a common Abrahamic origin.

Olivier Guyotjeannin

Bibliography

Cahen, C. *Orient et Occident au temps des croisades*, Paris, 1983 (with bibliography).

Cilento, N. "I Saraceni nell'Italia meridionale nei secoli IX e X," *Archivo storico per le provincie napoletani*, 77 (1959), 109–22, repr. in *Italia meridionale longabarda*, Milan-Naples, 1971, 135–66.

Toubert, P. *Les Structures du Latium médiéval*, Rome, 2 vols., 1973 (BEFAR, 221), 311–12, 970–3.

von Wartburg, W. *Franzözisches etymologisches Wöprterbuch*, 11 (1964), 217–21.

SCHISM. Throughout the history of the Catholic Church, and, as defined by it, schism has in its broadest sense meant a separation from the ecclesiastical communion. However, it differs from Apostasy and Heresy in that the separation does not involve a question of truth of belief or a doctrine demanding submission. In the restricted sense that has prevailed in canon law, the term signifies refusal to submit to the pope or to be in communion with the members of the Church subject to him (canon 751 of the 1983 CODE OF CANON LAW). In short, and as a practical matter, the offense of schism, for one baptized, consists in separating oneself from the unity of the Church. According to St. Thomas Aquinas, the unity of the Church comes about from the union of its members among themselves and their union with their head, the pope (*Summa theologica*, IIa-IIae. Q.39, art. 1). Therefore, a schismatic is one who separates himself from one or the other of these unions, and does so knowingly and doggedly (*pertinaciter*).

Thus, a clearly declared intention and a demonstration of seriousness are demanded. The baptized person must give evidence, by clear actions, of his desire for separation (unlike schismatic thinking, which is simply a fault, not an offense incurring censure), and he or she must express a repeated and systematic refusal to acknowledge the authority of the Church (unlike disobedience, which can be merely a transitory act). For Catholic schismatics, the penalty provided is EXCOMMUNICATION *latae sententiae* (today formulated in canon 1364 of the Code of 1983).

Schisms of the First Centuries

Schisms of the First Centuries A.D. The early centuries of the history of the Church were a time of considerable doctrinal and theological turmoil, in which orthodox opinion—which in those days was chiefly that of the most powerful—could be imposed only gradually. As it encountered the diverse ideas about heresy coming from many quarters, orthodox opinion was able to formulate a number of dogmatic positions; at the same time, it was obliged to describe its faith in detail. Certain heterodox movements, which gained strength as they gained numbers, had from the 2nd and 3rd centuries been able to find institutional expression and to form communities. Thus the first schisms came into being, some of which were far-ranging in effect.

Marcionism. Marcion (a. 85–a. 160) came from Asia Minor and taught in Rome. A complex personality, he espoused the ideas of the Docetics (from the Greek *dokein*, "to seem"), a fairly widespread movement at the time, according to which Christ's humanity was only apparent and he therefore did not effectively become incarnate. Marcion also confronted the contrast between the loving God of the Pauline epistles and St. Luke's gospel, and the terrifying God of the Old Testament. He was excommunicated in 144. The schismatic Marcionite church, which was well organized and preached a severe morality, included communities in Syria that persisted until around the 5th century.

Novatians. Theologians were divided on the proper treatment of the so-called *lapsi*, those Christians who had complied with Decius's edict of 250 laying down the obligation to sacrifice to the pagan gods. Some advocated the condemnation of the lapsed Christians, whereas others recommended their pardon or reintegration into the Church. The bishop of Carthage, St. Cyprian, believed that they should be reconciled, after a strict penance, basing his argument on the power Christ conferred on the Church to bind and unbind on earth. On this point, he opposed the Roman theologian Novatian, who advocated uncompromising severity. Condemned by a council summoned by Pope CORNELIUS (251–3) and held in Rome in 251, Novatian refused to submit and founded a schismatic Church that survived up to the 7th century, some of its communities extending to Alexandria.

Donatism. Bishop of Numidia in North Africa, Donatus disputed the validity of the accession of Caecilian to the bishopric of Carthage (312), accusing him of turning the Scriptures over to Emperor Diocletian during the persecutions of the early 4th century. Donatus had another bishop elected to the position, to which he himself soon succeeded. Condemned by the Council of Arles in 314, Donatus attracted a large part of the then important Numidian Church into a schismatic movement. This became even stronger after his exile and his death in 355. At a colloquy organized by Emperor Honorius in Carthage, St. Augustine won the debate with the Donatists, whose last remnants were annihilated in the Vandals' raids on North Africa from 430.

The Byzantine Schism

The Byzantine Schism. The first great historic rupture of the unity of the Church took place in the mid-11th century, when the Roman West and Byzantine East—the Latin and Greek Churches—broke apart. Even today the influence of the schism is still felt, despite the efforts made by ECUMENISM since the pontificate of JOHN XXIII (1958–63).

Deep cultural differences between the two groups—the use of the Latin or Greek language, the rise of a northwestern Europe that was largely alien to Byzantium, and the opposition of two societies that were closed and close to autarchy—unquestionably played a major part in this rupture. Yet they cannot be considered among the immediate causes for separation. These are to be found in the religious domain, both theological and canonical.

The conflict became crystallized over the question of the Procession of the Holy Spirit, which the ecumenical councils of Nicaea (325) and Constantinople (381) held to proceed from the Father alone. The Roman West later affirmed that the Spirit proceeded from the Father and the Son (*a Patre Filioque*), countering Photius, patriarch of Constantinople, who in the 9th century supported the decision of the earlier councils, thereby provoking a temporary schism with Rome. This episode followed a crisis pitting iconodulists against iconoclasts in 8th-century Byzantium, as well as many doctrinal debates over questions of liturgy (e.g., use of unleavened bread in the Eucharist) and ecclesiastical discipline (e.g., priestly celibacy, wearing of beards by clerics).

These disputes, which were later considered somewhat specious ("Byzantine quarrels"), nevertheless represented for contemporary thinkers fundamental issues whose solution came with the affirmation of Roman pontifical primacy. When Leo IX (1049–54) noted that the old slanders were being hurled against Rome with renewed vigor, probably at the instigation of the patriarch of Constantinople, Michael Cerularius, he sent Cardinal Humbert of Moyenmoutier as legate to the capital of Eastern Christianity. On 16 July 1054, the cardinal entered Santa Sophia in the middle of the mass and placed on the altar a bull of Leo IX excommunicating the patriarch. Shortly thereafter, Michael Cerularius called a council, known as the synod of Constantinople, which in a counterbalancing move issued a general excommunication of the "Latins." Despite several more attempts, two of which did lead to acts of union (council of Lyon, 1274; council of Florence, 1439), the separation remained in force; the exactions of the Fourth Crusade in 1201–4, in particular, engendered a lasting hatred of the Latins.

VATICAN II, to which observers from non-Catholic Churches were invited, and the meeting—at once hailed as "historic" by the media—between PAUL VI (1963–78) and Patriarch Athenagoras of Jerusalem (January 1964) certainly marked the beginning of a new era in Rome's relations with the Orthodox world. The solemn declaration that the two leaders pronounced on the eve of the close of the council (7 December 1965) officially lifted the reciprocal excommunications of 1054. Each side expressed regret for the "historic wrongs" done to the other, although agreement was not reached on the debate over the conception of the government of the universal Church.

The Great Schism of the West (1378–1417). In spite of the name by which it is still known, the Great Schism does not come under the strict definition of schism. At the time, there was no question of separation with the Catholic Church, but only a conflict over the legitimacy of the choice and election of those who claimed the papal see.

The Lutheran Reformation. This was initiated by Martin Luther, a German Augustinian friar and professor at the University of Wittenberg in Saxony, who in 1517 posted a declaration containing 95 points (or "theses"). This stigmatized, in particular, the traffic in indulgences that was practiced by Rome and designed especially to finance the building of St. Peter's basilica. Condemned by Pope LEO X (1513–21) in his bull *Exurge Domine* in 1520, and excommunicated the following year, Luther gradually adopted increasingly radical and uncompromising positions regarding the person of the pope and the institution of the Church in its Roman configuration. At the same time, he worked out a theology centered on

three points he considered fundamental: the unique authority of Holy Scripture (*sola scriptura*) as against tradition as the source of faith; justification of the Christian by faith alone (*sola fide*) and not by works; and the universal priesthood of Christians in place of bowing to a caste of priests.

The Anglican Reformation. England's geographical distance from Rome, together with notable differences in the matter of religion—for instance, the traditional independence of the English monarchy vis-à-vis the papacy, or the evangelical movements of Wycliffe and the Lollards in the 14th and 15th centuries—no doubt prepared favorable ground for the ideas of the Protestant Reformation. Nonetheless, the birth of the Anglican Church had little to do with theology. Rather, it resulted from a personal conflict between King Henry VIII of England and Pope CLEMENT VII (1523–34), from whom, despite repeated demands, Henry failed to obtain the annulment of his marriage to Catherine of Aragon. In 1533, Henry had his new union with Anne Boleyn blessed and his previous marriage pronounced null and void by Archbishop Cranmer, primate of England, who had been appointed to settle the question and was devoted to the king's cause. Excommunicated by the pope, who declared this second marriage invalid (1534), the king lost no time in arranging for Parliament to pass the Supremacy Act, whereby he appeared as the supreme head of the English Church. Schism occurred, despite Henry's personal loyalty to the Catholic faith. But Cranmer, who was imbued with Lutheran ideas, caused the Anglican Church to develop along Protestant lines.

In spite of a period of Catholic restoration under the reign of Mary Tudor (1553–8), followed by the search for a middle way with Elizabeth I (r. 1558–1603), relations with Rome came up against the question of Anglican ORDINATIONS. PAUL IV (1555–9) declared these invalid in 1555. Later attempts at reconciliation failed. Thus, when Lord Halifax and Abbé Portal put forward their proposals for reunion (1893–6), LEO XIII (1878–1903) confirmed the invalidity—and hence the unacceptability—of such ordinations within the Roman Church, in his encyclical *Apostolicae curae* (13 September 1896). Dialogue was later resumed on different bases; the latest development was a decision of the General Synod of the Anglican Church to admit women to the priesthood (11 November 1992), as a result of which some conservative Anglicans asked to be allowed to join the Catholic Church.

Old Catholics. On 6 December 1864, PIUS IX announced the First Vatican Council (VATICAN I). That was two days before the publication of the encyclical *Quanta cura*, which detailed a program for strengthening society against modern errors and was followed by the listing of the 80 theses of the *Syllabus Errorum*. In the pope's thinking, the council would complete the doctrinal work that he had initiated.

Controversy arose around the council's bull of convocation (*Aeterni patris*, 29 June 1868), which left out any reference to the issue of infallibility as a fundamental question that the Fathers should debate. Rome's silence was interpreted in various ways. Some deemed the proclamation of infallibility indispensable in order to defeat the demagoguery of the civil states, most of which held revolutionary principles and were proclaiming their hostility to the Church. Others, by contrast, saw in this idea the beginnings of a disguised dictatorship, doomed to the errors and excesses of despotism.

The debate aroused intense interest in countries of German language and culture. These were, although in different ways, all hostile to an ULTRAMONTANISM that exalted a medieval model of Christianity founded on the extreme principles of the bull *Unam Sanctam* regarding relations between the Church and the civil powers. Some evoked the humiliation of Henry IV at CANOSSA or "the specter of Charlemagne imposing baptism on the Saxons" (R. Aubert). A minority opposition to infallibility took shape as the debates continued at the heart of the council itself. Its leader was Cardinal von Schwarzenberg, archbishop of Prague, a friend of the theologian Johannes Friedrich, who himself had been the pupil of Ignaz von Doellinger (1799–1890), dean of the theological faculty of Munich and a distinguished intellectual figure of the time. The primate of Hungary, as well as the virulent Bishop Josip Strossmayer of Croatia, feared Roman centralism as a cause of dissension between Church and state in their respective countries. Others, like the German professors Carl Joseph Hefele and Wilhelm Ketteler, joined the minority out of a more objective conviction.

At first, the tone of the controversy was moderate. From February 1870, following discussion of the additional text to chapter XI of the schema *De Ecclesia*, which was directly concerned with the definition of infallibility, there was palpable agitation in Germany. The historian Janssen warned his Roman friends of the imminent danger of the rise of an "old Catholic community," which risked provoking "a great ecclesiastical catastrophe." Ignaz von Doellinger, who up to that time had stayed apart from the debate, emerged from silence by publishing a violent article against the planned definition of infallibility (21 January 1870). The submission of the episcopate of the German-speaking countries to the constitution *Pastor Aeternus* (voted 18 July 1870) followed soon after. It was motivated in part by the danger of depreciating ecclesiastical authority in the eyes of the faithful if there were prolonged doctrinal opposition.

The scene was not the same in the universities. Addressing the archbishop of Munich, Doellinger evoked the "old Church" and, with the help of a canonist from Prague, Johann von Schulte, encouraged a meeting of university representatives aimed at drawing up a declaration that would reject the decree regarding infallibility. The movement attracted few supporters, however, save among older priests; the young clergy, like the mass of the faithful, were touched only superficially. Seeing itself isolated and diminished, the university group resigned itself to witnessing the solemn excommunication of Doellinger (23 April 1871). At the congress of Munich, in May 1871, Doellinger opposed the constitution of schismatic communities, but the majority voted for the creation of parishes to harbor the few thousand Catholics who had refused to recognize the council. At the peak of its expansion, around 1877–78, the movement numbered 52,000 members in Germany and Austria, divided among 122 parishes, and in Switzerland, 73,000 supporters among 46 parishes. Rather than "Old Catholics," the latter called themselves members of the "Catholic Christian Church."

China. At a time when communist governments were urging the formation of "national churches" free of any Roman influence (Hungary, Poland, Czechoslovakia), in 1951 the media made much of rumors regarding certain maneuvers of the Beijing government. Under the leadership of Chou En-lai, it was exhorting Chinese Catholics to proclaim an independent Church. This would be done in the name of a threefold autonomy—economic (*tze-yang*), administrative (*tze-chich*) and missionary (*tze-ch'uan*). Underlying the movement was the desire to weaken the local Church in matters of doctrine (manifesto of Kuang-Yuan, 13 December 1950). In line with the communist policy of opposition to Western interference, Rome was charged with imperialist designs. Whereas the Chinese Protestant churches had quickly proclaimed their total independence of ties to any foreign government in matters of missionaries and money, thereby affirming their nationalist sentiments, the Catholics saw themselves accused of a lack of patriotism, with the consequences—loss of employment, police interrogations, imprisonment—that this implied.

The declarations that the Chinese government demanded of Catholics therefore took on a schismatic character. The apostolic internuncio in China, Msgr. Antonio Riberi, was suspected of unpatriotic dealings. At a trial organized in the presence of Protestant and Buddhist dignitaries (June 1951), he was supported by Father Tong Che-Tche, a priest from the diocese of Nanjing, who reproached the representatives of the other faiths for their compromises with the Chinese government. In his encyclical *Ad Sinarum gentem* of 7 October 1954, PIUS XII condemned the attempt to form parochial councils and local "reform committees" made up essentially of layfolk. In so doing, he alluded to those who, "seduced by new fallacious ideologies, have recently become followers of special and nefarious principles propagated by the enemies of all religion."

The pope emphasized both the need for obedience to the civil government, in spite of tortures and imprisonment, and the denial of the principle of Catholicity and universality contained in the aim of the creation of a "national" Church. The Congregation of Propaganda made public, on 17 March 1955, a decree of excommunication *latae sententiae*, drawn up on 1 February 1952 and brought against the person of the vicar general of Nanjing, the abbé Jean-Baptiste Ly Wei-kuang. To the Holy See, he was guilty of having convened a synod of priests from the entire ecclesiastic province of Nanjing and of having forced the participants to sign a formula of "peaceful coexistence" between the Roman Catholic Church and the Chinese state. Statistics from the beginning of 1955 indicated the expulsion of 79 bishops and 7,000 missionaries and nuns, the imprisonment of three bishops and 198 priests from 54 dioceses out of the 143 in all China, and the death of four bishops and 156 priests.

Pius XII issued a passionate warning against the claims of the "pseudo-patriotic" movement that it would proceed to elect and consecrate bishops on its own (encyclical *Ad apostolorum principis* of 29 June 1958). In a consistorial allocution of 15 December 1958, and later in a Pentecost message of 17 May 1959, John XXIII evoked the Chinese situation, stating that a "grievous schism" was in the making. Although there had been no actual formalization of schism, the *Annuario pontificio* indicates that the great majority of Chinese ecclesiastical districts (29 apostolic prefectures, one apostolic exarchate, and 20 metropolitan sees) today do not have clergy.

Msgr. Marcel Lefebvre. In 1965, even before VATICAN II packed its bags, Msgr. Pailler, the archbishop coadjutor of Rouen, had publicly called attention to "independent circles" which, at the instigation of certain unnamed individuals, ran the danger of refusing obedience. He feared that "the end of this year" would see a schism in the Church of France. Father Michonneau, considered the spokesman of the modernists and an ardent defender of the council's work, feared for his part "the schism of those who keep silent" and who, without necessarily encouraging open dissidence, "would leave the Church on tiptoe."

The rumors were particularly targeted at Mgr. Marcel Lefebvre, who was born 29 September 1905 in Tourcoing and was once archbishop of Dakar (appointed 22 September 1948, he was the first titular of that see). Shortly after that, he was named bishop of Tulle, in central France, and superior general of the congregation of the Fathers of the Holy Spirit, which he joined in 1935. Giving up his episcopal seat, in September 1968 he founded at Fribourg the St. Pius X International Priestly Fraternity, which received its provisional constitutional approval from the hands of the diocesan bishop of the see in 1970. In 1976, he was found guilty of ordaining 13 priests without the consent of the bishop of Sion, Switzerland, under whom he served. He was suspended *a divinis* on 22 July 1976 and was not granted renewal of the canonical approval conceded to the fraternity. Several proposals tending to steer the community toward an act of submission to the pope were made by the pontiff himself, in the form of personal letters bearing the respective dates of 29 June 1975, 8 September 1975, and 15 August 1976.

On 29 August 1976, a speech given in the Sports Palace of Lille made clear the Maurras-inspired monachist roots of the movement, as exemplified by other protesters, such as Jean Madiran and the abbé Georges of Nantes, who actually did not see eye to eye with Msgr. Lefebvre. The objections put forward by the movement officially concerned only two documents of Vatican II: the declaration on religious freedom, and that on the relations of the Church with other religions. The Vatican spokesman revealed, in a declaration of 27 August 1976, that Msgr. Lefebvre had signed almost all the council texts, in particular those on the liturgy and ecumenism. Msgr. Lefebvre had been one of the active members of the Coetus Internationalis Patrum uniting Fathers of the same way of thinking, and he had prepared a series of concerted actions, for example at the time of the tabling of modi, or when it came time to vote. First, he criticized collegiality (11 October 1963, from a somewhat pastoral viewpoint, and 10 November 1963, on its principle). Next, he questioned religious freedom (24 October 1964, 20 November 1965, petitioning for a delay, 17 and 19 November 1964). He synthesized these propositions in the form of a "profession of faith" (made public in Rome on 21 November 1974): "We refuse and have always refused to follow the Rome of neomodernist and neo-Protestant tendency which has manifested itself clearly in the Second Vatican Council and after the council in all the reforms that issued from it." After being received by Paul VI at Castel Gandolfo on 11 September 1976, he devoted himself to the leadership of his seminary at Écône, in the Swiss canton of Valais. Some of his supporters got into a dispute with Archbishop Lustiger of Paris by taking over, without permission, the parish church of St. Nicholas of Chardonnet in Paris, from 27 February 1977.

Defender of a tradition that derived its essential value from its unchangeability, Lefebvre was able to recruit sympathizers from among people attached to the liturgy in the Latin language, as contained in particular in the Mass according to the rite of St. PIUS V and the catechism of the council of Trent. He also drew on a latent anti-semitism by denouncing the "immeasurable and unprecedented scandal" of the visit of JOHN PAUL II to a Roman synagogue in 1986. Condemning, in the same order of ideas, the interreligious meeting in Assisi in 1987, he made the serious charge that "the throne of Peter and the positions of authority in Rome [are] occupied by antichrists." He insisted on risking the consequences by proceeding, on 30 June 1988 at Écône, to invest four bishops, despite a protocol of agreement that had been negotiated a few months earlier with Cardinal Ratzinger (5 May 1988), which stipulated the swearing of an oath of loyalty to the pope, respect for the ecclesiastical magisterium, and the opening of a positive dialogue on liturgical matters.

Lefebvre was excommunicated on 1 July 1988. Through his *motu proprio Ecclesia Dei afflicta* (2 July), JOHN PAUL II posited that "the Apostolic See [had] given proof of patience and indulgence to the limits of the possible" and called on theologians to deepen and tirelessly explain the spirit of the Second Vatican Council. A commission designed to retain the other members of the brotherhood within the Church was set up on 9 July, without much success. The death of Lefebvre in 1991 did not end the schism; the communities henceforth went under the vague name of "traditionalists" or "integralists" and numbered some 20,000 persons in the 1990s.

François Jankowiak

Bibliography

Anzavui, J. *Le Drame d'Écône: Analyse et dossier*, Sion, 1976.

Aubert, R. *Le Pontificat de Pie IX* (1846–1878) [Histoire de l'Église depuis les origines jusqu'à nos jours, ed. A. Fliche and V. Martin, XXI], Paris, 1952.

Bonnichon, A. "Naissance des schismes," *Études*, 1956. no. 4, 29–44.

Congar, Y. *La Crise dans l'Église et Mgr Lefebvre*, Paris, 1976.

Congar, Y. *Martin Luther: Sa foi, sa réforme*. Études de théologie historique, Paris, 1983.

de Boüard, M. *La France et l'Italie au temps du Grand Schisme d'Occident*, Paris, 1936.

Decarreaux, J. *Byzance ou l'autre Rome*, Paris, 1982.

Delaruelle, E., Labande, E.-R., and Ourliac, P. *L'Église au temps du Grand Schisme et de la crise conciliaire* (1378–1449) [Histoire de l'Église et la vie religieuse en Occident à la fin du Moyen Age, Paris, 1971.

Duchesne, L. *Autonomies ecclésiastiques: Églises séparées*, 2nd ed., Paris, 1905.

Dvornik, F. *Les Legendes de Constantin et de Méthode vues de Byzance*, Prague, 1933.

L'Église et les Églises (1054–1954). Études et travaux sur la douloureuse séparation entre l'Orient et l'Occident offerts à dom Lambert Beauduin, Chevetogne, 1954.

Gschwind, P. *Geschichte der Entstehung der christkatholischen Kirche der Schweiz*, 2 vols., Bern, 1904–10.

Heiler, F. *Urkirche und Ostkirche*, Munich, 1937.

Jugie, M. "Schisme byzantine," *DTC* XIV (1939), col. 1312–1468.

Nichols, A. *Rome and The Eastern Churches: A Study in Schism*, Edinburgh, 1992.

Pétré, H. "Haeresis, schisma et leur synonymes latins," *Revue des études latines*, 1937, 316–25.

Sherrard, P. *The Greek East and The Latin West: A Study in Christian Tradition*, Limini, Greece, 1992.

Villier, M. *La Question de l'union des Églises entre Grecs et Latins depuis le concile de Lyon jusqu'à celui de Florence*, Louvain, 1922.

SCRIPTOR. Scribes "of the Lateran palace," the scriptors (*scriptores domini pape, scriptores litterarum apostolicarum*) originally were engrossers of the pontifical documents drawn up in the chancery. Charged with setting up in definitive form documents, the text of which had been written by the ABBREVIATORS, to whom they were superior in the hierarchy, by the early 13th century they constituted a college proper. Appointed by the pope, they were directed by the rescribendarius, who supervised their output and provided them with imperfect documents (not suitable for a fair copy) to write out, whence their name. Other members of the college—one or two *distributores notarum grossandarum*—divided among themselves the minutes they had to engross (write in the legal style suitable for a fair copy of a document). The college reached the traditional number of 100 members by the 13th century; it was frequently exceeded, then stabilized at 101 in 1436. But in the pontificate of BONIFACE VIII, it was noted that out of a total of 110 scriptors in 1310, only about 50 were attested as producers of documents; thus, the title must have been an honorific one for the others.

Olivier Guyotjeannin

See also VATICAN LIBRARY.

Bibliography

Barbiche, B. "Les scriptores de la chancellerie apostolique sous le pontificat de Boniface VIII (1295–1305)," *Bibliothèque de l'École des chartes*, 128 (1970), 114–87.

Schwarz, B. *Die Organisation kurialer Schreiberkollegien von ihrer Entstehung bis zur Mitte des 15. Jahrhunderts*, Tübingen, 1972, Bibliothek des deutschen historischen Instituts in Rom, 37; "Der Corrector litterarum apostolicarum . . . von Innocenz III. bis Martin V.," *Quellen und Forschungen aus italienischen Archiven und Bibliotheken*, 54 (1974), 122–91.

SECRET, PONTIFICAL. The pontifical secret must be distinguished from many other kinds of secrets, such as the natural secret, which has to do with things whose divulging might prejudice the interested parties; the promised secret, which results from a commitment, whether or not accompanied by an oath; and the entrusted secret or *commissum*, otherwise known as the professional secret, which is received on the express condition that it not be divulged, because of the position or function exercised, with a view to obtaining counsel. An example of the last is the secret of the sacrament of confession, which every confessor must respect absolutely; its violation would make the confession odious and would thereby be punished by an excommunication *latae sententiae*, which can be carried only by the Apostolic See (c. 1388 1 of the Code of Canon Law of 1983).

In the Roman Curia, the common secret is automatically imposed for all matters having to do with the service of the universal Church; its moral obligation derives from the decision of the superior, or from the nature of things, or from the particular situation. Besides this, there exists another secret: the pontifical secret, or secret of the Holy Office, which must be observed in the case of certain very serious affairs and which always involves a grave obligation.

The pontifical secret of the Holy Office was defined by CLEMENT XI (decree of 1 December 1709) and CLEMENT XIII (decree of 1 February 1759). It was restated by PIUS X (*motu proprio Romanis Pontificibus*, 17 December 1903) before it passed into the Code of Canon Law of 1917 (c. 239 § 1 and 243 § 2).

Canon 243 § 3 established as a general rule that all those belonging to the congregations, tribunals, and offices of the Roman Curia are obliged to observe secrecy regarding matters they know by virtue of their function, and to do this within the limits and according to the manner established by the regulations of each dicastery. The secret of the Holy Office must be observed by the members of that congregation. It was extended to the members of the Consistorial Congregation in the matter of the nomination of bishops, and to those of the Congregation for Extraordinary Ecclesiastical Affairs (PIUS XI, letter, 5 July 1925, in *Acta Apostolicae Sedis* XIII [1926], 89). This was therefore a secret that must be kept under penalty of excommunication *latae sententiae*, to the extent that even the Penitentiary and the cardinal penitentiary could not dispense one from the penalty, except if one were at the point of death (Pius X, *motu proprio Romanis Pontificibus*, 17 December 1903). The secret of the Holy Office is now known as the pontifical secret, following an instruction from the Secretariat of State, dated 24 June 1968.

As for the secret known simply as common, it must be observed in the other dicasteries of the Curia. Confirmed by an oath, it concerns everything that the sacred canons or the superiors order to be kept secret; similarly, it must be observed when an ordinary imposes it, or when the parties or the Church might suffer damage as a result of divulging a fact. The cardinals, consultants, and officers of the Roman congregations must observe this secret regarding all printed matter and manuscript notes which they have by virtue of their functions, whether this secret be imposed by a positive order or by the particularly delicate nature of the business.

With regard to the use of means of communication in the life of the Church, it has been laid down that every time the business at hand demands secrecy, "the general rules in use in the civil institutions must prevail"; and that secrecy will be observed only "to preserve the reputation of another person as well as individual or collective rights" (Pontifical Commission of the Means of Social Communication, pastoral instruction *Communio et progressio*, 23 May 1971, note 121).

These provisions are not present in the Code of Canon Law of 1983; however, the obligation to observe secrecy has not ceased. After a preliminary instruction on the pontifical secret of 24 June 1968 (unpublished), the Secretariat of State put out a new instruction, dated 14 February 1974. In its preamble, it presents the secret not so much as a law imposed from outside as an "obligation proper to human dignity itself," because it is aimed at the public good.

The pastoral instruction prescribes the pontifical secret for 10 categories of situations (article 1): the preparation and editing of pontifical documents, for which this kind of secret is expressly demanded; affairs of the Secretariat of State or the Counsel for the public affairs of the Church, that are known because of the function involved and that need to be dealt with under the seal of the pontifical secret; the denunciation of doctrines and books and their examination by the Congregation for the Doctrine of the Faith; the denunciation of crimes against faith and morals, and against the sacrament of penitence and the procedures relative to it; the relations of legates with the Holy See on questions marked by the pontifical secret; information relating to the creation of cardinals; information relating to the nomination of bishops, apostolic administrators, and other ordinaries bearing the episcopal dignity, vicars, apostolic prefects, and pontifical legates; information relating to the nomination of superior prelates and leading officers of the Roman Curia; everything relating to the cipher and coded correspondence; and legal cases reserved for the Roman pontiff, the heads of dicasteries, or the pontifical legates calling for the pontifical secret.

The obligation to keep the pontifical secret is imposed (article II) on cardinals, bishops, higher prelates, officers major and minor, advisers, experts, and ministers of the lower order; legates of the Holy See, their collaborators and all those with whom they consult; all those on whom the obligation to keep the pontifical secret is imposed; and all those who wrongfully obtain knowledge of a document or a matter covered by the pontifical secret, or who obtain such knowledge through no fault of their own but knowing that it fell under the pontifical secret. The General Regulation of the Roman Curia in force since 7 June 1992 recalls the obligation for the whole staff of the Curia to keep the pontifical secret and, in particular, the pontifical secret according to the instruction *Secreta continere* (article XXXVIII).

In each case, there exists a serious obligation which persists even after the affairs for which the secret was imposed are closed. Anyone who infringes the secret externally must be judged by a special commission set up by the cardinal prefect of the competent dicastery, who must impose a penalty in proportion to the wrong committed. If the one who violates the secret works for the Roman Curia, he will receive the disciplinary penalties provided for in article III: suspension from office for violation of the professional secret (General Regulation of the Roman Curia, article LXIX, 5) or dismissal for violation of the pontifical secret (article LXXIII 1, 3). An appeal against these penalties is possible (article LXXVIII).

The individual who is bound by the pontifical secret must swear with these words (article IV): *Ego . . . constitutus coram . . . tactis per me sacrosanctis Dei Evangeliis, promitto me fideliter "secretum pontificium" servatum esse in causis et in negotiis que sub eodem secreto sunt tractanda, adeo ut nullo modo, sub quovis praetextu, sive maioris boni, sive urgentissimae causae, secretum praefatum mihi violare liceat. Secretum, ut supra, me servaturum esse promitto etiam causis et negotiis finitis, pro quibus tale secretum expresse imponatur. Quod si in aliquo casu me dubitare contingat de praefati secreti obligatione, in favorem eiusdem secreti interpretabor. Item scio huismodi secreti transgressorem peccatum grave committere. Sic me Deus adjuvet, et haec Sancta sua Evangelia, quae propriis manibus tango.*

The Secretariat of State (declaration, 29 December 1981) invited the prefect of the Roman dicasteries and the pontifical legates from the whole world to remind their coworkers of the strict obligation of the pontifical secret and to punish its violation (J.-B. D'Onorio, *Le Pape et le gouvernement de l'Église*, 501).

The General Regulation of the Roman Curia gives, in annex I, the text of the profession of faith that was enforced on 1 March 1989; in annex II, that of the oath of loyalty and the command of the same date to observe the professional secret, with a penultimate supplementary paragraph: "In addition I swear, I affirm and I promise to accomplish with diligence the tasks that are entrusted to me in this Office and to observe religiously the professional secret; I promise at the same time not to seek and not to accept presents in remuneration of my task, even in the form of a gift." (*Insuper spondeo, voveo ac promitto me ministeria mihi commissa in hoc Officio diligenter impleturum et secretum officii religiose servatum; simulque promitto munera mihi in remunerationem, etiam sub specie doni oblata, nec quaesiturum, nec recepturum.*)

Last, annex III includes a promise that must be made by the clerks, ushers, and auxiliaries: "I . . . promise to God to be faithful to the sovereign pontiff and to his legitimate successors and rigorously to observe the professional secret; I promise to fulfill with diligence all my duties and to observe the orders which will be given me by my superiors."

Dominique Le Tourneau

Bibliography

Arias, J. "Las normas sobre secreto pontificio. Sistema de defensa," *Ius Canonicum*, XIV, 28 (1974), 332–50.

Cadène, F. "De secreto S. Officii," *Analecta ecclesiastica*, 5 (1897), 498–504.

d'Onorio, J.-B. *Le Pape et le Gouvernement de l'Église*, Paris, 1992.

Echappé, O. "Le secret en droit canonique et en droit français," *ibid.*, 29 (1985–6), 229–56.

Gennari, C. "Sul segreto del S. Officio," *Il monitore ecclesiastico*, 22 (1897), 174–86.

Lefebvre, C. "Le secret pontifical," *L'Année canonique*, 19 (1975), 164–7.

Naz, R. "Secret," *DDC*, Paris, 7, 1965, 895–99.

Pius X, Apostolic Constitution *Sapienti consilio*, 29 June 1908, *Normae peculiares*, IV, 5.

Secretariat of State, instruction *Secreta continere*, 4 February 1974, *Acta Apostolicae Sedis*, 76 (1974). 89–92; General Regulation of the Roman Curia, 7 June 1992.

SECRETARIAT OF BRIEFS. This is one of the offices of the Roman Curia responsible for the dispatch of documents known as "BRIEFS." Its origin is linked to the complications of assigning responsibility for the writing of briefs to various secretaries, depending on the contents or destination of the documents. Secret briefs—those having to do with political matters or ecclesiastical matters concerning important people—were entrusted by INNOCENT VIII (bull *Non debet*, 31 December 1487) to secretaries known as "domestics." During the years 1560–6, as their work became specialized, they were split into two distinct offices: the Secretariat of Briefs and the Secretariat of Briefs to Princes.

The Secretariat of Briefs was essentially responsible for graces and dispensations granted to cardinals, legates, nuncios, and other ministers of the Holy See. It also recorded certain bulls that were sent "by secret way"—that is, outside the DATARY—as the pope saw fit. BENEDICT XIV, with the bull *Gravissimum Ecclesiae* (26 November 1745), defined the duties of the Secretariat of Briefs and the Datary for the granting of graces, giving the former wide powers to grant graces in the ecclesiastical as well as the civil domain: government, private law (trusts, entailed properties, legitimations, etc.), worship, indulgences, appointments to civil and curial posts, granting of honorary titles, and all graces that the secretary of briefs could obtain directly from the pope during an audience. This secretary was often a cardinal, and always so from the 18th century on.

From the pontificate of PIUS VII the post became one for life. With the curial reform of 1908, PIUS X changed the secretariat into one section (section III) of the Secretariat of State and placed it under the authority of a prelate who retained the title secretary of briefs. This section disappeared in the reform of PAUL VI (1967), who passed its duties to the offices of the SUBSTITUTE OF THE SECRETARIAT OF STATE, but reserved to the chancery the sending of particularly important briefs. When the chancery was abolished (31 March 1973), the writing of briefs and bulls was entrusted to an office of the Secretariat of State called the Chancery of Apostolic Letters. (This name has never appeared in the *Annuario Pontificio*.)

In the 19th century, the Secretariat of Briefs was the great dispenser of pontifical graces to the Catholic world. Ecclesiastics applied to it to become protonotaries, prelates of the household of His Holiness, or assistants to the pontifical throne. Members of the laity applied to it to join the knightly orders of the Holy See, as knights or commanders, or to become "counts of the apostolic palace and the court of the Lateran," or, more briefly, counts of Rome.

The records of the Secretariat of Briefs were turned over to the Vatican Archives in 1908. The series begins in 1566 but underwent phenomenal growth during the papacy of SIXTUS V, when the organization, which lasted until the beginning of the 20th century, is generally believed to have been instituted. For each grace that was granted, the office preserved the petition, the draft of the brief, and a summary approved by the pope—who wrote the word *placet* followed by the initial of his baptismal name—and countersigned by the secretary of briefs. This archive is vast, containing no fewer than 6,217 volumes covering the years 1566–1908. Access to the documents would be impossible without the old indexes (150 volumes covering the years 1554–1872), which were arranged according to criteria that could vary depending on the era.

François-Charles Uginet

Bibliography

Laurain-Portemer, M. "Le Statut de Mazarin dans l'Église," *Bibliothèque de l'École des chartes*, 127, (1969), 355–419, 128 (1970), 5–80 [very useful presentation of the workings of the secretariat and its archives in the 17th century, together with a typical study based on this archive].

Moroni, G. *Dizionario di erudizione storico-ecclesiastica*, VI, Venice, 1840, 115–25.

Pásztor, L. *Guida delle fonti per la storia dell'America latina negli archivi della Santa Sede*, Vatican City, 1970, 112–19.

SECRETARIAT OF BRIEFS TO PRINCES. From the middle of the 16th century, around 1560–6, the pontifical secretaries responsible for writing so-called secret briefs were divided into two specialized sections. One became the Secretariat of Briefs, and the other the Secretariat of Briefs to Princes. The secretary of briefs to princes, a prelate who was a member of the papal family, drew up the *epistulae ad principes* (letters to princes), many of which were protocolar letters (letters of courtesy), whence the name *segretario dei complimenti* ("secretary of compliments"). These were destined for princes, a term that embraced not only the emperor and members of the reigning families but also cardinals, bishops, and other high-ranking ecclesiastics. The letters included, in the first instance, the official correspondence occasioned by an important event (accession to the throne, dispatch of legates and apostolic nuncios, baptisms of princes, condolences, etc.). But the pope also made this secretariat responsible for letters that were dispatched without passing through the diplomatic staff, and that concerned matters with which the sovereign pontiff wanted to deal directly. The text of these was often provided by the pope or the secretary of state; the task of the secretary of briefs to princes was to put it into good Latin. Thus, the secretary of briefs was often called on to write pontifical documents of all kinds (allocutions, decrees of canonization, homilies, etc.).

Custom, which by the contemporary era had become rule, decreed that the secretary of briefs to princes be responsible for pronouncing the *Oratio de eligendo pontifice* before the cardinals entered the CONCLAVE. The last such oration, pronounced at the conclave of 1963, aroused some excitement among the religious press, who thought they discerned an implicit criticism of the papacy of JOHN XXIII.

The Secretariat of Briefs to Princes dispatched not only briefs (sealed with the FISHERMAN'S RING) signed by the secretary, but also letters signed by the pope and bearing his private seal. Up to the curial reform of 1908, the secretariat was also responsible for matrimonial dispensations to members of reigning (and formerly reigning) families. This prerogative was then transferred to the newly created Congregation of Sacraments. At the time of the reform of the Curia in 1967, PAUL VI abolished the Secretariat for Briefs to Princes, and its duties were given to an office of the Secretariat of State responsible in particular for drawing up documents in Latin (*officium pro exarandis latina lingua litteris apostolicis, epistolis aliisve documentis a Summo Pontifice eidem commissis*). This body does not appear in the *Annuario Pontificio*, which makes no distinction between the various linguistic authorities that share the work of compiling the documents of the Secretariat of State.

The archives of the Secretariat of Briefs to Princes are kept, for the most part, in the *Epistulae ad Principes* section of the Vatican Archives (about 380 articles for the years 1560–1914). This contains the originals of letters sent to the pope by sovereign rulers, drafts of replies, records, and lists of the secretariat's audiences. There are many gaps in the series, since, aside from various losses, many documents have, for administrative reasons, been filed in other archives, such as the Armaria XVIX and XLV and the Archive Principi e Titolati of the Secretariat of State.

François-Charles Uginet

Bibliography

Del Re, N. *La curia romana*, 3rd ed., Rome, 1970, 453–4.

Moroni, G. *Dizionario di erudizione storico-ecclesiastica*, 62, Venice, 1853, 265–7.

Pásztor, L. *Guida delle fonti per la storia dell'America latina negli archivi della Santa Sede*, Vatican City, 1970, 120–2.

SECRETARIAT OF STATE. The Roman pontiffs have always had secretaries at their disposal to aid them in their apostolic mission. At the beginning of the 15th century, the Camera Secreta provided the pope with *secretarii* of various nationalities for the compiling of diplomatic dossiers. CALLISTUS III fixed their number at six (constitution *Decet Romanum Pontificem*, 1456). These became the *secretarii* and *numerarii*, from whom, under SIXTUS IV, there soon emerged one who would act as their superior. Not long afterward, INNOCENT VIII established a college of apostolic secretaries consisting of 24 members, some of whom were of archepiscopal or episcopal rank (constitution *Non debet reprehensible*, 1487). To these was added a *secretarius domesticus*, who resided in the pontiff's household and was entrusted with matters which the pope wanted to deal with personally. The domestic secretary was outside the hierarchy, being directly attached to the pontifical person and the sole executor of the pope's political wishes. Nevertheless, this figure was gradually eclipsed in the 16th century by the cardinal nephew, also known as "cardinal patron" (*cardinale padrone*). This office appeared during the pontificate of Sixtus IV (1471–84) with the popes' adoption of NEPOTISM; the pontiff now selected from his family a man in whom he could place absolute confidence. Before the office was abolished under SIXTUS V (brief *Romani Pontificis providentia*, 1586), the domestic secretary had acquired a competitor in the intimate, or major, secretary whom LEO X (1513–21) placed beneath the authority of the cardinal nephew and who had charge of all papal correspondence.

At the beginning of the 17th century, all those collaborating with the cardinal nephew in the diplomatic service had been appointed. It was in 1644 that the title "secretary of state" was for the first time given to a cardinal, by INNOCENT X. After the college of apostolic secretaries was abolished by INNOCENT XI in 1678, and nepotism suppressed by INNOCENT XII in 1692 (constitution *Romanum decet Pontificem*), the Secretariat of State acquired a central place in the diplomatic workings of pontifical government, with the internal affairs of the Papal States being handled by the Apostolic Camera. In 1833, GREGORY XVI paired this dicastery of external affairs with a secretariat for internal affairs of state. As soon as he was elected in 1846, PIUS IX abolished this dualism and created a single agency under the direction of his new secretary of state, Cardinal Pasquale Gizzi. However, it consisted of two sections: external and internal affairs. In 1847 the pope extended the function of his secretary of state naming him among other things, president of the council for ministers and minister of foreign affairs for the papal states.

With the ending of the popes' temporal power in 1870, the Secretariat of State inevitably saw its scope reduced. PIUS X, in his apostolic constitution *Sapienti consilio* (1908), restructured it in three sections: Extraordinary Ecclesiastical Affairs, for relations with foreign governments; Ordinary Affairs, for contacts with nunciatures and embassies as well as appointments of ecclesiastic dignitaries; and Apostolic Briefs, for the preparation of official documents. The writing of these documents was entrusted to two agencies connected with the Secretariat of State. One was the Secretariat of Briefs to Princes, which had been autonomous since the 14th century but in 1678 was divided into a Secretariat of Ordinary Briefs and a Secretariat of Briefs to Princes; under Pius X, the two were combined for the writing of Latin letters to heads of state which were signed by the pope (nuncios' letters of accreditation, replies to ambassadors' letters of accreditation), as well as encyclicals, apostolic letters and constitutions, consistorial allocutions, and canonization homilies. The other agency was the Secretariat of Latin Letters, whose task was to put into Latin, letters to members of the ecclesiastical hierarchy or lay officials (eucharistic congresses, episcopal jubilees, commemorations, speeches, congratulatory messages, etc.).

The reform of 1908 brought the disappearance of the Secretariat of Memorials, instituted in the 15th century to receive memoranda in the form of requests for favors which only the pope could grant by virtue of his sovereign powers in spiritual or temporal matters. The secretary of memorials, who from 1769 was a cardinal, saw his powers halved as a result of the loss of the Papal

States in 1870. His dicastery expired with its last office-holder, Cardinal Ricci, in 1894.

Although under the direction of the pope's primary collaborator, one of the four Palatine cardinals, the Secretariat of State had been placed last in the organization chart of the Curia that was drawn up according to the wishes of Pius X. Later, PAUL VI made a de facto situation de jure by promoting the Secretariat of State head of the Roman dicasteries (apostolic constitution *Regimini Ecclesiae universae*, 1967). At the same time, the secretariats of Briefs to Princes and of Latin Letters were absorbed into State, as were the Apostolic DATARY (abolished by a simple communiqué of 1 January 1968) and the Apostolic Chancery (*motu proprio Quo aptius*, 1973).

The new Secretariat of State, however, lost one area of diplomatic relations, which was given to a Council for the Public Affairs of the Church under the close supervision of the cardinal secretary of state who, by law, was its prefect. The two dicasteries were thus jointly governed by one person. In 1988, JOHN PAUL II decided to reunify his Secretariat of State by fully reintegrating into it the Council for Public Affairs, which now became simply Section II (apostolic constitution *Pastor bonus*).

Today, the Secretariat of State is divided into two sections, General Affairs and Relations with the States. It thus has the same configuration as it had before the council, the one difference being that with Pius X's reform, General Affairs (then called Ordinary Affairs) made up the second section, while Diplomatic (or Extraordinary) Affairs, made up the first. John Paul II thought it more logical that the religioius domain have precedence over the political.

The section of General Affairs, directed by the archbishop substitute aided by a prelate assessor, consists of eight linguistic divisions (Latin, Italian, French, English, Spanish, German, Portuguese, and Polish) through which passes all mail received and sent. Here translations and abstracts are written by the employees, both clergy and laity, men and women. Section I comprises a dozen specialized services: cipher, for coded diplomatic correspondence with nunciatures and embassies; chancery of apostolic letters, for shipping of papal documents; section for relations with the dicasteries, which examines all affairs handled by the Curia; juridical section; section of international Catholic agencies, both the movements of the lay apostolate with the official label of ICO—International Catholic Organization—and public international agencies (UN, UNESCO, CSCE, Council of Europe, etc.); section of personnel, in change of nominations and promotions within the Curia, the nunciatures, and apostolic delegations; section of protocol and ceremonial, for receiving heads of state, ministers, and ambassadors; section of information and documentation, for review and round-up of the international press; and section of honorary distinctions, in charge of titles of apostolic protono-

tary, prelate of honor or chaplain of His Holiness for the clergy, or gentlemen of His Holiness for the laity, and of pontifical decorations such as the Supreme Order of Christ, the order of the Golden Spur, orders of Pius IX, of St. Gregory the Great and Pope St. Silvester, order of the Holy Sepulcher of Jerusalem, the Pro Ecclesia et Pontifice cross and Benemerenti medal, excluding noble titles no longer conferred, as well as benedictions and papal autographs.

The section for Relations with the States is headed by a secretary archbishop who is aided by a prelate undersecretary and a council of cardinals and bishops, both curial and diocesan. This section dates back to the French Revolution of 1789, since it was because of that event that PIUS VII created the Congregation for French Ecclesiastical Affairs, which functioned up to 1798. In 1801, Pius VII restored the section, with wider powers, under the title of Congregation of Extraordinary Ecclesiastical Affairs, its primary task being the preparation of the concordat with Napoleon Bonaparte. In abeyance during the pope's captivity, this dicastery reappeared with his return to Rome in 1814. Now bearing universal responsibilities, it was called the *Congregatio Extraordinaria Praeposita Negotiis Ecclesiasticis Orbis Catholici.* LEO XII changed the title somewhat, placing the adjective "extraordinary" more logically next to "affairs" rather than the congregation itself.

Pius X placed the dicastery as it was in his curial chart of 1908, in which its political responsibilities were confirmed (concordats, state consultations for episcopal nominations, creation of dioceses, etc.). However, the congregation lost its jurisdiction over Latin America, Russia, and the Portuguese colonies in Africa and Asia, which were handed to the consistorial congregations and that of Propaganda Fide. Although under the direction of the cardinal secretary of state, the Congregation for Extraordinary Ecclesiastical Affairs was recognized as an autonomous dicastery within the Curia (letter of PIUS XI of 5 July 1925, published in the form of a notification). In his constitution of 1967, Paul VI emphasized the close connection of this political domain with the general activity of the Secretariat of State. He therefore reduced the congregation to a simple Council for the Public Affairs of the Church, paired with the Secretariat of State. Noting the overlap of the two structures, John Paul II decided to combine them officially, giving the new Section II the responsibilities of the former council (concordats and conventions, both bilateral and multilateral, political consultations, representation of the Holy See in international institutions and conferences, etc.).

Finally, the Secretariat of State includes a series of administrative services: typing and calligraphy, telegrams and benedictions by mail, diplomatic pouches, and archives. It also supervises the *Acta Apostolicae Sedis* (the Holy See's official journal), the *Osservatore Ro-*

mano (th Vatican's official newspaper), the *Amuario Pontificio* (administrative updating of the Church), the Statistical Office, Vatican Radio, Vatican Television Center, the Press Office of the Holy See, and the Ecclesiastical Pontifical Academy (the school for the nuncios). Structural ties link it especially with the Pontifical Commission for Russia, under the section for Relations with the States, and with the Pontifical Council of Justice and Peace as well as Social Communications, which have to obtain its endorsement before taking any important initiative.

The list of responsibilities of the Secretariat of State gives an idea of its overall powers, which make it the veritable staff officer of the Roman Curia. All business passes through it for the information of the pope and the smooth running of his pastoral government.

To this end, the role of the cardinal secretary of state is a leading one. Selected at the discretion of the sovereign pontiff, he does not come under the curial regulation of the five-year mandate, being entirely at the disposition of the pope. Thus, his duties automatically end with the reign of the pontif who appointed him. As head of papal diplomacy, he represents the Holy See in international relations and receives heads of state, ministers, and ambassadors after their audience with the head of the Church. He accompanies the pope on all his trips. On the pope's orders, he convenes the heads of the curial dicasteries in plenary session. His duties extend to the temporal domain because, since John Paul II's accession, he acts as regent of the Vatican City State in the name of the pope, who remains elective sovereign (chirograph of 6 April 1984).

Secretaries of State: Giovanni Giacomo Panciroli, 1644–51. Fabio Chigi (Alexander VII), 1651–5. Giulio Rospigliosi (Clement IX), 1655–67. Decio Azzolini, Jr., 1667–9. Federico Borromeo, 1670–3. Francesco Nerli, 1673–6. Alderano Cibo, 1676–89. Giambattista Rubini, 1689–91. Fabrizio Spada, 1691–1700. Fabrizio Paolucci, 1700–21. Giorgio Spinola, 1721–4. Fabrizio Paolucci, 1724–6. Niccolò Maria Lercari, 1726–30. Antonio Banchieri, 1730–3. Giuseppe Firrao, 1733–40. Silvio Valenti Gonzaga, 1740–56. Alberico Archinto, 1756–8. Ludovico Maria Torriggiani, 1758–69. Lazzaro Opizio Pallavicini, 1769–85. Ignazio Boncompagni Ludovisi, 1785–9. Francesco Saverio de Zelada, 1789–96. Ignazio Busca, 1796–7. Giuseppe Doria Pamphili, 1797–9. Ercole Consalvi, 1800–6. Filippo Casoni, 1806–8. Giuseppe Doria Pamphili, pro-secretary of state, 1808. Giulio Gabrielli, pro-secretary of state, 1808. Bartolomeo Pacca, pro-secretary of State, 1808–9. Ercole Consalvi, 1814–23. Giulio Maria della Somaglia, 1823–8. Tommaso Bernetti, 1828–9. Giuseppe Albani, 1829–30. Tommaso Bernetti, 1831–6. Luigi Lambruschini, 1836–46. Pasquale Gizzi, 1846–7. Gabriele Ferretti, 1847. Giuseppe Bofondi, 1848. Giacomo Antonelli, pro-secre-

tary of state, 1848–52, secretary of state, 1852–76. Giovanni Simeoni, 1876–8. Alessandro Franchi, 1878. Lorenzo Nina, 1878–80. Lodovico Jacobini, 1880–7. Mariano Rampolia del Tindaro, 1887–1903. Raphael Merry del Val, 1903–14. Domenico Ferrata, 1914. Pietro Gasparri, 1914–30. Eugenio Pacelli (Pius XII), 1930–9. Luigi Maglione, 1939–44. Domenico Tardini, pro-secretary of state, 1952–8 with Giovanni Battista Montini (Paul VI), pro-secretary of State, 1952–4. Domenico Tardini, 1958–61. Amleto Giovanni Cicognani, 1961–9. Jean Villot, 1969–79. Agostino Casaroli, 1979–90. Angelo Sodano, pro-secretary of state, 1990, secretary of state since 1991.

Joël-Benoît d'Onorio

Bibliography

Bertagna, B. "La Segretaria di Stato," *La Curia Romana nella Cost. ap. Pastor bonus*, Rome, 1990.

Buonomo, V. "La Segretaria di Stato: Competenze nella funzione diplomatica," *La Curia romana nella Cost. ap. Pastor Bonus*, Rome, 1990.

Del Ré, N. *La Curia romana: Lineamenti storico-giuridici*, Rome, 1970.

d'Onorio, J. B. ed., *Le Saint-Siège dans les relations internationales*, Paris, 1989; *Le Pape et le gouvernement de l'Église*, Paris, 1992.

Moersdorf, K. "Der Kardinalstaatssekretär; Aufgabe und Werdegand seines Amtes," *Archiv für katholisches Kirchenrecht*, 131, 1962.

Naz, R. "Secrétairerie d'État," *DDC* VII, 901–4.

Richard, P. "Origines et développement de la Secrétairerie d'État apostolique," *RHE*, 1910.

Serafini, A. "Le origini della pontifica Segretaria di Stato e la Sapienti consilio del beato Pio X," *Romana Curia a beato Pio X sapienti consilio reformata*, Rome, 1951.

SECRETARIATS OF THE ROMAN CURIA. Three secretariats are among the offices of the Roman Curia created during VATICAN II to establish a doctrinal dialogue and to enter into religious relations with non-Catholics. In PAUL VI's curial reform of 1967 (apostolic constitution *Regimini Ecclesiae Universae*), they were listed immediately after the Roman congregations and before the councils, commissions, and tribunals. They were raised to the level of pontifical councils by JOHN PAUL II during the 1988 restructuring of the pontifical administration (apostolic constitution *Pastor bonus*).

The first of these, the Secretariat for the Unity of Christians, was created by JOHN XXIII (*motu proprio Superno Dei nutu*, 1960) to encourage ecumenism—that is, interreligious relations with other Christians, Orthodox, Anglican, and Protestant. It was confirmed by Paul VI at the closing of the council (*motu proprio Finis concilio*, 1966) to develop the important domain of conciliar deliberations. The second, the Secretariat for Non-Christians, was created during the council (brief *Progrediente concilio*, 1964) to emphasize Paul VI's preoccupation with extending the Church's dialogue to non-Christians who nevertheless professed a religion or had some religious feeling. The third, the Secretariat for Non-believers, was created in April 1965 (without an official founding document) to begin discussions with atheists of all kinds (Marxists, humanists, positivists, etc.) and to study atheism and agnosticism from the viewpoint of history, philosophy, sociology, and psychology, with the idea of drawing from them viewpoints and trends useful for the cultural and spiritual pastoral service of the Church.

Joël-Benoît d'Onorio

Bibliography

Del Ré, N. *La Curia Romana: Lineamenti storico-giuridici*, 3rd ed., Rome, 1970.

d'Onorio, J. B. *Le Pape et le gouvernement de l'Église*, Paris, 1992.

Koenig, F. "Vatican II et le Secrétariat pour les non-croyants," *La Documentation catholique*, 1967, col. 1693–1706.

Rodé, F. "Les 25 ans du Conseil pontifical pour le dialogue avec les non-croyants: Un fruit du concile Vatican II," *La Documentation catholique*, 1982, 502–7.

Willebrands, J. "Les 25 ans du Secrétariat pour l'unité des chrétiens," *Osservatore Romano* (Fr. ed.), 30 July 1985, 4–5.

SEDE VACANTE. See See, Vacant and Impeded.

SEDIA GESTATORIA. The *sedia gestatoria* ("sedan chair") was a ceremonial piece of furniture used to carry the pope during his coronation and other solemn processions that took place in the midst of crowds. It seems to have been a descendant of the litter, a triumphal conveyance that was known in the Roman world and used throughout the Middle Ages, eventually being supplanted by the carriage in the 17th century. Affixed to poles, the *sedia gestatoria* exemplified the authority and prestige of the pope by the very circumstance of being raised up. At the same time, it allowed the crowds to see him all along the processional route. On these occasions, members of the pope's personal staff made up the *sediari pontifici*, who from PIUS IV's reign were a virtual cavalry corps, becoming a confraternity around 1565. The *sediari* consisted of 14 men; there was a functional distinction between them ·and the *flabelli*, who carried huge fans of peacock feathers, and the porters themselves. The few iconographic illustrations

of the ceremonial seat that have come down to us from early times show a finely carved wooden structure, not overly heavy and with simple lines, the top of the back being curved. The *sedia* used by PIUS XII (1939–58) had a panel in the back, also carved and stamped with the Vatican coat of arms. Use of the sedia was abolished by PAUL VI (1963–78), and JOHN PAUL I (1978) was the first to go to his coronation on foot. JOHN PAUL II, who succeeded him, completely gave up the *sedia*, preferring the popemobile, a raised AUTOMOBILE with bulletproof windows which was further improved after the assassination attempt on the pope's life (13 May 1981).

Philippe Levillain

Bibliography

Palazzini, G. "Sediari pontifici," *EC*, 11, 1953, 225–6.

Strauss, R. *Carriages and Coaches*, London, 1912.

Tardini, D. *L'incoronazione del Papa ed il solenne possesso del Laterano*, Rome, 1925.

Valentino Stivano, G. *De levatione seu portatione Pontificis*, Venice, 1578–9.

SEE, VACANT AND IMPEDED.

The Vacant See. Given that Christ left no indication as to what procedure to follow in the ELECTION of the Roman pontiff—at least, there is no trace in the New Testament—the popes have always considered it their prerogative, right, and duty to determine the best way of providing for the election of their successors. Originally, the papal election took place with the participation of the people and the clergy of Rome, along with the suburbicarian bishops. Little by little, election came to be reserved to the three higher orders of the Roman clergy, consisting of the bishops, priests, and deacons called "cardinals" by the Holy Roman Church (NICHOLAS II, decree *In nomine Domini*, promulgated at the Roman synod of 1059, which appears in Gratian's *Decree*, 23, c. 1).

At the Third Lateran Council, it was definitively established that the election belonged exclusively to the college of cardinals, all other parties being excluded (ALEXANDER III, constitution *Licet de evitanda*, 1179). This college was a stable body which could readily be convened the moment the Apostolic See became vacant. It was laid down that the pope's electors could not themselves be elected or designated as such electors during the vacancy of the Apostolic See.

During the 20th century, the norms concerning the election of the Roman pontiff underwent important modifications, at first under PIUS X (apostolic constitution *Vacante Sede Apostolica*, 25 December 1904, and apostolic constitution *Commissum nobis*, 20 January 1904), then PIUS XI (apostolic constitution *Cum proxime*, 1

March 1922) and PIUS XII (apostolic constitution *Vacantis Sedis Apostolicae*, 8 December 1945). The last document announced a diversification of the college of cardinals through the incorporation of a larger number of representatives of the various Churches of the Catholic world and different countries.

JOHN XXIII increased the number of cardinals (*motu proprio Summi Pontificis electio*, 5 September 1962), determining at the same time that they would all be elevated to episcopal dignity (*motu proprio Cum gravissima*, 15 April 1962). PAUL VI again altered the Sacred College (*motu proprio Cum gravissima*, 21 November 1972) by setting an age limit of 80 for taking part in a consistory. Most important, however, he revised the norms covering the election of Peter's successor (apostolic constitution *Romano Pontifice eligendo*, 1 October 1975).

The principal provisions of this apostolic constitution are as follows.

During the vacancy of the Apostolic See, the government of the Church is entrusted to the Sacred College of cardinals for expediting current business and business that cannot be deferred, as well as making all necessary preparations for the election of the new pontiff of Rome.

In this same period, the Sacred College has neither jurisdiction nor power of any kind concerning questions that had fallen within the competence of the pope during his lifetime, which must be reserved exclusively to the future successor of Peter. Such is the current doctrine of the Church. GREGORY X prohibited the cardinals from carrying out business during the vacancy, except for matters of extreme urgency (constitution *Ubi periculum*, 7 July 1274). CLEMENT V declared null any exercise of pontifical power by the cardinals during the interregnum (constitution *Ne Romani Pontifices*, 1311).

The cardinals also are forbidden to correct or alter laws promulgated by the Roman pontiffs, to add anything to them, or to dispense with them, especially with regard to the organization of the election of the Roman pontiff. Any such action would be null and void.

According to the norms currently in force (JOHN PAUL II, apostolic constitution *Pastor bonus*, 28 June 1988), on the death of the pope, all the moderators and members of the dicasteries of the Roman Curia cease their duties, including the cardinal secretary of state; exceptions are the cardinal camerlengo of the Roman Church and the cardinal Grand Penitentiary, who deal with ordinary affairs and hand over to the college of cardinals those matters that would have been referred to the sovereign pontiff. The secretaries provide for the ordinary government of the dicasteries. They must be confirmed in their duties by the new pontiff within the three months following his election (*ibid.*, art. VI).

Aided by three assistant cardinals, the cardinal camerlengo must first obtain the agreement of the college of cardinals for secondary affairs and its approval for each important business. He must officially affirm the death of the pope by arranging for the sepulcher in accordance with the *Ordo exsequiarum Summi Pontificis vita defuncti*, included in the apostolic constitution *Romano Pontifici eligendo*.

In accord with the dean of cardinals, the cardinal camerlengo must ensure that a conclave will be duly held for the election of the successor of the deceased pope (*Ordo sacrorum rituum Conclavis*, also an integral part of the constitution). He is responsible for the care and administration of the possessions and temporal rights of the Holy See.

The cardinal penitentiary expedites business in conformity with a tradition dating from the council of Vienne (1311–12) and with provisions put forward by Pius XI (apostolic constitution *Quae divinitus*, 25 March 1935).

The mission and powers of the pontifical legates do not cease during the vacancy of the See.

The pope's overall civil power over the government of Vatican City passes to the college of cardinals. The decrees it puts out, solely in cases of urgent necessity and for the duration of the vacancy, will remain valid beyond the said vacancy only if the new pontiff confirms them. As soon as the new pope is elected and has accepted his election, he at once takes over the government of the Church, and the rights conceded to the cardinals during the vacancy cease.

The ordinary duties of the congregations and tribunals of the Roman Curia are maintained, but only for the granting of graces of lesser importance.

The vacancy of the See can come about as a result of the death of the Roman pontiff or by the resignation of his office. Doctrine envisages other causes: insanity, certain and perpetual, which is equivalent to the death of the pontiff; heresy, notorious and openly divulged, which deprives the pope ipso facto of all jurisdiction, even before any declaratory sentence; and schism, which is the same as the preceding case.

If the Apostolic See becomes vacant during the celebration of a council, it is automatically interrupted (but not dissolved) until a new Supreme Pontiff orders it to be continued or dissolves it (c. 340). This situation arose during VATICAN II with the death of John XXIII (3 June 1963), its initiator. Paul VI, who was elected on 21 June, confirmed his intention to continue the work undertaken by his predecessor on 27 June (rescript *Ex audientia*).

The see may become vacant after a synod has been called, or during its celebration. In that case, the synod is suspended by the law itself, until the new pontiff decrees either that the session be dissolved or continued (c. 347 § 2). The duties entrusted to its members are likewise suspended.

The Impeded See. The impediment may be extrinsic to the person of the Roman pontiff: this is the case with captivity, imprisonment, or exile. It may also be intrinsic, through incapacity. In either circumstance, the pope must be wholly prevented from fulfilling his pastoral function for the good of the universal Church (cf. c. 412).

The reform of the Curia envisaged cases in which the Roman pontiff might have to be replaced during a prolonged absence. This provision was not retained in the apostolic constitution *Pastor bonus*. However, John Paul II granted the cardinal camerlengo, by chirograph, a broad delegation of powers on the occasion of his apostolic travels to Mexico (25 January–1 February 1979) and Poland (2–10 June 1979).

Special laws enacted for these circumstances are to be observed (c. 335); in this case, the provisions are in the apostolic constitution *Romano Pontifici eligendo*.

The Principle *Nihil Innovetur*. The CODE OF CANON LAW recalls (c. 335) the golden rule in case of vacancy or impeachment of the see of Rome: *Nihil innovetur in Ecclesiae Universae regimine*. That is, nothing is to be innovated in the governance of the universal Church, according to the principle laid down by LEO XIII: *Ne, Sede vacante, aliquid innovetur* (constitution *Praedecessores nostri*, 24 May 1882). At such times, it is forbidden to effect any innovation in the government of the Church. As is indicated above, the college of cardinals possesses only that power in the Church that is given to it in special law (c. 359).

Dominique Le Tourneau

SEMINARIES. This is the term used in the modern and contemporary era for establishments—colleges, schools, or communities—set up for the training of future ministers, especially those of the Catholic Church. The inauguration of seminaries was determined at the council of TRENT, with the decree of 15 July 1563. Nevertheless, some European countries did not actually put the decree into practice until later, even centuries after the council. In some cases, pre-conciliar practice remained in force; other countries preferred to use training methods that only partially applied the guidelines laid down by the council Fathers.

The effective realization of the wishes of the council of Trent came about only at the beginning of the 20th century, with the measures taken by PIUS X. Over the decades that followed, the institution of seminaries was called into question several times, on both theoretical and practical grounds, as a result of severe crises in the recruitment of priests. Nonetheless, VATICAN II confirmed their usefulness to the Church, while respecting a certain diversity of local opinion.

Antecedents of the Council of Trent. Over the centuries, methods of entering the priesthood had varied but

little. In small communities, youths met in the palace of the bishop, who prepared them for their future ministry. Then they began to be trained in parishes, which allowed candidates for the priesthood to receive practical training by doing pastoral work. Sometimes, however, this was done to the detriment of study and disciplined life. On several occasions, popes and councils attempted to set standards for preparation for the priesthood and criteria for spiritual training, as well as a minimal scholastic curriculum for all. However, abuses were far from rare, as were cases of young men who were ordained priest without preparation of any kind. This gave rise to behavior and ways of life that occasionally caused scandal, as can be deduced from the exhortations and even disciplinary measures to which bishops sometimes had to resort.

In some places, it was up to the cathedrals to try to solve the problem. It was their task to find and remunerate a teacher who would set up a free school for young clergy. This laid the foundations of the schools called *studium generale*, which were the ancestors of the later faculties of theology, the origin of the universities that would spring up in the 12th century.

Next, to enable youths to attend the faculties of theology regularly, university colleges were set up that were designed as student residences. The next step was to accept in these colleges only youths who were preparing for the priesthood, who were receiving spiritual and disciplinary training, and who were attending the schools of the *studium generale* or the university. This structure—the college as both residence and day school—would remain the training model for the German-speaking world, even after the decree of the council of Trent.

It was the colleges—which spread to Spain, France, and Italy in the 15th century—that would serve as models for the establishment of seminaries. This trend was due chiefly to the Roman Cardinal Capranica, founder of a college in the mid-15th century, and to Ignatius Loyola, the founder of the Society of Jesus, who set up, in Rome, first the Roman College (1551), and later the German College (1552). The Roman College soon attracted students through the fame and quality of its teachers; it later became one of the most renowned ecclesiastical universities, the Gregorian. This institution took its inspiration from the humanities schools and the university faculties.

The first real example of a seminary before the council of Trent came from the work of Cardinal Pole in England. In 1555, he convened a national synod with the precise aim of organizing a *reformatio Angliae*. In the chapter on the clergy, the final text suggested providing for the opening of schools from which, *tamquam ex seminario*, "as from a seminary," candidates could be selected for the priesthood. These schools were to be established in each diocese. The rules for living and the training programs were in large measure taken up, a few years later, by the council of Trent's decree on the institution of seminaries.

Institution of Seminaries. After much debate among the Fathers, the conciliar text was approved unanimously on 15 July 1563, and was confirmed by PIUS IV on 26 January 1564. Known by the Latin words of the exordium, *Cum adolescentium aetas*, it laid down the various norms that were to regulate life in the future seminaries. The dioceses were invited to open a college (*seminarium*) to take in and train future priests. Where dioceses were too small, these colleges could be provincial or interdiocesan. The colleges accepted boys of at least 12 years of age who were the offspring of legitimate marriages, who could at least read and write, and whose character inspired the hope that they would serve the Church through the exercise of the priestly ministry. The council also laid down rules concerning scholastic programs, religious and theological training, disciplinary regulations, supervisors responsible for correctly running and directing the college, and the obtaining of funds necessary for their existence.

Thus, the work of the council radically altered the history of the training of clergy. Based on experiments already in existence, it turned the colleges, which were already providing for the recruitment of future priests, into comprehensive, self-sufficient institutions. Cultural education was also provided for, so that there was no need to have recourse to external schools or university faculties.

After the council of Trent, for many years the Church offered three ways of attaining the priesthood. The first was the old two-entity college-university, separating residence and school, which grew considerably in Rome and continued to be applied in the German-speaking world. Next came the seminary on the model proposed by the council of Trent: a comprehensive institution designed to provide the future priest with a complete training; at a school where the students boarded, run by members of the secular and regular clergy. This institution spread widely in Italy and Spain, and later in France. Finally, there were nonresident students, who were far more numerous than is generally believed, and whose training derived from the preceding formulas. In the last case, the young boy lived at home and, as a day student, attended the faculty or the seminary school, or else was simply taught by a priest who presented him to the bishop for ordination.

During the 16th century, Rome saw the founding of several colleges. Those instituted by St. Ignatius of Loyola functioned according to the council's decrees. The German College was aimed at training young men of German origin; thereafter, they were supposed to return to their country with cultural and spiritual training that would allow them to stop the spread of the Lutheran Reforma-

tion. The Roman College was highly successful, but it did not provide a place for the seminarians to live in common, being simply a school of the humanities, philosophy, and theology. Out of this need, after the council of Trent, came the foundation of the Roman seminary. It had a large student body since, in a way, it set an example for the other dioceses—and not only in Italy—since the head of the Roman diocese was the sovereign pontiff himself. The seminary opened in 1565 under the direction of the Jesuits. Not only did the students attend courses at the Roman College; the seminary's superiors were also members of the Society of Jesus.

Over the following years, a large number of bishoprics followed the example of the German college and started colleges in Rome for their aspiring priests. In this way, there arose the Greek College (1577), the "venerable College for the English" (1579), and the Polish College (1583), which met with little success. Other colleges were opened as well, while the German College was combined with that of Hungary. These were independent institutions, extensions of national Churches rather than of particular dioceses, which conformed only in part with the decrees of the council of Trent.

The diocesan seminaries, in contrast, fulfilled the hopes of the council Fathers, especially of Charles Borromeo, who crafted the application of the council's decree. During the 1550s, a few Italian bishops opened residences for clerics, following the example of the Jesuit foundations, but it was the decree of the council of Trent that provided the impetus for these foundations. About one hundred of them sprang up in the 10 years following the council. Some came up against difficulties, while others had to close a few years after opening their doors. In the 40 years after the council, a few more than 20 seminaries were founded in Spain, and a dozen in France.

The chief impetus for this growth came from Charles Borromeo, nephew of Pius IV, who was the pope's secretary before being appointed to head the diocese of Milan. In 1564, he opened a seminary, then collaborated on the establishment of seminaries in outlying dioceses. Most important, he drew up a program of studies and a rule of life for the seminaries that inspired those of a large number of similar institutions, not only in Italy. These programs would even serve as a basis for programs later elaborated by the dicasteries of the Vatican, and the Roman Congregation for seminaries and Ecclesiastical Faculties which would be called on to organize the life of seminaries throughout the Catholic world.

The seminary as organized by Charles Borromeo was centered on three main stages of priestly training: the acquisition of a ritualized spirituality, linked to a series of pious exercises (prayer, both individual and communal, reading and meditation, spiritual exercises, service in the cathedral); a cultural education through humanist studies (chiefly Latin) and philosophy; and finally, the study of theology (dogma, morality, and law, as well as pastoral concerns such as liturgy, chant, and sacred eloquence). This was a scholarly curriculum whose application often depended on the potential and good will of the superiors and professors. A strictly disciplined way of life was designed to accustom the young man to personal asceticism and to help him avoid worldly temptations. Superiors oversaw the training under the direction of a rector, who had general responsibility for the seminary. A prefect of studies organized and supervised seminary life.

Borromeo's concept became a model for European seminaries. Similarly, in later years and on other continents, structures governing ecclesial life were exported through missionary preaching, so that young Churches came into being in the image of their mother Churches.

In France, little attention was paid to the decree of the council of Trent, and it was almost a century before the problem of training clergy was settled. The chief representatives of this French school of spirituality were Pierre de Bérulle, Charles de Condren, and François Bourgoing, who insisted on the need for residential colleges for the training of clergy. They embraced the idea, typical of the French school, that priestly spirituality was founded on the central figure of Christ the high priest. The training consisted of two stages: spiritual exercises for the priesthood, as conceived by St. Vincent de Paul; and parish work—preparation for the priesthood carrried out in the context of pastoral work in the parish, a concept derived from Adrien Bourdoise.

St. Vincent de Paul founded the charitable work known as the Priests of the Mission, or Lazarists, which was designed to supervise the training in doctrine, morality, and the spiritual life of future priests. It was soon realized that such short preparatory courses were insufficient, and that it was difficult to organize a program for living and training if young boys and men of different ages were grouped together in one building. Thus was born the division into two kinds of seminaries, based on age and type of study: the minor and major seminaries. The first provided young boys with humanist courses, while the second took in young men who wanted to pursue studies in philosophy and theology.

Those who institutionalized the training formula in France were Jean Eudes, who founded his first seminary in 1643, and Jean-Jacques Olier, who set up a broadly academic school. Appointed curate of St.-Sulpice in Paris, Olier took in young students there to prepare them for the priesthood. Some of them studied in the parish while others took courses at the nearby Sorbonne. Growth in the number of students led to their being housed in a residence set apart, and teachers being appointed to be responsible for their training. Thus arose the society known as the Sulpicians, who became a dominant influence in French priestly training. Olier himself defined the society's spiritual orientation and established rules aimed at producing a fruitful priestly life. Although inspired by the decree of the council of Trent as well as by Charles Borromeo's practical methods, the rules also introduced innovations, such as a communal life shared by directors and students, and the abolition of the rigid distinction of roles between those responsible for discipline and those providing spiritual training. Any director could not only teach but also act as a spiritual father to the young men. Olier's writings, which were completed by his successors (in particular M. Tronson), thus constituted the most significant model for the training of the clergy, in France and beyond.

Seminaries in the History of the Contemporary Church.

By the end of the 17th century, most countries of Europe had put into practice the decrees of the council of Trent, even though many dioceses also followed the old training methods; in the German-speaking world, there was still a separation between school and college, where the students lived. Interventions on the part of the Church authorities were constant, especially when synods and provincial councils were convened. A large body of information developed on various aspects of priestly training.

In each country, the rise of revolutionary ideas made for difficult situations, and local authorities were often forced to close the seminaries. It was not until the papacies of LEO XIII (1878–1903) and Pius X (1903–14) that any significant innovations took place. Leo XIII reorganized studies in the seminaries and, in particular, insisted that programs of philosophical studies return to the doctrine of St. Thomas Aquinas. Thomism was considered virtually the official philosophy of the Church, and an indispensable basis for those wishing to devote themselves profitably to the study of theology. Pius X put into practice what the council of Trent had suggested but not imposed. Under him, the seminary became the obligatory passage for a young aspirant to the priesthood. By setting forth various regulations, Pius X determined that no one could be ordained priest without spending an adequate period of time training in a seminary or, at the least, taking four years of theological studies. He also realized another of the council's wishes by encouraging the founding of regional seminaries in Italy. Thus, seminaries from a region or area that was relatively small—because of the small number of students or economic problems of small dioceses—were concentrated in one place. Later, these regional seminaries were placed under direct rule from Rome, thus reinforcing a certain centralizing trend in the government of the Church, a trend begun by PIUS IX.

The new norms were ratified by the CODE OF CANON LAW that came into force in 1917, after seminaries had gone through a particularly difficult time in the wake of the modernist crisis. Another important step was taken before the promulgation of the code. In 1915, a Roman congregation was set up to be responsible for overseeing seminaries and ecclesiastical faculties. The latter were completely brought up to date and reorganized a few years later through the constitution *Deus Scientiarum Dominus*, issued by PIUS XI in 1931.

Other changes were practically forced on the seminaries by the major transformation of civil society in the 20th century. One of these changes was mass education, which brought about a crisis in the minor seminaries. Another was the increase in adult vocations (more young people wanted to attend a seminary after studying in the public schools, up to university level). Finally, vocations appeared in more diverse strata of society, such as the working class, which forced a rethinking of the role and organization of the major seminary.

In addition, a solution had to be found to the problems posed by the sometimes very uneven distribution of clergy in various regions of a country. An example is the Mission of France, created to confront the problem of the evangelization of lapsed Christians. The mission set up a seminary to train priests who did not have to serve in their original diocese but were sent where there was the greatest need.

The problem of adult vocations also encouraged thinking about different ways of training, to suit the different educational levels of entering seminarians. During the 1950s and 1960s, as during the conciliar period, there was open debate on these questions, and a large number of dioceses experimented with new formulas. Some even raised doubts as to the expediency of continuing to think of seminaries as the sole place where future priests got their training. VATICAN II, however, confirmed the desirability of seminaries, especially the major ones, while allowing a greater freedom of choice for the training of young candidates in the minor seminaries.

With the 1970s came a grave crisis in vocations. Many dioceses were forced to close their seminaries or to concentrate young seminarians from several dioceses in one place. In recent years, the trend has reversed slightly, encouraging some bishops, with the support of Rome, once again to insist on the appropriateness of the traditional seminary, even in areas where the choice seemed to have been seriously called into question.

Maurilio Guasco

Bibliography

Balust, L. S., and Hernandez, F. M. *La formación sacerdotal en la Iglesia*, Barcelona, 1966.

Broutin, P. *La Réforme pastorale en France au XVIIᵉ siècle*, 2 vols., Tournai, 1956.

Conde, M. F. *España y los seminarios tridentinos*, Madrid, 1948.

Degert, A. *Histoire des Séminaires français jusqu'à la Revolution*, 2 vols., Paris, 1912.

Guasco, M. "La formazione del clero: I seminari," in G. Chittolini and G. Miccoli, eds., *La Chiesa e il potere politico dal Medioevo all'età contemporanea, Storia d'Italia, Annali 9*, Turin, 1986, 629–715.

Hernandez, F. M. *Los seminarios españoles: Historia y pedagogia (1563–1700)*, Salamanca, 1964.

O'Donohoe, J. A. *Tridentine Seminary Legislation: Its Sources and Its Formation*, Louvain, 1957.

Pelliccia, G. *La preparazione ed ammissione dei chierici ai santi ordini nella Roma del secolo XVI*, Rome, 1946.

Peri, I. *I Seminari*, Rome, 1985.

Roge, J. *Le Simple prêtre: Sa formation, son expérience*, Paris, 1965.

Sacra Congregatio pro Institutione Catholica. *Seminaria Ecclesiae Catholicae*, Vatican City, 1963; *Enchiridion Clericorum: Documenta Ecclesiae futuris sacerdotibus formandis*, Vatican City, 1975.

Sanchez Aliseda, C. *La doctrina de la Iglesia sobre Seminarios desde Trento hasta nuestros dias (desarollo y sistematización)*, Granada, 1942.

SENATE, ROMAN, AND THE PAPACY.

The senatorial assembly was the chief governing body of the Roman Republic. With the establishment of the imperial regime, its influence and powers were considerably altered. Under the reign of Augustus (27 B.C.–14 B.C.), authority was handed from this assembly to another, which entrusted the leader now known as the Roman emperor with wide personal power, at the expense of the preexisting institutions, though without abolishing them. This evolution had some effect on the Senate's powers; it changed its character and replaced the authority it had lost with new duties.

First in importance was the Senate's constitutional authority. It was the Senate that conferred on the emperor his legal powers: the imperium (military and judicial), the tribunician power (civil administration in the city), and the pontificate (high priesthood). Tradition and official ideology decreed that the *princeps* dispose of powers and titles that were nominally attached to the Republic, of which the Senate in fact remained the sole guarantor—even through the army played an increasingly important part in the process before making its dominant influence official toward the end of the 3rd century A.D.

For the assembly, this prerogative carried an incontestable moral prestige. It revealed for all to see that now it alone represented the ancestral tradition (*mos majorum*) and that it fulfilled the function of a constitutional council that was the guardian of that tradition. It was the Senate that, on the death of a ruler—and taking into account the attitude he had adopted toward it—granted him apotheosis, an act that allowed him to be equal to the gods. On the other hand, it could condemn a deceased tyrant so that coming generations would execrate his memory. The Senate served as a rampart to forestall or limit the reign of a despot and prevent a regime from becoming dictatorial.

There was another aspect that the Senate displayed even under the Republic, and which it retained and sometimes even reinforced. It served as a symbol, physical and concrete, of the affirmation of the social class its members and their families represented—the class of the greatest landowners, the richest of Rome's citizens. The few powers that the Senate retained under the emperors—administrative, electoral, financial, or judiciary—were of secondary importance compared with the influence that senators enjoyed in the conduct of their affairs.

Augustus limited the Senate's membership to 600. But as time passed, there were not sufficient senatorial families to ensure recruitment, so "new" men had to be called in—knights or local noblemen of Italy, then of the provinces. It is striking that in almost every case, the new members who were introduced from the outside and might have brought a different atmosphere with them soon fit into the existing structure and assumed its prejudices, habits of thinking, and ideology, even when they were Christians.

It can be said that the papacy and the Senate lived separate lives, with no actual connection up to the last quarter of the 4th century. The assembly played no real part in the persecutions of Christians. Constantine's reign marked a turning point. The emperor converted to Christianity; he reorganized the Senate by extending its membership to 2,000 and giving it a different status, perhaps because from then on he no longer resided in Rome. The Senate as a body certainly saw the number of Christians within it gradually increase, yet the pope had no dealings with it—only with the Christian senators, individually or as a group. By supporting Symmachus, the Roman rhetorician, the Senate played an important role in the affair of the altar of Victory. Nevertheless, Pope DAMASUS in 382–4 had but a shadowy part in the debate. He certainly handed over to the imperial court the Christian senators' petition against Symmachus's position, but it was Ambrose, bishop of Milan (where the emperor resided), who assumed leadership of the Christian party. Symmachus rightly affirmed that the pagans had a majority in the assembly when they deliberated and cast their votes. If Ambrose claimed the opposite, it was because he implicitly took into account those senators who lived in the provinces and were not actually based in Rome.

The first authentic contact between the assembly and the pope occurred in connection with the rebuilding of the basilica of ST. PAUL'S OUTSIDE THE WALLS, as we learn from a letter of Valentine II to the prefect of the city, Sallustius, in 383–4 or 386. The emperor made it clear that a preliminary inquest had been conducted "through the efforts of the prefect in collaboration with the venerable priest," and that the decisions contained in the document should be "brought to the knowledge of the most magnificent order [the Senate] and the Christian people" (coll. Avell., 3).

The Visigothic invasion of 408–10 forced the Senate and the pope to cooperate to some degree. Innocent I agreed to join a deputation of senators going to Ravenna to plead the cause of Rome before the emperor. At that time, Christians were certainly a majority in the assembly, although the pagans remained strong. After the death of Pope ZOSIMUS in 419, violence flared up between two rivals, Boniface and Eulalius; yet once order had been reestablished and Boniface was recognized thanks to Emperor Honorius's change of position, the Senate was involved in the decision. An imperial message was read in the Curia, and the prefect of the city had the solution approved by the assembly. These episodes show that pope and Senate never really worked together; each side acted within its own particular sphere, and the prefect could, if necessary, consult them separately on the same question.

When Odoacer became king of Italy in 476 and at once wanted to reconcile with the nobility, he allowed the Senate to play a more important part than in the past. Consequently, the assembly could then exercise a palpable influence on the affairs of the Holy See, in particular on the papal elections, as with the choice of FELIX III in 483. Relations became stable under the government of Theodoric and his successors. The Senate intervened to some degree in the relations with the East. After Theodoric, it even became an institution competent to legislate in religious matters, since it was associated with the pope's decisions. As Charles Pietri has observed, it is a paradox and a curious symbol that the last texts known to us that came out of the assembly have to do with quarrels of the "clerks."

The reconquest of Rome by the Byzantines in 536 saw the gradual decline of the Curia. Rome was besieged four times and passed from hand to hand during the long, atrocious Byzantine–Gothic war, followed by the Lombard invasion. At that time, the Senate acted as municipal council of a city of mediocre demographic importance. It also seemed like a civil council assisting the pope alongside the council formed by the clergy, for the bishop was obliged to take affairs in hand more often than in previous times.

The last testimonies date from the papacy of GREGORY I. In 593, the eminent bishop gave his homily on Ezekiel: "Where is the Senate? . . . The Senate is diminished," he cried. The last known mention of the Senate was made on 25 April 603. The affirmation of the body's disappearance in those early years of the 7th century is corroborated by a passage from Agnellus, who notes that, after the Lombard invasion, "the Roman Senate gradually faded away." Only the pope remained to represent the whole of Roman society.

See also ROME.

André Chastagnol

Bibliography

Arnaldi, G. "Rinascità, fine, reincarnazione e successive metamorphosi del Senato romano (secoli V–XII)," *ASR*, 1–5 (1982), 5–56.

Chastagnol, A. *Le Sénat romain à l'époque impériale: Recherches sur la composition de l'Assemblée et le statut de ses membres*, Paris, 1992.

Lécrivain, C. *Le Sénat romain depuis Dioclétien à Rome et à Constantinople*, Paris, 1888.

Pietri, C. *Roma christiana: Recherches sur l'Église de Rome, son organisation, sa politique, son idéologie de Miltiade à Sixte III (311–440)*, 2 vols., Rome, 1976.

Stein, E. *Histoire du Bas-Empire*, I, *De l'État romain à l'État byzantin (284–476)*, Fr. trans., 2 vols., Paris, 1959; II, *De la disparition de l'Empire de Rome, son organisation, sa politique, son idéologie de Militiade à Sixte III (311–440)*, Rome, 1949.

Stein, E. "La Disparition du Sénat de Rome à la fin du VIᵉ siècle," *Académie royale de Belgique. Bulletin de la Classe des Lettres*, 25 (1939), 308–22.

Talbert, R. J. A. *The Senate of Imperial Rome*, Princeton, 1984.

SERGIUS I. (*b. Palermo, ?, d. Rome, 9 September 701). Elected pope on 15 December 687. Buried in St. Peter's, Rome. Saint (ancient cult, appears in Ado's martyrology).*

Better known today as a result of improved documentation, Sergius I's long papacy makes it possible to measure the ground covered since the pontificate of Gregory I. CONON'S reign on the seat of St. Peter was too brief to allow for much change in the situation in Rome. There were two candidates to succeed him: the archdeacon Paschal and the archpriest Theodore. Once elected, each pope occupied part of the Lateran palace with his supporters; both are now regarded as antipopes. The intervention of the exarch John Platyn on behalf of Paschal only complicated the situation. As in 686, a compromise was reached by selecting a priest—which suited the clergy—but one of Eastern origin, to appease the civil and military functionaries. Sergius was born in Palermo to a family that originally came from Antioch. Under ADEODATUS II (672–6), he embarked on an ecclesiastical career in Rome in the Schola Cantorum before becoming titular priest of St. Susanna, on the Quirinal hill.

As soon as he became pope, Sergius carried on his predecessors' programs in the city of Rome. He enriched the liturgy, which became more and more distinctive of the Roman Church, by introducing the Agnus Dei chant into the Mass. When a fragment of the True Cross was discovered, it provided an opportunity to add, probably during his pontificate, a feast day complete with the lavish ceremonies typical of the time. Sergius also encouraged the embellishment of churches, endowing them with generous gifts. This arose not so much from a new—and hypothetical—prosperity as from the clergy's desire to affirm the splendor of the city. The pope's biography bears witness to that pride.

In his dealings with Constantinople, Sergius opposed the canons of the Quinisext council convened by the emperor Justinian II (692). The latter wanted to carry out the decisions of the fifth and sixth ecumenical councils—which had not promulgated disciplinary canons—by renewing the 28th canon of the council of Chalcedon (canon 36 of 692), which stipulated that Constantinople had the same privileges as Rome. It also sought to impose Greek customs throughout the Christian world, such as authorizing priests to marry—practices that the West rejected.

The *LIBER PONTIFICALIS* lays particular stress on the show of force that threatened Rome at the time. The emperor sent his general, Zacharias, under orders either to obtain the pontifical signature or to arrest Sergius. However, the situation had changed considerably since the papacy of MARTIN I (649–53). Now, the Italian forces, in particular those of Ravenna, rushed to the aid of the pope, who even had to intervene to save Zacharias's life. These confrontations heartened the military, who wanted to have as their chief a man familiar with the East and the imperial court. From a more distant perspective, they reveal growing differences between Rome and Constantinople in the interpretation of the Christian tradition.

At the same time, the pope increased his influence over the life of the Western Churches. In Italy, he consecrated the bishop of Ravenna, Damian, who thus acknowledged the authority of Rome. In England, he sent the *pallium* to the archbishop of Canterbury, ordered the archbishop of York to be restored to his see, and welcomed King Caedwalla, who had come to Rome to be baptized (10 April 689).

Most important, Sergius expressed more decisively than in the past, the claim of the Western patriarchate to act as a universal power by appointing Willibrord to head a mission to Frisia. The pope was responding to the wishes of the mayor of the palace of Austrasia, in eastern Gaul, who was taking advantage of the missionary zeal of the English. But the bishop, who was promoted archbishop of the Frisians in Rome on 27 November 695, was under the direct authority of the pope. The Romans failed to see the potential in the simple confirmation by their pontiff of decisions taken by the civil power; thus, the *Liber pontificalis* gives them no more than two sentences.

Jean Durliat

Bibliography

JW, I, 244–5; II, 699, 741.
LP, I, 371–82.
Bertolini, O. *Roma di fronte a Bisanzio e ai Longobardi*, Bologna, 1971, 398–409.

SERGIUS II. *(b. Rome, 785/95, d. 27 January 847). Elected pope in January 844.*

Through his mother, Sergius II belonged to a Roman lineage that produced two more popes in the 9th century (STEPHEN IV and HADRIAN II). He was orphaned by the deaths of both his mother and his father when he was 12. Later, on account of his parents' nobility, LEO III took him in at the Schola Cantorum at the Lateran, where he completed his studies. He soon became an acolyte and, under PASCHAL I, a priest of the titular church of St. Sylvester, situated at the heart of the aristocratic quarter of Via Lata. Finally, under GREGORY IV, he was appointed archpresbyter, thus reaching the pinnacle of the Roman ecclesiastical hierarchy.

Sergius's election to the papacy, at which the deacon John tried to have himself proclaimed pope, was obviously organized by the Roman lay aristocracy. But, in order to obscure collusion between the latter and the pro-imperial "party" of Rome, his election was not immediately relayed to Emperor Lothair, as had been the custom since 824. The emperor refused to wait and sent his son Ludovic, king of Italy, to Rome with an army and a large group of ecclesiastics and nobles led by the bishop of Metz, Drogo, with the aim of intimidating the pope and strengthening imperial power over Rome.

Sergius handled the crisis with great skill. He renewed his oath of loyalty to the absent Lothair but not to Ludovic, who was not yet emperor. The pope thus reaffirmed the special prestige of his office by rejecting any link of vassalage between Rome and the kingdom of Italy. Subsequently, Sergius fell ill and let his brother Benedict, bishop of Albano, govern in his place. Lothair had granted Benedict the title of imperial *missus* (representative of the Emperor) to Rome. If the papal biographer is to be believed, during this period the Church was stripped of its possessions for the benefit of Benedict's protégés, a measure that incurred divine punishment in the form of the invasion of the Saracens near Ostia on 23 August 846. In the absence of any serious Roman resistance or help from either Lothair or Ludovic, the Saracen bands reached Rome and sacked St. Peter's and St. Paul's, which were then unfortified. The raiders were eventually driven out by Duke Guido of Spoleto, but peace did not actually return until several months later, the pope having died in the meantime.

Federico Marrazi

Bibliography

JE, I, 327–9.
LP, II, 8a6–105.
PL, 106, 905–17, 115, 1399.
Barezzi, P. *Rome e l'Impero medievale*, Bologna, 1947.
Duchesne, L. *Les Premiers temps de l'État pontifical*, Paris, 1898.
Llewellyn, P. *Rome in the Dark Ages*, London, 1971.

SERGIUS III. *(d. Rome September 911). Elected pope on 29 January 904. Probably buried in St. Peter's, Rome.*

Sergius was elected pope at the end of 897 but was expelled by supporters of JOHN IX. Of aristocratic birth, he was the son of a certain Benedict probably (not, as some have claimed, Pope BENEDICT III). Ordained sub-deacon by Pope MARTIN I, deacon by STEPHEN V, and bishop of Caere (present Cerveteri) by FORMOSUS, he doubtless stopped exercising his duties as bishop in 896. Violently anti-Formosan and a champion of Pope STEPHEN VI, Sergius, like Stephen, did not recognize Formosus' ordinations and may have arranged to be reordained priest by Stephen VI. After being ousted by JOHN IX in 897–8, Sergius was deposed and excommunicated at a council held in Ravenna in 898 (c. 8), if we are to identify the "priest Sergius" cited in it as the rival of John IX. Liutprand of Cremona relates that Sergius was elected at the same time as Formosus in 891, but this story has a shaky basis.

Although deprived of power, Sergius III continued to consider himself the legitimate pope and consequently to regard all the other popes, from John IX to CHRISTOPHER, as usurpers (*invasores*). In 904, with the support of the margrave Adalbert (according to Liutprand) or else with the help of the Franks (according to Auxilius, who may have used this term to describe the house of Spoleto), he managed to eliminate both LEO V and Christopher (both of whom he imprisoned and had murdered) and finally seated himself on the papal throne. He is believed to have been consecrated pope on 29 January 904.

Sergius at once set about revoking, in a synod, the decrees concerning Formosus, most of which had been adopted during John IX's pontificate, as well as the ordinations he had granted, and to reaffirm the "cadaver synod" condemnation of Formosus pronounced by Stephen VI. Sergius intended to carry on Stephen's tradition—in fact, many sources confuse the two—and probably had his predecessor's bones transferred to below the porch of St. Peter's (907). He also undertook the rebuilding of the basilica of the Lateran, whose walls had crumbled during Stephen VI's pontificate.

The refusal to recognize ordinations conferred by Formosus entailed a large number of reordinations, which resulted in terrible confusion. The ensuing conflict was expressed in the lampoons of Auxilius of Naples and Eugenius Vulgarius (see also the *Invectiva in Romam*), which did not pose a real threat to the papacy of the anti-Formosan Sergius. After Sergius's reign, certain noble Roman families, particularly that of the consul and Roman senator Theophylact, exercised a direct and obvious influence on the papacy. Theodora, Theophylact's wife, is said to have influenced papal policy considerably. According to the no doubt polemical testimony of Liutprand of Cremona, Sergius even had a son by Marozia, Theodora's daughter, who would become Pope JOHN XI.

There is evidence of several plans to reinstall the empire during Sergius's pontificate, but they were not put into practice. Despite these restrictions, his pontificate once again set the papacy on a firmer basis. Documents note at least passive contacts with the Christian world—Italy and Germany, and especially France. In Byzantium, the obstacles placed in the way of the fourth marriage of Emperor Leo VI (886–911) provoked the tetragamy dispute, which Sergius III obligingly settled in the emperor's favor. Since an appeal had been made to the pope, this was one way to impose Rome's power in the East.

It is dificult to form an opinion of this pope, since all the critical sources come from the camp of the Formosans, who, being hostile to Sergius, gave a distorted picture of him. Certainly the elimination of two popes resulted in his pontificate's beginning under bad auspices. As for the council of 904, it does not show signs of a renewal but, rather, retrogression. Nevertheless, with Sergius, the Formosan quarrels did finally come to an end. The papacy as an institution emerged somewhat strengthened, despite the pernicious effects of the dominance of the Roman nobility and the influence of what was satirized as the "government of women." Contrary to the claim of Benedict of Mt. Soracte, Sergius III's death must be placed not in April but in September 911.

Klaus Herbers

Bibliography

JL, I, 445–7, II, 705, 746.

LP, 2, 236–8.

Carbonetti Venditelli, C. *Le più antiche carte del convento di San Sisto in Roma (905–1300)*, Rome, 1987 (Codice diplomatico di Roma e della Regione romana), 2–8.

Duchesne, L. "Serge III et Jean XI," *MAH*, 33 (1913), 25–55.

Dümmler, E. *Auxilius und Vulgarius*, Leipzig, 1866.

Fedele, P. "Ricerche per la storia di Roma e del papato nel secolo X," *ASR*, 33 (1910), 177–247; 34 (1911), 75–115, 393–423.

Hartmann, W. *Die Synoden der Karolingerzeit im Frankreich und in Italien*, Paderborn, 1989 (Konziliengeschichte, Reihe A, Darstellungen), 396.

Scholz, S. *Transmigration und Translation: Studien zum Bistumswechsel der Bischöfe von der Spätantike bis zum Hohen Mittelalter*, Cologne-Weimar-Vienna, 1992 (Kölner Historische Abhandlungen, 37), 228–32.

Zimmermann, H. *Papstabsetzungen des Mittelalters*, Graz-Vienna-Cologne, 1968, 64–5.

Zimmermann, H. *Papsturkunden*, 31–57.

SERGIUS IV. *Peter Os Porci (d. Rome, 12 May 1012). Elected pope 31 July 1009. Buried in St. John Lateran.*

It was undoubtedly only after the death of his predecessor, JOHN XVIII, that the bishop of Albano, Peter Os Porci (Bocca di Porco, or "Pig's Snout"), was elected pope under the name of Sergius IV, at the instigation of the Roman patrician John II Crescentius. Peter was the son of a Roman shoemaker in the area known as Ad Pinea, near the Via Lata, and his wife, Stephania. Through his mother, he may have been related to the Crescentii or to his predecessor. Like John XVIII, but more prudently, he sought to establish ties with the court of the king of Germany. It is in the context of this program that, shortly after he was raised to the pontificate in 1009, he caused to be erected in the basilica of the Lateran a funerary monument to Pope SYLVESTER II, a close friend of Emperor Otto III. Not long after the enthronement of Bishop Thietmar of Merseburg (21 May 1009), the pope confirmed the restoration of his bishopric and possessions. At the beginning of April 1012, Sergius sent legates to consecrate the cathedral of Bamberg—the favorite church of the German king, Henry II—and renewed the privilege set up for that foundation by John XVIII. Nothing is known of the other missions given to the legates, but it is likely that the king was invited to Rome to be crowned, an invitation rendered null and void by Sergius IV's sudden death in May 1012.

The story that Sergius IV called for a crusade after the destruction of the Church of the Holy Sepulcher in Jerusalem by the caliph Al-Hakim on 18 October 1009, and that the pope was planning to lead the army into the Holy Land in person, is spurious. Perhaps it should be linked to a reference, probably dating from the year 1010, to Sergius's attempts to form a coalition of Italian princes designed to expel the Muslim Saracens from Sicily. The contents of that reference are also disputed. Just as false, apparently, is the account according to which the pope is said, in 1009, to have sent the Byzantine patriarch Sergius II a credo with the highly controversial Filioque (stating that the Holy Spirit proceeds from both Father and Son) and thus to have provoked the excommunication by the patriarch of all the popes since Christopher and the erasure of their names from the prayer diptychs of the Roman Church in the East, the origin of the religious schism between the two Churches.

It is certain, however, that the granting of a privilege to the archbishopric of Benevento, which was under the nominal authority of Byzantium, helped give rise to long-lasting disputes. This suggests the true origin of the "change that occurred under Sergius IV in the relations between Rome and Byzantium" (H. Zimmermann).

The pope established relations with monasteries and religious institutions in Catalonia and the south of France, ties that were reinforced by his successor, BENEDICT VIII. Toward the end of his pontificate, there were apparently tentative, indirect contacts with the reforming monastery of Cluny, but like the even more hesitant contacts with the German court, they were inconclusive.

Sergius IV died 12 May 1012, perhaps violently in the course of conflict between the Crescentii and their Tusculan rivals. His epitaph is in the basilica of the Lateran.

Klaus-Jürgen Herrmann

Bibliography

JW, I, 504 ff.
LP, II, 266 ff.
Amann, E. "Serge IV," *DTC*, 14–2 (1941), 1021–2.
Schaller, H. M. "Zur Kreuzzugenzyklikta Papst Sergius IV." *Papsttum, Kirche und Recht im Mittelalter, Festschrift H. Fuhrmann*, Tübingen, 1991, 135–53.
Zimmermann, H. *Papstregesten*, 1036–74.
Zimmermann, H. *Papsturkunden*, II, 443–63.

SERVICES. See **Common and Small Services.**

SEVERINUS. *(b. Rome, ?, d. Rome, 2 August 640). Elected pope on 28 May 640. Buried in St. Peter's, Rome.*

This extremely ephemeral papacy shows how fully enmeshed the civil and religious sectors had become in Byzantum; it also illustrates the particularism of regions that were even less well controlled because of the Arab dismemberment of the Empire. To judge from his name, this son of a certain Avienus belonged to the ruling class of Rome, where he may have had an ecclesiastical career. His election by the clergy and the Roman nobles was doubtless submitted to the exarch Isaac of Ravenna, according to official procedure. The exarch seems to have insisted on the pope's approval of Emperor Heraclius's doctrinal ecthesis regarding the monothelite heresy, which had been sent by the patriarch Sergius of Constantinople. When the pontifical emissaries refused, Rome now being uncompromising, the matter was taken up by the court. The pope's apocrisaries (envoys) waited for imperial confirmation of Severinus from late 538 to the summer of 540. It was long in arriving, since Heraclius insisted that ecthesis be signed before he confirmed the election. He finally yielded, without obtaining any concession from Rome, thus recognizing Rome's autonomy, de facto if not de jure.

Meanwhile, the exarch, as the emperor's representative, was demanding that the pope, considered to be merely the manager of Rome's public finances, pay the military stationed in the city. Isaac sent one of his functionaries, the registrar Mauritius, to demand, by order of the Emperor himself, the monies that were kept in the papal treasury, and were owed to the soldiers—the *exercitus romanus*—who were included in the city of Rome's budget. Despite this dramatic twist, it is clear that the pope managed two budgets, one for ecclesiastical expenses and one for civil and military expenses of the city of Rome. It is certain that the wages were in fact paid by the services of the central administration, and that the seals placed by the exarch's staff made it easier to distinguish, among the monies deposited in the pontifical treasury, which went to which of the budgets managed by the bishop of Rome.

When the *LIBER PONTIFICALIS* states that after this inquiry "part of the resources was sent to the emperor Heraclius, in the capital; later, the most holy Severinus was consecrated and Isaac returned to Ravenna," there is no reason not to believe the writer. The Romans exerted pressure to obtain confirmation of their pope by not paying the wages. The emperor responded by delaying his confirmation for a year and a half. Everything ended in a compromise after various attempts at intimidation. For its share, the clergy received a year's salary on the pope's death, according to a custom that gradually became established.

Jean Durliat

Bibliography

JW, I, 227.
LP, I, 328–9.
PL, 129, 583–6.
Bertolini, O. *Roma di fronte a Bizanzio e ai Longobardi*, Bologna, 1971, 317–26.
Mansi, 675–80.

SICKNESS OF THE POPE, MIDDLE AGES. The history of medieval popes must include the history of their health. Not only did good or poor health influence the popes' activities, but it fed rumors and conjectures. Sometimes the poor health of a candidate for the papacy, paradoxically, was a decisive factor in his election, the cardinals wishing to elect a pope of transition who they thought would only occupy the apostolic see briefly.

In general, the illnesses of the popes of the Middle Ages are known to us through three types of documents: (1) biographies, especially those contained in the *LIBER PONTIFICALIS* or in the *Lives* written about saintly popes, (2) through their correspondence, quite abundant for certain popes, and (3) toward the end of the Middle Ages, through the reports made by ambassadors. Despite all these, for many popes we must resign ourselves to knowing practically nothing about their state of health.

If we examine the lives of the 163 popes from Gregory the Great to ALEXANDER VI, we first notice that a large number of them were elected at an advanced age. Therefore, they suffered from the illnesses caused by old age, and the role that they were able to play was accordingly reduced. For some, age only allowed them a few months or even a few weeks as pope. This was the case for an entire series of popes during the 7th century: SEVERINUS (639–40), AGATHO (678–81), JOHN V (685–6), and CONON (686–7) (of whom the *Liber pontificalis* says, that at the time of his election he was a very old and venerable monk). For the same reason, SISINNIUS, elected in 708, was only pope for 20 days; VALENTINE, elected in 827, had only one month's reign; BONIFACE VI, elected in 896, 15 days; and THEODORE II, elected in 897, 20 days. In 1187 GREGORY VIII was elected at age 87 and died two months later. CELESTINE IV was an old man living his final days when he was elected on 25 October 1241. He died on 10 November of the same year without having been crowned. Also, ADRIAN V was old and suffering from fevers at the time of his election in 1276 and only reigned for 5 weeks.

The handicap of age was, however, overcome by several popes and did not stop them, to the astonishment of everyone, from displaying an untiring level of activity. CELESTINE III (1191–8) was 85 when elected. He remained on the pontifical throne for 7 years and died at age 92. JOHN XXII (1316–34) was already in his seventies at the time of his election. He reigned for 18 years and, thanks to an ordered life, was able to display an astonishing resistance to fatigue and an exceptional level of work until the time of his death. Another example, CALLISTUS III (1455–8), was elected at age 77 because the conclave thought that he had only months to live. During the 3 years of his pontificate he showed invincible energy and displayed an inflexible will against the Turkish peril. One week before his death, he was still making important decisions. On the other hand, other popes, much younger, were perpetually ill. Gregory the Great (590–604) reveals, through his letters, his sufferings from the illness that he endured for most of his life. CLEMENT III (1187–91) had a heart condition, it seems, and was always sickly. Among the popes at AVIGNON, CLEMENT V (1305–14) and GREGORY XI (1370–8) were the youngest but also the most infirm. Their poor health slowed their pontifical activities in several cases. Gregory XI, the youngest of the popes at Avignon, died before he reached the age of 50. In the 15th century, NICHOLAS V (1447–55), only 49 at the time of his election, was in delicate health and, from 1450 on, continually ill. PIUS II (1458–64) was already a sick old man at the time of his enthronement, though he was barely 53 years old. Finally, INNOCENT VIII (1484–92) was, during his entire pontificate, a perpetual sufferer.

These elderly or ailing popes can be compared with other pontiffs who enjoyed vigorous good health until just before their death: ALEXANDER II (1061–73), URBAN II (1088–99), PASCHAL II (1099–1118), ALEXANDER III (1159–81), INNOCENT III (1198–1216), MARTIN V (1417–31), and EUGENE IV (1431–47).

What illness most frequently afflicted these popes? The imprecision of records keeps us, in many cases, from knowing. What should we conclude, for example, from texts saying that a particular pope had "pernicious fevers?" For several popes we have more precise information. Several of them suffered from gout, an illness that, while not mortal, caused a great deal of pain and rendered them invalids when it was chronic. Gregory the Great suffered from digestive troubles all his life and was afflicted with gout during the last years of his pontificate. He ended up spending his days in bed, only standing up for great occasions. MARTIN I (649–54) suffered from gout and dysentery. Others with gout were Sisinnius, SERGIUS II (844–47), Boniface VI, INNOCENT VI (1352–62), Nicholas V, and Pius II. Several other popes had kidney- or gallstones: CLEMENT VI (1342–52), URBAN V (1362–70), Gregory XI, BONIFACE IX (1389–1404). Several other illnesses are also named, or can be deduced from records. The serious digestive troubles of Clement V were perhaps due to liver or intestinal cancer. BENEDICT XII (1334–42) had to bear gangrenous ulcers on his legs, which ended up killing him.

To fight their illnesses, the popes very naturally turned to medicine. We know that at the end of the Middle Ages, like most European sovereigns the popes had their own medical service. We are well enough informed on those at the court at Avignon. The pope had, in principle, one or two appointed doctors permanently present with him, but, when ill, several doctors of good reputation were called in as consultants. In the accounts of the APOSTOLIC CAMERA, the rather considerable salaries paid to doctors and surgeons for the pope are noted. In 1385 the annual salary of the doctor Jean de Tournemire was as high as 400 gold francs. To the doctors of Italian origin were added, in a notable proportion, local doctors. It has been calculated that at least one out of five, and probably one in four, had done his medical studies at Montpellier. Among the most famous are Arnaud de Villeneuve, Guy de Chauliac, Jean de Tournemire, Raymond Calmel de Viviers, along with Italians Paolo Geminelli and Gandolfo di Cremona. The pope's apothecary specialized in furnishing medicines for the papal household. He prepared, according to doctors' instructions, the drugs prescribed for the pontiff. He also embalmed the pope's corpse after his death. In the 14th century one of the best known was Jacques Melior, succeeded after his death by his son, Agapitus Melior.

The state of the popes' health, especially in the case of an elderly pope or one in fragile health, was the object of constant rumors. Without doubt, during the time of the GREAT SCHISM, the health of the popes and antipopes was scrutinized attentively because the death of one of the popes could signal the end of the Schism. In August 1398 the rumor spread through Paris that BENEDICT XIII, the pope in Avignon, then around age 70, was seriously ill with a contagious, epidemic-causing disease. Soon a letter was written in the king's name recommending that the cardinals postpone any election, but Benedict XIII recovered and the letter was never sent. At the end of the 15th century, the always shaky health of Innocent VIII was the object of general preoccupation: several times, news of his death spread in Rome and everyone withdrew to their homes, fearing trouble. The 15th century was also a time when there was more information available regarding the popes' health than in previous centuries. The reason for this was the rise of diplomacy. The great European states and the principal Italian cities (Milan, Venice, Florence, Genoa, Naples) all had their ambassadors at the pope's court, who reported on the pope in regular dispatches covering the popes' activities and all pertinent information including his state of health, opening the door to speculations.

To what extent did the popes' illnesses influence their policies and their actions? Though it is difficult to answer such a question, it is certain that a constantly ill pope would have to slow his level of activity, and rely more on the zeal of his subordinates and the suggestions of his entourage. Sickness also made some popes more pessimistic and cowardly. Beginning in 1312 the illness that would cause his death two years later took hold of Clement V without respite. His will weakened, and his character became more bitter, erratic, and impulsive. The situation of Pope Nicolas V, in the middle of the 15th century, was similar: intellectually brilliant with a sensitive soul, he plunged into melancholy toward the end of his life due to his constant suffering and as a result of an assassination attempt. On the other hand, illness did not stop Pius II from expending his remaining strength on his plan for a crusade. On 18 June 1464, already quite weak, he insisted on leading the army. Traveling by water in small stages, he reached Ancona with the last of his vital energy, and died at the moment the Venetian fleet, long awaited, entered the port.

Elected sovereigns, the popes escaped several hereditary illnesses that affected certain kings, but their age, often advanced at the time of election, led many of them to suffer the usual afflictions of old age. The fact that they were elected was largely responsible for the numerous speculations made about their state of health.

Pierre-André Sigal

Bibliography

Aubert, R. (ed.), *DHGE*, Paris, since 1912.

Gagnière, S. "Les apothicaires à la cour des papes d'Avignon," *Revue d'Histoire de la Pharmacie*, 1976, 147–57 and 226–36.

Guillemain, B. *La Cour pontificale d'Avignon au XIVe siècle (1309–1376). Étude d'une société*, Paris, 1966.

Le Blévec, D. "Les médecins de l'université de Montpellier et la papauté d'Avignon," *Une université, ses maîtres et ses étudiants depuis sept siècles, 1289–1989*, Montpellier, 1992, 39–43.

Mann, H. K. *The Lives of the Popes in the Middle Ages*, London, 1906–32, 18 vol.

Marini, G. *Degli archiatri pontifici*, Rome, 1784.

Pansier, P. "Les médecins des papes d'Avignon," *Janus*, 1909, 405–34.

Pastor, 1.

See also PRIVATE LIVES, POPES'.

SIGNATURE (TRIBUNAL). See **Tribunals, Apostolic.**

SILVERIUS. *(d. Palmaria, 2 December 537.) Elected pope probably in June 536. Deposed on 25 March 537. Saint.*

The son of Pope HORMISDAS (514–23), Silverius himself wrote his father's epitaph, in which he celebrated the end of the schism between Rome and Constantinople. He was a subdeacon of the Roman Church when the Gothic king Theodahad thrust him forward as the successor of Pope AGAPITUS (536, in Constantinople). According to a passage in the *LIBER PONTIFICALIS*, which is hostile to him, the Roman priests who refused to sign his election decree were forcibly obliged to swear their allegiance after his ordination.

The new pope found himself in a precarious situation. His election frustrated the plans of Empress Theodora, who wanted to see on the throne a pope who would allow the monophysite bishop Anthimus, deposed by Agapitus, to be returned to the see of Constantinople. She persuaded the Roman deacon Vigilius by promising him the see of Peter in exchange for his accommodation of the monophysites.

Then Justinian's general, Belisarius, entered Rome in December 536. Although Silverius seems to have persuaded the citizens to yield to Belisarius, the pope was suspected of harboring sympathies for Theodahad's replacement, Witiges. The situation grew even more delicate when the chief of the Goths besieged Rome in 537. Silverius was soon urged to reestablish Anthimus, if not directly by Theodora then at least by Belisarius himself and especially by his wife Antonina, who was anxious to please the empress. But he refused, and a forged letter from him was written by Belisarius's entourage, in which the pope promised to hand Rome over to Witiges.

Belisarius, at first silent in the face of these accusations, finally summoned Silverius to justify himself. At the second interview, the disillusioned pope submitted, despite the warnings of those closest to him. Then, having been separated from his entourage, Silverius was stripped of the *pallium* in Virgilius's presence and forced by two Roman clerics to don a monk's habit. The next day (25 March 537), Belisarius had VIGILIUS elected pope, while Silverius was sent into exile to Patara in Lycia.

The bishop of Patara, indignant at the pope's fate, went to Justinian to protest. Despite the opposition of the Roman deacon Pelagius, who had sided with Theodora, the emperor decided to send Silverius back to Italy to be judged. If found guilty, he would be returned to his throne, but outside Rome. If found innocent, he could return to his see as well. In Italy, Silverius fell victim to the intrigues of Vigilius, who, under direct threat from the imperial decision, told Belisarius that he would not support the monophysite cause. He gained permission to have Silverius delivered to him. Exiled to the island of Palmaria, Silverius died there, probably of hunger. The sacrilegious crime perpetrated to Vigilius's advantage underlined the dependence of the Apostolic See on the imperial power and presaged the difficulties to be faced by later pontificates.

Christiane Fraisse-Coué

Bibliography

Amann, E. *DTC*, 14, 2, 2065–7.

Auctuarium Marcellini, A. 537, MGH, 9, *Chronica minora*, 2, 105.

Duchesne, L. *L'Église au VIe siècle*, Paris, 1925, 151–4.

Gaspar, E. *Geschichte des Papsttums*, II, Tübingen, 1930, 228.

Hildebrand, P. *Die Absetzung des Papsts Silverius, Historisches Jahrbuch*, 42, 1922, 231–49.

Liber pontificalis, I, 290–5.

Liberatus, *Breviarium causae Nestorianorum et Eutychianorum* 22, ACO, II, 136–7.

Procopius, *De bello gothico*, I, 25, ed. Haury, 125; *Historia arcana*, I, 14 and 27, Paris, 39 and 31.

SILVESTER I. *(b. Rome, ?, d. Rome, 31 December 335). Elected 31 January 314. Buried in the cemetery of St. Priscilla on the Via Salaria. Saint.*

Pope MILTIADES's successor had to administer his Church under changed conditions. It was during his episcopate, at 22 years one of the longest, that Christianity saw the realization of the changes begun by his predecessor in favor of freedom of worship, as well as the rise of the Donatist crisis and the Arian heresy.

That little is known of his role in such great ecclesiastical events as the establishment of the churches in Rome can be explained by the fragmentary surviving documentation. But it also resulted in some harsh judgments being made on Silvester's retiring character. He was, however, one of the first confessors whose cult was established in Rome, and hagiographical accounts have helped to elucidate his memory, though both enriching and distorting it.

Born in Rome—the son of a priest, Rufinus, according to the *LIBER PONTIFICALIS*—Silverster I is said to have been a priest under the episcopate of Marcellus. He inherited the Donatist affair, which the council his predecessor held in 313 had not been able to solve, since the Donatists again sought help from the emperor directly. Constantine decided to convene an important council in Arles on 1 August 314, and made the imperial postal system available to the bishops, as he indicated in a letter to Chrestos of Syracuse.

The council was to be held "in the presence of the bishop of Rome." It consisted of 33 bishops drawn from all over the West, several churches being represented by lower-ranking clergy. The pope did not attend. His recent consecration may have been one reason for his absence, but more likely Silvester was reluctant to go to a council convened by the emperor. He arranged to be represented by two priests, Claudianus and Verus, and two deacons, Eugenius and Quiriacus, who acted more as observers than as representatives of the Roman episcopal authority.

The council once again condemned the Donatists and confirmed the legitimacy of Caecilianus of Carthage. The bishops then sent the pope a highly deferential letter (*dilectissimus papa, gloriosissimus*) in which they regretted his absence. Sure of his agreement with the judgment, they surmised that the sentence would have been harsher had he been present. They informed him that they had pronounced judgment on a certain number of provisions on the organization of the life of the Church—such as the date of Easter, communion, and baptism—and hoped that he would make the legislation known to all the Churches. By asking him to fix the date of Easter in a global letter, they thereby recognized the primacy of the bishop of Rome over the West. The decisions of the council of Arles are to be found in a separate collection, edited as *Canones ad Silvestrum*. A century later, in 410–11, Augustine of Hippo would defend Silvester's memory as well as that of his predecessors, whom the Donatists accused of having surrendered the Scriptures at the time of the Diocletian persecution.

Parallel with Donatism in Africa, Silvester's pontificate saw the spread of the Arian HERESY in the East. It was Arius who, around 319, professed a doctrine of the Trinity that recognized the divinity of God the Father alone, the Son being the first of His creatures. After the council of Alexandria in 323, Bishop Alexander communicated to the pope the council's decisions excommunicating Arius. The emperor tried unsuccessfully to reconcile the two rivals, telling them in writing that they were disputing "over useless details" and sending Bishop Osius of Cordoba on a mission to Alexandria. In May 325, he held a general assembly of the whole episcopate in Nicaea, a city in northwestern Turkey that could easily be reached by the Italian and European bishops; however, those who attended, thanks to the *cursus publicus* (public transport) were mainly Eastern bishops.

Because of his age, according to Eusebius of Caesarea, or perhaps because this was a council convened by the emperor, Silvester again did not attend. He delegated two of his priests, Vitus and Vincentius, the future bishop of Capua, who followed the debates unobtrusively. Yet even though they were simply priests, they countersigned the documents immediately after Osius of Cordoba, who presided over the assembly. The title of "legate of the pope" given to that bishop was accredited by Gelasius of Cyzicus and repeated thereafter, perhaps to cover up Silvester's silence in this Eastern affair.

The legates reported to the pope the condemnation of Arius, the formula of the Nicaean creed, and some disciplinary and liturgical canons, including that dealing with Easter, which was to be determined by an agreement between Rome and Alexandria. Silvester's reaction to this dossier is not known, but a year later, in 326, the bishop of Rome announced a date for Easter that differed from the one put forward by Alexandria. The Arians, back in Constantine's graces from 328, undertook a purge in which several bishops who had defended the Nicene creed fell victim. Throughout this crisis, there was frequent criticism of Silvester's seclusion far from the troubled areas, as well as for his respect for the autonomy of the Eastern Churches in a Roman primacy that was in the midst of establishing itself.

More is known about the great building work undertaken in Rome thanks to imperial endowments. Silvester, in fact, was a witness to the building of Rome as a Christian city. The construction of many churches in Rome is attributed to Constantine, who paid for them by donating lands in his possessions in Italy and the East. In the case of some churches, epigraphic and archeological evidence confirm the list of churches in the *Liber pontificalis*. In Silvester's pontificate, Constantine caused to be built during the first 20 years of his reign the Constantinian basilica (ST. JOHN LATERAN), erected on the domain of the Laterani; the Sessorian basilica (St. Croce in Gerusalemme) next to Helena's Palace; the funerary basilica of the martyrs Sts. Marcellinus and Peter; ST. PAUL'S OUTSIDE THE WALLS; and the Laurentian basilica (St. Lawrence) on the Via Tiburtina. The second part of Constantine's reign saw work begin on St. Peter's of the Vatican, which probably started before 333 and was completed in 354.

All these churches were provided with oratories, liturgical trappings, and decoration. Silvester also was active in creating burial areas, in particular the cemetery of the Church on the Appian Way, where Pope EUSEBIUS is interred. To the north, he had an oratory built along the Via Salaria, dedicated to St. Priscilla.

In two instances, the *Liber pontificalis* reports that Silvester founded a church near the Domitian baths. This was the *titulus Equitii*, called *titulus Silvestri* at the end of the notice. The patrimonial list appended shows some discrepancies. Some have believed the references to these churches to be fabrications, because of the repetition of the evidence. However, the *titulus Equitii* was a church that was represented at the Roman synod of 499 by two priests, Sebastianus and Adeodatus. In Pope SYMMACHUS's time, this *titulus* became, against all probability, the *titulus sancti Silvestri*, after Symmachus had it restored in order to dedicate it officially to St. Silvester and St. Martin. There is in fact mention of a church *tituli sancti Silvestri* at the synod of Rome of 595. The discovery in 1632 of a lamp dedicated to *sancto Silvestro* in the garden adjoining the church of S. Martino ai Monti in Rome is an indication of the site of Silvester's church.

The pope died on 31 December 335, according to the *Liberian Catalogue*, the *Hieronymian Martyrology* (which qualifies him as *sanctus*), and the *Depositio episcoporum*, which was written less than a year after his death. He was buried in the Priscilla cemetery on the Via Salaria, and the name Priscilla ad s. Silvestrum was given to this cemetery in the 7th-century *Itineraries*. In this area, in 1890, J. B. de Rossi discovered a group of buildings including one which he took to be a *basilica Silvestri* and which may have contained Silvester's tomb, but there was no epigraphical evidence to confirm this hypothesis.

Perhaps because his reign is so little known and because he was pope in a period of transition, the gaps in Silvester's history have been filled by legend more than with any other pope. Three chief documents, examined briefly here—the *Vita Silvestri*, *Constitutum Silvestri*, and Donation of Constantine—have helped to give a false image of Silvester. The *Vita Silvestri*, probably written in Rome at the end of the 6th century and erroneously attributed to Eusebius of Caesarea, relates fictitious episodes on the persecution of Silvester by Constantine and the pope's baptism of the emperor at the Lateran.

The writer of the *Liber pontificalis* clearly drew his inspiration from this document, with a certain eclecticism. Introducing the pope's dogmatic activity—*Hic fecit constitutum de omni Ecclesia*—he lists the disciplinary and liturgical measures taken at a council in Rome of 270 bishops that was convened by Silvester after Nicaea. Such a council did not in fact take place, and its fabrication descends straight from the series of Symmachian apocryphal writings to which the *Constititum Silvestri* belongs. The Donation of Constantine, a document included in the Pseudo-Isodorian *Decretals* fabricated in the 8th century, is a purported copy of a letter from Constantine to Silvester in which he gives the pope spiritual primacy over all bishops and agrees to share temporal sovereignty with him. This supposed edict of Constantine inspired Pope HADRIAN I to confer on Charlemagne the bases of pontifical prerogatives over certain cities. The influence of the forgery lasted until the 16th century. The extensive iconography of this pope, one of the many examples of which is the frescoes in the church of the Quattro Sancti Coronati in Rome, was inspired by the Donation of Constantine and episodes of the *Vita Silvestri*.

Élisabeth Paoli

Bibliography

LP, I, 170–87; see L. Duchesne, notes 187–201 and Introduction, CIX–CXX, CXXXIII–CLIV.

Acta syn. rom., 1, 7, MGH AA 12, 413 = Symmachus, *Ep.* 1, 9, ed. Thiel, 652–53.

Amman, E. "Silvestre," *DTC*, 14, 7 (1941), 2068–75.

Amore, A. "Silvestro," *EC,*. 11 (1953), 596–7.

Augustine, *De unico baptismo*, 16, 27, and 30, *CSEL*, 53, 28, and 31; *Ep.* 53, 3, *CSEL* 34, 2, 153–4.

Caspar, E. *Geschichte des Papsttums*, I, Tübingen, 1930, 115–30.

Concilia Gallia, CC, 148, 9–25.

Epistula ad Silvestrum, in Optatus of Milevis, App. III, *CSEL*, 26, 206–8.

De Rossi, G. B. *Roma sotteranea*, Rome, 1867, II:, 195–210.

Depositio episcoporum, *MGH*, AA, 9, 70.

Eusebius of Caesarea and Jerome, *Chron.* a. 314, PL 27, 495.

Ewig, E. "Die Konstantin-Tradition im Kaiserlichen Italien und in der römischen Kirche," *Das Bild Constantins des Grossen im abendländlischen Mittelalter*, *Historisches Jahrbuch*, 75 (1956), 10–18.

Gregorius, *Decretum*, MGH, Ep. I, 366.

Leclercq, H. "Silvestre," *DACL*, 15, 1 (1950), 1455–8.

Levison, W. "Konstantinische Schenkung und Silvester-Legende," *Mélanges Ehle, Studi e Testi*, 38 (1924), 159–247.

Liberian Catalogue, ed. Duchesne, 9.

Martyrolog. hieronym., AASS, Nov. II, p. post. 17.

Mocchegiani-Carpano, C. "Silvestro," *BS*, 11 (1968), 1081–2 (iconography).

Picard, J. C. "Études sur l'emplacement des tombes des papes," *MEFR*, 81 (1969), 739 ff.

Pietri, C. *Roma christiana*, Rome, 1976, I, 14–21, 69–77, 168–87, and II, 1699.

Sozomen, HE, I, 17; GCS, 50, 36.

Vieillard, R. *Saint-Martin-aux-Monts à Rome*, Rome-Paris, 1931, 11 ff.

Vita Silvestri, ed. Mombaritius, *Sanctuarium*, II, 508–31 (ed. 1910) = *BHL*, 7725–35.

SILVESTER II. *Gerbert d'Aurillac (b. Aquitaine, mid-10th century, d. Rome, 12 May 1003). Elected pope on 2 April 999. Ordained on 9 April. Buried in St. John Lateran.*

Pope Silvester II's life, in some ways an extraordinary one, has fired many people's imagination. A monk, the head of a cathedral school, an abbot in Italy, once again a teacher in Rheims, then archbishop of that city and later of Ravenna, and finally pope in the year 1000, Silvester II was one of the great personalities of the early Middle Ages.

At a very young age, Gerbert was sent to the monastery of Saint-Géraud d'Aurillac. Attracting his abbot's attention because of his unusual intelligence, he was entrusted to the care of the count of Barcelona and for three years studied at the schools of Vich and Ripoli. Here he learned arithmetic, geometry, astronomy, and music, sciences which the Catalans knew through their contacts with the Arab world. In 970, Gerbert came to Rome, where he became acquainted with Pope JOHN XIII and Emperor Otto the Great. Declining to remain in their service, he left to study dialectics in Rheims, soon becoming head of the cathedral school and a friend of the archbishop, Adalbero. His teaching, which was based on experimental methods, attracted large numbers of followers; one was Richer, a monk of Saint-Remi of Rheims, his future biographer.

In 981 in Ravenna, Gerbert met Otto II, who bestowed on him the abbey of Bobbio with its famous library. But the opposition of the lay aristocracy and some monks forced him to leave Bobbio on the death of the emperor (983) and to return to Rheims, where he resumed his studies and teaching. There he assisted Archbishop Adalbero in his struggles against the Carolingian kings, Lothair and Louis V, and helped to secure the advent to the throne of Hugh Capet in 987.

Two years later, the archbishop died and Gerbert hoped to succeed him. But Hugh Capet was eager to give the archbishopric to a Carolingian prince in order to cement relations with his political rivals. However, Arnoul, the new archbishop, betrayed the king shortly after he was consecrated (August 989). After briefly hesitating over which choice to make, Gerbert sided with the king, who triumphed over the Carolingians and clapped Archbishop Arnoul into prison.

At this point, the king asked Pope JOHN XV for advice on how to deal with the felonious archbishop. The pope sent no reply. After waiting for 11 months, the king decided to have Arnoul tried by a national synod at Saint-Basle-de-Verzy, near Rheims. The bishop of Orleans, another Arnoul, and a friend of Gerbert's, took the part of accuser; Abbo, abbot of Fleury-sur-Loire, was one of the advocates. Thirteen bishops representing the four ecclesiastical provinces of the kingdom were present, and the archbishop of Sens, primate of both Gauls, presided over the debates.

Basing his argument on the canons of the "False Decretals," Abbo claimed that the synod had no power to judge an archbishop and that appeal should be made to the pope. Arnoul of Orleans replied that the pope had remained silent, and, moreover, the immorality and incompetence of the popes made them incapable of judging a case that the bishops could examine. Almost certainly on Gerbert's advice, Arnoul pronounced a violent indictment against the papacy, which became famous and was published by Protestant historians at the beginning of the 17th century.

Arnoul had numerous examples of dishonorable popes to choose from, even though he picked the notorious JOHN XII. "Can the bishops," he asked, "be legally subjected to such monsters, full of ignomy, devoid of divine and human knowledge?" The bishops assembled at Saint-Basle were then asked to observe the canons of the councils of Africa and those of Gregory the Great and to follow "the example of those who in the days of Louis the Pious deposed Archbishop Ebbo of Rheims, who was also guilty of treason."

Having acknowledged his wrongdoings, Arnoul of Rheims was deposed and shortly afterward replaced by Gerbert. A long conflict then ensued between the new archbishop and the papacy. John XV dispatched the abbot Leo to investigate the affair, ordering him to convene a council at Aix-la-Chapelle in 992. Hugh Capet invited the pope to come to France, or at least to the neutral territory of Grenoble, but John XV refused. The legate organized a council at Mouzon, in the Ardennes (June 995), which the king forbade the bishops to attend. Gerbert disobeyed in order to vindicate himself. He pleaded his case in a long speech, which has been preserved, and accepted the idea of a "national" council to be held in Rheims in July 995. Meanwhile, he published the documents of the synod of Saint-Basle, which he had written down and which contained the attacks on the papacy.

The legate Leo was shocked by this "veritable pamphlet, filled with insults and blasphemies against the Church of Rome," as he wrote Hugh Capet. He went so far as to call the bishops "antichrists." He took up their arguments point by point to justify the popes. Gerbert then wrote a long letter to Bishop Wilderod of Strasburg in which he laid out his "Gallican" ideas. For Gerbert, as for Hincmar, the the universal Church was made up of all the local Churches; all the bishops could share in the powers of Peter. "Arnoul has been condemned according to the rules of the Gospel and the precepts of the apostles and the prophets; in this matter we have observed the holy councils and the decrees of the bishops of Rome according to the advice and the decisions of the most learned and most eloquent bishops."

In a letter to Seguin, archbishop of Rheims, Gerbert defined the common law of the Catholic Church as "the Gospel, the apostles, the prophets, the canons inspired by the spirit of God and consecrated by the respect of the whole world and the decrees of the Holy See when they do not depart from those canons." The council of Rheims not having come up with a solution to the conflict, Gerbert decided to go to Rome to justify himself before the new pope, GREGORY V. It was there that he met the young Emperor Otto III. He became his friend and very soon his tutor.

The death of Hugh Capet (October 999) deprived Gerbert of an ally. His son Robert the Pious, who had married a cousin, thought it wise to negotiate the validity of the marriage in the time between Gerbert's departure and Arnoul's return to Rheims. The emperor, full of enthusiasm over his teacher's great learning, compensated him for the loss of Rheims by giving him the archbishopric of Ravenna (April 998). Gerbert carried out some reforms, ensured the application of measures taken by the synod of Pavia concerning the alienation of goods of the churches, and had Otto III grant a privilege for the abbey of Bobbio, of which he still considered himself abbot (October 998).

The sudden death of Pope Gregory V (18 February 999) opened up a new career for Gerbert: Emperor Otto III offered his teacher the see of St. Peter. Gerbert moved, as he said jokingly, "from R to R: Rheims, Ravenna, Rome." He was consecrated on 9 April, on Easter Day, under the name Silvester II. His taking that name suggests that he must have intended to work closely with the new Constantine, Otto III. In fact, relations between the old pope (he was almost 60) and the 19-year-old emperor were good.

Gerbert settled in the Lateran amid the books he had brought from Rheims—scholars have been able to reconstruct the catalog of the works, many of which are today in Bamberg—and filed his Rheims archives and his letters. He was a highly active pope. He accepted Otto III's denunciation of the false Donation of Constantine and affirmed his authority over Italy and the West (edict of January 1001). He strove to have the emperor apply philosophical principles favorable to the governing of the state. In this, he was attempting to emulate and even surpass his great model, Boethius. He encouraged Otto to create in Poland a national Church independent of that in Germany. The archbishopric of Gniezno, founded in the year 1000, had several suffragans, including the bishop of Cracow. Similarly, Silvester II sent Prince Stephen, the first Christian sovereign of Hungary, a royal crown, of which the present crown in Budapest is a copy. Thus Roman Christianity extended its frontiers to the Vistula and the middle Danube.

Silvester II sent dozens of letters and privileges to clergy, monks, and laymen throughout the Christian world. He settled current affairs, including that of the archbishopric of Rheims, by generously pardoning Arnoul. He agreed to allow the former legate, Leo, to be appointed archbishop of Ravenna, and the monk Petroald to be abbot of Bobbio. He confirmed the legality of Theotard's election to the see of Le Puy with a bull. He granted privileges to abbeys in Germany and Italy and settled various conflicts—for example, between the abbey of Lorsch and the bishop of Worms, and between the archbishop of Mainz and the abbess of Gandersheim. He also had good relations with his Catalan friends, as we know from bulls that have come down to us in favor of the churches of Urgel and Vich and the bishop of Barcelona.

Otto III and Silvester II spent the first months of the second millennium in Rome, but, faced with a Roman revolt, they had to leave the capital in February 1001 and move to Ravenna. In May, the emperor decided to reconquer his capital, but he died in January 1002 in the castle of Paterno, north of Rome. Once more Silvester II settled into the Lateran, where he died on 12 May 1003. He was buried in the basilica of St. John Lateran. His metric epitaph, which was written by Pope SERGIUS IV, can still be seen on the second column on the right in the basilica nave.

Silvester II was quickly forgotten, but Gerbert's scientific writings gained wide renown. By the end of the 11th century, legends began to arise about the "magician pope"—such a learned man could surely not have had such a magnificent career had he not entered into a pact with the Devil. These legends were reinforced by others concerning the year 1000 which circulated as late as the 19th century. In another, more serious sense, Gerbert was rediscovered in the 16th century by Protestants and Gallicans, who took advantage of the decrees of the synod of Saint-Basle and the letters of the archbishop of Rheims. In contrast, the Ultramontanists, loath to believe that a future pope had taken a position against the papacy, depicted the anti-Rome attacks as a Protestant forgery—an unacceptable argument, since the manuscript containing them dates from the 11th century.

Pierre Riché

Bibliography

LP, II, 263.

Erdoes, R. A.D. *1000: A World on the Brink of Apocalypse*, Berkeley, Calif., 1998.

Riché, P. *Gerbert d'Aurillac, le pape de l'an mil*, Paris, 1987, 2nd ed., 1990; "Les Églises de France occidentale et de Lotharingie à l'époque de Silvestre II," *L'Église de France et la Papauté, Colloque franco-allemand, Paris, 17–19 October 1990*, Bonn, 1993, 48–53.

Richer de Saint-Remi, *Histoire de France*, ed. and trans. R. Latouche, 2 vols., 1930, repr. 1964–7.

Zimmermann, H. *Papsturkunden*, II, 712–77.

SILVESTER III. *John (d. 1063). Elected pope on 20 January 1045. Deposed in December 1046.*

In September 1044, because of unrest aroused by the autocratic rule of the Tusculani, riots broke out in Rome. Part of the Roman citizenry sided with the Crescentii (Stephani) against the ruling pope, BENEDICT IX, forcing him after violent fighting to leave Rome and retire to his property near Frascati. In early January 1045, Benedict IX, accompanied by troops, managed to return to Rome, take over part of the Trastevere, and disarm the rebels on 10 January. On 13 or 20 January 1045, the rebels, with the aid of the Crescentii, chose as the new pope John, bishop of Sabina, who was attached to their house. He took the name Silvester III.

It is highly likely that corruption played a part in this election. "The Romans, for their part, hoped, by putting him on the throne, effectively to prevent the undesirable return of Benedict IX, and it is possible that Bishop John did not fall in with their plans in a totally spontaneous way" (H. Zimmerman). As a result, Benedict IX excommunicated Silvester III.

In May 1045, an arrangement was worked out. Benedict IX gave up the pontifical office in favor of the archpriest John Gratian, who took the name GREGORY VI. It appears that Silvester III definitely renounced his claims to the papal office and recognized Gregory's papacy as legitimate. In December 1046, at the synods of Rome and Sutri, Henry III, king of Germany, turned his attention to the fate of the three popes. According to accounts in some sources, Silvester III was deposed and condemned to be shut up for life in a monastery; however, the sentence was apparently not carried out, but quickly annulled.

In August 1047, the former pope resumed his duties as bishop of Sabina and, even under the reign of the next popes, gave no more evidence of pontifical ambitions. He is quoted in a document dated 1051, when he came to Rome before Pope LEO IX to express his grievances against the monastery of Farfa. This extremely wily prince of the Church seems to have served as bishop of Sabina until the end of his life. Mentioned for the last time in 1062, he died a natural death, sometime before October 1063.

Klaus-Jürgen Herrmann

Bibliography

JW, I, 523–5.

Amann, E. "Silvestre III," *DTC*, 14–2 (1941), 2083–4.

Herrmann, K. J. *Das Tuskulanerpapsttum 1012–1046*, Stuttgart, 1973, 152 ff.

Wolter, H. *Die Synoden im Reichsgebiet und Reichsitalian 916–1059*, Paderborn, 1980, 373 ff.

Zimmermann, H. *Papstabsetzungen des Mittelalters*, Vienna-Cologne-Graz, 1969, 121–34.

[SILVESTER IV]. *Maginulf. Antipope (18 November 1105–12 or 13 April 1111).*

After the death of the antipope CLEMENT III, his adherents elected the antipopes Thierry (1100–01) and Albert (1101), whom Pope PASCHAL II rapidly managed to eliminate. The election of a new antipope in November 1105 was evidently not the doing of Clement III's supporters but of the Roman aristocracy, whose loyalty toward the emperor was not returned in kind. Henry IV's role in the election of these three antipopes cannot be verified. A group of Roman barons, consisting primarily of members of the Varuncii family, ordained the archpriest of San Angelo, Maginulf, pope in the church of Sta. Maria Rotonda (Pantheon). They justified the procedure by claiming that Paschal II was guilty of simony and heresy. Nothing certain is known about Maginulf's life beyond these events.

The supporters of the antipope immediately turned for help to Marquis Werner of Ancona. Doubtless convinced he was rendering a service to his German sovereign, Werner lost no time in coming to Rome with a troop of soldiers. At this time Paschal II was outside Rome, in the Leonine City. Under Werner's protection, Maginulf left on 18 November 1105 for the Lateran, where he was consecrated and enthroned under the name Silvester IV. On Paschal's return, violent fighting flared up. At first, the antipope's side had the upper hand, but when they ran out of money, his adherents became few and far between. Silvester was forced to leave Rome before the end of November 1105. After a brief stay in Tivoli, he found refuge in Osimo in Ancona, where he lived, undisturbed, under Werner's protection. In the spring of 1111, Henry V had him brought to his camp near Rome to put pressure on Paschal II. His aim achieved, the emperor dropped the antipope. On 12 or 13 April 1111, Silvester had explicitly to resign and promise the pope obedience. He spent the rest of his life (the date of his death is unknown) under the benevolent protection of Marquis Werner.

Georg Schwaiger

Bibliography

JL, I, 773 ff.

LP, 298, 345 ff.

MGH, *Const. I*, 146, 98.

MGH, SS XIX, 281 ff.

Servatius, C. *Paschalis II (1099–1118)*, Stuttgart, 1979, 69–72, 339 ff.

SIMONY. The classic definition of simony relative to divine law is given by St. Thomas Aquinas: "The premeditated or deliberate desire to buy or sell a possession that is spiritual or linked to the spiritual" (*ST*, 2a, 2ae, q. 100). The term has in particular been used to designate the purchase or sale of ecclesiastical orders and positions. Pope URBAN II (1088–99) wrote the following in 1089: "The name simoniac is used for persons who are known to have bought ecclesiastical orders or positions, whether through money, through a promise, in exchange for favors or through a service rendered for a specific purpose" (*JL*, 5396).

The term comes from Simon the Magus, an ancient sorcerer from Samaria whose prodigies gained him the title of "power of God, the power called great." When his city was converted by Philip the evangelist, he too was converted and baptized. Then, when the apostles Peter and John came from Jerusalem to Samaria and carried out the laying on of hands for the gift of the Holy Spirit, Simon offered them money in return for that power. But Peter rebuked him severely: "Thy money perish with thee, because thou hast thought that the gift of God may be purchased with money" (Acts, 8, 9–24). Episodes prefiguring Simon's sin are to be found in the Old Testament, in particular in Balak's attempt to corrupt Balaam (Numbers 22, 15–19), Naaman's gifts to Gehazi, the servant of Elisha (2 Kings, 5, 19–27), and the presents given by Jason to King Antiochus Epiphanes for the high priests (2 Maccabees 4, 7–20). Such incidents show that simony could be committed by the clergy as well as by the laity.

In the 4th century, simony became a critical problem when the peace of the Church made possible the acquisition and exchange of property on an extremely large scale. The first conciliar legislation—the second canon of the council of Chalcedon (451)—prohibited bishops from ordaining or promoting anyone to a rank of holy orders or to a religious position in exchange for money. Soon, pontifical declarations were issued that vigorously reinforced the interdiction. In the declaration *Ventum est*, Pope INNOCENT I (401–17) did not use the term "simony" but cast doubt on ordinations made by "heretics": "Assuredly, what a man does not have, he cannot give" (*JK* 303). Pope GREGORY I (590–604) in his homilies (*Hom.* XL in *Ev.* 1, 17, 13; 2, 13, 9) and letters (*JK* 1743–4, 1737, 1859) defines the term "simony" as a heresy (*simoniaca haeresis*) consisting of selling the gifts of God; those who resort to this trade are like the money-changers whom Christ chased from the temple.

Gregory I also drew up a classification of the methods that could be used in simoniacal transactions. These were the *munus ab obsequio* (rendering of undue services), the *munus a manu* (monetary gift, or one calculable in money), and the *munus a lingua* (offer of praises, promises, or recommendation) (*Hom*, XL in *Ev.* 1, 4, 4).

The impassioned writings of Innocent I and Gregory I form part of the classic texts of medieval polemics against simony.

Between the 9th and 11th centuries, the problem of simony assumed major proportions. In the monastic orders, for example, gifts handed over on entrance became virtually obligatory because they ensured the material support of the monks and nuns, at the same time regulating the number and aptitude of the recruits for giving gifts. Long considered perfectly normal, these gifts came to be suspected of being simoniacal from the end of the 11th century.

The rise in power of the feudal order, the "system of ecclesiastical property," and lay investitures had greater repercussions for the regular Church. The lords treated "their" church as they did the rest of their patrimony. The clergy paid according to the benefices derived from their posts, just as vassals did with regard to their fiefs. As for the choice of bishops and abbots, Raoul Glaber complained that "the kings themselves, who should choose men appreciated for their faith, are corrupted by the granting of presents; to govern the churches and their souls, they appoint those from whom they can hope to receive lavish gifts" (*Hist.* 2, 6, 11). When the German emperor Henry III intervened in Rome in 1046, he dealt with two popes, BENEDICT IX (1032–45) and GREGORY VI (1045–6) who were both, in different ways, guilty of simony.

The legends that grew up about Simon Magus played just as important a role as these patent excesses in the reinforcing of opposition to simony. Some of them seem to be linked to Simon of Gitta, a heresiarch already evoked by the martyr Justin (c. 100–v. 165) who might possibly have been Simon Magus. The legends spread abroad, preserving the identification, in writings such as the *Clementis recognitiones* which circulated in the Latin translation of Rufinus (c. 450), and the *Passio ss. apostolorum Petri et Pauli* attributed to Marcellus (BHL, 6657). At the end of the 11th century, the legends were particularly current in southern Italy. In 1077–9, Amatus of Monte Cassino dedicated to Pope GREGORY VII his poem on St. Peter in which Simon Magus follows Peter's steps to Caesarea and Antioch, before finally fighting him and St. Paul before Emperor Nero in Rome. To establish his credibility after a long battle with St. Peter, Simon Magus tries to jump from a particularly high tower and falls to his death. Furious with this ending, Nero orders the apostles' martyrdom. Such legends identified the struggle between the pope and the emperor with that of St. Peter and Nero.

The popes of the Middle Ages carried out a serious campaign against simony from the papacy of LEO IX (1048–54), who combated it in his Roman councils as well as those of Pavia, Rheims, and Mainz. He extended simony to include the possession of ecclesiastic revenues by laymen, ordering that these revenues be returned to the clergy, to whom all tithes should also be paid. The decree on the pontifical election issued by NICHOLAS II (1058–61) in 1059 begins by recalling the "innumerable repeated blows and shocks dealt by the merchants of simoniacal heresy to the Apostolic See." The synodal letter *Vigilantia universalis*, issued by Nicholas II and summarized by ALEXANDER II (1061–73), forbade any simoniacal ordination or ecclesiastical promotion. The papal campaign against simony reached its peak under Gregory VII (1073–85) and Urban II. It was carried out both in the Church in general and against the German emperor Henry IV (1056–1106). The role that Gregory VII played in this conflict is made clear by the claim voiced in his last encyclical: "My major care has been that Holy Church, the bride of Christ, our lady and mother, should recover her true glory and be free, chaste and Catholic" (*Epp. vag.* 54).

The turbulent years of the papal reforms and the INVESTITURE CONTROVERSY (end of the period 1040–1120) saw a widening and deepening of the definition of simony. As a consequence of the clashes between the papacy and the kings and refractory bishops, highly placed people who accepted gifts were more severely denounced than those who, like Simon Magus, were in the position of petititioners. Free, canonical elections were called for in the papacy and, in 1059, in bishoprics and abbeys and even local parish churches. Any lay intrusion into these elections was expressly denounced as simoniacal. From the end of the 1070s, the practice of lay investiture such as the bestowal of the cross and ring upon bishops was increasingly stigmatized, until Emperor Henry V renounced it at the concordat of WORMS (1122 (*MGH, Const.* 1, no. 107–8).

A violent controversy broke out as a result of the ambiguous declarations of Innocent I and Gregory I, over the question of whether simony rendered ordinations totally null and void. Cardinal Humbert of Silva Candida argued in this sense with particular force and skill in his *Adversus simoniacos libri tres*, written around 1057–60. However, this text was not widely diffused, and the more moderate viewpoint of his contemporary, Peter Damian, finally prevailed. According to the latter, sacraments administered in simoniacal fashion were valid in themselves, but the ordinations had to be rehabilitated by bestowing the Holy Spirit through a special laying on of hands (*ex. Ep.* 46).

Much attention was also given to the reasons why simony had been defined as a heresy since the papacy of Gregory I. Peter Damian's argument was that, deriving from the Acts of the Apostles, simony was the most ancient of heresies, the one directed against the rules of the early Church. Humbert stressed the contradiction of the simoniacs who reduced the Holy Spirit to salable merchandise, thus making it inferior not only to the Father and the Son but also to themselves (*Adversus simoniacus* 1, 3). Such reflections led Gregory VII to the conclusion that simony must bring about the exclusion of the Catholic Church. Thus, according to the pope, the archbishop of Milan had "ventured to buy his church like an ordinary slave, to prostitute the bride of Christ to the devil, and by attempting to separate her from the Catholic Church, had sought to soil her with the crime of simoniacal heresy" (*Reg.* 1, 15).

After the mid-12th century, the resolution of the Investiture Controversy, the growth of a more rational scholastic way of thought, and above all the evolution of tradition and the methods of canon law made possible a more disciplined and sober approach to simony. The *Decretum* of Bishop Burchard of Worms (composed in 1007–14) had already spread abroad the texts of the council of Chalcedon and Pope Gregory I against simony (1, 112–3). In his *Decretum* dating to about 1140–2, the Bolognese jurist Gratian set forth, in admirably methodical and complete fashion, the problems and canonical texts referring to the texts (pars 2, caus. 1, qq. 1–7).

The fight between St. Peter and Simon Magus was still evoked, as in the mosaics of the Palatine chapel of Palermo (1132–40), but henceforth emphasis was placed on the adoption of legislation that was decisive but expressed with sobriety, after the example of the Second Lateran council (1139) of Pope INNOCENT II (canons 1–2, 24–5). The Third Lateran council (1179) (canon 10) under ALEXANDER III (1159–81) dealt with simoniacal gifts on the part of those entering the religious life. The Fourth Lateran council (1215) (canons 63–6) under INNOCENT III was a résumé of the preceding measures against simony in secular and regular orders. Together with the measures taken by the provincial councils, this legislation reflects the Church's gradual assimilation of the aims of the reformers from the late 11th century to the highest point of pontifical authority under Innocent III (1198–1216).

The modern era saw no diminution of papal vigilance, which was particularly noticeable during the Catholic and Protestant reformations. At the Fifth Lateran council (1512–7), JULIUS II (1503–13) published a constitution against simoniacal corruption in pontifical elections (sess. 5). In 1537, the cardinals gave PAUL III (1534–49) their opinions on reform, in which they referred to the "pestilential evil" of those clergy who were guilty of simony, purchased absolution, and kept the benefices they had bought. The decrees of the council of TRENT (1545–63) provided for severe legislation against simony (sess. 20, canons 1, 9; sess. 22 [Dec. de cel. miss.]; sess. 24, canons 14, 18.

Simony relative to divine law is distinguished from simony relative to ecclesiastical law in that it is a specific exchange of spiritual or temporal benefices attached to spiritual things.

Herbert E. J. Cowdrey

Bibliography

Amman, É. "Simon le Magicien," and A. Bride, "Simonie," *DTC*, 14 (1941), 2130–40 and 2141–60.

Leclercq, J. "Simoniaca heresis," *Studi Gregoriani*, I (1947), 522–30.

Lentini, A. *Il poema di Amato sus. Pietro apostolo*, 2 vols., Monte Cassino, 1958–9 (Miscellanea Cassinese, 30–1).

Lynch, J. *Simoniacal Entry into Religious Life from 1000 to 1260: A Social, Economic and Legal Study*, Columbus, 1976.

Mirbt, C. *Die Publizistik im Zeitalter Gregors VII*, Leipzig, 1894.

Saltet, L. *Les Réordinations, Études sur le sacrement de l'ordre*, Paris, 1907.

SIMPLICIUS. (*b. Tivoli,?, d. Rome, 10 March 483*). *Elected pope 3 March 468. Buried in St. Peter's, Rome. Saint.*

Simplicius's long pontificate made him a witness to the last years of the Roman Empire of the West and the first years of Odoacer's reign. But these important events left no trace in his actions, his reign being distinguished chiefly by the resurgence of monophysitism in the East and the early beginnings of the Acacian SCHISM. Simplicius—whose father, according to the *LIBER PONTIFICALIS*, was named Costinus—succeeded Hilarus on 10 March 483, after a vacancy of 10 days.

What we know of Simplicius's activity in the West had to do with ecclesiastical discipline. In 479, when addressing some bishops of the Picenum region who, as suburbicarian bishops, were directly responsible to him, he stripped Bishop Gaudentius of Altinum of the right to make ordinations. Conferring it on one of his colleagues, the pope recalled that the bishop had to be content with a quarter of the Church's revenues. This is the first explicit mention of that rule, later mentioned in Gelasius and on several occasions by Gregory the Great.

In 482, Simplicius wrote to the bishop of Ravenna, Iohannes, reproaching him sharply for consecrating bishop in Modena a cleric of Ravenna, Gregorius, who had not consented to it. By threatening Iohannes with the suspension of his metropolitan rights, Simplicius was exercising direct authority over Ravenna, but at the same time giving evidence that in that period the Ravenna see had acquired considerable ecclesiastical power. At some unknown date, Simplicius made Bishop Zeno (of Seville) vicar of the see of Rome (*vicaria sedis nostrae*).

Simplicius's activity in Rome was considerable. He caused the church of S. Stefano Rotondo to be built on the Celian. A private church built by Iunius Bassus and belonging to a certain Valila—who no doubt bequeathed it to the Church—was turned into one dedicated to St. Andrew. This church was near St. Mary Major and was destroyed in 1684. Next to St. Lawrence's Outside the Walls, he dedicated a basilica to St. Stephen, and he turned a grotto into a basilica dedicated to St. Bibiana (Sta. Bibiana on the Esquiline). Simplicius transferred to the three great basilicas outside the city walls (St. Paul's, St. Peter's, and St. Lawrence's) part of the clergy from the neighboring parishes, so that they would be sure to provide baptisms and burials, a move that no doubt reflects a modification of the Roman ecclesiastical geography.

The end of the Roman Empire in Italy left only a few vague traces in Simplicius's episcopate. He consecrated 58 priests, a particularly high number and one that may bear witness to a reorganization of the Roman clergy. The hypothesis is a shaky one, however, since it is not known whether the ordinations came before or after the deposition of Romulus Augustulus. In any event, the bishop of Rome was no enemy of the new regime. He came to an agreement with Odoacer that the king should confirm the election of the bishop of Rome, as was the custom with the emperor, according to the testimony of a council held after Simplicius's death.

Thus, the pope's essential concerns had to do not with the Arian king of Italy but with the East. Like his predecessor, HILARUS, Simplicius believed the victory at Chalcedon was definitive, and at the beginning of his papacy he wrote to Bishop Acadius of Constantinople protesting against the 28th canon of the council, which gave that see rights equivalent to those of Rome. Basiliscus's usurpation of Zeno's throne in 475 did not worry Simplicius unduly. In January 476, he sent a series of letters to the new emperor, to Acacius, and to the Constantinople clergy as a whole, encouraging them to resist monophysitism, to demand measures against Timothy Aelurus (bishop of Alexandria, very hostile to Chalcedon), and to urge the emperor to continue to uphold the policy of his predecessors Marcian and Leo.

However, Basiliscus's policy was exactly contrary to the pope's wishes. He published an encyclical "canonizing Ephesus 431 and Ephesus 449 and anathematizing the Tome of Leo." This rendered null and void the work of the council of Chalcedon, since it was precisely the many irregularities of the council of Ephesus of 449—known as the "Robber Council"—that brought about the council of Chalcedon and the composition of the Tome of Leo.

There was no time for this brutal change of policy in the East to affect Simplicius, however. In August 476, Basiliscus was overthrown, Zeno was restored as emperor, and Acacius, the patriarch of Constantinople, resumed control of religious policy. This restoration resulted in the expulsion of the monophysite Peter the Fuller from the see of Antioch and the replacement, in Alexandria, of Timothy Aelurus, who had died before the change, by Timothy Salofacius, the Chalcedonian candidate.

Acacius informed Rome of all—or almost all—this news, presenting it as a total victory for Chalcedonian orthodoxy and neglecting to mention the death of Timothy Aelurus. Simplicius replied by expressing his joy (April 477). At the same time, in a series of letters to Acacius and Zeno, he asked that severe measures be taken against Timothy Aelurus, Peter the Fuller, who had usurped the throne of Antioch, and Paul, who had taken over that of Ephesus.

Little by little, the situation deteriorated. In the East, Acacius, confronted with the obvious hesitations of the Monophysites, was at least embarrassed. Peter Mongo was stirring up trouble in Alexandria, while Timothy Salofaciolus, for the sake of conciliation, introduced Dioscorus's name into the diptychs. The pope revealed his anxiety to Acacius in several letters in March and in the autumn of 478. Before June 479, the Chalcedonian bishop of Antioch, Stephen, was assassinated. He was replaced by Calandion, a supporter of Chalcedon, but appointed and consecrated by Acacius himself, in conformity with canon 28 of the Chalcedonian council and thus in opposition to the traditions and rights of the patriarchal see of Antioch. In a letter of June 479, Simplicius expressed his embarrassment. He tolerated the procedure owing to the exceptional circumstances, but he reproved it in principle.

No documentation remains of the following years of Simplicius's correspondence with the East. Acacius and Zeno failed to keep the pope informed of developments paving the way for the reconciliation of the Church of Constantinople to the Monophysites and its consequent break with Rome. Calandion, bishop of Antioch, regularized his situation by having his election confirmed by a synod. He informed the pope of this measure through a courier who was passing through Constantinople. Acacius added a brief message of greeting to Calandion's letter.

Meanwhile, there had been important developments in Alexandria. Timothy Salofaciolus had died and been replaced by John Talaia. This Alexandrian priest, loyal to his bishop, had been sent to the emperor by Timothy to prepare an orthodox succession on the seat of Alexandria. After a cold reception by the emperor, John Talaia had been forced to promise not to claim the episcopate for himself. Then, on Timothy's death, John was elected to the see. In a letter of June 482, Simplicius reproached Acacius for not keeping him informed of events in the East.

A month later, Simplicius learned that John Talaia had been deposed by the emperor and his place taken by Peter Mongo. Again the pope sent urgent letters to Acacius, chiding him for his silence and expressing astonishment at the accusations against John Talaia; he also wrote to the emperor, begging him not to side with the opponents of Chalcedon. Simplicius seems not to have known that, in the meantime, Acacius and Zeno had been working toward a reconciliation with Peter Mongo. This would take the form of an edict of union, the Henoticon, which was made public in March 483.

The pope died on 10 March 483, leaving his successor, FELIX, with the responsibility for breaking off relations with the Eastern Churches.

Claire Sotinel

Bibliography

LP, I, 249–51.

Nautin, P. "Simplice," *DHGE*, XVI, 889–95.

Schwartz, E. "Publistische Sammlungen zum acacianischen Schisma," *Abhandlungen der Bayerischen Akademie der Wissenschaften*, 10 (1934), 202–19.

Simplicius, *Epistulae XXI*, Thiel, 175–214.

SIRICIUS. *(b. Rome, ?, d. 26 November 399). Elected pope in December 384 (date uncertain, 15, 22, or 29). Buried in the cemetery of Priscilla, in the basilica of St. Silvester. Saint.*

A Roman by birth and the son of Tiburcus, this pope's epitaph shows that he was first a reader then a deacon before becoming pope. He succeeded DAMASUS by unanimous vote, as is shown in a letter from Emperor Valentinian to Pinian, then prefect of Rome (February 385, extract cited in *PL*, XIII, 1147).

Siricius's first official act was to write to Himerius, bishop of Tarragona. This is almost certainly the first known decretal (a pontifical letter of general application written in response to a question). The question had been asked by the priest Bassian, who had been sent by Himerus to Damasus, and concerned various points of ecclesiastical discipline. Siricius, who had just acceded to the Apostolic See, sent him his reply. The letter (epistolae, *PL*, XIII, 1131–48) includes disciplinary prescriptions on baptism (1,1; 1,2–3), penitence (1,2; 1,5; 1,14), accession to orders (exorcism: 1,9; readership: 1,9–10; minor orders: 1,10), order (1,8; 1,10; 1,11; 1,14), and marriage of laymen and clergy (1,4; 1,8).

Siricius was not innovating here. Several of these regulations had been determined by the councils of Nicaea (325) and Sardica (343), others by the Roman council held under Damasus. His originality consisted in providing the Church with the means for imposing respect for its laws. In his decretal to Himerius, he combined his rulings with sanctions, at the same time striving to spread the information by suggesting that the bishop of Tarragona publish his decretal in the neighboring provinces. Similarly, he communicated to the African bishops the decisions of the Roman council held by Damasus and those of the council of Rome of 386, and urged their application (epistolae 5, *PL*, XIII, 1155–63). Here the question was the consecration of the bishop (5,2) and obliga-

tory continence on the part of bishops, priests, and deacons (5.3). In a second decretal (epistolae 6, *PL*, XIII, 1164–8), addressed to all the bishops of all the provinces, Siricius asked that a preliminary inquiry be made into the life of a candidate for orders (6,1), disqualifies soldiers and public functionaries from ordination (6,1), and refuses to recruit clergy whose past history is not known (6,2).

Such are the beginnings of a kind of papal legislation, for which Siricius provided a new literary form. His aim was to restore the purity of the Church, to affirm the primacy of the see of Rome at a time when the city was losing its capital status, and to ensure its independence vis-à-vis the temporal power. Thus, in reply to a letter (now lost), Emperor Maximus affirmed to him in connection with the question of Priscillianism that he would leave the judgment of religious matters to the Catholic bishops (epistolae 3, *PL*, XIII, 1148).

Siricius was just as zealous in his fight against heretics, but evidence of his activity is not as clear owing to the overriding presence of Ambrose, bishop of Milan, in religious matters during the last 20 years of the 4th century. Siricius condemned to exile Bishop Ithacus, who had been overzealous in his struggle against the Priscillianists. Siricius and Ambrose joined forces to heal the Melitian schism of Antioch. The council of Capua (392) condemned Bonosus, bishop of Naissus, for denying the perpetual virginity of Mary. In late 392, Siricius wrote Ambrose regarding Jovinian, a monk who went further than Bonosus by arguing that the virtue of virginity was valueless. Ambrose condemned Jovinian at the council of Milan. Siricius supported that decision (epistolae 7, *PL*, XIII, 1168–72). Siricius's writings (six letters) illustrate his personality: firmness when ecclesiastical discipline must be put into practice, respect for foreign Churches as in the Bonosus case, moderation and prudence with regard to Ambrose of Milan in light of his prestige, and foresight in the beginnings of the Origenist controversy.

Siricius was quoted by Prosper of Aquitaine (*Chron. MGH*, AA, 9, 461), described as *clarissimus pontifex* by Isidore of Seville (*Vir. Ill.*, *PL*, 83, 16), and praised by Ambrose for his role against heresies (*Epist.* 42). He is included in the *Hieronymian Martyrology* (p. 621) and the *Roman Martyrology* (p. 547).

Ghislaine de Senneville-Grare

Bibliography

PL, 13, 1131–94.

Budzin, A. J. "Jovinian's Four Theses on the Christian Life: An Alternative Patrisitic Spirituality," *Toronto Journal of Theology* 4 (1998), 44–59.

Duchesne, L. *LP*, L, 216–17, Paris, 1886.

Gaudemet, J. *l'Église dans l'Empire romain*, Paris, 1958.

Jaffé, P. *Regista pontificorum romanorum*, I, 40 (1885).

Mansi, J. P. *Sacrorum conciliorum nova et amplissima collectio* III, 653 ff.

Palanque, J. R. *Saint Ambroise et l'Empire romain*, Paris, 1933.

SISINNIUS. *(b. Syria, ?, d. Rome, 4 February 708). Consecrated pope on 15 January 708. Probably buried in St. Peter's, Rome.*

All that is known about this "20-day pope" is in the four lines devoted to him in the *Liber pontificalis*. Sisinnius was the son of a Syrian named John, about whom nothing else is known. The concision of his biography may be interpreted as the result of aversion to him on the part of the Roman clergy, or perhaps a reflection of the absence of anomaly in an ecclesiastical career that led naturally to the pontificate. The statement, "He took care of the inhabitants of our city" could not be used to characterize such a brief papacy but must refer to his life as a whole. The only evidence his biographer provides concerns an extremely ordinary activity for a bishop responsible for the municipal administration: he had whitewash prepared for the restoration of the walls. Because Sisinnius suffered from gout at his election, it was felt that his pontificate would be brief, and in fact he was soon replaced.

Jean Durliat

Bibliography

JW, I, 247.

LP, I, 338.

SISTINE CHAPEL. This building derives its name from its sponsor, Pope SIXTUS IV, who had it built between 1475 and 1481 for the celebration of liturgical ceremonies uniting the ecclesiastical and lay bodies comprising the papal chapel, and for CONCLAVES. The dedication took place on 15 August 1483 in honor of the Assumption of the Blessed Virgin.

The Sistine Chapel is situated between the palace of NICHOLAS V and the façade of the palace of PAUL II. On the outside it has the look of a fortress, with its machicolations, while on the inside, the layout, due principally to Mino da Fiesole, introduces decorative elements characteristic of the Florentine and Urbanite Renaissance with the choir screen and the cantors' loft. The nave (40.5 × 13.20 meters and close to 21 meters high) and the immense barrel vault were conceived from the beginning to receive painted decoration. The latter is composed of three cycles of frescoes commissioned by four sovereign pontiffs.

The Paintings of the Sidewalls. These paintings were undertaken as soon as the construction was finished. The contract is still extant, signed 27 October 1481 between the papal agent Giovanni De' Dolci and the most famous Tuscan and Umbrian artists of the day—Cosimo Rosselli, Sandro Botticelli, Domenico Ghirlandaio, Pietro Perugino, Luca Signorelli, Pinturicchio, and Bartolomeo Della Gatta.

The project, established during the reign of Sixtus IV (1471–84), has parallel biblical scenes following a traditional principle of association between the Old and New Testaments, with a treatment of great horizontal bands cutting the wall in a sequence of decorated panels linked together to form continuous cycles. The six great compositions are framed by pilasters that vertically accentuate the wall, and by cornices that subdivide the wall into three zones. On the south wall, starting at the altar, the following are represented: *The Journey of Moses into Egypt* by Perugino and Pinturicchio; *The Youth of Moses* by Botticelli; *The Crossing of the Red Sea and the Handing over of the Tablets of the Law to Moses on Mount Sinai* by Cosimo Rosselli; *The Punishment of Korah, Dathan and Abiram* is also Botticelli's, while *The Testament and the Death of Moses* is by Luca Signorelli, perhaps aided by Bartolomeo Della Gatta. On the north wall, accompanied by explanatory inscriptions in Latin, six other compositions illustrate scenes from the New Testament. Again, starting at the altar: The *Baptism of Jesus in the Jordan* by Perugino and Pinturicchio; the *Healing of the Lepers and the Temptations of Christ* by Botticelli; *The Calling of the Apostles Peter and Andrew* by Ghirlandaio; *The Sermon on the Mount* by Cosimo Rosselli aided by Bartolomeo Della Gatta or a follower of Signorelli; and finally, *The Last Supper* by Cosimo Rosselli. The first frescoes of the two cycles (*Moses Saved from the Waters* and the *Nativity*) disappeared during the creation of the *Last Judgment* by Michelangelo on the altar wall.

Between the bays, the portraits of popes standing in false niches are attributed to painters Fra Diamante, Ghirlandaio, Botticelli, and Cosimo Rosselli. The vault was, at the time, simply painted in blue and studded with gold stars following an ancient custom that considered it the image of the sky, while the lower part of the walls were decorated with false tapestry with the arms of Sixtus IV.

The Second Cycle. Further work was commissioned by Pope JULIUS II. In 1504, during the construction of the new St. Peter's Basilica, earth movements caused a long diagonal fissure in the vault of the chapel. It is a Roman vault, which is not constructed of masonry, but is poured onto a wooden counter-vault and composed of an agglomerate of tufa, lime, and pozzolana, on dry-built walls. It has the appearance of a surbased profile that rests on concave triangles.

After difficult negotiations, Julius II (1503–13) secured an agreement with Michelangelo to undertake the painted decoration of the lunettes of the chapel, where the 12 apostles were to be represented. However, some time after, the artist proposed a new project organically linking his decoration to that which already adorned the walls, and the sovereign pontiff gave him total freedom as to the choice of subjects. This original work, begun 10 May 1508, was partially unveiled at the end of the summer of 1510, on 14 August 1511, and finally on 31 October 1512. That is to say, in a little more than four years, a painting measuring 540 square meters, of absolute novelty in form and color and with which the pope was well pleased, was inaugurated in an extraordinary explosion of enthusiasm.

The execution of the early stages was slow, particularly because there were many figures in the scenes of the flood, but also because Michelangelo had fired (in January 1509) his four assistants who came from Ghirlandaio's studio (among them Giuliano Bugiardini and Francesco Granacci) whom he found incompetent. (They had already done the decoration of the cornices, the caryatid infants, the medallions, and the three Noah scenes.) The artist worked standing on scaffolding of his own design, which touched neither the floor nor the vault, and was adjustable according to the curvature of the roof. For the figures he made drawings, then traced them directly on the *intonaco* with the help of string and nails, ruler and compass, creating a complex, fake architectural structure that masks the nature of the vault by substituting a structure all the more strange because it is not entirely convincing and can only be observed in fragments.

The composition is the result of a singular invention that reveals Michelangelo's skill as architect, sculptor, and painter. The iconographic project, in broad outline, is understandable by all, but to grasp the details requires scholarship. In fact, it is drawn from the *Decachordum christianum* published in 1507, in which Marco Vigerio Della Rovere (d. 1516), cousin and treasurer of Pope Julius II, explains the *Tree of Life* of St. Bonaventure. This project is consistent with the purpose assigned to the chapel. In order to interpret the scenes, one must go from the altar toward the entrance, but to see them in chronological order one must walk backward, as Michelangelo painted the subjects in reverse order of the project. This was accomplished in a classic arrangement at three levels. On the arch of the vault, in rectangular panels, he depicted the *Twelve Prophets and Sibyls* (seven prophets and five Greco-Roman sibyls), images of inspiration and power of the spirit, acting as telemones. Above the windows, grouped together in triangular lunettes, are the *Ancestors of Christ*, images of the preparation for the coming of Christ, in grisaille. In the upper zone, limited by a heavy fake cornice, is the Revelation of God through the nine scenes of *Genesis*, on a pale sky-blue base. This begins at the side of the altar, but the chronological order is sometimes compromised: three scenes of the Creation of

the World, three scenes with Adam, and three scenes with Noah—before the enclosure, the scenes without God, linked by a scene above the enclosure, then the four scenes with God, soaring in the heavens—framed by the *Ignudi*, nude young men in sculptured relief, perched on marble cubes. For Vasari, they bear "festoons of oak leaves and acorns placed instead of the arms and symbols of Pope Julius, which indicated that at that time and under his government the golden age was located." Ram heads, a customary motif in Rome since antiquity, flank the great panels. Ram horns were equally an ornamentation of the Hebrew altar; in the *Sacrifice of Isaac*, one sees the ram, a foreshadowing of the sacrifice of Christ. Among the iconographic details, one must also observe the frames of false marble that encircle the medallions placed between the *Ignudi*: they are pierced with five slots, the five wounds of Christ on the cross; the bands of tissue recalling the shroud, and the oak tree of life.

The restoration of recent years, financed by Japan in exchange for video rights for the NTV chain on the procedure, and directed by professor Pier Luigi Colalucci, restored the original color to the frescoes. The frescoes had been obscured by the accumulation of stains and the inevitable assaults of time (seepage of water coming from the roof, smoke from oil lamps, candles and brazier, dust raised by the faithful). The cleaning also allowed the lifting of layers of varnish and adhesive, as well as the additions made during different restorations undertaken since the 16th century. It also gave the restorers the opportunity to study the technique of the fresco as practiced by Ghirlandaio's student, heir to a solid craft.

Remember that this type of painting is done by applying colors on fresh plaster (that is, wet), hence the name of the process, a *fresco*. The pigments crystallize on the lime carbonate plaster coating. Once the *intonaco* is dry, the painter can no longer intervene, except to cover part of his work with fresh plaster. The fresco therefore requires rapidity and simplicity of execution, with little or no retouching. The artist always works on fresh plaster, so it is easy to determine the space covered each day: the *giornate*. The painter obtains transparency only by applying, within a very brief space of time, a second color diluted on the first. No varnish is used and, therefore, no glaze is put on the first dry layer of pigment as is done in oil painting. The material in the fresco is perfectly cohesive; it scarcely changes during the course of time, and its colors stay clear and matte. If the work is altered over time, it can only be by foreign matter deposited on the surface as a thin film of blackish powder formed by dust, soot, and smoke.

The restoration facilitates a new appreciation of the chromatic unity and continuity of this very luminous painting due to the perfect carbonation of colors and the very great care taken in its execution. Heir of the

Florentine Quattrocento, Michelangelo, architect, arranged his composition with false moldings, a souvenir of Tuscan buildings. As a sculptor, he gave his painted figures an obvious living force by skillfully using shadows. As a painter, he arranged space by using a vivid, sharp palette with broadly modeled accents admirably adapted to the grandiose scale of the setting. However, at the center of the vault, the color is less startling than in the lunettes where it is intense, for the artist applied color in the natural light. The comprehensibility of the composition is due to the creative unity, graphic and chromatic, to the power of the imagination, to the energy of the design, and to the supernatural proportions. The restorers emphasized the rapid work of Michelangelo: the lunettes were painted directly without drawings. They estimate the work of actual painting at about one hundred *giornate*. For the figures, the contours were traced with a stylus and broad strokes of charcoal, then brush covered with coats of pigment. Violent hachures were used to form the contrasts in the drapery of the cloth. The singular vigor of contrasting tonalities was also noted, the use of oranges against blues and of reds near greens. The variable luster of the changing draperies made Michelangelo one of the great representatives of mannerism, above Pontormo or Rosso. For the flesh, he used matte variegated material, where the shadows and changes flow in infinite nuances of rose and golden light. His composition is notably transformed and developed during the work; he at first clustered several figures in a setting, then placed fewer figures, but of a gradually larger size.

The Third Cycle. This cycle, desired by CLEMENT VII in 1533, was finished in 1541 under the pontificate of PAUL III Farnese, who had gave the order to Michelangelo in 1534. This cycle involved ornamenting the east wall of the chapel, the altar wall. The conception of the fresco and the preparation of the wall lasted several months, and only in the spring of 1536 did the artist, then 60 years old, begin to paint, alone, the gigantic *Last Judgement*. A very great stylistic distance separates it from the vault.

To the spiritual crisis that tormented Michelangelo during these years of religious agitation and that intensified after the sack of Rome, we must add that the times required strong images and symbolic representations. The *Last Judgement* did not appear to anyone to be ill timed; on the contrary, according to Vasari, Rome was filled with "amazement and wonder." The artist manifested, through his tragic style, the exceptional experiences the people had lived through in 1527.

Very few sketches are extant today for the *Last Judgement*. The charcoal sketch at the Casa Buonarotti in Florence is especially well known, but it is not a complete design because parts of the composition are not precisely defined.

In contrast to the vault, no architectural frame encloses this fresco, and it covers the entire wall in one block. Michelangelo abandoned the principle of perspective construction from the unique point of view of the Quattrocento and organized the composition of the apocalyptic vision in horizontal zones divided around a central axis: in the lower zone, the resurrection of the dead; on the left, a few figures risen from the dead; and on the right, the damned descending into hell, all establish a link between the ascending and descending vertical movement of the chosen and the condemned situated in the middle zone. Around the figures of Christ and the Virgin, the prophets and saints brandish the instrument of their torment and the chosen gather together; the damned are thrown toward Charon's boat, which casts them into the river of hell. The whole is dominated at the top of the wall by the angels—without wings—who carry the instruments of the Passion, but the latter two parts are rather inappropriately situated with respect to overall composition.

The artist constructed this massive composition on the principle of consistency of the figures, however, the figure of the Virgin breaks the symmetry: a figure in serpentine form with clothes of striking colors creates dissonance. In the same register one sees prophets, confessors and martyrs, heroines of the Old Testament, sibyls, and virgins. A general tension emerges in the fresco, especially visible in the athletic energy of the angels of the lunettes, energy also expressed in the exceptional complexity of the foreshortening.

Once again Michelangelo accomplished an extraordinary revitalization of forms and motifs. The figures of the saints and of the patriarchs are divided in an elliptic movement around Christ, the Judge, who, in a terrible gesture, raises his right hand in an act of condemnation and with the right, beckons the chosen. The circle described by this movement of the hands confers majesty on him. The balance is achieved by the counterpoint between the upper and the lower limbs. This gesture of Christ justifies, on the stylistic plane, the universal movement of rotation, the principle of the greater part of the fresco; the vision of a heliocentric universe where Christ appears as the center of the solar system, according to Charles de Tolnay.

The emphasis is placed essentially on the dramatic aspect of the theme: salvation and damnation. The center, where one sees the flight of the chosen and the fall of the damned, presents the most diversity, although consistency is not sacrificed between the opposing zones. The figures maintain the clear allusion to the isolation of the plastic bloc, each of them is like a statue, perfectly defined by its own contours. The turning movements are similar to those in the unfinished *Captives* and are linked to each other by the exigencies of the expression and the drama.

The restoration, completed in 1994 under the direction of Fabrzio Mancinelli, facilitates the rediscovery of a luminous work where the figures stand out with assurance. Today, the work compels attention as a work of faith: Michelangelo's correspondence with the poetess Vittorio Colonna confirms it. The *Last Judgement* "announces the great art of the COUNTER REFORMATION through the unbelievable temerity with which he does not fear to represent the final reality of Christ judging mankind . . . Michelangelo offers, in contrast to his century, a powerfully colored representation, luminous and without equivocation of the Catholic doctrine on the end times" (O. Madelin).

The influence of these paintings was immense, but the fresco was heavily retouched in the 16th century and 18th centuries, especially in the time of PIUS IV (1559–65), who ordered the painter Daniele da Volterra to clothe the nude figures.

Sylvie Chambadal

Bibliography

Connaissance des arts, 454, December 1989.
De Tolnay, C. *Michel-Ange*, Paris, 1970.
Ettlinger, L. D. *The Sistine Chapel before Michelangelo*, Oxford, 1965.
Hartt, F., Mancinelli, F., and Mondzain, M. J. *La Chapelle Sixtine*, Paris, 1989, 2 vol.
Michel-Ange, l'artiste, sa pensee, l'ecrivain, Paris, 1976, 2 vols. (foreword by Mario Salmi).
Salvini, R. *La Capella Sistina in Vaticano*, Milan, 1965.
Vasari, G. *Vie des meilleurs peintres, sculpteurs et architectes*, IX, Paris, 1986.

SIXTUS I. *(d. ca. 125.) Elected pope ca. 115. Saint.*

The pontificate of Sixtus I (also called Xystus) is one of the least known of all. Sixtus was the sixth successor of Peter, being preceded on the throne of Rome by ALEXANDER I. Even the length of his pontificate is controversial: the Liberian Catalogue places his episcopate, according to the consular dates, from 117 to 126. Eusebius of Caesarea wrote that he died in the twelfth year of Hadrian's reign (128–9), after a 10-year pontificate (a timespan on which most of the sources agree). His feast is 3 April, but nothing is known of his activity.

He appears to have been of Roman origin (from the seventh region), the son of a man called Pastor. A decree is attributed to him that in fact could be understood only in the context of the 6th century; apparently it had to do with the sacred vessels, which could be touched only by members of the clergy. Another decree was said to have allowed the chanting of the Sanctus with the priest. He was represented as a martyr, though there is no historical evidence for this, and is said to have been buried near Peter in the Vatican, but here again, proof is lacking.

Jean-Pierre Martin

Bibliography

Amann, E. *DThC*, 1941, XIV, 2, col. 2193–4.
Eusebius, *HE*, IV, 42; 5, 5; v. 6, 4; 24, 14.
Irenaeus, *Adv. Haeres.*, III, 3, 3.
Weltin, E. G. *NCE*, XIII, 271.

SIXTUS II. *(d. 6 August 258.) Elected pope in September 257. Buried in the catacomb of Callistus.*

Sixtus II (also called Xystus) succeeded STEPHEN I, who had been deposed on 2 August 257 (*MGH*, AA, 9/1, 70). At that time, because of the severely uncompromising attitude of its head, the see of Rome was encountering opposition from many quarters in Africa and the East. The new bishop was of Greek origin (*natione Graecus*, according to the *LIBER PONTIFICALIS*, *LP*, I, 156 = *MGH*, GPR, I, 34, and had had philosophical training. He was ordained that August, at the time of Valerian's persecution of the Christians.

Compared to Stephen, Sixtus projected the image of a conciliatory pope. He was aided in his task of reunifying the Churches by Bishop Dionysius of Alexandria. The bishop had written Sixtus that Stephen's excommunication of the Churches of Asia Minor and Africa had been an excessive gesture, out of proportion with the offense that had provoked it; in short, it was right to take into account the diversity of traditions regarding the baptism of heretics, since in early times judgments had been made without entailing arguments or divisions (Eusebius, *HE*, VII, 5). Relations were soon resumed with Cyprian of Carthage and with the Asian Churches. From then on, unity was combined with diversity of practice. The Church of Africa, which baptized heretics, preserved its custom up to the council of Arles of 314, at which time it abandoned the practice without difficulty.

Above all, Roman Christianity had to face persecution. Whereas the first years of the reigns of Valerian and Gallienus had brought peace to the Churches, once the Empire had remustered its strength after the serious crisis of the years 250–3, in mid-257 everything turned upside down. The emperors may have been influenced by a concern for reinforcing conformity, or perhaps by the desire to find tax resources for the state. Eusebius of Caesarea, quoting Dionysius of Alexandria (*HE*, VII, 10) mentions the sinister part played by Macrian, the emperors' chief financial adviser. In August 257, the emperors put out an initial edict, decreeing that members of the clergy, bishops, and deacons must sacrifice to the gods of the state and prohibiting gatherings in the cemeteries. In Carthage and Alexandria, two of the greatest episcopal sees, Cyprian and Dionysius were brought before the governor and sentenced to exile for refusing to sacrifice; the Church of Rome, however, seems—paradoxically—not to have suffered unduly.

The second edict, was more ruthless. When Cyprian transmitted the contents of the imperial decree, he described the speed with which the new measures were applied: "Valerian, in a reply to the Senate, has ordered that the bishops, priests and deacons be executed on the spot, that the senators, nobles and Roman knights lose their titles and be deprived of their possessions; that if these latter, after the confiscation, persist in calling themselves Christians, they should be beheaded; that the matrons, too, be sent into exile after confiscation of their goods; that the servants of the palace and the administration who had confessed their faith before or who would confess it henceforth be deprived of their possessions and sent away in chains into the emperor's domains . . . Know that Sixtus was executed in a cemetery on 6 August, and four deacons with him" (Cyprian, *Epist.*, 80). The deacon Laurence, who had refused to hand over the treasury of the Roman Church, was burnt on a gridiron, if we are to believe a legend handed down with the account of his passion, 8 August 258. On 6 August 258, Sixtus II was taken by surprise and summarily beheaded. Cyprian of Carthage was executed the following 13 September.

The Roman Church's calendar for the liturgy of the martyrs, celebrated by the Christians of Rome in the 4th century, reflected the worship and pious customs of the Roman community. It gives the date of 29 June 258 ("under the consulate of Tuscus and Bassus") as that when the remains of Peter were placed in the catacombs and those of Paul in the cemetery of the Ostian Way (*MGH*, AA, 9/1, 71). The significance of that date in the evolution of the cult of the founders has been disputed. Some have taken it to refer to a removal of the relics of Peter and Paul to some other place to escape the persecution that had been raging for nearly a year (Duchesne, Lietzmann, Delahaye). But this hypothesis, based on a bold correction of the text handed down in the 354 calendar, comes up against numerous problems. It is preferable to presume that, in 258, the Roman Church under Sixtus II's pontificate chose for the commemoration of Peter and Paul an anniversary fixed as 29 June, and that the mention of that date in the calendar of holy days was designed to show the antiquity of an important passage of the apostolic liturgy (Pietri).

Michel Christol

Bibliography

Frend, W. H. C. *Martyrdom and Persecution in the Early Church*, Oxford, 1965, 421–9.

Lebreton, J. and Zeiller, J. *De la fin du IIe siècle à la paix constantinienne: Histoire de l'Église* (ed. A. Fliche and V. Martin II), Paris, 1943, 152055, 209–10, 416.

Pietri, C. *Roma christiana: Recherches sur l'Église de Rome, son organisation, sa politique, son idéologie de Miltiade à Sixte III (311–440)*, Rome, 1976, 365–89.

Vogel, C. *Liber pontificalis* (new ed. 1957), III, 75.

SIXTUS III. *(b. Rome, ?, d. 10 August 440). Ordained pope 31 July 432. Buried in St. Lorenzo, on the Via Tiburtina. Saint.*

Roman in origin, the son of a certain Sixtus according to the *Liber pontificalis*, Sixtus (also called Xystus) was a priest of the Roman Church under Pope ZOSIMUS (417–8). Suspected of Pelagian sympathies, he ostensibly distanced himself from those views, perhaps at the synod presided over in the summer of 418 by Zosimus, at which Pelagius and Celestius were again excommunicated. Sixtus then wrote two letters to Africa—one to Aurelius of Carthage, and the other to Augustine of Hippo—in which he defended himself against charges of collusion with the Pelagians. After September 418, Augustine first congratulated him in a brief note, then in a long missive urged him to exercise vigilance with regard to the Pelagians.

Elected bishop of Rome to succeed Pope CELESTINE I, from his consecration Sixtus found himself faced with the Eastern question. Two Egyptian bishops sent by Cyril of Alexandria informed him of the difficult negotiations between the Churches of Alexandria and Antioch to reestablish union, which had been broken since Nestorius, who represented Antiochene Christology, had been deposed by Cyril's supporters at the council of Ephesus (431). Sixtus took the position of one continuing Celestine's policy. He told Cyril and the Eastern bishops, to whom he gave notice of his accession, that he supported the reconciliation of the Churches on the basis of the recognition by John of Antioch of Nestorius's deposition, and that he was solidly behind the action of the bishop of Alexandria (*JK*, 389–90). He also congratulated the Illyrian bishop, Flavian of Philippi, one of the leaders of Cyril's party, on his attitude at Ephesus. Sixtus did not question, any more than did his predecessor, the part played at the Council of Ephesus by Cyril, whom he considered a saintly bishop. Sixtus participated in the negotiations toward reconciliation by writing to Bishop Acacius of Berea, a mediator in the affair, and, on several occasions, to Cyril of Alexandria. Like Celestine, however, he did not intervene to define the faith. The formula of union between the two great sees, based on the Profession of Faith drafted by the Antioch party, was elaborated in the East under pressure from the emperor. In the Christology that the two sides defined—recognition of the union of the two natures in one Christ—Rome did not take sides.

In 433, Cyril informed Sixtus of the conclusion of the negotiations and the difficulties he had met among his own followers. The pope also received two letters from John of Antioch. In one, which was read on 31 July 433 to the council on the day of the pope's *natalis* (the anniversary of his consecration as pope), John declared his acceptance of the formula of union. In the other, also addressed to Cyril and Maximian of Constantinople, John vowed to adhere to the deposition of Nestorius, to anathematize "what is defective" in the latter's writings, and to recognize Maximian as the legitimate bishop of the imperial capital.

Yet John of Antioch's reconciliation owed far more to the situation in the East than to the weight of pontifical power. The pope proved anxious to soothe feelings. On several occasions, he recommended that Maximian try to understand the dissidents who were obstinately refusing union. On 17 September 433, he congratulated Cyril on the new-found union (*JK*, 391) and informed John of Antioch that he accepted his profession of faith (*JK*, 392). He did not take into consideration the appeal (*supplicatio*) sent to him—very late—by two metropolitan bishops, supporters of Nestorius, who denounced Cyril's attitude at Ephesus and now asked Sixtus to reexamine the case of the former bishop of Constantinople. Unlike his predecessor, he did not call for new sanctions against the bishop.

In Illyricum, Sixtus had to act to maintain respect for the authority of the Apostolic See. He received an appeal from the new bishop of Thessalonica, Anastasius, whose rival, Bishop Perigenes of Corinth, wanted to exercise his metropolitan rights in Achaia uncontrolled. This attitude called into question the rights granted by the pope's predecessors to the bishop of Thessalonica as vicar of the Apostolic See. Sixtus intervened firmly. He despatched two legates to Illyricum and, on 7 August 435, sent the council of Thessalonica a letter confirming his vicar's privileges (*JK*, 394). He also reprimanded Perigenes, urging him to obedience within the framework of the institutions set up by Rome (*JK*, 393).

The pope also opposed attempts at encroachment on the part of the bishop of Constantinople, Proclus, who was eager to set himself up as a champion of orthodoxy—attempts encouraged, it seems, by the inclinations toward independence of some Illyrian metropolitans. On 18 November 437, Sixtus sent the bishop of the imperial capital a very firm statement (*JK*, 395). He stressed that he himself had refused to reconsider the sentence brought by Proclus against Bishop Idduas of Smyrna, who had appealed to Rome. He cited his vicar's powers, particularly in the matter of episcopal consecrations. Further, Sixtus sent to Illyricum a legate, the priest Artemius, with a decree addressed to all the bishops of the vicariate, who were called to a council and urged to observe canonical discipline (*JK*, 396).

In Italy, Sixtus may have encountered opposition from certain quarters, which are perhaps echoed in an apocryphal account dating from the 6th century—the *Gesta de Xysti purgatione*, the tale of a trial purportedly brought against the pope. His attitude toward the Pelagians was uncompromising. According to Prosper, in 439 the pope received from the Pelagian Julian of Eclanum a request for reconciliation, which he rejected on the recommendation of the deacon Leo (the future LEO I).

Sixtus carried out a remarkable building program in Rome. At St. Mary Major, a basilica dedicated to Mary, Mother of God, and at St. Peter's, St. Lawrence's Outside the Walls, and St. Paul's, he also concerned himself with restoring the liturgical trappings of the churches after the barbarian invasions.

Christiane Fraisse-Coué

Bibliography

Amann, E. *DTC*, 14, 2, 2196–9.

Caspar, E. *Geschichte des Papsttums*, I, Tübingen, 1931, 416–22.

Pietri, C. *Roma christiana*, II, BEFAR, 224, Rome, 1976.

Sixtus, *Epistulae*, 5–6, Coll. Veronens. 300–31, ACO, I, 2, 107–10; *Epistulae*, Coll. Atheniens 99–101, ACO, I, 1, 7, 143–5; *Epistulae 7–10*, Coll. Thessalonicensis, 11–4, ed. Silva-Tarouca, Rome, 1937, 36–43.

SIXTUS IV. *Francesco Della Rovere (b. Celle Ligure, Savona, 21 July 1414, d. Rome, 13 August 1484). Elected pope on 9 August 1471. Installed on 25 August. Buried in St. Peter's, Rome.*

Francesco was the son of Leonardo, a cloth-cutter and wealthy cloth merchant, and Luchina Monleone, a descendant of the old Genoese nobility. Information handed down by contemporary and later writers (humble birth, adoption by the wealthy Paolo Riario of Savona) is barely credible. Doubtful, too, is his kinship, later claimed, with the Della Rovere nobles of the Piedmont. Consecrated to St. Francis, at age nine he entered the monastery of St. Francis of Savona, where he began his studies and took his vows (1429). He then studied in Chieri (Turin), perhaps in Bologna and Pavia, and finally in Padua. After obtaining his degree (1444), he was regent and professor of theology, logic, and philosophy at Padua, Bologna (where he knew John Bessarion, henceforth his friend and supporter), Florence, Perugia, and Siena. He also distinguished himself as a preacher.

In the Franciscan order, Francesco Della Rovere became successively general bursar, minister of the province of Genoa, vicar general for Italy and the Roman province, and minister general (1464). Appointed in absentia as titular cardinal of S. Pietro in Vincoli (St. Peter in Chains, 18 September 1467), he left the generalate in 1469. He was elected pope after a four-day conclave with 12 votes out of 18, thanks to the support of the pro-Milanese group of cardinals (perhaps owing to the intrigues of his nephew, Pietro Riario), but also because of his theological knowledge, integrity, and gifts as a mediator.

The electoral capitulation foreshadowed the resumption of the war with the Turks, but, as with his predecessors, his urgings and dispatch of cardinal legates (Bessarion, Borgia, Barbo, Capranica, Carafa) were fruitless. The fleet, arduously assembled with the help of Naples and Venice, contented itself with overcoming the port of Satalia and taking Smyrna (1472). Equally unsuccessful was Sixtus's attempt at uniting the Orthodox and Catholic Churches through the marriage of Zoe Paleologus and Ivan III of Russia.

From the earliest days of his papacy, Sixtus IV had to confront the problem of the cohesion of the Papal States, often the source of disagreements with other states. He therefore strove to remain on good terms with each, seeking alliance with the European rulers, but especially the Italians—with Savoy, Milan, Florence (with which he had previously had good relations), Naples, and Venice—and even agreeing to compromises. Nevertheless, this program was hampered by dissension among the Italian powers and by the not always successful foreign policy of his nephews, Giuliano Della Rovere, Pietro Riario, and—after the latter's death (1474)—the greedy and conniving Girolamo. Expeditions against the rebellious Umbrian cities (1473) were not very successful, in particular that against Città di Castello and Niccolò Vitelli (supported by Lorenzo de' Medici), who was vanquished only with the aid of Federico da Montefeltro.

The year 1475 saw the celebration of the jubilee and the strengthening of an alliance with Ferrante of Naples, who had come in person to Rome. Relations among the Italian powers, however, went from bad to worse. Lorenzo, who aimed to conquer Umbria and Romagna, sided with Venice and Milan and continued to support the rebellious cities of the Papal States. Sixtus IV therefore made an alliance with Ferrante against Florence. Believing it indispensable to eliminate the Medicis, and badly advised by Girolamo Riario and Cardinal Salviati, archbishop of Pisa, he agreed to the formation of a league put together by a few Florentine families headed by the Pazzi—but only so long as no blood was spilled. At this time, acting on the pretext of the assassination of Salviati and the imprisonment in Florence of his nephew, Cardinal Sansoni Riario, the pope excommunicated Lorenzo and put an interdict on the Florentines—who shrugged it off.

An extremely difficult period ensued: the brutal breaking off of relations with the Medici states; dangerous tension with the king of France, Louis XI, who supported the Medici and threatened to convene a council; and the volte-face of the king of Naples, who had signed an accord with Lorenzo (December 1479) and with the new duke of Milan, Ludovico il Moro. Added to these problems were the conquest and sack of Otranto (11–14 August 1480) by the Turks. Forced to accept a peace treaty, the pope (fortuitously aided by the death of Sultan Ma-

homet II) succeeded in freeing Otranto (1481). He then sought an alliance with Venice (which was offered Ferrara), urged on by Girolamo Riario, who, not content with Imola, wanted to seize Forlì and Faenza.

This precipitated a new general war, this time, with its theater of operations in the Papal States and Rome itself, where fights between the Colonna and Orsini factions had broken out again with violence. The Neapolitan forces, led by Alfonso of Calabria and supported by the Colonna, invaded southern Latium and got as far as the Castelli Romani. The fleet seized Terracina, and the Florentines took Città di Castello, while the rebel bishop Andrea Zamometi of Basel hurled the threat of a schism and a general council. Thanks to the intervention of Roberto Malatesta, Venetian and papal troops finally routed the army of Naples at Campomorto (21 August 1482) in the Pontine marshes, but the pontiff derived no advantage. He was forced to sign a peace treaty (12 December 1482), to which Venice did not adhere. Meanwhile civil war continued to rage in Rome. The later treaty of Bagnolo (7 August 1484), drawn up without Sixtus IV's knowledge, was a hard blow for the pontiff. Already in poor health, he died six days later, filled with bitterness because of a peace he considered "shameful and dishonorable."

According to his wishes, Sixtus was buried in the Chapel of the Conception in St. Peter's. The bronze sarcophagus with a recumbent figure surrounded by allegorical figures, commissioned by Giuliano Della Rovere from Pollaiolo, is today in the treasury museum of the basilica.

Sixtus IV was a much disputed, controversial figure, even to his contemporaries. S. Infessura and Vespasiano da Bisticci pronounced negative judgments on him, while B. Platina and D. Domenichi spoke positively about the pope. The contradictions that are visible in his conduct—simple and straightforward before his election, then almost cynical and violent—were doubtless due in part to the harmful influence of his Riario nephews. But they were also due to the fact that he suddenly found himself hoisted out of the protected Franciscan environment and into the necessity of learning, as cardinal and (after only four years) as pope, what other pontiffs knew by dint of noble birth or a long career in the secular clergy. Nonetheless, even as pope he always preserved the mark of his Franciscan simplicity and his fine education.

One of the most serious criticisms against him is that of NEPOTISM, but this practice seems to have been an accepted part of the program of government. Its aim was not merely the promotion of the pope's family in society, but chiefly to turn the Papal States into a principality capable of rivaling the great Italian domains, to reinforce the power of the pontiff in a "monarchical" direction (the pope-king, inspired by God, as understood in the 16th and following centuries), and to guarantee his independence to make decisions within the Church. Finally, in his relations with the rulers, he sought to make the pope the absolute sovereign, both spiritual and temporal, of the greatest of kingdoms, the "scourge of the balance" of European politics.

Sixtus IV's papacy was thus a turning point. The communes enjoyed less and less autonomy. Rome was changed into a city-court, the capital of a principality, where the pope had charge of functions concerned with religion, politics, and war and enjoyed the support of trusted allies and the control exercised by loyal individuals linked through family or personal ties to the principal agencies: the college of cardinals, the magistratures, the administration, and the army (which was stable and no longer mercenary).

As soon as Sixtus IV was elected pope, a controversial consistory was held (December 1471) which appointed as cardinals Giuliano Della Rovere (later JULIUS II) and Pietro Riario (called by his contemporaries the pontiff's "tutor"). The latter already held several posts, including that of commander of the army. A few years later, Girolamo Basso Della Rovere, Raffaele Sansoni Riario, Cristoforo Della Rovere (1477), and his brother Domenico (1478) were also given the red hat. Girolamo Riario succeeded his brother Pietro as head of the army. He was given Imola and Forlì and married Caterina Sforza, the illegitimate daughter of Galeazzo Maria. Giuliano's two brothers, Leonardo and Giovanni, were made prefects of Rome (1472–5). The first, the duke of Sora, married a bastard daughter of Ferrante of Aragon, and the second a daughter of Federico da Montefeltro.

It appears that culture, too, was utilized in a political sense as an element of prestige: note the sumptuous feasts held by Pietro Riario, the modernization of the city, and the presence in Rome of noted men of letters (who were sometimes even employed at the Curia). Certain humanists (B. Fonzio, T. Gaza) left Rome after a few years, complaining of a hostile intellectual climate. Others remained—foreigners like I. Regiomonato and G. Fichet; Italians such as F. Filelfo, D. Calderini, and B. Platina, who were given the task of writing the lives of the pontiffs, and P. Leto, around whom the Academy of Rome, dissolved by Paul II, was resurrected. Sixtus IV aided both universities (Freiburg) and colleges (Rome, S. Bonaventura; Valladolid; Avignon), but monies for the *Studium Urbis* were often diverted to other ends. The pontifical chapel was rebuilt and enlarged. New singers and composers of talent were engaged, and polyphonic music introduced. Publication of texts, even Jewish, was subsidized and developed, and translations from the Greek were encouraged. The funds of the Vatican Library were particularly increased, and the collection was open to the public under the direction of Platina.

Sixtus IV was never a great writer, and his literary interest cast doubt on the breadth of his cultural education. His collection of books, today in the Vatican Library (on philosophy, logic, theology, largely of the Scotist school or linked to the history of the Church) shows an absence of the *humanae litterae*. He wrote very little. The attribution to him of an *Oratio de Conceptione B. Mariae Virginis* is uncertain. Three small works that predate his pontificate are linked to religious controversies: *De sanguine Christi*, on the hypostatic union of the blood of Christ (1463; text revised several times; Vat. Lat. 1051, 1052, with autograph notes; ed. de Lignamine, 1471); *De futuris contingentibus* (VAt. LSat. 1050; ed. 1473); and *De potentia Dei*, on the relation between the "ordered" and "absolute" power of God (ed. 1471).

The restoration of the city, which was embellished with commemorative epigraphs, gave rise to the Capitoline museums and the gift to the people of Rome of the bronze statues (notably the She-wolf) formerly in the Lateran (1471). Other works during his reign include the restoration of the Sixtus bridge (1475); the enlargement, opening, alignment, and paving of various streets, even through expropriations and demolitions (Via Recta, Via Sistina, Via Papale, Via Florea); the restoration of the Acqua Vergine aqueduct and the Santo Spirito hospital (perhaps the work of A. Bregno), with its frescoes of portraits of prophets and scenes of the life and deeds of Sixtus IV; the construction and restoration of many churches (St. John Lateran, S. Maria della Pace, S. Maria del Popolo, Sant'Agostino, the Chapel of the Conception in St. Peter's). But the most noteworthy achievement was the Sistine Chapel (1475–81; 1482 for the frescoes); its plans were drawn by G. de Dolci, while the walls were decorated notably by Perugino, Botticelli, and Ghirlandaio with portraits of the popes and parallel scenes from the lives of Moses and Christ, perhaps suggested by the pope himself and accompanied by titles. Finally, Sixtus completed premises designed for the Vatican Library (1475), decorated with frescoes by the brothers Ghirlandaio and by Melozzo da Forlì, and many palaces for his nephews (Chancery, Santi Apostoli, etc.).

In the ecclesiastical domain, Sixtus IV favored the Franciscans and protected the mendicants. He attempted in vain to reform the Conventuals and the Roman Curia. He clearly had a great veneration for the Virgin, and he was doubtless too generous in meting out indulgences, favors, and privileges. He persecuted heterodox and heretical sects, and he authorized the king of Spain (1478) to create the Inquisition against the Marranos and apostates and to appoint inquisitors, though Sixtus intervened later on several occasions to limit abuses.

Paola Placentini

Bibliography

Cenci, C. "Notizie su alcuni superiori generali O.F.M. (1398–1443)," *Le Venezie francescane*, 29 (1962), 76 ff.

Goffen, R. "Friar Sixtus IV and the Sistine Chapel," *Renaissance Quarterly*, 39 (1986), 218–62.

Infessura, S. *Diario della città di Roma*, Rome, 1890 (Fonti per la Storia d'Italia, 5), 74–169.

I Pontefici Sisto IV (1471–84) e Sisto V (1585–90), Rome, 1987 (extracted from *Miscellanea Francescana* 86 (1986), 195–1104.

Lee, E. *Sixtus IV and Men of Letters*, Rome, 1978 (bibliography on pp. 263–76).

L'età dei della Rovere: Atti del Convegno Storico Savonese, Savona, 7–10 November 1985, Atti e memorie della Soc. Savonese di storia patria, n.s. 24 (1988), 1–250; n.s. 25 (1989), 1–306.

Mannucci, U. "Le capitolazioni del Conclave di Sisto IV (1471): Con notizia di un codice fin qui ignorato sui Conclavi dei sec. XVe XVI," *Römische Quartalschrift für christliche Altertumskunde und Kirchengeschichte*, 29 (1915), 73*–90*.

Pastor, 4.

Piana, C. *Chartularium Studii Bononiensis S. Francisci (XIII–XVI sec)*, Ad Claras Aquas, 1970, 79*, 81, 83–85; *La facoltà teologaica dell'Università di Firenze nel Quattro e Cinquecento*, Grottaferrata, 1977 (Spicilegium Bonaventurianum 15), 93–4, 292–3, 296, 456.

Platino, *Liber de vita Christi ac omnium pontificum*, Città di Castello, 1913–32 (RIS/2, II:, 1), 398–420.

Sisto IV e Giulio II mecenati e promotori di cultura, Atti del Convegno Internazionale di Studi, Savona, 1985, Savona, 1989.

Un pontificato ed una città: Sisto IV (1471–84), Atti del Convegno, Rome, 3–7 December 1984, Vatican City, 1986.

Vespasiano da Bisticci, *Le vite*, I Rome, 1970, 174 ff.

SIXTUS V. *Felice Peretti (b. Montalto, 13 December 1520, d. Rome, 27 August 1590). Elected pope on 24 April 1585. Ordained 1 May. Buried in St. Mary Major.*

Sixtus V was one of the architects of the COUNTER-REFORMATION. His humble origins (born to small farmers near Ancona, in the Marches) would give rise to the legend of an adolescence spent keeping pigs, as if to underline the exceptional nature of his ecclesiastical career and his accession to the papal throne. Furthermore, such a career was rare among those who, like him, belonged to a religious order.

After entering the conventual Franciscans, Peretti took his vows in 1534. For about 20 years, he was a theologian and preacher in the context of his order until a seminal meeting in Rome, in 1552, with Michele Ghislieri, the future PIUS V. At that time a member of the Inquisition, Ghislieri would exempt him from all suspicion of heterodoxy. Peretti was given important duties at the heart of the Inquisition, in Venice (1557–60), where he violently opposed the Republic, and in Spain (1565), following the cardinal legate Boncompagni (the future GREGORY XIII) for a preliminary investigation of the case of Archbishop Carranza of Toledo. He was appointed consultant of the Roman Congregation of the Inquisition (1560) through the support of Cardinal Ghislieri. When the cardinal became pope, Peretti was named vicar general of the conventual Franciscans (1566–8), then bishop of Sant'Agata dei Goti in the kingdom of Naples (1566), and finally cardinal (1570). At the time he was a member of the Congregations of the Index, of Bishops, and of the special congregation that drew up the official condemnation of Archbishop Carranza.

Moved to the diocese of Fermo (1571), he left it in 1577 after a period of difficult relations with Pius V's successor, Gregory XIII, difficulties that went back to the legation to Spain. On the death of Gregory XIII, in 1585, his accession to the pontificate was made easier by the Spanish accord, which quashed the widespread resistance at the conclave and, in particular, opposition on the part of the Roman nobility.

The election of Sixtus V would be understood, both then and later, as the revival in the Church of the Counter-Reformation of a hegemony of the religious orders, chiefly the mendicants. These had already seen a Dominican accede to the papal throne in the person of Pius V; now it was the turn of a Franciscan to become pope. Cardinal Peretti took the name Sixtus in memory of another Franciscan, Sixtus IV, as if to signify the resumption of old positions of leadership after the struggle against the religious orders that took place before and during the council of Trent. Sixtus V took a keen interest in the orders as well as the regular congregations, although he was sometimes violently polemical regarding the methods of government within the framework of the Society of Jesus.

His concern for the episcopate was not so great. Nonetheless, he later used methods of controlling and restricting the Curia through the intermediary of the Congregation of the Council. His relations with the Inquisition were also fundamental, as they had been before he became pope, because of the exemplary character that the Congregation of the Holy Office had in his eyes. This idea had persisted in fairly coherent fashion from PAUL IV to Pius V, with the result that Sixtus would apply and generalize it at the time of the reform of the Roman Curia. Thus his pontificate should be understood not only as a renewal of traditional forces like the Franciscan order, but also as establishing the organic character of a plan linked to the nurturing of new institutions, henceforth stabilized and capable of playing an essential role in the life of the Catholic Church.

Beyond his combined interest in ecclesial organization and the tools of political government, there stands out his obvious determination to discipline violence within the state. Sixtus V would insist on more severe justice in the Papal States, so that criminals and bandits would be dealt with in an exemplarily harsh way, and on a more lasting and incisive campaign against banditry, especially from 1585 to 1587. If the results were not always decisive, they were certainly significant. Notably in the case of the parallel struggle the pope waged against the feudalism within the Papal States, the result of his policies would give his government a clearly absolutist stamp, which the more alert contemporaries—for instance, the Venetian ambassador, Paolo Paruta—recognized. The source of these autocratic tendencies is to be found not only in his background within a religious order, but also in his education. A sign of this is the singular presence of Machiavelli's *Prince* in Sixtus V's library, among more predictable juridical and political texts. The pontiff encouraged a policy of public works in Rome and the state (with attempts at improving the Pontine marshes), especially in order to make massive use of manpower in the context of the suppression of begging.

The Apostolic Camera took a large number of economic measures concerning the papal public debt, which had increased with the creation of 11 "Monti," or charitable lending institutions. From 1586 to 1588, Sixtus V restructured the central government by systematizing a process begun by PAUL II and enhanced considerably by Pius V. First the SACRED COLLEGE was reorganized with the bull *Postquam verus* (3 December 1586) and another bull (13 April 1587). Then the bull *Immensa aeterni Dei* (22 January 1588) set up a system of permanent CONGREGATIONS (see list following this entry). These were an ensemble of temporal and spiritual agencies (the Consistorial Congregation, for instance, alongside that of the Annona or Aqueducts), whose superimposition in the Papal States constituted a stage in the development of the modern state.

Yet Sixtus V's initiative was not merely the conclusion of a process initiated by others. The congregation system represented a substantial acceleration in the evolution of the papacy, from the aristocratic monarchy of the Renaissance—as seen in the dualism of the papal powers and the Sacred College in consistory—to an absolutist centralization of power in the person of the pope. This new historical phase of pontifical power was characterized under Sixtus V, on the external level, by an exaggerated NEPOTISM (particularly obvious in the case of the 15-year-old cardinal nephew, Alessandro), and by a policy of courting prestige on the financial level. This latter policy was given concrete form by the establishment of a "treasury" in the Castel Sant'Angelo (1586). By this move, the pope intended not so much to built up a reserve of gold as to convey an image of solidity.

To further this end, he encouraged extreme combativeness on the part of the militant Church. This was reflected in several moves: Sixtus's support of the Catholic coalition in France during the turbulent years just before Henry IV's accession; the massive financial interventions in favor of the Spanish Armada and Philip II's ambitions regarding England; the energetic relaunching of Catholic reconquest of the Protestant and Reformed regions in Germany and Switzerland; and the clever, modern use of means, both new and renewed, of cultural and religious propaganda. Despite the pontiff's personal intervention, after years of debate, the printing of the Vulgate (1587)—with the most accurate text possible, to further anti-Protestant ends—was a failure.

For this reason, Sixtus V's interest in creating cultural establishments for preservation and study that conformed to and were technically better suited to the service of the Church found its best expression in the Vatican Library, with the construction of the Sistine Hall (1587–9), by D. Fontana, and the almost simultaneous founding of the Vatican Press. Alongside the exceptional attempt to reorganize the state into a sort of ideal Catholic state of the Counter-Reformation—an attempt that was not pursued with the same determination by his successors—increased importance was given to Rome on the religious plane. This would set a seal, concretely and symbolically, on the work of Sixtus V.

The bulls *Decet Romanum Pontificem* (1587) and *Suprema cura regiminis* (1590) allowed for costly town-planning measures to be realized with remarkable speed. These measures were designed, on the one hand, to construct a network of streets directly connecting the principal churches of the center of Catholicism, and on the other, to set up an overall plan linking religious concerns to practical and material interests. In the building of roads and aqueducts (like the Felice, named after the pope), of markets and manufactures, there was—beyond the evident religious intent—a plan to urbanize the higher, less densely populated areas of Rome by connecting them to the lower areas and to the ancient consular roads. Thus created a new relation between city and countryside.

Sixtus V's program to make Rome a center of consumption, also designed to become a seat of trade and production, was not without its utopian aspects. An example is Fontana's strange plan of transforming the Coliseum into a huge factory for treating wool. Nevertheless, when one looks beyond the social and economic aspects of urban development, one sees a different picture. The Villa Montalto near St. Mary Major, where Sixtus lived when he was a cardinal and which he embellished still further when pope, as well as the creation of the Quirinal palace, can be said to reflect an ideal of late Renaissance magnificence. But it is the alteration of the Lateran area, the completion of St. Peter's dome, and the architectural and symbolic value of the obelisks the pope set up that display the peculiarly sacred aspect of his program. Unmistakable modern elements are mingled with the primordial affirmation of the pontiff's determination to restore Catholicism in the Counter-Reformation.

Congregations Instituted or Reorganized by Sixtus Quintus by the Bull *Immensa aeterni Dei* (22 January 1588).

Congregation of the Holy Office of the Sacred Roman and Universal Inquisition, already in existence, for the defense of the Catholic faith and the struggle against heresy.

Congregation of the Signature of Graces, for the examination of favors not dependent on the ordinary tribunals.

Congregation for the Erection of Churches and Consistorial Provisions, for the examination of requests concerning the erection of new Churches and new chapters and the granting of inherent benefices.

Congregation of the Abundance of the Ecclesiastical State, for the provisioning of the Papal States.

Congregation of Rites and Ceremonies, for liturgical questions and processes of beatification and canonization.

Congregation of the Navy, for the creation of a fleet of 10 galleys designed to defend the coasts.

Congregation of the Index, already in existence, for the condemnation or the correction of works that are heterodox or dangerous for faith and morals.

Congregation of the Council, already in existence, for the interpretation and application of the disciplinary decisions of the Council of Trent.

Congregation for the Disbursement of the Contributions of the Ecclesiastical State, for the needs of the communities of the state.

Congregation of the University of Rome, for the organization of the studies of La Sapienza.

Congregation for the Affairs of Regulars, already in existence, to accommodate the differences between the various religious orders.

Congregation for the Affairs of Bishops, already in existence, to resolve disputes between representatives of the diocesan hierarchy.

Congregation of Roads, Bridges, and Aqueducts, for the control of the road network and the supervision of aqueducts.

Congregation of the Vatican Press, for the supervision of the Vatican printing press.

Congregation of the Council of State, for the revision in final appeal of civil, criminal, and mixed trials, and for jurisdictional interventions on the territory of the State, with the exception of Rome, the Legations, Benevento, Spoleto, and Fermo.

Mario Rosa

Bibliography

Cugnoni, G. "Documenti chigiani concernenti Felice Peretti, Sisto V, come privato e come pontefice," *ASR*, V (1882), 1–32, 210–304, 542–89.

de Feo, I. *Sisto V. Un grande papa tra Rinascimento e Barocco*, Milan, 1987.

del Rè, N. "Sisto V e la sua opera di organizazzione del governo centrale della Chiesa e dello Stato," *Idea*, 36 (1980), 1, 41–53.

Gamrath, H. *Roma sancta renovata: Studi sull'urbanistica di Roma nella seconda metà del secolo XVI con particolare riferimento al pontificato di Sisto V (1585–90)*, Rome, 1987.

La Bibbia "Vulgata" dalle origini ai nostri giorni. Atti del Simposio internazionale in onore di Sisto V, Grottammare 29–31 agosto 1985, ed. T. Stramare, Rome, 1987.

Mandel, C. "Golden Age and the Good Works of Sixtus V: Classical and Christian Typology in the Art of a Counter-Reformation Pope," *Storia dell'arte*, n. 62, 1988, 29–52.

Ostrow, S. F. *Art and Spirituality in Counter-Reformation Rome: The Sistine and Pauline Chapels in S. Maria Maggiore*, Cambridge and New York, 1996.

Pastor, 21 and 22.

Penuti, C. "Aspetti della politica economica nello Stato pontificio sul finire del '500: le 'visite economiche' di Sisto V," *Annali dell'Istituto storico italo-germanico in Trento*, (1976), 183–202.

Prosperi, A. "Sisto V papa della Controriforma," in *IV centenario di Sisto V (1585–90). Le diocesi delle Marche in età sistina. Atti del Convegno di studi, Ancona-Loreto 16–18 ottobre 1986*, Fano, 1988, 19–35.

Schiffmann, R. *Roma felix. Aspekte der städtebaulichen Gestaltung Roms unter Papst Sixtus V.*, Bern-Frankfurt, 1985.

Spezzaferro, L. "La Roma di Sisto V," *Storia dell'arte italiana*, Part 3, *Situazioni momenti indagini*, V, Momenti di archittura, Turin, 1983, 365–405 (with bibliography).

SLAVERY. In theory, the Roman Church granted non-Christians the same right to freedom as it did to Christians. In reality, however, depending on times and circumstances, the right to freedom belonged to Christians alone. CANON LAW stated that only baptism could change a slave's social status. This practice was actually similar to that of Islam, in which conversion procured the freedom of a slave, the theory being that no Muslim could be the slave of another Muslim. According to the rigorist opinion expressed by BENEDICT XII, excommunication entailed the loss of personal freedom. After Europeans had settled in the Canary Islands (1436) and then in South America, EUGENE IV and, later, ALEXANDER VI forbade the reduction to slavery of Christian neophytes. The wars against the TURKS in the Mediterranean served as the occasion of the popes' enforcing the same prohibitions in favor of Christians, who could neither be taken as slaves, nor bought, nor sold, nor brought to the galleys. URBAN VIII and BENEDICT XIV extended these prohibitions in favor of non-Christians, thereby taking aim at the black slave trade. In practical terms, none of these measures had much effect, and slavery remained a common practice in Rome and the PAPAL STATES until the end of the eighteenth century. Only the republic of Ragusa in the Mediterranean forbade the buying and selling of slaves, whether Christian or not.

Documentation on slaves in Rome is rare for the period of the early Middle Ages. In 849 some were listed as working on the city fortifications. A decree of 863 permitted the exchange of slaves between the Church and members of the laity. In 1051, there were prostitute slaves in the Lateran Palace. During the following period, the Roman situation must not have been very different from that in better-known Italian regions (Sicily, Venice, Genoa, Florence). The most we can assume is that the slaves in Rome were primarily domestic slaves—which means they were a luxury, evidence of a certain social status—and not agricultural slaves. The fact that value was placed on slaves of color appears clearly in a fresco by Giotto (around 1330) in Assisi, *The Resurrection of Lazarus*, which shows a black man such as the painter must have seen at the court of BONIFACE VIII. Thanks to the archives, we know that slaves were also held in high repute in AVIGNON. Furthermore, it seems that around the middle of the 14th century, Italian families often had recourse to slaves to replace the domestics wiped out by the PLAGUE. In 1363, Florence made it legal to own slaves. Still, we can assume that during that same period there were fewer slaves in Rome than in Venice, Florence, Genoa, and Palermo. The flourishing of Roman society and the growing ostentation of the papal court following the return of the papacy to Rome gave rise to the practice of incorporating slaves as domestic servants. Slaves were purchased at the markets of Genoa, Venice, Palermo, and Ancona, and they were also accepted as gifts. We have only sporadic information on the subject, but we know of some slaves given to PIUS II and INNOCENT VIII, to Cardinal Ippolito d'Este and Lucrezia Borgia. That slaves of color were the most prized is evident from the fact that, owing to a shortage of black slaves to take part in the tournaments and triumphs at an Altemps-Medici marriage in 1555, some Roman pages had to be painted black.

The provenance of the slaves is varied. Recent research has shown that until the 13th century the majority of slaves were Muslims from the Iberian Peninsula. In the 14th century, they came from the eastern Mediterranean: often there were Greeks, which raised the question of whether, as schismatics, they should be considered Christians, that is, whether they were free or not. In the end, it was decided that those from north of Corfu were Christians, whereas those from south of Corfu could be forced into slavery! From the middle of the 14th century to the fall of Constantinople, the majority of slaves came from the Black Sea: Tatars, Circassians, etc. Later, the market gradually moved toward Maghreb and North AFRICA. Until the middle of the 16th century, slaves were purchased almost exclusively at the markets, usually from Genoese or Venetian merchants; after 1550, it was the turn of corsairs and pirates to offer their captives as slaves. Added to these were the Muslims (and sometimes the Christians) who were seized on ships during battles with the Turks or who were victims of raids. At the end of the 17th century, there was a considerable influx of prisoners, civilian and military, captured during the Venetian-Ottoman wars in Greece and Dalmatia. Thus, after the defeat of Modon, Coron, and Castelnuovo, the major part of the population—Muslims of recent date or Greek Christians—were reduced to slavery.

The figures available for the 16th century do not allow us to know with any precision the number of slaves living in Rome. We can assume, however, that it was not negligible, to judge by the foundation in 1543, by PAUL III, of the *Casa dei Catecumeni* for the instruction of Muslims and Jews in the Christian faith. The proportion at the *Casa* was two Jews for every Muslim. Given an estimated Jewish population of 5,000 for every of 80,000 to 100,000 persons, we must conclude that there were in Rome approximately 2,000 to 2,500 slaves, almost exclusively Muslims.

Different regulations applied to slaves, reflecting the legislators' uncertainties with respect to the freedom acquired through baptism and with respect to schismatic slaves. On 27 June 1545, Paul III reaffirmed to the Roman

SENATE and the conservators of Rome the ancient right of granting freedom and citizenship to every slave who succeeded in taking refuge at the Capitol. The religion of the slave was not mentioned. The confirmation of this privilege by PIUS V on 6 September 1565 limited the freedom in question "to the baptized and those who had already become Christians." This restriction opens the possibility that baptism did not free all slaves, and that Christian slaves did exist. Accordingly, cases are known of former slaves turned Christian who, detained in the kingdom of Naples, asked for letters of liberation from Rome. Occasionally, freedom was granted under the condition that a slave continue to serve his former masters for a certain time. A BRIEF of Paul III dated 8 November 1548 but published on the following 12 January, explicitly authorized the possession and the purchase of slaves "for the public utility and the good of all those who will acquire or already have acquired slaves." On the other hand, twenty years later Pius V renewed Pius II's prohibition of 1462 against reducing Christians to slavery, and ordered the liberation of all Christians made prisoner during the military operations against the Turks.

The pontifical brief of 1549 indicates that there were slaves in Rome belonging to private persons as well as to the state. In any case, they must have been numerous enough to justify the establishment of the *Casa dei Catecumeni*. The presence of female slaves is confirmed by the fact that in 1562 PIUS IV also founded a *Casa* for them: evidently the Muslim women all belonged to private persons. The archives of the *Casa dei Catecumeni*, which fortunately have been preserved, are the only source for the history of private slaves in Rome; the state slaves, especially those of the galleys of Civitavecchia, are known through the naval accounting documents deposited in the Archivio di Stato in Rome, which have not yet been thoroughly researched.

The records of the *Casa dei Catecumeni*—though they concern only a portion of those who, having declared their willingness to convert to the Christian faith, received religious instruction lasting at least forty days—allow some estimates to be made and some conclusions to be drawn. It must always be kept in mind, however, that the majority of slaves, especially the women and the children, would have been baptized in the homes of their masters, that others would have remained Muslims, and that still others would have obtained their freedom by paying the required ransom. Moreover, some of the slaves at the *Casa* belonged to foreigners passing through the city and not to Romans. Here are the figures provided in the records of the *Casa*:

	Total	Slaves Private	State	Men	Women
17th century (from 1614)	733	684	49	645	88
18th century (until 1768)	292	208	84	272	20
1800–1807	11	4	7	9	2

Of the 49 state slaves in the 17th century, 11 came from the papal NAVY, 10 belonged to the APOSTOLIC CAMERA, and the others came from other navies. In the 18th century, 46 of the 84 slaves belonged to the Papal States, and 8 of those 46 belonged to the Apostolic Camera. In the 19th century, all 7 slaves came from Civitavecchia. It should been noted, however, that 73 Muslims who had entered the *Casa* were not slaves, but are called "free": they were either merchants or, possibly, liberated former slaves.

The Private Slaves. The women and children were, as has been said, private slaves. The former represent about 15%, the children under 10 years 1%, and those between 10 and 20 years 20%, of the total number of slaves. But these percentages cannot be applied to the whole group of slaves living in Rome. Among the converted who did not pass through the *Casa*, women more or less young, made up the great majority, as proved by a partial examination of the parish registers. All the slaves seem to have been domestic servants. In some cases, it can be assumed that masters acquired them with the intention of having them baptized and liberating them after providing religious instruction themselves, thereby performing a meritorious deed.

On the other hand, the data supplied by the records of the *Casa* can be applied to the entire servant population of Rome. In the 17th century, one-third of the slaves came from Eastern Turkey, one-third from Africa, and one-third from the Balkan territories under Turkish domination. In the 18th century, North Africa supplied about two-thirds of the slaves. Over the course of two centuries, blacks represented about 15% of the total. As for the Roman masters, they belonged to all classes of society, and of the 20 women mentioned as owning slaves during the 17th century, 11 were Roman.

	Clerics	Ambassadors	Laypersons
17th century	14	8	63
18th century	4	1	7

Masters are nevertheless rarely mentioned in the records, in which slaves are designated simply by the word *mancipium*. Among the clerics are CARDINALS and PRELATES, and most of Rome's great families are mentioned among the lay owners.

Private slaves were normally bought, except in the case of certain military personnel who could have been made prisoner while at sea, or, for instance, during the Peloponnesian wars against the Turks. Sometimes things were done in a big way: in 1663, Prince Chigi offered the pope a hundred slaves to be enlisted as "volunteers" in the papal navy. In the 18th century, it was the papal navy that gave slaves to private citizens. Purchases of slaves were made at the markets, especially at

Malta, but in the 18th century the sellers were Christian privateers and pirates. The treatment of slaves in private homes seems not to have been very different from that of other domestic servants, and it often happened that slaves remained in their former owners' service even after being liberated.

State Slaves. While it is difficult to establish the number of private slaves, the collections of the Tresoreria Generale of the Archivio di Stato in Rome offer some precise data concerning the galley slaves of Civitavecchia, an inevitable consequence of the creation of a papal navy during the second quarter of the 16th century. Formerly, slaves of the state had belonged to the Apostolic Camera and been employed in urban construction works and even as soldiers at CASTEL SANT'ANGELO: 18 of this last group passed through the *Casa* during the 17th and 18th centuries. The crew of a galley was made up of approximately 250 to 400, not all of whom were slaves: on the five papal galleys in 1664, there were 946 condemned criminals, 15 vagrants, and 290 slaves. In the 18th century, these were joined by volunteers, often former slaves who had become Christians. Between 1570 and 1750, the number of slaves permanently manning the galleys can be estimated at between 300 and 400: allowing a period of service of some twenty years, that makes about 2,000 slaves per century. There had always been difficulties procuring slaves, as evidenced by Prince Chigi's offer to the pope. In 1645, the general of the galleys, Nicolò Ludovisi, bought 100 slaves *en bloc*. In 1723, the Order of Malta offered the pope 50. The rest were either bought at the market or taken prisoner during the wars or during excursions. The crew of a shipwrecked enemy vessel could be turned over to the galleys of Civitavecchia. The number of galley slaves greatly decreased after the middle of the 18th century. In 1723, 393 could still be found, but in 1789 there were only 47, and many among of these, being artisans, merchants, coffee shop owners in Civitavecchia, or loaned as servants to private people, actually enjoyed a kind of semi-liberty. In fact, some slaves, particularly the aged, had in the meantime bought their freedom or converted. The frequent misgivings with regard to conversions in the 16th and 17th centuries—there was evidently no wish to lose slaves who were useful, especially if the sincerity of their desire to become Christian was in doubt—ceased in the 18th century. The majority received instruction and were baptized on the spot by Capuchin friars. At that time, the conditions of life for the slaves had become easier: they could wear ordinary clothes, and the excursions were less and less frequent, as the ships did not put out to sea except in summertime. The slaves worked in the harbors, in the arsenals, on coastal fortifications, or in the garrison of Castel Sant'Angelo. After the disappearance of the papal fleet during Bonaparte's expedition in Egypt, the slaves who remained in the 19th century were all on land, some even being described as "pensioned slaves."

The Muslim slaves who converted became full-fledged subjects of the pope and generally received—an extra inducement—a bonus from the state or from their godfathers and godmothers, once they no longer remained purely and simply at the service of their former masters. From then on, however, it was necessary for a slave to have a family name. In most cases, a godfather or a godmother, often from an illustrious ecclesiastical or lay family, passed on to the slave his or her own name, sometimes in the form of an anagram (Filipani for Panfili, Rosini for Orsini), or the name of a personal landholding or coat of arms. With these new names, the descendents of the former slaves were incorporated in Roman society, which accounts for the great number of families today bearing the names of historical families to which they have no ties. Even in the 19th century, the sister of the Austrian emperor Francis I, the archduchess Marianna, who lived in Rome, transformed her little black servant Fatima into Maria Aloisia of Austria.

It could be said in conclusion that the condition of slaves in the Papal States in modern times was undoubtedly better than their condition elsewhere, above all because freedom was much easier to obtain: probably for that reason a great number of slaves from Genoa, Naples, Tuscany, and even France sought refuge in Rome, and there is no record of any movement in the opposite direction.

Wipertus Rudt de Collenberg

Bibliography

Maxwell, J. F. *Slavery and the Catholic Chuch: The History of Catholic Teaching Concerning the Moral Legitimacy of the Institution of Slavery*, Chichester and London, 1975.

Rudt de Collenberg, W. "Le baptism des musulmans esclaves à Rome an XVIIe et XVIIIe siècles," *MEFRM, Italie et Méeiterranée*, 101 (1989), 9–181 and 519–670.

SOCIAL COMMUNICATIONS. VATICAN II COUNCIL introduced the term "social communications" into the vocabulary of the Church with the decree *Inter mirifica (technicae artis inventa)*, which imposes the following definition, a norm for subsequent developments: "Among these inventions, a particular place must be assigned to the means which, by their nature, reach and influence not merely individuals but the very masses, and even the whole of humanity. Such is the case with the press, cinema, radio, television, and other techniques of like nature. These can rightly be called the means of social communication."

Borrowed from the Anglo-Saxon vocabulary of the sociology of communications, the term, coined around 1930, has been taken as the equivalent of the mass media, which in effect blurs the distinction made by PIUS XII in his 1944 Christmas message: "The people live in the plenitude of men who comprise it . . . The masses, on the contrary, await impetus from outside."

Four documents constitute the doctrinal corpus of Vatican II on social communications:

1. The draft constitution *De Instrumentis communicationis socialis*, that is, "means of social communication," was the subject of a provisional vote on 28 November 1962.

2. Reworked, this text became the decree *Inter mirifica*, promulgated by PAUL VI on 4 December 1963. In it "social communication" passed from singular to plural.

3. The *motu proprio In fructibus multis* of 2 April 1964 created the pontifical commission on social communications, assigned to put it into practice.

4. The pastoral instruction *Communio et Progressio*, drawn up by the commission and approved by Paul VI on 25 May 1971, explained the doctrinal bases and ideas for application of the concept. The French episcopate, in an assembly of November 1980, published "guidelines for a ministry of communication" based on the Roman documents.

Called at the time by a young historian, "a circular steeped in a romantic vision of information," this decree, from its inception, encountered numerous criticisms that never acknowledged its merits or its specific purpose. Conceptual thought suffered, on the one hand, from its daily encounter with the urgency of immediate application. On the other hand, the document did not take into account "communications'" own historical roles in the service of evangelization and a history that began with the written transcript of the first authentic or apologetic testimonies to the historicity of Christ, the Epistles and Gospels.

During Vatican II social communication was present, every day at midday at the doors of St. Peter's, in the clamor raised by the 1,500 representatives of the "means of communication." From the members of an assembly of whom the majority preferred the eternal to present reality, the journalists demanded precise information, almost in a raw state, concerning the morning discussions. Accredited by the Holy See to exercise their profession, they were not there as pilgrims to the tomb of the apostle.

These "mediators," by demanding the council render an account, forced it to demonstrate, instantly and without rehearsal, a readiness for speaking to the entire world in clear, simple language. The council fathers, the most traditional as well as those more aware of modern formulations of the message, had never so intimately faced the awesome and harsh character of the reality of communication. Did they make a proper distinction between "social communications" and apologetics and "religious information?" Paul VI, the first pontiff who granted an interview to a major neutral newspaper (to Alberto Cavallari of *Corriere della Sera*, on 3 October 1965), understood more clearly than any of them. On many occasions his recognition of the reality and needs of the media forced a reinstatement of the traditional defensive stance, or rather of strict control of the methods of dissemination.

In addition, not all of the reporters and bishops at the council judged the stakes on a historical basis. For example, the texts on marriage and the Christian family and the schema on social communications concerned modern questions "on which until then only the popes had decided and about which public opinion will demand much" (P. Levillain). These "modern questions" were actually but one: the limits of man's freedom in faith and morals, either in the area of his sexuality, or in the expression of his thought. These areas were always associated with each other in previous documents, generally written to curb tendencies classified under the umbrella of "liberalism."

Inter mirifica was promulgated exactly five centuries after Gutenberg installed (at Mainz) the first printing press to publish books, precursor of the modern "means of social communication." Other material support for the transmission of ideas and convictions then followed. In the 17th century the newspaper broadened access to the written word. Three centuries later, thanks to electricity, radio, television, and now the Internet can reach the whole of humanity capable of listening and seeing.

The introduction of printing did not catch the ecclesiastical institution napping. From the moment Christianity became a state religion (381), the propagation of its exclusive message—the "words of eternal life" confided to Peter—was accompanied by the repression of any divergent formulation, beginning with preventative control (censorship) of the sole means that allowed its reproduction, the written manuscript in howsoever many copies. The printing press changed the dimension, not the essence, of the control. The instrument of publication was by definition harmful if used for purposes other than those of the Church. All texts were subject to judgment. The explicit distinctions of the 20th century: type of "information" (ideas or opinions, simple facts, entertainment), choice of information to be transmitted, drafting of the message to be conveyed, reception of the message by the receptor, none of these stages was distinguished. Together and separately, they came under the principle of censorship and ecclesiastical review and penalty. Until Vatican II this practice was carried out in two ways: repression, which devolved from an inscription in the INDEX of Forbidden Books, and the printing and promotion of orthodox texts.

At first many ecclesiastics celebrated the new "divine art" with enthusiasm. At the end of the 15th century, more than a 1,000 printing presses were installed in Germany, and around 100 took root in Italy at Venice, Subiaco, then at Rome, which in 1475 already had more than 20 letter presses. The mistrust of the Church was at first directed against the press. The UNIVERSITY of Cologne in 1479, was encouraged by SIXTUS IV to censure the printers, sellers, and readers of writings contrary to faith and morals. The bishops of Mainz and Wurzburg established prior censorship of manuscripts. INNOCENT VIII extended the German measures to the entire Catholic world by the constitution *Inter multiplices* of 17 November 1487. The printing press was "very advantageous when it facilitates the diffusion of useful and approved books," but "very reprehensible if its artisans use it in a perverse way." From this sprang the institution of an apparatus of vigilance and repression destined to give the Holy See absolute control over all writings in the Christian world: prohibition, under pain of excommunication and prosecution, of printing without prior review by the bishop and his experts, followed by a "special and explicit" authorization "which will be granted for free." It involved detecting passages that were "contrary to the Catholic faith, impious, hostile, scandalous and offensive." The same penalties applied to anyone who "has the presumption to bind or posess these books." Recourse to the secular arm was recommended for recalcitrants. Everyone, printers and readers, were to deliver to the bishop works declared suspect, which were burned. Revived by ALEXANDER VI in 1501, this constitution was reproduced by LEO X in the decree of the LATERAN V Council *Inter sollicitudines* (1515), most often cited as the origin of the legislation of repression related to the REFORMATION and to the humanism of the Renaissance, which will be qualified as "indifferentism" three centuries later.

The repression had its instrument: The *Index of Forbidden Books*. The INQUISITION, reconstituted by PAUL III to this end on the eve of the Council of Trent, would later lose to the Congregation of the Index the power to draw up lists proscribing heterodox books. But before then its first list, in 1559, banned Machiavelli, deemed to be "impious and atheist." Without any real clout outside of the PAPAL STATES, the initiative also served to feed the controversies. SIXTUS V refashioned the Congregation with a single objective—the control, with three aims, of anything printed: destruction of heterodox books, suppression of the free opinions of publishers, and prohibition of the free circulation of publications. At the end of the century the index was extended to profane works. Princes helped in rigorous ecclesiastical repression, but the effects were quite limited. Braving the sanctions, publishers continued printing and circulating books that were "infectious and pernicious," particularly, foreign books, whose numbers, according to Bellarmine, continued to

increase at the Frankfurt book fair. For two centuries the policy scarcely changed, and was hardly relieved under BENEDICT XIV (1740–58). Threats and prohibitions multiplied on the eve of the FRENCH REVOLUTION with the flood of the Enlightenment, which encouraged "the contagious plague of books unleashed on the Christian people" (CLEMENT XIII, 1766). PIUS VI spoke of "the monstrous right to print with impunity on religious matters whatever they please" (Pius VI, 1791). The strategy of fear and repression found its formulation in a major text, the encyclical *Mirari vos* of Gregory XVI, of 15 August 1832. Heretics, said GREGORY XVI, were no longer outside the Church, but were camped within, minds that dreamed of modernizing the religious institution, of modifying the forms of modern apologetics, and of rendering it more accessible. "Staff in hand" against "the insolence of the tacticians," the pontiff, charged with guarding "the deposit of faith in the midst of this vast conspiracy of impious men," fulminated against the "temerity of the innovators," "the enemies of ecclesiastic celibacy," the partisans of the dissolution of marriage, put on the same level as the propagators of "this madness: that one should procure and guarantee to each one freedom of conscience, freedom of opinion without limit. . . ." "To that madness was attached freedom of the press, the most dangerous freedom, execrable freedom, for which one will never have enough horror." The pope even demanded the destruction of publications suspected of nourishing "a single weed. . . ."

Under PIUS IX followed *Quanta Cura* and the SYLLABUS (prop. 79), which explained the idea that freedom of expression stopped when it "propagates the pest of indifferentism" on matters of faith, and "promotes moral and spiritual corruption of the people" on matters of morals. The idea remained intact under the wave of "hypotheses"—conjectural interpretations that paralyzed the categorical commandment. It was continually reiterated in other terms. The Fathers of Vatican II, through the formation they had received, were cognizant of these basic texts, which influenced the debate at the Council. Embodying dogmatic rigidity in the service of the COUNTER-REFORMATION, consistency, and the hard line against "the modern spirit," the Congregation of the Index lasted until 1917 when its task was transferred to the Holy Office. It had delivered 4,000 to 6,000 misguided and fruitless condemnations such as that of the *The Spirit of Laws* by Beccaria in 1751.

Paul VI, changing the name and regulations of the Holy Office on 7 December 1965, substituted "promotion of doctrine" for judicial repression and "compassion" for sanctions. The Index of Forbidden Books, whose publication Pius XII had suspended in 1947, was totally abolished in 1966. The new CODE OF CANON LAW included six canons alluding to "social communications" and its pastoral use. The duty of approving "and even of condemning writings which harm true faith or good morals" remained with the pastors, but any idea of ecclesiastical or secular sanction is excluded, except a generic allusion to "just penalty" (unspecified) merited by those who use the means of social communication to "blaspheme, harm good morals or excite hate against the Church and religion."

Now let us turn to the positive aspects of the Church's attitude toward printing for the purposes of evangelization. Beginning in 1562, the pontiffs created three printing presses that were dependent on the Holy See: (1) the press of the Roman people to edit the works of the Council of Trent and correct the works tainted with heresy, (2) the "Oriental" press, which published 5,000 copies of the Gospel in Arabic for the purpose of an evangelization campaign in Islamic territories, and (3), in 1587, the Vatican polyglot letterpress, which published texts in all languages. The printery of the CONGREGATION for the Propagation of the Faith followed in the next century to publish missionary texts.

The line of action was clear: once the development of technical support allowed the freedom of expression to surmount every effort at condemnation, the Holy See accepted it as an instrument in service of the temporal powers, and charged it with the propagation of the Church's message.

After the book, a new type of publication became autonomous—the printed newspaper. Gregory XVI dreaded it and, like Pius VI before him, adopted it with severe measures of control. Pius IX embraced it after recognizing the influence of the hostile press in the revolutionary movements of 1849. He decided to use it as a tool in the struggle, and encouraged Father Curci, a young Neapolitan Jesuit, to found (1850) the CIVILTÀ CATOLICA to neutralize ideological poison and propagate healthy doctrines. On 1 July 1861, OSSERVATORE ROMANO appeared, an instrument "of the universal message of faith (charged) to lead the fight for truth, for peace, for charity and for the defense of human rights."

LEO XIII provided some reflection. At first (encyclical *Etsi nos*, 1882) he considered that the methods of communication could serve not only for combatting evil, but also for instruction in the "duties towards the Church." The development of a polemical Catholic press resulted, articulated with forceful national and diocesan plans because it was a time of political struggle between lay states and Catholic communities. In a second stage (*Libertas praestantissimum*, 1888), Leo XIII opened the door a little wider, but only succeeded in changing the problem: opinion and free expression became acceptable on "questions that God left to human debate." The debate, however, raged about the definition of these questions. This continued during Vatican II as a basis of the logical relationship between the authorities of the Holy See and the Catholic professionals in communications: on what would they be free to report and debate? Since the begin-

ning of the 20th century, the attack against the profane world had been effected with the utilization of the means of communication for apologetics. The "intransigent" press encouraged the repression of Modernism by PIUS X. The Assumptionists in France, between 1885 and 1900, established a very effective popular press, professional, remarkably organized, and of such polemic vigor against the "sectarian" government that Leo XIII ordered the congregation to abandon the newspaper and its approximately 100 associated regional publications. Their diffusion under the aegis of the "good press" came up against the fact that they had hardly been read by Catholics, to the advantage of neutral newspapers, which carried much more information and were detached from any preoccupation with religious instruction or moral pedagogy. The prohibition of "evil reading" institutionalized by the Code of Canon Law had at the same time been propagated by publications whose audiences did not share such a stance.

After WORLD WAR I, the Holy See, firmly fixed in a defensive position, saw the radio amplify the potential of free expression. At first there was total reserve or prohibition. The broadcast of mass and sermons was treated as an abuse before being accepted in 1939 as a messenger of evangelization. The Lateran agreements gave the Holy See the means, never before available, of broadcasting its own word to the entire world. They envisioned Italy connecting radiotelephonically and telegraphically with the other states and the Vatican constructing its own autonomous radio installation, the modern equivalent of the earlier Vatican letterpresses.

On 12 February 1931 PIUS XI inaugurated VATICAN RADIO, a realization directed by Marconi, the technical capacity and successes of which mark the full active acceptance of modern methods, crowned by the decision in June 1939 that the faithful who receive the papal benediction over the radio benefit from plenary INDULGENCES attached to the gesture. Pius XII, himself an assiduous radio listener, celebrated the radio, in December 1944, as "one of the most powerful means of diffusion of civilization and true culture."

The cinema was subject to the same evolution. A mosaic of "unhealthy" images, "passively" received, it was initially judged as "deleterious for morals," and was forbidden to clerics and placed under very strict censorship, until the ENCYCLICAL *Vigilanti cura* (29 June 1936), which deemed it an appropriate vehicle for "resuscitating virtue" and "contributing positively to the constitution of a just social order in the world."

Television experienced no such mistrust. Pius XII immediately welcomed the medium and gave his first televised message at Easter 1949, accepting the gift of a production station from the French Catholics. The choice of the French receiving station, rapidly abandoned, impeded development of the station.

In 1948 Pius XII created an Office for the Cinema, enlarged in 1954 to include radio and television, which JOHN XXIII transformed, in 1959, into a Pontifical Commission, the beginning of an organization that would soon be imitated by national episcopates. At the doctrinal level, constantly bearing in mind moral and pastoral preoccupations, Pius XII pronounced progressively decisive words which would direct conciliar and post-conciliar thinking. He stripped the Catholic press of its vocation of political combat, its amateurism, and ghetto spirit and instilled a sense of culture along with the permanent concern with moral education. He finally accepted, without reserve, the refinements of the technique. These teachings were collected in the encyclical *Miranda prorsus* (8 September 1957), which insisted on the need for the presence of the Church in communications. Pius XII in 1950 radically reversed earlier policy by recognizing the importance of "public opinion," which until then had been considered inconsequential: "Something would be missing in the life of the Church if public opinion were not taken into account."

The traditional restrictions appeared, however, in 1949 under the rubric of "apostolate" in the catalog of material to be considered by the council envisaged by Pius XII. It was merely a question of defining "clear norms for the correct usage of the instruments of the apostolate: press, cinema, theatre, sports events, etc., precautions on the utilization of cinematography."

In the spring of 1960 when the preparatory organs were established for the council, a "Secretariat for the Press and Entertainment" was created under the presidency of J. M. O'Connor, then president of the Pontifical Commission for cinematography, radio, and television. It comprised 19 members and 26 consultants from 21 nations. This secretariat, said O'Connor, "demonstrates the attention of the Church to anything which is good and useful in modern technical progress, especially through the methods of diffusion of ideas which have so much influence on the spiritual life of the faithful." The secretary of that body, André Deskur, was charged with preparing the dossier which "could serve the Holy Father for the council deliberations." But "the technical participation" of the press and the radio in the work of the council did not enter into the competence of the Secretariat. The main points of the dossier were detailed in the definitive booklet outlining matters to be treated by the preparatory commissions of the council. The Secretariat for the Press and Entertainment was responsible for the following subjects:

—proposal for a Church instruction on "the writings published by the press";

—promotion of works that would allow the conscience of Catholics to observe Catholic principles in utilizing these methods (of social communication);

—formation of a "correct conscience" in all Catholics working in these industries ("specialists, producers, artists, technicians, directors, etc.") so that they are both efficient and respectful of faith and morals;

—"presentation of the rules which will allow these methods to properly serve the works of the apostolate."

On this basis, the secretariat drafted a document in 6 fascicles of 84 pages, which were examined by the Central Commission of the council on 2 and 3 April 1962, and on 11 May by the Subcommission on Amendments. Its first part, divided into three chapters, dealt only with the Church, its discipline, its apostolate, and its authorities. The second, in a single title, resumed the previous positions on different means of communication including comic strips and advertising. It was the only text submitted to the council that enumerated the constitutive canons of the appropriate disciplinary rules. The attitude of warning remained in the background. On the 23, 24, and 26 November 1962, the General Congregation examined the amended schema. Stourm, Archbishop of Sens, reports on it. He gave the means of social communication, including the press, a definition, the singularity of which demonstrates how much the deliberation was limited, in spite of some previous papal texts:

> "[they are] for the modern world means of entertainment. . . . In its role as mother, the Church is concerned that the entertainment be not harmful to the conscience, the spirit, and the dignity of men. . . . They are never indifferent at the moral level, although they are considered as means of entertainment or as means of the communication of ideas and of culture."

The Church must use this "entertainment" for its mission of teaching the Gospel.

The majority of interventions criticized the form rather than the substance, sometimes proposing postponment of the subject to an extra-conciliar document. Cardinals Léger, Bea, and Suenens insisted on the urgency of a pastoral plan; the last did not hesitate to claim a "theology of actuality."

On 28 November, a first, quasi-unanimous vote approved the schema "in substance," sending it back, however, to the Secretariat for a shorter version. This new text came back before the council on 11 November 1963, reduced to 9 pages and 24 articles, and with a change of status: from a "constitution," it became a "decree." The 82 amendments it accepted gave the laity a much greater role in the competent ecclesiastical bodies, recommended more attention to youth, explicit support to the Catholic press, and mentioned the theater, forgotten in the first version.

Although the text was voted on without debate, it became the object of a strong and heterogeneous opposition movement. Three American journalists, supported by four experts of the council (Murray, Daníelou, Mesia, and Häring) circulate a brief note, labeling the draft, "a step backwards":

"It deals with a press which exists only in manuals, but which is hardly recognizable by us . . . , its moralizing emphasis is simplistic . . . it utters not a word about those who have obligations, of those who must be at the source of information . . . , it is a classic example of the way in which the Second Vatican Council was not able to fulfill its task of confronting the problems of the world which surround it."

At the doors of St. Peter on 25 November, before the final vote, a flyer calling for a *Non placet* vote was distributed to the council Fathers. It bore the signature of 6 archbishops, 18 bishops, and a superior general (that of the Society of the Divine Word). Cardinal Tisserant, in the name of the presidency, protested against this exceptional act, which he qualified as "an attack on the freedom of the council." Only one of the signatories claimed that his name had been inscribed without his knowledge. Of the 2112 voters, 503, nevertheless, voted against the decree.

There were still 164 votes against during the final solemn ballot on 4 December, before Paul VI promulgated the decree in a public session, but close to 200 fathers were missing from the final vote. The decree was not a reaffirmation of a state of mind attached to the letter of the disciplinary prescriptions, yet the majority of the actors and commentators failed to acknowledge that the precipitous path over the previous 30 years had resulted from 5 centuries of rigidity. This decree anchors within the Church a new institution clearly charged with implementing a change of direction desired by Paul VI and a part of the council. This was the task of the Pontifical Commission for Social Communications created by the *motu proprio In fructibus multis* of 2 April 1964. Composed of 20 new members, among them 4 laymen very close to the Vatican and 11 consultants, it had its first plenary meeting on 28 September 1964 in the presence of the pope.

What bases did the council use to develop the document and to put it into practice? The decree, after all, must be read in light of *Gaudium et spes* and *Lumen gentium*, the two great conciliar constitutions, which allowed for the articulation of a "theology of communications" still in its initial stages. Beyond the simple utilization of technical methods for evangelization, these documents define the involvement of the Church in culture. The right to culture of every human being includes his right to information.

"Information" was not always clear in every sense of the word. For a century and a half for the Church as for the entire intellectual class, printing, as an "instrument of communication," transmitted ideas and opinions. From the end of the 19th century, the "news," the "facts," seem to adulterate its nature, and even Zola deplored it. The two meanings that inspired the decree *Inter mirifica* were either ideas and, therefore, implicit pedagogical aims, or "entertainment" as Stourm called it at the council.

On 23 May 1971 Paul VI approved the pastoral instruction *Communio et progressio*, developed by the commission after long consultations with a number of lay experts. "The Church considers the means of communications as gifts of God" to inherit the earth, to unite man to his brothers, and to contribute to God's design in history. All the subjects, hitherto so suspect, are positively treated: public opinion, the right to information, freedom of expression, and the necessary professional formation of journalists. The third part, dedicated to the Church's use of the means of communication expresses, in an optimistic tone rarely achieved by such documents, the need to promote technical research in the media and "to establish a priority plan at the world level," for "the People of God anticipate the promises of a new age: that of social communications."

The pursuit of the "annual day of social communication" led, in all dioceses, to reflection on the matter. Subsequent directives detailed items that the instruction evaded. Thus, on 19 March 1986, the Congregation for Catholic Education published "guidelines for the formation of future priests in the means of social communication."

With JOHN PAUL II the media became a constitutive part of the life of the Church. His interventions were frequent, tending to reinforce particularly Catholic entities. Two documents published in the first semester of 1992 brought the doctrine of social communications up to date: the Pontifical Council for Social Communications published a pastoral instruction on 22 February, *Aetatis Novae* for the 20th anniversary of *Communio et progressio*. This account of achievements and principles is both open on the rights and dangers of information, and clear on the rights of the Church. It proposes that "the information era" and rapid technological changes give "new possibilities and pose new pastoral problems" to the Church's mission. Dialogue with the secular world "requires an anthropology and a true theology of communications," as well as the liberty to enjoy "freedom to communicate which is the right of all." There is urgency, concludes the document which, referring to John Paul II, notes that the "great contemporary 'Areopagus' of the media has been more or less ignored by the Church until now." The elements of a "pastoral plan, aimed at episcopal conferences and dioceses" were proposed in an annex.

The Congregation for the Doctrine of the Faith intervened on 20 March with an instruction on "certain aspects of the utilization of the means of social communications in the promotion of the doctrine of the faith." Cardinal Ratzinger recalled the disciplinary principles in the service of "care and vigilance." Bishops are responsible for judging writings related to faith and morals, of authorizing them or not, of giving clerics the permission to write in newspapers hostile to the Church, and of overseeing publishing houses dependent on religious institutions. The "*Nihil obstat*" and the "*Imprimatur*" were unmistakably restored, without their names being mentioned. No allusion was made to the reestablishment of the index.

This reminder of the traditional legislation (and possible sanctions) also concerned "advertisers" in general, told to "keep within the limits of professional ethics and to pay attention to principles concerning the manner of treating religious problems."

The new regulation of the Roman CURIA prohibits all "declarations and interviews" from DICASTERIES. They must pass through the Sala Stampa.

Jacques Nobécourt

Bibliography

Boullet, M. *Le choc des medias*, Paris, 1985.

Caprile, G. SJ, *Il Concilio Vaticano II*, Rome, 1965–8, 6 vols.

Cavallari, A. *La fabbrica del presente*, Rome, 1990.

Civiltà Cattolica, No. 2780 (1966), II, 127–37.

Documentation catholique, 30 July 1950, 1007–10, and 1964, 1425, 681–4.

Les Medias, textes des Eglises. Ed. Mediathec, Paris, 1990 (Les dossiers de la *Documentation catholique*).

Levillain, P. *La Mecanique politique de Vatican II*, Paris, 1975.

Naz, R. "Index," *DDC*, 5 (1953), 1318–30.

Pinto De Oliveira, C. J. OP, "Le premier document pontifical sur la presse," *Revue de sciences philosophiques et theologiques*, 50 (1966), 625–43.

Rotondò, A. "La censura ecclesiastica e la cultura," *Storia d'Italia*, V, Turin, 1973, 1401–92 [deals with the Italian situation, fixes the chronology and condemned subjects from the 16th century to the French Revolution].

Ruszkowski, A. "Vatican II et les communications sociales," *Le Concile revisite*, 235–52, Rome, 1986.

Sacrosanctum Oecumenicum Concilium Vaticanum II. Constitutiones, Decreta, Declarationes, Vatican City, 1966.

Wenger, A. *Le Cardinal Villot (1905–1979)*, Paris, 1989.

SOCIAL DOCUMENTS. The following are the principal documents of the SOCIAL TEACHING of the Church: LEO XIII, the ENCYCLICAL *Rerum novarum*, 15 May 1891, on the condition of workers; PIUS XI, the encyclical *Quadragesimo anno*, 15 May 1931, on the establishment of a new social order, for the fortieth anniversary of *Rerum novarum*; the encyclical *Mit brennender Sorge*, 14 March 1937, on the situation of the Catholic Church within the German Reich; the encyclical *Divini Redemptoris*, 19 March 1937, on atheistic communism; PIUS XII, a radio message on 1 June 1941, for the fiftieth anniversary of *Rerum novarum*; JOHN XXIII, the encyclical *Mater et Magistra* 15 May 1961, on the contemporary evolution of social life in light of Christian principles, for the seventieth anniversary of *Rerum novarum* the encyclical *Pacem in terris*, 11 April 1963, on peace between nations; the VATICAN II COUNCIL, pastoral constitution on the church in the modern world, *Gaudium et spes*, 7 December 1965; PAUL VI, the encyclical *Populorum progressio*, 26 March 1967, on the development of peoples; an apostolic letter to Cardinal Maurice Roy *Octogesima adveniens*, 14 May 1971, in response to the needs of a changing world, for the eightieth anniversary of *Rerum novarum*; JOHN PAUL II, the encyclical *Laborem exercens*, 14 September 1981, on human work, for the ninetieth anniversary of *Rerum novarum*; the encyclical *Sollicitudo rei socialis*, 30 December 1987, for the twentieth anniversary of *Populorum progressio*; the encyclical *Centesimus annus*, 1 May 1991, for the centennial of *Rerum novarum*.

To this may be added other documents, sometimes dealing exclusively with social problems, especially radio messages and speeches: Pius XII, speeches at Christmas, 1939 and 1940; radio message for Christmas, 1941 and 1942; a speech to workers about the social question (13 May 1943); radio messages for Christmas 1943; on the first of September 1944; and for Christmas 1944; worldwide radio broadcasts for Christmas—1949, 1950, 1951, and 1952; a speech to a group of workers marking the anniversary of *Rerum novarum* (14 May 1953); radio messages to the world for Christmas 1955 and 1956; John XXIII, a radio broadcast for Christmas 1959; John Paul II, a speech to the papal commission *Justitia et pax*, for the twentieth anniversary of *Populorum progressio* (24 March 1987). Numerous speeches given by the Roman pontiff during his apostolic travels on all five continents should also be mentioned, as well as his speeches on 19 March, the feast day of St. Joseph, the patron saint of workers.

Dominique Le Tourneau

Bibliography

Chabot, J. L. *La Doctrine sociale de l'Église*, 2nd ed., Paris, 1992.

SOCIAL TEACHING. The notion of social teaching in the Church was defined in a broad way as teaching discourse of the ecclesiastical magisterium, on the organization of political, social, and economic relations—

including the family—on the national and international levels and addressed to society. The frequent application of the term "doctrine" to this concept, seems, in view of Church, and particularly papal, practice, less indicative of dogma than of social teaching, to inform rather than strictly to bind the consciences of the faithful. The Latin terminology, it is true, does not distinguish clearly between these two types of discourse, the word *doctrina* meaning doctrine as well as instruction.

The value placed on the give-and-take of debate is especially apparent in a letter sent by PAUL VI to Cardinal Roy (*Octogesima Adveniens*, 19 May 1971), in which the pope indicated that "to propose a solution [to a widely varied set of social situations] that has universal value . . . is not our ambition, nor even our mission," thus rejecting the idea of a single world solution and encouraging Christians to analyze specific situations in their own milieu. This approach was maintained and confirmed by the instruction of the CONGREGATION FOR THE DOCTRINE OF FAITH (*Libertas christiana*, 1986), which renewed this appeal to conscience shaped by analysis and presumably steeped in biblical principles.

Despite previous attempts by the Church to analyze and reflect upon society—sometimes renounced by clerics in favor of a total rejection of the profane world—the "social subject" appeared at the end of the 19th century as "new things" (*Res novae*). It is well known, however, that much earlier—particularly in the 4th and 5th centuries—the FATHERS of the CHURCH had clearly advocated a communal disposition of worldly goods by showing extreme severity toward profiteers and not accepting the right of private property unless it was exercised carefully. Medieval society, such as that in France during most of the Ancien Regime, ascribed social organization to divine will, forbidding any emphasis on injustices and inequalities. Suffering was linked to work, based on—and even justified by—the Biblical injunction to "earn one's bread by the sweat of one's brow," a direct consequence of original sin (Genesis 3:17–19). The awakening of Catholicism to the modern world resulted from a new perception of the role of work and changed the Church's attitude toward the earthly aspects of its mission. The long silence of the institutional Church on these questions had helped throw it into disrepute, particularly in the 19th century. PIUS XI was obliged to stigmatize this "great scandal of the Church in the 19th century," the desertion of the working class, due as much to changing modes of production (the Industrial Revolution in its various forms) as to the financial and economic system (liberal capitalism), even though Catholic countries were the last to confront the social question raised by industrialization, as opposed to Germany and the Anglo-Saxon countries. Polarized over the defense of religious freedom and the fight against skepticism, Rome paid only scant attention to the initiatives of Villeneuve, Lamennais, Le Play (1806–82),

or Albert de Mun (1841–1914), or even Freppel (1827–91), the founder of the school at Angers, and Ketteler (1811–77), the bishop and Hessian deputy from Mainz who stood up to Marx and also vigorously protested against the "flagrant injustices" of capitalism.

Beginning in 1877, LEO XIII, then still bishop, put into effect a social policy that he continued after his accession to the pontificate within the Union of Freiburg, linking the three European centers of social action (Rome, Paris, and, Frankfurt) sensitive to Thomist thought (ENCYCLICAL *Aeterni Patris*, 1879). A "thunderbolt" (G. Bernanos), perceived more by its echo than its original impact, struck with the appearance of the encyclical *Rerum novarum* of 15 May 1891. Although restrained, it focused on the situation of the working class (the encyclical was subtitled "On the condition of workers"), clearly condemning the excesses of a system based upon the dominance of capital and consequently profit, but also rejecting the damaging effects of socialism and the theory of class struggle. While recalling, on the basis of principle, that "the Church does not recognize any right to involve itself without reason in the conduct of temporal business" (*Rerum novarum*, 13), the encyclical advocated, by virtue of its authority over moral issues, a reconciliation of social classes by the Christian use of wealth as private property "for common use," with the state having a duty to promote the common good and protect workers against excesses of any kind. In effect, "a complete perspective [did not allow] the separation of the temporal and the spiritual" (Émile Poulat) and grounded the right of the Church to express itself. Though it clearly denounced the abuses of the economic system, the papal text did not make any statement on the intrinsic nature of existing institutions, leaving to those working in the area the responsibility of determining the methods and pathways of reform. The mood remained conservative, concerned primarily with moral as opposed to structural reform. Yet even this moderate pronouncement was conspicuous within the broader context of the Church's "social indifference" (R. Aubest).

Despite a rather enthusiastic reception and much gratitude on the part of "social" Catholics, the text of the Leonine encyclical was not widely published. One explanation for this lies in the expectations of the liberal individualist mentality—an attitude that itself is subject to many interpretations. A number of allusions to the social question appeared during succeeding pontificates. PIUS X showed his concern when certain radical tendencies appeared within the *Azione Popolare cattolica* and went so far as to write, in a *motu proprio* dated 18 December 1903, that social inequalities were of divine law. A letter to the French episcopate on 25 August 1910 warned about the new Sillon, open to non-Catholics and favoring radical reforms. However, the proclamations of Pius X marked the end of an era, and the Church, by then irrevocably involved in the social realm had to adopt a clear approach to the world that resulted from WORLD WAR I. The weight of urgent matters hindered BENEDICT XV from preparing even a superficial written commentary on the topic. This was to be the privilege of Pius XI, who, in a text commemorating the fortieth anniversary of *Rerum novarum* (the encylical *Quadragesimo anno* on 15 May 1931), repeated the discussion of basic points begun by Leo XIII, engaging himself in a program of widespread reorganization of the economic system. The pope displayed his desire to promote a system of the corporate type, redefining the role of the state and the constitution of "professional bodies" in that context, but also in contrast to the Italian fascist corporatism then being developed. After June 1919, Pius XI took a position favoring freedom for trade unions, in a letter addressed to the bishop of Lille, Liénart. Echoing the text of *Quadragesimo anno*, as well as some 1,500 episcopal documents made public between 1891 and 1931, his encyclicals condemning totalitarian regimes (*Mit Brennender Sorge,*14 March 1937, on German national socialism, and *Divini redemptoris*, 19 March 1937, against the atheistic doctrines of communism) tried to help define a third way between liberalism and socialism, based on a reform that addressed morals, social justice, and charity. Restricted almost from the first days of his pontificate by the horrors of war, the social discourse of PIUS XII emphasized the rights of human beings, defining the social teaching of the Church as a common patrimony (speech of 1 June 1941 for the fiftieth anniversary of *Rerum novarum*, and the Christmas message of 1942) and warning against state takeovers in light of the German experience (letter to the Social Week of Strasbourg, 1946, on nationalization; speech of 19 June 1948).

The altered situation—this time worldwide in scope— that existed after WORLD WAR II required the promulgation of a new text that could serve as a reference "on recent developments of the social question in the light of the Christian teaching," the exact subtitle of the encyclical *Mater et magistra* published by JOHN XXIII on 15 July 1961, for the seventieth anniversary of Leo XIII's encyclical. Due to the necessity of making justice penetrate to sectors outside the boundaries of advanced industrial society, such as agriculture, the pope insisted on an internationalist approach to economic and social problems, among which were demographic growth and development. The text heralded a new spirit, that of the VATICAN II COUNCIL, by delineating the notion of "the signs of the times" (*signa temporum*), in tandem with the encyclical *Pacem in terris* (1963) which, aimed at promoting and defending international peace, inaugurated a consideration of the rights of man, including economic and social rights. Thus the natural right of workers to unite in collective bargaining was definitively sanctioned by the council (constitution *Gaudium et spes*, 68) as well as—

from a more pastoral than theoretical perspective—the idea that economic development should serve mankind, and not the reverse.

Another major step in the history of papal thought on the social question was the appearance of the encyclical *Populorum progressio* (26 May 1967), in which Paul VI was determined to consider issues whose significance stretched beyond the West (such as the binary opposites capital/labor) and extend them on a worldwide scale through a single unified vision encompassing all human attributes and activities, economic, cultural, moral, and religious. An apostolic letter addressed to Cardinal Roy on 9 May 1971 (*Octogesima adveniens*) invited Christians to get actively involved in addressing new challenges like urbanization, immigration, women's issues, and the environment, and embraced new ideas, in particular those that arose from the expansion of human sciences.

A similar viewpoint, arising from an anthropological vision also derived from an integral humanism, fills the five encyclicals of JOHN PAUL II, spread out over the first 15 years of his pontificate, that deal with the social question. The sensitivity of the pope to injustices and inequalities, derived from his past experience as a quarry worker in Poland (as noted by a number of biographers and commentators) is doubtless essential to the social teaching of this sovereign pontiff but is not the only factor to analyze. We can also see great continuity with the speeches of Paul VI, to which John Paul II made many allusions in orations given in Rome or during his travels throughout the world. After the encyclicals *Redemptor hominis* (4 March 1979), placing man as the "first, most basic" path of the Church, and *Dives in misericordia* (30 November 1980), placing love over and above distributive or commutative justice, the accent was placed on "the working man" (encyclical *Laborem exercens* of 14 September 1981; speech to the International Conference on Work in Geneva of 15 May 1982) and the planetary scale on which it is necessary to understand the social question and try to ascertain the place of the individual, including his rights and duties (encyclical *Sollicitudo rei socialis* of 30 December 1987). But Church discourse on society in the contemporary era found its apogee in the encyclical marking the one hundredth anniversary of *Rerum novarum (Centesimus annus*, 1 May 1991), published on May (Labor) Day and the feast of St. Joseph the worker, not on the actual anniversary (15 May). Along with an analysis of the collapse of the socialist regimes at the end of 1989 (Poland is the only state named specifically), the text urged a Christian vision of the economy challenging the remaining capitalist model, which was in the midst of great difficulties. The link was made to a form of democracy of the state which could only find its legitimacy and its "authentic foundation" in the recognition and service of the rights of man, another facet of an integral anthropology attempting to restore the total dimension of man. It was gradually becoming understood that social and economic problems had ramifications beyond the working world. The general approach of the Church's social teaching was exemplified by its making *Rerum novarum* the only encyclical, and even the only papal document, whose publication was periodically commemorated. This step paved the way for a social theology that is still evolving today, and demonstrates that the hopes of Leo XIII for the inauguration of a harmonious *ordo futurus rerum* have never been abandoned.

Philippe Levillain

Bibliography

Antonchich, R. *La Doctrine sociale de l'Église*, Paris, 1992.

Aubert, J. M., Metz, R., Sicard, G., Wackenheim, C., and Winninger, P. *Le Droit et les institutions de l'Église catholique latine de la fin du XVIIIᵉ siècle à 1978, Églises et sociétés (Histoire du droit et des institutions de l'Église en Occident*, XVIII), Paris, 1984.

Buchele, H. *Christlicher Glaube und politische Verkunft. Für eine neue Konzeption der katholischen Soziallehre*, Vienna, 1987.

Calvez, J. Y. *L'Économie, l'homme, la société: l'enseignement social de l'Église*, Paris, 1989.

Daujat, J. *L'Ordre social chrétien*, Paris, 1970.

De Clercq, V. *Les Doctrines sociales catholiques en France depuis la Révolution jusqu'à nos jours*, Paris, 1905.

Dorr, D. *Option for the Poor. A Hundred Years of Vatican Social Teaching*, New York, 1983, revised edition, 1992.

Dwyer, J. A., ed. *The New Dictionary of Catholic Social Thought*, Collegeville, Minn., 1994.

Gonzales, P. E. "La doctrina social de la Iglesia frente a las ciencias sociales: intentos y dificultades de un dialogo," *Theologica Xaveriana, Conflictos morales del cristiano*, 35/75 (1985), 235–89.

Le Discours social de l'Église catholique. De Léon XIII à Jean-Paul II, Paris, 1984.

Maugenest, C. (dir.), *Le Discours social de l'Église, de Léon XIII à Jean Paul II*, Paris, 1990.

Pluralité et cohérence du discours social de l'Église, special issue of the *Revue de l'Institut catholique de Paris*, December 1984.

Portelli, H. *Les Socialismes dans le discours social catholique*, Paris, 1987.

E. Poulat, "Le libéralisme économique entre deux encycliques. Cent ans de doctrine sociale catholique," *Foi et développement*, 208 (1992).

Rutten, C. *La Doctrine sociale de l'Église*, Juvisy, 1932.

Schasching, J. "Die soziale Botschaft der Kirche," *Theologisch-Praktische Quartalschrift* 138/1 (1990), 3–48.

Tosos, M. "Catechesi e dottrina sociale della Chiesa," *Orientamenti Pedagogici* 37, 221 (1990), 959–91.

Cardinal Verdier, *Problèmes sociaux, réponses chrétiennes*, Paris, 1939.

SOCIETIES, PONTIFICAL MISSION. There are four Pontifical Mission Societies: the Pontifical Society for the Propagation of the Faith, the Pontifical Society of the Holy Childhood, the Society of St. Peter the Apostle, and the Pontifical Missionary Union. With the exception of the last, they all originated in France.

"As institutions of the universal Church and of each particular Church, the Pontifical Mission Societies have as their goal to awaken and deepen the missionary awareness of the people of God, to inform the faithful concerning the life and needs of the universal mission, to encourage the Churches to pray for one another and to give one another mutual support by sending personnel and material aid, and thus to arouse a spirit of solidarity in the cause of evangelization" (*Statutes*, chap. I, n. 5).

The Pontifical Mission Societies must be established everywhere (VATICAN II council, decree *Ad Gentes*, n. 38), an injunction also found in the instruction *Quo aptius* (24 February 1969): "Pontifical Mission Societies must be established in all dioceses."

The societies have two principal characteristics. On the one hand, they are pontifical societies, that is, directly dependent on the Roman pontiff through the intermediary of the Congregation for the Evangelization of Peoples, even if "they are also those of the whole episcopate and all the people of God" (PAUL VI, *Message for World Mission Day of 1976*). On the other hand, the societies are universal, in 1) the collection of funds, which is carried out under the aegis of the HOLY SEE throughout the whole Catholic world and which is their primary objective; a central, pontifical solidarity fund helps ensure that certain Churches will not be left out; 2) their aim: the Pontifical Mission Societies come to the aid of all missions; 3) their juridical status: arising out of spontaneous Christian initiatives, the societies have all been raised to the privileged status of missionary action and of direct aid to the Congregation for the Propagation of the Faith, today called the Congregation for the Evangelization of Peoples (JOHN PAUL II, apostolic CONSTITUTION *Pastor bonus*, 28 June 1988, art. 91), leaving intact the powers of the Congregation for the Oriental Church. Brought under the protection of the Holy See in 1922, they are also dependent, at the local level, on the bishops' conference of each country and on the bishops of the particular Churches, in collaboration with the existing mission centers.

A supreme committee "sees to it that each Pontifical Mission Society develops steadily and effectively within its own sphere of action, and resolves difficulties that might arise among them" (PIUS XI, *motu proprio Decessor noster*, 24 June 1929). The members of this committee are the general secretaries and one delegate from each of the four societies.

The activity of the mission societies is under the direction of a higher council based in Rome. It is made up of the following members: president, general secretaries of the four societies, undersecretaries of section II of the SECRETARIAT OF STATE, of the Congregation for Bishops, and of the Congregation for the Oriental Church, the national directors of the four societies, and in certain cases counselors appointed by the Congregation for the Evangelization of Peoples. Each of the four societies has an international secretariat, the secretary being appointed by the congregation on consultation with members of the higher council.

In each country, there is a national council and a national board of directors of the four societies, headed by a national director appointed by the congregation at the suggestion of the conference of bishops.

This organization follows the directives of the Vatican II decree *Ad Gentes*, and of the *motu proprio* of Paul VI, *Ecclesiae Sanctae*, for the application of this conciliar decree (6 August 1966, part III). This latter document recalls that the four Pontifical Mission Societies are subordinate to the Congregation for the Propagation of the Faith (III, no. 13 § 2). But they remain autonomous and are governed by their own statutes. The general statutes of the societies were published by the Congregregration for the Evangelization of Peoples on 26 June 1980.

The role of this congregation and other bodies concerned with missionary activity was recalled once again by John Paul II, in the encyclical *Redemptoris missio* of 7 December 1990. The pope defined the functions of the Pontifical Mission Societies: besides collecting subsidies, they are to play a leading role in animating the missionary zeal of the people of God by promoting the universal missionary spirit, and to encourage lifelong vocations *ad gentes*, in all the Churches, young and old. In short, they bring to the Catholic world the spirit of universality and missionary service without which there is no authentic cooperation.

The Pontifical Mission Societies seek to bring about harmonious collaboration with the different mutual aid organizations grouped together in the Pontifical Council *Cor unum*, and with the mission institutes.

The CODE OF CANON LAW of 1983, in a canon which has no equivalent in the previous code but which repeats provisions of the *motu proprio Ecclesiae Sanctae* III, nos. 9 and 11, and of the instruction *Quo aptius* (24 February 1969), provides that, in order to encourage mission cooperation, each diocese must have a priest charged with effectively promoting works supporting the missions, "principally Pontifical Mission Societies" (c. 791.2). This last reference is an adjunct to the provisions of the *motu proprio Ecclesiae Sanctae* (III, no. 4), which is reproduced in number 2 of c. 791, the provisions themselves

implementing the conciliar decree *Ad Gentes*, no. 39. The *motu proprio* specifies that the priest will be part of the diocesan pastoral council (cf. c. 512 of the Code of 1983).

The Pontifical Mission Societies collaborate in a number of events:

1) The most important is World Mission Day, in October, instituted by Pius XI in 1926 at the request of the superior council of the Society for the Propagation of the Faith (today, it is often a World Mission Week). Until then, members' subscriptions and private gifts had been the principal source of revenue. The first members of the Society for the Propagation of the Faith were workers who paid a "mission penny" each week. Canon 791.3 makes the event obligatory in the dioceses, in accordance with the *motu proprio Ecclesiae Sanctae* (III, no. 3). This document specified that its goal was to encourage prayer during the mass, the offering of Holy Communion and sacrifices, the furthering of membership in the society, the collection of offerings for the missions, and, above all, the fostering of the missionary spirit.

2) The Mission Day of Priests, originally promoted by the Missionary Union of the Clergy and made official by the Congregation for the PROPAGATION OF THE FAITH (letter, 16 October 1946); henceforth its objective was to invite priests and religious to contribute as much as they were able to the mission cause, and to pray for the urgent needs of the missions in their pious practices and in their ministerial offices.

3) The Mission Day of the Sick, likewise organized in several countries on the initiative of private individuals or groups. The first was held in Rome, in 1931. This enterprise was soon taken over by the Congregation for the Propagation of the Faith. Its aim is to encourage the sick to offer their suffering for the transcendent cause of mission.

Dominique Le Tourneau

Bibliography

Annuario Pontificio per l'anno 2000, 1275–9.

Congregation for the Evangelization of Peoples, *Les Oeuvres pontificales missionnaires. Leur but. Leur importance. Leur actualité*, Vatican City, 1978.

Paventi, S. "Opere Pontificie Missionarie," *EC*, IX, 1952, 162–6.

Statutes, 26 June 1980, Vatican City, 1980.

SOTER. *(d. ca. 175.) Elected pope ca. 166. Saint.*

Very little is known about this pontiff. The *Liberian Catalogue* antedates him, since the consular dates cited for his reign would place him between 162 and 170. Because he was the eleventh successor of Peter and came immediately after PIUS I, the general chronology obliges us to place his pontificate from 166 and 175, since all the sources agree that Soter died in the eighth year of his reign. According to the *Liber pontificalis*, he came from Fundi, in Campania. Eusebius of Caesarea quotes a letter from Dionysius, bishop of Corinth, thanking Soter for help sent from the Church of Rome to that of Corinth; this shows the solicitude of the Roman community toward all unfortunate Christians. A letter written by Soter was purportedly read in the Church of Corinth. He is said to have taken a public stance against the Montanists and the Tertullianists, but this is an error, since Tertullian had not yet broken with the Church. The most important action of his pontificate was certainly the fixing of the feast of Easter on the Sunday following the fourteenth day of the month of Nisan—a move that would give rise to much controversy. Despite tradition, he was not martyred. His burial is supposed to have taken place in the Vatican, close to Peter, but there is no evidence to confirm this.

Jean-Pierre Martin

Bibliography

Amann, E. *DThC*, XVI, 2, 2422–3.
Eusebius, *HE*, IV, 19, 1; 22, 2; 30, 3; V, 6, 4; 14.
Ireneaus, *Adv. Haeres.*, III, 3, 3.
Richard, M. "La question pascale au IIe siècle," *L'Orient Syrien*, VI, 1961, 179–212.
Weltin, E. G. *NCE*, XIII, 444.

SPOIL. Spoils are the portable goods of a cleric provided with a BENEFICE, which were seized upon his death by the apostolic collector to add to the general treasury. This store of spoils occurred regularly during the time of the AVIGNON papacy and reached the height of its unpopularity during the Great SCHISM. The seizure, inventory, and sale of clothing, ornaments, and furnishings reserved for the Holy See was so time-consuming that the collectors were usually content to take one piece of furniture in the cases of wealthy men, and refused to take anything from the majority of those with benefices. The seizures made were only done when clerics had heavy fiscal debts to the APOSTOLIC CAMERA. Often denounced by polemicists who were looking for scandalous examples of fiscal persecution, the seizure of spoils brought practically nothing to the papacy.

Jean Favier

Bibliography

Williman, D. *The Right of Spoil of the Popes of Avignon, 1316–1415*, Philadelphia, 188 (*Transactions of the American Philosophical Society*, 78–6) [review by J. Jugie in *Revue historique*, July–September 1990, 1941–9].

STATIONS, ROMAN. The term "stations" originated in the military terminology of the ancient Roman Empire, where *statio* meant both the post of guard and guard duty, which was obviously performed awake and standing up—hence the root, *stare* ("to stand"). As happened with many profane words, the early Christian community adopted it to designate a particular moment of worship: the plenary assembly of the local community in the presence of its bishop and priests.

The early reasons for the choice of this military term must have been linked to the practice of fasting. The Christian community was pausing in its journey to the Heavenly Jerusalem and, by prayers and corporal mortification, was "mounting guard" against the enemy's attacks, against the spirit of evil. Jewish tradition prescribed fasting twice a week, on Monday and Thursday. The Christians took their inspiration from this tradition but, to set themselves apart from it, dedicated Wednesday and Friday to the fast. "Moreover, your fasts are not made at the same times as those of the hypocrites; indeed, they fast on the second and fifth days of the week; but you fast on the fourth day and on the day of preparation" (Didache, c. 8). In the Christian community, Wednesday was linked to the memory of Judas's betrayal; Friday (the eve of and preparation for the Jewish holy Sabbath) was clearly linked to the memory of Christ's death. In the early community, both these fast days were thus already observed at the end of the 1st century, but not during the 2nd century is there documentation showing that they were given the name *stationes* in Rome and elsewhere. According to the various testimonies, it seems that fasting was not obligatory, but it was strongly recommended and certainly observed by the most fervent Christians. Moreover, fasting on Wednesday and Friday was in practical terms a halffast, since it ended at the ninth hour—that is, in the middle of the afternoon, usually before the Eucharistic feast.

The connection between fasting and the Eucharist varied depending on the Church. As an eyewitness to the tradition of the African communities, Tertullian (155–222) reported that, even on fast days, celebration of the Eucharist took place in the morning, although some did not take part, convinced that communion broke the fast. In Alexandria, by contrast, these fast days were non-liturgical; fasting and the celebration of the Eucharist were mutually exclusive. The Church of Rome adopted the latter tradition, as is shown by a letter of the early 5th century (416) from Pope INNOCENT I to Bishop Decenzio of Gubbio.

The Quadragesimal Stations in Rome. This twice-weekly practice of fasting combined with worship in assembly, with or without communion, held a particular place of honor in Rome. It developed especially in the penitential context of Lent and owing to the unique presence of St. Peter's successor.

In Africa, from the 3rd century, the term "station" signified not only an assembly of worshippers, linked to fasting, but any other plenary liturgical assembly presided over by a bishop. Thus, it was the term used by Cyprian (210–58) to describe the assembly that met in Carthage under its bishop and in the presence of clergy, to hear the delegates of the antipope Novatian give their report. The term was used in the same sense toward the end of the 4th century, in Rome, in a text by an unknown writer. This relates that after the pseudo-bishop Felix had been expelled from Rome, he returned to celebrate a "station" with his disciples in the basilica of Sta. Maria in Trastevere.

It was as plenary assemblies presided over by a bishop that the stations, which first arose in Jerusalem, were greatly developed in Rome, and from there reached the new Western Churches. They were a visible, expressive manifestation of the local Christian community in its progress toward the Promised Land, representing a pause to affirm its approach to the holy table in a communion of faith around its bishop, the visible symbol of Christ the Shepherd. The earliest witness to offer a complete series of the Roman stations presided over by the pope throughout the liturgical year is a reader, (known as a *Comes*), from Würzburg that dates from the 7th century. The existence of these Roman stations is corroborated by the *Gregorian Sacramentary*, almost contemporary with the reader, aside from a few insignificant details. The ritual associated with these stations is described in the *Ordines Romani*, in particular in Ordines I, II, and III, as well as in the manuscript of St. Amandus.

The Roman stational system, therefore, had its roots in the phenomenon of the local Eucharistic assembly presided over by the bishop. Such an assembly was universally characteristic of the first urban communities, before Christianity spread into the countryside. It was not until the number of believers grew and the communities started to expand beyond the cities that places of worship multiplied. In Rome, these were known as *tituli* in the cities and as "parishes" in the rural areas. In the 3rd century, and therefore before the peace of Constantine, the Roman community experienced a significant increase, with the result that on Sundays and feast days it had to be divided. Smaller groups met in various centers of worship, at the homes of certain wealthy families that had large estates, of which the assemblies bore the title. It was from these that the particular places of worship derived their names. In Rome, the station for the most important liturgical assemblies was at the Lateran—that is, in the cathedral. However, on special occasions the pope would go from one parish church to another, since the Lateran assembly was the one that officially represented the whole city. The priests who resided in or were responsible for the other *tituli* were not obliged to take part in all the pontifical stations. Nevertheless, to preserve in some way the original idea of a single ecclesial community presided over by one bishop, there was instituted the custom of *fermentum*, by which the pope, as the symbol of unity and communion with the priests, sent each one a piece of the bread he had consecrated. The priests then added it to the Eucharistic species that they had consecrated at the mass celebrated in their churches.

In Rome, a particular ritual soon came to be associated with the station: the procession. This custom probably arose and evolved in the context of the feasts celebrating the birthdays of martyrs, when the faithful would gather around the tomb of the one who had given his blood to remain faithful to Christ and his Gospel, the pope participating with all the clergy of Rome. This procession was known as a *letania*, since the visit to the tomb ended with the singing of the litanies of the saints. The local community met in a predetermined place (*ad collectam*). From there, it made its way to the station church, where the pope solemnly presided over the celebration of the Eucharist.

GREGORY I the Great gave particular impetus to these processions, reorganizing them into a series for the liturgical year. The earliest testimony to describe in detail the procedures for these stational processions again is found in the *Ordo Romanus* I, written in the first half of the 8th century. The people were encouraged to meet around 3 o'clock in the afternoon in a specified place, to which the pope also came, accompanied by clergy. Before beginning the procession, the pontiff said a prayer (*oratio ad collectam*). Then the procession began with the cross at the head followed by the crowd, the pope, and behind him the clerics, carrying all the objects needed for the celebration of the Mass. All made their way to the stational church accompanied by the singing of psalms, anthems, and, finally, the litanies of the saints. At the church, the pope presided over the Eucharist, the priests concelebrating with him. After the communion, the archdeacon announced to the faithful where the next stational assembly would be held.

In the 8th century in Rome, there were daily stations during Lent. However, processions did not take place every day, but only on Monday, Wednesday, and Friday, according to the *Ordo Romanus* I. In Charlemagne's time, a procession was also added to the Saturday station. The organization of quadragesimal stations in Rome seems to have been done later, at three different periods. The earliest series of quadragesimal stations was clearly associated with the Sunday assemblies and the weekly fasts on Wednesday and Friday. Pope LEO I (440–61) added a Monday station. In the next stage, processions were held on the other days, with the exception of Thursday. The places were chosen, preferably, from among the 25 Roman titular churches. According to Callewaert, Pope

HILARUS (461–8) originated this innovation. Finally, Pope GREGORY II (715–31) appointed a stational Eucharistic liturgy on Thursday, which up to that time had had no assembly of worship attached to it. In fact, in pagan Rome, Thursday was consecrated to Jupiter, and because many Christians had not yet completely freed themselves from the old traditions, the churches remained closed on that day.

Decline, Present Situation, and Future. After the golden age, which may be situated from the 3rd to the 9th century, the Lenten stational processions survived under various guises until the Avignon exile (1305). Thereafter, the names of the old Roman stations were merely a historical memory in the Roman missal, at the beginning of the Lenten or Advent Masses. This continued until the reform of the missal effected by VATICAN II (1969). In fact, the Roman missal as revised by PAUL VI (1963–78) no longer refers to the specific Roman stations that had distinguished the Roman liturgy and the episcopal sees during the first millennium. Nonetheless, this same Roman missal encouraged the restoration of those quadragesimal stations best suited to the structure and life of the modern Church: "It is a good tradition that, especially during Lent, prayer meeting should be held in the local churches in the form of the Roman stations. It is to be recommended that this tradition be preserved and reinforced, at least in the principal cities, and in the most suitable way for each place. This assembly of faithful, particularly if it is presided over by the pastor of the diocese, may meet on Sundays and on weekdays that are most suitable, whether at the tomb of a saint, in the largest churches or sanctuaries of the city, or in an area of the diocese that is the goal of frequent pilgrimages." Paul VI himself set the example of this essential resumption of the ancient Roman stational tradition, brought up to date, when he once again began to preside over the ceremony of the ashes, which begins Lent, in the titular church of Sta. Sabina. Moreover, he brought new life to the centuries-old tradition by instituting the custom, especially during Lent, of celebrating Sunday by visiting the various parishes of the city. He thus brought together, at least in theory, the whole local community, conscious that in each particular assembly, however small—and particularly when it was presided over by its bishop—the entire universal Church (*LG*, 26) was present and manifest. That was especially valuable when the Church of Rome assembled around its bishop, the successor of St. Peter and guardian of the apostolic tradition.

Silvano Sirboni

Bibliography

Andrieu, M. *Les Ordines Romani du haut Moyen Age*, Louvain, 1960, II, 67–133; III, 247.

Baldovin, J. F. *The Urban Character of Christian Worship: The Origins, Development, and Meaning of Stational Liturgy*, Rome, 1987.

Berlière, U. "Les stations liturgiques dans les anciennes ville épiscopales," *Rev. Lit. et Mon.*, 1920, 213–16; 242–8.

Bo, V. *Storia della parrocchia*, Rome, 1988, I, 98–71.

Bonsirven, T. "Notre station liturgique est-elle empruntée au cule juif?" *Recherches de science religieuse*, XV, 1925, 258–66.

Borella, P. "Le stazioni quaresimali," *RL*, 45 (1958), 266–76.

Callewaert, C. "La Durée et le caractére du carême romain dans l'Église latine, " *Collationes Brugenses*, 18 (1913), 90–108, 311–23, 455–63.

Chavasse, A. "La Structure du carême et les lectures des messes quadragésimales dans la liturgie romaine," *LMD*, 31 (1952), 76–119.

Chavasse, A. *Le Sacramentaire gélasien*, Desclée Tournai, 1958, 75–86.

Chavasse, A. "L'organisation stationnale du carême romain avant le VIIIe siècle, une organisation pastorale," *Recherches de science religieuse*, 56 (1982), 17–32.

Denis-Boulet, N.-M. "Titres urbains et communauté dans la Rome chrétienne," *LND*, 36 (1953), 14–32.

Jungmann, J. A. *The Mass of the Roman Rite: Its origins and development (Missarum Sollemnia)*, New York, 1951–5.

Kirsch, J. P. "Origine e carattere primitivo delle stazioni liturgiche di Roma," *Rendic. della Pontificia Accad. di Archeol.*, III, 1925, 123–41.

Leclerq, H. "Stations liturgiques," *DACL*, XL, Paris 1953, col. 1653–57.

Mohrmann, C. "Statio," *Vigiliae Christianae*, VII (1953), 221–45.

Morin, G. "Liturgie et basiliques de Rome au milieu du VIIe siècle," *RB*, 28 (1911), 296–331.

Righetti, M. *Storia liturgica*, II, Milan, 1855 (2nd ed.), 115–20 (these pages aptly complement the *DACL* article).

Socratis, "Historia seu decretum Innocentii papae ad Decentium episcopum eugubinum," IV *PL*, 20, 556. *Epist.*, XLIII, Ad Correlium, II.

Tertullian, *De Oratione*, 19; *De Degunio*, 2, 10, 13.

Willis, G. G. "Roman Stational Liturgy," *Further Essays in Early Roman Liturgy*, London, 1968.

STEPHEN (POPES). Since he was never ordained, STEPHEN (II) was at first not fully regarded as having been pope. His successor of the same name (d. 757) was accordingly called STEPHEN II when the list of popes and their numbers was drawn up (see ONOMASTICS, Pontifical), and so on up to STEPHEN IX (d. 1058). In the modern era, and up until the 1960 *Annuario pontificio,* he was reintroduced into the official list of popes, thereby altering the numbers assigned to his successors of the same name, from STEPHEN III to STEPHEN X. Starting with the 1961 edition, he was once again deleted from the official list of popes in their order; the medieval system of numbering has thus been returned to, but now the ordinal number assigned in the modern era is shown in parentheses: we refer thus to Stephen (II) (d. 752), Stephen II (III) (d. 757), and so on up to Stephen IX (X) (d. 1058).

STEPHEN I. *Pope from 12 March 254 to 2 August 257.*

Stephen, of Roman origin (*natione Romanus,* according to *Liber pontificalis* I, 156 = *MGH, GPR,* I, 32), followed LUCIUS in 254 A.D. From the statement of EUSEBIUS that Lucius, "after fulfilling his ministry for slightly less than eight months, . . . passed, on his deathbed, his functions to Stephen" (*Ecclesiastical History* VII, 2), we can gather that the succession did not take place in difficult circumstances. In fact, the papacy enjoyed a climate of peace in imperial rule, since Valerian and Gallienus gave up the hostility of their predecessors, Decius and Trebonius Gallus, when they ascended to the throne.

Nevertheless, Stephen had to confront a number of difficulties within the Christian Churches. On the Iberian Peninsula, two bishops, Basilides of León and Martial of Emérita (in Asturias-Galicia and in Lusitania respectively), had procured certificates of sacrifice during the reign of Decius in order to escape condemnation: they ran into opposition from their faithful, who banished them, and subsequently they were deposed by the decision of an African COUNCIL and replaced (Cyprian, *Ep.* 67). Stephen heard their appeal, as was often the case with conflicts between bishops of the same province. At first he considered restoring them, but this aroused the indignation of Cyprian, who accused him of not following the teaching of Cornelius, who had "decided that such men could undoubtedly be allowed to do penance, but should be kept from clerical life and episcopal dignity" (*Ep.* 67).

To this question were added, in the West, the consequences of the schism of NOVATIAN, which had just been condemned under the episcopate of Cornelius, but which spread rapidly. In fact, Cyprian, ever solicitous for the unity of the Church, vehemently denounced the attitude of Bishop Marcian of Arles, who had "strayed from the truth of the Catholic Church and the unanimity of our episcopal body" (*Ep.* 68). In this letter addressed to Stephen, he pressed the pope to assemble the Gallic episcopate against the schismatic bishop and to come up with a choice for a successor. And when he asked the bishop of Rome to let him know who would be appointed to the see

of Arles, so that his African colleagues would know with whom they were in communion, he took up a theme already dear to him: harmony with the see of Rome is the best guarantee of legitimacy.

On the other hand, a third question, a pressing one at that time, gave rise to friction between these two strong personalities. Stephen clashed not only with Cyprian and the African bishops, but also with a number of important communities in the Roman East. The issue was the baptism of heretics. In the Roman Church, the baptism that heretics had received was traditionally admitted as valid. In AFRICA, such was not the case. In 255, a Carthaginian council adopted a categorical position (Cyprian, *Ep.* 70 and 71). Cyprian defended it at the risk of opposing Stephen. Cyprian was joined by an important figure in Christianity in the Roman East, Bishop Firmilian of Cappadocia, and around him a circle of several other bishops. For his part, Stephen reacted strongly, as Eusebius relates (*EH,* VII, 5): he "had . . . first written about Helenus, about Firmilian, and about all those of Cilicia and Cappadocia, and also, certainly, about those of Galatia and all the neighboring peoples, that he would no longer be in communion with them, for one simple reason: because, he said, they rebaptize heretics." He attracted the fulminations of his adversaries; Cyprian (*Ep.* 75) cites an exasperated retort by Firmilian on the occasion: "You thought you could excommunicate everyone, and it is yourself alone whom you have excommunicated." Stephen's death prevented an irreparable rift.

This last conflict brought to the fore a few strong personalities who were leaders in Eastern and Western Christianity. It also highlighted the place held by Rome, and the manner in which its bishop made use of the Roman see's past. In fact, when confronted by Cyprian, Stephen put forward the argument from Tradition; for him, it established the rule in matters of faith or discipline: "Let there be no innovation, rather let Tradition alone be followed . . .!" (according to Cyprian, *Ep.* 74, confirmed by Eusebius, *EH,* VII, 3). For Cyprian, the bishop of Rome holds a PRIMACY since he occupies the see of Peter; the Church of Rome is the heart and the source of the unity of the Church. It was thus that the granting and receiving of communion among colleagues placed Rome at the center of the relationships that laid the foundation of catholicity. But Cyprian had reason to be disturbed by this foundation, because Peter's successor was being solicited by schismatics on all sides and ran the risk of being circumvented by one or another of them. It was possible for him to make a mistake, as Stephen had done in the matter of the baptism of heretics. It was therefore important that the other bishops, who were also the inheritors of the apostolic teaching, make use of the right of warning or remonstrance to lead him back to the truth.

Stephen served as bishop from around 12 March 254 to 2 August 257 (*Liberian Catalogue, MGH, AA*, 9/1, 75). He was buried in the catacomb of Callistus on the Via Appia (*LP* I, 156 = *MGH, GPR*, I, 33).

Michel Christol

Bibliography

Danielou J. and Marrou, H. *Des origines à Grégoire le Grand (Nouvelle Histoire de l'Église*, I, under the direction of L. J. Rogier, R. Aubert, M. D. Knowles), Paris, 1963, 229–37.

Lebreton J. and Zeiler, J. *De la fin du IIe siècle à la paix constantinienne* (Fliche-Martin, 2), Paris, 1943, 197–209, 413–16.

Pietri, C. *Roma christiana. Recherches sur l'Église de Rome, son organisation, sa politique, son idéologie de Miltiade à Sixte III (311–440)*, Rome, 1976, 298–310.

Turner, C. H. "The Papal Chronology of the Third Century," *JThS*, 17 (1916), 343–5.

Vogel, C. *Le Liber pontificalis* (reed. 1957), III, 75.

STEPHEN (II). *(d. March 752). Elected pope in March 752, not ordained.*

On the death of Zacharias, a priest by the name of Stephen was elected; he was perhaps the deceased pope's envoy to Liutprand. But he died four days after his election, without having been consecrated pope. He was replaced by the deacon Stephen, who took the name STEPHEN II.

Jean-Charles Picard

Bibliography

JW, 1, 270.

Aubert, R. "Étienne," *DHGE*, 15 (1965), 1184.

STEPHEN II (III). *(b.?, d. 26 April 757). Installed as pope on 25 March 752. Buried at St. Peter's in Rome.*

Stephen was elected pope unanimously. He belonged to a family of the Roman aristocracy whose house stood in the Via Lata, the wealthy section of Rome. Raised at the Lateran after the death of his father, Constantine, he became deacon and played an important role in the administration of the hospices that took in pilgrims. His attention was first caught by the Lombard threat. He renewed the truce with Aistulf for a term of forty years, but the latter soon demanded that the Romans pay a head tax of one *solidus* per person: after he had received the rendering of the exarch of RAVENNA, Aistulf regarded the Byzantine provinces of central Italy as having passed under his sovereignty. The pope and the Romans had no desire to be subjects of the LOMBARDS. Roman sources describe the Lombards as barbarians, which certainly is inaccurate. The Lombards from that time on were orthodox Catholics, and the relatively numerous documents left to us for the 8th century show that they were at least as pious as, and certainly more cultivated than, the FRANKS. But the pope, holder of universal authority, did not want to be subject to a local power. More concretely, he preferred the distant and almost nonexistent authority of the emperor, who left him master in his own house, to that of the Lombard king: he feared being placed under tutelage. To oppose the Lombards, the emperor sent only a negotiator, the silentiary John. Stephen delegated his own brother, Paul, to accompany him to Pavia: Aistulf conceded nothing. The emperor then appointed the pope to negotiate with the Lombard king directly in his name: the pope henceforth considered himself in charge of imperial administration, not only in the duchies of Rome and Perugia, where he already held actual power, but also in the Exarchate and the Pentapolis. But he needed armed protection: the Franks were his only hope. Pepin had owed a debt to the papacy ever since Zacharias had given legitimacy to the overthrow of the Merovingians. Discreetly apprised of the situation, he sent the bishop of Metz, Chrodegang—on whom he relied in ecclesiastical affairs—and Duke Autcar, to escort the pope. Having set out on 14 October 753, Stephen II first had an interview with Aistulf in Pavia; but he lacked Zacharias's eloquence, and Aistulf had no intention of changing his position. Stephen then announced that he would make his way to Pepin, and Aistulf did not dare prevent him. In the middle of winter, the pope crossed the foothills of the Alps and reached the royal domain of Ponthion, in the Marne, where he arrived for Epiphany; he was welcomed by the king with the greatest show of respect, and settled in St-Denis for the winter. The Franks had the opportunity to witness the spectacle of the pontifical LITURGY, which was not without consequence for its later adoption in the kingdom. Plans for a war against the Lombards met some opposition among the Franks, who remembered the alliance forged between Charles Martel and Liutprand. To reinforce this inclination, Aistulf had Carloman sent for from Monte Cassino and dispatched him to his brother Pepin; but the latter had him locked up in a monastery at Vienne. Pepin overcame the opposition and, on 14 April 753, before the general assembly of the Franks meeting in Quierzy, he solemnly promised to restore St. Peter's rights to him, in the person of the pope. On 28 July, in St-Denis, the pope anointed Pepin once again, with his two sons, Carloman and the future Charlemagne. He also conferred on him the honorific title "patrician of the Romans," which was normally borne by the exarch, and which was designed here to concentrate the role it was hoped Pepin would henceforth begin to play, of defender of the papacy. After the failure of a number of ambassadors to Aistulf, Pepin reached northern Italy with his army and laid siege to

Pavia. Negotiations were opened, and a three-way treaty was signed by the Lombards, the Franks, and the Romans. Aistulf promised to restore "to the Romans" the cities of the Exarchate of which he had taken control, and never again to attack the territory of the empire; and he gave hostages to Pepin. But Aistulf had not spoken his last word; a few months later, he tried to force destiny by laying siege to Rome on 1 January 756, with the support of the duke of Benevento. It was the first time Rome had been under siege since the 6th century; and Roman sources give a horrific description of the siege, which lasted three months. The Lombards took advantage of the situation by withdrawing the bodies of saints from the CATACOMBS: the indignant Romans could not know that the Franks would end up doing the same thing. Stephen II managed to send an ambassador to Pepin by sea, to ask for help. The king of the Franks gathered his army together in May, and went back to lay siege to Pavia until Aistulf's surrender. Aistulf again promised to return the cities the Lombards had taken, and Pepin gave them to St. Peter in a written act. There was disagreement about the extent of the territory that was to be restored by the Lombards, and the pope subsequently complained that not all the cities to be returned to him had been given back. At all events, the abbot of St-Denis, Fulrad, was entrusted with taking possession of these territories, the KEYS of which he placed, along with the royal diploma, on the tomb of Peter. These arrangements created a new legal situation. Regarding himself as the inheritor of the powers of the exarch, the pope judged that he had the right to name all the local administrators of the Exarchate and of the Pentapolis, and he appointed two Romans, a priest and a duke, to manage the regions. This aroused the discontent of the archbishop of Ravenna, Sergius, who was of the opinion that the administration of the Exarchate fell under his purview, and the discontent of at least one segment of the local notables: Ravenna had a long history of fighting for its independence vis-à-vis Rome. Stephen II reacted strongly; he brought his opponents to Rome, where they spent the rest of their days, in prison, and he even had Sergius arrested.

Aistulf died in a hunting accident shortly thereafter. Part of the Lombard aristocracy was in favor of Ratchis's return to the throne, to which Desiderius, duke of Tuscany, also laid claim. Stephen II found himself in the position of an arbitrator; he supported Desiderius, who promised him some of the cities the pope was still claiming as his own. The negotiations were led by Paul, Christopher, and Fulrad, and Fulrad controlled the Frankish and Roman detachments that lent their support to Desiderius, the new king however, ended up ceding only some of the cities promised. Stephen, for his part, attempted to weaken him by granting his protection to the dukes of Spoleto and Benevento, who were taking advantage of the power vacuum to regain their independence;

the pope wrote to Pepin that they were ready to place themselves under his protection. The situation was still unclear at the time of Stephen II's death.

Jean-Charles Picard

Bibliography

JW, 1, 271–7; 2, 701.

LP, 1, 440–62.

MGH, Ep., 3, 487–507.

Bertolini, O. *Roma e i Longobardi*, Rome, 1972.

Duchesne, L. *Les Premiers Temps de l'État pontifical*, Paris, 1911.

Dumas, A. *DHGE*, 15 (1963), 1184–90.

Noble, T. F. X. *The Republic of St. Peter*, Philadelphia, 1984.

STEPHEN III (IV). *(b.?, d. 3 February 772). Elected Pope on 1 August, ordained on 7 August 768. Buried at St. Peter's in Rome.*

The candidate of the primicerius Christopher, who had just thrust aside CONSTANTINE and PHILIP, Stephen III was nominated in the Forum by a large assembly. A native of Sicily, he entered the clergy at a young age and became a priest of the TITLE of Sta Cecilia; he was known to be pious, but his pontificate was marked especially by the prolongation of the bloody rivalries that were setting the members of the papal court one against another. Christopher's son, Sergius, was sent to the FRANKS to inform them of events; Pepin had just died, and his two sons, Carloman and Charles (the future Charlemagne), who shared power, consented to send a delegation of thirteen bishops to Rome. A council was held at the Lateran in 769, the day after Easter. After condemning the ANTIPOPE CONSTANTINE, all of whose decisions were thrown out and it was decided to reserve thenceforth for the Roman clergy the right to elect the pope; members of the laity would be allowed only to ratify the choice after the fact. This measure was counter to tradition and served only to stir up the rancor of the lay aristocracy, which was deprived of all participation in the choice of the pontiff. The council likewise pronounced an anathema upon the canons of the iconoclastic council of Hiera, fifteen years after its meeting in 754, over which the emperor Constantine V had presided; this condemnation marked the final failure of the emperor's attempts to convert the Franks to his theological ideas.

Christopher's triumph was short-lived. He had made himself an enemy of Desiderius, the king of the LOMBARDS, who had come to his aid without profit. The hostility was intensified by a burgeoning rapprochement between the Franks and the Lombards. The queen mother, Bertrada, had Charles marry the daughter of Desiderius, having taken no account of letters in which the pope described the Lombards as savages. Christopher also had enemies in Rome, chief among whom was the papal chamberlain Paul Afiarta, and his dominance was beginning to weigh on the pope. In 771, Desiderius made a PILGRIMAGE to Rome for Lent: Stephen III left Christopher and his son Sergius to their enemies, led by the chamberlain Paul Afiarta. Their eyes were gouged out; Christopher died shortly thereafter, and Sergius was assassinated shortly before the pope's death. Stephen III must have feared Carloman's anger, since the latter's envoy had supported Christopher; counting on the enmity that reigned between the two Frankish kings, he wrote a letter to Charles and Queen Bertrada in which he justified his actions and praised the stance of King Desiderius. Carloman's death in 771 must have alleviated the pope's anxiety, but he survived him by only a few months.

Jean-Charles Picard

Bibliography

JW, 1, 285–8; 2, 701.

LP, 1, 468–85.

MGH, Ep., 3, 558–67, 713–15.

Duchesne, L. *Les Premiers Temps de l'État pontifical*, Paris, 1911.

Dumas, A. *DHGE*, 15 (1963), 1190–3.

Hallenbeck, J. T. Pope Stephen III: Why Was He Elected," *Archivium Historiae Pontifical* 12 (1974) pp. 287–99.

Noble, T. F. X. *The Republic of St. Peter*, Philadelphia, 1984.

STEPHEN IV (V). *(b. Rome, ca. 770, d. Rome, 23 January 817). Elected pope on 22 June 816 after the papal see had been empty for ten days, immediately crowned at St. Peter's in Rome, which is also his burial place.*

His pontificate, between those of LEO III and PASCHAL I, marks an interval in the struggle between the monarchical and centralizing tendencies of these two popes and the will of the Roman aristocracy to impose its control on the Church. Biographical notes on Stephen IV prior to his election are quite interesting. He was the son of a certain Marinus, and the biographer of the *LIBER PONTIFICALIS* describes him as *nobili prosapia atque clarissimo genere ortus*, a family that had considerable fortune during the second half of the 9th century, since it provided two other popes, SERGIUS II and HADRIAN II. In that respect also, Stephen differed profoundly from Leo III, who was of humbler origins. Under the pontificate of HADRIAN I, the future pope's father placed him at quite an early age in the care of the *patriarchum* of the Lateran, to be educated and, naturally, oriented toward an ecclesiastical career. His talents first led him to the subdiaconate, and then the diaconate, during the pontificate of Leo III. Upon Leo's death, he was elected pope, with the unanimous approval of the people of Rome, as the *Liber pontificalis* puts it.

This was the first election of a pope after the reestablishment of the Western Empire, and Stephen IV merely informed the emperor of the fact. The pope was just continuing, after all, the politics of formal dissociation from all other powers begun with the coronation of (741), ZACHARIAS, confirmation of whose election was not awaited from the emperor. On the other hand, a contrary tendency was shown in the first (and, in fact, the only) political acts of the pontificate. During the summer of 816, Stephen IV traveled to Reims to place the imperial crown on the head of Louis I the Pious and his wife Irmengard. The importance of this journey has perhaps not been fully recognized by historical criticism. In effect, on this occasion, Stephen IV obtained from the emperor the confirmation of the privileges and the autonomy of the PAPAL STATES granted by Charlemagne. This reinforced the pope's role as temporal sovereign. When he returned to Rome, Stephen IV agreed to have all those who had been forced to leave Rome and take refuge among the FRANKS after the riots against Leo III (in 799 or 815?) return with him.

Federico Marazzi

Bibliography

JE, 1, 316–18.

LP, 2, 49–51.

MGH, SS, 2, 593–4 and 597; *MGH, SS In usum scholar.*, 6, 144.

PL, 102, 1071–85.

Brezzi, P. *Roma e l'Impero medievale (774–1252)*, Bologna, 1947 (*Storia di Roma*, ed. Istituto di Studi Romani, 10).

Duchesne, L. *Les Premiers Temps de l'État pontifical*, Paris, 1888.

Dumas, A. "Étienne IV," *DHGE*, 15 (1963), 1193–4.

Llewellyn, P. *Rome in the Dark Ages*, London, 1971.

Noble, T. F. X. *The Republic of St. Peter: The Birth of the Papal State, 680–825*, Philadelphia, 1984.

STEPHEN V (VI). *(b. ?, d. 14 September 891). Elected pope in August or September 885, ordained before 20 November. Buried at St. Peter's in Rome.*

Born to a family of the Roman aristocracy, a relation of the pontifical librarian Zacharias and educated by him, Stephen was CARDINAL priest of the title of SS. Quatro Coronati when he learned of Pope HADRIAN III's death, near Modena, in August or September 885. He was elected immediately and, it is said, ordained rapidly, without trouble being taken to wait for ratification of the election by the imperial authority. Having been put in this position twice in a row, Charles the Fat was furious and sent his archchamberlain Liutward, bishop of Vercelli, on a mission to initiate the DEPOSITION of the pontiff, since he considered him illegitimate; subsequently on the strength of the transcript verifying unanimity in favor of Stephen, he ratified his election.

The relations between Charles the Fat and Stephen V were of short duration, since the emperor was deposed in November 887. The pope was then faced with the difficult question of choosing among claimants to the throne. To Guido of Spoleto, a neighbor much too close not to be a threat to papal independence (JOHN VIII, in his time, had had a number of dealings with him), Stephen V would gladly have preferred the more distant domination of the king of the German lands, Arnulf. While he dealt politely with Guido, it was to Arnulf that he appealed, in 890, to come to Rome to the assistance of Italy, menaced by the *mali christiani*, a term vague enough to include the SARACENS as well as the duke of Spoleto's people. However, Arnulf had worries at home, and Guido already had the legitimacy of his election as king of Italy in hand, after his fairly recent victory over Berengar (November 889). There was thus no other choice but to crown him emperor (21 February 891), which ended up having no injurious consequences for the integrity of the PATRIMONY OF ST. PETER.

A man with little luck in the realm of politics, Stephen V managed to assert himself in the internal administration of the Church by being ever careful to remind the upper clergy of his authority. Thus, the bishop of Bordeaux, Frotaire (or Frotier), who had taken it upon himself to assume the see of Bourges, saw this change of office refused him for non-respect for the canonical procedure. Similarly, the archbishop of Lyon, Aurelian, was called to order for having appointed a bishop to Langres without consulting either the clergy or the faithful of the region. Although less skillful, Stephen's behavior was just as vigorous vis-à-vis the problem of the evangelization of the Slavs. In Moravia, a conflict had arisen over what language to use in the liturgy: those who sided with the archbishop of Pannonia, Methodius, a defender of the use of Slavonic, which was clearly more within the grasp of the local population than was Latin, had won out over John VIII; but Stephen V, persuaded to the contrary by Methodius's successor, put an end to the experiment. The partisans of the deceased archbishop had to take refuge in Bulgaria, a land which, as a result, became the promoter of the Slavic liturgy and alienated a wide region from Roman influence, in the long term to the benefit of BYZANTIUM.

Relations with the East, for their part, were not going well. Emperor Basil I was still contesting the legality of the election of MARINUS I; pressured by the patriarch, Photius, he had sent Hadrian III a highly critical reply to the conciliatory justifications used by the pontiff. It was in fact Stephen V who received it, his predecessor having died in the meantime; he replied in his turn, passing the responsibility on to the patriarch. However, this correspondence had no lasting effect on relations between Rome and Constantinople, in that, upon the death of Basil I (29 August 880), his son, Leo VI, immediately opposed Photius, whom he forced to resign. In attempts to reconcile the two ("Ignatian" and "Photian") parties, who were fighting over the patriarchate, the Western Church once again found an essential role, but Stephen V had not resolved the problem by the time of his death. In any case, a sign of a return to good relations with the *basileus* could be seen in the help provided by Leo VI, upon the request of the pope, against the Saracens, who were once again threatening the principalities of southern Italy.

François Bougard

Bibliography

JW, 1, 427–35; 2, 705.
LP, 2, 191–8.
Dumas, A. "Étienne V," *DHGE*, 15 (1963), 1194–6.
Fliche-Martin, VI, 442–3, 462, 498.

STEPHEN VI (VII). *(b. Rome, ?, d. August 897). Elected pope in late April or early May 896.*

Stephen VI (who also appears under the name Stephen VII, because of the different ways of numbering Pope STEPHEN II, and who is also occasionally confused with Pope SERGIUS III), the son of a certain John about whose identity nothing further is known, was born in Rome. He was ordained bishop of Anagni by Pope FORMOSUS (891–6) and was probably elected pope in late April or early May. According to the sources, Stephen either replaced Pope BONIFACE VI or directly succeeded Pope Formosus. When Stephen was elected, the prohibition against translation was violated, as had also been the case for Pope Formosus's election. From the time of his election, Stephen probably no longer considered himself a bishop, since in the notorious "cadaver synod" he attempted, among other things, to declare the sacraments conferred by Formosus null and void. The only accounts we have concerning the judgment over Pope Formosus's cadaver (he died in 896), are furnished by one-sided sources favorable to Formosus, though they are probably correct in essentials. The synod, which lasted perhaps three days, took place in Rome, probably in the early days of 897. Pope Formosus's cadaver was placed on a throne before the assembled synod, and three bishops accused the deceased of having violated the prohibition against translation, of having disregarded the excommunication pronounced by JOHN VIII, and of having failed to honor the oath sworn at Troyes in 878 no longer to solicit ecclesiastical office. A DEACON had to take on the ungrateful task of his defense. The condemnation of Pope Formosus also had the effect of nullifying the sacraments he had conferred. The deceased pope was symbolically stripped of his vestments; two fingers from the hand with which he had taken the oath and given his blessings were chopped off. The political background of this affair remains obscure. The old theories that the Spoletan dynasty, especially Emperor Lambert (d. 898) and his mother, Ageltrude, provoked the synod have been largely abandoned on account of their unlikelihood. On the other hand, a conceivable motive is the interest Stephen might have had in his own legitimization. The pope's relations outside Rome, known via the acts, concern the entire kingdom of West Francia. Toward the end of the month of June, Stephen VI was taken prisoner, stripped of his dignity, and incarcerated. Some sources claim that he became a monk and that he was later strangled (toward the end of July 897) in his cell. In 907, Pope Sergius III is said to have had his cadaver transferred to St. Peter's. The collapse of the Lateran basilica, later reconstructed by JOHN IX and especially by Sergius III, could have appeared to the contemporaries of Stephen VI as divine punishment for acts contested from the time of his pontificate.

Klaus Herbers

Bibliography

JL, I, 439–40; II, 705.
LP, 2, 229.
Dumas, A. "Étienne VI," *DHGE*, 15 (1963), 1196–7.
Hartmann, W. *Die Synoden der Karolingerzeit im Frankenreich und in Italien*, Paderborn, 1989 (*Konziliengeschichte Reihe A, Darstellungen*), 388–90.
Scholz, S. *Transmigration und Translation. Studien zum Bistumswechsel von der Spätantike bis zum hohen Mittelalter*, Cologne-Weimar-Vienna, 1992 (*Kölner Historische Abhandlungen*, 37), 218–24.
Zimmermann, H. *Papstabsetzungen des Mittelalters*, Graz-Vienna-Cologne, 1968, 55–9.
Zimmermann, H. *Papsturkunden*, 3–9.

STEPHEN VII (VIII). *(d. late February 931). Elected pope in mid-January 929. Most probably buried at St. Peter's in Rome.*

Stephen VII was pope in Rome from mid-January 929 until the end of the month of February 931. He is believed to have been a native Roman, even if his father's name, Teudemundus, suggests Germanic roots. It is undoubtedly thanks to the decisive influence of the matron senator Marozia, who ruled over Rome at the time, that the CARDINAL priest of the title of Sta Anastasia was raised to the papacy while Pope JOHN X, imprisoned in 928, was still alive. Not one act of his brief pontificate has been transmitted. There is only some unconfirmed information about the granting of a privilege to an Italian monastery; two other concessions of privileges to monasteries are also attributed to this pope, but they are forgeries. At the request of its founder, Abbot Gerard, who

had come to Rome on PILGRIMAGE, the pope is said to have confirmed the creation of the reformed monastery of Brogne, near Namur. Stephen VII, who was probably a fairly elderly man when he acceded to this elevated office, like his predecessor, LEO VI, is thought to have occupied a throne being kept for Marozia's son, who was elected after Stephen's death under the name of JOHN XI.

Harald Zimmermann

Bibliography

Aubert, R. "Étienne VII," *DHGE*, 15 (1943), 1197–8.
Zimmermann, H. *Papstregesten*, 37–40.

STEPHEN VIII (IX). *(Rome, ?, d. Rome, late October 942). Elected pope in early July 939. Buried at St. Peter's in Rome.*

Stephen VIII was pope in Rome from the beginning of July 939 until the end of October 942. According to tradition, the election of this erudite Roman, a former CARDINAL priest of the title of SS. Silvestro e Martino, took place after only one day of vacancy of the papal throne, and certainly was the work of Prince Alberic II (932–54), who was ruler in Rome. From this brief pontificate three acts have been transmitted, all of them for monasteries. The reference to the old Roman right (*ad auctoritatem romanae legis*) makes one of these acts particularly interesting. It is the mandate established at the request of Abbot Odo of Cluny, at the time on PILGRIMAGE in Italy (940), respecting his other monastery of Déols, and addressed to Archbishop Gerontius of Bourges, to put an end to the litigation in process between the archbishop and the monastery, regarding a piece of land to which both parties laid claim on the strength of a testamentary donation. Odo also worked successfully on the pope for the ordination of the bishop of southern Italy, John of Nola, and in 942 he served as intermediary between Rome and King Hugh of Italy (926–48). A later act leads us to conclude the existence of an earlier one, now lost, concerning the abbey of St. Maurice of Magdeburg, which the king of the Germany lands, Otto the Great, had just founded, in 937. Moreover, it is reported that in 942 the pope dispatched Bishop Damasus to France as a papal LEGATE to lend support to King Louis IV d'Outremer (936–54), who was under attack by the French princes. In fact, at the end of 942, the Capetian Hugh the Great, duke of France, and Count Herbert II of Vermandois ended up surrendering after the Carolingian king also won over the German King Otto to his cause. In the struggle over the archdiocese of Reims, after the antiarchbishop Artaud, a partisan of the Carolingians, was discharged, Hugh of Vermandois was restored as archbishop and received the archbishop's *pallium* at the request of a delegation from Reims to Rome. Finally, according to some sources, the pope manifested sympathy for a Roman revolt against the powerful prince Alberic II, as punishment for which he is said to have had his body mutilated; these sources, however, are both late and less than completely trustworthy.

Harald Zimmermann

Bibliography

Zimmermann, H. *Papstregesten*, 911–1024, Vienna, 1969 (*Regesta Imperii*, II/5), 60–4.

STEPHEN IX (X). *Frederick of Ardennes (d. Florence, 29 March 1058). Elected pope on 2 August 1056, enthroned on 3 August. Buried in the cathedral of Florence.*

Although born into the noble class of the empire, this pope broke the very close ties of the papacy to the emperor and followed the path of reform, often exaggeratedly called Lotharingian reform since it had been conceived by LEO IX, who had had Frederick come to Rome and had placed his confidence in him.

A member of the powerful family of the counts of Ardennes, Frederick was the son of Duke Gozelon of Lotharingia (1023–44) and the brother of Godfrey the Bearded, duke of Upper Lotharingia (1044–7), marquess of Tuscany (1054–69), and duke of Lower Lotharingia (1065–9). He was educated in Liège, where he became archdeacon of the St-Lambert chapter. Called to Rome by Leo IX, he was head of the papal CHANCERY from 1051 to 1055 and participated in 1054 in the mission to Constantinople that led to the excommunication of the patriarch Michael Cerularius; he was made CARDINAL priest by VICTOR II on 14 June 1056, became abbot of Monte Cassino beginning on 24 June, and then was elected pope on the following 2 August, keeping his status as abbot during his pontificate. His enthronement took place on 3 August without any invitation to the German court—where Empress Agnes was regent during the minority of Henry IV—to offer its opinion. The presence of his brother Godfrey as marquess of Tuscany, who was capable of lending him military support, may have counted heavily in the choice of Frederick. In 1057, he convened a SYNOD in Rome in which he railed against married priests and pursued simoniacs; he forbade the election of a pope to succeed him upon his death before the king had delivered his opinion. He also intervened in favor of the tenants of the Milan reform (Pataria). Preoccupied by southern Italy, he dreamt of a new mission against the NORMANS and hoped for the support of his brother Godfrey. Having fallen ill and grown anxious over the succession, he insisted that all those concerned await the return of Hildebrand (the future GREGORY VII) before proceeding to a new election. His eight-month pontificate constituted a new step toward greater freedom for the papacy vis-à-vis the lay powers.

Michel Parisse

Bibliography

JW, 1, 553–6.
LP, 2, 278, 334, 356.
PL, 143, 865–84.
Despy, G. "La carrière lotharingienne du pape Étienne IX," *Revue belge de philologie et d'histoire*, 31 (1953), 955–72.
Michel, A. "Die Accusatio des Kanzlers Friedrichs in Lothringen gegen die Griechen," *Römische Quartalschrift*, 38 (1930), 153–208.
Robert, U. *Un pape belge. Histoire du pape Étienne IX*, Brussels, 1892.
Schmale, F. J. "Étienne IX," *DHGE*, 15 (1953), 1198–1203.
Watterich, 1, 188–204, 738, 748.

STYLE AND PRAXIS OF THE ROMAN CURIA. See **Curia**.

SUBCINCTORIUM. The subcinctorium is a liturgical ornament which the pope formerly wore to celebrate the pontifical Mass. It was a sort of large maniple, 55 centimeters in length, that was attached at the waist so that it hung down on the right side. Its color was dictated by the liturgical calendar. There have been various explanations of its symbolism: an echo of the alms-purse that the popes wore on the left side, to give charity to the poor who crossed their path; a reminder of the cloth with which Pilate washed his hands at the condemnation of Christ; a sign of humility, representing the cloth that Jesus used to wash his disciples' feet; or even, according to St. Augustine, a vestige of one of the ornaments of the Jewish high priest.

Originally worn by all priests, the subcinctorium came to be exclusively reserved to the sovereign pontiff in the Latin Church, but it is still part of the liturgical vestments of the bishops of the Greek rite. It was abolished in the Roman rite after the second Vatican council.

Joël-Benoît d'Onorio

Bibliography

Battandier, A. "Les ornements du souverain pontife," *Annuaire pontifical catholique*, 1907.

SUBSIDIARITY. Subsidiarity is a principle of political and social organization formulated by the social doctrine of the Church, but it goes back to a far older idea. It is generally ascribed to Aristotle and Greek thought, clarified and complemented by St. Thomas Aquinas and medieval scholasticism.

By virtue of this principle, each degree of authority is obligated to exercise all the duties entrusted to it without having recourse to the rank above. The intervention of the latter in the duties of the subordinate can be justified only as a supplementary or subsidiary measure—that is, in case of the default or failure of the lower rank. This principle regulating the relations between the state and its citizens is aimed at guaranteeing the rights of persons against the encroachments of public authorities, which, moreover, are bound to respect the intermediary bodies of natural law (families), public law (villages, provinces, regions), and private law (businesses, professional and trade-union associations, etc.).

The basis of the principle of subsidiarity lies in the dignity inherent in the human person, which comes from its quality of being a creature of God fashioned in His image. Because the individual is always the subject of law and never its object, he comes before the state. Therefore, the state must contribute to the realization of the human personality and not to stifling it by interventionism or, worse, totalitarianism. This is by no means to say that society is secondary or that the state is superfluous, for they are each elements of the natural order, since humans are by nature social beings, and some public authority is indispensable for any organized society. Subsidiarity merely postulates that the action of the society or the state is secondary in relation to that of the person. The idea of a subsidiary state is intellectually contradictory to that of a welfare state, but it is quite in keeping with that of a state of law, of which it indeed constitutes a more perfect form.

The idea of bringing government into the closest possible relationship with the governed may be traced as far back as the Bible. The book of Exodus shows that Moses' father-in-law counseled him not to govern the Israelites on his own, but to choose men who were competent and incorruptible in order to divide the leadership among "the rulers of thousands, and rulers of hundreds, rulers of fifties, and rulers of tens" (Exodus 18, 13–26). Although not explicitly formulated by this term, the notion of subsidiarity was present in Aristotelian thinking and later in Thomist philosophy. In France, it is associated with the idea of decentralization for which Robespierre laid the premises before the tribune of the Convention 10 May 1793 when he pleaded for the guarantee of individual, family, and communal liberties by the public authority (*Moniteur universel* of 13 May 1793, p. 363).

American democracy shares the same thinking, to judge from Abraham Lincoln's statement that "the legitimate aim of the government is to do for a community of people, whatever they need to have done, but cannot do at all, or cannot so well do, for themselves, in their separate and individual capacities. In all that the people can individually do as well for themselves, the government ought not to interfere." The principle of subsidiarity is also present by implication in solidarism and Christian personalism, as it is moreover in the idea of federalism—although the latter is not its exclusive realization. Thus it has been invoked in the debates on European institutions, and even explicitly mentioned—in the European Maastricht accords in 1992 (article 3B).

The first churchman to speak openly about subsidiarity was Wilhelm von Ketteler, bishop of Mainz and a deputy of the Reichstag (1870–1). The prelate had described suppletory state intervention as a "subsidiary right" (in *Die Katholiken und das Reich*). Along with the Jesuit Luigi Taparelli d'Azeglio (1793–1862) and his considerable study of the role of the state according to natural law, Bishop von Kettler was considered the precursor of the innovative ideas of LEO XIII's social encyclical, *Rerum novarum* (1891). In it the pope denounced both statism and liberalism: if the state has not the power to refuse private societies, "the right to existence which was granted them by nature herself," it nevertheless has the duty to intervene for the defense of the common good.

However, it was not until PIUS XI became pope that a definition of subsidiarity was officially pronounced. In his encyclical *Quadragesimo anno* of 1931, the pope, faced with the rise of Marxist and fascist totalitarianism, wrote: "That most weighty principle . . . remains fixed and unshaken in social philosophy: Just as it is gravely wrong to take from individuals what they can accomplish by their own initiative and industry and give it to the community, so also it is an injustice and at the same time a grave evil and disturbance of right order to assign to a greater and higher association what lesser and subordinate organizations can do. For every social activity ought of its very nature to furnish help to the members of the body social, and never destroy and absorb them.

"The supreme authority of the State ought, therefore, to let subordinate groups handle matters and concerns of lesser importance, which would otherwise dissipate its efforts greatly. Thereby the State will more freely, powerfully and effectively do all those things that belong to it alone because it alone can do them: directing, watching, urging, restraining, as occasion requires and necessity demands. Therefore, those in power should be sure that the more perfectly a graduated order it keeps among the various associations, in observance of the principle of 'subsidiary function,' the stronger social authority and effectiveness will be [and] the happier and more prosperous the condition of the State."

From then on, Catholic thought exercised all its influence on the German neo-liberalism of the period between the wars and on the economic and social theory of the *Ordo* put forth by W. Röpke. The Freiburg School also took its inspiration from it to give German policy of the post-Nazi period its founding principles. In his message of 1 June 1941 for the 50th anniversary of *Rerum novarum*, PIUS XII had, in fact, taken up the subject anew in these terms: "The right and the duty to organize the work of the people belongs above all to those who have an immediate interest in it: employers and workers. If thereafter they do not fulfill their task, or cannot do so as a result of extraordinary circumstances, then the state has a duty to intervene in this area, in the division and distribution of work, in the form and to the extent that the common good, rightly understood, demands." In his consistorial allocution of 20 February 1946, when the question was to provide the European nations with new bases, the pope again took up the principle of subsidiarity with these words: "What individuals can do for themselves, through their own efforts, must not be taken away from them and transferred to the community."

JOHN XXIII invoked the principle in his turn in his encyclical *Mater et magistra* (1961), to restrict the state's role to "encouraging, stimulating, coordinating, supplying and integrating," emphasizing at the same time, in his encyclical *Pacem in terris* (1963) that the public authorities must not thereby forget their essential duty to guarantee the "common good," which resides above all in "personal rights and duties." According to the pontiff, the same principle was valid in both the domestic and the international orders. For its part, VATICAN II evoked this pivotal principle of the social doctrine of the Church in two of its 16 documents. In the pastoral constitution *Gaudium et spes*, the council applied it to the international community for the sake of greater justice in world economic relations; in the declaration *Gravissimum educationis*, it referred to it twice in regard to the relations between parents and civil society in children's education. Thereafter, the papal magisterium would remain faithful to it, notably JOHN PAUL II in his two great social encyclicals, *Laborem exercens* (1981) and *Centesimus annus* (1991).

Pius XII ventured to extend the principle of subsidiarity to ecclesial society in his allocution of 20 February 1946 to the newly created cardinals. Quoting Pius XI's comments, the pope remarked: "These are truly illuminating words which are valid for social life at all levels and also for the life of the Church without prejudicing its hierarchical structure." However, this opening was followed only by silence on the part of John XXIII and Vatican II. It was not until the inauguration of the synod of bishops that the theme returned to the foreground of the ecclesiastical stage. At the first ordinary session of 1967, unanimously minus one vote, the bishops pronounced themselves in favor of the introduction of this principle in the structures of the Church. At the extraordinary session of 1969, PAUL VI unambiguously affirmed: "We do not hesitate to admit the principle of subsidiarity in its fundamental acceptance." The general report of the synodal session of 1974 repeated the wish that "the principle of subsidiarity be truly applied and that a decentralization take place so that

the local Churches may assume their rightful responsibilities." The idea reappeared in the catechetical plans put forward by the synod of 1977. Thus the CODE OF CANON LAW of 1983 mentions the principle in its preface, including it among those that guided the new codification.

A reconsideration of the question came to light at the extraordinary session of the bishops' synod of 1985, which had ordered a study of the possible applicability to the Church of the principle of subsidiarity. The synodal discussions revealed a division of opinion among the bishops, not all of whom used the same definition or even, at times, had a very clear idea of the notion under discussion. For some, subsidiarity seemed aimed at a revaluation of the local Church as a result of Vatican II, thus leading to a vast decentralization of the powers of Rome. For others, by contrast, this principle of social philosophy could not be transposed to ecclesial society, since it had always been taught by the magisterium as being applicable to civil society. In fact, the conciliar ecclesiology of Vatican II sufficed to guarantee the personality of the local Church within the universal Church. Furthermore, the Code of Canon Law is fairly generous as to the degree of autonomy of the powers peculiar to the diocesan bishops without falling into that "emphasis on the local Church" often denounced by John Paul II.

Most important, the universal Church (i.e., the Church as a whole, *Ecclesia universa*, according to the phrase used by the council and the code) is not subsidiary in relation to the local Church, since the unity of the Catholic Church precedes the plurality of its component parts. Thus the power of the pontiff of Rome is ordinary—and in no way subsidiary—over all the local Churches and within each of them (canon 333). Clearly, the governmental regime of the Church cannot be copied from that of the secular states. The specific mission of the Petrie ministry makes it present and active in the totality of the Church by virtue of its immediate, not mediate, power. These elements provide the reason for the restrictions that Pius XII expressed in his time, like Paul VI, when he counseled, in a similar vein, "a humble and wise prudence" (speech at the opening of the extraordinary synod of 1969). In fact, the doctrinal controversy over ecclesial subsidiarity calls directly into question the Roman pontiff's primacy of jurisdiction which is exercised over the entire Church, universal as well as particular, not in a subsidiary way but by its very essence, since it is, by divine right, its foundation.

Joël-Benoît d'Onorio

Bibliography

Bertrams, W. "De principio subsidiarietatis in jure canonico," *Periodica*, Rome, 1957: "Das Subsidiaritätprinzip in der Kirche," *Stimmen der Zeit*, 1957.

Beyer, J. "Principe de subsidiarité ou juste autonomie dans l'Église," *Nouvelle revue théologique*, Louvain,

1986; and "Le principe de subsidiarité: son application en Église," *Gregorianum*, Rome, 1988.

d'Onorio, J. B. *Le Pape et le gouvernement de l'Église*, Paris, 1992.

Komonchak, J. "Le principe de subsidiarité et sa pertinence ecclésiologique," *Les Conférences épiscopales: Théologie, statut canonique, avenir* (H. Legrand, J. Manzanares, A. Garcia, ed.), Paris, 1988.

Leys, A. *Ecclesiological Impacts of the Principle of Subsidiarity*, Kampen, 1995.

Metz, R. "La subsidiarité principe régulateur des tensions dans l'Église," *Revue de droit canonique*, Strasburg, 1972.

Milon-Delsol, C. *L'État subsidiaire*, Paris, 1992 (complete bibliography on politico-social subsidiarity).

von Nell-Breuning, O. "Subsidiarität in der Kirche," *Stimmen der Zeit*, 1986.

SUBSTITUTE OF THE SECRETARIAT OF STATE.

The position of substitute of the Secretariat of State of the Holy See was created on 3 August 1814 by Pius VII with the appointment of Carlo Mauri. The new duties included the already existing ones of Secretary of the Cipher, relating to diplomatic correspondence both received and expedited secretly in coded writing, according to the usage inaugurated in the chanceries under Innocent VIII at the end of the 15th century. A Service of the Cipher was created at the Holy See in the reign of Leo X at the beginning of the 16th century; the first to bear the title Secretary of the Cipher was Trifone Bencio, during the papacies of Paul IV and Pius IV (1555–65).

As the primary collaborator of the Cardinal Secretary of State, the Substitute has become the direct head of all the pontifical diplomats and occupies a key position in the Roman Curia, which Paul VI reformed in 1967 and John Paul II in 1988, since he is at the center of all the intricate machinery of administration. He is also the one who, at the death of a reigning pontiff, assumes direction of his dicastery, the duties of the Cardinal Secretary of State then ceasing automatically. Nevertheless, the Substitute must account for his activity to the College of Cardinals and must be confirmed in his duties by the new pope within the three months following his election.

In the past, the Substitute of the Secretariat of State ranked as a simple prelate (as was the case for della Chiesa, the future Benedict XV, under Cardinal Merry Del Val and Pius X, or for Montini, the future Paul VI, under Cardinal Pacelli and Pius XI). From the time of John XXIII, the substitute has been a titular archbishop becoming a cardinal when he leaves his post. He is helped in his task by an prelate assessor, a post that corresponds to the undersecretaries of the other dicasteries and was created by Paul VI in his curial reorganization *Regimini Ecclesiae Universae* of 1967.

List of Substitutes. Carlo Mauri (1814–30). Francesco Capaccini (1831–44). Vincenzo Santucci (1844–6). Giovanni Cordoli Bussi (1846–7). Vincenzo Santucci (1847–51). Giuseppe Berardi (1851–68). Marino Marini (1868–75). Vincenzo Vannutelli (1875–8). Serafino Cretoni (1878–80). Luigi Pallotti (1880–2). Mario Mocenni (1882–93). Aristide Rinaldini (1893–6). Luigi Tripei (1896–1901). Giacomo Della Chiesa (Benedict XV) (1901–7). Nicola Canali (1908–14). Federico Tedeschini (1914–21). Giuseppe Pizzardo (1921–9). Alfredo Ottaviani (1929–35). Domenico Tardini (1935–7). Giovanni Battista Montini (Paul VI) (1937–52). Carlo Grano (1952–3). Angelo Dell'Acqua (1953–67). Giovanni Benelli (1967–77). Giuseppe Caprio (1977–79). Eduardo Martini Somalo (1979–88). Edward Idris Cassidy (1988–9). Giovanni Battisa Rè (1989–2001). Leonardo Sandri (2001–).

Joël-Benoît d'Onorio

Bibliography

Del Rè, N. *La Curia romana: Lineamenti storico-giuridici*, Rome, 1970.

d'Onorio, J. B. *Le Pape et le gouvernement de l'Église*, Paris, 1992.

SUBURBICARIAN DIOCESES. See **Dioceses, Suburbicarian.**

SUBURBICARIAN ITALY.

Already in the years 281–9 two *correctores* shared the administration of the Italian peninsula: one for the northern provinces and the other for the center and south. In 297–8, the administrative reform of Diocletian regrouped the provinces of the Roman Empire into fourteen dioceses, each of them with a vicar as its head. Italy made up one DIOCESE, the vicar of which lived in Milan, and was divided into two vicariates. One covered the northern provinces, which paid property taxes on land and were called "annonarian regions"; the other covered the provinces of the center and the south plus the three islands of Corsica, Sardinia, and Sicily, and paid the tax only from 305–6. These were the "urbicarian" or "suburbicarian" regions. Around 313 (the date is still in dispute), an administrative document known as the "List of Verona" mentions this division, indicating for the "diocese of Italy" a *pars annonaria*, with Milan as its principal city, and a *pars urbicaria*, with Rome as its metropolis. Both were probably under the authority of a *corrector utriusque Italiae*. But between 306 and 320, two vicars appeared: the *vicarius Italiae* and the *vicarius in Urbe*.

These two vicars, one from Milan and one from Rome, divided the peninsula between them along a line that followed the course of the Rubicon and Magna rivers and extended to the outskirts of Populanium north of Ancona. During the 4th century, this border would shift a little, in the east and in the west.

At the beginning of the 4th century, the *regiones suburbicariae* (the expression "suburbicarian Italy", which would become current among modern historians, is never found in the ancient texts) included, besides the three island provinces, five provinces on the peninsula: Tuscany-Umbria, Flaminia-Picenum, Campania, Lucania-Bruttium, and Apulia-Calabria. During the course of the century, Samnium, detached from Campania, and then Valeria, detached from Picenum, were added. Accordingly, there were six suburbicarian provinces. Around 385–90 (?), Tuscany-Umbria was divided between the two vicariates by modifying the border between the two *partes Italiae*: Annonarian Tuscany belonged to the north, and Umbria to the south. Several years later, Picenum in its turn was divided in the same fashion into a Picenum *annonarium* and a Picenum *suburbicarium*, and in 398 Flaminia, detached from Picenum, would become an annonarian province. A constitution from 413 (*CTh.*, 11, 28, 7) is the only document to give an official list of the peninsular provinces belonging to the southern vicariate. After the 350s, the expression *regiones urbicariae* or *suburbicariae* (never *Italia urbicaria* or *suburbicaria*) was frequently used in administrative terminology. A constitution dated 23 February 359, addressed to the prefect of the praetorium of Italy, Taurus (*CTh.*, 11, 16, 9), established, "following the example of what is occurring in Africa," an exemption from the "extraordinary charges" benifiting the imperial territories: "throughout all of Italy," stating that this measure would apply "not only in Italy, but also in the urban regions and in Sicily" (on this mention of Sicily and the implications of it, see M. De Dominicis, *Regiones sububicariae*, 54 and no. 45).

The *regiones urbicariae* reappear in two constitutions of 365, one regarding the suppression of banditry (*CTh.*, 9, 30, 3) and the other (*CTh.*, 11, 1, 9) regarding the service of the *cursus publicus*. The latter sought to put an end to frauds uncovered in the *suburbicariae regiones*. A constitution of 383 (*CTh.*, 11, 13, 1) required the prefect of the praetorium to announce the termination of fiscal exemptions previously granted to imperial domains "throughout all Italy, including the urban regions, those of Africa, and all of Illyria" (that is to say, the three dioceses within the jurisdiction of this prefecture of the praetorium). A constitution of 377 to the prefect of the city (*CTh.*, 11, 2, 3) likewise mentions the *urbicaria regio* and in 423 (*CTh.*, 11, 28, 14), the *comes sacrarum largitionum* was given a constitution that extended the scope of fiscal exemptions granted *per urbicarias regiones*. Around 400, the *Notitia dignitatum* makes note of a diocese in Italy, but mentions two vicars, one for

Italy and the other for the *urbs Roma*, which corresponds to the situation found at the beginning of the 4th century. The fiscal administration mentions the same division. The *Notitia dignitatum* indicates three *rationales rei privatae*: one *per Italiam*, another *per urbem Romam et suburbicarias regiones cum parte Faustinae*, and the third for Sicily. There is likewise a *rationalis per Italiam* and another *per Urbem et per urbicarias regiones*. According to A. Piganiol, the vicar of the *urbs Roma* took the place of the prefects of the praetorium and should not be confused with another vicar who assisted the prefect of Rome. A new look at the sources led A. Chastagnol to amend these conclusions ("Administration du diocèse," 123). The vicar was responsible to the prefect of the city, then from 321 to 326, with the title of *vicarius praef. praetorio in urbe*, to the praetorium prefects, and then once again to the prefect of the city from 326 to 357 (with the title of *vicarius praefecti urbis*) and, after that date, and once and for all, to the prefect of the praetorium with the title of *vicarius urbis Romae* (a list of the thirty-seven vicars known up to 423 is found in Chastagnol, *Préfecture urbaine*, 463–5, and of five vicars for the period 423–536 in "Administration du diocèse," 123). After the middle of the 4th century, when the vicar of the urban prefecture disappears, the "vicar of Rome" inherits his functions, while remaining attached to the prefect of the praetorium of Italy-Illyria-Africa. He thus becomes "the support and rival of the prefect of the city." In a brief addressed to the Senate dated 11 February 376, the distinction is made, regarding "Italy," between the governors *de suburbanis provinciis*, who must defer to the prefecture of the city, and those *de ceteris*, who depend on the prefect of the praetorium.

This administrative organization would not survive the invasions, which ended in the establishment of the Ostrogoth kingdom of Theodoric at the end of the 5th century, and then the Lombard kingdom at the end of the 6th century.

During Justinian's reign, the "suburbicarian" zone was nothing more than a modest territory around Rome, wedged in among Etruria, Valeria, Campania, and the sea. At the beginning of the 7th century, the Lombard kingdom covered most of Italy, but it was cut in two by a zone that had remained apart and that extended from the Byzantine EXARCHATE OF RAVENNA to the Roman region (as far as Gaeta) with a thin corridor joining it to the upper valley of the Tiber.

The reference to "suburbicarian Italy" therefore is of no interest for the history of the secular administration after the end of the 6th century. But the language of the Latin Church would take the adjective and guarantee it a long life. "Suburbicarian" appears for the first time in the ecclesiastical language with an interpolation of canon 6 of the council of Nicaea in 325. The adjective is found in the *Versio prisca* of this canon. It says that "by virtue of ancient custom" the bishop of the city of Rome *suburbicaria loca et omnem provinciam sua sollicitudine gubernet* (*in suburbicaria loca sollicitudinem gerat* in the *Interpretatio Caeciliani*). The Greek text of canon 6 says nothing like this. At the end of the 5th century, Rufinus of Aquileia in his *Ecclesiastical History* (I, 6, *PL.*, 21, 475) gives canon 6 this form: *et in urbe Roma, vetusta consuetudo servetur, et [. . .]suburbicariarum Ecclesiarum sollicitudinem gerat.*

But the expression "suburbicarian churches (or dioceses)" no longer refers to the vast territory of the civil provinces of the *regiones suburbicariae*. Nevertheless, the administrative division of the peninsula under the management of two vicars, one living in Milan and the other in Rome, finds a parallel in the religious life of Italy, in the last years of the 4th century, when SIRICIUS occupied the see of Peter and Ambrose that of the Milanese "capital." A sort of sharing, sometimes even a collaboration, existed between the two prelates in their administrative and pastoral activity. But this *de facto* duality in the government of the Church in Italy never implies a duality in the civil administration. It was a simple geographical symmetry unsupported by any normative text or even by any personal claim. The strong personality of Ambrose and the *de facto* capital that Milan was contributed to this temporary sharing of Christian Italy. The very rich information available to us on the administration of the Church during the pontificate of GREGORY I (590–604), thanks to a collection of his letters, furnishes substantial proof of the persistence of a region (which is not expressly referred to as "suburbicarian") made up of central and southern Italy and the three islands, where the pope intervened in a more active and direct way. In fact, before the 10th century there are no metropolitans, in this vast area, exercising their authority over "suffragan" dioceses. The dioceses therefore depended directly on the Roman pontiff. Gregory's correspondence shows him intervening in Cagliari, Naples, Capua, Locres, Palermo, Syracuse, etc., in episcopal decisions. He oversaw the governing of the patrimony of the dioceses and abbeys, the consecration of churches, the provision of various church functions (priests, deacons, abbots, etc.), and he exercised his jurisdiction by appointing judges. In the absence of the hierarchical intermediary that the metropolitans usually constituted, a "suburbicarian" Italy (without the qualifier, which was never used) persisted in the vast central and southern regions of Italy and the three large islands. If the word was not totally forgotten (cf. Andrerecci, *De episcopis cardinalibus suburbicariis quaestiones selectae*, Rome, 1766), it disappeared nevertheless from the official language of the latin Church, to reappear only with the *motu proprio* of Pius X of 5 May 1914. It is found in the two Codes of Canon Law, that of 1917 and that of 1983. But these "suburbicarian" churches (or dioceses), which take up once again the administrative language of the Late Empire, have no connection with the *regiones suburbicariae* of the 4th and 5th centuries. They are small dioceses in the Roman countryside, still called suburbicarian sees today (cf. the *Annuario pontificio*). The determination of these sees over the course of history has seen many changes. The number of seven, already found in the *Liber pontificalis* of the 8th century, and found in 1587 in the constitution *De religiosa sanctorum* of SIXTUS V, is still found today: the sees of Ostia, Porto–Santa Rufina, Albano, Frascati (Tusculum), Palestrina (Praeneste), Sabina and Poggio Mirteto, and Velletri are "suburbicarian."

The particular condition of these sees goes back quite far. It has its origin in the participation of the bishops of these dioceses in the Roman liturgy in certain circumstances and in diverse capacities. These bishops, whom later language would call "suburbicarian," were long referred to as *episcopi Romani*, *vicarii Curiae*, and their dioceses as *laterales, domesticae, filiae*. These suburbicarian dioceses go back as far as the *regiones suburbicariae* of the 4th through the 6th centuries. They overlap with another geographical datum, much narrower, that of the hundred leagues around Rome. Already in the 3rd century, this zone was under the judiciary authority of the prefect of the city. In the following century, it fell likewise under his jurisdiction at the administrative level. It became a "suburbicarian" zone, reattached to Rome and overseen by the prefect of the city (see this distinction between *intra centesimum urbis Romae miliarium* and *per omnem vero Italiam* in CTh., 2, 16, 2 pr.; 319). The coexistence, in the vocabulary, of this suburbicarian zone and the *regiones suburbicariae* is a source of uncertainty for historians. Are they two distinct realities in administrative geography, or are the *regiones suburbicariae* the hundred miles around Rome?

The question was raised, with perhaps some ulterior motives, in 1618 by Jacques Godefroy in a work published in Frankfurt with no author's name, *De suburbicariis regionibus et ecclesiis, seu de praefectura et episcopi urbis Romae diocesi coniectura*. The title created a sort of amalgam of the territory of the pope and that of the prefect of the city during Roman times. Godefroy wished to show that, the jurisdiction of the prefect being limited to a hundred miles, the ancient jurisdiction of the pope, as patriarch, had the same limits (see also his commentary on CTh., 2, 16, 2 and 9, 1, 13). Taken up again by another Protestant, Claude Saumaise, a professor at Leiden, this thesis was disputed by several illustrious Catholic historians such as Archbishop Pierre de Marca and especially Fr. Jacques Sirmond. The latter demonstrated that, if there was some coincidence between the territorial extent of the competence of the prefect and that of the patriarchal jurisdiction of the pope, it was only verbal. BENEDICT

XIV (*De synodo diocesana*, Rome, 1748, II, c. 2, no. 2) echoed these debates. Removed from these backgrounds of religious controversy, the question has once again been taken up by several historians of our own day.

The assimilation of the *suburbicariae regiones* to the hundred miles has been maintained by M. De Dominicis. But A. Chastagnol has shown that the hundred miles around Rome must not be confused with the totality of the provinces of the center, of the south, and of the islands of the diocese of Italy. (In the same vein, Edgar Faure, "Italia annonaria," 165, no. 34, which contests the existence of different fiscal regimes, particular to each of the two parts of the peninsula, the annonarian and the suburbicarian.) The vast group that made up the *regiones suburbicariae* of the 4th and 5th centuries should therefore not be confused with the "suburbicarian" churches (dioceses) of the Roman countryside, whose titulars have long been associated in diverse capacities with liturgical life and with certain administrative tasks of the Church of Rome.

Jean Gaudemet

Bibliography

Andrerecci, *De episcopis cardinalibus suburbicariis quaestiones selectae*, Rome, 1766.

Cantarelli, L. *Le diocesi italiciane da Diocleziano alla fine dell'impero occidentale*, Rome, 1964.

Chastagnol, A. *Évolution politique, sociale et économique du monde romain*, Paris, 1982, 247–8.

Chastagnol, A. *La Préfecture urbaine à Rome sous le Bas-Empire*, Paris, 1960; "L'administration du diocèse italien sous le Bas-Empire," *Historia*, 1963, 348–79, repr. in *L'Italie et l'Afrique au Bas-Empire*, Lille, 1987, 117–48.

Claeys-Bouaert, "Vo Diocése suburbicaire," *DDC*, 4 (1949), 1267–70.

Clemente, G. "Due note sulla storia delle diocesi italiciane nee IV secolo," *Athenaeum*, 53 (1965), 355–68.

De Dominicis, M. "I distretti della prefettura urbana e le 'regiones suburbicariae,'" *Studi in onore di Guido Zanobini*, vol. 5, Milan, 1962, repr. in his *Scritti romanistici*, Padua, 1970, 45–67.

Faure, E. "Italia annonaria," *Revue internationale des droits de l'Antiquité*, 3rd series, XI, 1964.

Gregory I, *Registrum Epistolarum*, ed. P. Ewals and L. M. Hartmann, *MGH*, 2nd ed., Berlin, 1891–99.

Notitia dignitatum, ed. O. Seeck, XI, 8, 9, 10, 21, 22, 23.

Palanque, J. R. "Les métropoles ecclésiastiques à la fin du IVe siècle," in Fliche-Martin, 3, 1945, 477.

Philips, *Kirchenrecht*, II, Ratisbonne, 1846.

Pietri, C. *Roma christiana*, 1976, 888ff., 916, 923.

Pitz, E. *Päpstreskripte im frühen Mittelalter*, Sigmaringen, 1990.

Thomsen, R. *The Italic Regions from Augustus to the Lombard Invasion*, Copenhagen, 1947.

Turner, *Ecclesiae occidentalis monumenta iuris antiquissimi*, I, 2, 1904, 120–1.

Verzeichnis der römischen Provinzen aufgesetzt um 297," ed. T. Mommsen, *Abhandlungen der könlichen Akademie der Wissenschaften*, Berlin, 1862, 489–538.

SUPERINTENDENT OF THE ECCLESIASTICAL STATE.

The institution of superintendence of the Ecclesiastical State took shape when the Fathers of the council of Trent parted ways for good in 1563. The Church had just lived through some grim years, nor were its trials yet at an end. The seamless robe had been rent; the unimaginable had come to pass. In 1527 Rome the Magnificent, the marvel of the world, had for a week been the scene of the worst excesses, and for nine months it had been occupied.

First the confession of Augsburg (1530) and then that of Basel (1534) drew up the articles of the Lutheran faith. In 1534 came the Anglican schism. If in this dramatic period the sovereign pontiff managed to escape becoming subject to the universal monarchy with which the Habsburgs were threatening him, or become no more than the emperor's chaplain, it was because he was the ruler of a state. This state had been formed, and reformed, since the mid-15th century, through the efforts of NICHOLAS V, JULIUS II, and LEO X. At first made up of fragmentary, unconnected possessions, then of various annexations, the state in early times allowed the popes to triumph over conciliarism and, at a later stage, over external enemies. In a period bridging the Middle Ages and the modern era, the popes recognized that their territorial foundation assured them both survival and independence, on the spiritual as well as the political level.

The heavy taxes levied on the pope's subjects served to support wars against heresy and the infidel, besides encouraging Catholic renewal and the deployment of missionaries. Before the schism and the Reformation, Europe had supplied the papacy with the greater part of its resources; now the situation was completely reversed, and three-quarters of its revenues came solely from the Papal States.

This explains the importance of these possessions, without which Rome would have counted for little, in either the spiritual or the temporal domain. Thus, if the pope was to remain the uncontested head of Christianity, he was compelled to ensure the good management of the Papal States. Organizing the government on a new basis became a task of burning urgency.

The task fell to Michele Ghislieri, better known as PIUS V, (1566–72). Naturally, he did not create the government *ex nihilo*, but he did institutionalize a system that would last until 1691. The 60 years that preceded his accession were distinguished by a great variety of ways in which power was organized, yet there was an unmistakable trend toward personal government; beginning with Julius II's papacy, the old medieval formula of collegial leadership, that of government shared by the college of cardinals and the pope was abandoned.

Under PAUL IV (1555–9) and PIUS IV (1559–66), the future solution gradually took shape. Each pope shifted the responsibility of the temporalia to a relative—a nephew—who was made a cardinal. What happened at the top was a development peculiar to Rome, which consisted on the one hand in entrusting men of the Church with tasks formerly carried out by communes or feudal lords—that is, by the laity—and, on the other hand, ensuring that these clerics took on new duties henceforth considered as dependent on a modern secular state.

Pius V drew up a constitutive charter covering the division of tasks, thus setting up, not in principle but in practice, a separation between the affairs of the Church and those of the state. The preamble of the brief that he delivered on 14 March 1566 made plain his intentions. Anxious to devote his energies essentially to the realization of the principles of the council of Trent, he created the superintendence of the Ecclesiastical States in order that everything to do with management would be carried out, under his control, by a delegate whose duties he listed in detail.

The superintendence of the Ecclesiastical States was made up of a commission that appointed a prime minister (even a super-prime minister) and described in minute detail the temporal powers that he would exercise. By virtue of his delegation, the superintendent was responsible for the external domain: all negotiations, no matter how important, with the emperor and with kings, princes, and others powers. He had to take charge of correspondence with the legates, the nuncios, and all other persons sent on missions. In other words, it was he who managed the diplomatic services of the papacy. Thus, he oversaw the secretary of state.

Not only was the superintendent entrusted with the question of peace, but he was also responsible for matters of defense—everything to do with operations of war, recruitment, the billeting of troops (navy, infantry, cavalry), the commissariat, and protection of territory. That meant that he could create ports, build fortifications, and so on.

In the domestic domain, the superintendent had supreme control over the administrations, the legates, vice-legates, magistrates, officers of the Urbs, and governors of the towns and provinces. He could appoint, transfer, or dismiss anyone in authority in the Ecclesiastical States. Responsible for public order, he would be informed of all civil, criminal, and mixed civil/criminal affairs, without exception. He had complete freedom to impose sanctions, whether these consisted of fines, confiscation of goods, or severe punishment. He could—

as a manifestation of the mixed nature of the Roman principate—pronounce all ecclesiastical penalties and censures against the clergy, whatever their rank or jurisdiction.

Last, he could dispose of monies in any amount, depending on the needs of his task, and he could take all measures necessary for safeguarding the public health. Thus the powers granted him made the superintendent the pope's alter ego in the temporal domain. The sovereign pontiff wanted to shift questions of management onto an aide responsible for regulating in his name the temporal affairs that "each day came both from the universal Church and from the city of Rome and the States of the Church"—hence the division of tasks. The affairs of the Church were made distinct from the affairs of the state.

In another period, the superintendent would be described as a prime minister. This is the comparison that in 1670 occurred to the great justice de Luca, when he was writing his *Relatio Curiae Romanae*. He entitled an entire treatise *De cardinali supraintendente generali seu primo ministro papae*. In reality, the superintendent was a super-prime minister. In contrast to the prime ministers of secular states, the superintendent in Rome in effect had the right to sign all instructions. At any time, he could decide on any matter of litigation. He could condemn the convicted to death. Above all, he enjoyed the right of granting pardons, virtually treat of a sovereign, regarding pecuniary as well as corporal punishment. Finally, he was authorized to be accountable to God alone for his overall management the moment the pope who had appointed him died.

It should not be thought, however, that by endowing his second-in-command with unparalleled delegatory powers, the pope was abandoning the reins of his government. Nothing important was accomplished without a preliminacy conference between the two. The pope wanted, above all, to free himself of those daily tasks that would hinder him from devoting himself to spiritual matters. It was up to the superintendent to study dossiers, suggest solutions, supervise, encourage, and coordinate government action. The pope disposed, the superintendent proposed—and executed.

The choice of officeholder had to be made in such a way that the spiritual and the political powers would have no problem coexisting. For this reason, the superintendent had to meet three criteria.

In the first place, he was a man of the Church, vowed to celibacy. Thus we find, at the highest level of government, the phenomenon of clericalization in pontifical administration, which encouraged members of the clergy to carry out tasks which in other states were entrusted to laymen. During the century and a half under discussion, recourse to a lay superintendent was envisaged only once—in 1647, under INNOCENT X. At that time the institution experienced its first serious crisis, when the superintendent Camillo Pamphili resigned from his post in order to marry. Nevertheless, the pope resisted the temptation to keep his superintendent and did not set up a precedent for allowing the superintendent to be a noncleric, someone not vowed to celibacy.

Second, the superintendent was a cardinal. Once the trial-and-error stage was past, the custom became accepted of raising the superintendent to the purple very soon after the pope's election, even through a special promotion. Once installed in his post, the cardinal superintendent could deal at least as an equal with the legates, whether or not they were *a latere* (designated to represent the pope for a specific occasion), with his colleagues of the college of cardinals, and with the titulars of the great dicasteries. In particular, he was head of the Secretariat of State, with which he is too often confused in discussion of the years 1566–1691. During this period (except for the papacy of INNOCENT XI, who had no "prime minister"), the one responsible for the diplomatic services and correspondence was the superintendent. The secretary of state was merely his subordinate, a prelate monsignor, from 1566 to 1644. Innocent X was the first pontiff to appoint a secretary of state who was already a cardinal, in the person of his favorite, Cardinal Panciroli. It is apparent from the observations of the Venetian ambassador in this period, Contarini, that Cardinal Panciroli did not enjoy a superintendent's powers. Thus, until the abolition of the office, the superintendent assumed responsibility for relations with foreign powers. Under CLEMENT X (1670–6), the correspondence of the nuncio Spada, recently published, is proof of this.

Finally, the superintendent was the pope's "nephew" by agnation, kinship, or even, in Roman fashion, by adoption. At the beginning of his papacy, Pius V strove to follow the decrees of the council of Trent which, in its last session of 4 December 1563, had condemned NEPOTISM. The pope at first divided political affairs among four cardinals, none a member of his family. When this solution was found to lend itself to ambitions and intrigue, he acceded to the pleas of the college of cardinals and the Spanish ambassador and chose for his aide a "nephew," his sister's grandson, Michele Bonelli, soon better known under the name Cardinal Alessandrino. But in appointing him, Pius V was careful to draw up rules for the duties of the one who would become his superintendent. This was the goal of his brief of 14 March 1566. Shortly afterward, with the bull *Admonet nos* (29 March 1567), he prohibited the alienation of cities or territories belonging to the Holy See, thus eliminating all danger of enfeoffment.

Through these various precautions, relations of the Church with its political government came under harmonious regulation. The pope and the papacy derived unmistakable advantages from this. The pope now had beside him a loyal supporter, the most trustworthy possible according to the ideas of the time: a relative, whose loyalty and zeal were never-failing because both uncle and nephew were committed to the same lofty enterprise— the success of the pontificate, whose glory would reflect on the whole family. Moreover, these blood ties spared the pope the charge of favoritism, since the appointment of the superintendent supposedly depended not on partiality but on the mysterious decrees of nature. The papacy benefited because this nephew was a cardinal, who could not marry or found a dynasty, and because, however much power he had as the pope's lieutenant, he was revocable at any time and could automatically lose his position when his relative died.

Thus neither the Holy See nor the pope had any reason to fear a mayor of the palace; however, the superintendent's position was vulnerable to his uncle's death. The new pope might ask him to take over a post with crushing responsibilities. In a terrible precedent, Cardinal Carafa and his brothers, relatives of Paul IV, were tried in the next pontificate and severely punished on the order of Pius IV in 1559. The popes, mindful of the risks their superintendent ran after their death, were induced to draw up guidelines exonerative of responsibility that have no equivalent in contemporary monarchies, intrinsic differences apart.

This unusual mechanism took various forms on the diplomatic plane—briefs, bulls, and chirographs. Documents, called *quitus*, were drawn up designed to free the superintendent from responsibility. They applied either to an action carried out in a clearly circumscribed area, or to management as a whole, but they were valid only *usque in presentem diem, sino a questo giorno* (the date—year, month and day—being indicated). In the latter case, all the superintendent's activities were mentioned. Thus, just as the highly varied aspects of his duties were described, so the practical importance of the institution was revealed. These preventive measures, however, did not stop Cardinal Barberini from being anxious at the death of his uncle, URBAN VIII.

After years of intrigue, annoyances, and reversals, Innocent X came to understand the need to have done with all the contentiousness. Imprudently, he had infringed the *modus vivendi* according to which the wishes of the pope's predecessor were respected as well as the responsibilities of his superintendent. If the latter were harassed, criticized, or condemned, papal authority itself suffered.

A leadership post and not simply a provisioning sinecure as it has sometimes been described, the superintendence of the Ecclesiastical States was a living institution whose origin, growth, classical period, and decline took place between 1566 and 1691. It died, a victim of the blood ties that had given rise to it and because nepotism—nepotism of blood rather than that of the *cardinale nipote*—killed it with its excesses, while other formulas for succession came to the fore. Yet it had given Catholic Reform a solid logistical base. For 150 years it had created a famillial type of government, strongly personalized, tending toward egocentricity and, more often than not, quite brilliant.

Madeleine Laurain-Portemer

Bibliography

Laurain-Portemer, M. "Absolutisme et népotisme: La surintendance de l'État ecclésiastique," *Études Mazarines*, 1, Paris, 1981, 403–79; *Ministeriat, Finances et Papauté au temps de la Réforme catholique*, Paris, 481–92; "L'Église et le pouvoir politique . . . Rome pendant la Réforme catholique," *Églises et Pouvoir politique*, Angers, 1985, 233–44.

SUPREME PONTIFF. See **Titles, Papal.**

SUSPENSION. Unlike interdict or excommunication, suspension is a penal sanction ("censure") that affects only clerics. It consists in depriving the cleric of his office and/or benefice and ends when the offender mends his ways. It is therefore theoretically provisional, whereas deposition is definitive. Suspension traces its origin to the Old Testament; it was made specific in the last state of Roman law (Digest) and was not organized until the 12th century. It could be pronounced by the pope throughout the Christian world and by bishops within their dioceses. It is not as rigid a procedure as excommunication and not as radical as deposition, but its flexibility entails endless possibilities, some extremely subtle.

The most frequent forms are general suspension, in which the one on whom the sentence is imposed no longer exercises any power save that of administering his benefice; and suspension *a divinis*, which prohibits any exercise of sacramental power (administration of the sacraments—the Eucharist, marriage, confession, ordination of priests or bishops). In recent years, suspension *a divinis* has been imposed chiefly on Latin American priests who took part in progressive governments (the possibility was mentioned of imposing it on Father Jean-Bertrand Aristide, elected president of Haiti in December 1990), and on the Integrists, most notably Marcel Lefebvre (d. 25 March 1991), ex-archbishop of Dakar (suspended on 24 July 1976, before being excommunicated on 30 June 1988).

Gérard Giordanengo

Bibliography

Cimetier, F. "Suspense," *DTC*, 14/2 (1941), 2864–7.
Code of Canon Law of 1917, canons 2186–94, 2255, 2278–85.
Code of Canon Law of 1983, canons 1331–5.
Jombart, E. "Suspense," *DDC* 7 (1965), 1118–25.

SWADDLING CLOTHES, CONSECRATED. Consecrated swaddling clothes were a complete layette of baby linen (figuratively an infant's first garments), specially blessed by the popes in allusion to Christ's birth (cfr Luke 2, 7), and sent as a gift to the newly born children of reigning Catholic sovereigns.

Normally the swaddling clothes and covers for the crèche were made from rich materials, embroidered in gold thread and decorated with the finest lace and semiprecious stones. The components of the gift varied considerably from time to time with respect to their quantity or the value of the objects. The cost of the gift for the birth of Prince Charles Edward, heir to James III of Great Britain (1720) is said to have amounted to 6,000 *scudi*, giving an idea of the expenditure expected on these occasions.

This gracious gesture was introduced by CLEMENT VIII (1592–1605), apparently in response to a wish expressed by Queen Margaret of Spain during her pregnancy, that the pope, who had officiated at her marriage by proxy to Felipe III, should be the one to provide the *mantillas* for her firstborn child. Princess Anna-Mauricia was born on 22 September 1601. Almost contemporaneously, Marie de Medicis, queen of Henri IV of France, gave birth to the dauphin (the future Louis XIII) on 27 September, and the pope sent a similar gift to this royal infant, which was consigned to their majesties at the Louvre on 16 December by Maffeo Barberini, extraordinary nuncio. The practice was followed by GREGORY XV, URBAN VIII, ALEXANDER VII, INNOCENT XI, ALEXANDER VIII, CLEMENT XI, BENEDICT XIII, CLEMENT XII, BENEDICT XIV, CLEMENT XIV, PIUS VI, PIUS IX, and LEO XIII.

The earliest form of the ritual blessing has not survived, only that specially composed for Innocent XI in 1683, with its invocations for the child's longevity, and that he or she be adorned with all the princely virtues. It was imparted personally by the pope in one of the chapels, or in the *sala consistoriale* of the papal palace, or in one of the churches of Rome. Frequently, a special envoy was sent to deliver the gift, or the resident nuncio received an explicit mandate to present it with the accompanying brief, which was read as part of the simple consignment ceremony.

Bibliography

MacSwiney de Mashanaglass, P. *Le Portugal et le Saint-Siège*. II. *Les langes bénits envoyés par les Papes aux princes royaux de Portugal*, Paris 1899.
Moroni, G. *Le Cappelle pontificie, cardinalizie e prelatizie*, Venezia 1841, 133–4.
Palazzini, P. "Fasco benedette," *EC* 5 (1950) 1049–50.

SWISS GUARD. This armed body is composed exclusively of Catholic citizens of Switzerland; its purpose is to be in charge of the guard of honor and to protect the pope and the Holy See. This is not the same guard as the Swiss regiments that, of different times, were recruited by the pope or other sovereigns for the needs of their army. Although SIXTUS IV did employ soldiers from the confederated cantons for the protection of the papal palace, the origins of the permanent guard go back to the time of JULIUS II who, in 1506 recruited a force of two hundred *lansquenets*. During the SACK OF ROME, those guards who had not followed the pope to CASTEL SANT'ANGELO were massacred by maréchal Bourbon's troops (6 May 1527). The force was then disbanded, and CLEMENT VII rented Swiss and German *lansquenet* services. It was not until the end of PAUL III's papacy that, under the aegis of the canton of Lucerne, a capitulation was concluded with the Catholic cantons so that new recruits could be obtained. These capitulations prescribed specific conditions of service, particularly the fact that the guard had its own tribunal. Since that time, except for brief intervals in the 19th century, the Swiss Guard has not ceased to be at the service of the pope. It was let go in 1798 during the French occupation of papal lands, but reestablished by PIUS VII in March 1800, by recalling the former guards who had remained in the pope's states (some sixty men distributed between the Vatican Palace and the QUIRINAL). In 1803, Pius VII renewed the capitulations with Lucerne. The guard was once again disbanded in 1809, when the Papal States were reattached to the French Empire, although a certain number of soldiers—boasting of rights acquired—continued to reside in the Quirinal after the pope's departure (five of them were still there in 1813). The guard was reestablished in 1814, and in 1824 LEO XII concluded a final capitulation with Lucerne. This was confirmed by the new federal diet at the end of article 8 of the Federal Pact of 7 August 1815, which authorized the once again sovereign cantons to "treat in particular with foreign governments for military capitulations," provided these capitulations were brought to the attention of the diet. But internal revolutions in Switzerland soon made foreign military service less than popular, especially in the pay of sovereigns who oppressed liberal trends. Moreover, the confederation feared losing valuable bodies for its own army. The federal constitution of 1848, in its article 11, thus forbade foreign military service. When PIUS IX took refuge in Gaeta (November 1848), the guard was disarmed and needed to begin wearing civilian clothing. Some of the soldiers nevertheless joined the pope who, upon his return to Rome, quickly raised the guard to its former status. The capitulation of 1825 could no longer be renewed. It was thus replaced in 1858 by a regulation resulting from the accord between the Holy See and commander Leopold Meyer de Schauense. The latter no longer recruited in the name of the canton of Lucerne, which lost its right to present its commander, but as a representative of the guard, which was henceforth considered to be a simple police force in order to escape the demands of the federal constitution. Nomination of the commander became a sovereign right of the pope. The guards could come from any of the cantons, with the exception of Tessin (an exception which was later removed). The goal was to have a force of 133 men, including officers. Subsequently, this total has undergone a number of modifications; it is presently stable at about 100 men.

The guard is placed under the authority of the secretary of state. For daily service, it answered to the majordomo and the chamber master (today, to the prefect of the papal house). In the course of recent years, some of its elements have seen their responsibilities increased for the personal security of the pope, particularly during his TRAVELS or even during public AUDIENCES.

The pope's Swiss Guard is known throughout the world today because of its picturesque uniform symbolizing, in the eyes of many, the VATICAN CITY STATE. The early guard did not have a uniform of its own; its members wore clothing of the colors of the reigning pope (yellow and blue under Julius II; blue, red, and yellow under LEO X and Clement VII; green, white, and yellow under HADRIAN VI; yellow and blue under Paul III; white and red under PAUL IV). The colors of the Medici (Leo X and Clement VII) were gradually returned to, with forms and accessories (headwear, cuirasses) that varied depending on military styles of the time. The present uniform, which is modeled on Renaissance styles, was established by BENEDICT XV in 1914–5, on the advice of Jules Repond, who was commander of the guard from 1910 until 1921. The guard's flag was designed at the same time, by the Swiss archivist Robert Durrer. It was inspired by the flags of the old Swiss regiments in the foreign service. A white cross marks off four quarters: on the first is the coat of arms of the reigning pope, and on the fourth is that of Julius II, who was the guard's founder; the guard's colors (blue, red, and gold) are on the second and third quarters; in the middle of the flag a laurel crown surrounds the arms of the commander in office.

For a long time, soldiers and officers were almost exclusively natives of the German regions of present-day Switzerland. They thus managed, in 1520, to get from the Germanic brotherhood of the Pietà in Campo Santo Teutonico, their own chapel inside this church. From that time on they were able to bury their dead in the chapel or in the common cemetery, Campo Santo Teutonico. In 1568, PIUS V had the small church of Saints-Martin-and-Sebastian built for the guard next to his quarters; it is presently located to the right of the colonnade. But since the building was rather small in size and did not have a cemetery, the guard still went to Santa Maria della Pietà and Campo Santo Teutonico for important ceremonies and burials. Finally, in 1653, the commander negotiated with the chapter of St. Peter for the somewhat precarious concession of the church of San Pellegrino and its cemetery (presently inside Vatican City, behind the church of Sant'Anna dei Palafrenieri; the cemetery is no longer extant). The concession was made perpetual in a BRIEF on 16 July 1658. The sanctuary, administered by a congregation chosen from among members of the guard was then considered to be the "national" church of Swiss soldiers.

François-Charles Uginet

Bibliography

Castella, G. *La Garde fidèle du Saint-Père. Les soldats suisses au service du Vatican de 1506 à nos jours*, Lausanne, 1935.

Krieg, P. M. *Die Schweizer Garde in Rom,* Lucerne, 1960.

SWORD. See **Theocracy, Papal, Middle Ages.**

SYLLABUS OF ERRORS. The Syllabus of Errors, Published in Latin as an annex to the encyclical *Quantum cura* (8 December 1864), is a collection of propositions that Pope PIUS IX had previously criticized or condemned in his various encyclicals, allocutions, and letters during the previous 18 years of his pontificate. The compilation was made by several of his cardinals. It was not derived from answers to a questionnaire. Its intention was to call attention to all those "errors" to be rejected by Catholics. It was not subsequently modified, but was much discussed by the public. Much of it is now out of date.

Pantheism, Naturalism, and Absolute Rationalism.

1. There exists no Supreme, all-wise, all-provident Divine Being, distinct from the universe, and God is identical with the nature of things, and is, therefore, subject to changes. In effect, God is produced in man and in the world, and things are God and have the very substance of God, and God is one and the same thing with the world, and therefore, spirit with matter, necessity with liberty, good with evil, justice with injustice.

2. All action of God upon man and the world is to be denied.

3. Human reason, without any reference whatsoever to God, is the sole arbiter of truth and falsehood, and of good and evil; it is law to itself, and suffices, by its natural force, to secure the welfare of men and of nations.

4. All the truths of religion proceed from the innate strength of human reason; hence reason is the ultimate standard by which man can and ought to arrive at the knowledge of all truths of every kind.

5. Divine revelation is imperfect, and therefore subject to a continual and indefinite progress, corresponding with the advancement of human reason.

6. The faith of Christ is in opposition to human reason and divine revelation not only is not useful, but is even hurtful to the perfection of man.

7. The prophecies and miracles set forth and recorded in the sacred Scriptures are the fiction of poets, and the mysteries of the Christian faith the result of philosophical investigations. In the books of the Old and the New Testament there are contained mythical inventions, and Jesus Christ is Himself a myth.

Moderate Rationalism.

8. As human reason is placed on a level with religion itself, so theological sciences must be treated in the same manner as philosophical sciences.

9. All the dogmas of the Christian religion are indiscriminately the object of natural science or philosophy, and human reason, enlightened solely in a historical way, is able, by its own natural strength and principles, to attain to the true knowledge of even the most abstruse dogmas; provided only that such dogmas be proposed to reason itself as its object.

10. As the philosopher is one thing, and philosophy another, so it is the right and duty of the philosopher to subject himself to the authority which he shall have proved to be true; but philosophy neither can nor ought to be subject to any such authority.

11. The Church not only ought never to pass judgment on philosophy, but ought to tolerate the errors of philosophy, leaving it to correct itself.

12. The decrees of the Apostolic See and of the Roman congregations impede the free progress of science.

13. The method and principles by which the old scholastic doctors cultivated theology are no longer suitable to the demands of our times and to the progress of the sciences.

14. Philosophy is to be treated without taking any account of supernatural revelation.

Indifferentism, Latitudinarianism.

15. Every man is free to embrace and profess that religion which, guided by the light of reason, he shall consider true.

16. Man may, in the observance of any religion whatever, find the way of eternal salvation, and arrive at eternal salvation.

17. Good hope at least is to be entertained of the eternal salvation of all those who are not at all in the true Church of Christ.

18. Protestantism is nothing more than another form of the same true Christian religion, in which form it is given to please God equally as in the Catholic Church.

Errors Concerning the Church and Her Rights.

19. The Church is not a true and perfect society, entirely free, nor is she endowed with proper and perpetual rights of her own, conferred upon her by her Divine Founder; but it appertains to the civil power to define what are the rights of the Church, and the limits within which she may exercise those rights.

20. The ecclesiastical power ought not to exercise its authority without the permission and assent of the civil government.

21. The Church has not the power of defining dogmatically that the religion of the Catholic Church is the only true religion.

22. The obligation by which Catholic teachers and authors are strictly bound is confined to those things only which are proposed to universal belief as dogmas of faith by the infallible judgment of the Church.

23. Roman pontiffs and ecumenical councils have wandered outside the limits of their powers, have usurped the rights of princes, and have even erred in defining matters of faith and morals.

24. The Church has not the power of using force, nor has she any temporal power, direct or indirect.

25. Besides the power inherent in the episcopate, other temporal power has been attributed to it by the civil authority granted either explicitly or tacitly, which on that account is revocable by the civil authority whenever it thinks fit.

26. The Church has no innate and legitimate right of acquiring and possessing property.

27. The sacred ministers of the Church and the Roman pontiff are to be absolutely excluded from every charge and dominion over temporal affairs.

28. It is not lawful for bishops to publish even letters apostolic without the permission of the government.

29. Favors granted by the Roman pontiff ought to be considered null, unless they have been sought for through the civil government.

30. The immunity of the Church and of ecclesiastical persons derived its origin from civil law.

31. The ecclesiastical forum or tribunal for the temporal causes, whether civil or criminal, of clerics, ought by all means to be abolished, even without consulting and against the protest of the Holy See.

32. The personal immunity by which clerics are exonerated from military conscription and service in the army may be abolished without violation either of natural right or equity. Its abolition is called for by civil progress, especially in a society framed on the model of a liberal government.

33. It does not appertain exclusively to the power of ecclesiastical jurisdiction by right, proper and innate, to direct the teaching of theological questions.

34. The teaching of those who compare the Sovereign Pontiff to a prince, free and acting in the universal Church, is a doctrine which prevailed in the Middle Ages.

35. There is nothing to prevent the decree of a general council, or the act of all peoples, from transferring the supreme pontificate from the bishop and city of Rome to another bishop and another city.

36. The definition of a national council does not admit of any subsequent discussion, and the civil authority can assume this principle as the basis of its acts.

37. National churches, withdrawn from the authority of the Roman pontiff and altogether separated, can be established.

38. The Roman pontiffs have, by their too arbitrary conduct, contributed to the division of the Church into Eastern and Western.

Errors About Civil Society, Considered Both in Itself and in Relation to the Church.

39. The State, as being the origin and source of all rights, is endowed with a certain right not circumscribed by any limits.

40. The teaching of the Catholic Church is hostile to the well-being and interests of society.

41. The civil government, even when in the hands of an infidel sovereign, has a right to an indirect negative power over religious affairs. It therefore possesses not only the right called that of *exsequatur*, but also that of appeal, called *appellatio ab abusu*.

42. In the case of conflicting laws enacted by the two powers, the civil law prevails.

43. The secular power has authority to rescind, declare and render null, solemn conventions, commonly called concordats, entered into with the Apostolic See, regarding the use of rights appertaining to ecclesiastical immunity, without the consent of the Apostolic See, and even in spite of its protest.

44. The civil authority may interfere in matters relating to religion, morality and spiritual government: hence, it can pass judgment on the instructions issued for the guidance of consciences, conformably with their mission, by the pastors of the Church. Further, it has the right to make enactments regarding the administration of the divine sacraments, and the dispositions necessary for receiving them.

45. The entire government of public schools in which the youth of a Christian state is educated, except (to a certain extent) in the case of episcopal seminaries, may and ought to appertain to the civil power, and belong to it so far that no other authority whatsoever shall be recognized as having any right to interfere in the discipline of the schools, the arrangement of the studies, the conferring of degrees, in the choice or approval of the teachers.

46. Moreover, even in ecclesiastical seminaries, the method of studies to be adopted is subject to the civil authority.

47. The best theory of civil society requires that popular schools open to children of every class of the people, and, generally, all public institutes intended for instruction in letters and philosophical sciences and for carrying on the education of youth, should be freed from all ecclesiastical authority, control and interference, and should be fully subjected to the civil and political power at the pleasure of the rulers, and according to the standard of the prevalent opinions of the age.

48. Catholics may approve of the system of educating youth unconnected with Catholic faith and the power of the Church, and which regards the knowledge of merely natural things, and only, or at least primarily, the goals of earthly social life.

49. The civil power may prevent the prelates of the Church and the faithful from communicating freely and mutually with the Roman pontiff.

50. Lay authority possesses of itself the right of presenting bishops, and may require of them to undertake the administration of the diocese before they receive canonical institution, and the letters apostolic from the Holy See.

51. And, further, the lay government has the right of deposing bishops from their pastoral functions, and is not bound to obey the Roman pontiff in those things which relate to the institution of bishoprics and the appointment of bishops.

52. Government can, by its own right, alter the age prescribed by the Church for the religious profession of women and men; and may require of all religious orders to admit no person to take solemn vows without its permission.

53. The laws enacted for the protection of religious orders and regarding their rights and duties ought to be abolished; nay, more, civil government may lend its assistance to all who desire to renounce the obligation which they have undertaken of a religious life, and to break their vows. Government may also suppress the said religious orders, as likewise collegiate churches and simple benefices, even those of advowson, and subject their property and revenues to the administration and pleasure of the civil power.

54. Kings and princes are not only exempt from the jurisdiction of the Church, but are superior to the Church in deciding questions of jurisdiction.

55. The Church ought to be separated from the State, and the State from the Church.

Errors Concerning Natural and Christian Ethics.

56. Moral laws do not stand in need of the divine sanction, and it is not at all necessary that human laws should be made conformable to the laws of nature and receive their power of binding from God.

57. The science of philosophical things and morals and also civil laws may and ought to keep aloof from divine and ecclesiastical authority.

58. No other forces are to be recognized except those which reside in matter, and all the rectitude and excellence of morality ought to be placed in the accumulation and increase of riches by every possible means, and the gratification of pleasure.

59. Right consists in the material fact. All human duties are an empty word, and all human facts have the force of right.

60. Authority is nothing else but numbers and the sum total of material forces.

61. The injustice of an act when successful inflicts no injury on the sanctity of right.

62. The principle of non-intervention, as it is called, ought to be proclaimed and observed.

63. It is lawful to refuse obedience to legitimate princes, and even to rebel against them.

64. The violation of any solemn oath, as well as any wicked and shameful action repugnant to the eternal law, is not only not blamable but is altogether lawful and worthy of the highest praise when done through love of country.

Errors Concerning Christian Marriage.

65. The doctrine that Christ has raised marriage to the dignity of a sacrament cannot be at all established.

66. The sacrament of marriage is only something accessory to the contract and separate from it, and the sacrament itself consists in the nuptial benediction alone.

67. By the law of nature, the marriage tie is not indissoluble, and in many cases divorce properly so called may be decreed by the civil authority.

68. The Church has not the power of establishing diriment impediments of marriage, but such a power belongs to the civil authority by which existing impediments are to be removed.

69. In the course of the centuries the Church began to establish diriment impediments, not by her own right, but by using a power borrowed from the State.

70. The canons of the council of Trent, which anathematize those who dare to deny to the Church the right of establishing diriment impediments, either are not dogmatic or must be understood as referring to such power as borrowed from the State.

71. The form of solemnizing marriage prescribed by the council of Trent, under pain of nullity, does not bind in cases where the civil law lays down another form, and declares that when this new form is used the marriage shall be valid.

72. BONIFACE VIII was the first who declared that the vow of chastity taken at ordination renders marriage void.

73. In force of a merely civil contract there may exist between Christians a real marriage, and it is false to say either that the marriage contract between Christians is always a sacrament, or that there is no contract if the sacrament be excluded.

74. Matrimonial causes and espousals belong by their nature to civil tribunals.

Errors Regarding the Civil Power of the Sovereign Pontiff.

75. The children of the Christian and Catholic Church are divided amongst themselves about the compatibility of the temporal with the spiritual power.

76. The abolition of the temporal power of which the Apostolic See is possessed would contribute in the greatest degree to the liberty and prosperity of the Church.

Errors Having Reference to Modern Liberalism.

77. In the present day it is no longer expedient that the Catholic religion should be held as the only religion of the State, to the exclusion of all other forms of worship.

78. Hence it has been wisely decided by law, in some Catholic countries, that persons coming to reside therein shall enjoy the public exercise of their own kind of worship.

79. Moreover, it is false that the civil liberty of every form of worship, and the full power, given to all, of overtly and publicly manifesting any opinions and thoughts whatsoever, conduce more easily to corrupt the morals and minds of the people, and to propagate the pest of indifferentism.

80. The Roman Pontiff can, and ought to, reconcile himself and come to terms with progress, liberalism and modern civilization.

Bibliography

Denzinger, H. *Enchiridion symbolorum: Definitionum et declarationum de rebus fidei et morum*, 32nd ed. annotated by A. Schönmetzer, Barcelona-Freiburg-in-Brisgau, 1963, 577–84.

Martina, G. "Osservazioni sulle varie redazioni del Sillabo," *Stato e Chiesa nell'ottocento, Miscellanea in onore di P. Pirri*, Padua, 1962, II. *Nuovi documenti sulla genesi del Sillabo*, APH, 6 (1968), 318–69.

Raulx, *Recueil des allocutions consistoriales, encycliques et autres lettres apostoliques des souverains pontifes Clement XII, Benoit XIV, Pie VI, Pie VII, Léon XII, Grégoire XVI et Pie IX, citées dans l'encyclique et le Syllabus du 8 décembre 1864*, Paris, 1865.

SYMMACHUS. *(b. Rome, ?, d. Rome, 19 July 514). Elected pope on 22 November 498. Buried in St. Peter's, Rome. Saint.*

Symmachus's pontificate was troubled by a schism dividing the Roman clergy between his supporters and those of the priest Lawrence, elected at the same time as Symmachus. The events in Rome were sufficiently dramatic to receive mention in contemporary histories, but above all they inspired each candidate's followers to write long, colorful accounts that changed papal historiography. The text known as the Lawrentian Fragment is an early attempt at the *LIBER PONTIFICALIS*, which contains a lengthy article on Symmachus himself. After the pope's death, his supporters wrote a copious biography and published the first version of the *Liber pontificalis*. But contemporaries were so caught up in the struggle between Symmachus and Lawrence that other aspects of the pontificate were neglected. Since few of Symmachus's letters have been preserved, our information is highly fragmentary.

Baptized in Rome according to his own testimony, Symmachus was a deacon at the time of ANASTASIUS'S death. There was tension among the Roman clergy. One strong party reproached the late pope for his conciliatory policy with regard to Constantinople, which had been separated from the Roman communion since the papacy of FELIX III, while a minority of the clergy, with the support of several senators, favored pursuing that policy in hopes of a reconciliation between the Churches. While a majority of the clergy met at the Lateran and elected Symmachus, part of the clergy and of the Senate—a minority, according to the formal testimony of the Greek historian Theodore the Lector—assembled at St. Mary Major and chose the priest Lawrence as pope. Both parties asked King Theodoric—although he was Arian, it being impossible to refer the matter to the schismatic emperor—to decide between the two.

Theodoric declared himself in favor of the one who had been elected first or by the majority, thus deciding in favor of Symmachus. On 1 March 499, therefore, the new pope was able to convene a synod of the Roman clergy—including his unhappy rival, Lawrence, and several suburbicarian bishops—to pursue the return to order. This proved to be a dangerous move. In 501, breaking the custom of recent years, the pope fixed the date of Easter at 25 March, according to the old Roman computation, instead of following the Alexandrine computation of 22 April.

This choice was probably meant as a signal of hostility toward Constantinople. The Byzantine party in Rome was not deceived and took advantage of the occasion to relaunch the controversy by denouncing the pope to the king for having fixed Easter at a noncanonical date. Symmachus was summoned to Ravenna. He solicited financial help for the purpose, in particular from the bishop of Milan, another Lawrence, who lent him a large sum thanks to the intervention of the Milanese deacon Ennodius, a loyal supporter of Symmachus. Stopping at Rimini on the way to Ravenna, the pope learned by chance that what awaited him at the court was not merely a debate on the date of Easter, but accusations of simony and debauchery. In a panic, he rushed back to Rome, where Lawrence's partisans, sure of their victory, had already taken possession of all the city churches, including the Lateran. Symmachus took refuge in St. Peter's. It was an easy matter for his opponents to present his flight as a confession of guilt, and they presented the king with a petition of accusation against him, asking that a visitor be appointed to celebrate the Paschal feasts.

Theodoric acceded to their request, a move that amounted to a de facto deposition of the pope. At the same time, he demanded that a council be held to settle the problem once and for all. Symmachus agreed to the council but asked that the visitor, Bishop Peter of Altinum, be removed, and that his churches be given back to him. It is not known how the king replied to the first of these demands, but the churches remained in the hands of Lawrence's party. Symmachus at least yielded on the second point, and the council was convened after Easter 502 in S. Croce in Gerusalemme. Bishops from all over Italy attended, including from Liguria and Venice, together with many priests and deacons. Symmachus himself, still secure in St. Peter's, agreed to attend, but on the way to the church his escort was attacked by some of Lawrence's supporters. Two of the priests in his suite, Dignissimus and Gordianus (the father of Pope Agapitus), were killed, and Symmachus therefore gave up the idea of taking part in the council.

The council opened, nevertheless. It proclaimed its intention of restoring peace in Rome, where riots were raging, and declared itself incompetent to judge a pope's legitimacy, thus justifying Symmachus. This decision did not resolve everything: it did not disarm Lawrence's supporters, who had the support of a majority of the senate, led by Senator Festus; nor did it satisfy the king, who was displeased with Symmachus's attitude toward the visitor. Symmachus's rivals published a pamphlet, *Against the Synod of the Aberrant Absolution*, to which Ennodius, the deacon of Milan, replied with a text *pro synodo*. The pope deposed Lawrence from his see in Nuceria, in Campania, to which he had been raised by the assembly of 1 March 499, and which he had left to claim the see of Rome. Still, Lawrence continued to hold a large part of the churches of Rome and to enjoy the loyalty of part of the clergy and a majority of the Senate.

On 6 November 502, Symmachus assembled a new Italian council. A smaller number of bishops attended it compared with the preceding councils, a sign that he had not won every bishop's confidence. The council annulled the *scriptura* promulgated by the prefect Basilius after SIMPLICIUS'S death to regulate the management of ecclesiastical possessions. The pope's principal aim was to show his opposition to the intervention of the senatorial aristocracy in Church affairs. He caused the council to adopt a resolution almost equivalent to Basilius's text: the possessions of the Church were absolutely inalienable, except when they could not be maintained. As for Lawrence's supporters, Symmachus obliged them, as a condition of reconciliation, to subscribe to the condemnation of the antipope and the royal visitor, Peter of Altinum. Despite this severity, the situation gradually became calmer. The deacon Dioscorus, a shrewd negotiator, persuaded Theodoric to abandon his support of Lawrence. In 506–7 the king asked Senator Festus, the leader and patron of Lawrence's party, to end his support. From then on nothing more was heard of Lawrence, who had retreated to a monastery, or his last champions, who survived Symmachus.

There is not much to say about the remainder of Symmachus's pontificate. Emperor Anastasius seems to have much preferred Lawrence as a candidate, which explains the accusations he hurled against "this illegally consecrated pope," taxing him with Manichaeism. Symmachus replied to these accusations with an "apology against Anastasius," rather violent in tone. The *Liber pontificalis* also recounts that Symmachus ousted some Manichaeans from Rome and had their books publicly burnt.

Although this aspect of his pontificate is the best-documented, Symmachus kept a watchful eye over the other provinces. He strove to strengthen the primacy of Arles over Gaul, in conformity with his predecessors' policy, and tried to extend it to Spain. He also sent the *pallium* to Caesarius of Arles, the first non-Italian bishop to receive it. To the African bishops exiled to Sardinia by the Vandal king, Guntharic, he sent material and spiritual comfort. He also tried to buy back some Ligurian prisoners, perhaps the chosen method to reimburse monies formerly lent by the bishop of Milan, which the deacon Ennodius had for long and in vain demanded be repaid.

Finally, Symmachus achieved some outstanding building works in Rome. He devoted most of his efforts to St. Peter's, where he lived for seven years. Here he built a baptistry on the model of that at the Lateran, which he was not entitled to use. Some mausoleums adjacent to the basilica he made into a church, and he built a residence, the first papal palace, at the Vatican. He also erected a basilica (not identified with any existing site) dedicated to St. Agatha on the Via Aurelia, and another over the tomb of the martyr Pancras (S. Pancrazio). In Rome itself, he built a church dedicated to St. Martin of Tours. This was next to the church of St. Silverius, built by his remote predecessor, which he embellished. In an unidentified place outside Rome, he consecrated a church to St. Peter that had been built by the senators Albinus and Glycerius. Symmachus restored the apses of the basilicas of ST. PAUL'S OUTSIDE THE WALLS and St. Agnes, which were near ruin. He enlarged a church within the walls dedicated to the archangel St. Michael, and added an oratory to ST. MARY MAJOR. He gave liturgical furnishings to the church of SS. John and Paul on the Coelian hill and caused "small dwellings for the poor" (no doubt intended to house pilgrims) to be built close to the basilicas of St. Peter, St. Paul, and St. Lawrence.

This pope, controversial in his lifetime as after his death, inspired the writer of the *Liber pontificalis* to append a touching homage: *Amarit clerum et pauperes.*

Claire Sotinel

Bibliography

LP, I, 260–8 and 44–6.

Acta Synhodorum habitarum Romae, MGHAA 12, 399–455.

Amann, E. "Symmaque," *DTC*, 14, 2 (1941), 2984–90.

Anonymus Valesianus, 65, MGHAA 9, 324.

Ennodius, *Libellus pro synodo*, MGHAA 7, 48–67; *Ep.*, IV, I, 129; *Ep.*, IV, VIII, XXXII, 287; *Ep.*, VIII, XXXVIII, 290.

Llewellyn, P. A. B. "The Roman Church During the Laurentian Schism: Priests and Senators," *Church History* 45 (1976) pp. 417–27.

Pietri, C. "Le Sénat, le peuple chrétien et les partis du cirque sous le pape Symmaque (498–514)," *MEFR*, 78 (1966), 123–39; "Aristocratie et société cléricale dans l'Italie chrétienne au temps d'Odoacre et de Théodoric," *MEFRA*, 93 (1981), 417–67.

Symmachus, *Epistulare*, XXIV, Thiel, 641–734.

Theodorus Lector, *Historia ecclesiastica*, 2, 17, PG, 86, 192.

Victor Tonnenensis, *Chronica*, 497, 2, MGHAA, 11, 192.

SYNOD OF BISHOPS. *Synodos* is derived from a Greek word meaning "to walk together." The Synod of Bishops is like a road followed by the Bishop of Rome together with the representatives of the episcopate.

Analogies can be found in the Roman synods convened in antiquity by the sovereign pontiffs to examine the serious problems of the time, and in the CONSISTORY, which in medieval times fulfilled the function of consultative assembly to the pope. But the Synod of Bishops is new, having been forged in the atmosphere of the second Vatican council. Some of the propositions sent out during the ante-preparatory phase of VATICAN II suggested the creation of a new central organ of the Church that, alongside the Roman pontiff, would represent the episcopate. This idea can be found in the conciliar debates. It took shape in the schema sent in April 1963 to all the bishops by the secretary of state. PAUL VI took up the project in his turn, in two interventions, before the Roman Curia (allocution, 21 September 1963) and at the opening of the second session of the council (speech, 20 September 1963), in which he wished "in the case of certain questions, to associate representatives of the episcopate with the supreme head of the Church for the study and responsibility of the ecclesiastical government."

At the end of the second session, Paul VI indicated that it would be a task in the postconciliar period to determine how the new organism would function (speech, 4 December 1963). He returned to the question at the close of the third session (speech, 21 November 1964) and, even more explicitly, at the opening of the work of the fourth session (speech, 14 September 1965). The very next day, when agreement was nearly unanimous and a conciliar document had been drawn up (decree *Christus Dominus* no. 5), Paul VI created the Synod of Bishops (*motu proprio Apostolica sollicitudo*, 15 September 1965) as a "permanent council of bishops for the universal Church, subject directly and immediately to Our authority."

It is from this *motu proprio* that the definition of canon 342 of the Code of Canon Law derives: "The Synod of Bishops is that group of bishops who have been chosen from different regions of the world and who meet at stated times to foster a closer unity between the Roman Pontiff and the bishops, to assist the Roman Pontiff with their counsel in safeguarding and increasing faith and morals and in preserving and strengthening ecclesiastical discipline, and to consider questions concerning the Church's activity in the world." This shows the importance attributed to the new body.

The general regulation of the synod, the *Ordo Synodi Episcoporum celebrandae*, was published on 8 December 1966, and the *Ordo Synodi Episcoporum celebrandae recognitus et auctus* on 24 June 1969. In the meantime, Paul VI had welcomed the express desire of the first extraordinary assembly of 1969 (Vote of 27 October, in *La Documentation catholique*, LXVI [1969], p. 1034) and set up the Council of the Secretary General of the Synod of Bishops (23 March 1970). This council is composed of 15 members, 12 of them elected by the synodal fathers and three designated by the Roman pontiff. Its mandate ceases at the beginning of a new general assembly (canon 348 § 1). The *Ordo* was increased and amended 20 August 1971 (*Ordo Synodi nullis additamentis perficitur*); unpublished explications were added 27 September 1974 (*Explicationes quaedam*).

According to the norms in force, the Synod of Bishops can be defined as being: (a) essentially consultative; (b) a central organ dependent on the Roman pontiff; (c) belonging to the hierarchical structure of the Church; and (d) not permanent. But canon 342 of the Code does not describe it as representative of the whole of the episcopate (*totius catholici episcopatus partes agens*) in contrast to the *motu proprio Apostolica sollicitudo* and the decree *Christus Dominus* no. 5. Consulted by the secretariat of the synod on the reasons for this omission, the commission responsible for revising the code replied that, in conformity with the dogmatic constitution *Lumen gentium* no. 23, the diocesan bishop does not have jurisdiction over other Churches, nor over the Church as a whole (reply, 20 February 1983).

The goals of the synod are to encourage union and close collaboration with the pope and the bishops; to provide direct information on the problems of the internal life of the Church and its action in the world; to facilitate agreement on the essential points of the doctrine and the life of the Church; to exchange opportune news; and to expresss opinions on the questions for which it was convened (canon 342).

The Synod of Bishops is directly subject to the authority of the pope, who, as *suprema potestas*, presides over it in person or through others and decides its conclusion (usually at the end of one month), as well as its transfer (from one location to another), suspension, and dissolution (canon 344). It is "a particularly fruitful expression and the very valuable instrument of episcopal collegiality, that is to say, of the peculiar responsibility of the bishops around the bishop of Rome" (JOHN PAUL II, speech, 30 April 1983), and it thus has a part in the central government of the Church.

The synod's function is a consultative one. It is not its duty to decide on the questions it is asked to debate, nor to issue decrees. But the Roman pontiff may decide to grant it deliberative power in certain cases. At that time, the pope must ratify the synod's decisions (canon 343). In reality, certain synods have drawn up synodal documents, promulgated with the authority of the Roman pontiff (for example, the three *relationes* on the episcopal collegiality of the extraordinary synod of 1969; documents on the priesthood and social justice, synod of 1971). This is explained by the fact that the Synod of Bishops is not a form of exercise of collegiality in the government of the Church, but a collaboration of the Catholic episcopate in the pope's primatial function of the government of the universal Church. Moreover, such is the interpretation of its function given by the preparatory conciliar commission of the decree Christus Dominus. It is a peculiarly intense moment of communication among the bishops and between the bishops and the head of the Church. In other words, the synod is an instrument of collegiality and a powerful factor of communion to an extent different from an ecumenical council. The extent to which collegiality and communion are realized at a synod depends on the manner in which the pastors of the local Churches express their views of it. The Roman pontiff is not bound by the deliberations of the synod; for instance, on the occasion of the synod of 1974, he corrected and even refuted certain of its conclusions.

The Roman pontiff convenes the synod wherever it seems to him to be opportune. He decides on the questions to be dealt with as well as the order of the day, ratifies the choice of members to be elected and the regulation of the synod, and at times presides in person over the sessions.

The assemblies are of two types. "General" assemblies, which deal with questions directly concerning the general good of the Church, are subdivided into ordinary assemblies (every three years) and extraordinary assemblies, according to the number of participants. "Special"

assemblies study questions concerning one or several regions (such as the Synod of Bishops convened in Lebanon for 1994); the special assembly must absorb the "particular" assembly, such as the synod of Netherlands bishops of January 1980.

Those participating in the ordinary general session (canon 346 § 1) are as follows (1) for the Eastern Catholic Churches, patriarchs, major archbishops, and metropolitans who are not part of the patriarchates; (2) bishops elected by their own national bishops' conferences or their equivalents, according to the proportions of one bishop for any conference that includes not more than 25 members, two for the conferences not exceeding 50 members, three for those whose members do not exceed 100, and four for those with more than 100 members (but only the president of the conference participates in an extraordinary assembly); (3) 10 religious representing the institutes of clerical life, elected by the union of the major superiors; (4) the cardinals heading the dicasteries of the Roman Curia, when the general assembly is ordinary; and (5) a certain number of representatives amounting to 15 percent of the total number which the Holy Father may add, who are "members" of pontifical appointment. Some bishops are normally appointed who are not part of a conference: Oriental bishops outside their patriarchates and without a metropolis, or bishops and ecclesiastics expert in the subjects to be debated, and others for similar reasons. All members are bound to pronounce the profession of faith (canon 833, § 1).

The extraordinary assembly consists of the cardinals who head the Roman dicasteries, the presidents of the conferences of bishops, and three religious elected under the same conditions as for the ordinary assembly. The special assembly is composed of the representatives of the conferences of bishops concerned, two elected religious, the presidents of the interested Roman dicasteries, and, if need arises, members nominated by the pope.

For each session, the pope appoints president delegates (normally three) and a special secretary. There may be as many special secretaries as there are particular subjects to debate (canon 348 § 2). For the duration of the session, a legal commission is created composed of three members nominated by the Roman pontiff. Study commissions of 12 members may also be set up.

Since the synod of 1983, an antepreparatory document, known as the *lineamenta*, has been sent to the bishops' conferences to inform them of the future work of the synodal assembly. Later, the bishops from around the world receive the document of work, or *instrumentum laboris*, written by the secretariat of the synod based on the observations and desires of the conference.

The first synod approved the principles guiding the reform of the Code and dealt with atheism, liturgical reform, and mixed marriages (29 September–29 October

1967); the second (30 September–6 November 1971) covered the ministerial priesthood and justice in the world; the third (27 September–26 October 1974) covered evangelization; the fourth (30 September–29 October 1977), catechesis; the fifth (26 September–25 October 1980), the functions of the Christian family in the world of today; and the sixth (29 September–29 October 1983), reconciliation and penitence in the Church's mission. Recent synods have included the Tenth Ordinary Assembly on Ministry of Bishops (2001), Special Assembly for America (1997), Special Assembly for Asia (1998), Special Assembly for Oceania (1998), and Second Assembly for Europe (1999).

Extraordinary synods took place in 1969 (11–27 October) on the episcopate, collegiality, the pope, Rome and the local Churches; and in 1985 (24 November–8 December) on the occasion of the 20th anniversary of the closing of Vatican II. Because of this, the seventh ordinary assembly was carried forward to 1987 (1–30 October) and dealt with the vocation and mission of the laity in the Church and in the world, 20 years after Vatican II. The eighth (30 September–27 October 1990) covered the training of priests. The ninth assembly was convened for 1994, on the theme of "the consecrated life and its role in the Church and in the world."

John Paul II convened several special synods: one for the bishops of Europe, which was held in Rome in 1991 (28 November–14 December); another for the whole of Africa, convened for 6 January 1993; and a third for the bishops of Lebanon.

Since 1974, the synod has been prolonged under the form of a post-synodal pontifical exhortation, which was based on the proposals of the Fathers and, since 1980, written at the express request of John Paul II by the council of the secretariat of the synod: *Evangelii nuntiandi* (8 December 1975); *Catechesi tradendae* (16 October 1979); *Familiaris consortio* (22 November 1981); *Reconciliatio et paenitentia* (2 December 1984); *Christifideles laici* (30 December 1988); *Pastores dabo vobis* (25 March 1992).

The norms governing the ecumenical council in case of vacancy of the Apostolic See also apply to the synod (canon 347 § 2).

Dominique Le Tourneau

Bibliography

Antón, A. "Verso una collegialità più effetiva nel Sinodo dei vescovi," *La Rivista del clero italiano*, 64 (1983), 290–302; 482–98; 562–76.

Arrieta, J. J. *El sínodo de los Obispos*, Pamplona, 1987.

Bertrams, W. "Motu proprio Apostolica Sollicitudo (15/9/65): Synodus Episcoporum pro universa Ecclesia constituitur," *Periodica de re morali, canonica, liturgica*, 55 (1966), 108–32; "De Synodi Episcoporum potestate cooperandi in exercitio potestatis primatialis," *Periodica de re morali, canonica, liturgica*, 57 (1968), 528–49.

Caprile, G. *Il Sinodo dei Vescovi*, 1967, Rome (and the later volumes, for each synodal session).

Colella, P. "Colegialità episcopale e Sinodo dei Vescovi," *La Chiesa dopo il Concilio: Atti del Congresso Internazionale di Diritto Canonico (Roma 14–19.1.1970)*, Rome, 1972, 333–50.

Collective, *La Synodalité: La participation au gouvernement de l'Église. Actes du VIIe Congrès international de droit canonique*, Paris, 1992.

Congar, Y. M. J. "Synode épiscopal, primauté et collegialité épiscopale," *Ministère et Communion ecclésiale*, Paris, 1971, 187–227.

Delhaye, P. "L'Épiscopat et sa représentation d'après les textes juridiques du Synode," *Episcopale Munus: Recueil d'études sur le ministère épiscopal offertes en hommage à Son Excellence Mgr J. Gijsen*, Assen, 1982, 100–11.

d'Onorio, J. B. *Le Pape et le gouvernement de l'Église*, Paris, 1992, 402–16.

Fagiolo, V. "Il synodus episcoporum: origine, natura, stuttura, compiti," *La collegialità episcopale per il future della Chiesa*, Florence, 1969, 3–43.

Fernández, A. "El Sínodo de los Obispos y la colegialidad episcopal," *Scripta Theologica*, I (1969), 403–44.

Foley, D. *The Synod of Bishops: Its Canonical Structure and Procedures*, Washington, 1973.

Fürst, C. G. "Die Bischofssynode," *Handbuch des katholischen Kirchenrechts*, Regensburg, 1983, 272–7.

Johnson, J. G. "The Synod of Bishops: An Exploration of its Nature and Function," *Studia Canonica* 20 (1986), 275–318.

Laurentin, R. *Le Synode permanent: Naissance et avenir*, Paris, 1970; "Paul VI et l'après-concile, le Synode des évêques," *Paul VI et la modernité dans l'Église. Actes du colloque organisé par l'École française de Rome, 2–4 juin 1983*, Rome, 1984, 569–601.

Marcolino, V. "Origem do Sinodo dos Bispos," *Itinerarium* 17 (1971), 133–74.

Marranzini, A. "Sinodo dei vescovi e comunione ecclesiale," *Ecclesiologia e cultura moderna: Saggi teologici*, Naples, 1979, 1–34; "I Sinodi dei Vescovi, sevizio di unità dinamica nella vita della Chiesa," *Il concilio venti anni dopo*, Rome, 1984, 161–85.

Tomko, J. "Le Synode des évêques et la collégialité," *Studia Canonica* 18 (1984), 239–52; (ed.) *Sinodo dei vescovi: Natura, metodo, prospettive*, Vatican City, 1095.

Urru, A. "Istituti per l'esercizio della Collegialità e del Primato: Il Concilio Ecumenico e il Sinodo dei Vescovi," *Monitor Ecclesiasticus*, CXV (1990), 569–89.

Zizola, G. "Il Sinodo dei Vescovi," *Coscienza* 89 (1967), 242 ff.

Zurowski, M. "Synodus Episcoporum in quantum 'pars agens totius catholici episcopatus,'" *Periodica de re morali, canonica, liturgica*, 62 (1973), 375–91.

T

TAX / TITHE, CRUSADE. An exceptional imposition was placed upon church temporalities (revenues) to finance the CRUSADES. The belief was that clerics should contribute their part to this action involving the entire Christian world, to which the lay people contributed by fighting. Raised for the first time during the third crusade, "Saladin's Tithe"—not to be confused with the tithe paid *to* the clergy, even if the Latin word *decima* referred to both payments—was paid by the clerics to enable the temporal princes involved to finance the crusade. Very quickly, the crusade became a pretext for taxes that, supposedly permitting preparation for the crusade by a ruling applicable to various transactions in Europe, financed, in reality, the political policies and wars of Christian princes. A conflict arose between BONIFACE VIII and Philip the Fair, who wanted to collect the tax without the pope's agreement in order to make an example of the obligation of the clergy to contribute to the common costs of running the kingdom, but even before this no one was fooled by references to the crusade: this tax was a political concession made by the pope to the temporal princes. Most often the pope kept half of it for himself. This sharing guaranteed harmony between the pope and the sovereigns at the expense of the clergy. Similar levies followed one another throughout the 14th century, imposed on all western Christianity. Generally established for one year, they were sometimes set up in advance for two, three, or even six years. After the GREAT SCHISM in the west, this kind of tax would be dropped; other financial pressures then were weighing upon the clergy, who were more and more often required to contribute to the finances of temporal sovereigns in specified, but nonetheless oppressive, forms.

Jean Favier

Bibliography

Causse, B. *Église, finance et royauté: la floraison des décimes dans la France du Moyen Âge*, 2 vols., Paris, 1988.

Cazel, F. A. "The Tax of 1185 in Aid of the Holy Land," *Speculum*, 30 (1955), 385–92.

Constable, G. *Monastic Tithes from Their Origins to the Twelfth Century*, Cambridge, 1984.

Ladurie, S. L. R. *Tithe and Agrarian History from the Fourteenth to the Nineteenth Centuries*, trans. Burke, S., Cambridge, Paris, 1982.

TAXATION, PAPAL. See **Finances, Papal.**

TELEPHONE. The Vatican acquired its first telephone in 1886, when one was installed in the Apostolic Library. The technician responsible for the installation was a young Roman, Gian Battista Marzi, who set up a small telephone exchange with an automatic 10-figure numbering system, designed principally for internal calls. Use of the telephone took as long to become widespread in the Vatican as in civilian societies, where up to the end of WORLD WAR I it still had an air of strangeness and breeziness in social relations. Pope PIUS XI had a gold telephone at his disposal, which he did not use. In contrast, PIUS XII did not hesitate to make use of it, and Msgr. Montini (prosecretary of state), out of respect for the pope's person, would stand up to talk with him when he was called. (Pius XII did not personally answer the phone, which could result in surprises or misunderstandings.)

Today, the Vatican's switchboard is a modern system which has continually been improved from the time of JOHN XXIII and VATICAN II. The office telephones, however, tend to be old-fashioned. From Rome, one communicates with the Vatican by dialing the number 6982 to be connected to the switchboard, or else the number 6988 followed by the extension of the desired party. The phone system as a whole is under the care of religious of the Society of St. Paul, the main switchboard being operated by nuns of that society. A series of secondary switchboards, also reached by dialing 6988, has for some years made it possible to relieve congestion on the network. This has been of particular benefit to the Secretariat of State, the VATICAN LIBRARY, the St. Callistus Palace, the Lateran University, and other institutions. Proof of the cohesion of the VATICAN CITY STATE, with its adjoining palaces and extraterritorial buildings, can be seen in the fact that it is possible to communicate from outside merely by dialing 6988. To reach the Vatican from abroad, however, one has first to dial the number for Italy (39) followed by the number for Rome (6).

Today one can buy a telephone directory for the Vatican City State, a remarkable information source of fewer than 200 pages. It has three sections. The first contains general references concerning communications—national and international codes, time equivalents and ways of finding these out, in particular as regards liturgical celebrations in the Roman basilicas. The second section is an alphabetical listing of the persons working in the Holy See, with the extensions at which they can be reached and, in certain cases, their home telephone numbers. A third section lists the extensions, in alphabetical order, of the offices and the employees attached to them. In theory, it is thus possible to place a direct call to the home of a cardinal of the CURIA whose number is provided—for example, the cardinal secretary of state. In practice, however, the dicastery heads who agree to this listing are protected more or less permanently by the intermediary of a third person. Others request that their telephone numbers remain secret because they often answer the telephone themselves.

Philippe Levillain

Bibliography

Elenco telefonico, Vatican City.

TELESPHORUS. *(d. ca. 136). Elected Pope ca. 125. Saint.*

The seventh successor of Peter, Telesphorus was chosen as bishop of Rome on the death of SIXTUS I. Little is known of his pontificate. It is said to have lasted 11 years, but, although EUSEBIUS claims that he was martyred in the first year of the reign of Antoninus Pius (138–9), it is safer to place his pontificate from 125 to 136, rather than from 128 to 139. The *LIBER PONTIFICALIS* says he was of Greek origin, adding, quite anachronistically, that he was an anchorite. He is supposed to have decreed the singing of the Gloria at the Christmas midnight mass and at daily mass. Tradition, coming down to us from Irenaeus and Eusebius of Caesarea, makes him the first bishop of Rome, after Peter, to have suffered martyrdom, but historical evidence for this is lacking. He is also said to have been buried in the Vatican close to Peter, but again this is unattested. His feast is 5 January.

Jean-Pierre Martin

Bibliography

Amann, E. *DTC*, Paris, 1946, XV, 1, 82.
Eusebius, *HE*, IV, 5, 5; 10; V, 6, 4; 24, 14.
Irenaeus, *Adv. Haeres.*, III, 3, 3.
Weltin, E. G. *NCE*, New York, 1967, XIII, 982.

THEOCRACY, PAPAL, MIDDLE AGES. The idea of a Christian empire, as Constantine envisaged it, allotted the papacy its place in the organization of the world at that time. The Church looked after spiritual matters, the pope being guarantor of faith and morals, but it was the council, headed by the emperor, that had the supreme magisterium in matters of dogma. The pontifical power was sacramental and disciplinary.

Another concept was developed in the 5th century by St. Augustine (354–430) in his *City of God*. For the bishop of Hippo, Christianity had turned the social order on its head by finally setting up a parallelism between the Heavenly City, which is essentially supernatural, and the Earthly City, whose organization is within time and episodic like that of state temporal powers, but whose very existence is one of the givens of creation. The Earthly City has no reality save in relation to and in light of the Heavenly City. The Church, therefore, preexisted the princes who rule the world below. It has by its nature power over temporal societies, which exist for the ultimate goal of leading humanity to salvation. It is not merely a question of the superiority of the spiritual power over the temporal, but of an essential inclusion of the temporal power in the City of God. For St. Augustine, the two powers are distinct.

Pope GELASIUS (492–6) went further. He conceived a dual subordination: to the pope in spiritual matters, but to kings in temporal ones. The natural State, in this view, has no reason for being other than to promote salvation. The social organization that underlies temporal power loses its importance in the face of the concept of heavenly organization, which relegates to the background kings whose power is merely an earthly convention.

Such theories barely outlasted the breakup of the Roman Empire. In Byzantium the two powers, spiritual and temporal, continued their rivalry. In the West, spiritual authority was in practice wielded by national or provincial councils, usually dominated by kings. The Carolingian Empire represented an explicit contradiction of Augustinianism. Here spiritual power was subordinate to an imperial power which the pope represented at the coronation but which he did not possess. It was the emperor who made decisions in matters of dogma and the liturgy, while the councils more or less ensured orthodoxy, discipline, and morality.

Nevertheless, the theologians adapted Augustine's ideas to the concrete situation prevalent in the West. Church and Empire were fused, temporal power having no other aim than to govern Christian people in their march toward salvation. What the Church was recognized to possess was a power of definition, in practice limited to questions of morality. The competence of the pope in temporal affairs had a foundation, however, *ratione peccati*. The power of Peter thus justified its strict qualification: the "power of the keys." This power explains the intervention of the Church—the bishops more than the pope—in secular confrontations. This can be seen in connection with the depositions of Louis the Pious (830 and 833) and Charles the Fat (887). At that time, the bishops' authority was enhanced because of the difficulties and divisions of royal power. They interpreted the uncertainties of political history as the will of God.

In the second half of the 11th century, the papacy once again took the upper hand. The Gregorian REFORM—which actually began well before the papacy of GREGORY VII, after whom it was named—was a reaction against secular control over the Church and the local churches and against the disciplinary and moral consequences of that control. Combining the work of the provincial councils and that of the agents of pontifical power—the legates—with the new network of submission to the papacy represented by the Cluniac order, the reform began by ensuring the independence of the spiritual. Next, the reform saw to it that the pope's spiritual power could have some control over purely temporal affairs. In 1059, a decree of NICHOLAS II definitely entrusted the choice of pope to a college of cardinals, originally the bishops of the province of Rome.

It was at that time that the doctrine of theocracy was formulated by Gregory VII (formerly the legate Hildebrand, pope from 1073 to 1085) and his circle of canonists, notably Deusdedit and Anselm de Baggio. Basically, this doctrine is the affirmation of the Church's spiritual and temporal freedom. This freedom implies an absolute break with every natural or contractual link with secular and feudal society. The pope even refused to accept the notion that the clergy receive and hold their temporal power from a secular authority. This so-called INVESTITURE CONTROVERSY was decisive in all respects. It meant the removal of secular control, deriving from the assignment to the churches of revenues still under the control of the original donors or founders, owing to their inclusion in the feudal system. The pope would therefore refuse the emperor—and, naturally, all other sovereigns—the right of conferring on bishops and abbots investiture by crozier and ring; those emblems of authority could only be bestowed by canonical consecration through the liturgy of unction and the laying on of hands. The emperor, however, prized this temporal investiture as the highest expression of the "eminent" and historic right of those who had founded and endowed churches, or were reputed by tradition to have done so.

The forms that ecclesiastical independence took were as follows: canonical election of bishops and abbots by their cathedral or conventual chapters; the conferring of minor benefices—archdeaconates, parishes, priories, and canonical prebendaries—by way of the ordinary patrons, bishops, and abbots; the judicial immunity of the clergy with regard to all secular jurisdiction; and the inviolability of ecclesiastical revenues. All the reform councils of the second half of the 11th century insisted on these demands. In this, they were supported by the papal legates with plenary powers to pronounce canonical sentences against the unwilling temporal lords and offending benefice-holders. The fight against simony and Nicholaism—the purchase of benefices and their shift toward patrimonialism in a clergy heedless of chastity—is only one disciplinary aspect of this pursuit of ecclesiastical independence.

Gregory VII assiduously pursued his declarations, at the same time attacking the emperor's prerogatives and those of the council. Only he, he declared, could use the imperial insignia, claim a universal authority, or publish canonical texts. Raising the tone of debate in the conflict over investitures, which touched on principles only when faced with imperial authority, certain canonists drew from the Church's responsibility for the salvation of the world a principle of submission, *ratione peccati*, of the temporal power to the spiritual. At the same time, the success of reform in the disciplinary and moral domains effectively ensured the primacy of the papacy over the local Churches.

The Christianization of secular society—an increase in oaths, blessing of knights' arms, pious and charitable clauses in wills—and the efficiency of the peacetime institutions imposed by the provincial councils also encouraged an extension of ecclesiastical jurisdiction that translated these principles into everyday life. This led to the pope's having moral control of the government of the states, a control illustrated by the canonical penalties imposed on many rulers because of their political behavior, not just their private life. Despite CANOSSA (1077), Emperor Henry IV was excommunicated and deposed in 1080. The Church was equally formidable when it relieved, or theatened to relieve, vassals of their oaths of loyalty toward their temporal lords. From there the pope went on to claim that he was the judge of the royal elections, inasmuch as they imparted a social function willed by God and subject to the magisterium of the Church.

Around the same time, URBAN II attempted to make the crusades a way for the papacy to exercise temporal government over the Christian people. Although he failed in his political plan, since his legate did not succeed in imposing his authority on the fund-raising operation and subsequently on the government of Latin Christianity in the East, the pope nevertheless succeeded in turning a pontifical initiative into a united Western action. At the end of the long conflict over the right of conferring investiture of the spiritual powers through that of the temporal, the papacy emerged the winner (concordat of WORMS, 1122).

The first refutations of these theocratic arguments came, naturally, from the imperial side. They were based on the Church's historically secondary role in the genesis, revival, and transmission of imperial power. Even as conceived in an Augustinian view of the Earthly City, it was God—not the pope—who had charged the emperor to lead the Christian people. References to the restoration of the Roman Empire went along the same lines. All this led to the absolute independence of temporal power. The two opposing doctrines were shaped and refined in the 12th century, helped by an intellectual renewal which, in Bologna and elsewhere, was reflected in a more attentive reading of the fundamental texts of the law of the State and canon law, as well as by a new political literature often proceeding from theologians and logicians. Honorius of Autun, Hugh of Saint-Victor, and St. Bernard reduced the temporal rulers to the role of executants in a Christian society that, because of its unity, seemed one with the Church. The temporal princes were merely administrators. The canonists labored to put order into the law (GRATIAN's Decree), as well as the rules of the new monasticisms (Cîteaux, Prémontré, Chartreuse, etc.). They also ensured the independence of the spiritual power and the management of new forms of social organization—particularly the growth of cities and economic functions—which had exploded the purely land-based framework in which the Church had set itself up materially in its early days.

The idea arose that, in the Earthly City, there were areas that the Church could not control. True, the pope might have the right to judge a posteriori, in cases where faith and morals were involved, but that did not entail the right to govern a priori. Thus many Bologna canonists, faced with highly visible political and social realities in the Italian towns in the 12th century, toned down the theories that had been worked out at a time when secular power and the Christian empire were merged.

In the 13th century, great canonists occupied the see of St. Peter and adapted to the conflicts of the time arguments that seemed to buttress the primacy of the Holy See. In this period when heresies proliferated, the defense of orthodoxy called for a new coordination of the dogmatic magisterium and the secular branch. The actions of rulers had therefore to be subordinated to the authority of the Church. INNOCENT III (1198–1216) convoked the council, arbitrated the rivalries for the imperial crown and that of England, and so began to impose papal authority. The fact that he established Church suzerainty, in both the West and the Latin East, over several kingdoms gave his theocratic pronouncements a distribution quite different from that of scholarly writings on the subject.

Now the pope claimed a *plenitudo potestatis* that respected the independence of a temporal power inferior to the spiritual but equally essential to society. However, he reserved to himself the right to intervene when political decisions, in his judgment, had consequences for spiritual life and public morality (decretal *Novit*, 1204). At this point, though no longer basing its claim on the heritage of St. Peter, the papacy likened itself to St. Peter by claiming a mission directly entrusted to it by Christ. Now the vicar of Christ, no longer of St. Peter, the pope therefore exercised his powers by virtue of the authority granted by God. This authority gave pontifical sovereignty its sway over both the spiritual domain and the temporal. The independence of kings thus concerned only the material ordering of the world. The empire itself was merely a chance institution, granted by the Church for the convenience of political life (Deliberatio of 1199; decretal *Venerabilem*, 1202). Their final mission, to lead people to their salvation, naturally placed emperor and princes within the jurisdiction of the Church.

Taking up Innocent III's arguments, GREGORY IX (1227–41) and INNOCENT IV (1243–54) were in not so good a position, since they were confronted with the claims and later the rebellion of Emperor Frederick II, Hohenstaufen. The emperor was trying to unify his territories, Germany and Sicily, and thereby entered into conflict in Italy with the pope's temporal power. The confrontation of theocracy and natural State was reflected on the ground by that between the Guelphs, who supported the pope, and the Ghibellines, champions of the emperor. It was no longer a matter of distinguishing the spiritual from the temporal. This was a political struggle, and the European princes now found themselves in the astonishing position of arbiters. Developing the theory of *plenitudo potestatis*, Innocent IV affirmed the pope's permanent authority over temporal governments, an authority which Innocent III had claimed only in cases of urgency or necessity. For Innocent IV, this authority was essential, even if the pope made use of it only for spiritual reasons—the *peccati ratione* argument was developed and would be again by the commentaries of Hostiensis (Henry da Susa) in his *Summa aurea*—to avoid disturbing the ordinary functioning of the Respublica. In short, spiritual and temporal were distinct, but the pope was above them both.

Coming to the support of the rise of the monarchies, university Aristotelianism gave this period an interest in the idea of the natural State. St. Thomas Aquinas, for his part, recognized that the State had an origin and a legitimacy linked to the natural and substantial needs of society. The two powers, spiritual and temporal, were therefore both derived from God. But, contrary to Aristotle, Aquinas joined the temporal with the divine, thus entrusting the spiritual mission of this unity to the authority of the vicar of Christ. Like his predecessors, Aquinas unfortunately left vague the realm of the spiritual. In practical terms, that left the pontifical power to define its own limits. The Great Interregnum (1250–73) and the fading of imperial power toward the end of the century, as well as the alliance of the king of France with the Guelph and Angevin party, all reduced the question of theocracy for a time to scholarly debates.

By launching the affair of the TITHE, BONIFACE VIII (1294–1303) in 1296 once again set forth theocracy as one of the factors at stake in the life of the states. Initially, this was a reply to Philip the Fair of France, who with the consent of particularly complaisant provincial councils had just ordered a tithe to be raised on the French clergy, without the prior consent of the pope. The bull *Clericis laicos* (24 February 1296) laid down the principles at the same time as it detailed the practical significance of the move. Essentially, it was a question of determining whether the clergy had to bear their share of the universal tithe, paying out of their own revenues—in other words, whether they belonged to the kingdom at the same time as they belonged to the Church. The pope subjected to his authority all fiscal levies on the clergy, which were regarded as a diminution of the churches. When the king responded by forbidding all exports of monies, which directly affected the production of the annates garnered for the pope on the ecclesiastical benefices in the kingdom, Boniface VIII made his pronouncements more dogmatic. With the bull *Ineffabilis amor* (20 Septembr 1296), he recalled the superiority of spiritual authority and the responsibility of ecclesiastical independence entrusted to St. Peter's successor. Neither adversary at the time had the means to start a war, the pope being heavily engaged in Italy and the king of France in Flanders, and so a compromise was reached (bulls *Romana mater Ecclesia* and *Etsi de statu*, 7 February and 31 July 1297). The king could, in case of need, forestall pontifical agreement and would be the judge of this need.

The principle was sound, but it was a dead letter. A more pressing matter led to the struggle being resumed in 1302. The case of the bishop of Pamiers, Bernard Saisset, hounded by royal justice for treason, provided the pope with the opportunity to proclaim his supreme jurisdiction over the spiritual and the temporal and to put the king explicitly under that jurisdiction (bull *Ausculta fili*, 4 December 1301). Philip the Fair forbade the French clergy to go to Rome for a council actually convoked against him; Boniface VIII responded with the strongest definition of theocracy ever formulated by popes or doctors, in the bull *Unam Sanctam* (18 November 1302). The Church was one, and she was the City of God on earth. She had but one head, the vicar of Christ, and as such, the pope was master and judge of temporal princes. The independence of the temporal power would be heretical because it would imply a divided Church. With *Unam sanctam*, political Augustinianism went beyond the competence of the Church *ratione peccati* to give the *plenitudo potestatis* its supreme expression: government of the world by the clergy, who are themselves subject exclusively and in all things to the pope.

The replies to these arguments were diverse. In the 1240s, Frederick II's jurists turned to the tripartite division of society inspired by St. Augustine and developed in the 11th century by Adalberon of Laon and Gerard of Cambrai. The priest, the soldier, and the laborer each have their distinct places in the divine plan. Those who pray, therefore, have no authority over those who govern. As heir of the Donation of Constantine—a document forged in the 8th century to justify the territorial claims of the pope in Italy—the pope could not wear the imperial crown, while temporal power came from the emperor. As Jourdain of Osnabrück and Alexander of Roes wrote in the second half of the 13th century, the empire being universal by vocation, it is by nature independent.

The Aristotelians and French jurists referred to natural law. Christ never exercised any earthly power (*Dialogue of the Clerk and the Knight*, 1296). Before there were clerics, there were kings, affirmed jurists led by the chancellor Pierre Flote. The tone hardened: Christ died for all men; it was not only the clergy he set free. The liberties of the clergy are peculiar to them and granted, rather than inalienable.

The affair ended in a show of force in which William de Nogaret, breaking with Flote's politics, set up the king of France as a defender of the Church against an unworthy pope. The mention of the pope before the coming council, the tumult of Agnani—which was chiefly the result of the factional fights in the Roman region—and the death of Boniface VIII left CLEMENT V and his successors faced with the threat of a legal process against the memory of their predecessor, and later with the serious dissension of the Franciscan order (the affair of the Spirituals). They were incapable of taking up the matter of theocratic claims. The conflicts of the papacy with Henry VII of Luxemburg and then with Louis of Bavaria caused the resurfacing of the imperialist and pontifical argument (bulls *Romani principes* and *Pastoralis cura*, 1312). The *Defensor pacis*, written in 1324 by two members of the University of Paris, Marsilius of Padua and Jean de Jandum, for Emperor Louis of Bavaria, defined the State as a natural reality. It also formulated the thesis of the superiority of the council over the pope, which would be the guiding thread of reform literature up to the councils of Constance and Basel. The latter would benefit from the emergence of a new dogmatic and political authority, in the Church but outside the established hierarchy: that of the university men. As for the popes, their conflict with the temporal powers now went beyond the political order and took the form of tests of strength. After 1378 the roles would be reversed, with the popes seeking the alliance and support of the princes. The

Pragmatic Sanction of 1438 and the various concordats of the second half of the 15th century would be a negation of theocracy.

Jean Favier

Bibliography

Pacau, M. *La Theocratie: l'Église et le pouvoir au Moyen Age*, Paris, 1989 (Bibliothèque d'histoire du christianisme, XX).

Ullmann, W. *The Papacy and Political Ideas in the Middle Ages*, London, 1976.

[THEODERIC]. *(d. 1102) Antipope, September 1100–January 1101.*

Little is known about Theoderic. In 1084 he was cardinal-deacon of St. Mary's in the Via Lata. He was one of the chief supporters of the antipope CLEMENT III (Guibert of Ravenna), who made him cardinal-bishop of Albano—not of Santa Rufina. In 1098 he headed a legation to Germany. When Clement III died 8 September 1100 at Città Castellana, Guibert's partisans chose the nighttime to elect, consecrate, and enthrone Theoderic in St. Peter's of Rome (September 1100). Emperor Henry V did not take part in the ceremony. When Theoderic went to meet the emperor 105 days after the election, supporters of PASCHAL II seized him (probably in January 1101) and brought him to Rome. Held at the monastery of the Trinity at La Cava, in Apulia (a territory under Norman sovereignty), he ended his days in 1102, a date attested by a funerary slab.

Georg Schwager

Bibliography

JL, 1, 772, 345.

LP, 2.298.

Hüls, R. *Kardinale, Klerus und Kirchen Roms 1049–1130*, Tübingen, 1977, 92.

Servatus, C. *Paschalis II (1109–1118)*, Stuttgart, 1979, 69–72, 339.

[THEODORE]. *(b. Rome, ?, d. ?). Antipope in 687.*

This Roman priest was on two occasions an unlucky candidate for the papacy put forward by the Roman militia. On the death of John V (2 August 686), two factions formed: the clergy, which supported the candidature of the archpriest Peter, and a rival group—evidently made up of all the civil and military chiefs, at a time when the heads of the army were also those of the administration—who chose the priest Theodore. All that is known of him is that he was a priest of the Church of Rome, and that he may have been part of a Roman delegation sent to the council of Constantinople (680–1). As neither group was willing to yield, the choice fell on CONON (21 October 687), whose election was confirmed by the exarch of Ravenna.

Promoted archpriest by Conon, Theodore was once again the candidate of the militia after the death of that pope (21 September 687). His rival Peter having apparently died in the interim, the archdeacon Paschal was put forward as candidate. The result was the same as before. The Roman *populus*—that is, the leaders of the clergy and the civil and military administration—remained divided, so a third man was chosen—Sergius. Theodore, who had settled in part of the Lateran, gave up without resistance. Although he had not received the exarch's confirmation, he was, mistakenly, considered an antipope. This illustrates the ambiguity of this concept for historians.

Jean Durliat

Bibliography

JW, I, 243–44.

LP, I, 368, 371–72.

Bertolini, O. *Roma di fronte a Bisanzio e ai Longobardi*, Bologna, 1971, 329–33.

THEODORE I. *(b. Greece, ?, d. Rome, 14 May 649). Ordained pope on 24 November 642. Buried in St. Peter's, Rome.*

In an apparent paradox, this first Byzantine pope, who was almost certainly a member of the Byzantine clergy, strongly accentuated the division between Rome and Constantinople. Theodore was the son of a "bishop"—that is, a patriarch—of Jerusalem. His accession to the Western patriarchate has received a variety of interpretations. Some have imagined that the Roman clergy chose a *homo novus* skilled in Eastern theological debate and fluent in Greek, while others have seen the choice as a sign of the power of Eastern refugees, who were now able to set one of their own in the see of Peter. In fact, the growth of monothelitism, complicated by controversies over the succession after Heraclius's death (640) and the hostility of the Eastern Churches toward the patriarchate of Constantinople, called for a leader who was perfectly familiar with the concepts and power struggles in the East.

In 642, the situation was one of utter confusion. After the regent Martina had been eliminated, the patriarch Pyrrhus, a versatile schemer, had just been deposed in favor of Paul, who drew up an edict (*typos*) whereby the emperor forbade all theological discussion so as to avoid compromising the unity of the Empire. The Orientals, who chafed under imperial sway—especially that of a patriarch with no apostolic foundation—still continued their campaign against monothelitism, both in the name of monophysitism and in the name of what the council in Trullo (680–1) would proclaim as orthodoxy. The latter cause found its most ardent propagandist in Maximus the Confessor, a nobleman with close ties to the imperial family who had cut short a career as a high civil servant to take monastic orders shortly before 618. In 632, he was already living in Carthage, whence he directed the opposition to the imperial theology, strengthened by his local position and his connections with the ruling class. In particular, he managed to rally Pyrrhus to orthodoxy and accompanied him to Rome, where the fallen patriarch solemnly abjured heresy, in 645 or 646; but when summoned to Ravenna by the exarch, he returned to his original beliefs.

In 646 the pope, with Maximus's staunch support, received the backing of provincial synods organized by all the metropolitans of Byzantine Africa. One year before the first Saracen raid on the region, this part of the Byzantine Empire declared its solidarity with the patriarch against a sovereign who was clearly incapable of ensuring its safety. We do not know what would have ensued had Theodore lived longer.

At that time, the situation in Italy was so confused that no one seemed able to impose order, which partly explains the bitterness of the theological quarrels. The cartulary Maurice, after first following the exarch, rebelled against him, rousing the towns and fortified strongholds (castra) of Latium before he was captured and put to death. The episode made it clear that the Lombards were sufficiently docile that the Byzantine forces were able to start a civil war. Above all, the official biographer, who relates the events with a multitude of detail, makes no mention of any intervention on the part of the pope. He was a religious authority as well as a powerful lawgiver, but not yet a figure powerful enough to arouse the people in favor of one or the other camp. Likewise, the lack of any reference to relations with the West over a pontificate of nearly seven years—whereas John IV had been solicited on all sides in only two years—is a reminder that rulers turned to the pope when some internal need made his arbitration desirable; however, he was helpless to intervene on his own initiative. Despite growing prestige among his dependents and an ever-increasing boldness toward his sovereign, the Western patriarch remained the Byzantine bishop of the Byzantine city of Rome.

Jean Durliat

Bibliography

JW, I, 228–30; 2, 698.
LP, 331–35.
PL, 87, 71–102.
Bertolini, O. Roma di fronte a Bisanzio e ai Longobardi, Bologna, 1971, 329–33.

THEODORE II. (d. ca. December 897 or January 898). Elected pope at the beginning of December 897.

Of Roman origin, Theodore II was the son of Photios and brother of the bishop Theodosius. He was ordained priest by Stephen V and elected pope around the beginning of December 897, most likely because of the support of FORMOSUS's supporters. His pontificate, which lasted only 20 days, was marked almost exclusively by the rehabilitation of Formosus. Theodore annulled the "cadaver synod" which STEPHEN VI had organized, and he caused the ecclesiastics ordained by Formosus to be reinvested with their rights. Aside from the information provided by Auxilius, we can cite in this connection chapter 4 of a capitulary published in Ravenna in 898. Theodore had Formosus's body returned to Rome, giving it full honors before its burial at St. Peter's. The source mentioning Theodore's death leaves the date unclear and gives no precise indication of where he was buried.

Klaus Herbers

Bibliography

JL, I, 441.
LP, 2, 231.
MGH, Capit. II, 124–26.
Auxilius of Naples, ed. PL 129, 1073–1102, E. Dümmler, Auxilius und Vulgarius, Leipzig, 1866.
Hartmann, W. Die Synoden der Karolingerzeit im Frankenreich und in Italien, Paderborn, 1989 (Konziliengeschichte Reihe A, Darstellungen, 390).
Scholz, S. Transmigration und Translation: Studien zum Bistumswechsel des Bischöfe von der Spätantike bis zum Hohen Mittelalter, Cologne-Weimar-Vienna, 1992 (Kölner Historische Abhandlungen 37), 225.
Zimmerman, H. Papstabsetzungen des Mittelalters, Graz-Vienna-Cologne, 1968, 59–60.

THIRD ROME (MOSCOW). The student of Russian history cannot fail to wonder at the lasting preoccupation with eschatology expressed by the idea of the "Third Rome," as found in the letter from the monk Philoteus to Basil III: "It is fitting, Tsar, that you maintain the kingdom in the fear of God. . . . Do not go, Tsar, against the commandment of your ancestors, Constantine the Blessed, St. Vladimir, the great Iaroslav chosen of God, and the other Blessed Saints of the same family whence you yourself came. Hearken, and remember, most pious Tsar, that all the Christian kingdoms are met in your kingdom; that two Romes have fallen, but that the third is still standing and that there cannot be a fourth; your Christian kingdom will be replaced by no other" (V. Malinin, Starets Eleazarova monastyria Filofei i ego poslaniia, Kiev, 1901, p. 49). Or again: "Now, the Holy Church apostolic is the Church of the new and third

Rome—the Church of your all-powerful kingdom—which, more brilliant than the sun, causes the orthodox Christian faith to shine forth to the ends of the universe. May your sovereignty, most pious Tsar, know that all the states of orthodox Christian faith are met in your kingdom: you alone are Tsar for the Christians here below" (*ibid.*).

Even before the idea of a third Rome arose, it was the conviction of Russian holiness that prevailed and legitimized the theme of "Holy Russia." Two legends combined to give rise to this theme. The first, which is unverifiable, is the legend of the coming of the apostle Andrew to what would become Russian soil; this fable, through the person of St. Andrew, is linked to the apostles and Pentecost. The second legend, even less plausible, has to do with Kitezh, the city of the saints, which sank to the bottom of a lake to escape the hordes of the Khan Batu—that is, evil.

What were the paths that led from that mysterious city or from holy Russia to the third Rome? What bonds linked holy Russia to the Christian world of the West? Or was Russia alien to that world, as a solidly established tradition would have it? In fact, to understand how holy Russia became the third Rome, we must look at the historical circumstances, first internal, then external.

The Mongol yoke—said to have caused the mysterious city of Kitezh to vanish—was finally shattered in the 16th century. The union of Church and State was strong, and the sovereign claimed to be the guardian of the true faith. That is what Ivan IV, known as the Terrible, would proclaim at the council of the Hundred Chapters.

Yet beyond this Russia freed from the Mongol yoke—in Byzantium, from which Russian Christianity derived—the reverse was happening. Turkish domination, established in 1453, handed over to Islam the former Russian possessions in Byzantium. Therefore Russia, now victorious over Islam, appeared as the new center of the true faith. Thus there came to be accepted the idea of a holy Russia, refuge and guardian of the Christian world, in contrast both to a Christianity in retreat in the old Byzantine lands and to the "schismatic" Christianity of western Europe. Thenceforth, the bonds between Church and State grew ever stronger in Russia, since the State was linked to the Church in the battle against the Antichrist. Moreover, these bonds had a personal aspect: the first sovereign of the Romanov dynasty, Tsar Michael, elected in 1613, was the son of the patriarch Philaret. The Old Believers, whom the reforms of the patriarch Nikon—encouraged by Tsar Alexis—caused to break away from the Church took up this bond between State and Church in their own fashion by identifying both tsar and Church with the Antichrist. But both the Russian Church and Avakkum's schismatic disciples proclaimed that, in principle, Church and State were inseparable on Russian soil.

To what extent were relations between God's realm and Caesar's in Russia different from the tradition of Roman Christianity? If there really were a confusion of the two domains, this would have lent the theme of the Third Rome a peculiar force. In fact, the Byzantine tradition from which Russian Christendom sprang was, like that of Rome, founded on the imperative, "Render unto Caesar the things that are Caesar's, and unto God the things that are God's." In Rome, however, the tradition of Roman law, with its respect for the human person, was combined with the mandate of the Church to heed the theory of the "two swords." The spiritual and temporal realms organizing human life, each one perfect in its order, were both required to respect each other and maintain a balance. Despite inevitable encroachments and conflicts, for centuries this balance molded history and thinking in the Christian West. In the Christian East, the practical choice was somewhat different, attempting to achieve harmony and solidarity of the spiritual and temporal powers according to Justinian's theory: "The Church and the State. . . flow from one source, the will of God. . . , and must be in perfect harmony." In the Byzantine tradition, there was a gradual shift in favor of the imperial power. Here the emperor appeared as the "living law," the image of the "heavenly monarchy," and the hold of the temporal power over the Church grew ever stronger. There is no doubt that Russia was heir to that tradition.

Hélène Carrère d'Encausse

Bibliography

Dupuy, A. *La Diplomatie du Saint-Siège après le IIe Concile du Vatican*, Paris, 1980.

Milcent, E. *A l'est du Vatican*, Paris, 1980.

Morozzo della Rocca, P. "Santa Sede e Russia rivoluzionaria," in G. Rumi (ed.), *Benedetto XV e la pace—1918*, Brescia, 1990, 151–69.

Pollakov, L. *Moscou, troisième Rome*, Paris, 1989.

Riccardi, A. *Il Vaticano e Mosca*, Bari, 1992.

Stehle, H. *Die Ostpolitik des Vatikans, 1917–75*, Zürich, 1975.

Wenger, A. *Rome et Moscou 1900–1950*, Paris, 1987.

Winter, E. *Die Sowjetunion und der Vatikan*, Berlin, 1971.

Zemov, N. *Moscow: The Third Rome*, London, New York, 1982.

TIARA. In the tradition of the Roman Catholic Church, the tiara and keys signify the supreme pontificate. The use of the keys was abandoned long ago, while that of the tiara had over time become theoretical as it lost touch with people's awareness of its symbolism. Nevertheless, from the viewpoint of iconography, both tiara and keys are still universally recognized signs. Heraldry also keeps alive the image of the tiara, an attribute that is the sovereign pontiff's alone and an emblem of his supreme function in the Church, that of universal bishop and "high priest" of the New Alliance.

Although the use of the modern tiara, or triple crown, was suspended if not abolished from the time of PAUL VI's accession (1963), the emblem, which still appears on the papal seal and the heading of papal documents, remains the specific symbol of the Petrine function. In conformity with the spirit of VATICAN II, Paul VI abandoned the use of the tiara or triple crown, the illustrious, symbolic headdress that had become the exclusive emblem of a temporal power (the Papal States) and political powers (over princes and peoples). Each of these powers had become ever more illusory and appeared too closely tied to a recent past (16th–19th century) that had nothing to do with the modern age. The history of the modern tiara (mid-14th–mid-20th century) is a confused one; the prototype (probably from the 7th century) was itself repeatedly the victim of false claims that later were made concrete—chiefly the "interventions" of INNOCENT III and BONIFACE VIII.

The classic triple crown was a stiff tiara, at first conical, then bulbous in form, and finally balloon-shaped. It was worn by the popes on the day of their *possesso* (later, coronation) and came to replace definitively the former *mitra papalis*, becoming fixed in form at the end of the 14th century. Despite slight variations in the shape (the result of artistic fashion) and ornamentation (depending on the taste for ostentation), and despite three major aberrations—the "mad" triple crown of Paul II (c. 1465), the "atypical" one of Julius II (1503), and the "wretched" one of Pius VII (1800)—the pontifical triple crown was an object of fixed structure. Paul VI's tiara was a timid attempt to return to the medieval tiara, at least from a stylistic point of view. This article is restricted to a history of the conical tiara, from the "Greek" to the "French" popes, and to imagining the original form of the Roman pontiffs' triple crown.

In Eastern antiquity and up to the first centuries of Christianity, *tiara* was the generic name given to a group of divine, royal, priestly, and king-priestly headdresses. Depending on period and culture, the term covered a variety of dissimilar headdresses which had a family likeness, although they served a variety of functions and persons: Asiatic gods and kings; Oriental—proto-Semitic, for the most part—priests and high priests, especially Old Testament ones from the time of the Mosaic Revelation; and so on. In the history of the early Church, the word *tiara*, which means "helmet" or "cap," was applied to certain miters. In the first centuries, the word "miter" (*mitra*) designated a wide range of religious headdresses, from that of the Virgin Mary, consecrated matrons, and young girls, to that of the monks, priests, and bishops. In the medieval West, the bishop's miter, which was flexible

and bound with a rigid band, competed with the stiff miter up to around 1100.

The term "tiara" (*thyara, thiara,* or *tiara*) appeared late in Rome (1099), where it signified the *mitra papalis*. (Before the 12th or 13th century, there was no real distinction between the liturgical headdress and the civil one.) The choice of the term certainly did not stem from any wish to give the pope a crown of the Asiatic type or a true temporal king's crown. "Tiara" was simply the word that St. Jerome used, in the Vulgate, for the miter of Aaron and his successors, the high priests of Israel. It was chosen in the 12th century because of its strong echoes of archaic and Old Testament times, at a period when the Church no longer shunned its Hebrew roots but, on the contrary, was rediscovering them and adapting their symbols. This was the period when Rome was, in a novel way, affirming its dominant position in Catholicism and in relation to the world. Still, it was not until the beginning of the 14th century that the word "tiara" began to take hold as the name for the new pontifical triple crown.

The name should not be thought to denote a stable form of the article, let alone a symbolic conception or fixed function. "Tiara" is merely a generic name for the special miter of the sovereign pontiff, and later—up to the present—for his royal-priestly triple crown. It is first necessary to define the terms, whose great flexibility and expressive variety have too often led historians into error, created inextricable confusion, and encouraged the fabrication of far-fetched theories. From one era to another, the same word might be used to designate articles that were diverse though akin, while sometimes the same article would have different names. Between the 8th and 14th centuries, the papal tiara would be known, successively, as *frigium, regnum,* even *corona,* finally taking on the name *triregnum.*

Apart from the philological oddity *camelaucum,* the most precise Roman term for the tiara from the 8th century on was *frigium.* In the false Donation of Constantine, an 8th-century Roman text, *frigium* designated one of the imperial pseudo-crowns which the emperor was said to have bestowed on St. Silvester. If the writer of this text used this word for the papal head-covering, it was probably because it had long been employed in Rome and therefore readers could not possibly confuse it with other contemporary official headdresses. Its last known use dates from around 1185, in the writing of a pontifical historiographer. Later, *frigium* definitively gave way to *regnum* and *corona,* often used together, which were replaced at the beginning of the 14th century by the term "triple crown" (*triregnum*). The word *regnum* seems to appear in the mid-11th century: after his election, the new pope made his way to the Lateran; before mounting on horseback in the forecourt of the Vatican basilica, he was acclaimed, while on his head was placed the *regnum quod ad similitudinem cassidis ex albo fit indumento*. Around 1100, Bruno da Segni reflected the schema set up by the Constititum Constantini: the pope wears the *regnum*, for the emperor once bestowed it on the pontiff Silvester.

It is virtually certain that the specific headdress of the bishop of Rome, "the bishop of the bishops," took on its tall, stiff form in the 7th century. In older times, it seems that the popes, the patriarchs of the West, followed Alexandrian usage and wore either a low, flexible tiara or the ancient Levitical miter, which was worn over a skull-cap and held to the forehead with a *circulus*. Such a head-dress was in fact found in 1607 in the tomb of Pope Leo the Great, who died in 461. Lacking explicit Roman sources, one can conjecture that the popes adopted this type of headdress from the 4th century, if not in apostolic times. Its Christian origin traces to the miter worn by the evangelist Mark, "the spiritual son of St. Peter" and prob-ably the founder of the Church of Alexandria. This miter was identical to that of the apostle James, the bishop of Jerusalem after Peter. This apostolic miter of Levitical tradition is still used in the East by the Coptic, Egyptian, Syrio-Malabar, and non-Catholic Armenian bishops, as it was by the Maronite bishops before the adoption of the Latin miter (in the 16th century), as well as certain Span-ish bishops (8th–9th centuries). It is related to the special headdress of the Russian Orthodox patriarch, the Western monastic cowls of Eastern origin, and even the canonial amices of medieval times. Both pre-Carolingian papal coins and the early series of pontifical portraits at St. Paul's Outside the Walls may show the early use of this Levitical-apostolic tiara.

It was not until the beginning of the 10th century that papal iconography first evidenced the use of the tiara-helmet, but its existence was noted at least two centuries earlier. In 708 or 710, Pope Constantine went to Byzan-tium wearing a headdress that distinguished him from the dignitaries of the court and to which the *Liber pontificalis* gave the bastard name *camelaucum*. In Rome, the first mention of the tiara-helmet occurs a half-century earlier, in the Donation of Constantine. Even though the icono-graphic and textual testimonies are not synchronous, they agree and are complementary. It appears that the typolog-ical substitution of the *mitra papalis* took place in the pe-riod immediately preceding, when the papal throne was occupied by a long line of popes from the Byzantine and Eastern region, perhaps between 619 and 741 or, more likely, between 624 and 708. Thus, at that time the head-dress changed in shape from a low, flexible tiara, drawn from the Levitical-apostolic tradition, to a high, stiff one, from the Jerusalem tradition—a mutation that conformed to a change in ecclesial sensibility.

Indeed, it was during the Carolingian and pre-Carolingian period, with St. Germain of Paris and St. Isidore of Seville, that the reticence—or even repug-nance—toward everything reminiscent of Christianity's Judaic origins fell away for good; in particular, many prelates sported miters just like those of their own mystic ancestors, Aaron and Melchizedek. At the same time, Western liturgists stressed the resemblance between Christian priestly vestments and ornaments and the sa-cred vestments of the Old Covenant. This closer reading of Scripture most likely encouraged the sovereign pon-tiffs to give their miters the distinctive tall, stiff shape in-spired by a contemporary Byzantine helmet used by the bishops of the Near East. If the figure of the bishop of Rome was often compared to that of Moses, from the 6th and 7th centuries it was the image of the high priest of Old Testament times that came to the fore. From now on, the image was that of Peter–Aaron, and it was logical that the pope should be given a headdress similar to his ideal model. Flavius Josephus points out that the tiara of the Jerusalem high priest differed from the miter of the simple Levites in its height and ornamentation.

It is interesting to note that, before a clear distinction was made in the 12th century between the papal tiara and the bishops' miters and their civil and liturgical usage was regulated, the two traditions clashed with each other. Large numbers of Exulet scrolls in Byzantine and post-Byzantine Italy up to the 12th century attest to the use by certain bishops of a miter-helmet similar to the contemporary papal tiara. Conversely, at the same time the flexible miter was found in southern and central Italy, which had considerable numbers of Eastern monks. It survived in Spain and southern France until around 1100. This was the period in the West when the various ancient forms of the bishop's miter disappeared. The field was left exclusively to the kind of miter that was divided, with two points in front, to which around 1200 a gusset was added to allow it to be folded.

The first pope to wear a true episcopal miter in Rome was almost certainly LEO IX (1049). He was a bishop in the Empire when he was appointed. Once enthroned, he gave up the old tiara, known outside Rome as *mitra ro-mana* to distinguish it from the other prelatic miters. The popes gradually adopted the new miter as a liturgical head-covering, while increasingly reserving the tradi-tional tiara to official use. Thus, the latter gradually came to serve as a mark of sovereignty. In Rome the two forms were frequently confused, even in the 15th century. But shortly before 1200, an exceptional theologian, liturgist, jurist, and historian came to the papal throne. INNOCENT III reaffirmed the Gregorian principles of the independence and universality of the Roman pontificate. On the sym-bolic plane, he decided to confer on the bishop of Rome an emblem that would be an unmistakable indication of the supremacy of the spiritual over all temporal powers. To the Ordines Romani there were then added the Prayers for the Coronation, which declared that although the pope is *rector omnium fidelium*, he is also *pater regnum*.

By wearing the tiara, henceforth distinct from the miter, the pope now presented himself as a super-king and endowed himself with two powers combined as one. This arbitrary act, conditioned by historical circumstances, thrust the ancient tiara into a symbolic domain where it did not belong. The change that this pope intended led naturally to the invention of the triple crown, a symbol of the regalian supremacy of the bishop of Rome. One can only admire the systematic rigor of the jurist's art applied to liturgical matters. From the bipolar system invented or fixed by Innocent III there arose a confusion of symbols that finally killed the *mitra papalis*. From the *regnum*, the sign of papal sovereignty, the symbolism extended to the *corona*, the sign of temporal sovereignty—the pope-king. We do not know whether Innocent III was the victim of his predecessors' errors, or whether he voluntarily surrounded the tiara with confused symbols to erect his system. His decision regarding the papal headdress reflects his general efforts to reinforce the Roman pontificate. He wanted to fix the symbolism, and therefore the use, of an emblem capable of illustrating at the same time the functions of *Pontifex maximus* and *Summus sacerdos*, and the supremacy of the spiritual power (the Church) over every form of temporal power.

In the middle of the 12th century, the old term *frigium* for the tiara was replaced by *regnum*, which from being an adjective became a noun expressing the superiority of the papal miter over the episcopal miters, emblems of an apostolic function at once common to pope and bishop but different. The tiara being henceforth likened to regalia, in the 13th century the tiara's gilded *circulus*, a simple band woven of gold, quite naturally became a royal crown. Still a modest circlet, it was adorned with a row of embroidered fleurons sewn on the white bonnet. Thus the funerary statue of Gregory X (ca. 1278, in the cathedral of Arezzo) shows a tiara that in place of a *circulus* has an embroidered decoration of a veritable crown whose pointed rays, each topped with a trefoil, imitate those adorning the metal crowns of contemporary kings.

The next stage, the metal crown set in the base of the bonnet, came with NICHOLAS III. About 15 paintings done over 20 years show this tiara: a tall omphaloid shape surmounted by an apex in the form of an acorn, a gilded crown, and a wide circlet with tall, pointed rays, each topped with a pearl. The cone was covered with white fabric with an esparto design and two, three, or four sewn bands, superimposed one above the other and decorated with a Greek key design. This tiara was used until around 1300; BONIFACE VIII wore it at the beginning of his pontificate. HONORIUS IV wore a tiara of similar type but lower, richer, and more massive. From the three-dimensional effect of his funerary gisant (ca. 1288, today at Sta. Maria in Aracoeli), one can see that this was now a tiara enchased in a veritable royal crown, a heavy metal diadem ornamented with large cabochons and rays of pearl.

Nicholas III's tiara was employed in 1294 at the coronation of Boniface VIII. It appeared again in 1299 on the latter pope's head when he announced the first holy year. But from the end of the Jubilee, the Caetani pope wore only his new tiara, the direct ancestor of the classic triple crown. This is the tiara that is shown on his gisant, created that same year by Arnolfo di Cambio. Given the personality of Boniface VIII, it is easy to understand how, in order to reinforce the new importance that Innocent had given the ancient papal headdress, he was able to conceive such an obviously royal *regnum* whose "antiquity" was meant to guarantee an essential authenticity. His stratagem was to resurrect nothing less than the imperial diadem that Constantine had given St. Silvester.

Boniface VIII's second tiara was a sort of cloche of perforated silver-gilt, consisting of two crowns decorated with florets and precious stones and topped with a chape that supported an enormous floral apex. This disproportionate copy from one on Honorius IV's tiara 15 years earlier consisted of a ring set with pearls and cabochons from which emerged a crown of acanthus leaves made of gilded metal. At the very top of the corolla was a ring of pearls that held an enormous ruby, an acquisition of Boniface VII. These three superimposed metallic elements were linked by six vertical stems, also made of metal, which were fastened with rivets. Obviously, a light cloth bonnet could not bear the weight of the two crowns and the apex. This bell-shaped structure of perforated metal covered the actual tiara-miter. No contemporary text explains this curious two-crown tiara, but it must be the prototype of the *triregnum*, the *mitra papalis* adorned with crowns which, through a superimposition of symbolic objects, was intended to affirm the superiority of the bishop of Rome as king and priest. It was probably the reaction against the excesses of Boniface VIII's papacy that caused this "imperial" tiara to be withdrawn. In fact, the gentle-natured BONIFACE XI seems in his brief pontificate to have used only the classic type of tiara of the 1200s, adorned with the discreet crown—the *circulus*—which appears on his gisant in Perugia.

Boniface VIII's atypical tiara was transported to France after Benedict XI's death and Clement V's election, to serve in Lyon for the coronation of the new pope (1305). This extraordinary object was thenceforth called the "tiara" or "miter of St. Silvester." In Avignon it was imbued with a sort of veneration and served at the coronation of the French popes in that city. In 1377, when GREGORY XI returned to Rome to die, he brought back the pseudo-relic. After the illegal election of Robert of Geneva, the deceased pope's vestiary who had stayed behind in Anagni arrived in Avignon with St. Silvester's tiara, which he had not been able to bring to Rome for the coronation of URBAN VI. Thus, Boniface VIII's creation crowned the Avignon antipopes, Clement VII and Benedict XIII, who made off with it when going into exile in Catalonia. In 1429, the tiara was brought back to Rome, and thenceforth promoted to the rank of a paleo-Christian relic. In 1447, it was borne in solemn procession from the Vatican to the Lateran, to be placed reverently in the chapel of the Sancta Sanctorum. It served at the coronation of NICHOLAS V before being stolen in November 1485.

The triple crown, strictly speaking, was born out of the 1305 coronation in Lyon. With the huge Caetani ruby lost, and the floral apex made to hold it no doubt badly damaged, the next step was to repair the tiara and in doing so to modify its extreme height, as the paintings of Fra Angelico in the Vatican (ca. 1448) illustrate. The chape and apex were replaced with a tiny crown of gilded metal, a simple circlet with five small, low, pointed rays, each holding a miniature cone adorned with a huge pearl. The work was executed by a French jeweler. The idea came from some literary expert in Old Testament culture who wished to adapt the papal tiara as closely as possible to passages in Exodus and the Jewish Antiquities of Josephus describing the Jewish high priest's supreme headdress, which was adorned with three superimposed circlets. The one who inspired this symbolic change and the actual creation of the triple crown must have been JOHN XXII (elected 1316). He was a man of wide culture whose defense of the Church against the temporal powers and heresy was uppermost among his concerns. In a harangue he gave in 1322 against this pope, William of Ockham accused the pontiff of having added a third crown to his tiara—a proof, he claimed, of John XXII's arrogance and pretension. Not until the papacy of Clement VI (1342), however, did the triple crown take its final form.

Clement VI's customary tiara figures on the carved escutcheon over the Champeaux porch of the Palace of the Popes in Avignon, where he was the fourth pope. At Urban VI's election (Rome, 1378), being deprived of St. Silvester's tiara and of the new triple crown that had been in use in Avignon for 25 years, the pope had to commission a new emblem. This Roman triple crown was generally very close to that of Clement VI and his successors in the first version with its decoration of florets and foliage.

This synopsis of the origins and forms of the papal headdress would be incomplete without mentioning the existence of a tiara-miter, apparently the result of an attempt on the part of certain popes to restore the article's religious significance. Written sources of the 13th and 14th centuries refer to it as *mitra aurifrixiata, preciosa, solemnis,* or *nobilissima.* It became the most precious Roman miter, used by the bishops for solemn occasions and, most recently, by the pope on 16 and 17 October 1978. Experts on the tiara have systematically classed this category of papal headdress in the family of liturgical miters, without noting that a rich iconography shows this type of tiara to be halfway between the bishop's miter (divided) and the *tiara regnum* (closed). Only Eugène Müntz deduced, from the inventories of the pontifical treasury (from Gregory X to Callistus III), that there existed an intermediate papal headdress, probably created under CALLISTUS II before becoming the tall, bulbous Roman miter of the 15th century. It is a conical bonnet with a *circulus* and two *tituli,* or inscriptions (vertical orphreys: frontal and occipital), set with precious stones. Unlike the *tiara regnum,* it was never divided. This form represents the *frigium* genre of the tiara and attests to resistance on the part of certain popes (chiefly from the 13th and 14th centuries) to the change of the ancient sacerdotal *mitra papalis* into a para-imperial crown. After the troubled reign of GELASIUS II (1118), the choice fell on Callistus who, coming from the Cluniac milieu steeped in antiquity, seems to have adopted this new type of tiara (second Lateran council). It would survive the modifications arbitrarily decreed by Innocent III and even score a certain success with the popes of the 13th century. It is this *tiara a tituli,* the ancestor of the precious miters, that Honorius III wears in the mosaic medallion in St. Lawrence's Outside the Walls, which is worn by St. Callistus in the cathedral of Rheims, and which is depicted on the head of the gisant (1260–75) of Clement IV in S. Domenico of Viterbo.

Richard Bavoillot-Laussade

Bibliography

Andrieu, M. *Le pontifical romain du Moyen Age,* 1938–41.

Andrieu, M. *Les Ordines romani du haut Moyen Age,* 1931–65.

Baluze, E. *Vitae paparum Avenionensium, 1305–1394* (critical study of G. Mollat, 1917).

Batifol, P. *La Corona des évêques—du IVe au VIe siècle,* 1912.

Batifol, P. *La liturgie du sacre des évêques dans son evolution historique,* 1927.

Duchesne, L. *LP,* 1886.

Dykmans, M. *Le cérémonial papal de la fin du Moyen Age à la fin de la Renaissance,* 1977–83.

Dykmans, M. *L'oeuvre de Patrizi Piccolomini ou le Cérémonial papal de la première Renaissance,* 1980.

Fabre, P. and Duchesne, L. *Liber censum,* 1904.

Jaffé, P. and Wattenbach, W. *Regesta pontificium romanorum,* 1885–8.

Ladner, G.-B. *The Concept of Ecclesia and Christianitas and Their Relation to the Idea of Papal Plenitudo Potestatis, from Gregory VII to Boniface VIII,* 1954.

Ladner, G.-B. *Der Ursprung und die mittelalteriche Entwicklung der päpstlichen Tiara,* Tainia, 1978 (1980).

Ladner, G.-B. *Die Papstbildnisse des Altertums und des Mittelalters,* 3 vols., 1941, 1970, 1984.

Maccarone, M. *La teologia del primato romano nel secolo XI*, 1974.

MacPherson, D. C. *The Tiara of the Patriarch of Alexandria*, 1948.

Müntz, E. *La tiare pontificale du VIIIe au XVIe siècle*, 1898.

Pelzer, A. *Les 51 articles de Guillaume d'Occam*, 1922.

Piltz, E. *Kamelaukion et mitre—insignes byzantins impériaux et ecclésiastiques*, 1977.

Salmon P. *Analecta Liturgica/Les manuscrits liturgiques latins de la Bibliothèque vaticane*, 1968–74.

Salmon, P. *Étude sur les insignes du pontife dans le rite romain*, 1955.

Schramm, P. E. *Kaiser, Könige und Päpste, gesammelte Aufsätze zur Geschichte des Mittelalters*, 1968–71.

Schramm, P. E. *Zur Geschichte der päpstlichen Tiara*, 1953.

TITLES, CARDINALS'. The titles accorded to cardinals go back directly to the titular churches of Rome. Originally a term of the ordinary language of the law, the term *titulus*, first attested in a reference dating from 377, was applied to the churches erected after the great Constantinian foundations (the cathedral of the Lateran and the Palatine chapel of the Sessorianum) to serve the Christian community, a priest being attached to each church as a fixed post. According to the synodal documents of 499 and 595, there were 25 or 26 titular churches in Rome at that time, a number that rarely varied until the 12th century. When the custom arose in the late 7th century of naming as "cardinals" the principal Roman priests who assisted the pope, they naturally took the names of their titular churches. Over the centuries some exchanges also took place, temporary or not, between priestly titles and diaconal churches (see below), which explains fluctuations in the lists drawn up by various historians.

Cardinal's titles in the strict sense of the term in the Middle Ages were as follows (in alphabetical order, with indication where necessary of earlier names): S. Anastasia, SS. Apostoli, S. Balbina, S. Cecilia in Trastevere, S. Ciriaco nelle Terme, S. Clemente, S. Crisogono, S. Croce in Gerusalemme, S. Eusebio, SS. Giovanni e Paolo, S. Lorenzo in Damaso, S. Lorenzo in Lucina, SS. Marcellino e Pietro (formerly S. Matteo), S. Marcello, S. Marco, S. Maria in Trastevere (formerly SS. Giulio e Callisto), S. Martino ai Monti (formerly SS. Silvestro e Martino), SS. Nereo e Achilleo, S. Pietro in Vincoli, S. Prassede, S. Prisca, S. Pudenziana, SS. Quattro Coronati, S. Sabina, S. Sisto Vecchio, S. Stefano [Rotondo] in Monte Celio, S. Suzanna, S. Vitale. Titles, in the strict sense of *tituli*, pertained only to cardinals associated with the churches listed above. However, analogous relationships existed between cardinal-deacons and their deaconries, and between cardinal bishops and their bishoprics, within Rome and nearby Italian cities. These are discussed in the following sections.

Cardinal-Deacons. The regional deacons, who looked after liturgical matters and especially the administration of the temporal possessions, as well as charity and public welfare within each Roman deaconry, were named after the deaconries. The placing of deaconries in former houses of worship or in new churches goes back mainly to the 7th–9th centuries. Following is a list of the cardinal deaconries, which became more or less fixed in the 12th century and did not undergo any noticeable change until the 16th century (in alphabetical order, with indication where known of the date when the deaconry was created): S. Adriano (under Adrian I, 772–95), S. Agata (c. 800), S. Angelo in Pescheria (755), SS. Cosma e Damiano (under Hadrian I, 772–95), S. Eustachio (7th century), S. Giorgio in Velabro (before mid-8th century), S. Lucia in Orfea, or in Silice or in Capite (under Honorius I, 625–38), S. Lucia in Septisolio or in Settizonio (before 8th century), S. Maria in Aquiro (before Gregory III, 731–41). S. Maria in Cosmedin (6th century), S. Maria in Domnica (before 800), S. Maria Nova (formerly S. Maria Antica, second half of 6th century, rebuilt under Leo IV, 847–55, today S. Francesca Romana), S. Maria in Porticu, S. Maria in Via Lata (1st quarter of 7th century), S. Nicola in Carcere (9th century), SS. Sergio e Bacco (under Hadrian I, 772–95), S. Teodoro (mid-6th–early 7th century), and SS. Vito e Modesto (under Leo III, 795–816).

Cardinal-Bishops. From earliest times, the titulars of the bishoprics around Rome had close ties with the pope. Toward the end of the 4th century, the bishop of Ostia had the privilege of consecrating the newly elected pope, if he was not already a bishop, assisted by the bishops of Porto and Albano. The first cardinal-bishops, in the sense of suburbicarian bishops, were created under STEPHEN III (768–72): Albano, Gabii-Labicanum, Ostia, Porto, Praeneste (Palestrina), and Silva Candida. The list underwent several changes, some of them temporary, until under HADRIAN IV (1154–9) it was stabilized at a total of six: Albano, Ostia and Velletri, Porto and Santa Rufina, Praeneste (Palestrina), Sabina, Tusculum (Frascati). Among the principal changes were the following: around 1060, Gabii-Labicanum was replaced by Tusculum and Ostia was combined with Velletri; around 1062–3, the bishopric of Sabina joined the group; the see of Silva Candida or Santa Rufina, which had been vacant on several occasions, was definitively combined with Porto under CALLISTUS II (1119–24) and henceforth known as Porto and Santa Rufina; the vacancy was temporarily filled by Tivoli in 1123–5 and its separation from the group took place under HADRIAN IV (1154–9);

during the schism of Clement III (Guibert of Ravenna, 1098–9) and the ensuing events, the bishops of Segni (1059–1130) and Nepi (1098–1126) temporarily joined the cardinal-bishops.

Finally, from the 13th century, along with their own priestly title, deaconry, or bishopric, many cardinals received another cardinals' church, whose possessions they administered and whose revenues they collected.

Pierre Jugie

Bibliography

Eubel, K. *Hierarchia Catholica Medii Aevi*, 2nd ed., I, Münster, 1913, 1–60.

Hüls, R. *Kardinaläle, Klerus und Kirchen Roms, 1049–1130*, Tübingen, 1977 (Bibl. des Deut. Histor. Instituts in Rom, 48).

Klewitz, H. W. "Die Entstehung des Kardinalkollegiums," *ZRGKA* (1936), 115–222.

"Le droit d'option des cardinaux," *Annuaire pontifical catholique*, Paris, 1908.

"Les diaconies cardinalices," *Annuaire pontifical catholique*, Paris, 1913.

Pietri, C. "Régions ecclésiastiques et paroisses romaines [aux derniers siècles de l'Antiquité]," *Actes du XIᵉ congrès international d'archéologie chrétienne (Lyon, Vienne, Grenoble, Geneva and Aosta, 21–28 September 1986)* II, Rome, 1989, 1035–62.

Reekmans, L. "L'implantation monumentale chrétienne dans le paysage urbain de Rome de 300 à 850," *ibid.*, 861–915.

TITLES, PAPAL. The *Annuario pontificio* uses the following designations for the successor of St. Peter:

Bishop of Rome
Vicar of Jesus Christ
Successor of the Prince of Apostles
Sovereign Pontiff of the Universal Church
Patriarch of the West
Primate of Italy
Archbishop and Metropolitan of the Province of Rome
Sovereign of the Vatican City State
Servant of the Servants of God.

These nine titles and their singular history are summed up by the designation "pope" (or, in a more respectful version, Most Holy Father), which Peter's successor gradually appropriated between the 4th and 12th centuries.

Bishop of Rome. This formula describes the primary function of the pope, who is chosen from among the Roman clergy. The tradition behind it has been upheld down the centuries, with the cardinals meeting in conclave, each a titular of a church in Rome, representing the clergy. In the first centuries of the Church, the words *Urbis Romae* were specified after the title *Episcopus Ecclesiae catholicae*, which was conferred on these bishops, whose see—unlike others—was dependent on the apostolic succession. PAUL VI signed the promulgation of the conciliar constitutions and texts with the phrase *Episcopus catholicae Ecclesiae*, an inversion of the usual formula (*Ecclesiae catholicae*), to signify that the bishop of the local Church of Rome was the pastor of the universal Church.

Vicar of Jesus Christ. Whether used in the phrase *Vicarius Petri* or *Vicarius Christi*, the term *Vicarius* entered ecclesiastical Latin (St. Cyprian, 3rd century) in the sense of taking the place of or representing someone else. The expression *Vicarius Petri* appears with LEO I (440–61), the title being taken up by his successors in the 5th and 6th centuries. Before that time, emphasis was laid on the fact that the bishop of Rome occupied the *cathedra Petri*. The term *Vicarius Petri* could apply to all the bishops if one considered that Peter was *initium episcopatus*. The Roman synod of 495 acclaimed GELASIUS (492–6) with the formula *Vicarium Christi te videmus*. This did not define a power so much as indicate the manifestation of the transcendent action of Christ. The formula also applied to other bishops, and even to priests and kings. Y. Congar writes: "The idea at that time . . . was that the saint [St. Peter], and Christ, were [?] the true personal subject of a community or a function: it is their power and their virtue that are at work here in those who are visibly active."

In the 11th and 12th centuries, the title *Vicarius Christi* was increasingly used to refer to the pope, but the usual title remained *Vicarius Petri*. He was even called *Vicarius Apostolicae Sedis* or "Vicar of Peter and Paul" (John VIII, 872–2). The formula *Vicarius Christi* entered into the usage of theologians and the Papal Chancery with EUGENE III (1145–58), a disciple of St. Bernard, but it was not yet reserved to the successor of Peter in Rome. INNOCENT III (1198–1216) favored the term *Vicarius Christi* to express a radical, more far-reaching authority than that of the other bishops. INNOCENT IV (1243–54) went so far as to employ the words *Vicarius Dei*. The great theoreticians of pontifical power, Torquemada and Bellarmine (16th and 17th centuries), even insisted on the fact that the pope was not the vicar of Peter but the vicar of God, his power extending beyond the faithful.

This question concerned the origin of the power entrusted to Peter's successor. Authority arose from Christ. The link between this delegated jurisdiction and the Apostolic See of Rome was debated throughout the later Middle Ages. Should the pope—*caput Ecclesiae*—necessarily be bishop of Rome, or even bishop? (This was the argument of Agostino Trionfo in the 14th century.) VATICAN I established the primacy of the jurisdiction given to Peter and his successor bishops of the Holy Roman See. VATICAN II confirmed the title *Vicarius Christi*, coupled with those of *Successor Petri, Pontifex romanus.* However, the constitution *Lumen gentium* (21) affirmed the sacramental idea of the active presence of Christ for the episcopal body. "Today, many think that the title *Vicarius Christi,* taken separately, that is without being a simple consequence of the quality of *Pontifex romanus* (*Successor Petri*), is to be avoided" (Y. Congar).

Successor of the Prince of the Apostles. This title completes that of *Vicarius Christi;* it is the conclusion of the debate on the subject. It alludes to the specification of the Roman see (*cathedra romana*) in contrast to the other apostolic sees founded by an apostle or one of his disciples. During the first three centuries of the Church, *Sedis apostolica* "designated, in the West, the Roman community, whose faith and doctrine had an exemplary value" (A. Kröger, cited by Y. Congar). But at the same time, it designated any episcopal see, to express the unity of the episcopate in the succession of the apostles. The popes caused the equivalence between *cathedra Petri* and *sedis apostolica* to triumph by invoking in absolute fashion, in the 11th and 12th centuries, their designation of "apostolic" as the successor of the Prince of the Apostles.

Sovereign Pontiff of the Universal Church. The term *Pontifex* appears at the end of the 5th century as a synonym for "bishop." *Pontifex maximus,* a pagan title abandoned by emperors Gratian and Theodosus in the 4th century, "was never a title assumed by the popes themselves" (Y. Congar)—not even by Leo I, as is sometimes claimed. The expression reappears in the 15th century in a humanist context, describing popes on funerary inscriptions or coins, or as a form of address to the pope himself (Lateran council V).

Summus Pontifex. From the 5th century, this title "Supreme Pontiff," designated any bishop as superior in the priestly order, and especially the metropolitan order. Its use for the pope alone came about at the end of the 8th century, and it became a favored title in the late 11th century. The title figures in the signature of pontifical bulls from the year 900. St. Anselm and later St. Bernard employed it in all their letters to the popes. It is the title most frequently used to designate the pope. The addition of the term "Universal Church" (*Ecclesiae catholicae*) is recent.

Patriarch of the West. The pope was only rarely addressed as "patriarch," even after the Great Schism. The title entered the pontifical titulature with Vatican I.

Primate of Italy, Archbishop and Metropolitan of the Province of Rome. These terms are linked to the definition of the jurisdiction proper to the bishop of Rome after the Lateran Treaty.

Servant of the Servants of God. This formula is found in the writings of St. Augustine and St. Benedict. Until the beginning of the 13th century, its use was not reserved exclusively to the pope. "It is an admirable expression of the hierarchy as service" (Y. Congar). It is also a manifestation of pontifical primacy. The formula has been stressed by the papacy in the contemporary era, in particular with Vatican II, under the heading of collegiality.

Among the other official titles given to the pope, one should mention *Caput Ecclesiae.* Certain nonofficial titles, listed by Migne following St. François de Sales, are as follows: the most holy bishop of the Catholic Church (conc. Successionens); the most holy and most blessed Patriarch (*ibid.* I VII Concil.); the most blessed Lord (S. Aug. *Epist.* 95); the universal Patriarch (S. Leo, Papa, *Epist.* 62).

Philippe Levillain

Bibliography

Congar, Y. "Titres donnés au Pape," *Concilium,* 108, 1975, 55–64.
Krömer, A. *Die "Sedis apostolica" der Stadt Rom in ihren theologischen Relevanz innerhalb der abendländischen Kirchengeschichte bis Leo I,* Freiburg, 1972.
Levillain, L. "Servus Servorum Dei," *Le Moyen Age,* 40, 1930, 5–7.
Maccarone, A. *Storia del titolo papale,* Rome, 1952.
Migne, J. P. *Dictionnaire des Papes,* Paris, 1861 (Manevit).

TOMBS OF THE POPES.
Up to the Year 1000. The sites of the popes' tombs are known at least from the middle of the 3rd century, when the Church of Rome organized the celebration of the anniversary of a pope's death at his tomb. At that time, Church calendars carried notices of the anniversaries of the martyr popes beginning with CALLISTUS I (d. 222), and those of the non-martyr popes beginning with LUCIUS (d. 254). A 4th-century manuscript (the Calendar of 354) shows two lists of anniversaries which, together with similar information, went to make up the *Hieronymian Martyrology.* After that, information comes from the LIBER PONTIFICALIS, in which each notice ends with the subject's date of death and place of burial. After this source of information ceases around 867, we can derive a list of burial places based on other documents, in particular medieval or modern descriptions of the basilicas of St. Peter's and the Lateran.

Thus, nothing is known of the burial sites of the popes of the first two centuries, with the exception of St. Peter. The *Liber pontificalis* presumes that his successors were interred next to him in the necropolis of the Vatican hill, but that is merely hypothetical, since the writers knew as little about the matter as we do. The first pope whose tomb site is certain, because it has been found, is the martyr Callistus I. He was buried in the cemetery of Cale-podius on the Via Aurelia, in a loculus, a small niche hol-lowed out of the wall of the underground gallery. It is a type of tomb common in the period, with nothing about it to suggest that it contains the body of a pope and martyr, save that it is placed at the foot of the steps providing ac-cess to the catacomb. Some sources, obviously later, place the tomb of his predecessor ZEPHRINUS (d. 217) in a building constructed on the surface, over Callistus's tomb, and that of his successor URBAN (d. 230) in Prae-textatus's catacomb, but these statements are suspect.

With the popes buried in Callistus's catacombs we are on far surer ground. The adoption of burial in Rome led to the development of the catacombs, which made it possible to economize on space on the outskirts of the densely pop-ulated city. In choosing to be buried in the catacombs, the Christians were following the general custom. At the be-ginning of the 3rd century, the Church of Rome acquired some land to the south of the city, bordering the Via Appia, on which to create a necropolis, as was the practice of other professional or religious groups. This catacomb was named after Pope Callistus, who is said to have supervised the building of it when he was only a deacon. The popes from PONTIAN (d. 235) to GAIUS (d. 296) were all interred there. Most of them were placed in a collective vault which was the underground equivalent of the mausoleums on the surface and was known as the "popes' crypt." It was there, or nearby, that the funerary slabs were found which sealed the wall niche. They bore a very simple inscription giving the individual's name and title. Ordinary popes lay along-side martyrs, such as Pontian (whose body was brought to Rome after his death in the Sardinian mines), FABIAN, or SIXTUS II. However, not all the popes of the period were buried here. Cornelius, another martyr who died in exile (d. 253), was placed in another catacomb nearby, but later transferred to that of Callistus. Gaius was closer to his pre-decessors, in another vault in the catacomb. The placing of the popes' tombs together in the same catacomb, or even the same vault, clearly indicates a desire to stress the unity of the episcopate and the strength of the chain binding Peter's successors; nor should one dismiss reasons of con-venience. In the 4th century, however, the popes did not hesitate to abandon their collective sepulcher in Callistus's catacomb.

The great persecution of Diocletian caused deep unrest in the Church of Rome and the first abandonment of this catacomb. Both MARCELLINUS (d. 304) and MARCELLUS (d. 309) were buried in the catacomb of Priscilla, north of Rome on the edge of the Via Salaria. Marcellinus's tomb was in the "hypogeum of the Acilii," of recent creation, and that of Marcellus in a basilica erected on the surface, which in the 6th century bore his name. Not enough is known of this building to determine its origin or under-stand why Marcellus was buried there. Once calm was re-stored, EUSEBIUS (d. 309/310) and MILTIADES (d. 314)

were again placed in Callistus's catacomb. Eusebius may have rested in a vault facing that of Gaius.

The Peace of the Church and SILVESTER's pontificate marked, unmistakably, the beginning of a new period in the history of pontifical burial. This was characterized by the dispersal of the tombs and the gradual emergence of burial *ad sanctos* ("beside the bodies of the saints"). Sil-vester I (d. 335), LIBERIUS (d. 366), MARK (d. 336), and JULIUS I (d. 352) were placed in funerary structures (*cimeteria*) which they had caused to be built on the sur-face of the catacombs of Priscilla, Balbinus, and Cale-podius. It is not certain whether these included altars—they were actually large mausoleums—but they were almost certainly small in scale. At Calepodius's cata-comb a small, half-buried basilica has been found. Shaped like a Greek cross, with an apse, it could be the "cemetery" of Pope Julius I. These sepulchers, which were situated close to the martyrs, were not really "be-side the saints" (*ad sanctos*) insofar as they were not in-tended to be in the immediate proximity of the saints' tombs. Nevertheless, the desire to be buried as near as possible to saints developed in the later 4th century. DAMASUS I (d. 384) resisted it: in the inscription that he caused to be placed in the "popes' crypt," he declared that he did not wish to be buried there so as not to disturb the saints. He chose to be buried not far away with his mother and sister, in a basilica that he had had built on the Via Ardeatina. SIRICIUS (d. 399) was interred in the same place as Silvester. The sepulchers of ANASTASIUS (d. 401) and INNOCENT (d. 417) again recall those of the century before. Both were buried in the cemetery built over Pontian's catacomb, each in his funerary edifice.

It is the tomb of ZOSIMUS (d. 418), next to St. Lawrence's body, that marks the real turn of the popes to the practice of interment *ad sanctos*. To be close to the martyr, the pope arranged to be buried at the heart of the catacomb, whereas from the time that Callistus's cata-comb was abandoned, all the popes' tombs had been built on the surface. Two of Zosimus's successors, SIX-TUS III (d. 440) and HILARUS (d. 468), joined him. BONI-FACE I (d. 422) was buried beside St. Felicity, in an ora-tory he had built over her tomb. Zosimus's choice and that of his successors has far more general significance, since Lawrence was one of the greatest saints of Rome, and Prudentius in his *Peristephanon* (II) presents him as the city's protector.

Yet the popes would soon turn to an even more sym-bolic figure: Peter, the founder with Paul of the Church of Rome, the gatekeeper of paradise and prince of the apos-tles. It was not by chance that the first pope to be buried in St. Peter's was LEO I (461), who was the first Pope to put forward the theological arguments on which the claim of pontifical primacy was based. He did not immediately set a fashion. Hilarus was buried beside Lawrence; Simpli-cius (d. 483) joined Leo in St. Peter's, but FELIX III (d.

492) arranged to be buried with members of his family in St. Paul's Outside the Walls. It was from the reign of GELASIUS (d. 496) that all the popes whose burial places we know were interred in St. Peter's, up to ANASTASIUS III (d. 913). There were only four exceptions to this rule in four centuries: SILVERIUS (d. 537) and MARTIN (d. 653) died outside Rome, prisoners of the emperor, and political circumstances prohibited their bodies from being repatriated. VIGILIUS (d. 555) was placed in the basilica of St. Marcellus at the catacomb of Priscilla [p], perhaps because he was reproached for having finally yielded to Justinian and ratified the condemnation of the Three Chapters. HADRIAN III (d. 885) was buried at Nonantola in northern Italy, where he died. Tradition was apparently beginning to lose its vigor, since it would have been possible to bring his body back to Rome, as had been done in the case of some of his predecessors—JOHN I (d. 526), who died in Theodoric's prisons in Ravenna, AGAPITUS (d. 536), who died in Constantinople, or even Vigilius (d. 555), who died in Syracuse. Whereas the funerary practices of the bishops of Rome were not original, their collective burial in St. Peter's did enhance the apostolic succession, the uninterrupted link binding the reigning pope to St. Peter, making him the vicar of the chief apostle and thus the inheritor of his dignity and all his powers.

Inside Constantine's basilica of St. Peter, the site of the popes' tombs varied over these four centuries. The scant information we possess allows us to identify three phases. We know little about the earliest tombs. Leo I and BENEDICT I (d. 579) were placed in the original sacristy, a large chapel with an apse situated at the southeast corner of the basilica, which was reached from the portico of the atrium that served as the vestibule of the basilica. Setting aside its liturgical function, this annex is reminiscent of the great mausoleums placed at the time alongside all the suburban basilicas of Rome. The tombs of ANASTASIUS II (d. 498), JOHN III (?) (d. 574), and certainly GREGORY the Great (d. 604) were placed in the vestibule of the basilica. Apparently Gregory the Great, in a double show of humility, wished to lie both in front of one of the basilica doors and in front of the door of the sacristy containing Leo's tomb. Finally, contrary to a common assertion, some popes were buried inside the basilica, where we know there were a number of tombs. At least, this is the case for PELAGIUS I (d. 561) and BONIFACE IV (d. 615). It is not known where the tombs of the other 7th-century popes were located.

JOHN VII (d. 707) inaugurated a new phase by choosing as his burial place an oratory built in the northeast corner of St. Peter's and dedicated to the Virgin Mary. To the protection of St. Peter there now was added the protection of the saints to whom the oratory was consecrated. These oratories in St. Peter's were separated from the rest of the basilica only by a railing, but the wall or pillar against which the altar was set could be richly decorated, as was

the case with John VII's oratory. The oratory where GREGORY III (d. 741) was buried was also dedicated to the Virgin and contained relics of saints from throughout Christendom. It was situated at the foot of the triumphal arch in the southwest corner of the main nave. The following oratories were built against the walls in the south arm of the transept: that of PAUL I (d. 767) was again consecrated to the Virgin; that of HADRIAN I (d. 795) to his patron saint, an eastern martyr; that of PASCHAL I (d. 824) housed the bodies of SS. Processus and Martinian, which had been transferred from the catacombs, the saints having according to legend been St. Peter's jailers. But Paschal I's own tomb may have been in the other oratory he founded, in the middle of the transept. Here he caused to be placed the bodies of two martyr popes, Fabian and Sixtus II; this was also the burial place of Sergius II (d. 847). With LEO IV (d. 855) we return to the south arm of the transept; he was placed in the oratory to which the body of Leo I had been brought in 688. We know practically nothing about the tombs of the other popes of this second period. Leo IV's successors were buried either in the vestibule of the basilica or inside the edifice, in particular the southernmost part of the lower naves.

At the beginning of the 10th century, the tradition of burial in St. Peter's was abandoned. The sparse information about that century shows that once again the popes' burial places were dispersed. Certain popes did remain loyal to St. Peter's—for example, JOHN XIV (d. 984) and GREGORY V (d. 999)—while JOHN X (d. 928) was buried in St. John Lateran, which he had just had restored after an earthquake. He was joined there by AGAPITUS II (d. 955) and SILVESTER II (d. 1003). The popes gave up their individual funerary arrangements and for the most part arranged to follow the example of the other 10th-century bishops and to be buried in their cathedral or in the principal funerary church of the city. There were also isolated burial places: that of JOHN XIII (d. 972) in St. Paul's Outside the Walls, and that of BENEDICT VII (d. 983) in S. Croce in Gerusalemme.

From the 4th century, the popes' tombs were provided with epitaphs in verse that were sometimes very elaborate. These epitaphs were copied from the 7th century on by pilgrims who admired Latin poetry and by the writers of descriptions of St. Peter's and the Lateran. In these basilicas they were placed on the wall close to the tomb. One of them has come down to us, that of Hadrian I. Composed at the court of Charlemagne, it can still be seen below the vestibule of St. Peter's in the Vatican.

J. C. Picard

Bibliography

LP, passim.

Borgolte, M. *Petrusnachfolge und Kaiserimitation*, Göttingen, 1989.

Gregorovius, F. *Le tombe dei papi*, 2nd ed. by C. Hülsen, Rome, 1931.

Montini, R. U. *Le tombe dei papi*, Rome, 1957.

Nestori, A. "La catacomba di Calepodio al III Miglio el-l'Arelia vetus e i sepolcri dei papi Callisto e Giulio I," *Rivista di archeologia cristiana*, 47, 1971, 169–278; 48, 1972, 193–233.

Picard, J. C. "Étude sur l'emplacement des tombes des papes du IIIe au Xe siècle," *MEFRA*, 91 (1969), 725–82.

Reekmans, L. *La Tombe du pape Corneille et sa région cémétériale*, Rome, 1964.

Reekmans, L. "Le complexe cémétérial du pape Gaius dans la catacombe de Calixte," *Roma sotteranea cristiana*, VIII, Rome, 1988.

11th to 15th Centuries. From the beginning of the 11th century to the beginning of the 14th, all but two of the popes were buried in Italy. The proportion of burials outside Rome rose (by 58%) between 1185 and 1304, but the most favored places were still the basilicas of the Lateran and the Vatican. The former contained the tombs of the first three popes of the 11th century and ten from the 12th. After 1181, only two popes would be buried in the Lateran. The fires that destroyed the basilica in 1308 and 1361 left no pontifical funerary monument standing. Over the centuries, popes had chosen to be buried in the Vatican, close to the burial place of the first pontiff. Here, in the 11th and 13th centuries, their tombs were twice as numerous as in the Lateran. Because of the popes' move to Avignon, in the 14th century seven popes had their burial place in France, but later almost all the popes were buried in St. Peter's of the Vatican. Sadly, the work of rebuilding the venerable Constantinian basilica, which began in 1505 and was completed a century later, caused irreparable damage to the greater part of the medieval tombs.

Silvester II, who died in 1003, was interred below the portico of the Lateran (J. Diacre). After the fires in the 14th century, his tomb was moved, together with the remains of the popes buried beneath the portico, to a site in the interior of the basilica where SERGIUS IV's original epitaph commemorating his predecessor was set in a pillar (Lauer, 145–6, fig. 56; A. Silvagni, *Monumenta epigraphica christiana saeculo XIII antiquiora quae in Italiae finibus adhuc exstant*, I, Roma, Vatican, 1943, pl. IV, 2).

JOHN XVII was buried in the Lateran between the two doors of the west façade (J. Diacre). John XVIII was interred in St. Paul's Outside the Walls. The epitaph *domnus iohs XVIII papa* (Silvagni, pl. XVIII, no. 3), which used to be between the 18th and 19th columns of the nave on the same side as the statue of St. Paul, is today in the Museo Profano of the basilica (*LP*, II, 266; Montini, 170–1). According to John the Deacon, Sergius IV's

tomb was in the Lateran, near the doors, at the left when one went in. His epitaph, the first three lines of which have been restored, is set in the pillar next to the one bearing the epitaph of Silvester II (Lauer, 147–8, fig. 57; Silvagni, pl. IV, 3; Montini, 171–2, fig. 50 and fig. 51 for the modern mausoleum of F. Borromini).

BENEDICT VIII was buried in the Vatican (Chacon, I, 768; Papebroch, I, 182), as no doubt was John XIX (Chacon, I, 772; Montini, 174). Benedict IX probably rests in the abbey of Grottaferrata, even if the tomb discovered there in 1739 is not his; the monument erected for this pope in 1750 should be viewed with caution (Montini, 174–5, fig. 52; *Die mittelalterlichen Grabmäler in Rom und Latium vom 13. bis zum 15. Jahrhundert*, I, *Die Grabplatten und Tafeln*, ed. J. Garms, R. Juffinger and B. Ward-Perkins, no. 83, 338–40). Nor can one be certain in the case of the burial of GREGORY VI, who is said to have been interred in St. Peter's after his body, which was placed outside the basilica, was miraculously moved to the interior (Mann, 26; Montini, 177). When CLEMENT II died he was, according to his wishes, moved to his former see of Bamberg and buried in the choir of the cathedral. The present sepulcher dates from the 13th century or the beginning of the 14th. The bas-reliefs depict an angel visiting the dying pope, together with John the Baptist, allegories of the cardinal virtues and, it may be, of liberality or gentleness. Protestants in the 16th century smashed the lid of the tomb, which was replaced in 1741 by a slab bearing an inscription (Papebroch, I, 188, drawing; E. Müntz, "Les tombeaux des papes en Allemagne et en France," *Revue de l'art chrétien*, 45 (1896), 352–6; A. von Reitzenstein, "Das Clemensgrab im Dom zu Bamberg," *Münchener Jahrbuch der bildenden Kunst*, n.s., 6 [1929], 216–75; Mann, 26–7; Montini, 177–9, figs. 53–4).

DAMASUS II, who died at Praeneste, was buried in Rome in St. Lawrence's Outside the Walls. It is not certain whether the great sarcophagus placed beneath the outer portico is his (*LP*, II, 274; Montinio, 179–80, fig. 55). The original tomb of LEO IX was at St. Peter's, in front of the doors, near the tomb of Gregory I (Guibert of Toul, *AASS*, April, II, 663). In 1606 the marble tomb was moved into the new basilica, beneath the altar dedicated to St. Martial and St. Valeria (*LP*, II, 275–6; Papebroch, I, 191–2; Mann, 27; Montini, 180–1, fig. 56). VICTOR II died in Arezzo in 1057. His body was to be taken to Eichstätt, but the convoy was stopped and robbed near Ravenna, after which the body was placed in Theodoric's mausoleum, which had been changed into the church of St. Maria (anonymous writer of Haser, MGH, SS, VII, 266). Chacon and Papebroch have referred to a burial in the cathedral of Florence (*LP*, II, 277; Mann, 27–8; Montini, 182). This is, at least, the site of the tomb of STEPHEN X. When the old cathedral was rebuilt, the body was found intact, with an inscription giving the name Stephen. A new monument was erected to him, which was already lost in the 17th century (Papebroch, I, 194; U. Robert, "Le pape Étienne," *Revue des questions historiques*, 1876, 74; Mann, 28). Florence was also the burial place of NICHOLAS II (d. 1061), but his tomb has also been lost (Montini, 182–3). ALEXANDER II (d. 1073) was interred in the basilica of the Lateran, of which he had been canon, near the tomb of Sergius IV, according to John the Deacon (Chacon, I, 833).

Gregory VII, who had been forced to leave Rome, died in Salerno. His body was placed in the right transept of the cathedral of St. Matthew, which he had consecrated in the year of his death (1085), in a Roman sarcophagus adorned with bucrânes and festoons, to which were added the crossed keys. Five centuries later, the body was found intact. In 1605 the tomb was opened once again for the removal of some relics, and in 1614 the body was placed beneath the altar erected by John of Procida in the so-called Crusade chapel, with a statue of the holy pontiff over the altar. The chapel was restored by PIUS IX in 1854 and again in 1954, at the millenary of the translation to Salerno of St. Matthew's body. Below the gisant were inscribed what were said to be the pope's dying words: *Dilexi justitiam et odivi iniquitatem, propterea morior in exsilio* (*LP*, II, 290–1; Chacon, I, 854 and Oldoini, 860; Mann, 29; Montini, 183–87, figs. 57 and 58).

VICTOR III, once Abbot Didier of Monte Cassino, died in his former abbey and was buried there, as he wished, in the apse of the chapter house. In 1515, his remains were taken to the chapel of St. Berthaire, where Mabillon saw them and made a copy of the original epitaph. Victor III's remains were preserved in Rome and later brought to Monte Cassino (*LP*, II, 292; Mann, 29; Montini, 187–8). URBAN II was buried in St. Peter's, in the south transept; his sepulcher was one of the first to be destroyed during the building of the new basilica in 1505 (*LP*, II, 294–5; Mann, 30; Montini, 188).

PASCHAL II (d. 1118) heads the list of the many popes buried in the Lateran in the 12th century. Nothing remains of his marble tomb, which was situated in the right wing (John the Deacon), nor of those of eight other popes interred in the Lateran in that century—CALLISTUS II, HONORIUS II, INNOCENT II, CELESTINE II, LUCIUS II, ALEXANDER III, CLEMENT III, and CELESTINE III—although we know their places of burial thanks to John the Deacon's description.

GELASIUS II, who died in Cluny in 1119, was interred in the great abbatial "between the cross and the altar, behind the choir" ("Cluny Chronicle," *Recueil des historiens de France*, XII, 313). His tomb was destroyed in 1790.

The body of Innocent II (d. 1143) was first placed in the Lateran, in a porphyry urn which, according to Diacre, had been used in the burial of Emperor Hadrian. After the 1308 fire, the pope's remains were moved to a spot below the portico of the church of Sta. Maria in Trastevere, which he had completely renovated, as is shown in a contemporary epitaph that can still be seen. In 1657 the canons of this church restored the tomb, and in 1860 Pius IX created the last funerary monument, as inscriptions show (*LP*, II, a385; Lauer, 176; Montini, 190–5, fig. 59). ANASTASIUS IV (d. 1154) is the only 12th-century pope buried in the Lateran whose tomb has been preserved. His body was placed in a mausoleum of porphyry with a decoration of riders, formerly that of Helena, the mother of Constantine (J. Diacre). The sarcophagus, which was damaged by the 14th-century fire, was restored in the 18th century and moved to the Vatican museum (*LP*, II, 388 and 450); Lauer, p. 177; Montini, 196–9, figs. 61 and 62).

In the 12th century, only two popes were buried in the Vatican: EUGENE III (d. 1153) in front of the main altar (*LP*, II, 387 and 449), and HADRIAN IV (d. 1159), who was buried nearby in an ancient pagan sarcophagus of red Egyptian granite decorated with bucrânes and garlands. The sarcophagus was moved twice during the work of rebuilding and was opened in 1606—when the small body was found intact—and then placed in the Vatican crypts, together with the inscription *Hadrianus papa III* (*LP*, II, 397; Chacon, I, 1061 and Oldoini, 1063; Mann, 31–2; Montini, 19–200, fig. 63).

In the 17th century, ALEXANDER VII commissioned a large funerary monument for Alexander III (d. 1181) from Francesco Borromini (Montini, 200–3, fig. 64).

With LUCIUS III, two centuries begin during which more than two-thirds of the popes were be buried outside Rome. Lucius III died in Verona and was interred in the cathedral before the high altar. While the cathedral was being restored, Bishop Gian Matteo Giberti (1524–43) had the body placed beneath the choir floor, the tomb being covered with a slab of red marble. The slab was broken in a storm on 25 February 1879, which damaged the apse. At that time the original tomb was found, made of red Verona marble with the figure of the pope in strong relief. The tomb was left *in situ*, but the gisant was placed in the wall of the cathedral (*LP*, II, 451; Chacon, I, 112; Mann, 32; Montini, 203–5, fig. 65). URBAN III was buried in the cathedral of Ferrara, behind the high altar. In 1305 the red marble sarcophagus was mounted on four columns, also of red marble (Papebroch, II, 29, drawing). In 1636 the pope's remains were placed in an imposing monument, the work of G.B. Boffa, in the left wall of the choir (*LP*, II, 451; Mann, 33; Montini, 205–7, figs. 66 and 67). The great sarcophagus of white marble that contained the body of GREGORY VIII (d. 1187) in the cathedral of Pisa was destroyed in a fire in 1600; a new epitaph was dedicated to the pontiff's memory in 1658 (*LP*, II, 451; Papebroch, II, 30).

INNOCENT III was interred in 1216 in the cathedral church of St. Lawrence of Perugia, which also received the remains of URBAN IV in 1264 and those of the Franciscan MARTIN IV in 1285. During the rebuilding of the cathedral in the 14th century, the tombs of the three popes were destroyed and their remains enshrined in a reliquary in 1345. In 1615, Bishop Napoleone Comitoli placed them in a tomb surmounted with a tiara, which in 1730 was moved from the right to the left transept. In the late 19th century, LEO XIII, who had been bishop of Perugia, had the remains of Innocent III brought to St. John Lateran, so far as they could be distinguished from those of Urban IV (those of Martin IV were identifiable by the Franciscan habit in which he was buried). In 1891 Innocent III's remains were placed in a tomb created by Giuseppe Luchetti, which framed the door leading to the sacristy, to the right of the sanctuary and facing what would be Leo XIII's own mausoleum to the left. At the top of the mausoleum, above the gisant, Francis and Dominic are shown on either side of Christ (*LP*, II, 451 and III, 140; Papebroch, II, 34, drawing; Lauer, 194; Mann, 34–5; Montini, 210–1, fig. 68).

Nothing is left of the porphyry tomb in which HONORIOUS III was interred in 1227 at St. Mary Major, before the altar of the creche (Papebroch, II, 35; Montini, 211), nor of the tombs of GREGORY IX (Chacon, II, c. 70) or CELESTINE IV (*LP*, II, 454) in St. Peter's. Innocent IV died in Naples in 1254 and was buried in the cathedral of St. Januarius. Work began on the rebuilding of the cathedral in 1294, a new funerary monument being erected in 1311 by Archbishop Humbert of Ormont in the new edifice. The present mausoleum, built by Annibale of Capua at the end of the 16th century, has retained the 14th-century sarcophagus, gisant, and inscription, which were surmounted by a new inscription and a statue of the Virgin and Child between the pope and the kneeling bishop (*LP*, II, 454; Chacon, II, 103 and 111–2 drawing; Mann, 35, fig. 7; Montini, 212–5, fig. 69; Ladner, II, 122–5, pl. XXII, XXIII, and III, 52). ALEXANDER IV (d. 1261) was buried in the cathedral of St. Lawrence of Viterbo, but from 1683 (Papebroch, II, 50) the whereabouts of the tomb was lost. Urban IV, who is interred in Perugia, is referred to above together with Innocent III; fragments of his epitaph are in the Musei Civici of Perugia (Montini, 216, fig. 70).

CLEMENT IV (d. 1268) was interred in Viterbo in the Dominican church of Sta. Maria in Gradi, which he had chosen for his tomb. As a result of the miracles performed through his intercession, he was transferred to the cathedral, but GREGORY X made the canons return the body to the Dominicans. The mausoleum, the work of the marble mason Pietro di Oderisio, consisted of a sarcophagus with a gisant, a base, a smaller sarcophagus with another gisant, and a baldachin. In 1840 the French ambassador to the Holy See, La Tour Maubourg, restored the mausoleum of this French pope. Moved to the church of St. Francis in 1885, the mausoleum was damaged by bombs in 1944 and restored in 1946–9 (*LP*, II, 455; Mann, 36–9, fig. 8; Montini, 217–9, fig. 7; Ladner, II, 143–52, figs. 65–6, pl. XXX–XXXII, and III, 53, 375–6; A. M.

d'Achille, "Il monumento funebre di Clemente IV in S. Francesco di Viterbo," *Skulptur und Grabmal des spätmittelalters in Rom und Italien*, Vienna, 1990, 129–42, figs. 1–30 and pl. h.-t. A; P.-C. Claussen, "Pietro di Oderisio und die Neuformulierung des italienischen Grabmals zwischen opus romanum und opus francigenum," *ibid.*, 174–200, 12 pl.).

Gregory X's mausoleum in the cathedral of Arezzo consists of a sarcophagus borne by three pillars and decorated with the crucified Lamb surrounded by the four evangelists, with gisant and baldachin. This tomb would seem to be the work of a Sienese master rather than of Margaritone. It was moved in 1810 from the left nave to the beginning of the right one. Oldoini's original epitaph is known to us (Chacon, II, 189; Mann, 39–41, fig. 9; Montini, 220–2, fig. 72; Ladner, II, 168–75, fig. 72, pl. XXXV–XXXVI, and III, 54; G. Bardotti Biasion, "Il monumento di Gregorio X ad Arezzo," *Skulptur und Grabmal*, 265–73, figs. 1–34). HADRIAN V had asked to be buried in Genoa, but he died in Viterbo (1276), where he was interred in the church of the Friars Minor. The mausoleum—base, sarcophagus, gisant, and baldachin—which is situated in the right arm of the transept, was restored several times: in 1715, 1887–9 and 1947–9, after the bombing of 1944. It was probably carved by Arnolfo di Cambio rather than Vassalletto. The epitaph recalls that Hadrian V was of the Fieschi family of Genoa, and that he had been a cardinal with the titular church of S. Hadrian (*LP*, II, 457; Mann, 41–2, fig. 10; Montini, 224–27, fig. 74; Ladner, II, 185–94, figs. 79–82, pl. XXXVIII and XXXIX, and III, 56; T. Iazeolla, "Il monumento funebre di Adriano V in S. Francesco alla Rocca a Viterbo," *Skulptur und Grabmal*, pp. 143–57, figs. 1–31, pl. h-t.B).

JOHN XXI, who also died in Viterbo (1277), was buried near the high altar in the cathedral of St. Lawrence in a sarcophagus of porphyry, then moved in the 16th century to the back of the church. In 1886 the duke of Saldanha, the Portuguese ambassador to the Holy See, had a new mausoleum erected in the chapel of St. Philip of Neri, by F. Gnaccarini. Here the remains of his compatriot were placed, while the original sarcophagus was set up near the staircase leading to the sacristy (Mann, 43, fig. 11; Montini, 227–9, figs. 75–6; Ladner, II, 206–8, figs. 90–1, pl. XLIII).

NICHOLAS III was buried in St. Peter's in the chapel that he had dedicated to St. Nicholas. When the basilica was reconstructed, the sarcophagus was moved (1620–1) to the crypt at Cardinal Alexander Orsini's instigation, the pope's remains having first been reunited with those of two cardinals of the Orsini family (*LP*, II, 458; Mann, 44, fig. 12; Montini, 229–30, fig. 77; Ladner, II, 209–19, figs. 92–5, figs. XLIV and XLVa, and III, 56–8).

MARTIN V has been mentioned above in connection with Innocent III. HONORIUS IV (d. 1287) was interred in the Vatican. His monument was destroyed in 1545, except for the gisant, which was moved to Sta. Maria in Aracoeli, to the Savelli chapel where his relatives lie. The pope's statue is considered to be the work of Arnolfo di Cambio (*LP*, II, 466; Mann, 45–7, fig. 13; Ladner, II, 229–34, figs. 99–102, pl. XLVIII–XLIX, and III, 61, 375; Montini, 232–5, figs. 79–80).

The first Franciscan pope, NICHOLAS IV, was buried in St. Mary Major in Rome, which he had restored, beneath a floor-level slab near the door leading to Sta. Pudenziana. In 1574 the cardinal of Montalto, the future Sixtus V, had a superb monument constructed for Nicholas IV, like him a Franciscan and born in Piceno. Since the mid-18th century, it has stood at the left when one enters by the main door. The work was created by Domenico Fontana; the sculptures of the pope and of Justice and Religion are by Leonardo da Sarzana (*LP*, II, 467; Chacon, II, 258 and 263–4; Mann, 47–9; Montini, 235–8, fig. 81).

CELESTINE V was interred very simply in the church of Sant'Antonio di Ferantino, which belonged to the eponymous order he had founded. His remains were moved in 1327 to L'Aquila, to the church of Sta. Maria di Collemaggio, where today the mausoleum housing them is in the left nave. It was designed by Girolamo da Vicenza in 1517 (*LP*, II, 468; Papebroch, II, 65–6, drawing; Mann, 49–51; Montini, 238–41, fig. 82; Ladner, II, 255–6, fig. 125).

BONIFACE VIII has his tomb in St. Peter's of the Vatican, in the southeast corner of the nave, behind the altar consecrated to the martyr St. Boniface. He had commissioned Arnolfo di Cambio for the work (1300). In 1605 the tomb was opened; the body was found intact and then placed in the crypts (*LP*, II, 471; Mann, 51–3, fig. 14; Montini, 242–4, figs. 83–4; Ladner, II, 302–13, figs. 152–4, pl. LXX–LXXII, and III, 69–70, 375). For Benedict XI, who is interred in San Domenico in Perugia, a mausoleum was created where the pope's gisant is flanked by two angels parting curtains, with the Virgin between Benedict and Domenico above. A baldachin with twisted columns surmounts the whole. In 1700 this mausoleum was moved from the choir to the left transept. The attribution to Giovanni Pisano is much debated (*LP*, II, 472; Papebroch, II, 69–70, drawing; Mann, 53–4, figs. 15–6; Montini, 245–7, fig. 85; Ladner, II, 341–6, pl. LXXIX–LXXXII).

The first of the Avignon popes, CLEMENT V, was buried according to his wish in the church of Uzeste near Bazas (Gironde), which he had founded and endowed with a canons' chapter. Commissioned from the Orleans silversmith Jean de Bonneval, the tomb was not completed until 1359 (epitaph: Chacon, II, 360). It was despoiled by Protestants in 1577, the mausoleum being badly damaged and the head of the gisant broken. First placed in the choir and moved several times, since 1897 it has stood behind the altar (*LP*, II, 478; J. de Lauriére and E. Mäntz, "Le

tombeau du pape Clément V à Uzeste," *Mém. Soc. Nat. Antiq. France*, 5th s., 8 (1887), 275–92; Mann, 54–6; Montini, 247–8, fig. 86).

The tomb of JOHN XXII is important in that it inaugurated a new type of pontifical mausoleum in which the baldachin is replaced by a structure akin to a Gothic cathedral, with niches, statues, dais, and pinnacles. The design would be imitated on the other French popes' tombs. It was originally in St. Joseph's chapel of the cathedral of Avignon, and is again there today after various vicissitudes. The work of Jean Lavenier, said to be from Paris, the structure has lost its 64 statuettes, 6 of which adorned the pulpit of St. Peter's of Avignon while 2 are in the Calvet Museum (Papebroch, II, 79–80, drawing; E. Mäntz, "Les tombeaux des papes en France," *Gazette des Beaux-Arts*, 36, 1887, 280–4; Mann, 56–7, fig. 17; Montini, 249, fig. 87).

BENEDICT XII was also interred in the cathedral of Avignon (1342). His tomb, also designed by Lavenier, has been almost completely worn away by time (destruction of the dais in 1689) and, especially, by the hand of man: stone-cutters, in whose chapel the tomb stood, and revolutionaries. It is known to us from a 17th-century drawing (Papebroch, II, 85); its restoration by Casimir Poitevin in 1829–31 is in the Avignon museum (E. Mäntz, "Note sur le tombeau du pape Benoît XII à Notre-Dame-des-Doms à Avignon," *Mém. Soc. Nat. Antiq. France*, 5th s., 3 [1882], 261–3; L. Duhamel, "Le tombeau de Benoît à la cathédrale d'Avignon," *Bulletin monumental*, 6th s., 4 [1888], 381–412; Mann, 57–8; Montini, 250–2, fig. 88).

The tomb of CLEMENT VI in the abbey of La Chaise-Dieu, where he had been a monk, was executed during 1346–51 in the pope's lifetime by Pierre Roye and his assistants, Jean de Sanholis and Jean David. The black marble sarcophagus, erected in the middle of the choir, included the statues of 44 people, nearly all of them uncles, brothers, nephews, and cousins of the pope—4 cardinals, 5 archbishops, 9 bishops—a remarkable illustration of that pope's NEPOTISM. The pontiff's body was brought there in 1353. In 1562 Protestants damaged the mausoleum, but the head was restored. Today all that remains is the sarcophagus and the gisant in the middle of the nave (Papebroch, II, 89, drawing; M. Facon, "Documents inédits sur la Chaise-Dieu," *Bull. archéol. Comité trav. histor. et scientif.*, 1884, 416–28 and pl. h.-t., Mann, 59–60; Montini, 252, fig. 89).

INNOCENT VI was interred in the Carthusian monastery of Villeneuve-lès-Avignon, in the Chapel of the Holy Spirit, which he had caused to be built there. Created during his lifetime, his tomb is ringed with 8 pillars terminating in 8 pinnacle turrets. The three central turrets bear statues of Christ, Peter, and Paul, each surmounted by a perforated dais. The tomb is said to be the work of Thomas of Tournon, and the gisant that of Barthélemi

Cavalier. It was spared by the Protestants and then abandoned. In 1835 Mérimæee arranged for it to be set up in the chapel of the hospice of Villeneuve (Papebroch, II, 89, drawing; E. Múntz, "Les tombeaux des papes en France," 378–80; R. Michel, "Le tombeau du pape Innocent VI à Villeneuve-lès-Avignon," *Revue de l'art chrétien*, 1911, 205–10; Mann, 60; Montini, 253–4, fig. 90).

First buried in Avignon (1370), the body of URBAN V was brought in 1372 to St. Victor of Marseilles, of which he had been abbot. The tomb (Papebroch, II, 93, drawing) was badly damaged during the redesign of the choir when the church was secularized, and almost entirely destroyed during the French Revolution (*LP*, II, 494; Mann, 60–1, fig. 18; Montini, 255–7, fig. 91). A cenotaph was put up in their church of St. Martial by the Avignon Benedictines. Its statue was donated to the Calvet museum between 1835 and 1840 (E. Múntz, "La statue du pape Urbain V au Musée d'Avignon," *Gazette archéologique*, 1884, 98–104).

The last French pope before the Great Schism, GREGORY XI, was buried in Sta. Maria Nova (Sta. Francesca Romana) in Rome, of which he had been cardinal. The present monument, in the right transept, was erected on the orders of the Roman Senate by Pietro Paolo Olivieri in 1584. On it is illustrated the pope's return from Avignon in 1377, flanked by the statues of Faith and Prudence (*LP*, II, 495; Mann, 61–2, fig. 19; Montini, 258–9, fig. 92).

The two Avignon popes at the time of the Great Schism, CLEMENT VII (d. 1394) and BENEDICT XIII (d. 1424), were buried, the former in the Celestines' church at Pont de Sorgues (Chacon, II, 673 and 676; Papebroch, 2, 103, drawing), the latter at Peñiscola, in Spain, the fortress of the kingdom of Valencia where he had taken refuge. Later, his nephew had the body moved to his fortress of Illuesca (Chacon, II, 734; Oldoini, 736–7).

The two popes who came out of the council of Pisa, ALEXANDER V and JOHN XXIII, are not considered legitimate. Alexander's terracotta tomb in the church of San Francesco in Bologna underwent considerable renovation in 1584 and 1672 and was restored by Leo XIII (*LP*, II, 512; Chacon, II, 776–8, drawing; Papebroch, II, 109, drawing; Mann, 67–70, fig. 21). The tomb of John XXIII, who died in Florence in 1415, can still be seen in the baptistry in that city. It was financed by Cosimo de' Medici and is the work of Donatello and his pupil Michelozzi (*LP*, II, 519; Chacon, II, 794–6, drawing; Mann, 70–1, fig. 22).

From URBAN VI, with the exception of GREGORY XII and Martin V, the last medieval popes were interred in St. Peter's. The tomb of Urban VI, which is in the south nave, was transferred to the crypts in 1606. On the main surface of the sarcophagus is a bas-relief showing the pope kneeling before Peter, who hands him the keys. The original epitaph was noted before 1606 (Rossi, II, 1, 420; *LP*, III, 140; Mann, 62–3, fig. 61; Montini, 260–3, figs.

93–5). The tomb of BONIFACE IX, with mosaic decoration, used to stand near the preceding one but was destroyed during the rebuilding of the basilica in 1507. We know the epitaph from the account of Peter Sabinus (*LP*, II, 507–8; Chacon, II, 695–7, drawing; Mann, 63–5; Montini, 264–6, fig. 96; Kajanto, 20–3). The sarcophagus of INNOCENT VII was moved to the crypts in 1606. At the feet of the gisant is an inscription indicating that the mausoleum was erected by NICHOLAS V (*LP*, II, 509; Mann, 65–6; Montini, 266–7, fig. 97).

Gregory XII resigned at the council of Constance in 1415 and died two years later at Recanati, cardinal-bishop of Porto and legate of the March of Ancona. He was buried in the cathedral of St. Flavian, where his tomb can still be seen in a dark corner, along with its epitaph in Gothic characters, a rarity in Italy (*LP*, II, 513; Oldoini in Chacon, II, 761–2, drawing; Mann, 66–7; Montini, 267–9, figs. 98–9; Kajanto, 24–30, fig. 1).

Martin V was, according to his wishes, buried in St. John Lateran, in the middle of the central nave beneath a bronze slab bearing his effigy, the work of Simone Ghini. An inscription describes him as "the happiness of his time" (*temporum suorum felicitas*); it is one of the first examples of humanistic writing. In 1853 the tomb was transferred to the confession (*LP*, II, 523; Oldoini in Chacon, II, 827–30, drawing; Mann, 71; Montini, 270–3, figs. 100 and 101; Kajanto, 31–42, fig. 2).

The Venetian EUGENE IV was interred in St. Peter's, in the south lateral nave. When the basilica was demolished, the Venetian canons of St. George in Alga, of which he had been benefactor, rebuilt the tomb with the original marbles in the cloister of their Roman church of San Salvatore in Lauro. The mausoleum, created by Isaïe of Pisa, consists of a Virgin and Child flanked by two angels above the gisant and surrounded by statues of Ambrose, Augustine, Gregory the Great, and Bonaventura. The present inscriptions date from the translation (*LP*, II, 557; Mann, 71–2, fig. 23; Montini, 273–7, fig. 102). The antipope Felix V (d. 1451) was buried in the choir of the priory church of Ripallo (G. Mollat, *DHGE*, II, 1173).

The tomb of Nicholas V (d. 1455) was at the Vatican near that of his predecessor. When the basilica was torn down under JULIUS II, it was moved, then in 1606 it was placed in the crypt—the sarcophagus together with statues of Christ and 6 apostles. His epitaph, the last of a pope to be written in verse, adorns the principal face of the sarcophagus (*LP*, II, 558; Oldoini in Chacon, II, 965–8, drawing; Mann, 73–4, fig. 24; Montini, 277–9, figs. 103–4; Kajanto, 53–63, fig. 5; G. Zander, "Restituzione del monumento sepolcrale de Niccolò V," *L'arte degli Ani Santi, Roma 1300–1875*, Rome, 1984, 350–1).

Callistus III was interred in the old church of Sant'Andrea or Sta. Maria in Febribus adjacent to St. Peter's. Under SIXTUS V, the tomb was transferred to the St. Peter's crypts in 1605. In 1610 the popes' remains were placed in the church of the Spanish colony in Rome, Sta. Maria de Monserato, and in 1889 they were housed in a little monument in the San Diego chapel (*LP*, II, 559; Oldoini in Chacon, II, 986–8, drawing; Mann, 74–7, fig. 27; Montini, 280–4, figs. 105–8).

The tomb of PIUS II used to be in St. Peter's, below the south side nave. In 1608 it was placed in Sant'Andrea della Valle with the marbles of the original monument. His epitaph is known to us through Panvinio and Chacon (*LP*, II, 560; Chacon, II, 1004–5; Mann, 77; Montini, 285–9, fig. 109; Kajanto, 63–9).

PAUL II (d. 1471) was interred in 1474 in St. Mark's chapel in St. Peter's, in a splendid monument built by Mino da Fiesole and Giovanni Dalmata, which was moved in 1544 and destroyed at the beginning of the 16th century. We know of it from some fine drawings, notably from Oldoini (Chacon, II, 1092–4). At the base were statues of the theological Virtues, the creation of Eve, and the temptation. Above the gisant was shown the resurrection of Christ and, in the upper lunette, the Last Judgment. What is left of the monument is in the crypts (Mann, 77–9, fig. 28; Montini, 290–3, figs. 110–1; Kajanto, 69–73, fig. 6).

Cardinal Giuliano della Rovere, the future Julius II, commissioned a splendid mausoleum for his uncle SIX-TUS IV (d. 1484), the work of the Florentine Antonio Pollaiulo. Moved from the old to the new St. Peter's basilica, where it remained up to 1922, the monument finally ended up in the crypts after a stay in the museum (Mann, 79; Montini, 293–6, fig. 295; Kajanto, 74–85, figs. 9–12).

Robert Favreau

See also ST. PETER'S BASILICA.

Bibliography

Borgolte, M. *Petrusnachfolge und Kaiserimitation: Die Grablegen der Päpste, ihre Genese und Traditionsbildung*, Göttingen, 1989.

De Rossi, J. B., ed. *Inscriptiones christianae urbis Romae septimo saeculo antiquiores*, II–1, Rome, 1888.

Descriptions and drawings from the 16th–17th centuries are still valuable, in particular the *Vitae et res gestae Summorum Pontificum* by the Dominican Alsonon Chacon (Ciaconius), penitentiary at St. Peter's, Rome (d. 1599), in the greatly enlarged edition by the Jesuit Agostino Oldoini, Rome, 1677, 3 vols., and the *Conatus chronico-historicus ad catalogum pontificum*, pub. by the Jesuit Daniel Papebroch (d. 1714) in *Propylaeum ad septem tomos maii* of the *Acta sanctorum*, reed. Paris and Rome, 1868, 2 pts.

Forcella, V. *Iscrizioni delle chiese e d'altri edifici di Roma del secolo XI fino ai giorni nostri*, Rome, 1869–84, 14 vols.

Gregorovius, F. *Die Grabdenkmäler der Päpste: Marksteine der Geschichte des Papsttums*, 1881;

Kajanto, I. *Papal Epigraphy in Renaissance Rome*, Helsinki, 1982 (Annales Academiae Scientiarum Fennicae).

Ladner, G. B. *I Rittrati dei Papi nell' Antichita e nel Medioevo*, I, *Dalle origini fino alla fine della lotta per le investiture*, Vatican, 1941; *Die Papstbildnisse des Altertums und des Mittelalters*, II, *Von Innocenz II, zu Benedikt XI.*, and III. *Addenda et Corrigenda*, Vatican, 1970–84 (Monumenti di Antichità cristiana pubblicati dal pontificio Istituto di Archeologia cristiana, II, IV).

Lauer, P. *Le Palais de Latran: Étude historique et archéologique*, Paris, 1911, 391–409 and 410–90.

Liber Pontificalis (*LP*), ed. L. Duchesne, Paris, 1955–7, 3 vols.

Mann, K. T. Msgr. *Tombs and Portraits of the Popes of the Middle Ages*, London, 1929.

Montini, R. U. *Le tombe dei Papi*, Rome, 1957.

Schneider, F. "Die Epitaphien der Päpste und andere stadtrömische Inschriften des Mittelalters," *Texte zur Kulturgeschichte des Mittelalters*, VI, Rome, 1933 (62 inscriptions from 308 to 1181).

TRAVELERS' VIEWS OF ROME AND THE VATICAN. Longer analyses of travelers' writings generally concentrate on precise themes considered over a long span of time; here, we cannot do more than present a single example, though a highly significant one. This is the *Voyage d'un François en Italie dans les années 1765 et 1766* (A Frenchman's Journey to Italy) by J. J. Lefrançois de Lalande, which constituted a veritable Bible for French travelers in the peninsula. The book allows us to define the unique character of Rome, and more specifically of the Vatican. Quotations are taken from volumes 3–6 of the 1786 edition.

Lalande's curiosity and culture, those of a man of the ENLIGHTENMENT, are vast and his judgments well balanced, so that his text retains interest for the modern reader. In general, however, travel books of the period demand a grasp on the reader's part of historical issues (e.g., the French occupation of Rome) and of the author's personal viewpoint. The writers' personalities can be extremely colorful—for example, the President de Brosses, who provides piquant anecdotes but also some cavalier judgments. One must also consider the writer's background in terms of social class and religion—a Protestant is likely to have a critical opinion of the Vatican—as well as classical education (possessed by most of the early travelers, though not by some moderns), and finally, whether the book is aimed at a general or specialized audience.

Cultivated travelers of Lalande's day were thoroughly familiar with the ancient sources, but also with historical bibliography, older guides, and travel writings. Beyond his personal experience, Lalande had a large number of well-informed correspondents in Rome and elsewhere in Italy who showered him with economic statistics, among other things. One of his chapters deals with "writers who have provided descriptions of Rome and its Antiquities" and gives a "note of the best writers whom one may consult to obtain the most thorough details." Rubrics in the volumes concern observations on the lay of the land, hydrography, climate (the bad air), the site of a "superb" city, its walls, and its general fascination: "Rome's situation is advantageous; the small hills within it furnish a variety of levels, form agreeable viewpoints and enable those who inhabit the lower ground to take the air without leaving Rome by climbing up to the heights . . . , the city is cut through with large, straight streets." Other preliminary information concerns ancient, modern, and contemporary history (III, 369: history of the papacy, causes of temporal greatness).

On the Monuments. The traveler's attention is then directed to the monuments: those of Antiquity, with precise information on their history, present state, and EXCAVATIONS; and those still in use—the churches and, first and foremost, ST. PETER'S. Lalande writes, "the first object that strikes the eye, no matter from which direction one reaches Rome, even from a very great distance is the vast dome. . . . Unquestionably this is the greatest and finest church in all the world; no other edifice exists to equal it in grandeur, richness and taste. It is the masterpiece of Italy; one might even call it the wonder of the Universe [account of building work], grandeur, magnificence, taste, great beauties of the whole, true proportion, no object can compare with it . . . , the dome is the most astonishing part, the boldest piece of work . . . that architecture has attempted [full description]." Detailed notes are given concerning the other Roman churches, the itineraries also describe other points of interest:

Civic buildings, notably palaces (including that of the Vatican): "An atmosphere of grandeur prevails in Rome, which is derived from the fact that the principal facades always give on to the street; this air of magnificence also is due to the height of the edifices, which have to be built several stories above the insalubrious air. These various floors are used at different seasons of the year. . . . As for the first floor [U.S. second], which is commonly called the *appartamento nobile*, it is designed for feasts and extraordinary assemblies."

Ornaments of the city, particularly the fountains: "There are at the crossroads of Rome and in a large number of small squares, fountains which lend much pleasure and gaiety to this city."

Villas, their gardens and art collections (Villa Mattei, Villa Giustiniani, etc.). The life of the inhabitants is described, with observations on demography as a whole (population estimated at 170,000 to 180,000 inhabitants),

on the city sections (Trastevere, the Borgo), social classes (beggars and vagabonds, commoners, bourgeois and nobles, including the great houses of the Colonna, Orsini, Conti, and Savelli. "The magnificence of the great families consists in the main in having vast palaces, many pages, footmen, lackeys, horses and carriages; valuable paintings and beautiful statues, both ancient and modern. Their pomp is displayed neither in fine food nor in luxurious clothing. Company is invited to dine only rarely, and that on grand occasions; one must except their stays in the country, or parties in the nobles' country places; here friends are invited and some money is spent. Rich families are few" (on society life, see below).

Lalande describes foreigners' stays in Rome, with pointed remarks on "the spirit of the nations": they have to rent an apartment and hire a carriage (there being no public coaches here as in France and England, with a fixed schedule), accept the practice of New Year's gifts, and be at the mercy of the *ciceroni* (guides). "The best advice is to lodge with an Italian family." The writer passes a severe judgment on his compatriots: "The English enjoy a high reputation in Italy. They only leave their country when they are able to spend freely. . . , whereas the French, who are more easygoing, more frivolous, often go to Italy with few resources and do not give a good impression of France; vagabonds and exiles go there to seek asylum because of its proximity, and they cause their nation to be disparaged. Moreover, the presumptuous French always pour scorn on anything that does not originate in their country, and say so boldly, being forward with the women and inconsiderate with the men; the frequent wars that they have fought in Italy have left behind an unfavorable impression . . . , but people appreciate the wit of the French, their agreeable ways, their language, their books, their fashions. . . . The women dress in the French style; they follow as closely as possible French fashions, as regards coiffure and attire."

Economy. "In the Papal State, agriculture is the worst of all enterprises, so that where the land is not extremely fertile, it is practically desert," ruined by the restrictions on wheat (in contrast to France where, in 1764, exports were permitted). Lalande describes the crafts of mosaic and stucco. "In Rome many sacred urns and reliquaries are made; people fashion hats of beaver and silk, which are very fine; lambskins, treated in alum, go to make white, embroidered gloves; from catgut, artificial pearls are made. Colored clay is sold to decorate pottery. The pope gives much encouragement to the fabrication of linens and fabrics." People also make cosmetic powder (*cyprio*), perfumed pomade, and artificial flowers. One chapter is devoted to weights, measures, coins, trade ("very limited"), and prices: "Along the Tiber they export grains, wools, silks, spirits, alum, saltpeter, manna-ash, cakes of sulfur, porcelain, lumber for building. . . . Rome has a thriving trade in paintings, antiques, medals, and engraved or molded stones. One must be either a connoisseur or a dupe. The English take away many antiques. . . . In Rome everyone is concerned with paintings and claims to know about them. . . . Rome also trades in Italian marble, even ancient and Oriental marbles."

Civilization in All Its Aspects. Lalande has praise for papal diplomacy: "All the resources of spirit and the most refined politics are employed in this court. There is no republic in Europe that affords more opportunity to practice this difficult art, which consists in influencing minds and reconciling everyone to achieve one's goals. . . . Politics is cultivated in Rome, and many cardinals and prelates carry out, as in the past, a serious study of the interests of nations." The author gives full details on the cardinals' duties (nuncio), the majordomo, the congregations, chamberlain, consistory, *consulta*, Inquisition, and Congregation of the Index. (He describes the condemnation of Copernicus; however, in the latest edition of the Index it was agreed to remove the article covering all his books upholding the movement of Earth.) He lists the tribunals ("Rome, even more than France, suffers from the calamity of long trials"), the governor ("hampered in the exercise of his duties by the influence of powerful persons"), the senator, the conservators, the Apostolic Chamber, the troops (77,000 men, 2,000 to 5,000 of them effective), and revenues ("these are said to amount to 10 million francs, but more than half are given over to the payment of debts; the rest is dedicated in part to pious destinations").

Lalande envisages the possibility of reforms, in particular concerning the right of asylum: "A misguided respect for the externals of religion brought about its institution, and there is nothing more harmful to the political government, the safety of citizens, the policing of the states and the true respect due to religion. . . . That is why Rome has so many robberies and assassinations. . . . The murderers all take refuge in the churches, and it is impossible to seize them." In general fashion, the writer denounces Roman intrigue: "In a country where one so often changes masters, where change affords everyone hope, where people expect everything from solicitation and intrigue, where almost everyone has opinions and where no one thinks of remaining in his present station, one can but long for a new reign."

Religion. Lalande observes that ecclesiastical habits can be seen everywhere. He is particularly interested in the situation of the cardinals, "the most eminent persons of the court of Rome, the ordinary council of the pope, the trustees and ministers of his authority. Not only do they choose the sovereign; but they always choose him from

among their number; which gives them all a hope and a right which raises them at least above everyone who is not a cardinal. . . ." (The writer passes a prudent judgment on certain abuses, like "protection.") "The hope of becoming cardinal is the greatest driving force of conduct and politics for the Romans, because from there one can attain sovereignty. All the wishes, all ambitions, all maneuvers are directed to this goal, some reaching toward it through their talents, others through their virtue, many through their intrigues and wiliness. Yet the hope that a cardinal has to become pope comes down to a fairly slight probability [as a man of science, Lalande here proceeds to make learned calculations]. . . . One must omit all foreigners, all those who, through too wide an influence, too powerful enemies, too lively a character, manners that are too free, manage to exclude themselves, those who come from too powerful a house, who show too much attachment or too much hatred for a kingdom or for a party; in this a way the number of cardinals that appear eligible (out of 70) amounts to barely more than three or four in a conclave; even though the cardinals' seats are granted by preference to persons of higher social rank, men from lower strata often attain them by influence and merit; even the members of religious orders can hope to win a place."

The writer describes at length how the conclave functions (a little history of some elections, but without malice), the coronation ceremonies, the papal procession and its symbolism (*flabelli*, *sedia*, the ceremonial of the kissing of the pope's foot), the rites of presentation, and audiences. He provides details on the administration of the faith (indulgences, canonizations, and excommunications); he defines the role of the orders (the Jesuits) and gives a good idea of religious feeling and its manifestations: feast days, processions (like that of dowered girls), the ceremony of the palfrey, Holy Week, pilgrimages, penitents "who go to pray inside the churches so as to obtain remission of sins committed during carnival."

In contrast to certain rationalists (like de Brosses) or Protestants (such as F. J. H. Meyer), Lalande gives a balanced overall judgment on the papacy: "The union of temporal and spiritual power makes the pope the most absolute of all sovereigns and, his despotism being that of God, he never experiences either contradiction or obstacles, [but] the gentleness of this paternal government tends to communicate itself and the sovereign's great age impels him to seek help for such an immense administration. . . . The pomp which surrounds the pope and the ceremonies of the Roman Church are the most majestic, the most august and the most important that one can see. I know that a philosophy destructive of all inequality, all religion, all power, makes certain persons regard all ceremonies as a game, but in whatever way one considers those of the court of Rome, they can only be respectable. . . . I have heard it said in all parts that the pope's table is served in the most modest manner. . . . The character of the papacy demands a retinue, a constraint, a subservience, a display, for which the glory of this exalted rank can barely compensate. . . . As care has been taken to choose a pope who has no great passions, his authority cannot be subject to grave hindrances; moreover, the great age and the gentle nature of the popes who have reigned for many years have caused the ecclesiastical state to be regarded as a place where everyone commands and no one obeys."

Cultural Life. One chapter is devoted to the state of the sciences and the arts: "Erudition, languages, the antiquities, monuments, sculptured medallions have been cultivated, in all ages, far more in Rome than in any other place." The sciences are not forgotten (reference to the Academy of the Lincei). Rome includes many men of letters, poets (lists of names, enumeration of writers, journals, doctors, artists). "In the realm of the fine arts, Rome has truly been the capital of the world."

Lalande's comments in this area allow us to measure the relativity of our judgments and to be aware of the evolution of taste. A characteristic example is the *Last Judgment* in the Sistine chapel: "The general composition of this painting appears to be unsound. . . . It is nothing more than a pile of figures. . . . There is no variation in the expressions . . ., the whole has neither effect nor colors . . . the painting is badly faded, and spoiled by the draperies that have been placed over most of the naked figures. It is a madness of anatomical representation and draftsmanship. Michelangelo was a bad painter, but a terrible draftsman . . . a palette lacking in harmony, a certain overall coloring that is unpleasant, a mixture of blue and red. . . . The whole work creates a sensation, and amazes more than it gives pleasure. [But] the academic figures on the ceiling are very fine and great examples of drawing . . ., some of the representations of the Eternal Father are admirable. Michelangelo has depicted in a sublime manner God dispelling chaos." Lalande's impressions of Raphael's frescoes in the Vatican seem more subtle: "In general, the composition is beautiful, the figures are well conceived, but for the most part badly carried out, especially as concerns the color . . ., almost all the heads are ill chosen. [And yet] the *School of Athens* is a great subject rendered in a noble and skillful manner. Not only is Raphael admirable in the detailed composition of each of these various works, he is admirable, too, in his overall conception." He stresses the cultural role of the papacy: "Father Visconti, antiquary to the pope, buys from all quarters . . ., he causes the principal acquisitions to be recorded by painters and engravers in order to publish their description."

The writer turns to the place of music in churches, on the eve or the day of festivals: "There is little difference between sacred music and that in the theater," he says, insisting in regard to the latter: "The propriety of the ecclesiastical State even forbids the presence of actresses in Rome. Women's roles are played by young boys, who might easily be taken for girls because of their voices and their faces, which they have acquired at the cost of their virility (the castrati). . . . Shows continue from Christmas, or Epiphany, up to but excluding Ash Wednesday; they commence at 2 o'clock in the morning and continue for four or five hours. At other times the only stage shows are the marionettes, and in Lent none are put on at all. . . . There is much leaping about and there are almost always pantomimes, performed often with but little grace." Rome possessed eight theaters, including the Argentina, "one of the finest in all Italy, [but] it is poorly decorated and there is no stage machinery. . . . The pope grants a privilege for the productions. . . . The Italians have a great fondness for heroic comedy. The Italian people have little liking for a good tragedy." Lalande describes the festivals (other than religious ones): Carnival (with executions to instil fear in the people), masked promenades (two rows of coaches on the Corso), disguises (Punchinello, Shepherdess, Harlequins, Bacchantes), weeklong horse races in the Corso, and balls. The author regrets the absence of public promenades, but notes that most gardens are open to visitors.

National Temperament and the Romans' Way of Life. Some observations have to do with public opinion and the way it is manifested: "In Rome, the license to write is stretched to the limit; the liveliest satires are permitted as are the most atrocious libels, and often people pin up even on a cardinal's door the most hurtful thing they have to say to him. . . . There is no conclave but attracts the most dreadful satires, some of which are attributed to cardinals or other persons of the highest distinction, and which are read everywhere, with no disguising of names, so great is the freedom in Rome" (allusions to Pasquin, Marforio, hand-written gazettes). "The city of Rome, although very large, does not offer the tumultuous aspect of a capital; its inhabitants lead a fairly uniform life; Rome resembles our great provincial cities rather than Paris, where everything is moving. . . . In Rome, people see each other and know each other as in our provincial cities; each knows the other's ways; and everything is food for the gazette writers in this gentle, agreeable society." Of dining, "The Romans never give foreigners anything to eat. . . . In the *conversazioni* or receptions, one is offered preserves and ices; at morning visits, chocolate is generally served. . . ; the custom of French chefs has not yet reached Rome; yet one can still be very well treated when one dines at the table of the rich; but the seasonings always taste somewhat sweet and sugary. . . . However, they use many spices. . . . The grand lords live extremely simply; there are some very well-off persons who use the services of an innkeeper or a cook. . . . The people live even more frugally, often lacking a table or appointed kitchen; one finds very few inns, restaurateurs or cook-shop proprietors, but many bad cooks who set up great pots at the street corners and make communal stews, where cheese is the dominant ingredient; and macaroni which everyone buys for a couple of bajoccos, together with some fish and some hard-boiled eggs." And of spending: "One does not find in Italy such extraordinary, newly made fortunes [as in Paris], those huge inequalities that are so overwhelming for the public. . . . An Italian, after having amassed a large sum of ready money through living frugally, often spends it on the construction of some grand building, which, serving as the adornment or the utility of his fatherland, passes on to posterity, in a lasting manner, his name, his magnificence, and his taste."

The author includes an obligatory chapter on the *cicisbeo*, the Italian married woman's male companion. He is prudence itself on this delicate matter: "The *coquetterie* of our Frenchwomen, some of whom take pride in tormenting men and being followed by a great number of admirers, is regarded in Italy as the height of indecency and bad morals: on the other hand, the use of *cicisbei* is claimed to be highly respectable: their constant attention is, some say, merely an accepted custom, one of polite society, nor do they make any other claims; but there is no general agreement on the question. . . . The Italian women's pride ensures constancy, and consequently diminishes licentiousness. . . . The Roman is exceedingly gentle by nature; he is humanized by the general custom of currying favor with one greater than oneself, and by the continual society of foreigners. The Romans are full of cordiality and consideration, more obliging and more accessible than in any other part of Italy."

One chapter is devoted to the receptions known as *conversazioni*: "In Rome, assemblies are the principal resource for foreigners and the principal diversion in a city where theatrical productions are given only during a very limited part of the year. The 'conversations' that begin at the Ave Maria, or at 24 hours, are called those of the *prima sera*. . . . At 2 o'clock at night the great conversations begin; these continue until 5 o'clock. . . ." (Lalande points out that in Italy the 24-hour day ends 30 minutes after the apparent setting of the center of the sun.) "Foreign travelers gain easy access to these conversations." The gardens are bright with illuminations and fountains. The author emphasizes the grace and expressivity of people's gestures. At the conversations, the guests play cards and discuss "with much freedom, even when speaking about affairs of Rome, or even more about those in foreign countries; everyone has a taste for politics. . . . The women in general have an affected, stiff way about them, and the women of distinction who want to appear easy and free affect an air that we would call immodest." He emphasizes etiquette, *la dignità*. "The ladies never go out alone. . . , a young girl may not walk about alone." He points out some faults which strike him as systematic: "The women of the people are magnificent, willful and lazy. . . . Charity is given out frequently and often inappropriately; this is one of the government's vices, for the practice encourages idleness. [A dowried daughter] will spend all her time at her window looking at the passersby. . . . The large number of hospitals and the custom of having bread, soup and alms in the convents encourages begging. The number of domestics of the nobles, drawing people off the land, creates hunger in the city and contributes to idleness and mendicancy." Like most travelers, Lalande notes that the Trasteverians constitute "a nation apart," a rougher people. Rome is the scene of frequent murders ("2,000 a year throughout the ecclesiastical State"), brawls, and dangers of uprisings. "The churches' right of sanctuary and granting of immunity contribute much to the encouragement of riots. It is seldom that one sees a hanging or death by the *massola* [clubbing] in Rome; sometimes prisoners are condemned to the galleys. The most common torture is the *strappado*." The author notes the absence of night patrols.

A Look into the Future. "I doubt not but that one day the Vatican will acquire buildings and a street, worthy of announcing from an even greater distance the incomparable monument." Lalande mentions plans regarding the Vatican Library, and he wishes that the statues in the Vatican museum might be shown individually instead of being housed in niches so that it might be possible to "walk around them to enjoy their different aspects." For him, as for the majority of the travelers, the vital problem is that of the Roman countryside: "One is astonished to see to what point the vast plains around Rome are abandoned and uncultivated, those plains that were once so flourishing and so peopled. . . . The want of cultivation in a countryside ordinarily brings in its wake the want of salubriousness in the air." An admirable summing-up, which might deserve to be republished.

Raymond Chevallier

List of Travelers to Rome. Guidebooks are excluded from this list. Works are given in the alphabetical order of authors' names.

J. Addison, *Travels in Italy*, London, 1705. *Remarks on Several Parts of Italy in the Years 1701, 1702 and 1703*, London, 1705, 1718, 1733, 1736, 1745.

F. M. G. Alexis, *Rome et l'Italie: Souvenirs de voyage dedies à la jeunesse chrétienne*, Paris-Tournai, 1923.

J. J. Ampère, "Portraits de Rome à différents âges," *RDM*, 1835; *La Grèce, Rome et Dante*, Paris, 1859.

P. Barbier, *Italie: Souvenirs et impressions de voyage*, Paris, 1893.

J. J. Barthélemy (abbé), printed from the original letters written to the count of Caylus, Paris, 1901, 1802, 1803, 1810.

P. J. O. Bergeret de Grancourt, *Voyage d'Italie (1773–74)*, Paris, 1948.

J. J. Boissard, *Topographia urbis Romae*, Frankfurt, 1527.

C. V. de Bonstetten, *Voyage sur la scène des six derniers livres de l'Énéide ou voyage dans le Latium*, Geneva, 1800, 1804, 1971.

J. J. Bouchard, *Les Confessions de J.J.B. Parisien, suivies de son voyage de Paris à Rome en 1630*, Paris, 1881.

C. de Brosses, *Lettres historiques et critiques sur l'Italie*, Paris, 1799, 1836, 1858. *Lettres familières écrites d'Italie en 1739–1740*, Paris, 1856, 1857, 1858, 1869, 1881, 1883, 1885; Dijon, 1897.

G. Burnet, *Some Letters Containing an Account of What Seemed Most Remarkable in Travelling through Switzerland, Italy . . . in the Years 1685 and 1686*, London, 1724, 1750.

A. C. P. de Tubières, comte de Caylus, *Voyage d'Italie, 1714–1715*, Paris, 1914.

François-René, vicomte de Chateaubriand, *Voyage en Italie*, Paris, 1827 (Grenoble, 1921; Geneva, 1969); *Memoirs*, Eng. tr. of *Mémoires d'outre-tombe*, London, 1961.

B. P. Chérémétieff, *Journal du Voyage du Boyard B.P.C. à Cracovie, Venise, Rome et Malte (1697–9)*, Paris, 1859.

C. N. Cochin, *Voyage d'Italie ou Recueil de notes sur les ouvrages de peinture et de sculpture qu'on voit dans les principales villes d'Italie*, Paris, 1751, 1758, 1769; Lausanne, 1773; Nuremberg, 1776.

J. B. Colbert, marquis de Seignelay, *L'Italie en 1671*, Paris, 1867.

L. Colet, *L'Italie des Italiens*, Paris, 1862–4.

H. de Bourbon, prince de Condé, *Voyage de M. le P. de C. en Italie*, Bourges, 1624; Paris, 1634, 1635, 1666; Lyon, 1665.

T. Coryat, *Coryat's Crudities*, London, 1611, 1776.

P. L. Courier, *Lettres écrites de France et d'Italie (1787–1812)*, Paris, 1828.

G. F. Coyer (abbé), *Voyage d'Italie*, Paris, 1775, 1776, 1778, 1790.

A. F. Creuz, de Lesser (baron), *Voyage en Italie et en Sicile fait en 1801 et 1802*, Paris, 1806.

É. J. Delecluze, *Lettres: Le Vatican*, Paris, n.d.; *Carnet de Route d'Italie . . . Impressions romaines*, Paris, 1942.

F. Deseine, *Description de la ville de Rome*, Lyon, 1690, 1699, *Nouveau voyage d'Italie*, Lyon, 1694; *L'ancienne Rome*, Leyden, 1713; *Rome moderne*, Leyden, 1738.

C. Didier, *La Campagne de Rome*, Paris, 1842.

M. A. Lepage Figuet (Madame Du Boccage), *Lettres de Mme D. contenant ses voyages en Italie* [made during the years 1756, 1757 and 1758; from 1766 to 1768], Dresden, 1771 (Lyon, 1764; Paris, 1749–56).

C. Pinot, dit Duclos, *Voyage en Italie ou Considérations sur l'Italie*, Paris-Lausanne, 1791 (Œuvres, Paris, 1806).

A. Dumas, *Impressions de voyage en Italie*, Paris, 1832.

J. B. Mercier Dupaty, *Lettres sur l'Italie écrites en 1785*, Lausanne, 1789, 1796, 1800; Genoa, 1810, Paris, 1827.

P. Duval, *Le Voyage et la description d'Italie*, Troyes, 1756; Paris, 1660; *L'Italie et l'Allemagne*, Paris, 1668.

M. D. D. Farjasse, *L'Italie*, Paris, 1834; II, 1836.

C. Frescot, *Remarques historiques et critiques faites dans un voyage d'Italie. . . .*, Cologne, 1705.

J. J. Gaume, *Les Trois Rome: Journal d'un voyage en Italie*, Paris, 1867–8–76, 4 vols.

F. Baron de Géramb, *Voyage de la Trappe à Rome (1844)*, Paris-Laval, 1938.

E. Gibbon, *Journey from Geneva to Rome*, 1764, ed. G. A. Bonnard, London, 1961.

J. W. Goethe, *Italian Journey*, 1786–1788, London, 1962, Eng. tr. of *Italienische Reise* (1780).

É., princesse de Gonzague (née Rangoni), *Lettres écrites à ses amis pendant le cours de ses voyages d'Italie en 1779 et années suivantes*, Paris, 1790; Berlin, 1796; Hamburg, 1797.

J. Gorani, *Mémoires secrets et critiques des cours de l'Italie*, Paris, 1793.

A. Goudar, *L'Espion chinois ou l'envoyé secret de la cour de Pékin, pour examiner l'état présent de l'Europe*, Cologne, 1764.

J. Gourdault, *Rome et la campagne romaine*, Paris, 1889.

B. Grangier de Liverdis, *Journal d'un voyage de France et d'Italie fait par un gentilhomme français (1600–1661)*, Paris, 1667, 1670, 1679.

P. J. Grosley, *Nouveaux Mémoires ou Observations de deux gentilshommes suédois sur l'Italie et sur les Italiens*, London-Paris, 1764; London, 1770; Amsterdam-Paris, 1774.

J. B. Marie Guidi (abbé), *Lettres contenant le journal d'un voyage fait à Rome en 1773*, Paris-Geneva, 1783.

M. Guyot de Merville, *Voyage historique et politique d'Italie . . .*, The Hague, 1729; Frankfurt, 1736.

J. Hughetan and J. Spon, *Voyage d'Italie curieux et nouveau*, Lyon, 1681.

A. Jal., *De Paris à Naples*, Paris, 1836.

C. Jordan, *Voyages historiques de l'Europe*, Paris, 1693.

P. de Joux, *Lettres sur l'Italie, considérées sous le rapport de la religion*, Paris, 1815.

V. J. Étienne, dit de Jouy, *L'Hermite en Italie*, Brussels, 1824.

J. R. B. Labat (R.P.), *Voyage en Espagne et en Italie dans les années 1705 et 1707*, Paris, 1730; Amsterdam, 1731.

F. de La Boullaye Le Gouz, *Les Voyages et observations*, Paris, 1657.

J. J. Lefrançois de Lalande, *Voyage d'un Français en Italie fait dans les années 1765 et 1766*, Paris, 1768; Venice-Paris, 1769, 1786; Geneva, 1790.

F. de Lamennais, *Affaires de Rome*, Paris, 1839.

A. H. Lemonnier, *Souvenirs d'Italie*, Paris, 1832.

J. Le Saige, *Chy s'ensuyvent les gistes, repaistres et despens que moi, J. Le Saige . . . ay faict de Douay à Hierusalem*, Cambray, 1520, 1523; Anvers, 1581; Douai, 1851.

Lettres contenant le Journal d'un voyage fait à Rome en 1773, Geneva, 1783.

J. F. Lullin de Chateauvieux, *Lettres sur l'Italie*, Paris, 1834.

G. M. J. Mabillon and M. Germain, *Iter Italicum Letterarium (1685–86)*, Paris, 1687; *Museum Italicum*, Paris, 1687–9, 1724.

H. Maréchal *Rome, souvenirs d'un musicien*, Paris, 1904.

F. J. L. Meyer, *Darstellungen aus Italien* (1783), *Voyages en Italie*, Paris, 1802; *Tableaux d'Italie* (ed. Elisabeth Chavellier, Centre Jean-Bérard Naples, 1980).

J. Michelet and Th. Scharten, *Les Voyages et séjours de Michelet en Italie*, Paris, 1934.

A. L. Millin, *Lettres à Langlès sur le carnaval de Rome*, Paris, 1812; *Tablettes d'un voyage en Italie*, Paris, 1818.

M. Misson, *A New Voyage to Italy*, 4 vols., London, 1714, Eng. tr. of *Nouveau voyage d'Italie fait en 1688*, The Hague, 1691–4, 1702, 1713, 1717.

T. Mommsen, *Tagebuch der französisch-italienischen Reise*, Bern–Frankfurt-am-Main, 1976 (ed. G. and B. Walser).

B. de Monconys, *Journal des voyages de M. de M.*, Lyon, 1665–6, 1678; Paris, 1677, 1695.

M. de Montaigne, *Journal (1580)*, Rome-Paris, 1774; Paris, 1946 (ed. Ch. Dédéyan).

C. L. de Segondat, baron de Montesquieu, *Voyages*, Bordeaux, 1894–6 and *Œuvres*, Paris, I, 1949–58.

B. de Montfaucon, *Diarium Italicum*, Paris, 1702 and ed. A. Galliano, Geneva, 1987 (Biblioteca del Viaggio in Italia, 20).

Lady Sydney Owenson Morgan (Miss Owenson), *Italy*, 3 vols., London, 1821.

Moyne (abbé), *L'Italie: Guide du jeune voyageur*, Rouen, 1855.

F. Nodot, *Relation de la cour de Rome*, Paris, 1701; *Mémoires curieux et galants d'un voyage nouveau d'Italie*, The Hague, 1702; *Nouveaux Mémoires*, Amsterdam, 1706.

A. C. Pasquin (Valery), *L'Indicateur italien*, Paris, 1831–3; *Voyages historiques et littéraires en Italie* (1826–1828), Paris, 1831-2-3-5-8; Brussels, 1843; Eng. ed. 1834, 1852.

P. Petit-Radel, *Voyage historique, chorographique et philosophique dans les principales villes de l'Italie en 1811 et 1812*, Paris, 1815.

R. Pocock, *A Description of the East, and Some Other Countries*, London, 1743–5.

C. L. baron de Poellnitz, *The Memoirs of Charles Lewis, Baron of Pollnitz*, London, 1737–8; 2nd ed., 1739–40.

E. Polonceau, *Itinéraire descriptif et instructif de l'Italie en 1833*, Paris, 1835.

D. Possot, *Voyage de la Terre sainte*, 1532 (cf. Schefer, Paris, 1890; Geneva, 1971).

A. Potocka, *Voyage d'Italie (1826–1827)*, Paris, 1899.

E. Quinet, *Allemagne et Italie*, Paris, 1846 (2nd ed.).

F. Rabelais, *La Sciomachie et Festins faits à Rome*, Lyon, 1549; *Les Epistres escrites pendant son voyage d'Italie*, Paris, 1651; Brussels, 1710.

E. Renan, *Voyages (Italie, 1849)*, Paris, 1850.

J. Richard (abbé), *Description historique et critique de l'Italie, ou Nouveaux Mémoires sur l'état actuel de son gouvernement, des sciences, des arts, du commerce, de la population et de l'histoire naturelle*, Dijon, 1766; 2nd ed., Paris, 1769, 1770, 1794, 1799.

Rogissart (Sieur de), Havard (abbé), *Les Délices de l'Italie*, Amsterdam, 1700, 1743; Paris, 1700, 1707, 1725; Leyden, 1709.

Henri, duc de Rohan, *Voyage fait en l'an 1600 en Italie . . .*, Amsterdam, 1646; Paris, 1661.

Rolland (abbé), *Promenades en Italie*, Tours, 1885.

D. A. F., marquis de Sade, *Œuvres*, Paris, 1967 (*Voyage d'alie*, Rome, pp. 193–381).

C. H. A. Schefer (ed.), *Le Voyage de la saincte cyté de Hierusalem* (1480), Paris, 1890.

S. Sharp, *Letters from Italy (1765–1766)*, London, 1767.

L. Simon, *Voyage en Italie et en Sicile*, Paris, 1827–8.

L. de Sivry, *Rome et l'Italie méridionale*. Paris, 1843.

Souvenirs de voyage ou lettres d'une voyageuse malade, Paris-Lille-Lyon, 1836.

J. Spon, G. Wheler, *Voyage d'Italie, de Dalmatie, de Grèce et du Levant*, Lyon, 1678; Amsterdam, 1679; The Hague, 1680, 1689, 1724.

A. L. G. Necker, baronne de Staël-Holstein, *Corinne ou l'Italie*, Paris, 1807.

H. Beyle (Stendhal), *Rome, Naples et Florence*, Paris, 1817, 1826; *Promenades dans Rome*, Paris, 1858, 1893, 1926.

H. Taine, *Voyage en Italie*, Paris, 1884, 1901.

Vicomte C. Terlinden, "Le voyage . . . Rome du chevalier de Moreau de Bioul, 1791," *BIBR*, 1949, 243 ff.; "Voyage en Italie de trois gentilshommes flamands, 1724–1725," *BIBR*, 1958, 217 ff.

Une année en Italie, Journal d'une jeune fille, Paris, 1847.

L. Veuillot, *Rome et Lorette*, Paris, 1841; *Le Pape et la diplomatie*, Paris, 1861; *Le Parfum de Rome*, Paris, 1862; *Rome pendant le concile*, Paris, 1972.

Comte de Vienne, *Voyage*, Ms Dijon, 1774.

L. É. Vigée-Lebrun, *Souvenirs*, Paris, 1835–7, 1885.

J. seigneur de Villamont, *Les Voyages du Sr de V.*, Paris, 1596–1600–1602–1609; Arras, 1598; Lyon, 1605; Liège, 1608; Rouen, 1607–1608–1610–1613.

P. Faillant de Villemarest, *L'Hermite en Italie*, X, 1824.

E. E. Viollet-le-Duc, *Lettres d'Italie*, Paris, 1971.

J. J. Volkmann, *Historisch-Kritische Nachrichten von Italien*, Utrecht, 1773; Leipzig, 1776–8; Amsterdam, 1779.

Voyage depuis Lyon jusqu'à Rome, Dijon, 1672–3.

E. Warcupp, *Italy in Its Original Glory, Ruins and Revival*, London, 1660.

J. J. A. M., baron de Witte, *Rome et l'Italie sous Léon XIII*, Paris, 1893.

E. Wright, *Some Observations Made in Travelling through Italy, 1720–1722*, London, 1730, 2nd ed., 1764.

A. Young, *Voyage en Italie pendant l'année 1789*, Paris, 1795–6, 1860.

É. Zola, *Mes voyages*, Paris, 1958.

Bibliography

Bertaut, J. *L'Italie vue par les Français*, Paris, 1913.

Chevallier, É. and R. *Iter Italicum: Les voyageurs français à la découverte de l'Italie ancienne*, Paris-Geneva, 1984.

CIRVI (Centro Universitario di Ricerche sul Viaggio in Italia, Moncalieri, To.).

d'Ancona, A. *Saggio di una bibliografia di viaggi in Italia: L'Italia alla fine del secolo 16. Giornale di viaggio di M. di Montaigne*, Città di Castello, 1889.

Dumesnil, A. J. *Voyageurs français en Italie*, Paris, 1865.

Harder, H. *Le Président de Brosses et le voyage en Italie au 18e siècle*, Geneva, 1981.

Kanceff, E. *Bollettino* and publications.

Nenci, G. and Panessa, G. "Itineraria Archaeologica Italica (IAI)," *Annali della Scuola Normale Superiore di Pisa*.

Pollak, O. and Schudt, L. *Le guide di Roma . . .*, Vienna-Augsburg, 1930; Westmead, Farnborough, 1971.

Schudt, L. *Italienreisen im 17. und 18. Jahrhunderten*, Vienna-Munich, 1959.

See also IMAGE OF ROME IN LITERATURE.

TRAVELS OF JOHN PAUL II. Fifty-six journeys outside Italy in fourteen years as pope, or an average of four a year; among them five long tours of Africa, ten of Latin America, five of Asia and Oceania—together they represent more than a year away from Rome and more than one hundred countries visited, some of them on several occasions. To be sure, Paul VI had been a pioneer in the matter of papal travel. His surprise 1964 journey to Jerusalem had created a sensation; his lightning 1965 trip to the UN had made international news. But age did not leave him enough time to institutionalize grand sweeps across entire continents. These journeys, short or long, far or near, single or combined, it would be the task of John Paul II to carry out in a systematic way. They form an integral part of his papal style and his manner of governing the Church.

The Nature of the Journeys. The pope, who conceives his ministry as one great missionary pilgrimage on a world scale, continually insists on the pastoral dimension of his journeys. They are, he says, "visits to local churches and serve to show the place they occupy in the universal dimension of the Church, to stress their particular role in the construction of the universality of the Church." And he adds: "The pope travels, sustained, like Peter, by the prayer of the whole Church, to comfort the Church, to encounter man. They are voyages of faith, of prayer, centered on the meditation and the proclamation of the word of God, on the eucharistic celebration, the invocation of Mary. . . . They are opportunities for itinerant catecheses. . . . Such is the goal, and the only goal, of the pilgrim pope, even if some may attribute to him other motivations. . . . Among the various ways of realizing Vatican II, this one seemed to be fundamental and particularly important. It is the apostolic method, that of Peter and even more that of Paul. . . . The technical means that our age offers today facilitate this method and in a certain sense make it obligatory to pursue it."

The essential idea of the pope's travels is contained in this speech of 28 June 1980 from John Paul II to the Curia. In fact, great religious gatherings are always the high points of pontifical visits. They are occasions for beatifications, as in the Philippines, the scene of the first ceremony of this type organized outside Rome, in 1981; for canonizations, as in Korea; for continent-wide bishops' reunions, as at Puebla, Mexico, in 1979 or in Africa in 1988; for international eucharistic congresses, as in Kenya in 1985 or Colombia in 1987; or for commemorations of significant events in the religious history of the country being visited, like that of the fourth centenary of the death of Teresa of Ávila in Spain in 1982. It is obvious that in these travels meetings with the bishops occupy an essential place, along with other meetings with priests, religious men and women, and seminarians, all designed to stimulate the dynamism of local churches and reinforce their consciousness of being part of the universal Church.

This apostolic dimension must naturally be understood in a broad sense. The journeys are the favored means of translating the policy of a worldwide presence, the very basis of the existence of the Holy See. At the same time they serve as an opportunity to remind political leaders, especially, who might tend to forget it, of the need to respect religious freedom as well as the conditions for this respect. Where such freedom is lacking or insufficient, the visit may be postponed. In Haiti, before the pope arrived, the government had to give up its right to present candidates for the episcopate. In Cuba, although here political and religious obstacles were intermingled, discrimination against believers caused the journey to be delayed for a long time.

The ecumenical dimension is naturally an integral part of pastoral concerns. John Paul II met the ecumenical patriarch of Constantinople in Istanbul in 1979. He travels to countries that are mainly Protestant and meets Protestant communities in the countries he visits. The same is true in the case of Jewish communities.

In non-Christian countries, interreligious dialogue is never neglected. It is, moreover, considered more necessary than ever, not from the viewpoint of some kind of syncretism, which would certainly be alien to a pope so concerned with affirming Christian identity, but to try to answer the many problems assailing contemporary humanity. It is clear that John Paul's speech to young Moroccans at Casablanca in 1985 was more important than his encounters with the Christian community in that country. What is needed is to make believers conscious of the values they have in common and to mobilize them to build a more just and peaceful world by defining concrete objectives in the service of man.

Organizing the Journeys. When the Holy See has received an invitation from a local church as well as one from the political authorities, or at least the latter's authorization, and if the pontifical timetable allows it, a journey can be programmed. In close liaison with the local church, the journey can then begin to be organized down to the smallest detail—the operation may take up to two years—and with the strictest timing. Among many factors playing a role in such an operation, the following should be pointed out:

—the religious context. Countries with a Catholic majority have benefited from a real priority in the pontifical agenda. As more and more journeys are undertaken, this factor becomes less important. Still, the possibility of a pontifical visit can, as we have seen, be a way to act in the direction of greater independence or greater freedom on the part of the faithful.

—timing. It is important to tie the trip to one or more significant dates in religious history and at the same time to avoid any interference in local political life. For example, no journey would be scheduled during an election.

—presence of international organizations. Both the organizations of the UN and those of the European Parliament are favored forums since they allow the pope to address international leaders, with the certainty of being heard on every continent.

—historic places. These can be places associated with great eras of Christianity, like Santiago de Compostela, or with tragedies from recent times, like Hiroshima or Auschwitz. What is important is to trace the roots and in some way to exorcise the behavior behind such happenings.

—local concerns. Although he systematically meets religious, diplomatic, and political leaders, the pope also meets individuals from the various categories that make up the people of God. To all these, whether they govern or are governed, whether they are city or country dwellers, rich or poor, sick or healthy, both the Gospel and the Church's social doctrine have a message to convey, a message that will be transmitted in the specific context of each situation. The importance that John Paul II attaches to the social doctrine of the Church shows, moreover, that it is dangerous to give a narrow definition to what he means by pastoral action.

The influence of politics on the organization of these journeys cannot be underestimated. Without exception, the pope will not go to countries whose status is uncertain (for example, New Caledonia, which was removed from the Asian tour of 1984). He postpones visiting those whose policies are scandalous (for example, Indonesia, which was twice removed, in 1984 and 1986, because of its attitude toward East Timor, and until recently South Africa, because of its apartheid policy). It is not insignificant that John Paul II waited until his eighth visit to Latin America to visit the Chile of General Augusto Pinochet. A trip can also be put off because of political differences. This was long the case with Israel, but the situation has been normalized (agreement of 30 December 1993). Finally, journeys are never arranged in times of serious disturbances or war, civil or international, even if the exclusion is deplored, as it was in the case of Lebanon and Croatia, where visits were ruled out for obvious reasons of safety.

If the pope sometimes postpones his visit, for reasons that may be religious or political, there has never been an absolute refusal on his part to go to a country. His desire to bring the Christian message everywhere would condemn such an attitude, and the pope is merely limiting himself on occasion to accepting in a conditional way. On the other hand, certain countries set up obstacles to such visits. Communist countries like China, Vietnam, or the former Soviet Union (at least until the Gorbachev era) have done so for ideological reasons. Others have done so for religious reasons. This is the case with present-day Russia, because of the hostility of the Orthodox

Church, as well as with several Muslim countries, like Saudi Arabia, where the Christian religion is barely tolerated and the event would thus have hardly any pastoral significance.

Their Impact. Not surprisingly, the journeys attract some criticism. Certain Catholics object to their cost, which is indeed considerable (more than 4 million French francs for the journey to France in 1986; $20 million for the voyage to the United States in 1987), and believe that such sums would be better used for social works. Others think they distort the image of the Catholic Church by centering it on a pope who is excessively portrayed by the media. It is true that, except in countries under censorship, the journeys are televised at length (fifty-eight hours in Spain in 1982; one hundred hours in Canada in 1984). Others are skeptical of the effectiveness of these huge celebrations. John Paul II certainly attracts crowds in the millions. It has been estimated that in the Congo, in 1980, half the population came on foot to see him, and that in Brazil, in the same year, thirty to thirty-five million Brazilians saw the pope in person. Crowds of more than a million are not rare in Latin America, much less in Poland. But such celebrations, say detractors, are experienced as exceptional festivals rather than as spiritual gatherings, and are quickly forgotten. Although John Paul II always insists that he "visits" not political systems but Christian communities, others reproach him for compromising himself with dubious regimes and, especially in traditionally Catholic countries, for risking becoming party to political repression by not sufficiently denouncing certain injustices or scandals in economic and social life.

The diversity of these criticisms illustrates, if it were needed, the manifold implications of these journey-events. Undeniably, they have repercussions on the life of the Church and of Christians, on the pope's perception of the world and the world's of the pope.

The influences on the attitude of Christians in general and Catholics in particular are obviously hard to gauge. Surveys that might answer such questions are rare, and inconclusive since they are often contradictory, and any long-term analyses are premature.

On the other hand, it cannot be denied that the journeys are apt to change relations between the papacy and the local churches. No longer is it only the bishops who come to Rome every five years on their visit AD LIMINA, no longer only the leaders of an extremely ramified institution who inform the Holy See. Now the pope goes out to bishops and local churches. In this new type of dialogue, these churches, on which the success of a visit they have helped prepare actually depends, recognize more clearly what they represent within the universal Church of which they are part. They cannot but be invigorated by this public affirmation of faith inseparable from the celebrations accompanying the papal visit.

As for the pope, he himself gets to know local realities. Even if this perception is only a partial one, perhaps distorted because of the rarity of the event and the theatricality that is an inevitable part of it, it gives a better picture of complex realities than would abstract reports. He gains an impression of the extreme diversity at the heart of the Church, and consequently of the need to reconcile the oneness of this Church with the autonomy of those who belong to it, and the difficulty of doing so.

At times, working sessions with the bishops, the clergy, and certain parish leaders or leaders of charitable associations are organized. Such meetings have been set up, in particular, in the Netherlands, Switzerland, and the United States. Frequently, like the behavior of crowds, they reveal tensions and differences in analyzing the problems of today, at both the ecclesiological and the societal levels.

Such confrontations may cause anxiety as to the future of an institution in which diversity could get the better of unity in the interpretation and application of Christian doctrine, leading to new forms of centralization. But a new interpretation of Catholicity may also result in a strengthening of the collegial dimension of the Church. The role of the Curia, very much aware, it is true, of local realities (it should be remembered that many heads of congregations and other Roman institutions once held pastoral responsibilities in dioceses), can similarly be changed by this direct dialogue of the pope with local churches. At present, it is rather the centralizing trend that predominates, even though the standardization of regional synods can make for greater autonomy of the local churches. But if papal journeys become a customary way for pontifical power to be exercised, it is not out of the question that collegiality could come more vigorously to the fore.

It is not only the Church's leaders who are the subject of the pope's visits but the people of God. This people, very much present, expresses itself most of the time in a collective manner, through the vast crowds that welcome the bishop of Rome, and sometimes through representatives who do not hesitate to tell the world to its face about their worries, their bitterness, or their desires (the testimonies of certain American Indians are symptomatic in this connection). However fleetingly, John Paul II perceives in concrete form the way of life, the poverty of the people, or by contrast the wealth of some of those in power. There is no doubt that the papal journeys are the immediate cause of solemn appeals launched, notably in Africa, among the "have nots" but also in the "have" countries, for a more just distribution of human wealth. No doubt, too, the visits have had an influence on the formulation of the social doctrine of the Church, now more insistent on the duty of sharing, and in particular on the latest social encyclicals, *Sollicitudo Rei socialis* and *Centesimus Annus*.

Further, the images that the pope brings back are not limited to the Christian world. These are heterogeneous crowds that cheer him and live before him. Sometimes people who are strangers to Christianity receive the pope, allowing him to apprehend the authentic values of a spiritual universe not his own. There is no doubt, here too, that this openness to all dimensions of the planet has had an influence on interreligious dialogue and on the desire, more clearly affirmed than in the past, to define common goals for all believers. In other words, one can hope that this new form of dialogue with the world will result in the Church gaining a better perception of the world, whether on the part of the pope or of other leaders, so that social doctrine, of which the papacy claims to be the guardian, will conform more adequately to life today.

To the changing of the image that the Church has of itself and the one the Church has of the world, we should add the change, thanks to these travels, of the image that the world has of the pope and the Church. Because of John Paul II's personality—his great ease before the media, his frequent use of it during his journeys (he does not hesitate to speak by radio with peoples he cannot join in person)—there is certainly the risk of reinforcing the image of one man, perhaps open to modernity but alone and irreplaceable, both distant and close, and who in any case could not represent the whole Church.

Yet this pope manages to make himself understood the whole world over, thanks to the communications systems at his disposal. In the most diverse circumstances, he knows how to find the gesture that will touch the crowds, and will do so better than words. He does not spare pains or his strength to go to the farthest reaches of the world in order to grasp, not only ecclesial and sociopolitical realities—sometimes characterized by hostility to his person—but at the same time the problems of all and of each one. He thus gains credence for the image of a Church open to daily realities. Also, his popularity is probably greater with the crowds that welcome him than with religious leaders, who may be disturbed by some of the papacy's doctrinal or ethical views. This is especially true since the pope often transcends religious divisions and addresses the whole world. His speech at Casablanca insisting on the values common to Islam and Christianity seems to have had a very great impact in the Muslim countries.

The pope is not the only one to benefit from media visibility. His journeys are a sort of public relations exercise, not only for him but for the whole of the Catholic Church. They are the occasion of many publications, special magazine issues, and newspaper articles, often features, which provide information on the Church, the way it functions, its doctrine, its concerns, its plan for humanity. And in this spotlight local churches—their leaders and activities—also have their place.

In closing, it is important to go beyond the ecclesial point of view and emphasize that the journeys of John Paul II are not without influence on the vision the world has of itself, its rights and duties. The pope continually recalls the great principles of the social doctrine of the Church and judges situations according to these principles, sometimes severely. Certain speeches he has given during his travels have had an undeniable sociopolitical impact. There are some chronological coincidences that are unmistakable. Poland is an obvious example in this connection: No one can deny the comfort that, by calling into question the legitimacy of the Polish state, Karol Wojtyła as pope gave his compatriots in their struggle with the communist regime.

Of course, the example of Poland, strengthened in its aspirations to freedom by a pope who enjoys huge popularity in his homeland, and effectively freed from dictatorship during the few days of his presence on Polish soil, cannot be generalized. But Chile, Paraguay, or the Philippines also illustrate how moral authority may have influence in crises that call for radical political change. By understanding problems, channeling impatience, and legitimizing the aspirations of certain groups in sometimes conflict-filled circumstances, the pope can help nations assume their own destiny. By focusing attention on the countries he visits, insisting before the world on certain needs for justice or certain social priorities, John Paul II forces humanity to journey; revealing it to itself at times and making it face its responsibilities.

John Paul's journeys mark a stage in the history of the papacy and in the way in which it affirms its existence. The abolition of distance thanks to technological progress allows the head of the Catholic Church to go everywhere, to inaugurate a new type of magisterium where presence counts for more and where dialogue finds its place. Such itinerancy appears irreversible. Its importance, however, will certainly evolve. What has, not unjustifiably, been called exceptional may perhaps become banal, under a pontificate less charismatic than that of Karol Wojtyła; we have grown accustomed to the image of the man in white alighting from his plane. There is the risk of a certain desacralization of the papacy. Paul VI had foreseen that his successor would travel a great deal. John Paul II's successor will perhaps do the same, but the novelty will have vanished, together, it may be, with influence owed to that novelty. Journeys will then be no more than part of the normal functioning of an institution whose aim is a universal presence.

Christine de Montclos

Bibliography

Blanquart, P. "Le pape en voyage: la géopolitique de Jean Paul II," *Le Retour des certitudes*, Paris, 1987.

de Montclos, C. *Les Voyages de Jean-Paul II, dimensions sociales et politiques*, Paris, 1990.

Jennings, P. and MacCabe, E. *The Pope in Britain: Pope John Paul II British Visit 1982*, London, 1982.

Lemieux, R. and Montminy, J. P. "Le voyage de Jean-Paul II au Canada: message et médium," *Le Retour des certitudes*, op. cit.

Melody, M. B. *The Rhetoric of Pope John Paul II: The Pastoral Visit as a New Vocabulary of the Sacred*, Westport, 1990.

Norman, S. J. *Pope John Paul II: His Travels and Mission*, London; New York, 1982.

Salvinis, G. "I viaggi di Giovanni Paolo II, annunzio itinerante des Vangelo e 'segno' per il notro tempo," *Civiltà cattolica*, 1985, IV.

Seguy, J., Hervieu-Léger, D., ed. alt., *Voyage de Jean-Paul en France*, Paris, 1988.

The Visit of John Paul II to Yad Vashem, Jerusalem, March 23, 2000, Jerusalem, 2000.

Willaime, J. P. (ed.), *Strasbourg, Jean-Paul II et l'Europe*, Paris, 1991.

TRAVELS OF PAUL VI. On the day after the election of Paul VI, 21 June 1963, many commentators cast him in the role of "a pope of the new times." Indeed, the gradual buildup of his image as a pilgrim pope had its foundation in a new development in pontifical practice. The nine journeys that Paul made outside Italy, all charged with a particular meaning or even symbolism, contrasted with the two modest trips his predecessor John XXIII had made, to Loreto and Assisi on 4 October 1962. In addition, Paul's itineraries enjoyed ample media coverage, made possible by the important "instruments of social communication," whose usefulness and legitimacy the conciliar decree *Inter Mirifica* had just proclaimed. On the very day that this address was promulgated to the modern world, 4 December 1963, also the day of the close of the second session of Vatican II, the effect of surprise worked superbly when the pope announced his intention to visit the Holy Land: "The Successor of the first of the Apostles will return, after twenty centuries of history, to the place whence Peter left, bearer of the Christian message."

The journey to Jerusalem was conceived as exclusively a pilgrimage, with solely religious implications. Its practical modalities, entrusted to Msgr. Martin and the pontiff's secretary, Macchi, were worked out in the greatest secrecy. The journey, made from 4 to 6 January 1964, consisted of two phases, the first in Jordan (Amman, the Jordan, Bethany, the Holy Sepulcher, Gethsemane) and the second in Israeli territory (Nazareth, Cana, Tabgha, Capernaum, Bethlehem). Commentators dwelt on the tumultuous episode of Paul's arrival in Jerusalem by the Damascus Gate. Pressed by a crowd that overwhelmed security personnel, he seemed at one point in danger of being crushed, and prayed: "Lord, I am not worthy of the great grace that it would be for me to die here where you died." Finally he reached the end of the way of the Cross

that was laid out on the route (he could pause only once, at the sixth station), and celebrated Mass at the Holy Sepulcher. There, a short circuit in the electrical wiring in the dome, over Christ's tomb, caused the lights to go out amid a cloud of sparks and smoke, while the interruption of televised transmissions caused stupefaction among the assembled dignitaries. After the commotion, the pope had some difficulty restoring the necessary reflective atmosphere.

The next day, Paul VI had a long meeting with the Oriental, Catholic, and Greek Orthodox patriarchs in the person of Athenagoras I. Both men manifested their desire for progress in unifying the Church, along the lines of the orientations then being worked out by the council, for which Paul prayed several times in the course of his journey.

The pope's second journey outside Italy was to Bombay, from 2 to 5 December 1965, where the 38th International Eucharistic Congress was to be held. After stopping briefly in Beirut and addressing a greeting to Lebanon, the pope consecrated six bishops from each continent as well as representatives of Africa, Madagascar, Ecuador, Australia, and India. Receiving an exceptional welcome, in a country where Catholics were barely two percent of the population, Paul emphasized the universal intent—and intended influence—of this journey. It gave him the opportunity to speak about non-Christian communities, and Christian non-Catholic ones, as well as on the still tricky questions of the liturgy and acculturation, and to launch another appeal for peace, imploring the nations, in "an anguished cry," to give up the arms race. When he left he presented Mother Teresa, the superior general of the Missionaries of Charity, with the car he had used during his trip, a white Lincoln convertible, as a gift to benefit her work for the poor of India.

The theme of international peace was the essential aim of Paul's visit to the United Nations, on 4 October 1965, on the feast of St. Francis of Assisi and the twentieth anniversary of the founding of the United Nations. The impact was immense. The pope gave a speech in the early evening before "this auditorium unique in the world," which he called a "world institution for peace and cooperation among peoples." He recalled, rather strangely, that as a head of state he possessed "only a minute and quasi symbolical temporal sovereignty," and preferred to describe himself to the General Assembly as an "expert in humanity." As such he called for the integration or reintegration, as far as was possible, of countries that were not or were no longer members, and declared, in the most personal tone, "Never again war!"

After a conversation with President Johnson and a Mass celebrated at Yankee Stadium before 90,000 people, the pope presented a stone from St. Peter's basilica to be included in the foundations of the new seminary of the New York diocese, under the direction of Cardinal Spellman. Back in Rome, he addressed the council fathers in an allocution, declaring that "the Church's mission has never been justified by more compelling reasons," and sent a brief (*Nuntius Evangelii Pacis*) to the United Nations as a memento of his visit.

The fourth journey of Paul VI was planned around the pilgrimage to the Virgin of Fátima in Portugal. It took place on 13 May 1967, the fiftieth anniversary of the Virgin's first appearance there in 1917 (she was said to have appeared there every 13th day of the month, from May to October of that year). The pope came in for some criticism, certain parties seeing in his presence evidence of support of Antonio Salazar's authoritarian government. The conversation between Paul VI and the Portuguese leader lasted only nine minutes, however, and its contents were not reported. Others stressed the problems posed by popular Marian piety and possible deviations, bound up as it was with the question of the "third secret" of Fátima, which Rome had kept in confidence since 1917. This had been written about extensively; the leading interpretation said that it entailed the revelation of the end of the Church as an institution, sanctioned by the Second Vatican Council. Although considered a visible sign of "the Church of the poor," the pontifical pilgrimage to Fátima was on the other hand judged unacceptable by the Protestant churches.

The journey that Paul VI made to Turkey on 25 and 26 July 1967 was to honor the joint commemoration of the ecumenical councils (Constantinople and Ephesus) as well as the Virgin and St. John at Ephesus. It also coincided with the commemoration of the ninetieth centenary of the martyrdom of St. Peter and St. Paul as well as the pope's proclamation of a "year of faith." Decided on 5 July 1967 and announced on the 15th in consistory, the journey would have as its incontestable climax two meetings with the patriarch Athenagoras (the first at the Orthodox cathedral of St. George at Phanar, the second at the Cathedral of the Holy Spirit). The patriarch had been a friend of the pope's since their conversation in the Holy Land three years earlier and the reciprocal lifting of the excommunications of 1054 at the closing of the council.

Athenagoras welcomed the bishop of Rome as "the first in honor in our midst, the one who presides over charity." The two leaders promised to pursue an open dialogue and to meet again. The only official document, however, a joint communiqué of 6 July, noted that "this meeting can only be considered as a brotherly gesture," although the preamble stressed the impact of this "sign and prelude of things to come for the glory of God and the illumination of his faithful people."

Paul's journey to Colombia (22–4 August 1968) took place in the context of the Soviet invasion of Czechoslovakia, and was somewhat eclipsed by international news. It was occasioned by the holding of the 39th International Eucharistic Congress. As soon as he arrived, the pope followed the new ritual established by the council and ordained some hundred priests and four deacons, two of them married. The next day he was flown by helicopter to Campo San José to inaugurate the new premises of Acción Cultural Popular, a charitable organization devoted to evangelization and the elimination of illiteracy among the poor peasants (*campesinos*), which was equipped with broadcasting facilities. The pope gave a speech before a crowd of 200,000 on "the eminent dignity of the poor," an expression taken from the works of J.B. Bossuet, and denounced the methods of violence and revolution, which could well, against all expectations, "delay and not encourage the social progress" to which the poor "quite legitimately" aspired. Then, on 24 August in the cathedral of Bogotá, the pontiff opened the Second General Conference of the Episcopate of Latin America. (The first had been held in 1955 in Rio de Janeiro, on the occasion of the International Eucharistic Congress.)

The following year (10 June 1969) Paul VI went to Geneva for the fiftieth anniversary of the International Labor Organization. Recalling the great milestones of the formation of the Church's social doctrine, from the encyclical *Rerum novarum* of Leo XIII (15 May 1891) to *Populorum progressivo* (26 March 1967), the pope insisted on the primacy of man vis-à-vis technology and on the need to bring about universal peace through social justice. He took the opportunity to praise the activity of the Jesuit Joseph Joblin, the Church's representative at the ILO.

The pope's trip to Switzerland was also marked by a visit to the head office of the World Council of Churches, to which he addressed these first, highly symbolic, words: "My name is Peter." The novelty of the occasion was noteworthy, each of the participants knowing that when the council had been established in 1928, the Vatican had condemned the initiative and refused to take part in it. Next, the pope had a meeting with the emperor of Ethiopia, Haile Selassie, who was in Geneva at the time, and repeated to him the necessity for peace and cooperation. Many noted that the pope received a somewhat cool welcome from the inhabitants of "the city of Calvin," in comparison with the enthusiastic crowds in Palestine, Bombay, and Istanbul. However, 60,000 to 80,000 people attended the Mass celebrated in the La Grange park.

That same year provided the pope with the opportunity of addressing the Church of Africa, a young, expanding Christian organization. This was the motive for his journey to Uganda on 13 July 1969. Paul presided over the closing ceremony of the symposium of bishops of the continent, stressing the fact that henceforth "the Africans are their own missionaries." He proceeded that same day to the ordination of twelve bishops. The ceremony was linked to the pope's last visit, when he had prayed at the place of martyrdom of twelve Ugandan ecclesiastics who were canonized 18 October 1964. He voiced a solemn pledge of peace in the war between Nigeria and Biafra, encountering throughout his journey even greater enthusiasm on the part of the crowd than in Bombay (which had struck all present).

The last great journey of Paul VI outside Italy was also his longest (nearly 50,000 kilometers in eight days). In this it resembles more than any other the style adopted by John Paul II, which it clearly prefigured. Paul's destination was the Far East, with stops in Pakistan, the Philippines, Samoa, Australia, Indonesia, Hong Kong, and Ceylon (now Sri Lanka), from 26 November to 5 December 1970. At a stop in East Pakistan (now Bangladesh), not initially planned, the pope expressed his sympathy with the families of the one million victims of the cyclone that had ravaged the country on 13 November. In the Philippines, Paul escaped an assassination attempt at the hand of the Bolivian surrealist painter Benjamin Mendoza y Amor, who, disguised as a priest and armed with a dagger, flung himself at the pope. His arm was stayed by Macchi and Marcinkus and President Ferdinand Marcos in person subdued the attacker, who finally wounded himself and was led away without the pope's realizing the seriousness of the threat. In a general audience he gave on his return to Rome (6 December 1970), the pontiff thanked God for having preserved him "from the attack of a madman."

Paul VI was therefore able to preside normally over the ordination of more than two hundred priests at Luneta Park in Manila, before one million people. He also inaugurated the broadcasting station Radio-Veritas, from which he delivered a "message to the peoples of Asia," warning against atheism. From Pago Pago in Samoa he gave another "missionary message," this time intended for the whole world. In it he developed the themes of the unity of the Church, development and poverty, and Eastern spirituality against materialism. He then conferred episcopal ordination on the first indigenous bishop of New Guinea. Proceeding next to Hong Kong, the pope noted, in terms similar to those he used in Australia, "human, cultural, social and spiritual values" over and beyond purely economic concerns. Msgr. Casaroli, secretary of the Council for Public Affairs of the Church, declared that "what is new is the fact of the pope's coming to Hong Kong, not the contents of his message."

After that the pope never again undertook such a long trip. Nevertheless, he did go to Sardinia, on 24 April 1970, for the sixth centenary of the sanctuary of Our Lady of Bonaria. This was named after a much venerated statue near Cagliari, found in 1370, in honor of which Pedro of Mendoza, Charles V's cupbearer, gave the name Buenos Aires (from *bonaria*, good air) to the city he founded in Argentina. There was an inci-

dent when a small group of anarchists, probably from Milan, threw a few rocks at the pontifical procession, though without hitting the pope's car. Paul did not realize what had happened until later, when he protested against the way the press had blown up the incident. Later he traveled to Venice, on 16 September 1972, and was welcomed there by the man who would succeed him six years later, Albino Luciani. To the end of his pontificate, he made only one more journey, to Aquino for the seventh centenary of the death of St. Thomas.

A primary characteristic of the great journeys of Paul VI was surely the very small size of the group that accompanied him—about twenty at the most. Msgr. Villot, the Vatican secretary of state, took part only in the pilgrimage to the Holy Land, judging thereafter that it behooved him to stay in Rome in the pope's absence. The master of ceremonies, Msgr. Dante, along with Msgr. Virgilio Noè; Msgr. Martin, prefect of the Pontifical Household; the dean of the Sacred College, Cardinal Tisserant; the pope's private secretary, Don Macchi; Msgr. Marcinkus, in charge of the itineraries; and Camillo Cibin, head of security, took part regularly, as did the pope's physician, a few Swiss guards, and a representative of Radio Vatican. The emphasis was on simplicity and sobriety.

Thus during his travels, as throughout his pontificate, Paul VI seems to have made a series of "unique and extraordinary" gestures (J. Chélini), each journey having a precise purpose although all presented the pope with an opportunity to elucidate an overall action he had defined in his first encyclical, *Ecclesiam Suam* (6 August 1964). Seen in this light, the journeys of Paul VI seem like an arrangement of signs, perhaps comparable to the *signa temporum* dear to the spirit of the council and, in any event, creating an essential path for pontifical witness on the great questions that animated it: development and poverty (Bombay, Bogotá, Uganda, the Far East to a certain extent) and ecumenism (the Holy Land, Turkey, Geneva), while providing occasions for evoking the internal problems of the Church, in the new perspectives opened up by the council.

Philippe Levillain

Bibliography

Ambrogiani, P. *Paul VI, le pape pèlerin*, Paris, 1971.

Carrara, G. *Fioretti in Terra Sants*, Rome, 1964.

Chélini, J. "Les voyages de Paul VI," *Paul VI et la vie internationale, Actes des journées d'études d'Aix-en-Provence des 18 et 19 mai 1990*, Brescia, 1992, 156–72.

Martin, J. "Le voyage de Paul VI en Terre sainte," *Paul VI et la vie internationale Actes des journées d'études d'Aix-en-Provence des 18 et 19 mai 1990*, Brescia, 1992, 173–79.

Martin, J. "Les voyages de Paul VI," *Paul VI et la modernité* de l'Église, *Actes du colloque de l'École Française de Rome des 2–4 juin 1983*, Rome, 1984, 317–32.

TRAVELS OF POPES, 536–1809.

List of papal journeys outside Rome or the Papal States before Paul VI:

536	Agapitus I	Constantinople
547	Vigilius	Constantinople
633–4	Martin I	Constantinople
710	Constantine I	Constantinople
754	Stephen II	France (Ponthion, Saint-Denis)
799	Leo III	Germany (Paderborn)
804	Leo III	Germany and France (Rheims)
816	Stephen IV	Rheims
833	Gregory IV	France (Colmar area)
878	John VIII	France (Troyes)
1012	Benedict VIII	Germany
1019	Benedict VIII	Germany and Strasbourg
1040	Benedict IX	Marseilles
1049–54	Leo IX	Germany and France (several times)
1095	Urban II	Marseilles and Clermont (First Crusade)
1106	Paschal II	Germany and France
1118–19	Gelasius II	Provence, Mâcon, Cluny
1119–20	Callistus II	Dauphiné, heims, Autun, Toulouse, Cluny
1129–32	Innocent II	France
1147	Eugene III	Dijon, Rheims, Langres
1164	Alexander III	France
1195	Clement III	Montpellier
1244	Innocent IV	Lyon (ecumenical council), Cluny
1274	Gregory X	France: (Valence, Vienne); Switzerland: (Lausanne)
1309		Clement V installed in Avignon (until 1377); new installation in the reigns of the "Avignon" or "Clementist" popes of the Great Schism, from 1379
1417	Martin V	Constance
1533	Clement VII	Nice, Villefranche, Marseilles
1533	Paul III	Nice
1782	Pius VI	Austria: Vienna
1804	Pius VII	Paris
1809	Pius VII	France (enforced exile)

See also TRAVELS OF JOHN PAUL II, TRAVELS OF PAUL VI.

TREASURY, PAPAL. See **Finances, Papal.**

TRENT, COUNCIL OF. A widespread myth tends to attribute to the council of Trent (1545–1563) everything that constituted Catholicism up to the time of VATICAN II, including doctrine, institutions, liturgy, and morality. That is to give it too much credit. The council of Trent was certainly a decisive moment in the formation of modern Catholicism, but modern Catholicism has acquired many other accretions, both before and after Trent, that owe nothing to the council; examples are priestly celibacy and the cult of the Virgin Mary.

This makes it all the more necessary to ask what this council, paradoxical in many aspects, really was. First conceived in 1520, it met 25 years later, was suspended several times, and did not conclude until 1563. It was never officially "received" by the French Church. Intended to restore Christian unity, it deepened and hardened the division between Catholicism and the Protestant Churches. Yet this machinery conceived to challenge the papacy strongly reinforced the authority of Rome.

The Struggle for the Council. The early history of the council of Trent began in 1518, when Luther called for a council against the abuses of the Roman Curia. The scholar of Wittenberg amplified this appeal with incomparable brilliance two years later in his treatise "To the Christian Nobility of the German Nation," in which he drew up a complete plan of Christian reform to be put into practice by a council, in spite of the pope. His call was heeded. In 1523, the Imperial diet brought together the princes and free cities of Germany, both Catholic and Protestant. With ever-growing intensity, it demanded "a free council [i.e. independent of the pope], to meet on German soil." Moreover, Emperor Charles V rallied to the cause. For him and his ministers, a council was the only way to re-create a union between the Empire and

Christianity, not only by condemning Luther's errors but also by forcing the pope and the clergy to carry out reforms "at the head and in the members" and thereby to cripple the Protestant revolt. From 1529, the emperor used every method at his disposal to break the resistance of the pope, who would have nothing to do with such a council.

In fact, it was in Rome that the most stubborn opposition to the council plan was found. The popes had not forgotten the movement that arose in the 15th century, reinforced by the Great Schism, to assert the superiority of a council over the pope. The restored papacy energetically fought against the danger of the Church being changed into a sort of parliamentary monarchy. PIUS II, with his bull *Exsecrabilis*, which was confirmed by LEO X in 1513, threatened to excommunicate any Christian who would dare call for a council. CLEMENT VII was persuaded that any reform of the Church would be at his expense. The Curia upheld him in this conviction. It succeeded in suppressing the timid reforms decided on by the fifth Lateran council but was less certain of any future success after Luther's brilliant outburst.

The council had another opponent in the king of France, Francis I. He was only too happy to see the empire split by religious controversy, but he had no desire to see Charles V rise above it and increase his strength and prestige. This was to be a constant in the history of the council of Trent: the more the Habsburgs were for it, the more the French king would be against it, and vice versa. As for the opinion of the faithful—if one may use such an expression—it swung between excited expectation and disappointment, with an underlying skepticism that can be readily understood if one considers the legacy of Lateran V.

With the accession of Pope PAUL III, in 1534, the field was changed. The new pontiff was a resigned supporter of the council, and in 1534 he announced its convocation, meanwhile embarking on the work of preparation. The most famous of these preparatory moves was the *Consilium de emendanda Ecclesia* (Advice on the Reform of the Church), which was worked on by a commission of reform cardinals and prelates (Contarini, Carafa, Sadolet, etc.) who met from 1536 to 1538. After the convocation, ten years of laborious negotiations followed before the council began. One of the major difficulties was to decide on a site. The pope wanted the council to be held, if not in Rome, at least in Italy (Mantua and, later, Vicenza were possibilities) so that he could keep an eye on it. The imperials insisted that the council take place in a city in Germany. The solution that was finally decided on was Trent: a city in the empire, German-speaking but situated on the Italian side of the Alps. Another problem was to bring the king of France to the council. In the end, Charles V's armies had to march triumphantly to the outskirts of Paris, in 1544, before Francis I hastily signed the treaty of Crépy-en-Laonnois and promised to send bishops to the forthcoming council.

The council finally opened in Trent on 13 December 1545. Since 1520, half of Germany, the whole of Scandinavia, and parts of Switzerland and central Europe had gone over to Protestantism. Meanwhile, from Geneva Calvin was beginning to win over France and the Netherlands, while England had broken with Rome.

The Working of the Council. A "general and ecumenical" council, Trent never swarmed with participants. When it opened, it included 4 archbishops, 21 bishops, and 5 generals of orders. The most heavily attended sessions (in 1563) numbered scarcely more than 200 fathers. Under PIUS IV (in 1562–3), the total assembly was made up of 9 cardinals, 39 patriarchs and archbishops, 236 bishops, and 17 abbots or generals of orders, although they never attended all at the same time. In comparison, the Catholic episcopate of the time probably had about 700 members. Moreover, the attending prelates were a very uneven representation of Christianity, even that part that had remained loyal to Rome. Catholic Germany, England, and Poland were represented only patchily and by unusual personalities (the Englishman Reginald Pole, or Stanislas Hosius of Poland). France sent 4 prelates to the first sessions, around 20 to the last ones (led by the cardinal of Lorraine), but none during the period 1551–2. The Spanish formed a small group. The great majority of the council was Italian, but the Italian bishops were split into several factions, with the tightly held group of the pope's flock pitted against the subjects of the king of Spain (from the kingdom of Naples and the Milanese), along with a few independents (in particular the Venetians).

It was chiefly on account of the Italian bishops, who came from the Curia or were provisioned by it, that from the 16th century onward critical minds raised the question of the freedom of the council fathers vis-à-vis the papacy. It is true that, in all the thorny discussions, the papal legates made great efforts to back up the camp of the papalists and the supporters of the Holy See. Nonetheless, recent research has shown that the fact of being provisioned by Rome did prevent certain bishops from voting with the opposition.

Below the bishops operated the theologians, brought in as experts. They played an indispensable role, since the prelates—most of whom were graduates in canon law—usually had only a weak grounding in theology. Almost all these theologians belonged to the religious orders; the Dominicans, Franciscans, and Augustinians, along with a few Jesuits (e.g., Alphonsus Salmeron and Diego Laynez), who would play their first leading role in the life of the Church. The theologians prepared the documents that were studied, discussed, and amended by the prelates sitting in committees, or "congregations."

After that, they were submitted for the general approval of the fathers at solemn "sessions" (over 18 years, the council of Trent held 25 sessions, including some that were purely formal).

In the hall or in the wings, the princes' ambassadors worked as in a beehive. Their job was not only to keep their masters informed about the doings of the council but also to influence its workings in the direction of state interests. Thus, formal receptions, set speeches, peremptory orders, and secret negotiations all loomed large in the actions of the council. The laity, in the sense of the sovereigns, were far from absent from these activities.

In the midst of all this, an essential place was given to the legates whom the pope appointed to preside over the council. Five days from Rome by courier, their task was to apply papal directives and see to it that the work of the council progressed without in any way encroaching on Rome's authority. It was a delicate and exhausting task, in which such prelates as Cervini (the future Pope MAR-CELLUS II), del Monte (later JULIUS III) and Morone, to cite only the most outstanding, showed exceptional talent.

Finally, special mention should be made of the work of the council secretariat. An excellent team of notaries and clerks, led from start to finish by the same person, Angelo Massarelli, carefully recorded all the conciliar discussions, both in the congregations and in the public sessions. At the same time, Massarelli kept a day-by-day history of the council, a mine of information for modern historians and theologians.

On the material level, the council came up against not a few problems. Trent, was a small, cramped town, poorly connected to the outside world and with no intellectual infrastructure. The presence of the prelates and their attendants caused a skyrocketing of the price of lodging and provisions. Many complained of the "bad air" (although, despite false rumors, the plague was less prevalent there than elsewhere). As soon as they were able, the fathers ran off to more pleasant sojourns in Venice or Verona, whence the legates had to recall them with great difficulty (at least, those who voted with the papalists). Moving the council to Bologna, in 1547, may have angered the emperor, but it gladdened the hearts of many prelates and theologians, once again in a large city with wealthy monasteries and a complete university.

Twists and Turns. The turbulent history of the council was linked with the events of general history and to conflicts between the powers, in particular in Germany and Italy. The following discussion can only indicate the high points.

In the spring of 1547, when the council was progressing at full speed (crucial questions had been decided on, such as the respective authority of Holy Scripture and tradition, and justification; that of the Eucharist was being broached), the legates suddenly put to the vote the question of moving from Trent to Bologna. The sudden death of one bishop, attributed to a contagious disease, had created panic. But there were suspicions of a maneuver on the part of Roman interests intent on torpedoing a council that was succeeding too well. Although the pope approved the transfer, the emperor took it very badly. Just when he was winning a decisive victory over the Protestants at Muhlberg, this decision ruined his plans. He ordered all the bishops under his sway to stay in Trent, with the result that the council that had been moved to Bologna limped along until it was suspended in September 1548.

In 1550, JULIUS III resolved to reopen the council in Trent. The Holy Roman emperor, Charles V, then at the height of his power in Germany, urged him to do so and vowed to send representatives of the Protestant princes. The king of France, Henry II, seeing the transfer as a move on the part of his rival, precipitously boycotted the council, even threatening to hold a national council at the same time. In Trent, work went on no less assiduously, in particular on the sacraments. For the first—and only—time, Protestant delegates arrived from Würtemberg, Saxony, and several imperial cities, notably Strasbourg. But the council only listened to their confessions of faith and juridical protestations; there was no dialogue. Soon war resumed in Germany, inflamed by France. In the spring of 1552, when the Protestant forces of Maurice of Saxony took Augsburg and invaded the Tyrol, the panicked council decided once again to disperse.

During PAUL IV's pontificate, it was easy to believe that the pope had determined to reform the Church on his own authority, without the council. But the results were so controversial, even in Rome, that his successor, PIUS IV, was elected (1559) only on condition that he bring the council to a satisfactory conclusion. He might not have had the strength to undertake the task, still less complete it, without the energy of his young cardinal nephew, Charles Borromeo. By this time, the situation of the Catholic Church had gone from bad to worse. Under the powerful surge of Calvinism, Scotland had yielded; the loss of England was confirmed; France and the Low Countries were severely threatened; heresy had even reached Spain. The kings were perturbed. One of the clauses in the treaty of Chateau-Cambrésis, concluded in 1559 between Philip II of Spain and Henry II of France, provided for the two rulers to combine their efforts toward reconvening the council.

But would a new council be called, as many—and not only the Protestants—hoped, or would the old council inaugurated in 1545 continue? With Spain behind him, the pope decided for the second option, and the council reopened in Trent on 18 January 1562. However, not until the failure of the colloquy of Poissy (summer 1561) and the unleashing of civil war in France (April 1562) did Catherine de' Medici decide to let the French bishops take their leave to Trent. In the autumn of 1562, the bishops found the council embroiled in crisis. The majority of the council was on the point of breaking with the pope in the matter of bishops residing in their sees, which called into question the inveterate practices of the Curia. The skill of the legates—especially Morone—won the cardinal of Lorraine to their cause and overcame the opposition. The council fathers, in their eagerness to have done with the matter, hastened the conclusion of the council, which was announced 5 December 1563.

Nevertheless, the council of Trent demonstrated a spirit of unity at the closing session, when all the canons and decrees voted under Paul III and Julius III were reread and approved en bloc. Thus the council's work was indivisible.

The Work of the Council. In the official Rome edition, all the texts drawn up by the council are contained in a simple volume of 239 in-folio pages. Later editions, of which there were many—especially in the 19th century—fit easily in the pocket of a cassock. The following are the principal points of the texts.

From the beginning, the fathers of Trent decided to tackle simultaneously the two parts of their task, doctrine and reform. Therefore, each session had a dogmatic and a disciplinary section, which only rarely collaborated. Toward the end of the council, the reform decrees were issued in a rush, without any great concern for order.

The doctrinal work of the council of Trent was conceived essentially as a response to the Protestant theses. One should not, therefore, look for a complete résumé of the Catholic faith, since what was not contested by the great reformers was not mentioned (for instance, there is nothing on the divine Trinity, the mystery of the Incarnation, or Christ's resurrection). This being the case, the texts followed a fairly methodical program.

Beginning with the Protestant declaration *Scriptura sola*, the council's first concern was to define the authority of sacred Scripture. It determined the authentic contents by listing all the canonical books, including those that the Protestants rejected. It also declared authentic the traditional Latin version, the so-called Vulgate, which would therefore continue to be authoritative within the Church, even if the fathers hoped the text could be improved in an amended edition. No edition of the Bible, in whatever language, should from then on be circulated without prior examination by the ecclesiastical authority. Further, the council debated in lively fashion the opportunity to translate Scripture into the vernacular, finally reaching no conclusion.

The authority of the Bible being thus affirmed, the council nevertheless declined to accept it as embracing all the contents of faith. Scripture, it declared, was complemented by the "non-written traditions" of which the Church was the depository. Note the plural, "traditions," which posterity has tended to forget. The council of Trent upheld traditions, but only in a highly restrictive sense. Avoiding a broad definition that would have included all the "ecclesiastical traditions" that the Church had over the centuries retained by the workings of the Holy Spirit, the fathers said only that the Gospel of Jesus Christ is contained in the holy books "and in the non-written traditions which have been received by the apostles from Christ's very mouth and transmitted (*traditae*) by them, as dictated by the Holy Spirit, as it were from hand to hand."

What are these traditions? The council did not list them and probably did not have a very clear idea what they were. The modern theologian is sensitive, and rightly so, to the many prejudices that Protestants might harbor against the diffuse Catholic notion of tradition; but the historian is obliged to say that the limited acceptance adopted at Trent was not the one imposed on Catholic dogma, since, from 1564, Pius IV's profession of faith called for the firm acknowledgment of "the apostolic and ecclesiastical traditions."

In sessions V and VI, the council defined the doctrine concerning original sin and justification. Regarding the former, it affirmed, contrary to the Pelagians—and against contemporaries suspected of Pelagianism—that original sin was not just the imitation of Adam's sin but was its hereditary consequence. Against Luther, the council maintained that original sin was not to be confused with concupiscence. That was only an inclination to sin, the sign of a nature that was fallen but not irremediably corrupted. In short, Adam's first sin is handed down to all men, who are born deprived of original righteousness. Yet through the merit of Jesus Christ they are cleansed of this sin by baptism, which leaves them only with concupiscence, against which they can struggle victoriously through the grace of God. Despite the pressure of a large number of fathers, the council refused to define dogmatically the Immaculate Conception of the Virgin Mary, being content on this point to refer to a constitution of Pope SIXTUS IV.

Although the subject had already been dealt with in large measure in the canons on original sin, the council could not avoid addressing directly the question of justification, which since Luther had constituted one of the major themes of the Reformation. It was "a difficult article," as the legate Cervini acknowledged as he opened the discussions, "and one which has never been treated in any council." Clearly there were too many shoals to avoid, as well as the danger of not laying enough stress on the freedom of sinful man in relation to God's grace which saves and justifies.

After long, highly technical debates which extended from June to December 1546, the council's decree, voted in session VI, was presented in the positive form of an exposition of doctrine, couched in terms that were weighed with the utmost care. Chapter VII, the central text, defines justification as "a profound transformation through which man, enriched by the gift of God and by a free acceptance of grace and its bounty of gifts, becomes righteous, a friend of God, the heir of eternal life. He is justified, not by an outward influence of the merits of Christ, but by a justice that it is intrinsic to man and which the Holy Spirit implants in all hearts, as it wills and according to the free cooperation of each one. This justice remains within man as a permanent principle; it implies the presence of the three supernatural virtues of faith, hope and charity. Without hope and charity, faith alone cannot justify man or make him a living member of Christ."

The Tridentine view of man is an essential contribution to the history of humanity. Against the radical pessimism of the theologians of the Reformation, by stressing free will it preserved humanism's essential belief in man. Moreover, through the doctrine of justification it accepted a form of cooperation on the part of man in the working out of his salvation. But the impression of balance that these texts might give is in part deceptive, as history was to show: the ambiguities in the relations between divine grace and human freedom would relaunch the theological debate before the end of the 16th century and nourish the Jansenist controversy in the 17th; furthermore, there began a drift toward a purely secular moralism, surfacing especially in the 18th century.

From session VII, almost all the doctrinal work of the Council of Trent was concentrated on the sacraments. The aim was, first, to uphold the complete list of the seven sacraments in order to rebut the Protestants, who recognized only baptism and the Eucharist; and next, to affirm that the sacraments were effective in themselves (*ex opere operato*) and not only as a response to the faith of the one receiving them.

Among the sacraments, the Eucharist was the prime focus of attention because of the passionate disputes it aroused, not only between Catholics and Protestants at the council but also within the world of the Reformation. The Eucharistic presence of Christ was defined as substantial. What is seen on the altar is the appearances (*species*) of the bread and wine. That is why the council considered the most appropriate term to express this mystery was "transsubstantiation" (already used by Lateran IV). With regard to communion, it affirmed that communion in the form, or species, of bread is complete, but it did not close the door to the pope's granting communion with the chalice, as the Germans and the emperor demanded. As for the Mass, it was forcefully put forward as an actualization of Christ's sacrifice on the cross, a propitiation for the living and the dead.

Regarding the sacrament of Orders, the council countered the Protestant idea of the universal priesthood by af-

firming the specificity of the ministerial priesthood and the hierarchical nature of the Church. According to a famous expression taken from the Psalms, the Church was compared to an army arrayed for battle. The fathers heatedly discussed the episcopate in connection with the residential duty—a question that at first glance seemed disciplinary, but in fact involved a whole underlying ecclesiology. The council did not come up with a clear definition of pontifical power—a silence that, on the part of the papacy and the legates who tended to its interests, was deliberately calculated.

In its last session, the council quickly disposed of the question of Purgatory. This, it said, was a place outside this world where the souls of the dead finally were purified before they entered Heaven. Here they could be consoled by the suffrages of the living, in particular by masses. The council likewise justified the cult of the saints and the veneration of images and relics.

On most doctrinal questions, Trent used, in succession, two languages that overlapped and complemented each other. First, it exposed Catholic doctrine in didactic fashion, quoting arguments from Scripture. Next it took up, one after another, the propositions denying what it had just affirmed, and violently condemned them. Each canon hit like the crack of a whip: "If anyone dare say . . . , may he be [anathema]!" It is clear that the council worked long and hard on these matters of doctrine: the theologians above all, but also the prelates, who contributed a meritorious effort. The major writings of the reformers were sifted and dissected, the libraries and universities consulted. But it is equally certain that the council found its task in large measure already accomplished by a half-century of controversies and local councils. For instance, Trent drew largely on the documents of the council of Sens (actually held in Paris) of 1528, whose leading theologian was Josse Clichtove, as well as on those of the council of Cologne of 1536, headed by Johann Gropper, and the council of Canterbury, held in 1555 by Reginald Pole. But instead of diminishing its achievement, it in a sense enhances the doctrinal work of the council of Trent to see in it the fruit of two or three generations of Catholic theologians.

Disciplinary Work. Like the work on doctrine, the disciplinary work of the council of Trent was at bottom neither new nor original. Those who praise it the most often seem to overlook the fact that, on many points, it merely repeats some old rules—for example, reminding bishops and pastors that they must preach to the people entrusted to them and live in the midst of them, or regulating the recruitment, career, and way of life of ecclesiastics. The prescriptions were firm, but not new. Others that seem to be new are often wrongly interpreted. An example is the famous decree on seminaries (session XXIII). Aimed at ensuring the recruitment of clergy, this ordered the bishops to open institutions (which would become "nurseries," *seminaria*) that would take in poor students of around 12 years of age at no charge, and teach them grammar (i.e. Latin) while training them in piety. There is nothing revolutionary in that; nothing, moreover, that could profoundly change the corps of priests, given the conditions of the time. At the most, it was the equivalent of what would in the 19th century become the minor seminaries. Far more innovative was the institution of a competition to secure a post as a parish priest; but as this was a limitation of the right of the patrons of parishes, which would unduly upset custom, it was scarcely ever applied.

As for the decree that determined the rules of the validity of marriage (the decree *Tametsi*, coming out of session XXIV), it put an end to the confusion that permitted "clandestine" marriages. However, it did not solve the irritating question of parental consent.

What is left, then, of the disciplinary and reforming work of the council? As regards the letter, very little; the essence is in its spirit. First of all, Trent provided a fresh orientation for the whole ecclesiastical institution from the viewpoint of the salvation of souls. The clergy, in its nature and in its actions, is essentially defined by its pastoral function, in the service of the faithful. Thus there is nothing surprising in the fact that the canonical clergy, who were defined by their intercessionary function, felt instinctively that the council had been structured against them, and that they adopted a hostile attitude to its application. Second, Trent concentrated this entire pastoral mission in the hands of the bishops, whose obligations—and corresponding powers—were constantly affirmed. Once again, it was a case of episcopal power at the expense of the cathedral canons, but even more at the expense of the religious—who, unless they had taken the right course, like the Jesuits, were among the losers of the council. Bishops heading the diocese, pastors in the parishes—these were the two pillars of the Church as Trent defined it. There was no mention of laymen: they never came up except as possible usurpers of the rights of the Church. As for the pope, the council of Trent did not refer to him, yet he emerged the victor over conciliarism. In fact, at the conclusion of the council, everything depended on him.

After the Council. As they dispersed, the fathers of the council of Trent had decided to submit their work to the pope for his approval and confirmation. It was a highly risky procedure which on other occasions had allowed Rome to stifle reforms. But times had changed. In June 1564 (in a bull dated 26 January), Pius IV solemnly lauded the council in his role as "bishop of the universal Church." A few months later, the same pope published the text of a profession of faith that henceforth all members of the clergy and all teachers had to pronounce before they took up their duties. It contained all the dogmas defined by "the sacrosanct council of Trent."

Without question, the papacy had taken over the executive work of the council. The four tasks with which the council had formally entrusted it—an index of prohibited books, a catechism setting forth Christian doctrine, a reformed breviary, and a reformed missal—were performed with dispatch. March 1564 saw the appearance of the new index, which contained a highly restrictive rule on reading the Bible in the vernacular. Pius IV's successor, Pius V, published the Catechism for parish priests according to the Order of the council of Trent, also called the Roman Catechism (1566), an enterprise of which St. Charles Borromeo was the prime mover. This was followed shortly afterward by the new Roman Breviary (1568) and revised Missal (1570).

Far more protracted was the task of applying the work of the council in the local churches, one to which the popes of the late 16th and early 17th centuries devoted considerable energies. To this end, new congregations of cardinals were created: the congregation for the interpretation of the council, the congregation of the bishops, and the congregation of regulars. Further, the nuncios at the court of Catholic sovereigns had as their mission to persuade them to "receive" the council's decrees and then to see that they were applied. Everywhere they could—which meant especially in Italy—the popes sent "apostolic visitors," prelates granted extraordinary powers to inspect dioceses, correct abuses, and report back to Rome. The provincial councils that were supposed to adopt and transpose the Tridentine measures locally submitted their orders to the Holy See before publishing them. In sum, the council of Trent, so much dreaded by the papacy beforehand, resulted in a spectacular strengthening of Rome's authority and centralization. The sovereign pontiffs had been wise enough to back the success of the council; now they garnered the fruits.

Marc Venard

Bibliography

Alberigo, G. "The Council of Trent," *Catholicism in Early Modern History: A Guide to Research*, J. W. O'Malley, St. Louis, 1988, 211–26.

Alberigo, G. "Vues nouvelles sur le concile de Trente à l'occasion du centenaire," *Concilium*, 7, 1965, 65–79.

Chaunu, P. *Église, Culture et Société. Essais sur Réforme et Contre-réforme, 1517–1620*, Paris, 1981.

Concilium Tridentinum, ed. Görres-Gesellschaft, Freiburg-im-Breisgau, 1901, 14 vols.

Crimando, T. "Two French Views of the Council of Trent," *Sixteenth Century Journal* 19, no. 2 (1988), 169–186.

Delumeau, J. *Catholicism Between Luther and Voltaire*, trans. J. Moiser, Philadelphia, 1977.

Dupront, A. "Du concile de Trente," *Revue historique*, 75 (1951), 262–80.

Duval, A. *Des Sacrements au concile de Trente*, Paris, 1985.

Hefele and Leclerq, *Histoires des conciles*, IX and X.

Jedin, H. *Geschichte des Konzils von Trient*, 4 vols. in 5, Freiburg i/Br., 1949–75; only first 2 vols. in English, *A History of the Council of Trent*, London, 1957–61.

Pallavicini, G. *Istoria del Concilio di trento*, 1656.

Power, D. *The Sacrifice We Offer: The Tridentine Dogma and Its Reinterpretation*, New York, 1987.

Prodi, P., and Reinhard, W., eds. *Il Concilio di Trento e il Moderno*, Bologna, 1996.

Sarpi, P. *Istoria del Concilio Tridentino*, London, 1619, new ed. Florence, 1966.

Tallon, A. *La France et le Concile de Trente (1518–1563)*, Rome, 1997.

Tallon, A. *Le Concile de Trente*, Paris, 2000.

TRIBUNALS, APOSTOLIC. Canon 1442 of the Code of Canon Law of 1983 sets forth the traditional principle whereby "the Roman pontiff is the supreme judge for the entire Catholic world; he tries cases either personally or through the ordinary tribunals of the Apostolic See or through the judges delegated by himself." In his own person, the pope is canonically the only judge of the highest officials in a state, of the cardinals, the pontifical legates and, regarding penal affairs, the bishops. He always retains the ability to reverse the judgment of any other matter (canon 1405 § 1).

There are three tribunals of the Roman Curia: the Apostolic Penitentiary, the Roman Rota, and the Supreme Tribunal of the Apostolic Signatura. Their jurisdiction is universal, and they pronounce their sentences in the name of the Roman pontiff.

The Apostolic Penitentiary. This agency still heads the three apostolic tribunals, even though its true nature has been questioned because of its peculiar character, which allows it to grant graces in matters of the internal forum and not judiciary sentences of the external forum. Moreover, although it is mentioned in the apostolic constitution *Pastor bonus* of 1988 under the heading of tribunals, the Penitentiary does not itself bear the title of tribunal, as do the other two agencies.

This dicastery was instituted at the end of the 12th century to aid the pope in the absolution of the ever-increasing number of grave sins, an absolution reserved to the vicar of Christ. The pope therefore delegated a cardinal to hear confessions in his place. HONORIUS III conferred on him the title of cardinal penitentiary; depending on the period he was also called supreme penitentiary, or general penitentiary, major or great penitentiary. With the inauguration of holy years from 1300 (with the subsequent organization of great pilgrimages to Rome), the cardinal's duties were extended to include both the internal and external forums. Thus, minor penitentiaries appeared in the great Roman basilicas to hear pilgrims' confessions in their respective languages. Up to VATICAN II, they could be recognized by their long sticks, with which they touched the heads of the penitents who knelt before them to obtain 30 days' indulgence, or even 100 if the cardinal penitentiary himself wielded the instrument. This occurred in public on only four days in the year: Palm Sunday at St. John Lateran, Spy Wednesday at St. Mary Major, and Holy Thursday and Good Friday at St. Peter's at the Vatican.

The minor penitentiaries were organized into colleges attached to the three Roman basilicas. In 1570, PIUS V established the Franciscans at St. John Lateran, the Dominicans at St. Mary Major, and the Jesuits at St. Peter's. Faced with crowds of pilgrims, ALEXANDER VII added penitentiaries of various religious orders, although they were not arranged in colleges. After their Society was suppressed by CLEMENT XIV, the Jesuits were replaced by the Conventuals, but they did not see their function restored when their order was reestablished under PIUS VIII. The penitentiaries of the Vatican basilica, who were more numerous and better compensated than the others, were responsible for laying out the pope at his death and reciting ritual prayers at the foot of his bed before accompanying his body to the basilica for entombment. The cardinal grand penitentiary gave the pope assistance and absolution at his last breath.

PIUS V restricted the responsibilities of the Penitentiary; BENEDICT XIV restructured it in 1744, and PIUS X modified it slightly in 1908. After that time, its field was limited to the internal forum. In these questions of conscience between the believer and God, the Church's jurisdictional power was either sacramental or not, depending on the case. In 1917 BENEDICT XV decreed this power to cover matters related to indulgences, a policy that would be followed by all his successors. The major cardinal penitentiary is assisted in his task by a regent (who, although not a bishop, has the right to the title "excellency" by virtue of this important function), a theologian (by tradition, always a Jesuit), a canonist, and two counselors. JOHN PAUL II has maintained the Apostolic Penitentiary in its traditional duties: internal forum (both sacramental and nonsacramental), indulgences, absolutions, dispensations, commutations, validations, and censures of penalties and other graces. The most serious decisions, which are dependent on the personal power of the sovereign pontiff, are approved and signed by him in person. For other important cases, the Penitentiary enjoys pontifical powers, of which the pope must nevertheless be kept scrupulously informed.

The list of grand cardinals penitentiary is as follows: Giovanni di San Paolo (1193–1205), Tommaso Capuano (1219–43), Ugo di San Caro (1244–63), Guy Le Gros (Clement IV) (1263–5), Pierre of Tarentaise (Innocent

V) (1273–6), Bentevenga dei Bentevenghi (1279–89), Matteo di Acquasparta (1289–1302), Gentile da Montefiore (1302–5), Bérenger Fredol (1305–23), Gaucelme Jean Deuza (?–1348), Étienne Aubert (Innocent VI) (1348–52), Gil Albornoz (1357–8), Francesco degli Atti (1358–61), Guglielmo Bragose (1361–7), Étienne de Poissy (1369–73), Jean de Cros (1373–8), Giovanni de Amelia (1378), Elzéar de Sabran (1378–9), Luca Radulfucio de Gentilibus (1382–9), Niccolò Misquino (1389), Francesco Carbone (1389–1405), Antonio Caetani (1405–12), Giordano Orsini (1415–38), Niccolò Albergati (1438–43), Giuliano Cesarini (1443–44), Giovanni di Tagliacozzo (1445–9), Domenico Capranica (1449–58), Filippo Calandrini (1458–76), Giuliano della Rovere (Julius II) (1476–1503), Pietro Ludovico Borgia (1506–11), Leonardo Grosso della Rovere (1511–20), Lorenzo Pucci (1520–29), Antonio Pucci (1529–44), Roberto Pucci (1544–7), Ranuccio Farnese (1547–65), Carlo Borromeo (1565–9), Francesco Alciati (1569–72), Giovanni Aldobrandini (1572–3), Stanislao Osio (1574–9), Filipppo Boncompagni (1579–86), Ippolito Aldobrandini (Clement VIII) (1586–92), Giulio Antonio Santori (1592–1602), Pietro Aldobrandini (1602–5), Cinzio Aldobrandini (1605–10), Scipione Borghese Caffarelli (1610–33), Antonio Barberini (1633–46), Orazio Giustiniani (1647–9), Niccolò Albergati Ludovisi (1650–87), Leandro Colloredo (1688–1709), Fabrizio Paolucci (1709–21), Bernardo Maria Conti (1721–30), Vincenzo Petra (1730–47), Gioacchino Besozzi (1747–55), Antonio Andrea Galli (1755–67), Giovanni Carlo Boschi (1767–88), Francesco Saverio de Zelada (1788–1801), Leonardo Antonelli (1802–11), Michele di Pietro (1814–21), Francesco Saverio Castiglioni (Pius VIII) (1821–9), Emmanuele de Gregorio (1829–39), Castruccio Castracane Degli Antelminelli (1830–52), Gabriele Ferretti (1852–60), Antonio Maria Cagiano de Azevedo (1860–7), Antonio Maria Panebianco (1867–77), Luigi Bilio (1877–84), Raffaele Monaco la Valletta (1844–96). Isidoro Verga (1896–99), Serfino Vannutelli (1899–1915), Wilhelm Van Rossum (1915–18), Oreste Giorgi (1918–24), Andrea Fruhwirth (1925–7), Lorenzo Lauri (1928–41), Nicola Canali (1941–61), Aradio Larraona (1961–2), Fernando Cento (1962–7), Giuseppe Ferretto (1967–73), Giuseppe Paupini (1973–84), Luigi Dadaglio (1984–90), William Wakefield Baum (1990–).

Tribunal of the Roman Rota. This is the oldest of the tribunals. It grew out of the Apostolic Chancery, where certain contentious matters came gradually to be handed over to *auditores causarum* empowered from the early 13th century to give out judicial sentences. The tribunal was granted autonomy by JOHN XXII in 1331. In 1472, SIXTUS IV decreed that the number of its judges, known as auditors of the Sacred Roman Rota, should be no more than 12. The name, inadequately explained at the outset, has given rise to a variety of explanations. Some say it came from the church of St. Catherine called "della Rota," to which the auditors belonged. According to others, it originated in their meetings held in a circle (*rota*) or around a table with a mosaic decoration in the form of a wheel; still others claimed it came from the presentation of petitions and pleas which were rolled up like ancient scrolls (*rotuli*).

In session, the auditors sported the four-cornered doctor's cap and were entitled to wear the *cappa magna*, or great cloak. They also served as pontifical subdeacons in the papal chapels, where the youngest member carried the pontiff's cross in processions.

Restructured by the canonist BENEDICT XIV in the 18th century (constitution *Iustitiae et pacis*, 1747), the tribunal disappeared at the end of that century as a result of Italy's annexation of the Papal States. However, PIUS X reestablished it in 1908 (apostolic constitution *Sapienti consilio*) with a special law which was granted in 1910 and revised in 1934, 1969, and 1982.

The Rota consists of a college of judges—with the rank of apostolic protonotaries—who have from the beginning been chosen by the pope from among the best-known canonists from different parts of the world. The tribunal sits by "turns" of 3 prelates, or in plenary session. It is presided over by a dean chosen from among the members. This post was traditionally acquired by seniority and held until retirement, but JOHN PAUL II put an end to this system by providing that henceforth the dean of the Roman Rota be appointed by the sovereign pontiff for a fixed length of time (apostolic constitution *Pastor bonus* of 1988, art. 127). Until recently, the former dean was made a cardinal. John Paul II appeared to compensate for the cessation of this practice by raising the acting dean to the episcopate.

According to the Code of Canon Law of 1983 and the 1988 charter of the Roman Curia, the tribunal of the Roman Rota (now no longer called "sacred") gives pronouncements in three instances. In the first instance, it judges the following: bishops in contentious nonpenal cases; primatial abbots or abbots superior of monastic congregations, as well as superiors of religious institutes of pontifical right; those dioceses and other ecclesiastical persons (physical or juridical) directly dependent on the Roman Pontiff (canon 1405 § 3); and other cases entrusted to it by the pope on his own initiative or at the request of the parties (canon 1444 § 2). The Rota is principally the ordinary tribunal of appeal of the Holy See for affairs of the external forum (canon 1443), especially matrimonial matters of any rite. Thus, the cases that it judges in second instance are cases already judged by diocesan or interdiocesan ecclesiastical tribunals, and in the third instance, cases already dealt with by the Rota itself or another tribunal of second instance but without force of law (i.e. in a nondefinitive manner). This monopoly of principle that the Roman Rota enjoys carries three exceptions: a third local instance exists in Spain before the Rota of the Madrid nunciature, in Hungary before the primatial tribunal of Ezstergom, and in Poland before the primatial tribunal of Gniezno.

Supreme Tribunal of the Apostolic Signatura. Originally—that is, at the beginning of the 13th century—the Apostolic Signatura was an administrative body which the pope delegated to sign in his place certain documents written in response to petitions. At the end of the 15th century, SIXTUS IV created a single body of chief clerks who worked together within two new structures: the Papal Signature, to examine the dossiers to be submitted for the pontiff's decision, and the Common Signature, to regulate the dossiers delegated by the pontiff. Shortly afterward, ALEXANDER VI made a clear distinction between the Signature of Grace and the Signature of Justice. The first, which was presided over by the pope himself (whence its name, Signatura Sanctissimi), had wide powers, since it dealt with recourse against the sentences of the cardinal legates of the Papal States or the administrative acts of judges, besides resolving conflicts of competence between the Roman congregations. SIXTUS V promoted this Signature of Grace to the rank of congregation. However, in the 17th century it began to fall into disuse as its work was taken over by the Apostolic Datary, and it was abolished by LEO XIII in 1899.

The Signature of Justice, in contrast, functioned as an actual supreme court of appeal. It was manned by magistrates called "voting prelates," in contrast to the prelate "referees" who were given a simple consultative vote. PIUS VII changed this Signature of Justice into a temporal tribunal for the Papal States (bull *Quando per admirabile*, 1816), and GREGORY XVI reinforced its duties in this regard (*motu proprio Elevati appena*, 1834). The fall of Rome in 1870 brought with it that of the Signature.

In 1908, Pius X undertook to restore the tribunal (apostolic constitution *Sapienti consilio*), but under a new name and with entirely new duties. The supreme tribunal of the Apostolic Signatura was given ordinary power of jurisdiction over the judges and sentences of the tribunal of the Sacred Roman Rota. It also had power to resolve the inter-dicasteral conflicts of the Curia. In 1967, PAUL VI modernized this highest tribunal (apostolic constitution *Regimini Ecclesiae Universae*) by splitting it into two sections. The first retained the traditional duties of the Signatura, while the second was responsible for settling disputes of canonical administration, an area hitherto unknown in Church law. This responsibility was confirmed by the Code of Canon Law of 1983 and the apostolic constitution *Pastor bonus* of 1988. Henceforth, the supreme tribunal of the Apostolic Signatura has been active in three sectors, as follows.

In the judicial sector, the tribunal corresponds to a court of last resort. It deals with recourses against the sentences or judges of the tribunal of the Rota, and it settles any positive or negative conflicts of competence between local tribunals that are not responsible to the same tribunal of appeal.

In the administrative sector of disputes, the tribunal functions as the equivalent of a council of state. This is because it alone is entitled to judge recourses for violation of the law against a canonical administrative act rendered or confirmed by a dicastery of the Roman Curia, except where the matter concerns the secretary of state or an act approved "in specific form" (not simply "in common form") by the sovereign pontiff according to the traditional principle whereby the pope, as supreme judge, is logically judged by no one (*Prima Sedes a nemine judicatur*, canon 1404). Since 1988, the Apostolic Signatura has been empowered to pronounce, in addition, on reparation of damages entailed by an unlawful administrative act. It continues, as in the past, to settle adminisrative disputes within the Roman Curia and those referred to it by the Holy Father or the dicasteries.

In the uncontentious administrative sector, the Supreme Tribunal acts as a ministry of justice by supervising all the jurisdictions of the Church, particularly thanks to the quinquennial reports of the lower tribunals. It extends the competences of the local tribunals, approves the creation of interdiocesan tribunals, and may inflict penalties on advocates (clergy or laity) of ecclesiastical tribunals. Certain concordats have also empowered this tribunal to verify the respect of canonical norms of sentences of nullity of marriage or dispensations of unconsummated marriage before these were passed on to the state judges for the granting of civil effects.

The Supreme Tribunal is made up of a dozen cardinal-judges and bishop-judges who are nominated by the pope for five years, with one taking the role of prefect in charge. The latter is aided by an archbishop secretary as well as prelates who promote justice, a defender of the bond for matrimonial matters, and a chancellor (clerk). "Referendary" canonists give their expert opinion on current dossiers, on which other "voting" canonists cast their vote. Cases are customarily judged by the plenary Signature of all the judges (*videntibus omnibus*), of whom one is the *ponens* (reporter). This structure is decided on in the last instance, since this tribunal calls itself supreme. Most of the time, it strives to reach a prior agreement rather than maintain the dispute, following the spirit proper to ecclesial law and the dispositions of canons 1446 and 1713 on methods of avoiding trials.

The list of cardinal prefects is as follows: Vincenzo Vannutelli (1908–14), Michele Lega (1914–20), Augusto Silj (1920–26), Francesco Ragonesi (1926–30), Bonaventura Cerretti (1931–3), Enrico Gasparri (1933–46), Massimo Massimi (1946–54), Giuseppe Bruno (1954), Gaetano Cicognani, pro-prefect (1954–9), Francesco Roberti (1959–69), Dino Staffa, pro-prefect (1967–9), prefect (1969–77), Pericle Felici (1977–82), Aurelio Sabattani (1982–8), Achille Silvestrini (1988– 91), Gilberto Agustoni, pro-prefect (1992–99), Mario Francesco Pompedda (1999–).

Joël-Benoît d'Onorio

Bibliography

Del Ré, N. *La Curia romana—Lineamenti storico-giuridici*, Rome, 1970.

d'Onorio, J. B. *Le Pape et le gouvernement de l'Église*, Paris, 1992.

Grocholewski, Z. "I tribunali apostolici," *Le Nouveau Code de droit canonique*, Ottawa, 1986; "I tribunali," *La Curia romana nella Cost. ap. Pastor bonus*, Vatican City, 1990.

TURKS. It is difficult to summarize briefly relations between the papacy and the Turks. They varied a great deal over the centuries, owing in the main to mutual ignorance, gradual recognition, religious opposition, and political rivalries. From the victories of the CRUSADES in 1097 at Nicaea and Dorleas over Kiliç Arslan—the first real contact between the Catholic world and the Seljuks—to JOHN PAUL II's journey to Istanbul and Ephesus, a recent episode in the history of an often ambiguous relationship, there is a span of more than nine centuries, and a complex evolution in reciprocal perception.

Up to the 13th century, until the emergence of the idea of Turchia (a Turkish realm), relations between the Holy See and the Turks were characterized by an ambiguity fed by a mutual lack of knowledge, an ignorance that took a long time to dispel. At the time of the preaching of the First Crusade, there was confusion between the persecutions ordered against the Christians in Jerusalem by the caliph of Cairo, al-Hakim, and the return of the holy city to Abbasid obedience a few years later, owing to its reconquest by the Grand Seljuks. Likewise, and despite the harsh fighting against the Seljuks of Rum, the latter did not at first appear to pose a real threat to the Holy Places. Moreover, the Seljuks were involved in the internal problems of the basileus, the emperor of the Christian East especially since he himself had used large numbers of Turkmen troops to reconquer Anatolia. Furthermore, in their lands the Seljuks practiced remarkable tolerance vis-à-vis Jews and Christians. With the Seljuk victory at Myriocephalon and the danger of Byzantium's fall in Anatolia, and even more with the pressures on Little Armenia, politically close to the West, the Seljuk threat came to be taken more and more seriously, while the Turks' consciousness of their own identity became ever clearer.

However, another ambiguity loomed: the frequent confusion on the part of the West between the Turks and their cousins, the Mongols. The provisional establishment of friendly relations with the followers of Genghis Khan, the hopes of converting the Mongols, and the establishment of relations with the Seljuks of Rum—in total decline after the Mongol "whirlwind"—all encouraged hopes of rapprochement (Marco Polo's mission to the court of the Great Khan is an example) and shifted the Turkish military threat to the background.

In the mid-14th century, the situation underwent a brutal change. On the ruins of the sultanate of Rum, emirates were set up which developed at the expense of their neighbors—Byzantine, Turkmen, and also Latin. The campaign waged by the emir of Aydin, Umur Pasha, to the detriment of the islands of the Greek Archipelago and Crete was evidence of the revival of the spirit of *jihad* among the Turks and resulted in the crusade of Smyrna (1342–8). The real menace, however, lay farther north. The Ottomans seized Gallipoli in 1353 and were not expelled until the crusade of Amadeus of Savoy in 1366. Their conquest of Andrianople (1396) and their crushing successes in the Balkans made them henceforth the foremost Muslim threat against Christianity, at a time when the Muslims of Spain and the Maghreb, and even the Mamelukes, could no longer stand up to the naval power of the Latins in the Mediterranean.

From now on the Turk, in reality the Ottoman, was promoted to the rank of hereditary enemy of the whole of Christendom. One result was the efforts to save the remnants of the Byzantine Empire, the crusades that failed lamentably (Nicopolis, 1396; Varna, 1444) just as Ottoman domination was expanding in Rumelia, with only the invasion of Tamerlane to slow it down. At the same time, the terror of the Turk, the reverberation of the fall of Constantinople, and the vigor of the struggle organized by PIUS II to support Venice in the long war of 1463–79, together with the shock of the capture of Otranto, did not prevent the papacy from continuing to hope for the conversion of the sultan—an old dream encouraged by the multinational and multiconfessional character of the court of Mehmet II, his religious apathy, and his partly Christian ancestry. Moreover, frequent conversions from Islam encouraged the belief that a Christian Turkey was possible.

These dreams were constantly cherished up to the mid-16th century, both as regards the Ottoman princes, like Cem Sultan, and the sultan's admirals, like Barbarossa, Dragut, or Uluç Ali. Soon, however, under the dual influence of the struggle with Persia and the Shiite heresy and the conquest of the Mameluke empire and the three holy cities of Islam, the Ottoman Empire became the champion of Muslim orthodoxy and undisputed leader of the war against the infidel. Increasingly, the empire wrapped itself in religious conservatism, a presage of its decline. Peace was not foreseeable for a long time hence, especially with the Turks at the gates of Vienna and Italy.

But discreet arrangements were still possible, negotiated through the intermediary of the patriarch in Constantinople. All in all—even though Constantinople's Turkish regime was perfectly familiar with the papacy's role in the various crusades of the 16th and 17th centuries—the coasts of the Patrimony of St. Peter were rarely pillaged by the Ottomans, except where a promise had clearly been broken, as at the autos-da-fé of Marranos at Ancona in 1555. Moreover, at that time the Ottomans considered the pope to be head of a very important sect and also a rich temporal ruler, though lacking military power. However, this was regarded as the time for confrontation, especially throughout the prolonged struggle for control of the Mediterranean, which pitted the Spanish against the Ottomans of Rhodes (1522) at Lepanto and Tunis.

In the 17th century, despite the resumption of hostilities which in Rome took the form of the Holy Leagues for the wars in Candia (Crete), Hungary, and the Peloponnese, two factors encouraged the gradual development of papal policy with regard to the Ottoman Empire. These were, on the one hand, the decline of the Turkish military threat, and on the other, the success of papal missionary policy in the Americas and Asia (despite arguments arising from the Chinese and Malabar rites). The papal thinking was that the Catholics in the Ottoman Empire were not really threatened by the Ottoman authorities in their persons or their convictions, since the protection of the French and Viennese courts gave them privileged status. The hope of converting the Muslims had been abandoned long since; yet with the empire's ever-growing openness to Western ideas, in particular after the Treaty of Passarowitz (1718), there remained a possibility of linking the Eastern churches to obedience to Rome and thereby exerting influence over Ottoman society, where the minority populations were growing.

One illustration of this choice of policy is the increase in missions to the Levant in the first years of the 17th century. Sometimes the policy met with success, as in the return of the Maronite Church to the Roman fold. In the 19th century, when part of the political Ottoman elite wanted to westernize—provoking the Tanzimet, a political and social revolution almost comparable in influence to the French Revolution—the papacy continued its pacific policy by establishing large numbers of Catholic schools and hospitals, strictly maintained by diplomatic missions. The influence of the teaching establishments was considerable, since they trained a sizable part of the multiconfessional elite of the empire. This rapprochement through a policy of small steps finally became concrete with the establishment of diplomatic relations between the caliph and the pope. The Turkish Republic maintained excellent relations with the Holy See until the 1960s, when they cooled somewhat because of the Church's reconciliation with the Orthodox Church and conservative Islam's return in force to Turkey.

Bruno Simon

Bibliography

Lupprian, K. E. *Die Beziehungen der Päpste zu islamischen und mongolischen Herrschem im 13. Jahrhundert anhand ihres Briefwechsels*, Vatican, 1981 (Studi e testi, 291).

Richard, J. *La Papauté et les missions d'Orient au Moyen Age (XIIe-XVe siècles)*, Rome, 1977 (CEFR).

Setton, K. M. *The Papacy and the Levant (1204–1571)*, Memoirs of the American Philosophical Society, 161, Philadelphia, I, 1976, II, 1978, III and IV, 1984.

ULTRAMONTANISM. *Ultramontanus qui circa montes, hoc est Alpes, degit* ["ultramontane means one who lives on the other side of the mountains, that is to say, the Alps"], says Du Cange's *Glossary of Medieval and Modern Latin*. By this definition, and from the Italian point of view, Germans and French are both ultramontane, just as they were "transalpine" in Caesar's time. The fraternity of French and German students and artists at the university of Perugia was known as the *societas ultramontanorum*, and the Bavarian canonist Barthel, speaking of Gallican theologians of the mid-18th century, still referred to them as *ultramontani doctores, praesertim Galli*. It is plain that everything depends on the perspective, and each side of the Alps is always ultramontane to the other.

Nonetheless, the adjective "ultramontane" and the noun "ultramontanism" derived from it soon acquired an ecclesiastical and theological meaning that still clings to them, and this is important in the history of the often conflict-ridden relations which the capital of Catholicism maintained for centuries with the local or national Churches that had remained in communion with the Apostolic See. During the endless controversy in Catholic France in the 17th and 18th centuries that divided Jansenists, Jesuits, and Gallicans, the Jesuits were soon dubbed "ultramontanes"—that is, Italians. This occurred at a time (mid-17th century) when the image of a Christian and cultivated Italy, the mother of civilization, was beginning to fade throughout Europe, and when relations between the Christian king of France and the papacy were strained under the dual impact of monarchial absolutism and a more assertive ecclesiological particularism.

Thus, "ultramontane" was the description given to maxims or doctrines that, rightly or wrongly, were perceived by most French religious and civil authorities as foreign to the religious traditions of the kingdom, whether they concerned the primacy and jurisdiction of the Roman pontiff; the force and validity of his theological definitions and condemnations; his liturgical customs; his disciplinary rules; his privileges, exemptions and immunities; or his moral, spiritual, and devotional orientations. In a letter from Cardinal de Luynes, sent by the nuncio Giuseppe Doria to the secretary of state, Torrigiani, in 1761, one reads that the Jesuits professed "ultramontane maxims, opposed to the laws of this kingdom." In 1768, France's diplomatic representative to the elector of Trier denounced CLEMENT XIII's monitory letter annulling, on his own authority, the ecclesiastical reforms that had been carried out in the duchy of Parma as the result of "the fanatical and murderous doctrine accredited in Rome by GREGORY VII." "The pope," he went on, "has, with the publication of the edicts, revived the abuses of ecclesiastical immunities and the former excesses of ultramontane pretensions."

In the same period, the publication in 1763 of the treatise of Febronius (a pseudonym of the suffrogan bishop of Trier, von Hontheim), under the title *De statu Ecclesiae et legitima potestate Romani Pontificis*, an episcopalist and regalist manifesto, popularized the adjective *ultramontan* in Catholic Germany. It designated and precipitously attacked Jesuits and Italians, theologians of the Roman Curia, and German defenders of the primacy of the Roman pontiff. Febronius's supporters vehemently denounced the *ultramontani doctores* who supported the unity of the Church around the Roman papacy and were opposed to full episcopal jurisdiction, especially to the reform of the Church by the secular ruler, acting by the authority which, in the Constantinian tradition, he arrogated to himself as a "bishop to those outside."

There followed attempts at religious restoration during the early 19th century. From the 1840s on, in the age of liberalism and triumphant nationalisms—in Belgium, France, Germany, Ireland, and England, and Poland—these attempts brought about a profound devotional and intellectual renewal in the context of a strengthened feeling of unity around the Holy See and the person of PIUS IX and his successors. At the same time, it gave rise to a new attack on the Ultramontanists and their doctrine, systematized under the name *ultramontanisme* in France and *Ultramontanismus* in Germany. In France, the invectives of the Count de Montlosier against the Jesuits and the "dangers resulting from ultramontanism" under the Restoration, relayed under the July monarchy by the anticlericals Michelet and Quinet, developed in parallel with the resistance of a concordatory episcopate that had remained attached, against Rome, to the "Gallican liberties" and to its prerogatives in the matter of the government of priests and the faithful. In England, the reestablishment in 1851 of a hierarchy of Catholic archbishops and bishops gave rise to a strong national wave of antipapism, which benefited by taking up the continental arguments against the Ultramontanists. In Germany, the "Old Catholic" schism of Döllinger and his disciples, who were opposed to the proclamation of papal infallibility in matters of faith and morals (18 July 1870), and then the bitter struggle of the *Kulturkampf* unleashed from 1873 by Bismarck against the Catholic Church, brought to a climax the dispute over ultramontanism.

Even though the polemical intent behind the use of the term "ultramontane" in all these conflicts is plain, it would be difficult to give a precise definition of what the idea of ultramontanism covered from the 17th century to the 19th. None of the movements attacked as ultramontanist claimed to be under that banner. In this sense, ultramontanism was more an accusation with aggressive intent than an analysis of content. In fact, hostility to Roman centralization proceeded from different modes of logic: ecclesiological in Febronius's case or in the moderate Gallican episcopate of 19th-century France; dogmatic in the case of Döllinger and his champions; nationalist in the British and German empires; and anti-Christian with Ernest Renan or Paul Bert.

The same held true of the negation of pontifical power. This arose from a number of sources: from episcopal or conciliar doctrines argued theologically; from a notion of the life and organization of the Church derived from an implicit or explicit Protestantism; from a reflexive desire to preserve local or regional autonomy; from a state jurisdictionalism prolonged and complicated in the 19th century by the emergence of the nation-state; or from a liberal reaction of concern for protection and defense of the individual against any form of religious authority outside the sphere of free choice. Finally, hostility to Rome went in tandem with the implicit rejection of Italy, a rejection that was tinged, depending on the circumstances, with ignorance of the latter's religious and cultural traditions, or else with an ill-concealed contempt on the part of northerners for a south that was suspected of every kind of despotism and superstition. Historically, ultramontanism was made up of this mixture of protection and aggression, contradiction and resistance, fear, misunderstanding, and resentment.

The inconsistency of these definitions, determined by different historical circumstances and fluctuating ideas, would hardly matter if the terms "ultramontane" and "ultramontanism" did not still influence the field of contemporary historiographic thinking in terms of concepts or major categories of religious analysis. The two terms' historic appositeness cannot be denied, nor can their convenience; yet this cannot excuse their imprecision of content, their intrinsically polemical character, or their often manifest impropriety. Thus, the Jesuits of the 17th and 19th centuries were in fact religious people who had taken a particular vow of obedience to the pope and defended his prerogatives, rather than the supporters of a vague ultramontanism. The Roman theologians of the ecclesiological turn of the 18th and 19th centuries (Zaccaria, Marchetti, Cappellari—the future GREGORY XVI—or Anfossi) were, strictly speaking, "Curialists." Bonald, Maistre, and Lamennais, at the dawn of the 19th century, were traditionalists rather than Ultramontanists. The term "intransigent," used by Italian historiographers, was in many cases—notably after the proclamation of the SYLLABUS (1864)—a useful substitute for "ultramontane." For Catholic intransigence, according to PIUS IX, covered not so much a geography (even if an ecclesiological one) as a dogmatic and moral theology as well as liturgical and devotional forms and modes of behavior and sensibility at the heart of membership in the Catholic Church. "Ultramontanism" thus becomes a fallacious concept, to be shelved in a warehouse of accessories of historical polemics or a dictionary of antiquated concepts.

Philippe Boutry

Bibliograpy

Brown, M. L. *Louis Veuillot, French Ultramontane Catholic Journalist and Layman*, Durham, N.C., 1977.

Buchheim, K. *Ultramontanismus und Demokratie: Der Weg der deutschen Katholiken im 19. Jahrhundert*, Munich, 1963.

Costigan, R. F. *Rohrbacher and the Ecclesiology of Ultramontanism*, Rome, 1980; *Les Ultramontains canadiens francais*, Montreal, 1985.

Derré, J. R. *Le Renouvellement de la pensée religieuse en France de 1824 à 1834*, Paris, 1962.

Epp, R. *Le Mouvement ultramontain dans l'Église catholique en Alsace au XIXe* siècle (1802–1870), Lille, 1975, 2 vols.

Gadille, J. "Le concept de civilisation chrétienne dans la pensée romantique," *Civilisation chrétienne*. Paris, 1975, 183–209.

Gough, A. *Rome and Paris: The Gallican Church and the Ultramontane Campaign 1848–1853*, Oxford, Eng., 1986.

Izbicki, T. M. "Papalist Reaction to the Council of Constance: Juan de Torquemada to the Present," *Church History* 55 no. 1 (Mar. 1986) 7–20.

Martimort, A. M. *Le Gallicanisme de Bossuet*, Paris, 1953.

Raab, O. H. "Zur Geschichte und Bedeutung des Schlagwortes 'Ultramontan' im 18. und frühen 19. Jahrhundert," *Historisches Jahrbuch*, LXXXI, 1962, 59–173.

UNIATES. At the end of the 16th century, the Holy See had hopes of putting an end to the SCHISM that since 1054 had separated it from the Eastern Church. From 1570 to 1580, GREGORY XIII's legate, Antonio Possevins, concerned himself with an attempt reestablishing Rome's authority in eastern Europe, though in vain. Nevertheless, circumstances seemed to favor the plan. The Constantinople patriarchate, weakened from 1453 by Ottoman domination, was striving to reinforce its prestige by gaining the support of the Moscow tsars. As a result of this rapprochement, in 1589 the patriarch Jeremy encouraged the creation of the patriarchate of Moscow, something fervently desired by Tsar Feodor. Henceforth the ambition of the Russian patriarchate would be to have all Eastern Christendom under the control of the "THIRD ROME."

Faced with Constantinople's fiscal needs and the pressures of the Moscow patriarchate, which were undermining their authority, the Orthodox bishops of eastern Europe therefore turned to Rome and begged the pope to be admitted to the Catholic Church. On 23 December 1595, in St. Peter's, Pope CLEMENT VIII solemnly celebrated the end of the schism. In Russia, the Orthodox—both bishops and priests—were divided on the question of union with Rome. However, on 8 October 1596 a synod was held at Brest-Litovsk which brought together the Ruthenian Churches of Lithuania, Poland, and Ukraine. The synod officially proclaimed the union, which Rome took to mean confirmation of the decision of the preceding year. The Uniate Church was born. But what for Rome was the end of the schism was for the patriarchates of Constantinople and Moscow a real schism and a betrayal—an invalid decision.

The Uniate Church took the name Greek Catholic Church of Eastern Rite. Its members recognized the whole of Roman doctrine, including pontifical primacy and the authority of the Holy See, but they retained their rituals, their own hierarchy, and the right for their clergy to marry.

Uniates and Orthodox then set about reinforcing their local positions by arguing, often in pitched battles, over the sites and objects associated with their rites. A sign of the violence of the confrontation was the assassination of the Uniate archbishop of Polotsk, Josaphat Kuncewicz, who refused Orthodox peasants the right to be buried in Christian soil. But this was also a political conflict, in which the Uniate and Orthodox hierarchies strove to af-

firm their differences in order to broaden their authority. The metropolitan of Kiev, Piotr Mohyla (1596–1647), one of the most virulent opponents of the union of Brest, played a leading role in strengthening the Orthodox Church. Creating the Mohyla Academy in Kiev in 1632, he made it a center of theological thinking, the first in Slavic Christendom. By contrast, the Uniates found themselves weakened in Poland by their unequal politico-religious status (the Uniate bishops were not admitted to the senate, and the clergy and nobility suffered discrimination), and in Ukraine by a powerful Orthodox thrust. In the 17th century, large numbers of Uniates were sufficiently discouraged that they joined the Roman Catholic Church or else returned to Orthodoxy.

The 18th century was for the Uniates a century of terror when their Church was on the verge of disappearance. In this part of Europe, this was a time marked by Russian expansion, by the successive divisions of Poland, and by the growing authority that the Russian rulers exercised over the Orthodox Church. (In 1721, the patriarchate was abolished in favor of a Holy Synod totally dominated by the tsar.) It fell to Tsarina Catherine II to elaborate a wide-ranging religious policy; this was necessary because of the growing number of representatives of different religions within the empire, an increase linked to the territorial conquests of her reign. In her Great Instruction (1767–68), Catherine set forth her opinions on questions of religious politics: a "prudent tolerance" was called for, she said, in a multinational empire. This idea was reinforced on 13 June 1779 by a declaration of religious policy.

Yet if tolerance was the keyword of Russian relations with Jews and Muslims, it was not extended to relations with the Catholic Church, even less with the Uniates. The carving up of Poland had modified the religious composition of the empire. At the first division, in 1772, 100,000 Roman Catholics and 800,000 Uniates lived in Russia. At that time, Catherine made certain commitments with regard to her new subjects. In Belorussia, she promised to respect their faith; and in September 1773, by signing the treaty with Poland, she guaranteed that the status of the Catholic religion would not be called into question.

Uniates and Catholics still presented Catherine with two essentially political problems. The Orthodox religion in the empire was a constituent part of the ideology of the State, even if the formula "Orthodoxy, autocracy, nationality" was not coined until the 19th century. Bringing non-Orthodox subjects into the empire was already a problem, exacerbated by the fact that—unlike the Jews or Muslims, who faced the sovereign on their own—the Catholics were bound to an external authority with which the imperial power had to reckon.

In 1773, Catherine's relations with the Holy See were complicated by the papal suppression of the Jesuits. She decided to ignore, in her states, the bull *Dominus ac redemptor* (21 July 1773), suppressing the Society of Jesus, even going so far as to create a novitiate for the Jesuits in Polotsk in 1777. Not content with this flouting of pontifical decisions, Catherine regulated as she saw fit the fate of Catholics and their hierarchies throughout the empire, threatening purely and simply to liquidate the Catholics of the Eastern Rite. If her attitude to the Roman Catholics can be explained by her wish to stand up to Rome, with regard to the Uniates her reasons went deeper. For her, the Greek Catholic Church of Eastern Rite was a bizarre, unacceptable compromise between the dogma and ritual of two religions, and especially the product of a political maneuver designed to diminish Russian power over the peoples of Belorussia and Poland. After the first division of Poland, Catherine on her own initiative created a bishopric in Polotsk, situated in Russian territory, to remove the Uniates from the authority of their bishop, who had remained on Polish soil. The bishop of Polotsk was meant to have authority over all the Uniates of the empire. Next, she raised Mogilev in western Ukraine to the rank of archbishopric and forced Rome to confirm her candidate to the office, threatening that if this was not done every link between Rome and the empire would be cut off. She won her case.

After Poland was carved up for the second and third times, the Uniates' situation worsened further. Four Uniate bishoprics were absorbed by Russia, and their flocks, seeing their parishes close for lack of funds and finding themselves isolated and the target of persecutions, converted en masse to Orthodoxy. By the end of Catherine's reign, roughly 45% of the Uniates had returned to the Orthodox fold because they foresaw that the policy of "religious tolerance" in fact meant the liquidation of the Uniate community.

The last blows were struck by the tsars Nicholas I and Alexander II. Nicholas I ordered the unification of the Uniate dioceses with the Orthodox ones, and in 1839 he had a medal minted with the following inscription: "Separated by hatred in 1595, reunited by love in 1839." Union with Rome thus ended in a disunity imposed from above. Over the following years, the number of Uniates still attached to their faith numbered fewer than 200,000. The center of the Uniate Church at the time was in Galicia. The Ruthenian population was passionately devoted to it, making religion a symbol of national life and of preventive struggle against any ties binding the region to Russia, which would also have entailed a compulsory conversion to Orthodoxy. A striking example of the confusion of religion and nationalism is the case of Count Andrei Schepitski. In the late 19th century, he led the Ukrainian nationalist movement, becoming, in 1900, Greek Catholic metropolitan of Lemberg (later Lvov).

It was the internal problems of the empire that in 1905 would save what survived of the Uniate community. In April 1905, an edict of religious tolerance forbade the persecution of the Uniates. But at the same time, the rapid rise of the Ukrainian nationalist movement in Russia and in the Austro-Hungarian Empire convinced Tsar Nicholas II of the need to bring about the rapid conversion of the Uniates. In line with this determination were the reinclusion, in 1908, of the district of Kholm to the government of Kiev and, especially, the anti-Uniate campaign launched in 1914 in Galicia and Bukovina under the occupation of the Russian army. The Orthodox religion was then imposed in those territories where the Uniate Church had prevailed. The metropolitan Andrei Schepitski was arrested and exiled to Russian territory, increasing the disarray of the Uniates, who found themselves stripped of their parishes and their priests.

In the Russian Empire, which in 1917 was replaced by the Soviet state, the Uniates' fate appeared to be definitively settled, at least up to 1945. Yet on the frontiers of the U.S.S.R., Uniate communities persisted—in independent Poland, and particularly in western Ukraine. It is not surprising, therefore, that, having annexed western Ukraine at the beginning of the Second World War and retaken it at war's end, the Soviets carried out ruthless repression in these territories and strove to erase all traces of the Uniate Church. After Schepitski died (1 November 1944) the Soviets were able, with the help of clergy won over to their side, to destroy what remained of the Greek Catholic Church. On 11 April 1945, all the bishops, including Bishop Slipyi, were arrested, and terror was launched against priests and faithful. On 23 December 1945, PIUS XII published the encyclical *Orientalis omnes*, protesting against the forced combining of the Greek Catholic Ukrainians with the Orthodox Church. But the encyclical could not prevent either the growing terror or the final destruction of the martyred Church. A synod held in Lvov from 9 to 10 March 1946 claimed to be representative of the Greek Catholic Church. It annulled the act of union of Brest and placed the Uniate Church under the authority of the Russian Orthodox Church, which, from 1943, had regained its legal right to exist under the Soviet regime. In August 1949, a similar decision was taken in the case of the Greek Catholic Church from Transcarpathia to Mukachevo, and in April 1952, in the case of the Uniate Church of the region of Priachiv, in Czechoslovakia.

The years of thaw in the East that followed Stalin's death, and then the years of VATICAN II and its aftermath, encouraged a certain détente in relations between the Communist states and the Vatican. Though not a true reconciliation, a certain degree of religious life once again became possible in eastern Europe. Only the Uniates were excluded from this revival. In Poland, the bishopric of Przemyśl, which had survived the persecutions, had been vacant since 1946. Bishop Slipyi had been freed in 1963 and authorized to go to Rome, where he would be made archbishop of Lvov and then cardinal, but all that happened in Rome; his Church did not reap any benefit because in those years it did not exist. It is true that the fate of the Uniates believed to have been absorbed into the Orthodox Church, or else de-Christianized, may have seemed to the Holy See at the time to be less important than the new relations with the Communist states, since these made it possible to negotiate the status of the Catholic Churches, to reopen bishoprics, and even to develop religious teaching, as had been done in Poland from the late 1950s. At the same time, ecumenical progress suggested that it was in this domain that the end of the schism was to be sought. In face of hopes like these, no doubt the obscure fate of the Uniates was not an overwhelming concern. This may explain why Cardinal Slipyi was honored in Rome and why, once liberated, he could do no more than stay in the Vatican until his death, in 1984. Only in August 1992 were his remains moved to Lvov, to an independent Ukraine that finally recognized the existence of the Greek Catholic Church.

It was the fall of Communism and the breakup of the Soviet empire that made possible the restoration of the Uniate Church. In 1988, the U.S.S.R., whose political system was at its last gasp, triumphantly celebrated one thousand years of Christianization. The country's leaders noted at the time that, in the general confusion and the collapse of Marxist and Leninist ideology, religious faith was the last means by which to appeal to the moral sense and good citizenship of its citizens. This general perception was combined with the desire to satisfy rising nationalist aspirations which, as in Ukraine, were made up in large measure of religious sentiment. In this connection, 1989 was a decisive year. The Soviet authorities ratified the reconstitution of the Greek Catholic Church, to which most of the parishes in Galicia were immediately added. On 28 May 1991, the Greek Catholic Church was legalized. Nevertheless, nothing was simple. Parallel with this revival, Ukraine saw the emergence of the autocephalous Orthodox Church established in Kiev, which would be legalized in October 1990 and receive the reinforcement of the bishop of the Russian Orthodox Church of Zhitomir. Further, the exarchate of the Russian Orthodox Church in Ukraine changed its name to the Orthodox Church of Ukraine in March 1990.

This made for three great Churches in Ukraine, two of them Orthodox, many rivalries concerning congregations and possessions, and many more problems for the Uniate hierarchy. If the Greek Catholic Church has survived, it is above all because it was a symbol of national life, of reaction to Russification and Orthodoxy. Today the Church has a legal existence and a material means of existence, but it is not certain how easy it will be for it to maintain its position between Roman Catholicism and autocephalous Orthodoxy. Time alone will tell whether the Greek Catholic Church, deprived of its nationalist justifi-cation, has any chance of survival, or whether, as Catherine II believed, it is a negligible hybrid. Again, time alone will tell whether it can, in the normal conditions of existence it is experiencing for the first time in its long history, play its part in reducing the schism; or if, as the Orthodox are convinced, this is a genuine schism without the possibility of reunification.

Hélène Carrère-d'Encausse

Bibliograpy

Codevilla, G. *Religione e spiritualità in URSS*, Rome, 1981.

Del Rio, D. and Giacomelli, R. *San Pietro e il Cremlino*, Casale Monferrato, 1991.

Gudziak, B. *Crisis and Reform*, Cambridge, Mass., 1998.

Haijar, J. *Les Chrétiens uniates du Proche-Orient*, Paris, 1962.

Mailleux, P. "Catholics in the Soviet Union," *Aspects of Religion in the Soviet Union 1917–1967*, Chicago, 1971.

Pospielovsky, D. *The Russian Church Under the Soviet Regime, 1917–1982*, New York, 1984.

Struve, N. *Les Chrétiens en URSS*, Paris, 1963.

Zizola, G. *Dopo l'ateismo—Diario di viaggio nell'URSS religiosa*, Milan, 1990.

UNITY, ITALIAN.

Unity, Unification and Risorgimento: Problems of Interpretation and Definition. On 26 February and 14 March 1861, in Turin, the capital of Piedmont, the Chamber of Deputies and the Senate approved a motion giving Victor Emmanuel II and his dynastic successors the title king of Italy. On 27 March, the deputies decided that the city of Rome must become the Italian capital, even though at the time Rome and Latium, like Venice and its surrounding region, were still not part of the new kingdom. From December 1860 on, patriotic committees "for the liberation of Rome and Venice" (*comitati di provvedimento per Roma e Venezia*), made up of moderates and progressives, were charged with the task of raising forces from all over the country to win back the remaining provinces.

The pontifical Rome of PIUS IX (1846–78) and Austrian-held Venice thus found themselves reduced to the same level by unitary propaganda. These illustrious cities and their respective regions were in the hands of two opponents of unification—one internal and the other external—that stood in the way of territorial unity. On 2 October 1870, Rome and Latium were annexed to the kingdom of Italy, which had in the meantime reconquered Venice (1866); and on 23 December 1870, the capital was officially moved from Florence to Rome. With Rome, Italy achieved the geographical structure of its unity as a nation-state even as the papacy—which now considered itself stripped of its possessions—was entering into an open conflict with the new state that lasted until the statutory settlement known as the LATERAN PACTS (11 February 1929).

The phrase "Italian unity" denotes both a process and its result. The former is the military and political winning of the independence of Italy, which was now constituted as a 19th-century European unitary state with a territory covering the entire peninsula and a single central government. The latter is the unification—political, social, economic, and cultural—measured in terms of national integration within a new order set up by the monarchy of Savoy. These two chronological frameworks are superimposed. They are characterized by intense historiographical and ideological debate opened up by the various interpretations of Italian unity among which one may distinguish three modalities of a single historical reality: the Risorgimento ("revival") as ideology, territorial unity, and national unification.

During the period from the congress of Vienna (1815) to the proclamation of Rome as the Italian capital (1870), the territorial unity of Italy was consolidated after the "wars of independence" of 1848–49, 1859, and 1866 against foreign powers (Austria and France) and internal powers (the papacy, the Bourbons) that were hindering that process. In a wider perspective tying Italian unity to the Risorgimento, the chronological limits are both more extended and more problematic as regards the dual question of the origins and achievement of national unity.

The question of *terminus a quo* gave rise to an important historiographical debate from the end of the 19th century to the years after the Second World War. The renewal of this debate since the mid-1970s makes it easier to understand the place of the unitary ideal within the Italian culture of the Risorgimento. If, as de Sanctis wrote, "culture created Italian unity," the main problem is to identify the indicators of the progress from a tradition of thinking linked to the Enlightenment to the elaboration of a political program of opposition to the old order, and finally to the adoption of the nationalist cause.

Up to the fall of Fascism, the question of the intellectual and political origins of the Risorgimento was frequently posed according to a schema opposing "national tradition" and "foreign influence"—in particular from France and the revolution of 1789. Liberal historians like Benedetto Croce and Adolfo Omodeo attempted to free the history of the culture of national unity from two dominating influences. They analyzed the mechanisms of the rise of Fascism and nationalism, at the same time condemning the democratic and anti-Fascist opposition to a set of ideas wrongfully held responsible for the liberal crisis and the rise of totalitariansm.

The link between the terms "Risorgimento" and "unity" is merely one of interpretation and historiographical representation, elaborated in the late 19th century and based on a mythic rereading (S. Soldani) of Italian history. This view is what Benedetto Croce defined as "a unity *ab origine* of the history of Italy," which saw the territorial and political unity of Italy as the political translation of a vast ideological current of revival (*risorgimento*) of the ideals of a glorious nation temporarily enslaved.

Recent studies have stressed the necessity—at the risk of anachronism—of avoiding "giving a premature importance to the unitary ideal of the Risorgimento" (A. Scirocco). The plan for a united territory, they say, arose only late—between 1848 and 1860—in the consciousness of the ruling progressive and liberal classes, united from the beginning of the 19th century around "patriotic" and national ideas. This new view emphasized the internal dynamism of certain pre-unitary states of the Bourbon Restoration, heirs of the Enlightenment and Napoleonic reform. Their legislative and administrative vitality, so the theory went, encouraged—despite regional rivalries and European diplomatic interests—Italy's progress from a multi-state pattern to union under the leadership of Piedmont. In this way of thinking, the unitary idea was only one of the end results (and a somewhat accidental one) of the political tradition of the Risorgimento, made concrete by the territorial annexations laboriously realized between 1859 and 1870.

When was the unification of Italy actually achieved? The question of the *terminus ad quem* has been pertinent from time to time throughout all periods of social and political crisis in Italy since 1870. Fundamentally, it has its origin in an implied similarity between the French Revolution and the Italian Revolution, a notion that descends straight from the ideas Taine developed during his journey to Italy in 1864. For Antonio Gramsci, what stands in the way of the parallel between the Jacobin revolution of the French and the national revolution of the Italians is the impossibility of reconciling the various "regional motive forces" of Italian history and the unresolved agrarian question, the origin of the problem of the Mezzogiorno—whence the idea of a "betrayal of the Risorgimento" by the ruling classes allied around the "clerico-moderate bloc," despite the problem of Rome. Little by little, one arrives at the idea of the chronic incompleteness of Italian unity, the result of regional disparities and rivalries, the inefficiency of state structures, the difficult relations with the Church of Rome, and the absence of historical legitimacy of a national, non-totalitarian culture.

This helps to explain why recourse to the history of unity logically leads to views that are mainly anti-state. G. Enrico Rusconi's *Se cessiamo di essere una nazione* ("If We Cease to Be a Nation," 1993) confirms the tendency in times of crisis to regard unification as an impossibility. In this context, relations between the Catholic Church and proponents of Italian unity at the heart of the

Risorgimento have been the object of interpretations that have often favored the Church's doctrine, institutional organization, and temporal power as well as the social, cultural, and political roles of Italian Catholics.

We must go back to the political and doctrinal origins of Cavour's formula, "a free Church in a free State" (*libera Chiesa in libero Stato*), in order to understand the singularity of this united Italy. The state had built up its territory against the temporal power of a pope who proclaimed himself "a prisoner in his States." It was a secular kingdom whose rulers had been excommunicated but in private multiplied their declarations of faith and called for the sacraments, a country whose largely Catholic population risked anathema the moment it took part in political life. Church and State were linked during unity by a variety of bonds: the religious matrix of the Risorgimento; the radicalization of the conflict between the papacy and the forces of unification over the "Roman question"; relations among the Church, civil society, and the kingdom of Italy; and the weight of the Catholic movement as a process of both contestation and national integration.

The Religious Identity of the Risorgimento: The Weight and Ambiguities of Christianity. Recent scholarship on enlightened absolutism in Italy has reacted against a tradition that too exclusively links the Enlightenment (*l'Illuminismo*) with Italian unity. The newer view holds that it is useless to look earlier than the French occupation and the Napoleonic period to discover the origin of the unifying ideals of the Risorgimento or the first systematic signs in Italy of 19th-century liberal constitutionalism and juridical thinking. Nonetheless, experiments in enlightened despotism in a number of regional states make it possible to stress the consequences of the intellectual awakening of the "philosophical" laity and Josephinist-inspired (see below) reformism on relations between Church and State in Risorgimento culture.

From the beginning of the 18th century, the cultural awakening of modern Italy illustrates the progress "of an urban culture to a regional culture" (Waquet), marked by the rise of the great state capitals (Naples and Milan, obviously, but also Florence and Bologna, now overtaking Siena and Ferrara). In these centers, the philosophical awakening of the Enlightenment was accompanied by brilliance in letters and the arts, an attraction to scientific progress, and an openness to foreign influences—especially from France and England—which provided rationalist bases of thinking founded on law.

This thinking, which originated with active commitment among intellectuals (often with ties to the Freemasonry of Naples, Tuscany, and Romagna), produced two principal evolutionary ferments. First, these thinkers prized absolute power, which alone had the ability to oppose the privileged—for example, the aristocracy and the regular clergy (notably the Jesuits) who favored the creation of states within a state—and owed its subjects the duty to oppose their oppressor. Further, the philosophers favored the principle of law and the economy, transcending boundaries, as a means of improving the lot of societies outside regional jurisdictions (cf. the works of Galiani, Genovesi, and Filangieri). These ideas have been interpreted as the origin of a juridical and economic philosophy of Italian unity; in fact, they conveyed principally the extraregional preoccupations of their promoters. Thus, out of the Enlightenment came a form of deist or rationalist MODERNISM, not so much antireligious as secular and anticlerical, which came into open conflict with the Society of Jesus up to the early 1770s. The theological consequences of this modernism within the clergy were violently denounced by a young professor of theology from Rome, Fra Mauro Cappellari—the future Pope GREGORY XVI—who in 1799 published "The Triumph of the Holy See and the Church against the Attacks of Innovators" (*Il Trionfo della Santa Sede contro gli assalti dei novatori*).

In the same period, new ties between the Church and secular rulers were established in the states under Austrian control: the Lombardy and Tuscany of the Habsburg-Lorraines, but also the Este states influenced by the "jurisdictionalist" and Josephinist model. The religious policy of Maria Theresa (1740–1870) and Joseph II (1765–90) reinforced the control of the state over the teaching of the clergy, its hierarchical and territorial organization (bishops' powers, ecclesiastical divisions), and the liturgy (fixing of feast days). Josephinism developed the earlier theses of "jurisdictionalism"—a system aimed at separating Church and State to the advantage of the State in the case of conflicts over rights and powers laid down after the council of Trent. Josephinism used these measures to redefine the Church's place in society and to submit its hierarchy to the civil political power, at the risk of straining organic ties with Rome.

In Milan, the 1757 concordat, which had already set certain limits to clerical power, was considered obsolete. After 1767, the ecclesiastical tribunals—including the Inquisition—were abolished, and state censorship was set up to rule on the publication of papal documents (the *placet*), while control over the regular clergy, numerically restricted by the civil power, was reinforced.

The Tuscany of Peter Leopold I (1765–90), brother of Joseph II, underwent the same evolution: confiscation of the possessions of the Society of Jesus (1768), grandducal censorship of pontifical documents (1769), abolition of the Holy Office, and the splitting up of former clerically held lands, which were redistributed to "communities" (municipalities) and the secular clergy of the grand duchy (1784). In Tuscany, Peter Leopold's Josephinist policy relied on the Jansenist tendencies of part of the clergy, even as it manipulated them.

Taking the opposite tack from the Italian historian Carlo Arturo Jemolo, who argued that the "second Jansenism" of the 18th century was a collection of anachronistic theses bypassed by the political evolution of pre-Risorgimento ideas, Maurice Vaussard traced the religious path of the Risorgimento back to JANSENISM and GALLICANISM (*Jansénisme et gallicanisme aux origines religieuses du Risorgimento*, 1959). How is one to account for the coming together of these religious arguments and the patriotic and unitary reawakening in Italy? As a result of their hostility toward the Jesuits and their concern with reducing the role of the Roman Curia and limiting papal prerogatives, the French Jansenists set a fashion in certain clerical milieus in Italy that were backing a return to the democratic customs of the pre-Tridentine Church. Even in Italy, they called for the protection of the civil power in the defense of the rights of priests vis-à-vis Rome, and for the creation of a "national Church" on the French Gallican model, the "spiritual fatherland" of the religious reformers. In western and central Italy (Tuscany, Lombardy, Piedmont, and Liguria), some representatives of the upper clergy and certain intellectual clerics were won over by these arguments, among them the bishop of Pistoia, Scipione de' Ricci, and the abbot Degola in Genoa. The synod of Pistoia (18–29 September 1786), convened by Ricci, followed the Leopoldian model in Tuscany in approving the subordination of Church to State regarding any problem of organization or regulation, recognizing the usefulness of the royal *placet*, and denying the bases of papal primacy. These theses, taken up and argued over by the theologians of Pavia, were eventually condemned by the bull *Auctorem fidei* (1794) of PIUS VI (1775–99).

During the French occupation and the Napoleonic period, the Italian Jansenists were influenced by a twofold movement. First encouraged in their stance favoring the Civil Constitution of the Clergy by the presence of French Revolutionary troops, the Jansenist prelates condemned counter-revolutionary intrigues in the countryside (autumn 1797) and enthusiastically defended the work of the French in all areas (Ricci, de Vecchi, Alpruni). But at the same time, the Jansenist, Josephinist, and regalist tradition, which was very strong in Lombardy, combined its hatred for the Roman Curia with its hostile defiance of the French, enemies of the Habsburgs (Palmieri). It is easy to understand the difficulty of assimilating the two movements from the late 18th century. On the one hand, there was a heterogeneous movement whose common denominator was, in the phrase of one of its representatives, Msgr. Campodonico, "the limitation of the authority of the Church, the prerogatives of the Holy See and the absolute power of the sovereigns"; on the other hand, there was the birth of a political movement of national emancipation directed first and foremost against the *ancien régime*. It is at the level of personal influence over thinkers and future statesmen of the Risorgi-

mento, like the Tuscans Lambruschini and Ricasoli—staunch defenders of the autonomy of religious thought and the prerogatives of a liberal progressivist state—that Jansenism's political imprint is most clearly visible, even surpassing the dreams of reconciliation of neo-Guelphism.

At the beginning of the 19th century and during the Restoration following the last act of the congress of Vienna (June 1815), the Church's place in the national Risorgimento movement was affirmed in a way quite different from the anticlerical laicism typical of the late Enlightenment. True, the papacy confirmed its condemnation of political and religious liberalism, as is clear in the encyclical *Mirari vos* of GREGORY XVI (1832). During the papacies of LEO XII (1823–29), PIUS VIII (1829–30) and GREGORY XVI (1831–46), preference for the conservative legitimism of the European sovereigns, though not abandoned in practice, yielded place officially to the desire to preserve the pontifical State, Rome's temporal and territorial power, and the sovereignty of the pope in Italy, even at the cost of some minor internal concessions. In this climate, the many attempts at rebellion against the authorities in the Papal States—in 1817–18 and from 1821 to the revolution of February 1832—were doomed to failure, harshly suppressed as attacks on the Church's temporal power and obstacles to the functioning of the representatives of its government, as to any other state of the Restoration.

Nonetheless, the growth of sympathy for Italian unification and independence in the 1830s and the concentration of such forces against Italy's external enemies led to the development of federalist groups in the which the papacy could assume an active, positive role. The neo-Guelph position gave this movement its conceptual and political legitimacy. Vincenzo Gioberti (1801–52), a priest since 1825, first taught at the faculty of Turin. Compromised by his direct ties to Mazzini's revolutionary movement Young Italy (*Giovine Italia*), he was subsequently exiled to Belgium and France. The publication of his work *Del primato morale e civile degli Italiani* (1843) gained him notoriety and made him one of the principal champions of Italian liberation, along with Luigi Torelli and Cesare Balbo, author of *Speranze d'Italia* (1844). Reflecting the part played by the Guelphs against the imperial pretensions of the Hohenstaufen and their Ghibelline supporters, neo-Guelphism arose out of the encounter of a Romantic tradition and a political hope. Its twin aims were to reform the Church and to revive the ancient freedom of the Italian communes.

Tradition exalts the memory of the struggle against the German emperor, made even more important by Austria's presence north of the Italian peninsula. It also affirms the historical "particularism" of Italy, arising from its plurality of states which, according to Gioberti, was preserved by the role played by the papacy. (Gioberti adopted arguments proposed in the 16th century by the Tuscan Guichardino.) At the heart of the mobilization machinery of the Risorgimento—which arose from nostalgia for a sublime and forgotten past—neo-Guelphism resurrected the historic grandeur of the Italian people, incarnated in the glory of ancient Rome, the Italy of the free medieval communes, the Rome of the popes, and the epic of the anti-Austrian patriots by way of the anti-Spanish rebel movement. (Alessandro Manzoni made the rebels the symbolic fathers of the Lombard Catholic Risorgimento in his novel *The Betrothed* [*I promessi sposi*], published in June 1827.)

The neo-Guelphs' idea was to form a confederation of the Italian states, autonomous but united under the effective presidency of the sovereign pontiff. This confederation was conceived as the only possible structure that would allow the Italian nation to win back its freedom by ousting the Austrians. The program of Gioberti and his supporters implicitly subjected the papacy to two conditions governing its internal and external policies: constitutional monarchy—in keeping with the rise of constitutionalism in other states—and commitment to the anti-Austrian struggle.

At first, PIUS IX (1846–78), who favored Gioberti's ideas, seemed to follow the path of parliamentarism and liberalism. He announced a partial amnesty of political prisoners one month after his accession to the pontificate (July 1846), ordered reforms of his civil administration (1847), created a civil guard, and even (under the strain of political pressures created by the precedent of the Piedmontese constitution) promulgated a constitution in the Papal States on 14 March 1848. Soon, however, even before the revolutionary events that reversed his power in Rome (winter 1848–9), Pius IX distanced himself by refusing to declare war on Catholic Austria. This dashed the hopes of those who wanted to make the pope "the president of some new republic that was to be formed with all the peoples of Italy" (pontifical allocution of 29 April 1848).

The failure of the experiments of 1848 in Italy also marks the end of the neo-Guelph dream of reconciling national independence, Romantic liberalism, and the role that Italian history had bequeathed to the papacy. From that time, a distinction was made between, on the one hand, respect for Christianity among many patriots, from moderates to revolutionaries—a majority of the workers' groups and craftsmen's fraternities (*società operaie* and *fratellanze artigiane*) inspired by Mazzini were placed under divine protection—and on the other hand, the necessary opposition to the interference of the Roman Church when it hindered the internal spread of political liberalism and the progress of political unity in an Italy that had regained its liberty. Cavour's compromise enacted these new, dominant trends with the withdrawal to Piedmont of the neo-Guelphs, who henceforth abandoned all hope of a confederation directed from Rome.

Profoundly influenced by the neo-Guelph positions, the Piedmontese Camillo Benso, count of Cavour and founder in 1847 of a newspaper, *Il Risorgimento*, early declared himself in favor of a clear separation of Church and State. Adopting some conclusions from a work by the Swiss Protestant Alexandre Vinet, *Essai sur la manifestation des convictions religieuses et sur la séparation de l'Église et de l'État* (1842), he associated the national role of the Savoy monarchy, the driving force of territorial unification, with his aim to give up all state control over the Church.

The formula "a free Church in a free State" (*libera Chiesa in liberto Stato*) immediately fell prey to a variety of interpretations. According to the author's close friends and supporters, such as Pier Carlo Boggio and Marco Minghetti, the principle was one of disconcerting simplicity: the coexistence of the forms of individual freedom (including religious freedom) and of public freedoms must be guaranteed by the State. In addition, it was the duty of the public power to stand aside so this right could be fully exercised. In practice, the government had to ensure that freedom and plurality of worship were respected and all regalist initiatives inspired by Josephinism or Gallicanism abandoned. At the same time, the Church was sovereign in matters of ecclesiastical organization and liturgy, but it had to give up all territorial control of a temporal nature. Moreover, as the first article of the Piedmontese constitution affirmed, recognition of the Catholic religion as the state religion in no way prohibited religious freedom and the protection of other beliefs. This passage from theory to practice, when extended beyond Piedmont, quickly met serious obstacles that arose from the close links between Cavour's religious plan and the process of national unification.

Literal respect for Cavour's formula implied that the pope willingly agreed officially to renounce his political authority as a sovereign head of state. At the end of 1860, Cavour sent two emissaries to the Curia, Carlo Passaglia and Diomede Pantaleoni, to attempt to persuade the pope to agree to end his temporal power in exchange for a guarantee of the independence of the Church and the maintenance of a certain number of the sovereign pope's honorific prerogatives within the new state. The opposition of the Curia, notably Cardinal Antonelli, was already well known when the pope expressed his official rejection of the "conciliatory" proposals (consistory of March 1861).

From that time on, some historians developed an argument reducing Cavour's plan to a felicitous, skillful formula that had only tactical content and was designed to leave open the way to compensations to the pope, now deprived of his possessions and the exercise of his temporal power by the unification process. This argument was refuted by the historian Carlo Arturo Jemolo—citing Cavour's sincerity of conviction—and moderated by Ettore Passerin d'Entrèves and Pietro Scoppola. For these men, the famous formula marked both the conclusion of a diplomatic transaction and a "turning point in Cavour's ecclesiastical policy" represented by "the new recognition of certain demands of the Catholic conscience and the papacy of Rome." In this spirit, it is easier to understand how the seemingly impossible reconciliation polarized both the opposition of the intransigents in the Curia and that of the Hegelian-influenced liberals who were denouncing the submission of the State to the Church. By 1861, Italy's territorial unity was well launched, and the papacy represented a military and diplomatic obstacle to its conclusion.

The Territorial Unity of Italy Against the Papacy. In 1815, Italy as drawn by the congress of Vienna consisted of ten states of unequal geographical size. The three smallest ones—the principality of Massa (with Carrara and Lunigiana) and the duchy of Lucca, the first annexed to the duchy of Modena (1829) and the second to the grand-duchy of Tuscany (1847), along with the little republic-city of San Marino—were situated in the west central section of the peninsula. The seven other states were to the north and south: the kingdom of Sardinia, consisting of Piedmont (with Savoy), Sardinia and Liguria, governed by the House of Savoy; the Lombardy-Veneto kingdom (with Valtellina, Trentino, and Trieste), possessed and administered by the Austrians; the duchy of Parma, Piacenza, and Guastalla, ruled by Maria Louisa of Austria; the duchy of Modena, Reggio, and Mirandola, ruled by the Este family; the grand duchy of Tuscany, under the domination of the house of Habsburg-Lorraine since 1738; the Papal States; and the Bourbon kingdom of the Two Sicilies, consisting of southern Italy—south of the Marches and Latium—and Sicily.

The proclamation of the restoration of the Papal States (Stato della Chiesa) dates from the treaty of Paris (10 May 1814). It was confirmed a year later in Vienna (9 June 1815). With 259,000 inhabitants at the end of the 1820s, this possession comprised a quarter of the Italian population, the largest after the Two Sicilies, Lombardy-Veneto, and Piedmont. The sovereign pontiff's temporal authority extended over a great variety of territories and administrative jurisdictions which justified the frequent use of the plural in "States of the Church" or "Papal States." Besides Latium, the pope's possessions embraced the Romagna, Umbria, and the Marches, thus extending from the central to the southern Apennines and linking the Tyrrhenian Sea to the Adriatic. In 1815, the Papal States—henceforth without Avignon or the Venaissin—were divided into 11 provinces grouped in "delegations" (*delegazioni*). These were in three categories: "first class" for the provinces of Bologna, Ferrara and Romagna; "second class" for the Patrimony of St. Peter

and the Marittima and Campagna provinces; and "third class" for the provinces of Urbino, Sabina, Umbria, Camerino, the Marches, and Benevento. A system of differentiation between delegations and legations (*legazione*) was then drawn up. It distinguished four legations governed by cardinal legates or prelates vice-legate (Bologna, Ferrara, Forlì, and Ravenna) and 14 delegations (Urbino and Pesaro, Ancona, Fermo, Frosinona, Macerata, Perugia, Spoleto, Viterbo, Ascoli, Benevento, Camerino, Civitavecchia, Rieti, Comarca of Roma) administered by prelates who were apostolic delegates (except for Comarca, which was governed by two lay jurists).

After various territorial redistributions carried out by Leo XII in 1827, the last great reform was in the reign of Gregory XVI, who fixed the number of provinces at 21. Outside the territory of Rome and Comarca and the district of Loreto, these were as follows: six legations (Velletri, Urbino and Pesaro, Ravenna, Forlì, Bologna, Ferrara) and 13 delegations (Frosinina and Pontecorvo, Civitavecchia, Viterbo, Orvieto, Rieti, Spoleto, Perugia, Camerino, Macerata, Fermo, Ascoli, Benevento, Ancona). In the political vocabulary of the time (though not in administrative or juridical usage), there was often confusion between the various types of jurisdictions, which were frequently designated by the word "legations" meaning everything that did not belong to Rome or the Patrimonio.

The pontificates of Leo XII (1823–9) and Pius VIII (1829–30) saw the continuation of the policy of administrative rigor and political repression of Cardinal Consalvi, secretary of state under Pius VII (1800–23). Patriotic agitation took the form of crimes and conspiracies fomented by secret societies linked to Freemasonry and the Carbonari and supported by the Bonapartists in Romagna and the Marches. Echoes of the Paris revolts of 27–30 July 1830 encouraged a great revolutionary uprising in Bologna (4 February 1831). At the end of February, the fall of pontifical power was even proclaimed by an assembly in the Romagna capital, made up of deputies representing the various provisional governments that had been set up in the papal provinces.

Thus an experiment in liberal and constitutional revolution came about: the insurgents convoked a constituent assembly for 20 March. The power of the pope was replaced by an executive that federalized all the provisional governments and abolished all the pontifical administrative bodies. The Austrians had to intervene in Bologna and the French in Ancona before the pope could restore order. Gregory XVI (1831–46) inaugurated his pontificate with a policy of repression that encouraged the two opposition forces, one born of national anti-Austrian patriotism and the other of constitutional liberalism, to combine forces. This union found full expression in the confusion of ideas and events of the Romantic revolution, which began in Italy with an outburst of fervor for the new pope, PIUS IX, elected in 1846.

In June 1846, with the papal election of Cardinal Mastai Ferreti as Pius IX, for the first time since 1815 a pope's name was associated with hopes for political change and the dream of national independence. After the various punctual reforms concerning the liberty of press and the functioning of local ecclesiastical structures and the Curia, the pope satisfied the aspirations of both liberals and nationalists by protesting publicly against the presence of the Austrians in Ferrara (1847) and by granting a bicameral constitution to the Papal States (March 1848). Symbolic acts ensued: the adoption of the tricolor ribbon of green, white, and red, inherited from the French occupation, to adorn the pontifical banner; and the despatch of Roman troops to protect the Romagna from possible Austrian attack. These made Rome, with Turin, one of the hotbeds of patriotic enthusiasm on the eve of the "first war of independence." This was attested by the publication in Milan, by Vincenzo de Castro, of a patriotic review entitled *Pius IX* (25 March 1848).

The war with Austria arose at the heart of the revolutionary outbreak known as the Lombard Quarantotto ("movement of 48"). After a Venetian revolt on 17 March 1848, on 18 March Milan was the scene of a genuine patriotic uprising which, after five days of fighting, forced Radetzky's Austrians to evacuate the city. On 23 March, Charles Albert, king of Sardinia, decided to come to the aid of the Lombards who had revolted against Austria, thus marking the beginning of the first "war of independence." Besides the Piedmontese and the Lombard-Venetian insurgents, the revolutionary forces included patriotic contingents from all the regional states, including the kingdom of the Two Sicilies (under General Guglielmo Pepe). After the Piedmontese defeat at Custoza (25 July 1848), Charles Albert negotiated with Marshall Radetzky the provisional ending of military operations. Three days before the signing of the armistice (9 August) and the Piedmontese retreat beyond the Ticino, the Austrians had already reentered Milan and proclaimed a state of siege. After the final defeat at Novara (23 March 1849), peace was concluded on the basis of a return to full Austrian domination, and Charles Albert abdicated in favor of his son, Victor Emmanuel II.

In Rome, Pius IX's refusal to declare war on Austria (April 1848) had upset the course of events and rendered even more tenuous relations among the pope, parliament, and the constitutional liberals grouped around Terenzio Mamiani. In November 1848, after the assassination of the conservative jurist Pellegrino Rossi, the pope's influential minister, a popular insurrection forced the pope to flee to Gaeta (24 November). On 9 February 1849, the constituent assembly declared the end of the pope's temporal power and proclaimed the Roman Republic. Once again the pope had to appeal to his Catholic allies, both in Italy and abroad, to restore order in his states. The Austrians and the Bourbons of Naples invaded the Papal States and put down the supporters of the Roman Republic from north to south. Meanwhile, a French expeditionary force commanded by General Oudinot landed at Civitavecchia in an attempt to reconcile the demands of the triumvirate of the Roman Republic—Mazzini, Armellini, and Saffi—with those of Pius IX. The French—with the efforts of Prince-President Louis Napoleon Bonaparte, who was anxious to retain the support of Catholic conservatives—espoused the pope's cause and opposed the Roman Republic. Despite the heroic defense of Garibaldi's troops at the battle of the Janiculum (30 April 1849), the French forces, breaking a truce with the Roman Republic, penetrated the city on 1 June and subdued it after a month's fighting.

On 4 July 1849, the Roman Assembly was dissolved and pontifical power restored. On 12 April 1850, Pius IX returned to Rome under French and Austrian escort. Henceforth, Italian unity could only be achieved against Rome and with the hegemony of the only state capable and willing to oppose foreign forces: the kingdom of Piedmont-Sardinia.

In the late 1850s, the achievement of territorial unity in Italy depended on diplomatic relations between France and Piedmont. At a secret meeting at Plombières in the Vosges (20–21 July 1858), Cavour obtained the support of the French emperor in case Austria declared war. In return, Napoleon III received the assurance that Nice and Savoy would be ceded to France. He also imposed on Cavour his plan for an independent, federal Italy composed of the states friendly to France: a kingdom of Upper Italy (Piedmont, Liguria, Lombardy, Venezia, and the northern duchies), a kingdom of central Italy (Tuscany), a kingdom of Southern Italy (the Two Sicilies), and the Papal States, which were left to the pope under French protection. On 23 April 1859, Austria gave the kingdom of Sardinia an ultimatum, enjoining it immediately to dissolve its corps of armed volunteers. On 27 April, one day after the ultimatum had been rejected by Turin, there began the second "war of independence," called in France the "war with Italy." Spring was marked by the Franco-Piedmontese victories of Magenta (4 June) and Solferino and San Martino (24 June), with enormous human losses on both sides. On 8 July 1859, the coalition of the Franco-Piedmontese and the Austrians met at Villafranca and drew up an armistice. The "preliminaries to peace" of Villafranca (12 July), signed by Francis Joseph and Napoleon III, provided for the cessation of hostilities—much desired by Napoleon, who wanted to appease French Catholic opinion, which did not look kindly on a long conflict with Austria. In return, Austria ceded Lombardy—but not Mantua—to France, with the mission of handing it over to Piedmont-Sardinia.

At the news of the launching of the war and after the Austrian defeat at Mentana, patriotic revolutions exploded in several states. On 27 April 1859, the Tuscans ousted the grand duke and set up a provisional government in Florence. At the beginning of June, the rulers of Parma and Modena were forced to abandon their duchies. After the Austrians had left the occupied legations, the patriots, with the support of the majority of the population, drove out the pontifical administrators. From spring 1860 to spring 1861, the buildup of the territory of the new Italian kingdom took place in three stages.

On 11 and 12 March 1860, Emilia and Tuscany were once again brought into the kingdom of Piedmont-Sardinia. This was based on the results of plebiscites organized on universal suffrage and in spite of the anti-unitary electoral propaganda of the legitimists and the clericals.

In May 1860, on the pretext of an appeal by Sicilian insurgents, General Garibaldi disembarked at Marsala at the head of about a thousand volunteers. After the defeat of the Bourbons at Calatafimi (15 May), he became dictator of Sicily in the name of King Victor Emmanuel. Victorious after their passage through Calabria, Garibaldi and his "Red Shirts" entered Naples (7 September), while the Piedmontese troops received the king's order to cross the Papal States (Umbria and the Marches) in order to "restore order" and join Garibaldi's volunteers. At the battle of Castelfidardo (17 September), an army of the pontifical zouaves commanded by the legitimist French general de Lamoricière was defeated by the Piedmontese.

The first phase of unification concluded with the annexation of the Two Sicilies after plebiscites on 21 October 1860, and of the Marches and Umbria after a vote on 4 and 5 November. In the Papal States, too, the population gave a loud "yes" to the plebiscite question: "Do you want to be part of the constitutional monarchy of Victor Emmanuel?" On 17 March 1861, the kingdom of Italy was proclaimed in Turin, its capital. All that was left under the territorial jurisdiction of the pope was Rome and Latium.

Now Venice in Austrian hands and Rome still governed by the "pope king" were the last two obstacles on the path of territorial unification. The new kingdom of Italy thus had to face two distinct types of political, diplomatic and military problems.

In October 1866, Venice was conquered and made part of the kingdom in the wake of the third "war of independence." In April 1866 an alliance had been signed—on the initiative of Napoleon III—between Prussia and Italy, in exchange for the promised prize of Venice in case of victory over Austria. Encouraged by both France and Prussia, Italy declared war on Austria (20 June). The Italians experienced a reversal at Custoza (24–28 June) and then a great naval defeat at Lissa (20 July). On 23 August, the treaty ending the war was signed in Prague, and on 3 October the Peace of Vienna decreed that Austria would

keep Trentino and the Venezia of the Julian Alps but would leave to France the task of returning to Italy Venice and its surrounding area. These were officially included in the new kingdom after a plebiscite on 21 October.

From the Garibaldians' cry "Rome or death!" to the official motion of the sub-Alpine parliament decreeing that Rome should be the capital of the new kingdom, the desire to reconquer Rome created unanimity in nationalist opinion and the ruling factions of the new Italy. The papacy, highly conscious of this, refused to recognize the Italian kingdom even after England, France, Russia, and Prussia crossed that threshold between spring 1861 and summer 1862. Though Rome aroused the covetousness of all patriots, the paths leading to it diverged.

In June 1862, Garibaldi—representing the extremist party favoring the immediate annexation of Rome—landed in Calabria with the firm determination to march on Latium to the cry of "Victor Emmanuel and Italy, Rome or death!" However, he was arrested by government troops at the battle of Aspromonte (29 August), following the king's official repudiation. The "September convention" was signed in Paris (15 September) between Italy and France. Italy promised to ensure that the present boundaries of papal Latium would be respected and to move its capital from Turin to Florence, while France undertook to evacuate its troops, which were still in Rome. In autumn 1867, the Garibaldians made another attempt to seize Rome and were beaten at Mentana (4 November) by the French and pontifical forces led by Failly and Kranzler, a few weeks after the failure of a patriotic uprising by the Roman Serristori barracks (22 October).

With the outbreak of the Franco-Prussian War (19 July 1870), the "Roman question" was once again at the heart of diplomatic negotiations. After the French refused to accept the Italians' proposals, Italy declared its neutrality, as did Austria, and France recalled its troops from Rome and Latium (August). After the French defeat at Sedan (2 September 1870), the Italian government launched its men in an assault on papal territory (10 September). Finally, on 20 September, the 39th infantry battalion and the 34th batallion of *bersagliere*, or sharpshooters, penetrated Rome by a symbolic breach made by the artillery at the Porta Pia. On 2 November, the inhabitants of Latium agreed by plebiscite to rejoin the Kingdom of Italy, of which Rome now became the new and definitive capital.

A Difficult Unification: The Pope, the Catholics and the Italian State. "It is easier to free a nation from the foreign yoke than suddenly to heal its economic and moral infirmities," declared Luigi Luzzati, the economist and politician, when he was newly elected as moderate representative of the Italian parliament in 1871. Without doubt, the relations among the new state, the papacy, the clergy, and the mass of Catholics were significant signs of these lasting "moral infirmities."

One historiographical view of the "Roman question" makes it the focus of crystallization, over more than a century, of opposition at the very heart of the Catholic Church and Catholic thought on the part of liberal and reforming trends. These trends corresponded broadly with two movements: first, criticism of the pope's temporal power; and second, conservative and authoritarian tendencies that confused the defense of this temporal power with the dogmatic affirmation of his primacy, as expressed in the proclamation of papal INFALLIBILITY at the council of VATICAN I. This religious dimension should not obscure the fact that the "Roman question" was posed first and foremost in statutory and political terms for the Italian state.

The "law for the guarantees of the prerogatives of the sovereign pontiff and of the Holy See and for the relations of the State with the Church," commonly known as the Law of Guarantees, was published in the *Official Gazette* (*Gazetta ufficiale*) in May 1871. It stipulated that the Italian State would ensure the pope the "prerogatives of his sovereignty," a sovereignty that was no longer exercised over territory, and provide him an annual financial settlement of more than 3 million lire. In the spirit of La Guéronière's pamphlet, with its axiom "The smaller the territory, the greater the sovereign" (*Le Pape et le Congrès*, 1860), the Italian government granted the pope possession of the Vatican, the apostolic palaces of the Lateran and the Chancery, and the summer residence of Castel Gandolfo. Under international law and the law of May 1871, the pope retained the "presidency of honor of the Catholic sovereigns," which allowed him to establish bilateral conventions with sovereigns—concerning religious and nonpolitical matters—and guaranteed diplomatic immunity for representatives of foreign governments to the Holy See. Nevertheless, the papacy, which had a "diplomatic pouch," did not enjoy the status of extraterritoriality in Rome.

Pius IX immediately rejected the Law of Guarantees and declared himself a prisoner of the king of Sardinia in his city of Rome. LEO XIII (1878–1903) reaffirmed the untenable character of the pope's position: deprived of his territory, he was condemned to be "the subject of another sovereign power." The seeming denial of pontifical status, linked with the abolition of Rome's temporal power, gave rise to a dual condemnation of the political legitimacy of the new State. Anathema was hurled in the highest symbolic way when the sovereigns Victor Emmanuel II (1861–78) and Umberto I (1878–1900) were excommunicated, though retaining the ability to carry out their religious duties in private.

If Italian Catholics thus could no longer recognize themselves in the image of an excommunicated monarch,

they were also enjoined from taking part, actively and individually, in the political life of their country. On 10 September 1874, one of the high apostolic tribunals (*penitenzieria apostolica*) declared that "it is not fitting" (*non expedit*) that Catholics participate in the political elections of the country, thus intensifying an earlier formulation issued in 1863 by Margotti's *Unità Cattolica*: "Neither elected nor electors." The interdiction did not apply to administrative (municipal and regional) elections, and it would be further attenuated in 1905 by the encyclical *Il fermo proposito* of PIUS X (1903–14). In 1913, the "Gentiloni pact" lifted the veto in order to block the progress of socialism by means of the Catholic vote, and BENEDICT XV (1914–22) definitively removed the interdiction in 1919. In fact, after the electoral reforms of 1882 (Depretis law) and the establishment of universal suffrage (1912), a large part of the Catholic voters had not obeyed the papal interdiction.

The "Roman question" and its implications would be settled with the signing of the Lateran pacts (11 February 1929) between Mussolini, in the name of King Victor Emmanuel III, and Cardinal Gasparri, in the name of Pope PIUS XI. Three documents were devoted to the question: a concordat between the Holy See and the Italian State which again made Catholicism "the State religion," officially privileged with regard to the other faiths; a political treaty; and a financial arrangement establishing the sovereignty of a new national territory in Rome, the Vatican City State.

After the proclamation of the kingdom of Italy in 1861, relations between the clergy and the representatives of the State were not nearly so conflict-ridden as might be supposed. At the local level in the annexed regions, priests and religious often joined with municipal and prefectoral authorities in great national celebrations—for example, the commemorative festival of the Statuto in June 1861, anniversary masses for the dead of the "wars of independence" (Curtatone and Montanara, San Martino), or blessings at official inaugurations of Garibaldian shooting ranges. At times conflict erupted between the local clergy, who would willingly side with the local representatives who supported the unitary State, and the episcopal hierarchy, which prohibited participation in national ceremonies, basing its arguments on reasons tied to the "purity of worship" (e.g. the refusal to allow National Guards, with arms and uniforms, to come to the altar). In June 1861, the organization in Piedmont, Tuscany, and the Romagna of masses for the repose of the soul of Cavour—who had been excommunicated—summed up the ambiguity of the situation at the birth of the kingdom.

Nonetheless, opposition between clergy and State had more and more opportunities to manifest itself. This happened first in the southern states, where the struggle against political brigandage revealed the complicity of a relatively poor clergy and an anti-unitary aristocracy. Throughout the country, the years 1860–80—with an acceleration resulting from the capture of Rome—saw the development of a form of clerical opposition (initially led by the regular clergy) that combined political legitimism and anti-unity struggle and that persuaded the rural population to use old anti-state tactics: refusing taxes and conscription, resistance to police authority. This movement, while officially frowned on because of its frequently violent and illegal character, was partly compensated for by Catholic *intransigentismo*, and even by such associations as the Opera dei Congressi (Work of Congresses), founded in September 1875. This trend was pitted against the liberal Catholic *transigente* tradition, which championed the reconciliation of Church and State through positions defined by the writers of the *Annali Cattolici* from 1862.

In Italian political thinking, "civil society" was defined by, among other attributes, the means that citizens had at their disposal to define their personal freedoms and their place vis-à-vis the State and the Church. In its task of secularizing Italian society, the Civil Code of 1865 stripped religious marriage of any legal value, although marriage could still be celebrated without preliminary recourse to the civil power. Whereas in 1871 the State gave up all its rights in ecclesiastical affairs having to do with citizens' individual relations with their Church (waiving of the bishop's oath of loyalty, of control over Church laws), it retained control over ecclesiastical benefices and possessions, usually those set up in public areas. On 15 August 1867, Florence passed a law abolishing ecclesiastical goods and domains, which were sold at auction or confiscated by the public powers. In 1890, the law was complemented by another law covering *opere pie* (charitable works), which was designed to establish strict state control over charitable brotherhoods.

The Italian penal code that came into force on 1 January 1890 (the Zanardelli code) was considered one of the most liberal in Europe. It abolished the death penalty, modified "crimes against property," and legitimized political opposition within strict constitutional limits. In the religious domain, it is significant that the code no longer referred to Catholicism as a "state religion," merely mentioning the existence of Catholic "worship" with its own "ministers" and "ceremonies." That same year (in October), the eighth Italian Catholic Congress, meeting in Lodi, did not reach agreement after heated debate on the contents of the petition it hoped to send the Chamber of Deputies in favor of the "reconstitution of the Pontifical State."

These examples show that, at the turn of the century, relations between Church and State continued to make it difficult to conceive of Italian unity. On the one hand, there persisted the inheritance of the "Roman question," but with the feeling that its mobilizing force was more symbolic than real in the ranks of Italian Catholics, who were divided over the birth of political radicalism and the worker and peasant movement. On the other hand, the civil powers believed they had settled the problem by legislating on the respective limits of the rights of individuals and of the State. The freedom of ministers of worship and their flocks was tolerated only if it did not infringe on public order. This harks back to the fluctuating understanding from one ministry to another of the limits of subversion and of political peril. Thus, the police authorities denounced and pursued the dangerous "maneuvers" of the clericals on the same grounds as they did the actions of socialist extremists. The situation with regard to the doctrinal debates symbolized by the "Roman question," the adversarial stance of the State, and the wish for integration in political and social life (later exploited by Christian Democracy and the lay apostolate) constitute three of the heterogeneous component parts of Italian Catholic opinion that were inherited from the first days of national unity. The effectiveness of the unification process derives from the interrelationship among these three facets of Italian Catholicism.

Gilles Pécout

Bibliography

Baroccini, F. *La "Roma dei romani,"* Rome, 1971.

Corrias Corona, M. *Stato e Chiesa nella valutazione dei politici sardi (1848–1853)*, Milan, 1972.

D'Amelio, G. *Stato e Chiesa. La legislazione ecclesiastica fino al 1867*, Milan, 1963.

Demarco, D. *Una rivoluzione sociale. La repubblica romana nel 1849*, Naples, 1944, 1992; *Pio IX e la rivoluzione romana del 1848. Saggio di storia economico-sociale*, Naples, 1947, 1992; *Il tramonto dello Stato pontificio. Il papato di Gregorio XVI*, Naples, 1949, 1992.

La formazione dello Stato unitario, Milan, 1963.

Ghisalberti, C. *Unità nazionale e unificazione e unificazione giuridica in Italia*, Rome-Bari, 1979.

Jemolo, C. A. *L'Église et l'État en Italie du Risorgimento à nos jours*, Paris, 1960.

McIntire, C. T. *England Against the Papacy, 1858–1861*, New York, 1983.

Marongiu Bonaiuti, C. *Gerarchia e laicato in Italia nel secolo ottocento*, Padua, 1969.

Martina, G. *Pio IX (1846–1850)*, Rome, 1974.

Martina, G. *Pio IX (1851–1866)*, Rome, 1986.

Mollat, G. *La Question romaine de Pie VI à Pie XI*, Paris, 1932.

Mori, R. *La questione romana (1861–1865)*, Florence, 1963.

Passerin d'Entreves, E., and Repgen, K. *Il cattolicesimo politico e sociale in Italia e in Germania*, Bologna, 1977.

Passerin d'Entreves, E. "I precedenti della formula cavouriana 'libera Chiesa in libero Stato,'" *Religione e politica nell'ottocento europeo*, Turin, 1993, 207–23; "Ancora sulla formula cavouriana 'libera Chiesa in libero Stato,'" *Religione e politica nell'ottocento europeo*, 242–52; "L'eredità della tradizione cattolica risorgimentale," *Religione e politica nell'ottocento*, 210–331.

Pellegrino, B. *Chiesa e rivoluzione unitaria nel Mezzogiorno. L'episcopato meridionale dall'assolutismo borbonico allo Stato borghese (1860–1861)*, Rome, 1979.

Ragionieri, E. *"La questione romana," L'Italia giudicata 1861–1945*, 1, *Dall'Unificazione alla crisi di fine secolo 1861–1900*, Turin, 1976; 50–125.

Romeo, R. *Dal Piemonte sabaudo all'Italia liberale*, Turin, 1963.

Romeo, R. *Il giudizio storico sul Risorgimento*, Catana, 1987.

Rossi, M. G. *Le origini del partito cattolico*, Rome, 1977.

Scoppola, P. *Chiesa e Stato nella storia d'Italia. Storia documentaria dall'Unità alla Repubblica*, Rome-Bari, 1961.

Scoppola, P. *Dal neo-guelfismo alla D.C.*, Rome, 1963.

Scoppola, P. ed. *I discorsi di Cavour per Roma capitale*, Rome, 1971.

Scott, I. *The Rise of the Italian State. A Study of Italian Politics during the Period of Unification*, Meerut, 1980.

Soldani, S. "Risorgimento," F. Levi, U. Levra, N. Tranfaglia, *Il mondo contemporaneo. Storia d'Italia*, III, Florence, 1978, 1132–66.

Spadolini, G. *L'opposizione cattolica da Porta Pia al 1898*, Florence, 1974.

Spadolini, G. *Cattolicesimo e Risorgimento*, Florence, 1986.

Tamburini, F. "Il Non Expedit negli Atti della Penitenzieria Apostolica (1861–1889)," *Rivista di storia della Chiesa in Italia*, 1987, 128–51.

Traniello, F. *Cattolicesimo conciliatorista. Religione e cultura nella tradizione rosminiana lombardo-piemontese (1825–1870)*, Milan, 1970.

Traniello, F. "Questione romana," F. Levi, U. Levra, N. Tranfaglia, *Il mondo contemporaneo. Storia d'Italia*, III, Florence, 1978, 984–96.

Vaussard, M. *Jansénisme et Gallicanisme. Aux origines religieuse du Risorgimento*, Paris, 1959.

Verucci, G. *L'Italia laica prima e dopo l'Unità 1848–1876. Anticlericalismo, libero-pensiero e ateismo nella società italiana*, Rome-Bari, 1981.

UNIVERSITIES, CATHOLIC. Concern with the higher education of Christians is part of the Church's mission. From the beginning of church history, education has been important and has included the preparation of catechumens, preaching, commentaries on Holy Scripture, and treatises on theology. The catechetical schools of Alexandria and Antioch were renowned. The turn of the 12th to 13th centuries saw the birth of universities under the influence of two overriding factors, on the one hand the growth of liberal studies and learning and, on the other, the trend toward corporatism. Added to these were the encouragement given to ecclesiastical, theological, juridical, and philosophical studies after the Lateran Council of 1179; the thirst for culture of nobles and merchants; and the attraction for the Christian kingdoms of the cultural institutions of the Arabs, where academic titles were conferred.

The universities all arose as a natural extension of cathedral schools, and in some cases of monastic schools. They were therefore initially designed for the training of clergy. But the interest of an ever-growing sector of the laity changed the cathedral school into a *studium generale* that was also open to laymen.

Up to the 14th century, universities were under Church law and thus shared in the Church's unity and universality. Fourteen universities were created in the 13th century. Among the oldest and most important were the two prototypes of Paris and Bologna.

In the 12th century youths flocked to Paris to hear the masters (William of Champeaux; Abelard) of the school of the cathedral of Notre-Dame or of the monasteries of Ste.-Geneviève and St.-Victor. The university was in fact constituted when the increasingly important professorial body decided to organize in order to assert its rights, especially as regards the bishop's delegate (the *cancellarius*), who alone granted the right to teach (the *licentia docendi*). The Studium of Paris was officially recognized in 1229 as a *universitas magistrorum et scholarium Parisium commorantium*. It became a university of pontifical right in 1231 (bull *Parens Scientiarum*). Its common "trunk" was the faculty of arts, through which all students of the other faculties—those of theology, law, and medicine, and eventually philosophy—had to pass. The University of Paris was famous above all for its faculty of theology, with such outstanding teachers as St. Thomas Aquinas and St. Bonaventure.

The University of Bologna emerged not out of a corporation of teachers but one of students. Alongside the cathedral schools and the monastic schools Bologna had long had prestigious municipal ones, essentially schools of civil law; this accounted for the great solidarity of the student body. On the other hand, most students came to Bologna to study civil or canon law, or both; their average age was well over thirty, which also explains how they were able to organize the nucleus of the budding university.

In Bologna, the theologian Gratian oriented his teaching toward the law, whereas in Paris Peter Lombard did not deem it necessary to depart from theology to give his opinion on the law governing the Church. Each one influenced the other. But it is interesting to note that at the time of the great debate on the efficient cause of marriage the Paris theologians won the day; Peter Lombard established the principle of consensualism as against the theory of sexual union defended by Gratian. It was the school of Bologna, however, which, thanks to its juridical expertise and to the revival of Roman law there, would give this principle its legal form, something the theologians of Paris were not able to do.

The University of Naples was founded (1224) by Frederick II, that of Salamanca (1243) by Ferdinand III the Holy. The University of Toulouse dates from 1229, and received the *ius ubique docendi* from Gregory IX in 1233. Oxford also acquired its university in the 13th century, as did Montpellier, Angers, and Coimbra. The University of Perugia goes back to 1308, that of Prague to 1348, and that of Heidelberg to 1385.

A second period of progress of the ecclesiastical faculties came about with the revival of theological and philosophical studies in the humanist period and under the Tridentine reform. Famous from that time on were the universities of Salamanca, Alcalá (founded in 1505), Valladolid (1346), Coimbra, and Louvain (1425). After the Lutheran schism, some German universities remained Catholic: Cologne, Mainz, Trier, Freiburg im Breisgau, Dillingen, and Ingolstadt.

In the Americas, the University of St. Thomas Aquinas was founded in Santo Domingo in 1538; that of Mexico in 1551, and, in the same year, that of San Marco in Lima. The first colleges in North America appeared in the 17th century (Harvard 1636; William & Mary 1693), with more founded in the early 18th century (Yale 1701; Princeton 1746), but they did not become universities until after American independence.

The century of the Enlightenment brought about the suppression of the ecclesiastical faculties in certain civil universities. From the 15th century a parallel process of secularization had been taking place with the rise of nation-states. The universities split away from ecclesiastical authority to become dependent on the civil authority in each country and acquired a national identity. The French Revolution and Napoleon instituted a system of education that was entirely dependent on the state, a model which, under the influence of the Enlightenment, would spread to Europe and America. It entailed the abolition of faculties of theology and canon law in many countries, relegating those disciplines to seminaries and centers for training priests. These faculties did survive, however, in Germany, Great Britain, and the Scandinavian countries.

The Church reacted by creating centers of higher learning and by guaranteeing the independence of those centers not taken over by the state. This is the origin of the Catholic universities, that is, centers of higher learning founded and directed by ecclesiastical authority to teach highly diverse branches of knowledge: law, medicine, philosophy, etc. For France, this was the period of the creation of the Catholic University of the West in Angers (1877) and the Catholic Institutes of Paris (1876), Lille (1876), Lyon (1876), and Toulouse (1879), and, in Belgium, the Catholic University of Louvain (1883).

LEO XIII (encyclical *Aeterni Patris*, 4 August 1879) encouraged the study of theology and philosophy, emphasizing the enduring pertinence of the philosophy of St. Thomas Aquinas. PIUS XI organized ecclesiastical faculties (apostolic constitution *Deus Scientiarum Dominus*, 24 May 1931), making them subordinate to the Congregation of Seminaries and Universities. All existing establishments had to submit to it their statutes, programs, etc. to be able to continue to confer academic degrees. The faculties of theology and canon law of the state universities had the same obligation.

The Code of Canon Law (1917) established the right of the Church to organize its own universities for the teaching of religious studies, and its own universities for teaching the secular sciences where the public universities were not imbued with a Catholic spirit (c. 1379, paragraph 2). The creation of Catholic universities and faculties was reserved to the Apostolic See, which gave them their statutes (c. 1376). PIUS XII created the International Federation of Catholic Universities (apostolic letter *Catholicas Studiorum Universitates*, 1950).

VATICAN II dealt with higher ecclesiastical education in the decree on the training of priests *Optatam totius*, no. 18, and the declaration on the education of Christian youth *Gravissimum Educationis*, no. 10. Under PAUL VI, the Congregation of Seminaries and Universities was renamed the Congregation for Catholic Education (apostolic constitution *Regimini Ecclesiae universae*, 15 August 1967), which in 1968 made changes in the studies and training offered by the ecclesiastical universities (*Normae quaedam*, 20 May 1968). During the pontificate of JOHN PAUL II, this became the Congregation of Seminaries and Teaching Institutions (apostolic constitution *Pastor bonus*, 28 June 1988), even though it was authorized to continue to use its old name. It was entitled to set up or approve universities and ecclesiastical institutes, to ratify and ensure their management, and, in the case of the Catholic universities, to resolve questions under the competence of the Holy See.

The apostolic constitution *Sapientia Christiana* (15 April 1979), prepared by Paul VI and promulgated by John Paul II, and the norms of application of the Congregation for Catholic Education (29 April 1979) appeared to consider the ecclesiastical universities a species within the genre of the Catholic universities. The 1983 CODE OF CANON LAW, however, treats the Catholic universities and the other higher institutes of study (c. 807–14), on the one hand, and the ecclesiastical universities and faculties (c. 815–21), on the other, separately.

First of all, the Code reaffirms the Church's right to establish and manage universities "which contribute to a higher human culture, to a fuller advancement of the human person, and also to the fulfillment of the Church's teaching office" (c. 807). These establishments would be able to call themselves Catholic universities only with the consent of the competent ecclesiastical authority. But, by contrast, there may be truly Catholic universities that are not so called and therefore are not formally Catholic, but are centers of higher education established according to civil law (c. 808).

The bishops' conferences were given the role of supervising the universities, or at least faculties, suitably distributed in their territories, where the various disciplines would be taught, while respecting their legimate scientific autonomy (c. 809), and with respect of the principles of Catholic doctrine (c. 810, paragraph 2). Catholic universities must include at least one faculty, institute, or chair of theology, independent of the courses in theology on those questions connected with other disciplines (c. 811).

Having solved the problem of the ecclesiastical universities and faculties (including the ecclesiastical faculties that were part of a Catholic university) with the constitution *Sapientia Christiana*, John Paul II gave a charter to Catholic universities and Catholic institutes of higher learning with the apostolic constitution *Ex Corde Ecclesiae* of 15 August 1990. Its aim was to ensure a Christian presence in the university milieu; to qualify for the title a Catholic university must be distinguished by a Christian spirit on the part of the individuals and the university community as such; a reflection of the light of faith on the knowledge acquired, which it helps to enrich; faithfulness to the Church's message; and an institutional commitment to the service of the people of God and the human family.

The creation of a Catholic university may be effectuated by the Apostolic See, a bishops' conference, another assembly of the Catholic hierarchy, or a diocesan bishop; by a religious institute or other public juridical person with the diocesan bishop's agreement; or by other ecclesiastical or lay persons with the agreement of the competent ecclesiastical authority. Every Catholic university must be in communion with the universal Church and the Holy See, and with the local church and the diocesan bishops of the region where it is situated.

In 1992, worldwide, the Church had under its jurisdiction 191 Catholic universities, 526 university institutes, 218 institutes of higher education, and 139 ecclesiastical universities and faculties (of which 103 were independent of the Catholic universities). The geographical distribution was as follows: 345 in Asia, 253 in North America, 149 in Europe, 132 in South America, 34 in Central America, 10 in Oceania, 6 in the Middle East, and 5 in Africa.

Rome deserves a special mention. The University of the Roman Curia was founded in 1244, and that of La Sapienza in 1303, by BONIFACE VIII. In the 16th century the Roman Seminary was also set up, and later the Angelicum and the College of the Propaganda Fide. Today there are sixteen Roman Atheneums:

1) The Pontifical Gregorian University, founded by St. Ignatius Loyola in 1553, through a concession granted the year before by Julius III. It is named after GREGORY XIII, who endowed it with donations and buildings. Pius XI, by motu proprio *Quod maxime* (30 September 1928), added to it the Pontifical Biblical Institute founded by St. Pius X (7 May 1909) and the Pontifical Oriental Institute founded by BENEDICT XV (15 September 1917). A faculty of Eastern canon law was inaugurated in 1971.

2) The Pontifical University of the Lateran, which dates back to 1773, when Clement XIV entrusted the faculty of theology and philosophy of the College of Rome to the Roman clergy. It was given its current title by John XXIII (motu proprio *Cum inde*, 17 May 1959), with the incorporation of the Pontificium Institutum Utriusque Iuris (1937) and the Pontifical Pastoral Institute (Pius XII, apostolic constitution *Ad uberrima*, 3 June 1958). Next to it, John Paul II founded the Pontifical Institute for the Study of Marriage and the Family (apostolic constitution *Magnum Matrimonii Sacramentum*, 7 October 1982). A section of the university was established in Washington, D.C. (Congregation for Catholic Education, decree of 22 August 1988).

3) The Pontifical Urbanian University, founded by Urban VIII (bull *Immortalis Dei Filius*, 1 August 1627). Associated with it are the Pontifical Scientific Missionary Institute (Congregation of Seminaries and Universities, decree of 1 September 1933) and numerous other institutes throughout the world. Since 1949 it has included a section for language study, particularly Oriental, and more recently a modern language section; since 1960 the Higher Institute for the Study of Atheism; since 1975 the Center of Chinese Studies and the "Cardinal Newman" Study Center. It also incorporates the Institute for Missionary Catechesis (Congregation for Catholic Education, decree *Cum Cathechesis*, 25 May 1980). Adjoining it is the International Center of Missionary Animation (CIAM). Many other institutes are linked to it throughout the world.

4) The Pontifical University of St. Thomas Aquinas, created by Gregory XIII in the 1580s under the name College of St. Thomas. The Angelicum was given its present name by JOHN XXIII (motu proprio *Dominicanus Ordo*, 7 March 1963). The Institute of Social Sciences was founded in 1955, becoming a faculty with the approval of new university statutes (Congregation for Catholic Education, 25 November 1974). In 1972 the "Mater Ecclesiae" Higher Institute of Religious Sciences was created.

5) The Salesian Pontifical University was created by the Congregation of Seminaries and Universities (de-

cree of 3 May 1940). PAUL VI granted it its university title (motu proprio *Magisterium Vitae*, 24 May 1973). The Congregation for Catholic Education inaugurated the Higher Institute of Pedagogy (decree, 2 July 1956), which became the Faculty of Education Sciences; it also incorporated within the university the Faculty of Christian and Classical Letters (letter, 4 June 1971), created the Higher Institute of Religious Sciences "Magisterium Vitae" (decree, 29 June 1986) and approved the creation of the Institute of Social Communication Sciences (17 December 1988).

6) The Pontifical Atheneum of St. Anselm was founded by INNOCENT XI in 1687. After various vicissitudes it was restored to the order of St. Benedict by LEO XIII. It became pontifical by decree of the Congregation of Seminaries and Universities (15 January 1933). Since 1952 it has included the Institute of Monastic Studies, and since 1961, the Pontifical Institute of Liturgy, becoming a faculty in 1978.

7) The Pontifical Atheneum Antonianum was created 17 May 1933 by the Congregation of Seminaries and Universities, which gave it its pontifical title 14 June 1938. With the approval of the new statutes (28 February 1989), the Studium Biblicum Franciscanum of Jerusalem was set up as a section of the faculty of theology. The atheneum also includes a Higher School of Medieval and Franciscan Studies and the "Redemptor Hominis" Higher Institute of Religious Sciences (Congregation for Catholic Education, decree, 31 July 1986).

8) The Roman Atheneum of the Holy Cross, originally established as the Roman Academic Center of the Holy Cross (Congregation for Catholic Education, decree *Dei Servus*, 9 January 1985), became an atheneum by decree of the same congregation 9 January 1990. A Higher Institute of Religious Sciences is part of the faculty of theology.

9) The Higher Pontifical Institute of Latin was established by Paul VI (motu proprio *Studia Latinitatis*, 22 February 1964) at the Pontifical Salesian University, into which it was incorporated 4 June 1971.

10) The Pontifical Institute of Sacred Music, founded by St. PIUS X in 1911, is included among the pontifical universities and faculties, having received its present denomination 24 May 1931 (apostolic constitution *Deus Scientiarum Dominus*).

11) The Pontifical Institute of Christian Archaeology was created by PIUS XI (motu proprio *I primitivi Cemeteri*, 11 December 1925).

12) The Pontifical Theological Faculty "St. Bonaventure" is derived from the *studi generali* of the 13th-century Order of Conventual Friars Minor and more particularly the Pontifical College of St. Bonaventure founded by SIXTUS V (bull *Ineffabilis divinae Providentiae*, 18 December 1587). Its title was conferred on it by a decree of 3 January 1955. The Congregation for Catholic Education approved its new statutes 19 December 1986.

13) The Pontifical Theological Faculty and the Pontifical Institute of Spirituality "Teresianum" were created 16 July 1935 and 8 September 1964 respectively. The faculty became pontifical 23 May 1963. It comprises the Pontifical Institute of Spirituality (8 September 1964) and the Institute of Medical Pastoral Theology "Camilianum" (Congregation for Catholic Education, decree, 28 April 1987).

14) The Pontifical Theological Faculty "Marianum." In 1398, BONIFACE IX empowered the Order of Servites to give academic degrees in theology. The Enrico Gandavense College was created in 1666. Abolished after the loss of papal temporal power, it was revived in 1895 under the name Sant'Alessio Falconieri. The faculty was given its pontifical title by the Congregation for Catholic Education (decree *Theologicas Collegii S. Alexii Falconeri Scholas*, 1 January 1971).

15) The Pontifical Institute of Arabic and Islamic Studies, created in 1926 near Tunis. In 1960 it was given the name Pontifical Institute of Oriental Studies. Its present name came from the apostolic constitution *Sapientia Christiana* (15 April 1979).

16) The Pontifical Faculty of Education Sciences "Auxilium," established at the Institute of Daughters of Mary the Helper (Congregation for Catholic Education, decree of 27 June 1970), has links with the Pontifical Salesian University of Rome. The Congregation for Catholic Education created the Higher Institute of Religious Studies "Auxilium" (decree, 25 July 1986).

Civil universities that include faculties of theology include the following: in Germany: Breslau (1581), Freiburg im Breisgau (1581), Munich (1459), Münster (1780), Tübingen (1476), and Würtzburg (1459); in Switzerland: Freiburg (1890); in Austria: Graz (1586), Innsbruck (1857), Salzburg (1623), and Vienna (1384); in France: Strasbourg (1621); in Canada: Montreal (1927) and Quebec (1853); in Peru: the University of San Marco of Lima.

Among the centers devoted exclusively to ecclesiastical studies—aside from the earliest, St. Mary's Faculty of Theology of Baltimore (1822)—are Washington (1887); Milan (1850) and Naples (1918); Paderborn and Trier; Kandy (1926) in Sri Lanka and Poona in India; Sydney; Heythrop in the United Kingdom.

Some of the Catholic universities that include a faculty of theology are the following: Louvain, Belgium (1425); the University of Comillas in Madrid (1904), St. Thomas University in Manila (1619), the Pontifical University of Salamanca, Pontifical Javeriana University in Bogotá, and the Catholic Universities of Buenos Aires, Kinshasa, Santiago de Chile (1888), Ottawa (1889), Lublin (1918).

Dominique Le Tourneau

Bibliography

Aigrain, R. *Les Universités catholiques*, Paris, 1935.

Annuario Pontificio per l'anno 1991, 1748–55.

The Application of Ex corde Ecclesiae for the United States, Washington, D.C., 2000.

Bride, A. "Universités," DTC, XV, 2230–68.

Calogero, G. "Università," *Enciclopedia Italiana*, 722–9.

Cecchetti, I., and Paschini, P. "Università," EC, XII, 1953, 857–64.

D'Irsay, S. *Histoire des universités françaises et étrangères des origines à nos jours*, Paris, 1933–5.

García y García, A., ed. *Collective, La Universidad Pontificia de Salamanca. Sus raíces. Su pasado. Su futureo*, Salamanca, 1989.

Gemelli, A., and Schrijnen, J., *Annuaire Général des Universités catholiques*, Nijmegen-Utrecht, 1927.

Haab, R. *Die geistige Haltung der katholisches Univ.*, Fribourg, 1952.

Haskins, C. H. *The Rise of Universities*, New York, 1957.

Hervada, J. "Sobre el estatuto de las Universidades católicas y eclesiásticas," *Raccolta di scritti in onore di Pio Fedele*, Perugia, 1984, 491–511.

John Paul II, apostolic constitution *Sapientia Christiana*, 15 April 1979; apostolic constitution *Ex Corde Ecclesiae*, 15 August 1990.

Langan, J. P., ed. *Catholic Universities in the Church and State: A Dialogue on Ex Corde Ecclesiale*, Washington, D.C., 1993.

La Magna Charta delle Università Europee, Bologna, 1988.

Manzanares, J. "Las Universidades y Facultades Eclesiásticas en la nueva Codificación canónica," *Seminarium*, 35 (1983), 572–90.

Pieronek, T. "Lo 'status' degli atenei pontifici in Polonia," in *Ius Ecclesiae* II (1990), 497–521.

Pius XI, apostolic constitution *Deus Scientiarum Dominus*, 24 May 1931.

La Universidad Católica hoy en Latinoamérica, Bogotá, 1985.

L'Université catholique dans le monde moderne, Rome, 1972.

Urrutia, F. J. "Ecclestical Universities and Faculties (Canons 815–21)," *Studia Canonica* 23, 459–69.

Valdrini, P. "Les universités catholiques: exercice d'un droit et contrôle de son exercice (canons 807–14)," *Studia Canonica* 23 (1989), 445–58.

UNIVERSITIES, MEDIEVAL. From the 6th century, with the disappearance of the ancient types of schools, education in the West became practically the monopoly of the Church. Schools scarcely existed except within monasteries and cathedrals. Most of the teachers were clerics, and their pupils themselves were almost all destined for a career in the Church. However, it was not until the 12th century that the papacy began to take a serious interest in the problems of the schools. This new attitude can be explained by the desire of the so-called Gregorian popes to have at their disposal a secular clergy that was more worthy of its calling, better educated and better prepared intellectually for its tasks (defending the rights of the churches against lay encroachments, preaching to the faithful, and refuting heresies). From the 1130s, moreover, even the Curia and the Sacred College included a growing number of clergy, theologians, and jurists who were trained in the best schools in Christendom, in Paris or Bologna. With them there grew the idea of a close collaboration between the papacy and these centers of scholarly excellence.

Throughout the 12th century, the popes took various steps that confirmed their respect for university teachers (thus, in 1159 ALEXANDER II personally informed the learned doctors of Bologna of his forthcoming visit) and their solicitude for students (ceiling on rents in Bologna from 1176; dispensation of residents to collect taxes on ecclesiastical benefices in Paris from 1178). Particularly important was canon 18 of Lateran III (1179). This prescribed that every cathedral should maintain a school where pupils would be admitted free of charge. In addition, at the end of their studies, those students who wished to start a school in the diocese should receive, from the cathedral scholasticus or the chancellor of the cathedral school, also free of charge, the "license to teach." But at the same time as they encouraged the rise of cathedral schools, too often neglected by apathetic prelates, the popes strove to keep them firmly within the ecclesial institution, opposing all the secularizing trends that could sometimes appear in those schools. From 1130 to 1139 (canon 5 of the Council of Clermont, canon 9 of Lateran II), monks and regular canons were forbidden to study the lucrative secular disciplines of civil law and medicine. CELESTINE III (1191–8) would issue a reminder that all the Paris students were clerics, under ecclesiastical justice.

The great popes of the first half of the 13th century—Innocent III, himself a former student of the schools of Paris (1198–1216); HONORIUS III (1216–27); GREGORY IX (1227–41); and INNOCENT IV, a renowned canonist (1243–54)—would continue the policies of their predecessors. Like them, they were eager to develop clerical education the better to meet the new needs of the Church (reinforcement of urban pastoral care; the fight against heresy). Also like them, they themselves were men of high culture, surrounded by cardinals and curialists most of whom were schoolmen. But the problem took on another dimension with, on the one hand, the triumph of the Church's monarchical centralization (from INNOCENT III to BONIFACE VIII) and the extreme exaltation of the pontifical *plenitudo potestatis*, and, on the other, the appearance in the scholastic world of the universities.

Although it is not possible to give a precise date for each one's founding, between 1200 and 1220 the first universities (Bologna, Paris, Oxford, Cambridge, the university of medicine at Montpellier) made their appearance. Undeniably, the creation of these first universities can be explained first of all by the changes in the schools themselves. These changes—a growing social demand for men of superior education, the considerable enriching of the actual bases of knowledge (through translation from the Arabic and Greek and the rediscovery of Aristotle) together with a keener self-awareness on the part of teachers and students—all combined to bring about the creation of those autonomous corporations that were the first universities. They took charge of their own recruitment, organized by themselves mutual help among their members as well as internal discipline, and decided freely on programs and teaching methods along with procedures of examination and the conferring of degrees, matters formerly determined by the chancellor and scholasticus of the cathedrals. Nevertheless, this desire for emancipation would not have won the day had it not found support on the outside. In spite of what has been written, local authorities, both ecclesiastical and lay, were not uniformly hostile. The princes were generally accommodating. But certain it is that the decisive move came from the papacy.

Very early on, the popes of the 13th century grasped that, compared with the traditional scholarly institutions—those of the cathedral schools within the framework of the diocese—the universities represented something fresh and important from which the Church and, first and foremost, the papacy could reap advantage. It must be said that teachers and students were often the first to turn to the papacy to solicit its help against local resistance and obtain its guarantee of their autonomy. The popes, for their part, willingly acceded to these demands, which allowed them to extend their authority still further throughout Christendom.

The first years of the 13th century thus saw the popes receiving delegations from the universities and responding favorably to their requests. Either directly or through their legates, they decided conflicts that had arisen even within the young universities, or between them and external authorities. They guaranteed the personal status of the scholars and granted the first statutes and privileges (in 1214 to Oxford, 1215 to Paris, 1217-20 to Bologna, 1220 to Montpellier). In so doing, the popes solemnly recognized the existence and autonomy of these communities of masters and students, placed them under their direct protection, and in a certain way made them pontifical institutions, at the heart of the ecclesial system, whose eminent role justified the exceptional situation.

Over the next years of the century, papal beneficence with regard to the universities did not flag. In 1231, after a particularly brutal struggle with the royal government and the bishop, Gregory IX sent the University of Paris the bull *Parens scientiarum*, which confirmed and extended all the liberties and franchises previously granted,

and proclaimed, with exceptional solemnity, the pontifical attachment to the institution of the university. This text would serve as a reference for a number of future foundations. In 1245, Innocent IV granted the same benefits to the university recently founded in Toulouse after the crusade against the Albigensians. Throughout the 13th century, in Bologna, Oxford, Cambridge, and Montpellier, one papal intervention after another took place, helping to confirm the privileges and strengthen the autonomy of the university.

The 13th century also saw the establishment of more new universities. If few of these can be attributed to the papacy alone (besides Toulouse, there was only the short-lived university of Piacenza, in 1248, and that of the pontifical court itself, or *Studium Curiae*, created in 1240–5), it should nevertheless be noted that almost all the founders of universities—cities or princes—took pains, even if belatedly, to request from the pope solemn confirmation of their foundation. One example was in the Iberian peninsula, where the popes confirmed the royal foundations of Salamanca (foundation ca. 1218; pontifical confirmation 1290), Coimbra (1228; 1290) and Valladolid (before 1300; 1346). In France, on the other hand, the doctors themselves asked the popes to set up as universities the schools of law of Montpellier (1289) and Orléans (1306).

Concurrently with the bulls of foundation or confirmation, canon law worked out a juridical definition of the university that was expressed in the concept of *studium generale*. A *studium generale* was an establishment of higher education founded by the pope (we may disregard here the very modest competition of the *studia generalia* founded by the emperors), whose members enjoyed privileges that were also guaranteed by the pope and whose degrees (bachelor's, master's, and doctorate) were, by virtue of this papal guarantee, recognized throughout Christendom.

We can deduce two things from the success of the concept of *studium generale*, certainly in evidence by the second half of the 13th century. First, that the idea had now taken root that papal confirmation was indispensable for the schools to have university status. Schools that lacked that confirmation were unfit to confer the recognized degrees and would have only local influence and little social and intellectual prestige.

Second, we can deduce that the medieval universities were "universal" and "Christian" institutions. In theory at least, they were not tied to a particular city or region. This was reflected in their recruitment—they could take in students of any geographical origin—and their teaching, which was based everywhere on the use of Latin and on the same authorities. The universities spread abroad a learning that combined the legacy of the ancients with Christian revelation and was thus a universal learning, the expression of one culture and civilization. Thus, like the papacy itself, they exercised their influence throughout Christendom. In practice, obviously, this universal outlook could be seen most clearly in the most prestigious and oldest centers of learning (Paris, Bologna).

For the papacy, at any rate, this universality justified both the university's autonomy, which freed it from local constraints, and limitations on that autonomy. These very soon became apparent. Since the university teaching "spread in all parts like a flood, irrigating and making fertile the universal Church," as Honorius II said in 1219 apropos of Paris, it was important for the papacy to control the orthodoxy of that doctrine and the loyalty of the men who imparted it or were trained in it. Addressing the schools of Bologna in 1210 with the official text of the canonical collection he had just published (*Compilatio tertia*), Innocent III began a practice that was followed by his successors and is a good indication that the pope thought of the universities as aides and relays of the Roman magisterium. It was therefore essential to ensure that none of the ferments of error or even "profane" doctrines invade the universities. In 1219 Honorius III prohibited the teaching of civil law in Paris. In 1219 and 1220, when the same pope raised the largely secular schools of Bologna and Montpellier to the status of universities, he submitted them to the control of local ecclesiastical authorities. It will also be noted in this connection that the pontifical policy was not so much to systematically deprive these authorities of all right of control over the universities as to in some way allow them to exercise this right from then on in the name of the pope.

This control over what was taught was not synonymous with obscurantism. On the contrary, the popes of the 13th century were able, with an exceptionally broad outlook, to take a risk on modern thinking and allow highly innovative doctrines (for example, Thomism) to develop in the universities, because they judged them pastorally effective and favorable to Roman primacy. But at the same time they did not hesitate to hound and condemn all writers of suspect philosophical or theological teaching, especially in Paris and Oxford.

To help the universities achieve their special goals, the popes began in the 1220s to send them the papacy's most zealous helpers—members of the new mendicant orders, Dominicans and Franciscans, in whose training and spirituality learning had an essential place. This policy is evidence of the high regard the popes had for university teaching. But it soon aroused the discontent of secular teachers faced with colleagues who were brilliant but who clearly put loyalty to their orders and the service of the pope before respect of university privileges. This discontent would often degenerate into violent conflicts, both in Paris (particularly from 1250 to 1260) and Oxford (in the early 14th century). But the papacy remained intransigent and the laymen had to give in. Neither the intellectual brilliance of the universities

nor even the way they functioned day by day really suffered, but they did get a taste of the limits the popes would set to the *libertas scolastica* they had granted.

On the 14th and 15th centuries there is not so much to say. The juridical framework fixed in the 13th century had hardly evolved. Of the numerous universities founded in this period (around sixty from 1300 to 1500), practically all received a pontifical bull of foundation or confirmation. The popes, especially the Avignon popes, continued to have a highly benevolent attitude toward the universities and the schoolmen, with the same determination to encourage studies and promote a well-educated clergy. They set up colleges for poor students in Toulouse and Montpellier and distributed ecclesiastical benefices by the thousands to nonresidential students by way of scholarships. From 1360, in Toulouse, Bologna, Padua, and other places, they established new faculties of theology to encourage the spread of a discipline in which Paris and Oxford had hitherto had a monopoly.

But in spite of all this the universities gradually eluded pontifical control. More and more students, trained in civil law or medicine, embarked on secular careers. The princes and cities, veritable founders and protectors of the new universities, while officially respecting their nature as ecclesiastical institutions, imposed an increasingly strict supervision on them in their turn, controlling the exercise of their traditional privileges and even meddling in the recruitment of students and the appointment of professors.

This is obviously but one aspect of the decline, by the end of the Middle Ages, of Christian universality when confronted with the rise of modern states along with their national churches. The crisis of the Great Schism (1378–1417) is exemplary here, marking as it does a turning point in the history of relations between the papacy and the universities, as in many other domains. Despite the favors the Avignon popes heaped upon them, a large number of university men, especially in Paris, sided with the council. No doubt they hoped to play a role in it that would be commensurate with the intellectual authority the papacy itself had formerly acknowledged they possessed. In fact their influence was limited. And, caught themselves in the manifold rifts splitting the Church, incapable of escaping the new political and national groupings, the university men thus helped burst apart the old unity of medieval Christianity, of which in the past they had, under the inspiration of the great Gregorian popes, been one of the most fruitful manifestations.

Jacques Verger

Bibliography

Bellone, E. *La cultura e l'organizzazione degli studi nei decreti dei concili e sinodi celebrati tra il "con-*

cordato" di Worms (1122) ed il concilio di Pisa (1409), Turin, 1975.

Bernstein, A. "Magisterium and License: corporate autonomy against papal authority in the medieval university of Paris," *Viator*, 9 (1978), 291–307.

Classen, P. "Rom und Paris: Kurie und Universität im 12. und 13. Jahrhundert," *Studium und Gesellschaft im Mittelalter*, ed. J. Fried, Stuttgart, 1983, 127–69.

Cobban, A. B. *The Medieval Universities: Their Development and Organization*, London, 1975.

Courtenay, W. J., ed. *Universities and Schooling in Medieval Society*, Leiden and Boston, 2000.

De Ridder-Symoens, H., ed. *A History of the University in Europe, I, Universities in the Middle Ages*, Cambridge, Eng., 1991.

De Ridder-Symoens, H., ed. *Universities in the Middle Ages*, 2 vols., Cambridge, Eng., 1992–95.

Delaruelle, E. "La politique universitaire des papes d'Avignon—spécialement d'Urbain V—et la fondation du collège espagnol de Bologne," *El cardenal Albornoz y el Colegio de España*, II (*Studia Albornotiana*, XII), Bologna, 1972, 8–39.

Knoll, P. W. "The Papacy at Avignon and University Foundations," "The Church in a Changing Society. Conflict, Reconciliation or Adjustment?" Uppsala, 1978, 191–6.

Maleczek, W. "Das Papsttum und die Anflänge der Universität im Mittelalter," *Römische historische Mitteilungen*, 27 (1985), 85–143.

Miethke, J. "Die Kirche und die Universitäten im 13. Jahrhundert," *Schulen und Studium im sozialen Wandel des hohen und späten Mittelalters*, ed. J. Fried (*Vorträge und Forschungen XXX*), Sigmaringen, 1986, 285–320.

Rashdall, H. *The Universities of Europe in the Middle Ages*, 3 vols., London, 1936.

Swanson, R. N. *Universities, Academics and the Great Schism*, Cambridge, 1979.

van Engen, J., ed. *Learning Institutionalized: Teaching in the Medieval University*, Notre Dame, Ind., 2000.

Verger, J. *Les Universités du Moyen Age*, Paris, 1973.

URBAN I. *(Pope 222–30). Most likely buried in the cemetery of Callistus (Rome).*

The pontificate of the sixteenth successor of Peter remains very obscure, as he is barely mentioned in surviving sources. He is said to have been born in Rome to a father named Pontianus. Eusebius of Caesarea credits him with an episcopate of eight years, the *Liberian Catalogue* one of eight years, eleven months, and twelve days, giving dates that do not correspond to the length of time cited. The decision to replace patens of glass with patens of silver in certain liturgical ceremonies is attributed to him. However, this does not appear accurate since the *Liber pontificalis*, which quotes it, also describes Urban as a confessor of the faith in Diocletian's time (284–305). In fact, Urban I was pope during a period of peace when the emperor Alexander Severus was tolerant in matters of religion, the Adoptionists and Montanists were behaving less aggressively, and the schism of HIPPOLYTUS was continuing but not growing. It was a period of calm in the Church of Rome, which is the reason we have little information. The story of Urban's martyrdom is certainly apocryphal. He almost certainly was buried in the cemetery of Callistus, where a stone found in the crypt bore his name in Greek capitals and his office: "OYPBANOC E (miskomos)." His feast is 25 May.

Jean-Paul Martin

Bibliography

Amann, E. *DTC*, Paris, 1950, XV, 2, 2267–68.
Eusebius, *HE*, VI, 2, 2; 23, 3.
Weltin, E. G. *NCE*, New York, 1967, XIV, 477.

URBAN II. *Eudes of Châtillon or Lagery (ca. 1035–Rome, 29 July 1099). Elected pope and consecrated at Terracina 12 March 1088. Buried in St. Peter's, Rome. Feast day 29 July.*

Born around 1035 into a noble family of Châtillon-sur-Marne, he received his clerical training in Reims at the school of Bruno the Carthusian, where he was first canon and then archdeacon. Between 1067 and 1070 he was a monk in Cluny, of which he was grand prior (around 1074–9) under Hugh's abbacy. When Gregory VII summoned Cluniac monks, Eudes was transferred (ca. 1080) to Rome, where the pope named him cardinal-bishop of Ostia. In 1084–5, Gregory VII entrusted his faithful follower with a legation to Germany. On 20 April 1085 in the Saxon town of Quedlinburg, in the presence of Herman von Salm, the German anti-king who had the support of the papacy, Eudes headed a synod that adopted rigorous decrees against the champions of the emperor Henry IV and the antipope Clement III (Guibert of Ravenna).

At the end of Gregory VII's pontificate, the crisis of the Gregorian reform burst into the open, and flared again after the brief reign (1086–7) of Victor III. After the See had remained vacant for at least six months, cardinal-bishop Eudes was elected pope, taking the name Urban II, and was consecrated 12 March 1088 in Terracina (near Gaeta).

Urban had been one of the staunchest supporters of Gregory VII. Now that he was pope he immediately adopted the program of Gregorian reform. But it was clear he did not share Gregory's rigor; as a skilled and, if need be, unscrupulous diplomat, he allowed for realism in politics. His personality was marked by the ideals of Cluny and by those of the Gregorian reformers as well as by the canons' spirit of reform. But it was also determined by his chivalric origins and the political thinking of his native country, France. An example is seen in his handling of the contemporary movement for peace, as seen in the episcopal peace councils and in the aptly named Truce of God (*treuga Dei*) (mandating protection of the unarmed population, clergy and monks, and beasts of burden, and cessation of hostilities during holy days and certain periods of the religious year). As pope, Urban II expressly confirmed the *treuga Dei* at the synods of Melfi in 1089, Troia in 1093, and especially Clermont (1095), where it was immediately associated with the crusades.

Urban II managed to soothe antagonisms, finally displaced the antipope Clement III, and led Gregorian reform to its triumphant conclusion by developing pontifical centralism as well as the Roman Curia and by favoring Benedictine monasticism in its commitment to reform, without neglecting the care of souls or the reform of chapters. The main pillars of his authority were the Norman sovereigns of southern Italy and Sicily and the nobility of France and Lorraine.

Two aspects of his pontificate stand out: the restoration of religious unity with Byzantium and the Greek Church (aided, from 1088 until the last phase of the crusade, by the emperor Alexis I); and the crusade, which was his own creation. The two are linked, proceeding as they do from the ecclesiology and theology of Urban's background. His actions were based on the idea of the fundamental unity of the Latin and Greek churches, then in the process of being restored. It was not the schism with Byzantium—which was never considered definitive—that disturbed this process, but conflicts caused by the reform of the Western Church, especially the pontifical schism in the INVESTITURE CONTROVERSY. The unity and restoration of Christianity on the outer frontiers became of concrete importance for Urban in the Christian Reconquest of lands lost to Islam's advance in the Mediterranean basin. Urban carried eastward this movement that had come out of the west (Spain; Sicily); this was the origin of his crusade.

During his first years, Urban II had to confront a highly complex situation. He found himself faced with an emperor (Henry IV) who was hampered in his sovereignty and an antipope (Clement III) who had prestige and was bent on reform. Clement, with his supporters, governed Rome. A majority of the cardinals was for him, together with a sizable part of Christendom. Urban could not stay long in certain parts of Rome, and spent most of the time in Norman territory. In Melfi (September 1089), he began talks with the Greeks. He renewed Gregory VII's legislation against NICHOLAISM, simony, and lay investiture, but he gave the legates in Germany, the bishops Altmann of Passau and Gebhard of Constance, relatively flexible guidelines. His conciliatory stance vis-à-vis bishops and priests who, to his way of thinking, had received legitimate ordination caused him to be criticized by intransigent Gregorians like Bonizo of Sutri, Deusdedit (ADEODATUS I), Bruno of Segni, and Bernold of St. Blaise, who at the time were seeking theological solutions to the problem of ordination. In fact, thanks to his particular modus operandi, the pope softened opposition as he gradually strengthened his position.

At first, it was impossible to defuse the German situation, Henry IV and the leading bishops having sided with Clement. Urban's reaction was to encourage the somewhat unlikely marriage (1089) of Matilda, countess of Tuscany, then no longer young, and the young Guelph (V), who was only seventeen and whose father, Duke Guelph IV of Bavaria, had been deposed by the emperor. The emperor's Italian campaign, which began in 1090, continued well into 1092, when reversals of fortune and political impotence turned the situation around. With papal support, the Lombard cities of Milan, Cremona, Lodi, and Piacenza banded together against Henry IV. In 1093 his oldest son, Conrad, king of Germany, was persuaded to defect. Conrad had himself crowned king of Italy in Milan; in April 1095, at Cremona, he took on the *officium stratoris* for Urban II and swore to protect the pope. In 1094 Henry's second wife, Eupraxia (Praxedes, the daughter of the grand-prince of Kiev), who was obviously ailing, went over to Henry's enemies and brought ignominious accusations against the emperor before Urban. Henry's misfortune was the pope's good fortune, for at the end of 1093 he was finally able to return to Rome. By bribery he was able to take possession of the Lateran in 1094 and the most important fortress of Rome, the Castel Sant'Angelo, four years later.

His political realism and diplomatic skill won Urban II success in a variety of countries. England presented severe problems. At the death of William I (1087), his sons divided his lands, Robert receiving Normandy, which favored Urban II, and William II England. William II at first maintained a neutral stance in the pontifical schism, controlled the English church in a most high-handed way, and soon (from 1089) came into open conflict with Anselm, archbishop of Canterbury. The cardinal-legate, Gautier of Albano, no doubt persuaded the king to recognize Urban II, but was forced to grant him significant concessions. Anselm had to leave England. The dispute was debated at the pontifical synods of Bari in 1098 and Rome in 1099, but, fearing that England would side with (antipope) Clement III, Urban refused to settle the matter.

Urban II acted with similar circumspection in the case of Philip I of France when that king in 1092 repudiated his wife Bertha and with the help of a complaisant bishop wed Bertrada, wife of Count Foulques of Anjou. Bishops who protested were intimidated; Yves of Chartres was even incarcerated. Archbishop Hugh of

Lyon, an uncompromising Gregorian, named papal legate to France in 1094, finally (synod of Autun, 1094) pronounced the king's excommunication, which Urban renewed at the Council of Clermont (1095).

At this time Urban significantly increased and asserted his authority, aiming to be more than a reformer at the heart of the Church. At the two brilliant councils of 1095, at Piacenza and Clermont, his authority was plain to see. The synod of Piacenza, in Lombardy (March 1095), pronounced invalid all ordinations performed by Guibert of Ravenna (Clement III) after his condemnation. Also invalid were ordinations carried out by his supporters, who were cited by name, and—with exceptions—those of bishops who had taken over the diocese of a bishop loyal to Urban. By contrast, ordinations performed by legitimate bishops, who had subsequently become schismatic, remained valid. Simoniac ordinations were invalid, unless the cleric ordained knew nothing of the simony involved. The eucharistic doctrine of Berengar of Tours was once again condemned. In answer to an appeal by the Byzantine emperor Alexis I, those fighting for Christendom were exhorted to defend the Christians of the East.

Urban II had already confirmed Gregory VII's interdiction (1075) of investiture at the synod of Melfi in 1089. He again took up the subject at the great council of Clermont (18–28 November 1095). This council renewed the interdiction but went further than Gregory by forbidding all bishops and clergy from rendering loyalty and homage to the king or any other lay person. Several French synods, such as those of Rouen in 1096, Poitiers in 1100, and Troyes in 1107, repeated this interdiction, as did Urban himself at the synod of Rome in 1099, although with certain modifications.

The conflict between the spiritual and the temporal power had been further aggravated by the question of investitures. At the synods of Melfi in 1089 and Troia in 1093, Urban had extended the Truce of God, which originated in France, to southern Italy. At Clermont the Truce became universal, and clergy, monks, and women, as well as the crusaders' persons and goods, were placed under its protection. In 1088 Urban had pursued a policy of rapprochement with Byzantium to restore the unity of the Church. This did not achieve its goal, however, and subsequently the schism was even deepened by the crusades. In Clermont, on 27 September 1095, the pope enthusiastically preached the first crusade and, without weighing the consequences, inaugurated the entire historical crusading movement. Now the pope appeared, on both the spiritual and the political level, at the head of Western Christianity; Henry IV found himself reduced to political helplessness in a corner of Italy, excommunicated like King Philip I of France. In the following months, Urban traveled in the south and west of France, zealously pursuing reform of the Church and the opening of the crusades. Philip I, eager to make peace with the Church, promised to separate from Bertrada and was (briefly) absolved from excommunication.

In 1098, Urban envisaged separating from Denmark the metropolis of Bremen-Hamburg (the ecclesiastical province of Lund was established for Denmark in 1104). In Melfi, in 1089, needing the Normans' aid, he had given Apulia in fief to Robert, son of Norman prince Robert Guiscard. Now, on 5 July 1098, he granted Count Roger I of Calabria and Sicily and his heirs a power of control similar to a legate's over the Church of Sicily. (This privilege would later be known as the *Monarchia Sicula*, a name that would survive until 1867.) In the Spanish kingdoms, he successfully supported the reconquest (*reconquista*) of lands occupied by the Moors, and extended his protection and sovereignty over Aragón, Navarre, and Catalonia (Barcelona), besides affirming pontifical authority in ecclesiastical reorganization. (In 1088, he had seen to the restoration of the archbishopric of Toledo, whose incumbent was named primate of Spain, and in 1089 to the restoration of that of Tarragona, with promises of indulgence for the crusade for the liberation of the Holy Places of Palestine.)

At Clermont, Urban had fixed the launching of the first crusade for 15 August 1096 and had entrusted direction of the enterprise to the bishop Ademar du Puy, whom he had appointed his legate. Military command fell to the powerful Count Raymond IV of Toulouse. On 25 July 1099, Jerusalem was captured after exhausting effort and at the price of atrocities. Victory over the Egyptian army at Ascalon (12 August 1099) temporarily ensured this first success. Urban had died in Rome 29 July 1099, before news of these events could reach him. The schism of Clement III persisted, and the problem of investitures had not yet been settled, but at the death of Urban II, the papacy and the Church of Rome had reaffirmed their authority, fortified by Gregorian principles.

Georg Schwaiger

Bibliography

LP, 293–5.

PL, 151, 9-582.

JL, I, 657–701.

Amann, E. "Urban II," *DTC*, 15–2 (1950), 2269–85.

Becker, A. *Papst Urban II.*, 2 vols., Stuttgart, 1964–88.

Blumenthal, U. R. *The Investiture Controversy*, Philadelphia, 1988.

Fuhrmann, H. *Papst Urban II. und der Stand der Regularkanoniker*, Munich, 1984.

Hehl, E. D., Seibert, H., Staab, F., ed. *Deus qui mutat tempora. Festschrift für Alfons Becker*, Sigmaringen, 1987: especially M. Larisse, "Urbain II et la Lorraine," 115–27; Ringel, I. H. "Ipse transfert regna et mutat tempora, Beobachtungen zur Herkunft von Dan. 2,21 bei Urban II.," 138–56; Fuhrmann, H. "Das Papsttum zwischen Frömmigkeit und Politik: Urban II.

(1088–1099) und die Frage der Selbstheililgung," 157–72.

Hüls, R. *Kardinäle, Klerus und Kirchen Roms 1049–1130*, Tübingen, 1977.

Morris, C. *The Papal Monarchy. The Western Church from 1050 to 1250*, Oxford, 1989, 109–53.

Robinson, I. S. "Bernold von Konstanz und der gregorianische Reformkreis um Bischof Gebhard III.," *Freiburger Diözesan-Archiv*, 109 (1989), 155–88.

Schwaiger, G. "Kirchenreform und Reformpapsttum (1046–1124)," *Münchener Theologische Zeitschrift*, 38 (1987), 31–51.

Sommerville, R. *The Councils of Urban II* (Annuarium Historiae Conciliorum, Suppl. I), Amsterdam, 1972.

Sommerville, R. "Mercy and justice in the early months of Urban II's pontificate," *Chiesa, diritto e ordinamento*, 1986, 432–46.

Sommerville, R. *Pope Urban II, the Collectio Britannica, and the Council of Melfi (1089)*, Oxford, Eng., 1996.

Sommerville, R. "Papal Excerpts in Arsenal MS 713B; Alexander II and Urban II,: *Proceedings of the Ninth International Congress of Medieval Canon Law*, ed. P. Landau et al., 1997, 138–54.

Sommerville, R. "Pope Urban II and the canons of St-Jean-des-Vignes at Soissons," in *From Byzantium to Iran*, ed. J. Mahé et al., Atlanta, 1997, 229–42.

URBAN III. *Umberto Crivelli (d. at Ferrara, 20 October 1187). Elected pope in Verona 25 November 1185, consecrated 1 December. Buried in Ferrara.*

Urban III was the scion of an important Milanese family, which was in avowed opposition to the emperor Frederick I (Barbarossa). A canon regular, he began his ecclesiastical career in France as archdeacon of the church of Bourges, where he sought refuge from the threat of the Hohenstaufen and was a member of the entourage of Thomas à Becket. He studied both canon and civil law and was active in teaching; Peter of Blois is attested as his *socius et discipulus*. Back in his own country, he became an archdeacon of the Milanese church. Next, having been named bishop of Vercelli, in early September 1182 he appeared as cardinal-priest of the title of St. Lawrence in Damaso. In 1183-4 he was appointed pontifical legate in Lombardy, before being appointed (at the beginning of January 1184) archbishop of Milan, while remaining a cardinal. Elected pope, he retained that archiepiscopal seat, having it administered by procurators, in defiance of Barbarossa's regalian right. But he could prevent neither the ever-closer rapprochement—reinforced by supplementary tribute—between Milan and the emperor, nor the decline of Cremona, which, following the pact between the Empire and Milan and the resumption of the conflict concerning the rebuilding of the commune of Crema, was forced to capitulate.

Tensions were exacerbated by the pope's support of Cremona, and by complaints concerning the emperor's failure to provide the promised protection of the PATRIMONY OF ST. PETER—Frederick's son Henry VI, who had been entrusted with this task, was actually encroaching on the lands. The prospect of reconciliation thus became more and more remote. The dispute over the inheritance of Matilda of Canossa moved to another stage when Urban III insisted, forcefully and quite unrealistically, that all unlawfully occupied possessions be restored; moreover, by demanding that Roman law be respected and written title-deeds provided, the pope confronted the imperial side with insurmountable difficulties. Urban then tried to reinforce Curial administration. He thus saw to exact recording of rents and expenses, which naturally brought about the systematic recording of title-deeds. In this situation, it is not surprising that the pope never gave a moment's thought to the crowning of Henry VI and that when the coronation of Frederick's son and his wife Constance was celebrated (1186) in Milan by the patriarch of Aquilea, without papal consent, tensions were aggravated anew.

Nor was Urban III prepared to accept a compromise with the emperor in the matter of schismatic consecration. In the competition for the archiepiscopal see of Trier, he gave up any attempt at reconciliation. Repudiating the election of the emperor's candidate, he argued that the latter had agreed to be invested by Frederick Barbarossa before he had made his own decision known. Actually, on 1 June 1185 his predecessor Lucius III had consecrated Volkmar, who was staying at the Curia, and given him the powers of a pontifical legate so that he could regain his archbishopric. Urban III thus pushed the conflict to the utmost, giving it a dangerously theoretical twist that risked calling into question the achievements of the imperial episcopate in the wake of the Investiture Controversy. This danger finally enabled the emperor to win to his cause the majority of the German bishops at the Diet of Gelnhausen (28 November 1186). Frederick managed to convince them of the merits of his position in the Cremona affair and to justify the harshness of his conduct vis-à-vis the Curia (the occupation of Church lands in western Italy and the military blockade of the Curia). In the end, all the pope could do was flee to Venice, whence he might have been able to reinforce his position. He died, however, on the road to Ferrara. It is not known if the news of the capture of Jerusalem by Saladin's armies (2 October 1187) reached him first.

As for ecclesiastical policy, Urban III's chief concern was to multiply DECRETALS—instruments of direct pontifical intervention—and restore strict discipline, in matters regarding not only vestments but also the abolition or absence of the tonsure and disregard of the rule of celibacy. He granted a general dispensation to the Cistercian order, which shielded it from episcopal jurisdiction. The pope also reinforced the authority of the great sees, such as Bourges, Toledo, and Canterbury.

Ludwig Vones

Bibliography

PL, 202, 1331–1534.

JL, 492–528, 726, 769–70.

LP, 2, 451.

Amann, E. "Urbain III," DTC, 15 (1950), 2285–8.

De Fischer-Reichenbach, M. C. *Urbain III et Barberousse et les trois cardinaux Crivelli*, Bern, 1940.

Fliche-Martin IX, 2 (1953), 196.

Kaufmann, H. *Die italienische Politik Kaiser Friedrich I. nach dem Frieden vom Konstanz* (1183–9), Diss. Greiswal, 1933.

Sauerwein, E. *Der Ursprung des Rechtsinstituts der päpstlichen Dispens von der nicht vollzogenen Ehe. Ein Interpretation der Dekretalen Alexanders III. und Urbans III*, Rome, 1980.

Watterich, *Vitae*, 663–83.

URBAN IV. *Jacques de Troyes (Troyes ca. 1185–Perugia, 2 October 1264). Elected pope 29 August 1261 in Viterbo, consecrated 4 September. Buried in Perugia.*

This pontificate marked a profound change in the history of the papacy. The solutions set in place to resolve the succession to the Kingdom of Sicily and to restore papal power in the States of the Church are the most visible aspects of this change.

Of humble origins, Jacques de Troyes grew up in the shadow of the abbey of Notre-Dame-aux-Nonnains in Troyes, and received his first schooling there. Later, the canons sent him to the University of Paris to pursue studies in arts and then in canon law, in which he obtained the degree of *magister*. He seems also to have received training in theology. During this period he formed a friendship with Hugh of St. Cher. Around 1215, his compatriot Anselm of Mauny, who had just been elected to the episcopal see of Laon, invited him to follow him as chaplain. Jacques bought a canonical house in 1223, which suggests he was then already a member of the cathedral chapter. Here he served as procurator for more than ten years (1226–37). When Robert de Thourotte, his former colleague, was elected to the archbishopric of Liège, he invited the canon Jacques to join him as archdeacon of Campine (1242). It was then that, together with Hugh of St. Cher, he declared himself in favor of devotion to the Blessed Sacrament, instituted in the diocese as a result of the visions of Julienne of Mont-Cornillon.

In Lyon, where a council was held in 1245, Jacques de Troyes met INNOCENT IV, who made him his chaplain before entrusting him in 1247 with a legation to Poland, Prussia, and Pomerania. In 1251 the pope sent him to Germany on the death of Frederick II, to encourage the candidature of William of Holland to the imperial succession. In the meantime he was appointed bishop of Verdun, but, taken prisoner in Germany, he did not make his solemn entry into Verdun until Christmas 1253. The short period he spent in his bishopric was devoted to regulating relations with the community. Named to the patriarchal see of Jerusalem in 1255, he had to settle the conflict between the Genoese and the Venetians and attempt to calm the rivalry between the Templars and Hospitallers. Diocesan interests took him to the Curia before the death of Alexander IV (12 May 1261) in Viterbo. At that time, bitter debate split the seven members of the Sacred College met in conclave. The heads of the two sides, John of Toledo and Ottaviano Ubaldini, confronted one another over the English candidature and over what position to adopt vis-à-vis the antipapal forces of Manfred, king of Sicily. They reached a compromise in the person of Jacques de Troyes, who was unanimously elected 29 August 1261.

Being neither Italian nor a cardinal, Urban IV presented himself as a fresh face who was a member of no party, one with good political experience in Germany and a knowledge of the Holy Land, but little acquainted with Italian problems or the cardinals' cliques. The most urgent problems facing him were the succession to the Kingdom of Sicily and the regaining of control over the Papal States. As a good canonist, Urban set himself up as a scrupulous defender of the rights of the Church, with documents at hand, never yielding the juridical point of view. To finance the war in the Papal States he appealed to Sienese banks rather than the moneylenders of Rome. He was also able to put pressure on the communes by using both financial (the blocking of bank credits) and political (blockade of external magistratures, withdrawal of episcopal rank, and manipulation of intercity rivalries) measures.

Under Urban IV, the staff of the pontifical entourage was significantly changed. Two promotions of cardinals reinforced the Sacred College while maintaining the fragile balance among its electors. Two members of the Orsini family were raised to the purple: Giacomo Savelli, the future HONORIUS IV, and Matteo Rosso, nephew of Cardinal Giangaetano, the rival of Riccardo Annibaldi. Annibaldi's influence was strengthened by the presence of another Riccardo Annibaldi and Goffredo d'Alatri, both of whom claimed to be his nephews. The number of Roman cardinals thus grew to seven, while in Rome much intrigue pitted the two most influential groups, the Annibaldi and the Orsini, against each other. Ottaviano Ubaldini and John of Toledo were in disgrace, so no political responsibility was entrusted to them. Among the seven French newcomers to the cardinalate, three had distinguished themselves in the service of Louis IX, the French king; Guy Foulques, the future CLEMENT IV; Simon de Brie, the future MARTIN IV; and Raoul Grosparmi. The pope also promoted Henri de Suze, author of the famous *Summa hostiensis*, and his nephew Ancher.

In order to effectively combat the forces dividing the Papal States and the whole of Italy, Urban IV summoned energetic personalities, like Giscardo di Pietrasancta of Milan and Manfredo di Roberti of Reggio Emilia, who were familiar with the communal magistratures and had already taken part in the struggle against Frederick II. The pope's intellectual gifts and keen religious sensibility rested on a solid juridical culture and a great openness to liturgical concerns, to the religious orders and the new forms of piety, in particular the devotion to the Blessed Sacrament and the feast of Corpus Christi, which he made universal definitively with the bull *Transiturus* of 11 August 1264. In each domain the pope's behavior was always firm, even authoritarian. Counsel and hesitation hardly slowed down the working out of decisions, as is attested by the portrait of Urban painted by the Sienese ambassadors at the beginning of his pontificate.

The restoration of the Papal States at first took the form of a tenacious fight against every type of alienation of papal rights: enfeoffments agreed to by Urban's predecessor and improper seizures of strongholds, mainly in three regions—southern Latium, the region of Lake Bolsena, and the Terra Arnulforum, that is, the territory shared by Orte, Rieti, and Spoleto. In the Marches, forces of the vice-emperor Perceval Doria had occupied almost the whole region in 1262. The rector Manfredo di Roberti succeeded in retaking most of the occupied towns before he was himself taken prisoner, in 1264. Thereafter the pope was directly threatened by the advance of Sicilian troops in the Duchy and the Campagna and by the support they received from Pietro IV di Vico to the south of the Patrimony. The murder (September 1264) of the rector of the province of the Patrimony, Giscardo di Pietrasancta, was crucial; it forced Urban to leave Orvieto for Perugia, where he died a month later. The imminence of danger hastened talks with Charles of Anjou to obtain his armed intervention with the least possible delay.

The instability of the Roman situation, which was dominated by a popular party violently opposed to the nobility, (itself highly fragmented), was exacerbated by external pressure brought by the candidates to the throne of Sicily. They hoped to accede to the Roman senate, considered the first step toward official recognition. But the pope did not relinquish his rights over senatorial election. The threat that Manfred caused to hang over central Italy persuaded Cardinal Riccardo Annibaldi, on his own initiative, to have Charles of Anjou elected perpetual senator in August 1263—without the knowledge of the pope or of Charles himself. Despite his surprise and annoyance, Urban IV was astute enough to take advantage of this in the last negotiations with Charles of Anjou when Charles sent Jacques de Gantelme to Rome (April 1264) to carry out his duties as vicar. The Angevin candidature, however, presumably had the indispensable agreement of the French king, (St.) Louis IX. In Louis's mind, the Sicilian plan was linked to the question of the Latin empire of Constantinople and the crusades. The fall of Baldwin II and Michael VIII Palaeologus's capture of Constantinople in 1261 had changed the diplomatic situation. Up to 1263, Louis and the pope hoped to win back the Latin Kingdom. But the king's decision not to put further obstacles to his brother Charles's candidature, in May 1263, caused an abrupt change in the situation. The pope replied favorably to Michael Palaeologus's offers to reconcile the Greek and Latin churches, and promised to send a legation to work out the conditions. A plan to cede the Kingdom of Sicily to Charles of Anjou as legitimate sovereign was drawn up in June 1263, then amended several times up to the legation of Cardinal Simon de Brie to Louis, in May 1264.

Letters to his legate reveal the anguish that dominated the last months of Urban's life. After fighting his rival Manfred, the pope died without having seen the conclusion of the latest negotiations in France or having witnessed the reversal brought about by the arrival of Charles of Anjou. His personality, nevertheless, left its stamp on a renewal of pontifical dignity.

Thérèse Boespflug

Bibliography

De Vaucouleurs, T. *Vita Urbani, Rerum italicarum scriptores*, ed. L. A. Muratori, 416–17.

Forey, A. J. "The military orders and holy war against Christians in the thirteenth century," *English Historical Review*, 104 (Jan. 1989), 1–24.

Foviaux, J. "Les sermons donnés à Laon en 1242 par le chanoine Jacques de Troyes, futur Urbain IV," *Recherches augustiniennes*, 20 (1985), 203–56.

Georges, E. *Histoire du pape Urbain IV et de son temps (1186–1264)*, Paris-Troyes, 1866.

Guiraud, J., and Clémencet, S., ed. *Les Registres d'Urbain IV (1261–4)*, 4 vols., Paris, 1899–1958.

Jordan, E. *Les Origines de la domination angevine en Italie*, Paris, 1909, 291–513.

Lamberts, J. "The Origin of the Corpus Christi Festival," *Worship*, 70 (Sept. 1996), 432–46.

Martinet, S. *La Fête-Dieu, Jacques de Troyes et l'école de théologie de Laon*, Laon, 1965 (Fédération des sociétés d'histoire et d'archéologie de l'Aisne, Mémoires, 11).

Paracivini Bagliani, A. "Gregorio da Napoli, biografo di Urbano IV," *Römische historische Mitteilungen*, 11 (1969), 59–78.

Pico, F. *The Cathedral Chapter of Laon (1155–1318)*, Multigraphed biographical index, n.d. [ca. 1975].

Potthast, 1474–1541, 2129–30, 2138.

Schneider, F. "Beiträge zur Geschichte Friedrichs II. und Manfreds," *QFIAB*, 15 (1913), 50–2.

Souplet, M. *Jacques de Troyes le "pacificateur,"* Verdun, 1954.

URBAN V. *Guillaume de Grimoard (Grisac, in the diocese of Mende, ca. 1310–Avignon, 19 December 1370). Elected pope 28 September 1362, consecrated 6 November. Buried in St. Victor, Marseilles. Beatified 10 March 1870.*

While continuing his predecessors' policy of centralization, Urban V broke to a certain extent with the traditional character of the Avignon popes in his preoccupation with restricting the greed of the clergy by recalling it to its duties and, especially, residence, as well as in his distrust of the cardinals. It was against the cardinals' advice that he reestablished the seat of the papacy in Rome, an attempt that ended, however, in failure.

The son of a nobleman from (and named) Gévaudan, and of Amphélise of Montferrand, he first studied in Montpellier and Toulouse, then entered the Benedictine order at the priory of Monastier-Chirac, making his profession at St. Victor of Marseilles. In 1352 he became abbot of St. Germain of Auxerre, and in 1361 of St. Victor of Marseilles. Meanwhile, however, CLEMENT VI and INNOCENT VI entrusted him with four diplomatic missions to Italy, where he found himself at the time of his election. Although he was not a member of the Sacred College, his name was probably put forward by Guillaume d'Aigrefeuille to the cardinals, who could not agree on which of their number to propose.

Deeply religious, Urban V continued to observe the Benedictine rule as far as the demands of his office allowed, devoting much time to prayer and living simply. Like his predecessors, he did not give up the idea of encouraging Edward III and Charles V to take part in a crusade, as is shown by the plan first outlined in the spring of 1363, in Avignon, with John the Good of France and the kings of Cyprus and Denmark. In Rome in 1369 he received the submission of the Greek emperor, John V Palaeologus, who had returned to Catholicism.

Urban V waited four years before carrying out the first of his four consistories creating cardinals. Six of his candidates, out of a total of fourteen, belonged to religious orders. He gave the cardinal's hat to only one member of his family, his brother Anglic, who had ably administered the bishopric of Avignon. In his day-to-day life, the pope surrounded himself with a small group of collaborators, of relatively modest rank, either from the Benedictine order (like the referendary Pierre de Banhac, whom he made abbot of Montmajour) or like him from the diocese of Mende (his cubicular and confidant, Bernard de Saint-Étienne).

A scholar and former teacher, he strongly encouraged sound learning on the part of the clergy, and founded two colleges in Montpellier for Benedictine monks and physicians. He also maintained, at his own expense (in Trets, then Manosque, at St.-Germain-de-Calberte, etc.), *studia* designed to prepare youths for university life. Moreover, his pontificate would see the foundation of the universities of Orange, Cracow, and Vienna.

His replies to the petitions presented to him daily, of which only those of the first four years have been preserved, bear witness to his strictness (he made it obligatory to give up benefices before receiving new ones), his great lucidity, and also at times a certain humor. Little by little pastors were ordered to leave court to go and live in their parishes, and functionaries were forced to choose between office and benefices, while the constitution *Horribilis* (lost) decreed severe penalties against pluralism. But overall reform was beyond the strength of Urban V, and the particular measures were only partially applied in the troubled times at the end of his pontificate. General impoverishment due to continuing wars necessitated a reduction by half of the tithe in the provinces of northern France.

The Hundred Years' War experienced a respite, but great companies of soldiers had fanned out to pillage the southern regions. The pope, who had hoped to send the mercenaries out to fight the Turks, condemned them on several occasions, when they refused, and in 1364 excommunicated them. He formally forbade any communication with them and encouraged the formation of leagues against them. The clergy had to contribute financially to protection measures taken in the face of the dangers that often threatened Provence and the Comtat Venaissin (the region around Avignon). On one occasion, after Urban had left for Italy, the Duke of Anjou tried to seize (1368) Queen Joanna's lands, and the rector of Venaissin, Philip Cabassole, had to purchase the withdrawal of the great military leader Bertrand Du Guesclin.

Italy was scarcely less troubled. When Bernabò Visconti, lord of Milan, seized some Bolognese castles, Urban summoned him to appear in Avignon, then condemned him for heresy 3 March 1363, and promulgated a crusade against him. The cardinal-legate Gil de Albornoz, leader of the papal forces, was preparing to crush him when the pope, to hasten the conclusion of peace on conditions less distressing for Visconti, stripped Albornoz of his powers, to the benefit of the mediocre Androin de la Roche. Nevertheless, Urban V soon restored his trust in Albornoz, now a legate to Queen Joanna. Joanna continued to play a role in Tuscany, smoothing dissensions between towns, aiding the struggle against the great companies, and pacifying the Papal States, until her death in 1367.

By 1365 Urban had begun making ready to return to Rome, arranging for the Vatican palace to be repaired. In June 1366 he announced his decision to leave Avignon, a plan that was cheered in Italy, as witness, for example, the testimony of the Florentine ambassador, Lapo da Castiglionchio, but ardently opposed by the French court, which vainly dispatched the representative of Charles V, Ancel Choquart, to attempt to restrain the pope. Urban quit Avignon 30 April 1367, embarked at Marseilles 19 May, and in the beginning of June reached Viterbo, where his stay was disturbed by clashes between the cardinals' entourages and the citizens. On 16 October, to the acclamation of crowds, Urban V brought the papacy back to Rome after an absence of nearly three quarters of a century. In the spring of the following year he welcomed to Rome the king of Cyprus and Queen Joanna of Naples, on whom he bestowed the Golden Rose, and then, in the autumn, the Emperor Charles IV, who had visited him in 1365 in Avignon. The pope spent the summers in Montefiascone, however, which he made a bishopric.

Yet problems had resurfaced in the Papal States with the rebellion of Francesco di Vico, who was allied with the Perugians. Viterbo, where the pope had taken refuge, was threatened by the bands of Sir John Hawkwood. In France, Anglo-French hostilities had resumed and Urban, already disappointed by his time in Rome, deemed it his duty to attempt to reconcile the enemies. On 5 September 1370 he set sail at Corneto. He entered Avignon on the 27th, only to die there a few weeks later, on 19 December, in his brother's house, where he had retired out of humility. According to his wishes, his body was moved to St. Victor of Marseilles, while his reputation for holiness spread throughout Christendom, as is attested by the tales of numerous miracles recorded a few years later.

Anne-Marie Hayez

Bibliography

Amarghier, P. *Urbain V. Un homme. Une vie (1310–1370)*, Marseilles, 1987.

Balmelle, M. "Iconographie du pape Urbain V," *Bull. de la Soc. des lettres de la Lozère*, 1964 [–1966], 73–88.

Baluze-Mollat, E. *Vitae paparum Avenionensium*, I, Paris, 1916, 349–414.

Cretoni, A. "Il Petrarca e Urbano V," *Studi Romani*, 9 (1961), 629–46.

Fierens, A., ed. *Suppliques [intéressant la Belgique]*, Rome-Brussels-Paris, 1924 (*Analect a Vaticano Belgica*, 7). *Relevé alphabétique des noms de personnes et de lieux contenus dans les suppliques . . .*, Paris, 8 vols.

Fierens, A., and C. Tihon, ed. *Lettres [intéressant la Belgique]*, Rome-Brussels, 1928–32 (*Analecta Vaticano-Belgica*, 9, 14).

Genèse et débuts du Grand Schisme d'Occident, Avignon 25–28 septembre 1378, Paris, 1980.

Guillemain, B. *La Cour pontificale d'Avignon*, Paris, 1962.

Hayez, M. "Un domaine rural universitaire à l'époque du pape Urbain V: le compte de Meynes (Gard)," *Revue du Gévaudun*, 18–19 (Mende, 1972–73), 163–90.

Hayez, A. M. "Les Rotuli présentés au pape Urbain V durant la première année de son pontificat," *MEFRM*, 96 (1984), 327–94.

Hayez, A. M. "A la Cour pontificale d'Urbain V, réceptions et déplacements," *Annuaire de la Soc. des Amis du Palais des Papes*, 63–4 (1986–87), 15–24.

Hayez, A. M. "L'entourage d'Urbain V: parents, amis et familiers," ibid., 1988–89, 31–45; "La personnalité d'Urbain V d'après ses réponses aux suppliques," *Aux origines de l'État moderne: le fonctionnement administratif de la papauté d'Avignon*, Avignon, 22–24 Jan. 1988, Rome, 1990, 7–31.

Kianka, F. "Demetrios Kydones and Italy," *Dumbarton Oaks Papers*, no. 49 (1995), 99–110.

Laurent, M. H., ed. *Lettres communes*, members of the French School in Rome and M. and A. M. Hayez, Paris, 1955–89 (ibid.).

Lecacheux, P. and Mollat, G., ed. *Lettres secrètes et curiales se rapportant à la France*, Paris, 1902–55 (*BEFAR*, 3rd series).

Mezzanotte, F. "La pace di Bologna tra Perugia e Urbano V (23 nov. 1380)," *Boll. d. Deputazione di storia patria per l'Umbria*, 74 (1977), 117–74.

Mollat, G. *The Popes of Avignon*, New York, 1963.

Prou, M. *Étude sur les relations politiques du pape Urbain V avec les rois de France*, Paris, 1888 (*Bibl. de l'École des Hautes Études*, 76).

Sabbadini, E. "Un pontefice avignonese pacificatore dell'Italia: Urbano V (Benedettino)," *Rivista Cisterciense*, 2 (1985), 241–57.

Schwaiger, G. "Urban V," *LTK*, 10 (1965), 545–6.

Stouff, L. "Une création d'Urbain V. Le studium papal de Trets, 1364–1365," *Provence historique*, 16 (1966), 528–39.

URBAN VI. *Bartolomeo Prignano (Naples, 1318 or 1320–Rome, 15 October 1389). Elected pope 8 April 1378, consecrated 18 April. Buried in St. Peter's, Rome.*

Urban VI played a leading, albeit controversial, role in the unleashing of the Great Schism of the West (1378-1417). Rarely has a pontiff aroused such violent and contradictory emotions. Known for his learning, his austerity, and his experience of the Curia, Prignano was accused after his election of fickleness, cruelty, and mental imbalance—both by his contemporaries and by historians, long influenced by nationalist passions. Relying on anti-Urban sources, many scholars, in the past, failed to observe neutrality, dismissing testimony that upset their thesis, differing on fundamental matters, and thus, as Noël Valois has pointed out, prolonging the uncertainties and disagreements that already afflicted contemporary accounts.

At the dawn of his career, Prignano was a doctor *in utroque iure*. He was an intimate of the French cardinal Guy of Boulogne. Promoted archbishop of Acerenza (1363), then of Bari (1377), he followed GREGORY XI to

Rome (1377). Here he was made head of the Apostolic Chancery, where he worked from 1368, replacing the vice-chancellor Pierre de Monteruc, who had remained in Avignon.

On the death of Gregory XI, the sixteen cardinals held a conclave at the Vatican on 7 April 1378. The Romans, anxious to profit from the commercial exploitation of pilgrimages and the presence of the Curia within their walls, tried clamorously to influence the electors' choice in favor of a Roman or, if that failed, an Italian. The next day, Prignano carried the vote. For six centuries, the conclave of April 1378 and the election of Urban VI, seminal events in the history of the Great Schism, have exercised a veritable fascination over historians. When one realizes that the story of the genesis of the Schism was built upon the basis of countless literary sources (more than six hundred) that are partial, partisan, contradictory, and suspected of exaggerations, omissions, and inaccuracies, one can better understand the perplexity, the confusion, and even the disarray of specialists who today, in the absence of new and convincing arguments, essay to solve the question: Was Urban VI's election free, regular, and valid?

Prignano had never been a cardinal. He therefore did not feel bound to the interests of the Sacred College. He at once adopted the stance of a reformer of the hierarchy and in unprecedented fashion clashed with the cardinals, who were already confused by the return to Rome. At the end of April he roundly reproached them for absenteeism, for a luxurious way of life hardly compatible with the Gospels, for the excessive number in their entourage, for simony, for accumulation of benefices, and even, in certain cases, for misappropriation of funds from his treasury.

The cardinals, shocked and enraged, touched to the heart of their interests, bear heavy responsibility for the unleashing of the crisis. At the end of June, the dissidents met at Anagni, except for three hesitant Italians, Orsini, Corsini, and Borsano; on 2 August they called on Urban VI to abdicate, calling him "Antichrist, demon, apostate, tyrant." On 5 August the three Italians proposed to the French that they have recourse to a general council—to no avail. At the end of the month all the cardinal-electors went to Fondi, where they placed themselves under the protection of Count Onorato Caetani. Judging Urban incompetent, they then exploited the events of the April conclave to bring about a reversal, which culminated, on 20 September, in a new election. They claimed to have voted five months before under duress and even threats of death by the Roman mob, disavowed their votes as invalid, and then proceeded to a new vote. Unanimously, save for the abstention of the Italians, they picked a man who occupied a central place within the Sacred College and enjoyed a large clientele and a vast network of alliances in the ecclesiastical hierarchy and the secular courts. This was the cousin of France's Charles V, Robert of Geneva, who was crowned 31 October as CLEMENT VII. The schism was created. Was it premeditated, or a conspiracy? Or was it the simple result of a series of errors and misunderstandings between Urban and his college? In the present state of research the question remains unsolved.

After the election of (antipope) Clement VII, allegiances quickly formed and Christianity split in two. The young emperor Wenceslas of Luxembourg and the kingdoms of England (1378), Hungary, Poland, Scandinavia (1379), and Portugal (1383) rallied to Urban's camp. Urban VI piled up "Crusade" bulls from February 1383. Italy was turned into a battleground; a theater of violence, the peninsula sank into anarchy and chaos. The pope plunged into the affairs of the Kingdom of Naples. At war with his rival's partisans, for five years he wandered from city to city seeking a refuge. By turns, Nocera (1385), Salerno (1385), Genoa (1385–6), Lucca (1386–7), and Perugia (1387–8) took him in. Faced with political problems from the beginning of his reign, Urban quickly betrayed his convictions and adopted authoritarian behavior, blundering into fiscal confusion and nepotism to strengthen allegiance to him. In 1385 he did not hesitate to have some of the rebellious cardinals, accused of plotting against him, tortured and put to death. His ambition to restore pontifical authority came up, though, against not only the opposition of the cardinals but also worse material difficulties: the dismantling of the Chancery, the lack of qualified curial staff, and a crushing lack of financial resources. Deprived of his working tools, Urban VI moved urgently to reconstitute his own college. In September 1378, he appointed twenty-five new cardinals, including Pileo da Prata, who subsequently changed allegiance. The four series of cardinal promotions from 1378 to 1385 reflect the pope's desire to once again bring Italians into the leading ranks of the Church. A chancery was reestablished from 1378 and almost completely renovated in 1386.

Urban VI decided prematurely to hold a jubilee in 1390. He even considered reducing to thirty-three years the length of time between two jubilees, as a reminder of the life of Christ. He instituted the feast of the Visitation, which the Council of Basel extended throughout Christendom. Finally, two universities, one in Germany and the other in Italy, owe him their foundation: Cologne and Lucca.

Monique Maillard-Luypaert

Bibliography

Bliemetzreider, F. "Die Kardinäle Peter Corsini, Simon de Borsano, Jakob Orsini und der Konzilsgedanke," *Studien und Mitteilungen aus dem Benediktineordern*, 24 (1903), 360–77, 625–52, "Über die Konzilsbewegung zu Beginn des grossen abendländischen Schismas . . . ," ibid., 31 (1910), 44–75, 391–410.

Brandmuller, W. "Zur Frage nach der Gultigkeit der Wahl Urbans VI. Quellen und Quellenkritik," *AHP*, 6 (1974), 78–120.

Brezzi, P. "Il regno di Napoli e il grand Scisma d'Occidente (1378–1419)," *Annali del Pontificio Istituto Superiore di Scienze e Lettere "Santa Chiara,"* 12 (1962), 9–32; *Studi di storia cristiana ed ecclesiastica*, 2, Naples, 1966.

Dykmans, M. "La troisième élection du pape Urbain VI," *AHP*, 15 (1977), 217–64.

Eubel, K. "Das Itinerar des Päpste zur Zeit des grossen Schismas," *Historisches Jahrbuch*, 16 (1895), 545–64.

Fink, K. A. "Zur Beurteilung des Grossen Abendländischen Schismas," *ZKG*, 73 (1962), 335–43.

Fliche-Martin, 14.

Fodale, S. *La politaica napoletana di Urbano VI, Caltanissetta.* Rome, 1973.

Franzen, A. "Zur Vorgeschichte des Konstanzer Konzils. Vom Ausbruch des Schismas bis zum Pisanum," *Das Konzil von Konstanz*, ed. A. Franzen and W. Müller, Freiburg (1964), 3–35.

Gastout, M., ed. *Suppliques et lettres d'Urbain VI (1378–1389) et de Boniface IX (1389–1404)*, Brussels, 1976. (*Analecta Vaticano-Belgaica. Documents relatifs aux anciens diocèses de Cambrai, Liège, Thérouanne et Tournai. Documents relatifs au Grand Schisme, 7*).

Hauck, A. *Kirchengeschichte Deutschlands*, 5, 5th ed., Leipzig, 1953.

Lindner, T. "Papst Urban IV," *ZKG*, 3 (1879), 409–28, 525–64.

Mollat, G. "Urbain VI," *DTC*, 15 (1950), 2302–5.

Prerovsky, O. *L'elezione di Urbano VI e l'insorgere dello Scisma d'Occidents*, Rome, 1960 (*Miscellanea della Società Romana di Storia Patria*, 20).

Schwaiger, G. "Urban VI," *LTK*, 10 (1965), 546–7.

Souchon, M. *Die Papstwahlen in der Zeit des grossen Schismas. Entwicklung der Verfassungskämpfe des Kardinaltes von 1378 bis 1417*, 2 vols., Braunschweig, 1898–99.

Tellenbach, G. *Repertorium Germanicum, 2. Verzeichnis der in den Registern und Kamerlakten Urbans VI., Bonifaz' IX., Innocenz' VII. und Gregors XII, 1378–1415*, Berlin, 1961.

Ullmann, W. *The Origins of the Great Schism. A study in XIVth century Ecclesiastical history*, 2nd ed., London, 1967.

Villiger, J. B. "Abendländisches Schisma," *LTK*, 1 (1957), 21–6.

URBAN VII. *Giovan Battista Castagna (Rome, 4 August 1521–Rome, 27 September 1590). Elected pope 15 September 1590; not consecrated. Buried in Sta. Maria sopra Minerva (Rome).*

Born into a noble Roman family originally from Genoa, Giovan Battista Castagna studied law at Perugia and Bologna, after which he entered the service of his uncle, Cardinal Verallo, accompanying him as datary of his legation in the kingdom of France (1551–2). Julius III made him referendary of the Signatura of Justice, and through the resignation of his cousin Paolo Emilio Verallo he became archbishop of Rossano (1 March 1553), on which occasion he took orders.

For some time governor of Fano, he next settled in his diocese, where he distinguished himself by his desire to be worthy of his charge and his eagerness for reform, principles that would dominate his whole life. From November 1561, until its close, he attended the COUNCIL OF TRENT and was a member of the commission for Church reform, where he took part in the debates on marriage, residency, and communion besides having extremely close contact with St. Charles Borromeo.

Hardly had he returned to his diocese when PIUS IV called on him to accompany Cardinal Boncompagni (later GREGORY XIII), the legate to Spain. He stayed there for seven years as nuncio at the court of Madrid. In 1573, after resigning his diocese, whose direction he claimed he could no longer conveniently handle, he was sent as nuncio to Venice, then as governor to Bologna. In 1578 he tried to arrange for a peace treaty between the United Provinces of the Netherlands and Philip II. He was consultor of the Holy Office and was promoted to the cardinalate by Gregory XIII on 12 December 1583. Highly esteemed within the SACRED COLLEGE, a moderate pro-Spain advocate, he was one of those favored at the conclave that led to the election of SIXTUS V. Then, on the death of that pope, after a conclave agitated by Spanish pressure in favor of certain candidates, the cardinals agreed on his nomination.

As soon as he was elected, Urban VII undertook the relief of poverty in Rome, gave a number of audiences, and commissioned Fontana to place the arms of Sixtus V in the Quirinal Palace. His discipline and honesty are shown by his refusal to favor the members of his family. Very soon, however, he fell ill, and died thirteen days after his elevation to the pontificate, at the age of sixty-five. He left his fortune to a charitable sisterhood at Sta. Maria sopra Minerva, where his remains were moved in 1606.

Because of the brevity of his reign Urban VII was unable to appoint any cardinals.

Anne-Cécile Tizon-Germe

Bibliography

Moroni, G. *Dizionario di erudizione storico-ecclesiastica*, 86 (1857), 37–41.
Pastor, 22, London, 1928.

URBAN VIII. *Maffeo Vincenzo Barberini (Florence, baptized 5 April 1568–Rome, 29 July 1644). Elected pope 6 August 1623; consecrated 29 September. Buried in St. Peter's, Rome.*

At the end of his twenty-one-year-long pontificate, Urban VIII bequeathed to the Romans the hateful memory of a pope who was manipulated by his family, greedy for money, and quick to raise taxes. To the Europeans of the time, embroiled in the Thirty Years' War, he was seen by all camps as a traitor. Today many people remember him as the pope who condemned Galileo and launched the long Jansenist crisis. He is also recognized, however, as the protector not only of Bernini but also of Pietro da Cortona and of Borromini. In fact, Urban VIII put his talents and authority to the service of what he judged to be the interests of the pontifical state and the Church in a period that was hardly lacking in dangers or threats.

The fifth of the six children of Antonio Barberini (d. 1571) and Camilla Barbadori (d. 1609), Maffeo was born to a Florentine merchant family that had made its fortune in the Eastern fabric trade at the beginning of 16th century with his great-grandfather, Francesco. The business flourished and after 1540 spread throughout Europe, with branches in Lyon, Paris, Antwerp, and London. In Rome, family interests were represented by one of Francesco's sons, Antonio, who was assassinated in 1559, and then by one of his nephews, also Francesco (1528–1600), who thanks to his uncle's connections and fortune became apostolic protonotary.

This Francesco took Maffeo, who had lost his father, under his protection. He arranged for him to enter the Roman College at the age of twelve to pursue his studies, begun with the Jesuits of Florence. Next, he sent him to Pisa to study for a *làurea* in civil and canon law, which he obtained in two years (in 1589) and which won him the title of doctor. In October of that same year, his uncle bought him, for 8,000 crowns, an office of apostolic abbreviator, where he was made a clerk. Maffeo then became referendary at the Signatura of Justice and thereafter that of Grace, posts which promoted him to the rank of prelate. His uncle Francesco resigned as protonotary in his favor in October 1593, and, in 1599, bought him the highly prized position of clerk of the Apostolic Camera.

This rapid rise founded on his uncle's fortune and connections was consolidated by the friendship and trust granted him by the popes. CLEMENT VIII, like him a Florentine, had named him governor of Fano in 1592—at which time he received minor orders—and then entrusted him with various missions, for example, one to regulate the waters of Lake Trasimene, another to convey Clement's congratulations to Henry IV on the birth of the dauphin in 1601. In October 1604 Clement named him archbishop *in partibus* of Nazareth—major orders were now conferred—and, in late 1604, ordinary nuncio to Paris, where he upheld the Jesuits but did not succeed in

official reception of the decrees of the COUNCIL OF TRENT.

Under PAUL V his career accelerated. Created cardinal 11 September 1606, at the age of thirty-eight, he received the red hat from the hands of Henry IV, returned to Rome in September 1607, and became protector of the kingdom of Scotland. Promoted in October 1608 bishop of Spoleto, he inaugurated a synod there and undertook the restoration of the cathedral, meanwhile acquiring the legation of Bologna from 1611 to 1614. In 1617 he gave up his episcopal position for that of prefect of the Signatura of Justice, the tribunal where he had started his career as curialist twenty-seven years before. After failing at the conclave of 1621, he embarked on a totally different career when the conclave of 1623 elected him pope 6 August, at the age of fifty-five, thanks to his friendship with Cardinal Maurice of Savoy, spokesman for the French side.

No sooner was he crowned than Urban VIII began handing out posts and revenues to his family. In 1624 he removed his younger brother Antonio (1569–1646) from his monastery and made him, against his wishes, cardinal grand-penitentiary and librarian. In 1623 his elder brother Carlo (1562–1630) was promoted general of the Church and given the title of Duke of Monte Rotondo. In October 1623 Carlo's son Francesco (1597–1679) was launched, at the age of twenty-six, as cardinal-nephew, as well as general superintendent and governor of Tivoli; he subsequently became librarian, vice chancellor, abbot of Grottaferratta, archpriest of St. Peter's, and prefect of the Holy Office. Antonio (1607–71), his brother, was made a cardinal in his turn in 1629, took on the positions of legate of Avignon and Bologna, abbot of Tre Fontane, camerlengo (1638) and prefect of the Signatura. Taddeo, their brother who had remained a layman, became general of the Church on his father's death, then prefect of Rome (1631), governor of the CASTEL SANT'ANGELO and prince of Palestrina.

This division of spoils among the members of the clan has given rise to many a historiographical debate. L. Pastor (1928) dismissed Urban VIII's nepotism by positing that the Barberini had only a secondary influence on the pope's policies except in the last years of his life, when he yielded to their pressure in the disastrous affair of the duchy of Castro. A. Kraus (1964–9) and M. Laurain-Portemer (1973), by contrast, have both shed light, with different emphases, on the not insignificant political role of Francesco, the cardinal-nephew. P. Prodi (1982), for his part, tried to interpret this nepotism as the specific form that centralizing absolutism took in the 17th century in the elective, nonhereditary regime of the papacy, where a sweeping "spoils system" functioned as it does in the presidential systems of today.

In fact, in his governance of the Church, Urban VIII appears as an absolute ruler. He wanted to control everything, read everything that he signed (this was a first), and left those around him with little power—except, at the beginning, his friend Lorenzo Magalotti (d. 1637), who was raised to the purple in 1624 and was secretary of state until 1628. The other cardinals, too closely tied to the European powers, were kept from political matters; to compensate for this loss of influence, in June 1630 he gave them the title of Eminence and the rank of Prince of the Church. Moreover, out of seventy-eight cardinals he created in nine consistories, aside from the Barberini few personalities stand out from a somewhat colorless group, among them Harrach (cardinal 1626; d. 1667), Berulla (cardinal 1627; d. 1629), Pamphili (cardinal 1627; the future INNOCENT X), Pázmány (cardinal 1629; d. 1637) and Mazarin (cardinal 1641; d. 1661). Sixty-three were Italians, four French, and three Spaniards. Thirty were members of the Curia, fifteen nuncios or former nuncios, and fourteen resident bishops.

This high proportion of nuncios among the cardinals reminds us that the great question of Urban's pontificate was the Thirty Years' War (1618–48), which by itself virtually monopolized his energies.

Throughout the conflict, the pope tried to defend the sometimes contradictory interests of the Papal States and Catholic Reform, which was taking place in both France and the Empire, hereditary rivals. As in the affair of Valtellina (1624–6), he aimed to free the Catholic inhabitants of the valley in Lombardy from the domination, encouraged by France, of the Protestant Grisons. But he feared that in so doing he would reinforce an already too genuine Habsburg domination in Italy. Hence his satisfaction at the conclusion of the treaty of Monçon, in March 1626, which restored Catholicism while at the same time prohibiting Spanish troops from entering the valley. Likewise, in the Mantuan war of succession (1627–31), again to protect himself from Habsburg hegemony, he recognized the legitimacy of the French candidate, the Catholic Charles of Nevers, without, however, taking the risk of giving him military aid against the emperor.

For in the meantime, Catholic renewal was taking place in the Empire. The two pillars of this movement were, in Bohemia-Moravia, cardinal Ernest von Harrach (1598–1667), archbishop of Prague from 1623 to 1667, and, in Hungary, Peter Pázmány (1570–1637), bishop of Gran (now Esztergom) and Hungarian primate from 1616 to 1637; Pier Luigi Caraffa, nuncio to Cologne from 1624 to 1634, was working in the same direction in Germany. Urban had to restrain the enthusiasm of the emperor Ferdinand II, who wanted to use the Edict of Restitution (1629) to give back to the Church those possessions secularized in the preceding century, at the time of the Reformation. With France not lagging in this area, the pope was able to celebrate the fall of La Rochelle in 1628, seeing it as the beginning of the final defeat of Protestantism, although he had refused to help Richelieu when the city was besieged. He was also able to give papal recognition to new French religious congregations working for the Counter Reformation, such as the Visitandines and the Lazarists (1632). In the same spirit, he supported Catholics who were being persecuted in Scotland and England.

The pope's balancing act became more difficult to maintain from February 1635, when Richelieu, a cardinal of the Church, decided to bring France into the war on the side of the German and Swedish Protestants. Urban then opted for a neutrality that condemned him to helplessness, caught as he was between the Spanish, who were calling for the excommunication of Louis XIII, and Richelieu, who brandished the threat of a Gallican schism. In 1635, however, Urban led intensive diplomatic activity by regularly renewing his appeals to bring the Catholic princes to the conference table. His efforts ended on the eve of his death, when talks began at Münster in April 1644.

The only dividends of this policy were the following: Urban VIII succeeded in keeping Italy out of the conflict, as well as the Papal States, several cities of which (Loreto, Ancona, Senigallia, Pesaro, Rimini, Civitavecchia) he had fortified. He converted the Castel Sant'Angelo into a citadel, and ringed the Vatican with a high wall. In this Italian climate of peace, in 1625–31, without striking a blow he annexed the duchy of Urbino and its dependencies: this allowed him to unite the Papal States by linking the Marches to the Romagna. By contrast, his attempt in 1641–4 to use force to strip the Farnese of their duchy of Castro, under the pretext of a matter of debts, proved a crushing failure. By the time of Urban's death the Papal States were left drained, while the Barberini had to flee to France to escape the exceptionally diligent investigation by Innocent X of their financial practices.

In his governance of the Church, Urban VIII paid particular attention, as with the inner mission of Catholic reconquest in Europe, to distant missions. He gave momentum to the Congregation of Propaganda Fide, created by Gregory XV in 1622, providing it with a multilingual printing facility, building it a palace (begun in 1642), and setting up next to it the Urbaniana College, which he founded in 1627 to welcome young Orientals to Rome. The Congregation proved an effective tool in the service of Roman centralization, while missions grew or were reinforced in China (where there began a controversy over rites) and in Japan, the Moluccas, India, Ethiopia, Egypt, Syria, Lebanon, and Constantinople. In these last regions of the East—as in Eastern Europe, where the Brest accords of 1596 had been called into question in 1620—several attempts at a union of the Churches had only temporary success.

The centralizing tendencies of Urban's papal absolutism appear also in the decrees of 1625 and the brief of

1634, prohibiting public worship of persons not beatified by the Holy See and defining a strict, universal procedure for the processes of beatification and canonization. This procedure remained virtually unchanged up to 1983. Urban himself celebrated only two canonizations, those of Elizabeth of Portugal in 1626 and Andrea Corsini in 1629, but he did beatify several venerable souls, among them Maria Maddelena de' Pazzi in 1626.

Finally, Urban's absolutism extended to culture. In 1633 he left his old friend Galileo in the hands of the cardinal-nephew, the new prefect of the Holy Office and a onetime disciple of the scholar at the Academy dei Lincei. Accused by the Roman Jesuits of having, in his *Dialogue on the Two Great Systems of the World* (1632), broken the 1616 interdiction against defending Copernican theses, Galileo was forced by the Holy Office, under threat of torture, to abjure the theses and live under supervision in Rome and later in Arcetri, where he died without the sentence having been lifted by the pope.

In 1642, other Jesuits denounced to the Holy Office the *Augustinus*, a posthumous work by Jansenius, bishop of Ypres, which had appeared the preceding year. This work contravened an interdiction of 1611, repeated in 1625, not to publish anything on the subject of grace, and in addition, took up some arguments of Michael Baius, which had been condemned in 1567. Urban condemned and proscribed the work with the bull *In eminenti*, signed 6 March 1642 but not published until January 1643 (and which therefore was for a fairly long time taken for a fake, both in Louvain and Paris). Jansenius's followers, in particular Antoine Arnauld, took advantage of the lapse of time to organize a defense of the book and launch the Jansenist controversy, which had barely begun at the pontiff's death.

In spite of everything, Urban VIII, who was highly literate and a polyglot (he knew Latin, Greek, and Hebrew), proved a generous and shrewd benefactor of the arts who was able to use art in the service of the Counter Reformation. In 1617, on his return to Rome while he was still only a cardinal, he began to surround himself with painters, composers, writers, and scholars like Holstenius (1596–1661), his librarian, Gabriel Naud (1600–53), and Jean-Jacques Bouchard (1606–44). He himself wrote poetry (*Poemata*, 1620), created one of the richest libraries in Rome, and founded the Barberini chapel in the church of S. Andrea della Valle. As pope, he had Campanella freed (1629) from prison, welcoming him and helping him escape to France when the Inquisition again threatened him in 1634. He reformed the breviary (1631) and the missal (1634), regulated sacred music, and himself composed certain liturgical hymns.

His stroke of genius was to call on Bernini (1598–1680) to complete the new St. Peter's basilica, which he consecrated on 18 November 1626. Undertaken for the 1625 Jubilee Year, Bernini's baldachin with its twisted columns, a monumental reaffirmation of the eucharistic dogmas of the Council of Trent, was completed in 1633. The tomb of Countess Matilda, a legendary defender of the Papal States and the temporal power of the popes, was completed in 1635; the Chair of St. Peter, the foundation of the papacy's spiritual power, which had still not found its final place in the basilica, in 1636; the four loggias that surround the choir and invite the worship of the basilica's four principal relics in 1640; and the two campaniles of the facade (which then had to be destroyed) in 1642. Bernini also built Urban and his family the church of Sta. Bibiana (1624–6), the Triton fountain (1642–3), and that of the Bees (1644), the palace of Propaganda, and the Barberini palace (1629–32). The latter two buildings were collaborations with Borromini (1599–1667), who at the same time designed the church of S. Carlo alle Quattro Fontane (1634–46) and drew the plans for that of S. Ivo alla Sapienza in the shape of a bee, the Barberini arms. Urban VIII also used the talents of Carlo Maderno (1559–1629), who had just finished building St. Peter's, to erect his palace of Castel Gandolfo, as well as those of Pietro da Cortona (1596–1669). He commissioned a large number of foreign painters who came to Rome to study the triumphant baroque, among them Van Dyck (up to 1627), Poussin (from 1625), Velasquez (from 1629 to 1631), and Claude Lorrain. It is in the tomb that he commissioned in 1628 from Bernini (not completed until 1647) that Urban VIII rests in St. Peter's.

The news of his death, in July 1644, after a reign of almost twenty years—one of the longest in history—gave rise to riotous public rejoicing. The Romans did not forgive him the harsh fiscal oppression due to his refusal to allow grain from Castro to be imported to Rome, dubbing him forever the "salt tax pope":

Han' fatto più danno
Urbano e nepoti
che Vandali e Gothi
a Roma mia bella
o Papa gabella.

Christian Renoux

Bibliography

Barberini, M. *Poemata*, Paris, 1620 (Naples, 1624; Rome, 1631, etc.); *Decreta et ordo conficiendi processus in causis beatificationis et canonizationitis sanctorum S.D.N. Urbani PP. VIII. iussu editus*, Rome, 1642.

Bullarum Romanum, Rome, 1868, XIII, XIV and XV.

Ciasca, R. "Urbano VIII," *Storia dei Papi da San Pietro a Giovanni XXIII*, Milan, 1966, 4, 221–68.

Gregorovius, F. *Urban VIII im Widerspruch zu Spanien*, Stuttgart, 1879; *Urbano VIII e la sua opposizione alla Spagna e all'Imperatore*, Rome, 1879.

Grisar, J. "Päpstliche Finanzen, Nepotismus und Kirchenrecht unter Urban VIII.," *Xenia Piana*, Rome, 1943, 207–366.

Kirwin, W. C. *Power Matchless: The Pontificate of Urban VIII, the Baldachin, and Gian Lorenzo Bernini*, New York, 1977.

Kraus, A. *Das päpstliche Staatssekretariat unter Urban VIII. 1623–1644*, Freiburg, 1964; "Der Kardinal-Nepote Francesco Barberini und das Staatssekretariat Urbans VIII," *Römische Quartalschrift für christliche Altertumskunde und Kirchengeschichte*, 64 (1969), 191–208.

Laurain-Portemer, M. "La surintendance de l'État ecclésiastique," *Bibliothèque de l'École des chartes*, CXXXI (1973), 487–568.

Lavin, M. *Seventeenth-century Barberini Documents and Inventories of Art*, New York, 1975.

Leman, A. *Urbain VIII et la rivalité de la France et de la Maison d'Autriche de 1631 à 1635*, Lille, 1919.

Leman, A. *Recueil des instructions générales aux nonces ordinaires de France de 1624 à 1634*, Lille, 1920.

Magnanimi, G. *Palazzo Barberini*, Rome, 1983.

Moroni, G. "Urbano VIII," *Dizionario di erudizione storico-ecclesiastica*, 76 (1857), 41–73.

Nicoletti, A. *Della vita di Papa Urbano VIII*, MS., Vatican Library, Barb. lat. 4730–9.

Nussdorfer, L. *Civic Politics in the Rome of Urban VIII*, Princeton, 1992.

Pecchial, P. "I Barberini," *Archivi*, 5 (1959).

Pollak, O. *Die Kunsttätigkeit unter Urban VIII*, Vienna, 1927.

Prodi, P. *The Papal Prince*, New York, 1987.

Quazza, R. *La guerra per la successione di Mantova e del Monferrato*, Mantua, 1926.

Redondi, P. *Galilée hérétique* (Fr. trans.), Paris, 1985.

Repgen, K. *Die Römische Kurie und der Wesfälische Friede*, Tübingen, 1962–5.

Rice, L. *The Altars and Altarpieces of New St. Peter's: Outfitting the Basilica, 1621–1666*, New York, 1997.

Scott, J. B. *Images of Nepotism. The Painted Ceilings of Palazzo Barberini*, Princeton, 1991.

Simonin, É. *Sylvae urbinianae, seu Gesta Urbani VIII*, Anvers, 1657.

Strozzi, C. *Discorso della familia Barberinia*, Rome, 1640.

Ubaldini, F. *Vita d'Urbano VIII*, MS., Vatican Library, Barb. lat. 4901.

Von Pastor, L. *Geschichte der Päpste*, Freiburg, 1028, XIII, 225–980; *Storia dei Papi*, Rome, 1931, XIII, 227–1061.

Weech, W. N. *Urban VIII*, London, 1905.

Wright, A. D. *The Early Modern Papacy: From the Council of Trent to the French Revolution, 1564–1789*, New York, 2000.

URBANISM. See Monumentality and Roman Urbanism (1848–1922).

[URSINUS]. *(September 366–November 367; d. ca. 385).*

Ursinus's story can be understood only in light of the divisions in the Roman Church during Liberius's papacy and the nomination at that time of another pope, Felix, who died before his rival. We know this story from three different sources: the histories of Ammianus Marcellinus, written at a critical distance from the quarrels of the Church; the Liber pontificalis, Jerome, and the historian Rufinus, all hostile to this pope; and finally, a dossier compiled by Ursinus's supporters and published in the Collectio Avellana. Provided one overlooks its exaggerations, it is this last document that seems closest to the truth.

A deacon of the Roman Church, Ursinus was elected bishop and consecrated in the Julian basilica in Trastevere 24 September 366, the day of Liberius's death. Whatever his rivals may have said, this seems to have occurred before the election, in the basilica of St. Lawrence in Lucina, of another bishop, Damasus, a candidate of the aristocracy (and presumably also of Felix's former supporters). The resultant conflict was settled both by force and by law. Damasus soon persuaded the authorities to send Ursinus into exile, and, thanks to his ability to mobilize tough henchmen, he also defeated his rival's priests. The attack on the Liberian basilica of 26 October 366, according to the sources, left between 137 and 160 of Ursinus's adherents dead. Still, the affair was not resolved. Damasus was accused of excessively currying favor with the great, and an uncompromising minority rose up against him, violently opposed to the evolution of the Church that Damasus's election consecrated.

The conflict resumed in earnest the next year with the short-lived return of Ursinus (15 September 367), followed, two months later, by another exile in Gaul and then by the banishment of his clergy and the handing over of the Liberian basilica to Damasus (12 January 368). This, however, did not prevent Ursinus's supporters from meeting with laymen—*sine clericis*—in the cemeteries, and in particular in the church of St. Agnes, where Damasus again sent in his henchmen. New administrative measures had to be taken against the Ursinians over the following years. Now cut off from suburbicarian Rome, they acted behind the scenes (one suspects them of having a hand in Isaac's accusation—of adultery?—against Damasus), although they still continued to plead their case at court. As late as 381, the fathers of the council of Aquileia were writing to the emperors to forestall a change of policy, asking them to expel from Rome the eunuch Pascasius, one of Ursinus's agents. This is the last mention of his name.

Thus Ursinus must have been an indomitable adversary throughout—or almost throughout his rival's long pontificate (Damasus died in 384). That may be why in his poems Damasus so warmly evokes his predecessors Eusebius and Marcellus, both of whom had to face stubborn competitors—not to mention Hippolytus, whose final reconciliation with his bishop he celebrated in writing (see epigrams 18, 35, and 40 in the edition by A. Ferrua).

Jean Guyon

Bibliography

Collectio Avellana, I., passim, CSEL, 35.

Duchesne, L. *Histoire ancienne de l'Église*, II, Paris, 1908, 455–8.

Duchesne, L., ed. *Liber pontificalis*, I, Paris, 1886, 202.

Jerome, *Chronique*, 366, *CB,* 24, 244.

Marcellinus, A. *Rer. Gest.*, XXVII, 3.

Pietri, C. *Roma christiana*, I, Rome, 1976, 408–18.

Rufinus, *Hist. Eccl.*, II, 10, *PL*, 21, 521.

V

VALENTINE. *(Rome, ?–September 827).*

Elected pope in August 827. We cannot be precise about Valentine's pontificate, which lasted only forty days. Valentine succeeded EUGENE II after a vacancy of the pontifical throne of which the duration is not known. We do know that his father was one Leonzio and that his family lived in the regio via Lata, also the home of the families of popes STEPHEN II, PAUL I (Stephen's brother), and HADRIAN I. This area was the aristocratic quarter of the Rome of that time. Valentine's biographers insist on his goodness, his prudent words, his understanding of others, and his simple, profound faith.

Valentine's actual ecclesiastical career started under PASCAL I, when *perfectae initium sumpsisset aetatis*, that is, when he reached the age of twenty-five. His rise was swift. Appointed subdeacon, he won the trust of the pope, who rapidly elevated him to the deaconate and then the archdeaconate. The *Liber pontificalis* adds the interesting detail that the latter promotion was essentially due to the fact that Valentine could be considered an accessible interlocutor, within the clergy, both for the people and for the *inclitus coetus* of the nobles. Given the problems that Pascal I, in particular, faced with regard to the Roman aristocracy, this well-born young deacon must have been a valuable connection. Following a custom of which we find traces from the first half of the 8th century, this personal connection was reinforced by the granting of *beneficia*, or the benefices of landholdings from the Patrimony of the Church, which was a special favor. The election of Eugene II seems to have confirmed Valentine's privileged position, for he was held in fatherlike affection by the pope.

Valentine's biography concludes with his election, uninterestingly as it happens, since this follows the usual pattern. The Romans receive the sign of his name by divine intervention, and the newly elected pope tries to refuse, but eventually accepts, an honor he had not sought. Finally, the joyous procession of the people and the *utriusque militiae* (clergy and nobles) bring him to the Lateran and, a few days later, to the Vatican for the *consecratio*.

Federico Marazzi

Bibliography

LP, 2, 71–2.

Arnaldi, G. "Rinascita, fine, reincarnazione e successive metamorfosi del Senato romano (secoli V–XII)," *ASR*, 105 (1982), 5–56.

Krautheimer, R. *Rome. Profile of a City, 312–1308*, Princeton, 1980 (on the regio via Lata).

VATICAN I (ECUMENICAL COUNCIL OF). The plan for an ecumenical council of the whole Church, the first to be convened since Trent, germinated quite early on in the mind of PIUS IX (1846–78), who announced it, albeit in a confidential way, only to the cardinals attending a session of the Congregation of Rites, on 6 December 1864, that is, two days before the promulgation of the SYLLABUS. In early 1865, the pope launched a series of consultations with a certain number of bishops of the Latin rite (including nine Frenchmen) on precise points of ecclesiastical discipline. On 28 June 1867, vigil of the feast of Sts. Peter and Paul, Pius solemnly proclaimed his intention to hold a general assembly of the entire Church. That year, the feast was celebrated in Rome in the presence of a crowd of bishops and marked by the canonization of certain figures who were put forward as models of Christian life and who served as so many spiritual presences sustaining the huge enterprise.

These Roman solemnities afforded the prelates who had made the journey the opportunity to give the pontiff their replies to a questionnaire concerning the state of the Church, which had been distributed on their arrival. These observations (*animadversiones*) were striking in their precision and general attitude—a resolutely practical one, even as an unmistakable trend, toward the internationalizing of problems relating to Christianity, to the detriment of national concerns and local needs, was becoming evident.

Impelled by the French Revolution and the spirit of the Enlightenment, with its crusade against "fanaticism" and intolerant obscurantism, an entirely new picture had developed, usually by fits and starts, of the situation of the Roman Catholic Church in Europe. Aside from the restoration of the hierarchy in England and the Netherlands, and the hope arising from the Oxford Movement and its possible repercussions in the German-speaking countries, the decline of clerical privileges was a common concern. In one country after another, the bishops found themselves subject to "heretical or unbelieving" rulers, according to the words used by Cardinal De Luca in 1866.

Some bishops also worried about the peculiar situation of the Church of France. This was governed by Napoleon's Organic Articles of 1802, which were undermining the provisions—actually mutually binding—laid down in the Concordat of 1801. The quasi-discretionary power given to the bishops was barely tolerated by the lower clergy. Always suspected of Richerism, its members soon took refuge in an often ardent Ultramontanism which, although it had been initiated by F. R. de Lamennais, the Holy See was reluctant to encourage openly for fear of directly confronting the secular governments concerned. In a general way, the attitude of "benevolent neutrality" (R. Aubert) characteristic of the Second Empire favored the success of Ultramontane movements. These were most evident in the victorious campaign waged by Dom Guéranger, abbot of Solesmes, in favor of a return to the Roman liturgy, and in the "Romanizing" evolution of the Society of St.-Sulpice, a training ground for a large part of the French clergy.

The idea of papal primacy (the term "infallibility" was not yet used) had experienced a revival some years earlier in milieus linked to the Roman Curia and the Gregorian University, and had been spread abroad and amplified by *Civiltà Cattolica*, which was run by members of the Society of Jesus. In 1854 the proclamation of the dogma of the Immaculate Conception had affirmed the pope's personal authority, as opposed to the "spirit of conciliarity" (J. Gadille) of an institution—the council—that had fallen into disuse after three centuries of inactivity. Practices observed in this period of the Holy See's international and diplomatic activities showed signs of centralization, which was employed as a technique for concentrating power as well as for designating the places where decisions were reached. Examples were the imposing on bishops of AD LIMINA visits and the plenipotentiary nature of the tasks given to the nunciatures, charged with ensuring respect, in both spirit and letter, of a specifically and exclusively Roman canon law. Some would even call for the law to be codified.

Most of the prelates consulted in the preconciliar phase took cognizance of this development, although they expressed some reservations. Bishop Pecci of Perugia, the future LEO XIII (1878–1903), suggested three essential points that needed to be examined by the council fathers: the defense of the purity of the Catholic faith, consolidation of the peace and unity of the Church, and reform of discipline and morals. In fact, the bull of indiction (*Aeterni Patris*), promulgated 29 June 1868 by Pius IX, set as a priority the solemn affirmation of the truth against the errors of the time (rationalism and naturalism, already stigmatized in the Syllabus) and the actualization, adapted to the new times, of the legislation inherited from Tridentine reform. The council itself was convoked for 8 December 1869.

Invitations to take part in the work of the council were sent to large numbers of prelates, including the dignitaries of the Orthodox churches, who did not follow them up. At this time Protestants were also asked to examine if they were not in error. Some Catholic bishops were unable to attend. The Polish hierarchy, in particular, victim of the uprising of 1863 and the deportation of more than four hundred ecclesiastics, was forbidden to travel to Rome by order of the government. In all, the council managed to assemble some seven hundred bishops, or roughly two-thirds of those entitled to attend. Most came from Europe (35 percent Italians, 17 percent French, together with seventy-five bishops from Germany and Austria), complemented by about sixty prelates representing Eastern Catholic Churches and 200 members from outside Europe (121 came from North America, but only nine from Africa, none of them indigenous).

Europe, more particularly the Latin countries, being politically dominant, provided the Holy See with a point of reference that was in some way cognate with the institution of the Church. Moreover, this geographical restriction could not but accentuate the impression of a council convened by Rome to deal with concerns that were, if not strictly those of the Vatican, then at least solely European. This was the basis for the disappointment later expressed by the Orientals who attended (but took such a minor part in) Vatican I.

Similar observations could be made on the makeup of the commissions set up to carry out the council's work. The eighteen months that followed the promulgation of the bull *Aeterni Patris* were devoted to the general preparation of the council. A committee of cardinals, created in March 1865, soon decided to distribute the tasks among five specialized commissions—a commission on politico-ecclesiastical relations, one on matters of faith (dogmatic theology), one on discipline, one on religious orders, and one on the Eastern churches and missions—assisted by the commission on rites or liturgy.

The first consultors to be appointed (sixty), all theologians or canonists resident in Rome, were joined, little by little and in highly controlled fashion, by foreigners who had been contacted by the leading European nunciatures, the choice falling on individuals not suspected of liberalism. J. H. Newman declined the invitation ostensibly for reasons of health. Among the criticisms heard at the time, those articulated with spirit by the renowned Munich professor Johann Döllinger drew most attention. He feared that the bias in this form of recruitment would impose a sifting *sub secreto*, as a result of which only the Curia's point of view would prevail. *Civiltà Cattolica* had published a text, at once provocative and indicative of the predominant thinking, on 6 February 1869, which suggested that a definition of papal infallibility would come by direct acclamation, removing all possibility of the fathers' debating it or softening its tone. In reaction to that article, Döllinger, under the eloquent pseudonym Janus, published a cutting lampoon against the authority of the pope. Certain French bishops, including Msgr. Maret, dean of the faculty of theology of Paris, Msgr. Darboy, archbishop of Paris, and Msgr. Dupanloup, the well-known bishop of Orléans, did not disguise their uneasiness. Thus the debate on infallibility, which had not been included in the council's initial program, found itself propelled to the forefront of the Church's preoccupations.

After a year of inactivity, the general commission reconvened on 22 November 1868. A consultor was the council historian Hefele, professor at the University of Tübingen, who saved precious time by settling several technical questions (such as matters of precedence and procedure) that had impeded the smooth working of almost all previous councils. With the bull *Inter multiplices*, dated 27 November 1869, Pius IX approved this regulation of the council. Retaining the suggestions of the cardinalitial commission as well, the pontiff had agreed to an extraordinary Jubilee that would open on 1 June 1868 and would embrace all the council sessions. At the same time, among other supplicatory measures, a novena was decreed in all the churches of Rome. On 8 December, the blessed Sacrament was exposed in St. Peter's basilica and the fathers, assembled in the transept, awaited the entrance of the pope, borne on the *sedia gestatoria*. After the Mass, which was celebrated by the cardinal-dean of the Sacred College and left a lasting impression on those present, approval of the decrees opening the council was voted by acclamation. Work could now begin.

The liturgical unanimity, if one may use that expression, achieved at the moment of the chanting of the *Veni Creator* at the opening ceremony did not prevent the rapid resurgence of controversy over infallibility. The latter was supported by a majority motivated by sometimes widely diverse considerations, who nevertheless agreed on the principle of a definition of papal authority. Its force, in the

view of some, would avoid disastrous tendencies for the Church, such as a loss of power in countries undermined by democratic principles. A minority of bishops maintained, on the other hand, that a Church presenting an autocratic appearance would seem forbidding, particularly with regard to a possible development of relations between the Catholic faithful and members of the other Christian confessions. This group, called simply the "minority," was led by the Austrian cardinal Rausscher, a determined opponent of Josephinism and a recognized specialist in patrology. It included in its ranks a sizable fraction of the French episcopate, including the archbishop of Paris, as well as the archbishop of Milan and several American prelates. Among these were Kennick, archbishop of St. Louis, whom Dom Cuthbert Butler recognized as "the most aggressive enemy of infallibility."

At the first general congregation, held on 10 December, the cardinal-president, De Luca, announced the creation of a central commission of twenty-six members under the presidency of the pope, who had decided on the immediate examination of questions of dogma. These were actually fairly uncontroversial, in the sense that they were a refutation of the errors of rationalism and modern philosophical-political doctrines. However, it was noted that the fathers gave a largely unfavorable reception to the schema *De Doctrina catholica*, which consisted of eighteen chapters. Cardinal Rausscher regretted that the fathers were handed "theological theses, an outline for the use of professors," while Msgr. Strossmayer, bishop of Dakovo in Bosnia and the "*enfant terrible* of the council" (H. Rondet), objected to the opening lines of the *schema*, which, under the formula *Pius servus servorum Dei, sacro approbante Concilio*, insisted overmuch, in his view, on papal primacy.

The detailed drafts (*schemata*) of the decrees, printed out and distributed to the council fathers, were, according to procedure, discussed within the framework of the "deputations" (specialized commissions) and then debated in general congregation, commented on—in Latin, exclusively—by the orators, in strict order of rank. These interventions, which were not at first recorded, were soon brought into order, after several fathers had voiced criticism of the general confusion of the discussions and the lack of interest of certain speeches. For instance, on 19 January 1870, Msgr. Darboy could affirm that for forty days the fathers had devoted their time to questions "without order or connection," for lack of even the most general work plan for the council. An addition to the conciliar regulations, promulgated on 22 February, simplified procedure by forcing the fathers to put their observations in writing and giving them strict time limits.

The results of this reform were not noticeable until much later. In the meantime, in fact, a collective petition signed by 450 fathers of the group known then by the somewhat restrictive label "majority" requested that the pope include the question of pontifical infallibility in the order of the day of the council, which would introduce it into the discussion of the *schema* on the Church handed out to the fathers on 21 January 1870. The "minority" attempted to put forward an opposing manifesto, managing to collect 136 signatures (29 January). After a discussion in the commission, the fathers' desiderata were transmitted to Pius IX, who gave his approval on 1 March through the intermediary of the council secretary, Msgr. Fessler, an Austrian (actually the only non-Italian nominated to a responsible position). The news alarmed a number of governments. The French statesman Émile Ollivier curbed extraconciliar agitation by allaying the fears of Count Daru, Napoleon III's minister of religion.

This new first plan for updating the council continued to arouse passionate reactions among many whose lack of accurate information fed rumors that were always uncontrolled and sometimes concocted. It was decided that the passage on infallibility that was the subject of so much attention would be inserted at the end of chapter XI of the *schema De Ecclesia*, devoted to the primacy of the Roman pontiff. The airing of the controversy gave the minority a margin for maneuver. It now organized around Dupanloup and an English lay Catholic who had the support of many international personalities, Lord Acton. This fussy phase of "salon agitation" (R. Aubert) on the part of the chanceries and the press came just after that held in the council *aula* (hall). During the month of March 1870, new demands were circulated by the majority requesting that chapter XI be studied immediately after the adoption of the constitution *Dei Filius*, which received solemn approval on 12 April and was promulgated on the 24th of that month. One of the cornerstones of Catholic theology, this had no equivalent, since the decisions of the Council of Trent, in its aloofness from rationalism and pantheism as well as from traditionalism and fideism.

In the interests of efficiency and perhaps exasperated by the reticence of the minority, Pius IX approved the idea of an early general debate on the question of infallibility, which opened on 13 May. The discussion very soon centered on the opportuneness of such a definition. Its recognition required no fewer than fifteen sessions of strenuous, painstaking work, the minority demanding at least the affirmation of episcopal dignity. Fifty-seven speeches, of uneven quality, were counted on the subject. Under the dual pressure of corridor dealings between the attending groups and the stifling Roman summer heat, many fathers, particularly the Italians, insisted that the council quickly reach agreement on a compromise formula. This would, in the view of the supporters of this late-constituted "third way," have the important advantage of avoiding a public display of the dissensions of the Church on a question that was unanimously recognized as essential.

Pius IX's intransigence no doubt crystalized opposition, despite the negotiators' last-minute efforts to rally all the members of the council. Some sixty council fathers, including the three Melchite, Syriac, and Chaldean patriarchs, who were already objecting to the exaggerated trend toward the Latinization of the Church and noting the obvious neglect on the part of most of the European fathers with regard to the East, preferred to leave the council rather than vote no. On 13 July, the vote on the constitution as a whole counted 451 *placet*, 88 *non placet*, and 66 approvals with reservations (*placet juxta modum*), out of a total of 601 ballots. Definitive approval, which called for only a "yes" or "no" vote, was obtained on 18 July 1870, by 533 votes against two. A precise formula was adopted for the future, according to which "the pope's definitions, when he speaks ex cathedra, that is, when he . . . defines a doctrine regarding faith or morals, are irreformable of themselves, and not from the consent of the Church."

The promulgation of this constitution, entitled *Pastor Aeternus*, was the most striking document of an ecumenical council that left pending fifty-one *schemata* relating to such questions as the life of the clergy and the religious, the catechism, and eligibility for ordination. It took place during a violent storm which some commentators saw as evidence of divine disapproval, while others likened it to the *tremendum* that had accompanied the giving of the Law to Moses on Mount Sinai.

After that the council pursued its work at a slower pace, troubled by the declaration of war between France and Germany on 19 July, which relegated to the background the question of the reception of the conciliar constitutions. Only Döllinger showed an immediate, and particularly violent, reaction, leading away some of his friends—despite personal reservations—toward the schism of the so-called Old Catholics.

The entrance of Italian troops into Rome on 20 September, followed by the plebiscite linking the Papal States to the kingdom of Italy (9 October), put an end to the council. It was officially adjourned *sine die* by Pius IX in a letter dated 20 October, when many of the fathers had already gone home.

Although unfinished, the First Vatican Council, with its more than eighty-nine ordinary sessions and four public sessions, gave the papacy the spiritual weapons that Pius IX's successors would use as they attempted to counterbalance the loss of the Church's temporal sovereignty, accentuating the Holy See's identification with the Church Universal. This council, held in a period of contraction and concentration of the ecclesial institution around the papacy in the face of external and internal dangers, also bequeathed to the future the outlines of debates which, less than a century later, would preoccupy participants in the Second Vatican Council. Thus the council was, somewhat paradoxically, without roots yet putting forth branches.

Philippe Levillain

Bibliography

Aubert, R., Guéret, M., and Tombeur, P. *Concilium Vaticanum I: Concordance, Index, Listes de fréquence, Tables comparatives*, Louvain, 1977.

Bellone, B. *I Vescovi dello Stato Pontificio al Concilio Vaticano I*, Rome, 1966.

Butler, C. *The Vatican Council*, 2 vols., London-New York, 1930.

Cecconi, E. *Storia del Concilio Vaticano*, 4 vols., Florence, 1873–9.

Collectio Lacensis. Acta et decreta sanctum concilorium recentiorum, VII (ed. T. Granderath, Freiburg-im-Breisgau, 1890).

Colombo, C. "La Chiesa e la società civile nel Concilio Vaticano I," *La Scuola Cattolica*, 89 (1961), 323–43.

Conzemius, V. *Katholicismus ohne Rom. Die altkatholische Kirchengemeinschaft*, Zurich, 1969.

Conzemius, V. "Pourquoi l'autorité pontificale a-t-elle été définie précisément en 1870?" *Concilium*, 64 (1971).

Croce, G. M. "Una fonte importante per la stocia del pontificato di Pio IX e del Concilio Vaticano I: I manoscritti inediti di Vincenzo Tizzani," *Archivum Historiae Pontificiae*, XXIV (1986), 273–363.

Feliciani, G. "Il Concilio Vaticano I e la codificazione del diritto canonico." *Studi in onore di U. Gualazzini*, II, Milan, 1982, 35–80.

Gadille, J. "Vatican I, concile incomplet?" *Le Deuxième concile du Vatican*, Actes du colloque de l'École Française de Rome, Rome, 1989, 33–45.

Gomez Heras, J. M. G. *Temas dogmaticos del Concilio Vaticano I*, 2 vols., Vitoria, 1971.

Granderath, T., and Kirch, K. *Geschichte des Vatikanischen Konzils*, 3 vols., Freiburg-im-Breisgau, 1903–6.

Heft, J. L. "From the Pope to the Bishops, Episcopal Authority from Vatican I to Vatican II," *The Papacy*, 1 765 (1983), 55–78.

Kulcsar, P., ed., *Mythographi Vaticani I et II*, Turnhout, 1987.

Maccarone, M. *Il Concilio Vaticano I e il "giornale" di Mons. Arrigoni*, 2 vols., Padua, 1966.

Mansi, J. D. *Sacrorum concilorium nova et amplissima collectio*, 49.53 (ed. P. Petit and J. B. Martin, Arnhem-Leipzig, 1923–5).

Martina, G. "La storiografia italiana sulla chiesa dal Vaticano I al Vaticano II," *Problemi di storia della Chiesa. Dal Vaticano I al Vaticano II*, Rome, 1988, 15–105.

O'Gara, M. *Triumph in Defeat: Infallibility, Vatican I, and the French Minority Bishops*, Washington, 1988.

Ollivier, E. *L'Église et l'État au concile du Vatican*, 2 vols., Paris, 1879.

Pastor, L. "Il Concilio Vaticano I nel diario del card. Capotti," *Archivium Historiae Pontificaiae*, 7 (1969), 401–90.

Petuzzi, P. *Chiesa e società civile al Concilio Vaticano I*, Rome, 1984.

Rondet, H. *Vatican I. Le Concile de Pie IX. La préparation, les méthodes de travail, les schémas restés en suspens*, Paris, 1962.

Thils, G. *Primauté pontificale et prérogatives épiscopales. "Potestas ordinaria" an concile du Vatican*, Louvain, 1961.

Thils, G. *Primauté et infallibilité du Pontife romain à Vatican I et autres études d'ecclésiologie*, Louvain, 1989.

Torelli, J. P. *La Théologie de l'épiscopat au premier concile du Vatican*, Paris, 1961.

Valentini, D. "Il Papato e il Concilio Vaticano I," *Il vescovo di Roma nelle Chiesa universale*, Rome, 1987, 5068.

von Der Horst, F. *Das Schema über die Kirche auf dem I. Katholischen Konzil*, Paderborn, 1963.

VATICAN II (ECUMENICAL COUNCIL OF).

The Second Vatican Council was held in St. Peter's basilica in Rome from 11 October 1962 to 8 December 1965, in four plenary sessions (that is, attended by all the council fathers): (1) from 11 October to 8 December 1962; (2) from 29 September to 4 December 1963; (3) from 15 September to 21 November 1964; and (4) from 14 September to 8 December 1965. These were complemented by other meetings of various types.

Over four years, Vatican II mobilized close to 2,500 council fathers representing the five continents. It produced sixteen conciliar documents voted on by the council fathers and promulgated by the pontiff (see list below). On the twentieth anniversary of its closing an extraordinary synod (24 November–8 December 1985) was convoked by JOHN PAUL II. Since its closing, the council has constituted an ecclesiological reference point in the history of Christianity. It created a crisis in the Church that some claim was predicted by the third secret of Fátima (Portugal), a place of pilgrimage associated with the cult of Mary and later visited in turn by PAUL VI (11–14 May 1967) and John Paul II (12–14 May 1982).

A huge amount has been written about Vatican II. Covered animatedly by the Catholic and non-Catholic media, described on the scene by large numbers of council fathers, experts, and observers, and commented on in later years by the papacy, bishops, theologians, and churches, its essence may be conveyed in one question: Did Vatican II present a closed or an open point of reference for the future? Or, did Vatican II pave the way for a Vatican III, or did it solve the problem of relations between the Church and the world in the second part of the 20th century? The sheer number of council fathers, the presence of non-Catholic churches, the growing interest that public opinion showed in the work of the council, gave rise to a kind of free interpretation that had never before been seen in the Roman Church.

From Vatican I to Vatican II (1870–1962). On 29 October 1870, PIUS IX gave notice of the "suspension" of the First Vatican Council, citing the special circumstances created by the Franco-Prussian War and the capture (20 September 1870) of Rome. A self-styled prisoner in the Vatican (until the Lateran treaty), the pope could not guarantee the assembly "the liberty and tranquillity" indispensable to its debates. By convoking an ecumenical council in 1868 (the first meeting was held 8 December 1869), Pius IX had revived an institution "sunk in lethargy for three hundred years" (Princess Carolyne of Sayn-Wittgenstein to Émile Ollivier, letter of 7 August 1877), that is, since the COUNCIL OF TRENT (1545–63).

Vatican I had lasted eight months. Its task was important, particularly in the domain of examination of the Church of Christ. The insistence of Pius IX on prior debate, in the schema *De Ecclesia Christi*, of chapters IX and XI, which dealt with the infallibility of the Church and the primacy of the pope, and the rewording of chapter XI to accommodate papal infallibility, had led to the sifting out of the question of the jurisdiction of the bishops working together with the pope. In the ecclesiological sense, the First Vatican Council was unfinished. The circumstances of its suspension, the ending of the pontiff's temporal power, the climate of apocalypse in which Pius IX and the Roman Curia lived through this period, the interpretation of infallibility as the affirmation of a spiritual authority superior to any other, all hid from view the modern aspects of the questions the council could have dealt with (on relations between the Church and the states; the training of the clergy; the social mission of the Church; etc.). Instead, the image left was that of a pessimistic council and a reactionary papacy under siege.

Even though, with the Law of Guarantees (May 1871), the unified Italian state ensured the pontiff freedom of movement, the idea of continuing Vatican I did not occur to Pius IX's successors LEO XIII (1878–1903), PIUS X (1903–14), and BENEDICT XV (1914–22): "Everything suggests that these popes, shut up in their palace at the Vatican, believed with all their hearts that the 'iniquitous war' ceaselessly denounced by Leo XIII would one day be over, that 'modern civilization' would repent and find its way back to the Church and that — who knows? — Rome would be returned to the Holy See" (P. Boutry).

The institution of the ecumenical council (twenty councils had been recognized by the Church since that of Nicaea) seemed to have fallen into disuse. Nevertheless, in 1899 (28 May to 9 July), Leo XIII did hold a plenary council of Latin America, at the Latin American College in Rome. And in 1911, again in Rome, an Armenian council took place at which, among other questions, the delicate one of the election of the patriarch was resolved.

Yet these particular councils that the Holy See convoked, far from calling into question the authority of the pope, reaffirmed it. Nonetheless, the 1917 Code of Canon Law (articles 222–9) described the canonical conditions in which an ecumenical council might be held. It was on those articles that John XXIII would base his thinking in convoking the Second Vatican Council on 25 December 1961 (bull *Humanae Salutis*).

When, on 25 January 1959, JOHN XXIII announced to the Sacred College his proposal to hold an ecumenical council, he apparently did not know of the unfinished plans of his two predecessors, Pius XI and Pius XII. It would seems he was only informed of them during 1959. Thanks to the research carried out by Father Caprile, editor of *Civiltà cattolica*, who combed through the archives of the Secretariat of State in the case of Pius XI and through those of the Holy Office in the case of Pius XII (the research was published in 1966), as well as the recollections of certain individuals (e.g., Carlo Cardinal Confalonieri, who was sixty-six in 1959 and had been close to both pontiffs), it was possible to pinpoint the dates and ways of exploring the idea of an ecumenical council between 1922 and 1948.

The Plan of Pius XI. Pius XI (elected 6 February 1922) explicitly mentioned the possibility of convening the whole of the Catholic episcopate in Rome on the occasion of the holy year (1925), in a document preparatory to the encyclical *Ubi Arcano*. When this came out on 23 December 1922, it merely noted the interruption of Vatican I and declared that a sign of the divine will was expected before such a decision could be taken. In April 1923 the pope gave orders that the archives of Vatican I be put in order. In May he entrusted three religious, Fathers Hugon (O.B.), Lépicier (Servites of Mary), and Tacchi Venturi (S.J.), together with a secular priest, Msgr. Bianchi Cagliesei, with the task of "summing up the First Vatican Council and indicating what questions were still in abeyance" (F.C. Uginet).

The material they found (essentially negligible printed matter) turned out to be disappointing. Fathers Hugon and Lépicier apparently sought the advice of various experts and proposed to the pope a list of questions to be examined in council. Subjects concerned with contemporary problems (war; the League of Nations; Catholic Action; religious education of children [catechism]; women's role in modern society) predominated over those regarding the examination of the intimate nature of the Church (in particular, relations between the contents of faith and the Church's mission). A circular letter was drawn up for the use of various experts, but it is not known whether it was sent out. At the same time, in a letter of 22 October 1923, Pius XI solicited the advice of the cardinals, archbishops, and resident bishops as well as prelates and abbots nullius, on the opportuneness of holding a council in 1925. They were asked to reply within six months. In all, 1,165 letters were sent out; 154 were unanswered. This procedure was repeated in 1959 by John XXIII.

The idea of convening a council in the near future was received favorably by nine-tenths of those who replied to Pius XI's letter. The pope seems to have personally studied the rarer (256) suggestions added to the agreement, while the cardinals' responses were minutely analyzed by Father Caprile. The Roman question weighed heavily. But the pope was also informed by Cardinal Ehrle of the small numbers of theologians, especially in Rome, who were familiar with the early theological tradition and versed in both "the positive and speculative functions." "He also deplored the harm caused by champions of 'strict obedience' who, by enforcing pontifical directives on the teaching of Thomist doctrine, considered all those who did not strictly conform to it rebels against the Holy See" (F. C. Uginet).

Pius XI gave up the idea of a council at the beginning of 1924. We cannot tell if his decision was influenced by the many debates aroused by the suggestions and observations made to him as well as by the prospect of an early settlement of the Roman question. The fact is that many questions that would be raised at Vatican II had thus been raised early, however unrepresentative they sometimes were, particularly those regarding tradition within the Church and the pontifical magisterium, or Christian unity. Furthermore, Pius XI, who was authoritarian, may have hesitated at the idea of a Church "Estates General" in the political climate of Italy, where fascism was gradually coming to the fore.

The Plan of Pius XII. At the electoral conclave of 1939, Msgr. Celso Constantini, secretary of the Congregation of Propaganda Fide, wrote a memorandum in which he expressed the wish to see a general council held during the forthcoming pontificate. Was the idea circulated? We cannot know for certain. But it clearly reflected "a current of opinion widely held in the Roman Curia, which was conscious of the lacunae in the Code of Canon Law and the problems in the current administrative style and practice" (F. C. Uginet). On 4 March 1948, Pius XII asked Alfredo Ottaviani, assessor of the Holy Office, about the feasibility of convoking a council. Study of the question was entrusted to a special commission of the Holy Office, which was bound to the strictest secrecy. This consisted of seven members, five of whom were members of religious orders. The first meeting took place 15 March 1948. A central commission was created to coordinate the work of five preconciliar commissions: a theological commission for questions of dogma; a theological commission for questions of practical theology, in two sections, one for moral theology, the other for social teaching; a canonical commission concerned with discipline (and liturgy); a commission on the missions; a commission for culture and Christian action.

Research was then carried out in the archives of Vatican I to make an inventory of the questions that had been held in abeyance at Vatican I. The documents of the Holy Office were also examined for any useful indications regarding contemporary problems, discussion of which might justify a council (F. C. Uginet). In June 1948 the central commission selected (in a provisional manner) thirty-six persons eligible to join the preparatory commissions, according to their abilities but also taking into account geographical balance. But it was agreed that each commission should be headed by a member of the Roman Curia on the central commission, whose work was supervised by the Holy Office.

In February 1949, Pius XII appointed Borgongini Duca (the nuncio to Italy) as president of the central commission and Father Charles (S.J.), professor at Louvain, as secretary. The number of members of that commission grew to eleven (cf. Caprile and Uginet). Six meetings took place between February and July 1949. It was decided to write a letter to some members of the episcopate requesting suggestions, but the Holy Office, in plenary session, voted against this on 6 June 1949, and Pius XII approved that decision on 28 June. From that point, the work of the central commission bogged down, and the differences among its members grew wider.

Suggestions were made for an extremely short council—three or four weeks—"bringing back to the fold the dissidents and infidels of the whole world" (B. Duca), or else one of indeterminate length. Pius XII was by then seventy-five years old. The logistical difficulties of such an assembly (and his role in it) worried him: The cold war was at its height; resistance to communism was his essential concern. In 1950, with the encyclical *Humani Generis*, the pope condemned—without, however mentioning infallibility—theological and liturgical studies (notably French) that proposed new ways of looking at tradition—the *nouvelle théologie* largely of patristic and directly biblical inspiration. In January 1951 he put an end to the work of the central commission.

From Vatican I to Vatican II, there is a thread that runs through the two unfinished projects of Pius XI and Pius XII, namely, that a council in every case constitutes a frightful trial for pontifical authority; the pope must prepare the event either by the vast study of precedent and through the choice of the subject matter to be studied. To this must be added the question of the date and duration of the council. Canonically, it is up to the pope to call the convocation. The beginning of a pontificate (1922, 1939) was ideal. But the moment could awaken the demons of conciliarism. John XXIII was able to escape this thanks to the unexpected character of his initiative, which transformed into a popular act, deserving of respect, a gesture of canonical authority. Paul VI, on the contrary, was confronted by this.

One finds that from Vatican I to Vatican II, the relations between the doctrine of the church, speculative and practical theology, and the contemporary ways of the visibility of the Church remain in force. It concerns the nature of the magisterium which, since the end of the 18th century, is concentrated in the specific powers of the sovereign pontiff but reinforced by Vatican I.

From Vatican I to Vatican II, the problem of the relations among three things—Church doctrine, speculative and practical theology, and the Church's visibility in the modern world—remained posed. The problem lay in the nature of the magisterium, which since the late 18th century had been concentrated in the specific powers of the pontiff, more recently reinforced in Vatican I. In the ten years that separated Pius XII's plan and John XXIII's decision, one sees how "certain men of the council" (P. Rocco Caporale) associated with Pius XII's plan—Msgr. Ottaviani; Father Tromp, S.J.; Father Bea, S.J.; Father Browne, O.S.B., among others—became leaders in furthering John XXIII's undertaking. One sees, also, that the importance of the Holy Office (Msgr. Ottaviani) had been accentuated by Pius XII's plan and by the theological debate that resulted.

Vatican II: A Council Unexpected Yet Desired (1959–62).

John XXIII was elected on 28 October 1958. On 25 January 1959, the anniversary of the conversion of St. Paul, he announced to the Sacred College the launching of three great plans, which seemed disparate and hazardous in view of his age (he was entering his seventy-seventh year). These were the holding of a Roman synod, reform of the 1917 Code of Canon Law, and an ecumenical council. The pope aired the idea of a council to a few people, but his mind was apparently already made up.

In retrospect, one notes that John XXIII had used the word *council* nearly eight hundred times in his previous writings (counting articles published in the *Vita Diocesana* of Bergamo, his birthplace), 15 percent in reference to the Council of Trent and its modalities of application. In so doing, Angelo Roncalli "intended essentially to stress that [the Council of Trent represented a] revitalizing force for the life of the Church, a force that he saw exemplified in Charles Borromeo, the pastor who began the application of the council in his Church and who became the 'model' of the modern Catholic bishop" (G. Alberigo). It is still a fact that the announcement of the pope's plan was received "like a thunderbolt" (P. Rocco Caporale). It went out to a Christianity that in perceptive quarters was disillusioned with the Holy See, the last years (1954–8) of Pius XII's pontificate having been spent in almost complete silence and having ended in spectacular agony (the photographs of the pope on his deathbed). Paradoxically, John XXIII's advanced age gave the forthcoming council increased credibility regarding the future of the Church.

25 January–18 June 1959.

The period from 25 January to 18 June 1959 is the least known in the history of Vatican II, its archives remaining closed to researchers. We know nothing of the researches John XXIII set in motion, as had Pius XI and Pius XII, on the questions left unanswered in September 1870. On 18 June 1959, the day of the Feast of the Sacred Heart, Cardinal Tardini, secretary of state (raised to the cardinalate at the consistory of 15 December 1958), sent a letter to all the cardinals, archbishops, and bishops of the Church of Rome, residential and titular, and to all the superiors general of the religious orders. They were asked to send in their *vota* to the Secretariat of State by 30 October 1959. From this consultation, which John XXIII intended to be "free and spontaneous," terms that were picked up by the media, it was gathered that the program of the council was left to the future council fathers. This was not untrue, since a centrifugal principle is part of the very notion of Catholicity. The pope was breaking with the method of selective consultation employed by Pius IX with the convocation of Vatican I in 1868, and with those of his two predecessors, most notably Pius XII in his vacillation between 1948 and 1951.

But two phenomena of the period 25 January to 17 May 1959 need to be noted. First, John XXIII, though never fixing a program for the council, expressed himself on many occasions as to the spirit in which it should set to work. Two major themes were stressed: it would be a council of union, and it would be a council designed for the Christian people—a pastoral council, that is, devoid of anathemas and geared toward a unity in faith and morals.

On 17 May 1959, John XXIII appointed an "antepreparatory" commission. The secretary of state was made president. Ten prelates representing the dicasteries were named to work with him, not only to collect the *vota* that would be solicited on 18 June, but also to make suggestions as to the various agencies needed to prepare for the council itself. Thus it was that the Curia was given a central position, whose importance would become clear over time. This happened unnoticed. The designated prelates held all the official posts, as secretaries or pro-secretaries. They were younger than the presidents of the dicasteries to which they belonged. Most of them were later given the cardinal's hat. John XXIII was thus creating a conciliar Curia within the Curia, caught between obedience to the views of the pontiff and the vigilance of their hierarchical superiors. The council was thus centralized before it was decentralized.

The Antepreparatory Phase (18 June 1959–30 May 1960).

From 18 June 1959 this conciliar policy seemed to be more conciliarist than Roman. The image it suggested was a complex one. Even the pope's democratic type of consultation did not make fully manifest his subtle purpose. Yet by his behavior John XXIII gave out all the signs making clear the ideas set forth in his speeches, which were probably (as always) little read. In his warm relations with couples, children, old people, and communities; in his public audiences; and in his "sociological" interest in the Christian people, seen in his words at the Sunday Angelus and during his parochial visits, people saw an engaging, friendly pope. This was a sort of exemplum of the pastoral mission that it would fall to the council to elaborate and announce to the world. Such an attitude was in complete contrast, characteristic by characteristic, with the hierarchism of the shy patrician Pius XII. The daily life of this pontiff engendered a pious attitude toward "Good Pope John" that set the tone, albeit still a faint one, of a purely personal sanctity. The spontaneity asked for in Cardinal Tardini's letter of 18 June 1959 was thereby evinced; it set a papal model for "democracy."

The term *aggiornamento* served to link a principle of centralized organization, a programmatic deconcentration with uncertain results, and a new pontifical style. This was a far cry from the memory of a pastor-pope such as Pius IX had been before his monarchical image, unyielding in the face of the loss of the Papal States, had been imposed. The meaning of *aggiornamento* was not precise. It was far from mere inspirational fervor, and constituted a subtle amalgamation of the terms "reform" and "self-criticism," which in Catholicism were unusable. It gave the Church a way in which it could reflect on itself. It suggested a council that would not be directed against anyone, because it would challenge the Church itself to distinguish within its tradition the fundamental from the transistory and the culturally conditioned.

The word caught on. First of all, it made it possible to gradually dispel the initial mistrust of the Protestant and Orthodox churches. The principle of a council of union had, for most non-Catholic churches, suggested a trap. They feared the consecration of the monarchical primacy of the pope, the impossibility of participation as equals. They had doubts about a plan with as yet no program, and to which from February 1959 the Protestant churches opposed a radically different ecclesiology, which excluded neither sympathy toward the plan nor encouragement of its purpose, given that this was a Roman Catholic council. Behind the goal of unity, they feared unification. When analyzed by them closely, John XXIII's allocution of 25 January 1959, which was published officially in the *Acta Apostolicae Sedis* of 27 February 1959, seemed to the clergy of the separated communities to stress the idea of "following" the papal initiative.

In a certain sense, the success of the council depended on the replies of those solicited through Cardinal Tardini's letter. There was no better way of setting up an interpersonal link between the Holy See and the future council fathers, each of whom was free to seek advice. The timing turned out to be good. The deadline (30 Octo-

ber) was met. The proportion of replies was staggering: 1,998 *vota* were sent to Rome within the stated time, representing over 77 percent of the persons concerned. Some *vota* continued to flow in after 30 October, reaching a figure of 2,900. The "plebiscitary character" of the result was emphasized by the secretary of the antepreparatory commission, Msgr. Felici, the future secretary of Vatican II.

No systematic study of the desiderata expressed by the episcopate has ever been made. However, in light of certain partial analyses, one can tell that John XXIII's complex proposals were answered by an ideological approach to social reality, one that it would behoove the council to take into account from a pastoral perspective. Clearly, a council that condemned was not called for. But errors such as atheism were pointed out; causes for concern, such as the status of the clergy, notably in France, were noted; and hopes were expressed, on the part of the British episcopate in particular, for an emphasis on Church law. These examples show that a good many council fathers leaned toward a normative council, of which the reform of the Code of Canon Law would be an extension. The American episcopate expressed a desire for a consideration of the relations between church and state and the question of religious tolerance. Defense of the Church characterized the interests of those countries where Catholicism was in the minority and where establishing an identity was more difficult in the face of abuses of power. Ecumenism captured little attention. By contrast, many Europeans favored the idea of a repeat of Vatican I on the question of the nature of episcopal jurisdiction as against the primacy of Rome, a question left unanswered in 1870.

What was sent to Rome was like a mirror in tiny pieces, and a limited one at that. The voices of Eastern Europe and the Asian continent were unrepresented. Father Daniel Stiernon pointed this out: "Bulgaria, Lithuania, Romania, Ukraine, not to mention Russia, have not been called upon. On the other hand, Yugoslavia, Latvia . . . and especially Poland . . . have been able to say something. . . . As regards the world of Asia, the spokesmen for China . . . are for the most part exiles who are tasting the delights of communist jails." It would be up to Vatican II to correct these imperfections. But it is clear that the wide variety of requests and their fragmentary nature gave the antepreparatory commission great freedom in directing the commissions that were to handle the preparatory phase. The antepreparatory phase ended on 30 May 1960. The preparatory phase began on 5 June 1960 with the motu proprio *Superno Dei Nutu*. The convocation of the council and the opening date still had to be determined. On 25 December 1961 and 2 February 1962 these tasks were completed.

The Preparatory Phase (14 November 1960–28 June 1962).

This phase was opened by John XXIII in the presence of thirty-three cardinals and several hundred bishops. It served to draw up the program of Vatican II, through preconciliar commissions that had been conceived in June 1959.

The term *commissions* disguised a structure modeled on the organization of the Roman Curia. The results of the consultation in the antepreparatory phase were put into the hands of the Vatican offices. The "democratic" phase was followed by a phase whose organization and technique was monarchical in type. Immediately, this move aroused much criticism. First, it seemed surprising that de-Italianizing the council's objectives, a goal of the antepreparatory consultation, was left to the care of agencies that embodied Rome's predominance in Catholicity. One vigilant observer, Father Congar, remarked, on 3 June 1961, "In Rome, the Church still is under the impression that it is in possession. This being so, it is not surprising that it is hard for a thoroughly Roman prelate to view the de-Christianization and irreligiosity of the contemporary world in as anguished a way as a Frenchman or a German."

It might have been feared that the state of the Church as presented in the eighteen volumes of the collected documents would appear warped by an unrealistic perspective. But the example of Vatican I gave rise to a different apprehension: that of a choice of objectives which would deflect the council from its goal. Dom Olivier Rousseau recalled in this connection the permanent, structural divorce between congregations and councils, particularly at Vatican I: "General and ecumenical councils are regulated in somewhat the opposite way from the [congregations], since they empower those whom, precisely, it is the Curia's task to . . . restrain and direct. People used to quote the words of a Curia cardinal, Cardinal Pitra, when he learned of Pius IX's decision to convoke the First Vatican Council: 'What, a council? But the French and German theologians will turn our congregations upside down!'"

From the start, however, Vatican II differentiated itself from Vatican I because of the size of the staff called on to work on the preparation of the council. Ninety-six persons had been distributed throughout six commissions to launch the program of Vatican II. Sixty consultants had been picked on the spot, from the Roman offices, and thirty-six summoned from outside. The commissions set up were the following: one on questions of dogma, one on ecclesiastical discipline and canon law, one on the religious orders, one on missions and the Oriental Churches, one on relations between church and state, and one on ceremonial. They were presided over by four Roman congregations: the Holy Office; the Congregation of Ecclesiastical Affairs; that of Propaganda and Rites; and that of Bishops, the Regulars, and the Council. The addition of the commissions to the congregations was justified on the basis that these were the repositories of the tradition of the Holy See, suitable for incorporating the subjects that the theologians and canonists might propose. A supervisory congregation had the task of coordinating their activities.

The motu proprio *Superno Dei Nutu* of 5 June 1960 set up eleven preparatory commissions and three secretariats:

The theological commission, presided over by Cardinal Ottaviani, secretary of the Holy Office;

The commission on Bishops and the Governance of the Church, presided over by Cardinal Mimmi, secretary of the Consistorial Congregation, who was replaced, after his death on 6 March 1961, by Cardinal Marella;

The commission for the Discipline of the Clergy and the Christian People, presided over by Cardinal Ciriaci, prefect of the Congregation of the Council;

The commission for the Religious, presided over by Valerio Cardinal Valeri, prefect of the Congregation of Religious;

The commission for the Sacraments, presided over by Aloisi Cardinal Masella, prefect of the Congregation of the Sacraments;

The commission for the Liturgy, presided over by Gaetano Cardinal Cicognani, prefect of the Congregation of Rites;

The commission for Studies and Seminaries, presided over by Cardinal Pizzardo, prefect of the Congregation of Seminaries and Universities;

The commission for the Oriental Churches, presided over by Amleto Cardinal Cicognani, secretary of the Congregation for the Oriental Churches, who was replaced on his nomination to the Secretariat of State, on 12 August 1961, following the death of Cardinal Tardini, by Cardinal Coussa;

The commission for the Missions, presided over by Cardinal Agagianian, prefect of the Congregation of Propaganda;

The commission for the Apostolate of the Laity, presided over by Cardinal Cento;

The commission for Liturgy presided over by Cardinal Tisserant, dean of the Sacred College;

The secretariat of the Press and of Spectacles presided over by Msgr. O'Connor, president of the Pontifical Commission for the Cinema, Radio and Television;

The secretariat for the Union of Christians, presided over by Cardinal Bea;

The Administrative secretariat, presided over by Msgr. Di Jorio.

These fourteen agencies were headed by the central commission (presided over by John XXIII himself), which had as its aim "to follow and coordinate the work of the various commissions, of which it will bring Us the conclusions, in order that We may set up the subjects to be dealt with in the ecumenical council. It is also the duty of the central commission to propose regulations concerning the progress of the future council."

As opposed to the preparatory phase of Vatican I, where the commissions that were set up arose from a selection a priori of certain momentous issues of doctrine or ecclesiastical politics, this phase in Vatican II was selective in the proper sense of the term. Most noteworthy was the determining role given to the Roman offices. In fact, it seems that in the lengthy process of conciliar *aggiornamento*, no dicastery was excluded from the preparation of plans to be presented to the central commission. What was taken to be a way of gaining the consultors' *vota* might be regarded as a shrewd tactic on the part of the pope. It is certainly clear that the drawing up of these desiderata, left to the dicasteries, was to be the occasion of very uneven efforts, and that there was a great danger of proceeding to the preparation of an interior reform of the Church through the very authorities whose task it was to direct and govern the church the way it was.

To justify this procedure, it was certainly possible to cite the theory upheld in the case of Vatican I. This is what W. d'Ormesson, for one, did. Writing in the *Revue de Paris*, he said, "The Holy Father has determined that it was best for the efficient organization of the preparatory work that the council commissions be broken up in such a way that their members might have access to information and documentation that had existed for centuries in each of the congregations."

But the idea of establishing a perfect coherence through *aggiornamento* could very well encounter strong resistance, which is what happened. What could not have been foreseen was that the council provided an opportunity for reform of the Curia, whose role in the preparatory phase seemed to presage the reinforcement, rather than the decline, of its traditional form. The wishes that were expressed at that time tended toward an internationalization of the Curia, which would in fact occur. But few realized that in giving it the task of preparing the council, the pope was forcing the Curia to reform itself or undergo a metamorphosis imposed from above. Doubts regarding the formula adopted for preparing the council were equivalent to requesting a head of government to make an abrupt change of majority by relying on an opinion poll, without putting forward any new policies or new personalities. Quite to the contrary, Rome would act like those strong executives who change government in response to a difficult period. The preparation of the council by the Curia was equivalent to an Estates-General planned by the nobility.

The First Session of Vatican II (11 October–8 December 1962).

The solemn opening of Vatican II took place on Thursday, 11 October 1962. It was broadcast by television. The assembly, which did not set to work until the next day, consisted of 2,778 persons who were entitled to speak and vote, namely: 80 cardinals; 7 patriarchs; 1,619 archbishops and residential bishops; 975 titular bishops; and 97 nonepiscopal superiors of orders or congregations.

The council fathers belonged to 93 nationalities and came from 136 nations. Their numbers were two-and-a-half times greater than those of Vatican I, to which 1,080 fathers had been invited. Slightly more than two-thirds of the members entitled to speak and vote had been in Rome in 1869, at the peak of participation (704) in the council. Five-sixths of the persons called to Vatican II came to Rome. On 23 October 1962, the assembly included 2,363 persons. Even at times of low participation, Vatican II was attended by not less than three-quarters of its members.

The Personnel of Vatican II. A comparison between the way the world was represented at Vatican I and at Vatican II is statistically interesting. Vatican I was the last council all of whose members were of the white race, the majority European-educated. Vatican II was the first council where all the races were represented. Most of the bishops from overseas had received their training in Europe, often in Rome. A study could be made of the careers of the council fathers, particularly those of the bishops of the local hierarchies in Asia, Africa, and Latin America, created by John XXIII between 1959 and 1962.

One statistic provided by *L'Osservatore Romano* in 1961 revealed the relative weight of the white and nonwhite episcopates. Europe, with 289 bishops in the mission countries, had a leading presence in overseas countries. Out of these 289 bishops, France alone had 151 bishops in Africa. After Europe came the Americas, from which only 54 bishops were in mission countries. The nonwhite episcopates were divided as follows: Asia, 73; Africa, 32; Oceania, 28.

John XXIII's establishment of local hierarchies explains the relative decline of European representation at the council. Looking at a breakdown by continent of the number of fathers called to the council, we note that Europe is represented by 38 percent (15 percent being Italians); North and South America contributed 31 percent; Africa sent 10 percent; and Asia and Oceania contributed the remaining 21 percent.

One notes first a clear difference between the preparatory phase (71 percent European) and the actual council. The schemata of the preparatory phase, which were drawn up by a European staff directed by the Curia, were summoned for examination by an assembly in which Europe would only represent a little over one-third of the members.

Next, it should be pointed out that this distribution was equivalent, for Europe and the two Americas, to a correlation of the legal Church with the real Church, that is to say, the percentage of Catholics in each continent: The 38 percent who were European fathers corresponded to the 47 percent of Europeans who were Catholics, the 31 percent of fathers from the two Americas to the 43 percent of the continents' inhabitants who were Catholics.

By contrast, Africa and Asia-Oceania were overrepresented: The 10 percent of the fathers who were from Africa corresponded to 3 percent of Africans who were Catholics, the 21 percent of the fathers who were from Asia-Oceania to only 7 percent of the people of those regions who were Catholics.

Nevertheless, from Vatican I to Vatican II there was a continuous evolution. At both councils the bishops, and especially the residential bishops, constituted by far the largest bloc of members of the assembly. Theologians and canonists, solicited during the preparatory phase of Vatican I and included in the assembly at Vatican II, therefore gave way to the bishops. The same went for abbots and religious superiors, who were now only a handful. This tendency to bring the council to its fundamental reality, that is, to represent it as an expression of collegiality, was voiced in the motu proprio *Cum gravissima* of 5 April 1962, in which John XXIII decided that all the members of the Sacred College would from then on be invested with episcopal dignity. Thus the obscuring of the council's function, owing to the importance of the numerical criterion in the notion of the universality of the Church, went in tandem with a return to the original sociology of an ecumenical assembly.

Only a rough statistical understanding of differences between the members of Vatican I and Vatican II is possible, since Vatican I recorded those attending and Vatican II those who were members by right. However, it is proper to point out that on 23 October, the day when, at its first session, Vatican II reached its maximum number of attendees, 2,269 bishops, residential and titular, were counted, out of the 2,381 fathers registered. For Europe, the national representation of bishops at the council, by decreasing numerical importance, was as follows:

Europe	Present	Convoked
Italy	385	430
France	122	159
Spain	84	95
Germany	58	68
Great Britain	39	42
Portugal	23	27
Belgium	21	27
Ireland	20	33
Austria	13	15
Netherlands	10	19
Switzerland	10	11
Greece	5	5
Turkey	3	14
Totals:	793	945

We can compare this with the total present at Vatican I on 24 April 1870:

	Bishops present
Italy	122
France	61
Spain	31
Austria-Hungary	18
Ireland	16
England and Scotland	11
Turkey and Greece	9
Switzerland	7
Belgium and Holland	5
Portugal	2
Total:	282

It will be seen that out of the four nations that have attended councils since the Middle Ages—Italy, France, Spain, and Germany—the first three have retained their traditional predominance. Even before the Council of Trent, it was they that gave the ecumenical assemblies their Mediterranean character. But from Vatican I to Vatican II there was a rise of German influence. Germany, where the announcement of Vatican I had caused a violent commotion, and which in the 19th century had a viewpoint more pastoral than dogmatic, in Vatican II expressed a theology that was rigorous and Christocentric and that gave it a prominent role.

From Vatican I to Vatican II, the retreat of the Latin nations accelerated. At Vatican I, 120 bishops, or nearly 20 percent of the total, came from countries of the British Empire, whereas at Trent only four English-speaking bishops had attended—a fact that should be borne in mind to appreciate fully the small number of bishops at Vatican I, only eleven, from England itself and Scotland. At Vatican II, the breakup of the British Empire did not prevent Britain's traditional ties with Australia, or countries like India, from playing a role. And on its own, with thirty-nine bishops, Great Britain now ranked fourth among the European nations. In addition, the North Sea countries, which had been marginal in Vatican I, saw their influence increase.

Nonetheless, from one council to the next the share of the various countries that made up 19th-century Europe decreased. They represented no more than 33 percent of the assembly at Vatican II, as against 44 percent at Vatican I. The new rift that would characterize the Europe of Vatican II was not the one between Latin and Teutonic countries, but the one that reflected the political division of postwar Europe. Eastern Europe was barely present at the council. Germany was represented by West Germany alone. Out of sixty-four Polish bishops convoked, only seventeen received permission to travel to Rome. Albania, Latvia, Lithuania, Romania, and the Soviet Union (the Ukraine) withheld their bishops. Only Yugoslavia, among Eastern European Countries, authorized most of the bishops invited (seventeen) to take part in the council (twenty-four were present on 23 October).

In all, on 23 October, Europe had 853 bishops, representing thirty-three states. But Eastern Europe had sent to Rome only a third of its bishops. Compared with Europe, the four other continents were represented by 1,416 persons: North America by 325 bishops; Central America, 58; South America, 407 (including 171 Brazilian bishops); Asia, 290 bishops (none came from the People's Republic of China, out of the 24 entitled, but 14 came from Taiwan, of 14 convoked); Oceania, 63. Vatican I, on 24 April 1870, had at the heart of its assembly only seventy-two bishops from the Americas, nine from Africa, forty-six from Asia, and thirteen from Australia. Non-European countries, which sent only 30 percent of the fathers at Vatican I, sent a majority of 62 percent at Vatican II.

Up to now, we have concerned ourselves with those persons whom John XXIII convoked to the council in conformity with the dispositions of canon 223, and those entitled to speak and vote. Canon 223 allowed the pope a number of ways in which to add persons from categories that the law did not provide to be members of a council. John XXIII made use of them all.

He summoned to the council all the titular bishops. By letter, dated 3 October 1962, he likewise convoked all the superiors general of the nonexempt religious families, who numbered some one thousand. Ninety superiors general out of ninety-seven who were invited joined the assembly at the opening of the first session.

To this universality in the representation of nations and continents, Rome added universality in representation of the many divisions within ecclesial society. All the theologians appointed by the pope as experts had the superior of their order or congregation in the *aula*. From the antepreparatory phase to its opening, the council called on the whole Church, save for the laity, to accomplish *aggiornamento*.

The Edges. The objectives that John XXIII had conceived for the council obliged him to open it up to the outside world. The papacy took up the custom at councils past of having witnesses from the rest of Christianity, who had been symbolized in medieval times by the presence of the princes. This was accomplished by inviting to the council (article 18) observers from the separated Christians, a disposition that followed logically from the ecumenical perspectives proposed to the council. Apparently, the inviting of observers as well as the drawing up of their statutes were done very early on. On 25 April 1962, in a lecture to the Foreign Press Association in Rome, Cardinal Bea was able to make public the ways in which the observers would be called on to participate in the work of the council. They were authorized

to attend public sessions and general congregations "except in particular cases that will be determined by the Presidential Council" (article 18, para. 1). Their presence therefore was not by right. They were not entitled to speak or vote "at the discussions of the council." This detail perhaps left the door open to admitting observers to the voting at public sessions, but this never happened. They did not attend commission sessions "unless the competent authority [that is, the Presiding Council] authorized them." Although bound to secrecy, like the other council fathers, they had a right of contact with their community (article 18, para. 2). Finally, the Secretariat for Unity had the task of creating a link between the directing organs of the council, the council fathers, and them.

A summons from the papacy was one thing, but one of the tasks of the Secretariat for Unity was to negotiate with the various Christian communities the appointment of delegates to the council. At the opening of Vatican II, fourteen of these communities had sent twenty-five delegates. While certain communities welcomed the pontifical invitation, others were racked with doubts regarding the turmoil that would be aroused in their groups by the prospect of "going to Canossa." A statement of 22 September 1962 from Pastor Roux, who was sent to Rome as an observer of the World Reformed Alliance, is a fairly good testimony that many delegates went to the council with only the "wish to observe." The leading Protestant communities were present at the opening of the council, along with the Old Catholic Church, the Coptic Church of Egypt, the Church of Armenia, and others. But the absence of a delegate from the Jewish religion was noted. A problem arose, the import of which the council would perceive at the third session, with the draft on non-Christian religions and then with that on religious freedom. For among the states not represented at the council, for a variety of reasons, in general reasons of their own, only one was excluded according to the Vatican's wishes: Israel. The KNA agency, in an explanatory note of September 1962, explained the reason for this absence: "The state of Israel, as a secular state, cannot appoint an observer."

Together with the observers, we should emphasize the "participation" at the council of guests not mentioned in the regulations. On 29 September 1962 there were six: Brothers Roger Schutz and Max Thurian, from the Taizé community (near Cluny); Dr. Oscar Cullmann; Canon Bernard Pawley, representative of the Anglican archbishops of Canterbury and York; G. C. Berkouwer, of the Protestant University of Amsterdam; and P. Alexander Schmemann, vice rector of the Orthodox Seminary of St. Vladimir in New York. Unlike the observers, guests had usually received a personal invitation from the pope—that is, a guest represented only himself, or else the papacy invited him as an individual from within his community, not as a representative. The distinction was often hard to make, but it existed. Still, the status of guest paralleled that of the observer; he had neither more nor less right than they.

If one had to describe this status, which was an "innovation according to usage," one might say that it was that of a specialized consultative voice. It gave few rights but did allow every kind of influence, and often in a more effective way than a consultative voice by right.

However unequal the rights of those invited to take part in Vatican II, this was still a council of the teaching Church. Despite much urging, no representative of the laity was called to take part in it. It was only on 19 November 1962 that, to use Henry Fesquet's words, "a breach opened up" in the assembly with John XXIII's invitation to Jean Guitton. He, too, was sworn to secrecy. By virtue of this disposition, the representatives of the press, about whom the regulations said nothing, were admitted only to the public sessions. This statute reflected the reality of the council debates. The recognition of public opinion in the work of the council was only possible at the time of the passage from the draft to the conciliar text, from the vote to the promulgation. For the press this was, as it turned out, an untenable situation. Having arrived in Rome en masse, the press realized, immediately after the solemn opening session of 11 October 1962, that its role would be limited to reportage.

The Conciliar Commissions. Vatican II opened with an unexpected debate, the stakes of which would affect its future, on the appointment of the conciliar commissions, which, it was clear given the number of council fathers, would control the editing of the *modi* (amendments) suggested by the assembly as the votes came in. The elections set for 13 October seemed bound to confirm the preconciliar commissions. An unexpected, though prepared, intervention, from Cardinal Liénart, bishop of Lille and member of the presidency council, upset the timetable. The difference between preconciliar and conciliar commissions was not considerable. But between 13 and 16 October, through much consultation and compiling of lists, the assembly turned its attention to the ulterior methods behind the consensus sought on the schemata to be discussed. Held amid certain confusion (owing to the vagueness of the conciliar regulation: one round or two?), the elections to the commissions should have given the assembly its shape for the council. There was only one round, on 16 October. In each commission, after those elected by an absolute majority, those who had the next-largest number of votes were appointed by a plurality—through a decision of John XXIII—to give sixteen members elected by the commission.

The Results. On 16 October, 2,381 fathers voted. Just as presence at the council was obligatory, so participation

in the voting was a duty. Abstention was only allowed in the case of departure or a well-founded absence, of which the council president had to be informed (articles 41 and 42). This rule was more flexible than that of Vatican I, whose regulations stipulated that no father could leave the council without prior authorization (section IX), but it existed. This meant the only way to abstain was to hand in a spoiled ballot. All the votes taken together totaled close to 24,000 ballots with 400,000 names.

The pope's resolution suggested that those elected by an absolute majority, on the first round, would be so numerous that complementing the members of the commissions with those elected by plurality would gain precious time, so cumbersome was the procedure. This came to nought. The members appointed by an absolute majority represented 34 percent of those elected. Each commission included between six and fourteen members appointed by plurality, which meant that more than two-thirds of the members of the commissions were given their jobs with a vote less than the majority required to pass on the adoption of amendments and drafts. Those last on the list (fifteenth and sixteenth places) were sometimes elected with even less than one-third of the votes. Elections to the commissions did not in any way reflect a majority in the council. They never implied any delegation of power to persons representing the essential tendencies of Vatican II. They bore witness instead to a balance in the representation of the universal Church at the council. In this sense, they were appropriately parliamentary, since they conformed to the structure of the conciliar assembly.

Each continent was represented more than once. Europe had eighty-four members, that is, more than an absolute majority of the whole; North America had twenty-six members; South America, twenty-six members; Asia and Oceania, sixteen members; Africa, seven members. So we see that one member out of two was European; one out of five American (North or South); one out of ten Asian; one out of twenty African.

Among the European countries, only Italy was represented on all the commissions. Italy had twenty-two electees, that is, numerically, more than a third of its slate, and from one to three representatives per commission. It was never a majority party. Only seven Italians obtained an absolute majority. None was at the top of the list, while seven were between thirteenth and sixteenth place. The most successful was Msgr. Rossi, bishop of Biella, a member of the preconciliar liturgical commission, with 1,954 votes. The least successful was Msgr. Peruzzo, bishop of Agrigento, in sixteenth place on the Doctrinal commission with 741 votes, the fourth-lowest plurality. Out of the twenty-two elected, the majority had taken part in the preparatory phase. But only twelve stayed in the same commission. The ten others, both old and new, were drafted to another commission. Finally, the average of the votes the Italians garnered was higher than an absolute majority, rising to 1,482.

The European list produced thirty-nine electees—as with Italy, a little over one-third of the designated candidates; claims of European success in the elections should therefore be tempered. Rather, the results show European influence in the council: twenty-two European members were elected by absolute majority. The least successful candidate in the majority was Msgr. Laszlo, bishop of Eisenstadt, who was chosen for the commission for the apostolate of the laity in fifth place with 1,246 votes, or 50 more than an absolute majority (1,196). Sixteen "Europeans" were elected by plurality, between thirteenth and sixteenth place. Of the twenty-two elected by an absolute majority, twelve found themselves on the same commission as during the preparatory phase; ten had come from another commission or were new.

On the other hand, out of the sixteen elected by plurality, two were confirmed in their place and fourteen changed positions, or else were newcomers. But most significantly, in six commissions out of ten, the European candidates were at the top of the lists. And, except on the commission for the Discipline of the Clergy and the Christian People, all the top-ranking ones had been voted by more than two-thirds majority (1,528). Msgr. Zauner, bishop of Linz, who was already a member of the preconciliar commission, was confirmed to the commission for the Liturgy with 2,231 votes, or 61 fewer than unanimity (2,292).

The two European countries that stood out at the elections were France and Germany. France, with sixteen members, was represented everywhere, except on the commission for the Oriental Churches. The other commissions included from one to three Frenchmen. Exactly half had gained an absolute majority; three were at the head of the list. Five were in the same commission.

Germany had eleven representatives, nine of whom gained an absolute majority. It was absent only on the commission for the Missions. The commissions for the Discipline for the Sacraments and the Religious included two Germans, the seven others having one each. Out of the eleven Germans, three served on the same commission. The eight others were mainly newcomers.

Together France and Germany contributed approximately 76 percent of the electees from the European list. After them came Austria (three elected by absolute majority), Belgium (four elected by plurality), Switzerland (one elected by an absolute majority), Yugoslavia (three elected by plurality), and the Netherlands (two elected by plurality). Except for the Scandinavian nations, all the countries on the list were represented on the commissions.

Spain, which had not proposed a slate, nevertheless had ten electees, four of them with an absolute majority. Save for the Doctrinal commission, the Spanish had one member elected everywhere, and two on the commission for Missions.

Finally, Great Britain, which was the odd man out, had four elected, all by plurality.

In the majority, Europe nonetheless found itself split into two blocs, whether it liked it or not. Italy was on one side, the eight countries on the European slate grouped around France and Germany, on the other. These three countries by themselves had forty-nine commission members. The myth of the Franco-German axis at the council had just been shown to be based in fact. If the sociological representation of Vatican II had not been universal, the council would have been over. But actually the division of Europe opened the way for other nations to influence the council.

South America (including Mexico), with twenty-seven electees, lagged far behind Europe but had an important place in the council. By itself, Brazil, although it had not presented a slate, had seven members distributed among seven commissions, including the one on Doctrine, whose Msgr. Scherer, bishop of Porto Alegre, a member of the preparatory theological commission, received 1,465 votes. The countries of South America properly speaking, who had presented thirty-five commission candidates in random order, had thirteen electees among the eight who had set up slates. Ecuador, which had stayed on the sidelines, had one candidate on the commission on the Religious. Three South Americans were appointed by an absolute majority, the eleven others by plurality. Per country, not counting those that put forward lists, the results were as follows:

Argentina:	three electees (to the commission for the Discipline of the Clergy and the Christian People, one with an absolute majority; to the commission for the Religious, one with a plurality; to the commission for the Liturgy, one with a plurality.)
Chile:	three electees (to the commission for Seminaries and Studies, one with an absolute majority; to the commission for the Apostolate of the Laity, two with a plurality)
Paraguay:	two electees (one to the commission for Seminaries and Studies, one to the commission for the Discipline of Sacraments; both with a plurality)
Colombia:	one electee (to the commission on Bishops and the Governance of the Church, with a plurality)

Venezuela: one electee (to the commission for the Sacraments, with a plurality)

Uruguay: one electee (to the commission for the Discipline of the Clergy and the Christian People, with a plurality)

Bolivia: one electee (to the commission for the Apostolate of the Laity, with an absolute majority).

These eight Latin American countries had candidates voted to seven commissions, all pastoral.

North America (Canada and the United States) was represented by twenty-six electees: eighteen from the United States, eight from Canada. Eleven (nine Americans, two Canadians) won an absolute majority. Americans twice came at the head of the list: for the commission of Oriental Churches, where Msgr. Senyshyn, Ukrainian archbishop of Philadelphia, won 1,432 votes, and for the commission of Seminaries and Studies, where Msgr. O'Boyle, archbishop of Washington, was confirmed by 2,059 votes. By itself, the United States made up one-quarter of the doctrinal commission, with Dearden, archbishop of Detroit, Wright, bishop of Pittsburgh, and Griffiths, auxiliary bishop of New York, voted respectively to eighth, tenth, and twelfth place. With Italy, the United States was the only country represented on all the commissions. Six of the American members sat on the same commission as earlier, three of them on Doctrinal; the twelve others changed commission or were newcomers.

Asia-Oceania, with sixteen members, was represented on every commission except for that for the Discipline of the Clergy and Christian People. India, on its own, had six electees, all with a plurality, five of whom polled between thirteenth and sixteenth place; of these five, two were in sixteenth place and one in seventh. The other electees from the Asian countries broke down as follows: China two; Japan two; Philippines two; Indonesia one; Australia three.

Africa, with seven commission members, including one electee (Cardinal Rugambwa) who headed the list of the commission for Missions, was represented on only five commissions, all pastoral. Nigeria and Madagascar, which had presented slates, had no national electee. Tanganyika and Congo-Léopoldville were represented twice; Tunisia, Cameroon. and the Republic of South Africa, once.

The Oriental Rites countries had four electees to the commission for the Oriental Churches.

Religious orders had three, of whom two were on the commission for the Religious, one on that for the Oriental Churches.

No country had an absolute majority inside a commission. Aside from Africa, each continent was represented on at least nine committees. Europe was absent from the commission for Missions, to the benefit of Asia, Africa, and Latin America. On the Doctrinal commission, Europe shared influence with North America. The number of U.S. members was equivalent to two-thirds of the total of German and French electees combined, and 80 percent of the total of those from Italy. Alone among the European countries, Spain maintained its traditional weight in the commissions, with ten electees. Two countries from the Third World affirmed their presence in the Church despite a very different percentage of Catholics: Brazil and India. From this we can gauge the role of the episcopal conferences and their limitations. India, which had created one, probably benefited from a certain voting discipline in favor of the slate it had drawn up. Brazil, whose ties between its national conference and the CELAM were loose, had seen six of its bishops elected, without presenting a slate. It is doubtful if the neighboring countries put all theirs on their lists. Brazil's success was in proportion to the high number of its bishops, together with an influence it exercised at the council from the preparatory phase onward: four of its electees were on the same commissions.

Africa, whose episcopal hierarchies were often relatively new, had a total number of electees higher by a unit than the Brazilian episcopate. But many African votes went to non-African candidates: the African episcopate was serving its apprenticeship at the council and, as many observers noted, its members possessed great humility.

Finally, the elections brought to the commissions members of the council without distinction of rank—cardinals, archbishops, residential bishops, titulars, coadjutors, auxiliaries. Only the regulars were not a group. Regulars and bishops of the Oriental Rites had joined the commissions that dealt with their concerns, but even here they did not have a majority. The commission for Missions alone had a certain sociological specialization—the role the Third World countries played in it in fact made its name anachronistic. But as a rule there was still nonspecialization of the commission personnel, at two levels: nonspecialization of the national groups, and nonspecialization of individuals.

And yet, out of the 160 electees, sixty ended up in the same commission as during the preconciliar phase. Twenty-nine had been named by an absolute majority and thirty-one by a plurality. If one considers the only members who had obtained an absolute majority, it is clear that the personnel of the preparatory phase predominated: 70 percent of the electees had taken part in it. Only 30 percent of members represented renewal.

The fathers elected by a plurality, by contrast, were distributed roughly half and half between members of committees in the preparatory phase and new members. It should be remembered that in theory, the elections were meant to incorporate several rounds. But it is noteworthy that the council had naturally relied on those fathers who had been involved in preparing for it. This fact confirms two hypotheses put forward above. The elections gave rise to selection and redistribution of members involved in the preparatory phase rather than to a renewal of personnel. On the whole, the percentage of fathers coming from the preconciliar commissions (either the same commission, another one, or the Central commission) was higher than that of the new members by 14 percent.

It would be tempting to believe that the breakdown of the two percentages within the ten commissions corresponded, more or less, to reliance placed by the council in the preconciliar commissions and to a first judgment on the schemata. This is by no means the case. The commission for the Liturgy, the schema of which was the result of a process of exceptionally intense consultations, it will be recalled, saw only 44 percent of its preconciliar personnel brought back. Nor was this a sign of distrust. After the commission on Bishops and the Governance of the Church, that of the Liturgy ranked second in the number of electees with an absolute majority (50 percent). The first five on the list of nominees were brought back onto this commission. Their average majority was the highest of the ten commissions. The first six were all Europeans, a reflection of Europe's role in the liturgical movement over the previous twenty years, of which the schema *De Liturgia* took note. The "European list" had five electees, one each from five nations (Austria, Belgium, France, Germany, Yugoslavia). Italy had three, including the second-highest and the lowest vote-getter; it benefited from manipulation of the rule at article 38. Three other European countries were represented: Great Britain, Poland, and Spain. The four other continents held five seats, the United States and Canada both being represented. Seven members of the commission had taken part in the preparatory phase; six were already on the commission on Liturgy, and only one came from another commission. Elections to the liturgical commission were therefore the occasion of selection without any dilution, given the quality of work of the preconciliar commission, and of representation that was faithful to the makeup of the assembly, with a European preponderance that had been responsible for the actual substance of the schema.

By contrast, the commission on Bishops and the Governance of the Church saw 81 percent of the members of the preconciliar commission confirmed in their task. A noteworthy point: this percentage was matched by the highest number of bishops elected with an absolute majority (ten out of sixteen). Seven of these ten had belonged to the preparatory commission, as had four out of the six electees by a plurality. All the way down to fifteenth place, the commission members received higher votes than did the first fifteen members of the other commissions. A very slight drop was noticeable to the fifteenth member (an Indian bishop), who among those

elected by a plurality was the first who had not been part of the preparatory personnel. He was separated from the fourteenth by 173 votes.

This commission's task was a fundamental one. The schemata that the preparatory commission had worked on constituted the extension, on structural and practical levels, of the general principles contained in *De Ecclesia*. The definition of the bishops' power, which complemented that of papal power, elaborated at Vatican I, represented the grand task of Vatican II in 1962. Indisputably, retaining a large proportion of the members of the preparatory commission on the commission on Bishops reflected concern for in-depth study. This did not necessarily mean trusting the schemata of the preparatory commission, since they were not well known, but rather accepting the procedure of amendments on a subject the council wanted to see through, and relatively quickly, to the final stage of conciliar text. Acceptance of the preparatory procedure for Vatican II and of the regulations is here plain to see. All the national groups represented on the commission had set up an episcopal conference. Fifteen members out of sixteen, all except the member from Spain, represented countries that had presented slates at the elections. In the designation of the members of this key commission, the electoral system had eliminated all the countries whose episcopates were unorganized. Thus Africa was not represented. The only Asian country that had an episcopal conference was India. And the Spanish bishop found himself sixteenth on the list, with 722 votes. The commission's structure prefigured the growing influence of episcopal conferences in the life of the Church.

The composition of the commission of Bishops must be seen as parallel with that on Doctrine, which was responsible for *De Ecclesia*. On the commission on Doctrine, only 62 percent of the preparatory personnel were reelected: 38 percent, from the preparatory theological commission and 24 percent from another commission or from the Central commission. Two bishops from the preparatory theological commission were elected with an absolute majority: the first on the list was Msgr. Schröffer, the bishop of Eichstadt; the fifth was Msgr. Scherer, a Brazilian of German origin. The counterweight to the Italian influence, exercised by the "terrible" Cardinal Ottaviani, was provided, not by Europe, but by North America, from which six bishops were elected to the commission. Europe made only a limited effort to sit on the commission on Doctrine, being content to be represented by four candidates from the "European list." Many non-European bishops elected to the commission were of Ruthenian origin. The withdrawal of Italy (two members) seemed to work to the benefit of internationalization, more apparent than real. The problems with selecting the personnel of the theological commission, the feeble attempt at achieving a "mix," and the facade of renewal, revealed the "doctrinal" crisis of the council, which, for good measure, professed to be pastoral. The European list, for example, preferred to be sure of a place on the Bishops' commission as more practical and concrete. One of the major problems of the council would arise from this.

In the other commissions, the changing of the personnel from the preparatory phase, ranging from five members (commission for the Discipline of the Clergy and the Christian People) to nine (commission for Seminaries and Studies), worked as a general rule to the advantage of the non-European continents, which had been underrepresented and hardly active in the preparatory period. The decline in European dominance, however, did not work to the disadvantage of France, Germany, or Italy, but to that of the other countries on the European list or of individual countries, except for Spain. France and Germany therefore ensured that the list would be created around them in the commissions. Two commissions—Missions and Oriental Churches—saw a reclassification of the preparatory personnel, linked to the mixing of the elections. This reclassification was combined with the introduction of jurisdictions to their area of competence into these commissions.

With the elections, the definitive makeup of the commissions did not cease, since, according to the regulations, the pontiff had a right to nominate eight members. In case of defection of a member of a commission, the papacy was in a more comfortable situation than the assembly; it was easy for it to proceed to another nomination. The council, for its part, had only theoretical recourse to a partial election, a procedure that implied a technical and psychological mobilization disproportionate to the stakes. The regulations established no guidelines in this regard. It is strange that there was no provision for means of making a substitution, although that had been traditional in the Church since the 18th century; provided for in the great conclaves of the assembly, with limited rights of proxy, it was even more important for the life of the commission. One should probably interpret this silence on the part of the regulations as meaning that the replacement of an elected member would be accomplished by following the results of the voting in the elections of 16 October. The question did not really arise, since the complementary elections took place in 1963, and the commissions did not experience any defections among electees. Proceeding to its nominations after the elections, the papacy, as abbé Laurentin stressed, gave moral precedence to the electees of the assembly. "By force of circumstance, the others appeared to have been fished out." The elections, however, took place between two series of nominations: those to directive or administrative tasks of the council, carried out beforehand; and those complementary to the elections. Despite its clearheadedness in designating its electees, the council had elected in third place to the commission for the Apostolate of the Laity Cardinal Wyszynski, member of the secretariat for Extraordinary Affairs, and in ninth place to the commission for the Oriental Churches Father Minishi, member of the secretariat for Christian Unity. Both being ineligible, because of the prohibition of plurality, they were replaced by the candidate with the highest place after them. India and Ireland each gained a representative here. By reserving its nominations to itself, the papacy retained the right to change the profile of the elections. Did it do so?

The Pontifical Nominations. The papacy had the right to appoint one-third of each commission's members, or eight out of twenty-four. It should be remembered that it had already nominated the presidents of commissions, all Curial cardinals who were already directors of the preparatory commissions. Each commission was therefore expected to include nine members appointed by the pontiff, that is, no longer a third but 36 percent.

The definitive constitution of the commissions, beginning with that of the Liturgy, of which the draft was to be brought before the council on 20 October, was an urgent matter. On 22 October Msgr. Felici presented the definitive list of the commission members and announced to the fathers nine, not eight, pontifical nominations. The pope was breaking the regulations for the second time; the members he had named reached 38 percent. In the early afternoon, in an attempt to explain this violation of the regulatory norms, the Press Office revealed that it was a question of creating an uneven number (twenty-five) in the commissions so as to make it easier to determine the majorities. But the commissions were bound by the rule of the so-called two-thirds majority, and with their president, who naturally had a major vote in the third ballot, the number of their members had already jumped to twenty-five. Chroniclers of the council, without exception, agree that this twisting of the regulations was due to John XXIII's forgetting, repaired in extremis, Enrico Dante, secretary of the Congregation of Rites, who had been promoted to the episcopate shortly before the council, along with all the secretaries of the Roman congregations. But by raising a particular case to the level of regulation, according to the principle of numerical equality of the commissions, the papacy allowed ten more council fathers to join them. It would be useless to try to determine who benefited most from this violation of the rules: all national groups and all categories of council fathers gained from it indirectly. Still, it might be noted that twenty-seven of the ninety members nominated by the pope were Italians.

On the whole, the nominations made by the pontiff, taken in themselves, matched the distribution among the personnel of the preparatory phase and the new members among the electees with an absolute majority: 70 percent old and 30 percent new. The result was that the proportion of preconciliar personnel increased in all the commissions, from 57 percent to 62 percent following the elections. The change was not large; in each commission, this increase maintained the balance established by the elections between the two categories of members.

The shift in favor of the preconciliar personnel ranged from 1 percent to 12 percent. But we should distinguish between fathers nominated in the same commission as during the preparatory phase, and those belonging to another, especially the Central commission. At the elections, this last category was a minority (thirty-one members). With the pontifical nominations, it had a majority (thirty-seven persons out of sixty-three from the preconciliar period). Thus, if one does not go into detail, the percentage of shift per commission is not significant. At the commission for Oriental Churches, it was only 2 percent. But five of the members nominated by the pope belonged to the Central commission. With an equal percentage of shift, or thereabouts, we note the same number of members of Central brought into Doctrinal and the commission on Bishops. Thus the papacy used the nominations to carry out a reclassifying of certain bishops whom the disappearance of Central would have removed from the commissions.

The papacy likewise brought in nations whose candidates had been defeated or neglected in the elections. In Europe, it boosted Poland, Switzerland, Ireland, and Portugal. It gave one representative each to Greece, Lithuania, and Czechoslovakia. It increased the share of all the Third World countries. The losers were the countries on the European list and in North America.

Nevertheless, the papacy did not proceed systematically to internationalize the commissions. It respected the balance set up by the elections, restricting itself to perfecting it in two cases. It named an African bishop to the commission on Bishops, to give a presence to the only continent not represented there, and did the same for Asia on the commission for Seminaries and Studies.

Two countries saw their role enhanced by the pontifical nominations: Spain and Italy.

Spain, which had only ten electees, benefited from eight nominations. It joined the Doctrinal commission, and was henceforth present everywhere. Its influence was doubled on three commissions (Bishops and Governance of the Church; Discipline of the Clergy and the Christian People; Liturgy).

In all the commissions, the Italians were henceforth no fewer than three, that is, four with the president, thus 15 percent. In five commissions, counting the president, their total rose to seven, or 27 percent. This situation was analyzed by a shrewd observer of Vatican II (Father Rouquette, *Études*, 7 December 1962): "In fact, this seesaw policy shows John XXIII's resolve not to impose his personal thinking on the council, as well as the desire to keep a strong check on the possible initiatives of the assem-

bly." The usefulness of this precaution was not immediately apparent.

The first session of Vatican II opened amid enthusiasm and ended in a mixture of hope and anxiety. The draft on the liturgy, which had seen some fierce opposition, was passed on 14 November by 2,162 votes against 46, a 97 percent majority. It would be promulgated, after some editorial modifications, in 1963. But on the same day, the assembly embarked on the thorny discussion of the schema on revelation, and the debate bogged down on the question of the two sources (*De duobus Fontibus*). The draft favored the pontifical magisterium, in post-Tridentine tradition, and did not respond to the findings of contemporary exegesis. A skillful use of procedure allowed the minority, which defended the schema, to win in a confused vote. John XXIII exercised his power as arbiter in favor of the defeated majority and handed the revision of the text to a mixed commission. It was clear from then on that Vatican II would include a second session to put the council's program on the agenda and would refine it during the intersession. The first session ended with the critical examination of the draft on ecumenism and the more or less indifferent examination of that on social communications. No text was promulgated.

Did John XXIII believe, as some have said, in a relatively brief council of only one session? The fact is that his interventions all tended toward granting the assembly the greatest freedom of judgment vis-à-vis the preparatory documents. Vatican II was not to be a registration chamber. The council broke down into two tendencies, identified by the media as "majority" and "minority." They were clearly observable but were not fixed on the same objective, except for the conservative stream, which had a post-Tridentine, Curialist rigidity.

On 3 June 1963, John XXIII died. By virtue of article 33 of the constitution *Vacantis apostolicae Sedis*, the council was suspended.

The Second, Third, and Fourth Sessions (1963–5). The near certainty that G. B. Montini would, without hesitation, proceed to a new convocation of Vatican II influenced his election at the conclave of 21 June 1963. On 27 June, with the rescript *Ex audientia*, Paul VI fixed the continuation of Vatican II for 29 September. On 12 September he wrote to Cardinal Tisserant defining the aims the council should set itself and outlining a reform of the conciliar rules of 6 October 1962.

On 14 September, with the letter *Horum temporum*, the council fathers were convoked to the second session: on the Church, the bishops, and ecumenism. The question of collegiality aroused extremely heated discussion. The moderators installed by the pope to serve as a link between the assembly and the directorial committees (the presidential council, the coordinating commission—a new entity—and the council secretariat) were hard put to win acceptance for the principle whereby the assembly would have specific questions put to it.

Five questions on the subject of collegiality were passed easily on 29 October 1963. But the vote was effectively contested by the minority as early as 7 November. More than five hundred bishops signed a petition in favor of a future synod and about one hundred for a reform of the Holy Office. Complementary elections to the commissions were held 28 November. On 4 December the constitution on the liturgy was promulgated, and on the same day the decree on social communications.

The second session was the one in which Paul VI remained very much removed from the activity of the council, even if he followed the course of the discussion in the minutest detail. On 29 November Msgr. Felici, secretary of the council, announced the probability of a third session beginning 14 September 1964. On 11 March 1964 an article by Msgr. Vallaine, head of the press office, was published in *L'Osservatore Romano*, implying that the third session would be the last.

In the intersession, the council program was worked over a second time. The number of schemata was brought to eighteen. Eight of these were pared down, suggesting that the voting would be carried out without lengthy discussion (a plan of Cardinal Döffner, archbishop of Munich). Paul VI exerted his authority by insisting that the views of the minority be taken into consideration to reach a consensus rallying the conservatives (notably Curialists) and the progressive wing of the assembly around the hope of concluding the council.

During the third session all the texts of the program of Vatican II were examined. Two short schemata were recast as long ones: that concerning priests (19 October) and that concerning missions (9 November). The schema on the laws governing mixed marriages (important for Christian unity) was eliminated. The constitution on the Church (*Lumen Gentium*), the decree on ecumenism, and the decree on the Oriental Catholic Churches were promulgated 21 November 1964. The vote on religious freedom was adjourned on 19 November 1964.

In the intersession, the texts not voted on were once more reworked, taking into account proposed amendments (*modi*).

The fourth and final session of Vatican II was the most complex and the most closely observed. Everyone knew that a great phase in the history of the 20th-century Church was coming to an end. At the opening, Paul VI announced the creation of a synod of bishops designed to assist him in the postconciliar period. The schema on the Jews aroused unexpected antagonisms, in light of preceding discussions on the question of deicide. The schema on the relations between the Church and the world of today raised passions. Paul VI used his authority and efficient diplomacy as he identified the resolutions of the mi-

nority in order to reconcile it with the majority. He reserved to himself the question of birth control, on which he would intervene with the encyclical *Humanae Vitae* in 1968.

This fourth session was a triumph. Paul's journey to the United Nations in October, the closing session of Vatican II, on 8 December 1965, the speeches to the laity and the nations, all created the feeling that the Church had entered the 20th century and that the postconciliar commissions would finish its work.

The Ecclesiology of Vatican II. The coherence of the sixteen documents comprising the work of Vatican II revolved around an axis proposed in November 1962 by Cardinal Suenens (archbishop of Malines) and Cardinal Montini: a reflection on the part of the Church on its own intimate nature (*ad intra*) and on the mission, conferred upon it by this mystery, to the various societies (both religious and civil) with which it was confronted. In this sense, Vatican II brought about a veritable "sociological revolution" (a term that some attribute to Msgr. Moeller, others to Msgr. Haubtmann).

At Vatican II the post-Tridentine legacy of a Church constituting a perfect society (the neo-Thomist *societas perfecta*) confronted an external world it invited to conversion through its doctrine and its leadership role.

The work of Vatican II thus was organized around the two poles presented by the constitution *Lumen Gentium* and the constitution *Gaudium et Spes*. The first recentered the Church on Christ as its foundation and set its face to the world. *Lumen Gentium* hoped to put an end to triumphalism through its identification with Christ, placing the Church at the service of Christ and urging it to humility in the face of His teaching and example: "Just as Christ carried out the work of redemption in poverty, so the Church is called to follow along the same way in order that it may communicate to humanity the fruits of salvation" (*LG*, 8).

This recentering constitutes the key (O. Cullmann) to ecumenism, that is to say, to brotherhood between the Catholic Church and the other Christian religions. In pursuance of this, Vatican II broke with the classic distinction, accentuated after Vatican I, between hierarchy and laity, Church and people. The Church was no longer defined by its juridical structure but by the communion of faith, hope, and charity that is given to all Christians: "There is not a specifically different Christian life on the one side for the hierarchy and the religious and on the other for simple Christians. The whole people of God is a holy, messianic and missionary people. In its entirety it benefits from the Holy Spirit and its charismata" (P. Laurentin, *Bilan du concile*, Paris, 1966).

Thus all Christians have a responsibility for the whole of the Church's mission. This responsibility is inscribed in the history of salvation, that of a progress toward a future that began with Israel. The institutional structure of the Church was rethought, based on the people of God, "a messianic people, although in fact it does not include everybody, and more than once may appear as a 'tiny flock' " (*LG* 9, 3). Rome remains at the center, as befits a community needing an authority. But the local churches take part in the mystery of the universal Church: Catholic, that is to say, decentralized, yet centripetal because based upon Christ. Rome's mission is not to establish uniformity but to maintain unity within diversity.

That is the basis of the conciliar texts on the bishops, the Oriental Churches, and the missions. The episcopate remains supreme on the level of the sacraments. The pope (the bishop of Rome) is superior to the bishops not on the sacramental level but on that of the jurisdiction defined at Vatican I. Infallibility remains, but it does not reside exclusively in the pope. It also belongs to the "body of bishops." It is placed in a new perspective by the affirmation of collegiality, by virtue of apostolicity, which strengthens the role of the local churches. "Just as St. Peter and the other apostles constitute one apostolic college, in a similar way the Roman pontiff, Peter's successor, and the bishops, successors of the apostles, are joined together. . . . However, the college or body of bishops has no authority unless this is understood in terms of union with the Roman pontiff, Peter's successor. . . ." (*LG*, 22).

The jurisdiction proper to the pope, which was wrested by Peter's successors from the successors of the other apostles, and by Rome from the other churches, thus finds a new balance in a dialectic between the growing ascendency of the supreme authority of Peter, and the apostolic tradition of the disciples surrounding Christ, which can claim equivalent sacramental jurisdiction.

The affirmation of collegiality, as the apex of the ecclesial communion which has as its source a people marching toward salvation, following Christ's example, is also rooted in a modern understanding of the transmission of revelation (constitution *Dei Verbum*). This constitution restores the active dimension of revelation, which is no longer exclusively dependent on the magisterium, especially on that of the pontiff. "As they hold, practice and witness to the heritage of the faith, bishops and faithful display a unique harmony" (*DV*, 10; *LG*, 25). The Christian experience of the laity takes on a dimension that post-Tridentine theology had left in the shadows. The separation between Tradition, what is transmitted "from mouth to ear," and Scripture (the revelation of Christ) is now abolished—not without lengthy debates, notably in 1962—in favor of an organic unity. Scripture and Tradition both proceed from the revelation of Christ, in a privileged written form, and from the Spirit through the apostolic tradition. "Consequently, the Church's certainty about all that is revealed is not drawn from holy Scripture alone" (*DV*, 9).

This ecclesiology of an open community whose diversity is centered on Christ as well as on Peter's successor and the apostolic college was the fruit of four years of conciliar work, which gave rise to complex, bitter debates that eventually moved toward clear majority resolutions, in a great freedom of spirit that John XXIII and Paul VI, each in his own way, guaranteed. The constitution on the liturgy, first discussed in 1962, then voted on and promulgated (21 November) in 1963, kept the argument alive. It differentiated the liturgical languages, entrusted to the episcopal conferences the responsibility for this differentiation, proclaimed the equality of rites, and gave new life to the particular churches. It proposed a fully developed, living theology of the people of God, who are the reason for the liturgical act, not merely the "clientele" (Y. Congar) of the priest. The priest recovered his original function: the sacramental service of the people of God. The theology of the word again recovered its honored place. And the Eucharistic meal once more became the central event of the liturgical celebration.

This was the axis around which the dialogues of Vatican II were organized: on ecumenism (dialogue with non-Catholic Christians); on the non-Christian religions; on the Church and the world; and on religious freedom. But there remained the test of reality, the putting into practice of conciliar texts by public opinion. The public had followed the council with hopes for immediacy no document, beginning with the constitution *Gaudium et Spes*, could satisfy. Paradoxically, the council's thirst to establish doctrine was about to collide with the response of a world that awaited freedoms, both general and individual, and would interpret in its own way a set of decrees that few actually read.

List of Promulgated Documents.

4 December 1963
    Constitution on the Sacred Liturgy *Sacrosanctum Concilium*
    Decree on the Instruments of Social Communication *Inter mirifica*
21 November 1964
    Dogmatic Constitution on the Church *Lumen Gentium*
    Decree on the Eastern Catholic Churches *Orientalium Ecclesiarum*
    Decree on Ecumenism *Unitatis Redintegratio*
28 October 1965
    Decree on the Bishops' Pastoral Office in the Church *Christus Dominus*
    Decree on the Appropriate Renewal of the Religious Life *Perfectae Caritatis*
    Decree on Priestly Formation *Optatam totius Ecclesiae renovationem*
    Declaration on Christian Education *Gravissimum Educationis Momentum*

28 October 1965
Declaration on the Relationship of the Church to Non-Christian Religions *Nostrae Aetate*
18 November 1965
Dogmatic Constitution on Divine Revelation *Dei Verbum*
Decree on the Apostolate of the Laity *Apostolicam Actuositatem*
7 December 1965
Declaration on Religious Freedom *Dignitatis humanae*
Decree on the Church's Missionary Activity *Ad Gentes divinitus*
Decree on the Ministry and Life of Priests *Presbyterorum Ordinis*
Pastoral Constitution on the Church in the Modern World *Gaudium et Spes*

Philippe Levillain

Bibliography

Alberigo, G., ed., *Storia dei Concili Ecumenici*, Brescia, 1990.

Alberigo, G., and Komonchak, J., eds. *History of Vatican II*, 3 vols. to date, New York, 1995–.

Beyer, J. *Du Concile au Code de droit canonique: La mise en application du Vatican II*, Paris, 1985.

Blasquez, R. *La Iglesia del Concilio Vaticano II*, Salamanca, 1988; *The Reception of Vatican II*, Washington, 1988.

Chadwick, H. "Paul VI and Vatican II," *Journal of Ecclesiastical History*, XVI (1990), 463–9.

[Collective] "Neu im Blick: Das Konzil," *Theologisches Jahrbuch* (1987), 68–232.

Cronache del Concilio Vaticano II, ed. G. Caprile, Rome, 1965–67, 4 vols.

Documents of Vatican II, trans. W. M. Abbot, SJ, and J. Gallagher, London, 1966.

Enebral Casares, A. M. *Como interpretar el Concilio Vaticanon II*, Madrid, 1986.

Grootaers, J., and Soetens, C., eds., *Sources locales de Vatican II*. Symposium Leuven/Louvain-la-Neuve 23–25.X.1989, Leuven, 1990.

Hauer, N., and Zulehner, P. M. Aufbruch in den Untergang" *Das II. Vatikanishe Konzil und seine Auswirkungen*, Vienna, 1991.

La synodalité, La participation au gouvernement dans l'Église, Actes du VIIe Congrès international de droit canonique, l'Année canonique, 2 vols., Paris, 1992.

Latourelle, René, ed. *Vatican II: Assessment and Perspectives, Twenty-Five Years After (1962–1987)*, 3 vols., New York, 1988–9.

Le deuxième Concile du Vatican (1959–1965). Actes du colloque de l'École Française de Rome, Rome, 1989.

McCarthy, T. G. *The Catholic Tradition: Before and After Vatican II, 1878–1998*, Chicago, 1994.

Melloni, A. "Per un approcio storico-critico ai 'Consilia et Vota' della fase antepraeparatoria del Vaticano II," *Rivista di storia e letteratura religiosa*, 26 (1990), 556–76.

Melloni, A. "Tensioni timori nella preparazione del Vaticano II. La 'Veterum sapientia' di Giovanni XXIII (22 febraio 1962)," *Critica Storica*, XI (1990), 275–307.

O'Malley, J. W. *Tradition and Transition: Historical Perspectives on Vatican II*, Wilmington, Del., 1989.

Richard, L. ed., *Vatican II: The Unfinished Agenda. A Look to the Future*, New York, 1987.

Sullivan, F. A. "Il Vaticano II e il Papo oggi," *Il vescovo di Roma nella Chiesa universale*, Rome, 1987, 69–78.

Vatican II commence . . . Approches francophones, E. Fouilloux, ed., Louvain, 1993.

Vatican Council II: More Post-Conciliar Documents, A. Flannery, OP, ed. Grand Rapids, Mich., 1982.

Vatican II: The Conciliar and Post-Consiliar Documents, A. Flannery, OP, ed., Grand Rapids, Mich., 1975.

Wiltgen, R. M. *Der Rhein fliesst in den Tiber. Eine Geschichte des Zweiten Vatikanischen Konzils*, Feldkirch, 1987.

Wycislo, A. J. *Vatican II Revisited. Reflection by One Who Was There*, New York, 1987.

VATICAN CITY STATE. The Vatican City State was born of the political treaty included in the LATERAN PACTS of 1929 between the Holy See and Italy to provide territorial setting for the sovereign government of the Catholic Church.

This tiny state, however, represents only a segment of the pontifical domain in Rome, which in fact is far more extended. It consists of Vatican City proper, which is bounded by its walls and placed under the exclusive jurisdiction of the Vatican government, with the exception of St. Peter's Square, which, although an integral part of Vatican territory, remains open to the public and therefore is under Italian police protection as far as the bottom of the staircase leading up to the basilica (except in the case of outdoor masses, processions, or papal audiences, when the Italian police withdraw to the borders of the piazza, marked by the exterior line of Bernini's colonnade); and a series of landed properties dispersed throughout the city of Rome or its environs which do not belong to Vatican territory but are the property of the Holy See. Some of these properties are considered both extraterritorial and exempt from taxation and expropriation (the basilica, the palace, and the buildings annexed to ST. JOHN LATERAN and the nearby Scala Santa; the basilica and adjacent buildings of ST. MARY MAJOR; the basilica and monastery of ST. PAUL'S OUTSIDE THE WALLS; the buildings and parks of the Urbanian University on the Janiculum; the buildings of the congregations on both sides of Pius XII Square in front of St. Peter's Square; the palaces of the DATARY, of the CHANCERY, of the PROPAGANDA on Piazza di Spagna, of S. Callisto in Trastevere, of the Convertendi on the Via della Concili-azione, of the HOLY OFFICE next to the Vatican and of the Vicariate on the Via della Pigna, of the domain of Castel Gandolfo, and of those of Sta Maria di Galeria [1,100 acres/400 hectares] and of Castel Romano [180 acres/117 hectares] for the technical installations of VATICAN RADIO). Others do not have extraterritorial status but are exempt from taxation and expropriation (the buildings of the Gregorian University, the Lombard and Russian colleges, the palace of the SS. Apostoli, of S. Apollinare, of S. Andrea della Valle, of S. Carlo ai Catinari, and the priests' house at SS. Giovanni e Paolo). These properties situated outside the Vatican are not under the jurisdiction of the Vatican City government, except for Castel Gandolfo, the pope's summer residence.

The constitution of Vatican State is the fundamental law promulgated by Pius XI on 7 June 1929 and according to which the Roman pontiff is its sovereign. Vatican City is therefore a religious monarchy, with a ruler elected for life. It can be described as an absolute monarchy to the extent that the supreme pontiff enjoys, in law, a plenitude of legislative, executive, and judiciary powers, even though the Vatican State is also a legal state subject to the primacy of the law (law no. 2 of 7 June 1929 on the sources of law), to the principle of equality (art. 2 of law no. 4 of 7 June 1929 on administrative organization), and to respect for individual rights. During a pontifical inter-regnum, the monarchic power becomes collegial in that it passes to the college of CARDINALS, which, however, can exercise only limited legislative power since it can act only in a case of emergency and only temporarily, while awaiting confirmation from the new pope to be elected.

The supreme pontiff ensures the diplomatic representation of the Vatican State through the SECRETARIAT OF STATE of the Holy See. We have here, then, the phenomenon of a personal union together with a certain real union between Vatican City and the Apostolic See since, although the two are juridically distinct, the former needs the latter in order to have access to the international scene. The instrumental character of the Vatican State must be seen clearly: its only end is to serve the Church and the papacy. Its mission, therefore, is religious: to manifest the sovereignty of the Apostolic See in international law and its independence with respect to every other instituted power. For that reason, the Lateran pacts state that the Vatican City State has been created for "special purposes" (art. 3). It is therefore a sort of "supporting state" or "instrumental state" absolutely unique of its kind.

That explains why its description as a "state" has often been contested in legal doctrine. In the opinion of some, the three elements constituting a state (namely, territory, population, and sovereign power) were in this case too far out of keeping with common law. Although the territory is tiny and its enclave of 110 acres/44 hectares seems to make it something of an ordinary Roman quarter, international law has never established a minimum surface for qualification as a state, as evidenced by the proliferation of mini-states that are members of the United Nations enjoying the same legal rights as the great powers. As is true for every other state, the Vatican jurisdiction, according to the rules of public law, extends to the soil, the subsoil, and the airspace above (aircraft activity over Vatican City is actually forbidden according to article 7 of the Lateran treaty). The fact that this domain is considered Church property does not in the least diminish its nature as a state, as it did not for the former Papal States of the Italian peninsula.

As far as the population is concerned, the criticism that Vatican "nationality" is merely functional does not take into account the fact that, both in actuality and in law, the question is one of simple CITIZENSHIP (art. 9 and 21 of the treaty and law no. 3 of 7 June 1929). It is true that this is most often auxiliary and temporary because attached to certain functions, such as those proper to cardinals of the Curia residing either in Vatican City or in Rome, or to papal diplomats on assignment abroad. In general, it was meant for the benefit of persons who, by virtue of their rank, their office, their service, or their employment, live either permanently or temporarily in Vatican City, as well as for the benefit of members of their families (parents, children, spouses, relatives) living under the same roof and being supported by them (art. 1 to 5 of law no. 3 of 7 June 1929 concerning citizenship and right of residence). This citizenship, which most often is superimposed on the nationality of origin, is lost when the function for which it was required comes to an end, when authorization is withdrawn, or when residence in Vatican City is terminated (owing to the age limitation—twenty-five years for the children, unless they remain in their parents' care for reasons of health that prevent them from working—or upon marriage, for the daughters of citizens or in the case of a cardinal's transfer from Rome). Obviously, this population does not constitute a nation because its citizenship is founded neither on *jus soli* nor on *jus sanguinis* but principally on *jus officii*, since all active members work together on the same religious mission of the State. But the law also provides that the pope, in his sovereign authority, may grant Vatican citizenship to persons regardless of any official function (art. 1 *c*). Nevertheless, beyond the specifically legal nature of the question, the population of the Vatican is not limited to its citizens (in March 1993 there were 456, of whom 223 were outside Vatican City), and includes also some residents (311) living in the City without being citizens. In spite of its smallness, it is a human population living under the jurisdiction of a government as real as that of any other state.

As far as the sovereign power is concerned, it is important to keep in mind the Vatican's situation of dependency with regard to Italy. The tiny Vatican State does have its own railroad station (built by Italy) and its own railroad cars and locomotives (essentially for commercial transportation and only in exceptional cases for passengers), but the system is clearly a minimal one and is directly linked to the Italian San Pietro station only a short distance away. When the pope travels by plane or helicopter, he uses Italian aircraft. It is likewise from Italy that the Vatican receives its supply of water, gas, and electricity. Its currency, while carrying the image of the reigning pope, must have the same denomination ("lire vaticane") and the same value as the Italian lira. It is issued on order by the official Mint (the *Zecca*) of the Republic of Italy, where it is legal tender. The Vatican's postal organization is partly a tributary of Italy's. Furthermore, the Vatican has no direct or indirect system of taxation (it is exempt from customs duty by virtue of the Lateran pacts). But these are only constraints similar to those binding all mini-states or enclosed states such as the principalities of Monaco, of Andorra, and of Lichtenstein or the Republic of San Marino, to say nothing of other young and sometimes vast states that are legally independent but economically very dependent for their survival on former colonial powers. Still, the Vatican City State does have its own banking system, its network of international telecommunications, its sanitary installations, a special registration number for its automobiles ("SCV"), and its own newspaper (*L'OSSERVATORE ROMANO*). It has an internationally recognized flag (two vertical bands, one yellow and one white, with the crossed KEYS of St. Peter in the middle surmounted by a TIARA), its own legal system, and its own police force. It could even have a NAVY at its disposal, as international law allows every state without a coastline the right of navigation by sea (the Barcelona declaration of 1921); the ships, furthermore, could fly the papal flag and navigate according to the terms of the Vatican decree of 15 September 1951. The Vatican is also a member of several international governmental organizations: the Universal Postal Union, the International Telecommunications Union, the International Council of Wheat Production, the World Intellectual Property Organization, the International Union for the Protection of Literary and Artistic Works, the International Union for the Protection of Industrial Property, the International Telecommunications Satellite Organization (INTELSAT), the European Conference of Postal and Telecommunications Administrations, and so on. It is likewise a signatory member of different international conventions: the London protocol of 1936 on submarine warfare; the Geneva convention of 1949 on prisoners of war, civilians, the sick, and the wounded; The Hague convention of 1954 on the protection of cultural goods in case of war; the convention on maritime law of 1965–7; and so on. In addition, it is implicitly but necessarily committed to all international documents signed by the Holy See as the supreme government of the Church.

The fact that the Vatican has no military defense (the SWISS GUARD does not depend on the State and in any case remains highly symbolic in terms of its numbers and equipment) is no obstacle to its independence but a consequence of its neutrality, since, in the terms of the Lateran pacts, it constitutes "a neutral and inviolable territory" (art. 24, § 2). In fact, the Holy See intends to remain "a stranger to the temporal competitions among the other states [. . .] unless the litigating parties unanimously appeal to its mission of peace, retaining the right in each case to exercise its moral and spiritual power" (ibid). It is true that during the Second WORLD WAR this principle of neutrality was at times violated by third states (the encampment of German soldiers in St. Peters' Square from 8 September 1943 to 4 June 1944, the dropping of a bomb on Vatican City, the Allied bombardment of Castel Gandolfo), but most often it has been effective (the commitment of President Roosevelt to respect Vatican neutrality when American troops landed in Sicily, the asylum granted to thousands of Jewish or political refugees in Vatican City and the locations benefiting from extraterritorial status in Rome and its environs). Still, the neutrality of the Vatican should not be interpreted as indifference, and even less as a kind of paralysis on the part of the Holy See, which refrains from intervening unless the mission of the Church, the moral and spiritual interests of the faithful, or indeed the fundamental rights of the human person are at issue. In 1955, Pius XII explained clearly that the Church "remains neutral or, better still, since this term is too passive and ambiguous, impartial and independent. The Holy See will not allow itself to be taken in tow by any power or group of political powers, even if the contrary has been stated a thousand times. It may happen from time to time that, as a consequence of circumstances, the road taken by the Holy See falls in with the one taken by a political power. But as far as the point of departure or the ultimate goal is concerned, the Church and her supreme head follow exclusively their own law, the mission they have inherited from their divine Founder."

The Lateran pacts cannot be likened to an occupancy agreement consented to by the Italian government, such as that of the United Nations buildings in New York, which receive the benefits not of any sovereignty but only of extraterritoriality. Solemnly recognized by Italy, Vatican independence also comes into play in its dealings with third countries, whose approbation has been manifested both explicitly in CONCORDATS (1953 with Spain, 1954 with the Dominican Republic, 1964 with Venezuela) and implicitly by diplomatic gestures (communication of the Lateran pacts of 7 February 1929 to all embassies and legations to the Holy See, the special papal audience on the following 9 March for the entire diplomatic corps making solemn acknowledgment of the new temporal sovereignty of the pope). However, the 1929 treaty never mentions the sovereignty of the Vatican State but indicates, in article 3, that "Italy recognizes the Holy See's full ownership of, exclusive and absolute power over, and sovereign jurisdiction over the Vatican [. . .] thus creating a kind of Vatican City for the special ends and with the terms contained in the present treaty," and article 4 specifies, "The sovereignty and exclusive jurisdiction over Vatican City that Italy recognizes as belonging to the Holy See implies that no interference on the part of the Italian government may be manifested and that there will be no authority there other than that of the Holy See." Likewise, article 26, § 2 states that "Italy recognizes the Vatican City State under the sovereignty of the supreme pontiff." It is actually to the Holy See and not to the Vatican that the diplomats of some 140 states are accredited, and moreover their residences are all located in the city of Rome outside the walls of the Vatican; their immunity has been sanctioned by the Lateran pacts, which guarantee freedom of access to Vatican City and free passage on Italian territory, even in time of war, to all diplomatic agents of the Holy See or of the other states, even if these have no official relations with Italy (art. 12, § 2). This was not fully observed by the Fascist Italian state, which, during the Second World War, issued a warning that it could not ensure the protection of embassies of states hostile to or at war with Italy, a development that prompted the French, British, Belgian, and Polish diplomats to take refuge inside the Vatican, where they were soon followed by the Americans, the Bolivians, the Brazilians, the Chinese, the Colombians, the Cubans, the Ecuadoreans, the Peruvians, the Uruguayans, the Venezuelans, and the Yugoslavians, whose embassies and archives were entrusted to the legal guardianship of the apostolic NUNCIO in Italy. After the liberation of Rome, in a reverse movement, they were replaced by the Germans, the Japanese, the Hungarians, the Finns, the Romanians, the Slovaks, etc.

Since then, the whole territory of Vatican City has been entered in the international register of UNESCO as a cultural domain (18 June 1960) and accordingly placed under the special protection of the 1954 convention of The Hague for the safeguarding of cultural treasures in case of armed conflict (Italy is internationally bound not to use the Via Aurelia, which borders Vatican City, for military purposes). Moreover, on 31 October 1984, the Buenos Aires conference unanimously declared that the entire Vatican belonged to the artistic patrimony of humanity by virtue of the 1972 UNESCO accord for the protection of the world's cultural and natural patrimony.

This unique international status is the result of the absolutely specific nature of the Vatican State, which carries a particular sovereignty beyond its territorial limits. Pius

XI accounted for it as follows as far back as 1929: "There is no cupidity in the Vicar of Jesus Christ [. . .] A certain territorial sovereignty is a condition universally recognized as indispensable to every true jurisdictional sovereignty: a minimum of territory is therefore sufficient for the exercise of sovereignty, only as much territory as is needed for subsistence, and without which it would have nothing propping it up [. . .] We are pleased to see this landed domain reduced to such minimal proportions that it could and must itself be considered as spiritualized by the immense, sublime, and truly divine spiritual power which it is destined to support and to serve." Twenty years later, in an address to the diplomatic corps on 28 December 1949, Pius XII declared: "Is it not very significant, this trust on the part of so many heads of state, who have sent you here as ambassadors [. . .] to the apostolic Holy See in [. . .] this State of Vatican City, whose importance cannot be illustrated by statistics, measured by its territorial extent, or evaluated according to the power of its armed forces? Its territory, on which you are now assembled, is nothing but an imperceptible point on the globe and on the maps of the world. In the spiritual order, nevertheless, it is a symbol of high value and universal extent, for it guarantees the absolute independence of the Holy See for the accomplishment of its mission in the world." From the tribune of the United Nations in New York thirty years later, JOHN PAUL II recalled that the presence of a pontifical observer within the UN "finds its raison d'être in the sovereignty with which the Apostolic See has been clothed for many centuries. That sovereignty is limited, as regards territorial extent, to the small Vatican City State, but it is motivated by a requirement binding upon the papacy, which must carry out its mission in full freedom and which, in matters concerning its partners in dialogue, must deal with each of them independently of other sovereign powers" (talk of 2 October 1979).

So we can conclude that the debate on the statehood of Vatican City is now outdated. Because the state for so long had constituted the sole category of subjects in public international law, it was necessary to resort to the solution of statehood to establish the sovereignty of the Church. Later, the notion of international personality having been extended to international governmental organizations, it was possible to find in the broader conception a status appropriate to the papacy—all the more so in that the state symbolism of the Holy See's sovereignty accords with a certain legal fiction acknowledged by Archbishop Casaroli himself, who saw in this territorial foundation "a psychological rather than a legal condition" (talk of 10 December 1974). Moreover, it is obvious that the official reception given by states to the pope during his numerous TRAVELS around the world is offered to the supreme Head of the Church rather than to the ruler of Vatican City. Nevertheless, the notion of international personality alone does not sufficiently account for the sovereignty inherent in the Apostolic See. If the notion of statehood is no longer needed in support of the international activity of the Church, it remains indispensable for the geographical locating of the papal government, which it is certainly preferable to have under no sovereign authority other than that of the Holy See. The pope is sovereign not because he rules over Vatican City; he rules over Vatican City because he is sovereign.

Regarding the actual government of the City, the fundamental law of 1929 had provided that the supreme pontiff could delegate the regular exercise of government to a governor general entrusted with executive power and some legislative power, while the judicial power was placed in the hands of the Vatican tribunals. Appointed and recalled by the pope, to whom he was personally, directly, and exclusively responsible, the governor had to be a citizen of the Vatican and to reside within its walls. This position, however, has been held only by one person, the marquess Camillo Serafini (1929–52), who has been without a successor. But following his accession to the throne of St. Peter in March 1939, Pius XII instituted a Pontifical Commission of three cardinals to preside in his name and in his place, over the government of the Vatican State; this entity supplanted, in fact, the authority of the governor general (and of the central Council that had been grouped around him for a decade) and in a way proclaimed his demise in favor of the new triumvirate of cardinals. The same thing happened thirty years later, to the position of general counselor of the Vatican City State, another position created by the fundamental law of 1929: appointed and recalled by the supreme pontiff, to whom he too was personally, directly, and exclusively responsible, the general counselor was expected to advise in all areas provided for by the law and on all questions referred to him by the pope; he was not required to be a citizen or resident of the Vatican, and since he was compensated merely by expenses and an honorarium, he was not considered an employee of the new Vatican State. The post of general counselor has been held by only two persons: from 1929 until his death in 1935, by the marquess Francesco Pacelli, brother of the future Pius XII, one of the compilers of the Lateran pacts, and, later, principal editor of the Vatican's constitutional laws; and by his son, Prince Carlo Pacelli, who replaced his father in 1938. As happened with the position of governor general this position was doubled after 1969 by a State Advisory Committee established by Paul IV to study certain particular dossiers and to contribute advice or suggestions useful for the proper government of the State. So effective was it that at present the governmental hierarchy of Vatican City is as follows:

The cardinal secretary of state, who, from JOHN XXIII to John Paul II, has presided over the Pontifical Commis-

sion for Vatican City State. He received, by virtue of the papal chirograph of 6 April 1984, the special mandate to represent the supreme pontiff in the civil government of the pontifical state and to exercise, in his name and place, the prerogatives of the temporal sovereign power, on the condition, of course, that this power is attributed wholly to the pope, whose sovereignty is inalienable. It is therefore the cardinal secretary of state to whom the Pontifical Commission applies on all questions that depend on the personal decision of the supreme pontiff. In establishing the office, the pope sought to free himself of all temporal cares, even of those greatly reduced cares attached to his now-minuscule State, so that he could devote himself fully to his spiritual charge as head of the universal Church. Long before John Paul II, St. PIUS V had taken a similar step in creating the office of superintendent of the ecclesiastical state, which was entrusted to the CARDINAL NEPHEW and was a prefiguration of the office of cardinal secretary of states; more recently, the same motivation prompted Pius XII to provide Vatican City with a Pontifical Commission of three cardinals to represent him in the City. It can be said, therefore, that the cardinal secretary of state in a sense has become the regent of the Vatican State.

The Pontifical Commission for Vatican City States, instituted, as we have seen, by Pius XII with a simple note of the SECRETARIAT OF STATE dated 20 March 1939, was reformed by Paul VI (law of 24 June 1969), who expressly delegated to it the exercise of legislative and executive power. A permanent organism, the Commission is made up of a restricted number of cardinals of the Curia (between five and seven, depending on the era) appointed by the pope for a five-year term. Under Pius XII, it was one of the member cardinals who acted as president of the Commission; John XXIII replaced him with his secretary of state, who from that time was assisted by a pro-president (Cardinals Alberto di Jorio, 1961–9 and Sergio Guerri, 1969–80; Archbishop Paul Marcinkus, 1980–90); since 1984, however, one of the member cardinals has presided once again, since the secretary of state exercises the regency. The presiding cardinals, in succession, have been Nicola Canali (1939–61), Amleto Giovanni Cicognani (1961–9), Jean Villot (1969–79), Agostino Casaroli (1979–1984), Sebastiano Baggio (1984–90), Rosalio José Castillo Lara (1990–7), and Edmund C. Szoka (since 1997). This Commission meets three or four times a year, or more if necessary.

The Special Delegate of the Pontifical Commission of Vatican City State, a position created in 1939 at the same time as the aforementioned Commission, received, in 1969, the exercise of administrative power. At first a liaison agent between the Commission and the governor general, in the end it came to assume the greater part of the powers of the latter (whose post has been vacant for half a century), except for the enactment of regulations issued by the Commission. This function seems to belong to members of the LAITY, since, to date, the only two persons who have held the office have been Count Enrico Galeazzi, from 1939 to 1968 (who also held the title of architect of the sacred Apostolic Palaces), and Marquess Giulio Sacchetti, since 1968. The special delegate participates in the meetings of the Pontifical Commission, but only as a consultant. He presides, by right, over the State Advisory Committee.

The State Advisory Committee is an organism created by Paul VI (*motu proprio Una struttura particolare*, 28 March 1968) and normally made up of twenty-four members of the laity whose usual place of residence is Rome. These persons—of whom in fact there have been only half a dozen for the last few years—are chosen for their competence in the various fields of interest to the government of Vatican City. The Committee usually also includes six non-Roman honorary consultants (though currently there is only one), who enjoy the same voting rights as the others, the only difference being that they are not subject to obligatory attendance, as are the Roman consultants. In a spirit of clear separation of functions, officials or other permanent dependants of the Vatican State or of the Roman CURIA cannot serve on the Advisory Committee. Appointed by the pope for a five-year, renewable term, the consultants make their contribution gratis, and, as stated in the official text, their places on the Committee are "non-hereditary." As members of the papal FAMILY, they may participate in civil ceremonies in an official character, but not in the papal cortege formed for the sacred rituals of the papal CHAPEL—this, in order to distinguish clearly between the temporal and the spiritual activities. Charged with advising the Commission in the administration of the Vatican State, the Advisory Committee is convoked by its president, the special delegate, at least once every three months, or more often in case of emergency; half the members form a quorum at these meetings, and resolutions must be passed by an absolute majority of those voting. The office of secretary is held by the head of the State's Legal Office, whose duty it is to draw up the reports of the Committee and submit them to the cardinals of the Pontifical Commission. If necessary, the Advisory Committee can create special internal subcommittees to address particular issues.

The Governatorato is the umbrella over the administrative services of the Vatican State, which are concentrated in the imposing building of the same name that dominates the City in the shadow of the dome of St. Peter's. At present, its organizational chart, which has been redrawn several times, is as follows: the management of the Vatican administration is entrusted to a General Secretariat (*Segreteria generale*), responsibility for which is entrusted to the General Secretary of the *Governorato* (*Segretario generale del Governatorato*), who is appointed by the supreme pontiff. He may replace the

special delegate in case of the latter's absence or incapacity; he also takes care of the secretariat of the Pontifical Commission. He exercises, furthermore, disciplinary power over the Vatican's entire administrative staff (as of September 1992, 1,267 persons). This position, with the title Secretary of the Commission, was first held by a prelate (raised to the rank of archbishop in 1956), Archbishop Primo Principi (1939–69); then, with the title General Secretary of the *Governorato*, by a layman, the attorney Vittorio Trocchi (1969–90) then again by a titular bishop, Bishop Bruno Bertagna (1990–6); and then by Bishop Granni Danzi (since 1996). The competence of the General Secretariat is evident in its composition: seven offices (*Uffici*) are under the direct authority of the secretary general, and eight other areas have been set up in directorates. The seven offices are as follows: the Legal Office covering legal affairs of the State, of its administrative personnel, and of Vatican citizens; proposals for new laws and City regulations and preparations for international conventions in which the State is a participant; real estate matters, and so on; the head of this office is also in charge of representing the *Governorato* before the judicial and administrative organs of Vatican City and of the Republic of Italy; the Personnel Office; the Office of Vital Statistics; the Office of Systems and ARCHIVES; the Office of Central Accounting; the Office of Philatelics and Numismatics; and the Post and Telegraph Office.

The eight directorates are as follows: the General Directorate for Pontifical Monuments, MUSEUMS, and Galleries; the General Directorate for Technical Services (roads, VATICAN GARDENS and plantations, parking, etc.); the Directorate of Economic Services; the Directorate of Health Services (medical staff and pharmacy); the Directorate of General Service; the Directorate of the Vatican Observatory (whose administrative headquarters, since 1934, in fact has been at Castel Gandolfo, from which, the Observatory itself was moved in 1984 to Tucson, Arizona, on account of the clearer sky there); the Directorate of Archaeological Studies and Research; the Directorate of Pontifical Villas (The palace of URBAN VIII, Villa Cibo, and Villa Barberini at Castel Gandolfo). Furthermore, there are four other components: the Directorate of the Police of the Vatican City State (the force serving the territory of Vatican City with the exception of St. Peter's Square which is under the protection of the Italian police); the Vatican Pharmacy, the Personnel Commission; and the Disciplinary Commission.

The judiciary power, belonging by right to the supreme pontiff, is delegated to TRIBUNALS instituted for Vatican City by the fundamental law of 7 June 1929. John Paul II added an ecclesiastical tribunal of the city proper (*motu proprio Quo civium iura*, 21 November 1987) on the model of the diocesan tribunals, presided over by a judicial vicar assisted by three judges, by a promoter of justice, by a defender of the bond, and by a notary (clerk); all are clergymen appointed by the pope for a five-year term. This tribunal, with competence only in affairs of the ecclesiastical forum, is dependent for appeal upon the Roman ROTA. It is located in the same building as the civil tribunals of the Vatican State. Those, established for the judgment of cases belonging to the temporal order, have been reformed several times, by Pius XI (*motu proprio Ab fine*, 21 September 1932), by Pius XII (*motu proprio Con la legge*, 1 May 1946), and, finally, by Cardinal Casaroli by virtue of his powers as regent (law of 21 November 1987). The Vatican legal jurisdictions are articulated on four levels: first, the single judge, who, required to be a Vatican citizen, is assisted by a notary-chancellor (clerk); second, the tribunal, which, made up of a president, three judges, a promoter of justice and a notary-chancellor, must judge through a college of three magistrates; third, the court of appeals, which has the same composition and the same method of functioning as the tribunal; fourth, the Court of Cassation, which is presided over, by right, by the prefect of the supreme tribunal of the apostolic Signatura (the supreme court of the Church) and which includes two other cardinals, judges of the same Apostolic Signatura appointed by the president at the beginning of each judicial year (1 October); likewise, the promoter of justice is chosen annually by the president from among the Signatura's voting prelates.

All the magistrates (judges and promoters of justice) of the first three levels are appointed by the supreme pontiff (for five years at the court of appeal). Even though the law of 1987 is silent on this point, the single judge and the tribunal judges are, in fact, lay persons, and those of the court of appeal are prelates of the tribunal of the Roman Rota. One and the same notary-chancellor exercises his powers over the four degrees and holds his appointment from the Pontifical Commission for Vatican City State. The magistrates and the notary-chancellor of the first two levels receive indemnities for their services (reduced to half if they already receive a salary from the Holy See or from the Vatican State), and regular remuneration is given to those of the court of appeal; on the contrary, no allocation is made to the cardinals of the Court of Cassation, where only the promoter of justice receives remuneration at the end of the year. The single judge, the tribunal, and the court of appeal sit in the Vatican's Palace of Justice, whereas the Court of Cassation meets in the Hall of Congregations of the Apostolic Palace. The names of the attorneys qualified to handle cases are registered in a listing held by the chancellor. They could be advocates of the Roman Rota holding the title doctor of civil law, or other competent persons accepted by the president of the court of appeal, in some cases even jurists not inscribed on the roll; in the Court of Cassation, the defense lawyers must all be advocates of the Roman

Curia (at one time called consistorial advocates), or professors or former professors at ecclesiastical or secular universities. The Vatican administration is defended by its own consulting barristers or jurists designated by the Legal Office of the *Governorato*.

The spiritual government of the inhabitants of Vatican City falls, of course, to the pope, but in reality to a VICAR general delegated by him and independent of the *Governorato*. Pius XI decided that Vatican territory, while part of the diocese of Rome, should be entrusted to the sacristan of the apostolic palaces, guardian of the pontifical sacristy. This office, assigned since Alexander VI to a religious of the order of St. Augustine, and since Clement VIII to one of episcopal rank, was joined with that of parish priest of the apostolic palaces beginning in 1824; having received the new title of vicar general of His Holiness for Vatican City at the time of the reorganization of the pontifical House (*motu proprio Pontificalis domus*, 1968), this prelate extended his jurisdiction over the Lateran Palace and over the entire domain of Castel Gandolfo; however, the Vatican BASILICA and the adjoining canons' house depended on the authority of the cardinal archpriest of St. Peter's. It was this latter who benefited from the reform of John Paul II, whose chirograph report of 14 January 1991 unified the religious administration of the entire Vatican territory by allowing the same cardinal to hold the two offices of archpriest of St. Peter's and of vicar general of the City and its outbuildings at Castel Gandolfo (but without the Lateran Palace, which was logically entrusted to the jurisdiction of the cardinal vicar of Rome, as the seat of the city's vicariate). The apostolic sacristy from then on has been entrusted to the master of liturgical ceremonies of the supreme pontiff, the Augustinian religious retaining pastoral responsibility, in the City, only for St. Anne's parish across from the barracks of the Swiss Guard.

The cardinal vicar of Rome is also president of the permanent Commission for the Protection of the Historical and Artistic Monuments of the Holy See, of which the special delegate and the general directors of pontifical monuments, museums, and galleries and of technical services are members. Established in 1923 by Pius XI and reorganized in 1963 by Paul VI, this commission is charged with overseeing the maintenance and construction of buildings situated within the Vatican enclosure or outside of it but with extraterritorial status.

Finally, two social institutions are common to the Vatican State and the Roman Curia. The first is the Health Care Fund (FAS), created by Pius XII (rescript of 25 July 1953) and placed under the authority of the ADMINISTRATION OF THE PATRIMONY OF THE APOSTOLIC SEE to ensure the social coverage (health insurance, surgery, pharmacy, etc.) of all ecclesiastical and lay personnel (with their families) working in the central government of the Church as well as in the Vatican State administration.

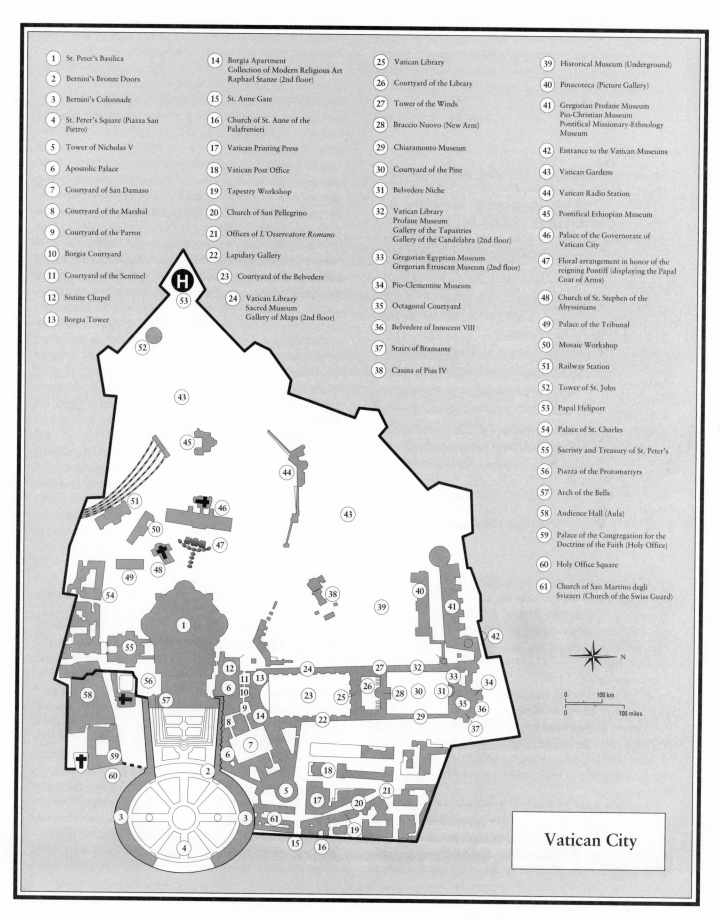

1. St. Peter's Basilica
2. Bernini's Bronze Doors
3. Bernini's Colonnade
4. St. Peter's Square (Piazza San Pietro)
5. Tower of Nicholas V
6. Apostolic Palace
7. Courtyard of San Damaso
8. Courtyard of the Marshal
9. Courtyard of the Parrot
10. Borgia Courtyard
11. Courtyard of the Sentinel
12. Sistine Chapel
13. Borgia Tower

14. Borgia Apartment
    Collection of Modern Religious Art
    Raphael Stanze (2nd floor)
15. St. Anne Gate
16. Church of St. Anne of the Palafrenieri
17. Vatican Printing Press
18. Vatican Post Office
19. Tapestry Workshop
20. Church of San Pellegrino
21. Offices of *L'Osservatore Romano*
22. Lapidary Gallery
23. Courtyard of the Belvedere
24. Vatican Library
    Sacred Museum
    Gallery of Maps (2nd floor)

25. Vatican Library
26. Courtyard of the Library
27. Tower of the Winds
28. Braccio Nuovo (New Arm)
29. Chiaramonto Museum
30. Courtyard of the Pine
31. Belvedere Niche
32. Vatican Library
    Profane Museum
    Gallery of the Tapastries
    Gallery of the Candelabra (2nd floor)
33. Gregorian Egyptian Museum
    Gregorian Etruscan Museum (2nd floor)
34. Pio-Clementine Museum
35. Octagonal Courtyard
36. Belvedere of Innocent VIII
37. Stairs of Bramante
38. Casina of Pius IV

39. Historical Museum (Underground)
40. Pinacoteca (Picture Gallery)
41. Gregorian Profane Museum
    Pio-Christian Museum
    Pontifical Missionary-Ethnology Museum
42. Entrance to the Vatican Museums
43. Vatican Gardens
44. Vatican Radio Station
45. Pontifical Ethiopian Museum
46. Palace of the Governorate of Vatican City
47. Floral arrangement in honor of the reigning Pontiff (displaying the Papal Coat of Arms)
48. Church of St. Stephen of the Abyssinians
49. Palace of the Tribunal
50. Mosaic Workshop
51. Railway Station
52. Tower of St. John
53. Papal Heliport
54. Palace of St. Charles
55. Sacristy and Treasury of St. Peter's
56. Piazza of the Protomartyrs
57. Arch of the Bells
58. Audience Hall (Aula)
59. Palace of the Congregation for the Doctrine of the Faith (Holy Office)
60. Holy Office Square
61. Church of San Martino degli Svizzeri (Church of the Swiss Guard)

N

| 0 | | 100 km |
| 0 | | 100 miles |

Vatican City

The other is the Labor Employment Office of the Apostolic See, established by John Paul II (*motu proprio Nel primo anniversario*, 1 January 1989) to settle all individual or collective labor disputes involving employees of any administration belonging to the Holy See, including those of Vatican City.

Joël-Benoît d'Onorio

Bibliography

Cammeo F. *Ordinamento giuridico dello Stato della Città' del Vaticano*, Florence, 1932.

de la Brière, Y. "Le fonctionnement du nouvel État pontifical. La Cité du Vatican," *Études*, July 1933.

Domestici-Met, M. J. "La Cité du Vatican," *L'Administration des grandes villes dans le monde*, Paris, 1986.

Gallina, E. *Il Vaticano è di tutti*, Libreria vaticana, 1991.

Guiho, P. "La citoyenneté vaticane," *Études offertes à Jean Vincent*, Paris, 1981.

Levillain, P., and Uginet, F. C. *La Vatican ou les frontières de la grace*, Paris, 1984.

d'Onorio J. B. "Le Saint Siège et le droit international," *Le Saint-Siège dans les relations internationales*, Paris, 1989.

d'Onorio. J. B. *Le Pape et le gouvernement de l'Église*, Paris, 1992.

Ripert, G. "La législation maritime de l'État du Vatican," *Le droit maritime français*, Paris, 1952.

Schulz, W. "Lo Stato della Citta' del Vaticano e la Santa Sede," *Apollinaris*, Rome, 1978.

Schulz, W. *Leggi e disposizioni usuali dello Stato della Citta' del Vaticano*, 2 vols., Rome, 1981 and 1982.

Walsh, M. J. *Vatican City State*, Oxford and Santa Barbara, 1983.

VATICAN GARDENS. Vatican Hill, located on the right bank of the Tiber, was outside the confines of the city for a long time. During the Roman Empire, it was covered with gardens, either small enclosed ones (*hortuli*) or larger gardens, those of the first Agrippina (wife of Germanicus) and of Domitia Lepida, Nero's aunt, all later absorbed into various imperial estates. This site was chosen in part for the views it offered of the Tiber valley, in part for the ease of access to it, across from the Campus Martius. Two roads bordered by tombs crossed through it. At the end of the 5th century, Pope SYMMACHUS had a modest home built there, which remained uninhabited for a long time and had to be restored in the middle of the 12th century.

When GREGORY XI returned to Rome in 1377, the traditional residence of the Lateran was abandoned. The pope went to live in the Vatican, in large part to escape the pressure of the "Roman people" and to ensure his own safety. At that time, the area surrounding the Basilica of CONSTANTINE was occupied by natural thickets and fallow fields. The story of the Vatican gardens is that of the gradual occupation of this land. It is inseparable from that of the pontifical palaces themselves.

Pope NICHOLAS V (1447–55), a great builder, took the initiative because he thought that only grandeur and magnificent buildings could instill in simple souls a feeling for the divine eternity and majesty of the Church. Nicholas V was only able to begin these grandiose projects, which did not include gardens. The great Roman villas of the Renaissance did not exist yet. There was no "modern" garden in all the buildings constructed during the first half of the 15th century. In what would become the courtyard of St. Damasus was a medieval garden like those described by Pietro de' Crescenzi in book VIII of his *De agricultura*, written around 1370: a flat piece of land, not large, surrounded by high walls against which trees were espaliered, and planted with grass (*prato*); at the center of this lawn was a basin with a fountain at its center. But unlike the gardens described by Pietro de' Crescenzi, the Vatican garden does not seem to have included plantings of fruit trees. Orange, citron, and other trees were located on the slopes of what would become the courtyard of the Belvedere. It was INNOCENT VIII (pope from 1484 to 1492) who created the first beginnings of a "villa" in what was then called la Vigna del Palazzo. He chose a high spot, north of the natural groves that extended around the palace and this hill, and built a "small summer palace" there, called *pulchrum videre Pontificis*, in Italian, *Belvedere*. Mantegna was put in charge of decorating the interior, beginning in 1488. By choosing a high location and emphasizing the views thus obtained, Innocent VIII was using the "modern" aesthetic formulated by Pietro de' Crescenzi, taken, in reality, from the theory illustrated by Pliny the Younger, who insisted upon the advantage of setting the villa above the plain. Besides, the villas of Tuscany, also built upon heights, provided examples, as did Bernardo Rucellai's garden at Quaracchi, near Florence.

The medieval aesthetic was still there: the predominance of straight lines and geometric shapes; but this geometry was not gratuitous. It imposed "reason" on the freedom of nature, according to the spirit of the Hypnerotomachia Poliphili that Francesco Colonna published at this time. The garden created between the pavilion of Innocent VIII and the palaces at the back of ST. PETER'S replaced the "Vineyard of Nicholas V," which had received only scattered, poorly coordinated development, the main item being a fountain fed, it seems, by rainwater and natural springs. A plan for a garden had been commissioned from Leon Battista Alberti (1414–72). Plantings of all sorts of plants and trees had been planned, with fountains of fresh water. But this project was never realized, and all possibilities were open when the Belvedere was first built. Following the tradition of classical antiquity, the Florentine architects erected statues there, the two most famous being the *Nile* and the *Tiber*. During the pontificate of JULIUS II (1503–1513) the improvement of this garden was actively implemented under the direction of Bramante, who began work on it shortly after 1503. Bramante's plan, only partially completed, was to transform the entire site into a "villa" worthy of the name by building two long, low walls—one to the west and the other eastward, so as to form terraces—as well as several monumental stairways and, at the foot of the Belvedere itself, a large grotto completing the axial view. Half of the Belvedere garden, which is enclosed between the two walls and the facade of the pavilion, was then planted with laurels, mulberries, and cypress trees while the other half was paved with terra cotta slabs between which orange trees were planted in a geometric pattern. This was a design carried out in accordance with the aesthetic principles of Francesco Colonna.

In the center of the garden were the statues *Nile* and *Tiber*, and, in niches built along the enclosing walls, other famous statues: the *Apollo Belvedere*, the *Laocoon*, the *Venus of Cride*, etc. These were the characteristic elements of a classical garden. A basin taken from the baths of Titus served as a fountain in the middle of the garden. Under the reign of Julius II, other gardens were added on to those of the Belvedere. They seem to have been made up of thickly wooded groves, half of them natural. Thus, the Belvedere and its garden appeared like an "enchanted" glade in the midst of this untamed natural vista, which calls to mind certain episodes of Orlando Furioso and the atmosphere of medieval romances. CLEMENT VII (1523–34) added another, similar grove along the other side of the western arm, oriented toward Monte Mario. The final modification to the Belvedere, the construction of the "braccio delle Bibliotheche" was done during the reign of Sixtus V (1585–90). Thus Bramante's aesthetics of an enclosed garden, enriched with elements from classical antiquity and the Platonizing intellectualism of Colonna, came to an end. From now on, the two halves of Bramante's garden would be only two palace courtyards. During the rule of Paul III (1534–49) work was begun to consolidate all the lands beyond the via delle Fondamenta on the slopes of the hill by the Belvedere. This garden included two old-fashioned pergolas forming a vault and placed at right angles to each other. At their intersection is a small cupola (a familiar theme of Florentine architects of the preceding century) like that built in Florence by Niccolo Pericoli for Cosmo I in 1549 for the Boboli gardens.

After the crisis brought on by the sack of ROME in 1527, the modernization and the development of the Vatican gardens was resumed, with little interruption. In the middle of the century, under Paul IV, the foundations of a pavilion (casino) were laid in the uncultivated field beyond the enclosure of the Belvedere, to the west, on the slopes of the hill. The architect given the assignment for this project was Pirro Ligorio. The work continued after the death of PAUL IV and was completed under PIUS IV in 1561 by the same Ligorio. From Pius IV it received the name frequently used for it, "villa Pia." In reality it is not a villa, but a simple pavilion, which clings to the very skip hillside, and dominates the entire site. This casino is made up of two *loggie* placed side by side, one facing the southwest and the other facing the northeast and with no actual connection to the Belvedere garden. Between the two *loggie* is a small oval courtyard paved with marble. In the middle of this courtyard is a fountain whose water is collected in a marble basin shaped like a bathtub. Two children riding dolphins embody an old pagan symbol, salvation sent by the gods (the dolphin was sacred to Apollo) during the passage of the soul leaving this world for the lands across the Ocean, where the Islands of the Blessed were. The resemblance to the design of the inner facade of the Medici villa, which was created at the same time, is obvious down to the importance given to the loggia, which opens up the living quarters to the gardens and create an exterior area to be used for entertainments. There is also a resemblance in the décor of the facades. As at the Medici villa, there are reliefs in the antique style half recessed in the walls. At each end is a statue that seems to emerge from the wall, through a door flanked by two columns and topped by a curved pediment. An overhead grid shaped like a barrel vault and shown in perspective, perhaps a vestige of old-style pergolas, seems to open out into these porchways, giving an impression of depth. This pavilion, built at approximately the same time as the Spada palace (constructed in 1540) uses the same theme, that of an illusion of depth created by the deceptive use of perspective.

With the pavilion of Pius IV, the pontifical residence is modeled on the great villas like that of Pope Julius III (the villa Giulia) or the villa Madama (begun under Clement VII but continued and completed after the sack of 1527). The influence of the COUNTER-REFORMATION is not to be felt there. This pavilion is often called "a pagan dream," but, in reality, in the Vatican as elsewhere, the gardens reflect an esthetic that was born and developed during classical antiquity, and for a long time some tension prevailed between the gardens and Christian sensibility. It was only in the 19th century that a grotto of Lourdes was added to the Vatican gardens, and this is an exception to the rest of the whole. After their creation by Pius IV, the Vatican gardens continued to evolve in the same spirit that had presided over their beginning. SIXTUS V (1585–90) created the "bracchio nuovo," which split in two the Belvedere garden and caused the ensemble to lose its unity. Under the rule of CLEMENT IX (1667–69) the fishpond created by JULIUS III a century earlier was transformed into a "picturesque" fountain representing a warship, with sails, anchors, and cannons ("fontana del Vascello"); it is only a curiosity.

No major modification was made until the time of GREGORY XVI (1831–46) other than various plantings, notably of citrus trees, and the addition of several small fountains. Gregory XVI heightened the enclosing wall and also added some fountains. On the unused portion he had an English-style garden planted, a fashion that was spreading throughout Europe, and lowered the level of the garden "della Pigna" (Pine Cone), which is the part of the Belvedere garden that lies in front of the Belvedere itself. Since then, with the establishment of the Vatican as a state, several bits of land still vacant along the wall bordering the viale del Vaticano have been used for various constructions that rise among the surviving thickets. The Vatican gardens are no longer, as they were intended to be from the 15th century on, comparable to those built by the cardinals near Rome or in the city itself. They have become a true museum of an art that reached its peak during the 16th century, with the pavilion of Pius IV.

Pierre Grimal

Bibliography

Cecchelli, C. *Il Vaticano . . . I Giardini*, Milan, 1927.

Dami, L. *Il giardino italiano*, Milan, 1924.

Friedlander, W. *Das Kasino Pius der Vierten*, Leipzig, 1912.

Gregorovius, F. *Geschichte der Stadt Rom im Mittelalter*, ed. Kampf, 4 vols., Munich, 1978.

Jung-Inglessis, E. M. *A Stroll in the Vatican Gardens*, Vatican City, 1995.

VATICAN LABOR UNION. The term "Syndicate of the Vatican" is commonly used to designate the Association of the Lay Dependents of the Vatican (Associazione Dipendenti Laici Vaticani), or ADLV, which was created in the spring of 1981 on the initiative of employees of Vatican City who were dissatisfied with their wages. The protest movement had begun two years before when, on 18 April 1979, 92 workers of Vatican Radio (then employed by Vatican State) wrote to the pope to request a considerable increase in their remuneration. After being received in audience by JOHN PAUL II on 6 April 1981, the ADLV acquired statutes, which were approved by its delegates' counsel on 19 May and by its general assembly on 3 June. These statutes, since amended, were officially recognized by the ecclesiastical authority on 11 October 1993.

The goal of the association is to defend the professional, juridical, moral, individual, and collective interests of its members and to improve their conditions of life and work according to the principles of the Church's social doctrine, and on the basis of relevant international conventions and Italian laws. Administered from its head office in Vatican City, the ADLV includes a large number of lay employees, both active and retired (700 out of 1,800 employees, according to its estimates), both in the Roman Curia and other pontifical institutions and in the administration of Vatican State (with the exception of the police and Swiss Guard, who cannot be unionized).

The ADLV is structured on two levels: the sector assemblies, set up in the various pontifical organizations; and the annual general assembly, which exercises deliberative power at the highest level of the association, especially for the elaboration of the platform of claims. Between the two general assemblies, the decision-making power falls to the council of delegates, which usually meets once a month. The direction of the ADLV is headed by a secretary general elected by the delegates, as is the executive council of eight members. The general vice-secretary and treasurer are elected by the executive council from within, on the proposal of the secretary general. In the case of important decisions, recourse may be had to a general referendum of all members.

On 29 February 1988, the functionaries of Vatican State experimented with a new form of manifestation: the "active strike," consisting in offering the pope three hours of nonremunerated work in the guise of a gift toward mitigating world hunger. On 28 May 1990, 500 employees organized a silent procession in the papal city against the insufficiency of salary increases. Their protests chiefly had to do with the indexing of salaries, benefits, and pensions.

The ADLV was expressly mentioned in the papal letter of 20 November 1982 to the cardinal secretary of state on the working community of the Holy See, in which John Paul II described it as an "initiative conforming to the social doctrine of the Church" and considered it as "one of the appropriate instruments for providing a better guarantee of social justice between workers and employers." Nonetheless, the pope wished to stress at the same time the "peculiar character of the Apostolic See" and the absolutely original nature of the Vatican State, unique of its kind because specially instituted for the exclusive service of the Church. Those who work there have committed themselves voluntarily and in full awareness of the uniqueness of Vatican City and consciousness of the duties that result from this. That is why the ADLV's activities may not be equated with those of the trade unions of political societies or go beyond certain limits, recalled by John Paul in these words: "But there is one thing that does not correspond to the social doctrine of the Church, and that is the shifting of this type of organization onto the terrain of all-out conflicts or class struggle. Nor must they be political in nature or serve, openly or in secret, the interests of parties or other entities aimed at objectives very different in nature." These terms were largely explicated in appendix II of the apostolic constitution *Pastor bonus* of 28 June 1988, reforming the Roman Curia. The cardinal secretary of state would take it up again in a circular letter of 11 July 1990.

It was with a view to improving the condition of the papal employees (clergy and laity) and work relations within the Vatican that the Ufficio del Lavoro della Sede Apostolica was instituted (*motu proprio Nell' primo anniversario* of 1 January 1989). The new General Regulation of the Roman Curia of 4 February 1992 echoed this concern by issuing the Statutes of Personnel of the Dicasteries. This was followed on 30 September 1994 by the *motu proprio La sollecitudine*, which reaffirmed the function and attributes of the Ufficio and its specific institutional identity.

Joël-Benoît d'Onorio

Bibliography

d'Onorio, J. B. *Le Pape et le gouvernement de l'Église*, Paris, 1992.

Schulz, W. *Leggi e disposizioni usuali dello Stato della Città del Vaticano*, II, Libreria Editrice della Pontificia Università Lateranense, Rome, 1982.

VATICAN LIBRARY.

History. Undoubtedly from the beginning the Roman pontiffs kept close at hand the books and documents they would need. But apart from occasional fleeting references to collections that seem to have been often dispersed and reassembled, only in the 13th century is there clear evidence of a true pontifical library, that of BONIFACE VIII; an inventory from 1294 has survived, showing that there were 442 volumes, 419 in Latin and 23 in Greek. Transferred to Perugia and then to Assisi, while the papacy was taking the road to France, the library, which had 645 volumes in 1311, was subsequently broken up: very few manuscripts reached AVIGNON.

But in the papal palace at Avignon a new library took shape, expanded in part by the right to the SPOILS, which allowed the pope to seize the property of deceased clerics *apud Sedem apostolicam*. By 1369, there were 2,059 volumes. However, left in Avignon when GREGORY XI returned to Rome and the GREAT SCHISM began, the library was transferred for the most part to Peñiscola by BENEDICT XIII. Collected by the cardinal LEGATE Pierre de Foix, in 1429, when he secured the renunciation of CLEMENT VIII, the successor of Benedict XIII, the ANTIPOPE'S volumes later formed the nucleus of the library of the College de Foix, founded in 1457 at the University of Toulouse by the former legate; what remained of it was bought at the end of the 17th century by Colbert and today belongs to the Bibliothèque Nationale in Paris.

The books left at Avignon—648 of them, according to a 1411 inventory—found their way back to Rome only a few at a time over the following centuries. In 1607, there was still a considerable batch of manuscripts on the banks of the Rhône, which was given by PAUL V to his nephew, CARDINAL Scipione Borghese, then legate at Avignon; these manuscripts remained in his family for many years, but eventually made their way back to the HOLY SEE, after they were bought from the heir by LEO XIII in 1891.

The present Vatican Apostolic Library was assembled around another nucleus. After the council of Constance and the end of the Great Schism, the popes, though back in Italy, continued to travel a good deal, which did not encourage the building up of a collection of books. MARTIN V, and especially EUGENE IV, collected some volumes; but NICHOLAS V is the pope responsible for setting the papacy in a palace adjacent to St. PETER'S at the Vatican and for planning a real library. A humanist, Nicholas V had copies made of many manuscripts, often richly illuminated, stored them in his apartments, and named a librarian in the person of the humanist scholar Giovanni Tortelli. By the time of his death, Nicholas V had collected more than 800 Latin and 353 Greek manuscripts.

Although librarians were named under succeeding popes, including the humanist bishop Giovanni Andrea Bussi (d. 4 February 1475), the library was still not institutionalized and the collections remained scattered around the papal palace. To the Franciscan SIXTUS IV goes the honor of having really founded the library. He began after Bussi's death by designating a new librarian, the learned historian Bartolomeo Platina (1421–81), who soon established a system for lending the books entrusted to him. On 15 June 1475, by the BULL *Ad decorem militantis Ecclesiae*, the papal collections were united in one library properly so called, located in three (and soon four) rooms of the Apostolic PALACE recently built at the Vatican, financed by fixed revenue grants, and entrusted to a specialized staff under the direction of Platina, *gubernator et custos* of the new establishment. The goal of the institution was affirmed clearly: to open a public library intended for use by scholars, and to make available to intellectuals—to humanists—the books of the papal palace.

Since then, the Vatican Library (Bibliotheca Apostolica Vaticana) has continued to grow. Only the major stages of its evolution can be recalled here.

Although the title "custodian" had been conferred on the one principally responsible for the Library, that designation later came to be reserved for assistants. Platina and his successors were called "librarians." Beginning with Marcello Cervini (the future Pope MARCELLUS II), named a cardinal in 1550, those in charge were cardinal librarians, always assisted by custodians (and soon first and second custodians), who were themselves later surrounded by *scriptores* (conservators, especially of manuscripts); this organization of the institution lasted—with the exception of the period of the revolutionary and imperial disturbances—until the end of the 19th century and the reforms of Leo XIII.

Problems of space arose as a result of the constant growth of the Library. The four rooms laid out by Sixtus IV—the Greek Room, the Latin Room, the Secret Library (precious holdings), and the Papal Library (archives)—were insufficient. Pope SIXTUS V had a building erected in 1587 that cut in two the vast courtyard conceived by Bramante, thereby separating the Apostolic Palace from the Belvedere pavilion. In 1589–90, manuscripts and printed books were moved into this building, into the large upper room (*Salone Sistino*) and its vestibule, space that was soon expanded by the addition of the rooms adjacent to the PIUS IV wing. In a section of these rooms, in 1612, Paul V installed the pontifical ARCHIVES, which he separated permanently from the Library.

The names of all the scholars appointed by the popes to the guardianship of the collections, either as cardinal librarians or as custodians, cannot be reviewed here. Only those who left the greatest mark can be mentioned. The librarians of the 16th century, besides Cervini, included Cardinal Sirleto and, at the turn of the next century, Baronius, while a veritable dynasty of custodians, the family of the Ranaldi, kept the collections in order and drafted inventories that are still used. In the 17th century, Cardinals Scipione Borghese, Francesco and Antonio Barberini, and Fabio Chigi, named to the post because they were relations of the popes, were nonetheless active administrators, attentive to the growth of the Library; they were also able to assemble personal libraries of a high quality that, after remaining in their families for many years, in the end made their way to the Holy See. The notable custodians included the scholars Lucas Holstenius and Leone Allacci, and the Belgian historian Schelstrate. In the next century, Cardinals Querini, Passionei, Albani, and Zelada were brilliant librarians, and a new dynasty of custodians was born, the Assemani, a Maronite family of scholars who procured many Eastern manuscripts for the Vatican Library.

The period of the French Revolution and Empire brought great disorder. The pope was required by the treaty of Tolentino (19 February 1797) to pay a tribute of 500 Vatican manuscripts, chosen by the commissioners of the Directory. A new seizure was made the following year, of 138 incunabula, 6 manuscripts, and, in particular, a quantity of coins and medals; the numismatic collection was also subjected to pillaging by the French military. Order had scarcely been restored under the authority of Cardinal Consalvi when Napoleon's seizure of the PAPAL STATES overthrew Roman institutions once again. The Library, however, did not suffer much damage and, after the fall of the emperor and the reestablishment of PIUS VII, almost all the manuscripts were returned from France; only 36 of them, either abandoned by the pope in the Bibliothèque Royale in Paris or lost, were not returned to the shelves at the Vatican.

Angelo Mai was the dominant figure at the Library in the 19th century. From the Ambrosiana in Milan, where he made his start in library work, this former JESUIT came to the Vatican as first custodian in 1819. His work on the manuscripts, his studies of palimpsests (notably the discovery of Cicero's *De re publica*), and his numerous editions of texts made him famous, and a pioneer of the new science of philology. Mai left his position at the Library in 1833, but he continued his labors, and returned as cardinal librarian before his death in 1854.

A new era for the Vatican Library began with Pope Leo XIII, who was highly literate and keenly attentive to scholarship and methods of research. He reformed the administrative structures of the Library, so that the cardinal librarian's role was now only that of "protector of the Vatican Library"—a reduced role, essentially honorary, but carrying a prestige that could be amplified by the personal prestige of the one who held the title. Effective responsibility was entrusted to the first custodian, who was soon designated by the title "prefect." Moreover, a physical reorganization of the buildings resulted in the opening of the *Sala Leonina*, situated in a former arms factory and one story below the *Salone Sistino*; 185,000 printed volumes were transferred to it from the Borgia apartments, where, for want of space, they had been stored under GREGORY XVI, and where they had been inaccessible to readers, who thus had been obliged to limit themselves to the study of manuscripts.

Not the least of Leo XIII's accomplishments is having made the Jesuit Franz Ehrle head of the Library. Ehrle not only assumed most of the responsibility for the work of reorganization, but also provided vigorous leadership for the staff's scientific work. A new series of catalogues of manuscripts, applying carefully elaborated norms, was issued, including that of the *Studi e testi* collection and another of editions of facsimiles of manuscripts (*Codices e Vaticanis selecti*). Continuing his work under the pontificate of PIUS X, Ehrle rearranged the premises by housing the manuscripts in new halls and by making available reading room in which they could be consulted on the same level as the *Sala Leonina*. The *Salone Sistino*, thus freed, could be opened to the public touring the Vatican Museums; later, it was turned into the site for exhibitions mounted by the Library.

Ehrle was succeeded by Achille Ratti (1914–19) and then Giovanni Mercati, whom Eugene Tisserant assisted as pro-prefect. Ratti, named pope as PIUS XI, did not forget his past as librarian. He freed up still more space for the library, allowing for a major expansion of its collections and improvements in its old buildings. That work is still going on. In the 1980s a new building was provided, for the printing department and a new computerized information service, with a basement storage space for manuscripts. In 1992, a second consulting room for printed materials, reserved for periodicals, was opened.

During recent years, the following have served, successively, as prefects: Giovanni Mercati (1919–36), Anselm Maria Albareda (1936–62), Alfons Raes (1962–71), Alfons Maria Stickler (1971–83), Leonard E. Boyle (1984–96), Raffaele Farino (1996–). Cardinal librarians, several of whom served earlier as prefect, include: Aidan Gasquet (1919–29), F. Ehrle (1929–34), G. Mercati (1936–57), E. Tisserant (1957–71), Antonio Samore (1974–83), A.M. Stickler 1983–8), Antonio Maria Javierre Ortas (1988–92), Luigi Poggi (pro-librarian, 1992–98), Jorge Maria Mejia (1998–).

The Collections. They are divided into three conservation departments.

1. *Manuscripts*. There are about 70,000 manuscripts, properly so called. Those that came to the library a few at a time are called "Vaticans" and are classified by language or system of writing. There are the Vaticano greco and the Vaticano latino (all those written in Latin letters, including Italian, French, etc.), and also Arab, Armenian, Copt, Ethiopian, Georgian, Hebrew, Persian, Slav, Syriac, etc. Collections that came to the library as entire lots, whether as legacies or purchases, have retained their former names. So there are Palatinates (from the library of the Palatinate electors of Heidelberg, received in 1622), *Urbinates* (from Frederick of Montefeltro, duke of Urbino, and his successors, 1657), "*Reginenses*" (from Queen Christina of Sweden, 1689), Ottoboni (1748), Borghese (1891), Barberini (1902), Borgia (1902), Rossi (1921), Chigi (1923), Sbath (1926), Chapter of St. Peter (1940), Patetta (1945), etc. To all these are added an almost equal number of bundles and registers of archival documents which keep the names of the collections from which they originated: Barberini, Chigi, Chapter of St. Peter, St. Mary Major (1931), and some other Roman churches. Finally, there are collections of personal papers, such as the papers of Paul Liebaert or Guiseppe Toniolo, and also collections of personal writings (Ferraioli, Patetta . . .).

2. *Printed materials*. These number about one million (of which 80,000 are available to readers by direct access). The books are divided in different sections according to material. Among others, one precious holding is made up of the Incunables (about 7,000), the Aldines (editions of Aldus Manutius and his descendants at Venice), the "Raccolta prima," the oldest printed collection in the library, etc. Finally, as with the manuscripts, block collections have been respected and keep the names of their former owners: Barberini, Chigi, Ferraioli, Capponi, Chapter of St. Peter, Cicognara, Mai, Rossi, etc. The periodicals are part of the print collection, as are the stamp collections (including the designs of the Ashby collection, acquired in 1933), and the geographic maps.

3. *Objects*. This department has various sections:

Indirizzi. These include dispatches of all kinds by the pope, articles, addresses, books of signatures, photographs . . . indications of the piety of Catholic people, classified by each pontificate.

Medagliere. The library's numismatic cabinet, reconstituted in the 19th century after the serious losses of 1798, enlarged again in the 20th by the acquisition of entire collections, or coins found in the excavations of St. Peter's, containing nearly 400,000 pieces: ancient, mediaeval or modern monies (especially Roman coins from the republican period, and papal coins), medals, coins, antique leads, seals and lead bulls, and an important collection of precious stones.

Museo sacro. Created by Benedict XIV and Cardinal Passionei, later expanded, it contains articles from the catacombs, ancient glassware, enamels, ivories, crystals, silver pieces. . . .

Museo profano. Clement XI instituted it to house articles from Greek and Latin antiquity. It was pillaged by the French in 1798, later reconstituted, and contains Etruscan and Roman artifacts: ivories, glassware, mosaics, mirrors, arms. . . .

Finally, the library has a regularly updated copy of the Princeton University *Index of Christian Art*, as well as a photography workshop and a restoration laboratory, and it looks after the direction and teaching at its school for librarians instituted in 1934.

Louis Duval-Arnould

Bibliography

Bignami Odier, J. *La Bibliothèque vaticane de Sixte IV à Pie XI. Recherches sur l'histoire des collections de manuscrits*, Vatican City, 1973.
Jullien de Pommerol, M. H., and Monfrin, J. *La Bibliothèque pontificale à Avignon et à Peñiscola pendant le Grand Schisme d'Occident et sa dispersion. Inventaires et concordances*, 2 vols., Rome, 1991.
Muntz, E. *La Bibliothèque du Vatican au XVIe siècle*, Paris, 1886.
Muntz, E., and Fabre, P. *La Bibliothèque du Vatican au XVe siècle d'après des documents inédits. Contributions pour servir à l'histoire de l'humanism*, Paris, 1887.
Ruysschaert, J. "Sixte IV, fondateur de la Bibliothèque vaticane (15 June 1475)," *AHP*, 7 (1969), 513–24.
Vian, N. "Vaticano. VI. La Biblioteca Vaticana," *EC*, 12 (1954), 1123–1130.

VATICAN PALACE. See **Residences, Papal.**

VATICAN RADIO. The idea of a radio station at the Vatican grew out of the LATERAN PACT of 11 February 1929, which sealed the reconciliation between the kingdom of Italy and the Holy See. Pius XI at once entrusted the realization of the idea to Guglielmo Marconi, the Italian scientist who founded the technology. With Marconi at his side, on 12 February 1931, the pope and his secretary of state, Cardinal Eugenio Pacelli (the future Pius XII), inaugurated the studio and first radio broadcast of the young VATICAN CITY STATE. The pontifical message *Omni creaturae* was broadcast via a 10-kilowatt transmitter over two short wavelengths that was set up in the medieval tower on the Vatican Hill, restored by Leo XIII in the late 19th century. In 1933, the pope attended the broadcast of the world's first radio link, formed by a permanent link by microwave between the Vatican Palace and the summer residence of Castel Gandolfo. In 1936, the International Radio Union recognized the "special case" of the universal purpose of the Vatican radio, authorizing it to broadcast without any geographical limits. On 25 December 1937, improvements were made to the technical installations by the incorporation of a Telefunken 25-kilowatt transmitter and two directional antennas transmitting over 10 frequencies.

In the first years of the SECOND WORLD WAR, news broadcasts—which by now were sent by pontifical radio in four languages over medium wave—were regarded with suspicion by the Nazis and, on Goebbels's orders, silenced in Germany. Throughout the war, Vatican Radio pursued its humanitarian task of uniting dispersed families, making a total of 12,105 hours of broadcasts and 1,240,728 transmitted messages. When peace came, the programs progressively reflected the universality of the Church, broadcasting in 19 languages from 1948 on and including, from 1957, a radio journal on commentary.

Nevertheless, to ensure the growth indispensable for a modern radio station, Vatican City's slender resources forced the authorities of the Holy See to acquire a 440-hectare area situated 18 kilometers north of Rome, toward Lake Bracciano. On 24 July 1952, this property, known as Santa Maria di Galeria, was granted extraterritorial status by the Italian Republic. Thanks to the generosity of Catholics, a large broadcasting center was built which Pius XII inaugurated on 27 October 1957. Linked by Hertzian wave to Vatican City, at the time the center consisted of a Philips 100-kilowatt shortwave transmitter, two 10-kilowatt shortwave transmitters, and one 120-kilowatt medium-wave transmitter, together with 24 metal towers arranged on three axes and supporting 21 shortwave directional antennas, complemented by one omnidirectional medium-wave antenna 98 meters high.

Next, Vatican's Radio transmission power was reinforced by two transmitters of 100 kilowatts each for Africa and Oceania, one 250-kilowatt transmitter for medium-wave broadcasts to Europe, and another of 500 kilowatt with a gyrating antenna for links with the Far East and Latin America. The present infrastructure represents, in short- and medium-wave facilities, a 1,700-kilo-

watt power reaching all parts of the world, with over 15,000 hours annually of broadcasts in 34 languages, including Esperanto. Vatican Radio uses three types of waves: short waves, covering almost the entire globe; medium waves, reaching the whole of Europe and all the Mediterranean Basin; and frequency modulation, for the city of Rome and the Roman Campagna. In this connection, it has been said that the only war the Vatican now wages is the war of waves. Its millions of listeners sometimes make their voices heard, as evidenced by the avalanche of mail, which reached 96,000 letters in 1990 (of which 62,000 came from Eastern Europe). Vatican Radio is a member of the European Union of Broadcasting (UER), the Catholic International Association of Broadcasting (UNDA), and the International Radio and Television University (URTI).

Since January 1970, Vatican Radio's central office has occupied the whole of the Palazzo Pio, an imposing building erected by Pius XII facing the Castel Sant'Angelo at the beginning of the Via della Conciliazione. Here are housed the technical transmission center, 14 broadcasting studios, two listening rooms, two libraries, all the offices and, naturally, a chapel from which Mass is broadcast each day. On the Leo XIII tower, a 10-story antenna has been installed, along with four Yagi antennas per story for FM (50- kilowatt) broadcasts, and two parabolic antennas to ensure a direct link with Santa Maria di Galeria. This center has two OC Telefunken 500-kilowatt transmitters connected to two gyrating antennas, two automatic 250-kilowatt Brown Boveri transmitters with a single lateral band, and five 100-kilowatt transmitters feeding 25 fixed antennas; one 600-kilowatt transmitter for medium waves is connected to a directional antenna consisting of four 94-meter-high towers. An omnidirectional antenna completes the installation. For grand pontifical events, Vatican Radio also makes use of transmission points inside St. Peter's basilica and on St. Peter's square, in the Hall of Benedictions over the basilica atrium, in the great general audience hall (Aula Paul VI), and in the synod hall. The content of the progams is, of course, mainly centered on religious news, but political, cultural, and social news is also treated from a Christian perspective. Doctrinal, spiritual, and liturgical education is another preoccupation of Vatican Radio, while its Roman network ("Rete romana") broadcasts cultural news and programs 20 hours a day. These offer a wide range of music (classical, sacred, rock, pop, jazz, etc.).

Administratively, Vatican Radio is no longer one of the nine services of the *governatorato* (government) of the Vatican City State. From 1 January 1986 on, it has had an autonomous administration, which the apostolic constitution *Pastor bonus* of 28 June 1988 included among the "Institutions linked to the Holy See." Its financing comes almost exclusively from public funds (a global endowment is paid each year to the General Direction of Radio by the financial services of the Holy See), supplemented, as always in the Church, by gifts of generous Catholic listeners. Thus, in the 1950 Holy Year, Catholics of the Netherlands offered Pius XII a 100-kilowatt shortwave Philips transmitter; in 1962, the Australians and New Zealanders presented John XXIII with a Telefunken transmitter of the same power, as did the U.S. Knights of Columbus in 1966. Individuals also make their own private contributions; for example, Cardinal Joseph Frings, archbishop of Cologne, and Cardinal Francis Spellman, archbishop of New York, each offered 100-kilowatt transmitters in 1961 and 1966, respectively. The customary state dues do not exist at the Vatican. Most of the reporting of papal ceremonies is exempt from fees, according to the system of free exchange between radio stations that belong to the European Broadcasting Union; other programs pay only transmission costs. Nor are there any authors' rights over production, since every broadcast may be recorded by anybody and freely rebroadcast. There is no advertising because Vatican Radio is not a commercial enterprise and does not aim to make a profit. Cassettes of various recordings are sold to the public practically at cost. Similarly, possessors of receivers do not have to pay dues. This explains Vatican Radio's chronic deficit (calculated at 7 billion lire in 1988); its expenses for 1993 totaled over 3 billion lire, half of it for staff salaries.

For the control of its general policy, the management of Vatican Radio from the outset was entrusted to the Society of Jesus but at first depended directly on the sovereign pontiff (regulation of 5 December 1932, art. 39). The radio station was, in fact, conceived as being above all authority but that of the pope. As a result, it had a mandate to inform the world in general, and the Catholic world in particular, of the Holy Father's words, actions, and gestures, and in so doing to reflect all the activity of the Apostolic See as it serves the universal Church. Since 1966 (letter of 23 December 1966 from cardinal secretary of state Amleto-Giovanni Cigognani to Father Pedro Arrupe, superior general of the Society of Jesus), Vatican Radio has remained a pontifical fief through the intermediary of the Secretariat of State. This office is responsible for checking programs, in particular from the point of view of doctrine, in order to provide listeners with information in conformity with the Church's teaching. Vatican Radio is governed like a monopoly, but this state monopoly is according to law and not in fact, since the many Italian radio and television stations, both public and private, can obviously all be picked up inside Vatican City. Even in the contents of Vatican Radio's programs, religious pluralism can be seen in the place given to ECUMENISM and the numerous non-Catholic guests who express their views.

Responsibility for Vatican Radio is entrusted to four directors under the authority of the president of the coordinating committee, who is a Jesuit, as are the following three principal directors.

(a) The Director General, appointed by the pope on the proposal of the superior general of the Society of Jesus, answers to the Secretariat of State of the Holy See. He is responsible for general coordination of the activities and initiatives of the whole radio operation—programs, news, and technical installations. It is his duty to keep the Secretariat of State well informed about the functioning of the radio station, its plans, and possible problems. His decision-making power is always subject to the Secretariat of State, but is exercised over the three other directors, of whom he is the hierarchical superior. Of his closest collaborators, one is responsible for international relations and another for promotion and development of the radio.

(b) The Director of Programs, nominated by the Secretariat of State on the proposal of the Society of Jesus, is directly responsible for the content, organization, and improvement of the programs, which vary considerably from one linguistic area to another because sensibilities and concerns are not the same in every country. The political and religious situations of the various regions must also be taken into account. Except for its broadcasts in Latin (daily Mass and rosary), Vatican Radio divides its programs into two categories: programs of an international nature that are translated in the same form into several languages (daily news and commentary and religious reports of important ecclesiastical events) and ethnic and linguistic programs, which vary among the 34 languages used. These broadcasts, which are designed for the information and spiritual and moral training of listeners, have religious content (papal discourses and teachings, along with commentaries and analysis) or a cultural content (progress in the sciences and the arts, music, peace, development, international solidarity, etc.). The Director of Programs oversees all aspects of production and coordinates the work of the language sections, ensuring their administrative links with the various sources of documentation (libraries, recording libraries, files, written or sound archives, etc.). As for program content, control is more or less nonexistent, insofar as no text is sent to the authorities before it is broadcast; the account of the broadcasts that each language section has to draw up each day is intended, like all the texts read over the radio, for the radio archives, where it can be looked up if need arises for control *a posteriori*. There is, however, no record of such a situation arising. Sometimes the Secretariat of State may ask to see a text after receiving letters of protest, so that it can verify the exact contents of the incriminated remarks. It is usually a case of wrongful accusation, because Vatican Radio, which never engages in polemics, hardly lays itself open to controversy.

(c) The Director of Technical Services is appointed by the Secretariat of State on the proposal of the Society of Jesus. It is his task to supervise the technical installations in general, as well as their maintenance and their development, which is decided by the authority exercising oversight. From the technical viewpoint, he is responsible for broadcasting pontifical radio messages and papal ceremonies, for which Vatican Radio enjoys the privilege of exclusivity without prior authorization. However, those foreign radios and television stations that are interested in an event, with or without the pope's presence, in areas directly dependent on the Holy See must obtain permission from the Pontifical Council for Social Communications. According to a regulation of 1964 aimed at "an exact and suitable informing of public opinion" and intended to "avoid excessive disturbance in the sacred functions, ceremonies or activities of the offices of the Holy See" (art. 1), authorization is dependent on the prior submission of a detailed request (list of individuals and materials, intentions, communication of the scenario in the case of a film, or text in the case of a disk, nature of the broadcast, which must not be used as commercial advertising, etc.). After conferring with the Secretariat of State, the Pontifical Council for Social Communications may agree. It will inform the authorities of the Holy See and Vatican City, and grant those requesting permission adequate religious assistance throughout the event. A rigorous respect for the limits of this permission is entrusted to the pontifical police force. In return, the interested party must promise in writing to observe a number of regulations: respect for the sacred places and the person of the sovereign pontiff; submission to the Pontifical Council of films or disks made before they are circulated; deposit of one copy of the film in the Vatican Film Library, and strict adherence of the film or sound recording to the aim for which it was authorized (art. 8 of 1964 regulation).

(d) The Administrative Direction, made up of merely 10 functionaries, sees to the regular management of Vatican Radio.

Vatican Radio is manned by a staff of more than 400 individuals working full or part time, together with about 200 occasional workers. Nearly 150 of these work for the technical section and about 40 for general management, but over half the radio's employees are engaged in the program division. These are men and women representing 55 different nationalities, the majority of them layfolk (355 out of 400 in 1992), alongside 52 priests and monks and 13 nuns. All are under the Personnel Office of the radio's general direction. This mosaic of languages and cultures gives Vatican Radio a specific character, not international but supranational—a supranationality which, far from erasing national particularities, embraces them and spreads them abroad.

The majority of Radio Vatican's employees come under the rules of common law applicable to all functionaries of the Vatican City State, namely the decree of 1 July 1969, General Regulation of Titular Personnel. A few exceptions have been added to this common-law statute through the decree of the Pontifical Commission for the Vatican City State dated 30 December 1981, which concerns only lay personnel and secular clergy, except for monks and nuns.

The staff may be divided into four juridical categories: (1) The Jesuits (34 in 1992) have no legal connection with Vatican Radio, since they are delegated to it by their order to see to its management and general workings, according to the wishes of the Holy See. (2) The regular staff (known as *di ruolo*) includes, without distinction, journalists and administrative and technical agents ranked as public functionaries of the Vatican State (25 in 1992). (3) Contractual personnel are under common law for the execution of full- or part-time functions provided for by open-ended contracts (25 in 1992). (4) Collaborators, who are recruited only in the information section, are divided into internal collaborators, the first stage before the category of regular or contractual workers, and external collaborators, who work only occasionally.

The Vatican's radio system regularly brings its installations up to date. For example, since 1 January 1993 it has been making broadcasts 10 hours a day by means of the Eutelsat II-Fl satellite, which is received throughout Europe and in Africa as far as Chad, using a parabolic antenna. The Vatican has also shown its ability to adapt to progress in the audiovisual field, for instance in the creation of the Centrum Televisificum Vaticanum (22 October 1983), designed to distribute films made of important ecclesiastical events.

The importance of radio communications for the Church's apostolate did not escape the fathers of the VATICAN II. They dedicated to it one of the 16 conciliar documents (decree *Inter mirifica* on means of social communication, 4 December 1963, following Pius XII's *Miranda prorsus* [8 September 1957] on the cinema, radio, and television). Radio communication has in fact proved to be a remarkable instrument for carrying out the papacy's universal mission—so much so that it is impossible nowadays to imagine the supreme pontiff performing this function without the aid of these techniques of social communication.

Joël-Benoît d'Onorio

Bibliography

Bea, F. *Mezzo secolo della Radio del Papa: Radio Vaticana 1931–1981*, Vatican City, 1981.

d'Onorio, J. B. "Radio Vatican," *Annuaire Européen d'Administration publique*, VII, 1984.

Matelski, M. I. *Vatican Radio: A Propagation by the Airwaves*, Westport, 1995.

Radio Vaticana 1931–1991, Vatican City.

VATICAN SECRET ARCHIVES. (Archivi Segreti del Vaticano—ASV).

This institution is one of the essential bodies of the Holy See and is meant to serve the sovereign pontiff and the CURIA in the pastoral government of the universal Church (Apostolic Constitution *Pastor bonus*, art. 187). All aspects of this ministry are reflected in the doctrinal, canonical, constitutional, judicial, and also purely administrative character of the archives, which originated in various departments of the central government over the centuries and are conserved *ad perpetuam rerum memoriam*. The Vatican Archives are only called "secret" because the original center of the present institution was SIXTUS IV's *Biblioteca secreta*. The same qualifier was applied to all the other archives of other sovereigns of Europe whose records could not, due to their nature, be consulted by outsiders. Their interest resides less in their "secret" characters than in the fact that they constitute the main, if not unique, source for the history of the papacy and the Church from the Middle Ages to the present day and are, therefore, an essential resource for scholarship.

Although in the past only hand-picked scholars were admitted to work in the archives, since LEO XIII's decision (1880) authorizing the open consultation of the papal archives, they have become the rallying point for countless researchers seeking useful sources for the ecclesiastical, social, and political history of their respective countries.

The international value and sheer abundance of the documentation contained in the collections led to the creation of many institutions based in Rome between 1880 and the end of the 19th century. L'Ecole Francaise de Rome, which preceded this movement, was inaugurated in 1873, followed by the Österreichische Historische Institut in 1881, then by the Preussische (later the Deutsche) Historische Institut and the Historische Institut der Görresgesellschaft in 1888. The publication of Vatican documents was almost exclusively handled by these establishments and by numerous other national institutions created afterwards. Unfortunately, there has never been any true institutional coordination between organizations or researchers, and this has provoked inevitable redundancies in their work as well as a waste of energy. Attempts to collaborate among these institutions, such as the Commission for the Coordination of Research at the Vatican Archives, created in 1928, have not been successful. On the other hand, a parallel project conceived to facilitate the use of published works has been edited in several volumes and entitled *Biografia dell'Archivio Vaticano*, a pioneering enterprise in this area.

The direction of the Vatican Archives is entrusted to the cardinal archivist of the Roman Church (a title held by Aidan Gasquet, the English Benedictine scholar, from 1917 until 1929), and to a prefect assisted by specialized personnel and services. Qualified researchers are admitted without discrimination with respect to their nationality or religion. Requests to consult the archives must be supported by a written recommendation from a cultural institution or another recognized authority. The reading rooms are open every day from 16 September through 15 July, except Sundays and holidays. The entrance to the Vatican Archives is through the Belvedere Court and one is allowed access through the St. Anne Gate upon the presentation of a reader's card. The Vatican School of Paleography, Diplomacy and Archival Documentation, founded by Leo XIII in 1884, is attached to the archives.

The Holy See is the only contemporary institution whose activities have continued uninterrupted since antiquity. Even within the early Church, archives were kept before the reign of Constantine (d. 337). Although we have no direct proof, several examples attest to the fact that popes were able to cite precedents and to utilize these in applying their decisions. This is why we are able to assume that pontifical decrees were copied early on at the seat of the central authority to be conserved there, akin to what occurred with imperial archives of the day.

The existence of such official archives in the *chartarium* is clearly in evidence as of the end of the 4th century. In the 5th century, there is an allusion to the recording of papal letters, that is, to the chancellary's habit of conserving in registers copies of correspondence emanating from the pontiff. It appears that for GREGORY I's reign (590–604), there were 14 volumes of papyri, one volume per year as pope. These were filed according to indictions, with the table of contents of each volume divided into 12 parts for the 12 months of the year. It is clear that this system left nothing to chance.

The *chartarium* or *scrinium sanctae ecclesiae* was used both as an archival depository and as a library. Although it was located in the Lateran, part of the archives were deposited *iuxta Palladium*, next to Titus's triumphal arch on the Palatine Hill, until the 11th century. There is almost nothing extant from this period and the Vatican Archives possess only one copy on parchment from the 11th century [letters written by JOHN VIII (872–82)] and 381 letters by GREGORY VII (1073–85).

The pontifical chancellery took a long time to move from the traditional use of fragile papyrus to more durable parchment. This explains why these first archives have not generally survived. Additional disappearances were probably caused by the extensive damage suffered by Rome during the Middle Ages.

The regular series of the *Registra Vaticana* that have come down to us begin with the reign of INNOCENT III (1198–1216). There are, however, significant missing pieces for the 13th and 14th centuries due to the mobility of the popes. A part of the archives was carried along with INNOCENT IV (1243–54) to the first council in Lyon (1245) and was then deposited for a time at the Cluny

Abbey. During other prolonged papal absences, the archives followed the itinerant CURIA and were moved from Viterbo to Anagni to Orvieto, Montefiascone, and Perugia, until CLEMENT V decided to leave the entire archive in Assisi for safekeeping. The registers of his two immediate predecessors were, along with his own, used in the very lively debate with Philip the Fair, and were deposited temporarily in the city of Carpentras and recovered only with difficulty after his death. Once the popes had established their long-term residency in Avignon, all the pontifical archives were gathered there in 1339. During this period, the chancellery's system of conservation was extended to the other offices of the Curia, such as the APOSTOLIC CAMERA, the DATERY, the PENITENTIARY, the ROTA, and the new secretariats. The original documents issued by the Holy See were then conserved and registered. The GREAT SCHISM OF THE WEST (1378–1417) was a time during which three rival obediences emerged, each generating its own lot of parallel archives. When Christianity was reunified under MARTIN V (1417–31), the pontifical archives had been dispersed to the four corners of southern Europe, and much effort was required to recover and transport this mass of documents to Rome.

It was in the 16th century, under PIUS IV (1559–65) that the idea of a central archive of the Holy See came to be, but the pope died before his plans had been carried out. It was not until PAUL V (1605–21) that the archives were finally established. The first transfer of holdings from the secret library to the new secret Vatican Archives began in 1610. Significant texts, particularly documents from the Apostolic Camera, were registered in the following years. The initial phase, the actual constitution of the archives, was completed in 1656 with the transfer of numerous registries from the SECRETARIAT OF STATE to the secret archives. For a century following, no significant acquisition occurred, until the documents that had remained in Avignon were sent to Rome in 1783. In 1798 the very important Treasury of Charters, until then deposited in the Castle of Saint Angelo, was moved to the Vatican for safekeeping.

The archives suffered serious damage under the Napoleonic occupation of the Papal States, because of the decision made in 1810 to transport to Paris some 200,435 bundles of wrapped papers in 3,239 cases, weighing more than 400 tons. Some were lost along the way and many other bundles disappeared in France. In addition, there were entire documents deliberately destroyed on the order of pontifical commissioners committed to organizing the return of the archives to the Vatican (1817) after the Congress of Vienna.

The papal archives briefly resided at the Hôtel de Soubise, which had some beneficial results. Pierre-Claude Daunou personally directed the reclassification of several collections which, in conformity with the pre-scriptions of the *Tableau systématique des archives de l'Empire* [Systematic Table of the Empire's Archives] were cataloged as follows: A. charters; B. registers of bulls, briefs, and petitions; C. privileges, goods, and holdings of the court of Rome; D. Legations and nunciatures; E. Secretariat of State; F. Datery; G. Chancellery; H. Penitentiary; I. Congregation of the Council of Trent; K. Congregation of Propaganda; L. Congregation of the Holy Office; M. Congregation of Rites; O. Administrative Archives—*Buon Governo*; P. legal archives; Q. inventories, tables, and repertories.

The catalog numbers attributed by the Parisian archivists remained attached to many of these documents and volumes. Of capital importance was the fact that the wealth of the collection had been made available to scholars for the first time. This eventually led to a change in the Vatican's policy regarding access.

Even though access to these documents was facilitated, it was not until the end of the 19th century, in 1880, that LEO XIII (1878–1903) formally decided to open the entire Vatican Archives to competent researchers, an innovation universally welcomed. The archives granted access to the existing Vatican collections, which had been considerably enlarged, and the original idea of a central archives of the Holy See was made effective. This development led to extension of the space occupied by the archives, which are today conserved on several floors of a long wing of the palace, between the Belvedere Court and the Vatican Gardens, as well as in recently constructed underground spaces beneath the Courtyard of the Pine.

Not all documents of historical interest emanating from the offices of the Roman Curia have been transferred to the Vatican Archives. Certain collections have remained autonomous and in the care of their department of origin. These include the following: the second section of the Secretariat of State handling relations with the States, known as the Department of Public Affairs, formerly the Department of Extraordinary Ecclesiastical Affairs; the Congregation for the Evangelization of Peoples or *Propaganda Fide*; the Congregation for the Doctrine of the Faith (previously the Holy Office); the Congregation for Catholic Education (formerly for seminaries and universities); the Congregation for Eastern Religions, the Congregation for Holy and Apostolic Life (formerly for the clergy); Fabric of St. Peter's; the Office of Pontifical Ceremonies; and the Police of the Papal House. Other departments, such as the Congregation for the cause of Saints (originally for apostolic rites and penitence) transferred significant portions of their archives to the Vatican Archives.

The first vicissitudes of this tumultuous past are still reflected today in the classification of the collections of the Vatican Archives, which were assembled over the centuries without any preconceived plan respecting the archival principles of provenance. For example, the artificially created series of *Registra Vaticana* include archives belonging to the Chancellery, the Apostolic Camera, and the secretariats. Moreover, materials partially belonging to the Chancellery and partially to the Camera must be researched in another catalog, the *Registra Avenionensia*. Other collections formed more recently also constitute a whole, although they are divided into subseries corresponding to the somewhat confusing branches of the Curia. In general, the Vatican's Secret Archives contain the archives of the papacy and the Roman Curia emanating from the following sources:

1. The major services, such as the Apostolic Chancellery, the Datery, and the Apostolic Camera, whose acts are contained in the series of Vatican catalogs or registers; the Avignon registers; the Lateran registers; and the registers of petitions and briefs from the Datary; *Introïtus et Exitus, Obligationes et Solutiones, Obligationes communes, Collectoriae, Diversa Cameralia*;

2. The Tribunals of the Rota, the Penitentiary, and the Signature of Justice;

3. The Secretariats of Briefs, of Briefs to Princes, the Latin Letters, and the Memorials.

4. Numerous congregations (now extant) such as Avignon, Bishops and Regulars, Discipline of Regulars, State of Regulars, Ecclesiastical Immunity, Indulgences and Sacred Relics, Rites, Sacraments, Council;

5. The financial management of the apostolic palaces.

The vast collections of the Secretariat of State are divided and subdivided into several sections:

1. Before the French Revolution: various correspondence arranged in several series according to the dignity of the correspondent (cardinals, bishops, prelates, princes, individuals, soldiers of the pontifical army).

2. Correspondence between the Secretariat of State and the nuncios (Germany, England, Spain, Flanders, Florence, France, Genoa, Malta, Munich, Naples, Poland, Portugal, Savoy, Switzerland, Venice, etc.).

3. The very rich collection of Miscellanea.

Other collections include:

1. *Epoca Napoleonica* (1798–1815).

2. After 1815 through 1978, cataloged according to modern archival principles.

3. Archives of the papal diplomatic missions, including the apostolic nunciatures, the internunciatures and delegations, including the first diplomatic missions in Europe (Madrid, Paris, Vienna, etc.).

4. The personal papers of several popes, such as Paul V, Clement XI, Pius IX, and Pius X.

5. The archives of the College of Cardinals and the consistory.

6. The acts of the ecumenical councils of Trent and Vatican I.

7. Several special collections, such as those of Castel Sant'Angelo and the *Instrumenta Miscellanea* containing numerous original documents of exceptional importance for Church history.

8. Many other archival collections without a direct relationship to the Holy See but somehow connected to it, such as the *Fondo Domenicani*, the *Fondo Veneto*, the archives of several brotherhoods and families of Roman nobility, such as the Boncompagni and the Borghese.

Charles Burns

Bibliography

Boyle, L. E. *A Survey of the Vatican Archives and of Its Medieval Holdings*, Toronto, 1972 (Pontifical Institute of Medieval Studies: Subsidia Mediaevalia).

Brom, G. *Guide aux Archives du Vatican*, Rome, 1911.

Favier, J. *Les Archives*, Paris (1965), 120–26; "Saint-Siège. Archivio Segreto Vaticano," *Archivum*, 15 (1965), 305–10.

Fink, K. A. *Das Vatikanische Archiv*, 2nd ed., Rome, 1951.

Fish, C. R. *Guide to the Materials for American History in Roman and Other Italian Archives*, Washington, D.C., 1911.

François, M. "Les sources de l'histoire religieuse de la France au Vatican," *RHEF*, 19 (1933), 305–46 (reprinted in V. Carrière, *Introduction aux études d'histoire ecclésiastique locale*, 1, Paris, 1940, 377–434).

Gachard, M. *Les Archives du Vatican*, Brussels, 1874.

Gualdo, G. *Sussidi per la consultazione dell'Archivio Vaticano*, Vatican City, 1989 (Collectanea Archivi Vaticani 17).

Macfarlane, L. J. "The Vatican Archives: With Special Reference to Sources for British Medieval History," in *Archives* (Journal of the British Records Association), 4 (1959), 29–44, 89–101.

Pasztor, L. *Guida delle fonti per la sotria dell'America latina negli archivi della Santa Sede e negli archivi ecclesiastici d'Italia*, Vatican City, 1970 (Collectanea Archivi Vaticani 2).

VATICAN TELEVISION. The Vatican Television Center (Centrum Televisificum Vaticanum) was instituted by JOHN PAUL II on 22 October 1983, in the form of an autonomous foundation endowed with juridical personality under canon law and placed under the supervision of the cardinal secretary of state. The Television Center is administered by a council of 11 members, including two laymen who act as president and vice president and are aided by a secretary general, an administrative secretary, and three comptrollers. Its finances come from its activities as well as from various donations. The center is not, strictly speaking, a local television station, but it ensures the production, diffusion, and distribution, by cable or videocassette, of programs on the activities of the pope and the Holy See in religious, cultural, scientific, and artistic matters.

Joël-Benoît d'Onorio

VATICANIST. The Italians, whose practical sense balances any temptation to indulge in theorizing, use the term "Vaticanist" (*Vaticanista*) to describe someone who because of his profession (e.g., a journalist) or intellectual interest (e.g., a teacher or private individual) devotes himself to observing and commenting on the activity of the Holy See. Usually, a Vaticanist is a newspaper correspondent in charge of religious news, either general or having to do specifically with the Vatican, in the broadest sense of the term. He may live in Rome or go there regularly. He may write for a national or a local paper, either regularly or occasionally.

Over time, he therefore builds up a close, quasi-conspiratorial relationship with the object of his observation, which does not necessarily lead to apologetics—far from it. He is a professional who has his own information network and knows those of others. But, beyond these normal journalist's tools, he knows how to interpret—either directly or indirectly, in the course of everyday life in Rome—the hidden meaning of seemingly insignificant events. Such little things as bumping into a Curial cardinal in a clerical suit at dinnertime, when he is ringing the doorbell of people whose position in Rome the journalist knows well; reading the *Annuario pontificio* the moment it comes out; the daily perusal of the *Osservatore Romano*; appreciation of the place so and so occupies in a papal audience photograph; and so on, all make the Vaticanist a professional who produces news through a ceaseless scrutiny of the world of the Vatican.

He becomes a great professional when the quality of his information, which is then basically irreproachable, is both guided and interpreted by intuition. From that moment on, people speak to him and leave him free to say what he will, trusting his Vaticanist discipline, which consists in not constantly thinking of himself as a crusader, and in showing that he has a sense of the relative.

Such is the ideal, but not rigid, portrait of the Vaticanist, who, in his professional work, sees the apologist as almost the devil. In short, what he dreads is seeming to defend the system, and this dread can even make him determined to show that transmitting information also implies a critical spirit. A cleric, former cleric, former seminarian, or the product of a Catholic education, in Italy the Vaticanist is rarely a layman, pure and simple. It is not a question of nationality but rather the effect of the mysterious power exercised over minds by an acculturation of which one is the product, and in which fascination has as its obverse side fear or repulsion.

This climate of mind appears also in foreign countries, even those whose civilization is not, as in Italy, domi-nated by Catholicism. A non-Catholic Vaticanist, well known in Rome and in his own country, can, for example, quickly shed his apologist complex with an irreverent book that he wants to be a best-seller. Or the reverse can happen: A religious who has left his order amid scandal may become a dedicated, recognized papal biographer. His subject will be endowed with every virtue and will cause all the popes to blend into the same monochrome, beginning with the contemporary pontiff.

Or, the Vaticanist may be a specialist whose surveillance of a key subject such as the Marian cult, canonization, the pontifical court, or the activity of the Congregation for the Doctrine of the Faith serves as a balance for assaying the general conduct of the Holy See. This is a question of personality; each journalist measures the value of a policy using the yardstick of his specialty and his preferences.

The Vaticanist may be a Vaticanologist and vice versa, just as, in the old days, the Kremlinologist might be a Sovietologist. It would be a mistake to think that the change from one to the other, or constant shifting, is a move from a practical to a mere scholarly approach. The Vaticanologist claims that he speaks methodically about Church history by analyzing its central government at the Vatican, with its human and historical realities, which are indissociable from the nature of the Holy See linked to the Vatican City State, just as the Sovietologist would speak about the Communist revolution using the example of the U.S.S.R., centered on the Kremlin. The Vaticanologist, like the Sovietologist, thus borrows from political science theoretical models, which allow him to take into account relations between ideology and history. As a result, the Vaticanologist has less obvious complicity with the object of his study than the Vaticanist—and if he has it, he does not want to use it, because he does not observe, he studies. Even more than the student of politics, who may be a constitutionalist dabbling in history or a historian with a smattering of constitutional law, the Vaticanologist must be at the same time a historian, sociologist, canonist, and theologian, among other things. Such is the ideal portrait, which may be confused with that of the Vaticanist in the best cases, when sensibility and culture are put to the service of historical explanation that takes into account the history of the Church and its nature so as to explain the twists and turns of contemporary history.

It is just as hard for the Vaticanologist as for the Vaticanist to give up his prejudices; again, this is very human. If the Vaticanist's political commitments are necessarily compromised in his news stories, which must impart information, the Vaticanologist, whose obligations do not arise so frequently, cannot disguise his methodological premises. There again, much depends on nationality.

In Italy, the history of Christian Democracy counts for more in discussions than in France, in Germany, and *a fortiori* in the English-speaking countries. The Italian Vaticanologist knows what it reveals of a pope and his pontificate to analyze the intellectual influences of his youth, the milieu in which he developed, the men he has chosen to work closely with him. The French or American Vaticanologist reasons more in terms of political systems—but there has been a papacy in Avignon, never in Washington. And like the Vaticanist, which he may be also, the Vaticanologist may present, as a scientific key to understanding, individual inclinations. One thing is certain, and that is what makes him a poor relation of the political economist: he cannot be a structuralist. And, besides, is not the structuralist bowled over before the facade of St. Peter's, where, as Barthes says, he invokes its immediate physical fascination to explain his awe?

Philippe Levillain

VESTMENTS, POPE'S LITURGICAL.

Falda. The falda is a liturgical vestment worn by the Roman pontiff until the VATICAN II council. It was a long, flowing skirt of cream-colored silk which the pope wore over the alb and under the chasuble or cope. There were two categories of falda, of which the common characteristic was disproportion, for the garment was uneven in length: The falda worn in secret CONSISTORY hung down 9.75 inches/25 centimeters in front and more than 19 inches/50 centimeters behind; the one worn in solemn ceremonies, 19 inches/50 centimeters in front and 4 feet/1.25 meters behind. That meant that when he moved the pope had to rely on the assistance of chamberlains whose special task was to hold the falda out from the pope's body. The garment also draped the pontiff's body when it lay in state and was placed in the casket.

The origins of the falda go back at least to the 15th century, for masters of the papal ceremonies at that time mention its being worn in their registers (*diarii*). According to some, the fullness the skirt created around the person of the vicar of Christ symbolized his charity toward the universal Church.

Fanon. This liturgical vestment is worn only by the Roman pontiff. It resembles a cape 19 inches/50 centimeters wide and 35 inches/90 centimeters in diameter, made of white silk with stripes of gold at right angles with delicate bands of purple. Edged with gold braid, the fanon is decorated in front with a radiating cross embroidered in gold thread. For solemn masses, the pope puts on this vestment after the alb and pectoral cross; over it, he wears the stole, the tunicle, the dalmatic, and, finally, the chasuble, over which the outer part of the fanon is made to extend; here is affixed the *pallium* with three gold pins.

The pontifical fanon is of ancient origin. At the beginning of the 13th century, INNOCENT III mentioned the use of this garment, then known as the "orale." BONIFACE VIII was known to wear the back part of the fanon tucked under his miter, not only during services but also at grand dinners. His seventh successor, URBAN V, did the same. Moreover, certain popes were buried wearing the fanon (CLEMENT IV in the 13th century and PAUL III in the 16th). Up to and including JOHN XXIII, the fanon was one of the pope's mortuary vestments.

The significance of the fanon is hard to ascertain. For some historians, it comes from the ritual practiced by Eastern bishops of covering the head with a veil for sacred ceremonies; it would thus derive from the amice, which before saying mass the priest placed on his head and then attached to his shoulders to signify the helmet of salvation. For others (including Innocent III), it recalled the *ephod* worn by the Jewish high priest when he offered to God the twelve tribes of Israel, since the pope carries upon himself the whole Church when he wears the fanon, whose three colors symbolize the Church triumphant in heaven (gold stripes), the Church militant on earth (white stripes), and the Church suffering in purgatory (purple stripes). The fanon was thought to have disappeared completely after the Vatican II council (PAUL VI no longer wore it during the second half of his reign), until JOHN PAUL II appeared wearing it once again on 22 November 1984 in the Church of Sta. Cecilia in Rome.

Joël-Benoît d'Onorio

Pallium. From the time of the drawing up of the *ordines* of pontifical consecration in the 12th century, the *pallium* has symbolized the plenitude of the pope's episcopal office (*plenitudo pontificalis officii*). It formed the pendant of the TIARA, which signified the pope's temporal power. Woven of white lamb's wool, the *pallium* in those days was a narrow band embroidered with small black crosses, which was passed around the back of the neck and which draped the torso. Over time, the garment often changed in appearance. Here will be described merely the origin of this sign of office, its liturgical and juridical function for the pope, and its use in papal ecclesiastical policy.

It was most likely in the 5th century at the latest that the *pallium* was added to the pontifical vestments. In fact, texts from the beginning of the 6th century give evidence of its use. Its actual origin is contested. Because a garment of the same name figures in the *Imperium romanum* as part of the emperor's Greek costume and was worn by him and by high officials, two possibilities arise. Either the emperor ceded the wearing of the *pallium* to the pope as a sign of honor, or the pope usurped it toward the end of the 5th century when the emperor's influence over Rome begun to wane. The frequent tensions between the pope and the Eastern Roman Empire at that time point to the second hypothesis as the more likely.

From the beginning, the *pallium* was and remained a purely liturgical garment. The pope wore it only during solemn offices and in processions. Before the miter, which did not become customary until the 11th century, the *pallium* was the only indication of his exalted rank. Thus, in 530 FELIX IV designated his successor, BONIFACE II, by bestowing on him the *pallium*. By contrast, to signify that a pope was being deposed, he was stripped of the *pallium*: that was the case with SILVERIUS in 537, and there is still evidence of the practice in the early 12th century. The formula of investiture cited at the beginning of the ordination of the pope is proof that the *pallium* continued to have great importance. In 336, Pope MARK is said to have conceded the *pallium* to the bishop of Ostia. In spite of its anachronism, the legend shows that by the time the story arose, in the early 600s, the bishop of Ostia, who was the chief ordainer in the pope's consecration and the most eminent bishop, after the pope, of the ecclesiastical province of Rome, was wearing the *pallium*. It also shows that from that period on, the pope permitted other bishops to wear the *pallium*. Those who received it in preference to others were his "vicars"—the metropolitans of Arles and Thessalonica—but also other bishops of these vicariates, of Sicily, and of the ecclesiastical province of Rome, and, finally, the metropolitan of RAVENNA. All belonged to domains already subject to the bishop of Rome or the subordination of which he was seeking. The concession of the *pallium* therefore served to strengthen and extend papal power. Accordingly, from the 7th century on, whoever received the *pallium* had to swear loyalty to the pope, who determined on which feast days the wearing of this sign of office was authorized. Unlike the pope, the bishops could wear the *pallium* only during the mass, and not in processions.

Like the suburbicarian bishops, the Anglo-Saxon Boniface II had also sworn fidelity on receiving the *pallium* and had thereby submitted to Roman authority. This highly significant action, together with the ever closer relations between the pope and the FRANKS, explains why certain leading bishops of the Frankish kingdom received the *pallium* from the pope, as in time did all the holders of the newly created archdioceses. Insofar as each archbishop had to ask for the *pallium* to be bestowed on him—generally by the pope's own hands—for the first time a personal and relatively close institutional bond was created between the papacy and the principal representatives of a national Church. Despite the resistance offered by some archbishops, such as Hincmar of Reims, as late as the 9th century, it soon became standard for archbishops to receive the *pallium* from the pope in order to exercise their rights and carry-out their duties legitimately.

From the 10th century on, this norm was transferred to other countries and other newly created archdioceses; from the time of the INVESTITURE CONTROVERSY at the latest, it was still in force throughout the lands of the Latin Church, where it was visible proof of their subordination to the pope. By modifying the formulas, the pope could, as he saw fit, strengthen or weaken the position of one archbishop in relation to others, elevate such and such an archbishop, or, when bestowing the *pallium*, establish a whole canon of obligations. GREGORY VII's action in this regard can be taken as an example. Gradually, the archbishops did not merely make their way to the TOMB of St. Peter (where the pallium was consecrated) in order to receive the *pallium*, but had to repeat their visits at regular intervals, a requirement that further strengthened the pope's control over the universal Church. To be sure, from the 11th century the *pallium* could be bestowed by LEGATES and the visit to Rome made by representatives; yet the idea remained that a personal visit was the norm. Finally, one result of the personal character of this "AD LIMINA" is that, in our era, not only archbishops but also the bishops belonging to their ecclesiastical provinces regularly visit the pope to inform him about the state of their churches. The *pallium* has therefore contributed largely to reinforcing the ties between the pope and the episcopacy.

Bernard Schimmelpfennig

Bibliography

Brau, 642–51.
DACL XIII 1, 932 ff.
LP I, 81, 202 ff.
LP I, 282, 293, 2, 345; I, 81, 202 ff.
Liber diurnus, 101–7, 200–5, 299–309.
Mayo, J. *A History of Ecclesiastical Dress*, London, 1984.
Noonan, J. C., Jr. *The Church Visible: The Ceremonial Life and Protocol of the Roman Catholic Church*, New York, 1996.
Santifaller, 119 ff., 198 ff., 223 ff., 252–4.

VETO. With the veto, also known as the EXCLUSION a temporal sovereign officially signaled his opposition to the election of a cardinal to the supreme pontificate. It thus differed from the imperial approval of the first centuries, which was bestowed, after a freely executed pontifical election. However, this preventive political intrusion in ecclesiastical affairs was a power enjoyed by only three monarchs: the emperor of Austria, the king of Spain, and the king of France, who granted themselves the privilege for reasons more political than historically justified. The Apostolic See could not be occupied by someone who did not agree with their views.

First to submit the conclave to such pressures was Charles V who, with a large part of Europe under his dominion, was the sovereign of the majority of the cardinals of his time. However, although he prided himself on his title of "advocate of the Roman Church," which he claimed to hold from Charlemagne, he only exercised his influence in an official manner through his ambassadors or the cardinals in his proximity. On the other hand, at the conclave of 1590 his son Philip II leaned all his royal weight on the vote because he was not satisfied with signifying his opposition to particular members of the Sacred College. He clearly indicated by name the seven cardinals from among whom the pope should be chosen, thus implying a veto against all the others, and, in fact, GREGORY XIV was elected from among those favored by His Most Catholic Majesty. A year later, the election of INNOCENT IX was a result of the same procedure.

Despite the importance of the Spanish crown for the life of Catholicism in the world—and in particular its expansion in the new world just being discovered—the papacy of CLEMENT VIII, on the cusp of the 16th and 17th centuries, saw some small signs of emancipation from Spanish protection, which the theologians of the court nevertheless hastened to justify. The papacy, for its part, had adopted an ambiguous attitude in this regard. In his bull *In eligendis* of 1562, PIUS IV mentioned these interventions, which he tolerated, but only as recommendations. In his constitution *Aeterni Patris* of 1621 GREGORY XV had scarcely been elected when he prohibited election cabals, but without taking direct aim at what he called the "inclusions or exclusions of one or more persons."

In the next century, CLEMENT XII's bull *Apostolatus officium* of 1732 followed the same line, not expressly condemning, but never approving. The great powers could thus continue meddling with impunity. This was primarily the case with Spain, and later, from the conclave of 1655, with France. However, France did not want to avail itself of a right or even openly use a veto in the proper form. For the Most Christian King, the important thing was to maintain good relations between the elder daughter of the Church and the Apostolic See, to their mutual advantage. Thus Louis XIV allowed some cardinals to accede to the TIARA against whom he nevertheless had a few prejudices, such as Chigi, who became ALEXANDER VII in 1655, or Odeschalchi, who became INNOCENT XI in 1676, to whom France would be the cause of many a difficulty.

The conclave of 1691 marked a turning point in the history of the veto with the unavowed but stubborn veto of Cardinal Barbarigo by the emperor of Austria. In fact, until that time the procedure could not succeed unless it was supported by a substantial group of electors who were more or less convinced of the reasons put forward by the sovereigns. This marked the period during which only the sovereign's wish would be taken into account as a right that Spain, France, and Austria implicitly possessed. The cardinals put up with it, even though they limited its effects to just one name for each of the three powers. Moreover, this would soften the declarations of official hostility (that is, those directed expressly to the Sacred College), the monarchs preferring from now on to act by means of unofficial warnings so as not to be caught powerless in the face of new candidates after using their one formal veto.

Throughout the 18th and 19th centuries the veto was subtly wielded, officially or unofficially, explicitly or by threats by Madrid (1724, 1730, 1829, 1831), Paris (1700, 1758, 1829, 1831), and especially Vienna (1700, 1721, 1730, 1800, 1823, 1829, 1846, 1903). To this end the sovereigns used the services of their ambassadors at the Roman court, and for greater safety, members of the Sacred College who were their subjects (cardinals Bentivoglio in 1730 and Marco y Catalan in 1831 for Spain, Luynes in 1758 and Isoard in 1831 for France, and for Austria, von Altham in 1721, Herzan von Harras in 1800, Albani in 1823, 1829, and 1831, Gaysruk in 1846, and Puznya in 1903).

Nevertheless, because of his repeated interventions and abuse of the veto, His Imperial and Royal Majesty would be the cause of the abrogation of this irregular privilege. Franz Joseph's veto of Cardinal Rampolla del Tindaro at the conclave of August 1903 is famous. Because of it, one of the first decisions of Cardinal Sarto, who emerged as PIUS X, was to prohibit this practice for good with the constitution *Commissum Nobis* dated 20 January 1904, but published in 1906, in which the new pope rejected this claim of privilege as baseless and unambiguously prohibited any and every "civil veto . . . even in the form of a simple wish, as well as any intervention or intercession, in order to prevent the heads of State from interposing or interfering under any pretext" in the election of the pontiff of Rome. That is the reason he threatened with automatic excommunication, absolution from this being reserved to the pope, all those—cardinals or conclavist prelates—who agreed, directly or indirectly, to receive or reveal the opposition of any power to any candidate whatever to the throne of St. Peter. This disposition was henceforth included in the oath of observance of every new cardinal receiving the Roman purple, as well as in the conclave regulations. It would naturally be upheld by all the successors of Pius X.

Joël-Benoît d'Onorio

Bibliography

Battandier, A. "L'exclusive dans l'élection des souverains pontifes," *Annuaire pontifical catholique*, 1910.

Blet, P. "La diplomatie française et l'élection de Pie X," *Pro fide et iustitia (Mélanges pour le 70e anniversaire du cardinal Agostino Cararoli)*, Berlin, 1984.

Engel-Janosi, F. *Österreich und der Vatikan 1846–1918*, Vienna, 1964.

Landrieux, M. "Le conclave de 1903," *Études*, 299, 1958.

Lector, L. *Le Conclave*, Paris, 1894.

Mathieu, F. D. "Les dernier jours de Léon XIII et le conclave," *Revue des Deux Mondes*, 74, 1904.

Molien, A. "Conclave," *DDC*, III.

VICARIATE, APOSTOLIC.

VICARIATE, APOSTOLIC. Two apostolic vicariates, which were roughly contemporary and presented certain similarities, existed in late antiquity. These were the vicariates of Arles and Thessalonica. The reasons for their creation, and with their histories, are sufficiently different that they should be examined separately.

The Vicariate of Arles. At the end of the year 407 Arles became the center for three agencies: the prefecture of the praetorium, which had previously been in Trier (the prefecture of the praetorium of the Gauls had been there since 395), the vicar of Aquitaine or the five (seven) provinces, who had resided previously in Bordeaux, and the governorship of Viennois.

This regrouping of three administrative services in the south of Provence was provoked not only by German pressure on the Rhine but also by the conquest of the greater part of Gaul in the summer of 407 by the usurper Constantine III, who also set himself up in Arles. This concentration in Arles would continue up to the 5th century.

Thus Arles had an important place in the administrative life of the Western Empire. For a brief period (409–11) it was Constantine III's capital. It was also, together with Marseilles, an important economic center. In the last years of the 4th century its bishop had been at loggerheads with the metropolitan of Vienne, each one claiming primacy. To end the disputes, the Council of Turin (held in 398 according to J. R. Palanque, "Les dissensions des églises des Gaules à la fin du IVe siècle et la date du Concile de Turin," *Rev. hist. Égl. de France*, 1935; in 491–501, according to Louis Duchesne; or in 417 according to C. Bahut, *Le Concile de Turin*, 1904, a date confirmed by André Chastagnol) had proposed a compromise solution, giving each of the two sees authority over the churches nearest to it.

This compromise did not solve the conflict. Patroclus, who occupied the see of Arles, obtained from Pope Zosimus a letter to the Gaulish episcopate (22 March 417, *PL*, 20, 642–5) insisting, on penalty of excommunication, that every Gaulish cleric going to Rome should obtain *litterae formatae* from the bishop of Arles. This gave Arles control over the Gaulish clergy. Further, the letter sacrificed Vienne's rights by entrusting the bishop of Arles with ordination of the bishops of the Viennois province and the two Narbonnes.

The motive invoked was the tradition of St. Trophimus, who was sent from Rome by St. Peter and who founded the church of Arles. Thus religious antiquity and Roman filiation helped reinforce the argument that Arles's political situation could have provided. The pontifical letter affirmed Rome's desire to give Arles a preeminent role. As Caspar has shown, it was in fact a matter of creating an apostolic vicariate. This did not sit well with the Gaulish clergy. Threatened with excommunication for defending the rights of his see, Hilary of Narbonne was forced to give in (letter of Zosimus of 26 September 417, *PL*, 20, 667). Proculus of Marseilles, who was more stubborn, was deposed (letter of 29 September 417, *PL*, 20, 665). Faced with the opposition of the clergy and the local population at Lodève, however, Patroclus was unable to install a bishop. The new pope, Boniface, who had more doubt about Patroclus, did not support him (*Ep.* 12, *PL*, 20, 772–4; 9 February 422).

By contrast, the imperial power seems to have implicitly ratified Arlesian primacy. A constitution of Valentinian III (in fact drawn up by his mother Galla Placidia, who was regent for her underage son), which was addressed in the summer of 425 to the prefect of the praetorium of the Gauls when Boniface was no longer supporting Patroclus, entrusted Patroclus with the fight against Pelagianism in Gaul (constitution of Sirmond 6 = CTh. 16, 2, 46 and 47). Was this deliberate, or done in ignorance of the pope's about-face? Caspar defends the latter interpretation, Völker the first. The following year, Patroclus was assassinated.

The vicariate of Arles survived him. After being occupied by Honoratus (426–7), the founder of Lérins, the see of Arles passed to his disciple Hilary (430–49). In 443–4, struck by the complaints of the people of Besançon against their bishop Chalidonius, Hilary caused that prelate to be deposed by a council. But Leo I denounced Hilary for assuming authority (*Ep.* 10, *PL*, 54, 628–36). When Hilary named as successor to the see of Besançon Projectus of Poitiers, who because of his age could not fulfill his duties, Leo kept Projectus at his post and reproached Hilary for intervening outside his province (*ibid.*, 2–6). He stripped Hilary of all authority even over the Viennois bishops, leaving him only his duties as bishop of Arles (*ibid.*, 7). To the emperor he denounced the "abominable tumult" aroused by Hilary's encroachments on the Gallic churches.

Next, Valentinian III joined in criticizing Hilary, intending in so doing to use his secular authority to reinforce the Roman pontiff's rebukes (17 November, 8 July 445). In 450 there were further infringements on Hilary's part as he produced a successor to the see of Vaison. The bishop of Vienne protested. But some bishops from the Viennois, the Narbonnes, and the maritime Alps intervened with the pope, supporting Hilary by invoking the tradition of Trophimus and the political situation of Arles (in the letters of St. Leo, *Ep.* 65, *PL*, 54, 879 ff.).

Leo refused to heed them. He made a division between Vienne and Arles. The former would be the metropolitan see for Valence, Grenoble, Geneva, and the Tarentaise, in fact regions occupied by the Barbarians. Arles retained authority over those still belonging to Rome, the rest of the Viennois, the second Narbonne, Uzès (Narbonnaise I), and the maritime Alps (*Ép.* 66, 2; 5 May 450, *PL*, 884).

Juridically, this put an end to the vicariate of Arles. In fact, however, if Arles was no longer privileged, the pope's friendship with the bishop Ravennius won the Arlesian see certain favors. The bishop of Arles intervened in several matters, beyond his fixed jurisdiction.

With the Visigothic occupation (476) and later that of the Franks (536), all traces of the vicariate disappeared.

The Vicariate of Thessalonica. If the history of the vicariate of Arles is reflected in facts more than in formal texts, if it depended to a great extent on the personalities of Patroclus and Hilary and the situation of the churches of Viennois-Provence, the vicariate of Thessalonica appears to have been more clearly desired by Rome and supported by official texts.

The territory in which it was situated, Illyria, was a frontier zone between West and East. Politically and religiously it was the object of a sort of competition, if not conflict, between Rome and Constantinople. Administratively, Illyria belonged to the *pars occidentalis* and was under the sway of a prefect of the praetorium of Italy, Illyria, and Africa. A short-lived prefecture of the praetorium of Illyria was even established by Gratian from 376 to 379, and may have been for a brief period restored by Theodore I in 387. But in the late 4th century, eastern Illyria (the diocese of Macedonia and Dacia) became a prefecture of the praetorium proper attached to the *pars orientalis* of the Empire. From the ecclesiastical viewpoint, Illyria belonged to Rome. But a struggle for influence between Rome and Constantinople would erupt on several occasions.

By perhaps the 4th century Thessalonica, a civil metropolis, enjoyed a preeminence over the dioceses of the region. The first juridical manifestations of the vicariate remain little known. Two letters from Damasus to Acholius of Thessalonica mention nothing of a delegation of power to a vicar (*Ep.* 5 and 6, *PL* 13, 365–70). This changed with Siricius. The pope submitted episcopal consecrations to the agreement of the bishop of Thessalonika, Anysius (*Ep.* 4, *PL*, 13; 1144 ff.). The prerogative was similar to those given to the bishop of Alexandria for Egypt and to the bishop of Rome for suburbicarian Italy.

Was this a protective measure against Constantinople? Possibly; in any case the motive was strictly personal. The measure benefited Anysius, not his see. In 412, in a letter to Rufus, Innocent I went further (*Ep.* 13; *PL*, 20, 515). He defined the territory and the powers granted to the bishop of Thessalonica, whose jurisdiction extended over the civil dioceses of Macedonia and Dacia. He was responsible for convoking councils, judging cases on his own, or forwarding them to Rome. He represented the pope, whom even the bishops could not address without his consent. The pope gave the bishop of Thessalonica the power of a vicar. Thus INNOCENT I is considered the creator of the vicariate. But perhaps it was a matter of the official consecration of a *fait accompli*.

Rome exercised its authority over the vicariate. The decree of 13 December 414 addressed to Rufus of Thessalonika and the Macedonian bishops is evidence of this (*Ep.* 17, *PL*, 20, 526). Boniface would maintain this policy toward the vicariate (*Ep.* 4 and 5, *PL*, 20, 760, and 761; *Ep.* 13, 14, and 15; 3 and 11 March 411, *PL*, 20, 774–84; 1120–30).

Despite the attempts of the patriarch of Constantinople, Atticus, to control Illyria, and the support given him by the young Theodosius II (CTh., 16, 2, 45, to the prefect of the praetorium of Illyria, 14 July 421, repeated in the code of Justinian 1, 2, 6 and 11, 21, 1), Boniface, who was supported on his side by Honorius, defended the vicariate (cf. Honorius's letter to Theodosius and the latter's reply in *Ep. Bonifacii, Ep.* 10 and 11, *PL*, 20, 769–70). Some letters of Celestine I (*Ep.* 3; 424; *PL*, 50; 427) and Sixtus III (*Ep.* 7 and 8: *ibid.* 610; 611) confirm the vicariate by setting forth the vicar's powers.

When, in 437, the patriarch of Constantinople, Proclus, tried to gain supreme control of eastern Illyria after its reincorporation into the *pars orientalis* of the Empire, the move met with a strong reaction on the part of Sixtus II (*Ep.* 9 to Proclus and 10 to the Illyrian episcopate, 18 Dec. 436, *PL*, 50, 612, and 616). The vicariate continued through the pontificate of St. Leo (440–61). In his letters, the pope very clearly specifies its definition and jurisdiction (*Ep.* 5, 6, 13, 14, *PL*, 54, 614–20; 663–77). However, when the pope met with certain hesitations on the part of the Illyrian episcopate, which was jealous of its prerogatives, in particular concerning episcopal consecrations, he had to urge the vicar to show discretion in the exercise of his jurisdiction (*Ep.* 13 and 14). At the same time he strengthened Roman authority over its vicar, with the result that the vicariate of Thessalonica was confirmed and controlled. It would survive until the 8th century, when, with the images controversy, eastern Illyria was placed under the jurisdiction of the patriarchate of Constantinople.

Jean Gaudemet

Bibliography

Caspar, E. *Geschichte des Papsttums*, 2 vols., Tübingen, 1930–3.

Chastagnol, A. "Le Repli sur Arles des services administratifs gaulois en l'an 407 de notre ère," *Rev. Hist.*, 505, 1973.

Fuhrmann, H. "Studien zür Geschichte mittelalterlichen Patriarchate," *Zeit des Savigny Stift. Kan. Abt.*, 1953.

Gaudemet, J. *L'Église dans l'Empire romain*, 1989.

Grumel, V. "Les origines du Vicariat Apostolique de Thessalonique," *Actes du XIIe congrès international des études byzantines*, 2, 1964.

Länggartner, G. *Die Gallienpolitik der Päpste im 5. und 6. Jh. Eine Studie über den Apostol. Vik. v. Arles*, 1964.

Parlatto, V. "Il Vicariato di Tessalonica (IV-VIIe siècle)," *SUSG*, 49–50, 1980–82.

Pietri, C. "Roma Christiana," *BEFAR*, 224, 1976.

Streichlan, F. "Die Anfänge des Vicariats von Thessalonick," *Zeit. des Savigny Stift. Kan. Abt.*, 12, 1922.

Völker, "Die Gründung des Primats von Arles und seine Aufhebung durch Leo I.," *ZKG*, 46, 1927.

VICTOR I. *(189–99).*

All our sources, except the *Liberian Catalogue*, give a length of ten years to the pontificate of this thirteenth successor of Peter. Even if these dates are to a certain extent problematic, his episcopate has to be placed between 189 and 199. The *Liber pontificalis* gives him an African origin and claims that his father was named Felix. Based on this fact, he would be the first pope of the Latin tongue and would have accelerated the Latinization of the Church, so strongly marked by its Greco-Oriental origins even in Rome itself.

One of the great acts of his pontificate involved the problem of the date of the feast of Easter. Since Soter's pontificate, relations between Rome and the Asian communities had been poisoned by this question. In fact, in Asia Minor Easter was celebrated at the full moon of the first month (the 14th of Nisan), following the system adopted by the Jews. In Rome, by contrast, the feast was now immutably celebrated on a Sunday, that closest to the Jewish festival, but always after 14 Nisan and not earlier than the day after it. Hitherto a mutual tolerance had allowed each group to respect its custom (Anicetus never wanted to impose anything on Polycarp). Still, the question divided the Church, and the controversy spread through the East and to Rome itself, where some championed the Asian Quartodeciman rite. Victor wanted to put an end to this regrettable state of affairs, which revealed divisions among Christians.

He initiated several bishops' reunions and asked Polycrates to convene those of Asia to debate the problem. Letters were exchanged between Victor and the Christian communities, even that of Egypt or Africa. A majority seemed to have formed to fix the date of Easter on Sunday, but the bishops of Asia Minor maintained their position in favor of the Quartodeciman rite. Polycrates of Ephesus sent an explanatory letter to Victor, who received it with great disfavor. Believing the Asians quite isolated, he decided to excommunicate them. Irenaeus of Lyon and many others who had recognized the validity of the Dominical rite were opposed to this measure and wrote in that vein to Victor. Understanding that this was a question that might entail a definitive rupture within the Church, the pontiff reconsidered his decision. He knew that unity in the Dominical observance would be achieved sooner or later, when the Asian bishops who were repositories of the apostolic traditions died off.

Victor thus affirmed the right of the bishop of Rome to intervene in the other churches. He acted with the same vigor against the first representative of an Adoptionist trend (Jesus is an ordinary man whom God adopted as His son; He is only God by name); Theodotus of Byzantium was excommunicated. A Gnostic, Florinus, was stripped of his priesthood. Victor was also, it appears, the first bishop of Rome to have genuine relations with the imperial household. He begged Marcia, Commodus's mistress who may herself have been a Christian, to have the Christians who had been sent to the Sardinian mines brought back; they were freed thanks to her intervention. Victor is also said to have written some treatises, in Latin, including one on the date of Easter. He is purportedly buried in the Vatican near PETER (the last to have this honor), but no evidence for this has come to light. This energetic, realistic pope did not suffer martyrdom, despite tradition. His feast is 28 July.

Jean-Pierre Martin

Bibliography

Amann, E. *DThC*, Paris, 1950, XV, 2, 2862–3.

Eusebius, *HE*, 22; 24, 1; 24, 9–11; 28, 7.

Irenaeus, *Adv. Haeres.*, III, 3, 3.

Jerome, *De vir. ill.*, 34.

Mohrmann, C. *Vigiliae Christiane*, Amsterdam, 1962, XVI, 154–71.

Richard, M. "La lettre de saint Irénée au pape Victor," *ZNTW*, LVI, 1965, 260–82.

Weltin, E. G. *NCE*, New York, 1967, XIV, 646.

VICTOR II. *Gebhard (ca. 1022–Arezzo, 28 July 1057). Appointed pope September 1054 in Mainz, consecrated 13 April 1055. Buried in Sta. Maria Rotonda, Ravenna.*

Victor II is the last of the so-called German popes, who were appointed by the Emperor and at the same time kept their bishopric until their death. He was always very close to the imperial court and concerned himself apparently more with Germany than with Italy. His pontificate is characterized by closeness of relations with the imperial power.

Of Swabian ancestry and a member of the royal family, Gebhard was bishop of Eichstätt in 1042, when he was not yet of canonical age. Considered by all to have a brilliant mind, he quickly became a close adviser to the king and administrator at the court. He often accompanied the sovereign on his travels, notably in Italy in 1046, at the time of the deposition of the three popes SILVESTER III, GREGORY VI, and BENEDICT IX (at the synods of Sutri and Rome). In 1053, Henry III named him regent of Bavaria for his son Henry (IV). This devotion was largely rewarded by rich concessions made to the church of Eichstätt. Gebhard did not leave written traces of his management of the diocese.

On the death of LEO IX (April 1054), a Roman embassy came to ask the Emperor for a new pope. In Mainz, in September 1054, Henry III named the bishop of Eichstätt, who needed time for thought and did not accept his nomination until March 1055. Victor II finally traveled to Rome to be enthroned there on 13 April. Assisted by Peter Damian, Frederick of Ardenne, and Hildebrand (the future GREGORY VII), he continued the policy of Leo IX, holding several synods. That of Florence, in June 1055, which Henry III attended, was said to have brought together 120 bishops and reiterated the injunctions dear to Leo IX. Others took place in April 1057 in Rome and in July 1057 in Arezzo.

Victor II carried out a policy of consolidation of the Patrimony of St. Peter, notably in Romagna, Fermo, and Spoleto, and tried to create a counterbalance to the power of the new marquis of Tuscany, Godfrey the Bearded, whose brother Frederick the pope appointed abbot of Monte Cassino and cardinal-priest of the titular church of St. Crisogono. Becoming tutor of the young king Henry IV on the death of Henry III (5 October 1056), he went to Germany to settle the succession, remaining several months. On his return to Italy he again presided over the paschal synod of Rome, then in July over another at Arezzo, where he died. His entourage attempted to have his body brought back to Eichstätt, but in the end he was buried in Ravenna.

Michel Parisse

Biliography

JW, 1 549–53; 2, 710–11, 750.

LP, 2, 277, 333.

Goez, W. "Gebhard I., Bischof von Eichsätt als Papst Viktor II. (ca. 1020–1057)," *Fränkische Lebensbilder*, 9 (1980), 1–21.

Kehr, P. *Vier Kapitel aus der Geschichte Kaiser Heinrichs III*, Berlin, 1930 (Abhandl. Akad. Wissensch. phil.-hist. Klasse, 3).

Kloos, R. M. "Päpste aus Bamberg und Einchstätt," *Bayerische Kirchenfürsten*, ed. L. Schrott, Munich, 1964, 84.

Riezler, J. "Über die Herkunft des Bischofs Gebhard I. von Eichstätt, Papst Viktor II," *Forschungen der deutschen Geschichte*, 18 (1878).

Watterich, 1, 177–88, 739.

Weinfurter, S. *Die Geschichte der Eichstätter Bischoffe des Anonymus Haserensis,* Regensburg, 1987 (Eichstätter Studien NF, 24), passim.

VICTOR III. *Dauferius; as a monk, Didier or Desiderius (Benevento, ca. 1027–Monte Cassino, 16 September 1087). Elected pope 24 May 1086, consecrated 9 May 1087; buried in the Abbey of Monte Cassino.*

Victor III is better known for his long, remarkable work as abbot of Monte Cassino than for the brief and troubled period when he was pope. Born in a Lombard family of the dukes of Benevento, he lost his father in 1047 at the hands of the Normans, who would later, however, become his staunch supporters. As a monk Didier made several sojourns at La Cava, Benevento, and Tremiti, and was for a short time a hermit before attracting the attention of LEO IX (1049–54); in 1055 he entered Monte Cassino. Cardinal Frederick of Lorraine, who in August became Pope STEPHEN IX (1057–8), was his abbot from June 1057. When Frederick fell ill, Desiderius was named prior, then abbot at his death. Cardinal Humbert da Silva Candida was present when he took over the office.

In Rome in 1059, the new pope, NICHOLAS II (1059–61), named him cardinal-priest of the titular Church of St. Cecilia and enthroned him as abbot of Monte Cassino. He attended the council convoked by Nicholas II in April 1059 in Rome and signed his decree on pontifical elections (*MGH*, Const. I, 382, 383). In August he was with Nicholas II in Melfi when the Norman chiefs, Robert Guiscard of Apulia and Richard of Capua, became the pope's vassals. Through this diplomatic revolution, in which Archdeacon Hildebrand—the future GREGORY VII—was involved, the papacy, the Normans, and Monte Cassino established a relationship that despite its frequent difficulties would be essential to the realization of Desiderius's plans.

Desiderius remained abbot until he died, retaining the office even while pope, as had Frederick of Lorraine. This period has rightly been described by the Monte Cassino historians as "the golden age of Father Desiderius." He extended the *terra sancti Benedicti*, on which the abbey was situated, to the sea and rebuilt much of the abbey church and monastery buildings. In this undertaking the tombs of St. Benedict and St. Scholastica were uncovered beneath the church. When ALEXANDER II visited Monte Cassino in 1071 to consecrate the new church, it attracted a huge crowd of people from Rome and the south of Italy, including the archdeacon Hildebrand. Desiderius headed a remarkable community of nearly two hundred monks, including scholars of high repute. His scriptorium produced manuscripts of the highest importance and quality. Besides his position as cardinal-priest, he was linked to Rome through the dependent church of Sta. Maria a Pallara, which was attached to his abbey. Under ALEXANDER III, he served the papacy on several occasions.

In 1073, Gregory VII told him of his election and called him to Rome "for you must know to what extent the Church of Rome needs you and trusts your judgment" (*JL*, 4722). Over the next ten years, however, relations between the two men were difficult. In large part this was because of Robert Guiscard, a leading benefactor of Monte Cassino, who was excommunicated three times by Gregory, and because of the destruction the Normans caused in the Patrimony. The situation improved in 1080 when, thanks in particular to Desiderius's good offices, Robert Guiscard and Jordan of Capua swore loyalty to Gregory at Ceprano.

Between 1076 and 1079 Desiderius wrote his only surviving work, the *Dialogi de miraculis sancti Benedicti*, inspired by the Dialogues of Gregory I (590–604). The first two of three extant books recount miracles concerning the abbey of Monte Cassino while the third is devoted to the first reformist popes. Desiderius praises the Emperor Henry III for purifying the papacy in 1046 and for limiting clerical marriage and, particularly, simony. Leo IX appears as his model; "A man apostolic in all things, of royal stock, full of wisdom, religiously noteworthy, extraordinarily erudite in the matter of Christian doctrine," he (according to the writer) "began to invoke the name of the Lord." He reformed and reestablished all ecclesiastical matters and "one saw a new light rise on the world" (3, Prol.) Desiderius's enthusiastic account of Peter of Albano's torture by fire in Florence in 1068, in which he reveals the bishop's simony (3,4), agrees with Hildebrand's controversial appreciation (MGH, SS 30/2, 1095). He refers to GREGORY VII as "occupying the apostolic throne in the city of Rome and illuminating the Church by his words and his example" (3, 1).

The years between the oaths of Ceprano and the death of Gregory VII on 25 May 1085 were marked by the development of the schism of Guibert of Ravenna (the antipope Clement [III;]), the expeditions to Rome of the German king Henry IV, the long, exhausting campaigns of Robert Guiscard against Byzantium, and Jordan of Capua's political untrustworthiness. In 1082 Henry IV, embarrassingly, put direct pressure on Desiderius to obtain his support, but the abbot apparently managed to put him off. According to the *Chronicle of Monte Cassino* (3, 50), he adopted a distinctly Gregorian stance in a debate in Albano with Cardinal Eudes of Ostia, the future URBAN II. In 1084, when Henry entered Rome and was crowned Emperor by the antipope Clement [III], Gregory was forced to withdraw together with Robert Guiscard, who finally came to his aid, after the Normans had pillaged much of the city. On his way to Salerno, it is almost certain that Gregory passed through Monte Cassino, whose resources were put at his and his supporters' disposal. Desiderius was in Salerno during Gregory's final illness, but we cannot be sure that he was present when he died.

Victor III has sometimes been criticized for his inappropriateness and indecision, in total contrast with his achievements as abbot. But things should surely be seen in a different light. Gregory probably did not appoint him as his successor, and up to the end of 1085, as chief cardinal-priest, Desiderius seems to have carried out his wishes loyally. But Bishop Anselm of Lucca, almost certainly Gregory's first choice, died on 18 March 1086. On 24 May, although he had himself proposed Eudes of Ostia, Desiderius was against his wishes elected pope in Rome. No doubt because of the Normans' lack of unity, he quickly left the papal insignia and returned to Monte Cassino, where he continued to concern himself actively with the question of the succession.

Norman unity was achieved by Lent of 1087. Despite the opposition of a few extreme Gregorians like Hugh of Lyon, Victor III finally accepted his election on Palm Sunday (21 March) in Capua. He spent Easter at Monte Cassino and then left for Rome. His Norman allies seized St. Peter's. On 9 May he was enthroned by four bishops, including Eudes of Ostia and Pietro d'Albano.

In spite of his illness, the 131 days before his death were full and eventful. In Rome, thanks to the support of Countess Matilda of Canossa, the supporters of Victor III were able to fight Clement [III] for control of the city. On 30 June he celebrated Mass in St. Peter's, then returned to Monte Cassino. In late August, before he fell seriously ill, he convoked a council in Benevento which was attended by the bishops of Apulia, Calabria, and the Principality.

While pope, Victor III wrote a number of letters and charters, particularly for the establishment of a new see in Ravello, near Amalfi, and to try to protect the pilgrims to Rome from being charged huge fees by Byzantium. Likewise, in Monte Cassino he took a tirelessly active interest in the running of his abbey. His strength as pope was recognized by friend and foe alike. The Roman cardinal-priest Deusdedit dedicated to him his very Gregorian *Collectio canonum*, while the anonymous monk of Hirsau, the author of the *Liber de unitate ecclesiae conservanda*, shows the impact he had on Germany by the hostility he evidently bore him under the pen name Sergius. Later writers associated his name ("Victor") with the "victories" represented by the arrival of the relics of St. Nicholas in Bari the day of his enthronement in Rome, and the expedition launched in August by Pisa and Genoa to Madhia in northern Africa. On his deathbed, Victor III recommended that Cardinal Eudes of Ostia succeed him. Thus Urban II (1088–99) was able to declare himself designated by both Gregory VII and Victor III (*JL*, 5348–9, 5351).

Herbert E. J. Cowdrey

Bibliography

Bloch, H. *Monte Cassino in the Middle Ages*, 3 vols., Rome, 1986.

Chronica monasterii Casinensis, ed. Hoffmann, *MGH*, SS, 34.

Cowdrey, H. E. J. *The Age of Abbot Desiderius. Montecassino, the Papacy and the Normans in the Eleventh and Early Twelfth Centuries*, Oxford, 1983.

Desiderius, *Dialogi de miraculis sancti Benedicti*, ed. G. Schwartz and A. Holfmeister, *MGH*, SS 30/2, 1111–51; Letters and charts: *PL* 149. 961–4.

[VICTOR IV]. *Gregory Conti (b. Ceccano?). Antipope elected mid-March 1138; abdicated 29 May 1138.*

Cardinal-priest of the titular Church of the Holy Apostles, in 1112 he was one of the severest critics of PASCHAL II. No doubt fallen from grace at that time, he was again named cardinal by CALLISTUS II in 1122. Elected to succeed the antipope ANACLETUS II (who died in January 1138) by the remaining cardinals hostile to INNOCENT II, he was left with no other support than that of the Norman ruler Roger II, conqueror of Sicily and southern Italy. At the same time, Roger was negotiating with Innocent II the recognition of the royal title he had obtained from Anacletus II; he soon withdrew his support from Victor, forcing him to abdicate. Despite his early promises, Innocent II stripped Victor of all his dignities at the second Lateran Council, held a year afterward. Nothing is known of his later life.

Olivier Guyotjeannin

Bibliography

JW, 1, 919.

Schmale, F. J. *Studien zum Schisma des Jahres 1130*, Cologne-Graz, 1961.

[VICTOR IV (V)]. *Ottaviano de' Monticelli (?–Lucca, 20 April 1164). Antipope elected 7 September 1159, consecrated in Farfa 4 October 1159.*

When this antipope was elected in 1159 he took the name Victor IV, since he and his supporters considered the preceding Victor IV (1138) an antipope and had eliminated him from the official pontifical list. Ottaviano was descended from a branch of the powerful Roman family of the counts of Tusculum. Cardinal-priest of the titular church of St. Cecilia, before his appointment he had headed the pro-imperial faction inside the Sacred College. Its members had been divided since the accession, as governor of the kingdom of Germany and the Empire, of Frederick Barbarossa, of the dynasty of the Staufen dukes of Swabia (1152). Before his arrival, Barbarossa had in fact undertaken to restore imperial power and, more particularly, impose his authority and control over Italy. With this in view, in March 1153 he had concluded an accord (the treaty of Constance) with EUGENE III. By its terms he promised to force the Roman rebels to submit to the pontiff and, in a general way, protect the Holy See from its enemies (Sicily and others). In exchange, the head of the Church would cooperate with him against their common enemies and would give him the imperial crown—which was done in Rome in 1155.

Even before this consecration, however Frederick's interventions in Italian affairs had caused great anxiety to HADRIAN IV and certain cardinals, who in any case were disappointed that the papacy had not obtained the promised aid and protection. In 1156, when the Papal States were threatened by the new king of Sicily, William I, the pontiff was forced to negotiate with him. But he took advantage of the situation to settle (Treaty of Benevento) all the disputes between them. This the Emperor took to mean a rupture of the alliance of Constance and their collaboration.

Tension became even more acute following the Diet of Besançon, where, according to the imperial chancellor's tendentious translation, the pontifical legates claimed that Frederick had received the Empire from the pope as a "benefice" (October 1157). The situation grew especially tense when the Emperor began effectively (Diet of Roncaglia, 1158) to extend his dominion over Italy. Hadrian IV then hardened his attitude, renewed the treaty with Sicily, and conveyed to the anxious Italian cities, including Milan, his active sympathy. This behavior, however, was not approved by all the cardinals. A bitterly anti-Sicilian group, led by Ottaviano, still championed the agreement with the Empire, with Frederick assiduously favoring and maintaining it by sending members of his entourage to Rome and the surrounding area.

When Hadrian IV died on 1 September 1159, the rift in the Sacred College became irreparable. On the one side was Cardinal Ottaviano, on whose family the Emperor had just lavished gifts, and on the other Orlando Cardinal Bandinelli. The election was tumultuous. At the beginning the votes were most probably split between the two protagonists and a third party. Finally, however, Orlando won a strong majority. But Ottaviano refused to give in, supported by a large section of the clergy and the Roman people, who favored their compatriot. His partisans remained masters of the terrain. Orlando having had himself crowned 20 September under the name of ALEXANDER III, Ottaviano followed suit at Farfa 4 October, taking the name of Victor IV.

Immediately, Frederick's representative in Rome recognized him as the true pope and treated Alexander III, who had excommunicated him, as an enemy. To ensure victory, the Emperor decided to convoke a council in Pavia, on his own authority. It proclaimed the legitimacy of Ottaviano's election and solemnly recognized it by stressing Orlando's refusal to come and present his defense. Unfortunately, not only were the arguments invoked in Ottariano's favor highly specious, but the bishops attending the council were mainly from Germany and northern Italy, very few from France or England.

In the ensuing months, the king of Sicily, those of France and England, and then the rulers of the Iberian Peninsula and the other kingdoms all joined Alexander's side. Victor IV, once again excommunicated, therefore contented himself with being the pope of the Emperor, who was anathematized in his turn, and had no choice but to throw in his lot with the Staufen ruler. In 1162, Barbarossa tried to intimidate Louis VII, beset by certain powerful French lords, by proposing they meet with the purpose of recognizing one and the same head of the Church. But at the Diet of Dole he made the error of having Victor IV's legitimacy proclaimed even before his meeting with Louis. This upset the French king, who had also been very cavalierly treated by the Emperor's representatives when they met him on the bridge of St.-Jean-de-Losne.

Shortly afterward Victor's party dwindled still further as a result of several defections in Italy and second thoughts on the part of some German bishops and clergy. Leaving the kingdom of Burgundy, to which he had followed the Emperor in the summer of 1163, Victor IV spent several months in Lombardy, but without succeeding in reversing the situation or rallying support, despite the efforts of the imperial chancellor, Rainald of Dassel. From there he proceeded to Tuscany and fell ill at Lucca, where he died 20 April 1164. The canons of the cathedral refused to bury him there, but Rainald, who had rushed to the scene, managed to convince his cardinals to name a successor to Victor, the antipope PASCHAL III.

Marcel Pacaut

Bibliography

JW, 2, 418–26, 725.

VIGILIUS. (*Rome, ?–Syracuse, 7 June 555*). *Buried in the church of St. Silvester on the via Salaria.*

Vigilius was a complex character, who became pope at a time when the Byzantine emperor Justinian's successful reconquest of Italy was creating profound changes in relations between the Church and the political power. Both pope and Emperor intended to set up a true Christian empire, but they had different ideas of what it should be. This misunderstanding would lead the bishop of Rome into appalling difficulties, for he was incapable of mastering the subtle theological disputes in which he was embroiled, or the complexity of relations with Constantinople.

Vigilius came from an aristocratic senatorial family. His father Iohannes was prefect of the praetorium and his brother Reparatus prefect of the city. Both men served the Gothic monarchy. Vigilius himself was a deacon during the pontificate of BONIFACE II, a pope favored by Theodoric. In 530 Boniface attempted to repeat the gesture of FELIX III (IV) by appointing a successor, in the person of Vigilius. But most of the Roman clergy were opposed to this decision and made Boniface retract his gesture. This was done during a solemn council, with the Senate taking part, at which the document appointing

Vigilius was thrown into the fire. No doubt this move was aimed both at the procedure itself and at Vigilius's candidacy. In fact, if the pope himself were to name his own successor, both clergy and Senate would lose most of their influence, and we know to what extent the accession to the papal throne entailed passionate struggles. But on the other hand Vigilius, named by Boniface, appeared to be the monarchy's candidate, in an age when, with the ending of the Acacian schism, more and more senators hoped for a Byzantine restoration.

On Boniface's death, the choice fell on the priest John, and after the latter's tragic death, on Agapitus. It is not known if Vigilius played a part in the intrigues surrounding both elections. In any case he continued his clerical career; in 536, when Agapitus was making his way to Constantinople, Vigilius was in the imperial city, with the title of apocrisiary according to certain sources, archdeacon according to others. Apparently he was still there when the pope died, during the council of the spring of 536 affirming the deposition of Anthimus, bishop of Constantinople (although he did not attend it), and stayed on after the legation had left.

In Italy Byzantine forces were fighting the Goths, and on 8 June, in Rome, which was in the power of King Theodahad, the clergy elected as pope SILVERIUS, the candidate of the Gothic party. Vigilius returned to Italy sometime in the summer or autumn of 536 and met with the Byzantine general in chief, Belisarius. No doubt this did not take place until November, by which time Naples had at last been seized. Vigilius was with Belisarius when in December of that year he recaptured Rome, now abandoned by the Goths. But Theodahad's troops returned to the attack and besieged the city. In March 537 Silverius was accused of treason. Summoned by Belisarius, he was deposed and sent into exile, and Vigilius took his place, becoming pope eleven years after his designation by Boniface.

These are the events that can be established with certainty, relying on documentation that is extremely unwieldy—both abundant and constantly involving harsh polemics, besides being always very hostile to Vigilius. The writers that we turn to for information (Facundus of Hermiane, Liberatus of Carthage, Victor of Tunnunna, Pelagius, the *Liber pontificalis*) tell us considerably more about him. When Vigilius was in Constantinople, he is said to have had the ear of the empress Theodora, promising her over a long period of time that he would reverse Agapitus's policy and favor the restoration of the Monophysites. According to certain writers, he obtained money from the imperial couple to stage a conspiracy against Silverius, caused faked letters to be written to bolster the accusation of treason, and then, not content with deposing and exiling Silverius, caused him to die of starvation. These accusations are not all based on fact— far from it—and rigorous scrutiny makes it possible to show their internal contradictions and improbabilities. But they do not contradict Vigilius's ambitious politics, and they especially reflect the hostility he later aroused in the affair of the Three Chapters.

The first years of Vigilius's pontificate were actually peaceful ones. The war gave him three years during which he could avoid any contacts with Constantinople. Indeed, in 540 Justinian reproached him for his silence, and it was not until September of that year that he sent the Emperor and Bishop Menas the profession of loyalty that popes traditionally swore at the beginning of their pontificate. From 538 to 544 Vigilius benefited, in Rome, from the support of Belisarius, who promoted the pope's brother, one of the few Roman senators surviving in Italy, to the post of prefect of the praetorium. He took advantage of the peace to set about organizing the churches of Gaul, also striving, with his vicar Auxanus, bishop of Arles, to develop enthusiasm for the Empire in the Frankish kingdom. He restored the Spanish vicariate, entrusting it to Bishop Profuturus of Braga. In Rome itself he restored several sanctuaries in the catacombs of the via Salaria as well as the decoration of St. Hippolytus's basilica on the via Tiburtina. In 544, very likely on the occasion of the anniversary of his accession to the papacy, he received the homage of the work of the poet Arator, who had put the Acts of the Apostles into verse, magnifying the glory of Peter and Paul and, thereby, that of the see of Rome.

But Vigilius would not long absent himself from matters connected with the East. In 542 he handed his apocrisiary Pelagius the dossier of the condemnation of Origenism, after which he was obliged to concern himself more closely with that of the Three Chapters.

In late 544, Justinian published an edict condemning Theodore of Mopsuestia, the writings of Theodoret of Cyrrhis against Cyril of Alexandria, and the letter to Bishop Maris attributed to Ibas of Edessa. (From then on, this dossier was known as the Three Chapters.)

Justinian wanted to contribute to the elaboration of Christology and to the unity of believers by condemning teachings too close to Nestorianism, arguments particularly hateful to the Monophysites. But the incriminated bishops had all long been dead in the peace of the Church, and two of them had been solemnly rehabilitated by the council of Chalcedon, after being deposed by the "brigandage of Ephesus." Justinian's edict was therefore at once understood as an attack on the council of Chalcedon, thus on the memory of Leo I and on orthodoxy. Even the Eastern bishops who agreed to sign only did so subject to the agreement of Rome, while a lively opposition formed in Africa, in Illyricum, and among the Roman clergy at Constantinople. Whether he wanted to or not, Justinian would have to obtain Vigilius's agreement.

His method was not the most delicate. He had the pope seized while he was celebrating Mass in the church of St.

Cecilia in Trastevere, on 25 November 545. Vigilius was taken to Sicily, where he stayed several months, trying from afar to continue to govern the Roman Church. He carried out several consecrations, entrusting temporal administration to the deacon Ampliatus and spiritual government to the bishop Valentinus. Vigilius despatched them to Rome at the same time as a convoy laden with provisions, but the Goths intercepted them and massacred all the clergy, except for Valentinus, who had his hands cut off. In Sicily, and later during his voyage to the East, in the autumn of 546, Vigilius learned the extent of the hostility of the provinces of Africa and Illyria toward the condemnation of the Three Chapters.

The pope reached Constantinople on 25 January 547. He was lavishly received by Justinian, but was at once plunged into theological debate, as his apocrisiary Stephanus had excommunicated the patriarch of Constantinople, Menas. Vigilius confirmed the sentence. On 28 May 547 the Emperor sent the pope the Latin translation of two letters from Constantine justifying the Emperor's intervention in questions of faith. In June Vigilius is said to have written two secret letters to Justinian and Theodora pledging to have the Three Chapters condemned, letters whose authenticity was contested by the West.

In the beginning of 548 Vigilius consulted one by one the bishops present in the capital, thus weakening the position of the defenders of the Three Chapters, who were more vulnerable to imperial pressure. After this consultation, which was vigorously reproved by Facundus of Hermiane, the pope gathered seventy signatures favoring condemnation. On 11 April 548 Vigilius wrote a *iudicatum* known only by the quotations the Emperor made from it when the council opened, in 553. Vigilius condemned the Three Chapters, but at the same time expressed his respect for the council of Chalcedon. This text aroused increasingly loud opposition in Illyria, Gaul, and Africa, where the pope was excommunicated by a council, and in Italy, where the Roman deacons Rusticus and Sebastianus started the most injurious rumors regarding the pope's orthodoxy.

In August Vigilius excommunicated the rebellious deacons. He also gained the Emperor's agreement to return his *iudicatum* in exchange, according to Justinian, for a most solemn promise to do all in his power to have the Three Chapters condemned. For his part the Emperor promised, according to Vigilius's testimony, not to intervene again in the debate.

In July 551, however, Justinian published a fresh edict condemning the Three Chapters. Vigilius threatened to excommunicate all those who subscribed to the edict, pronounced these excommunications on 14 July, and left the palace of Placidia where he was residing, seeking refuge in a church. On 14 August he wrote out the sentence of excommunication of 14 July, but still abstained from publishing it. He had it signed by members of the clergy accompanying him, in particular the apocrisiary Stephanus and the bishop of Milan, Datius.

Not long afterward, troops were sent to seize the pope. The soldiers penetrated the church, grabbed Vigilius by the beard and feet, and tried to wrest him from the columns of the altar to which he was clinging. But the altar collapsed, an angry crowd intervened, and the soldiers gave up their attempt. The Emperor, forced to carry out negotiations of which we do not know the contents, had the pope returned to his residence, but not for long. Feeling threatened once again, Vigilius escaped through the window on 23 December 551 and took refuge in Chalcedon, in the church of St. Euphemia. Justinian's attempts to negotiate or uproot the pope from his symbolic refuge by force were of no avail. On 5 February Vigilius published an encyclical in which he recounted all the recent happenings, demanded respect for the pontifical decisions and the council of Chalcedon, and entrusted Datius of Milan with further negotiations. A little later he had the sentence of 14 August made public. In particular it concerned Theodore Askidas, bishop of Caesarea in Cappodocia, who was in good standing at court.

In the spring of 552, the pope finally obtained substantial concessions from his opponents, in particular a promise to demand the annulment of the imperial edict of 551, to condemn violent actions against the pope, and to reject those who were excommunicated. Before August 552 Vigilius returned to Constantinople, though without his companion the bishop Datius, who died before the month of July.

On 6 January 553, Menas's successor, Eustachius (Menas having died 24 August), proposed that an ecumenical council be held to settle the question. Vigilius accepted this proposal with joy, but did not obtain from the Emperor satisfactory representation from the western provinces. Only a few African bishops, meticulously chosen by Justinian from among the rare supporters of the condemnation of the Three Chapters, were convoked to Constantinople. On 20 April 553 Vigilius asked the Emperor for a twenty-day delay to formulate his advice based on the documents assembled for the council.

The council opened on 4 May, six days before the expiration of the delay, but without the pope or any Latin bishop. In spite of legations sent to them on 6, 7, and 8 May, they refused to come and take their seats. On 9 May, the deliberations were put off until later, and on 12 and 13 May, after the expiration of Vigilius's requested delay but before the pope had rendered his verdict, the council condemned Theodore and Theodoret. On 14 May Vigilius finished his second great text on the Three Chapters, the *constitutum*. In it he condemned the texts incriminated by the imperial edict but refused to condemn the persons, both because they had died in the peace of the Church and because the condemned formulas had been employed

in good faith. An ancient tradition, malicious so far as Vigilius is concerned, attributes the writing of this text to the deacon Pelagius.

Nevertheless, the council proceeded without taking cognizance of Vigilius's text, which was abruptly rejected by the Emperor. On 25 May the latter declared it superfluous if it was condemning the Three Chapters, perjury if it was defending them. The next day, in its seventh session, the council at Justinian's request ordered the pope's name to be struck from the diptychs, claiming to make a distinction between the man and the office. At its last session, on 2 June, the council published its decrees. Repression came down on the pope's entourage and on those defending the Three Chapters. The pope's companions were interned and exiled, while he stayed on alone in Constantinople.

Which should astonish us more, that after six months of this treatment Vigilius yielded and agreed to condemn the Three Chapters, or that for six months this old man— over seventy—resisted imperial pressure before agreeing to subscribe to the condemnation? On 8 December 553, in a letter to Eutyches of Constantinople, Vigilius surrendered to due self-criticism and accepted the condemnation of the Three Chapters. On 23 February 554 he published a final text, the *iudicatum* of the second indiction, virtually repeating the terms of Justinian's encyclical. The pope's name was then reinserted in the diptychs of the Byzantine Church.

Vigilius took advantage of his return to grace to cause the emperor to issue a body of laws designed to reorganize Italy, now conquered by Byzantine forces. These laws are the so-called Pragmatic Sanction. He also won the right to return to Italy, in particular to Rome, from which he had been absent for nine years. But on the homeward journey he died in Syracuse, of the gallstone disease from which he had long suffered. His body was brought to Rome, but he was not buried in St. Peter's, the first sign of a *damnatio memoriae* carefully nurtured by his successor, PELAGIUS I.

Vigilius does not deserve all of the opprobrium that has been heaped on him. If he was unable to control the difficult political situation in which he found himself, he was constantly preoccupied with trying to obtain for Italy a worthy place in Justinian's empire, and for the Church an independence the Byzantine Empire begrudged it. The fall of Vigilius illustrates the incompatibility of two divergent visions of the world.

Claire Sotinel

Bibliography

Amann, E. "Trois Chapitres," *DTC*, 15, 2, c. 1868.

Duchesne, L. "Vigile et Pélage," *Revue des Questions Historiques*, 1884, 36, 369.

Facundus Episcopus Hermianensis, *Pro defensione Trium Capitulorum libari XII, Contra Mocianum*

Scholasticum, Epistula fidei catholicae in defensione Trium Capitulorum, CC 90a.

Liberatus Carthaginensis Diaconus, *Breuiarum Causae Nestorianorum et Eutychianorum.*

Pelagius Diaconus, *In defensione Trium Capitulorum*, Studi e Testi, 57, Rome, 1932.

Schwartz, E. *Acta conciliorum aecumenicorum*, IV, 1.

Sotinel, C. "Autorité pontificale et pouvoir impérial sous le règle de Justinien: l'exemple du pape Vigile," *MEFRA*, 204, 1, 439–63.

Victor Tonnennensis Episcopous, *Chronica, MGH*, AA, 11, 179–206.

Vigilius Papa, *Epistulae, CSEL*, 35; "Vigiliusbriefe," *Sitzungsberichte der Bayerischen Akademie der Wissenschaften, Philosophisch-historische Abteilung*, 1940, 2; *ACO*, IV, 2; *PL*, 69.

VITALIAN. *(Segni, in Campagna, ?–Rome, 27 January 672). Consecrated pope 30 July 657. Buried in St. Peter's, Rome. Saint (included by Baronius in the Roman Martyrology).*

Vitalian occupied the Roman see longer than any other Byzantine pope. He received the last Emperor who affirmed his authority over Rome, greatly enhanced relations with the kings of the West, in particular the English kings, and increased papal power over the Roman people.

The *Liber pontificalis* reveals the major preoccupations of the Roman clergy who supervised its compilation. In this case it deals exclusively with the link with imperial power. As soon as he was elected, Vitalian restored good relations between Rome and Constantinople. Without giving way on fundamentals, he avoided any reference to the Lateran Council and sent the Patriarch Peter a synodique that satisfied both him and the Emperor Constans II. This meant that the pope's name was once more included in the diptychs of the Church of Constantinople and that Roman privileges were confirmed. The Emperor also showered him with lavish gifts.

The truce enabled the parties to present a common front to the Lombard Rothari, who, particularly with the annexation of Liguria, was reducing the imperial possessions in Italy as well as threatening Rome. Constans II's reconquest of 663 brought about a twelve-day visit to Rome, where he was very well received by Vitalian, and later the establishment of the court in Sicily.

In 668 the Emperor was assassinated. The pope vigorously championed his son, Constantine IV (668–85), thus allowing his name to be kept on the Constantinople diptychs despite his opposition to Monothelitism and the hostility of the Patriarch John (669–75). The development of a balance of power gave the pope autonomy. However, the Emperor granted the bishop of Ravenna the privilege of autocephaly. Like the pope, he would be chosen by the clergy, with the Emperor's direct confirmation, and consecrated (666) by three of his suffragans.

Nevertheless, the Roman clergy, still absorbed in the struggles for influence among the patriarchates within the traditional Empire, were slow to realize the papacy's newly won advantages. The western kings were calling for missionaries and the confirmation of privileges and exemptions granted to churches and monasteries. The prestige of the Roman shrines grew rapidly, attracting pilgrims and scholars, especially from England.

However, the phenomenon did not escape men like the Venerable Bede, who wrote at length about the links that were developing between the kings and the pope. The kings hoped to take advantage of the high religious culture of the Italian and Eastern clergy living in Rome. The pope profited from these demands to increase the influence of his see. In particular, Vitalian supported the efforts of Oswy of Northumbria (655–70) at the synod of Whitby (664) to establish a common date for Easter and do away with Celtic practices.

On 26 March 668, the pope consecrated the Greek monk, Theodore of Tarsus, as archbishop of Canterbury, at the request of the kings of Kent and Northumbria. He was assisted in his task by the African abbot Hadrian and by Benedict Biscop, a Northumbrian noble who had completed part of his studies in Rome. The English Church broke away definitively from Irish influence, acquiring a cohesion and an influence that very soon made it the most dynamic in Europe. At the time, English missionaries became the best propagandists for Roman authority of all the Western Churches.

Relying on his prestige in the West, which helped consolidate his independence vis-à-vis Constantinople, Vitalian established his authority more solidly over Rome, where all profited from its newfound influence. Constans II had been able to strip the Pantheon dome of its bronze tiles as well as to carry off other monuments and precious objects; it was the last pillage Rome would have to suffer. Meanwhile the pope developed the Lateran school of chant, doubtless created by Gregory the Great. The choristers, called *vitaliani*, took part in the richer liturgy, which showed the influence of Constantinople's grandiose ceremonies but more and more affirmed its own individuality. At the same time it displayed to pilgrims and other visitors the rediscovered grandeur of Rome, no longer an imperial but a pontifical city.

Jean Durliat

Bibliography

JW, 1, 235, 237; 2, 699, 740.

LP, 1, 343–5.

PL, 87, 999–1010.

Bertolini, O. *Roma di fronte a Bisanzio e ai Longobardi*, Bologna, 1971, 355–64.

VITERBO. Today the capital of one of the five provinces of Latium, Viterbo shares with a few other cities of central Italy, like Anagni, Perugia, and Orvieto, the privilege of having been in the 13th century one of the favorite residences of the pontifical court. The leading city of the Patrimony of St. Peter in Tuscia, it was an effective if not always official capital of what was, until the abolition of the popes' temporal power, one of the six great provinces of the Papal States. Yet Viterbo was long a restive city, one that rebelled even against pontifical authority. It was not until the middle of the 15th century that the Church was able to definitively impose its dominion over a city long sunk in torpor, as were almost all the other cities of the Papal States. Its key period is therefore a brief one, barely one hundred years, a period that was naturally exceptional for Viterbo, whose history was then closely tied to that of the papacy, but one that was also characterized by episodes rich in meaning for the evolution of the fundamental structures of the papacy.

In the 12th century, Viterbo, situated a few days' walk from Rome, served from time to time as a residence for several popes, as well as for the antipopes PASCHAL III and CALLISTUS [III]. But if these settled in Viterbo, it was chiefly because the vicissitudes of the struggle between Empire and Church prevented them from residing in Rome. In the next century, by contrast, everything leads one to suppose that when the papacy settled in Viterbo, or in some other city in the Papal States, it was in response to new requirements on the part of the Roman pontiffs. We should therefore place it in the context of that itinerancy of the pontifical court that was long attributed to political causes but that, as A. Paravicini Bagliani has recently shown, should be seen rather as a social phenomenon, linked to the new thinking about the body and health that was developing in precisely this period in the popes' and cardinals' entourages.

The figures provide an explanation. With 3,319 days of pontifical presence *intra muros* between the pontificate of INNOCENT III and that of BENEDICT XI, Viterbo leads Anagni (3,214 days)—a city where, however, BONIFACE VIII alone resided more than three years—as well as Orvieto (2,806 days) and Perugia (1,770 days). Moreover, from Innocent III to MARTIN IV (elected in Viterbo in 1281), all the popes, except INNOCENT IV, resided there for long periods of their pontificates. Four of them died and were buried there: ALEXANDER IV (1261), CLEMENT IV (1268), HADRIAN V (1276), and JOHN XXI (1277). No fewer than five conclaves took place in Viterbo, where URBAN IV was elected and crowned in 1261, GREGORY X in 1271, JOHN XXI in 1276, NICHOLAS III in 1277, and MARTIN IV in 1281.

These conclaves sometimes lasted an exceedingly long time—nearly three years were needed to choose the successor of Clement IV, who died on 29 September 1268. Often they were tumultuous, giving rise to episodes that varied between the prankish—as, for example, when the communal authorities decided to remove the roof of the hall where the cardinals were sitting in order to hurry their decision (1270)—to the violent, as when these same authorities had two cardinals of the Orsini family imprisoned and prevented another Orsini from participating, during the long conclave of 1281. This episode actually encouraged the new pope, Martin IV, to abandon Viterbo, swearing that he would never set foot in the city again. In fact, after him no pope ever did stay long in Viterbo.

All the dicasteries of the pontifical court, beginning with the Chancellery and the various offices of the Apostolic Camera, accompanied the pontiff on his journeys. Thus they settled in Viterbo for stays that lasted an average of a few weeks to a few months and usually took place during the best season. Suddenly, Viterbo, which at that time had hardly had more than fifteen thousand inhabitants, saw several thousands of new arrivals stream inside its walls. Moreover, these were people whose demands in the way of shelter and provisions were certainly above average. On several occasions, the communal authorities and the papacy exchanged agreements, trying to solve in advance the manifold problems the influx of such a singular crowd must entail. Today, these documents, painstakingly edited by papal historians, remain one of the richest sources of information on the conditions of life of the pontifical court in the Middle Ages.

Jean-Claude Maire Vigueur

Bibliography

Ladner, G. B. "Die Statue Bonifaz' VIII. in der Lateranbasilika und die Entstehung der dreifach gekrönten Tiara," *Images and Ideas in the Middle Ages, Selected Studies in History and Art*, I, Rome, 1983, 393–426.

Pinzi, C. *Storia della città di Viterbo*, 3 vols., Rome, 1887–99.

Radke, G. M. *The Papal Palace in Viterbo*, New York [cf. Diss. Abst., 41 A (1980–1), 6, 2335].

Signorelli, G. *Viterbo nella storia della Chiesa*, 3 vols. in 5, Viterbo, 1907–64.

WARS OF ITALY, FRENCH (16TH CENTURY).

Under this heading are grouped expeditions led into Italy by the kings of France, Charles VIII, Louis XII, and Francis I, for the purpose of conquering land between 1492 and 1518. Because the House of Anjou's rights over the kingdom of Naples, a feudal holding of the Holy See, had come to the king of France via the will of Charles of Maine, nephew of René of Anjou (10 December 1481), Charles VIII decided to claim them to the detriment of the House of Aragon, which had been established in Naples since 1442. In 1493 he called upon pope ALEXANDER VI Borgia for his investiture as king of Naples, but the pontiff was allied with the House of Aragon: at the death of Ferrante of Naples (25 January 1494), he conferred this investiture upon Alfonso of Calabria, who took the name Alfonso II.

Forced to resort to the use of force to exert his rights, Charles VIII got the support of Ludovico Sforza, called the Moor, who took hold of power in Milan to the detriment of his nephew Giangaleazzo, the husband of Isabella, the daughter of Alphonse II of Naples. Cardinal Giuliano Della Rovere, an enemy of Alexander VI, sought refuge in the court of France and proposed to depose the Borgia pope so that he, once pope himself, might give the crown of Naples to Charles VIII.

The French made their way into Piedmont on 3 September 1494 and, welcomed by Ludovico Sforza, crossed into Milanese soil. The Aragonese fleet did not manage to stop the French fleet off the coast of Genoa. Pietro de Medici, a Neapolitan ally, handed over his border territory to the French. The Florentines were indignant and overthrew him, receiving Charles VIII as their liberator from tyranny, as the Dominican Savonarola encouraged them to do. Pisa, detached from the Florentine state, passed under French protection. Nothing further could stop Charles VIII's march toward Rome, where he made his entrance on 31 December 1494. Despite Giuliano Della Rovere and the prelates from his party, the king pledged allegiance to the Borgia pope. He left again, without having obtained the investiture of Naples, but accompanied by the Turkish prince Djem (up to that point held in the Vatican), whom he was hoping to use in a future CRUSADE, departing from the kingdom of Naples: this hope was dashed by the sudden death of the hostage.

Upsetting his Aragonese competitor, Charles VIII entered the southern capital on 22 February 1495, but a league was formed against him in Venice on 1 April, composed of the Venetians, the pope, Maximilian of Austria, the Catholic king and queen of Spain, and the duke of Milan. Charles VIII retreated toward France to avoid being surrounded. On 5 July he forced a passage at Fornoua, but his garrisons left in the kingdom of Naples surrendered one after the other. Charles VIII died accidentally on April 1498 while he was preparing a new expedition.

As soon as he ascended to the throne, Louis of Orleans, now king Louis XII, prepared to leave for Italy to take from Ludovico Sforza the duchy of Milan, which he claimed through his inheritance from his grandmother Valentina Visconti. Pope Alexander VI, who was anxious to form closer ties with France, charged his son, Cesar Borgia, with taking a dispensation to Louis XII after the canonical dissolution of his marriage to Jeanne of France, to allow him to marry Anne of Brittany, his predecessor's wife. Cesar, named duke of Valentinois by the king, participated in the conquest of the Milanais, Ludovico Sforza's duchy; the conquest was complete in October 1499. After a short counteroffensive led by Ludovico with troops furnished by Maximilian of Austria in February 1500, Louis XII took the duke prisoner and firmly established his domination in Milan, where Cardinal Georges of Amboise was carrying out the duties of lieutenant general of the king and LEGATE to the pope. While Ferrara, Mantua, Bologna, and Siena established ties with France, Cesar Borgia took control, with the help of the French army, of Imola and Forli (1499), and then of Pesaro and Rimini (1500). These cities, taken away from local lords, formed the duchy of the Romagna with which Alexander VI invested his son.

Louis XII formed an alliance with king Ferdinand of Aragon through the treaty of Granada (11 November 1500) to conquer Neapolitan territory.

The assassination of the Neapolitan prince Alfonso of Aragon, duke of Bisceglie and husband of Lucretia Borgia, on the order of Cesar Borgia, allowed Cesar to join the invaders when he had just annexed Faenza, Piombino, and the island of Elba to his States. In June 1501 Pope ALEXANDER VI made public his alliance with France and Spain, and pronounced the downfall of king Frederick of Naples who, after the surrender and sacking of Capua in July 1501, was transported to France, where he received the duchy of Anjou as compensation. Nevertheless, division of the zones of occupation set the duke of Nemours' Frenchmen against the Spaniards of Gonzalvo of Cordoba. In the spring of 1503 the Spaniards were victorious in Seminara and Cerignola. Louis XII dispatched an army against them in August; it stopped outside Rome where Alexander VI had just died. But the presence of these troops did not advance the candidacy of Georges of Amboise, who was pushed back twice, first to the benefit of PIUS III Piccolomini, and then to that of Giuliano Della Rovere, who became Pope JULIUS II in November 1503.

Placed facing the Spaniards at the mouth of the Garigliano, the French army retreated toward Gaeta where it surrendered in January 1504. In March the King made a three-year truce with Ferdinand of Aragon, before signing an accord in September 1504 in Blois with Maximilian of Austria and his son, Philip the Fair, the husband of Joanna, the daughter of Ferdinand of Aragon and Isabelle of Castille: Philip and Joanna's heir, Charles of Gand, who was also heir to Spain, was to marry Claude of France, the eldest daughter of the king and Anne of Brittany. One of the newlyweds would receive the kingdom of Naples, and the other, Milan, Genoa, and the county of Asti, as well as Burgundy, Brittany, and the county of Blois. After a period of illness, Louis XII broke off the engagement to order (31 May 1505) the marriage of his daughter Claude to François of Angoulême.

The breaking of the Blois accords, the death of Philip the Fair (25 September 1506), and the assumption of supervision of Philip's heir, Charles, by Marguerite of Austria, governess of the Netherlands, stirred up rivalry between France and the Empire just at the time when the revolt in Genoa broke out (February 1507) against France; revolt was secretly favored by Julius II.

Louis XII marched against the city with a considerable army, forcing it to surrender in April 1507. This victory was followed by a meeting in Savoy between the king and Ferdinand of Aragon.

To oppose collusion between the two powers, Maximilian of Austria penetrated into Italy, but the Venetians forced him to return to Germany. This failure brought him closer to Louis XII, as well as to Julius II. Both felt that Venice had become too powerful and joined with the emperor against it. In Cambrai, under the aegis of Marguerite of Austria, a treaty between Maximilian and Louis XII was signed on 10 December 1508. It was apparently aimed at the struggle against the TURKS, but it contained hidden clauses specifying that the alliance was directed against the Venetians. Julius II and the king of Aragon adhered to the secret accord that called for the return (by Venice) of Verona to the emperor, Brescia to the king of France, RAVENNA to the pope, and Otranto to the king of Spain.

After Julius II launched the INTERDICT against Venice in 1509, Louis XII went to war. The Venetians opposed him with 40,000 men and a considerable amount of artillery, but the French bested them at Agnadello on 14 May. The fortresses on land surrendered one after the other. The king gave Treviso, Padua, and Verona to the emperor. Venice returned the cities of the Romagna to the king and the ports of Apulia that it occupied to king Ferdinand.

Fortune again smiled upon the vanquished. The subjects on the mainland called the Venetians back. Emperor Maximilian, who had entered the campaign, had to give up his siege of Padua. In November 1509 he was forced to negotiate in Mantua. In July the pope received Venice's plenipotentiaries, who had come to beg for peace. On 24 February 1510 he raised the interdict against the republic. Thereafter he concentrated on eliminating France from Italian soil. He counted on the armed force of the Swiss cantons which, in 1510, through the intermediary of Mathias Schinner, bishop of Sion, began to provide mercenaries to the papacy. Henry VIII of England and a great number of Italian princes supported the pope.

Hostilities began with a Swiss attack against duke Alfonso of Ferrara, an ally of France (August 1510). The French and the papal armies clashed in the Romagna. Louis XII, who had obtained the support of his clergy in the war against the pope, had a general council called by the cardinals of the French party to have the pope condemned. Julius II, in turn, called a general COUNCIL at the Lateran in 1512. On 4 October 1511 he signed an alliance, called the Holy League, with Spain and Venice, aimed at driving out the French from Italy. The kings of England and Aragon adhered to the treaty. Among the great European princes, only the emperor remained beside Louis XII.

The young French general Gaston de Foix, the sovereign's nephew who was successor to Chaumont of Amboise as the king's lieutenant, drove out the pope's Swiss mercenaries from Milan, and then in February 1512 confronted the Venetian, Aragonese, and papal forces surrounding Bologna and forced them to raise their siege. He then freed the fortress of Brescia and went off to lay siege to Ravenna, forcing the Spaniards under Pedro Navarro and Ramon of Cardona into combat on 11 April. The French, with whom a contingent of Germans had joined, were victorius, but Gaston de Foix and a great number of his valiant warriors lost their lives on the battlefield.

After Ravenna's surrender, the Romagna submitted to the conquerers, but a new Swiss army raised by Julius II obliged the French to withdraw to the Alps. The council called by France in Pisa withdrew to Milan, then dispersed after having sentenced Julius II to be suspended. But the condemnation was in vain. The Lateran council, to which the remainder of Christendom adhered, lent its support to the pope. The defection of the emperor, who in November 1512 rejoined the Catholic League, marked the complete isolation of France.

Maximilian Sforza's reestablishment in Milan took place on 29 December 1512. Julius II died shortly thereafter on 20 February 1513. He was replaced on 11 March by Giovanni de Medici, who took the name LEO X. Disturbed by the pope's closer ties with the emperor, Venice formed an alliance with France on 14 March 1513. Louis XII again invaded the Milanais, but on 6 June his troops were put to flight in Novara by a large Swiss army. In the north and the east, France was invaded by English, Flemish, German, and Swiss forces. In September, through the treaty of Dijon, La Trémoille agreed to abandon Milan and Asti, and to return to the pope, the emperor, and their allies, all the lands that had been taken from them, and to pay a heavy fine to the Swiss cantons. Although he refused to ratify the treaty, Louis XII did agree to make concessions: he adhered to the Lateran Council in January 1514, in March he signed a treaty with Ferdinand of Aragon, and on 7 August a peace treaty with Henry VIII of England, whose sister, Marie, he married after he was widowed.

Only the Austro-Hispano-papal coalition was left to face France. Such was the situation when Francis I ascended to the throne on 1 January 1515. By spring, the new king was already preparing to reconquer the Milanais, occupied by Swiss troops. Crossing the Alps in August, he took Novara. He forced the Swiss to withdraw into Milan. Led by the papal legate cardinal Mathias Schinner, they went out to confront the French in Marignano. The battle ended with the French king's victory on 12 September 1515. After taking Milan, Maximilian Sforza gave up his rights over the Milanais (4 October), in favor of the king of France. The pope recognized the treaty in exchange for the return of Parma and Piacenza to the Holy See. On 11 December, Francis I met Leo X in Bologna to discuss the terms of an agreement aimed at ending the Pragmatic Sanction of Bourges (1438), which

had been a continual source of conflict between France and Rome. The CONCORDAT promulgated by the pope in August 1516 preserved some of the Holy See's privileges, but the majority of the ecclesiastical nominations passed into the king's hands.

After a fruitless campaign by Emperor Maximilian to drive out the French from Milan, a league was formed in Rome in November 1516 between France, the pope, the republic of Florence, the duke of Urbino, and the members of the house of Medici. The *Perpetual Peace*, a treaty signed with the thirteen Swiss cantons in Freiburg on 29 November 1516, indemnified the cantons for expenses accrued during their battles with France. In exchange they were to return, with the exception of Bellinzona, those locations they occupied at the borders of the Milanais, and were to be engaged in the service of no power hostile to the kingdom of France or the duchy of Milan.

Assured of possession of the Milanais, Francis I signed the treaty of Cambrai (11 March 1517) with representatives of Emperor Maximilian and his grandson Charles, who had become king of Spain upon the death of Ferdinand of Aragon (23 January 1516). The treaty recognized that Lombardy belonged to France, while Central Italy was placed under imperial care and the kingdom of Naples under Spanish domination. Thus, in 1518, the wars of Italy were ended, but the peninsula was soon to become the theater for almost continual hostilities between the houses of France and Austria, which again called into question how Italian soil was to be allocated.

After the death of Emperor Maximilian (12 January 1519), lively competition arose for election to the Empire between Francis I and Charles of Spain. The latter, elected on 28 June 1519 became emperor Charles the Fifth. By 1521 the two princes were at war. In the Milanais Marshal de Lautrec, under attack by imperial troops, beat his retreat. Francesco Maria Sforza, the last duke's brother, took advantage of the situation to enter Milan and reclaim the title of duke. Obliged to wage war by his own Swiss mercenaries in La Bicoque, Lautrec was defeated (29 April 1522) and the Imperials took back Genoa.

It was at this time that the French supreme commander Charles de Bourbon violently clashed with the king's mother, Louise of Savoy, over questions of inheritance. Given the impossibility of entente, he betrayed Francis I and, in September 1523, went into the service of Charles the Fifth. In 1524 he invaded Provence at the head of imperial troops, but he did not succeed in taking Marseille in August. Francis I recovered and crossed the Alps in mid-October. He reclaimed Milan (26 October) and went to lay siege before Pavia, where his enemies commanded by the viceroy of Naples, Charles of Lannoy, and Bourbon, were assembled. Despite a papal attempt to secure peace on the basis of sharing the duchy of Milan, the two armies confronted one another during the night of 23 to 24 February 1525. Francis I was taken prisoner. Taken off to Spain, he signed the treaty of Madrid (14 January 1526) through which he abandoned all his rights over Italy, returned Burgundy to Charles the Fifth, and restored Bourbon and his associates, but gave his two elder sons to the emperor as hostages. When he returned to France he denounced the commitments that had been extorted from him and mounted an offensive alliance, the league of Cognac (22 May 1526), with Venice, Florence, pope CLEMENT VII, and even the duke of Milan. Under seige by the Imperials, Francesco Sforza was forced to return the duke's castle (24 July 1526), while the Colonna party, pushed by the emperor's agents, rose up against the pope in Rome. Since Clement VII had engaged in strict repression against the Colonnas, Charles the Fifth launched a punitive expedition against Rome formed of Germans and Austrians, commanded by George von Frundesberg. This army joined with that of supreme commander Bourbon, stationed in Milan. South of Rome, the viceroy Lannoy crossed over the border of the PAPAL STATES. Deprived of pay, Frundsberg's troops mutinied after the sudden death of their leader (March 1527), taking de Bourbon's mercenaries with them. Unable to keep his troops in line, Bourbon lead them to the walls of Rome. On 6 May 1527 the city was taken. The assailants began to sack it viciously. The pope, who had managed to take shelter in CASTEL SANT'ANGELO, gave in to his victors' demands (6 June 1527), and then fled the city. To create a diversion, Lautrec's French troops attempted an expedition into the north of Italy, and then toward Naples, but Florence rose up against the Medicis and reestablished the republic. Andrea Doria soon seceded in Genoa and went into the service of Charles V.

It seemed clear that the French were no longer able to assure the pope's protection and on 29 June 1529, Clement VII reconciled with the emperor, agreeing to crown him and to give him the investiture of Naples. The pope's bastard son, Alessandro de Medici, was to marry the natural daughter of Charles V. The emperor committed to assist the pontiff in overturning the republic of Florence, and to set the Medicis in power. For France this situation constituted a veritable new abandonment of Italy, which was confirmed by the peace of Cambrai, or Ladies' Peace, concluded between Louise of Savoy and Marguerite of Austria on 3 August 1529. Charles V, who had disembarked in Genoa the same month, met the pope in Bologna in November to work out litigious questions in Italy. On 22 February 1530 he received the iron crown from the pontiff, in the church of San Petronio, and the imperial insignias on 24 February. The ceremonies were followed by reconciliations with the princes formerly allied with France. Alfonso d'Este, whose son, Ercole, had married Renée of France, received from the emperor the investiture of Modena and Reggio. The duke of Milan, Francesco Sforza, saw the duchy of Milan recognized as his; it would go to Charles V after his death (1535). The marquis of Mantua received the duccal dignity for the price of his rallying. After a second meeting with Charles V in Bologna (December 1532–January 1533), the pope, who was concerned about having a counterbalance given the crushing imperial power in Italy, negotiated the marriage of his cousin Catherine de Medici with Henry of Orléans, the second son of Francis I, and he went in person to Marseille to celebrate the union (27 October 1534), which reserved new reasons for future French intervention in Italy.

Upon the death of Francesco Sforza, Francis I, who had not secured the duchy of Milan for Henry of Orléans, went to war and occupied the States of Savoy and the Piedmont. From 1540 to 1545 a number of incidents kept the Milanais from being returned to Charles, Francis I's third son: it was finally Philip of Spain who was invested with it by his father the emperor. Henry II began his reign with a trip to Turin (1548) to affirm his possession of the Piedmont. The support he gave the Farnese family, relatives of pope PAUL III, preceded the return to war by Charles V, a war that was marked notably by the proclamation of the union of the republic of Siena with France (1552), soon reduced to nothing by the Spaniards (1555). Despite the attachment of Corsica to France and pope PAUL IV Carafa's support of French interests, the expedition of duke Francis of Guise failed in Naples at the end of Henry II's reign and the treaty of Cateau-Cambrésis (1559) obliged France to evacuate all territory it still held in Italy, with the exception of five locations (Turin, Piginerol, Chieri, Chivasso, and Villanova d'Asti), and the marquisate of Saluces.

Ivan Cloulas

Bibliography

Cloulas, I. *Henri II*, Paris, 1985; *Charles VIII et le mirage italien*, Paris, 1986; *Jules II*, Paris, 1990.

Delaborde, H. F. *Histoire diplomatique et militaire de l'expédition de Charles VIII en Italie*, Paris, 1889.

Jacquart, J. *François Ier (1492–1547)*, Paris, 1981; *Bayard*, Paris, 1987.

Knecht, R. J. *François Ier*, Cambridge, 1982.

Lemonnier, H. *Les Guerres d'Italie. La France sous Charles VIII, Louis XII et François Ier (1492–1547)*, Paris, 1903 (*Histoire de France*, dir. E. Lavisse, V).

Quilliet, B. *Louis XII, Père du Peuple*, Paris, 1986.

WORLD WAR I. On a number of occasions, BENEDICT XV condemned the conflict, each time more firmly and with less reserve. The day after his election to St. Peter's throne, the pope called the war a "monstrous spectacle" and, later, in other speeches and documents, he used expressions like "frightful scourge," "horrific carnage," "the suicide of civilized Europe," "tragedy of human dementia," and, in August 1917, "useless massacre."

In his first ENCYCLICAL, *Ad Beatissimi*, Benedict XV affirmed that "Each day the earth flows with new blood, it is covered with the dead and the wounded. Who could believe that these people who are fighting against one another come from the same ancestor, that we are all of the same nature, and that we all belong to the same human society? Who would recognize in them the brothers, the sons of the same Father who is in heaven?"

Based on such clear and forthright judgments, Benedict XV has been considered the first pope to reject the traditional Catholic doctrine of a just war. In reality, he never did so officially, but the widespread opinion is not without foundation. Benedict XV always believed firmly that the Catholic Church should irrevocably condemn the dramatic conflict. Academic discussions on the more or less just nature of the war would have been inappropriate.

In the case of Benedict XV, this condemnation of the war was accompanied by a rigorously neutral behavior of the Holy See. The pope avoided explicit condemnation of the specifically destructive actions of either side, or of obvious violations of international law, which the warring parties urgently demanded. He preferred to limit himself to constantly demanding that the universal and natural laws that the war was violating be respected. The German invasion of Belgium was a case in point. Benedict XV did not denounce Germany's action, as the allies wished. The Holy See remained neutral as any judgment ascribing culpability to one of the warring parties would have incited the adversary's war propaganda to refer to the pontiff's moral authority.

On the other hand, the Holy See's position *super partes* did not devolve solely from a clear-cut moral judgment on war or giving in to the facts, but rather, once again, from doctrine, from the theory of a just war. Actually, there were masses of committed Catholics in both camps. It was in Europe, Christian territory par excellence, that the Catholic faithful were doing battle and killing one another.

In his address to the consistory on 22 January 1915, Benedict XV affirmed:

We greatly condemn any injustice on whichever side it might have been committed. But to implicate pontifical authority in the specific differences between the warring parties would certainly be neither appropriate nor useful.

Anyone who judges with a balanced view cannot but understand that, in this frightful struggle, the Holy See, while it is greatly concerned, should remain perfectly impartial: the Roman Pontiff, as Vicar of the Christ who died for men as a whole and for each man individually, must embrace all the combatants in a feeling of charity, and since he is also the common Father of Catholics within both warring parties, he has a great number of sons about whose salvation he must equally and indescriminately, be concerned.

Some feel that the neutrality of the Holy See came out of political opportunism, but it is difficult to hold that the Vatican's pacifism from 1914 to 1918 was inspired by anything but faithfulness to principles and the need to avoid dividing the Catholics belonging to the different armies. If Benedict XV had not repeatedly and radically condemned the war, he would certainly have gotten a clearer agreement from the European governments at war and public opinions in prey to unbridled nationalism. Diplomacy would have had the pope either maintain silence or align himself with the winners, which did not occur.

Actually, in each of the parties at war, Catholics would have wanted Benedict XV to bless the armies and the flags of their nations. There were unfailing hawkish spirits everywhere. The socialists were no exception: "The *Internationale* was made for peacetime," said Kautski. Catholic intellectuals from both warring parties prayed for divine assistance for their armies to be victorious. Such was the tone of the well-known declarations of the 76 German Catholic notables and the pubications of the Catholic committee for French Propaganda Abroad. In Germany, in France, in Italy, everywhere, the clergy, Catholic associations, and a number of bishops burned with the flame of patriotism.

Some German and Austrian Catholics felt it their duty to do battle against a secularized France and an Anglican England. On their side, French Catholics saw in Prussia the spirit of Lutheranism and an anti-Latin paganism that did not respect the natural law that authentic Christianity defended. All Catholics, especially at the beginning of the war (since after 1917 all remaining illusions were dissipated), tended to believe that the war was stirring up a great religious awakening, especially among soldiers. The most nationalistic Catholics and the military chaplains were either silent on, or censured the pope's positions on war. Léon Bloy compared Benedict XV to Pontius Pilate for his apparent insensibility to the sufferings of those—his compatriots—who were fighting on the side of justice.

The pontiff's interventions naturally were less respected outside Catholic circles. Most often, the Holy See's position of neutrality was misunderstood. Some saw a "Kraut Pope" in Benedict XV, while others saw a friend of the Habsburgs, and still others an Italian patriot or an ally partisan. The pope's actions and those of his entourage were interpreted with the hope of drawing from it a motif of support for one of the parties and, if possible, some respective elements of blame and justification. If a *Te Deum* was sung in Rome to celebrate the taking of Jerusalem, Berlin saw a gesture hostile to the central empires, while the instructions published by the *OSSERVATORE ROMANO* on the nature of religious offices in time of war were interpreted in Paris as a disavowal of the prayers and ceremonies ordered by bishops in favor of a victorious peace. Moreover, there were Benedict XV's "silences" regarding the war crimes of which each side accused the other—a matter which, in some ways, is reminiscent of Pius XII's situation, the difference being that in the latter's case it broke out after his death while Benedict XV found it daily in the international press he read with the greatest of attention. In 1917, André Tardieu wrote concerning him: "The first duty [of the pope] consists in choosing between good and evil," meaning siding with the warring party that is on the side of justice.

After all was said and done, Giuseppe De Luca (a close observer of the Vatican) was not far from the truth when he wrote: "The Holy See was neutral, but its neutrality may have cost it a double war: a war with one side, and one with the other. The Holy See could do nothing good without it being immediately taken amiss."

Benedict XV was particularly unpopular in France, and not only in government circles where it seems that Clemenceau abhorred him. In reality, his diplomatic experience under LEO XIII was characterized by an ongoing struggle against the Triplice and the search for an understanding with republican France. When he became pope, Benedict XV immediately sought a detente with Paris, in contrast to his predecessor, by multiplying goodwill gestures. His actions were in vain; the only thing French opinion wanted of him was a condemnation of the central powers. The war had hardly come to an end when Henri Le Floch published an essay in which he attempted to raise the pope's status in the eyes of the French, by taking a new perspective on *La Politique de Benoit XV*. He placed less emphasis on the pontiff's impartiality than he did on his clear favoring of France and his distancing himself from Germany. Le Floch apparently felt the pope's best defense lay in his expressions of sympathy to one of the warring parties.

Benedict XV was a "political pope," although this term should not be viewed as being in conflict with the spiritual nature of the pope's responsibilities. He had real political talents that came from his juridical and diplomatic formation and his extensive experience in the SECRETARY OF STATE's office under cardinal Rampolla's guidance. For the pope, although a frank condemnation of the war was a matter of principle, he did not hesitate to exercise political action and to make choices. Throughout the conflict, the Holy See's neutrality was not passive.

This neutrality was understood and interpreted in a variety of ways (not only during the time of the war) because of the positions taken by the warring parties. It is true that some of the Holy See's political initiatives can be interpreted in more than one way. One case in point was the mediations undertaken to keep Italy out of the war. In early 1915, when Italy was still neutral, the Holy See made several attempts to reach an agreement between Italy and Austria based on territorial compensations granted in exchange for maintaining neutrality. This was a means of determining the alliances of war and to prevent the ruin of the Habsburg Empire. For the Roman CURIA, these mediations, which aimed above all at safeguarding peace and, in a wider sense, the Church's interests and those of both Italian and Austrian Catholics, did not appear to compromise the Vatican's neutality.

In the spring of 1916, another, lesser-known episode took place. At the time, Vatican diplomacy asked the Kaiser to stop, eventually by military operations, all Russian advance in the direction of Constantinople. This represented a real intervention in the war's development, one the Vatican justified recognizing by the "nightmare" it would have been to see the Cossacks as masters of Santa Sophia and, consequently, the fear of a union between the second and third ROME against the first. However, a few days after this request was made to William II, the Holy See withdrew it, probably because it realized at the time that it went beyond the principle of noninterference that had previously been followed. Moreover, it is revealing that the papers concerning this matter were for the most part burned.

On the whole, the orders for neutrality were strictly respected. It must however, be made clear that this was primarily due to Benedict XV's firmness of resolve. Opinions about the war were not unanimous in the Roman Curia. In general, the prelates were inclined to take sides, with varying degrees of passion, in alliance with the country of their national origin. Among the Holy Father's closest collaborators, in the secretary of state's office there was real respect for the pope's wishes, but with less intransigence than he demonstrated. While for Benedict XV the question of war and reaching peace was more important and took priority over all the other matters that might have come before the Vatican, for the secretary of state, Cardinal Gasparri, resolving the Roman question remained of utmost importance.

A year after the war broke out, Benedict XV opened his series of attempts to impose a negotiated peace. The papal note of 28 July 1915 reiterated denunciation of the war and asked that diplomacy and the affirmation of law, rather than arms, be used to solve it. The text of the note is equally significant for the way the Vatican conceived of nations and nationalities. In it, Benedict XV sadly affirmed that "nations do not die," clearly not in order to glorify them, but rather to avoid bloody excesses of nationalism:

Let it not be said that the frightful conflict cannot be resolved except through the violence of arms. It is necessary that mutual determination to destroy one another be abandoned and that consideration be given to the notion that nations do not die. Humiliated and oppressed, they tremblingly bear the yoke that is placed upon them, preparing for revolt and transmitting from generation to generation a sad heritage of hatred and revenge. Why not recognize serenely the rights and the just aspirations of peoples from the very beginning? Why not resolutely attempt an exchange of views, direct or indirect, with the aim of taking into account as much as possible these rights and aspirations, and arrive at putting the horrible conflict to an end, as has been done in other, similar, circumstances?

One subsequent attempt at mediation on the part of the Vatican involved a plan to return to the previous status quo ante. This plan was doomed to failure from the very beginning based on the negative opinions expressed by the two prelates (Cardinal Mercier, Archbishop of Malines, and Msgr. Baudrillart, rector of the Institut Catholique de Paris) to whom it had been entrusted. Their inquiries, in Belgium and France, had not produced favorable results, and the allied governments decided to fight to the point of diplomatic defeat, searching for overtures for peace proposals.

After this first failure and realization of the radical and almost insurmountable opposition of the warring powers, the Vatican primarily oriented its action toward assisting the war's victims. The humanitarian aspect of the Holy See's activity from 1914 to 1918 is worthy of treatment in itself, due to the importance and the variety of interventions undertaken. Vatican diplomacy, the high and low clergy, and Catholic organizations attempted to collect news of the wounded, the dead, and the missing. It also attempted to help prisoners, to repatriate the mentally ill and the sick, to assure that mail and food were reaching their destinations, and to help the civilian populations directly affected by the conflict, as well as oppressed peoples and minorities. This was the case, especially, for the Christians in the Ottoman Empire—Armenians, Assyrians, Chaldeans, Greeks, and Lebanese, whether they were Catholic or orthodox—because in 1915 and thereafter, they suffered genocides and massacres. The Holy See attempted to save those who could be saved and to relieve the suffering of the survivors. In a distressed tone, Benedict XV wrote twice (1915 and 1918) to the sultan on behalf of the Eastern Christian subjects of the Sublime Door.

In late 1916 the Holy See again took up activity aimed at a negotiated settlement of the conflict. Germany and Austria-Hungary had proposed, albeit in general, peace talks on 12 December 1916, a few days after Wilson's appeal. On the other hand, the general atmosphere in 1917 was one of weariness and defeatism among both soldiers and civilians. These were a few of the reasons that pushed the Holy See to begin diplomatic initiatives again. This action was aimed especially at Germany, not because William II's empire was the privileged partner of the Holy See, but rather because, in a sense, it was at the center of both Europe and the conflict and was the most militarist of the powers. In other words, Benedict XV paid greater attention to Germany because he judged that peace negotiations could not be launched unless Germany's intentions were made clear. It is of some significance that beginning on May 1917, the new nuncio in Bavaria was Eugenio Pacelli, the Vatican diplomat who was closest to the pope. The nuncio discussed a detailed plan for peace with the German government that went beyond the latter's more general proposal made the previous December. Benedict XV's note for peace of 1 August 1917 came after Rome's determination that Pacelli's activities had opened the door for Germany's agreement. Rome undoubtedly underestimated the influence of German military circles that had, during the summer of 1917, increased their power at the expense of political forces that were ready for peaceful compromises.

Benedict XV's note was addressed to chanceries with the hope of remaining secret, although a few days after it was sent to representatives of the warring powers, it appeared in newspapers. This made attempts at negotiation more difficult, and ultimately impractical.

In addition to a total condemnation of the war, the note expressed "more concrete and practical proposals" for ending hostilities. It expressed a wish for general talks based on the affirmation of law and not on arms. This entailed a reduction in arms and the institution of an international system of arbitration with responsibilities for keeping peace. The conditions for peace were as follows: reciprocal payment for war damages; mutual return of occupied territories, whether these be Belgian and French territory occupied by the Germans or German colonies occupied by the Allies (no mention was made of the territory that formerly belonged to the czars which was, six months after the February revolution, still in the hands of the German armies, although the note did make specific mention of the problem in Poland); examination "in the spirit of conciliation" of the territorial disputes existing between Italy and Austria, as well as between Germany and France; and an equally fair examination of the "territorial and political questions" relating to "Armenia, the Balkan States, and the countries forming part of the old kingdom of Poland."

Replies from the governments disappointed the Holy See. No one accepted what seemed to be a peace without compensation for the sacrifices made. Germany showed no intention of making concessions regarding Belgium, like those Cardinal Gasparri was insistently requesting, referring to tendencies that, before the note, had been shown by the Germans. Likewise, Austria was in no way disposed to make the slightest concession toward Italy. The central empires and the Allies dropped the papal initiative, each blaming responsibility for the failure of the 1 August 1917 note on the other party for refusing to take the first step. Actually, the note did not please the English government, either, in the sense that it looked like a mixture of morals and politics. It was neither a simple call to peace nor a proposal with detailed items for negotiation. The note was based on Wilson's idea of "peace without victory," but the American president did not recognize himself in it: he also sent out the call for German soldiers to withdraw to within the boundaries of prewar Germany as a condition to be met before peace talks could open. Italy, which had wanted the treaty of London to see to the Holy See's exclusion from the peace talks after the end of the war so that the Roman question would not be discussed, was particularly upset by the Vatican's initiative. Minister of Foreign Affairs Sonnino, the strong man in the cabinet, declared in a forcefully worded speech to the Chamber that some of the papal note's proposals looked as though they were "somewhat inspired by Germany."

More generally, the press everywhere reflected the irritation of governments and nationalist currents in regard to the pope who, with his talk of "useless massacres," cast doubt upon all the efforts, sacrifices, and propaganda for the war. The most patriotic Catholics joined with their governments. "Holy Father," the Dominican Sertillanges preached, expressing the views of a good number of French Catholics, "we do not want your peace." Nevertheless, among the different populations the pope's call for peace, which passed from the secrecy of the chanceries to the publicity of the newspapers, caused quite a sensation, especially in its allusion to the "useless carnage" and, as has been said, "in a different sphere, it gave the pontiff a moral prestige which, diplomatically, had met with hard failures."

The negative result of the August note encouraged Vatican diplomacy not to undertake any other important peace initiatives until the end of the conflict. Nevertheless, the Holy See did pay the greatest attention to all possibilities for overtures in this direction. Thus, Benedict XV, in his private correspondence with Charles I of Habsburg, did not fail to discuss the possibilities for peace talks throughout 1918. But on the whole, the Vatican had to maintain its silence, forced to defend itself against accusations of partiality toward one of the warring parties or the other, something of which it was victim quite often after 1 August 1917.

Whatever the case, the Vatican's humanitarian intervention for victims of the war did continue, while politically and diplomatically the Holy See prepared to face the new postwar Europe. Until the summer of 1918, it was difficult to foresee who would be the winner of the conflict, but on both sides the principle of nationality was increasingly important: among the Allies as a goal of the war, and among the central empires about Eastern Europe, which were already under Russian domination. Given the probable birth of new States based on nationality, the Vatican did not wait until the end of the hostilities to act. In May 1918, Ratti was sent as an apostolic visitor to Warsaw, where he was able to observe the uprisings of the Eastern nations. The Holy See considered Bolshevism as a passing phenomenon (had any revolution ever lasted?) and what it retained from the Russian crisis was primarily the explosion of nationalities and nationalisms: an explosion in which a considerable number of Catholics were implicated. In fact, national groups (the Poles, the Lithuanians, and the Ukrainians, among others) who aspired to independence were increasing their appeals and requests for audiences with the pope. In the Vatican, the arrival of a central and Eastern Europe no longer of empires, but rather of nations, was already sensed, albeit somewhat diffusely.

Roberto Morozzo della Rocca

Bibliography

Actes de Benoît XV, 3 vols., Paris, 1924–1926.

Benedetto XV e la pace—1918, published by G. Rumi, Brescia, 1990.

Benedetto XV. I cattolici e la prima guerra mondiale, published by G. Rossini, Rome, 1963.

De Rosa, G. "Benedetto XV," *DBI*, VIII, Rome, 1967, 408–417.

Garzia, I. *La Questione romana durante la prima guerra mondiale*, Naples, 1981.

Levillain, P. "Le Saint-Siège et la Première Guerre mondiale," *Les Internationales et le problème de la guerre au XXe siècle*, Rome, 1987, 123–137.

Monticone, A. *Il pontificato di Benedetto XV*, in Fliche-Martin, Italian ed., XXII/1, Alba, 1990, 155–200.

Morozzo della Rocca, R. *Le Nazioni non muoiono. Russia rivoluzionaria, Polonia indipendente e Santa Sede*, Bologna, 1992.

Pollard, J. *The Unknown Pope: Benedict XV and the Pursuit of Peace*, London, 1999.

Steglich, W. *Der Friedensappell Papst Benedikt XV. vom 1. August 1917 und die Mittelmächte*, Wiesbaden, 1970.

WORLD WAR II. When the Second World War broke out on 3 September 1939, the Holy See found itself protected, for the first time, by a negotiated juridical instrument that stipulated its international character. The Lateran treaties of 11 February 1929 assured that, due to its spiritual sovereignty, it enjoyed temporal sovereignty within the VATICAN CITY STATE. By virtue of this sovereignty "that belongs to it, even in the international arena," it declared its neutrality of principle regarding "temporal competitions among other States and international meetings called for this purpose" and its tendency being well disposed to "assert its moral and spiritual power," if the parties in litigation addressed "a unanimous appeal to its mission of peace" (Lateran treaty, art. 24 (*DC*, 1929, col. 1605–17). Consequently, Vatican City would always be considered neutral and inviolable territory, the article specified, reinforcing the stipulation in article 8 that "The person of the pope is sacred and inviolable."

The Second World War provided a reality test for the effectiveness of the Lateran treaty on two fronts. In the matter of the Holy See, a spiritual and moral power, it specified the scope of its relations with warring governments: interventions to end the hostilities, refusal to recognize new territorial statutes, and assistance to civil victims and combatants.

Because the war was the result of the confrontation of nationalisms that involved territorial conquests, the classical definition of neutrality remained valid, and the Church did not take part. Pius XII specified this in January 1943 in a letter to the archbishop of Munich: his line of conduct was defined "by the word impartiality and not by the word neutrality, [which] might be understood in the sense of a passive indifference unbefitting the head of the Church in the face of such events."

In contrast to World War I, the second appeared as a clash of ideologies upon which the Catholic magisterium had already made pronouncements. Since 1933 the Third Reich had been persecuting the Church in the name of the values of National Socialism, a pagan doctrine condemned as such. Since 1917 the Soviet regime had been pursuing religion in the name of historical materialism. In 1937 the two encyclicals, *Mit brennender Sorge* and *Divini Redemptoris*, had proclaimed the doctrinal incompatibilities, reaffirmed by the encyclical *Summi Pontificatus*, of 20 October 1939, which placed the Holy See in the camp hostile to totalitarianism.

In 1929, the course of operations highlighted the one event regarding the status of the Holy See that might have seemed unlikely: the threat of immediate aggression, beginning with a general blockade of communications and means of existence crossing Italian land or air space (i.e., sound waves), leading to the use of armed force (fighting at its doors, or aerial bombardments). In addition to the fact of peril, what was even less probable, the peril would come from each of the camps present. They respected the Holy See's neutrality, not out of principle, but with an eye toward using it to their benefit and to the detriment of the adversary. Between the Allies and the Axis there were, nevertheless, degrees in form if not in firmness. If the most avowed threat was the presence of the German and Italian dictators, British politics never did deprive itself of the means of pressure that a permanent defiance in-

spired. After all was said and done, the Holy See's "impartiality" had a number of meanings: charitable and geographical when it was a question of the classical events of war, but "benevolent" for the Western democracies, and "critical" toward the totalitarian states when the political stakes and the principles of peace were evoked (a distinction proposed by Pastorelli).

Its implementation resulted from a fragile internal balance, perhaps even from a certain distribution of tasks, according to the personal inclinations of the actors in the drama. The main players, Tardini, secretary for the Extraordinary Ecclesiastical Affairs, and Cardinal Maglione, the secretary of state, by role and by temperament, easily played the third parties. They were first and foremost politicians who placed Nazism and communism on the same plane, "both materialistic, antireligious, totalitarian, tyrannical, cruel, [and] militaristic" (*ADSS*, 7, p. 378). They proffered their personal analyses, while the substitute, Montini, kept in the background. They clearly stopped the pope from intervening, either publicly or in terms that were too precise. Tardini liked to reply by saying "The facts speak for themselves." Unofficially certain individuals assured unofficial communication: the Jesuit father Tacchi-Venturi with Mussolini; Hudal, the rector of the German seminary L'Anima, (manifestly, close to Nazism) with the German authorities; fathers Pfeiffer and Leiber, closely tied to Pius XII, were the correspondents of Hitler's opposition. Some Italian cardinals remained close to Fascism out of patriotism, hence the friction within the Vatican itself. This "team," whose homogeneity Pius XII assured, empirically invented and gained acceptance for its own ways of applying neutrality, taking advantage of the polyvalence of Rome's name, expressed by the topographical complexity of the Vatican's placement and that of its dependencies within the Italian capital. The clearly articulated juridical formulations in the Lateran treaty had not been made with the twists and turns of wartime in mind. This was never so clear as when the proposal came from the Americans to light the Vatican by night so that it would not be bombed. Cardinal Maglione made the somewhat tongue-in-cheek remark that the suggestion was tantamount to asking Italy for electric current to help mark the target of Rome by plunging it into darkness.

A War Pope. Immunity was thus conditioned by neutrality. As head of the Church and a spiritual power, the pontiff reserved the right to intervene by his words alone, provided he was asked to do so by all the antagonists. These principles were unilaterally underwritten by Italy alone, outside of international guarantees, but they had "international significance" (J. M. Mayeur).

These clauses were the fruit of recent experience. One was positive, practiced twice during times of peace: in

1885 the Holy See had acted as a diplomatic mediator at the request of the parties in the matter, Germany and Spain; and in 1905, it did likewise for Brazil, Bolivia, and Peru. The other was aborted when, acting on his own initiative, Benedict XV intervened in the European war, and twice met with failure. On 15 January 1915, he suggested in vain to emperor Franz Joseph that Trentino be returned to Italy in exchange for its neutrality. Three months later, in April, by the London accords, Italy added to the price of its entrance into war the elimination of the Holy See from future conversations on peace. In the spring of 1917, Benedict XV met a clear rejection from the English and the French for his plea to put an end to "useless massacres" and to his proposal for a general peace settlement.

On these two occasions the Holy See had suggested territorial concessions, thus exposing itself to complaints that it favored political demands, as well as to the rebellious attitude of Catholics who had been wounded in their nationalism. Benedict XV moved his field of action. In his note of 1 August 1917, he constructed his admonition upon general principles: disarmament, international arbitration, freedom of the seas, war damages, and restoration of occupied territories, without really taking any practical action or expounding a doctrine.

Removed from the League of Nations immediately after the conflict, the Holy See had to endure, at the same time, disregard for both the intentions behind its proposed mediations and the distance it had put between itself and the Europe of Versailles. Together with implications of national battles, these intentions engendered prejudices and polemics that surely weighed upon Pius XII's papacy from the very beginning.

The Lateran treaty thus broke with an outdated idea of the Holy See's place among nations at war. Eugenio Pacelli, secretary of the Congregation of Extraordinary Ecclesiastical Affairs, had been the artisan and messenger of Benedict XV's proposals since 1915; he then was the primary architect of the new doctrine under the papacy of Pius XI, who made him his cardinal secretary of state in 1929. When he became Pius XII, he had to put it to the test, to interpret it to bring about forms of intervention that would be justified, and even required, by his spiritual power.

It was from this perspective that the unusual naming of his successor by Pius XI was explained, expressing as clearly as the reserve of language would allow, the wish for continuity that "the state of danger of war" in Europe justified. The collection of the Holy See's documents for the period 1939–45 officially recognized the episode in its introductory commentary, which also attests to its scope. In his last CONSISTORY, Pius XI said "*Medius vestrum stet quem vos nescitis*," according to the OSSERVATORE ROMANO of 17 December 1937, allowing us to understand that the pope had expressed his views before the whole SACRED COLLEGE. At that time, he only expounded

the obvious. The authenticity and the specificity of the speech which, after the fact, was understood as an order, were faithfully rendered by a direct witness, cardinal Tardini, in his *Pius XII*.

The scene took place on 15 December 1937. Pius XI addressed only the five newly created cardinals upon whom he was going to place the birretta: Piazza, Pizzardo, Hinsley, Gerlier, and Pellegrinetti. They were accompanied by a sixth, Secretary of State Pacelli. Pius XI's designation then became much more explicit, except perhaps for Cardinal Pizzardo. *L'Osservatore Romano* was given the task of making the pope's remarks less pointed.

Pius XI had thus advocated the future pope as clearly as he was authorized to do, and broken the four-century tradition that excluded the cardinal secretary of state's access to Peter's throne. The German and French cardinals persuaded the CONCLAVE to vote according to the deceased pontiff's wish because, at the human level, no other *porporato* appeared to be as qualified by his experience to be the pope for the coming war.

In this spirit, the Holy See entered the period of the Second World War, and the way of thinking that devolved from it, on the date of the election (3 March 1939). The beginnings of the new papacy preceded Hitler's entering Prague by 12 days. For the Church, the war included the six months preceding the opening of hostilities in the European theater.

Direct Interventions for Peace. On 3 March 1939, the day after his election, Pope Pius XII, who had taken as his motto *Opus Justitiae Pax*, addressed a radio message to the Catholic and non-Catholic world formulating his "wish for peace and invitation to peace," particularly "peace between nations through fraternal assistance founded on exchanges, amicable collaboration, and cordial understanding for the higher interests of the great human family." The text of the formal act, composed in general terms, opens the edition of the *Acts and Documents of the Holy See Relative to the Second World War* published starting in 1965. From the beginning of his papacy, even though he was not invited by unanimous agreement of the powers, the pontiff played a personal role in attempts for peace, despite the German violations of the Munich Accords. In early May 1939, he got dilatory responses—courteous but negative—and, in vain, proposed that he act as mediator between Berlin and Warsaw. During the summer of 1939, the pope increased his interactions with Mussolini, and up to the very last he gave a solemn warning:

Nothing is lost with peace. All can be lost with war. Justice finds its way not with armed force, but with the force of reason [. . .] May the strong hear us and not thus become weak through injustice. May the powerful hear us, if they wish their power to be not destruction, but rather support for the peoples and protection of tranquility in order and work.

On 31 August, Cardinal Maglione delivered a message to ambassadors, "begging the governments of Germany and Poland to do whatever is possible to avoid any incident, and to abstain from taking any measure that might aggravate the present situation."

During those days, Pius XII returned twice to the line of conduct defined by Benedict XV. He acted as mediator to support concrete solutions: first, negotiations on the status of Danzig and the reciprocal treatment of Polish and German minorities. Then he proposed a specific plan: a truce of 10 to 14 days, to be spent in a general conference for the revision of the Versailles Treaty and the creation of a collective nonagression pact. Once the war broke out, the pope no longer took territorial stakes into consideration. His efforts were solely to keep Italy neutral, and he no longer associated himself with compromise proposals for peace coming from any of the warring parties. Then there was a period of strict reserve. His message on peace to the cardinals (24 December 1939) defined the conditions for a "just and honorable peace": the right to life and independence for all nations, mutually agreed upon disarmament, supranational institutions, respect for the just claims of minorities, recognition of the "holy and unwavering [norms] of divine law" above human laws and conventions.

Irrespective of exhortations and necessary procedures based on principle, Pius XII took at least one peace initiative upon himself. During the winter of 1940, setting aside cardinal Maglione, the secretary of state, and his adjunct Tardini, who were normally entrusted with such missions he received from his secretary, Leiber, inquiries from the German Catholic and military opposition, and personally transmitted them to Francis d'Arcy Osborne, the British minister. In the spring of 1943, when Italy's fate was at stake, Pius XII made no explicit offer of intervention toward negotiations. Hindered by the extreme defiance of the British in his regard, he limited himself to two indirect gestures: a suggestion to Mussolini that it was time to end everything, and to Roosevelt that Italy be treated "with clemency and consideration." Contacts with Mussolini's opposition movements were entrusted to Tardini, who through Osborne, attempted to persuade the Allies to tone down their demand for unconditional surrender as far as Italy was concerned. Other inquiries, originating in Germany, passed through the secretary of state's office without personally implicating the pope. Roncalli, a nuncio in Ankara, thus made himself the intermediary in measures attempted by his German colleague, von Papen.

Until the end of the conflict, the numerous documents on peace remained limited to general principles, with no proposal for territorial concessions. In the same spirit,

and conforming to doctrine, no canonical change would be allowed until the end of the war in the territories conquered by the Reich, where episcopal sees remained vacant, despite Berlin's demands as it imposed a forced Germanization. The same approach was used in opposition to the British initiative to expel Italian missionaries in occupied Africa.

A double exception was, nevertheless, necessary. The persecution of Polish Catholicism brought on the naming (19 November 1939) of the German bishop of Danzig as a provisionary administrator of the diocese of Chelmno, and of the Polish bishop Dymek to the Poznan diocese, although these precedents were never repeated, despite the urgency. Cardinal Kaspar, archbishop of Prague, had no successor, and the sees of Metz and Strasbourg were not filled with German bishops, since their holders had not resigned. Diplomatically, while it respected the doctrine of nonrecognition of the new states before any peace treaty, the Holy See exchanged representatives without diplomatic status with the two new Catholic nations: Burzio was chargé d'affaires in Slovakia (under German jurisdiction) directed by Abbot Tiso, whose prelature had not been renewed by Pius XII. In Croatia, (under Italian jurisdiction) the papal LEGATE in Zagreb, the Benedictine dom Marcone, had unofficial, unpublicized status. His mission was to restrain the Croatian bishopric in the anti-Serb struggle.

Ideological hopes remained. The two simultaneous encyclicals in March 1937 regarding pagan National Socialism and atheistic Communism formalized categorical warnings against the two forms of doctrinal hegemony. On these bases, the Holy See would continually refuse to recognize the "crusading" nature of the war against the Bolsheviks and the anti-Nazi offensive. It would never go back on these condemnations, but remembered them when called upon: for example, when pressure was applied (September 1941) by the ambassadors of Germany and Italy in favor of declarations of war against the USSR, and when Roosevelt attempted to get the war against Nazism declared "just." The American president later made another attempt at this, maintaining that the USSR had changed. In March 1943 London would also try to reassure the Holy See regarding the Soviet government's objectives.

In his homilies and speeches, delivered as reminders of moral rules and conditions for justice, Pius XII continually reaffirmed his compassion for "the people," never to be confused with regimes that dragged their victim populations behind them, regardless of the vicissitudes of the war. Since the summer of 1941, he never mentioned the words "communism" or "West" (as was underscored by J. M. Mayeur), nor did he generally identify the opposing camps.

In the daily practice of papal diplomacy, the two principal actors, Tardini and Maglione, showed they were convinced that under ideological proclamations, the traditional national ambitions persisted and dictated the real aims. They quickly turned their thoughts to the postwar period. Concerned about the implications of a soviet victory for Europe as a whole, refusing to take at its word a Reich that was presenting itself as the defender of civilization, and uncertain of America's postwar intentions, they actually counted—albeit silently—on the Allied strategy being upset.

In the spring of 1943, when Osborne left for London and as Italy was falling apart, Tardini gave him an analysis that in no way sugarcoated his ulterior motives: the Allies were "exasperating 'the people' by demanding unconditional surrender," a practically meaningless phrase, "since there will always be conditions, even if they are imposed by violence.

> While the Allies would have every interest in not prolonging the war, in not prejudicing the future, they are doing just the opposite: they are inciting their adversaries to stiffen in their resistance, to close themselves up in their resentment, making it possible for destructive communism to march on triumphantly. (*ADSS*, 7, 282–283).

This political argument, in the secrecy of a face-to-face meeting, had no equivalent in the discussions with the German ambassador. Between 1944 and 1945, Weiszäcker increased his inquiries for an eventual mediation on the part of the Holy See, to convince the Allies that the Reich would soon find itself backed into a corner where it had to choose between East and West. Tardini listened, showed his skepticism, and said no more than what might be considered a judgment-free recognition of the Allied positions.

When the end of the hostilities drew near, the pope reminded the public that at Christmas in 1939 he had wished for the creation of international bodies "truly able to preserve peace according to the principles of justice and equity against any possible threat for the future." The papacy had not participated in the 1919 peace conference, nor had it in the League of Nations. Pius XII did not ask to participate in the San Francisco conference, nor was he invited.

His last message, on 9 May, the day after the signing of the armistice, made no mention of the victors, the defeated, the victims, or the executioners. His aim was to give the survivors a message from the deceased: "Be the architects of a new and better Europe."

In his radio messages and speeches during these years, Pius XII developed a detailed doctrine on the organization of peace and international relations. He called for an international order to assure the independence of states, one capable of stifling any threat of aggression. The idea of a "just war" consequently disappeared.

Relief Effort. Even more than his diplomatic interventions and his ideological condemnations, which were always judged partial by one camp and hostile by the other, the Holy See's assistance work met the paradoxical fate of being poorly received by the parties at war, or totally rejected. Their scope was nevertheless immense, and included all military and civil victims, who were helped by the work of nunciatures and charitable organizations, depending on what new needs arose, and with means that came exclusively from funds given to the pope, without the participation of international organizations.

Beginning in September 1939, Pius XII entrusted his deputy, Montini, who was to be the architect of this assistance until shortly after the end of the hostilities, with the organizing of a Bureau of Information. The Bureau of Information was responsible for liaison between prisoners of war and their families, through the work of nuntios. The warring powers were united in their opposition to this initiative, arguing that the Geneva Convention of 1929 had given the international Red Cross exclusive rights to such a mission. The Germans, the English, and the Americans, more or less tactfully, refused to communicate their lists of prisoners of war. To the best of its ability the Bureau of Information improvised means for answering the hundreds of thousands of individual requests to the Holy See to pass on news, or to give assistance. Pius XII, despite the difficulties of cooperation, continually affirmed the independence and autonomy of the charitable works of the Holy See, whose spiritual assistance, through the work of priests and nuncios, met with considerable obstacles that it had not encountered in the First World War.

Diplomats, Guests, and Hostages. In principle, the Lateran treaties had provided for all the details of freedom of movement and communication controlled by the Italian state, between the State of Vatican City and the outside world, including those with Italy's enemies. This included freedom to enter and leave Italy, to transmit and receive information, and to exchange diplomatic representatives by using the rights of active and passive legation.

From the time Italy entered the war, despite the stipulations of Article 12 of the Lateran treaty, the diplomats of countries at war with Italy who were authorized by the Holy See found themselves deprived of privileges of residence on Italian soil. The Holy See first suggested that they go reside in Switzerland, as the representatives of the Triple Alliance had done during the war. It then allowed the head of the mission, his family, and a secretary, to be taken in at the convent of Santa Marta, inside the Vatican. The English and French representatives, Francis d'Arcy Osborne and Wladimir d'Ormesson, joined the Polish Ambassador Casimir Papée there on 13

June 1940. The ambassador from Belgium, a state with which Italy did not consider itself to be at war, came only at the end of the German occupation. Not being a delegate of the Belgian government in London, he represented no one. As a matter of fact, during the entire war the Vatican was totally cut off from Belgium and the Netherlands, as well as from Poland, except through the intermediary of the nuncio in Berlin. In all, representatives from a dozen countries were harbored. Léon Bérard, the ambassador of the Vichy government, came to live as a guest after his resignation on 25 August 1944. An "observer" from the committee of Algers was unofficially accepted after the spring of 1943. For the duration of the war, three powers succeeded one another outside the white line that marked the official border on St. Peter's Square, between the two sides of Bernini's colonnade. The police or the armed forces of the legal Italian government patrolled across from the papal gendarmerie until 8 September 1943. They were followed by the German occupation troops until 4 June 1944, and those of the Allied military government whose authority substituted for that of the royal Italian government in accordance with the armistice agreements.

The Lateran stipulations were violated only by Italian power. Both the Germans and the Allies let it be known on a number of occasions that since they were not parties in an international guarantee, they were not under the treaty's obligations. For this very reason, nothing obliged the Holy See to offer protection to their representatives. It had not done so in 1915 under the regime of the Law of Guarantees. Nor was Italy forced to tolerate this unprecedented asylum, but the two signatories of the treaty had every interest in it. The Holy See was able to pride itself on the fact that Paris and London had accepted the gesture, and claimed this was tantamount to an international guarantee given to the status of the Vatican State. Italy accused the Vatican of holding hostages.

Italy took every possible advantage of the situation by formalizing its permanent hidden control of the Holy See's political neutrality. The ambassadors closely connected to Cardinal Maglione, Attolico Guariglia (starting in February 1942) and Ciano (in the spring of 1944) took the place of diplomatic jailers. In the subordinate ranks, a network of agents of the OVRA, which seemed to be directed by a prelate-journalist who looked suspicious to all the diplomats, infiltrated the Holy See's administration by appealing to the patriotism of the lower level Italian staff. Rome maintained control of the free working of the instruments of daily life: electric lines, water conduits, banking circuits, provisions for the bursar's office, and transmissions of various kinds. It really was a blockade, ready to work through progressive retaliatory measures, stifled to the extent of the Holy See's nonintervention in the area where Mussolini considered forbidden to it. The substitute Montini continually worked to unmask the

clandestine agents of this system of blackmail. The Gestapo itself had its man in the secretary of state's office, a former Estonian seminarian of the Russicum who had become a translator, to keep his eye on relations with the German bishops. He was discovered by the Italian secret service, who suspected him of working for the Russians.

On the whole, however, despite incessant skirmishes, the pontiff's freedom was basically preserved, as much by his firmness on principles as by the prudence of all the opposing camps and the balance in their methods of reciprocal pressure and the instinct for their tactical interests. On both sides of the Tiber, the interplay was extremely subtle, and based, as always, on personal relationships, the family relationships of the men of the Church and Italian political personnel. This is why so little evidence of it is available. Behind violent public confrontations in the press, there occured an exchange of unwritten concessions that showed consideration for Pius XII's moral prestige and saved face for Mussolini. For example, even though Mussolini easily obtained from Cardinal Canali (president of the papal commission for the Vatican State, who passed for a pro-fascist) agreement that refugee diplomats would have only the most precarious existence (in fact they lived quite poorly), the pope, on the other hand, was able to receive Italians who were hounded by the Fascist regime, like Alcide de Gasperi, the director of the popular party and an employee in the Vatican library, or count Della Torre, the manager of *L'Osservatore Romano*.

Communication between the refugee diplomats and their governments benefitted from their status as hostages. Contrary to the Italian administrative staff's convictions, the British representative d'Arcy Osborne had refused, despite the foreign office's insistence, to use a radio transmitter, even though the Holy See had not formally forbidden it. Ernst von Weiszäcker, the Reich's ambassador, brought one in the summer of 1944, when he also took refuge in the Vatican. In principle, these exiles were subject to the strictest censure of private and diplomatic correspondence, composed without code and passing over Italian soil. The pontiff's diplomatic portfolio soon accepted coded documents from them, which nuncios passed to their colleagues in the nations at war.

In theory, the exiled diplomats in the Vatican were authorized to cross Italian territory to leave and return. Mussolini ordered that this commitment be respected by authorizing Osborne to spend some time in Switzerland in the summer of 1942. The British representative did not benefit from this arrangement, but encouraged by the precedent, he went to London via Seville and Lisbon on 8 April 1943. He returned on 18 June. Myron Taylor, President Roosevelt's personal representative, who was absent from Rome when Italy declared war on the United States, returned for a few days at the end of September 1942, after the Allies' entrance. His adjunct Tittmann continually resided in the Vatican. Foreign cardinals and bishops, most notably Spellman, came in the Vatican without difficulty.

After the Allies entered Rome on 4 June 1944, the Reich's ambassador, Ernst von Weiszäcker, remained in his residence, Villa Bonaparte, for several weeks. The British government wanted to see him received by the Vatican in Osborne's company, since the latter would, in turn, watch over his activities, albeit against his will. "It was one or the other," the Holy See said. Roosevelt went along with this view and called for Tittmann's departure. Eden then consented to allow Sir Francis d'Arcy Osborne to transfer his domicile and chancellery to Rome. For the Reich's ambassador, Santa Marta was an asylum, both from the Allies and from his own government. The name Weiszäcker was mentioned by one of the conspirators in the plot against Hitler (20 July).

Direct Threats Against the Vatican. Pius XII quickly took note of the possibility of direct aggression against his person. The only way seen to foil the plan was to face it directly, by letting it be known that he was aware of it. The rumor returned a number of times, always filtering from the Vatican. The pope was adamant from the moment of the German offensive in the West: "We are not afraid. We are not even afraid of going to a concentration camp," he stated to the Italian Ambassador Dino Alfieri, on 13 May 1940. In front of Ciano on the previous evening, Mussolini had maintained he was ready to go to extremes "to liquidate the papacy once and for all, that cancer eating away at the life of the nation." His rage came from the publication of the pope's telegrams to the sovereigns of Belgium, the Netherlands, and Luxemburg, on the day after the German invasion. The Fascist squads booing the pontiff had spilled out into the streets of Rome. From the Chigi palace to the Vatican, it was not unlikely that Il Duce's words spread within a matter of hours. The dialogue was indirect; Alfieri spoke of serious events to come. Pius XII gave no indication of how much credit he gave the boast. At most he added a shadow of irony by warning that he would not take part in an abduction which, in Italy's situation, would have been a sudden impulse rather than a political calculation, neither the initiative nor the timing of which would have been appreciated by the German ally.

On four different occasions in the following years, the same rumor resurfaced, always placed in circulation by the Vatican as a preventive measure. In late April 1941, early in 1942, and again toward the end of the year, and in the spring of 1943, the secretariat of state, still citing German sources, inquired among Fascist leaders about how well founded they were. In relative confidentiality, it foresaw the transfer of certain papal powers to the representatives of the Holy See abroad, "in case it is no longer possible to communicate with them." The *minutanti* were advised to prepare light baggage to accompany the pope. In the summer of 1943, the pope had his papers hidden in the tilework, the archives were scattered, and the refugee diplomats were encouraged to burn their documents. Files on relations with the Third Reich were sent to the United States on microfilm.

Up to that time, it appears as though the rumor placed its origins among the leaders of the Nazi party, as a vague threat rather than an elaborate project. They were considering an abduction and transfer of the pope into any of a number of fortified places within the Third Reich: Wartburg, Wurtemberg, Würzburg, Lichstein, or Lichtenstein. These similar names show evidence of their being passed by word of mouth. These rumors tended toward strengthening the blockade of the Vatican.

Hitler seemed to take responsibility for the plan during his evening speech of 26 July 1943, in the aftermath of Mussolini's fall. The occupation of Rome by parachutists and tanks would make taking over the Vatican, capturing the pope and diplomats, and seizing the archives easier. Nevertheless, no detailed instructions for the plan's execution were transmitted. From that point on, the information that reached the Vatican showed the German leaders to be divided. It was discovered after the war that Ribbentrop encouraged the plan, while Goebbels was opposed to it. From the start, those who were to carry out the plan were busy warning the Holy See. At the time all the survivors—generals, officers close to the oppositon, diplomats who were faithful to the ambassador, and even SS generals—fought to assure that each of them was responsible for saving the pope. Concerns sprang up each time. Some of Pius XII's apologists (e.g., Padellaro) revealed that after an ultimatum by Weiszäker, the pope held a farewell consistory on 9 February 1944, to say once again that he would give in only to violence and would leave the cardinals free to "take shelter." In any case, the consistory left no record, either in the acts of the Holy See or in Pius XII's speeches.

In November 1943 English radio mentioned these rumors, which allowed those who were supposed to carry out the operation to give it up, discrediting it as a fabrication of enemy propaganda. Fear of repercussions among German Catholics was the most likely reason for filing away a plan that was more hypothetical than carefully elaborated. At least this is Father Graham's ultimate conclusion regarding this episode of psychological warfare (Robert Graham II, "Voleva Hitler allontanare da Roma Pio XII?" *Civiltà Cattolica*, I, 1972, 319 ff., 454 ff.).

The Italian armistice (8 September), transforming Italy from an ally to an enemy of the Reich, made Rome a city occupied by the Germans from 8 September 1943 to 4 June 1944; the Vatican State was surrounded by a cordon of troops. Keeping the Holy See safe from 8 September 1943 to 4 June 1944 was accomplished by the different authorities present: operational staffs, a local commander, embassies of the Third Reich, expanded by a number of liaison bodies, and each of these with a representative at the Vatican. There were two kinds of relations: the appearance of coexistence, where German soldiers occasionally even visited St. Peter's as pilgrims, and where the pontifical gendarmerie kept watch lest desertions be encouraged. Simultaneously, the pressure of a specifically Nazi police force (Gestapo, S.D.) was overtly felt. The police, enjoying considerable autonomy, used Italian republican fascists, regrouped into the "Koch gang," to carry out their operations.

In the daily uncertainty about what the future would bring, these months of German occupation in Rome were also months of a profuse Roman clandestinity, which the pope was unable to either protect explicitly or to control. This evolved into networks of nonuniformed, noncredentialed combatants who were able to get various individuals recognized by the Holy See: Italian or allied information agents, escaped prisoners of war, German deserters, and Italians in rival resistance groups (especially those in Communist patriotic action groups, who were determined to fight openly). Other networks joined them, those of spontaneous agents of assistance and reception, generally connected with ecclesiastics or religious houses whose canonical enclosure the Holy See had raised, or Vatican prelates acting on their own, knowing that they were protected by a papal "silence" that was tantamount to encouragement and assurance of nonobstruction.

On two occasions, the Roman Jewish population was threatened. On 20 September a ransom in gold was demanded under the threat of deportation. Pius XII paid the sum that had been asked. Then, during the night of 15–16 October, SS units that had come from the Third Reich began a house-to-house roundup that had been planned to take place for three days, seeking 8,000 Roman Jews. The following day, 1,000 of those arrested were sent to Auschwitz, where almost all perished. The hunt was not continued after the first day.

In the following months, SS commandos and the "Koch gang" made forays into a few buildings belonging to the Holy See, searching for refugees, prisoners of war, members of the Italian political opposition, and Jews. The most famous of these was aimed at the monastery of ST. PAUL'S-OUTSIDE-THE-WALLS, during the night of 3–4 February 1944, and concluded with a formal pillaging and several hundred arrests.

The attack on 23 March 1944, where 32 German soldiers were killed in an explosion, engendered the execution of 335 hostages by the chief of the SS police in the Adreatine ditches. The event took place so quickly that the Holy See was unable to intervene.

However, Berlin modified its instructions and the local German police services did not follow to the end the well-known trails leading to their victims' hiding places. Thus, in the LATERAN PALACE, land under Vatican sovereignty, just a few hundred meters from the Gestapo headquarters, the main political figures of the left and the future members of the first Italian Liberation government lived the nine months of the occupation without peril, while maintaining relations with the resistance and the Bari royal government.

Rome, an Open City. Even before Rome was caught in the line of operations, the armed threat carried by aircraft bombers was considered as soon as Italy entered the war. That same day, Paris and London were asked to refrain from such activities, and France gave its assurance. Great Britain refused, offering to spare Rome throughout the war on one condition: It would agree if the Italian government did so, too; Rome was, first and foremost, the capital of a nation at war, as was the case for London. The Holy See objected, since it was the city of the pope, filled with art treasures, venerated throughout the world, a "sacred city," a "holy city." The foreign office saw only a mask for Italian interests in this, and made the observation that the bludgeoning of English cities by the Luftwaffe had never been condemned. The confusion of military targets and religious edifices, and the Vatican's location in the heart of the Italian capital, made the exchange of diplomatic documents that had been carried on for three years ineffective. The threat of a papal protest in the event Rome was hit was not completely ineffectual, especially for Roosevelt, who had his Catholic electorate in mind. London consistently held to its refusal to refrain from bombing, in the strongest terms. The inevitable came in the spring of 1943, when the Allies prepared to disembark on the Italian coast. On 16 May, an incursion into Ostia, without bombs, served as a warning. The high command was authorized to take aim at marshaling yards, avoiding religious monuments. On 19 July, 500 planes attacked railway installations for five hours, hitting areas where the working class lived. There were 1,500 dead and 500 wounded. Pius XII went to San Lorenzo-fuori-le-mura. The same neighborhoods were targeted once again on 13 August. The pope's protests were accompanied by insistent steps to get Rome declared an "open city." Badoglio's Italian government agreed on 16 August, but the subject was lost in the confusion of negotiations of an armistice.

During the evening of 5 November 1943, one isolated aircraft dropped four bombs on the Vatican itself, although they caused no damage. The warring parties all denied responsibility, and the rumor was that the pilot had been Farinacci, a fascist dignitary known for his hostility to the Holy See.

After the war, these realities as a whole were addressed through the efforts of different governments and a number of individuals, some Catholics and others not, to get from Pius XII explicit words of condemnation of the enemy for the "anti-Nazi crusade," for the "anti-Bolshevik crusade," or a denunciation of the extermination of the Jews. In the years after the war, Pius was accused of silence and of non-assistance to the Jews who were hunted down. From 1965 to 1980, in response, the Holy See published its "Acts and Documents" for the period during the war, which refuted the accusations.

Jacques Nobécourt

Bibliography

AAS: Acta Apostolicae Sedis.

ADSS: Actes et documents relatifs à la Seconde Guerre mondiale, ed. P. Blet, R. A. Graham, A. Martini, B. Schneider, Vatican City, 1965–1981, 11 vols. (see: V. Conzemius, "Le Saint-Siège et la guerre mondiale, deux éditions de source," Revue d'histoire de la Seconde Guerre mondiale, October 1982).

Becker, J. "Der Vatican und der II. Weltkrieg," Katholische Kirche im dritten Reich, ed. D. Albrecht, Mayence, 1976.

Blet, P. Pius XII and the Second World War: According to the Archives of the Vatican, trans. L. J. Johnson, New York, 1999.

Chadwick, O. Britain and the Vatican During the Second World War, Cambridge, 1986 (based on Osborne's papers).

Charles-Roux, F. Huit ans au Vatican, 1932–1940, Paris, 1947.

Chelini, J. L'Église sous Pie XII, I. La Tourmente, 1939–1945, Paris, 1983.

Cianfara, C. The War and the Vatican, London, 1945.

Civiltà Cattolica, 1961, 4 March, 1 July, 2 September.

Cornwell, J. Hitler's Pope: The Secret History of Pius XII, London, 1999.

Coste, R. La Doctrine de la paix chez Pie XII, Paris, 1962.

de Montclos, X. Les Chrétiens face au nazisme et au communisme. L'épreuve totalitaire, 1939–1945, Paris, 1983.

di Nolfo, E. Vaticano e Stati Uniti, 1939–1952, Milan, 1978.

D'Ormesson, W. De Saint-Pétersbourg à Rome, Paris, 1969.

Duclos, P. Le Vatican et la Seconde Guerre mondiale, action doctrinale et politique en faveur de la paix, Paris 1955.

Giordano, I. Vita contro morte, la Santa Sede per le vittime della Seconda Guerre mondiale, Milan, 1956.

Giovanetti, A. Il Vaticano e la guerra (1939–1040), Vatican City, 1960; French trans. L'Action du Vatican pour la paix, Paris, 1962.

Graham, R. A. The Vatican and Communism in World War II: What Really Happened?, San Francisco, 1996.

Graham, R. A. Vatican Diplomacy, Princeton, N.J., 1959; articles in Civiltà Cattolica, 1970, 1971, 1972, 1973, 1974, 1976, 1978, 1984.

Hill, L. Die Weiszäcker-Papiere 1933–1950, Frankfurt, 1974.

Mother Lehnert, P. Erinnerungen an Papst Pius XII, Würtzburg, 1982.

Maccarone, M. Il nazionalsocialismo e la Santa Sede, Rome, 1947.

Marchione, M. Yours Is a Precious Witness: Memories of Jews and Catholics in Wartime Italy, New York, 1997.

Mayeur, J., et al. Histoire du Christianisme, XII, Guerres mondiales et totalitarismes (1914–1958), Paris, 1990.

Padellaro, N. Pius XII, French ed., Paris, 1950.

Papeleux, L. L'Action caritative du Saint-Siège en faveur des prisonniers de guerre (1939–1945), Rome, 1991.

Phayer, M. The Catholic Church and the Holocaust, 1930–1965, Bloomington, Ind., 2000.

Phayer, M. "Pope Pius XII, the Holocaust, and the Cold War," Holocaust and Genocide Studies 12 (Fall 1998) pp. 233–56.

Pichon, C. Le Vatican devant la guerre et la paix, Paris, 1960.

Pius XII, Discorsi e radiomessagi, Vatican City, I–VII.

Rhodes, A. The Vatican in the Age of Dictators, 1922–1945, London, 1973.

Riccardi, A., et al. Pio XII, Bari, 1984.

Roma città aperta, Milan, 1962.

Cardinal Tardini, D. Pio XII, Vatican City, 1960.

Taylor, M. C. Wartime Correspondence between President Roosevelt and Pope Pius XII, New York, 1947.

Von Weiszäcker, E. Erinnerungen, Munich, 1950.

Weisbord, R. G., and Sillanpoa, W. P. The Chief Rabbi, the Pope, and the Holocaust: An Era in Vatican-Jewish Relations, New Brunswick, N.J., 1992.

Zucotti, S. Under His Very Window: The Vatican and the Holocaust, New Haven, Conn., 2000.

WORMS, CONCORDAT OF (1122). Following Leibniz, we call the documents exchanged on 23 September 1122 near Worms, in the Rhineland-Palatinate, by three legates of Pope CALLISTUS II and the Emperor Henry V (1106–25), "the Concordant of Worms." This exchange put an end to the INVESTITURE CONTROVERSY, which dated back to the reign of GREGORY VII, and to the schism in the Church, finally reestablishing peace between the Church and the monarchy. The original deed of Henry V is still preserved today in the Archivio segreto vaticano. In his time, Callistus II had a fresco painted in the new St. Nicholas chapel at the Lateran Palace showing Henry V handing the pope the document, which is even legible.

It was a triumph for the papacy. Henry V renounced investiture of bishops and abbots by the ring and crozier and consented to canonical election and the free consecration of those elected. In 1122 the Emperor also promised to restore all the Church's possessions and the *regalia beati Petri*, which he or his supporters had garnered during the Investiture Controversy. The "privilege" that Callistus II established for the Emperor in exchange is known to us only through copies, which vary in form. The pope authorized election of bishops and abbots in the German Empire to take place in the presence of the Emperor, who would give the newly elect the regalia by the scepter, that is, before consecration. In the rest of the Empire, the prelates were to receive their temporal possessions from the Emperor and by the scepter, that is, within six months after consecration. All ecclesiastics were to fulfill those obligations to their sovereign that resulted from the investiture with regalian rights (*quae ex his jure tibi debet faciat*). In the Empire, in the case of litigious elections, the Emperor also preserved a certain power of decision. Finally, the two parties pledged mutual pacts.

These two documents, no doubt deliberately couched in imprecise terms, represented a compromise, based on the pope's concessions. The clear separation between spiritual and temporal rights, as it appears in the documents, was opposed above all to an idea bitterly defended from the mid-11th century by Gregorian reformers: that the bishopric, made up of the office, possessions, and rights, forms an indissoluble entity. This idea was further reinforced by the ancient precept of the Church according to which everything that had once been ceded to the Church was a possession for all time. Up to 1119, at the synod of Mouzon, negotiators representing the pope, like William of Champeaux, bishop of Châlons, still wanted to abolish the German sovereigns' right of investiture, without any other form of compensation. The distinction of the notion of bishopric (*episcopatus*) was the result of a long evolution. Concrete examples of this are to be found in the letters of Bishop Ivo of Chartres, in the *tractatus de investituris*, and especially in the accords between Pope Paschal II and Henry V in 1111 and between Paschal and Henry I of England in 1107.

The determining factor in the case of the concordat of 1122 was Callistus's recognition of a royal right, defined without any further precision, over the goods, possessions, and rights handed over to the Church and the authorization given the Emperor to exercise this supremacy within the framework of the elections of bishops and abbots by means of investiture by the scepter. The text of the pontifical document mentions the regalian rights that had been defined in publications and synods in Paschal II's time. But in practice, all the Church's possessions and the temporal goods of the bishopric were conceived as regalian rights. Henry renounced investiture by the religious symbols of the crozier and ring, a clear distinction being made between temporal and spiritual goods. This distinction, which complied with the English agreement of 1107 (which had been limited in time), was rejected by the first Lateran council (1123) in favor of Henry V.

As PASCHAL II had done in his day, Callistus II imposed the Worms document by way of tolerance. However, and despite different interpretations of the pontifical documents, in particular under the emperors Lothair III (1125–37) and Frederick I (Barbarossa) (1152–90), in the long term the Concordat of Worms created the juridical basis regulating relations between the German monarch and the Church. The handing over of temporal goods was conceived as a purely feudal act. Thus, feudal right, which was still recent in Germany (unlike England and France), became "the foundation of all the temporal rights of the imperial Church and all the rights of the Empire" over the possessions of the Church (P. Classen).

After the Concordat of Worms, the imperial bishoprics and part of the imperial abbeys became elective principalities, fiefs of the Empire. In addition, the Concordat of Worms, established through the cooperation of the Emperors, anchored their participation in the government of Germany, which was henceforth officially designated, in the spirit of Gregory VII, *regnum Teutonicum*.

Uta-Renate Blumenthal

Bibliography

MGH Legum sectio IV Constitutiones, I, 107 ff., 159 ff.

Buttner, H. "Erzbischof Adalbert von Mainz, die Kurie und das Reich in den Jahren 1118 bis 1122," *Investitursstreit und Reichsverfassung*, ed. P. Classen, Sigmaringen, 1973, 395–410.

St. Chodrow, A., "Ecclesiastical Politics and the Ending of the Investiture Contest," *Speculum* 46 (1971), 613–40.

Classen, P. "Das Wormser Konkordat in der deutschen Verfassungsgeschichte," *Investitursstreits*, 411–60.

Fried, J. "Der Regalienbegriff im elften und zwölften Jahrhundert," *Deutsches Archiv* 29 (1973), 450–528.

Herklotz, I. "Die Beratungsraeume Calixtus' II. im Lateranpalast und ihre Fresken. Kunst und Propaganda am Ende des Investiturstreits," *Zeitschrift für Kunstgeschichte* 52 (1989), 145–214.

Hofmeister, A. *Das Wormser Konkordat*, ed. rev. R. Schmidt, Darmstadt, 1962.

Ladner, G. "I mosaici e gli affreschi ecclesiastico-politici nell'antico palazzo Lateranense," *Rivista di archeologia cristiana* 12 (1935), 2669–80.

Minninger, M. *Von Clement zum Wormser Konkordat*, Cologne-Vienna, 1978.

Schieffer, T. "Nochmal die Verhandlungen von Mouzon (1119)," *Festschrift E. Stengel*, Münster-Cologne, 1952, 324–41.

Z

ZACHARIAS. *(?–22 or 23 March 752). Elected pope 3 December, consecrated 10 December 741. Buried in St. Peter's, Rome. Saint and confessor (early cult).*

Zacharias is the last of the Greek popes. We know nothing of his life up to his election, which took place when the adventurous policies of his predecessor, GREGORY III, had brought down on Rome the ire of the Lombard king Liutprand. Zacharias poured oil on troubled waters. Abandoning an alliance with the Duke of Spoleto, Trasimund, he sought close ties with Liutprand, who was stronger and more to be trusted. Liutprand accepted the help of the Roman army to seize the duchy of Spoleto, which he wanted to make part of his kingdom, and promised in exchange to give back the towns he had captured in *Tuscia romana*.

After the Lombard king had seized Spoleto, aided by Roman arms, Zacharias decided to meet him in person, in an attempt to settle all the matters in dispute between them. This "summit meeting" took place in Terni in August 742. Never before had a pope and a Lombard king met face to face. The two men took a liking to each other, and the meeting was a success. Liutprand agreed to restore not only the cities of the duchy of Rome and the pontifical lands in Sabina, but also the cities of Pentapolis, which he had seized earlier. He finally made peace with the pope, a peace that was to last twenty years.

Accompanied by Liutprand's representatives, Zacharias personally took possession once more of the towns of Tuscia, then returned in triumph to Rome. Liutprand therefore gave up the idea of incorporating in his kingdom the Byzantine kingdoms administered by the pope. But he believed he still had a free hand in northern Italy, and the following year attacked Ravenna. The exarch Eutychius and the archbishop John implored the pope to come to their aid. As his embassies were to no avail, Zacharias made his way to Ravenna, whose civil and religious authorities welcomed him at l'Aquileia, hailing him as the good shepherd who rescues his lost sheep.

This was tantamount to admitting that Ravenna depended on Rome, politically and religiously, whereas the archbishops had fought since the 6th century to win their independence. Later, the people of Ravenna would regret the move.

Next, Zacharias reached Pavia, where he met the king on 29 June 743, obtaining from him a pledge to give back most of the conquered towns. Liutprand died the following year. His successor, Ratchis, confirmed the truce in favor of the duchy of Rome, but soon laid siege to Perugia, thus cutting off relations between Rome and Ravenna. Zacharias caught up with him and, by naming his price, won the king's agreement to abandon his plans. Shortly afterward, Ratchis abdicated and entered a monastery, together with his wife and children. This would be the final coup of Zacharias's policy of direct negotiation. Ratchis was succeeded by his brother Aistulf, who, for his part, was determined to achieve the unification of Italy even if it meant flying in the face of the pope. In 750 Aistulf seized Ravenna, where he accepted the surrender of the exarch Eutychius. He then placed the duchy of Spoleto under his direct control. The situation was a tense one when the pope died.

If Zacharias's relations with the Lombards were far from easy, he did not have to suffer the hostility of the Emperor. Early in his pontificate, the pope had been led to hope that the victory of Artavasdus—the son of the Emperor LEO III, who favored the cult of images—over his brother Constantine would mark the ending of iconoclasm. But in the end Constantine V was the victor, in September 732. Despite this, the Emperor and the pope had a courteous relationship, doubtless because each man knew he had nothing to fear or to hope from the other.

If they remained totally at loggerheads on the theological level, here too Zacharias's attitude had none of the aggressiveness of his predecessor's. The letters he exchanged with Byzantium essentially concerned relations with the Lombards, but the pope knew he could not rely on the Emperor for protection. Constantine even presented him with two imperial domains close to Rome, Ninfa and Norma, as compensation for the confiscations of Leo III.

Zacharias took advantage of these donations, and those of certain members of the Roman aristocracy, to reorganize the government of the Patrimony of St. Peter in Latium. He set up the first five *domus cultae*, contiguous estates covering a vast area, which were worked by a group of clergy settled on the lands. Their products were shipped directly to Rome. The Church of Rome, which heretofore had lived mainly on financial resources from its possessions in the south, now wanted to count on a steady, direct supply of agricultural products.

Parallel with this, Zacharias still pursued the traditional policy of renting lands at long lease and on advantageous terms. Its chief benefit was to create a clientele among members of the Roman aristocracy. The pope made use of part of his resources to embellish the palace of the Lateran. Like his predecessors, Zacharias was unstinting in his support of Boniface. He encouraged him to direct the program of reform of the Frankish church. Charles Martel having died in 741, his two sons, Carloman and Pepin (the future king), divided power in the Frankish kingdom between them.

Carloman was a pious man who in 747 would retire to Monte Cassino. Realizing that the Church could not be left in the disorganized state into which his father had sunk it, he asked Boniface to hold a series of councils from 742 to 745. We know that Boniface thought of Rome as the source and guarantee of the rights of the Church. This may explain why Pepin, seeking to legitimize his coup d'état, consulted the pope to find out who should bear the title of king, the one who effectively held royal power or the one who held it no more. By lending his support to Pepin the Short, Zacharias put him under fealty to the papacy. This obligation would enable Stephen II, in his struggle with the Lombards, to obtain the Frankish support that Charles Martel had refused to give.

Jean-Charles Picard

Bibliography

JW, 1, 262–70; 2, 700, 742.
LP, 1. 426–39.
MGH, Epist., 3, 479–87, 709–11.
Bertolini, O. *Roma e i Longobardi*, Rome, 1972.
Davis, R., trans. *The Lives of the Eighth Century Popes*, Liverpool, 1992.
Duchesne, L. *Les premiers temps de l'état pontifical*, Paris, 1911.
Noble, T. F. X. *The Republic of St. Peter: The Birth of the Papal State, 680–825*, Philadelphia, 1984.
Richards, J. J. *The Popes and the Papacy in the Early Middle Ages, 476–752*, London, 1979.

ZEPHYRINUS. *(199–217).*

The *Liberian Catalogue* gives Peter's fourteenth successor an eighteen-year pontificate. Eusebius of Caesarea and other sources provide little information on his actions. Apparently he was a Roman, the son of one Habundius. HIPPOLYTUS presents him as a man of little culture, inexperienced, incapable of making decisions influencing the future of the Church, and, for good measure, avaricious in the extreme.

His era was characterized in Rome by an intense doctrinal struggle known to us through Hippolytus's *Philosophumena*. Two opposing trends gradually came to the fore: adoptionism, according to which Jesus had been an ordinary man until his baptism, and modalism, which made no distinction between the Father and the Son. This latter doctrine was defended by Praxeas, Noet, Epigonus, and his disciple Cleomenus. According to Hippolytus, around 215 Zephyrinus encouraged modalism under the influence of his archdeacon Callistus. Hippolytus attributes to him an ambiguous credal formula: "I acknowledge one God, the one who was born, suffered and died." In fact, Zephyrinus seems to have tried to define an intermediate position that maintained the unity of God without denying the distinction of the hypostases. But this did not clarify the debate.

The *Liber pontificalis* attributes to him a constitution on the concelebration of priests with the bishop. Another of his decisions seems to have been concerned with the publicizing of ordinations, but this matter probably goes back to the earliest days of the Church. Zephyrinus was not a martyr, nor is there any solid proof for to the tradition whereby he was the first to be buried in the small basilica near the entrance to the cemetery on the Appian Way known as that of Callistus. His feast day is 26 August.

Jean-Pierre Martin

Bibliography

Amann, E. *DTC*, Paris, 1950, XV, 2, 3690–1.
Capelle, B. "Le cas du pape Zéphyrin," Rev. B, n, d., 38, 1926, 321–30.
Eusebius, *HE*, V, 28, 7; VI, 21, 1.
Hippolytus, *Refutations*, IX, 7–12.
Weltin, E. G. *NCE*, New York, 1967, XIV, 1118–19.

ZOSIMUS. *(?–26 December 418). Consecrated pope 18 March 417. Buried in St. John Lateran on the via Tiburtina.*

Zosimus, who according to the *Liber pontificalis* was of Greek origin and the son of a certain Abraham, succeeded Innocent I (d. 12 March 417). Throughout his brief pontificate he practiced an authoritarian policy that spawned serious conflicts within the Church. On 22 March 417 Zosimus intervened in a controversy in Gaul.

Here Bishop Patroclus of Arles, a protégé of the patrician Constantius (brother-in-law of the Emperor Honorius) was vying with his colleague Proculus of Marseilles for the jurisdiction of two villages. Without even summoning Patroclus to Rome, Zosimus impetuously decided in his favor, investing him with wide-ranging powers and establishing a sort of vicariate in his favor. He gave him sole authority, for the Gauls and the seven provinces, to grant letters of credence allowing the clergy to travel throughout the Christian world, as well as the right to consecrate bishops in the province of Vienne and the two Narbonnes. He also gave him authority over these two disputed territories.

Zosimus justified granting these privileges to Patroclus personally (*specialiter*) because of the latter's merits and the tradition whereby the Church of Arles was the mother Church of Christianity in Gaul (JK, 328). This policy, which undermined acquired rights, aroused the protests of Hilary, bishop of Narbonne, who claimed the right to ordain bishops in the two Narbonnes, as well as the open resistance of Proculus of Marseilles. In defiance of canon law, Proculus proceeded to consecrate two bishops in the disputed areas. Warned by Patroclus of Arles, Zosimus, who in September 417 was attending the council in Rome, had the bishop condemned in absentia. He also loudly reaffirmed his policy favoring the primacy of Arles through a series of letters (22–9 September 417, *JK*, 331–4) addressed to the Churches of Africa and the whole of Gaul and Spain, as well as to the adamant Hilary of Narbonne, now threatened with excommunication, to Bishop Patroclus himself, who was confirmed in his powers, and to the churches of the Second Narbonnaise and the Viennois.

When Proculus of Marseilles initiated a schism, the pope was forced to intervene again in Gaul, in March 418. He reproached Patroclus of Arles for having allowed a condemned bishop to retain his see despite the privileges he had been granted. He told the clergy and faithful of Marseilles that, Proculus no longer being their bishop, they should bow to the authority of Patroclus of Arles, who would give them a bishop (*JK*, 340–1). This was a waste of time, as Proculus still held the see of Marseilles when Celestine I was pope.

Zosimus was also greatly preoccupied with the Pelagian controversy. He agreed to revise the condemnations issued in January 417—on the complaint of the Church of Africa—by Innocent I against Pelagius and his disciple Celestius, both of whom had been excommunicated because of their position on original sin, baptism, and redemption. Before 21 September 417, Zosimus had Celestius brought before a Roman tribunal, which declared him guilty of the accusations. The tribunal also agreed to reexamine the case of Pelagius, who, shortly before the death of Innocent I, had appealed to Rome against his condemnation. After a public reading of the letter and of Pelagius's profession of faith, Zosimus in his turn declared the latter's faith to be above reproach. He sent the African bishops two successive letters (JK, 329–30) informing them of the pontifical decisions and blaming them for being overhasty in their actions against the Pelagians since 411. In the first letter, before 21 September 417, the pope summoned the Milanese deacon Paulinus to Rome, giving him two months to prove his accusations against Celestius. In the second, he invited Pelagius's detractors to bow to the pontifical sentence.

Zosimus's decisions received the support of the Italian bishops and the Roman clergy—including the priest Sixtus (the future Sixtus III)—and encouraged the diffusion of Pelagian ideas in Rome. On the other hand, in Africa they were met with fierce opposition. In November 417 the deacon Paulinus let it be known that he would not accede to the Roman summons. For their part, the African bishops, assembled in Carthage, sent Zosimus a letter (described by the pope as an *obtestatio*) in which they accused him of standing surety for Celestius's ideas and disputed the judgment. They also appealed to the court of Ravenna.

The pope therefore backed down. On 21 March 418 he wrote to the African bishops reminding them that pontifical authority could not brook the slightest delay but agreeing to review Celestius's case (*JK*, 432). The concession did not go far enough. On 30 April 418 Zosimus was disavowed by the Emperor Honorius, who, pronouncing on the root of the problem, issued a rescript condemning Pelagius and Celestius for their errors and ordered their supporters to be hounded down. Furthermore, on 1 May 418 an African council of two hundred bishops meeting in Carthage again condemned Pelagius and Celestius and demanded that the pope uphold the sentences brought against them by Innocent I, even if it meant a public retraction. This twofold opposition forced the pope to capitulate. He called on Celestius to appear before a plenary synod. When Celestius failed to do so the pope declared both him and Pelagius excommunicated in absentia until resipiscence, the sentence being pronounced in a synod of bishops.

Before September 418, Zosimus solemnly confirmed the condemnation of Pelagius and Celestius in an *epistula tractoria* (preserved only in fragments) addressed to all the Churches, chiefly those of Constantinople, Alexandria, Thessalonica, and Jerusalem, and inviting them to confirm the pontifical sentence. Against the Pelagian doctrines, the pope declared himself *instinctu Dei* on the existence of original sin, the necessity for baptism of little children, and the need for divine grace to accomplish good. He would hold a synod around autumn 418 against any bishops who refused to sign the *tractoria*.

The pontiff was also concerned with African affairs. He intervened indirectly in Caesarean Mauretania, where he ordered Augustine of Hippo and his colleagues to settle the problems of the Donatist bishop, Emeritus of Caesarea (*JK*, 344). He received the appeal of a bishop of Byzacena who had been condemned in a fiscal matter by a council attended by lay assessors; on 16 November 416 he violently reprimanded the bishops of the province for irregularities, without however settling the controversy himself (*JK*, 346). By contrast, he intervened directly in the affair of Apiarius, priest of Sicca Veneria, who had been excommunicated by Bishop Urbanus. On receiving Apiarius's appeal he despatched three legates—Bishop Faustinus of Potentia and the Roman priests Philip and Asellus—to Africa, with instructions and a dossier justifying the right of appeal to Rome. The dossier was based on canons he believed were derived from the council of Nicaea (but in fact came from the Sardica council). The legates were ordered to discuss with the African episcopate the question of appeals to Rome and visits to the bishops' court, as well as that of the judging of excommunicated priests and deacons by their bishop, and finally the matter of Urbanus, who had been threatened with excommunication or a summoning to Rome. The legates were met with reserve on the part of the African episcopate, from which Zosimus received a protest disputing the canons invoked by Rome and declaring that it would agree to observe them only provisionally.

In Illyria, Zosimus maintained links with Bishop Rufus of Thessalonica, to whom he sent his *tractoria* against the Pelagians. He did not, however, seek to impose his authority directly. He acted at the request of Bishop Hesychius of Salona to restore ecclesiastical organization to order. On 21 April 418 he issued a decretal condemning the usages whereby monks and even members of the laity had direct access to the episcopate. He defined the ecclesiastical *cursus* as well as canonical impediments to ordination, and forbade the multiplying of episcopal sees (*JK*, 339).

For reasons that are not clear, the pope clashed with certain members of the Roman clergy, who brought complaints about him to the court of Ravenna. The pontiff, recalling that these approaches were contrary to canon law, on 3 October 418 sent his representatives in Ravenna a letter informing them that he was excommunicating the rebels. When his envoys returned, he reserved the right to enter proceedings against their supporters (*JK*, 345).

Zosimus fell dangerously ill, with brief returns to health, a situation that appeared to have favored intrigue. Through his authoritarian, somewhat incoherent policies, which were often contrary to those of his predecessor Innocent I, he helped to weaken the authority of the Apostolic See and provoked the Emperor's intervention in matters of faith. In later years he was described by the African Churches as a pope *non beatae memoriae*.

Christiane Fraisse-Coué

Bibliography

LP, 225–6.
Amann, E. *DTC*, 15, 3708–16.
Caspar, E. *Geschichte des Papsttums*, I. Túbingen, 1930, 343–60.
Duchesne, L. *Fastes épiscopaux de l'ancienne Gaule*, I, Paris, 1907, 95–108.
Histoire ancienne de l'Église, III, Paris, 1911, 227–57.
Pietri, C. *Roma Christiana*, II, *BEFAR*, 224, 2976, 1000–21; 1101–5, 1212–54.
Zozimus, *Epistulae*, *PL*, 20, 642–86; *Epistulae* 2–3 and 12, *Collectio Auellana* 45–6, 50, *CSEL*, 35, 1, 99–108; 115–16.

ZOUAVES, PONTIFICAL. Created just after the French army had seized Algiers by order of General Clausel on 1 October 1830, confirmed by royal ordinance dated 21 March 1831, the battalion of Zouaves (from the name of the Berber tribe of the Zwawa, or Zouaoua) was originally a troop of light infantry made up of native auxiliaries, mainly Kabyles. Based on this model, battalions of French Zouaves were formed over the following years. Under the July monarchy and the Second Empire, they took an active part in the bloody conquest of Algeria, the Crimean War, the Italian campaign of 1859, and finally the Franco-Prussian War of 1870–1.

Characteristic of the Zouave regiments was their uniform, which was of Oriental inspiration. "The Zouaves wear the Moorish costume," wrote the Grande Encyclopédie at the end of the 19th century, "a dark-blue jacket and vest of Arab cut, decorated with red braid, a dark-blue hooded collar, a girdle of sky-blue cashmere, baggy trousers of Arabian style with dark-blue braiding, and shoes with great white gaiters to the knee. . . . On their heads the Zouaves wear a cap of lightweight red wool called a *chéchia*, to the top of which is attached a tassel fringed with blue. For full dress, this *chéchia* is wound around with a length of rolled white stuff known as a turban."

The huge popularity of the Zouaves in the mid-19th century was linked to the prestige of the colonial wars and the heroic aura that surrounded these infantry troops who were assigned to the fiercest fighting (the siege of Constantinople; the capture of the Smala, or retinue, of the emir Abd El Kader; the battle of Alma in the Crimea, commemorated in Paris by the statue of the Zouave on the Pont de l'Alma). Also contributing to their popularity was a way of life and behavior apt to arouse youthful enthusiasm and flatter virile imaginations, as well as their magnificent moustaches, their pointed beards "in the imperial manner," long pipes, their only half-tolerated indiscipline and plundering, and, finally, the whole laxity of clothes and morals that was part of barracks life in peacetime.

Thus it was natural that the volunteers, mostly French and Belgian, who enlisted to defend the Papal States in the summer of 1860 should adopt the celebrated uniform of the Zouaves. (In the opposing camp, also in 1860, Major Falcone, fighting alongside Garibaldi in Calabria, formed a battalion of *zuavi calabresi*.) Had not Lamoricière, the general in chief of the pontifical army that was crushed by that of the Piedmontese, distinguished himself at the head of the Zouave battalion in Algeria in the 1830s? It was natural, too, that the battalion of Franco-Belgian riflemen in the service of the pope should adopt a name "which public opinion and the Piedmontese had already given the combatants of Castelfidardo," as its first chief, Lieutenant-Colonel Louis-Aimé de Becdelièvre, recalls in his memoirs.

The creation of a battalion of Pontifical Zouaves (*zuavi pontifici*), formed from the remnants of the Franco-Belgian riflemen and enlarged with new volunteers, took place officially on 1 January 1861. The battalion was at once put to work restoring order in what, for ten more years, remained of the former Papal States (the five provinces of Rome and Comacchio, Civitavecchia, Frosinone, Velletri, and Viterbo) and putting down banditry in the *cioriara* (southern Latium). Originally consisting of eight companies, it was raised to regimental rank from 1 January 1867, comprising two battalions of six companies and one supply company. The increase in the number of recruits at the time of the fighting at Mentana (3 November 1867) brought the strength of the Pontifical Zouaves to four battalions of six companies and four supply companies. In 1870, the last year of existence of the Papal States, out of the 13,157 men (and 1,206 horses) making up Pius IX's army, 2,901, or 22 percent, belonged to the regiment of the Pontifical Zouaves and 1,110, or 8.5 percent, to the *Legione romana* (or Legion of Antibes), consisting of volunteer soldiers of the regular French army.

The regiment of Pontifical Zouaves was disbanded on 21 September 1870, in the wake of the collapse of the Papal States. It numbered officially 10,920 enrollees, counting many re-enlistments (for six months, a year, or more), and approximately 7,000 officers, noncommissioned officers, and soldiers. The influx of volunteers was constant although irregular. There were 1,015 enlisted men in 1861, but only hundreds in each of the following years (186 in 1862, 217 in 1863, 213 in 1864, and 289 in 1865). Soon, however, the abolition of the regular French army, written into the Convention of 15 September 1864, and the rise of new threats against the last temporal possessions of the popes mobilized Catholic opinion and brought about a rise in manpower. A total of 1,463 enlisted in 1866, 3,274 in 1867 (the year of Mentana), 1,654 in 1868, 1,382 in 1869, and 1,227 in 1870.

The national distribution shows the wide geographical range of recruitment. No fewer than twenty-two nations were represented, including Canada and the United States. The French and Dutch predominated, followed by the Belgians, Swiss, Germans (the majority Bavarians), and Italians. Out of the 3,000 French registered, the west (with roughly a thousand), the north (the dioceses of Cambrai and Arras), the uplands of the Massif Central, but also the large cities (Lyons, Marseilles, Paris) drew a map of Catholic loyalty, intransigent and Roman in sensibility, that cut across all classes, from the aristocracy (at the officer level) to the peasantry (the simple soldiers).

The command reflected and accentuated these characteristics. The 170 officers included 111 French, 25 Belgians, 7 Dutch, 6 Swiss, 5 Germans, and 5 Romans (including Prince Rospigliosi). Leadership of the Zouaves, however was not given to a volunteer officer but to a member of the regular pontifical army, Colonel Joseph-Eugène Allet (1814–78), a Swiss soldier (originally from Loèche) who entered the pope's service at the age of eighteen in 1832 and was placed at the head of the battalion on 21 March 1861. Lieutenant-Colonel de Becdelièvre (1826–71), former head of the Franco-Belgian Riflemen, then commander-in-chief of the battalion of the Pontifical Zouaves, resigned on 23 March. He was replaced as head of battalion (16 March 1861) and then as lieutenant-colonel (16 December 1866) by the man who would, on the French side, symbolize the Catholic and monarchical dimension of the enrollment of large numbers of zouaves, Athanase de Charette de La Contrie (1832–1911). He was the grand-nephew of the renowned leader from the Vendée, the son of a peer of France of the Restoration who had fought in 1815 and 1832 for the Bourbons, and of an illegitimate daughter of the Duc de Berry. He had had a legitimist upbringing outside France at the military academy of Turin, becoming an officer of the Duke of Modena and later fighting at Castelfidardo, all the while remaining a loyal supporter of the Count of Chambord (Henry V, the pretender to the French crown).

Also among the regimental officers were ninety-five nobles (56 percent of the officers from the rank of sub-lieutenant) who helped make the command a heraldic armorial with rank upon rank of names from one section of the French legitimist party: de Lambilly, Le Caron de Troussures, d'Albouisse, de Sairy, de Cordon, de Goesbriand, de Kermoal, de Montcuit de Boiscuillé, de Villèle, de Kersabiec, de Bourbon-Busset, du Réau, de Peytes de Montcabrier, etc. The regimental chaplain, Jules Daniel (1825–79), who was from Nantes, assisted by two Belgian ecclesiastics (Sacré and de Woelmont), held a decisive place at the heart of this troop, united as it was by strong religious conviction.

Thus the regiment of the Pontifical Zouaves formed an original microcosm not reducible to its purely military role, which in any case was hardly significant except for its part in the fighting at Mentana. Rather it was the visible—and highly controversial—incarnation of the stubborn resistance with which the Holy See tried vainly to oppose the irresistible aspiration of the Italian people to national unity and constitutional government, using even military force to defend its temporal sovereignty. Glorified as new crusaders by Catholic opinion, denounced as stateless mercenaries by the Italian press, the Pontifical Zouaves represented first and foremost a championing of the Church and a stake in diplomacy.

The recruitment of the Pontifical Zouaves came in response to an unprecedented effort to mobilize Catholics in favor of the pope, who had been stripped of the greater part of his States and resources and faced the threat of being deprived of any territorial base. The "Roman campaign" of the 1860s represented a close combination of devotion to the person of Pius IX, loyalty to the Church, financial effort (through collections for Peter's pence and subscriptions for soldiers' equipment), the personal commitment of young volunteers and their families, denigration of the national and liberal aspirations of the young kingdom of Italy, and growing hostility to the policies of the Emperor Napoleon III.

In Flanders, Brittany, and far-off Quebec, a concerted, militant, and effective organization of propaganda and recruitment was set up around the episcopate, the clergy, and the Catholic nobility. The aim was to use preaching and teaching, solemn appeals and public demonstrations, religious ceremonies in honor of the new Maccabees and latter-day martyrs of Castelfidardo or Mentana (such as the seminarist Joseph Guérin of Nantes), newspapers, and brochures—among which the novel of Father Antonio Bresciani, *Olderico, ovvero Il Zuavo Pontificio* (1861), would be the most popular—to raise the manpower and money necessary to organize the army of the pontifical volunteers. One single parish, that of Campbon (4,500 souls), near Nantes, answered its curé's appeal by providing twenty-nine zouaves.

The letters the zouaves wrote to their families, which were spread around widely by the clergy, overflowed with religious ardor and soldierly emulation. "I told myself, being a young man of twenty with a little good old blood in my veins, it is my duty to respond to the call of the vicar of Jesus Christ," declared Henri Le Chauff de Kerguenec, a future Jesuit, in May 1862. "I am leaving, and am ready to sacrifice my life for the defense of the Holy Father. Pray for me and ask that I gain martyrdom," wrote a law student in November 1865. This was Joseph Rialian of Ploërmel, who would die at Mentana.

The solemn oath sworn on the Piazza of St. John Lateran before Msgr. Daniel summed up this profession of faith by developing the whole argument justifying of the temporal sovereignty of the Holy See in a spirit of devotion and sacrifice: "I swear before almighty God to be obedient and faithful to my sovereign, the Roman Pontiff, Our Most Holy Father the Pope, Pius IX, and to his legitimate successors. I swear to serve him with honor and loyalty and even to sacrifice my life for the defense of his august and sacred person, in order to uphold his sovereignty and to maintain his rights."

The influx of young recruits into Pius IX's city resembled a "ninth Crusade," as the fiery abbé Jules Delmas would write in 1881. Echoing this is the speech the pope himself gave to the officers of the pontifical army on 18 December 1864: "There is but one army that has never drawn the sword and that will never draw it save in the cause of justice and truth, and that is you."

The actual commitment of the Pontifical Zouaves in the battle for the survival of the pontifical state, however, depended on considerations—diplomatic, military, political, and religious—which largely escaped the comprehension of the enthusiastic volunteers who had flocked to offer their lives for the defense of Pius IX. For, once the proclamation of the kingdom of Italy (28 February and 14 March 1861) had realized the almost complete unity of the peninsula, with Victor Emmanuel II at its head, the fate of the ecclesiastical state was virtually sealed. Rome would be the capital of a resurrected Italy as history, geography, reason, and sentiment demanded. Cavour had had the first parliament of the kingdom vote on this promise on 27 March 1861, a few months before his death. The papacy, for its part, which claimed with total conviction the integrity of the "Patrimony of Peter" as the inalienable legacy of ages past and the guarantee of the independence and liberty of the Apostolic See, was deeply wounded by this process of "sacral hardening" (A. Omodeo). Thanks to this process, since Consalvi's reinstatement of 1814–15 the Papal States, restored with great difficulty after the French Revolution, had become a diminished power where the needs of the state were gradually sacrificed to ecclesiastical logic. The pope-king (*il Papa-Re*) to whom the zouaves pledged allegiance became each day more pontiff than sovereign.

Two decades earlier, Pius IX in his allocution of 29 April 1848 had refused to wage war with Austria. Moreover, he had reproved the very principle of participation of the Papal States in a war as being contrary to the universal mission of the supreme head of the Church, thus disappointing all the national hopes of the patriotic neo-Guelph movement. True, the papacy fought, late in the day, in 1860 as it would again in 1867, to affirm before Europe the principle of pontifical sovereignty. But, Pius IX, a prisoner of the sacral dimension, could never, even if he had wished to (and this was never the case) henceforth act like Julius II.

Deep inside the Curia, two tendencies confronted each other in the pope's immediate entourage. The cardinal secretary of state, Giacomo Antonelli (1806–76), who had been directing pontifical diplomacy since the autumn of 1848, was eager above all to preserve the international importance of the Holy See. Immediately after the defeat of Castelfidardo, which entailed the papacy's definitive loss of the Legations, the Marches and Umbria, Antonelli declared to the Duke of Gramont, the French ambassador to Rome, that "so far as external aggression is concerned, the strength of the small states lies entirely in the guarantees of international law, and their armies can have no other goal or effect than to maintain internal order" (telegram of 26 September 1860).

Antonelli's diplomacy was aimed at humoring Napoleon III, who favored Italian unity but was concerned with accommodating French Catholic opinion and at awakening Europe's interest in the preservation of an ecclesiastical state, albeit a diminished one. Antonelli reproved the imprudence of the intransigent Catholics and bemoaned Austria's enfeeblement vis-à-vis France, Prussia, and Italy. Thus—for reasons also connected with obscure power struggles within the Curia—he vigorously opposed the bellicose ardor of the impetuous, energetic Xavier de Mérode (1820–74). A Belgian aristocrat, Mérode was a former officer in the Algerian campaign and the brother-in-law of Montalembert. He had been ordained a priest in 1849 and was a secret chamberlain and influential counselor to Pius IX, who on 21 April 1860 promoted him pro-minister of war (*pro-ministro della Armi*) of the Papal States. De Mérode was the one responsible for the Holy See's military mobilization. In the spring of 1860 he chose to summon General Lamoricière—a convinced legitimist and declared enemy of the Empire—to command the army that would be crushed at Castelfidardo. Over the following years he determinedly inspired the Papal States' policy of rearmament, encouraged the recruitment of the zouaves, and ardently defended the argument of all-out resistance to threats of Italian annexation.

It happened that de Mérode's intransigent, bellicose line—the one most closely in tune with the religious and political program that the Pontifical Zouaves and their legitimist officers had rushed to defend—suffered a decisive defeat in the autumn of 1865. The most immediate dangers seemed at the time, however, to have been averted. In the Franco-Italian convention of 15 September 1864, Italy had pledged to respect what remained of the Papal States and to set up its capital in Florence. France, meanwhile, had promised to withdraw its troops from Rome within two years. A reaction against the radical wing of the Risorgimento led to the defeat of the champions of Rome as the capital, and to Garibaldi's retreat to the island of Caprera. Moreover, the policy of rearming the Papal States was proving very onerous, while the recruitment of volunteers throughout Catholic Europe worried or irritated cabinets, particularly in France, where the causes of the pope and dynastic legitimism appeared very closely bound together.

Finally, by his frankness and impetuosity (also because he was a foreigner) de Mérode alienated the greater part of the Curia, along with the whole of the diplomatic corps. Also, with the death of General de Lamoricière (10 September 1865), he lost his most precious ally. On 20 October 1865, Pius IX dismissed de Mérode from the ministry of war "out of concern for his health" and on 27 October he replaced him with a placid, disciplined Swiss from Baden, Hermann Kanzler (1822–88), an officer in the pontifical army since 1845. The new crusaders, although never disavowed by Pius IX, henceforth had lost their principal political and ideological support in the court of Rome.

It is in this new context that we should appreciate the meaning and influence of the action at Mentana, the principal military episode of the history of the Pontifical Zouave regiment. The cession of Venezia to Italy through the mediation of Napoleon III just after Austria's defeat at the hands of Prussia (Treaty of Vienna, 3 October 1866) and the partial retreat of the French army from Rome by the terms of the convention of 15 September 1866 caused the radical wing of the Italian patriots to revive the plan of annexing Rome to the kingdom. Raids by armed groups on the provinces of Viterbo and Frosinone multiplied in the summer of 1867, while muffled agitation surrounded Pius IX's capital. Yet the hoped-for insurrection did not take place, being limited to the heroic episode of the resistance of the brothers Cairoli at Villa Glori (23 October).

Garibaldi, who had reached Florence on 22 October thanks to the ambiguous policy and tacit connivance of the Rattazzi government, resolved to make for Rome, in an attempt to repeat the bold enterprise that been so successful in Sicily in 1860. He assembled up to 8,000 volunteers and on 26 October seized the stronghold of Monte Rotondo, at the gates of Rome. At the same time, the pontifical army was mobilizing, while a French expeditionary corps of 22,000 men hurriedly disembarked at Civitavecchia on 29 October. Under the orders of General Kanzler, the pontifical counteroffensive began on 3 November in the area of Mentana, where the Pontifical Zouaves, the pontifical *carabinieri*, the soldiers of the legion of Antibes, and the regular French troops broke through the Garibaldian lines at the cost of violent fighting. The nationalists were forced to retreat in haste. The day ended with 172 dead on the pontifical side (including 39 Frenchmen), and 1,400 prisoners and close to a thousand dead on the Garibaldian side. "Our Chassepot guns have done wonders," General de Failly wrote cynically in the *Moniteur* of 10 November.

Although of little military significance, the Mentana action had immense importance in the realm of politics and diplomacy. It ensured the Papal States a three-year respite, which would allow the Holy See to convoke the First Vatican Council in Rome and proclaim the dogma of papal infallibility (constitution *Pastor Aeternus* of 18 July 1870), conceived as the absolute guarantee, on the ecclesiological level, against any collapse of the temporal sovereignty of the popes. Because of Mentana, all the political benefits that France had in Italy were withdrawn— as were the sympathies arising from its intervention against Austria alongside Piedmont in 1859—depriving France of a potential ally in its coming conflict against Prussia. Mentana caused immense religious confusion among Catholics; the Vicar of Christ had caused blood to be shed in order to preserve his territory. Also, in 1870 the Papal States had a permanent army of 13,000 men for a population of some 700,000 inhabitants, or one soldier for 53 inhabitants—which would be proportionately equivalent to a permanent army of 600,000 men in Italy and more than a million in France (A. Vigevano). This transformed the Papal States into another Prussia, or Piedmont, yet without giving it the slightest hope of providing an effective counterbalance to Italian power. In spite of the influx of volunteers, the presence of the Pontifical Zouaves thus tended to lose its significance in contrast with the mobilization of the Church around the pontiff. The "wonders" of the Chassepot would give way to the ecclesiological claim of the "Martyr Pope."

The launching of the invasion of the Papal States by an Italian corps of 50,000 men under the orders of General Cadorna, taking advantage of the retreat of the forces of France, which had now been conquered by Prussia, sounded the knell of the Pontifical Zouaves—hardly a glorious one at that, militarily speaking. The zouaves had visions of going into battle again, but the Realpolitik of Cardinal Antonelli would attempt to cool their ardor. Realizing the disproportion of forces, and the futility of a resistance that could only harm the effectiveness of protests based on principle, the cardinal secretary of state imposed on the docile General Kanzler a strategy aimed at "reducing confrontation to the minimum necessary to allow the use of force to be noted" (P. Dalla Torre). The price of this policy would be 56 dead and 141 wounded on the Italian side, 20 dead and 49 wounded on the pontifical side, as well as a breach in the Aurelian Wall, a little to the west of the Porta Pia.

The capitulation of Rome was signed 20 September 1870 at the Villa Albana, by generals Primerano and Rivalta, and countersigned by generals Cadorna and Kanzler. Charette's troops, who had withdrawn in orderly fashion from the province of Viterbo, where they were stationed, in order to come down to Rome, exchanged only a few shots with the temporizing attackers. On 21 September 1870 the regiment of the Pontifical Zouaves was disbanded, and its men embarked at Civitavecchia for an invaded France.

The French segment of the regiment would write the final page of its history during the Franco-Prussian War of 1870–1. Reconstituted in the form of a Legion of Volunteers of the West (7 October 1870–31 March 1871) under the command of General de Sonis and Lieutenant-Colonel de Charette, both convinced legitimists, the regiment took part in the battles of Orléans (11 October 1870) and Patay (2 December 1870) against the Prussian army. Next, it participated in the second siege of Paris and helped crush the workers' uprising of the Commune (March–May 1871). Thus, in the context of the policy of moral order of the years 1871–7, the Pontifical Zouaves again took up the indissolubly military, religious, and political mission originally assigned to them. Through commemorations, friendly societies, and historical and military publications, for more than half a century they were called on to serve as a mobilizing force and unifying agent for intransigent Catholic opinion. In intending to defend pontifical sovereignty, they had grasped the logic of a now hopeless struggle against the Revolution, or, in the case of the most devoted, perceived the opportunity for an exemplary sacrifice.

Philippe Boutry

Bibliography

Abbé Allard, *Le Volontaire Joseph-Louis Guérin du corps des zouaves pontificaux*, Nantes, 1862.

Abbé Allard, *Les zouaves pontificaux, ou Journal de Mgr Daniel*, Nantes, 1880.

Andreotti, G. *La sciarada di Papa Mastai*, Milan, 1967.

Aubert, R. "La chute de Monseigneur de Mérode en 1865. Documents inédits," *Rivista di storia della Chiesa in Italia*, IX, 1955, 331–92; "Mgr de Mérode, ministre de la guerre sous Pie IX," *Revue générale belge*, 1956, 1102–43 and 1316–34.

Briollet, M. "Les zouaves pontificaux du Maine, de l'Anjou et de la Touraine," *Province du Maine*, LXV, 1963, 185–98, and 261–70; LXVI, 1964, 59–77, 136–55, and 285–98; LXVII, 1965, 79–88.

Cerbelaud-Salaganac, C. *Les zouaves pontificaux*, Paris, 1963.

Charette de La Contrie, A. C. M. *Souvenirs du régiment des zouaves pontificaux, Rome, 1860–1870, France, 1870–1871. Notes et récits*, Tours, 1875.

Cicconetti, L. *Roma o morte. Gli avvenimenti nello Stato Pontificio nel 1867*, Milan, 1934.

de Barral, E. *Les zouaves pontificaux, 1860–1870*, Paris, 1932.

de Becdelièvre, L. A. *Souvenirs de l'armée pontificale*, Paris, 1867.

Della Torre, P. *L'anno di Mentana*, Turin, 1938.

Delmas, J. *La neuvième Croisade*, Paris, 1881.

Hardy, R. *Les zouaves. Une stratégie du clergé québécois au XIXe siècle*, Montreal, 1980.

Jacini, S. *Il tramonto del potere temporale nelle relazioni degli ambasciatori austriaci a Rome (1860–1870)*, Bari, 1931.

Lagrée, M. "Les zouaves," *Religion et cultures en Bretagne, 1850–1950*, Paris, 1992, 158–65.

Launay, M. "Le denier de Saint-Pierre et les zouaves pontificaux," *Fidélités, solidarités et clientèles. Centre de recherches sur l'historie du monde atlantique. Enquêtes et documents* (Nantes), XI, 1985, 275–303.

Le Chauff de Kerguénec, F. *Souvenirs des zouaves pontificaux*, Poitiers-Paris, 1890–1, 2 vols.; *Les Français zouaves pontificaux, 5 mai 1860–20 septembre 1870*, by two veterans (G. de Villèle and C. de La Noue), Saint-Brieuc, 1903.

Lodolini, E. "I volontari del Canada nell'esercito pontificio," *Rassegna storica del Risorgimento*, LVI, 1969, 641–87.

Mancini Barbieri, A. "Nuove ricerche sulla presenza straniera nell'esercito pontifico," *Rassegna storica del Risorgimento*, LXXIII, 1986, 161–86.

Marraro, H. R. *Canadian and American Zouaves in the Papal Army*, Toronto, 1945.

Martin, J. "Pie IX et monseigneur de Mérode," *Pio IX*, 1975, 3–27.

Martina, G. *Pio IX*, Rome, 1974–90, 3 vols.

Maurain, J. *La politique ecclésiastique du Second Empire de 1852 à 1869*, Paris, 1930.

Mehier de Mathuisieux, H. *Historie des zouaves pontificaux*, Tours, 1913.

Régiment des zouaves pontificaux. Liste des zouaves ayant fait partie du régiment du 1er janvier 1861 au 20 septembre 1870, Lille, 1910–20, 2 vols.

Trinquier, J. "Le Rouergue et les zouaves pontificaux," *Revue du Rouergue*, 1986, 1–24.

Vigevano, A. *La fine dell'esercito pontificio*, Rome, 1920.

Chronological List of Popes

Peter, *30–64*

Linus, *64 (?)–76 (?)*

Anacletus, *76 (?)–88 (?)*

Clement I, *88 (?)–97 (?)*

Evaristus, *97 (?)–105 (?)*

Alexander I, *105 (?)–115 (?)*

Sixtus I, *115 (?)–125 (?)*

Telesphorus, *125 (?)–136 (?)*

Hyginus, *136 (?)–140 (?)*

Pius I, *140 (?)–155 (?)*

Anicetus, *155 (?)–166 (?)*

Soter, *166 (?)–175 (?)*

Eleutherius, *175 (?)–189 (?)*

Victor I, *189 (?)–199*

Zephyrinus, *199–217 (18 years)*

Callistus I, *217–222 (5 years)*

[Hippolytus], *217–235*

Urban I, *222–230 (8 years)*

Pontian, *21 July 230–28 September 235 (5 years, 2 months)*

Anteros, *21 November 235–3 January 236 (6 weeks)*

Fabian, *10 January 236–20 January 250 (4 years, 10 days)*

Cornelius, *March 251–June 253 (2 years 3 months)*

[Novatian], *251*

Lucius I, *25 June 253–8 March 254 (8 1/2 months)*

Stephen I, *12 May 254–2 August 257 (3 years, 2 1/2 months)*

Sixtus II, *30 August 257–6 August 258 (11 months, 1 week)*

Dionysius, *22 July 259–26 December 268 (9 years, 5 months)*

Felix I, *5 January 269–30 December 274 (6 years)*

Eutychian, *4 January 275–7 December 283 (8 years, 11 months)*

Gaius, *17 December 283–22 April 296 (12 years, 4 months)*

Marcellinus, *30 June 296–25 October 304 (8 years, 4 months)*

Marcellus I, *27 May 308–16 January 309 (7 1/2 months)*

Eusebius, *18 April 309–17 August 309 (4 months)*

Miltiades or Melchiades, *2 July 311–11 January 314 (2 years, 6 months, 1 week)*

Silvester I, *31 January 314 –31 December 335 (21 years, 11 months)*

Mark, *18 January 336–7 October 336 (8 months, 3 weeks)*

Julius I, *6 February 337–12 April 352 (15 years, 2 months)*

Liberius, *17 May 352–24 September 366 (6 years, 4 months)*

[Felix II], *355–22 November 365*

Damasus I, *1 October 366–11 December 384 (18 years, 2 months, 10 days)*

[Ursinus], *366–367*

Siricius, *December 384–26 November 399 (14 years, 11 months)*

Anastasius I, *23 November 399 –19 December 401 (2 years, 1 month)*

Innocent I, *22 December 401–12 March 417 (15 years, 2 months, 3 weeks)*

Zosimus, *18 March 417–26 December 418 (1 year, 9 1/2 months)*

Boniface I, *28 or 29 December 418–4 September 422 (3 years, 8 months, 1 week)*

[Eulalius], *27 or 29 December 418–419*

Celestine I, *10 September 422–27 July 432 (9 years, 10 1/2 months)*

Sixtus III, *31 July 432–19 August 440 (8 years, 3 weeks)*

Leo I (the Great), *29 September 440–10 November 461 (21 years, 6 weeks)*

Hilarus, *19 November 461–29 February 468 (6 years, 3 months, 10 days)*

Simplicius, *3 March 483–10 March 483 (15 years)*

Felix III, *13 March 483–1 March 492 (8 years, 11 months, 20 days)*

Gelasius I, *1 March 492–21 November 496 (4 years, 8 months, 3 wks)*

Anastasius II, *24 November 496–19 November 498 (2 years)*

Symmachus, *22 November 498–19 July 514 (15 years, 8 months)*

[Lawrence], *498–501*

Hormisdas, *20 July 514 –6 August 523 (9 years, 15 days)*

John I, *15 August 523–18 May 526 (2 years, 9 months)*

Felix IV, *12 July 526–22 September 530 (4 years, 2 months, 10 days)*

Boniface II, *22 September 530–17 October 4532 (2 years, 1 month)*

[Dioscorus], *22 September 530–14 October 530*

John II, *2 January 533–8 May 535 (2 years, 4 months)*

Agapitus, *13 May 535–22 April 536 (11 months, 1 week)*

Silverius, *1 June 536 –11 November 537 (2 December 537) (1 year, 5 months, 10 days)*

Vigilius, *29 March 537–7 June 555 (18 years, 2 months, 1 week)*

Pelagius I, *16 April 556–4 March 561 (4 years, 11 1/2 months)*

John III, *17 July 561–13 July 574 (13 years)*

Benedict I, *2 June 575–30 July 579 (4 years, 2 months)*

Pelagius II, *26 November 579–7 February 590 (10 years, 2 months, 10 days)*

Gregory I (the Great), *3 September 590–12 March 604 (13 years, 6 1/2 months)*

Sabinian, *13 September 604–22 February 606 (1 year, 5 months, 10 days)*

Boniface III, *19 February 607–12 November 6 or 7 (9 months)*

Boniface IV, *25 August 608–8 May 615 (6 years, 8 1/2 months)*

Adeodatus I (Deusdedit), *19 October 615–8 November 618 (3 years, 3 weeks)*

Boniface V, *23 December 619–10 June 625 (5 years, 10 months)*

Honorius I, *27 October 625–12 October 638 (13 years)*

Severinus, *28 May 640–12 October 640 (2 months)*

John IV, *24 November 640–12 October 642 (1 year, 9 months, 3 weeks)*

Theodore I, *24 December 642–14 May 649 (6 years, 5 months, 3 weeks)*

Martin I, *July 649 –16 September 655 (6 years, 3 months)*

Eugene I, *10 August 654 –2 June 657 (2 years, 9 months, 3 weeks)*

Vitalian, *30 July 657–27 January 672 (14 1/2 years)*

Adeodatus II, *11 April 672–17 June 676 (4 years, 2 months)*

Donus, *2 November 676–11 April 678 (1 year, 5 months, 10 days)*

Agatho, *27 June 678–10 January 681 (2 years, 6 1/2 months)*

Leo II, *17 August 682–3 July 683 (10 1/2 months)*

Benedict II, *26 June 684–8 May 685 (10 months, 10 days)*

John V, *23 July 685–2 August 686 (1 year, 10 days)*

Conon, *21 October 686–21 September 687 (11 months)*

[Theodore], *687*

[Paschal], *687*

Sergius I, *15 December 687–8 September 701 (13 years, 9 months, 3 weeks)*

John VI, *30 October 701–11 January 705 (3 years, 2 months, 10 days)*

John VII, *1 March 705–18 October 707 (2 years, 7 1/2 months)*

Sisinnius, *15 January, 708– 4 February 708 (20 days)*

Constantine, 25 March *7 or 8 –9 April 715 (7 years, 15 days)*

Gregory II, *18 March 715–11 February 731 (15 years, 8 months, 3 weeks)*

Gregory III, *18 March 731–November 741 (10 years, 8 months)*

Zacharias, *10 December 741–22 March 752 (11 years, 3 months, 10 days)*

(Stephen II, *died 3 days after his election, before even being ordained bishop, therefore not considered pope*)

Paul I, *29 May 757–28 June 767 (10 years, 1 month)*

[Constantine], *28 June 767–5 July 767*

[Philip], *31 July 767 (resigned the same day)*

Stephen III, *1 August 768 –24 January 772 (3 years, 5 months, 3 weeks)*

Hadrian I, *1 February 772–25 December 795 (23 years, 11 months)*

Leo III, *26 December 795–12 June 816 (20 years, 5 1/2 months)*

Stephen IV, *22 June 816–24 January 816 (7 months)*

Paschal I, *25 January 817–11 February 824 (7 years, 15 days)*

Eugene II, *11 May 824–August 827 (3 years, 3 months)*

Valentine, *August–September 827 (5 weeks)*

Gregory IV, *827–January 844 (16 years)*

[John], *January 844*

Sergius II, *January 844–27 January 847 (3 years)*

Leo IV, *1 April 847–17 July 855 (8 years, 4 1/2 months)*

Benedict III, *29 September 855–17 April 858 (2 years, 6 months, 18 days)*

[Anastasius Bibliothecarius], *August–September 855 (d. 880)*

Nicholas I (the Great), *24 April 858–13 November 867 (9 years, 6 months, 17 days)*

Hadrian II, *14 December 867–14 December 872 (5 years)*

John VIII, *14 December 872–16 December 882 (10 years)*

Marinus I, *16 December 882–15 May 884 (1 year, 5 months)*

Hadrian III, *17 May 84–November 885 (18 months)*

Stephen V, *November 885–14 September 891 (5 years, 10 months)*

Formosus, *6 October 891–4 April 896 (4 years, 5 months)*

Boniface VI, *April 896*

Stephen VI, *May 896–August 897 (15 months)*

Romanus, *August–November 897 (3 months)*

Theodore II, *December 897 (20 days)*

John IX, *January 898–January 900 (2 years)*

Benedict IV, 1 *February 900–July 903 (3 years, 5 months)*

Leo V, *July–September 903 (3 months)*

[Christopher], *August 903–January 904*

Sergius III, *29 January 904 –14 April 911 (7 years, 2 1/2 months)*

Anastasius III, April *911–June 913 (2 years, 2 months)*

Lando, *July 913–February 914 (6 months, 10 days)*

John X, *March 914–May 928 (14 years, 2 months)*

Leo VI, *May–December 928 (7 months)*

Stephen VII, *May 928–February 931 (2 years, 8 months)*

John XI, *March 931–December 935 (4 years, 9 months)*

Leo VII, *3 January 936 –13 July 939 (3 1/2 years)*

Stephen VIII, *14 July 939–October 942 (3 years, 3 months)*

Marinus II, *30 October 942–May 946 (3 1/2 years)*

Agapitus II, *10 May 946–December 955 (9 years, 7 months)*

John XII, *16 December 955–14 May 964 (8 years, 5 months)*

Leo VIII, *4 December 963–1 March 965 (15 months)*

Benedict V, *22 May 964 –4 July 966 (2 years, 6 weeks)*

John XIII, *1 October 965–6 September 972 (6 years, 11 months, 1 week)*

Benedict VI, *19 January 973 –June 974 (17 months)*

[Boniface VII], *June–July 974 and August 984–July 985*

Benedict VII, *October 974–10 July 983 (8 years, 9 months)*

John XIV, *December 983–20 August 984 (8 months)*

John XV, *August 985–March 996 (10 years, 8 months)*

Gregory V, *3 May 996–18 February 999 (2 years, 9 1/2 months)*

[John XVI], *April 997–February 998 (10 months)*

Silvester II, *2 April 999–12 May 1003 (4 years, 1 month, 10 days)*

John XVII, *June–December 1003 (6 months)*

John XVIII, *January 1004–July 1009 (5 1/2 years)*

Sergius IV, *31 July 1009–12 May 1012 (2 years, 9 1/2 months)*

Benedict VIII, *18 May 1012–9 April 1024 (11 years, 10 months, 3 weeks)*

[Gregory], *1012*

John XIX, *14 May 1024–1032 (8 years)*

Benedict IX, *1032–1044 (12 years)*

Silvester III, *20 January 1045–10 February 1045 (3 weeks)*

Benedict IX (second time), *10 April 1045–1 May 1045 (3 weeks)*

Gregory VI, *5 May 1045–20 December 1046 (7 1/2 months)*

Clement II, *24 December 1046–9 October 1047 (9 1/2 months)*

Damasus II, *17 July 1048–9 August 1048 (22 days)*

Leo IX, *12 February 1049–9 April 1054 (5 years, 2 months)*

Victor II, *16 April 1055–28 July 1057 (2 years, 3 months, 10 days)*

Stephen IX, *3 August 1057–29 March 1058 (8 months)*

[Benedict X], *5 April 1058–24 January 1059*

Nicholas II, *24 January 1059–27 July 1061 (2 1/2 years)*

Alexander II, *1 October 1061–21 April 1073 (11 years, 5 months, 3 weeks)*

[Honorius II], *28 October 1061–1072*

Gregory VII, *22 April 1073–25 May 1085 (12 years, 1 month)*

[Clement III], *1080–1084 (8 September 1100)*

Victor III, *24 May 1086–16 September 1087 (16 months)*

Urban II, *12 March 1088 –29 July 1099 (11 years, 4 months, 10 days)*

Paschal II, *13 August 1099–21 January 1118 (18 years, 5 months, 1 week)*

[Theoderic], *1100 (d. 1102)*

[Albert], *1102*

[Silvester IV], *1105–1111*

Gelasius II, *24 January 1118–28 January 1119 (1 year)*

[Gregory VIII], *1118–1121*

Callistus II, *2 November 1119–13 December 1124 (5 years, 5 weeks)*

Honorius II, *21 December 1124–13 February 1130 (5 years, 1 month, 23 days)*

[Celestine II], *1124*

Innocent II, *14 February 1130–24 September 1143 (13 years, 7 months, 10 days)*

[Anacletus II], *1130–1138*

[Victor IV], *1138*

Celestine II, *26 September 1143–8 March 1144 (5 months, 1 week)*

Lucius II, *12 March 1144–15 February 1145 (11 months)*

Eugene III, *15 February 1145–8 July 1153 (8 years, 4 months, 3 weeks)*

Anastasius IV, *12 July 1153–3 December 1154 (1 year, 5 months)*

Hadrian IV, *4 December 1154–1 September 1159 (4 years, 9 months)*

Alexander III, *7 September 1159 –30 August 1181 (21 years, 11 months, 1 week)*

[Victor IV], *1159–1164*

[Paschal III], *1164 –1168*

[Callistus III], 1168–1178

[Innocent III], *1179 –1180*

Lucius III, *1 September 1181–25 September 1185 (4 years, 3 weeks)*

Urban III, *25 November 1185–20 October 1187 (23 months)*

Gregory VIII, *21 October 1187–17 December 1187 (2 months)*

Clement III, *19 December 1187–March 1191 (3 years)*

Celestine III, *30 March 1191–8 January 1198 (6 years, 9 months, 1 week)*

Innocent III, *8 January 1198–16 July 1216 (18 years, 6 months, 1 week)*

Honorius III, *18 July 1216–18 March 1227 (10 years, 8 months)*

Gregory IX, *19 March 1227–22 August 1241 (14 years, 5 months)*

Celestine IV, *25 October 1241–10 November 1241 (16 days)*

Innocent IV, *25 June 1243–7 December 1254 (11 years, 5 1/2 months)*

Alexander IV, *12 December 1254–25 May 1261 (6 years, 5 months, 3 wks)*

Urban IV, *29 August 1261–2 October 1264 (3 years, 1 month)*

Clement IV, *5 February 1265–29 November 1268 (3 years, 10 months)*

Gregory X, *21 November 1271–10 January 1276 (5 years)*

Innocent V, *21 January 1276–22 June 1276 (5 months)*

Hadrian V, *11 July 1276 –18 August 1276 (5 weeks)*

John XXI, *8 September 1276–20 May 1277 (8 months, 3 weeks)*

Nicholas III, *25 November 1277–22 August 1280 (2 years, 9 months)*

Martin IV, *22 February 1281–28 March 1285 (4 years, 1 month)*

Honorius IV, *2 April 1285–3 April 1287 (2 years)*

Nicholas IV, *22 February 1288 –4 April 1292 (4 years, 1 1/2 months)*

Celestine V, *5 July 1294–13 December 1294 (d. 19 May 1296) (5 months)*

Boniface VIII, *24 December 1294–11 October 1303 (8 years, 1 month, 3 weeks)*

Benedict XI, *22 October 1303–7 July 1304 (7 1/2 months)*

Clement V, *5 June 1305–20 April 1314 (8 years 10 1/2 months)*

John XXII, *7 August 1316 –4 December 1334 (18 years, 4 months)*

[Nicholas V], *1328–1330 (d. 1333)*

Benedict XII, *20 December 1334–25 April 1342 (7 years, 4 months)*

Clement VI, *7 May 1342–6 December 1352 (10 years, 7 months)*

Innocent VI, *18 December 1352–12 September 1362 (9 years, 9 months)*

Urban V, *28 September 1362–19 December 1370 (8 years, 2 months, 3 weeks)*

Gregory XI, *30 December 1370–26 March 1378 (7 years, 3 months)*

Urban VI, *18 April 1378–15 October 1389 (11 years, 8 months)*

Boniface IX, *2 November 1389–1 October 1404 (14 years, 11 months)*

Innocent VII, *17 October 1404–6 November 1406 (2 years, 3 weeks)*

Gregory XII, *30 November 1406–4 July 1415 (d. 18 October 1417) (8 years, 8 months)*

[Clement VII], *20 September 1378–16 September 1394*

[Benedict XIII], *28 September 1394–23 May 1423*

[Alexander V], *26 June 1409–3 May 1410*

[John XXIII], *17 May 1410–29 May 1415, deposed on that day by Council of Constance (d. 22 November 1418)*

Martin V, *14 November 1417–20 February 1431 (13 years, 3 months)*

Eugene IV, *3 March 1431–23 March 1447 (16 years)*

[Felix V], *5 November 1439–7 April 1449 (d. 7 January 1451)*

Nicholas V, *6 March 1447–24 March 1455 (8 years, 15 days)*

Callistus III, *8 April 1455–6 August 1458 (3 years, 4 months)*

Pius II, *19 August 1458–15 August 1464 (6 years)*

Paul II, *30 August 1464–26 July 1471 (6 years, 11 months)*

Sixtus IV, *9 August 1471–12 August 1484 (13 years)*

Innocent VIII, *29 August 1484–25 July 1492 (7 years, 11 months)*

Alexander VI, *11 August 1492–18 August 1503 (11 years)*

Pius III, *22 September 1503–18 October 1503 (25 days)*

Julius II, *31 October 1503–21 February 1513 (9 years, 3 months, 3 weeks)*

Leo X, *9 March 1513–1 December 1521 (8 years, 8 months, 3 weeks)*

Hadrian VI, *9 January 1522–14 September 1523 (20 1/2 months)*

Clement VII, *19 November 1523–25 September 1534 (10 years, 10 months)*

Paul III, *13 October 1534–10 November 1549 (15 years, 1 month)*

Julius III, *7 February 1550–23 March 1555 (5 years, 6 weeks)*

Marcellus II, *9 April 1555–1 May 1555 (3 weeks)*

Paul IV, *23 May 1555–18 August 1559 (4 years, 3 months)*

Pius IV, *28 December 1559–9 December 1565 (5 years, 11 months, 10 days)*

Pius V, *7 January 1566–1 May 1572 (6 years, 4 months)*

Gregory XIII, *13 May 157 2–10 April 1585 (12 years, 11 months)*

Sixtus V, *24 April 1585–27 August 1590 (5 years, 4 months)*

Urban VII, *15–27 September 1590 (12 days)*

Gregory XIV, *5 December 1590–16 October 1591 (10 months, 10 days)*

Innocent IX, *29 October 1591–30 December 1591 (2 months)*

Clement VIII, *30 January 1592–3 March 1605 (13 years, 1 month)*

Leo XI, *1–27 April 1605 (26 days)*

Paul V, *16 May 1605–28 January 1621 (15 years, 8 1/2 months)*

Gregory XV, *9 February 1621–8 July 1623 (29 months)*

Urban VIII, *6 August 1623–29 July 1644 (21 years)*

Innocent X, *15 September 1644–7 January 1655 (10 years, 3 months, 3 weeks)*

Alexander VII, *7 April 1655–22 May 1667 (12 years)*

Clement IX, *20 June 1667 0 9 December 1669 (2 1/2 years)*

Clement X, *29 April 1670–22 July 1676 (6 years, 3 months)*

Innocent XI, *21 September 1676–12 August 1689 (13 years)*

Alexander VIII, *6 September 1689–1 February 1691 (16 months)*

Innocent XII, *12 July 1691–27 September 1700 (9 years, 2 months)*

Clement XI, *23 November 1700–19 March 1721 (20 years, 4 months)*

Innocent XIII, *8 May 1721–7 March 1724 (2 years, 10 months)*

Benedict XIII, *29 May 1724–21 February 1730 (5 years, 9 months)*

Clement XII, *12 July 1730–6 February 1740 (9 1/2 years)*

Benedict XIV, *17 August 1740–3 May 1758 (17 years, 9 months)*

Clement XIII, *6 July 1758–2 February 1769 (10 years, 7 months)*
Clement XIV, *19 May 1769–22 September 1774 (5 years, 4 months)*
Pius VI, *15 February 1775–29 August 1799 (24 ½ years)*
Pius VII, *14 March 1800–20 August 1823 (23 years, 5 months)*
Leo XII, *28 September 1823–10 February 1829 (5 years, 4 months)*
Pius VIII, *31 March 1829–30 November 1830 (20 months)*
Gregory XVI, *2 February 1831–1 June 1846 (15 years, 4 months)*
Pius IX, *16 June 1846–7 February 1878 (31 years, 7 months)*
Leo XIII, *20 February 1878–20 July 1903 (25 years, 5 months)*
Pius X, *4 August 1903–20 Aug, 1914 (11 years)*
Benedict XV, *3 September 1914–22 January 1922 (7 years, 5 months)*
Pius XI, *6 February 1922–10 February 1939 (17 years)*
Pius XII, *2 March 1939–9 October 1958 (19 years, 8 months)*
John XXIII, *20 October 1958–3 June 1963 (4 years, 7 months)*
Paul VI, *21 June 1963–6 August 1978 (15 years, 2 months)*
John Paul I, *26 August 1978–28 September 1978 (1 month, 2 days)*
John Paul II, *6 October 1978–*

Martyred Popes

Names of popes whose martyrdom is uncertain or dubious are printed in italics.

Peter, ca. 64. Rome; Nero's persecution.

The martyrdom of all the popes from Linus (78) to Sixtus I (ca. 125), obligatory territory for hagiographical legend, is uncertain.

Telesphorus, ca. 235. Martyrdom attested by Irenaeus of Lyon a half century later.

The martyrdom of all the popes from Pius I (ca. 155) to Urban I (230) is uncertain.

Pontian, 235. Died deported to Sardinia at the same time as the antipope Hippolytus and after abdicating; persecution of Alexander Severus.

Anterus, 236.

Fabian, 250. Rome; Decian persecution.

The martyrdom of the popes from Cornelius (253) to Stephen I (257) is uncertain.

Sixtus II, 258. Rome; Valerian's persecution.

The martyrdom of the popes from Dionysius to Marcellinus (304) is uncertain.

Eusebius, 310.

John I, 523–526.

Silverus, 536. Classed as a martyr (Eastern Church) because deported by Justinian.

Martin I, 649–655.

Popes Who Are Saints

Names of popes who do not appear today in the Roman Proper are in italics.

From Peter to Gelasius I (492–496), all the popes are saints.

Gregory I, 590–604. Confessor and doctor; venerated from his death. About fifty years after death his tomb was moved to St. Peter's cathedral and placed beneath an altar dedicated to him. His name was added to the Hieronymian martyrology by the end of the 7th century.

Boniface IV, 619–625. Confessor. His cult was promoted by his homonymous successor Boniface VIII (1294–1303), who uncovered his tomb.

Adeodatus I (Deusdedit), 615–618. Included in the Roman Martyrology by Baronius (16th century).

Martin I, 649–653. Last pope celebrated as a martyr. His cult, also developed in the East, predates Ado's martyrology (9th century), which changes the date of his feast under the influence of that of St. Martin of Tours.

Eugene I, 654–657. Included in Roman Martyrology by Baronius (16th century).

Vitalian, 657–672. Included in Roman Martyrology by Baronius (16th century).

Agatho, 678–681. His cult, which is ancient, is also attested in Constantinople.

Leo II, 682–683. Confessor. His cult, attested in the martyrologies of Bede (8th century) and Ado (9th century), may derive from shifting of one of feasts of Leo I (the Great). In any event, as with his homonym Leo III, it grew after Paschal II arranged for his remains to be transferred and combined with those of Leo I. His name no longer appears on Roman Proper or calendar of the universal Church.

Benedict II, 684–685. His cult, which is ancient, is attested in Ado's martyrology (9th century).

Sergius I, 687–701. Early cult attested in Willibrord's calendar (8th century) and Ado's martyrology (9th century).

Gregory II, 715–731. Cult attested in Ado's martyrology (9th century).

Gregory III, 731–741. Cult attested in Ado's martyrology (9th century).

Zacharias, 741–752. Confessor. Cult appears to be ancient.

Paul I, 757–767. Cult not attested until the 14th century. Pope's name included in martyrologies in 15th and 16th centuries (Baronius).

Leo III, 795–816. Object of ancient local cults (Brittany from the 10th century; see the entry on Leo II above) that developed in the 14th century, Leo III was included in the Roman Martyrology in 1673. His name was removed from Roman Proper in 1963.

Paschal I, 817–824. Listed in the Roman martyrology by Baronius (16th century). His name was removed from Roman Proper in 1963.

Leo IV, 847–855. Cult developed after his remains were moved during papacy of Paschal II. Listed in Roman Martyrology, he was removed from the Roman Proper in 1963.

Nicholas I, 858–867. Cult attested from 868 in the West and 869–870 in the East, but pope's name is not included in the Roman Martyrology until 1930.

Hadrian III, 884–885. Local cult (diocese of Modena), confirmed in 1891.

Leo IX, 1049–1054. Confessor. His cult, virtually immediate, was recognized by Victor III in 1087 when his remains were transferred and was attested at Toul (France) in 1091. In 1762 the city of Benevento adopted him as protector.

Gregory VII, 1073–1085. Confessor. Clergy favoring Gregorian reform reported several miracles over his tomb in Salerno, and the Norman Hugh de Flavigny named him martyr and confessor. However, this does not constitute proof of a special cult of the pope. His real "rediscoverers" were the Protestant polemicists who condemned his anti-imperial actions. His cult developed as a reaction (two recognitions of his tomb, in 1578 and 1605, one translation in 1614). The pope was beatified in 1584 and canonized in 1606. A Proper of the saint was granted to the church of Salerno in 1609, and to the Cistercians in 1705 (similarly, Proper lectiones in 1673 to Vallombreuse, who managed for a time to pass off the pope as a member of the order). His feast was extended to the whole of Christianity in 1728, despite protests of the Gallican church. In a final metamorphosis, the pope became a symbol of Roman centralization, and as late as 1810 the French minister of cults of the empire asked Italian bishops to follow the example of their French colleagues by omitting Gregory VII's name during the mass.

Victor III, 1086–1987. Blessed. His cult, which is local (Monte Cassino), was confirmed in 1887.

Urban II, 1088–1099. Blessed and confessor. Cult confirmed in 1881.

Eugene III, 1145–1153. Blessed. Beatified in 1872 (cult considered immemorial by Benedictines and Cistercians).

Gregory X, 1271–1276. Blessed. His cult, which is local (his birthplace of Piacenza, also Arezzo, Liège and Lyon), was confirmed in 1713 as immemorial and he was listed in Roman Martyrology by Benedict XIV.

Innocent V, 1276. Blessed, doctor *spectabilis*. Beatified in 1898, he was included in Roman and Dominican Propers.

Celestine V, 1294. Confessor. Canonized in 1313 under the name Peter Celestine; however, the king of France, enemy of Boniface VIII, was not able to have him recognized as a martyr.

After 1294, Pius X (1903–1914) is the only pope who is a saint.

Index

Page numbers in **boldface** indicate entry titles. Antipopes are shown in [brackets].

A quo primum (1751 encyclical), 170

Abbo of Fleury-sur-Loire, 65, 592, 646, 843, 1043, 1421; canonical collection, 224, 225

abbreviator, **1**, 293, 451

abdications, papal. *See* resignations, papal; *specific popes*

Abdul Mejid, Ottoman sultan, 711

Abelard, Peter, 701, 1543; apologetics, 76; Bernard of Clairvaux and, 275, 276, 277, 450; consistory confirmation of trial of, 414; Curia as doctrinal arbitrator and, 450

Abercius, 1164

abortion, 1150

About, Edmond, 756

absolution: indulgences and, 775; for medicinal penalty, 1149; Penitentiary and, 1523–1524; Pius VI and, 1179; for plague victims, 1221; reserved cases, 1298

absolutism: *auctoritas* doctrine vs., 21; Boniface VIII as last defender of, 191; Counter Reformation and, 704, 1109; *Defensor pacis* against, 131–132; Dominicans and, 510; Donation of Constantine and, 103; Gregory VII on, 650–651; Gregory XVI and, 670, 671; Innocent III *plenitudo potestatis* philosophy, 786; liberalism vs., 943–944; monarchical, 93–94, 803; over Rome, 103; papism and, 1109; Paul II and, 1121; Pius V and, 1176; Sixtus V and, 1437; Urban VIII and, 1560–1561, 1562

Abyssinian Church, 664

Acacian schism (484–519), 35, 44, 48, 49, 200–201, 564, 621–622; ending of, 502, 573; Felix III and, 572–573; Simplicius and, 1425

Acacius, patriarch of Constantinople, 44, 200, 563–564, 622, 737, 1391; Felix III reciprocal excommunication, 572; Simplicius and, 1426; Sixtus III and, 1432

academies, pontifical, **1–2**, 171, 1206; artists in Rome, 118–121; list of, 2

Academy of France, 101, 118–119, 121, 304, 1345

Academy of Rome, 1435

Academy of St. Luke. *See* Accademia di San Luca

Academy of St. Thomas Aquinas, 2

Academy of Sciences, 2, 498, 1206, 1562

Academy of Social Sciences, 2

Acadius of Constantinople, 1426

Acarius. *See* Curia

Accademia dei Lincei. *See* Academy of Sciences

Accademia del nudo (Rome), 120

Accademia di San Luca (Rome), 118, 119–120, 1092–1093, 1117, 1269

Acciaiuoli, Angelo, 192, 359

Acciaiuoli banks, 82, 137

Acción Cultural Popular (Colombia), 1515

Accotti, Benedetto, 345

"Achilles' Shield," 1022

Achilleus of Spoleto, 184, 1164, 1165

Acholius of Thessalonica, 1611

Acquasparta, Matteo d', 280

Acre, 439, 501; siege and fall of (1290–1291), 440, 722, 988, 989, 1028, 1039

Acta Sanctae Sedis (later *Acta Apostolicae Sedis*; newspaper), 228, 1236

Action Française, 512, 614, 1198, 1205, 1208, 1236

Acton, Lord, 1568

Acts of Paul, 3, 631

Acts of Peter, **2–4**, 947, 1160

Acts of the Apostles, 2–4, 554, 696, 1617; on Antioch, 69; on papal office development, 1244; on Paul, 1117, 1118, 1119, 1372; on Peter, 1157, 1158

Acuto, Giovanni. *See* Hawkwood, Sir John

Ad Beatissimi (1914 encyclical), 173

"ad limina" visits, **4–5**, 465, 503, 992, 1167, 1304, 1512, 1566; Gregory VII initiation, 1245, 1283; *pallium* and, 1608; Sacred College and, 1356

Adalberon of Laon, 1485

Adalbert (antipope). *See* [Albert]

Adalbert, archbishop of Mayence, 732

Adalbert-Atto (builder of Canossa fortress), 237, 238

Adaldag Hamburg-Bremen, 155

Adam, Robert, 120

Adam's sin, 429, 1520

Adar, Gustave, 175

Adelaide, dowager queen of Italy, 237

Adelchis, king of the Lombards, 957

Adenauer, Konrad, 309

Adeodatus I, **5–6**, 187, 495, 736, 940, 1111, 1551; oldest known bull by, 195

Adeodatus II, **6**

Adhemar de Monteil, 112

ADLV. *See* Vatican labor union

Administration for the Patrimony of the Apostolic See, 583–584

administration, papal, **6–8**; apostolic constitutions and, 421; Avignon papacy's legacy, 130; cardinal nephew role in, 245, 1341; career and, 247–248; Clement VIII centralization of, 347; consistory, 413–416; Damasus I development of, 479; Fabian's early organization of, 557; Gregory I skills in, 639, 640; Gregory XIII centralization of, 664; Gregory XVI reform edict, 672–673; Palatine application, 1094–1095; Paul II bureaucratic reforms, 1122; Roman government and, 1341; Secretariat of State duties, 1403–1404; Sixtus V reforms, 1437, *See also* congregations, Roman; Curia; dicastery; Sacred College

administrative offices, Roman, **8–12**; *Annuario pontificio* (directory), 12, 62–63; Apostolic Camera, 80–84, *See also* camerlengo; chamberlain; chancellors and vice-chancellors; Chancery, papal

Adolph of Nassau, 190

Adoptionism (theological doctrine), 599, 681, 698, 701, 1550, 1640; Victor I action against, 1612

Adrian. *See* Hadrian

adultery, 1249

Advent, 194, 210, 295

Aelfric of Canterbury, 646

Aelurus of Alexandria, 44

Aeneas, 441

Volume Key: Volume 1, pages 1–614; volume 2, pages 615–1266; volume 3, pages 1267–1637.

1659

Aetius, 699

"Affair of the Ambassadors," 350–351

Affairs of Regulars, Congregation for the, 1438

Affre of Paris, 954

Africa and the papacy, 13; Agapitus I and, 14; Anastasius I and, 43; apologetists, 75; barbarian invasions, 140, 545, 572; bishop of Carthage authority, 250; bishops' conferences, 401, 404–405; Boniface I policy and, 184, 185; Byzantium and, 1318; canonical collections, 231; Celestine I and, 273; concordats, 398, 399, 400; Donatist heresy, 13, 698, 993, 1418; evangelization, 410, 544, 545; Felix III and, 572; Gregory I and, 640; Gregory XIII and, 664; Gregory XVI and, 675; Innocent I and, 783, 1641; John II and, 833; John XXIII and, 853; John Paul II special synods of bishops, 1479; John Paul II tours of, 1510, 1512; Julian the Apostate and, 882; legates and, 908; Leo I and, 915, 917; minor basilica, 144; missions, 664, 1004, 1130, 1343; monasticism, 1011; Novatian and, 1055, 1394; papal patrimony and, 576; papal primacy and, 1108; Paul VI travels in, 1515–1516; Pelagianism and, 251, 1147, 1641; provincial councils, 430; Roman medieval Church in, 156; Roman persecutions in, 966, 1155 (*see also lapsi* controversy); schism, 1147, 1394, 1617; Sixtus III and, 1432; slave trade, 1439, 1440; station and, 1453; Stephen I and, 1431, 1455; Symmachus and, 1476; synod (1994), 144; Three Chapters and, 1147, 1617; Vandal control, 915, 1318; Vatican I and, 1566; Vatican II representation, 1143, 1575, 1576, 1577, 1578, 1580, 1583; Vigilius and, 1618; Zosimus and, 1641–1642, *See also* Alexandria; Carthage; Egypt; North Africa; *specific countries*

Agagianian, Cardinal, 368, 370, 854, 1574

Against the Galileans (Julian the Apostate), 882

Agapitus I, **13–15**, 35, 141, 503, 1019; Arianism and, 833; Byzantium and, 14–15, 198, 201, 564; death and burial of, 1497; legates of, 909; Pelagius I and, 74, 1145; Vigilius and, 1616

Agapitus II, **15–16**, 840, 1497; Dioscorus rehabilitation by, 71

Agatha of Catania, St., 1391

Agatho, **16–17**, 153, 202, 429, 835

Agça, Ali, 123

Age of Lights. *See* Enlightenment

Ageltrude, 1460

Agilulf, king of the Lombards, 142, 187, 957, 1047

Agliardi, Antonio, 364

Agnadello, battle of (1509), 271, 885, 898

Agnellus, 1047, 1411–1412

Agnes, St., 24, 1012, 1019, 1156

Agnes, Mario, 1083–1084, 1164

Agnes of Poitou (regent), 17, 18, 159, 328, 648, 731, 1461

Agobard of Lyon, 223, 615, 870–871

Agony and the Ecstasy, The (film), 322, 323

Agostini, Philippe, 322–323

Agricola, Filippo, 1125, 1372–1373

Agrippa of Augigné, 67, 1095

Agrippina, 1374, 1594

Aguati, 1022

Agucchi, 1090, 1093

Ailly, Pierre d', 164, 213, 242, 777; conciliarism treatise, 390

Aimeric, 42, 275, 276, 732–733, 783, 784, 959

Aistulf, king of the Lombards, 1120, 1273, 1354, 1456, 1457, 1639

Aix-la-chapelle, Peace of (1748), 170

Alaleone, Paolo, 285

Alanus Anglicus, 390

Alaric, king of Visigoths, 75, 140, 260, 781, 1046, 1318, 1327

Albani, Alessandro, 361, 672, 1092, 1117, 1191, 1270, 1598

Albani family, 694, 931, 1090

Albani, Giovanni Francesco. *See* Clement XI

Albania, 638, 787, 1084, 1122

Albergati, Niccolò, 911, 1040, 1171

Alberic II of Spoleto, 15, 122, 225, 226, 922, 970, 1097, 1332, 1460

Alberico, Gregory di, 159

Alberoni, Giulio, 353, 354

[Albert] (Adalbert), **17**, 70, 72, 1112, 1423

Albert of Austria, 190

Albert of Bavaria, 170

Albert of Brabant, 278

Albert of Brandenburg, 927, 1286, 1287

Albert of Pisa, 593

Albert of Prague, 843

Alberti, Aldo, 761

Alberti banks, 82, 136, 137

Alberti, Giovanni and Cherubino, 1269

Alberti, Leon Battista, 104, 107, 255, 1594

Alberti, Nicolas, 508

Albertus Magnus (Albert the Great), 774, 847, 1204

Albigensian crusade, 127, 702, 787–788, 989–990

Albigensian heresy, 702, 787, 897

Albinus, Caecina, 331, 831, 940, 1045

Albizzi, F., 29, 823, 824

Alboin, king of the Lombards, 957

Albornoz, Gil de, 1, 110, 129, 132, 801, 1028, 1048, 1556; cross and keys emblems, 689; expenses of campaigns, 795; legation of, 911; papal lands reorganization, 1101, 1102; political skills of, 796; Roman political organization and, 1338

Albrecht. *See* Albert

Alcalá, University of, 1544

Alcántara Order, 989

Alcazar, Luis de, 68

Aldobrandini, Cinzio Passeri, 347

Aldobrandini family, 247, 667, 1032, 1130; Curia nepotism and, 466; painting collection, 1090, 1092

Aldobrandini, Gian Francesco, 347

Aldobrandini, Giovanni Giorgio, 668

Aldobrandini, Ippolito. *See* Clement VIII

Aldobrandini, Olimpia, 801

Aldobrandini, Pietro, 297, 347, 668, 1129, 1130; painting collection, 1091, 1092

Aldrovandi (prodatory), 168–169, 170, 469

Alessandri, Antonio d', 1163

Alessandrini, Federico, 1083, 1237, 1239

Alexander I, **17**, 1431

Alexander II, **17–19**, 72, 211, 1036; antipopes to, 109, 731; banner, 689; benefices and, 765–766; crusades and, 18, 111–112, 437, 711; Gregorian reforms and, 1278; Gregory VII and, 648, 649; health and vitality of, 1416; Jewish legal/political status and, 871; legates and, 240, 909; liturgy and, 953; Norman alliance, 17, 18, 1053; reforms, 1280; simony condemnation, 1424; theocracy doctrine and, 1483; tomb of, 1499; universities and, 1547

Volume Key: Volume 1, pages 1–614; volume 2, pages 615–1266; volume 3, pages 1267–1637.

1660

Alexander II, tsar of Russia, 1532

Alexander III, **19–22**, 23, 196, 211, 534, 788, 1304; "ad limina" visits and, 1304; antipope to, 20, 72, 217, 684, 1114, 1615–1616; canon law and, 225; canonization and, 233, 268; cardinalate and, 241; Celestine III and, 277; Chancery, 289; conclave rules, 392, 1356, 1405; decretals, 22, 85, 773, 774, 897, 910; dispensations, 504–505; exemptions, 553; film portrayal of, 322; Frederick Barbarossa confrontation, 19–21, 109–110, 217, 313, 715, 785, 1021, 1334, 1615–1616; as Gratian disciple, 489; Gregory VIII and, 652–653; health and vitality of, 1416; indulgence decretal, 773, 774; judges delegate and, 453, 880, 881; Lateran III and, 22, 429, 901, 1027, 1425; as legate to Germany, 684; legates of, 910; Lucius III and, 960; military orders and, 989; monasticism and, 1015; mosaics of, 1021; naval voyages by, 1028; Pantheon restorations, 1096; pavilion and, 692; Propaganda Fide and, 1254; register of, 1293; St. John Lateran restoration, 1363; tomb of, 1499; travels by, 1015; Victor III and, 1613

Alexander IV, **22–24**, 655, 1554; "ad limina" visits and, 4; Antichrist charges and, 66; appointment of bishops and, 93; Franciscans and, 593, 792; Guelphs and, 629; Inquisition and, 812, 813, 814; literary witticism by, 743; nepotism and, 22–23, 24, 685, 1031; Nicholas III and, 1037; tomb of, 1500; Viterbo residence, 1304

Alexander V, **24–25**, 70, 798; as antipope, 72, 132, 242, 636, 661, 662; apostolic almoner bull, 37; arms, 114; conciliarism and, 390; embalming of, 486; Franciscans and, 24, 25, 594; [John XXIII] and, 130, 132, 137, 238, 662; Martin V and, 974; papal household, 738; tomb of, 1502

Alexander VI, **25–28**, 58, 798; accusations and enemies of, 28; Apostolic Camera functions and, 9; arms, 114, 1368; arts patronage, 1340; banner and keys, 138; Calatrava Order and, 989; Callistus III and, 218, 1032; cardinal protector abuse remedies by, 247; Castel Sant'Angelo reinforcements and, 255; censorship and, 1443; collectors and, 463; corruption by, 393, 1246; Curia and, 462, 471; Dumas portrayal of, 758; Eugene IV and, 537; Franciscans and, 595; French alliance, 1064, 1621–1622; heresy charges against, 27; Holy Sepulcher Order and, 723; Holy Year, 726, 983; humanism and, 1295; imprimatur and, 763, 770; Julius II opposition, 26, 27, 28, 884–885, 1621; medallion, 983; military orders and, 989; museum collection, 1026; Naples and, 1621; naval defense and, 1030; nepotism, 25–28, 218, 1032; New World division by, 26, 27, 96, 999–1000; nunciature, 1056–1057, 1057; painting commissions, 1089; Papal States and, 1102; Paul III and, 1124; penitentiaries and, 1152; Savonarola trial and, 509; Signatura Apostolic and, 1525; simonical election of, 393; slavery regulation, 1439

Alexander VII, **28–31**, 802; architectural projects, 30, 1089, 1116, 1383–1384; arms, 115; beatification and, 145, 269; camauro shape, 620; Chair of St. Peter, 286, 1379; chamberlains, 288; chaplains, 301; Church-State conflict, 617; Clement IX and, 349; Clement X and, 350; coins, 375–376; Curia nepotism and, 467, 468; Dominicans and, 510; heraldry, 696; Index updating, 29, 770, 772; Jansenism and, 354, 808, 824; Jesuits and, 827; legate of, 913; libraries and, 30, 467–468, 1598; missions and, 1001; monument for Alexander III and, 1499; obelisks of Rome and, 1061; papal chapel musicians, 298, 299; Peace of West-

phalia and, 802; penitentiaries, 1523; Quirinal and, 1269, 1271, 1272; simony and, 393; tomb of, 1344, 1386

Alexander VIII, **31–32**, 256, 807, 808; annona, 61, 62; arms, 115, 693; beatification and, 146; canonizations by, 235; cardinalate and, 243; Clement XI and, 352; coins, 376; infallibility and, 778; missions and, 1003; nepotism, 32, 468; papel chapel and, 295

Alexander of Alexandria, 33

Alexander of Antioch, 183

Alexander of Roes, 1509

Alexandre, Noël, 511

Alexandria, **32–36**, 176, 198–199; Anastasius II and, 44; as anti-Chalcedonian, 563, 564; apoligists, 74; Arab conquest and, 318; Arianism, 33–34, 419, 562, 698, 699, 1418–1419; Celestine I and, 275; Church unity and, 318; Clement VIII and, 348; conflict with Constantinople, 563, 564; Congregation for the Eastern Churches and, 407; crusade against, 440; Easter date, 517; eastern cults, 442; Fathers of the Church, 562, 563, 564; Isis cult, 442; Leo I and, 917–918; Liberius and, 946; major basilica, 144; Mark as apostolic founder, 32, 33; Nestorianism and, 274; Novatianism and, 1394; papal evangelization and, 545; papal primacy and, 502, 1108, 1245; patriarchs, 86, 572, 737; power under Dioscorus, 34, 200, 563; Simplicius and, 1426–1427; Sixtus II and, 1431; Sixtus III and, 1432; tiara and, 1490, *See also* Athanasius of Alexandria; Coptic Church; Cyril of Alexandria; Dioscorus

Alexandrine Way, 28

Alexis, St., 748, 749

Alexis I, emperor of Byzantium, 206–207, 1112, 1552

Alexis II, patriarch of Moscow, 523

Alexis IV, prince of Byzantium, 438

Alfama Order, 989, 990

Alfanus, 152

Alfarano, Tiberio, 559, 1375

Alfieri, Dino, 1634

Alfonso I, king of Portugal, 349

Alfonso II, king of Aragon, 27, 1621

Alfonso III, king of Aragon, 1039

Alfonso V, king of Naples and Aragon, 217, 218, 303, 974; Eugene IV and, 536, 537, 1041

Alfonso IX, king of Léon, 787

Alfonso X, king of Castile and Léon, 315, 628, 716, 973, 990

Alfonso, duke of Ferrara. *See* Este, Alfonso d'

Alfonso of Calabra, 1434

Alfrink, Cardinal, 863, 1140, 1142

Algardi, Alessandro, 803, 1362, 1386

Algardi family, 927

Algarotti, Francesco, 170

Algeria, 675, 1642, 1643

Algiers, toast of (1890), 934

Alidosi, Francesco, 885

All Saints' Day, 913

Allacci, Leone, 30, 1598

Allegra, Antonio, 299

Allegra, Salvatore, 744

Allegri, Gregorio, 298

Allet, Joseph-Eugène, 1643

allocution by the Pope to the Roman Rota, **36–37**

Volume Key: Volume 1, pages 1–614; volume 2, pages 615–1266; volume 3, pages 1267–1637.

1661

allocution, consistorial, **37**

Allucingoli, Ubaldo. *See* Lucius III

Almain, P., 616

Almoner, Apostolic, **37–38**, 454, 458, 473, 559, 741, 990, 1094, 1095 (*see also* chaplain, papal; military ordinariates)

almonry, 37–38, 454, 458, 1225

Alphonse. *See* Alfonso

Alphonsus of Vadaterra, 162

Alps: Henry IV's penitential crossing of, 238, 239; Ultramontanism, 1529–1531

altar, papal, **38**, 107, 144, 549, 1090, 1341

"alternative pope," 283

Altieri, Emilio. *See* Clement X

Altieri family, 694, 1052

alum of Tolfa/Tolfa alum, **38–39**, 137, 578, 581; banking activity and, 39, 137, 885; crusades financing from, 373, 1122; Paul II and, 1121, 1122; Pius II and, 1172

alumbrados, 818, 1268

Alvarez, Juan, 709

Alvarez, Rodrigo, 989

Alviano, Bartolomeo, 885

Amadeus VI of Savoy, 440

Amadeus VIII of Savoy. *See* [Felix V]

Amand of Elnone, St., 598

Amandus, St., 1166

Amanieu, A., 71

Amaseo, Romolo, 1126

Amatus of Monte Cassino, 1424

Amauritans, 701

Amaury de Bène, 702, 897

ambassadors. *See* diplomatic corps accredited to the Holy See

Ambrose of Milan, St., 75, 172, 181, 199, 622, 747, 947, 1364, 1375, 1427; angelology, 49; canonical collections, 223; Church influence by, 478, 479; on dissolution of marriage, 1249; as Doctor of the Church, 287, 568; fall of Rome and, 986; as Father of the Church, 566, 567, 568; just war doctrine and, 98; liturgy, 949, 952; Lombards and, 1036; on monasticism, 1012; naming as bishop, 92; on persecutions, 1230; pilgrimage description, 1164; as Pius XI influence, 1200, 1202; on primacy of Peter, 1160; Roman emperors and, 1317; Roman Senate and, 1411; Siricius and, 1466; theological orthodoxy and, 986

Ambrosian Church, 17, 34

Ambrosian liturgy, 949, 952

Ambrosiaster, 1249

Ameilh, Pierre, 485, 486

American Revolution, 991

Americanism, **39–41**, 326, 935

Americas. *See* Latin America; New World; North America; *specific countries*

Amette, Cardinal, 512

Ammannati, Iacopo, 983, 1173, 1340

Amomoeans, 699

Amphilochius of Iconium, 567

Anabaptists, 704, 816, 1287

Anacletus I, **41–42**

[Anacletus II], **42–43**, 70, 72, 450, 733, 961; Castel Sant'Angelo fortress and, 254; as Innocent II antipope, 42, 72, 254, 276, 732–733, 783, 784, 785, 900, 959; Norman alliance, 313, 1053, 1615; register of, 1293; [Victor IV] as successor, 1615

Anagni affair (1303), 160, 191, 334, 1049

Anagni, Peace of (1176), 190, 1334

Anagni, Peace of (1295), 190

Anastasio, Lodovico Agnello, 70

Anastasios of Thessalonica, 915, 1433

Anastasius I, **43**, 154, 770, 906–907; Innocent I and, 781; monastic movement and, 1011; tomb of, 1496

Anastasius I, emperor of Byzantium, 44, 141, 622, 907, 1318, 1476

Anastasius II, 35, **44**, 141, 600, 622, 942; Dante's consignment to Hell, 481; false document of, 589; tomb of, 1377, 1497

Anastasius II, emperor of Byzantium, 420, 737

Anastasius III, **44–45**, 839, 1497

Anastasius IV, 19, **45–46**, 683, 1499

[Anastasius Bibliothecarius], **46–47**, 70, 71, 600, 681–682, 1303, 1393

anathema, **47–49**; Anastasius Bibliothecarius followers as, 46; Cathars as, 901; Constantinople II and, 428; Cyril of Alexandria espousal of, 34, 275, 833, 1146; of Damasus I, 479; definition of, 47; Dioscorus as, 14, 185, 503; excommunication relationship and differentiation, 47–48; Freemasons as, 934; Gelasius I treatise as first on, 624; Hadrian I's political use of, 680; iconoclasm as, 205; Italian kingdom sovereigns as, 1541; John II on twelfth, 833; Lateran IV pronouncements, 897; lay intervention into bishops' election as, 91; lifted between Rome and Constantinople (1965), 430, 521; Montanism as, 698; Nicholas (deacon) as, 1043; Twelve of Cyril, 34, 833

Ancona, 168, 314, 613, 672, 675, 1029, 1538; as free port, 376; Napoléon's occupation of, 1103, 1186; papal fleet at, 1028, 1030; in Papal States, 1098, 1104, 1342; Pius II in, 1173, 1174, 1417; slave market, 1439; Turks and, 1527, *See also* Marches of Ancona

Anderson, James, 602, 603

Anderson, Michael, 322

András of Hungary, 53

André, J. F., 228

Andre of Hungary, 337

Andrea, Giovanni d', 242

Andreotti, Giulio, 310

Andrew (St. Andrew the Apostle), 207, 1157, 1378, 1385–1386, 1488; Eastern Church veneration of, 202, 206, 1389, 1391

Andrew II, king of Hungary, 734, 1220

Andrew of Gorze, 15

Andrew of Rhodes, 508

Andrew of Thessalonica, 44

Andrieu, Michel, 955

Andronicus II, emperor of Byzantium, 208, 973

Androse, Johannes, 227

Anerio, Felice, 297, 298

Angeli, Nicolò d', 1360

"angelic seat" (expression), 49

Angelicals, 1126

Angelico, Fra, 295, 509, 1042, 1091, 1492

Angelini, Giuselppe, 1083

Angellus of Ravenna, 1274

angels, **49**

Angelus, 27, **50**, 569, 1275; bells, 152, 249; text of, 50

Angers, University of, 1544

Angevins, **50–54**, 131, 160; Aragon rivalry. *See under* Sicily; Avignon papacy and, 50–54, 132, 337, 633; Clement VI and,

Volume Key: Volume 1, pages 1–614; volume 2, pages 615–1266; volume 3, pages 1267–1637.

1662

337; genealogical chart, 52; Ghibelline/Guelph conflict and, 53, 628, 629, 630, 676, 716; Gregory X and, 316, 658; Hadrian V and, 685; Holy Roman Empire and, 316, 716; Honorius IV and, 736; Innocent V and, 794; Martin IV and, 972–973; Nicholas III and, 51, 972, 973, 1037, 1038; Nicholas IV and, 1038, 1039; Roman aristocratic families and, 1048; Roman government and, 1337; Sacred College factions and, 280; Sicilian kingdom and, 50–54, 676, 716, 973

Angilbert of St.-Riquier, 599, 920

Angles, 140, 1108, 1318 (*see also* Saxons)

Anglicanism, **54–57**; ecumenism, 519–520, 521, 522, 865, 934, 1075–1076, 1395; inception of, 1288–1289, 1395, 1518; liturgy, 955; ordination, 55–56, 934, 1072–1077, 1395; ordination of women, 56, 1076, 1395; Oxford Movement, 55, 955, 1074, 1086–1087; reestablishment of (1559), 1128; Vatican II and, 1577

Anguillara family, 1048, 1121

Angus Dei, 948, 1412

Anibaldi family, 387

Anicetus, **57**, 523, 1244; Easter-date controversy, 517, 561, 1612; papal altar, 38

Anicii family, 1045

animals, **57–59**; bullfights, 58, 249; chinea offering, 303–304; Curia services, 458; Leo X hunting expeditions, 59, 927; taurobolium (bull sacrifice), 441–442

Anjou, house of, 189, 190, 662, 676; Guelphism and, 676; Honorius IV and, 736; Martin V and, 975; War of Spanish Succession, 353; wars in Italy, 1621–1624

Annales de Fulda, 188

Annales ecclesiastici, 1296

Annali Cattolici (journal), 1542

Anna-Mauricia, princess of Spain, 1470

annates, **59–60**, 136, 293, 464, 578, 611, 1266; abolishment of, 60, 581, 1116; Boniface IX and, 192; as common and small services, 389

Anne, St., 37, 194

Anne of Brittany, 885, 1621, 1622

Annibaldi, Annibaldo, 735, 1554

Annibaldi family, 1047, 1048

Annibaldi, Riciardo, 24, 451, 791, 973, 1360, 1554, 1555

Annibale of Capua, 1500

Anno II of Cologne, 17, 18, 731

annona, **60–62**, 1341, 1353; Byzantine popes and, 196; Gregory I and, 576; Gregory XI policies, 659; Gregory XIV policies, 666; Innocent XIII and, 810; Pius VI reform, 1180

Annuario pontifico (directory), 12, **62–63**, 1095; list of popes and antipopes, 70, 1065; Vaticanists and, 1606

annuary, telephone. *See* telephone

Anouilh, Jean, 322

Anse, Council of (995), 900

Ansegius of Sens, 837

Anselm of Baggio. *See* Alexander II

Anselm of Canterbury, 822, 1113, 1551

Anselm of Lucca, 224, 329, 495, 649, 1036, 1111, 1614; canonical collection, 231

Anselm of Mauny, 1554

Anselm of St. Rémy, 924

Anselmo dedicata, 231

antechamber. *See* apartments, papal

Anterus, **63–64**, 557, 1155

Anthemius, emperor of Byzantium, 707

Anthimus, patriarch of Constantinople, 14, 15, 564, 1145, 1417–1418

Anthoninus of Florence, 218

Anthony of Massa, 594

Anthony of Padua, St., 655

Antichità romane (Piranese), 171

Antichrist, **64–68**, 69, 513, 633, 703, 899, 1010; Lefebvre characterization of papacy as, 1398; Reformation characterization of papacy as, 1287, 1354; Russian Church-State bonds against, 1488

anticlericalism: of Arnold of Brescia, 701; Christian Democracy as response to, 304, 305, 308; Enlightenment, 528, 1181, 1535–1536; Flagellants and, 703; French Revolution, 612; in Germany, 218; Great Schism effects on, 633; Leo XIII efforts against, 934; liberalism and, 944; modernism and, 1007; of Nazis, 1110; Pius X efforts against, 173; Pius XI efforts against, 1208, 1209; prejudices of, 1232–1233; Roman monumentality and, 1018, *See also* papism; secularism

antiliberalism. *See* liberalism

Antimoderne (Maritain), 1010

antimodernist oath (1910), 1251

Antimus, 1012

Antioch, **69**, 176; Alexandria and, 34–35; Arab conquest and, 318; Athanasius condemnation by, 269; Byzantium and, 198–199, 200; canonical collection of, 230–231; Church unity and, 314, 1426, 1432; Congregation for the Eastern Churches and, 407; ecumenical councils, 427; Fathers of the Church, 562, 563, 564; Gregory XIII and, 664; Innocent I on Rome's primacy to, 782; Julian the Apostate and, 882; Leo I and, 917; major basilica, 144; Nestorius and, 1432; Novatian and, 1055, 1056; papal evangelization and, 545; papal primacy and, 1108, 1245; patriarchates, 86, 737; Paul and, 1118–1119; Peter in, 1158; provincial councils, 430

Antioch, synod of (268), 561, 570

Antioch, synod of (341), 91, 198

Antioch, synod of (379), 34

antipope, **69–72**; art portrayals, 1284; clerical status of, 181; definition of, 69; deposition of, 495; Felix numberings and, 1065; first John XXIII as, 854; Great Schism and, 130, 632–638, 1109, 1417; Hippolytus as, 707; investiture controversy and, 238–239; list of, 70–72; military conflicts, 109; Normans and, 1053; Novatian as, 698; Prophecies of Malachy and, 1262; Roman nobility's use of, 1333, *See also* specific names (enclosed in brackets)

antipopism. *See* anticlericalism; papism; Reformation

anti-Semitism: Benedict XIV encyclical on, 170; ghetto establishment, 374, 873, 874, 876, 932, 1188, 1310; Jesuit publications, 874; John Paul II condemnation of, 876; John XVIII mandate against, 845; John XXIII efforts against, 853, 875; Lefebvre schism and, 1397–1398; Nazi policy, 853, 874, 877 (*see also* Holocaust); Pius XI condemnation of, 875; segregation and forced conversions, 870–873; *Sicut iudaeis non* doctrine, 872

Antonelli, Giacomo, 324, 582, 1094, 1107, 1324, 1537, 1644–1645, 1646; Pius IX and, 1191, 1193, 1195, 1196, 1326

Volume Key: Volume 1, pages 1–614; volume 2, pages 615–1266; volume 3, pages 1267–1637.

Antonelli, Leonardo, 930, 1184

Antonini, Gino, 322

Antoninius of Fussala, 865

Antonino of Florence, 1223–1224, 1275

Antoninus of Fussala, 13, 273, 662

Antoninus Pius, emperor of Rome, 1314

Anulinus, 993

Anulus Piscatoris. *See* Fisherman's Ring

Anysius, 1611

apartments, papal, **72–73**; floreria (warehouse), 588; Julius II improvements, 869; Palatine Guard and, 1095; papal court and, 436; Sunday noon Angelus from, 50

Apiarius, 13, 184, 251, 273, 1642

Apion family, 639

Apocalypse, 64, 65, 66, 67, 631, 698; image of Rome, 747, 750, 1354; sack of Rome (1527) and, 1354, *See also* eschatology; millenarianism

Apocraypha, 202; Gospel of Peter as, 631

apocrisarius, 35, **73–74**, 1056, 1058, 1148

Apollinaris, Sidonius, 905, 906

Apollinarism, 34, 35, 567, 699

Apollinarius of Laodicia, 35, 479, 699

Apollo Belvedere (statue), 1025, 1177, 1595

Apollonius, 1154

apologetic, **74–79**; Benedict XIV promotion of, 170; Clement XIV and, 360; evangelization, 544; by Fathers of the Church, 77, 567; Hippolytus and, 707–708; Napoleonic invasion and, 670–671

Apology Against the Arians (Julius I), 883

apostasy, **79**; camerlengo, 219–221; Christian persecutions and, 1155; indulgences for, 773; Inquisition and, 813; modernism as, 1008–1009; schism vs., 1393–1394, *See also lapsi* controversy

apostolic blessings. *See* benedictions, papal; blessing

Apostolic Camera, **80–84**, 196; administrative offices, 8–10; animal expenses, 57, 58; annona, 61; *Annuario pontificio* (directory), 63; archives, 83, 1604, 1605; Avignon period, 130; camerlengo, 219–221; camerlengo's ferula, 575; cardinal camerlengo list, 10; Celestine V reorganization of, 281; clerks, 220; collectors, 378, 464, 466; common and small services obligation to, 389; Curia and, 8, 449, 455, 459–460, 464; death of the pope and, 9–10; documents and, 282, 459–460; Eugene IV and, 535; financial management, 171, 464, 578–581, 584; Honorius III and, 733; Innocent III structuring of, 788; *Liber censum* and, 940, 941; money changer of, 136–137; nuncios, 80, 81–82, 1058; papal household and, 739; Papal States and, 1098, 1102; pavilion, 1145; photography regulation, 1162; Pius VI and, 1179; protonotary, 517; Sixtus V and, 1437; slave ownership, 1440, 1441; Tolfa alum production/sales, 37, 39; Tridentine reforms, 465; Urban II and, 449; Vatican headquarters, 452

apostolic chaplaincy. *See* Almoner, apostolic

apostolic constitution. *See* constitution, apostolic

apostolic cursor. *See* cursor, apostolic

apostolic datary. *See* datary, apostolic

Apostolic Hospice, 739, 741

apostolic notary. *See* notary, apostolic

Apostolic Palace. *See* Palace, Apostolic

Apostolic Penitentiary. *See* Penitentiary, Apostolic

apostolic poverty. *See* poverty ideal

Apostolic See. *See* Holy See

Apostolic Signatura. *See* Signatura Apostolic, Supreme Tribunal of

apostolic tradition: Alexandria-Rome relationship, 32; Byzantium and, 200–208; deacons and, 484; Fathers of the Church and, 566; St. Peter's basilica and, 1377; Vatican II on, 1585

Apostolic Tradition (Hippolytus), 90, 223, 283

apostolic tribunals. *See* tribunals, apostolic

apostolic vicariate. *See* vicariate, apostolic

Apostolics (herectical sect), 702, 736

apothecary, papal, 486, 1416–1417

apparel. *See* clothing

appeal to the Pope, **84–85**, 1283; Byzantium and, 199–200; Curia and, 450

Appian Way, 214, 418, 548, 836; catacombs, 257, 258, 423, 1159, 1160, 1419, 1496, 1640; pilgrimages to, 1164; veneration of Peter and Paul, 1159, 1160

appointment of bishops, **85–90**

appointment of bishops, history, **90–95**; Concordat of Worms on, 1637; Gregory VII theocratic doctrine and, 1483; Lateran II Canon 28, 901; Lateran pacts and, 902; Lefebvre irregular appointments, 1398; Leo IX stand on, 91–92, 924; Napoléon-Pius VII conflict, 1187–1188; Paschal II and, 1113; regalia and, 1290–1291, *See also* investiture controversy

approbations, papal, **95–98**

APSA (Administration for the Patrimony of the Apostolic See), 583–584

Apulia, 1052, 1053, 1124

Aquilas, 1153

Aquileia, 1147, 1148

Arab League, 713, 847

Arab-Israel wars, 713

Arabs: Aristotelianism and, 132–133; British Palestinian mandate and, 712; Jewish homeland and, 713–714; rise of universities and, 1543, 1548, *See also* Islam; Saracens

Arachetti, Giovanni Andrea, 1179

Arafat, Yasser, 865, 877

Aragon, 162, 165, 167, 189; Angevin conflict over Sicily, 51–52, 54, 160, 280, 628, 735–736, 973, 975, 1038, 1039; appointment of bishops, 93; cardinals from, 451; crusades and, 973; French wars in Italy and, 1621–1624; Ghibellines and, 629; Great Schism and, 340, 637; Inquisition in, 812, 815–816; Martin IV and, 440, 973; in Naples, 1621; Nicholas V and, 1041; Peter's Pence payment, 577

Arator (poet), 1617

arbitration, papal, **98–100**; Avignon popes, 127, 129, 130; Curia reorganization and, 453; Holy See actions, 718–719, 720; list of good works, 99, *See also* diplomacy

Arcadelt, Jacques, 297, 298

Arcadius, emperor of Byzantium, 183

archaeology, Christian, **100–102**; Benedict XIV and, 171; Castel Sant'Angelo, 255; catacombs, 100, 171, 260, 1016, 1296; classical sites and, 108, 1345; Clement XII interest, 357; humanist scholarship, 1296; mosaics and, 1021; papal commission, 389; photography, 1162; Pius VI and, 1180; pontifical academy, 2, 101; relics and, 262; Roman monumentality and, 1016, 1017, 1122; St. Peter's excavations, 547–549, 1375–1376; Vatican museum collections, 1027, 1117

Volume Key: Volume 1, pages 1–614; volume 2, pages 615–1266; volume 3, pages 1267–1637.

1664

archconfraternities. *See* Roman confraternities

architecture, papal, **102–108**, 1089; Alexander VII projects, 30, 1089, 1116, 1383–1384; Castel Sant'Angelo changes, 28, 254, 255; Catholic reform, 1277, 1340, 1341; Constantine the Great and, 418; gardens, 1594–1596; Julius II projects, 104–105, 885, 886, 1117; Julius III projects, 887; monument restorations, 1016–1017; mosaics, 1022; museums, 1025, 1026; patronage, 1116–1117; Paul II and, 1121; Paul III and, 1123; Paul V and, 106, 1130; Pius IV and, 1176; post-Counter Reformation, 1344, 1345; Quirinal, 1269–1272; Sixtus V projects, 1437–1438; Urban VIII projects, 1562, *See also* residences, papal; St. John Lateran, basilica of; St. Mary Major, basilica of; St. Paul Outside the Walls, basilica of; St. Peter's basilica

architecture, Roman. *See* mountality and Roman urbanism

Archivi Segreti del Vaticano. *See* Vatican Secret Archives

ARCIC (Anglican Roman Catholic International Commission), 1076

Aretino (Pietro Bacci), 1127, 1366

Arezzo, Lorenzo d', 389

Arezzo, Tommaso, 1187

Argellata, Pierre, 486

Argenti, Bonaventura, 871

Argentina: election of bishops, 89; papal arbitration, 720; papal concordats, 397; Pius XI legate to, 1213; Vatican II representation, 1579

Argrinus of Langres, 154

Arianism, 199, 566, 571, 698–699; African Church and, 14, 33–34, 572, 573, 833; Alexandria and, 33–34, 419, 562, 698, 699, 1418–1419; Antioch and, 69; barbarians and, 140, 141, 142, 573, 575, 699, 831, 832; Christology, 33, 140, 419, 698–699, 1418; Constans II policy toward, 881; Constantine the Great and, 419; Damasus I countermeasures, 477, 479; Gregory I missions against, 1108; Hilarus and, 707; John II and, 833; Julius I policies, 882, 883; Justin I campaign against, 831, 832; Leo I and, 914; Liberius policies, 945, 946, 947, 1012; Lombard converts and, 140, 142, 957; Milan and, 986; Nicaean Council condemnation of, 428, 1316; papal evangelization and, 545; Roman Empire and, 477, 1316, 1317; Silvester I and, 1418–1419

Ariosto, 238, 927, 1269

Aripert, king of the Lombards, 142–143

Aristide, Jean-Bertrand, 1470

Aristides, 74

aristocratic families. *See* nobility, Roman

Aristotle, 132–133, 702, 847, 861, 1548; Clement VI arguments against, 336; Jesuits and, 867; John XXI commentary on, 847; Lateran V and, 899; natural state concept and, 1484, 1485; scholasticism and, 1296; subsidiarity concept, 1461, 1462

Arius, 33, 140, 419, 698, 699, 770, 1418

Arles, 184, 185, 187; Gregory I and, 598; Holy Roman Empire and, 716; Leo I and, 915; Symmachus and, 1476; vicariate of, 1610–1611

Arles, Council of (314), 85, 907, 986, 1297, 1394, 1418, 1431

Arles, Council of (455), 551

Armada, Spanish (1588), 55

Armellini, Carlo, 1323, 1324, 1529

Armenia, 176, 429, 536, 787; canon law, 370; conferences of bishops, 404; Congregation for the Eastern Churches and, 407; Dominicans in, 508; evangelization of, 508, 545, 659, 998, 1039; patriarch, 86; Pius IX conflict with, 1196; Vatican II representation, 1577

Armenian College, 662

armies, papal, **108–112**; Castel Sant'Angelo fortifications, 254–255; Comacchio retreat by, 1103; financial drain of Great Schism, 661; financial expenditures for, 110, 111, 578, 799; Gregory IX and, 110, 654–655; Gregory XI and, 659; Gregory XIV and, 666; Gregory XV and, 668; heraldry, 689; Innocent IX and, 800; Julius II and, 885, 1471; mercenaries, 109, 110, 111, 129, 132, 157, 659, 1052; revolutions of 1848 and, 1098; Zouaves, 1107, 1643–1646, *See also* Noble Guard; Swiss Guard

arms, papal, **112–116**, 693; keys position and colors, 690, 891; keys with pavilion, 691, 693; list, 113–116; majordomo of household, 739; pavilion, 1145; tiara and, 692; titles and, 1050

arms, private, 694–695, 1091

army. *See* armies, papal

army chaplains. *See* military ordinariates

Arnau, N. Jubani, 368

Arnaud. *See* Arnold; Arnoul

Arnauld, Antoine, 29, 704, 803, 806, 824, 1562

Arnauld family, 704

Arneil, Pierre, 284

Arnobius, 75

Arnold of Brescia, 109, 450, 533, 534, 683, 701–702, 901, 1096, 1133; Abelard defense by, 277; view of Donation of Constantine, 513

Arnold of Liège, 830

Arnold of Lübeck, 963

Arnold of Pellegrue, 335, 848

Arnold of Villeneuve, 1416

Arnold of Wion, 1261

Arnold the Souab, 66

Arnolfo di Cambio, 1039, 1360, 1366–1367, 1371, 1372, 1373, 1379, 1491

Arnoul of Reims, 646, 842, 1420–1421

Arnulf of Milan, 821, 1227

Arpadian Kingdom, 52

Arpino, Cavaliere d', 1090, 1091, 1092, 1269, 1341, 1362, 1369, 1383, 1385

Arsenius of Orta, 681

art: baptistry designs, 138–139; Canossa confrontation depictions, 239; cardinal nephew patronage, 245; cardinalate patronage, 242; coin portraiture, 375, 376; foreign artists, 116–121, 1092, 1180, 1345; Golden Rose, 1347–1348; Gregorian reform and, 1284–1285; medallions, 981–984; *possesso* iconography, 1229; Quirinal, 665, 1269, 1270, 1271, 1272; Roman architecture and, 107–108, 1344, 1369; St. John Lateran, 1360–1364; St. Mary Major, 1367–1368, 1369; St. Paul's Outside the Walls, 1372–1373; St. Peter's basilica, 1378, 1379, 1380–1381, 1385; Sistine Chapel, 1428–1431, 1435; of 17th-century Rome, 1340–1341, 1344–1345; traveler's view of, 1506; Vatican gardens statuary, 1595; Vatican mural maps, 252–253; in Vatican museums, 1024–1026, 1117, *See also* frescoes; iconoclasm; iconography; mosaics; painting; papal patronage

Artaud, A. G., 1183

Volume Key: Volume 1, pages 1–614; volume 2, pages 615–1266; volume 3, pages 1267–1637.

1665

Artaud of Reims, 15, 840, 970

Artavasdus, 1639

Arthur, King (legendary), 749

artists, foreign, in Rome, **116–121**, 1092, 1180, 1345; etchings of chinea fête, 304; papal medallions, 982; papal patronage, 1117, 1340; Paul V commissions, 1130; Urban VIII commissions, 1562

Ascalon, battle of (1099), 1552

Ascension, 194, 913

asceticism: antique monasticism and, 1011, 1012; Catherine of Siena and, 266; Celestine I on, 273; laity and, 895–896; [Lawrence] and, 906; penance and, 773

Ascoli, Girolamo da. *See* Nicholas IV

Ash Wednesday, 211, 952

Asia: communism in, 1218; indigenous clergy training, 1373–1374; John Paul II tours of, 1510, 1511; missionizing in, 1343; Paul VI tours of, 1143, 1514, 1515; Portuguese holdings, 29, 999, 1000, 1002; Propaganda Fide and, 1255; Vatican II representation, 1575, 1576, 1577, 1578, 1580, *See also* Chinese rites; *specific countries*

Aspromonte, battle of (1862), 1540

assassination attempts against the pope, **121–124**; antiquity, **121–222**, 838, 1432; Middle Ages, **122**; modern period, **122**; contemporary period, **122–124**; John Paul II, 50, 860, 865, 1170, 1248, 1384; Leo III and, 79, 122, 599, 920, 1320; popemobile security, 1405

Assemani family, 1598

Association of the Lay Dependents of the Vatican, 1596–1597

Assumption of the Virgin Mary, **124**, 1367; dogma definition (1950), 421, 519; feast of, 124, 212, 569, 913, 1096; Jesuits and, 828

Assumptionists, 1444

Astalli, Camillo, 802

asterisk. *See* Mass, papal

Astesan bank, 137

Astolf, king of the Lombards, 599

Astros of Toulouse, 954

ASV. *See* Vatican Secret Archives

asylum, right of, **124–125**, 666

Atargatis of Hierapolis, cult of, 442–443

Athalaric, king of Ostrogoths, 186, 832

Athanasius of Alexandria, St., 33, 34, 35, 198, 199, 419, 622, 699, 986; Chair of St. Peter and, 287; condemnation of (355), 945; as Father of the Church, 562, 566, 567; Holy Spirit definition and, 428; Julian the Apostate and, 882; Julius I and, 432, 882–883; Liberius and, 34, 199, 571, 881, 945–946; monasticism in the West and, 1011; on Roman prefecture, 1230

atheism, 1006, 1573

Athenagoras I, patriarch of Jerusalem, 520–521, 1514, 1515; Paul VI meeting, 1140, 1245, 1395

Attendolo, Francesco, 975

Attendolo, Muzio, 975

Atticus, patriarch of Constantinople, 183, 567, 1611

Attila, 140, 914, 986, 1046, 1318

Atto of Vercelli, 1043

Aubert, Arnaud, 219, 459

Aubert, Étienne. *See* Innocent VI

auctoritas vs. doctrine, 21

audience, **125–126**, 130, 739; Chancery and, 452–453; datary and, 483; Holy Year pilgrims, 729; newspaper daily listing of, 1082; open-air, 127; papal court and, 436–437; by Paul VI, 1139; photographs of, 1163; as pilgrimage culmination, 1170; pontifical blessing and, 177; Pontifical Gendarmes and, 626

Audience, The (film), 323

auditor, Rota, **126**, 130, 415, 1094; Alexander VIII as, 31; camerlengo and, 220; datary and, 483; First French Empire and, 1349–1350; keys on seal of, 690; responsibilities, 80, 81, 460, 461

Aufklärung (Catholic Enlightenment), 169, 705, 825, 954

Auger, Emond, 263

Augsburg Confession, 891, 1288

Augsburg, diet of (1077), 238

Augsburg, diet of (1530), 1287

Augsburg, diet of (1548), 1288

Augsburg Interim (1547), 1125

Augsburg, Peace of (1555), 936, 1128, 1288

Augustine of Canterbury, St., 142, 641, 996–997, 1076

Augustine of Hippo, St., 3, 135, 181, 184, 273, 522, 543, 619, 698, 700, 783, 850, 942, 1161; on Antichrist, 65; apologetics, 75; bishop of Rome's primacy and, 1108; canonical collections and, 223; on complete conversion, 1345; on dissolution of marriage, 1249; as Doctor of the Church, 287, 568; Donatist debate with, 1394; fall of Rome and, 986, 1318; as Father of the Church, 567, 568; on grace, 210, 823; as Gregory VIII influence, 652; image of Rome and, 747; as Jansenite influence, 704, 823, 824, 867; just war doctrine and, 98; Laurentius and, 446; liturgy and, 948; Miltiades and, 994; monasticism and, 1011, 1012, 1013; on monks' pilgrimages, 1164; Pius XI encyclical on, 1204; pontifical title used by, 1495; rule of, 722, 987, 988, 989, 1013, 1015, 1044, 1280; Silvester I defense by, 1418; Sixtus III and, 1432; theocratic doctrine of, 1482, 1484, 1485; Zosimus and, 1642, *See also* Rule of St. Augustine

Augustinians, 348, 664, 732, 788, 976; colleges, 379; at Council of Trent, 1518; Paul III and, 1126

Augustinus (Jansen), 28–29, 704, 808, 823, 824, 1562

Augustus, emperor of Rome, 253, 1095, 1229, 1313, 1411

Aurelian, emperor of Rome, 254, 543, 570–571, 1156, 1315

Aurelius of Carthage, 43, 251, 784, 1432

Auschwitz, 496, 876, 1511, 1635

Austerlitz (film), 322

Austerlitz, battle of ((1805), 1186

Austria: Anabaptists, 704; Anschluss, 1212; appointment of bishops and, 93; Benedict V and, 174–175; Benedict XIV and, 169, 170; bishops' conferences, 401; Catholicism in, 174–175, 891–892; Clement XIII and, 358; crusades and, 333; crypto-Protestants in, 869; Enlightenment, 530; exclusion right, 550, 551; French wars in Italy and, 1622; Gregory XVI and, 394, 672; Italian unity and, 1324, 1535–1540; Jansenism in, 867–868; Jesuits and, 358, 361; Josephism and, 674, 867–869, 1109, 1179; *Kulturkampf* in, 891, 893; Leo IX and, 1194; Munich Accords (1938), 1206, 1213, 1630; Napoleonic wars and, 1183–1184, 1185, 1186; Old Catholics, 1396; papal concordats, 397–398; Papal States and, 1103, 1104, 1183; papal support by, 1189; Paul V and, 1130; Pius VI and, 1179; Pius IX concordat with, 397, 1194; Pius XI and, 1206–1207, 1212; temporal veto,

Volume Key: Volume 1, pages 1–614; volume 2, pages 615–1266; volume 3, pages 1267–1637.

1666

1608–1609; Thirty Years War and, 669; Vatican I and, 1566, 1567; Vatican II and, 1579, 1581; World War I and, 174–175, 1625–1627, 1630, *See also* Holy Roman Empire; Vienna

Austrian Succession, War of the (1740–1748), 169–170, 1103, 1345

Ausukimono seminary, 664

autocephaly privilege, 1273

automobiles, papal, **126–127**, 1405, 1588; *possesso* ceremony, 1229

Auxanus of Arles, 1617

Auxentius of Milan, 986, 1364

Auxilius of Naples, 590, 1414

Avars, 997, 1319

Avenir, L' (newspaper), 306, 673, 674, 1191

"Aventino" (pseudonym), 1236

Averlino, Antonio (Filarete), 537, 1380

Averroes, 133, 702, 847

Avezzano earthquake (1915), 174

Avicenna, 133, 847

Avignon: bishopric of, 160–161; Clement VI purchase of, 337, 1220; French post-Napoleonic control of, 1189; French Revolution and, 611–612, 613, 1103, 1104, 1181; history of city, 127–128; Inquisition in, 812, 813

Avignon, papacy of, **127–133**; almonry, 458; Angevins and, 50–54, 132, 337, 633; animals and, 58; annona, 60; Antichrist charges and, 67; archives, 1604; banking and finances, 136, 137; Benedict XII and, 161; [Benedict XIII] and, 25, 132, 162, 660, 661; benefices collation, 1266; Black Death epidemic, 1221–1222; Boniface IX and, 192; camerlengos and, 219, 220; canonical collections, 226–227; cardinalate power and, 241, 393; Catherine of Siena and return from, 266; Catholic reform and, 1274; ceremonial, 284; Chancery activity, 128–129, 292–293; chaplains and, 457; chef, 302; Clement V establishment of, 102–103, 127, 128, 136, 481, 632, 1246, 1304; Clement VI court, 103, 127, 129, 336, 337–338, 1220–1222; [Clement VII] and, 163, 192–193, 1558; coins, 373; conclave site, 392; consistory, 415; Curia and, 455–456, 457, 458, 460; Dante's condemnation of, 481; datary, 483; doctors and surgeons, 1416–1417; Dominicans and, 507–508; effects on Rome, 1330; expectative abuse, 555; financial management, 80–81, 82, 578, 579–580, 581, 1246; French ties with, 1109; geographic situation of, 102–103; Ghibelline-Guelph conflict and, 628, 676; heraldry, 689, 690; heresies, 703; Holy Year pilgrims and, 724, 725; Jewish expulsion and, 872; John XXII and, 456, 848–851; Julius II and, 884–885; legacy of, 130; legates and, 911; library, 1597; liturgy, 953; military expenses, 110; naval forces, 1028–1029; nepotism, 336, 1031–1032, 1048, 1049; Nicholas V ending of (1449), 1040–1042; papal arts patronage, 1116; papal chaplain role, 300–301; papal coronation and, 426; papal family and, 559–560; papal real estate and, 1101; papal tomb sites, 1498, 1501–1502; plague epidemics, 1220–1222; popes during, 128–130; regalia and, 1291; registers, 1293; residences, 102–103, 128; return to Rome from, 103, 104, 266, 659–660; Roman papacy and, 1338; Sacred College composition, 1356; slavery and, 1439; spoils and, 1452; tax collectors, 378; tiara, 1491–1492; universities and clerical education, 1549; Urban V and, 1556–1557; vacant benefices and, 179, *See also* Great Schism of the West

Avignon, University of, 128, 129

Aviz (Evora) Order, 988

Avvenire d'Italia, L' (newspaper), 1205

awards and honors. *See* decorations; titles, pontifical

Aycelin, Hugues, 280, 281

Azzo II of Ostia, 647

Azzolini, Decio, 349, 468, 802

Azzuri, Franco, 1017

Baal cults, 443

Baalbek temple, 443

Babylon: patriarch of, 86; Rome stereotyped as modern, 1232

Bacchanals (Titian), 1092

Bacci, Antonio, 1135

Bacci, Pietro (Aretino), 1127, 1366

Bacon, Roger, 213, 333

baculum. See ferula

Baden, fourteen articles of (1832), 674–675

Baggio, Anselm de. *See* Alexander II

Baglione, Giovanni, 1341, 1342, 1362

Baglioni, Giampaolo, 885, 1090

Baglioni of Perugia, 928

Bagnolo, treaty of (1484), 1434

Baini, Giuseppe, 257, 297, 298

Baius, Michael, 823, 1562

Bajazet, Ottoman sultan, 799

bakeries, 457, 458

Balbinus's catacomb, 1496

Balbo, Cesare, 1536

Baldwin II, king of Jerusalem, 333, 1555

Balfour Declaration (1917), 712

Balkans, 30, 542, 638; Clement XI evangelization, 355; diplomatic ties with Holy See, 503; evangelization, 997; John IV and, 1360; Leo I and, 915; Leo XIII and, 934; remains of Roman Empire in, 1319; Sixtus III and, 1433; slaves from, 1440; Turks in, 638, 1526; Vandals and, 1318; vicariate of Thessalonica, 1611; Zosimus and, 1642, *See also* Illyricum Church; *specific countries*

Balmes, Jaime, 78

Baltimore, Md., 401, 1344

Balue, Jean, 1122

Banco Ambrosiano (Milan), 583

Banco di Roma, 582

Bandi, Giovanni Carlo, 1178

Bandinelli, Orlando (Roland). *See* Alexander III

banditry, 665, 666, 1437, 1643

Bank of the Santo Spiritu, 376

banking and the papacy, **135–137**, 376, 580; antiquity, **135**; Middle Ages, **135–137**; modern era, 582, 583, 1352, 1588; Avignon popes and, 132; Benedict XIV policies, 169, 170–171; coins, 373; collectors, 82, 378; Corsini family, 356; Curia residency, 452; farm loans, 62; Gregory XVI and, 673; Innocent III and, 373; Innocent VIII and, 799; Julius II and, 885; Templars and, 136, 988; Tolfa alum sales, 39, 137, 581; Vatican City State, 1588

bankruptcies, 136

banners, **137–138**; Apostles Peter and Paul figures on, 138, 693; cross on, 688–689; crusades and, 18, 688; cursors and, 475; gonfalonier, 694–695; keys emblem, 138, 689,

Volume Key: Volume 1, pages 1–614; volume 2, pages 615–1266; volume 3, pages 1267–1637.

1667

891, 1588; Noble Guard and, 1052; pavilion, 1145; pontifical fleet, 1028

banquets, papal, 302

baptism, 138–140, 1286; of heretics, 1455; slave status and, 1439, 1440, 1441

Baptist Church, 904

baptistry, **138–140**, 1377

Barat, Madeleine Sophie, St., 1204

barbarians, 124, **140–143**, 1046, 1047, 1317; Arianism and, 140, 141, 142, 572, 573, 575, 699; Catholic conversions of, 36, 141–142, 545, 597; control of Rome by, 563; convert pilgrimages to Rome, 1166; Leo I and, 913, 914, 1354; Milan and, 987; papal finances and, 575; Roman Empire infiltration by, 1315–1316, *See also specific groups*

Barbarigo, Gregorio, 358, 807, 1609

Barbaro, Marcantonio, 937

barber, pope's, **143–144**

Barberini, Antonio, 256, 801, 802, 1469, 1560, 1598; arts patronage, 1091, 1092; Propaganda Fide and, 1254

Barberini, Carlo, 1560

Barberini family, 30, 356, 802, 804; nepotism, 466, 467, 1032; Noble Guard commander, 1052; painting collections, 1090, 1091, 1092

Barberini, Francesco, 243, 245, 801, 912, 1032, 1092, 1560

Barberini, Maffeo Vincenzo. *See* Urban VIII

Barberini Palace, 1091, 1271, 1344, 1562

Barberini, Tadeo, 1560

Barbier, Emmanuel, 944

Barbier de Montaul, Xavier de, 1162

Barbo, Pietro. *See* Paul II

Barbo, Pietro (cardinal nephew), 1121

Barcelona, treaty of (1287), 736

Bardas, 1034

Bardi banks, 82, 136, 137

Bardo of Mainz, 845

Barlaam of Calabria, 75, 208

Barlic, Carlo, 2

Barlow, William, 1073

Barnabas, 566, 1118

Barnabites, 1126, 1177, 1276, 1277

Baroncelli, Francesco, 1338

Baronio, Cesare, 467, 664, 1296

Baronius, 514, 1129, 1130, 1598

Barrot, Odilon, 1326

Barruel, Augustín de, 603

Barth, Karl, 519

Bartholomew of Brescia, 227

Bartholomew of Ravenna, 192

Bartholomy of Odessa, 76

Bartolo de Sassoferato, 628

Bartolomasi, Angelo, 175

Bartolomeo of Capua, 281

Barzotti, B., 1022

Basel, Council of (1431–1449), 196, 429, 616, 1040–1041, 1101, 1558; annates abolishment, 60, 581; benefices decrees, 1266, 1298; calendar reform, 213; canon law and, 227; cardinal protector restrictions, 247; conciliarism and, 389, 391, 1109; Eugene IV and, 535, 536, 537; [Felix V] and, 574; Martin V and, 975, 976–977

Basil, St., 33, 34, 69, 199, 566, 638, 1015

Basil I (the Macedonian), emperor of Byzantium, 46, 47, 198, 837, 969, 1459

Basil of Ancyra, 571, 881–882, 946

Basil of Caesarea, 562, 567, 699

Basil of Ochrida, 206

Basile, E., 1018

Basileus, 1013

Basilians, 156

basilicas, major, **144**; cardinals under, 144, 239; Carnival procession and, 248; jubilee pilgrims and, 726, 729; painting commissions, 1090–1092; papal altar, 38, 144; papal cermony, 103, 283–284, 1117; papal patronage, 1116; pavilion, 1145; penitentiaries, 454, 1151, 1152, 1523; pilgrimages to, 1169, 1170; protonotaries, 1264; Vatican City and, 1592, *See also* St. John Lateran; St. Mary Major; St. Paul's Outside the Walls; St. Peter's basilica

basilicas, minor, **144**, 1116, 1148–1149; veneration of saints and, 1388

Basilides of León, 1455

Basiliscus, emperor of Byzantium, 1426

Basilius (praetorium), 179, 736, 1046

Basseville assassination (1793), 1181

Bassus, Junius, 1045, 1230, 1365, 1425

Bastia, Giuseppe, 1082

Batiffol, Pierre, 954, 1008

baton. *See* ferula

Battista, Franceschetto, 798, 799

Battista, Giovanni. *See* Innocent VIII

Battista, Giovanni Pianciani, 324

Baudoin I, patriarch of Jerusalem, 722

Baudrillard, Jean, 1010

Bautain, Louis-Eugène, 78

Bavaria, 399, 401, 598, 997, 1189; concordats with, 1189, 1207

Baviera, Augusto, 1082

Bayle, Pierre, 77

Baylot, J., 609

Bea, Augustin, 434, 855, 875, 1139, 1445, 1572, 1574, 1577

beards, popes with, 143

beatific vision doctrine, 133, 268, 850–851

beatification, **144–151**; Middle Ages, **144–145**; modern and contemporary eras (list), **145–151**; auditor and, 126; canonization vs., 144, 145, 234, 268, 269; cases for modern popes, 865–866; consistorial advocates, 413; Holy Year, 728; proof of miracles and, 884; statistics (by century), 885; time limit, 884; Urban VIII procedural regulation, 145, 884, 1562, *See also* Causes of Saints, Congregation for the

beatii (blessed), 145

Béatrice de Provence, 127

Beatrice of Lorraine-Tuscany, 17, 238

Beauduin, Lambert, 519, 521, 955

Beaufort, Pierre-Roger de, 1222

Beauharnais, Josephine de, 1022, 1187

Becdelièvre, Louis-Aimé de, 1643

Becket (film), 322

Becket, Thomas, St., 21, 652, 725, 880, 1114, 1553; canonization of, 268

Beda (monk), prophesy of, 387

Volume Key: Volume 1, pages 1–614; volume 2, pages 615–1266; volume 3, pages 1267–1637.

1668

Bede, Venerable, 65, 142, 152, 942; on Doctors of the Church, 568; on links between kings and popes, 1619; Paschal Tables, 518

Bees fountain, 1562

beggars. *See* poor relief

Beghards and Beguines, 131, 703, 811, 813, 849, 896, 1268

Belarus, 522

Belgium: artists in Rome, 117, 118, 119; bishops' conferences, 400; Catholic university, 675, 1541, 1544; Christian Democracy, 306, 307, 309; churches in Rome, 316; congregation of exempts, 553; founding as nation, 1190, 1191; Freemasonry, 604, 607; Great Schism position, 633, 661; Jansenism, 803, 808; Latin Monetary Union, 377; Leo XII and, 932–933; Leo XIII and, 933; liberalism, 672, 674; papal nunciature, 933, 1059; Pius XI and, 1205; Vatican II representation, 1579, 1581; World War I and, 173–174, 175, 1628; World War II and, 1633; Zouaves, 1643

Belgrade, 218, 375

Belisarius, 141, 1273, 1318, 1328, 1417–1418, 1616, 1617

Bellarmine, Robert, 68, 467, 827, 1031, 1129, 1443; as Doctor of the Church, 1204; papal candidacy, 667; on poor relief, 1226; small catechism, 263

Bellegarde, Dupac de, 867

Bellemère, Gilles, 227

Belli, Guiseppe, 143

Belli, L., 1016

Belli, Pasquale, 1025, 1372

Belli, Valerio, 375, 982, 983

Bellicard, Charles, 304

Bellori, 1093, 1341

bells, **151–152**; Angelus, 50; Carnival and, 249; minor basilica, 144; St. Peter's tower, 152, 1378

Belorussian Uniates, 1531, 1532

Beltoft, John, 111

Beltrami, Luca, 1026

Belvedere (Vatican), 886, 1176; artists, 800, 1092; gardens, 1594–1596, 1598; as museum, 1024, 1025, 1026; Terza Loggia, 252, 253, 1176; Vatican Archives and, 1604

Bembo, Pietro, 1295

Bencio, Trifone, 1464

Benedict, St., 142, 539, 540, 541, 1013; Gregory I biography of, 639, 1013; pontifical title used by, 1495; tomb of, 1613, *See also* Rule of St. Benedict Benedict the Levite, 231

Benedict I, **152–153**, 1497

Benedict II, 143, **153**, 180

Benedict III, **153–154**; Anastasius Bibliothecarius imprisonment of, 46, 73, 600; bull design, 195; iconoclast controversy, 207; Nicholas I and, 601, 1033

Benedict IV, **154–155**, 268, 372

Benedict V, **155**; Church-State conflict and, 71, 648, 1541; deposition of, 495, 575, 923, 1305

Benedict VI, **155–156**; assassination of, 71, 155, 188

Benedict VII, **157**, 188, 251, 372, 1497

Benedict VIII, **156–157**, 1279, 1333; antipope to, 647; Apostolic Camera, 8; arms, 114; canonization and, 232; clerical marriage opposition, 1043; John XIX as successor, 845, 846; military activity, 109, 647, 1393; tomb of, 1498; unpopularity of, 529

Benedict IX, **157–159**, 688, 703; competing popes, 71, 72, 158, 328, 481, 495, 647, 648, 1305, 1422; deposition of, 495,
1612; Franciscans and, 594; mediocrity of, 1333; reserved case and, 1298; resignation by, 158, 647, 1305; simony and, 1424; tomb of, 1498

[Benedict X], 70, 72, **159–160**, 329, 1035, 1036

Benedict XI, **160**; arms, 113; as Dominican, 507; dying ritual for, 485–486; tomb of, 1501

Benedict XII, 110, 132, **160–162**, 1041; abbreviators for, 1; arms, 113; Avignon residence, 103, 128–129, 456, 1116; beatific vision controversy, 850; benefice reserves withdrawn from, 1298; chaplaincy and, 457, 1152; Church-State conflict and, 316; Clement VI and, 336; consistorial advocate, 413; doctrine and, 133; Dominicans and, 161, 508; expectative annulment and, 555; finances, 578; Franciscans and, 594; health problems of, 1416; heraldry, 690, 693; Inquisition and, 812; Jewish persecutions and, 976; masters of Ceremonies, 284; menegerie, 58; nepotism rejected by, 241; papal chaplain and, 300; reforms of, 128, 300; Rota member numbers, 1349; Sacred College and, 1356; slavery view, 1439; tomb of, 1501

[Benedict XIII], 70, **162–165**, 284; Aragon support, 974; datary, 482; deposition of, 661, 852, 1305, 1492; Dominican support, 508; Great Schism and, 25, 72, 130, 132, 163–164, 167, 193, 341, 508, 634, 635, 636, 637, 660, 661, 797; library, 1597; military forces, 111, 1029; tiara, 1491–1492; tomb of, 1502

Benedict XIII, 72, **165–167**, 217, 376, 810, 1210, 1558; "ad limina" visits and, 4; annona, 62; arms, 112, 115, 693; arts patronage, 1117; banner, 689; beatification, 146; Benedict XIV relationship, 168; canonizations by, 235; Church-State relations and, 469; coins, 376; Curia and, 469; Dominicans and, 165–166, 511; Enlightenment and, 528, 529; Franciscans and, 594; Jansenism and, 825; Jewish status and, 872; military orders and, 989; poor health rumor about, 1417; Quirinal and, 1271; St. Paul's Outside the Walls rebuilding, 1372; tomb of, 1386

[Benedict XIV], 70, 72, **167**

Benedict XIV, 143, **168–172**, 668, 1091; academies, 120; "ad limina" visits and, 4; apostasy decretal, 79; arms, 115; beatification and, 145, 530; beatification of, 146; bell ringing, 152; [Benedict XIV] and, 167; as Benedict XV influence, 173; camerlengo powers and, 220; canonical collection of, 228, 232, 363, 366; canonization canonical treaty of, 232, 268, 269; canonizations by, 27, 235–236; chamberlains, 288; Chinese rites denial, 1003, 1004, 1255, 1345; Christmas Cantata abolishment, 299; Clement XIII and, 358; Code of Canons of Eastern Churches and, 370; coins, 376; Colosseum and, 388; consistorial advocates and, 413; Curia and, 469–470; cursor numbers reduction, 475; datary reduction, 483; Dominicans and, 511; election of, 167, 529; encyclical list, 524; encyclicals, 169, 530; as Enlightenment pope, 169, 170, 529–530, 1345; Fabric of St. Peter and, 558; Freemasonry condemnation, 170, 602, 605; heraldry, 690, 696; on images in churches, 1090; imprimatur, 763; Index revision, 170, 171, 530, 709, 772, 1443; Jesuits and, 827; liturgy and, 954; martyrology, 210; military chaplaincy and, 990; mosaics and, 1022; museum collection, 1025, 1026, 1117; nepotism reforms by, 243; painting commissions, 1090, 1117, 1372; Penitentiary restructuring, 1152, 1523; Pius VI and, 1178–1179; *possesso* ceremony, 1228; Quirinal and,

Volume Key: Volume 1, pages 1–614; volume 2, pages 615–1266; volume 3, pages 1267–1637.

1669

1269, 1271; registry of noble Roman families, 1049–1050; St. Mary Major restoration, 1367, 1370; Secretariat of Briefs, 1400–1401; slavery prohibitions, 1002, 1439; Spanish concordat with, 483, 1002; suburbicarian Italy and, 1466–1467; Trevi fountain project, 1117; tribunal of Roman Rota and, 1524

Benedict XV, **172–177**, 1211; arbitration by, 99; arms, 116; beatification, 148, 271; blessing *urbi et orbi* and, 177; camauro use, 620; canon law and, 435; canonizations by, 236, 271; Catholic University founding, 177, 1545; Christian Democracy and, 307–308, 1023; Code of Canon Law (1917), 228, 232, 243, 366, 395; congregations and, 472; Dante homage by, 482; dicastery elimination, 772; dispensation codification, 505–506; Dominicans and, 512; encyclical list, 525; encyclicals, 482, 1205, 1625; episcopate meetings and, 401; financial management, 582; Gentlemen of His Holiness ranking and, 627; Holy Office and, 710; Holy Places status and, 712, 723, 874; Italian People's Party and, 305; Italian unity and, 1570; Jewish restrictions and, 873, 874; League of Nations and, 1077; legislative derogations and, 406; Missionary Union and, 996; modernism and, 172, 173, 1110; native clergy training and, 1004, 1110, 1257; *Osservatore romano* and, 1083; Penitentiary duties and, 1523; Pius XI relationship with, 1200–1201, 1202, 1206; Pius XII as nuncio for, 1211–1212; Propaganda Fide and, 1257; Prophecy of Malachy motto, 1261, 1263; as Substitute of the Secretariat of State, 1464; Swiss Guard uniform, 1471; on unionism over ecumenism, 518–519; Vatican museum collection, 1026; World War I and, 172, 173–175, 307, 512, 539, 540, 582, 1110, 1211–1212, 1624–1628, 1630, 1631

Benedict Biscop, 142, 1166, 1619

Benedict of Albano, 1413

Benedict of Aniane, 952, 1014

Benedict of Nursia. *See* Benedict, St.

Benedictine Rule. *See* Rule of St. Benedict

Benedictines, 156, 1013, 1015; Benedict XII and, 161; Celestine V and, 280; founding of, 1013; Hadrian IV and, 683; Honorius II and, 732; Innocent III and, 788; Leo VII and, 922–923; liturgy, 952, 954; Paul VI and, 1133–1134; Pius VII and, 693, 1182–1183; St. Paul's Outside the Walls monastery, 1373; unionism and, 519, 539; Urban II favoring, 1551; Urban V and, 1556; Victor III and, 1613–1614, *See also* Benedict, St.; Rule of St. Benedict

benedictions, papal, **177–178**; for hat and sword gifts, 182; as pilgrimage culmination, 1170

benefaction, **178–179**; animal gifts, 58; blessed hat and sword, 182; consecrated swaddling clothes, 1470; by Constantine, 178, 1045–1046; by converted Christian nobles, 1046; keys as gift, 598; to national cleric, 1027; papal gifts of relics, 1389; spoils, 1452, *See also* nepotism; simony

benefices. *See* finances, papal

benefices, vacant, **179–180**, 577–578, 579–580, 1266; expectative grace and, 555; reserve of, 1298–1299; Urban V and, 1556

Benelli, Cardinal, 858, 863, 864

Beneventan rite, 948, 951

Benevento, 51, 141, 166, 196, 643, 667, 925, 1052, 1054, 1319, 1538; Charlemagne and, 599, 680; Gregory VIII and, 652; Hadrian IV and, 683, 684; Lombards and, 958, 1120, 1393; Papal States and, 1102, 1189

Benevento, battle of (1266), 315, 332, 440

Benevento, concordat of (1156), 278, 684, 960, 961, 1053, 1054, 1615

Benevento, Peace of (1128), 732

benevolence. *See* poor relief

Benigni, Umberto, 614, 1009–1010, 1110, 1199

Benso, Camillo. *See* Cavour, Conte di

Bentivoglio, Giovanni, 885

Bentivoglio, Guido, 466

Benvenuti, Cardinal, 672

Beorhtweald of Canterbury, 835

Beran, Bishop, 1085, 1086, 1215

Beraud of Lyon, 334

Berbers, 143

Berengar I, king of Italy, 154, 838, 839, 923, 924

Berengar II, king of Italy, 172, 840, 851

Berengar of Tours, 701, 1036, 1552

Bergerre, Max, 1236

Bergier, Nicolas-Sylvestre, 77

Bergson, Henri, 1008

Berkouwer, G. C., 1577

Berlin, Congress of (1878), 711, 712

Berlin Wall, 859, 865, 1086

Bermejo, Louis, 764

Bernadette, St., 1204

Bernadot, M. V., 512

Bernard Delicieux, 849

Bernard di Porto, 277, 438

Bernard, François, 1237

Bernard of Clairvaux, St., 72, 111, 414, 450, 701, 750, 850, 1348; [Anacletus II] deposition by, 42, 900; attacks on Abelard by, 275, 277, 450; canonical collections and, 226; canonization of, 268; Celestine II and, 275–276; Eugene III and, 496, 532, 533; Innocent II support by, 784–785; Lucius II and, 959; Lucius III and, 960; Malachy and, 1261

Bernard of Menthon, St., 1168

Bernard of Montemirat, 227

Bernard of Parma, 227

Bernard of Toledo, 651

Bernardino of Siena, St., 67, 725, 976, 1041

Bernetti, Cardinal, 672, 932

Berni, Francesco, 464

Bernier of Orléans, 585, 586

Bernini, Gian, 30, 38, 547, 549, 569, 694, 753, 803, 1062, 1270, 1386, 1586; architectural projects, 104, 106, 107, 1089, 1116, 1344, 1383–1384; Chair of St. Peter, 286, 287, 1159, 1379; Clement X projects, 351; major works, 1344; painting commissions, 1090; papal tombs, 1344; St. Mary Major, 1369; St. Peter's basilica redesigns, 1371, 1383–1384, 1562; Urban VIII commissions, 1091, 1383, 1560, 1562

Bernini, Pietro, 1369

Bernis, Cardinal de, 611, 612

Bernold of St. Blaise, 1043, 1551

Bernon of Cluny, 839

Bernward of Hildsheim, 1280

Berruyer, Philip, 233

Berteloot, Father, 608–609

Bertha of Turin, 18

Volume Key: Volume 1, pages 1–614; volume 2, pages 615–1266; volume 3, pages 1267–1637.

1670

Berthe of Bourgogne, 646

Berthier, Alexander, 122, 613, 1320

Berthier, J., 512

Bertrada, queen of the Franks, 599, 1457, 1458, 1551, 1552

Bertram, Cardinal, 1201, 1204

Bertrand, Pierre, 227

Bertrand de Got. *See* Clement V

Bertrand de Got (uncle), 334

Bertrand of Pavia, 226, 231, 266, 663

Bertrand of St. Martin, 657

Bérulle, Pierre de, 1409

Besci, Francesco Antonio (Finaia), 256

Besozzi, Cardinal, 171

Bessarion, 208, 537, 1122

Bessarion, Cardinal, 1172, 1294

Bethlehem, 711, 729

Bethlehem (Our Lord) Order, 990

Bevilacqua, Cardinal, 243, 1135, 1137

Bianchi, Gerardo, 280, 282

Bianchi, S., 1017

Bianchini, Francesco, 1024

Bibbiena, Bernardo, 926, 927

Bibbiena, Il (G. Battista Galli), 1363

Bible: Antichrist in, 64, 65; humanist textual criticism of, 1294; irrenancy position, 176; Luther on primacy of, 1286, 1287, 1395; Lutheran, 1354; Marcion heresy and, 697; modernism and, 1006, 1008; painting illustrations, 1090; prophecies in, 1261; rational criticism of, 1007; Roman breviary, 193–194; of St. Paul's, 1370, 1373; subsidiarity concept in, 1462; tiara and, 1489, 1490, 1492; translations, 169, 1522; Trent on authority and interpretation of, 1277, 1520; Vatican II and, 1585; Vulgate, 194, 348, 388, 1296, 1437, 1520, *See also* Gospels, the, and papal authority; New Testament; Old Testament; *specific gospels*

Biblical Commission, Papal, 388, 407, 981

Biblical Institute, Pontifical (Rome), 1545

Bibliothèque Nationale (Paris), 1597

Bibliothèque Royal (Paris), 1598

Bigard, Jeanne, 1373–1374

Bigard, Stéphanie, 1373–1374

Bilhères, Jean, 1378

Bilio, Cardinal, 1195, 1196

billets de confession, 171

Billot, Cardinal, 944

biographies, pontifical. *See Liber pontificalis*

Biondo, Flavio, 1173

Biordi, Giovanni, 298

birds, 58–59

biretta, cardinal's, **180**; caudatary and, 267; Noble Guard and, 12, 1051, 1052; nuncio and, 1057

Birot, Louis, 1007

birth control, 1110, 1132, 1140–1141, 1141–1142, 1143, 1247

Bisceglie, Alfonso da, 27

Biscop, Benedict. *See* Benedict Biscop

bishop: "ad limina" visits, 4–5, 465, 503, 992, 1167, 1245, 1283, 1512, 1566; appointment of, 85–95; canon law and, 787; Catholic reform and, 1276; collegiality, 385–387, 1129, 1242–1243, 1277, 1584, 1585; conference of, 400–405, 431, 432, 1243, 1292; confraternity oversight, 1309; deacons and,

484; diocese, 499–500; dioceses *in partibus*, 500–501; dispensation, 505; Dominican, 506, 507, 512; ecclesiastical province, 1264–1265; first Chinese, 1257; lay investiture issue, 1424; *pallium* and, 1608; regalia, 1290, 1291; reserved cases, 1298; seminaries, 1408; simony prohibition, 1423; synod, 1477–1479, *See also* Bishop, Congregation for

bishop of Rome, 90, **180–181**, 199, 1156; anathema power of, 624; Angelus and Sunday blessing, 50; catacombs and, 261–262; Clement I in chronology of, 327; "crypt of the popes," 258; differences with Eastern Churches, 200, 208, 1034; ecumenism vs. primacy of, 521, 522; election hierarchy, 1036; excommunication power, 48–49; Frankish relationship, 1319; Gregory I and status of, 640; John Paul II and status of, 865; John XXIII and status of, 854; *lapsi* treatment and, 968; Lateran as seat of, 1300, 1304, 1363; Lateran synod election decree of 1059, 1035–1036; Linus as Peter's successor, 947–948; monasticism and, 1011, 1012; Nicholas I and status of, 1035; perpetual succession, 1241; Peter as first, 1108, 1157, 1159, 1160; as pontifical designation, 1494; pope as title for, 1227; primacy of, 480, 1108, 1241–1242, 1244; Roman Empire reorganization and, 564; Roman nobility and, 1047; Roman persecutions and, 1155, 1156; scriptural foundation for, 631–632; tiara, 1490; ties with Italy, 538; titles for, 1109, 1494–1495; veneration of, 1391–1392

Bishops and Regulars, Congregation of, 247, 401, 411

Bishop's Ceremonial (1600), 348

Bishops, Congregation for, 411, 435, 469, 675; on "ad limina" visits, 5; creation and function, 408–409, 415, 465, 1178; military ordinariate and, 992; personal prelatures, 1235; Sixtus V and, 1438; Vatican II and, 1574

Bismarck, Otto von, 891, 892, 893, 1104, 1530; Canossa allusion by, 237, 239; Leo XIII and, 934, 1196

Bisticci, Vespasiano da, 218, 1434

Bizzarri, Msgr., 1192

Black Death, 129, 336, 337, 508, 703, 1275; Avignon papacy and, 1220–1222; Rome and, 1329

black Guelphs, 481, 677

black nobility, 627, 1050

Black Plague. *See* Black Death

black slavery, 1439, 1440, 1441

blacksmith shop, 457, 458

Blado, Antonio, 968

Blanche of Bourbon, 796

Blanche of Castille, 910

Blesilla, 1013

blessed, declarations of. *See* beatification

Blessed or Holy Hat and Sword, **182–183**

blessing, 38, 126, 177, 182, 1233; Angelus recitation with, 50; Golden Rose, 1348; St. Peter's basilica and, 1384; with swaddling clothes gift, 1470

Blet, Pierre, 496, 1214

Blondel, Maurice, 78, 1008

blood libels, 360–361, 871, 872, 873, 874

Bloy, Léon, 1625

Bobbio (monastery), 142, 156, 552, 730, 1420

Bobola, Andrea, St., 1204

Bobone, Giacinto/Hyacinthus. *See* Celestine III

Boboni family, 277, 451, 1048

Volume Key: Volume 1, pages 1–614; volume 2, pages 615–1266; volume 3, pages 1267–1637.

Boccamazza family, 1047

Boccamazza, Giovanni Cardinal, 736

Boccamazza, Pietro, 280

Boccasini, Niccolò. *See* Benedict XI

Bockenheim, Jean de, 302–303

Bodin, Jean, 391

Boegner, Marc, 520

Boethius, 831, 832, 847, 1046, 1421

Boff, Leonardo, 764

Boggio, Pier Carlo, 1537

Bohemia: Austrian Catholicism and, 669, 1130; blessed hat and sword gift to, 182; Calvinism in, 1288; crusades and, 333; crypto-Protestants in, 869; Great Schism and, 636; Holy Roman Empire and, 717; Hussite heresy and, 703–704, 775, 1130; missions to, 997; in papal early 15th-century domain, 661; Paul II and, 1122, *See also* Czechoslovakia

Bohemond of Tarento, 1112

Bohic, Henri, 227

Boito, Camillo, 1018

Boldetti, Marc'Antonio, 100

Boleslaw Chrobry, ruler of Poland, 844

Boleyn, Anne, 345, 1288–1289, 1395

Bolgi, Andrea, 1383

Bolivia, 398, 1580

Böll, Heinrich, 1142

Bollandists, 169, 872

bollatica, **183**, 293

Bologna: cardinal protectors for, 246–247; Council of Trent moved to, 429, 1125, 1519; Gregory XV and, 667; Italian unity and, 672, 1535, 1538; Julius II conquest of, 885; legation, 672; Martin V and, 111, 975; Napoleonic occupation of, 1103, 1183; painting school, 2, 1091, 1092; in Papal States, 1102, 1104, 1105(map)

Bologna, Concordat of (1516), 397, 616, 1266, 1298

Bologna, Council of (1547–1548), 886

Bologna, Gregorian College of, 246–247

Bologna, University of, 19, 171, 379, 655, 1543–1544, 1547, 1548, 1549; canonical collections, 225, 226; conciliarism and, 390; Curia career and, 451; dissection prohibition, 1221; Gratian and, 225; Great Schism and, 635; Gregory XV degree from, 667; Innocent III decretals collection, 789

Bolsena massacre, 659

Bolshevism. *See* Marxism and the papacy

Bombay, Paul VI visit to, 1139, 1514, 1516

Bonaccolsi, Rainaldo (Passerino), 629

Bonagrazia of Bergamo, 850

Bonaparte, Carlo, 1324

Bonaparte, Joseph, 586, 613, 1320

Bonaparte, Louis. *See* Napoléon III

Bonaparte, Napoléon. *See* Napoléon I

Bonaventure, St., 234, 593, 657, 685, 774, 1038, 1429, 1543

Bonaventure of Bagnoregio, 657

Boncompagni, Eleanora, 1226

Boncompagni family, 694, 1032

Boncompagni, Ugo. *See* Gregory XIII

Bonelli, Michaele, 346, 510, 1178, 1469

Bönhoffer, Dietrich, 1006

Boniface, St.: Easter date, 518; missions, 997; papal relations, 643, 644, 1640; pilgrimage to Rome, 1166

Boniface I, **183–185**, 198, 251, 1046; Celestine I and, 273; election of bishops and, 91; Eulalius as antipope, 72, 183, 184, 538, 1230; evangelization and, 545; as former deacon, 484; legates and, 908; military expenditures, 110; monasticism and, 1013; on primacy of Peter, 1160; tomb of, 1496

Boniface II, 14, **185–186**, 832; Byzantium and, 202; Dioscorus schism and, 71, 502, 503; *pallium*, 1608; Vigilius and, 1616

Boniface III, **186**, 268

Boniface IV, **186–187**, 254, 1328; Anglo-Saxon Church and, 142, 188; Franks and, 598; Pantheon consecration, 1096; plague and, 1220; tomb of, 1497

Boniface V, 142, **187–188**, 730

Boniface VI, **188**

[Boniface VII], 70, 71, **188–189**; arms, 112, 113; assassination of, 122; Benedict VI and, 155, 188; Benedict VII and, 156; John XIV imprisonment death by, 842; *maleficius* epitaph of, 189

Boniface VIII, 127, 186, **189–191**, 334, 848, 973; Angevins and, 53; annona, 60; arms, 113, 693; banks and, 452; Benedict XI as successor, 160; canonical collection, 226, 231, 1109; cardinalate and, 241, 242, 267; Catholic university founding, 128, 379, 1545; Celestine V resignation and, 282, 1305; Church-State conflict and, 131, 160, 189–191, 615, 1291, 1481; Clement V and, 334, 335; crusades and, 685, 1481; Dante's consignment to Hell, 481; dissection prohibition, 1221; Doctors of the Church and, 568; Dominicans and, 506–507; exemptions curtailment, 190, 594; fanon, 1607; finances management, 80, 190, 579; first Holy Year (1300) proclamation, 190, 724, 774, 1169; Franciscans and, 594; Guelphs and, 481, 676; heraldry, 689; heresy and, 702, 703; indulgence revocations by, 281; Latium Palace, 1303; library, 1597; menagerie, 58; nepotism and, 1031, 1038, 1049; Nicholas IV and, 1039; non-Roman residence, 1302; papal primacy and, 676; Papal States codification, 1101; pavilion, 822; pet parrot, 58; pilgrim penitentiaries and, 1151; pontifical gloves, 620; resignation, 1305; Roman family rivalries and, 280; Rota member numbers, 1349; St. John Lateran basilica and, 1360, 1361; St. Peter's basilica and, 1379; scriptors, 1398; slavery and, 1439; theocracy definition by, 496, 1109, 1485; tiara, 1489, 1491–1492; tomb of, 486, 1501; vacant See and, 486

Boniface IX, **192–193**, 851, 1371; Angevins and, 53; [Benedict XIII] and, 164; brief origination, 194–195; Castel Sant'Angelo fortification by, 254–255; Catholic university founding, 193, 1546; Fisherman's Ring, 587; Great Schism and, 192–193, 634, 635, 661; Holy Year and, 192, 725; hunting as sport of, 58; Innocent VII and, 797; Inquisition and, 703; military forces, 111; Roman government and, 1338; scriptors, 459; tiara, 1491; tomb of, 1379, 1502

Boniface of Canossa, 238

Boniface of Tuscany, 481

Bonifician fourth, 507

Bonizo of Sutri, 224, 1551

bonnet of the Holy Spirit. *See* Blessed or Holy Hat and Sword

Bonvicino, Alessandro, 1383, 1385

Bonzagna, Gianfederigo, 982

Book of Common Prayer (Anglican), 55, 1086

Book of Hours, 1275

Book of Pastoral Rule, The (Gregory I), 641

Volume Key: Volume 1, pages 1–614; volume 2, pages 615–1266; volume 3, pages 1267–1637.

1672

Boretti, Guidobaldo, 256

Borghese, Camillo. *See* Paul V

Borghese family, 247, 667, 1032; Curia nepotism and, 466; increased holdings under Paul V, 1130; painting collection, 1091, 1092

Borghese, Marcantonio, 1130

Borghese Palace, 1130, 1229

Borghese, Paolo, 801

Borghese, Scipione, 256, 667, 668, 1597, 1598; painting collection, 1091, 1092, 1369

Borgia, Cesare, 25, 27, 884–885, 926, 1102, 1174, 1621–1622

Borgia family, 138; arms, 1145; "legend of," 28; nepotism, 25–28, 218, 1032

Borgia, Francesco. *See* Borgia, Francis, St.

Borgia, Francis, St., 351, 726, 827, 1000, 1545

Borgia, Joffrey, 25, 26

Borgia, John, 25, 26, 27

Borgia, Lucrezia, 25, 26, 27, 1269, 1439, 1622

Borgia, Pietro-Luigi, 218

Borgia, Rodrigo. *See* Alexander VI

Borgia, Stefano, 1001, 1254

Boris, khan of Bulgaria, 205, 682, 836, 969, 997, 1034

Borja, Alfonso de. *See* Callistus III

Borja, Rodrigo. *See* Alexander VI

Borromeo, Carlo. *See* Borromeo, Charles, St.

Borromeo, Charles, St., 168, 358, 379, 666, 906, 1177, 1559; canonization of, 1130, 1137; church architectural requirements, 1341; Curia reforms, 465; on jubilee pilgrimage (1575), 727; as patron saint of Lombards, 569; Pius IV reforms and, 1175–1176; as Pius XI influence, 1200, 1202; poor relief and, 1224; Roman Catechism and, 263, 1522; seminaries and, 1408–1409; Tridentine reforms and, 1277, 1408, 1519, 1572

Borromeo, Frederick, 350, 1175, 1176

Borromini, Francesco, 107, 803, 1117, 1344, 1360, 1361, 1362–1363, 1370, 1383, 1499, 1560, 1562

Bosco, John, St., 1204

Bosio, Antonio, 100, 260

Bosnia, 659, 1567

Boson, 450, 452, 940

Bossuet, Jacques-Bénigne, 77, 808, 1268

Botticelli, Sandro, 104, 1091, 1428, 1435

Bouchard, Jean-Jacques, 1562

Boucicaut, Marshal, 634

Boulanger, F., 1362

Bourbons, 347, 530, 824, 1534, 1539–1540; chinea tribute, 303, 304; Clement XI support for, 1103; conflict with Jesuits, 828; definitive fall in France, 1190; jurisdictional conflict, 888; in Naples, 357, 1623, 1624

Bourdarias, Jean, 522

Bourdon, Sabastien, 117

Bourges, assembly of (1438). *See* Pragmatic Sanction

Bourget, Paul, 759

Bourgoing, François, 1409

Bourguerol, Sicard de, 82

Bouvier de La Motte, Jeanne. *See* Guyon, Mme.

Bouvines, battle of (1214), 314

Boveschi family, 1049, 1098

Boxadors, Jean-Thomas de, 511

Boy Scouts, French, 955

Boyl, Bernard, 27

Brabant, 633

Braccio Nuovo gallery, 1025

Bracciolini, Francesco, 1091

Brahe, Tycho, 213

Bramante, Donato, 255, 549, 885, 926, 982, 1029, 1344; St. Peter's basilica rebuilding, 104–105, 106, 107, 1382; Vatican gardens and, 1595, 1598

Brandt, Willy, 1084

Braschi family, 1049, 1180, 1181, 1182, 1184

Braschi, Giovanni Angelo. *See* Pius VI

Braschi, Luigi Onesti, 1181

Braschi Palace, 1181

Braschi, Romualdo Onesti, 1181, 1184

brass band, 299

Braulio of Saragossa, 143

Brazil: Catholic missions, 932, 1343; John Paul II visit to, 1512; papal concordats, 398; Vatican II representation, 1579, 1580

Breakspear, Nicholas. *See* Hadrian IV

Breisgau, University of, 1544

Bremond, Henri, 1008

Brent, Charles, 518

Bresciani, Antonio, 324, 325, 1644

Brest-Litovsk, synod of (1596), 1344, 1531

Brethren of the Free Spirit, 1268

Breviarium Extravagantium (Bernard of Pavia), 655

breviary, Roman, **193–194**, 213, 951, 954; Benedict XIV reform of, 169, 530; Clement VIII and, 348; liturgical music revisions and, 298; Pius X and, 1198; registers of, 1293; Tridentine (1568), 193, 194, 954, 995, 1109, 1130, 1175, 1178, 1277, 1289, 1522; Urban VIII reform of, 298, 1562

Breviatio canonum, 231

Briand, Aristide, 309

Briçonnet, Guillaume, 1276

Bridget of Sweden, St., 144, 162, 896; Avignon papacy and, 266; canonization of, 193; St. Paul's statue of, 1373

Brie, Simon de. *See* Martin IV

brief, **194–195**; cardinal nephew office and, 245; Curia and, 292–293, 460, 461, 463–464; decorations and, 487–488; seal, 196, 293, 587, *See also* Secretariat of Briefs

Brienne, Gauthier de, 1054

Briganti, G., 1272

Brigette of Sweden. *See* Bridget of Sweden, St.

Britain. *See* England; Ireland; Scotland

Britannica collection (ca.1090), 1283

broadcasting. *See* media, communication, and the Vatican; Vatican Radio; Vatican Television

Brossard de Beaulieu, Geneviève, 120

Brosses, Charles de, 1344, 1345

Brother Son, Sister Moon (film), 323

brotherhoods. *See* Roman confraternities

Brothers of the Militia of the Poor Knights of Christ. *See* Templars, Knights

Brunelleschi, Filippo, 103, 104

Brunet, Jacques, 256

Brunetta, Gian Piero, 322

Brunetti, Angelo (Ciceruacchio), 1018, 1324

Volume Key: Volume 1, pages 1–614; volume 2, pages 615–1266; volume 3, pages 1267–1637.

1673

Brunhild, queen of the Franks, 597, 598

Bruno, Giordano, 348, 1018, 1344

Bruno de Segni, 111, 625, 962, 1490, 1551

Bruno d'Egisheim. *See* Leo IX

Bruno of Carinthia. *See* Gregory V

Bruno of Holstein-Schauenberg, 657

Bruno of Trier, 1113

Buccapeccus, Theobaldus. *See* Celestine (II)

Bucer, Martin, 1289

Budes, Sylvester, 659

"buffoons" (Lollards), 703

Bugenhagen, Johann, 1287

Bugiardini, Giuliano, 1429

Bugnini, Annibale, 956

Buhrig, Marga, 522

Bulgaria, 522, 590, 787; John VIII and, 836; John X and, 839; Marinus I (Martin II) and, 969; *ostpolitk*, 1084; Rome-Constantinople conflict over, 205, 318, 969, 997; Slavonic liturgy, 1459

bull, **195–196**; *bollatica* and, 183, 293; brief vs., 194, 195; on causes of canonization, 268; Chancery and, 292, 293–294, 1282; crusade model, 438; death of the pope, 485; on Dominicans, 506; forgeries, 589; Leo IX design forms for, 195, 925

Bullan, B., 1223

Bullarium (Benedict XIV), 363

bullfights, 58, 249

Bultmann, Rulf, 1006

Buonaiuti, Ernesto, 1008

Buonarroti family, 695

Buondelmonti family, 629

Buonsignori banks, 136, 452

Burckard, Johannes, 284, 285

Burchard of Worms, 224, 231, 871, 1279, 1280; *Decretum*, 231, 1279, 1425

Burckhardt, Jacob, 1355

Burdinus, Mauritius. *See* [Gregory VIII]

Bureau, Lawrence, 1276

Burgundio of Piso, 534

Burgundy, 140, 714, 715, 716, 732; fall of western Roman Empire and, 1318; Holy Roman Empire and, 313, 1624; investiture controversy and, 215–216, 821

burial sites, papal. *See* tombs of the popes

Burney, Charles, 298

Bussi, Corboli, 1193, 1324

Bussi, Giovanni Andrea, 1597

Butler, Cuthbert, 1567

Butor, M., 751, 754, 760

Buzio, Ippolito, 1369

Byzantine Church. *See* Eastern Churches; Constantinople

Byzantine popes (534–715), 141, **196–197**, 201–203; Martin I as, 971–972; Ottoman conquest (1453), 208; Theodore I and, 1486–1487; Vitalian as, 1619

Byzantium and the papacy, **197–208**; African Church and, 13; Agapitus I and, 14, 198, 267; Alexander III support by, 20; Alexandria and, 32–34; Anastasius Bibliothecarius and, 46–47; apostolic legend of Andrew and, 202, 206; Benedict IX and, 158; Benedict VII and, 156; Benedict VIII and, 157, 846; Boniface V and, 187, 188; [Clement III] and, 329; con-quest by Turks (1453), 208, 218, 319, 440, 1041, 1526–1527, 1531; conquest by Turks and Normans (1071), 206–207; Constantine I and, 420; control of Constantinople by, 1319 (*see also* Constantinople); crusaders and, 206–207, 437, 438, 440, 973, 1112, 1319; Damasus and, 479–480; Donus and, 514–515; ecumenical councils, 198, 200, 201, 202–203, 204, 206, 427–428; fall of empire in West and, 1318; Felix III and, 572–573; Gothic wars and, 1327–1328, 1330; Gregory I and, 639, 640, 641; Gregory II conflict with, 642–643; Gregory III and, 644; Gregory X and, 1038; Hadrian III and, 682; Hormisdas and, 737–738; iconoclast controversy, 197, 198, 203–205, 1394; imperial coronation and, 424; imperial mourning duration, 486; Islam and, 202, 203, 204, 206, 1319; John I and, 564, 831–832; John III and, 833; John VI and, 835; John VII and, 835–836; John VIII and, 836–837; John X and, 839; John XIX and, 846; Julian the Apostate and, 881–882; Lateran Palace seizure by, 1354; Leo I and, 915–918; Lombard invasions response by, 1115; Martin IV crusade against, 973; Nicholas IV and, 1038; Normans and, 18, 206–207, 318, 684, 1036; Ottoman domination of, 206–208, 1531; papal legates to, 909; Paschal II and, 1112; Paul I and, 1120; primacy of Rome recognized by, 201, 202, 207, 317, 318, 563, 564, 1245; Ravenna and, 203, 546–547, 1115, 1273, 1319, 1331; reconquest of Italy by, 318, 564, 1096, 1273, 1330, 1411, 1616; Russian Church and, 1488; Saracens and, 1392, 1393; schism with West. *See* Eastern Churches; Sergius IV and, 1414–1415; Silverius and, 1417–1418; Simplicius and, 1426–1427; Stephen I and, 1455; Stephen V (VI) and, 1459; Symmachus and, 1475–1476; tetragamy crisis (906–920), 45, 206, 839; Thessalonica and, 1611; tiara, 1490; Turks and, 1526; Urban II and, 1551, 1552; Vigilius and, 1616–1618, *See also* Byzantine popes; Roman Empire; *specific emperors and prelates*

Cabassole, Philip, 1556

Cabrini, Frances, St., 270

Cabrol, Father, 954

Cacciaguerra, Bonsignore, 1309

Caccianemici, Gherardo. *See* Lucius II

Cadalus of Parma. *See* [Honorius II]

"cadaver synod" (Formosus exhumation), 1459–1460

Caecilianus of Carthage, 993, 1394, 1418

Caecilianus of Spoleto, 945

Caeionii family, 1045

Caelestius, 251, 783

Caesar, Julius, 213, 1313, 1374

Caesarius of Arles, 14, 181, 185, 573, 597, 833, 1476

Caesestius, 700

Caetani, Benedetto. *See* Boniface VIII

Caetani family, 189, 282, 692, 1047, 1049, 1303

Caetani, Leone, 285

Caetani, Loffredo, 1039

Caetani, Onorato, 1558

Caetani, Pietro, 1303

Caffarelli, Scipione, 1129–1130

Caius, **209**, 1496

Cajetan, Thomas, 509, 778, 899, 927, 1128, 1286

Calabria, 203, 318, 638, 644

Calais, Peace of (1347), 1221–1222

Volume Key: Volume 1, pages 1–614; volume 2, pages 615–1266; volume 3, pages 1267–1637.

1674

Calandion of Antioch, 1426

Calandrelli, G., 1062

Calandrini, Filippo, 1041

Calasanz, José, St., 360, 1226

Calatafimi, battle of (1860), 1540

Calatrava Order, 989, 990

Caldera, Rafael, 310

Calderini, Guglielmo, 1372

calendar, **209–211**, 995, 1062, 1366, 1461; anniversaries of popes' deaths, 1495; apostolic constitutions dating, 421–422; cycles of the year, 210; Easter-date controversies, 517–518, 561, 562, 563, 707, 1612; feast days, 209, 210–212, 569, 1388; French Revolutionary changes, 612; Gregory XIII reform. *See* calendar, Gregorian; liturgical cycle listing, 211–212; liturgy of martyrs, 1432; papal death commemoration, 1391–1392, 1495; saint veneration, 1388; stations, 1452–1454

calendar, Gregorian, 51, 209, **212–214**, 612, 665; Easter date, 518

Calepodius's catacomb, 1391, 1496

Caleppi, Lorenzo, 1181

Caligula, emperor of Rome, 64

Calini, Muzio, 263

Calistus. *See* Callistus

Calixtus. *See* Callistus

Callistus (slave martyr), 1154

Callistus I, 63, 70, **214–215**, 1045; banking activity, 135; catacomb, 258, 261, 557, 1496; Hippolytus opposition, 707, 708; martyrdom of, 121–122; tomb of, 1391, 1496; Zephyrinus and, 214, 1640

Callistus II, 42, 152, 172, **215–217**, 275, 959; Apostolic Camera and, 449; Burgundian cardinals and, 732; canonization and, 233, 268; cardinalate and, 450; Cathars and, 702; Concordat of Worms signing, 397, 428, 1281, 1284, 1636–1637; expulsion of antipope by, 109, 215–216, 626, 652, 1281; Honorius II and, 731, 732; Lateran I and, 428, 900; Paul II and, 1121; St. Peter's basilica altar and, 38, 549; suburbicarian dioceses, 501; tiara, 1492; tomb of, 1499; [Victor IV] and, 1615

[Callistus III], 70, 72, **217**, 313, 785, 901; Viterbo residence, 1620

Callistus III, 104, 112, **217–219**, 1114; abbreviators for, 1; advanced age and energy of, 1416; Alexander VI and, 25, 26, 537, 1032; Angelus recitation, 50; arms, 114; datary, 482; master of the Sacred Palace, 981; naval fleet, 218, 1029; nepotism and, 218, 1032; Pius II and, 1171, 1172; secretaries, 1402; tomb of, 1502–1503

Calmel de Viviers, Raymond, 1416

calotte (skullcap), 619, 620

Caltabellota, Peace of (1302), 190

Calvetti, Giuseppe, 325

Calvin, John, 68, 1288, 1518; catechism, 262, 263

Calvinism, 595; Eastern Churches and, 1000; in England, 55, 1519; in France, 663, 1518; Inquisition against, 817; John Paul II and, 865; Josephism and, 868, 869; on nonexistence of female pope, 830; Pius V campaign against, 1177; in Scotland, 1519; spread of, 1288; Thirty Years War and, 669

Camaldolese order, 246, 670, 671, 693

camauro (headdress), 620

Cambarou, Etienne, 219

Cambarou, Stephen, 459

Cambi, Pasquale, 324

Cambio, Arnolfo di. *See* Arnolfo di Cambio

Cambrai, Peace of (Ladies' Peace; 1529), 1624

Cambrai, treaty of (1517), 1623

Cambridge, University of, 749, 1548

Camelio (Vittore Gambello), 981

Camera. *See* Apostolic Camera

Camerino, Giusto da, 1192

Camerino, Jacopo da, 1360, 1361, 1363

Camerino, Rodolfo da, 110, 1538

camerlengo, **219–221**, 240, 483; coin issuance, 376; conclave and, 392; lay vs. ecclesiastical, 626–627, 739–740; in Middle Ages, 219, 452; of papal chapel, 298; pavilion, 1145; role in death of the pope, 221, 485, *See also* chamberlain

Cameroon, 398

Camillians, 1224

Camp David accords (1976), 858, 877

Campagna, 196, 1345, 1538, 1555; first bells, 151; papal patrimony, 576; Papal States and, 1102; Saracen threat and, 1393

Campanella, 1562

Campano, G. A., 1173

Campeggi, Lorenzo, 912

Campo Marzio, 1327, 1328

Camporese, 1016

Campori, Pietro, 667, 668

campsor camerae, 452

Campus Martius, 253, 442, 1095

Camuccini, Vencenzo, 1372–1373

Canada, 351, 675; French Catholic missions in, 1000, 1130, 1255; John Paul II visit to, 1512; Vatican I and, 1566; Vatican II representation, 1578, 1580, 1581

canaries, 59

Canary Islands, 98, 999, 1439

Candidus (Candide), Hugo (Huguges), 18, 649

Canfeld, Benoît de, 1267

Canisius, Peter, 263, 827, 1000, 1204

Cano, Alonso, 1123

Cano, Melchior, 778

canon, **221–222**; clerical celibacy promotion, 1044; Congregation for Bishops and, 409; election of bishops by, 92; first preserved Latin collection, 201; forgeries, 589; of minor basilicas, 144; monasticism and, 1015; papal reform and, 1280; simony and, 1281; theocracy doctrine and, 1483, 1484

canon law, **222–230**, 1543; Alexander III training in, 19, 21; *Apostolic Tradition* (Hippolytus), 90, 223; appeal to the pope, 85; auditors (papal advisors), 126, 460; beatification and, 145, 234, 268; biretta and, 180; canonical collections, 223–225, 230–232, 507; canonization and, 232, 233, 234, 268, 269–271; censure, 283; codification completion (1917), 175; concordats, 396–400; consistorial advocate, 413; Curia and, 451; custom and, 476; decretals, 488; dispensations, 504–505; divine vs. disciplinary, 222; Eastern Churches, 370–371; ecclesiastical penalties, 1149–1151; election of bishops, 86–87, 89, 90–91, 92, 93; episcopal reform of 13th-century, 787; forgery definition, 588; function of bishop and, 787; Gratian influence, 21, 84; Gregorian reform, 224–225, 1283; Gregory IX and, 226, 655; Gregory VIII training in, 652; Gregory XIII and, 665; Innocent II and, 785; inquisitory procedures development, 810–812; judges delegate and, 224, 453; judiciary function. *See* Rota, tribunal of the; Lat-

Volume Key: Volume 1, pages 1–614; volume 2, pages 615–1266; volume 3, pages 1267–1637.

1675

eran IV and, 897; legates and, 224, 909, 910; Lucius III and, 960; master of the Sacred Palace and, 981; Nicaean Council and, 222; nunciature and, 1056–1058, 1566; Penitentiary and, 1152; on pilgrimages, 1170; pontifical councils and commissions, 435; simony and, 1425; slave status and, 1439; sources and history, 222–223; tribunal of Roman Rota, 1524–1525; Tridentine reforms, 1109; university definition, 1548, *See also* Code of Canon Law

canonical censure. *See* censure, canonical

canonical code. *See* Code of Canon Law

canonical collections, **230–232**; Church primacy and, 1109; *Corpus juris canonici* (1580), 231, 363, 665; custom and, 476; decretals and, 488, 507; on deposition of pope, 495; *Dictatus papae* and, 499; Dominicans and, 507; Donation of Constantine in, 513; of Eastern Churches, 370–371; Gregorian reform and, 1283; Gregory IX and, 224–225, 231, 490–492, 507, 653, 1109; Honorius III and, 734; legates and, 908; Pius V and, 363; Propaganda Fide and, 1256; Rota decisions and, 1349, 1351, *See also* Code of Canon Law; Decretum of Gratian

canonization, **232–237**; auditor and, 126; beatification vs., 144, 145, 234, 268, 269; Benedict XIV history and critical study of, 168, 530; campaign for Celestine V, 282–283; cases for modern popes, 865–866; causes of, 268–272; consistorial advocates, 413; feast events, 570; first of modern Christianity, 667, 669; historical background, 268–269; by Holy Office, 268, 406; Holy Year, 728; of Jesuits, 827; of layman, 896; list of saints (by pope), 234–237; liturgical calendar and, 211; of Pius V, 496; statistics (by century), 271; of Thomas Aquinas, 508; Urban VIII's uniform procedures, 1562, *See also* saints, veneration of

canons regular, 732, 1044, 1276

Canossa (fortress), **237–239**; Henry IV pilgrimage to, 237, 238–239, 650, 1280, 1386, 1483; symbolic meaning of, 237, 239, 1280, 1577

Canossa, Mathilde de. *See* Matilda (of Canossa)

Canova, Antonio, 1025, 1117, 1272, 1345

Canterbury, 142, 188, 519–520, 521, 522; pilgrimages to, 725

Canterbury, archbishop of: Anglican communion united under, 54, 56; Anglican ordination and, 1073–1074, 1395; dialogues with pope, 1075, 1076; establishment of, 997; Henry II confrontation, 1114; Innocent III appointment of, 93; investiture controversy, 1113; John VI and, 835; Vigilius and, 1619

Canterbury, Council of (1555), 1521

cantors. *See* chaplain, papal; music

Canute, king of England and Denmark, 846

Cap of the Holy Spirit. *See* Blessed of Holy Hat and Sword

cape. *See* *cappa magna*; fanon

Cape Colonna, battle of (1982), 156

capellani papae. *See* chaplain, papal

Capetians, 278, 332, 440, 970, 1291

Capistrano, John, 594, 1041

Capitol, 1327; architectural renovation, 107, 976, 1116, 1127; bells and bell ringing, 152, 249; city planning around, 1121; Marcus aurelius statue, 1362; museum collection, 1026; *possesso* ceremony and, 1228, 1229, 1364; revolutionary occupation of, 1016; as slave refuge, 1440; stauary museum, 357

Capitoline Museum, 1092

Capitulary on Images, 428, 681

Capitulations (1517–1917), 711, 712

Capocci, Angelo, 1336

Capocci family, 451, 1047

Capocci, Ranuccio, 791

Caponi bank, 137

cappa magna, 144, 267

Cappadocians, 33, 34

cappellani. *See* chaplain, papal

Cappellari, Caterina, 670

Cappellari, Mauro. *See* Gregory XVI

Capponi, Alessandro, 357

Capranica, Cardinal, 379, 1407

Caprara, Cardinal, 913, 1186, 1187

Caprile, Father, 1570, 1571

Caprogrossi, Balthazar, 365

Capuchins, 595, 596, 664, 669; Barbarini family and, 1091; colleges, 1343; Jesuit conflicts with, 827; missions, 1000; Paul III and, 1126; Paul V and, 1130; plague and, 1222

Caput Ecclesiae (papal title), 1495

Caracalla, emperor of Rome, 1095, 1315

Caraciolo of Naples, 1267

Caradosso, 982, 983

Carafa, Alfono, 1175, 1469

Carafa, Antonio, 1177, 1469

Carafa, Carlo, 465, 466, 663, 1126, 1276, 1469; Paul IV and, 1128, 1175

Carafa family, 1269; Pius V and, 1176–1177; trial of, 1175

Carafa, Gian Pietro. *See* Paul IV

Carafa, Oliviero, 1121, 1127–1128

Carafa, Pier Luigi, 1561

Caravaggio, 1022, 1025, 1092, 1341, 1344

Carbonari, 605, 626, 932, 1189, 1538

Cardella, Valeriano, 325

Cardi, Ludivico (Il Cigoli), 1369, 1383

cardinal, **239–244**; up to Council of Trent, **239–243**, 449–450, 1056; after Council of Trent, 242, **243–244**, 467; arms of patronage, 695; biretta, 180; camerlengo, 219, 221, 240, 392, 452; camerlengo, list of, 10; caudatary for, 267; ceremonials, 294, 299, 569; as Chancery head, 293, 451; conclave, 392–395; conclavist assistance, 396; congregation, plenary, 405–406, 471, 1341; congregation prefects, lists of, 407–408, 409, 410–411, 412; consistorial allocutions to, 37, 240, 413, 414, 415, 456; crown, 241; Curia residency by, 451, 456, 462; datary, 483–484; death of the pope and, 9–10, 485; dicastery heads, 1283; Dominican, 507, 508, 511, 512; election of the pope and. *See* conclave; ferula, 575; finances, 80, 241, 242, 1246; first Jesuit, 827; funerary rites, 485; garb within Vatican, 619–620; Great Schism effects, 242, 393; humanist, 1295; internationalization, 244, 1357; legates, 240, 1058; librarians, 1597; lost prerogatives of, 467; major basilicas and, 144, 239; nepotism and, 241, 242, 243, 1032–1033, 1356, 1357; Noble Guard and, 12, 1051, 1052; non-Roman, 451; number limit, 465, 1357; origins, 239–240, 242; painting patrons, 1090–1092; Palatine, 1094; papal chapel and, 294, 296, 453; penitentiary, 454, 1523–1524; as Propaganda Fide prefects, 1256; red hat, 792; St. Peter's basilica burials, 1386; Secretariat of State, 1402–1403, 1404; superintendent of Ecclesiastical State, 1469; three orders of, 239–240; titles, 1493–1494; tombs in St. John Lateran, 1361, 1362–1363; Vatican citizenship of, 324, *See also* Sacred College

Volume Key: Volume 1, pages 1–614; volume 2, pages 615–1266; volume 3, pages 1267–1637.

1676

cardinal bishop, 239, 240, 243, 414; coronations and, 424, 426; overview, 1493–1494

Cardinal Bishops, Congregation of, 664

cardinal deacon, 239–240, 243, 1358; overview, 1493

cardinal "in petto," **244–245**

cardinal judges, 1525

cardinal nephew, **245–246**, 462, 463, 1033, 1590; career and, 247–248; Christmas Cantata responsibility, 299; conclave and, 394; Curia and, 466, 468; datary and, 483; diplomatic service, 1402; Enlightenment reforms and, 529; office establishment, 1402; painting collections, 1091–1092; Palatine, 1094; in papal hierarchy, 1341; as superintendent of Ecclesiastical State, 245, 1468, 1469, *See also specific popes*

cardinal penitentiary (list), 1523–1524

cardinal priest, 239, 240, 243, 244

cardinal protector, 241, **246–247**, 462, 475; for Dominicans, 246, 507; for papal chapel singers, 296

cardinale padrone. See cardinal nephew

Cardinal's salt, 1027

career, **247–248**; Curia advantages, 451; simony and, 463

Caresina, Father, 1133

Carey, George, 1076

Carit, Bernard, 82

caritas (concept), 871

Carloman (son of Pepin the Short), 1319, 1320, 1456, 1640; Hadrian I and, 679–680; Stephen III (IV) and, 1457, 1458

Carloman of Austrasia, 598

Carmelites, 351, 379, 734, 1001; Black Death epidemic and, 1221; reforms and growth, 1276, 1343

Carmina Burana, 750

Carnival, **248–250**, 1121, 1506

Caro, Annibale, 968

Carolingian renaissance, 681, 1300

Carolingians, 15, 124, 970; action against monastic exemptions, 552; appointment of bishops and, 91; canonical collections, 223, 224, 231; Church relations, 821, 1320, 1331, 1378–1379, 1425, 1482; coins, 372; collapse of empire, 1245; Donation of Constantine forgery hypothesis, 513; fragmentation of, 601; Holy Roman Empire and, 600, 601, 714, 715, 842; iconoclast controversy and, 600, 681, 701; liturgy, 952; Lombards and, 957, 958; monasticism and, 1013; Nicholas I and, 1033–1034, 1035; papal administration under, 600; papal arbitration and, 98; papal armies and, 109; papal finances and, 577; papal protection by, 1245; Paschal I and, 1111; pilgrimages to Rome, 1165, 1166, 1167; relic traffic to, 261; Roman Church influence on, 418; Roman rebuilding and, 1328; St. Peter's basilica and, 1378–1379; sainthood recognition, 233, *See also* Charlemagne

Carpegna, Gaspare, 350

Carpentras (Elzear Genet), 297, 298

Carpophorus, Marcus Aurelius, 135

Carracci, Annibale, 1092

Carracci, Antonio, 1091, 1270

Carracci gallery, 1089, 1344–1345

Carranza, Bartolomé, 818

Carrara, Francesco de, 983

Carrero, Porto, 1369

Carrier, Jean, 165, 167, 1236

Carroll, John, 94

Cartagena Order, 990

Carter, Jimmy, 858

Cartesianism. *See* Descartes, René

Carthage, **250–252**; bishop as primate of Africa, 13, 250; bishop of Rome election and, 181; Celestine I and, 273; Donatist schism and, 419, 993, 1394; ecumenical councils, 427; evangelization, 544, 545; *lapsi* schism and, 232, 422–423, 1155, 1156; loss of (698), 203; martyrs, 1316; monasticism, 1012; Novatian and, 1055; Pelagian heresy, 700; Pelagius I and, 1146; provincial councils, 430; Sixtus II and, 1431; Vandal occupation of, 1318, *See also* Cyprian, St.

Carthage, Council of (256), 251

Carthage, Council of (401), 233

Carthage, Council of (411), 993

Carthage, Council of (416), 251

Carthage, Council of (418), 1641

Carthage, Council of (419), 13, 273, 908

Carthage, Council of (525), 551

Carthusians, 553, 952

cartography, **252–253**

Carus, emperor of Rome, 543

Carushomo, Benedetto, 1334–1335

Carvajal, Cardinal, 1172

Casanata, Cardinal, 29, 827

Casaroli, Agostino, 368, 1085, 1086, 1589, 1592

Casimirri, Luciano, 1236

Casoni, Filippo, 1187

Casoni, Giovanni Battista, 586, 1082–1083

Casoni, Vannicelli, 1326

Caspe, compromise of (1412), 165

Cassagnes, Jesselin de, 227

Cassel, Odo, 955

Cassetta, Francesco, 364, 1210

Cassian, John, St., 913, 1013; as Father of the Church, 567, 568

Cassianus (deacon), 993–994

Cassidy, Edward Idris, 434

Cassiodorus, 179, 832–833

cassock, 619

Castagna, Giovan Battista. *See* Urban VII

Castaldi, Giolamo, 166

Castel Gandolfo, 104, 668, 1093, 1541, 1562, 1587; death of the pope and, 10; *Gendarmeria*, 626; musical instruments, 299; Observatory telescope, 1063; papal apartments, 72, 73; peacocks, 59; Pius XI redevelopment of, 583; Vatican City and, 1592; Vatican Radio link, 1600; World War II bombardment of, 1588

Castel Sant'Angelo, 218, **253–256**, 666; administrative offices, 9, 1341; Benedict VI imprisonment in, 155, 188; Boniface IX reconstruction of, 193; coin repository, 374; Gregory VII imprisonment in, 329, 650; imperial Roman origins, 1314; John XIV imprisonment in, 189; Leonine City area, 921, 1302; Napoleonic control of, 1187; Nicholas V building plan, 1042; papal improvements, 255; as papal refuge, 109–110, 254–255, 1302, 1354, 1355, 1471, 1624; Pierleoni control of, 330; Pinturicchio paintings of, 28; Pius IV fortifications, 1176; as political prison, 254, 255; revolutionary occupation of, 1016; Sixtus V gold reserve in, 359, 1437; slaves, 1440, 1441; Sunday papal blessing and Angelus, 50; surrender to France (1798), 1320; Urban II and, 1551; Urban VIII and, 1560, 1561

Volume Key: Volume 1, pages 1–614; volume 2, pages 615–1266; volume 3, pages 1267–1637.

1677

Castelbolognese, 982

Castelfidardo, battle of (1860), 1195, 1540, 1645

Castelman, Pierre, 787

Casti connubii (1930 encyclical), 1141, 1204

Castiglionchio, Lap da, 1556–1557

Castiglione, Baldassare, 344, 1355

Castiglioni, Francesco Saverio. *See* Pius VIII

Castiglioni, Goffredo da. *See* Celestine IV

Castile, 162, 163, 165; Great Schism position of, 340, 632–633, 637; Inquisition in, 815–816

Castillo Lara, R., 368, 1292

Castor and Pollux (statue), 1269

castrati of the papal chapel, **256–257**, 297, 298

Castro, Alphonso de, 778

Castro and Ronciglione, 1049, 1342

Castro, Giovanni de, 38

Castro, Vincenzo de, 1539

Castro war (1649), 802, 1560, 1562

catacombs, **257–261**; archeological interest in, 100, 171, 260, 1016, 1296; baptistry remains, 139; Callistus I and, 258, 261, 557, 1496; Christian persecutions and, 1152, 1155; Constantine the Great and, 418, 1419; Holy Year pilgrims, 729; Peter and, 1159, 1160, 1161, 1165; saint veneration and, 1388, 1391, *See also* tombs of the popes

catacombs, saints' bodies in the, 250, **261–262**, 557; Clement X regulations, 351; Damasus I tomb building, 478; Paul I and, 1120; pilgrimages and, 729, 1164, 1165, 1170; protection of, 1389; St. Peter's basilica and, 547–549, 1376, 1378

catalogues of martyrs. *See* martyrologies

Cateau-Cambrésis, treaty of (1559), 1102, 1519, 1624

Catechism for Adults, 264

Catechism of Montpellier, 867

Catechism of Pius X, 1197, 1198

Catechism of the Catholic Church, 264

Catechism, Roman, **262–264**, 265, 1000, 1175, 1522

Catechism, Roman (1992), **264–265**, 410, 1142, 1178, 1277, 1289

Catechisme (Auger), 263

Catharism, 21, 133, 701, 702, 788, 962; as Antichrist, 65; crusade against (1208), 438; Inquisitors and, 812, 813, 814, 815; Lateran III and, 901; Lateran IV and, 897; military orders against, 987

Cathars. *See* Catharism

cathedral schools, 23, 1543, 1547–1549; as seminary antecedents, 1407

Catherine II, empress of Russia, 361, 1179, 1531–1532, 1533

Catherine de Médicis, queen of France, 345, 704, 928, 1064, 1520, 1624

Catherine of Aragon, queen of England, 54, 345, 1073, 1288, 1395

Catherine of Siena, St., **265–267**, 340, 508, 569, 660, 896, 1173

Catholic Action, 307, 308–309, 519, 902, 903, 955, 1142; dissolution of, 1008; fascist challenge to, 1135, 1136, 1207; Pius XI and, 1203, 1204–1206, 1207, 1209; Pius XII and, 1217

Catholic Christian Church. *See* Old Catholics

Catholic Education, Congregation for, 472, 1544, 1546; as Congregation for Studies, Seminaries, and Universities, 176–177, 411, 1408–1409, 1544, 1545–1546; founding and functions, 411–412; social communications, 1446

Catholic Emancipation Act of 1829 (United Kingdom), 94

Catholic Enlightenment. *See* Enlightenment

Catholic Institutes of Paris, 954, 1008, 1544

Catholic League, 1623

Catholic modernism. *See* modernism

Catholic Movement. *See* Movimento Cattolico

Catholic Reform. *See* reform, catholic

Catholic Religion, Academy of, 2, 671

Catholic renewal (1840s), 675

Catholic universities. *See* universities, Catholic

Catholic University of America, 40, 41

Catholic University of the Sacred Heart (Milan), 177

Catholic University of the West (Angers), 1544

Catholic University Students Federation. *See* FUCI

Catholic workers associations, 935

Catholicisme, 944

cats, 59

caudatry, **267**

causes of canonization, **268–272**; congregations and, 234, 408; consistory and, 413, 414; current procedures, 269–271; definitions, 268; historical background, 268–269; Holy Office and, 268, 406; statistics, 271

Causes of Saints, Congregation for the (formerly Congregation of the Rites): beatifications, 145, 268–269; Benedict XIV and, 168, 269; canonization and, 234, 268–269; cardinalate and, 243–244; Jews and, 875; liturgical movement and, 955; missal reform and, 995–996; objective and function, 270, 271, 408, 410; Sacred Heart feast days, 360; Sixtus V and, 268; Theologian of the Papal Household and, 981; Vatican II and, 1582

Cavagnis, Felice, 364, 1211

Cavallari, Alberto, 1442

Cavallini, Pietro, 1039, 1116, 1370, 1371

Cavelier, Barthélemi, 1501–1502

Cavicchioni, Beniamino, 364

Cavino, Giovani, 982

Cavour, Conte di (Camillo Benso), 889, 1195, 1535, 1537–1538, 1539, 1541, 1644

CCEE. *See* Episcopal Conferences of Europe, Council of

CD. *See* Christian Democracy

Ceccarelli, Guiseppe, 257

Cecilian of Carthage, 251, 698

CELAM, 401, 541, 1580

Celani, Enrico, 284

Celestine I, **273–275**, 567; Council of Ephesus, 199, 428, 563; election of bishops, 91; liturgy, 949; monasticism and, 1013; successor Sixtus III, 1432

Celestine (II), 70, 72, 109, 251, **275**, 940; chaplain, 300; Honorius II and, 275, 732, 733; Normans and, 1053

Celestine II, **275–276**, 277, 282, 959; tomb of, 1499

Celestine III, **276–279**, 1037; advanced age of, 1416; Byzantium and, 207; decretals attributed to Clement III, 331; Holy Roman Empire and, 314; Innocent III and, 278, 786; military orders and, 989; monasticism and, 1015; Normans and, 277–278, 1054; Papal States' borders and, 1098; St. John Lateran bronze doors, 1360; Vatican Palace residency, 1301

Celestine IV, **279**, 655, 1500

Celestine V, **279–283**, 284; abdication by, 189, 281, 282, 283, 481, 1305; Angevins and, 52; arms, 113; canonization of [as Morrone], 282, 283, 334, 1380; Dante's consignment to

Volume Key: Volume 1, pages 1–614; volume 2, pages 615–1266; volume 3, pages 1267–1637.

1678

Hell, 481; Franciscans and, 280, 281, 702; residence in Sicily, 1302; senility of, 282; tomb of, 282; vacant See and, 486

Celestines, 280, 281, 282, 849

Celestius, 1432, 1641

celibacy, 1036, 1517, 1553; Enlightenment critique of, 528; first papal decisions favoring, 1043; Gregorian reforms and, 1282; Gregory II and, 643; infractions linked with simony, 1043; John Paul II on, 863; nicolaism and, 1042–1044; Paul VI on, 1110, *See also* clerical marriage

Cellini, Benevenuto, 374, 375, 982

Celse, St., 233

Celsius (pagan), 544

Celsus, 1157

Celts. *See* Ireland

cemetery. *See* catacombs

Cencius, Cardinal, 940, 941, 1360

Cennini, Francesco, 801

cenobitic monasticism, 33, 1012

Cenred, king of Mercia, 421

censorship: art, 359, 1093, 1177, 1341, 1342, 1431; cinema, 320, 1444; of *The Deputy*, 496; imprimatur, 763–764; in Milan, 1535; press office, 1239; printing press invention and, 899; Roman Republic (1849) easing of, 1323, *See also* Index; Index, Congregation of the; press freedom

censure, canonical, **283**; Apostolic Penitentiary, 1151; suspension, 1470, *See also* penalties, ecclesiastical; reserved cases and causes

censure, clerical, 1470

census taxes. *See* Peter's Pence

Center for Liturgical Pastorate (CPL), 955

Centesimus annus (1991 encyclical), 1447, 1463

Cento, Cardinal, 1574

Centurione, Zaccaria, 1029

Centurioni banks, 137

Cerdo, 57, 744

Ceremonial (Piccolomini engraving), 294

Ceremonial Congregation, 11, 12

ceremonial, papal, **283–286**, 569; bell ringing, 152; cardinalate participants, 294, 299, 569; floreria (warehouse) storage, 588; Mass, 294; Middle Ages, 284; post-Vatican II, 285

Ceremonial papale (de Grassi), 294

Cerretti, Bonaventura, 175, 901, 1212

Cerri, Urbano, 1001

Cerularius. *See* Michael Cerularius

Cervini, Marcello. *See* Marcellus II

Cervole, Arnaud de, 129

Cesarini, Giuliano, 440, 976, 1171

Cesarini, Sforza, 535, 536, 1050

Cesena massacre (1377), 659

Cesi, Federico, 668

Cesti, Antonio, 298

Ceyssens, L., 823–824

Chaco, Pedro, 213

Chair of St. Peter, **286–287**, 1378–1379, 1382; completion under Urban VIII, 1562; feast of, 1159; papal coronation and, 426

Chalcedon, Council of (451), 14, 15, 198, 199, 201, 203, 204, 207, 552, 706; Alexandrian Church and, 34, 35; canonical collection, 231; Christology, 219, 428, 563, 572, 699, 897,

916, 1108, 1146, 1318; Eastern Churches and, 35, 200, 317, 737; Ephesian (449) irregularities and, 1426; incardination prohibition, 765; Justinian edict and, 251, 1617; Leo I and, 916, 917, 918, 1108; opponents, 563; overview, 428; papal primacy and, 427, 480, 1426; Pelagius I and, 1147; simony prohibition, 1423, 1426; Three Chapters schism and, 1146–1147; Vigilius statement on, 1617, 1618

Chalcedon, Council of (479–480), 915

Chalcedonians, 563, 564, 572, 737, 1145

Chaldean Church, 86, 176, 404, 998; Pius IX conflict, 1196

Chalidonius of Besançon, 1610

Chalon, Philibert de, 1355

chamberlain, **287–289**; cardinals and, 452; as chaplain, 301; closeness to pope, 459; duties, 452, 457, 459, 941; financial management, 80–81, 372, 578; first, 449; honorary, 288; papal household, 288, 739–740, *See also* camerlengo

chancellors and vice-chancellors, **289**, 460; Alexander III prior post as, 19; canon law and, 226, 451; Gregory VIII prior post as, 653; influence decline, 462; list of, 289; papal family and, 451, *See also* Chancery, papal

Chancery, papal, 8, **289–294**, 447, 449, 451, 460, 464, 471, 1541, 1587; abbreviators, 1, 293; Alexander VII reorganization of, 29–30; archives and, 1604, 1605; Avignon, 128–129, 292–293; *bollatica*, 183; as bureaucracy, 463; Byzantium and, 204; couriers, 460; dispensation letters, 505; expansion of, 1282; Gelasius II and, 625; Honorius III and, 733; Innocent III and, 451, 452–453, 788; Latinity and, 906; legates and, 911; Leo IX and, 925; Leo X and, 927; loss of influence of, 462; Middle Ages, 1331; notary and, 293, 446, 447, 460; Paul III reform commission, 1127; Paul VI abolishment of, 294; petition annotations, 1161; protonotary, 1263, 1264; registers, 1293; Roman populace sacking of (1405), 797; Rota as outgrowth of, 1524; scriptors, 455, 460, 1398; Urban II and, 449, 1282; Urban VI dismantling of, 1558

chansons de geste, 749

chant. *See* liturgical chant, Roman

chapel, papal, **294–300**; castrati of, 256–257, 297, 298; chaplain, 300–302; historical, **294–295**, 449, 451, 457, 1282–1283, 1380; liturgical objects, 980, 1461; liturgy, 953; music, 256–257, **295–300**, 457, 1340, 1341 (*see also* as separate listing); Palatine cardinals and prelates seating, 1094; Palatine Guard and, 1095; St. Peter's, 1380; Sixtus IV rebuilding of, 1435, *See also* chaplain, papal; Sistine Chapel

chaplain, military. *See* military ordinariates

chaplain, papal, 126, **300–302**, 498; Middle Ages, **300–301**, 415, 449, 453, 454, 457, 460; 16th century onward, **301–302**, 740, 741, *See also* Penitentiary, Apostolic

chaplaincy. *See* almoner, apostolic; chaplain, papal; military ordinariates

Charette de la Contrie, Athanase, 1643

chariot races, 618

charity. *See* poor relief

Charlemagne, king of the Franks, 47, 103, 109, 122, 152, 156, 204, 205, 318, 518, 577, 679, 1456; calandrical dating and, 210; canonical collections and, 223, 231; canonization and, 233, 1114; clerical training and, 379; conversion of Saxony by, 997; cross processional and, 437; Gregorian chant and, 950, 952; as Holy Roman Empire ancestor, 600, 714, 715; Holy Sepulcher guardianship by, 722; on iconoclast contro-

Volume Key: Volume 1, pages 1–614; volume 2, pages 615–1266; volume 3, pages 1267–1637.

1679

versy, 599, 680–681, 701; kingdom expansion by, 1320; Leo III and, 254, 424, 437, 600, 920, 1108, 1320; Lombard conquest by, 957; on monastic exemptions, 552; monasticism and, 1014; as new Constantine, 513; papal relations, 599–600, 920, 1097, 1111, 1245, 1319, 1320, 1331, 1420, 1458; *possesso* ceremony and, 1228; relics and, 261; Roman coronation of, 254, 372, 424, 586, 600, 714, 920, 921, 957, 1108, 1320; St. Peter's basilica and, 1328; St. Peter's basilica statue of, 1386; Stephen III (IV) and, 1457–1458; trips to Rome, 569, 599, 600, 680, 1301

Charles, Father, 1571

Charles I, king of England, 55

Charles I (Charles of Anjou), king of Naples and Sicily, 51, 52, 127, 190, 208, 628, 656–658, 685, 689, 716, 735, 794, 1037, 1038, 1555, 1556; Aragon crusade and, 973; chinea tribute and, 303; Clement IV and, 332, 333; crusade privileges and, 440; Martin IV and, 972, 973; possession of kingdom by, 315, 440; Roman senator title, 1336

Charles II, king of England, 55

Charles II (Charles of Anjou), king of Sicily, 280, 281, 282

Charles II (Charles of Salerno), king of Naples, 52, 53, 127, 628, 735–736, 1039; John XXII and, 847–848

Charles II (the Bad), king of Navarre, 163

Charles II (the Bald), Holy Roman emperor, 91, 223, 552, 681, 682, 1033–1034; Saracen threat and, 1393; throne and Bible bequest by, 287, 1370, 1373, 1378

Charles III, king of Naples, 53

Charles III, king of Spain (Charles VII of Naples), 303, 359, 361, 1346

Charles III (the Fat), Holy Roman emperor, 682, 837, 970, 991, 1483; Carolingian collapse following, 1245; invasion of papal land by, 1103; Stephen V (VI) and, 1458–1459

Charles III (the Noble), king of Navarre, 163, 192

Charles III (the Simple), king of France, 839

Charles IV, Holy Roman emperor, 130, 132, 716, 717, 796; Clement VI and, 336, 337; Golden Bull of, 316, 337; Great Schism and, 340

Charles V, Holy Roman emperor, 54, 99, 569, 659, 686, 717, 816, 928; censure of Luther and, 1286; Clement VII and, 344, 345; coronation of, 424; Council of Trent and, 1125–1126, 1289, 1517–1518, 1519; election of Julius III and, 886, 887; Farnese family and, 1123, 1124–1125; French wars in Italy and, 1124–1125, 1623, 1624; Index and, 770; Inquisition and, 817; military ordinariates and, 991; Paul III and, 1124–1125, 1126; Protestantism and, 1125, 1287, 1288; sack of Rome and, 255, 345, 374, 726, 1124, 1296, 1340, 1354, 1355, 1624; temporal veto, 1608

Charles V, king of France, 340, 716, 1029, 1556–1557, 1558; Clement VII and, 343; St. John Lateran restoration, 1361

Charles VI, Holy Roman emperor, 166, 182, 810

Charles VI (the Mad), king of France, 24, 163–164, 192–193; Great Schism and, 132, 341, 633, 634, 660, 974

Charles VII, king of France: Nicholas V and, 574, 1040; Pragmatic Sanction issuance, 536, 1041

Charles VII, king of Naples. *See* Charles III, king of Spain

Charles VIII, king of France, 26, 27, 884, 1064, 1174; Italian wars of, 1102, 1621

Charles IX, king of France, 1291

Charles Albert, king of Sardinia, 1194, 1324, 1539

Charles de Bourbon, constable of France, 884, 1354–1355, 1623

Charles Emanuel I (the Great), duke of Savoy, 667

Charles Martel, 52, 598, 643, 644, 957, 997, 1319, 1456, 1640

Charles of Anjou. *See* Charles I, king of Naples and Sicily

Charles of Durazzo, 341

Charles of Gand, 1622

Charles of Habsburg, 353

Charles of Maine, 1621

Charles of Nevers, 1561

Charles of Valois, 51, 334, 440

Charles the Gimp, duke of Clabria, 51

Charles-Roux, Cardinal, 1208

Chartres canonical collections, 224–225, 228

Chastellain, Pierre, 725

chastity vow: dispensation, 505; monastic, 1011

Chateaubriand, F. R., 78, 757–758, 759, 933, 1186, 1191, 1372

Chaucer, Geoffrey, 1169

chef, pope's, **302–303**, 457–458

Cheli, Giovanni, 435

Chenaux, Philippe, 310

Chenu, M. D., 512

Chiaramonti, Barnaba (Gregorio). *See* Pius VII

Chiaramonti Museum (Vatican), 1272

Chiarenti banks, 452

Chigi, Cardinal, 912–913

Chigi, Agostino (Agostino the Magnificent), 39, 137, 885

Chigi, Fabio. *See* Alexander VII

Chigi family: alms emblem, 694; banking activity, 39, 136, 137

Childebert I, king of the Franks, 597, 1147

Childeric III, king of the Franks, 599, 1319

Chile: John Paul II travel to, 1511, 1513; papal arbitration, 720; papal mission to, 932; Pius IX pre-papal mission to, 1192; Vatican II representation, 1579

China: Catholic mission destruction, 355, 529; Catholic missions, 335, 348, 998, 1002, 1003, 1004, 1561; Catholic schism, 1396–1397; communist expulsion of Catholic missions, 1218; election of bishops, 87, 1257; Gregorian calendar delayed adoption in, 213; Holy Childhood Society, 708–709; Jesuit missions, 664, 827, 1343; Pius XI ordination of bishops, 1205; Propaganda Fide and, 1254, 1255, 1256, 1257; Vatican II representation, 1580; Vatican information agency in, 984, *See also* Chinese rites

chinea, **303–304**, 689, 1180

Chinese Patriotic Church, 1218

Chinese rites, 169, 529, 810, 1002–1004, 1345; Alexander VII toleration decree, 29; authorization of (1939), 1257; Benedict XIV condemnation of, 1003, 1004, 1345; Clement XI and, 355; Innocent X condemnation of, 802; Jesuits and, 29, 169, 327, 355, 529, 802, 810, 1002–1003, 1345–1346; Propaganda Fide and, 1255, 1257

chinoiserie, 1271

chivalry, 182, 688, 1050; Holy Sepulcher and, 723; military orders and, 987

Choquart, Ancel, 1556–1557

Chosroes II, king of Persia, 1319

Chou En-lai, 1396

Christ Order, 990

Christ Washing the Feet of the Apostles (Landini), 1270

Christian III, king of Denmark, 1287

Volume Key: Volume 1, pages 1–614; volume 2, pages 615–1266; volume 3, pages 1267–1637.

1680

Christian Archaeology, Pontifical Institute of, 2, 101

Christian cemetery. *See* catacombs

Christian Democracy, **304–312**, 1542; origins to World War II, 305–309; World War II and aftermath, 309–310, 1141; from 1978 onward, 311–312; assassination of Moro and, 305, 310, 311, 859, 864; *Civiltà Cattolica* condemnation of, 310, 326; Gregory XVI condemnation of, 670, 673–674; John XXIII dissociation from, 854; Movimento Cattolico and, 1023–1024; Paul VI and, 1134; Pius X and, 306, 1197; Pius XII and, 305, 309, 310, 1136, 1215; social liberalism linked with, 944; Vaticanists and, 1606–1607

Christian Democratic People's Party (Switzerland), 309

Christian Doctrine (confraternity), 263, 1309, 1310, 1311

Christian Era, concept introduction, 517

Christian of Mainz, 217, 960–961

Christian People's Action, 306, 307

Christian Social Party (Belgium), 309

Christina, queen of Sweden, 30, 375, 569, 1345; painting collection, 1089; St. Peter's burial site, 1386

Christlich-Demokratische Union, 309

Christmas, 182, 194, 568, 913; calendar cycle, 210; coronation of Charlemagnes and, 424, 1108, 1320; papal ceremonials, 299; papal chaplain, 300; papal radio messages, 1447; papal Vatican residency site, 296

Christmas Cantata, 299

Christology, 738; Abelard heresy and, 701; adoptionism vs. modalism, 1640; Adoptionist, 599, 701, 1612; Antiochan-Alexandrian union formula, 1432; Arian, 33, 140, 419, 698–699, 1418; Chalcedonian, 219, 428, 563, 572, 699, 897, 916, 1108, 1146, 1318; of Cyril of Alexandria, 274, 275, 1146; Damasus I and, 479; Dionysius of Rome and, 33, 502; Fathers of the Church and, 566; Flavian and, 563; *Henoticon* and, 572; Hilarus and, 705; Hippolytus, 708; John II and, 833; Justinian edict, 832–833; Lateran IV creed, 897; Leo I and, 914, 915, 916, 917, 1147; Monophysite, 35, 572, 699, 730; monothelite, 16–17; Nestorian, 913; Nicaea and, 1316; Nicene Creed, 428, 479, 657, 698, 699, 738, 836, 897, 945, 946, 986, 1419; Novatian, 1055; Roman and Alexandrian, 33–34, 35; Theopaschite, 832; Victor I and, 1612

[Christopher], 70, 71, **312**, 417, 1162, 1413; Stephen III (IV) and, 1457–1458

Christus medicus (concept), 847

Chrodegang of Metz, 599, 950, 952, 1456

Chronique des pontifes romains et des empereurs (Martin the Pole), 830

Chronograph (324), 942

Chrysogonus of Aquilea, St., 1389

Chrysostom, John, St., 183, 198, 534, 670, 727; apologetics, 75; Chair of St. Peter and, 287; cult veneration of, 268; as Father of the Church, 563, 567; on Peter in Rome, 1158; on pilgrimages, 1164; Theophilus of Alexandria rivalry, 782

Church of England. *See* Anglicanism

Church of Gesú, 106, 107

Church Triumphant, age of the, 1270

churches, national in Rome, **316–317**; conflict with pontiffs, 153, *See also* Febronianism; Gallicanism; Josephism

Churches of Silence, 1085

Churches of the Orient (antiquity and Middle Ages), **317–320** (*see also* Eastern Churches)

Churchill, Sir Winston, 712, 859

Church-State conflict, **312–316**; absolutist monarchies and, 93; Alexander II and, 18; Alexander III and, 19–22, 109–110, 217, 313; Alexander IV and, 23; Alexander VII and, 30; Alexander VIII and, 31; Angevins and, 51–54; Anglican schism as, 54–57, 1395; antipopes and, 69–72, 131, 313; Avignon papacy and, 131–132; Benedict V and, 155; Benedict XII and, 316; Benedict XV and, 173, 174–176; bishops' appointments and, 91–92, 93–94; Boniface VIII and, 160, 189–191, 615, 1481; Byzantine popes and, 197; Byzantium and, 14–15, 206; Catholic universities and, 1544; Clement III and, 330–331; [Clement III] as antipope prototype for, 329–330; Clement V proclamation, 131, 796; Clement VII and, 343–345, 1395; Clement X and, 350–351, 352; Clement XI and, 166, 353–354, 528; Clement XII and, 357; Clement XIII and, 358–360; conclave intervention and, 394, 1036; Concordat of Worms and, 1637; crusade tax/tithe and, 1481; crusades and, 438, 439–440; *cujus regio ejus religio* principle and, 801; in England, 21, 131; Enlightenment and, 528–531; Eugene IV and, 535–536, 616, 1041; exemptions and, 552–553; First French Empire and, 584–587; France and, 30, 31, 160, 528, 805, 1109; French Revolution, 611–613; Gallicanism as, 615–618; Gelasius I and, 21, 621–623; Ghibellines and Guelphs, 627–631, 676–677; Gregorian reforms and, 650–651, 1278–1285; Gregory II and, 642–643; Gregory IX and, 315, 653, 654–656, 1484; Gregory V and, 646; Gregory VII and, 21, 72, 109, 313, 329, 649–650, 1053, 1108–1109, 1483; Gregory XVI and, 671, 1536, 1538–1539; between Henry II of England and Thomas Becket, 21, 652–653; Holy Roman Empire and, 1–22, 128, 131, 154, 155, 158, 313–316, 683, 684, 715–717, 1039–1040, 1053, 1109, 1615–1616; Innocent III's *plenitudo potestatis* approach, 786–787; Innocent IV view of, 439–440, 791; Innocent XI and, 805, 806; investiture dispute as, 66, 91–92, 215–216, 312, 820–822, 1109, 1636–1637; Italian political participation and, 175–176; Italian unification and, 1533–1542; John XII and, 841–842; John XXII and, 128, 131, 316, 676, 850, 1039, 1040; John XXIII withdrawal from, 854; Lucius III and, 961–962; Nicholas I and, 1035; Nicholas II and, 17, 1036; Nicholas III and, 1037–1038; Nicholas V and, 1041–1042; Normans and, 1053–1054; papal armies and, 110–112; papal theocracy and, 1483–1486; Pius IX and, 1110; Pius VI and, 1179; Pius VII and, 1185–1187; Pius X and, 173; Reformation and, 1286; regalia and, 1291; Roman nobility and, 536–537, 1048–1049; sack of Rome (1527) and, 1354–1355; Sicily and, 166, 313–315; simony issue and, 1424; Urban II and, 1551; Urban III and, 1553, 1554–1555; [Victor IV (V)] and, 1615–1616; Viterbo as papal escape from, 1620, *See also* Pragmatic Sanction (1438)

Church-State relations: Benedict XIII and, 469; cardinal protector and, 462; Charlemagne–Leo III model for, 1320, 1331; Civil Code of 1865 and, 1542; concordats, 396–400, 1266; Constantine the Great and, 419–420; Dominicans and, 510–511; first known letter from emperor to pope, 993; French separation from Church (1905) and, 1007, 1110, 1198; imperial

Volume Key: Volume 1, pages 1–614; volume 2, pages 615–1266; volume 3, pages 1267–1637.

coronation and, 423–425; Jansenists and, 171; Jesuit suppression and, 528; Josephism and, 867, 868–871, 869; jurisdictionalism and, 357, 888–889; *Kulturkampf* and, 891–893; Lateran pacts on, 902, 903–905; liberalism and, 943, 1537–1538, 1539; medieval papal theocracy and, 1482–1486; papal gifts to royalty and, 1389, 1470; Papal States and, 1102–1104, 1106; Pius V constitutive charter on, 1468; Pius VIII and, 1191; Pius X view of, 173, 1110, 1198; pre- and post-Gregorian reforms, 1278–1285, 1284; in Russia, 1488; Secretariat of Briefs to Princes and, 195, 1400, 1401–1402; superintendent of the Ecclesiastical States and, 1468–1470; Syllabus of Errors on, 1473–1474; temporal veto in, 1197, 1608–1609; Ultramontanist view of, 1396; World War I and, 173; Worms concordat basis for, 1278, 1281, 1627

Ciampelli, Agostino, 1091

Cibo, Caterina, 595

Cibo family, 1032

Cibo, Franceschetto, 26

Cibo, Giovanni Battista. *See* Innocent VIII

Cibo, Innocenzo, 927

Cibo, Lorenzo, 800

Cicero, 1044, 1598

Ciceronianism, 906, 1295

Ciceruacchio (Angelo Brunetti), 1018, 1324

cicisbeo (male companion), 1507

Cicognani, Amleto, 1138, 1237, 1574

Cicognani, Gaetano, 1574

Cigoli, Il (Ludovico Cardi), 1369, 1383

cinema, popes and, **320–323**, 1163; filmography, 323; Pius XI concerns, 320, 322, 1205–1206; Pius XII concerns, 1444, 1445; pontifical council and, 435–436; portrayals of popes, 321–323; social communications and, 1441, 1444

circus, Roman, 619, 1374

Ciriaci, Pietro, 367, 368

Cistercians, 103, 128, 160, 161, 196, 438, 732, 1553; Alexander III and, 20; almonry and, 458; cardinal protector and, 246; Eugene III and, 532, 533, 1016; exemptions and, 553; founding of, 1015; Innocent II and, 785; Innocent III and, 788; liturgy, 952; Lucius III and, 960; military orders and, 987, 989, 991; missions, 998; rosary recitation and, 1346

citizenship, Vatican, **323–324**, 1587; passport, 1115

Cittadino, Il (publication), 172

City of God (Augustine), 75, 747, 1318, 1482, 1484

Cividale del Friuli, Council of (1409), 661–662

Civil Code of 1805, 1186, 1188; Rota decisions and, 1349–1350

Civil Code of 1865, 1542

Civil Constitution of the Clergy (France; 1790), 530, 611, 612, 617, 1181, 1291, 1321, 1346, 1536

civil law, 1547, 1548, 1549; auditors (papal advisors), 126; canon and, 221; *Code of Justinian*, 1319; codifications, 227; German and Austrian marriage, 892, 893; Honorius III ban against study, 734; master of the Sacred Palace and, 981; Syllabus of Errors on, 1473; Theodosian Code (426), 1318, *See also* Civil Code of 1805; Civil Code of 1865; Roman law

Civil War, British, 55

Civil War, Spanish, 978, 1070, 1209

Civiltà Cattolica (Jesuit publication), **324–326**, 828, 829, 855; anti-Semitic attacks by, 874; Christian Democracy attacks by, 310, 326; on Code of Canon Law (1983) development, 369;

founding of, 1194, 1444; infallibility definition and, 1196; on Lateran pacts, 902; Movimento Cattolico and, 1023; on papal primacy, 1566; press office of Holy See and, 1239, 1240; Vatican I and, 1567

Civitas Leonina. *See* Leonine City

Civitate, battle of (1053), 1053

Civitavecchia: Clement VII and, 345; galley slaves, 1440, 1441; Gregory IV fortifications, 645, 1393; Napoléon's occupation of, 575, 1103, 1186; naval defense, 1028, 1029, 1030; Tolfa's alum discovery, 581

Clamanges, Nicholas de, 164

Clare of Assissi, St., 24, 591

Clarelli, Paracciani, 672

Clarendon, Constitutions of, 21

Clareno, Angelo, 282, 594, 849

clarissimi, 1044, 1045, 1046

Clarizio, Emmanuele, 435

classical art, 1089, 1090, 1092, 1122, 1345; Christian archaeology and, 108, 1345; Pius V campaign against, 1177, 1342; Roman monuments, 1329

classical Latin. *See* Latinity

classical logic, 847

Claude of France, 1622

Claudian, 747

Claudio di Torino, 701

Claudius, emperor of Rome, 1152–1153, 1313–1314

Clavasio, Angelo de, 777

Clavius, Christof, 213

Clemenceau, Georges, 174, 1626

Clement (Soissons heretic), 701

Clement I, 98, **327–328**, 329, 566, 1054, 1244; as apologist, 74; Christian persecutions and, 1154; election of bishops, 90; Peter and Paul martyrdom and, 1119, 1159; relics of, 682; veneration of, 1390

Clement II, 70, 72, **328**, 329, 480, 495; assessment of pontificate, 529; election of, 158, 648, 924; pre-Gregorian reforms and, 1278, 1280; tomb of, 1498

[Clement III], 18, 66, 70, 110, **328–332**, 653, 940; as antipope, 69, 72, 109, 650, 1112, 1614; antipopes following, 1423; cardinal priests and, 240, 1356; Innocent III and, 785, 786; investiture controversy and, 822; Judaizing fears, 872; Normans and, 1053; Ravenna and, 1274; [Theodoric] support for, 1486; Urban II displacing, 330, 1112, 1550, 1551, 1552

Clement III, **330–332**, 372–373; crusades and, 438; military order and, 989; Papal States and, 1098; supremacy over Rome by, 1334; tomb of, 1499

Clement IV, **332–333**, 658, 1037, 1554; Angevins and, 628, 716; arms, 113; chinea tribute to, 303; fanon, 1569; Fisherman's Ring, 485, 587; Hadrian V and, 685; non-Roman residence, 1302; papal vacancy following, 392, 656, 657; pontifical gloves, 620; reserval of benefices, 1297–1298; Rota member numbers, 1349; Sacred College and, 1246; Sicilian kingdom and, 440; tomb of, 1500

Clement V, 161, **333–335**; annates, 59; arms, 113; Avignon papacy established by, 102–103, 127, 128, 136, 481, 632, 1246, 1304; banking and, 136; Boniface VIII heresy and, 191; canonical collection, 231; canonization of Celestine V [as Morrone] by, 282, 283, 334, 1380; chamberlains, 287; chaplaincy and, 457; chefs, 302; coins, 373; Corpus Christi

Volume Key: Volume 1, pages 1–614; volume 2, pages 615–1266; volume 3, pages 1267–1637.

1682

feast and, 1275; Council of Vienne and, 429; Curia and, 455, 456, 459; cursor, 475; Dante's consignment to Hell, 481; Dominicans and, 508; Franciscans and, 235, 592, 594; heresy and, 703; Holy Roman Empire and, 316; John XXII and, 848, 849; Lateran rebuilding, 1360; military forces, 110, 132; military orders, 990; missions and, 998; nepotism, 241, 335; on papal supremacy, 131, 796; Penitentiary and, 1151; Saracens and, 440; sicknesses of, 1416, 1417; Templars conflict, 131, 333, 334, 429, 988, 989; theocratic doctrine and, 1485; tiara, 1491; tomb, 1501; vacant Holy See provision, 1406; Vatican archives and, 1604

Clement VI, **335–338**; annates, 59; arms, 112, 113; Avignon court of, 103, 127, 129, 336, 337–338, 456; cardinals created by, 336–337; chaplains of the chapel, 300, 457; chef, 302, 458; collectors, 82; conclave rules, 392; crusade against Turks, 440; Curia and, 456; Dominican plague service and, 508; English conflict with, 131, 338; Flagellants and, 129, 337, 703, 1221; heraldry, 689, 690, 691; Holy Places and, 711, 722; Holy Year and, 337, 724, 774; Innocent VI and, 794, 795; Jewish protective measures, 129, 337, 1221; keys on family shield of, 891; menegerie, 58; military expenditures, 110, 132; missions, 999; nepotism, 129, 336, 658, 659; personal physician, 486; plague relief measures, 1221–1222; reputation of, 337; Roman government and, 1338; scholasticism and, 336; tiara (triple crown), 1492; tomb of, 1501; universities and, 379; Urban V and, 1556

[Clement VII], 53, 67, 70, **338–343**, 659; annona, 61; arms, 113; [Benedict XIII] and, 162, 163; Boniface IX and, 192, 193; breviary reform, 193; death of, 341; election of, 130, 132, 162; England and, 54; Great Schism inception and, 24, 72, 132, 163, 192–193, 266, 339–342, 632–633, 634, 1558; Holy Year and, 725, 726; Leo X and, 1032; military forces, 110, 111, 342; naval forces, 1029; nepotism, 1032

Clement VII, **343–346**, 686, 928, 1471; Anglicanism and, 1289, 1395; anti-Masonry, 602; arms, 114, 693; Capuchins and, 595; Charles V sack of Rome and, 255, 345, 374, 464, 1124, 1354, 1355, 1624; coins, 374, 375; *conversos* and, 816; Dominicans and, 507–508, 509, 510; film portrayal of, 322; Fisherman's Ring, 587; French wars in Italy and, 1624; heraldry, 689–690; humanists and, 1295–1296; Index revision, 770, 772; kidnapping of, 374; Leo X and, 926, 927; medallions and, 982; naval forces, 1029; papal chapel singers of, 296; Paul III and, 1124; plague epidemic and, 1225; reform avoidance by, 1125, 1276, 1518; Reformation and, 596, 1285, 1287; reforms and, 596, 1123; St. Peter's basilica altar, 38; St. Peter's basilica rebuilding, 104, 105, 558; Sistine Chapel restoration, 1430; tiara, 1491; tomb of, 1502; Vatican gardens, 1595; villa and gardens of, 1595

Clement VIII, **346–348**, 801; abdication by, 217, 941; Angevins and, 53; annona, 61, 62; as antipope, 72, 132; Aragon support for, 974; arms, 114, 115; banner of, 138; beatification, 145; [Benedict IV] as antipope, 72, 167; bishop authority bull, 1309; breviary reform, 194; canonizations by, 235; cardinalitial titles regularization, 243; catechism, 263; celebration of end of Eastern schism and, 1531; Church-State relations and, 1470, 1609; coins, 374, 375; congregations and, 407, 408, 409; Curia and, 466, 471; Dominicans and, 510; Fabric of St. Peter and, 558; Gregory XV and, 667, 668; heraldry, 690; hu-

manism and, 1296; Index rules, 770; indulgences and, 775; Innocent X and, 801; Jesuits and, 827; Jewish expulsion by, 873; Leo XI as advisor to, 929; missions and, 409, 1000, 1001; mosaics and, 1021; nepotism, 466; nunciature, 664; painting commissions, 1089, 1090, 1092; Pantheon pillage by, 1096; papal chapel musicians and, 297; Paul V and, 1129, 1130; poor relief, 1308; Quirinal gardens and, 1270; Recollects and Reformati and, 596; reserved case, 1298; St. John Lateran decoration and, 1090; St. Peter's basilica and, 549, 1021, 1382, 1383; tomb of, 1369; Urban VIII and, 1560; Vulgate revision and, 1296

Clement IX, **349**, 467; Alexander VII and, 29; arms, 115; banner of, 138; beatifications and, 145, 349; canonizations by, 235, 349; Clement X and, 350; Golden Rose and, 1347; indulgences and, 775; Jansenism and, 824; Judaism and, 863; legate and, 912; nepotism, 468; tomb of, 351; Vatican gardens and, 1595–1596

Clement X, **349–352**, 411; Alexander VIII and, 31; arms, 115; arts patronage, 1092; beatifications and, 145–146, 269; Benedict XIII and, 166; camauro shape, 620; canonizations by, 235, 351; chamberlains, 288; cursors, 475; false cardinal nephew and, 468; St. Peter's basilica projects, 1384; superintendent of the Ecclesiastical State, 1469

Clement XI, **352–356**; academy founding, 2, 1092; Anglican ordinations and, 1073–1074, 1075; anti-Jansenist bull, 167, 354, 528, 529, 617, 810, 824, 825; arms, 115; beatifications and, 146; Benedict XIII policies vs., 166, 167; Benedict XIV and, 168; as Cardinal Albani, 352, 672, 1270; cardinal protector role clarification, 247; cardinalate and, 243; Carnival suspension by, 248; Chinese rites condemnation by, 827, 1003, 1255; Church-State relations and, 1103; Clement XII and, 357; coins, 376; crusades appeal by, 1000; Curia and, 469; Enlightenment and, 528, 529; Innocent XIII and, 809; missions and, 1001–1002, 1003; mosaics and, 1021; obelisks of Rome and, 1061; papal authority bull (1714), 511, 617, 824–825, 1246, 1345; pilgrimage indulgences, 1170; plague relief, 1222; pontifical secret definition, 1399; *possesso* engraving, 1229; problems of pontificate, 353–355, 809; St. Mary Major restoration project, 1369; St. Peter's basilica projects, 1384; statuary collection, 1024; Turkish threat and, 375

Clement XII, 168, 170, **356–358**; arms, 115, 692; beatifications and, 146; canonizations by, 235; chaplains, 301; Chinese rites and, 1003; coins, 376; conclave reform, 394; Curia nepotism, 469; Dominicans and, 511; Freemasonry condemnation bull, 49, 357, 602–603; honorary private chaplain, 301; military ordinariates, 991; museum collection, 1025, 1092, 1117; painting commissions, 1090; papal household, 738; *possesso* ceremony, 1228; Quirinal and, 1269, 1271; St. John Lateran facade and, 1363; temporal veto and, 1609; tomb of, 1363, 1386; Trevi fountain project, 1117

Clement XIII, 170, **358–360**; arms, 115; beatification, 146; canonizations by, 235; Clement XIV and, 362; Curia and, 470; encyclicals, 360; Enlightenment as challenge to, 358, 359–360, 470; Enlightenment condemnation by, 1443; Fabric of St. Peter and, 558; Jesuit expulsions and, 359; Michelangelo's *Last Judgment* and, 1093; military ordinariates, 991; museum collection, 1025; Pius VI and, 1179; portrait commission, 1117; Portuguese Jesuits and, 359, 530, 827–828; tomb of, 1345; Ultramontanism, 1529

Volume Key: Volume 1, pages 1–614; volume 2, pages 615–1266; volume 3, pages 1267–1637.

Clement XIV, **360–362**; arms, 112, 115, 693; beatifications and, 146; Catholic University founding, 1545; chamberlains, 739; Enlightenment and, 361, 362, 528, 530; Franciscans and, 528, 596, 693; Jesuit suppression by, 360, 361–362, 470, 528, 530, 828, 1179, 1189, 1260, 1346, 1523; Jewish policy, 361, 873; Pius VI and, 1179; portrait commission, 1117; prophecy of death of, 1260; Roman nobility and, 1049; tomb of, 1345, 1386; Vatican museum collection, 1025, 1092, 1117

Clement of Alexandria, St., 327, 696

Clement of Rome, 1153

Clementines, 226, 227, 231, 849

Cleomenius, 214, 1640

Cleopatra Dying (statue), 1024, 1025

Clergy, Congregation for the, 410–411

clerical censure, 1470

clerical marriage: Anglican Church and, 54; Augsburg Interim permission, 1125; Greek rite, 638; Gregorian reform and, 1282; Henry III limiting, 1614; Lateran II (1139) invalidation, 901; Lateran synod decree against (1059), 1036, 1037, 1043; nicolaism and, 1042–1044; simony linked with, 1043; Tridentine decree against, 666, 1176; Uniate, 1043, 1531, *See also* celibacy

clerical morality, 1281–1282 (*see also* concubinage, clerical)

clerical training. *See* seminaries

Clermont, Council of (1095), 65, 1547, 1551, 1552; bell ringing at dusk, 152; crusades and, 112, 437, 711, 722; first papal reserve, 1298; Gregorian reforms, 1282; investitures interdictum, 821; Truce of God and, 900

Cletus. *See* Anacletus I

Clichtove, Josse, 1521

Climent, Francesco, 164

Cloche, A., 510

Clodion, 119

Clodomir, 597

Clotaire, king of the Franks, 598

Clothilde, queen of the Franks, 597

clothing: consecrated baby linens, 1470; ecclesiastical within Vatican, 619–621; Genlemen of His Holiness, 627; Jewish distinctions edicts, 332, 870; legate, 911; papal burial, 486; of pilgrims to Rome, 1168, 1169; pope's liturgical vestments, 1607–1608; Swiss Guard uniform, 1471; Zouaves uniform, 1642, 1643, *See also* headdress

Clovis, king of the Franks, 589, 597, 1064, 1108, 1318, 1319

Cluny: Apostolic Camera ties, 449, 450; Callistus II and, 216; exemptions, 552, 553, 840, 845; as Gelasius II tomb site, 1499; Gregory VII and, 1016; Honorius II and, 732; John X and, 839; John XI and, 840; John XIX and, 845; liturgy, 952; monasticism, 1015; reforms, 1275, 1276, 1279, 1280; Urban II and, 449, 1016, 1281, 1550; Vatican Archives and, 1603–1604

Cluny movement, 430

coats of arms. *See* arms, papal

Cochin, Augustin, 603

Codde, Pietro, 354

Code of Canon Law (1917), **362–366**, 558, 1142; on "ad limina" visits, 4; on appointment of bishops, 85, 89, 94; asylum right, 129; Benedict XV promulgation of, 173, 366, 395, 1110; bishops' conferences, 401; cardinal "in petto" and, 244; cardinal protector function, 247; on cardinal status, 243; cardi-nalate, 244; on cardinal's biretta, 180; Catholic universities creation, 1544; on causes of canonization, 270; on censure, 283; Chancery and, 293; on conclave, 395; concordats and, 396, 397; on conditions for ecumenical councils, 1570; con-fined to Roman Church, 370; consistories and, 416; on Curia reform, 243, 472; on Curia style and praxis, 474; custom and, 476; on datary powers, 483; Decretum of Gratian inclu-sions, 492–493; development of, 228–229, 232, 362–366; on dispensation, 505–506; dogmatic constitution, 422; ecclesi-astical penalties and, 1149, 1151; on ecclesiastical provinces, 1264; on exemptions, 555; on imprimatur, 763, 764; on incardination, 766–767; Index updating, 770; John XXIII revision initiation, 855, 1572; John Paul II and, 862; Lateran IV teachings and, 897; on Masonic membership, 608; nunciature and, 1057, 1060; on oath of fidelity, 1253; papal appeals and, 85; on papal approbations, 96; papal legates and, 1087; on papal resignation, 1305; Pauline privi-lege and, 1249; Petrine privilege and, 1250; on pilgrimage, 1170; plenary council and, 431; pontifical secret and, 1399; post-Vatican II changes, 366–367, 1573; prelatures and, 1233, 1234; Propaganda Fide and, 1256; provincial councils and, 430, 431; pseudodecretals and, 589; reserved cases and causes and, 1297–1299; Rota tribunal and, 1350, 1351; Sa-cred College and, 1357, 1358, 1359; on seminary norms, 1409–1410; suburbicarian Italy and, 1466; territorial prela-tures and, 1233; Trent teachings and, 897; updating of. *See* Code of Canon Law (1983)

Code of Canon Law (1983), 362, **366–370**; on "ad limina" visits, 5; on appointment of bishops, 89, 94; on bishops' confer-ences, 402–404; on canonization, 232, 408; cardinal "in petto" and, 244; on Catholic universities vs. ecclesiastical universities, 1544–1545; on censure, 283; conclave and, 395; concordats and, 396; congregations and, 411; consisto-rial allocutions and, 37; on Curia style and praxis, 474; cus-tom and, 476; Decretum of Gratian inclusions, 493–494; de-velopment of, 229; dissolution of marriage and, 1249, 1250; on ecclesiastical penalties, 1149; ecclesiastical provinces and, 1264, 1265; ecclesiastical region and, 1292; on exemp-tions, 554; Freemasonry and, 610; on Holy See, 717; impri-mateur and, 763; on incardination, 769; John Paul II and, 865; judges delegate and, 266; nonmention of biretta in, 180; oath of fidelity and, 1252; on offenses against the pope, 1063–1064; papal appeals and, 85; Pauline privilege and, 1249; Penitentiary references, 1152; on pilgrimages, 1170; Pontifical Mission Societies and, 1451; on reserved cases and causes, 1297–1299; Sacred College and, 1358; on schis-matics, 1394; Signatura Apostolic and, 1525; social commu-nications and, 1443–1444; subsidiarity principle and, 1463; suburbicarian Italy and, 1466; Synod of Bishops and, 1477; tribunals and, 1523, 1524

Code of Canons of the Eastern Churches, **370–371** , 435; election of bishops and, 85–86; simplified outline of, 371

Code of Justinian, 1319

Codex canonum ecclesiae africane, 13

Codex Iuris Canonici. See Code of Canon Law

Codici Iuris canonici Orientalis recognoscendo. See Code of Canons of the Eastern Churches

Coétivy, Alain de, 1041

Coetus Internationalis Patrum, 1397

Volume Key: Volume 1, pages 1–614; volume 2, pages 615–1266; volume 3, pages 1267–1637.

1684

Coeur, Jacques, 112

Coghetti, Francesco, 1372–1373

Coimbra, University of, 1544, 1548

coins, papal, **371–378**; Hadrian I and, 680, 1097; keys on, 689, 690; papal arms on, 693; pavilion on, 1145; Pius VII and, 1184; *possesso* ceremony and, 1228

Cola di Rienzo, 1109, 1337–1338

Colalucci, Pier Luigi, 1429

Colbert de Croissy, Charles Joachim, 867, 1345, 1597

cold war: Helsinki Conference and, 687–688; John XXIII and, 852, 853, 855, 859; papal policies and, 540, 1084–1086; Paul VI and, 1140, *See also* ostpolitik

Colisum. *See* Colosseum

Collectio Avellana, 231, 1563

Collectio Dionysio-Hadriana, 223, 224

collectorie series, 83

collectors, **378**; Apostolic Camera and, 81–83, 464, 466; diplomatic missions, 1058; election and duties, 80, 81–83, 378, 459; of indulgences, 463, 774–775; spoils seizures, 1452

college. *See* collegiality; colleges of Rome

College of Cardinals. *See* Sacred College

College of Enrico-Gandavense, 379

College of France, 944, 1008

College of St. Norbert, 379

College of St. Patrick, 379

College of the "English" (Rome), 1408

colleges of Rome, 375, **378–385**, 667; architecture, 1340; Austrian Catholic reforms and, 867; Gregory XIII and, 465, 664; Jesuits and. *See* Roman College of the Society of Jesus; list of, 380–385; missionary, 378–379, 1001, 1002; seminary, 1342–1343, 1407–1408; Sixtus IV and, 1435, *See also* seminaries; universities, Catholic

collegiality, **385–387**; cardinals in conclave, 239; conferences of bishops, 400–405; five patriarchates and, 318; John Paul II view of, 863, 1247; papal primacy and, 385, 1242–1243, 1244, 1247; Paul VI view of, 1139, 1091386; Sacred College, 1357; Tridentine reforms and, 1277; Vatican II on, 385, 1129, 1584, 1585

Collegio Romano. *See* Roman College of the Society of Jesus

Collegio Teologico Anselmiano, 1373

Collegio Urbaniano, 668, 1002, 1254, 1257, 1561

Colleoni, Bartolomo, 1122

Collezione di Arte Religiosa Moderna, 1026

Collin, Michael, 70

Collins, Anthony, 77

Collivaccinus, Petrus, 789

Colocci, Angelo, 968

Cologne, University of, 193, 1544, 1558; papal censorship and, 1443

"Cologne affair," 674

Colombanus, St., 142, 552

Colombia, 398, 932, 1515, 1579

Colombo, Carlo, 864, 1137

Colombo, Giovanni, 1137

colonialism: missions separated from, 176, 1002; papal distancing from, 1005; Portuguese in India, 1193, 1194–1195; Propaganda Fide and, 1255, 1343; slavery prohibitions, 510, 1439; Zouaves and, 1642, *See also* decolonization; New World

Colonna, Ascanio, 1049

Colonna, Aspreno, 1050

Colonna family, 160, 189, 190–191, 451, 798, 928, 1048, 1337, 1340; Celestine V and, 280, 282; Church conflict with, 110, 242, 344, 1048–1049, 1342, 1354; Clement VII and, 344–345; Eugene IV and, 122, 535, 536; excommunication of cardinalate members, 242; heraldry and, 691; Julius II and, 884; Ludovisi acquisitions from, 668; Martin V nepotism and, 535, 975–976, 1032; Nicholas IV and, 1038, 1039; Nicholas V and, 1042; Orsini rivalry, 11, 280, 799, 976, 1048, 1049, 1434; papal chapel and, 740; Roman insurrection and, 797, 1624

Colonna, Francesco, 1594, 1595

Colonna, Giacomo, 190, 280, 281, 1038

Colonna, Gilles, 131

Colonna, Giordano, 975

Colonna, Giovanni, 451, 1039, 1221

Colonna, Jacopo, 1367

Colonna, Marcantonio, 569–570, 937

Colonna, Oddone di Giordano, 1335

Colonna, Odone (Ottone). *See* Martin V

Colonna, Pietro, 190, 280, 1039, 1367

Colonna, Pompeo, 1048

Colonna, Prospero, 976–977

Colonna, Sciarra, 160, 191, 316

Colonna, Stefano, 190

Colonna, Vittorio, 1431

Colosseum, **387–388**; earthquake damage, 1329; literary images of, 751, 753, 754; Sixtus V conversion plan, 388, 1437

Columbanus, St., 142, 156, 187, 730, 1014

Columbus, Christopher, 26, 27

columns (orders), 107–108

Comacchio, 469, 672, 810, 1103

comatesque paving, 1363

Combe, François de La Combe, 1267–1268

Comitoli, Napoleone, 1500

commedia dell'arte, 249, 250

commissions, papal, **388–389**, 407, 416; Paul III appointments, 1126–1127; Paul VI on family and population control, 1140–1141; for Vatican City State, 1590–1591, 1592; Vatican II and, 1574, 1578–1582, *See also specific commissions by key words*

committees, papal, **389**

Commodus, emperor of Rome, 135, 523, 1154, 1315, 1612

common and small services, **389**; financial distribution, 80, *See also* annates

communcal burial grounds. *See* catacombs

commune of Rome. *See* Rome

communes: Guelphism and, 676–677; power of, 1048

communication. *See* media, communication, and the Vatican; social communications

Communications of the Council, Center for Coordination of, 1239

communion. *See* Eucharist

Communist countries: Chinese schism, 1396–1397; Church status in, 541, 542, 1532–1533; diplomatic relations with Holy See, 503; election of bishops, 87; evangelization of, 522–523; fall of Communism (1989), 311, 542, 865, 977, 979; Helsinki Conference and, 687–688; John XXIII and, 854–855, 859; John Paul II and, 860, 862–863, 864, 865, 979, 1511; nonrepresentation at Vatican II, 1573,

Volume Key: Volume 1, pages 1–614; volume 2, pages 615–1266; volume 3, pages 1267–1637.

1576–1577; papal anti-Marxism and, 977; papal *ostpolitik* and, 1084–1086; Paul VI policies, 1137; Pius XII and, 540, 1137, 1215–1216, 1218; religious freedom curbs, 687; Third World advances, 1218; Vatican Radio programs directed to, 984, *See also* cold war; Marxism and the papacy

Communist Party Manifesto (Marx and Engels), 977

Compeggio, Tommaso, 1125

Compilatio Quinta (Tancred), 734

composers. *See* music

conciliar movement, **389–392**; Council of Constance and, 974–975, 1101, 1246; dispensation and, 505; dispensation criticism by, 505; Dominicans and, 508; Donation of Constantine critique, 514; Great Schism ending by, 1246; papal condemnations of, 1101, 1109, 1518; papism vs., 1109; pope's personal authority vs., 1109, 1566, 1571; precedents, 390; Vatican II and, 1578, *See also specific councils, by place name*

conciliarism. *See* conciliar movement

conclave, **392–395**; conclavist, 396, 1356; cursors and, 475; definition of, 392; *habermas papam* announcement, 679; longest of 16th century, 1175; press coverage, 1236; Sacred College and, 10, 239, 1280, 1356, 1357, 1358, 1405–1406; secrecy of, 392, 393, 395; Sistine Chapel and, 1428; temporal veto, 1608–1609; time-lapse requirement, 394, 486; two-thirds majority requirement, 22, 392, 901; two-thirds plus one vote requirement, 22, 395; vacant see and, 1405–1407, *See also* coronation, papal

conclave, before Council of Trent, **392–394**; Alexander III two-third majority vote requirement, 22; cardinal participants, 240, 241, 242, 393; controversial election of Celestine V, 280–281; controversial election of Innocent II, 42, 45, 783–784; controversial election of Urban VI, 1558; effort to end Great Schism, 661; establishment of, 241, 392; Lateran III regulations, 241, 429; longest of 15th century, 272; Lyon II procedural regulation, 241, 657; Nicholas II procedural decree, 42, 240, 649, 783; nonresident cardinal voters, 244; simonical corruption prohibition, 393, 1425

conclave, since Council of Trent, **394–395**; antipopes, 70; camerlengo and, 221, 392; cardinal maximum voting age, 245, 395, 1357, 1358, 1406; conclavist elimination, 396; disappearance of antipopes, 70; exclusion right, 550–551; length of (18th-century), 528–529; Pius XII two-thirds plus one vote requirement, 22; reforms, 232, 395, 667, 668; site requirements, 394

conclavist, **396**, 1356

concordat, 85, **396–400**, 1299; Benedict XIV and, 169; benefice division and, 1266; conferences of bishops and, 404; datary and, 483; first. *See* Worms, Concordat of; list of, 397–400; origin of word, 974; Pius XI and, 1110, 1206–1207; Vatican City State and, 1588, *See also* Lateran pacts

Concordat of 1802, 1566

Concordat of Bologna. *See* Bologna, Concordat of

Concordat of Worms. *See* Worms, Concordat of

Concordia canonum, 231

concubinage, clerical, 157, 1043–1044; children of popes, 25–26, 663, 681; Gregorian reform and, 1282; lay investiture and, 91; Leo IX measures against, 1245

concupiscence, 1520

Condillac, Abbé de, 1182

Condren, Charles de, 1409

Condulmaro, Francesco, 122, 536

Condulmaro, Gabriele. *See* Eugene IV

Confalonieri, Carlo, 1201, 1570

conference of bishops, **400–405**, 431, 432, 1243, 1292; existing (list), 404–405

Conference of Christian Churchs, 522–523

Conference on Security and Cooperation in Europe (CSCE). *See* Helsinki Conference

confession, 171, 1341; abuses of, 669; Apostolic Penitentiary and, 1151–1152; Holy Year pilgrims, 726; papal confessor office, 457; pastoral reform and, 1274, 1275; Tridentine work on, 1289

confessional altar. *See* altar, papal

Confessions (Augustine), 619

confirmation, papal. *See* approbations, papal

confratelli. *See* Roman confraternities

confraternities. *See* Roman confraternities; military orders

Confucius, 29, 355

Congar, Yves, 56, 512, 520, 568, 1035, 1494, 1495, 1574

Congo, 1343

Congregation (for or of). *See* key words for specific organizations

Congregation of the Council, 469, 583; "ad limina" visits and, 4; Benedict XIV and, 168; creation of, 415, 471, 1357; Sixtus V and, 1436, 1438; Tridentine reforms, 465, 1175

congregation, plenary (congregatio plenaria), **405–406**, 1341; consistorial advocate and, 413

congregations, Roman, **406–412**; Benedict XIV and, 469–470; conclave and, 394; consistory effects, 242, 413, 415, 471, 1356–1357; as dicasteries, 498; first, 415; John Paul II Curia reforms, 472–473; list of, 1438; liturgy and, 953–957; organization of, 465, 666, 1341–1342, 1437, 1438; Pius X Curia reform and, 472; Rota functions and, 1349; Sixtus V and, 1437, 1438; Tridentine, 410, 471, 1522; Vatican II participants, 1574, *See also specific congregations, by key word*

Congress of. *See* key words

Conon, **412**, 1111, 1486

Conra, Sebastiano, 1363

Conrad I, king of Germany, 1551

Conrad II, Holy Roman emperor, 158, 845, 846, 960, 1053; Leo IX relationship to, 924

Conrad III, Holy Roman emperor, 313, 424, 533–534, 732

Conrad IV, Holy Roman emperor, 315, 716

Conrad of Marburg, 702, 812, 813

Conrad of Mure, 196

Conrad of Subura. *See* Anastasius IV

Conrad of Urach, 989

Conradin (German prince), 23, 51, 332, 440, 628, 658, 1336

Consalvi, Ercole, 55, 585, 586, 671, 672, 929, 930, 931, 932, 933, 1016, 1103, 1104, 1190, 1538, 1598, 1644; Pius VII relationship, 1182, 1184–1185, 1186, 1187, 1188, 1189

conscience, 1009

consecration of pope, 425, 426

conservatism. *See* fundamentalism; Syllabus of Errors

Consilium de emendanda Ecclesia (1537), 464, 1518

consistorial advocate, **413**, 740

consistorial allocution, 37, 465–466

Consistorial, Congregation of the, 416, 1437; "ad limina" visits and, 4; pontifical secret, 1399

Volume Key: Volume 1, pages 1–614; volume 2, pages 615–1266; volume 3, pages 1267–1637.

1686

consistory, **413–416**, 456, 1341; before Council of Trent), 130, 240, 242, **413–415**, 462, 471; following Council of Trent, **415–416**; allocutions to, 37; cardinal "in petto" and, 245; consistorial advocate and, 413; Gregorian reforms and, 449–450; peak of influence of, 413–414; Sacred College and, 413–414, 1356, 1406; Sixtus V reforms, 466, *See also* congregations, Roman

Constance, Council of (1414–1418), 72, 137, 162, 165, 196, 553, 616, 703, 786; calendar reform and, 213; canon law and, 227; cardinalate privilege and, 393; conciliarism and, 390–391, 974–975, 1109; Curia reform and, 460–461; Dominican plenipotentiary, 508; Franciscan reforms and, 594; Great Schism ended by, 130, 132, 636–637, 662, 974, 1101, 1246; Great Schism exemptions revocation, 1233; Hus condemnation by, 775; indulgences and, 774, 775; [John XXIII] deposed by, 851, 852, 974; Martin V participation in, 974, 975; on national churches in Rome, 316; overview, 429; papal chaplain and, 301; papal tax system and, 580; plague as threat to, 1222; provincial councils and, 430

Constance, Peace of (1183), 313, 315, 715, 716

Constance, queen of Sicily, 51, 313, 314, 735, 961, 1052

Constance, treaty of (1153), 19, 46, 534, 683, 684

Constans I, emperor of Rome, 417, 1375

Constans II, emperor of Byzantium, 75, 198, 202, 531, 562, 881, 882, 972; autocephaly privilege and, 1273; Donus and, 514; pillage of Pantheon by, 1096, 1354, 1619; Vitalian and, 1619

Constantina, 418

[Constantine], 70, 71, 180, **416–417**, 1162

Constantine (the Great), emperor of Rome, 199, **417–420**, 424, 1044, 1319, 1482; apologetics and, 75; army chaplains and, 990; benefaction and, 178, 1045–1046; Bernini statue of, 1384, 1386; Christian conversion of, 140, 417, 418, 513, 545, 993, 1045, 1116, 1316; division of empire following, 882, 1316–1317; ecumenical councils and, 198, 419, 427–428; empire bequest to Silvester I, 1294 (*see also* Donation of Constantine); gladiator ban, 619; Greek Fathers of the Church and, 561–562; heresies and, 698, 699; Holy Places and, 711; Julius I and, 882; Milvian Bridge victory, 417, 418, 993, 1156, 1316; prefecture of Rome and, 1230; Roman building projects, 1419; St. John Lateran basilica and, 1359, 1360, 1362, 1375; St. Peter's basilica construction, 38, 418, 548, 549, 1120, 1374–1375, 1378, 1382; Senate reorganization by, 1411; tiara, 426

Constantine I, 203, **420–421**, 642

Constantine II, emperor of Rome, 6, 34, 883, 986

Constantine III, emperor of Rome, 1610

Constantine IV, emperor of Byzantium, 16, 202, 428, 546, 919, 1619; Donus and, 514–515

Constantine V, emperor of Byzantium, 203, 204, 680, 1120, 1639

Constantine VI, emperor of Byzantium, 204, 920

Constantine IX Monomachus, emperor of Byzantium, 206, 711

Constantini, Celso, 1205, 1218, 1571

Constantinian donation. *See* Donation of Constantine

Constantinople: apostolic origin legend, 202, 206, 207; apostolicity principle, 200; Byzantine popes and, 196–197; Catholic missions, 1561; Chalcedonian precedence claim for, 200; Church unity and, 314; Constantine the Great and, 418, 420, 1316; crusader capture of (1204), 207, 319, 438, 1319; fall to Turks (1453), 208, 218, 319, 440, 1041, 1526–1527, 1531;

founding of (330), 418; Gregory I and, 639, 641; Holy See representation, 1058; John I embassy to, 831, 832; John Paul II travels to, 1511, 1526; Leo I and, 914–918; Leo III and, 203, 920; Leo IX and, 925; major basilica, 144; as New Rome, 317, 428, 562–563; papal primacy and, 1245; patriarchate, 202, 204, 207, 737; Pelagius I and, 1145, 1146; Pius IX apostolic delegate to, 1193; as Roman emperor's seat, 140, 197; Roman Senate and, 1045; Saracens and, 1393; Theodosian Wall, 1318; Thessalonica and, 1611; Three Chapters schism and, 1146–1148; Turkish regime, 208, 1527, 1531; Vigilius in, 1616, 1617; Vitalian and, 1619; World War I and, 1626, *See also* Byzantium and the papacy; Eastern Churches

Constantinople, Council of (360), 882

Constantinople, Council of (450), 916

Constantinople, Council of (691), 837

Constantinople I, Council of (381), 34, 198, 199, 699, 737; on Constantinople as New Rome, 317, 428, 562–563; Damasus I hostility toward, 480; on Holy Spirit procession, 1394; overview, 428; Theodosius convocation of, 1317; trinitarian creed, 897

Constantinople II, Council of (553), 35, 141, 201, 700; overview, 428; Vigilius and, 1618

Constantinople III, Council of (680–681), 16–17, 143, 420, 701, 730, 835; overview, 428; refusal to rehabilitate Martin I, 972, *See also* Quinisext Council

Constantinople IV, Council of (869–870), 46, 91, 682, 836–837, 969, 1034; overview, 428

Constantius I (Chlorus), emperor of Rome, 1316–1317

Constantius II, emperor of Rome, 199, 477, 571, 945, 946, 1230, 1641

constitution, apostolic, **421–422**; as anti-Freemasonry, 601; Assumption of the Virgin Mary dogma, 124; on Catholic universities, 1545; Curia and, 460; dogmatic constitution vs., 422; Penitentiary and, 1152; Secretariat of State changes, 1402; vacant Holy See provision, 1406; Vatican I and, 429

constitution, dogmatic, **422**

Constitution of the Apostles, 91

consubstantiality, 33–34, 428, 699

Contarini, Gasparo, 464, 968, 1124, 1125, 1276, 1288, 1296

Conti de Segni family, 653–654, 1098; Innocent III and, 785

Conti de Segni, Hugo (Ugolino) ei. *See* Gregory IX

Conti family, 627, 1047, 1048, 1049; arms, 694

Conti, Gregory. *See* [Victor IV]

Conti, Michelangelo. *See* Innocent XIII

Conti, Nicolas, 735

Conti, Stephen, 791

Continental Blockade, 586

Continental System, 930

contraception. *See* birth control

Contumeliosus of Riez, 14, 833

convents. *See* monasticism; religious orders; *specific orders*

conversazioni (receptions), 1507

conversions. *See* evangelization; missions

conversos, 799, 815, 816, 818, 870–871

Conzié, François de, 80, 220, 284, 485

cook books, 302–303

Copernican theses, 530, 1562

copper coins, 375, 376

Volume Key: Volume 1, pages 1–614; volume 2, pages 615–1266; volume 3, pages 1267–1637.

1687

Coptic Church, 86, 348, 536, 664; canon law, 370; conferences of bishops, 404; Vatican II representation, 1577

Cordes, Paul Joseph, 434

Cordier, Charles, 239

Cordier, Nicolas, 1364, 1369

Cordoba, Gonzalve de, 27

Cormier, H., 512

Cornelius, **422–423**; Carthage and, 13, 250; Curia and, 444; elected bishop of Rome, 90, 180, 181, 1055; exile of, 1155; Fabian and, 557; *lapsi* treatment and, 250, 422–423, 1155, 1455; Lucius as successor, 959; necropolis, 258, 1496; Novatian schism, 71, 422–423, 698, 959, 1055–1056, 1155, 1394, 1455

Cornelius (centurion), conversion of, 544, 1158

Cornwell, John, 1214

coronation, imperial, **423–424**; Church-State conflict and, 313, 316; coronation in Reims, 424, 600, 1458; coronations in Rome, 313, 600, 715, 716, 1108, 1111; of Napoléon, 423, 586, 1103, 1186

coronation, papal, **425–427**; imperial coronation paralleling, 424–425, 1283; *pallium* replacement for tiara, 244; as papal chapel occasion, 295; *possesso* ceremony and, 1228; processional music, 299; route, 829, 1228, 1353–1364; sedia gestatoria, 1405; symbolism, 1283; tiara and, 1283, 1489–1492

Corpus Christi, feast of, 211, 569, 588, 1555; importance in Middle Ages, 1275; papal Mass preceding, 296

Corpus juris canonici. See canonical collections

Corradino (son of Conrad IV), 315

Correction of Eastern Books, Congregation for the, 1001

corrector litterarum apostolicarum, 294, 460

correctores romani, 363

Correr, Angelo. *See* Gregory XII

Correr, Antonio, 534, 535, 661

Corrigan, Michael, 40

corruption. *See* simony

Corsi, Cardinal, 1194

Corsica, 1098, 1393, 1624

Corsini, Andrea, St., 1562

Corsini, Bartolomeo, 357

Corsini, Cardinal, 1021, 1558

Corsini family, 356, 469; arms, 694; paintings collection, 1090

Corsini, Filippo, 356

Corsini library, 356

Corsini, Lorenzo. *See* Clement XII

Corsini, Neri, 168, 356, 357, 469

Corsini, Ottavio, 356

Corsini, Piero, 340

Corsini, Tommaso, 1324

Cortese, Gregorio, 1124

Cortesi, Paolo, 1295

Cortona, Pietro da. *See* Pietro da Cortono

Coscia, Niccolò, 166, 357, 376, 529

Cosma, Deodato di, 1360

Cosma, Giovanni di Maestro, 1368

Cosmas, St., 1390, 1391

cosmatesque style, 1368

Cossa, Baldassare. *See* John XXIII

Cossa, Gaspar, 1029

Costello, Matteo, 665

costume. *See* clothing

Cottolengo, Joseph Benedict, St., 1204

Council, Congregation of. *See* Congregation of the Council

Council of... *See key word, e.g.* Trent, Council of

Council of State, Congregation of the, 1438

councils, ecumenical, **427–430**; bishop of Carthage and, 13, 250; Byzantium and, 198, 200–204, 206, 427–428; canonical collections and, 230; Constantine the Great and, 419; criticism of papal appeals, 85; disuse of, 1570; Fathers of the Church and, 561–564, 566, 567; first in West. *See* Lateran I; legates and, 908; as papal authority threat, 1572; particular vs. universal, 427; Paul VI commemorative visit, 1515; Pelagius I and, 1145–1147; Pius IX revival of, 1195–1196, 1565, 1570; plague effects, 1222; western vs. eastern, 1245, *See also* Lateran councils; Trent, Council of; Vatican I; Vatican II; *specific other councils, by place name*

councils, particular or local, 427, **430–433**; antisimony measures, 1425; pre-Gregorian, 1281–1282; provincial, 429, 431–432, 1522; Tridentine reforms and, 1522

councils, pontifical, **433–436**, 474; commissions and, 388; Curia and, 447; as dicasteries, 498; dogmatic constitution and, 422

Count of Monte Cristo, The (Dumas), 758–759

Counter Reformation. *See* reform, Catholic

couriers. *See* cursor, apostolic

Court of Rome. *See* court, papal; Curia

court, papal, **436–437**; Apostolic Camera function, 8; caudatary, 267; cursors and, 475; expansion of (15th century), 462–464; Gentlemen of His Holiness, 626–627; master of the Sacred Palace, 457, 627, 980–981; musicians, 299; residences outside Rome, 1302; Roman nobility and, 1050; simony and, 463; Viterbo residence, 1620

Couturier, Paul, 519

Cracow, archbishop of, 862–863, 876

Cracow, University of, 1556

Cranach, Lucas, 67, 1288

Cranmer, Thomas, 1395

Credo, 948

Creed. *Se* Nicene Creed

Cremer, Bruno, 322

Cremona, 20, 1551, 1553

Cremonese union. *See* Lombard League

Crescemzo, Ottaviano, 159

Crescentii family, 71, 155, 156, 158, 188, 646, 647, 648; Benedict IX opposition by, 158, 1361; John VII and, 844; John XIX and, 845; John XV support by, 842, 843; John XVIII and, 844, 845; papal domination by, 254, 842, 1332–1333; revolt in Rome (974), 155

Crescentius II Nomentanus (John), 156, 645, 647, 842, 843, 844, 845, 1414

Crescentius of Theodora, 155, 188

Crescenzi, Pier Paolo, 262

Crescenzi, Pietro de', 1594

Crescenzio, Alessandro, 350

Crescenzio, Giovanni (father), 1332–1333

Crescenzio, Giovanni (son), 1333

Crescenzio, Marcello, 887

crest, 690, 691, 692–693

Crete, 203

Crimean War, 1642

Crispi, Francesco, 889

Volume Key: Volume 1, pages 1–614; volume 2, pages 615–1266; volume 3, pages 1267–1637.

1688

Crispolti, Cesare, 1082

Cristofari, Pietro Paolo, 1021

Crivelli, Arcangelo, 298

Crivelli, Umberto. *See* Urban III

Croatia, 225, 523, 688, 997, 1215; World War II and, 1631

croccia, 267

Croce, Benedetto, 1534

Croix, La (newspaper), 1205, 1236, 1237

Cromwell, Oliver, 55, 802

crosier, 821

Crosparmi, Raoul, 332

cross, 437; as crusader emblem, 437, 688, 689; as ferula replacement, 575; as Holy Sepulcher insignia, 723; on papal shoe,
621; pectoral, 619, 620; St. Paul's Outside the Walls basilica,
1372; St. Peter's basilica, 1344, 1382, 1383; symbolism of,
688–689; *via crucis* rite and, 388

cross processional, papal, 138, **437**

crown cardinals, 241, 393, 394

crusades, **437–441**; Alexander II and, 18, 111–112, 711; Alexander III and, 21, 22; Alexander VI and, 27; Antichrist concept
and, 63; Avignon papacy and, 127, 130; Callistus III and,
218; Celestine III and, 278; Clement III and, 330, 331;
Clement IV and, 332, 333; Clement VI and, 335, 337–338;
Clement XI and, 375; code for, 439; conquest of Constantinople (1204), 207, 319, 438, 1319; Counter Reformation
and, 936; credibility loss by, 440–441; cross emblem, 437,
688, 689; Eastern Churches and, 998; Eastern Churches-
Roman schism and, 206–207, 1395; Eugene III and, 533,
534, 536, 997; financing of, 136, 189, 373, 375, 438, 439,
440, 509, 578–579, 787, 1122, 1481; forced Jewish conversions and, 871, 872; Frederick II and, 315, 439, 734; against
Manfred (Ghibellines), 676, 685; Gregory IX and, 654–655;
Gregory VIII and, 653; Gregory X and, 656, 657, 658, 685;
Guelpism and, 676; Hadrian V and, 685; Hadrian VI and,
686; for Holy Places, 711; Holy Sepulcher order and, 722;
Honorius III and, 734, 736; indulgences, 18, 439, 440–441,
509, 724, 774, 792; Innocent III and, 207, 438–439, 701,
702, 734, 787–788, 789, 896; Lateran I and, 216, 428; Lateran IV and, 429, 897–898; legate leadership, 910; Leo X
and, 509, 928; Lyon II and, 429, 440; against Manfred (Ghibellines), 332, 333, 440, 676, 685, 973; Martin IV and, 973,
974; medallion commemorating, 982; military orders, 987,
988, 989, 1016; missionizing and, 1000; naval forces, 218,
375, 1028, 1029; Nicholas III and, 1038; papal armies and,
111–112; as papal theocracy, 1483–1484; Paschal II and,
1112; Paul II and, 1122; Pius II and, 38, 1172–1173, 1417;
Pius V and, 1177; political, 439–440; against Saracens, 1393;
Sixtus IV and, 26; tax/tithes, 136, 189, 1246, 1481; theology
evolvement, 811; Tolfa alum financing, 38–39, 1122; against
Turks, 375, 440, 1122, 1124, 1125, 1172, 1177, 1526; Urban
II and, 65, 112, 711, 774, 1483–1484, 1551, 1552; Urban IV
and, 1555

Crux Vaticana, 1378

Crypto-Judaism. *See conversos*

Cuba, Holy See diplomatic relations, 503

Cuban Missile Crisis (1962), 855, 1085

cuisine. *See* chef, pope's

Cullmann, Oscar, 1139, 1577

cult of saints. *See* canonization; saints, veneration of

cults, eastern, **441–444**

Cultural Property of the Church, Papal Commission for the, 389

Culture, Pontifical Council for, 435

Cuoroe di Gesú, Maria Teresa del, 1259

Curci, Carlo Maria, 325, 1194, 1444

Curia, **534–475**; administration, 6–8; administrative offices,
8–12, 80–84, 130; *Annuario pontificio* (directory), 62–63;
apostolic almoner status, 37–38; Apostolic Camera and, 8,
1283; archives, 1603–1605; banking and finance, 135–137,
452; breviary, 193; camerlengo, 220, 221; canonization
process and, 232, 234; career and, 248, 451; Church-State
conflict and, 676, 1537–1538; commissions, 388–389; Congregation for the Doctrine of the Faith, 406–407; congregations, 406–412; datary, 482–484; dicasteries, 416, 498–499;
domestic offices, 457–458; Dominicans and, 507, 508; Fabric of St. Peter and, 448, 472, 558; feudal oath and, 18; finances, 549, 582; Holy Office, 709–710; Holy See and, 717;
Jesuits in, 827, 828; liturgy, 953; media relations regulation,
1447; Moroni history of, 143; notaries, 1054–1055; oath of
fidelity, 1253; papal approbations and, 96; papal chapel,
294; papal committees, 389; papal court and, 436; papal
household administration, 738; Propaganda Fide and,
1253–1254; protonotary, 1263–1264; Roman nobility and,
1048; Sacred College as nucleus of, 1280, 1356; Secretariat
of Briefs, 195, 461, 1400–1402; Secretariat of State,
1402–1404; Secretariats, 1404–1405, 1404–1407,
1574–1575; secrets, 1399–1400; simony and, 463, 468; Substitute of the Secretariat of State, 1464; tribunals,
1348–1351, 1523–1526

Curia, origin to Gregory the Great, **444–446**

Curia, 6th to 10th centuries, **444–448**

Curia, 11th to 13th centuries, **448–455**; Apostolic Camera initiation, 8, 1283; benefice vacancies, 577–578; camerlengo responsibilities, 219, 452; cardinalate residency obligation,
241; Celestine III structural reforms, 278; Clement III and,
331; crusades contribution, 439; documents, 291–292; Dominican procurator in, 507; Eugene III and, 533, 534; expansion of, 1282, 1333; Fieschi family and, 793; Gregory IX
and, 655; Gregory X ceremonial of, 284; Innocent III structuring, 300, 451, 452–453, 788, 1301; Innocent IV and,
791–792, 793; Lateran I and, 216; Lateran III and, 897; Leo
IX reorganization, 924–925; Lucius III and, 960; monasticism and, 1015; papal chaplain, 300; papal family, 455,
559–560; Penitentiary and, 454; relocations in Papal States,
1302–1304; Urban II and, 449, 1282, 1283, 1551

Curia, 14th to 15th centuries, **455–461**; brief, 292–293; Dominican posts, 508; expenses as princely court, 799; Great
Schism and, 340; Innocent VI and, 795; Latinity and, 906;
papal chaplains, 300–301; papal family, 455, 559–560; Paul
II and, 1122

Curia, 15th century, 137, **462–464**, 975, 1263

Curia, 16th to 18th century, **464–471**; Alexander VII career in,
28; Alexander VIII career in, 31; Benedict XIV reforms,
469–470; breviary, 193–194; cardinalate and, 242, 243,
1357; Clement VII and, 344; humanist employees, 1294,
1295; indulgences and, 775; Josephist conflict with, 869;
Lateran V reforms, 899; Luther's attack on abuses of, 1517;
nepotism, 466, 467, 468; Paul IV reforms, 464–465; Petrine
privilege and, 1249–1250; Pius IV reforms, 465; Pius V re-

Volume Key: Volume 1, pages 1–614; volume 2, pages 615–1266; volume 3, pages 1267–1637.

1689

forms, 1178, 1349; protonotary, 1263; Sixtus V reforms, 242, 247, 293, 465, 467, 471–472, 1277, 1357, 1437

Curia, contemporary era, **471–474**; "ad limina" visits, 5; cardinal residency, 244; internationalization of, 1232; Italian fascism and, 308; John Paul II reorganization, 472–473, 710; John XXIII and, 854, 855; minutate status, 994–995; Paul VI pre-papal service, 1136; Paul VI reform, 472, 473, 710, 1141, 1258, 1401, 1404; Penitentiary, 1152; Pius X reform, 1, 7, 8, 10, 11, 12, 243, 472, 1197, 1257, 1349, 1357, 1403; Pius XII and, 1218; protonotary, 1263–1264; reforms of 1967, 125, 294, 406–407, 1142, 1234; World War I and, 1626

Curia, style and praxis, **474–475**

curial minuscule, 1282

"Curialists," 1530

Curran, Charles, 764

currency. *See* coins, papal

cursor, apostolic, 452, 459–460, **475**

custom, **476**

Cybele, 441–442

Cyprian, St., 13, 181, 908, 1055; apologetics, 75; on Christian apostasy, 1155; collegiality and, 385; on Cornelius, 422–423; election of bishops and, 90, 91; as Father of the Church, 561, 567, 568; *lapsi* policy, 250–251, 423, 1394; liturgy and, 948; martyrdom of, 1316; persecution of, 1431–1432; on prefecture role in persecutions, 1230; Roman Church and, 250–251; on Rome as Chair of St. Peter, 1159–1160; Sixtus II and, 1431; station and, 1453; Stephen I and, 1455

Cyprian, Senator, 831

Cyprus, 340, 440, 536, 1556, 1557; Chaldean Church, 998; Lepanto victory and, 936, 937–938; Templars withdrawal to, 988; Turkish seizure of, 1177

Cyriacus, 251

Cyril of Alexandria, St., 34–35, 36, 200, 519, 915; Celestine I and, 275; Christology of, 274, 275, 1146; as Father of the Church, 563, 567; Julian the Apostate and, 882; opposition to Nestorius, 199, 274–275, 563, 567, 699, 1432, 1443; Paschal Tables, 517; Sixtus III and, 1432; Theodoret writings against, 1146, 1617; Twelve Anathemas of, 34, 833

Czechoslovakia: election of bishops, 88; German invasion of, 1213; Holy See diplomatic ties with, 503; Munich Accords (1938), 1206, 1213, 1630; Old Catholics, 1396; *ostpolitik*, 1084, 1085, 1086, 1215; Soviet domination of, 863, 1216; *See also* Bohemia

Dabenton, Jeanne, 703

Dacheriana, 223, 231

Dacia, 967, 1611

daily life of the pope. *See* private lives, popes'

Dalla Costa, Elia, 1213

Dalmata, Giovanni, 1380, 1503

Dalmatia, 688, 834

Damasus I, 32, 34, 72, 178–179, 181, 199, 428, **477–480**, 624, 1045, 1230, 1563; Antioch and, 69; calendar and, 210; catacombs and, 260, 261, 1160; Christianization of Roman nobility by, 1317; Curia and, 444; Eastern Churches and, 477, 479–480, 562, 699; episcopal ordinations by, 500; as Father of the Church, 568; as former deacon, 484; Latinity and, 905; *Liber pontificalis* and, 941; long pontificate of, 477; on Marcellus I, 967; martyriums, 478–479, 1388; monastic move-

ment and, 1011, 1012; papal office and, 1244; poem on Eusebius, 543; St. John Lateran and, 1364; St. Peter's basilica and, 549, 1375, 1377; saint veneration, 478–479, 1389, 1390; Siricius and, 1427; Symmachus and, 1411; Thessalonica and, 1611; tomb of, 479, 1496

Damasus II, 158, **480–481**, 495, 924, 1280, 1498

Damian, St., 1390, 1391

Damian, Peter, 158, 159; Alexander II and, 17, 18, 731, 909; on cardinalate origins and powers, 240; Clement II and, 328; on Clement III, 69; Gregorian reform and, 1280, 1281, 1282; Gregory VII and, 648; on investiture formula, 821, 1424; Nicholas II and, 1035, 1036; nicolaism condemnation by, 1043–1044; on papal military expenditures, 111; on papal venality, 750; pilgrimages and, 1167; on simony, 1280, 1281, 1424–1425; Victor II and, 1613

Dance, George, 120

Daniel, Book of, 64, 65

Dante, **481–482**, 703; on Anastasius II as heretic, 44; on Celestine V abdication, 282; "Ghibelline State" reference, 629, 630; on Nicholas III nepotism, 1031, 1038; popes consigned to Hell by, 481; popes consigned to Purgatory by, 481–482; as white Guelph, 481, 677

Dante, Enrico, 285, 1582

Dante, Francesco, 325

Danti, Ignazio, 213, 253, 1025, 1062

Danzig (World War II status), 1631

Darboy, archbishop of Paris, 1567

Dardani, Jacopo, 83

Daru, Count, 1568

datary, apostolic, 471, **482–484**, 1094, 1587; abuse reforms, 273, 1126, 1128; brief drafting by, 195; duties, 461; Julius III reforms, 887; petitions and, 461, 1152, 1162; Pius X changes in, 293–294; Secretariat of Briefs, 1400–1401; simony and, 463; spoils and, 466

dates. *See* calendar; Easter-date controversies

Dati, Leonardo, 508

Datius of Milan, 987, 1618

Daughters of Charity, 1343

Daunou, Pierre-Claude, 1604

David, Jacques-Louis, 120, 1501

Davy du Perron, Jacques, 347

day, liturgical, 209

Dayan, Moshe, 877

DCI. *See* Christian Democracy

De Angelis, G., 1018, 1225

de Buck, Victor, 1074

De cardinalatu (Cortesi), 1295

De Gasperi, Alicide. *See* Gasperi, Alcide de

de Gaulle, Charles, 853, 859, 1141, 1214

De Grandis, Vincenzo, 298

De Lellis, Camillo, 1309

De Luca, Giuseppe, 468, 1083, 1566, 1567, 1626

De Marinis, J.-B., 510

De Ricci, Scipione, 670

De Rossi, Giovanni Battista, 100, 101, 947, 967, 994

De Rossi, Giovanni Giacomo, 1229

De Statu Ecclesiae (Febronius), 358, 359

De Sutrio, Antonio, 661

De Waal, A., 1311

Volume Key: Volume 1, pages 1–614; volume 2, pages 615–1266; volume 3, pages 1267–1637.

1690

De Zelada, F.-S., 1062

Dea Syria cult, 442

deacons, **484–485**; cardinal, 239–240, 243, 1358, 1493; Curia and, 448; elected bishop of Rome, 180, 181, 642

death of the pope, **485–487**; camerlengo certification of, 221, 485; Capitol bell ringing, 152; caudatary role, 267; chamberlain appointment and, 452; chaplains' duties, 454; conclave site and, 2102; conclave time lapse and, 394, 486; embalming procedure, 486; Fisherman's Ring and, 10, 221, 485; majordomo's duties, 739; Middle Ages, **485–487**; mortuary vestments, 1607; novendials, 1056; as papal chapel occasion, 295; pillaging of palace and, 486–487; press coverage, 1236, 1248; public display of remains, 486; Sacred College and, 9–10, 485; vacant See and, 486, 1405–1407, *See also* tombs of the popes

death penalty abolishment, 1542

debt. *See* public debt; usury

Decentius of Gubbio, 782

Decii family, 1046, 1055

decima (10 percent tax). *See* tax/tithe, crusade

Decius, emperor of Rome, 250, 422, 423, 557, 561; persecutions by, 501, 967, 1155, 1316, 1394, 1455

Déclaration des Quartre Articles (1682), 615

Declaration of Indulgences (1687; England), 55

decolonization, 852, 1005, 1217–1218; indigenous churches and, 1257–1258; John XXIII and African/Asian, 853

decorations, **487–488**

decretals, **488**; Alexander III and, 22, 85, 774, 897, 910; on apostasy, 79; apostolic constitution and, 421; appeal to the pope and, 85; asylum right, 124; on bishops' election, 92, 93; Boniface VIII and, 190; canonical censure, 283; as canonical collections basis, 223, 226, 230, 231, 363; Celestine III attributions to Clement III, 331; of Clement V, 235; commentary on (14th-century), 133; Curia and, 278; decretists, 225; dispensation, 505; Dominicans and, 507; Donation of Constantine and, 513; false. *See False Decretals*; forgeries; first collection, 734; first known, 1427; of Gratian. *See* Decretum of Gratian; of Gregory IX. *See* Decretals of Gregory IX; indulgence definition, 773, 774; of Innocent III, 786, 789, 910; of Innocent IV, 793; judges delegate, 453, 880; Lateran IV, 897; legates and, 910–911; *Liber pontificalis* use of, 942; of Lucius III, 897; provincial councils and, 430; simony condemnation, 1425; Urban III and, 1553; Urban VI's election and, 162, *See also False Decretals*

Decretals of Gregory IX, 85, 227, 231, 256, 257, 266, 421, 490–492, 507, 513, 589, 770, 793, 910

Decretum of Burchard of Worms, 231, 1279, 1425

Decretum of Gratian, **488–495**, 652; as canonical collection basis, 221, 225–226, 227, 228, 229, 231, 495, 1109, 1283; Codes of Canon Law (1917) inclusions, 492–493; Codes of Canon Law (1983) inclusions, 493–494; commentary on, 227; conciliarism and, 390; on dispensations, 505; on dissolution of marriage, 491, 1249; Donation of Constantine and, 513; Gregory IX concordances, 490–492; on legates, 908; Lucius III view of, 960; "private" laws and, 363; on simony, 1281, 1425; summary, 489–492

Decretum of Yves of Chartres, 224, 225, 231, 489

deer park, 58

Defensor pacis (1324 treatise), 131, 133, 850, 1485

defensores (defenders), 447–448

Degli Andalo, Brancaleone, 373

Dehon, Leon, 306

deism, 77, 1535

del Monte, Antonio, 887, 968, 1092

del Monte, Giovan Maria Ciocchi. *See* Julius III

del Monte, Innocenzo, 887

Delfini, Giles, 595

Della Chiesa, Giacomo. *See* Benedict XV

Della Francesca, Piero, 1091, 1368

Della Gatta, Bartolomeo, 1428

Della Genga, Annibale. *See* Leo XII

Della Porta, Ardicino, 26

Della Porta, Giacomo, 106, 107, 665, 1126, 1340, 1362, 1382

Della Porta, Guillelmo, 1126

Della Rovere, Cristoforo, 1435

Della Rovere, Domenico, 1435

Della Rovere family, 694, 799, 1342

Della Rovere, Francesco. *See* Sixtus IV

Della Rovere, Francesco Maria, 885, 927, 1103

Della Rovere, Giovanni, 799

Della Rovere, Girolamo Basso, 1435

Della Rovere, Giuliano. *See* Julius II

Della Rovere, Giulio, 911

Della Rovere, Marco Vigerio, 1429

Della Rovere, Vittorio, 1162

Della Scala family, 629, 676, 677, 695

Della Scalla, Cangrande, 850

Della Somaglia, Cardinal, 931, 932

Della Torre, Giuseppe, 1083, 1633

Dell'Acqua, Angelo, 325

Delmas, Jules, 1644

Delzant, Antoine, 764

Demetrios Chomatenos, 207

Demetrios Kydones, 208

Demetrios of Alexandria, 561

Demetrius, 1222

Demisas preces (Benedict XIII), 167

demiurge, 697

democracy. *See* Christian Democracy; Roman Republic of 1849

Démocratie chrétienne, La (magazine), 306

Democrazia Christiana Italiana, 309

Denis le Chartreux, 76

Denis of Alexandria, 423

Denis of Corinth, St., 385

Denis of Paris, St., 952

Denis the Carthusian, 777

Denis the Little. *See* Dennis the Small

Denmark, 1556; artists in Rome, 121; evangelization, 997; Hadrian IV in, 683; Reformation, 1287; Urban II and, 1552

Dennis the Small (Denys le Petit), 210; canonical collection, 223, 231

Denon, 1272

Denys le Petit. *See* Dennis the Small

Denys of Milan, 945

Denza, Father, 1062–1063

Déon, Michel, 68

deposition of a pope, **495**; list of, 495

Deputy, The (Hochhuth), **495–496**, 875, 1141, 1214

Derizet, Antoine, 1363

Désaguliers, Jean-Théophile, 602

Volume Key: Volume 1, pages 1–614; volume 2, pages 615–1266; volume 3, pages 1267–1637.

1691

Descartes, René, 76–77, 867, 1006, 1170

Descent from the Cross (Caravaggio), 1022

Désenchantement du monde crise moderniste, Le (Gauchet), 1006

Desiderius, king of the Lombards, 680, 1120, 1162, 1457, 1458

Desiderius of Monte Cassino. *See* Victor III

Deskur, Andre, 1445

Despuig, Antonio, 1184

Deusdedit. *See* Adeodatus I

Deusdedit, Cardinal (1083–1087), 224, 1483, 1614

Deutsche Historische Institut, 1603

Devotio Moderna, 1275, 1276

devotion to the pope, **496–497**; pilgrimages and, 1169, 1170

Di Campello, Pompeo, 1324

Di Giussano, Casati, 1362

Di Jorio, A., 1574

Di Pietro, Michele, 1181, 1186, 1187

Di Vico family, 1048

Di Vico, Francesco, 1557

diabolism, 1268

diaconia, **497–498**

Dialogue with Non-Believers, Pontifical Council for, 435

Dialogues (Gregory I), 639, 641, 1614

Diamante, Fra, 1428

Diane of France, 1126

Diario di Roma (official bulletin), 984

dicastery, 125, 416, **498–499**, 668; administrative offices, 8–12, 221, 463, 464, 1283; causes of canonization and, 269; congregation, plenary, 405–409; datary, 482–483; Index and, 772; Inquisition tribunals and, 406–404, 816; list of presiding officers, 407; Penitentiary, 1523–1524; Propaganda Fide and, 1254–1257; Vatican II and, 472

Dickens, Charles, 751, 752, 753, 760

Dickson, William K. L., 321

Dictatus of Avranches, 499

Dictatus papae, **499**; dispensation, 504; of Gregory VII, 224, 499, 650–651; papal resignation, 1305

Didaché, 223, 283

Didaskleion of St. Justin, 378–379

Diderot, Denis, 77, 359, 527, 1182

Didier, king of the Lombards, 109, 417, 599, 957

Didier, Charles, 751, 752, 754, 757, 759, 760

Didier of Monte Cassino. *See* Victor III

Diego of Toledo, 506

Digest of Justinian, 225, 1319

Dignissimus, 1476

Dillignen, University of, 1544

Dimitri of Russia (False Dimitri), 1130

diocese. *See* province, ecclesiastical

diocese of Rome, **499–500**

dioceses *in partibus*, **500–501**

dioceses, suburbicarian, **501**

Diocletian, emperor of Rome, 209, 251, 1044, 1550; diocese of Rome and, 500; imperial government reorganization by, 417, 1156; persecutions by, 966, 967, 993, 1156, 1230, 1316, 1394, 1496

Dionysiana/Dionysiana III, 231

Dionysio-Hadriana, 223, 224, 231

Dionysisus of Milan, 986

Dionysius, **501–502**, 560, 1056; Alexandrian theology and, 33, 502; elected bishop of Rome, 180, 502, 1244; Felix I and, 570; persecution of, 1431; Sixtus II and, 1431; veneration as saint, 1121

Dionysius Exiguus, 84, 210, 223, 517, 621; canonical collection, 231; Easter date computation, 831

Dionysius of Corinth, 327, 560, 1159

Dionysius the Carthusian, 76

Dioscorus, 44, 70, 72, 185, 186, **502–503**, 560, 737; Acacian schism ending and, 503, 573; Alexandria and, 33, 34, 35, 200, 563; anathema against, 503; anathema retraction, 14, 71, 503; Boniface II schism, 71, 502, 503; Chalcedonian deposition of, 916, 917; Ephesian council (449) and, 428, 705–706, 916; Flavian controversy and, 563; *lapsi* controversy and, 561; Leo I and, 915; Symmachus-Lawrence schism, 502, 1476

Dioscuri (statue), 1269, 1272

diplomacy: by Anastasius Bibliothecarius, 46–47; arbitration by pope, 98–100; audiences with pope, 125; cardinal nephew and, 1402; by Clement VI, 337; concordat, 396–397; in contemporary Europe, 541; Curia and, 447; by Gregory VIII, 652–653; by Gregory IX, 654; Gregory XI and, 659; by Gregory XV, 667, 669; by Hadrian V, 685; Helsinki Conference, 687–688; by Innocent IV, 792; by Innocent VIII, 799; Israel-Arab conflict and, 877; Italian unity movement, 1645; legates and, 910, 911, 912–913; by Leo XII, 929, 930; by Leo XIII and, 933; mail preparation, 461; nunciature, 1056–1058, 1058–1060; origins of, 1058; *ostpolitik*, 1084–1086; Papal States and, 1103; Paul VI pre-papal career in, 1134–1135; by Pius VI, 1179–1180; by Pius XI, 1202; Pius XII pre-papal career in, 1211–1212; pontifical academy, 2; by Substitute of the Secretariat of State, 1464; Vatican City State representation, 1587; World War I, 1626, 1627–1628, 1630, 1631; World War II, 1212–1214, 1588, 1589, 1630–1635

diplomatic corps accredited to the Holy See, **503–504**, 718–720, 1589; countries represented, 718; Innocent XI restraints and, 805; Secretariat of State and, 718, 1402–1404

Directory (France), 612–613, 1103, 1185, 1346, 1598; Roman Republic and, 1320–1322

Disbursement of the Contributions of the Ecclesiastical State, Congregation for the, 1438

Discalced Carmelites, 664, 1000

Discalced Friars, 595, 596

disciplinary law. *See* canon law

dispensation, **504–506**; until 15th century, 453–454, **504–505**; since 16th century, **505–506**; Congregation for Divine Worship and the Discipline of the Sacraments, 408; Curia and, 453–454; datary and, 482, 483; exemption vs., 551; Julius II selling of, 885; reserved to Holy See, 1299

dissection, 1221

ditheism, 214

Dives in misericordia (1980 encyclical), 1449

Divina Pietà (confraternity), 1310

divination, 1274

Divine Comedy, The (Dante), 44, 282, 481–482, 1038

divine law. *See* canon law

Divine Love, Society of, 1225

divine right, 943, 1108, 1280

Divine Worship and Discipline of the Sacraments, Congregation of, 407, 408, 410

Volume Key: Volume 1, pages 1–614; volume 2, pages 615–1266; volume 3, pages 1267–1637.

1692

Divini Redemptoris (1937 encyclical), 305, 1208, 1209, 1447, 1449, 1629, 1631

Divjak, J., 135

divorce: Henry VIII of England and, 343, 345; John Paul II opposition to, 857–858; Pauline and Petrine privileges and, 1248–1250

Dizionario d'erudizione storico-ecclesiastica da S. Pietro ai nostri giorni (Moroni), 143, 294–295

Dobrin Order, 990

doctors. *See* medicine

Doctors of the Church, 265, 568; Chair of St. Peter and, 287; Congregation for the Causes of Saints and, 408; Pius XI candidates, 1204; Thomas Aquinas, 510

Doctrine of the Faith, Congregation for the, 410, 710, 763, 770, 819; dissolution of marriage, 1250; oath of fidelity, 1252–1253; overview, 406–407; Paul VI and, 1141; pontifical councils and, 434, 435, 473; profession of faith, 1251–1252; social communications and, 1446–1447; Theologian of the Papal Household and, 981

Doctrine of the Twelve Apostles, 223

documents: abbreviators, 1; Chancery, 289–294; couriers, 452, 460–460; datary, 480–482; decretals, 488; *Dictatus papae*, 224, 499, 650–651; diplomatic mail, 461; letters to the pope, 939–940; master of the Sacred Palace and, 981; minutante as record-keeper, 994–995; notary, 1050, 1054–1055; petitions, 1161–1162; pontifical, 289–294; registers, 1293; scriptors, 452, 1398; Secretariat of Briefs, 1401; Secretariat of Briefs to Princes, 195, 1400, 1401–1402; social, 1447; Vatican Library collections, 1599; Vatican Secret Archives, 1603–1605, *See also* printing press

Dodici Apostoli (confraternity), 1310

dogmatic constitution. *See* constitution, dogmatic

dogs, 59

Dolci, Giovanni de', 104, 1428, 1435

Dolcino of Novara, 702, 703

Dollfuss, Engelbert, 397, 1206

Döllinger, Johann Ignaz von, 674, 778; Old Catholic schism, 778, 779, 1396, 1530, 1567, 1568

Dombres Group, 519

Domenichi, D., 1173, 1434

Domenichino, Il, 668, 1090, 1091, 1092, 1383

Domenico of Pescia, 509

Dominic, St., 569, 593, 654, 655, 734, 788, 1282; Dominican order and, 506, 507; as first master of the Sacred Palace, 981

Dominican Republic, 398

Dominicans, **506–513**; 13th century, 160, **506–507**, 553, 1549; 14th and 15th centuries, **507–509**; 16th through 18th centuries, 165–167, **509–511**, 1346; 19th and 20th centuries, **511–513**; archaeology and, 101; Avignon papacy and, 507–508; beatific vision controversy, 850; Benedict XI and, 160; Benedict XII and, 161, 508; Benedict XIII and, 165–166, 511, 693; cardinal protector and, 246, 507; catechism, 263; Catherine of Siena and, 266, 508; clerical privileges, 593; complete conversion belief, 1345; at Council of Trent, 1518; Easter-date controversy, 517; exemptions and, 553; feasts of patron saints, 569; Franciscan ministerial parity with, 593; grace vs. free will dispute, 348; Gregory IX and, 654, 655, 734; Gregory XI and, 659; Gregory XV and, 669; Honorius III recognition of, 506, 511, 734, 788; Hono-

rius IV and, 736; Index trials and, 771, 772; Innocent IV and, 792; Innocent V and, 793–794; Innocent VI and, 795; Inquisition and, 322, 332, 507, 509, 799, 816, 817; Jewish persecution by, 871–872; liturgical movement, 955; as masters of the Sacred Palace, 507, 508, 512, 981; military orders and, 987; missions, 509–510, 998, 999; nuns, 507; penitentiaries, 454, 1153, 1523; Pius V and, 510, 1176, 1177; popes, 507, 511, 794; reforms, 508, 509, 510, 1275–1276; rosary and, 1347; schools, 379; university teaching and, 593, 812, 1549

Dominici, John, 508, 509, 662

Dominicus, 13, 251

Domitian, emperor of Rome, 387, 1095, 1154, 1314

Domitilla, 258, 549, 1045, 1064, 1154

Domnio, 1013

Donatello, 977, 1380, 1502

Donation of Constantine, 54, 103, 447, 464, **513–514**, 577, 589, 599, 600, 1052; Donation of Pepin and, 513, 1320; falsity of, 447, 513, 514, 1294, 1296, 1300, 1420, 1421, 1485; Papal States and, 1098, 1101; Patrimony of St. Peter and, 1115; St. John Lateran basilica and, 513, 514, 1359, 1419; St. Peter's basilica and, 513, 1374, 1419; Silvester I and, 513, 514, 1294, 1300, 1320, 1374, 1419, 1420; on tiara, 1489

Donation of Pepin, 513, 1097, 1319–1320

donations. *See* benefaction

Donatism, 13, 43, 432, 567, 698, 783, 1087; Carthage and, 419, 993, 1394; Constantine the Great and, 419; Miltiades and, 993, 1156; persecutions and, 251; Silvester I and, 1418; Zosimus and, 1642

Donatus. *See* Donatism

Doncoeur, Paul, 955

Donin, Nicolas, 792

Donizo da Canossa, 238

Donoso Cortès, Juan, 78

Donus, **514–515**, 1065

doppia romana (coin), 376–377

Dori, Alessandro, 1025

Doria, Andrea, 937, 1030, 1124, 1624

Doria, Antonio, 1030

Doria, Girolamo, 345

Doria, Perceval, 23, 1555

Dorso, Conrad, 812

Dostoyevsky, Fyodor, 68

Dottrina Cristiana (confraternity), 1310

Douai rosary, 1346–1347

dove symbolism, 182, 693, 1020

Drewermann, Eugen, 764

Drey, Johann Sebastian, 78, 674

Dreyfus affair, 307, 873, 874, 934

Drogon, bishop of Metz, 600

Drogon, count of Melfi, 1053

Du Prat, Antoine, 912, 927, 1169

Dubois, Pierre, 111

Duca, Borgongini, 1571

Duchesne, Louis, 101, 707, 830–831, 1074–1075, 1211; *Liber pontificalis* and, 941; liturgical studies, 954; on Marcellinus, 967; modernism debate and, 1007, 1008

Duchesne, Theodore, 5

Volume Key: Volume 1, pages 1–614; volume 2, pages 615–1266; volume 3, pages 1267–1637.

1693

Duèse, Jacques. *See* John XXII

Dufay, Guillaume, 297, 298

Dufilho, Jacques, 321

Dugnani, Antonio, 1181

Dulcinians, 429

Dumas, Alexandre, 752, 757, 758–759

D'un pays lontain (film documentary), 323

Dupanloup of Orléans, 778, 1195, 1196, 1567, 1568

Duphot, Léonard, 1103, 1181, 1320

Duplessis-Mornay, Philippe, 67

Duployé, Pius, 955

Duquesnoy, François, 1383

Dura Europes (Syrian baptistry), 138

Durand, Guillaume (William) the Younger, 390, 615–616, 910, 953; Martin IV and, 973

Durand of Huesca, 788

Durand of Saint-Pourçain, 850

Durazzo family, 633

Durazzo, Ladislas, 25, 636

Dürer, Albrecht, 755

Durrer, Robert, 1471

Dutch Catechism, 264

Duval, Noël, 101

Duvergier de Hauranne, Jean, 704, 806

E venne un uomo (film documentary), 323

Eadmer, 1303

earthquakes, 174, 248, 387, 1329, 1388

Easter, 194, 568; Eucharist, 1274; papal chaplain, 300; papal Vatican residency for, 296; Symmachus and, 1475

Easter cycle, 210, 211

Easter-date controversies, 430, **517–518**; Anicetus and, 57, 561; calendars and, 209, 210, 213; Constantine the Great and, 419; Eastern Churches and, 561, 562, 563; Eleutherius and, 523; Hilarus and, 706; Ireland and, 834; John I and, 831–832; Leo I and, 917; Nicholas I and, 1034; Silverster I and, 1419; Symmachus and, 517, 1475; Victor I and, 430, 517, 561, 1108, 1612; Whitby synod and, 1619

Eastern Churches: Acacius and. *See* Acacian schism; Agapitus I and, 14; Anastasius Bibliothecarius and, 46; anathema lifting with Rome, 430; anti-Latin reaction, 1000; apologetics, 75; apostolic principle of Roman primacy and, 201, 207–208; Assumption celebration, 124; Balkans and, 915, 997, 1459; Benedict XV and, 176; Byzantium and, 198–208; canonical collection, 230–231; Celestine I and, 274, 275; Chair of St. Peter and, 287; Christology. *See* Chalcedon, Council of; [Clement III] and, 329; Clement VIII and, 348; Clement XI evangelization of, 355; clerical training colleges in Rome, 664; Code of Canon Law (1917) and, 362; Code of Canon Law (1983), 368; Code of Canons of, 370–371; conferences of bishops, 404; Constantinople as de facto head of, 318; crusades and, 437, 438, 440, 998; Damasus I and, 477, 479–480, 562, 699; Easter-date controversy, 517, 518, 561, 563, 1612; ecumenical councils and, 427–428; ecumenical movements and, 518, 519–521, 539, 542, 1086, 1394; election of bishops, 85–86, 91; end of schism with (1595), 1531; Epiphany, 210; Eugene III and, 533; Eugene IV and, 536, 537, 998; Fathers, 560–565; Felix III break with, 572–573, 1427; Gregorian calendar opposition, 213; Gregory XIII reconnection

moves, 664; Hilarus and, 706; Holy Places, 711; Hormisdas and, 737–738; iconoclasm controversy, 197, 198, 203–205, 600, 643, 701, 1394; Innocent III and, 787; John Paul II travels and, 1511; John XXIII and, 853, 1237; Josephist tolerance edict, 868; Leo I and, 915–918; Leo IX relationship, 925, 1280; Leo XIII and, 934; Lyon II and, 657–658; Monothelitism controversy, 16–17; of the Orient, antiquity and Middle Ages, 317–320; orthodoxy development, 34; papal evangelization and, 545; papal legates to, 909; papal primacy and, 1245; Paschal II and, 1112; patriarchate principle vs. primacy of Rome, 1108; patriarchs of, 86; Paul VI and, 1140, 1245, 1357, 1514, 1515; Pelagius I and, 1145; Pius IX and, 1193, 1196; Pius XI and, 1204, 1208; Pius XII and, 1216; Propaganda Fide and, 1255, 1256, 1257; Protestantism and, 1000; Quinisext Council, 203; Roman cardinalate and, 1358; Roman Church and, 14, 200, 201, 207, 317–319, 521, 531, 536, 561–564, 572–573, 621–622, 736, 1038, 1060, 1108; Roman missions to, 998, 1000; Roman schism with, 141, 153, 154, 184, 186, 187, 197, 198, 199, 205–208, 216, 287, 319, 480, 513, 521, 572–573, 622, 638, 644, 925, 1034, 1046, 1245, 1280, 1394–1395, 1427; Roman union edict, 44, 200, 563, 564, 572, 622, 658; Russia and, 1487–1488; saint veneration, 1391; Simplicius and, 1426–1427; Sixtus III and, 1432–1433; tiara, 1490; Uniates, 176, 208, 1531–1533; unionism and, 519, 522, 657–658; Urban II and, 1551, 1552; Vatican I and, 1566, 1568; Vatican II and, 370, 1580, 1584. *See also* Alexandria; Antioch; Constantinople; Jerusalem; *other specific churches*

Eastern Churches, Congregation for the, 176, 407–408, 409, 472, 519; "ad limina" visits and, 5; pontifical council and, 434

eastern cults. *See* cults, eastern

Eastern Europe. *See* Communist countries; Europe

Eastern Roman Empire. *See* Byzantium and the papacy; Constantinople

Eastern-bloc countries. *See* Communist countries

Eban, Abba, 877

Ebionism, 698

Ecclesia (periodical), 1083

Ecclesia Dei Papal Commission, 388–389

Ecclesiastical Affairs, Congregation of, 1574

ecclesiastical centralization. *See* reform, Gregorian

Ecclesiastical History (Eusebius), 199

ecclesiastical law. *See* canon law

ecclesiastical penalties. *See* penalties, ecclesiastical

Ecclesiastical Pontifical Academy, 2

ecclesiastical province. *See* province, ecclesiastical

ecclesiastical region. *See* region, ecclesiastical

ecclesiastical universities. *See* universities, Catholic

Ecclesius of Ravenna, 573

Ecco, Umberto, 68

Eck, Johann, 1286

Eckhardt, Meister, 508

École Biblique, 101

École Française. *See* Academy of France

Economic Commission, 470

economic materialism, 943

Economy, Congregation of the, 409

Ecuador, 398

ecumenical councils. *See* councils, ecumenical; *specific councils*

Volume Key: Volume 1, pages 1–614; volume 2, pages 615–1266; volume 3, pages 1267–1637.

1694

ecumenism, **518–523**; Americanism and, 40–41; Anglicanism and, 56, 934, 1075–1076, 1395; conciliar movement and, 389–391; Eastern Churches, 518, 519–521, 539, 542, 1086, 1394; John Paul II and, 521–522, 523, 539, 542, 863–864, 865, 1110; John Paul II travels and, 1511; John XXIII and, 56, 520–521, 539, 855, 856, 858, 1005, 1394; Lateran pacts and, 904; Paul VI celebration of, 1141; Paul VI travels and, 1141, 1515; Pontifical Council for the Promotion of Christian Unity and, 434; as prejudice dispelling, 1232; Secretariat of the Roman Curia, 1404–1405, 1574–1575; Vatican II and, 56, 430, 520, 521, 1075, 1076, 1232, 1247, 1584

edia gestatoria, 740

Edict of Milan. *See* Milan Edict of Tolerance

Edinburgh Missionary Conference (1910), 518

education: academies, 1–2; Americanism and, 40; cathedral schools, 23, 1407, 1543, 1547–1549; colleges of Rome, 378–385; by confraternities, 1310; convent schools, 1343; Enlightenment reforms, 869; French secularization of, 1544; German and Austrian secularization of, 869, 893; Jesuit schools, 362; Lateran pacts on, 902; Leo XII secondary school reorganization, 932; monastic schools, 379, 1543; Pius XI encyclical, 1206, *See also* Catholic Education, Congregation for; seminaries; universities, Catholic; universities, medieval

Education and Censorship, Commission on, 869

Educational and Religious Films, Commission on, 984

Edward I, king of England, 315, 657, 736

Edward III, king of England, 268, 338, 1221–1222

Edward VI, king of England, 54, 887, 1073, 1075, 1289

Edwin, king of Northumbria, 142, 188

efficacious grace, 167

Egidian constitutions, 1102

Égletons, Roger Rosiers d'. *See* Gregory XI

Egypt: Catholic missions, 1561; Copts, 86, 348, 370, 404, 536, 664; crusades and, 439; Isis and Serapis cults, 442; Islamic conquest of, 318, 1319; Leo I and, 917; monasticism, 33, 34, 1011, 1012, 1013; Monophysites, 36, 202; obelisk in Rome, 1062, 1362, 1374; Vatican museum collection, 1026, *See also* Alexandria; Antioch

Egyptology, 1026

Ehrle, Franz, 1598

Eid, Emile, 370

Eight Saints, War of the (1376), 136

Einhard (Charlemagne biographer), 261, 645

Einsiedeln Itinerary, 1328

Elah-Gabal (god), 443

Elchasaism, 697

Elder Daughter of the Church. *See* Oldest Daughter of the Church

Eleanor of Portugal, 1171

elections of bishops. *See* appointment of bishops

elections of the pope. *See* conclave

Eleutherius, 5, 180, 187, **523–524**, 546, 948

Elias of Cortona, 593

Eliot, George, 755, 760

Elipand of Toledo, 599

Elizabeth I, queen of England, 54–55, 348, 663, 938, 1073; Anglican reform, 1289, 1395; excommunication of, 55, 1177

Elizabeth of Portugal, St., 1562

Elizabeth of Thuringia, St., 655

Elizabeth of York, 799

Elprand of Toledo, 701

emblems. *See* heraldry

Emeritus of Caesarea, 1642

Emesa (Homs), cult of, 443

Emilia, 599, 1540

Emiliani, Jerome, 1276

Empire, Knights of the, 1287

employees of the Vatican. *See* administration, papal

Enckenvoirt, Willem von, 686

encomienda system, 1002

Encratism, 700

encyclical, **524–527**; anti-Masonic, 601, 605–607; apostolic constitutions vs., 421; characteristics, 524; dogmatic constitution vs., 422; Enlightenment period, 529; first, 530; list of (principal), 524–525; magisterium of, 524, 965; medallion commemorating, 983; social teaching, 1447–1450; subsidiarity principle, 2462–2463, *See also specific popes and topics*

Encyclopédie (Diderot and d'Alembert), 77, 170, 359, 1169, 1182

Engels, Frederick, 977

Engeltrudam Canon, 48

England: Adeodatus II and, 6; Agatho and, 16; Alexander III and, 20; Anglicanism, 54–57, 1072–1073, 1128, 1177, 1288–1289, 1395; Anglo-Saxon Church, 141, 142, 143, 197, 545, 643; antipapism, 1530; apologists, 77, 78; appointment of bishops, 92, 93, 94; artists in Rome, 120, 121; barbarian invasion, 140; blessed hat and sword gifts to, 182; Boniface V and, 142, 188; Boniface VIII conflict with, 190; break with Rome, 1518 (*see also* Anglicanism); canonical collections, 225, 226; Catholic persecution in, 802, 1130, 1177, 1561; Catholic restoration in, 887, 1289, 1395; Celestine II and, 276; Clement VI and, 131, 338; Clement VII and, 343, 344, 345, 1289; Clement VIII and, 348; Council of Trent representation, 1518; crusades and, 438; diplomatic ties with Holy See, 503; Easter-date controversy, 93, 517; Eugene III and, 533; fall of Roman Empire and, 1318; Freemasonry and, 601–602, 604, 607, 609; Great Schism and, 632, 633, 634–635, 636; Gregorian calendar delayed adoption by, 213; Gregory I evangelization of, 142, 152–153, 188, 545, 597, 641, 895, 996–997, 1108, 1166; Gregory II and, 643; Gregory VII and, 649, 822; Gregory VIII and, 652–653; Gregory XIII and, 663; Gunpowder Plot, 1130; Hadrian IV as only pope from, 683; Hadrian V and, 685; Henry II–Thomas Becket conflict, 21, 652–653; Holy Land protectorate, 712–713; Honorius I and, 730; Hundred Years War, 1556–1557; indulgences critics, 775; Innocent III and, 787; Innocent VIII and, 799; intellectuals in Curia, 450; investiture controversy, 821, 822, 1637; Italian kingdom and, 1540; John VI mediation, 835; John XIX and, 846; John XV mediation, 842; judicial appeals and, 880–881; Julius III and, 886; Leo IV and, 921; Leo XII and, 933; Leo XIII and, 934; Lucius II and, 960; medieval anti-Roman satire in, 750; military order, 989; missions to, 996–997; modernism, 1008; monasticism, 1015; Napoleonic war, 586; Norman conquest of, 18; Oxford Movement, 55, 1074, 1086–1087, 1566; in papal early 15th-century domain, 661; papal tax collectors, 378; [Paschal III] and, 1114; Paul III and, 1124, 1125, 1289;

Volume Key: Volume 1, pages 1–614; volume 2, pages 615–1266; volume 3, pages 1267–1637.

1695

Peace of Calais (1347), 1221–1222; persecution of Catholics, 802; Peter's Pence origination, 372, 577, 582, 846; pilgrims to Rome, 1166; Pius V and, 1177; Protestantism in, 1128, 1288–1289, 1519 (*see also* Anglicanism); provincial councils, 431; Sergius I and, 1412; Ultramontanism and, 1530; Urban II and, 822, 1551; Urban VI support by, 1558; Vatican II, 1579, 1581; Vatican II and, 1573, 1576; Vitalian and, 1619; World War II and, 1632–1633, 1634, 1635

Enguerrand of Coucy, 659

Enlightenment, **527–531**; anticlericalism, 528, 1181, 1535, 1536; apologetics and, 77–78, 670–671; Benedict XIV relations with, 169, 170, 529–530, 1345; Church status following, 1566; as Clement XIII challenge, 358, 359–360, 470; Clement XIV and, 360–361, 362, 528, 530; Curia reaction to, 470; Freemasonry and, 601–602; Italian unity and, 1535, 1536; Jansenist ideas and, 527–528, 825, 867, 869; Jewish freedoms and, 874; Josephism and, 867, 868, 869; liberalism and, 943, 944; modernism and, 1007; papal battle against, 1010, 1443; papism vs., 1109; as philosophical-theological conflict, 1009; pietism and, 705; pilgrimage critique, 1169; Pius VI condemnation, 528, 530, 671, 1178, 1179, 1181; Pius VII and ideas of, 1182, 1183, 1185; socialism linked with, 980; traveler's view of Rome, 1503–1507; university secularization, 1544

Ennodius, 135, 502, 736, 737, 987, 1475, 1476

Enrico da Susa, the Ostiense, 390

Enrico Gandavense College, 1546

enthronement, papal. *See* coronation, papal

entourage. *See* family, papal

envoy. *See* legate; nuncio

Eon de l'Étoile, 66, 533

Ephesus, Council of (431), 34, 198, 199, 204, 274–275, 432, 563, 567, 699, 700, 1020, 1365, 1366, 1617; Cyril of Alexandria and, 1432, 1433; overview, 428; Simplicius and, 1426

Ephesus II, Council of (449), 34, 563, 705–706, 916; Chalcedon and, 1318, 1426; irregularities of, 1426; Simplicius and, 1426

epidemics. *See* Black Death; malaria; typhus

Epigonius, 214, 391, 1640

Epiphanius, St., 218, 832, 1043

Epiphany, 194

Episcopal Conferences of Europe, Council of, 541

episcopal miters, 1490–1491

Episcopates of the European Community, Commission of, 396

Epistle of Clement to the Corinthians, 90

Epistles of Paul, 327, 1248–1249

Erasmus, Desiderius, 429, 726, 906, 928, 1169, 1225, 1355, 1520; papal relations, 1295; works on Index, 1296

Erection of Churches, Congregation for the, 1438

eremitic monasticism, 33

Erfurt, University of, 193

Eric, king of Sweden, 233

Erlembaldo, 18

eschatology, 899, 1181, 1487, 1584–1585; prophetism and, 1260; Roman persecutions and, 1261; sack of Rome (1527) and, 1354, *See also* Apocalypse

Escrivá, Josémaria, 1070–1071

Eskil de Lund (archbishop), 683, 684

Eskirch, Peter, 252

Esposito, A., 1308

Esposito, Rosario, 609

Essenes, 696

Establishment of Churches, Congregation for the, 415

Estaing, François d', 1276

Este, Alfonso d' (duke of Ferrara), 27, 344, 885, 1269, 1342, 1354, 1622, 1624

Este, Alfonso II d', 347

Este, Azzo d', 23

Este, Ercole d', 1624

Este family, 629, 667, 676, 1270, 1535, 1538; arms, 694; Canossa possession, 238; Ferrara possession, 1103

Este, Ippolito d', 1269, 1439

Este, Luigi d', 1269

Estonia, 997, 998

Estouteville, Guillaume d', 26, 1041, 1368

Estrées, Cesar d', 351, 805

Etchegaray, Roger, 434, 541

Ethelbert, king of the Anglo-Saxons, 142, 641, 997

Ethelred II, king of England, 842

Ethelwulf, king of Wessex, 154

Ethiopia, 545, 998, 1561

ethnological artifacts, 1026

Étienne of Muret, 331

Étienne of Tournai, 488

Etruscan antiquities, 1026

Eucharist: age at first communion, 1198; Anglican, 56, 1076; doctrine, 1036; excommunication from, 47, 48, 49; fasting and, 1452; heresy, 701; Jewish segregation and, 870; liturgical movement and, 956; Luther on, 1286; medieval elaboration, 1275; Pius X changes, 1198; pontifical gloves for, 621; salvation based on obligatory, 1274; stational liturgy, 1454; Tridentine dogma decrees, 429, 887, 1176, 1277, 1289, 1521; Vatican II emphasis on, 1585, *See also* Mass

Eudes de l'Étoile, 701

Eudes, Jean, St., 1409

Eudes of Acquitaine, 643

Eudes of Châtillon. *See* Urban II

Eudocia, empress of Byzantium, 917

Eugene, St., 952

Eugene I, 71, **531–532**, 600

Eugene II, **532**, 600, 645

Eugene III, 66, 450, **532–534**; Alexander III and, 19; Anastasius IV and, 45, 46; apostasy decretal, 79; Bernard of Clairvaux and, 496, 532, 533; Byzantium and, 207; canonization and, 233, 268; Cistercians and, 532, 533, 1016; consistory, 414; crusades and, 438; Curia and, 450; exemptions and, 553; Gratian and, 489; Hadrian IV and, 683, 684; heresies and, 450, 701; judiciary and, 1348; missions and, 997; monasticism and, 1015; Normans and, 1053; Papal States development by, 1098; pontifical title, 1494; residence outside Rome, 1303; Roman government and, 1334; tomb of, 1499; Vatican Palace and, 1301

Eugene IV, 128, 138, 182, **534–538**; Angevins and, 54; arms, 114, 692, 693; Calatrava order and, 989; camerlengo, 220; cardinal "in petto" and, 244; Carnival and, 248; Chancery and, 293; Church-State conflict, 535–536, 616, 1041; coins, 373; conciliarism opposition by, 1101, 1246; conclave site, 392; confraternities and, 1307; Council of Florence and, 429, 508–509; crusade to aid Constantinople, 440; Curia and, 461; death ritual for, 485; deposition of, 122, 255, 536, 574, 1171; Dominicans and, 508–509; Eastern Churches

Volume Key: Volume 1, pages 1–614; volume 2, pages 615–1266; volume 3, pages 1267–1637.

1696

and, 536, 537, 998; Fisherman's Ring, 587; Franciscans and, 594–595; health and vitality of, 1416; Lateran rebuilding and, 1360; library, 1597; master of ceremonies, 284; military forces, 111; missions in New World and, 999; monument to, 537; naval protection, 1029; nepotism, 534, 535, 536–537, 1032, 1048, 1121; papal primacy and, 1246; Paul II and, 536, 1032, 1121; penitentiary and, 1152; plague and, 1222; poor relief, 1307; portrait commission, 1117; St. Peter's basilica commissions, 1380; shield crest, 690; slavery regulation, 1439; tax collection, 378; tomb of, 1380, 1502

Eugenius Vulgarius, 590, 1414

Eugippius, 1013

Eulalius, 70, 72, 181, 184, **538**, 1046, 1230

Eulogius, 33, 35

Eunomius, 479, 699

eunuchs. *See* castrati of the papal chapel

Euphemia, St., 1391

Euphemius, 622, 737

Eupraxia (Praxedes), 1551

Europe, **538–542**; balance of power (17th-century), 30; Catholic unionism in, 539–540; Church antiliberalism and, 943–944; concordats with papacy, 396, 397; Enlightenment (18th-century), 527–531; evangelization (20th-century), 522–523, 542; Helsinki Conference, 541, 686–688; national identities and, 542; *ostpolitik*, 540, 1084–1086, 1215–1216; papal power reassertion (1846), 39; patron saints of, 539, 540, 541; Pius XII policies, 1216–1217; political integration moves, 540–541, 1079, 1216–1217; rise of secular politics (1648), 99; Vatican I representation and, 1566, 1575; Vatican II representation, 1576–1577, 1578, 1579, 1581, *See also specific countries*

Europe, Council of, 1080

European Churches, Conference of, 541

European Community, 396, 1079

European Parliament, 1511

Eusebius, **543**; on councils, 430; tomb of, 1419, 1496

Eusebius of Caesarea, 42, 57, 199, 327, 523, 543, 546, 744, 986, 1043, 1563–1564; on Acts of Peter, 3; apologetics, 74; on Christian martyrs, 1154; on Constantine the Great, 417–418, 419; on Cornelius/Novatian schism, 423, 1055; on evangelization of Italy, 545; on Fabian, 557; Gospel According to Peter reference, 631; on Linus, 948; on Mark as Alexandrian Church founder, 33; on persecutions, 63, 1154, 1155, 1156, 1431; on Peter in Rome, 1158; pontifical lists, 942

Eusebius of Milan, 914

Eusebius of Nicomedia, 562, 883; baptism of Constantine by, 417

Eusebius of Vercelli, 199, 479, 945, 986, 1012

Eustachius of Antioch, 428, 1618

Eustathius of Rome, 1097

Eustorgius of Milan, 986

Eutelsat agreements, 1080–1081

Eutyches, 200, 563, 699, 705–706, 737, 914–917, 1618

Eutychian, **543**

Eutychius, exarch of Ravenna, 643

Evangelical Lutheran Church of Italy, 904

evangelization (early centuries of the Church), **543–546**; of barbarians, 141–142, 545; by English missionaries, 1619; by Gregory I, 142, 152–153, 188, 545, 597, 597–598, 641, 895, 996–998, 1108, 1166

evangelization (Middle Ages onward). *See* missions

Evangelization of Peoples, Congregation for the (since 1967): "ad limina" visits and, 5; establishment and functions, 409–410, 1001, 1258; finances, 583; military ordinariates and, 992; Missionary Union and, 996

Evaristus, **546**, 1244

Evora (Aviz) Order, 988

ex cathedra, **546**; encyclicals vs., 524

Ex omnibus Christiani orbis (1756 encyclical), 171

Exarchate of Ravenna, **546–547**, 642, 643, 730, 986–987, 1064, 1273–1274; Byzantine control of, 203, 546–547, 1115, 1273, 1319, 1331; Constantine I and, 420; Donus and, 514; establishment of, 1318; Gregory III election and, 643, 644; Lombards and, 546–547, 599, 643, 644, 1273, 1274, 1319, 1331, 1639; Martin I and, 972; papal coronation and, 425; papal legates to, 909, 1097; Papal States and, 1097, 1098; Patrimony of St. Peter and, 1115–1116; Paul I and, 1120; restoration to pope, 841–842, 1274; Sergius I and, 1412; Severinus and, 1415; Simplicius and, 1425; Stephen II (III) and, 547, 1064, 1097, 1273, 1274, 1456–1457; suburbicarian Italy and, 1465; Zacharias aid to, 1639, *See also* Ravenna

excardination, 767

excavations in St. Peter's, **547–550**

exclusion, **550–551**; excommunication as, 47–48

exclusive voice. *See* veto

excommunication: anathema vs., 47–48; apostasy and, 79; Carthagian appeals to Rome, 13; causes and effects of, 1150–1151; as censure form, 1149; consistory meetings on, 413; definition of, 1150; degrees of, 48; Freemasonry and, 608, 609, 609–610; of Italian kingdom sovereigns, 1661; Italian unification and, 1195; of Lefebvre, 1398, 1470; of Luther, 1286, 1354, 1395; Movimento Cattolico and, 1023; of Napoléon, 123, 586, 587, 1187; pope/patriarch reciprocal, 206, 1245, 1395, 1461; of Savonarola, 27; of schismatics, 1394; suspension vs., 1470

exemption, **551–554**; Boniface VIII and, 190, 594; Cluny and, 552, 553, 840, 845; conciliar decisions on, 1233; Franciscans and, 593–594; Fraticelli and, 702; Honorius I and, 552, 730; opponents, 615; Propaganda Fide privilege, 1254; Teutonic knights and, 988, *See also* dispensation

exempts, congregations of, 553–554

expectative grace, 293, **555**

expiatory penalty, 1151

Explication des Maximes des Saints (Fénelon), 1268

Exsuperius of Toulouse, 782

Extraordinary Ecclesiastical Affairs, Congregation for, 1211, 1236, 1257; pontifical secret, 1399; Secretariat of State, 1403

Extravagantes, 226–227, 231

Eybel, Valentin, 1179

Eymerich, Nicolas, 659, 789, 872

Ezzelinio da Romano, 21

Fabian, **557**, 708, 1223; Cornelius as successor, 422; Curia and, 444; election as bishop of Rome, 180–181, 1155; martyrdom of, 422, 557, 1055, 1155; notaries and, 1054; Novatian ordination by, 1055; Origen disagreement with, 33, 561; tomb of, 1497

Fabius of Antioch, 423, 1056

Fabre, Paul, 941

Fabric of St. Peter, 448, 472, **558–559**, 1022, 1095, 1341, 1382; photography commissions, 1162

Volume Key: Volume 1, pages 1–614; volume 2, pages 615–1266; volume 3, pages 1267–1637.

1697

Fabris, Giuseppe, 1026

Fabroni, C.-A., 824

Facchinetti, Antonio (cardinal nephew), 243

Facchinetti, Giovanni Antonio. *See* Innocent IX

Facundus of Hermiane, 1617

Fagiolo, V., 368

Faith and Constitution (Lausanne; 1927), 518

Faith of Jesus Christ Order, 989–990

faith, profession of (text), 1251–1252

Falcone, Major, 1643

Falconieri, Costanza, 1181, 1192

falda, 1607

Faletti, Bartolomeo, 995

Falkenberg libel, 976

False Decretals, 85, 223, 224, 231, 489, 589, 921, 923, 1034, 1283; *Dictatus papae* and, 499, *See also* Donation of Constantine

false documents. *See* forgeries

Famagusta, fall of (1571), 937

family, papal (Middle Ages), 455–456, 462, 466–467, **559–560**

family, papal (modern). *See* household, papal

family policy: Paul VI and, 1110, 1132, 1140–1141, 1141–1142, 1143, 1247, 1584; Pius XI and, 1204

Family, Pontifical Council for the, 434

famine: of 546, 1146; of 605, 1353; of 1250, 703; of 1361, 1222; of 1374, 659; of 1766, 359, 1179

fan. *See flabellum*

fanon, 1607

Fanucci, Camillo, 1307

Farald, Jean, 167, 1030–1031

Farfa, abbot of, 1111, 1112

Farnese, Alessandro. *See* Paul III

Farnese, Alessandro (cardinal nephew), 346, 968, 982, 1032, 1124, 1126; art collection, 1127

Farnese, Antonio, 357

Farnese, Constanza, 1124

Farnese family, 238, 667, 1269, 1561; arms emblems, 694; career and, 247; French support, 1624; nepotism, 1032, 1049, 1102, 1103, 1123; paintings collection, 1090, 1091, 1092, 1127; Parma and, 887, 1102, 1126; Urban VIII and, 1342, *See also* Paul III

Farnese Gardens, 1127, 1228

Farnese, Giulia, 26

Farnese, Odoardo, 695, 1342

Farnese, Orazio, 1124, 1125

Farnese, Ottavio, 887, 1124–1125

Farnese Palace, 105, 106, 107, 503, 570, 1089, 1091, 1123, 1127, 1340, 1341, 1344, 1362, 1384

Farnese, Paolo, 1124

Farnese, Pier Luigi, 1049, 1102, 1103, 1124, 1125

Farnese, Ranuccio, 1124, 1126

Fasanus, John. *See* John XVIII

fascism, 864, 1083; Church responses to, 305, 308, 310, 1135–1136, 1207; Italian unity and, 1534; jurisdictionalism and, 275; Lateran pacts and, 901–904; papal concordats and, 397; Paul VI pre-papal position on, 1135; Pius XI and, 305, 308, 524, 874, 902, 1205, 1206, 1207, 1462; Pius XII and, 1634; Vatican status and, 1633–1636, *See also* Nazism

Fassini, Vincenzo, 77

Fassoni, Liberato, 77

fasting, 1452–1453

Fate-Bene-Fratelli, 1224

Fathers of the Church, Greek, 197, 199, **560–565**; canonical collections and, 1283; Chair of St. Peter and, 287; Easter-date controversy, 561; heresy and, 696, 697; image veneration and, 680; monasticism and, 1011

Fathers of the Church, Latin, **565–568**; apologetics, 77, 567; canonical collections, 223, 224; Chair of St. Peter and, 287; chronology, 568; definition of, 567; Doctors of the Church, 568; four criteria, 568; heresy and, 696, 697; monasticism and, 1011

Fátima holy site (Portugal), 1170, 1569

Faulhaber, Cardinal, 1209

Faustina, empress of Rome, 1314

Faustinus of Lyon, 1056

Faustinus of Potentia, 13, 273, 622

Faustus, 179, 738

favoritism. *See* nepotism

Fawtier, Robert, 266

Faydieu, Father, 955

Fayet of Orleans, 954

Fea, Carlo, 1372

feasts of papal Rome, 176, 530, **568–570**; Assumption, 124, 212, 569, 913, 1096; breviary reform, 194; calendar, 209, 210–212, 1388; chinea ceremony, 303; Corpus Christi, 211, 296, 569, 588, 1275, 1555; major basilica consecration anniversaries, 144; Pantheon fetes, 1096; papal chapel use, 296; St. Peter, 1159–1160; saint veneration, 1388–1389; stational processions, 1453; Transfiguration, 218, 832; traveler's views of, 1506

feathered fan. *See flabellum*

Febronianism, 511, 617, 778, 779, 868; dispensation, 505; Enlightenment thought and, 358; Josephism and, 1179; jurisdictionalism and, 888, 1180; papism vs., 1109, 1345

Febronius (von Hontheim), 358, 359, 360, 505, 1529, 1530

Federicis, Francesco de, 1163

Federigo of Parma, 982

Felbiger, Ignace, 869

Felice Società dei Balestrieri e Pavesati, 1338

Felici, Giuseppe, 1163

Felici, Pericle, 368, 679, 857, 858, 864, 1237, 1584

Felicity, St., 1389, 1391, 1496

Felipe. *See* Philip

Felix I, 140, 543, 567, **570–571**, 622, 946, 947, 1065

[Felix II], 70, 71, 432, 477, **571–572**, 882

Felix III, 70, 72, **572–573**, 1065, 1616; on excommunication, 49; as former deacon, 484; Gelasius and, 573, 621, 622; as Gregory I ancestor, 572, 639; tomb of, 1496–1497

Felix IV, 70, 71, 141, 185, 186, **573–574**, 1065; Agapitus I and, 13; Dioscorus and, 503; *pallium*, 1608; Roman nobility and, 13, 1046, 1047

[Felix V], 54, 70, 72, **574**, 621, 1065, 1101; arms, 114; Curia and, 460; datary, 483; Eugene IV deposition and, 72, 536, 574, 1171; Pius II and, 1171; surrender of, 574, 1040–1041

Felix of Ravenna, 420

Felix of Rugen, 701

Felix of Urgel, 599

Fellini, Federico, 323

Volume Key: Volume 1, pages 1–614; volume 2, pages 615–1266; volume 3, pages 1267–1637.

1698

female pope. *See* Joan

Fénelon, François de Salignac de La Mothe, 77, 617, 808, 1268

Feodor, tsar of Russia, 1531

Ferderzoni, L., 902

Ferdinand I, Holy Roman emperor, 424, 1176

Ferdinand I, king of Naples, 26, 798, 1434

Ferdinand II, Holy Roman emperor, 1561

Ferdinand II, king of Naples, 1104

Ferdinand II (the Catholic), king of Aragon (Ferdiand V of Castile), 26, 303, 723, 799, 815, 885, 989, 1622

Ferdinand III (the Holy), king of Castile and Léon, 93, 1057, 1544

Ferdinand V, king of Aragon, 217

Ferdinand VI, king of Spain, 483

Ferdinand d'Antequerra, 165

Ferdinand of Tyrol, 182

Fermano, Gianfranco, 285

Fermin of Belleval, 213

Ferrabosco, Martino, 1270

Ferrand, Fulgence, 231

Ferrandus (Carthaginian deacon), 1146

Ferrante of Naples. *See* Ferdinand I, king of Naples

Ferrara, 672; Clement VIII and, 347; Hadrian IV claims to, 1098; Italian unification and, 1538; Napoleonic occupation, 1103; in Papal States, 1102–1103, 1105(map), 1342

Ferrara-Florence, Council of (1438–1447), 429, 998

Ferrari, Ettore, 1018, 1201

Ferrata, Domenico, 364

Ferrattini Palace, 668

Ferrer, St. Vincent. *See* Vincent Ferrer, St.

Ferrer-Benimeli, José A., 602–603

Ferreti, Mastai. *See* Pius IX

Ferretti, Cardinal, 1193

Ferrini, Contardo, 1024

ferula, 426, 427, **575**, 1228

Fesch, Cardinal, 990, 1186–1187

Fesquet, Henry, 1139, 1578

Festa, Costanzo, 297, 298

festivals. *See* feasts of papal Rome; Carnival

Festus (Roman senator), 44, 502, 907, 1476

feudal system, 18, 27, 1048; Angevin, 50, 51, 52, 973; bishops' elections, 91, 92; Church dissolution of (post-1818), 1189; Church use of, 50, 53, 277–278, 315, 331, 577, 578, 579, 582, 736, 973, 1483, 1621; Condordat of Worms and, 1637; fête of the chimea and, 303; heraldry, 688; Holy Roman Empire and, 715; Normans and, 684, 689; papal army and, 109; papal relocations and, 1303; Papal States and, 1098, 1342, 1437; simony and, 1424–1425

Février, Albert, 101

Ficino, Marsilio, 509

fidelity, oath of. *See* profession of faith and oath of fidelity

Fidenzio of Padua, 440

Fides (international agency), 984

Fieschi family, 451, 790, 793

Fieschi, Ottobono. *See* Hadrian V

Fieschi, Sinibaldo. *See* Innocent IV

Fifth Crusade (1217–1221), 439

Figaro, Le (newspaper), 1238

Filarete (Antonio Averlino), 537, 1380

Filareto, 1361

Filioque, 206, 207, 208, 318, 657, 836, 920, 1394

Filippini, Giuseppe, 321, 1163

Filippini, Lucia, St., 1204

Fillon, Artus, 262

Film, Papal Commission on, 321

films. *See* cinema, popes and

Filocalcus, Furius Dionysius, 478

Filopanti, Quirico, 1323

finances, papal, **575–584**; 6th to 12th century, 153, 448, **575–577**; 13th to 15th centuries, 136, 336, 464, **577–581**, 927, 1246; modern era, 375–376, **581–584**; Administration of Apostolic See, 10; Alexander VII and, 30; alum of Tolfa discovery, 38–39, 373, 578, 581, 885; animal expenses, 58; annates, 59–60, 136, 389, 578, 581; annona, 60–62, 576; Apostolic Camera management of, 8, 80–84; Avignon papacy spending and, 80–81, 82, 130, 578, 579–580, 581, 1246; Avignon period legacy, 130; Benedict XIV reforms, 170–171, 376; benefaction and, 178–179; benefice vacancies, 179–180, 555, 577–578, 579–580, 1556; Boniface VIII and, 190, 579; Boniface IX and, 192; camerlengo and, 219, 220; cardinalate and, 80, 241, 242, 1246; Celestine III and, 278; Clement III and, 331; Clement IV problems, 332; Clement VI and, 336, 337–338; Clement VII reforms, 344; Clement XII reforms, 376; Clement XIII reforms, 359; Clement XIV reform, 362; coins, 371–378; collectors, 378; common and small services, 389; crusades and. *See under* crusades; Curia and, 459, 582; datary and, 482–483; expectative abuses, 555; Great Schism's drain on, 80–81, 82, 342, 578–579, 580, 661; Gregory I and, 575, 576, 640; Gregory VII and, 449; Gregory XI and, 659, 660; Gregory XIII drains on, 665; Gregory XVI and, 673; Innocent VI and, 795; Innocent VIII and, 799; John VIII and, 836; John XXII and, 849; Julius II expenditures, 885; Leo X extravagances, 344, 374, 927; *Liber censum* report of, 940–941; military expenses, 110, 111, 578; nepotism and, 1031, 1033; Nicholas V and, 1041; Paul V expenses, 1130; provisions and, 1265–1266; public debt and, 30, 1130, 1340, 1345, 1437; for Roman city planning and construction, 1340; Sixtus V economies, 1437; vacant benefices, 179–180; Vatican Radio financing, 1601, *See also* banking and the papacy; taxation, papal

Finland, 1287

Firmilian of Caesarea, 561

First Amendment (U.S. Constitution), 40

first communion, lowered age for, 1198

First Crusade (1095–1099), 65, 112, 1526, 1551–1552; conquest of Jerusalem, 437, 711, 722, 1112, 1552

First French Empire and the papacy, **584–587**; castrati ban, 257, 298; Colosseum and, 388; French Church effects, 1185–1186, 1566; Gallicanism and, 585, 586, 618; Gregory XVI and, 670–671; monasticism suppression, 670; occupation of Rome, 122–123, 138, 530, 1187, 1272; occupations of Papal States and, 1103–1104, 1187–1188; papal chapel musicians, 297, 298; Papal States and, 1103–1104; Pius VII and, 496, 1186–1189; Propaganda Fide status and, 1255; regalia ending, 1291; removal and restitution of Vatican museum collection, 1025; Roman nobility and, 1050, 1185; Rota decision and, 1349–1350; Vatican Archives damage, 1255, 1604; Vatican Library effects, 1598

First Letter of Peter, 197–198

Volume Key: Volume 1, pages 1–614; volume 2, pages 615–1266; volume 3, pages 1267–1637.

1699

First Vatican Council. *See* Vatican I

First World War. *See* World War I

Fisher, Geoffrey, 56

Fisher, John (Jean), 522–523, 778, 1124

Fisherman's Ring (Anulus Piscatoris), 195, 196, 292, 693, 739; as briefs seal, 1401; death of the pope and, 10, 221, 485

fistula. *See* Mass, papal

Fitzherbert, William, archbishop of York, 46, 533

Five Propositions (Jansenius), 616

flabellum, **588**

flag, Vatican City State, 1588

Flagellants, 129, 337, 703, 1221

flagellations, 169

Flaminio, Marcantonio, 1310

Flanders. *See* Belgium

Flavian dynasty. *See* Domitian; Titus; Vespasian

Flavian of Philippi, 1432

Flavian, patriarch of Constantinople, 34, 200, 563, 705, 706; Council of Chalcedon and, 1318; deposition of Eutyches, 915; Leo I support for, 916

Flavius Claudius Julianus, emperor of Byzantium, 881

Flavius Clemens, 1154

fleet. *See* navy, papal

Fleming, 1075

Fleury-sur-Loire, 552, 1015

Fliche, Augustin, 1278

Flodoard of Reims, 748, 923

Florence: architecture, 103, 104, 1594–1595; artists from, 1117; as banking center, 82, 132, 136, 137; Charles V seizure of, 344; Church-State separation, 1542; Clement VII and, 345; collectors, 82; Dante exile from, 481; Dominicans and, 508–509; Eugene IV arts patronage, 509, 537; expatriate Roman confraternity, 1308–1309; French wars in Italy and, 1624; Great Schism and, 661; Guelphs and Ghibellines, 160, 628, 629, 658, 676–677; Innocent VIII entente, 798–799; Inquisition abolishment, 819; Italian unity and, 1533, 1535, 1645; jurisdictionalism and, 888; Martin V and, 975; Medici family and, 926–927, 929; nunciature, 1059; Opera dei congressi founding in, 1023; in papal early 15th-century domain, 661; papal relations resumption with, 1041; Papal States and, 1342; papal tombs, 1499; Paul II and, 1122; Pius VI exile in, 1181; rebellion against Gregory XI, 659; rebellion against Medici, 1624; Sixtus IV interdict on, 1434; slave ownership, 1439

Florence, Council of (1438–1445), 429, 508, 1222, 1380

Florence, Union of (1439), 208, 319, 440, 1395

Florensz, Adriaan, **686**

floreria, **588**

Flores, Bartolomeo de, 255

Florian, emperor of Rome, 543

Florinus, 1612

Flote, Pierre, 191, 1485

fly-chasing funerary rite, 485

Fogazzaro, Antonio, 758, 760, 1008, 1199

Foix, Gaston de, 1622–1623

Foix, Pierre de, 1597

Foley, John, 985

Fondi, conclave of (1378), 162

Fonsgrieve-Lespinasse, Georges-Pierre, 78

Fontainebleau agreement (1813), 1188

Fontana, Carlo, 559, 1369, 1386

Fontana dei Quattro Fiumi (Rome), 1062

Fontana, Domenico, 106, 107, 108, 1062, 1089, 1269, 1271, 1340, 1559; St. John Lateran rebuilding, 1359, 1362, 1363, 1364; St. Mary Major design, 1369; St. Peter's basilica obelisk, 1383; Vatican Library Sistine Hall, 1437

Fontana, Philip, archbishop of Ravenna, 23

Fontenelle (canon of St. Peter's), 1236

Food and Agricultural Organization, 1079

food provisions: almonry, 458; animals, 58; annona, 60–62, 1353; chefs of popes, 302–303; for conclave participants, 396; Curia, 457–458; grain, 60–62, 659, 666; for Roman poor, 681; shortages, 659, 666; traveler's view of Roman cuisine, 1506–1507, *See also* famine

foot-kissing custom, 621

footwear, papal, 620, 621

forbidden books. *See* Index

Forbin-Janson, Charles de, 31, 708, 709

Foreign Missions, Seminary of, 1000

Foreign Press, Association of, 1239

Foreiro, Francesco, 263

forfeiture, ecclesiastical, 439

forgeries, **588–589**, 598; canonical collections, 231; decretals, 85, 223, 224, 1034; Donation of Constantine, 447, 513, 514, 1294, 1296, 1420, 1421, 1485; "false documents" of Leo VIII, 923; indulgences, 774

Forli, Melozzo da, 672, 1091, 1435

Formosus, 154, **590–591**, 837, 838, 997, 1327; Boniface VI as successor, 188; [Christopher] and, 312; John X and, 838, 839; legates of, 909; Marinus I (Martin II) rehabilitation of, 970; rehabilitation of, 1460, 1487; Sergius III and, 1413–1414, 1459, 1460; trial of cadaver of, 590, 1413, 1459, 1487

Fornari, Matteo, 256

Fornici, Giovani, 285

Fortebraccio, Niccolò, 111

Forteguerri, Niccolò Cardinal, 1172, 1173

Fortunata (Pietro di Macerata), 281, 282

Fortunatus of L'Aquila, 945, 946

Forty Hours' Devotion, 1277

Forum, 1327; Christian churches, 1328; churchs in, 1318, 1344; *possesso* ceremony and, 1228, 1229; Trajan's building of, 1314

Forum Boarium, 1272

Foscarini, Egidio, 263

Fossombrone, Ludovico and Raffaele da, 595

Fossombrone, Pietro di, 281

Foucois, Gui. *See* Clement IV

Foulques, Guy. *See* Clement IV

Foulques of Neuilly, 438

Fountain of the Four Rivers, 1344

Four Articles (1682; Gallican), 617, 932

Fournier, Arnaud, 848

Fournier, Jacques. *See* Benedict XII

Fournier, Paul, 1283

Fourteen Points (1918), 1077

Fourth Crusade (1202–1204), 207, 338, 701, 724, 787, 1395

Fragni, Lorenzo, 982

Volume Key: Volume 1, pages 1–614; volume 2, pages 615–1266; volume 3, pages 1267–1637.

Fragonard, Jean Honoré, 1345

France: Albigensian crusade and, 787–788; Alexander III and, 20; Alexander V and, 24–25; Alexander VII and, 30, 913; Alexander VIII and, 31, 32; anticlericalism, 528; anti-Romanism, 1345; apologetics, 76–77, 78; apostolic regions, 1293; appointment of bishops, 88–90, 92, 93, 94; artists in Rome, 116, 117, 118–120, 1345; Assumption holiday, 124; auditors of the Rota, 126, 1349; Benedict IX and, 158; Benedict XIV and, 171; Benedict XV and, 1626; bishops' conferences, 400; blessed hat and sword gifts to, 182; Boniface VIII conflict with, 160, 190–191; breviary, 194; Calvinism, 663, 1288; as cardinalate influence, 241; Catholic renewal, 674; Catholic universities, 1543, 1544, 1548; Christian archaeology in, 101; Christian Democracy in, 305, 306, 307, 309; church in Rome, 317; Church-State conflict, 30, 31, 131, 132, 160, 528, 615, 1185; Church-State separation, 1007, 1110, 1198; Clement VIII and, 347; Clement X and, 350–351, 352; Clovis conquests and dominance of, 1319; concordats with papacy, 397, 398; congregation of exempts, 554; Council of Trent and, 887, 1518, 1519–1520; crusades and, 437, 438, 533; devotion to the pope, 496; diplomatic relations break, 503; Directory, 612–613, 1103, 1185, 1320–1322, 1346, 1598; Dominicans, 510–511, 512; exclusion right, 550–551; exemptions and, 553, 554; Franciscans, 594, 596; Freemasonry and, 603–604, 606, 607–608, 609, 610, 1345; fundamentalism, 614; Gallicanism. See Gallicanism; Ghibelline opposition to, 630; Great Schism and, 163–164, 340, 616, 632, 634–635, 636, 660–661, 974; Gregory V conflict with, 646; Gregory VII and, 649; Gregory XIV and, 666; Guelphism and, 676; heresies, 701, 702, 703, 704; Holy Land status and, 711, 712, 713; Holy See jurisdictional conflict with, 31; Holy Sepulcher order and, 722, 723, 724; Hundred Years War, 1556–1557; Innocent XI and, 805; Innocent XII rapprochement with, 808; Inquisition and, 507, 812, 813, 814, 816; investiture controversy, 821, 822, 1113; Italian unity and, 1107, 1533, 1535–1536, 1538, 1539, 1540, 1645, 1646; Jansenism. See Jansenism; Jesuit expulsions, 1004, 1346; Jesuits, 359, 362, 828; Jews in, 845; John VIII and, 837; John XIX and, 845; John XVIII and, 844–845; John XXIII and, 853, 1217; Julius II and, 885, 886; Lateran V and, 898, 899; Latin Monetary Union and, 377; Lefebvre schism, 1397–1398, 1470; Leo X and, 927; Leo XII and, 932–933; liturgy, 954; Martin IV and, 973–974; medieval anti-Roman satire, 750; military chaplaincy, 990–991; military orders, 989–990; minor basilicas in, 144; modernism and, 1006–1008; monastic reforms, 157; monasticism, 1014–1015; national cleric post, 1027; "new theology," 1217; as Oldest Daughter of the Church, 1064, 1378; Organic Articles (1802), 585–586, 1186, 1566; papal finances and, 580, 581; papal nunciature in, 1058, 1059–1060; papal ties with, 450–451, 1109, 1246; papal titles in, 1051; Paschal II and, 1113; patron saints, 569; Paul II and, 1122; Paul VI anticontraception encyclical and, 1142; Peace of Calais (1347), 1221–1222; Pius V and, 1176; Pius VII concordat with, 398, 1185–1186, 1189; Pius VIII and, 1191; Pius IX and, 1192; Pius X and, 1198; Pius XI and, 1207–1208; Pius XII and, 1213, 1214, 1216, 1217, 1218; Pontifical Mission Societies, 1450; post-Napoleonic status of, 1566; post-Revolutionary Catholic restoration struggle, 1185; Pragmatic Sanction, 536, 581, 616, 927, 1041, 1266; Protestantism in, 347, 663, 938, 1128, 1177; provincial councils, 431; Quietism and, 805–806, 808, 1267–1268; regalia and, 1290–1291; religious holidays, 124, 913; revolution of 1830, 672; Roman Republic of 1849 and, 1323, 1325–1326; sack of Rome (1527) and, 1354, 1355; St. Bartholomew Massacre (1572), 663; St. John Lateran gift by, 1364; secular education, 1544; seminaries, 1409; Sixtus V and, 1437; temporal veto, 1609; Thirty Years War, 1560, 1561; traveler's views of Rome, 1503–1507; Truce of God, 158; Turks and, 936, 937; Ultramontanism and, 1529, 1530, 1566; Urban II and, 1015, 1550, 1551–1553; Urban VIII alliance, 1000; Vatican I and, 1566, 1567, 1568; Vatican II and, 1143, 1573, 1576, 1579, 1581; War of Spanish Succession and, 353; wars of Italy, 1102, 1621–1624; Wars of Religion, 348, 663, 666, 807–808, 1288, 1342; World War I and, 174, 176, 1625–1627; World War II and, 1214, 1632–1633; Zouaves, 1642, 1643, 1646, See also Avignon, papacy of; First French Empire and the papacy; Franco-Prussian War; Franks; French Revolution and the papacy; Napoléon I

Frances of Rome, St., 376, 1130

Francesco di Bernardone, 591

Francese, Stefano, 252

Francia. See France

Francis I, king of France, 93, 616, 711, 926, 927, 928, 968, 1124, 1289; Clement VII and, 343, 344, 345, 1029; Holy League and, 1354; Italian wars of, 1102, 1124, 1621, 1623–1624; opposition to Council of Trent, 1518; Paul III conflict with, 1124, 1125

Francis II, Holy Roman emperor and emperor of Austria, 1184

Francis Borgia, St. See Borgia, Francis, St.

Francis de Sales, St., 269, 1204

Francis Joseph, emperor of Austria, 397, 893, 1194, 1211, 1539, 1630; temporal veto by, 1197, 1609

Francis of Assisi, St., 24, 654, 655, 1037; cardinal protector and, 246, 247; coin depiction of, 375; film depiction of, 323; Franciscans and, 591, 592, 595, 788; liturgy and, 953; Pius XI encyclical on, 1204; poverty ideal of, 133, 849, 1223; stigmata of, 266

Francis of Conzie, 459

Francis of Guise, 1624

Francis of Lorraine, 170

Francis of Paola, 1276

Francis of Sales, St., 30

Francis Xavier, St., 669, 827, 999, 1001; beatification and canonization of, 1130; missionizing by, 1343

Franciscans, 131, 160, **591–597**; absolute poverty issue, 133, 591, 592, 594–596, 702, 813, 830, 849–850; Alexander III and, 23; Alexander IV and, 24, 593, 792; Alexander V and, 24, 25, 594; Antichrist charges and, 66; archaeology, 101; Benedict XII doctrinal bull and, 133, 161; branches of, 595–596; breviary and, 193–194; cardinal protector for, 246, 247; Catholic reform and, 1274; Celestine V and, 280, 281, 282; Clement XIV and, 528, 596, 693; clerical apostolate and, 593; colleges, 379; complete conversion belief, 1345; at Council of Trent, 1518; division of, 133, 592, 594–596 (see also Spirituals); Fraticelli heresy, 133, 702, 850; Gregory IX and, 591–592, 593, 653, 655; Holy Land province, 711, 722; Honorius IV and, 736; indulgences and, 775; Innocent III

Volume Key: Volume 1, pages 1–614; volume 2, pages 615–1266; volume 3, pages 1267–1637.

1701

and, 788; Innocent VI and, 129, 792, 795; Innocent VII reform attempt, 798; Inquisition and, 133, 507, 812, 813, 814, 817; Jesuit conflicts with, 827; Jews and, 872; Joan (female pope) story, 830; John XXII and, 813, 849–850; Leonine union (1897), 596–597; liturgy, 953; Martin IV and, 974; Martinian Constitution and, 594; ministerial parity with Domicans, 593; missions, 998, 999, 1130; missions in Balkans and Near East, 1039; missions in Mexico and South America, 1343; missions in Philippines, 664; Nicholas III and, 592, 1037, 1038, 1040; Nicholas IV and, 593, 1038, 1039, 1040, 1360, 1366, 1501; [Nicholas V] and, 1040; Observant Reform, 594–596; papal ceremonials, 284; penitentiaries, 454, 1152, 1523; Pius XI and, 1200; reforms, 1276; Sixtus V and, 1436; Sixtus IV and, 1433, 1434, 1435; Tridentine missal and, 995; university teaching and, 593, 1549, *See also* Capuchins; Francis of Assisi, St.; Poor Clares; Rule of St. Francis

Franck, César, 954

Franco, Francisco, 397, 1070, 1209, 1216, 1218

Franco of Perugia, 508

François. *See* Francis

François de Meyronnes, 336

Franco-Prussian War (1870), 99, 718, 1540, 1642, 1646; Italian unity movement and, 1107; Vatican I suspension from, 1568, 1570

Franco-Roman rite, 948, 951

Frangipani, Cencius, 625, 732–733, 1306

Frangipani family, 42, 109, 451, 652, 731, 732, 1035, 1048, 1333; Callistus II/Pierleoni alliance against, 216; Colosseum and, 387; Innocent II–Anacletus contested election and, 783, 784, 900

Frangipani, Leo, 625

Frangipani, Robert, 109, 275

Frankfurt, Council of (794), 599, 681, 701

Franks, **597–601**; Arles occupation by, 1611; Benedict III and, 154; Christian conversion of, 597, 1108, 1318; crusade failure in Holy Land (1187), 438; Easter-date controversy, 517, 518; fall of western Roman Empire and, 1318, 1319; *Filioque* in creed and, 920; Gaul controlled by, 1318; Goths alliance, 833; Gregory I and, 136, 141, 597–598, 640–641, 1108; Gregory II and, 643; Gregory III and, 644; Gregory IV and, 645; Hadrian I and, 680, 681; Hadrian III and, 682; Holy Roman Empire formation, 714; Leo III and, 920; Leo IV and, 921; liturgy, 948, 950–951, 952; Lombards and, 957; Martyrology of Ado, 210; migration, 140; missions and, 997, 1108; Muslim defeat by, 1319; Nicaea II contestation, 428; *pallium* and, 1608; papal alliances, 109, 143, 204, 547, 597–600, 1064, 1097, 1456–1457; papal rapprochement with, 421; Papal States and, 1097, 1331; Paschal I and, 1111; patron saint, 1378; Pepin's kingdom division, 1320 (*see also* Charlemagne); pilgrimages to Rome, 1166; relic traffic to, 261; Stephen II (III) and, 1319, 1331, 1378, 1456–1457, 1640; Vigilius and, 1617; Zacharias and, 1319, 1331, 1640, *See also* Carolingians; Merovingians

Fransoni, Cardinal, 675, 1256

Franz Joseph. *See* Francis Joseph

Fraticelli, 133, 702, 850

Fraticelli della opinione, 1121

Fratres Milicie Christi de Livonia. *See* Sword Bearers Order

Frauitas, 622

Frederick, duke of Austria, 850

Frederick I, king of Denmark, 1287

Frederick I, king of Sicily. *See* Frederick II, Holy Roman emperor

Frederick I (Barbarossa), Holy Roman emperor, 330, 534, 652, 960, 962, 1054, 1637; Alexander III conflict, 19–21, 109–110, 313–314, 715, 831, 1021, 1615–1616; Alexander III recognition, 313, 785, 1334; Anastasius IV support for, 45–46; [Callistus III] aid to, 217, 313, 901; Ghibelline/Guelph conflict and, 627, 628; Hadrian IV and, 313, 683, 684, 715, 1098, 1615; imperial coronation and, 424; independence from papacy declaration (1156), 313, 1615; Lucius III and, 960, 961; [Paschal III] and, 1114; pavilion and, 692; Roman prefecture and, 1334; royal rights and, 313, 715, 960, 961, 962, 1109; Third Crusade and, 330, 438; Urban III conflict, 653, 1553

Frederick II, duke of Swabia, 732

Frederick II, Holy Roman emperor, 23, 50, 51, 242, 715, 1028, 1054, 1544, 1554, 1555; as Antichrist, 66, 703; Canossa and, 238; crowning as emperor, 424, 716; crusades and, 315, 439, 734; Ghibelline/Guelph conflict and, 315, 628, 629, 676; Gregory IX conflict, 110, 429, 439, 653, 654–656, 701, 716, 1484; Honorius III indictment against, 315, 734; Innocent III and, 314–315, 787, 1379; Innocent IV and, 315, 791, 792; Innocent IV deposition of, 439, 716; Inquisition and, 813; John XXI pre-papal career and, 846; as king of Sicily, 190, 715; Lyon I and, 791; Roman administration and, 1335; theocracy arguments and, 1109, 1485

Frederick II (the Great), king of Prussia, 170, 361, 868

Frederick III (Frederick-Wilhelm), emperor of Germany, 893

Frederick III, Holy Roman emperor, 536, 716, 1041, 1122–1123, 1171, 1172, 1347

Frederick III (the Simple), king of Naples, 628, 659

Frederick V, elector of the Palatinate, 669

Frederick Augustus of Saxe (king of Poland as Augustus II), 808–809

Frederick of Antioch, 629

Frederick of Ardennes/Lorraine. *See* Stephen IX

Frederick of Mainz, 923, 970

Frederick–William IV, king of Prussia, 674

Fredol, Berenger, 848

Free Spirit sect, 633

free will, 348, 573, 700, 803, 806, 823; Tridentine view of, 1521

free zone, 805

freedom: errors in Pius IX *Syllabus*, 1195; liberalism and, 943–944, *See also* censorship; slavery

freedom of information. *See* press freedom

freedom of religion, 673, 1537, 1542; Americanism and, 40; Communist countries and, 541, 542; as error in Pius IX *Syllabus*, 1195; Helsinki Conference and, 687–688; Josephism and, 170, 528, 868–869; Judaism policies and, 870–871; Vatican II and, 1397

Freemasonry, **601–611**, 1232, 1345; Benedict XIV bull condemning, 170, 602, 605; Clement XII bull condemning, 49, 357, 602–603; Code of Canon Law (1983) on, 229; Gregory XVI condemnation, 601, 605, 672; Italian unity and, 605, 1535, 1538; Leo XII condemnation, 605, 932; Leo XIII anathema against, 601, 605, 606–607, 874, 934; Pius VII condemnation, 605, 1189

Volume Key: Volume 1, pages 1–614; volume 2, pages 615–1266; volume 3, pages 1267–1637.

1702

Frei, Eduardo, 310
Freiburigm, University of, 1462, 1544
Freising canonical collection, 223, 231
French Academy. *See* Academy of France
French Revolution and the papacy, **611–613**; apologetics and, 78; Christian Democracy as response to, 304, 305; confraternity suppression, 1310; Curia effects of, 470; educational secularization, 1544; Freemasonry and, 603; fundamentalism as reaction to, 613, 825; Gallicanism and, 618; Holy Year pilgrims and, 727–728; liberalism and, 943–944; papal conservatism and, 1203; Papal States restoration following, 1103, 1644; Pius VI and, 122, 470, 530, 611–612, 613, 1010, 1178, 1181–1182; Propaganda Fide suppression, 1255; prophetism and, 1260; Risorgimento and, 1191, 1534, 1536; traumatic effects of, 943, 1010, 1182, 1185, 1186, 1193, 1566; Vatican Library effects, 1598, *See also* First French Empire and the papacy; Napoléon I; Roman Republic
French School of Rome, 101, 954, 1603
Freppel, Charles-Émile, 1448
Frequent Communion (Arnalud), 704
Fréret, Nicolas, 77
Frescobaldi banks, 136
frescoes, 665, 1026, 1127, 1301, 1506; black slavery depiction, 1439; Lateran, 1301, 1361, 1363; pontifical family commissions, 1091; St. Mary Major, 1340–1341, 1367, 1368, 1369; St. Paul's Outside the Walls, 1372–1373; St. Peter's basilica, 1378; Silvester I iconography, 1420; Sistine Chapel, 1066, 1340, 1429–1431, 1435; Vatican, 1089, 1354; Vatican Library, 1435
Friars Minor. *See* Franciscans
Fribourg, Union of, 513
Friedberg, E., 225
Friedrich, Johannes, 1396
frigium. See tiara
Frisia, 598, 997, 1166
Frohschammer, Jacob, 78
From a Far Country (film), 323
Froude, Richard Hurrell, 1086
Frühwirth, A., 512
Frutaz, A. P., 71
FUCI (Federation of Catholic University Students), 1024, 1135, 1136, 1137, 1207
Fuga, Ferdinando, 1271, 1363, 1369–1370
Fulbert of Chartres, 1043
Fulda monastery, 1013, 1015
Fulrad, abbot of St. Denis, 1457
fundamentalism, **613–615**, 825
funerals, papal. *See* death of the pope
Furno, Carlo, 723
Fürstenberg, Maximilian de, 728
Fusconi collection, 1025

Gabriel, Archangel, 49
Gabriel of Alexandria, 348
Gabrielli, Giulio, 1187
Gaddi, Gaddo, 1367
Gaddi, Nicolo, 345
Gaetana family, 1037
Gaetani, Giovanni, 1370
Gaetani, Honorat, 193

Gaetano of Thiene, St., 351
Gagliardini, Pietro, 1372–1373
Gagnon, Edoaurd, 434
Gaius (pope). *See* Caius
Gaius (priest), 261, 548, 549
Galatinus, Petrus, 872
Galdin of Milan, 20
Galeazzi, Enrico, 1591
Galerius, emperor of Rome, 1156, 1316
Galganus (hermit), 962
Galicia, 869, 1532
Galilei, Alessandro, 357, 1363
Galileo, 1560, 1562; Inquisition trial of, 467, 819, 1137; John Paul II rehabilitation of, 2
Galla Placidia (mother of Valentinian I), 914, 1610
galleons, 937, 938
Gallery of Geographical Maps, 253
Galletti, Pierluigi, 285
galley slaves, 1440, 1441
Gallican Articles (1682), 528, 778
Gallicanism, 132, 358, 430, 468, **615–618**, 673, 808; Anglicanism compared with, 1289; anti-infallibility position, 616–617, 618, 777, 778, 779; anti-Jesuit campaign, 359; appeals to the pope and, 85; conciliarism and, 390; dispensation criticism by, 505; Dominicans and, 511; four articles of, 31; French Revolution and, 611; Great Schism historiography and, 637; Jansenism and, 616–618, 823, 824, 825; jurisdictionalism and, 888; Leo XII and, 932; liturgy and, 948, 949, 952, 954; Napoleonic Empire and, 585, 586, 618; papism vs., 1109; Pius IX and, 1191, 1196; Pragmatic Sanction and, 899; as Propaganda Fide obstacle, 1255; Risorgimento and, 1536, 1537, *See also* Jansenism
Gallienus, emperor of Rome, 502, 986, 1045, 1156, 1315, 1431, 1455
Gallipoli, 1526
Gallo, Cardinal, 256
Galloni, Grancesco, 1134
Gallus, Trebonianus, emperor of Rome, 423, 1056, 1155, 1455
Gamaliel, 1118
Gambello, Vittore (Camelio), 981
game parks, 58
games, Roman Empire, **618–619**
Gance, Abel, 322
Gandolfo. *See* Castel Gandolfo
Gandolfo di Cremona, 1416
Ganganelli, Lorenzo [Giovanni Vincenzo Antonio). *See* Clement XIV
Gantelme, Jacques de, 1555
Gantin, Bernardin, 434
garb, ecclesiastical, within the Vatican, **619–621**; camauro, **620**; mule, **621**; pontifical gloves, **620–621**
Garcia de Parérèdes, B., 512
Garcia y Garcia, A., 227
Gard, Roger Martin du, 1007
Garden of Gethsemane, 631
gardens. *See* Vatican gardens
"Gardens of St. Philip of Neri," 935
Gargari, Teofilo, 298

Volume Key: Volume 1, pages 1–614; volume 2, pages 615–1266; volume 3, pages 1267–1637.

Garibaldi, Giuseppe, 760, 1107, 1323, 1539, 1540, 1643, 1645; monument to, 1018, 1323

Garnier, Bernard. *See* [Benedict XIV]

Gasbert of Laval, 459

Gasparri, Pietro, 1075, 1083, 1541; Benedict XV and, 173, 174, 175, 1211; canon law and, 228, 363–364, 365, 366, 1211; Christian Democracy and, 308; Holy Land and, 712; Lateran pacts signing and, 901, 902, 1363; papal candidacy of, 1201; Paul VI and, 1134, 1136; as Pius XI secretary of state, 1202–1203, 1207, 1212; World War I and, 512, 1628

Gasperi, Alcide de, 309, 310, 326, 1633

Gasquet, Aidan, 1075, 1603

Gaston de Foix, 886

Gastriota, George, 218

Gatti, Raniero, 1304

Gattico, 285

Gauchet, Marcel, 1006

Gaudemet, Jean, 367

Gaudenti, 987

Gaudentius of Altinum, 1425

Gaudium et spes (1965 pastoral constitution), 1447, 1463

Gaul: barbarians, 140, 141, 142; Boniface I policies, 184, 185; canonical collection, 223, 231; Celestine I and, 273; Christian urban topology, 101; Cybele cult, 442; Donation of Constantine and, 513, 514; Easter date, 517, 706; ecclesiastical provinces, 1264; Frankish control of, 598–601, 1318, 1319; Hilarus and, 707; Hormisdas and, 738; Irish monastic missions to, 552; Leo I and, 915; monasticism, 1011, 1012; Novatian and, 1055; papal patrimony and, 576; Pelagius I and, 1147; pseudodecretals, 589; semi-Pelagianism and, 700; Vandals and, 1318; vicariate of Arles and, 1610; Zosimus and, 1640–1641

Gautier of Albano, 1551

Gautier of Châtillon, 75, 750

Gautier of Ravenna, 959, 1274

Gavardini, Carlo, 1372–1373

Gazali, al-, 847

Gebhard. *See* Victor II

Gebhard of Eichstätt, 1280

Gedda, Luigi, 1137

Gelasian Sacramentary, 951–952

Gelasius I, 432, **621–625**, 738; Anastasius II and, 44, 600; apostolicity principle, 200, 564; barbarian defeat under, 141; benefaction rules, 178, 179; canonical collections and, 223; censorship by, 770; Church-State relations and, 21, 200–201, 621–623; Curia and, 446; excommunication distinctions, 48, 49; Fathers of the Church and, 567; Felix III and, 573, 621, 622; finances, 575, 576; liturgy, 951–952; *Polyptique*, 940; Roman nobility and, 1046; saint veneration, 1391; theory of two powers, 108, 1108, 1482; tomb of, 1377, 1497; as Vicar of Jesus Christ, 1494

Gelasius II, **625–626**; Anastasius IV and, 45; antipope to, 72, 215, 652, 1281; Chancery and, 449, 1282; Frangipane abduction of, 1306; Honorius II and, 731; Latinity and, 906; naval voyages, 1028; tomb of, 1499

Gelnhausen, Conrad von, 390, 633

Gelnhausen, Diet of (1186), 1553

Gemelli, Father, 1206

Geminelli, Paolo, 1413

Gendarmes, Pontifical, **626**

Genet, Elzear (Carpentras), 297, 298

Geneva conventions (1949), 1081

Genghis Khan, 1526

Genigni, Msgr., 1211

Gennadios Scholarios, 76

Gennadius of Marseille, 223

Gennaric, Casimiro, 363, 364

Genoa: as banking center, 136, 137, 581; crusades and, 653; Guelphs and Ghibellines, 685; naval defense by, 1028; outside of papal domain, 661; rebellion and surrender to France, 885; slave market, 1439

genocide. *See* Holocaust

Genseric, king of the Vandals, 140, 914, 1327, 1354

Gentile da Fabriano, 537, 1361, 1380

Gentileschi, Orazio, 1270

Gentili banks, 137

Gentilly, Council of (767), 204

Gentiloni pact (1913), 1023

Gentlemen of His Holiness, 288, 437, **626–627**, 1052

Geoffrey de Beaulieu, 657

Geoffrey of Trani, 451

Geoffroy of Poitiers, 655

Geoffroy of Vendôme, 225, 1167, 1281

George IV, king of Great Britain, 933

George V, king of Great Britain, 174

George of the Aventine, 682

George of Trebizonde, 76, 1294

George Podiebrad, king of Bohemia, 983, 1122, 1172

Georges of Amboise, 1621, 1622

Georgia, f, 545

Gerard of Angoulême, 42, 784

Gerard of Borgo San Donnino, 593

Gerard of Cambrai, 1485

Gerard of Florence. *See* Nicholas II

Gerard of Galeria, 159, 731

Gerard of Parma, 51

Gerard of Sabina Croce, 189, 276

Gerbert d'Aurillac. *See* Silvester II

Gerbert of Ravenna, 646–647, 1274

Gerbert of Reims. *See* Silvester II

Gerdil, Hyacinthe, 1184

Geremek, Bronislaw, 1223

Gerhard, J., 565

Gerhard of Mainz, 870

Gerhard of Toul, 924

Gerhoh of Reichersberg, 45, 66, 534, 959, 1043

Germanic College of Jesuits (Rome), 379, 826, 887, 1342, 1407, 1408

Germanic language, 140

Germanic Roman Empire. *See* Holy Roman Empire

Germanus, patriarch of Constantinople, 519, 643

Germanus II, patriarch of Constantinople, 207

Germany: Alexander II and, 18; apologetics, 77–78; appointment of bishops, 87–88, 91, 94, 238; artists in Rome, 120, 121; *Aufklärung*, 169, 705, 825, 954; Benedict IX and, 158; bishops' conferences, 400–401; Catholic modernism defense, 1008; Catholic renewal, 674; Catholic universities, 1544, 1558; Christian archaeology, 101; Christian Democracy,

Volume Key: Volume 1, pages 1–614; volume 2, pages 615–1266; volume 3, pages 1267–1637.

1704

305, 308, 309, 891–893, 1141; church in Rome, 317; Church organization, 30; concordat with (1933), 397, 398, 1207, 1209, 1212; confraternity studies, 1311; Council of Trent representation, 1518, 1519; crusades and, 533; Enlightenment thought and, 530; evangelization in, 545, 997–998; Febronianism, 358, 617, 778, 779, 868, 888, 1109; Freemasonry, 607, 609; Great Schism and, 340, 633, 636, 662; Gregory VII and, 649; Gregory IX arbitration offer, 654; Hadrian IV and, 684; Holy Sepulcher order, 722; imprimatur, 763; indulgences preaching, 509; investiture controversy, 821; Jesuit college, 379; *Kulturkampf*, 891–893, 1110, 1530; Leo XII and, 930, 932–933; liturgy, 954; Lombard origins and, 957, 958; Luther's Ninety-five theses. *See* Luther, Martin; medieval anti-Roman satire, 750; national cleric post, 1027; Nicholas II conflict, 1036; Old Catholics, 1396; papal monastic exemptions, 156; Paul VI anticontraception encyclical and, 1142; pietism, 704–705; Pius XI policy, 1206–1207, 1212; Pius XII postwar policy, 1216; Pius XII pre-papal diplomacy with, 1211–1213; Protestantism in, 1125, 1130, 1288, 1518; provincial councils, 431; Reformation inception and spread, 1286–1287, 1290; Teutonic order, 987, 988; Ultramontanism and, 1529, 1530; Vatican I and, 1566; Vatican II and, 1143, 1576, 1579, 1581; witchcraft trials, 799; World War I and, 174, 1107, 1625–1628; World War II and, 1212–1214, 1600, 1629–1636, *See also* Holy Roman Empire; Nazism; Prussia

Gerson, Jean, 164, 262, 777, 1168–1169, 1275

Gesta Romano, 748

Gestapo, 1635

Geta, emperor of Rome, 1315

Geymin, prince of Lithuania, 998

ghettos, 374, 873, 874, 876, 932, 1188; Jewish confraternities and, 1310

Ghezzi, Pier Paolo, 1363

Ghibellines, 131, 132, **627–631**, 973, 1048, 1536; Alexander IV and, 23; Angevins and, 53, 628–30, 676, 716; Canossa and, 238; Clement VI and, 337; common characteristics, 629–630; Gregory X policies against, 658; Guelphs vs., 315, 316, 627–631, 676–677, 685, 707, 716, 794; Holy Roman Empire and, 236, 315, 316, 627–631, 716; military orders against, 987; theocratic arguments and, 1484

Ghiberti, 537, 1127, 1380

Ghini, Simone, 1361

Ghirlandaio, Domenico, 1428, 1429, 1435

Ghislieri, Michele (Antonio). *See* Pius V

Giangaetano, Cardinal, 1554

Giannone, Pietro, 888

Giaquinto, Corrado, 1091

Giardino Quadrato, 1026

Gibbons, James, 40, 41

Giberti, Gian Matteo, 1276, 1499

Gichtel, Johann-Georg, 704

Gide, André, 761

Gierek, Edward, 1086

gifts. *See* benefaction

Giglio, Antonio, 213

Gilbert de la Porrée, 414, 450, 533

Gilbert of Tournai, 657

Giles of Rome (Egidio Collona), 131, 233, 242, 282

Giles of Viterbo, 799, 898, 927

Gillet, M., 512

Ginetti, Cardinal, 912

Giobbe, Paolo, 484

Gioberti, Vincenzo, 1193, 1536–1537

Giocondo, Fra, 1382

Giolitti, Giovanni, 901

Giornale di Roma, 984

Giornale ecclesiastico di Roma, 670–671, 1179

Giotto, 692, 1361, 1380, 1385, 1439

Giovannelli, Ruggiero, 298

Giovanni, duke of Paliano, 1175

Giovanni da Montecorvino, 1039

Giovanni di Castrocoeli, 281, 282

Giovanni of Santa Prisca, 278

Giraud de Bari, 749

Giraud of Cambrai, 454

Girodon, Victor, 1259

Girolamo, Cardinal, 801

Giustiniani, Tommaso, 898

Gizzi, Pasquale, 1193, 1402

Glabert, Raoul, 1424

gladiators, Roman, 387, 618, 619

Glenville, Peter, 322

Gli uomini non guardano il cielo (film), 322, 323

Glorious Revolution (1688–1689), 55

gloves, papal, 620–621

gnosticism, 57, 523–524, 561, 697, 1159; angelology, 49; Hyginus and, 744

Goa, 1193, 1256, 1343

Gobelinus, Johannes, 1173

Godefroy, Jacques, 1466

Godfrey of Bouillon, 722

Godfrey of Lorraine-Tuscany, 17, 238, 1035

Godfrey of Trand, 227

Godfrey of Tuscany, 1461

Godfrey the Bearded, 924

God's peace. *See* Peace of God

God's truce. *See* Truce of God

Goebbels, Joseph, 1600, 1634

Goethe, Johann Wolfgang von, 249, 753, 755, 759, 1170, 1345

Gogol, Nikolai, 751

gold: coins, 373, 374, 376, 377; medallions, 982, 983; from New World, 28, 104; ransom for Roman Jewish population, 1635; rose sacred ornament, 1347–1348; Sixtus V reserve, 359, 1437

gold bulls, 196

Golden Bull of 1356 (Holy Roman Empire), 132, 316, 337, 717, 796

Golden Host, Order of, 487, 488

Golden Militia, Knight of the, 694, 1050

Golden Rose. *See* Rose, Golden

Golden Spur, Order of, 487

Gomez, Gutierre, 163

gonfalon, gonfaloniere. *See* banners; pavilion

Gonfalone (confraternity), 1308–1309

Gontran, king of the Franks, 597

Gonzaga, Aloysius, 827

Gonzaga, Ercole, 1127

Volume Key: Volume 1, pages 1–614; volume 2, pages 615–1266; volume 3, pages 1267–1637.

Gonzaga, Ferrando, 1125

Gonzaga, Louis, St., 569, 596

Gonzaga, Valenti, 469

Gonzales, Tirso, 809

Good Friday penitentiaries, 1523

Good Government, Congregation for, 467, 1103

Good News, proclamation of. *See* evangelization

Gordianus, 1476

Gordon, John Clement, 1073–1074

Gospel of Peter, **631**

Gospel of Saint Mark Silver, 750

Gospels, the, and papal authority, **631–632**; Peter and, 1157–1158, 1160; principle of succession, 1241

Gothic wars (535–553), 957, 1327–1328, 1330

Goths, 140, 699, 781; assaults on Rome, 254, 914, 1146, 1317, 1318, 1377, 1616; evangelization of, 545; Frankish alliance, 833; in Italy, 1318; Leo I and, 914; Milan and, 987; Vigilius and, 1617, *See also* Ostrogoths; Visigoths

Gotti, Girolamo, 364, 1256

Gottifredi, Giacomo, 59

Gouffier de Boissy, Adrien, 927

Gounod, Charles, 299, 744

Gouyon of Rennes, 864

government (central government of the Church). *See* Curia

Gozlin of Bourges, 157

Gozzadini, Giovannia, 391

Gozzoli, Benozzo, 1042

Gracchus, Furius Maaecius, 1230

grace, doctrine of, 354, 573, 704, 803, 806, 823, 825, 865, 867; Council of Trent and, 1520–1521; for crusaders, 438; expectative, 293, 555; Jesuits and, 348; works vs., 429, 438

Graham, Robert, 496, 1636

grain provision, 60–62, 659, 666

Gramsci, Antonio, 1534

Granacci, Francesco, 1429

Grand Almoner, 990

Grande Loge de France, 607–608, 609

Grandi, Francesco, 1363, 1372–1373

Grandmaison, Léonce de, 1008

Granvella, Nicholas, 1125

Grassi, Paris de, 284–285, 294, 621

Gratian (jurist), 19, 21, 84, 92, 124, 1543–1544; background, 488–489; *Decretum. See Decretum of Gratian*; on dispensation, 504, 505; on dissolution of marriage, 1249; on election of bishops, 92, 93; just war doctrine and, 98; on legates, 908; on simony, 1425

Gratian, emperor of Rome, 199, 479, 700, 986, 1230, 1317, 1611

Gratian, John. *See* Gregory VI

Gravina, concordat of (1192), 277–278, 1054

Great Britain. *See* England; Ireland; Scotland

Great Instruction (1767–1768), 1531–1532

Great Interregnum (1257–1273), 315–316, 716, 1485

Great Schism of the West (1378–1417), **632–638**; Angevins and, 50–54; Antichrist charges and, 66–67; antipopes and, 70, 72, 130; archives and, 1604; Avignon papacy and, 130, 132, 632–636; beatification and, 145; [Benedict XIII] and, 25, 72, 130, 132, 163–164, 167, 193, 341, 508, 634, 635, 636, 637, 660, 661, 797; Boniface IX and, 192–193, 634; canon law and, 227; cardinalate powers and, 242, 393, 1356; Catherine of Siena and, 266, 340; characterized as conflict, not schism, 1395; Clement VII and, 266; coin commemorating end of, 373; conciliarism and, 390, 1101, 1109, 1246; conclaves during, 393; consistory decline and, 415; council ending. *See* Constance, Council of; Curia organization, 460–461; deposition of popes, 495; Dominicans and, 508; exemptions revocation, 1233; financial management, 80–81, 82, 578–579, 580, 661; Franciscans and, 594; Gallicanism and, 616; Gregory XII and, 266, 660–662; health of popes and, 1417; Holy Years and, 725; indulgences and, 774; initiation of, 1246; Innocent VII and, 797–798; Inquisition and, 813; Joan (alleged pope) argument about, 830; legates and, 911; Martin V election marking end of, 429, 974, 1101, 1246; military forces, 111, 1029; nationalist factions in, 131, 132, 632–637; naval forces, 1029; nepotism's function in, 1032, 1049; papal administration in Rome and, 104; papal tombs, 1502; papal-university relations and, 1549; as reform hindrance, 1275; Rome rebirth following, 1339–1340; Sacred College split from, 242, 339–340, 342, 1356; tax collectors, 378; Urban VI role in, 24, 25, 266, 339, 1557–1558; vacant benefices and, 179

Great Synagogue (Rome), 521

Greece: Christian archaeology in, 101; remains of Roman Empire in, 1319; Roman Catholics in, 523, *See also* Greeks in Italy

Greek Catholic Church of Eastern Rite. *See* Uniates

Greek College (Rome), 1000, 1408

Greek Fathers of the Church. *See* Fathers of the Church, Greek

Greek Orthodox Church: Josephism and, 868, 869; Lyon II and, 429

Greek studies, 47, 1548

Greeks in Italy, 562, 563, **638–639**; monasticism and, 638, 1011; as slaves, 1439

Grégoire, Henri, 611, 1183

Gregorian calendar. *See* calendar, Gregorian

Gregorian chant, 298, 948, 950–951, 952, 954, 1619; Pius X restoration of, 1198

Gregorian reform. *See* reform, Gregorian

Gregorian Sacramentary, 951, 952

Gregorian University (Rome), 380, 583, 664, 828, 1343, 1407, 1545, 1566

Gregoriopolis, founding of, 645

Gregorovius, 182

Gregory I (the Great), **639–642**, 649, 671, 834; "ad limina" visits and, 4; African Church and, 13, 33; angelology and, 49; as apocrisarius, 74, 1148; army of, 108; banking and, 135; barbarians and, 141–142; basilica construction, 1388; as Benedict's biographer, 1013; benefaction and, 179; bishops' election and, 91; Boniface III and, 186; Boniface IV and, 186–187; British evangelization by, 142, 152–153, 188, 545, 597, 641, 895, 1166; Byzantium and, 202, 639, 640; canonical collections and, 223; Carthage and, 251; chamberlain duties, 287; chronic illness of, 1416; consistorial advocate and, 413; Curia and, 446, 447, 451; *Dialogues*, 141, 142, 1614; as Doctor of the Church, 568; Felix III as ancestor, 572, 639; finances, 575, 576, 640; as former prefect of Rome, 1231; Franks and, 136, 141, 597–598, 640–641, 1108; iconoclast controversy and, 600; Jewish relations, 870, 871; John I and, 832; as last Father of the Church, 567–568; legates of, 909; liturgy, 298, 949, 950, 951, 1619; Lombard response

Volume Key: Volume 1, pages 1–614; volume 2, pages 615–1266; volume 3, pages 1267–1637.

1706

by, 957; missions, 142, 641, 996–997, 1108; monastic exemptions, 5, 551–552; monasticism and, 1013; nepotism and, 1031; Order of, 487; on papal supremacy, 650, 1245; patrimonies, 1115; Pelagius II and, 1148; pilgrimages to Rome and, 1165, 1166; plague relief by, 1220; plague vision by, 254; registers, 1293; relics and, 261; Roman college and, 379; Roman Senate and, 1047, 1411; Roman services by, 1319, 1330; Sabinian and, 1353; St. Peter's basilica and, 38, 547, 549, 1378; simony definition, 1423–1424, 1425; stational processions and, 1453; tomb of, 1497, 1498; veneration of saints and, 1389, 1390, 1391; Victor III praise for, 1614

Gregory II, 197, 420, 552, **642–643**, 644; Byzantium alliance and, 206, 546; finances, 576, 577; Franks and, 598; iconoclast controversy and, 203, 598, 643, 701; Lombard threat and, 108–109, 643, 1245

Gregory II of Tusculum, 157

Gregory III, 552, **643–644**, 1097; coins, 372; Franks and, 598; iconoclast controversy and, 203–204, 644; Lombard threat and, 109, 598, 644, 957, 1245, 1331; Pantheon roof replacement, 1096; St. Peter's basilica and, 549; tomb of, 1497; Zacharias contrasted with, 1639–1640

Gregory IV, 71, **644–645**, 681, 1393; antipope following, 830; Carolingians and, 600; headdress, 620; Lateran Palace reconstruction, 1300; missions, 997; mosaics, 1019

Gregory V, **645–647**; antipope to, 122, 646; Cluny bull, 1015; exemptions and, 552, 844; tomb of, 1497; use of Italian language by, 905

[Gregory VI], 70, 71, 72, 156, **647**

Gregory VI, 70, **647–648**; Benedict IX's resignation and, 158, 647, 1305, 1422; deposition of, 328, 495, 1305, 1612; Gregory VII friendship, 648, 649; residence outside Rome, 1303; Silvester III recognition of, 1422; simony and, 1424; tomb of, 1498

Gregory VII, 19, 159, **648–651**, 653, 671, 785; African Church and, 13; Alexander II and, 17, 18; antipope to, 238, 240, 329, 650; banner, 688; bishops' elections and, 92; canonical collection, 224–225, 231; Carthage and, 251; Castel Sant'Angelo refuge, 1301, 1354; Church-State conflict, 21, 72, 109, 238–239, 240, 313, 329, 649–650, 651, 1053, 1108–1109, 1483, 1637; [Clement III] and, 329; collection of taxes and, 1283; conciliarism and, 390; coronation of pope symbolism, 1283; crusades and, 437; *Dictatus papae*, 224, 499, 650–651; election as bishop of Rome, 180; exemptions and, 552; exile of, 239; with Gregory VI in exile, 648; Henry IV confrontation with, 237, 238–239, 240, 254, 329, 587, 649–650, 651, 1053, 1329; heresy condemnation, 701; Holy Roman Empire and, 715; imperial coronation and, 313; investiture controversy, 18, 66, 69, 92, 238–239, 649, 649–650, 821–822, 900, 1109, 1280, 1636, 1637; Islam and, 1393; Latinity and, 906; legates and, 909, 910; Leo IX and, 449; letters in Vatican Archives, 1603; liturgy and, 951, 953; military forces and, 109; monasticism and, 1016; Nicholas I prefiguring, 1035; Nicholas II and, 1035, 1036; nicolaism condemnation, 1043, 1044, 1282; Normans and, 109, 239, 1053, 1329, 1354; nuncio and, 1058; *pallium* and, 1608; on papal primacy, 650, 676, 1279; Paschal II and, 1112; on pope as title, 1227; reforms of. *See* reform, Gregorian; register of, 1293; St. Paul's Ouside the Wall basilica door commission, 1370; simony

condemnation, 1424, 1425; theocratic claim of, 496, 1278, 1280, 1284, 1333, 1483; tomb of, 486, 1499; Ultramontanism charges and, 1529; Urban II and, 1550, 1551, 1552; Victor II and, 1613; Victor III and, 1613–1614; William I of England and, 649, 822

[Gregory VIII], 70, 72, 109, 215–216, **651–652**; coronation of Henry V by, 1114; Gelasius II and, 1281

Gregory VIII, 111, 625, **652–653**; tomb of, 1499

Gregory IX, **653–656**; Alexander IV and, 22–23; antiheretical laws, 701; on apostolic constitution, 421; armies, 110, 654–655; arms, 113; asylum decretals, 124; canonical collection, 224–225, 226, 227, 231, 513, 1109; canonizations by, 655; cardinalate and, 451; Catholic universities and, 655–656, 1544, 1547, 1548; Celestine IV and, 279; crusades and, 439; Curia and, 452; cursor, 475; decretals. *See Decretals* of Gregory IX; Dominicans and, 507, 654, 655, 734; elections of bishops and, 92, 93; exemptions and, 553; as first cardinal protector, 246; Franciscans and, 591–592, 593, 653, 655; Frederick II conflict with, 110, 315, 439, 653, 654–656, 716, 1484; French alliance, 1064; heresies, 702, 812; hunting sport, 58; Innocent III and, 788; Innocent IV and, 790–791, 793; Inquisition and, 507; judges delegate and, 453; Latium residence, 1303; Lyon I and, 429; military orders and, 987, 989, 990; missions and, 998; naval forces, 1028, 1029; nepotism and, 1031; notaries and, 451; Papal States and, 1098; regalia and, 1291; Roman conflict and, 1335; St. Peter's redecoration, 1378; Talmud inquiry and, 792; theocratic arguments of, 1484; tomb of, 1500; universities and, 507

Gregory X, 51, **656–658**, 848, 1037; on apostolic almoner duties, 37; Apostolic Camera functions, 8, 655; arms, 113; bankers, 452; bull design, 196; Byzantium union and, 657–658, 1038; canonicalal collection, 226; ceremonial of Roman Curia, 284; conclave rules, 241, 280, 392, 657, 846, 1356; crusades and, 438, 440, 656, 657, 658, 685; film portrayal of, 318; funerary rites, 486; Holy Roman Empire and, 316, 658, 685; Innocent V and, 794; Lyon II and, 429; mendicant orders and, 280, 593; nepotism, 1031; Papal States and, 1098; tiara, 1491; tomb of, 1500; vacant Holy See provision, 1406; Viterbo refuge, 102

Gregory XI, 58, 458, **658–660**, 690; annona, 60; Avignon papacy, 129–130, 131, 132, 266, 559–560, 1246; [Benedict XIII] and, 162; cardinal protectors and, 246–247; chamberlains, 287; chef for, 302; Clement VI nepotism and, 129, 336; [Clement VII] and, 338, 339, 340, 342; coins, 373; Curia and, 455; Dominicans and, 508; heraldry, 690; Hospitallers and, 988; Inquisition and, 703; Lateran rebuilding, 1360; military expenses, 110, 659; papal chaplain, 301; poor health of, 1416; return to Rome by, 103, 130, 132, 162, 659–660, 1246, 1338; Roman populace attacks on, 254; tiara, 1491; tomb of, 1502; Urban VI and, 1557–1558; Vatican residence of, 1362, 1594

Gregory XII, 535, **660–663**, 798; abdication of, 662; annona, 61; arms, 114; Avignon registers, 1293; [Benedict XIII] and, 164, 660, 661; Council of Pisa and, 25, 72, 132, 137, 636, 661; cursor, 475; defects of, 661; Dominicans and, 508; Fisherman's Ring, 587; Great Schism and, 635, 636, 637, 660–662; Holy Year, 727; hunting sport, 58; [John XXIII] and, 851; resignation by, 1305; return to Rome decision, 266; tomb of, 1502

Volume Key: Volume 1, pages 1–614; volume 2, pages 615–1266; volume 3, pages 1267–1637.

Gregory XIII, **663–666**; Anglican schism and, 55, 663; annona, 61; arms, 114; arts commissions, 1090, 1091, 1092; breviary and, 194; calendar reform, 51, 212–214, 518; canonical collection, 231; Capuchins and, 595; cardinalate and, 241; Catholic colleges and universities founded by, 465, 664, 1545; Catholic scholarship and, 1296; Clement VIII and, 346; coins, 375; Congregation for the Eastern Churches and, 407; congregations and, 471; Discalced friars and, 595; efforts to end Eastern schism, 1531; financial problems, 374; Gregory XIV and, 666; Gregory XV and, 667, 668; Holy League and, 938; Holy Year, 726–727; Index rules and, 770, 772; Innocent IX and, 800; Jesuit interventions by, 826–827; Jewish forced conversion policy, 873; jurisdictional conflicts, 888; legate of, 912; martyrology and, 210; medallions, 982; as "missionary pope," 348, 664, 669, 1000, 1001; mosaics and, 1021; mural map, 252–253; nunciatures, 465, 664, 1057; papal chapel singers, 297; Petrine privilege and, 1250; Quirinal and, 665, 1269, 1270; Reformati and, 596; reforms by, 1246; St. Peter's chapel and, 1382; Sixtus V and, 1436; statuary removal by, 1024; tomb of, 1386; Urban VII and, 1559; Vatican Observatory and, 1062

Gregory XIV, 346, 467, **666–667**, 800; arms, 115; breviary reform, 194; conclave electing, 1609; expenditures, 374; Gregory XV and, 667; jurisdictionalism, 469, 888; papal chapel singers, 296; Paul V and, 1129; Prophecy of Malachy motto, 1261

Gregory XV, 467, **667–670**; apostolic constitution and, 421; arms, 115; arts patronage, 1092, 1383; arts projects, 1090, 1093; beatification, 145; camerlengo powers, 220; canonizations by, 233, 667, 669; Discalced friars and, 595; Dominicans and, 510; expenditures, 374; Innocent X and, 801; Jesuits and, 827; missions and, 1000; nepotism, 668, 1032; papal funeral rules, 1056; Propaganda Fide founding, 57, 348, 409, 667, 668–669, 1001, 1253–1254, 1561; relics and, 262; temporal veto and, 1609; Tridentine reforms and, 667

Gregory XVI, 78, 89, 143, **670–676**, 932; academies and, 2; apologetics, 78, 670–671, 1535; Apostolic Camera functions, 9; arms, 112, 116, 693; attack on liberalism by, 306, 605, 1109, 1193; attack on modernism by, 78, 670, 673–675, 1104, 1109, 1193, 1443, 1535; beatifications and, 147; brief and, 195; cardinalate and, 245; Castel Sant'Angelo and, 255; chamberlains, 288, 739; Church-State powers and, 671, 1536, 1538–1539; coins, 377; conclave electing, 394; as "Curialist," 1530; Dumas audience with, 757; encyclical list, 524–525; Fabric of St. Peter and, 558; Freemasonry condemnation, 601, 605, 672; Gentlemen of His Holiness and, 627; heraldry, 696; hereditary nobility ban, 488; Leo XIII and, 933; missions and, 1004; Moroni history of Church and, 143, 294–295; Papal States territorial redistribution and, 672, 1247, 1538; photograph of, 1162; Pius IX and, 1192, 1193; printing press and, 1444; Propaganda Fide and, 1256; protonotaries of, 1263; Roman monuments and, 1016; Rota tribunal ended under, 1350; St. Paul's Outside the Walls restoration, 1190, 1372; Secretariat of State, 1402; Signatura Apostolic and, 1525; uprisings against, 1104; Vatican gardens and, 1596; Vatican Library and, 1598; Vatican museum collections, 1025–1026

Gregory Asbestas of Syracuse, 206

Gregory of Nazianzus, St., 34, 198, 199, 765; as Father of the Church, 563, 566, 567; Holy Spirit definition, 428; relics of, 253

Gregory of Nyssa, 34, 567

Gregory of St. Crisogono, 1283

Gregory of Sant'Angelo, 277

Gregory of Tours, 145, 942, 1165, 1166

Gregory the Illuminator, 545

Grescentzi, Giovanni, 1332

Grescenzio II, 1333

Grève, Philippe de, 750

Griffi, Orazio, 256, 298

Griffini, Michelangelo, 77

Grimoard, Anglic, 1556, 1557

Grimoard, Guillaume de. *See* Urban V

Gromyko, Andrei, 1140

Groote, Gerhard, 633

Gropper, Johann, 1521

Grosparmi, Raoul, 1554

Grosseteste, Robert, 213

Grossi, Giovanni Francesco (Siface), 257

Grotius, 99

Grottaferrata, 158–159, 638

Gruber, Herman, 608, 609

Guaccialotti, Andrea, 982

Guarantees, Law of (1871), 436, 583, 718, 889, 1077, 1107, 1541; papal nonacceptance of, 901; Rota decisions and, 1350; Vatican I suspension and, 1570

Guardaroba maps, 253

Guardian of Holy Relics and Cemeteries, 262

Guelph IV, duke of Bavaria, 1551

Guelphs, 160, **676–677**, 732, 1048; Alexander IV and, 23; Boniface VIII and, 481, 676; Ghibellines vs., 315, 316, 627–631, 676–677, 685, 703, 794; Gregory X and, 658; Hadrian V and, 685; Lombard League as basis, 20; neo-Guelphism, 676, 1536, 1537, 1644; Orsini family and, 1037; position of, 676; Sicilian kingdom and, 280, 315, 628, 629, 676, 716; split among, 676, 677; theocratic arguments and, 1484; Urban II and, 1551; Urban IV and, 314

Guenée, Antoine, 77

Guéranger, Prosper, 674, 954, 955, 1373, 1566

Guercino, 668, 1025, 1090, 1091, 1345, 1386

Guérin, Joseph, 1644

Guerra, Giovanni, 1362

Guesclin, Bertrand du, 1556

Gui. *See* Guy

Gui, Bernard, 18, 813, 814

Guía espiritual (Molinos), 1267

Guibert of Nogent, 65, 75–76

Guibert/Wilbertus, archbishop of Ravenna. *See* [Clement III]

guides to Rome, 774, 1166, 1167, 1168, 1170, 1328

Guidiccioni, Bartolomeo, 1124

Guido II, bishop of Assisi, 591

Guido da Baiso, 227

Guido di Busco, 284

Guido di Città de Castello. *See* Celestine II

Guido, Filippo, 512

Guido of Crema. *See* [Paschal III]

Guido of Milan, 1036

Volume Key: Volume 1, pages 1–614; volume 2, pages 615–1266; volume 3, pages 1267–1637.

1708

Guido of Pisa, 152
Guido of Spoleto, 1459
Guido of Tuscany, 838, 839
Guillaume de Aigrefeuille, 1556
Guillaume of Brescia, 486
Guillaume of Champeaux. *See* William of Champeaux
Guillaume of Mandagout. *See* William of Mandagout
Guinigi bank, 82, 137
Guiscard. *See* Robert Guiscard; Roger I Guiscard
Guitry, Sascha, 322
Guitton, Jean, 1132, 1578
Gundlach, G., 1214
Gunpowder Plot (1605), 1130
Guntharic, king of the Vandals, 1476
Günther, Anton, 78, 674
Gustav I Vasa, king of Sweden, 1287
Gutton, J.-P., 1223
Guy de Chauliac, 486, 1221, 1222, 1416
Guy de Montpellier, 1307
Guy of Boulogne, 53, 339, 658, 659, 1557 (*see also* Callistus II)
Guy of Burgundy, 333
Guy of Ferrare, 330
Guy of Spoleto, 970
Guyon, Mme (Jeanne Bouvier de La Motte), 808, 1267–1268

habermus papam, **679**
Habsburg-Lorraine, 1538
Habsburgs, 30, 658, 717, 867, 1246, 1561; Council of Trent and,
    1518; Curia and, 469; Josephism and, 1179; War of Spanish
    Succession and, 353; World War I and, 1626
Hadrian, emperor of Rome, 253–254, 255, 1095, 1096, 1153,
    1314
Hadrian, St., 683
Hadrian I, 181, 204, **679–681**, 683, 968, 1331; army troops, 109;
    calendar, 210; canonical collections, 223, 231; Charlemagne
    and, 599, 1320, 1420; coins, 372, 1097; Colosseum and, 387;
    diaconiae, 498; exemptions, 552; Frankish alliance, 1320;
    Lateran reconstruction, 1300, 1359; Leo III and, 919, 920;
    liturgy, 952; Nicaea II and, 701; Roman building projects,
    1328; Stephen IV (V) and, 1458; tomb of, 1374, 1497
Hadrian II, 590, 601, **681**, 836, 1413, 1458; Anastasius Bibliothe-
    carius and, 46–47; Byzantium and, 206; Marinus I (Martin
    II) and, 969; Moravian apostles and, 837; Slavonic liturgy ap-
    proval by, 997
Hadrian III, **682–683**, 1458, 1497
Hadrian IV, 450, **683–685**; Alexander III and, 19; Curia and, 450,
    464; Eugene III and, 533, 534; Gregory VIII and, 652; Holy
    Roman Empire and, 313, 715, 1098, 1615; Lucius III and,
    960; military forces of, 109; Normans and, 19, 1053; Papal
    States development, 1098; Scandinavian churches and, 46,
    533, 683, 684; tomb of, 1499; Vatican Palace and, 1301
Hadrian V, **685–686**, 846, 1037; arms, 113; Boniface VIII and,
    189; Clement IV and, 332; conclave rule abrogation by, 280,
    392–393; Dante's consignment to purgatory, 481, 482; as
    Innnocent IV cardinal nephew, 793; tomb of, 1500
Hadrian VI, **686**, 927, 928; Antichrist charges and, 67; arms, 114,
    693; Clement VII as successor, 344, 1124; humanists' dislike
    of, 1295; Inquisition and, 817; military orders and, 989; naval
    forces, 1029; Reformation challenge to, 1246, 1285, 1287

Hadrian of Canterbury, 142, 1619
Hadrian's Villa, 1021, 1026, 1345
Hagen, J. G., 1063
Hague Peace Conference (1898), 719
Hail Marys, 1346–1347
Haile Selassie, emperor of Ethiopia, 1515
Haimeric, 450
Haiti, 398, 1470
Hakim, al-, caliph, 711, 1414, 1525
Half-bull, 195–196
Halifax, Lord, 934, 1076, 1395
Hallmayr (Austrian composer), 744
halo (in saint iconography), 145
Hamao, Stephen Fumio, 435
Hamerani family (papal engravers), 983
Hammer, Jérôme, 1239
Hammerstein, Irmingard von, 157
Harisson, Thomas, 120
Harnack, Adolf, 1006
Harold, king of England, 18, 111
Harrach, Ernest von, 1561
Harrison, Rex, 322
Hartmann, Felix von, 363
Harvard College, 1544
Hasler, August Bernhard, 1196
hat. *See* Blessed or Holy Hat and Sword; headdress
Hattin disaster (1187), 438
Havas agency, 1236
Havet, Julien, 589
hawks, 59
Hawkwood, Sir John de, 110, 339, 659, 1557
Hayes Code (film), 320
Haymo of Faversham, 594
headdress: biretta, 180; Blessed or Holy Hat, 182–183; ecclesias-
    tical within Vatican, 619, 620; tiara, 1488–1492
Health Care Funds, 1592
Health Workers, Pontifical Council of the Apostate for, 435
Hébert, Marcel, 1007
Hecker, Isaac, 41
Hedwig of Poland, 333
Hefele, Carl Joseph, 1396, 1567
Hegesippus, 57, 942, 1244
Heidelberg, University of, 193, 1544
Heim, Bruno, 688
Heimburg, Gregory von, 1172
Heine, Heinrich, 239
Heinrich of Langenstein, 390, 633
Helena, St., 417, 418, 722, 1025; statue of, 1383; tomb of, 1499
Hell, popes consigned by Dante to, 44, 282, 481, 1038
Helleputte, Georges, 306
Helsinki Conference (1975), 541, **686–688**, 720, 1085
Helvétius, 77, 359, 362
henotheism, 443–444
Henoticon (483), 44, 200, 563, 564, 572, 622, 1377, 1427
Henri. *See* Henry
Henricians, 701
Henrietta of France, 55
Henry (the Navigator), prince of Portugal, 21, 999

Volume Key: Volume 1, pages 1–614; volume 2, pages 615–1266; volume 3, pages 1267–1637.

1709

Henry I, king of England, 42, 784–785, 822, 1113, 1637; Gregorian reforms and, 1281

Henry I, king of France, 924

Henry II, Holy Roman emperor, 109, 513, 647, 844, 1043, 1052; Benedict VIII and, 156–157; canonization of, 233, 268; Church reforms and, 1279, 1280; Papal States' borders and, 1097; Tusculum and, 449

Henry II, king of England, 21, 313, 322, 485, 880–881, 1114; Becket conflict with, 21, 652; sanctioned for Becket murder, 652

Henry II, king of France, 816, 886, 887; Council of Trent and, 1519; marriage to Catherine de Medicis, 1624; Protestantism and, 1288

Henry III, Holy Roman emperor, 17, 109, 426, 688, 714, 1053; Church reforms and, 1278, 1279, 1280, 1284, 1333; competing popes and, 158, 495, 648, 1422, 1424; Leo IX relationship to, 924, 925; naming of Clement II, 328; naming of Damasus II, 480–481; papal depositions by, 495; Victor II and, 1612, 1613; Victor III praise for, 1614

Henry III, king of England, 685

Henry IV, Holy Roman emperor, 1423; abdication by, 900, 1483; Agnes as regent, 328, 1461; Alexander II and, 17, 18, 731; Canossa pilgrimage by, 237, 238–239, 650, 1280, 1386, 1483; [Clement III] as antipope, 1274; Gregory VII conflict, 21, 66, 69, 109, 254, 329, 587, 648, 649–650, 651, 1053, 1329; investiture controversy and, 238–239, 432, 649–650, 821–822, 900, 923, 1112–1113; occupation of Rome by, 329, 650; papal antisimony campaign and, 1424; papal election rights, 240, 1036; Paschal II and, 1112–1113; Urban II confrontation, 1550, 1551, 1552; Victor II and, 1612, 1613, 1614

Henry IV, king of England, 799

Henry IV, king of France, 666, 667, 1470, 1560; Catholic conversion and absolution of, 347, 348, 929, 1344; gift to St. John Lateran, 1364; mediation between Paul V and Venice, 1131; papal legate and, 912

Henry V, Holy Roman emperor, 215–216, 513, 625, 715, 731, 732; antipope Gregory VIII and, 651–652, 1114, 1281; Canossa and, 238; Concordat of Worms signing, 397, 1284, 1424, 1636–1637; investiture controversy and, 900, 1113, 1424; Paschal II conflict, 1113, 1114, 1281, 1423

Henry VI, Holy Roman emperor, 51, 715, 786, 1052, 1054, 1098, 1553; Celestine III and, 277, 278; coronation of, 330, 653; Lucius III and, 961, 962; mysterious "great offer" to Curia by, 278; Sicilian kingdom and, 313, 314, 331, 961

Henry VII, Holy Roman emperor, 131, 316, 334, 513, 628, 629, 716, 717, 850, 1337, 1485; Colosseum and, 387; imperial coronation and, 424

Henry VII, king of England, 799

Henry VIII, king of England, 54, 322, 770, 799, 1073; Anglicanism and, 1288–1289, 1395; Clement VII and, 343, 344, 345, 1395; French wars in Italy and, 1622, 1623; Leo X and, 928; Paul III and, 1124, 1125

Henry of Albano, 331, 438, 653

Henry of Castile, 332, 1336

Henry of Dinant, 702

Henry of Lausanne, 701

Henry of Saxony, 714, 1125

Henry of Suses. See Hostiensis

Henry of Villars, 954

Henry of Waiblingen, 627

Henry the Lion, duke of Saxony, 277, 314, 961

Heraclea, Council of (517), 737

Heraclius (defender of lapsi), 543

Heraclius, emperor of Byzantium, 187, 202, 484, 1319

Heraldic Capitoline Congregation, 1050

heraldry, 688–696; arms and, 112–116, 693–694; banners and, 138, 688–689; crusader, 437, 688, 689; Holy Sepulcher, 723; keys and, 689–692, 1588; mosaics, 1020; pavilion and, 692–693, 1145; tiara and, 692, 1488–1489, 1492

Herbert II of Vermandois, 839

Hercules (Roman deity), 443

Heredia, Jean Ferdinand de, 110

hereditary nobility. See decorations; titles, pontifical

heresies, 696–705; Acts of Peter and, 3–4; Antichrist charges and, 66, 67, 68; apostasy vs., 79; consistory and, 414; etymology of word, 696; Fathers of the Church and, 567, 696, 697; Index and, 770–771; Inquisition and, 406–407, 810–820; Judaism not covered by, 258; schism vs., 1393–1394; torture authorized against, 703

heresies, early, 696–700; African Church and, 1431; Apollinarism, 34, 35, 567, 699; Byzantium and, 198–200; Celestine I prosecutions, 273, 274; Damasus I and, 479–480; ecumenical councils on, 198; Hilarus condemnation, 706; Hippolytus refutation, 707–708; Leo I and, 913, 914, 915, 916, 917; Marcionism, 523–524, 697, 1394; Montanism, 48, 523, 698, 1550; persecutions of, 545; Pricillianism, 700, 773, 782, 1427; semi-Pelagianism, 573, 700; Siricius campaign against, 1427, See also Arianism; Donatism; gnosticism; iconoclasm; Manicheism; Monophysitism; Monothelitism; Nestorianism; Novatianism; Pelagianism

heresies, 8th to 13th centuries, 700–702; of Abelard, 701; Alexander III and, 21; crusade against, 438; evangelical, 701; Ghibelline identification with, 676; iconoclasm, 204, 680, 701; Innocent III and, 896; Lateran II and, 429; Lateran III rulings, 901; Lateran IV and, 896, 897; Lucius III bull against, 962; nicolaism seen as, 1042, 1043; simony seen as, 1281, See also Adoptionism; Albigensian heresy; Catharism; Waldensianism

heresies, since the 14th century, 702–705; apostolic poverty seen as, 574, 1096, 1121, 1122; charges against Alexander VI, 27; Clement VIII prosecutions, 348; Curia appeals and, 450; Gregory XI prosecutions, 659; Holy Office prosecution, 709–710, 1177; Lateran V and, 898; master of the Sacred Palace trial role, 981; modernism seen as, 1198–1199; Reformation and, 1289; Roman Inquisition against, 1128; Tridentine responses to, 1277; witchcraft, 799, See also Anabaptists; Beghards and Beguines; Flagellants; Hussites; Jansenism; pietism; Quietism

Hering, Count, 174

Herman of Toul, 924

Herman von Salm, 1550

Hermann of Metz, 650

Hermann of Scheda, 75

Hermenegild, 141, 142

Hermes, Georg, 78, 675, 819

Hermesianism, 819

Volume Key: Volume 1, pages 1–614; volume 2, pages 615–1266; volume 3, pages 1267–1637.

1710

Hermits of St. Augustine, 24
Herriot, Edouard, 1206
Hersfeld, Lambert von, 238
Hervet, Gentien, 968
Herzan, Cardinal, 1184
Herzl, Theodore, 874
Heston, Charlton, 322
Hezius, Dirk, 686
Hiereia, Council of (754), 204
Hieronymian Martyrologue, 261, 1388, 1495
Higher Institute of Pedagogy, 1546
Higher Pontifical Institute of Latin, 1546
Hilanius of Narbonne, 185
Hilarius. *See* Hilarus; Hilary
Hilarus, 450, **705–707**, 945, 946, 1013; benefaction and, 179; as
    former deacon, 484; pilgrimaages and, 1095; stational pro-
    cession, 1453–1454; successor Simplicius, 1425, 1426; tomb
    of, 1391, 1496
Hilary of Arles, 273, 915, 1610, 1611
Hilary of Narbonne, 1610, 1641
Hilary of Poitiers, 199, 479, 883; as Doctor of the Church, 568; as
    Father of the Church, 567, 568; Liberius and, 945, 946
Hildebert of Lavardin, 225, 748
Hildebrand. *See* Gregory VII
Hildegard of Bingen, St., 65, 533, 655
Hilduan of Milan, 840
Himerius of Tarragona, 1427
Hincmar, archbishop of Reims, 74, 154, 600, 615, 681, 1034,
    1035; canonical collection, 224, 225; on dissolution of mar-
    riage, 1249; John VIII and, 839; Leo IV and, 921; *pallium*
    and, 1608
Hincmar, bishop of Laon, 681–682
Hippolytus, 63, 181, 517, 699, **707–708**, 1550, 1564; *Antichrist*,
    64; as antipope, 70–71, 1222; *Apostolic Tradition*, 90, 223,
    283; basilica of, 1390, 1617; on Callistus I, 214–215; Christ-
    ian cemetery reference, 258; Christian persecutions and, 63,
    1154, 1155, 1223; *Liber generationis*, 942; on papal cere-
    monies, 283; *Philosophumena*, 1640; rival Callistus, 135,
    1045
Hiroshima, 1511
Hispana Gallica, 223, 224, 231
Hispanic rites, 948, 951, 953
Hispanus, Petrus. *See* John XXI
Historical Sciences, Papal Committee of, 389
Historische Institut de Görresgesellschaft, 1603
History of Seven Sages of Rome, 748
Hitler, Adolf, 397, 874, 1110, 1206, 1207, 1209, 1634
Hitler's Pope (Cornwell), 1214
Hittorp, Melchior, 954
Hochhuth, Rolf, 495–496, 875, 1141, 1214
Hohenstaufens, 533, 627, 653, 676; crusade against, 440; extinc-
    tion of male line, 628, 629; Hadrian V opposition to, 685;
    Holy Roman Empire, 313, 424, 439, 715, 897, 961; in south-
    ern Italy, 278, 315, 1037, 1039
Holland. *See* Netherlands
Holocaust, 875, 876, 877; *Deputy* (Hocchuth) play about,
    495–496, 1141, 1214; Pius XII and, 495–496, 875, 876, 877,
    1214, 1636; Roman Jews and, 1635
Holstenius, Lucas, 30, 1562, 1598

Holy Alliance, 394, 673
Holy Childhood, Pontifical Society of the, **708–709**, 1450
Holy College. *See* Sacred College
Holy Cross, Knights of the, 488
Holy Cross, Pontifical University of, 380
Holy Crusade, Brotherhood of the, 928
Holy Door (major basilica), 144, 729
Holy Hospice, 627
Holy Lance, 799
Holy Land: Capitulations, 711, 712; Christian archaeology in, 101;
    crusades and, 437, 438, 439–441; dispensations on pilgrimage
    vows, 505; fall of last Latin settlements, 1039; first Islamic at-
    tacks on (630), 1319; Holy Places (until 1917), 711–712;
    Holy Places (since 1917), 712–714; Holy Sepulcher order,
    722–724; indulgences for travel to, 774; Islamic conquest of,
    318, 438, 711, 712, 722; Jerusalem's status, 877; Jewish-papal
    relations and, 874, 875; jubilee 2000 pilgrims, 729; military
    orders and, 987, 988; Nicholas IV and, 13; papal navy voy-
    ages, 1028; Paul VI visit to, 1170, 1510, 1514, 1516; pilgrim-
    age to, 724, 1163, 1165, 1167; Turks as threat to, 1526; Urban
    IV and, 1554, *See also* Jerusalem; *specific crusades*
Holy League, 528, 1527, 1622; founding and purpose, 26–27,
    886, 937, 1177, 1179, 1354; Lepanto and, 937, 938; sack of
    Rome and, 1354, 1355
Holy Office, Congregation of the, **709–710**; abolition in Tuscany,
    1535; causes of canonization and, 268, 406; Counter Refor-
    mation and, 1276; Curia responsibilities transferred to, 465;
    on dissolution of marriage, 1249; establishment of, 242,
    415, 416, 471, 509, 816, 817–820, 1341, 1443; as first per-
    manent congregation, 415, 464; Galileo condemnation,
    1562; Gregory XVI and, 671; Index and, 472, 772, 1443; in-
    dulgences and, 775; Italian unification and, 1535; Jansen
    condemnation, 803, 824; missionizing and, 1001, 1004;
    Molinos condemnation, 1267; Paul III and, 509, 1123, 1126,
    1357; Paul IV as member of, 465, 709, 1128; Paul VI reform
    of, 171, 772, 1141, 1443–1444; Petrine privilege and, 1250;
    Pius V career in, 1176, 1177; pontifical secret and, 1399;
    Propaganda Fide and, 1254; repression of liberals, 673; re-
    served cases and, 1298; Sixtus V and, 1436–1437, 1438;
    usury rejection by, 1191; Vatican II and, 1571, 1574, *See
    also* Doctrine of the Faith, Congregation for the; Inquisition
Holy Places, **711–714**; until 1917, 437, **711–712**, 722–723, 874,
    987, 988; since 1917, **712–714**, 723–724, 729, 875; pilgrim-
    age to, 1163–1171, *See also* crusades; Holy Land; Jerusalem
Holy Redeemer, Hospital of. *See* Montegaudio (Mons Gaudii)
    Order
Holy Roman Empire, **714–717**; Alexander II and, 18; Alexander
    VIII and, 31–32; Augsburg, Peace of, and, 936, 1128, 1288;
    banner, 688; Benedict VII close relationship, 156; Benedict
    VIII close relationship, 156–157; Blessed or Holy Hat and
    Sword bestowals to, 182; Boniface VIII conflict with, 190;
    Canossa and, 238; cardinalate and, 241; Carolingians and,
    600, 601; Catholic-Protestant division of, 1288; Church re-
    forms and, 1278; Clement VII and, 344–345; coronation of
    pope and, 426; coronations of emperors in Rome, 313,
    423–425, 600, 715, 716, 1041; Council of Trent and, 1125,
    1517–1518, 1519; dismantling of (1806), 99, 930, 1186;
    election of bishops and, 91–92; election of pope and, 240,
    328; elective monarchy, 716; enlargement of, 716, 717; Eu-

Volume Key: Volume 1, pages 1–614; volume 2, pages 615–1266; volume 3, pages 1267–1637.

1711

gene III and, 534; Frederick I (Barbarossa) view of, 313; German crown linked with, 840; Ghibelline backers, 627–631, 716, 850; Golden Bull (1356), 132, 316, 337, 717, 796; Great Interregnum (1257–1273), 315–316, 716, 1485; Great Schism of the West and, 340, 634, 635; Gregory IV and, 560; Gregory VII and, 648–649, 1637; Gregory IX and, 653, 654–656; Gregory X and, 658; Honorius III and, 314–315; Honorius IV and, 736; Innocent III and, 733–734, 735, 786–787; Inquisition and, 703; investiture controversy, 92, 238–239, 821, 1113, 1114, 1636–1637; John XXII/Louis IV conflict and, 128, 676, 850, 1039, 1040; king of the Romans as prior title, 313; last imperial crowning in Rome, 1041; liturgy, 952–953; Louis of Bavaria/Frederick of Austria conflict, 850; Luther under ban of, 1286; monasticism and, 1015; Nicholas III and, 1037–1038; Nicholas V antipope and, 1039–1040; as nonhereditary, 961; Normans of Sicily and, 961; in papal early 15th-century domain, 661; papal election ratification by, 154, 155, 158, 204; papal nunciature in, 1058; Papal States and, 1097; Paschal II and, 1112, 1113, 1114; [Paschal III] and, 1114; Paul II and, 1122–1123; Paul III and, 1124–1125; pontifical seminaries, 1343; Protestantism and, 936, 1125, 1128, 1287, 1288; Reformation as threat to, 1287, 1288; Roman commune and, 1334, 1335; sacking of Rome by (1527), 255, 345, 374, 726, 1354–1355; Thirty Years War and, 669; Victor II and, 1612; war with Turks, 30, 31, See also Church-State conflict; Germany; specific emperors

Holy Roman Universal Inquisition, Congregation of the, 406

Holy Russia, 1488

Holy Sacrament and the Five Wounds, Archbrotherhood of, 475

Holy Sacrament, Company of, 1000

Holy Sacrament confraternities, 475, 1309–1310, 1311

Holy Sacrament, devotion to, 1555

Holy See (or Apostolic See), 717–722; academies, 1–2; administrative offices, 8, 10–12; administrative structure, 80–84, 545, 1333 (see also Curia); Alexandrian See relationship, 32–36; Annurio pontificio (directory), 12, 62–63; apostolic tradition and, 199; appeal to, 84–85, 1283; archives, 1593–1605; artist commissions, 1089–1093; audiences, 125–126; bankers, 136–137; Blessed Hat and Sword symbolizing defense of, 182–183; briefs, 194–195; budget, 584; bulls, 195–196; canonization reserved to, 144, 145; career and, 247–248; censures reserved to, 1299; Clement VII weakening of, 343; concentration of power in 19th century, 1566; concordats, 396–400, 404; congregations, Roman, 406–412; creation of Catholic universities by, 1544, 1545; crusades and, 437–438; Curia, 444–475; decoration awards, 487–488; diplomatic powers, 190, 503–504, 718, 1056–1057, 1541; domain (in early 15th century), 661; ecclesiastical provinces and, 1264, 1265; exemptions authority, 190; fascism and, 308; filling of vacancy in. See conclave; financial institutions, 583–584; French Revolution and, 611–613; Fundamental Agreement with State of Israel (1993), text of, 878–880; Guelph backers, 627–631; as head of all Churches, 14, 15, 186; Helsinki Conference participation, 687–688; heresy trials, 981; historical development of papal office, 1244–1251; Holy Places and, 713–714; Holy Sepulcher order and, 723; impeachment provision, 1406–1407; independence from Roman Empires, 204; international organizations and, 718, 1077–1081; Josephist conflict with, 869; judiciary. See Rota, tribunal of the; Lat-

eran pacts and, 582–583, 901–905, 1541, 1586; legitimacy of, 33; library, 1597–1599; media and communication by, 984–985; monastic relations, 1015–1016; national churches in Rome and, 317; Nazi intrusions into, 1635; nepotism and, 1030–1033, 1049; neutrality of, 1211, 1588, 1620–1630, 1625–1626, 1633; newspaper, 1081–1084; Noble Guard and, 1052; nunciature and nucio, 1056–1060; organizational diagram, 721; ostpolitik, 24–26; painting patronage, 1091–1093; palatine designations, 1094–1095; papal hymn, 744–745; Patrimony of St. Peter, 1115–1116; pavilion symbolism, 1145; Peter as founder, 1157; petitions to, 1161–1162; press office, 984, 985, 1083–1084, 1236–1240; reestablishment in Rome (1375), 162; Roman nobility and, 1047–1051; Roman properties of, 1586–1587; Rota as tribunal of appeal, 1524–1525; states of. See Papal States; Vatican City State; stereotypes of, 1232–1233; Swiss Guard, 1471–1472; tribunal. See Rota, tribunal of the; vacancy provision, 1406, 1479; vassal taxes, 577, 578; Vatican City State relationship with, 1587; Vatican Secret Archives, 1603–1605; Vaticanist commentary on, 1606–1607; World War I status of, 174–176, 1211, 1625–1626, 1627–1628; World War II status of, 1213–1214, 1588, 1628–1629, 1633, See also primacy, papal

Holy Sepulcher (Jerusalem), 711, 722, 1514

Holy Sepulcher of Jerusalem, Knightly Order of the, 488, 722–724, 987

Holy Spirit, 281, 1244; Byzantine schism over doctrine of, 1394; causes of canonization and, 268; conciliarism and, 391, 1317; Constantinople I definition of, 428, 897; Council of Trent on, 1520, 1521; simonical investitures and, 1424–1425; symbol of, 1020; symbolism of, 182, 693, See also Filioque

Holy Spirit, Confraternity of, 537

Holy Thursday, 248, 1523

Holy Trinity, Hospital of (Rome), 1225

holy war, 18, 109, 1181; Byzantine rejection of, 206; crusades as, 437; Islamic, 207

Holy Wednesday, 1523

Holy Week: bell silence, 152; confraternity as lay patron, 1308; liturgy, 949, 955, 1217; music, 257, 298; Tridentine Missal, 996

Holy Year, 724–730; Middle Ages, 724–726; modern era, 27, 28, 726–728; contemporary era, 519, 728–729, 775; list of, 729–730; Alexander VI (1500), 27, 28; Carnival suspension during, 248; Clement VIII and, 347; Clement X and, 351; coin commemoration, 373; Counter Reformation restoration of, 1340; exceptional, 728, 745; feast days, 569; first (1300), 190, 316, 724, 774, 1151, 1168, 1169, 1361, 1379; Gregory XIII (1575), 665, 727; indulgences collection, 724, 725, 726, 728, 1196; Innocent X and, 803; John Paul II apology to Jews and, 877; Jubilee of 2000, 729, 745, 877; Leo XII renewal of, 932; medallion commemorations, 983; millennium, 729; painting commissions, 1090, 1091; papal hymn, 745; papal Mass and, 296; Paul VI and, 1143; photography, 1163; pilgrimages, 569, 724–730, 932, 1169–1170, 1225, 1340; Pius VIII and, 1191; Pius XI and, 728, 1203; Pius XII and, 1215; Vatican I and, 1567

Homeousians, 699

Homer, 1227

Volume Key: Volume 1, pages 1–614; volume 2, pages 615–1266; volume 3, pages 1267–1637.

1712

Homobonus of Cremona, 896

Hondius, Jodocus, 691

Honor Guard of His Holiness. *See* Palatine Guard

honorary awards. *See* decorations

Honoratus, 1610

Honoré, Jean, 264

honorific titles. *See* titles, papal

Honorius, emperor of Rome, 184, 538, 781, 1046, 1165, 1318; Donatist debate and, 1394; mausoleum, 1377; Zosimus disavowed by, 1641

Honorius I, 5, 143, 181, 202, **730–731**, 1116, 1354; last prefect of Rome under, 1231, 1330; monastic exemptions, 552, 730; Monothelitism and, 16, 701, 834, 919; Normans and, 1053; Pantheon closure by, 1095; prohibition of gladiators by, 387; Rome upkeep and, 1330

[Honorius II], 18, 70, 72, 329, **731**

Honorius II, 276, **731–733**, 959; [Anacletus II] and, 42; Anastasius IV and, 45; conflict over successor, 783; election of, 275; Holy Roman Empire and, 313, 716; judges delegate and, 453; military support for, 109; monasticism and, 1015; Templars and, 988; tomb of, 1499; university teaching and, 1548

Honorius III, **733–735**, 788, 900; Alexander IV and, 22; as camerlengo, 219, 451, 452; cardinal penitentiary post, 1523; cardinal protector and, 246; cardinalate and, 451; chaplains, 300; clerical education and, 734, 1541, 1548; crusades and, 439; Curia and, 452; Dominican recognition by, 506, 511, 734, 788; as former camerlengo, 8; Gregory IX and, 653, 654; Holy Roman Empire and, 314–315; *Liber censum* and, 940, 941; master of the Sacred Palace origins, 980; military orders and, 989–990; missions and, 997–998; naval forces, 1028; Penitentiary and, 1151; Roman law study ban, 226, 734; St. Paul's Outside the Walls mosaics and, 1370; Teutonic knights and, 988; tiara, 1492; tomb of, 1500

Honorius IV, **735–736**, 1039, 1554; Angevins and, 52; arms, 112, 113; bells and, 152; conflict over successor, 1038–1039; heresy and, 702; Nicholas III and, 1037; regalia and, 1291; residence, 1302; tiara, 1491; tomb of, 1500–1501

Honorius of Autun, 284

Hontheim, Johann Nikolaus von. *See* Febronism

Hormisdas, 15, 141, 567, **736**, 831, 832, 1145; Acacian schism and, 502, 573; on apostolic principle of Roman primacy, 201, 564, 736, 738; Frankish gift to, 597; relics veneration, 1389; son Silverius's pontificate, 1417–1418

horses, 58, 463; chinea offering, 303–304

Horus, cult of, 442

Hosius, Stanislas, 778, 1518

hospices, Roman, 316–317, 448, 1170, 1225, 1226, 1301; confraternities and, 1307–1308, 1310

Hospitallers, Knights, 129, 440, 987, 988, 989, 990, 1016, 1028, 1554; banking activity, 136; Clement V and, 335; Gregory XI and, 988; Paul III and, 1126; Pius V and, 1177; Templars controversy and, 131

hospitals. *See* hospices; *specific hospitals by key word*

Hostiensis (Henry of Suses), 451, 1304, 1349, 1484

Hôtel de Soubise, 1604

Houdon, Antoine, 119

household, papal, **738–742**; administration, 7; animals and, 57–59; apostolic palaces and, 1093; arms of patronage, 695;

camerlengos, 221, 627; chamberlain members, 288, 739–740; chapel inclusion, 740; chaplain, 301; Curia workers, 457, 466–467; history of, 455–456, 738–740; humanists employed in, 1294–1295; Palatine, 1094; papal court and, 436; Pontifical Gendarmes, 626; prefecture, 6–7, 738, 739, 1231; Tridentine reforms, 465; Vatican II and, 301, 740–742, *See also* family, papal

housekeeper, pope's, 457

Houtin, Albert, 1007

Howard, Henry, 174

Howard, Phillip, 55

Hrabanus Maurus, 870

Hubert of Pirovano, 451

Huet, Daniel, 77

Hügel, Friedrich von, 1008

Hugo, king of Italy, 839, 840, 922, 1460

Hugh Capet, 224, 842, 1420–1421

Hugh de Payns, 988

Hugh Geraud of Cahors, 848

Hugh of Arles, 839

Hugh of Cluny, 233, 238, 651, 1550

Hugh of Fleury, 1113

Hugh of Lyon, 909, 1113, 1551–1552, 1614

Hugh of Provence, 254, 1332

Hugh of St.-Cher, 451, 1151, 1554

Hugh of Vaucemain, 161, 508

Hugh of Vermandois, 1460

Hugo of Cluny. *See* Hugh of Cluny

Hugolino dei Segni. *See* Gregory IX

Huguccio of Pisa, 225

Huguenots, 347, 663, 938, 1177

Hugues de Die, 910

Hulst, Maurice d', 1007

human rights, 541; Helsinki Conference, 687; Holy Places and, 714; John Paul II defense of, 860; Pius XII and, 1449

Humanae vitae (1968 encyclical), 1110, 1132, 1141–1142, 1143, 1247

Humani generis (1950 encyclical), 1136, 1217

humanism. *See* Renaissance humanism and the papacy

Humanum genus (Leo XIII encyclical), 606–607, 608

Humber of Moyenmoutier, 924

Humbert II of Viennois, 440

Humbert da Silva Candida, 92, 206, 701, 925, 1043, 1245, 1280, 1281, 1282, 1283, 1613; Donation of Constantine and, 513; on simonical investitures, 821–822, 1424

Humbert of Ormont, 1500

Humbert of Romans, 208, 657, 871

Hume, David, 603

humor, **742–744**; medieval anti-Roman satire, 749–751

Hundred Years War, 632, 975, 1556

Hungary: Angevins and, 52–53; Austrian Catholicism and, 669; Blessed Hat and Sword gifts to, 182; Calvinism, 1288; concordat with papacy, 399; crusades and, 333; diplomatic ties with Holy See, 503; evangelization, 997; failed revolution (1956), 540; first cardinal, 451; Great Schism and, 632, 636, 660, 661; Holy Roman Empire and, 714, 717; Josephism and, 869; *Kulturkampf* and, 893; missionaries in, 998; *ostpolitik*, 1084, 1085–1086; in papal early 15th-century domain, 661; Paul II support to, 1122; Pius XI legate to, 1213; Pius XII

Volume Key: Volume 1, pages 1–614; volume 2, pages 615–1266; volume 3, pages 1267–1637.

1713

and, 1215; Roman seminary, 1342; Silvester II and, 1421–1422; Turkish threat to, 375, 928, 1122; Urban VI support by, 1558

Huns, 140, 200, 1317–1318

hunting (sport), 58–59, 927

Hus, Jan, 67, 535, 637, 703, 775; infallibility criticism, 777

Hussites, 373, 530, 703–704, 775, 976, 983, 1130; Lateran V and, 898; Pope Joan story and, 830

Hutin, François, 304

Hutten, Ulrich von, 514

Huyghebaert, N., 514

Hyginus, **744**, 1171

hymn, papal, **744–745**, 949; Urban VIII compositions, 194, 1562

Ibas of Edessa, 201, 1146, 1147, 1617

Iceland, 1287

iconoclasm: Byzantine controversy, 197, 198, 203–205, 600, 643, 701, 1394; Charlemagne and, 599, 680–681, 701; Frankish theologians and, 600; Greeks in Italy and, 638; Gregory II/Emperor Leo III conflict over, 203, 598, 642–643, 701; Gregory III and, 203–204, 644; Hadrian I and, 680; as heresy, 204, 372, 680, 701; Illyricum Church and, 203, 318, 643; Italian art and, 1116; Nicaea II refutation of, 428; papal arts patronage and, 1090, 1117

iconography: apostolic imagery, 1160–1161; of bankers, 138; Gregorian reform and, 1284–1285; of keys, 891, 1488; of saints vs. blessed, 145; of tiara, 1488–1489, 1492, *See also* painting

Idduas of Smyrna, 1433

idolatry controversy. *See* iconoclasm

Ignace de Laubrussel, 77

Ignacius, St., 69

Ignano, Giovanni da, 1336

Ignatius of Antioch, 385, 566, 664, 1157, 1159; on Church organization, 1244; on deacon ranking, 484

Ignatius of Constantinople, St., 205, 206, 560, 682, 836, 1034; Leo IV and, 921; poor relief and, 1225

Ignatius of Loyola, St., 569, 669, 704, 726, 1373, 1545; beatification and canonization of, 827, 1130; Counter Reformation and, 1125; crusade missions and, 1000; Jesuits founding by, 826, 827, 1125, 1276; Marcellus II relationship, 968; Roman College founding, 379, 1343, 1407, 1408; Roman confraternities founding, 1309

Ildephonse, St., 952

illnesses of popes. *See* sickness of the pope

Illustrazione Vaticana, L', 1083

Illyricum Church, 184–185, 318, 563, 737, 782–783; Church of Rome quarrels with, 318; iconoclast controversy, 203, 381, 643; under patriarch of Constantinople, 200, 201, 203, 205, 644, 997; Slavonic liturgy, 682, 837, 997, 1459; Three Chapters schism and, 1617

Illyricus, Thomas, 778

image of Rome in literature, **747–762**; Middle Ages, **747–751**; modern and contemporary eras, **751–762**, *See also* traveler's views of Rome and the Vatican

image veneration. *See* iconoclasm

Immaculate Conception: Alexander V dogma development, 24; Alexander VI support, 27; *Civilita Cattolica* support, 326; Clement XIII and, 360; Council of Trent and, 1520; dogma definition and proclamation (1854), 39, 524, 1194, 1372,

1566; dogma preparation, 675; dogma proclamation significance, 1566; Dominicans and, 669; feast of, 1141; Spanish Square column honoring, 303

immanence, 79

Immigrants, Office of Spiritual Aid to. *See* Pastoral Care of Migrants and Itinerants, Pontifical Council of the

immortal soul, 899

immunity, ecclesiastical, 469

Imola, 1192, 1193

impeded See. *See* See, vacant and impeded

imperial benefaction, 178

imperial coronation. *See* coronation, imperial

imprimatur, **762–765**, 770

In Emineti (1738 bull), 602–603, 604

incardination, **765–770**

Incarnation, 897, 917

Independent Catholic Action, 1137

Index, **770–771**, 819; Alexander VII updating, 29, 770; Alexander VIII and, 31, 32; Benedict XIV and, 170, 171, 530, 772; catalogs of prohibited books, 771; Clement VIII and, 348; Clement XIII and, 359–360; discontinuance (1966), 710, 763, 770, 772, 1443; Holy Office and, 406, 472, 709, 710, 772; humanist works and, 1296; imprimatur, 763–764; Jansenist works listed on, 704, 824; Lateran V and, 899, 1443; *Liber Septimus Decretalium* on, 363; modernism and, 1008; Paul IV and, 770, 771–772, 1128, 1175; Pius IV revision, 770, 772, 1175, 1296; Pius VIII and, 1191; printing press and, 1442, 1443; Quietist works listed on, 1267; suspension of, 1443; Tridentine revision, 666, 1175, 1289, 1296, 1522

Index, Congregation of the, 469, **771–773**, 819; activity resumption (1758), 359–360, 362; antiliberalism support by, 943; expansion of activities (1840s), 675; initiation of, 415, 465, 471, 770, 1178, 1179, 1341, 1357, 1443; purpose of, 1444; reform of, 171, 1443; Sixtus V and, 770, 772, 1438, 1443; termination of (1917), 1443, *See also* Holy Office, Congregation of the

Index of Christian Art (Princeton University), 1599

India: Catholic missions, 669, 675, 1002, 1003, 1004, 1343, 1561; native clergy training, 1004; Paul VI travel to, 1139, 1514, 1516; Portuguese colonialism in, 1193, 1194–1195; Propaganda Fide and, 1254, 1255; Vatican II representation, 1580

Indian rites. *See* Chinese rites

indiction. *See* acts, pontifical

indifferentism, 1472

indigency. *See* poor relief; poverty ideal

indigenous clergy, 1002–1005, 1110, 1218, 1255–1258; Society of St. Peter the Apostle and, 1373–1374

individualism, 823

Indochina, 827, 1255, 1343

Indonesia, 1580

indulgences, **773–776**; Alexander VI grants, 27; for Angelus recitation, 50; Boniface IX and, 192, 193; Celestine V and, 281; Congregation for the Doctrine of Faith grants, 406; to crusaders, 18, 439, 440–441, 507, 724, 774, 792; Fabric of St. Peter's and, 1382; Flagellants' condemnation of, 703; Gregory XI grants, 659; guides to Rome listings, 774, 1168; Holy Office and, 710; Holy Year, 724, 725, 726, 728, 1196;

Volume Key: Volume 1, pages 1–614; volume 2, pages 615–1266; volume 3, pages 1267–1637.

1714

Julius II and, 885; Leo X abuses, 374, 509, 775; Luther's condemnation of, 926, 927–928, 1286, 1382, 1395; medallion exchanges, 983; for missionizing, 999; Penitentiary and, 1523; for pilgrimages, 519, 724, 725, 774, 1165, 1168, 1169, 1170; for plague care workers, 1221; pontifical blessing and, 177; rosary recitation and, 1347; Tridentine reforms and, 1289

Industrial Revolution, 1225

Inerius, 652

infallibility, **776–781**; in canonization, 268; *Civiltà Cattolica* support, 326, 1567; Clement VI defense of, 336; defenses of, 777–778; dogmatic constitution and, 422; Dominican support, 512; ecumenism movement and, 519–520; encyclical, 524; as *ex cathedra*, 546; on factual questions, 29; Gallican challenge to, 511, 616–617, 618, 777, 778; Gregory XVI and, 671; Jansenism vs., 511, 778, 823, 825; *Kulturkampf* reaction to, 779, 892, 893; Luther's challenge to, 1286; magisterium, 776, 780, 963–966; Old Catholics schism and, 778, 779, 1396, 1530, 1567, 1568; of papal dispensation, 505; Pius IX and, 778, 1194, 1196, 1396; "real" vs. "false" popes and, 830; Sacred College effects, 1357; Vatican I dogma proclamation of, 39, 429, 519, 618, 776, 777, 778–779, 855, 860, 892, 1110, 1196, 1247, 1541, 1567, 1568, 1570, 1645–1646; Vatican II on, 779–780, 1585

Infenssura, St., 1434

Inferno (Dante). *See Divine Comedy, The*

information offices. *See* media, communication, and the Vatican; press office of the Holy See

Ingelheim, synod of (948), 909

Ingelis, Angelo, 1259

Inghirami, Tommaso, 250

Ingoli, Francesco, 668, 1001, 1254

Ingolstadt, University of, 1544

Innitzer, Cardinal, 1262

Innocent I, 183, 184, 538, 698, **781–783**; altar crosses and, 437; barbarian invasion of Rome and, 140, 1046, 1353–1354; Byzantium and, 198, 199; canonical collection, 231; on dissolution of marriage, 1249; on excommunication degrees, 48; monasticism and, 1013; mosaics and, 1020; Pelagian schism and, 1641; reserved causes and, 1297; Roman Senate and, 1411; saint veneration and, 1390; simony condemnation by, 1423, 1424; tomb of, 1496; vicariate of Thessalonica creation, 1611; Zacharias policies and, 1641, 1642

Innocent II, **783–785**; Abelard condemnation by, 450; Anacletus II as antipope, 42, 72, 254, 276, 732–733, 783, 784, 900, 959; Anastasius IV as partisan, 45; appointment of bishops and, 93; Celestine II and, 276; consistory functions and, 414; Gratian and, 489; heresies and, 701; judges delegate and, 453; Lateran II and, 429, 785, 900, 1425; Luicus II and, 959; Lucius III and, 960; monasticism and, 1015; naval voyages, 1028; Normans and, 313, 1053, 1615; Sacred College and, 240, 732; Templars and, 988; tomb of, 1499; [Victor IV] and, 1615

[Innocent III], 70, 72, **785**

Innocent III, 19, 70, 653, 656, **785–790**, 1037, 1038; alms distribution, 454; appointment of bishops and, 92, 93; Aragon as fiefdom of, 973; banner and keys, 689; canonization and, 233, 268; canonization of layman by, 896; cardinalate and, 451, 1356; as Celestine III successor, 278; censorship by, 770; coins, 373; coronation procession and, 426; crusades and,

207, 438–439, 701, 702, 734, 787–788, 789, 896; Curia reforms and, 278, 300, 451, 452–453; decretals of, 22, 897, 910; dispensations and, 505; Domincans and, 506, 511; exemptions and, 553; fanon, 1607; film depiction of, 323; forgery evaluation rule, 589; Franciscans and, 591; as Gregory IX model, 653, 654; health and vitality of, 1416; heresies and, 701, 811; Holy Roman Empire and, 314, 315, 715–716, 795–787; Honorius III and, 733–734, 735; imperial coronation and, 424; incardination and, 766; as Innocent XIII ancestor, 809; Inquisition inception by, 810–811; Jewish segregation policy, 870, 871, 872; judges delegate and, 453, 880; keys emblem, 891; Lateran IV and, 429, 896–897, 1425; Latium residence, 1303; literate witticism, 742; liturgy and, 953; Magna Carta annullment by, 787; on marriage of unbelievers, 1249; military forces, 110; military orders and, 989; mosaic, 1020; naval fleets, 1028; nepotism and, 1031; Normans and, 1054; papal chaplain, 300; on papal Mass, 284; papal primacy and, 676, 1109, 1246; Papal States territorties, 1098, 1100(map), 1101; Penitentiary and, 454; *plenitudo potestasis* claim, 786, 1246, 1484; pontifical title, 1494; poor relief, 1307; public viewing of remains, 486; regalia and, 1291; registers of, 1293, 1603; Roman prefecture and, 1335; Rota development and, 1348; St. John Lateran basilica dream of, 1359; St. Mary Major rebuilding and, 1366; St. Peter's basilica project and, 1379; *scriptores* and, 452; simony condemnation, 1425; theocratic pronouncements of, 1484; tiara and, 1489, 1490–1491, 1492; tomb of, 1499, 1500; universities and, 1547, 1549; Vatican Palace restoration, 1301

Innocent IV, 451, 655, 735, **790–793**; "ad limina" visits and, 1304; Alexander IV and, 22, 23; Antichrist condemnation by, 66; appointment of bishops and, 93; army forces, 110; banking activity, 136; canonical collections and, 226, 227; canonization and, 233; cardinalate and, 241, 451; chaplains, 300; clerical education and, 379, 1547, 1548; conclave and, 393; crusades and, 439–440; dispensations, 505; on Dominicans in Curia posts, 507; Franciscans and, 593; Frederick II deposition by, 315, 439, 716; Golden Rose and, 1347; Guelphs and, 629; Hadrian V and, 685; heresy prosecution and, 703, 793; Islamic trade and, 1393; Jewish protection policy, 871, 872; Lyon I and, 429, 655, 716, 791–792, 998; Lyon residence and court, 791–792, 1304; master of the Sacred Palace and, 981; naval forces, 1028; nepotism and, 685, 793, 1031; Nicholas III and, 1037; papal prestige decline under, 1246; plague epidemic and, 1222; *plenitudo potestatis* claim and, 1484; pontifical title, 1494; pope's treasure and, 452; residences outside Rome, 1303; Sicily reclamation by, 51; Talmud inquiry and, 792; theocratic arguments of, 1484; tomb of, 1500; Urban IV and, 1554; Vatican Archives and, 1603–1604; Vatican Palace and, 1302

Innocent V, 657, 685, **793–794**, 998, 1037; arms, 113; conclave electing, 392; as Dominican, 507

Innocent VI, **794–797**; arms, 113, 115; Avignon papacy, 129, 132; cardinalate capitulations and, 241; chaplains of the chapel, 300; conclavists and, 1356; Dominicans and, 508; heraldry, 690; military expenditures, 110, 129; nepotism, 336, 795; tomb of, 1501–1502; Urban V and, 1556

Innocent VII, 25, 82, 660, **797–798**; arms, 114; arts patronage, 1340; Fisherman's Ring, 587; Great Schism and, 635, 797–798

Volume Key: Volume 1, pages 1–614; volume 2, pages 615–1266; volume 3, pages 1267–1637.

Innocent VIII, 26, 105, 195, **798–800**; Apostolic Camera functions, 9, 799; arms, 114, 693; art and architectural patronage, 800, 1024, 1116, 1594; Calatrava Order and, 989; children of, 26, 798, 799; cursor, 475; datary and, 461; diplomatic representation, 799, 1056; Discalced friars and, 595; Holy Sepulcher order and, 722; humanism and, 1295; Index and, 1443; Inquisition and, 816; Julius II and, 884; liturgy, 953; military forces, 111, 799; naval defense, 1030; nepotism, 799, 801, 1032; papal funerary rites review, 485; Paul III and, 1124; poor health of, 1417; scriptors and, 463; secret briefs, 1400; secretariat, 1402; slave ownership, 1439; tomb of, 800, 1381; villa and gardens, 1594; witchcraft bull, 799

Innocent IX, 346, **800**; arms, 115; conclave electing, 1609; nepotism and, 243

Innocent X, **801–803**; Alexander VII and, 28, 29; architectural projects, 1117; arms, 115, 693; beatifications and, 145; Chinese rites condemned by, 29, 802; Clement X and, 350; coins, 376; Dominicans and, 510; heraldry, 696; Innocent XI and, 804; Jansenism condemned by, 29, 527, 616–617, 778, 803, 823, 824; Jesuits and, 827; military ordinariates, 991; obelisks erected in Rome, 803, 1061; *possesso* ceremony, 1229; Quirinal and, 1271, 1344; St. John Lateran refurbishing, 1362–1363, 1383; St. Peter's basilica restoration, 1383; Secretariat of State, 1402, 1469; superintendent of the Ecclesiastical State and, 1468–1469; tomb of, 1386; Urban VIII and, 801, 1561

Innocent XI, 29, 143, **803–807**, 1470; Alexander VIII and, 31, 32; Anglican schism and, 55; arms, 693; beatifications and, 146, 540, 806; Catholic University founding, 1546; coins, 375, 376; Dominicans and, 510, 511; European unity and, 540; Innocent XII and, 807; Jansenism and, 824; Jesuits and, 827; Louis XIV conflict with, 31, 118, 510, 528, 617, 805, 1267; missionizing and, 1003; nepotism rejection by, 468, 806; as own state secretary, 1469; Pius XII canonization suit, 1215; poor relief by, 1226; portrait commission, 1117; Quietism question and, 805–806; Quirinal and, 1271; reforms of, 1345; regalia and, 1291; rigorism of, 31, 32, 245, 468, 806; treaty of Westphalia and, 467; Turkish threat and, 375, 540, 795, 1369

Innocent XII, **807–809**; Alexander VIII and, 31; arms, 115; beatifications and, 146; canonizations by, 235; cardinal protector role clarification, 247; Clement X and, 350; Gallicanism and, 617; gonfalonier abolishment, 695; on incardination, 766; nepotism reform, 30, 394, 468, 807, 1033, 1402; poor relief and, 1226; Quietism and, 1268

Innocent XIII, 166, **809–810**; arms, 115; beatifications and, 146; as chamberlain, 288; coins, 376; Jesuit Chinese rites and, 827; length of conclave electing, 528–529; *possesso* engraving, 1229; Quirinal and, 1271

Inquisition, **810–820**; Middle Ages, **810–815**; modern era, **69–74**; abolishment in Milan (1767), 1535; Alexander IV and, 23; apostolic poverty debate, 849; Benedict XII and, 128; Benedict XIII and, 167, 810; Chinese rites condemned by, 1003; Clement IV and, 332; Clement VIII participation, 348, 471; Dominicans and, 322, 332, 507, 509, 799, 816, 817; Franciscans and, 133, 507, 812, 813, 814, 817; Galileo trial, 467, 819, 1137; Guelphism and, 676; heresy trials by, 701, 702, 703, 793; Holy Office control of, 242, 509, 709–711; humanist effects of, 1296; Jesuits and, 827; Jewish status with, 872;

Julius III and, 887; modernism as target of, 1199; Nicholas III and, 1037; Paul III reestablishment of, 1123, 1125, 1126, 1443; Paul IV and, 1126, 1128; Pius V and, 465, 1137, 1176; Quietists condemned by, 1267, 1268; as Reformation response, 1289; Sixtus IV and, 1435; Sixtus V and, 1436; Spirituals as target, 133, 813, 814; torture use by, 703, 793, 811, 814, 817–818; Urban VIII and, 1562; witchcraft repression by, 799, *See also* Doctrine of the Faith, Congregation for the; Index; Index, Congregation of the

insignia, papal. *See* heraldry

Institute for the Works of Religion. *See* finances, papal

Institute of Sciences, 171

Institutes (Justinian), 1319

Institutes of Consecrated Life and Societies for Apostolic Life, Congregation for the, 411

Integrists, 1470

Intelsat, 1080–1081

interdict, **820**, 888, 1151; causes of, 1149; on investitures, 821–822; suspension vs., 1370

interest (debt). *See* usury

International Academy of Mary, 2

International Association for Peace, 935

International Association for the Protection of Workers, 1077

International Association of Workers, 935

International Atomic Energy Agency, 1080

International Catholic Office of Film, 320

International Catholic Organization, 1403

International Congress on Canon Law (1968; Rome), 369

International Eucharistic Congresses, 1514, 1515

International Eucharistic Congresses, Papal Committee for, 389

International Federation of Catholic Universities, 1544

International Labor Organization, 1077, 1079, 1516

international organizations. *See* organizations, international, the Holy See and

International Radio Union, 1600

International Telecommunications Union, 1080, 1588

International Theological Commission, 388, 407

International Wheat Council, 1080

International Year of Peace (1986), 521

Internationale, 1208–1209

Internet, 985

Inter-religious Dialogue, Pontifical Council for, 435

inthronizatio, 426, 590

intransigence, 1530

Introitus et Exitus (Treasury records), 580

investiture controversy, 312, **820–822**; Antichrist invocation, 66; antipope and, 69, 238–239, 651–652; art portraying, 1284; Callistus II and, 215–216, 652, 1281; Canossa's significance to, 238–239; Concordat of Worms compromise, 92, 216, 239, 397, 715, 783, 900, 1281, 1484, 1636–1637; double investiture and, 1281; election of bishops as basis of, 91–92; false documents, 923; Gregory VII and, 18, 66, 69, 92, 238–239, 649–650, 1109, 1280, 1483; [Gregory VIII] and, 651–652; Henry I of England and, 1113; imperial coronation and, 424; Lateran Council of 1112 on, 900; Lateran fortifications and, 1301; military confrontations and, 109; mosaics and, 1021; papal coronation and, 426; papal victory in, 1281, 1484; Paschal II and, 109, 651–652, 1112–1113, 1281; regalia and, 1291; Roman councils and, 432; simony

Volume Key: Volume 1, pages 1–614; volume 2, pages 615–1266; volume 3, pages 1267–1637.

1716

condemnation and, 1424; temporal vs. spiritual distinction, 900, 1113, 1637; Urban II and, 1551, 1552; Urban III and, 1553

IOR (Institute for Religious Works), 583–584

Iran. *See* Persia

Ireland, 188, 533, 545; bishops' conferences, 401; Catholic colleges, 379; Catholic renewal (1840s), 675, 933; Celtic liturgy, 953; Celts, 142; Easter date, 834; evangelization of, 545; Great Schism and, 340; John IV and, 834; Leo XII and, 933; liturgy, 953; missionaries to England, 997; missionaries to the Continent, 1108; monk exemptions, 552; penitential tariff and, 1167; provincial councils, 431; Vatican II representation, 1582, 1583

Ireland, John, 40, 41

Irenaeus, St., 42, 57, 523–524, 544, 546, 560–561, 696, 942, 952, 1042, 1064, 1164; Easter-date controsvery, 1612; on infallibility, 776; on Linus, 947; martyrdom in Lyon, 1315

Irene, regent of Byzantium, 204, 205, 599, 680, 701

Irish Church. *See* Ireland

Irmengard, 1458

irony, humor vs., 742, 744

Isaac II, emperor of Byzantium, 207, 478

Isaac, Jules, 875

Isabella, queen of Castille, 799, 815, 1622

Isabelle of France, 634, 734

Isaia of Pisa, 537, 1361, 1363, 1380

Isenburg, Diether von, 1172

Isidore of Seville, 47, 537, 639, 952; canonical collections and, 221, 223, 231; on custom in law, 476; as Father of the Church, 567, 568

Isis, cult of, 442

Islam: Alexander II distinction between Judaism and, 871; as Antichrist, 65, 66; apologetics against, 75, 76; Church missions and, 998–999, 1000; Congregation of the Eastern Churches and, 407; crusades against, 437–441, 1526; Holy Land conquest by, 318, 438, 711, 712, 722; Holy Places, 711, 713; holy war, 207; invasion of Egypt, 36; invasion of Spain, 143, 1319; invasions of Byzantium, 202, 203, 204, 206, 1319; lunar calendar, 213; papal contacts with, 1393; papal view of, 871; Reconquest against, 871, 1551, 1552; slave converts from, 1441; slave status under, 1439; Turkish threat and, 1526–1527, *See also* Saracens

Isodoro de Sevilla. *See* Isidore of Seville

Isodorus, St., 669

Israel, State of, 713–714, 875, 876; diplomatic ties with Holy See, 503, 504; Fundamental Agreement with Holy See (1993 text), 878–880; John Paul II visit to, 877–878; Vatican II exclusion of, 1577

Istanbul. *See* Constantinople

Istituto Paol VI, 1132

Italia, L' (newspaper), 1205

Italian Catholic Action. *See* Catholic Action

Italian Meteorological Society, 1062

Italian People's Party (PPI; Populars), 175, 305, 307–308, 309, 901, 1023, 1134, 1135, 1207

Italic League, 1041

Italy: Alexander VI political involvement, 26–27; apologetics, 77, 78; Assumption holiday, 124; barbarian invasion of, 140–141, 196, 201, 1318, 1465; bishops' conferences, 400; Byzantine

popes, 196–198; Byzantium reconquest of, 318, 564, 1318–1319, 1616, 1618; Canossa as national monument, 237; Catholicism as state religion, 1207, 1541; Christian Democracy in, 306, 307–310, 311; Church of Rome's privileged place in, 538; crusades and, 533; early administration of, 1464–1467; Enlightenment, 530; evangelization of, 545; as Exarchate of Ravenna, 546–547; fascism in, 305, 308, 397, 524, 874, 901–904 (*see also* Lateran pacts); foreign brotherhoods and, 317; Franciscans, 594, 595; Freemasonry, 604, 607, 609; French wars in, 1102, 1621–1624; fundamentalism, 614–615; Ghibelline/Guelph conflict, 315, 316, 627–631, 676–677, 685, 707, 716, 794; Great Schism and, 636, 1558; Greek population in, 638; Gregorian calendar and, 213; Gregory VII and, 649; Holy Roman Empire and, 313, 715, 716; Holy See diplomatic corps and, 503–504; Holy See relationship, 719–720; iconoclast controversy and, 643; Inquisition in, 816, 817–820; Jews' status in, 874, 875; John XXIII and Church in, 854; jubilee 2000 pilgrims and, 729; jurisdictionalism, 888, 889; kingdom proclamation (1861), 1107, 1195, 1644; Latin Monetary Union, 377; Lombard invasion, 833, 834, 957–958, 1148–1149, 1319, 1331, 1465; modernism and, 1008; monasticism, 1011, 1013, 1015; Movimento Cattolico, 1023–1024; Napoleonic occupation, 670–671, 1183, 1263; normalization of Vatican relations. *See* Lateran pacts; papal patromonies. *See* Papal States; papal relations, 20th-century, 126–127, 175–176, 397, 399, 582–584, 718; papal titles in, 1051; Patrimony of St. Peter, 1115–1116; Pius V and, 1176; prejudices against, 1232; provincial councils, 431, 432; restitutions to Holy See, 10; saints from, 1391; Saracen raids, 1392–1393; secularization, 1542; seminaries, 1342; suburbicarian, 501, 942, 1464–1467; terrorists, 310, 859, 864, 1364; Ultramontanism and, 1529–1530; unification. *See* unity, Italian; Vatacanists in, 1606–1607; Vatican City State powers and, 1586–1594; Vatican II representation, 1576, 1578–1579, 1581, 1583; World War I and, 174, 175, 1628, 1630; World War II and, 1630, 1632–1636, *See also* Papal States; Rome; *specific areas*

Ithacus, 1427

Iulius Africanus, 1159

Ius novissimum, 363

Ivan III, tsar of Russia, 1434

Ivan IV (the Terrible), tsar of Russia, 664, 1488

Ivernel, Daniel, 322

Ivo of Chartres. *See* Yves of Chartres

Jacobite Syrian Church, 664

Jacques d'Amboise, 1275

Jacques de Vitry, 486, 655

Jadwiga, princess of Poland, 998

Jaffa, treaty of (1228), 439

Jagiello, prince of Lithuania, 998

James (St. James the Apostle), 1158, 1490; pilgrimages to shrine of, 1167

James I, king of Aragon, 332, 657

James I, king of England, 55, 348, 1130

James II, king of Aragon and Sicily, 628, 735, 990, 1039

James II, king of England, 55

James VI, king of Scotland. *See* James I, king of England

James, Henry, 759

Volume Key: Volume 1, pages 1–614; volume 2, pages 615–1266; volume 3, pages 1267–1637.

James of Aragon, 163

James of Compostela, St., 569, 725

James of Percorara, 655

Jandel, Vincent, 511–512

Janiculum, battle of the (1849), 1323, 1539

Jansen, Cornelius. *See* Jansenism

Jansenism, 704, 727, 805, **823–826**, 1255; Alexander VII and, 28–29, 30; Alexander VIII and, 32, 468; anti-infallibility position, 511, 778, 823, 825; anti-Jesuit position, 359, 527–528, 704, 824, 825, 867, 1536; attitudes and beliefs, 867; in Austria, 867–868; in Belgium, 803, 808; Benedict XIV encyclical on, 169, 171; Clement X and, 349, 351; Clement XI bull against, 167, 354, 469, 529, 617, 810, 1345; Clement XII and, 357; Clement XIII and, 360; Court of Rome's negative connotations and, 436; Enlightenment ideas and, 527–528, 825, 867, 869; Gallicanism and, 616–618, 823, 824, 825; Innocent X condemnation of, 29, 527, 616–617, 778, 803; Innocent XII and, 807–808; Innocent XIII and, 810; Josephism and, 867, 869; jurisdictionalism and, 889; liturgy, 954; in Netherlands, 354, 704, 803, 808, 824, 825; papal battle against, 467; penitent absolution case, 354; Pius IX condemnation of, 1194, 1196; Pius VI condemnation of, 470, 869, 1179, 1180; Pius VIII hostility toward, 1191; Pius X and, 1198; prophetism and, 1263; Risorgimento and, 1535–1536; Urban VIII and, 1560, 1562

Jansenius, Cornelius. *See* Jansenism

Janvier, M. A., 512

Japan: Catholic missions in, 348, 664, 1004, 1343, 1561; closure to European, 1255; Dutch Protestants in, 1000; Gregorian calendar delayed adoption in, 213; Jesuit missions, 664, 669, 827, 1000, 1001; persecution of Catholics in, 1000, 1345; Vatican II representation, 1580

Jaricot, Pauline, 708, 1259, 1347

Jaricot, Philéas, 1259

Jarlot, Georges, 307

Jean (*see also* John)

Jean III Vasa, king of Sweden, 348

Jean IV, count of Armagnac, 974

Jean de Bourbon, 1275

Jean de Brébeuf, St., 1204

Jean de Jandum, 131, 1485

Jean de la Grange, 339

Jean de Mailly, 830

Jean de Paris, 242, 615

Jean de Saint Marc, 331

Jean de Tournemire, 457, 1416

Jean des Murs, 213

Jean of Lorraine, 927

Jeanne I and II. *See* Joanna I; Joanna II

Jeanne d'Arc. *See* Joan of Arc, St.

Jeanne de Chantal, St., 360

Jedin, Hubert, 1274

Jemolo, Arturo Carlo, 325, 904, 1536, 1537–1538

Jena, battle of (1806), 1186

Jerome, St., 43, 199, 327, 1045, 1056, 1563; Alexandria and, 33; angelology, 49; canonical collections and, 223; as Doctor of the Church, 568; as Father of the Church, 567, 568; Hieronymian Martyrology, 210; on Peter in Rome, 1158–1159; pilgrimage by, 1164; Roman monasticism and, 1011–1013; use of word *tiara*, 1489

Jerome of Ascoli, 657

Jerusalem: Alexander III and, 20; Congregation of the Eastern Churches and, 407; diplomatic return to crusaders (1228), 439, 654, 722; fall to crusaders (1099), 437, 711, 722, 1112, 1552; fall to Islam (638), 1319; fall to Saladin (1187), 438, 711, 722, 1553; final destruction of Temple, 544; final fall of (1244), 501, 722; as First Crusade objective, 437; Holy Places, 711, 712, 713; Holy Sepulcher order in, 722–724; Ignatius and founding of Jesuits at, 826; Latin patriarchate restoration, 1193; Leo I and, 917; papal primacy and, 1245; patriarchate of, 318, 722, 723, 1193; Paul VI visit to, 1510, 1514; pilgrimages to, 1165; post-1917 status of, 713–714, 877; Roman conquest of, 1314; Templars and, 987, 988; Turks and, 1526; Urban IV and patriarchal see of, 1554

Jesuits, **826–829**; accomodation to local cultures by, 169, 355, 529, 1002–1004, 1345 (*see also* Chinese rites); Antichrist charges and, 68; anti-Semitic publications, 874; apologists, 77; Benedict XIV and, 169, 171, 530; brief suppressing, 195, 617; bull reestablishing, 195, 362, 828, 1189, 1523; catechism, 263, 265; Chinese rites and, 29, 169, 355, 529, 802, 810, 1002–1003, 1345–1346; church design, 106; Clement XIII protection of, 358–359, 360; Clement XIV dissolution of order, 362, 470, 1179, 1189, 1346; colleges. *See* Roman College of the Society of Jesuits; Council of Trent and, 1289, 1518, 1522; Counter Reformation and, 1125, 1177, 1289; Enlightenment and, 358, 359, 470, 527–528; expulsions of, 359, 360, 361–362, 828, 1004, 1131, 1260, 1346; feasts of patron saints, 569; founding of, 826, 829, 1125, 1276; Freemasonry and, 608; Galileo accusations by, 1562; grace vs. free choice dispute, 348; Gregory XIII support, 664; Gregory XIV and, 666; Gregory XV and, 667, 668, 669; Jansenist hostility toward, 359, 527–528, 704, 824, 825, 867, 1536; John Paul I and, 829, 859; Julius III favoritism toward, 885; laxist charges against, 827; missions, 169, 529, 664, 669, 827, 999, 1000, 1001, 1130, 1343; modernism and, 1008, 1535; Molinos condemnation by, 1267; papal authority diffusion by, 616; papal primacy and, 1566; papal supression of, 195, 528, 529, 530, 596, 1531–1532; Paul III bull establishing, 195, 826, 1000, 1123, 1125, 1126; penitentiaries, 1152, 1523; Pius VI view of, 1179; Pius VII reestablishment of, 362, 828, 1189, 1523; Pius XII and, 1212; prophetism and, 1260; publication. *See Civiltà Cattolica*; research on Pius XII Holocaust position, 1214; Risorgimento and, 1535, 1536; Roman confraternities and, 1309; Roman Seminary, 827, 1176, 1408, 1545; as ultramontane, 617, 1529, 1530; Urban VIII and, 1560; Vatican I and, 1196; Vatican Radio and, 984, 1601, 1602

Jesus, 202, 207; Antichrist concept and, 64–68; apostolic poverty ideal and, 336, 415, 849; cross symbolism, 688; dating of birth, 210; evangelization perspective, 543, 544; Gospel of Peter and, 631; Gospels on Peter's supremacy with, 631–632; Holy Places and, 711; mosaics and, 1019, 1020; nature of. *See* Christology; nepotism and, 1031; papacy instituted by, 1108; Passion and Resurrection, 631, 728, 1158, 1275, 1359; Peter and, 631–632, 1157–1158; rosary recitation and, 1346; as supreme doctor, 847

Jewish Agency, 712–713

Jews. *See* anti-Semitism; Judaism

Joachim II of Brandenburg, 1125

Volume Key: Volume 1, pages 1–614; volume 2, pages 615–1266; volume 3, pages 1267–1637.

1718

Joachim of Flora, 66, 76, 133, 281, 282, 331, 724, 770, 897
Joan (Pope), **829–830**
Joan I and II. *See* Joanna I; Joanna II
Joan of Arc, St., 167, 1275; canonization of, 176
Joanna I, queen of Naples, 53, 127, 129, 340, 341, 659, 1556, 1557, 1622; Clement VI's purchase of Avignon from, 337, 1220
Joanna II, queen of Naples, 54, 303, 537, 975
Joblin, Joseph, 1515
Johann Frederick, elector of Saxony, 1289
Johannes Teutonicus, 227
John (popes): choice of name, 854; list of, 1068; numbering of, 495, 846, 1066
John (St. John the Apostle), 64, 202, 561; Gospel of, 631–632, 1157–1158, *See also* St. John Lateran, basilica of
John (Lackland), king of England, 93, 314, 787, 897, 910
[John], 70, 71, **830–831**
John I, 141, 564, 573, **831–832**, 1046; death and burial of, 1497; St. Peter's basilica alterations, 1377
John I, king of Aragon, 163
John II, 13, 14, 201, 738, **832–833**
John II, king of Castile, 182
John II, king of France, 1222
John II Crescentius. *See* Crescentius II Nomentanus
John III, 152, 597, **833–834**; tomb of, 1497
John III (the Good), duke of Brittany, 1556
John III (the Scholastic), patriarch of Constantinople, 231
John III Wasa, king of Sweden, 663
John IV, **834**, 1360
John IV, count of Armagnanc, 167
John IV (the Faster), patriarch of Constantinople, 202
John V, 646, **835**
John V, king of Portugal, 1003
John V Palaeologus, emperor of Byzantium, 208, 440, 1556
John VI, 202, 203, **835**
John VII, **835–836**, 1300, 1373, 1378, 1497
John VIII, 47, 682, **836–838**, 1459; authority expansion by, 1245; Byzantium and, 205; coins, 372; excommunication of Formosus, 590, 1459; excommunication/anathema distinction, 48; Franks and, 601, 1378; letters in Vatican Archives, 1603; Marinus I (Martin II) and, 969, 970; military role of, 109, 645, 836, 837, 1393; register of, 1293
John VIII Palaeologus, emperor of Byzantium, 208, 536, 982, 1222
John IX, 154, 372, 590, **838**, 1413
John X, **838–839**, 1460; assassination of, 122, 838; deposition of, 495; Leo VI and, 922; naval defense against Saracens, 109, 1027, 1393; tomb of, 1497
John XI, 122, 206, **839–840**, 868, 1414; coins, 372; s Stephen VI (VIII) and, 1460
John XII, 180, **840–841**, 1332; Benedict V as successor, 71, 155; deposition of, 495, 923; Holy Roman Empire and, 714, 840–841, 923; legates from, 909
John XIII, **841–842**; Benedict VI as successor, 155; blessing of bells ceremony, 152; capture of, 122; tomb of, 1497
John XIV, **842**; assassination of, 71, 122, 189; deposition of, 495; tomb of, 1497
John XV, 645, **842–843**, 847, 882
[John XVI], 70, 71, 646, **843**; mutilation death of, 122

John XVII, **843–844**, 1498
John XVIII, 495, **844–845**, 1305, 1414, 1498
John XIX, 157, 158, **845–846**, 1333
John XX (name never taken), **846**
John XXI, 657, **846–847**, 1037, 1038; arms, 113; death in Viterbo, 1304; heresies and, 702; tomb of, 1500
John XXII, **847–851**; advanced age and energy of, 1416; Angelus recitation, 50, 152; Angevins and, 53; annates, 59; Antichrist charges and, 66; antipope against, 72, 128, 850, 1039; appointment of bishops, 93; arms, 112, 113, 693; auditors establishment, 126; Avignon papacy and, 128, 130, 131, 559, 676; Avignon residence of, 103, 456; Beguines and Beghards criticism by, 896; Benedict XII as successor, 161; benefices, 1041; canonical collections, 226, 227, 231; canonization of Thomas Aquinas by, 508; Chancery procedure and, 292; chaplaincy and, 457; Church-State conflict and, 128, 131, 316, 676, 850, 1039, 1040; coins, 373; conclave site, 392; consistorial controversies and, 415; Curia and, 455, 459, 460; decretals, 133; doctrine and, 133, 336; Dominican theological conflicts, 507–508; expectative abuse and, 555; feast of the Trinity, 211; financial management, 80, 82, 220, 578; Franciscans and, 592, 594; Guelphism of, 676; heresy and, 702, 703, 813; Holy Roman Empire and, 716; Inquisition and, 813, 850; Jewish expulsion by, 872; menagerie, 58; military forces, 110; military orders, 990; missions and, 998; nepotism and, 241, 848; papal chaplain and, 300; papal family size, 559; plague victim charity, 1221; plots against, 848; Rota member numbers, 1349; tiara (triple crown), 1492; tomb of, 1502; tribunal of Roman Rota and, 1524
[John XXIII], 25, 70, 72, 130, 132, **851–852**; banking irregularities, 137, 851; Catholic University and, 1545; *Civiltà Cattolica* and, 325; datary, 482; deposition and flight of, 662, 703, 777, 851, 852; Great Schism and, 636–637, 662; heraldry, 689; John XXIII's view of papacy and, 854; Martin V and, 974; tomb of, 1502; weaknesses of, 851, 852
John XXIII, **853–857**, 863, 864; academies and, 2; agenda of, 1572; allocution topics to Rota, 36; Angelus recitation at Sunday blessing, 50; Anglican dialogue, 56; Antichrist concept and, 67; arms, 114, 116; beatifications and, 149, 271, 865, 1140; camauro use, 620; canonizations and, 236, 271; cardinals "in petto" and, 245; on Chinese schism, 1397; Christian Democracy and, 309–310, 1024; cinema and, 323; Code of Canon Law (1983) and, 229, 366, 367, 368, 865; conclave electing, 852–853, 1232; conclave rules, 395; daily life coverage, 1248; death of, 1583; devotion to, 497; ecumenism and, 56, 520–521, 539, 855, 856, 1005, 1404; encyclical list, 526; encyclicals, 310, 367, 520, 856, 977, 1078, 1085, 1110, 1447, 1449, 1463; European unity and, 539, 540; fanon, 1607; film documentary of, 323; footwear, 621; fundamentalist reaction to, 614; Holy Sepulcher order and, 723; humor of, 743; Jewish policy, 875, 876, 877; letters to, 939, 940; liturgical movement, 955; Marxism rejected by, 977, 978–979; military forces, 111; modernity and, 853, 1247; as multilingual, 859; naval forces, 1049; onomastics and, 495, 637; Opus Dei organization, 1071; *ostpolitik*, 855, 859, 1085; papal apartments, 73; papal philosophy of, 854; pastoral emphasis by, 1110; Paul VI and, 1132, 1137, 1138, 1140; photographs of, 1163; pilgrims to tomb of, 1170; pon-

Volume Key: Volume 1, pages 1–614; volume 2, pages 615–1266; volume 3, pages 1267–1637.

1719

tifical councils, 434; pontifical gloves, 620; press relations, 985, 1236–1237, 1240; Propagation of the Faith and, 1205; radio messages, 1447; on Rota tribunal, 1351; Sacred College and, 1357, 1406; St. John Lateran and, 854, 1363; St. Paul's Outside the Walls and, 1373; social teachings, 309–310, 310, 856, 1078, 1085, 1110, 1217, 1447, 1449, 1463; spiritual journal of, 323, 852, 855, 856; subsidiarity principle, 1463; Substitute Secretariat of State, 1464; tomb of, 1384; travels of, 1514; United Nations and, 1078, 1079; Vatican II convocation, 370, 429–430, 779, 855, 856, 858, 1005, 1110, 1139, 1141, 1142, 1570, 1571, 1572–1583, 1585, 2647; Vatican City State and, 1590; Vatican museum collections, 1026; World War II and, 1631

John Cassian. *See* Cassian, John, St.

John Chrysostom. *See* Chrysostom, John, St.

John, Gospel of, 631–632, 1157–1158

John Kamateros, patriarch of Constantinople, 207

John Lateran, St., 144

John Mesarites, 208

John of Abbeville, 451, 655

John of Antioch, 275, 1432–1433

John of Austria, 937, 938, 1177

John of Bethancourt, 999

John of Brienne, 76

John of Cesena, 1280

John of Crema, 652, 732

John of Damascus, 76, 198

John of Gaeta. *See* Gelasius II

John of Holywood, 213

John of Illicitum, 738

John of Jandun, 850

John of Montecorvino, 998

John of Naples, 850

John of Nola, 1460

John of Paris. *See* Jean de Paris

John of Parma, 685, 792

John of St. Paul, 454, 591

John of Salisbury, 450, 533, 1053

John of San Paolo, 786

John of Segovia, 391

John of the Cross, St., 145, 351, 1204, 1343

John of the Walls, 213

John of Toledo, 24, 685, 792, 1554

John of Tournemire. *See* Jean de Tournemire

John of Trier, 331

John of Turrecremata. *See* Torquemada, Juan de

John Paul I, **857–859**, 864; arms, 116, 693; Catholic Democracy and, 310; *Civiltà Cattolica* and, 325; Code of Common Law (1983) and, 367; conclave electing, 858, 863; coronation of, 1405; ferula replacement by, 575; humor of, 743; illness and death of, 858–859, 1232, 1248; Jesuits and, 829, 859; *possesso* ceremony, 1229

John Paul II, 143, **859–867**; academies and, 2; "ad limina" visits and, 5; administrative offices, 12; African minor basilica consecration, 144; allocution topics to Rota, 37; Anglican relations, 56, 865, 1076; announcement of election of, 679, 864; Apostolic Camera functions and, 9; apostolic constitution and, 421; arbitration by, 720; arms, 116, 691, 693; assassination attempt on, 50, 122, 123, 127, 860, 865, 1248, 1384; as-

sessment of pontificate, 1247; audiences, 125, 127; automobile, 127, 1405; background and vocation of, 860–863; beatifications and, 149, 271, 865; canonizations by, 234, 236–237, 269, 270, 271, 408, 865, 876; cardinal "in petto" and, 245; cardinalate and, 244, 1358–1359; case for canonization, 865–866; Catechism and, 264; Catholic universities and, 1544, 1545; Christian Democracy and, 305, 311–312; *Civiltà Cattolica* and, 325; Code of Canon Law (1983) and, 229, 366, 367, 368–369, 1351; collection of letters to, 939; commissions, 388; conclave electing, 863–864; concordatory agreements, 397; Congregation for Bishops and, 409; congregations and, 407, 408, 409, 410, 411; conservatism of, 1110; consistories and, 416; Curia reorganization, 472–473, 710, 1152; daily life coverage, 1248; devotion to, 497; ecumenism, 521–522, 523, 539, 542, 863–864, 865, 1110; encyclical list, 527; encyclicals, 523, 524, 541–542, 865, 1010, 1247, 1449, 1463; European-Church relations and, 539, 541–542, 687, 1079; Fabric of St. Peter and, 558–559; fanon, 1607; ferula replacement by, 575; film biography of, 323; finances, 584; Galileo rehabilitation by, 2; Helsinki principles and, 541, 687; heritage and imprint of, 864–865; Holy Places status and, 714, 722; Holy See diplomacy and, 720; Holy Year and, 728–729, 745; imprimatur, 763; International Theological Commission, 388; Jesuits and, 829, 859; Jewish relations, 876–878, 1397–1398; Lefebvre schism and, 1397–1398; Marxism denunciation by, 977, 979, 980; media usage by, 984–985, 1239–1240, 1446, 1447, 1605; missionary activity, 996, 1005, 1451; modernity approach, 1010–1011, 1247; mosaics commission, 1020; Opus Dei and, 1069, 1071; papal apartments, 73; papal hymn, 744, 745; papal liturgical processions, 741; papal powers delegation by, 1407; papal titles and, 1050–1051; Paul VI compared with, 1132; Penitentiary, 1523; persona of, 864; photographs of, 1248; Pius XII Holocaust position and, 1200; Polish background, 686, 863–864; pontifical councils, 433, 434, 435; press office and, 1239–1240; Propaganda Fide and, 1258; Prophecy of Malachy motto, 1261–1262; radio message, 1447; Sacred College plenary meetings, 1358–1359; Secretariat of State, 1403; Secretariats of the Roman Curia, 1404; social documents, 1447, 1449, 1463; socialism critique by, 980; special synods of bishops, 1479; Sunday blessing and Angelus, 50; travels of. *See* travels of John Paul II; tribunal of Roman Rota and, 1351, 1524; United Nations and, 1079, 1589; Vatican II and, 859, 860, 862–863, 865, 866, 1569; Vatican City and, 1384, 1591–1592, 1594; Vatican labor union and, 1596; Vatican museums and, 1026

John Philagathos. *See* [John XVI]

John Talaia, patriarch of Alexandria, 564, 572, 1426

John the Baptist, St., 706, 1157

John the Deacon, 1148, 1353, 1388, 1498, 1499

John the Evangelist, St., 706

John the Good, 1556

John Tiniossus, 1035

John Vekkos, 208

Johnson, Lyndon B., 1514

Jonas of Orleans, 209, 895, 1167

Jonathan of Tusculum, 1098

Jordan, 713, 714

Volume Key: Volume 1, pages 1–614; volume 2, pages 615–1266; volume 3, pages 1267–1637.

1720

Jordan of Capua, 1053, 1614

Joseph (biblical), 854

Joseph I, Holy Roman emperor, 353, 375

Joseph II, emperor of Austria and Holy Roman Emperor, 361, 528, 553, 828, 888, 1535; closure of monasteries, 1346; Pius VI conflict with, 1179, *See also* Josephism

Joseph, Father, 1000

Joseph Napoleon, 1186

Josephini, 702

Josephism, 511, 611, 674, **867–871**, 1567; Austrian secularism and, 868, 893; Gallicanism and, 617; Italian unity and, 1535, 1536, 1537; jurisdictionalism and, 867, 868–869, 888–889; papism vs., 1109; Pius VI campaign against, 1179, 1180; Pius IX Austrian concordat and, 1194

Josephus, Flavius, 1490, 1492

Jouenneaux, Guy, 1275

Jouffroy, Jean, 1122, 1172

Jourdain of Osnabrück, 1485

Journal de Rome, 1082

Journal des Débats, 1236

Journal of a Soul (John XXIII), 323, 852, 855, 856

journalism. *See* media, communication, and the Vatican; *specific publications*

Jovian, emperor of Rome, 1317

Jovinianus affair, 1013, 1427

Juan of Austria. *See* John of Austria

Jubilee. *See* Holy Year

Judaism, **870–880**; up to 1870, **870–874**; after 1870, **874–878**; Fundamental Agreement with Holy See, **878–880**; [Anacletus II] family background and, 42, 900; anathema practice, 47; Antichrist and, 64, 65, 66; apologetics against, 75; Benedict XIV relationship with, 168, 170; blood libels and, 871, 872, 873; Carnival and, 863, 1121; Clement IV measures against, 332; Clement VI protective measures, 129, 337, 1221; Clement XIV view of, 360–361, 873; converts, 75, 815, 816, 818, 870–871; Easter-date controversies, 517, 1612; evangelist progressive split with, 544–545; exclusions, 47; ghettos, 374, 873, 874, 876, 932, 1188; heresies and, 696, 698; Holy Land and, 712–713, 874, 875; Holy Year and, 724; Innocent IV condemnation of Talmud, 792; Jerusalem Holy Places, 711, 713; John XVIII protective measures, 845; John Paul II dialogue with, 876–878, 1397–1398; Josephist toleration of, 869; Lateran IV measures against, 429; Lateran pacts and, 902, 903, 904; Leo VII and, 923; Leo XII measures against, 932; lunar calendar, 209, 213; Martin V protective measures, 976; Nazi genocide program. *See* Holocaust; Nazi occupation of Rome and, 1214, 1635; nonrepresentation at Vatican II, 1577; papal rapprochement, 521, 876–878; Paul IV ghettoization, 872–873, 1310; Paul (St. Paul the Apostle) and, 1118–1119, 1120; as Peter's background, 1157; pilgrimage derivation from, 1163; Pius II defense of, 1173; Pius V repressions, 374, 1177; Pius VI repressions, 1179; Pius VII ghettoization, 1188; Pius XII and, 1214, 1635, 1636; plague blamed on, 1221; pontifical council and, 434; *possesso* ceremony and, 1228; Roman confraternities and, 1308, 1309, 1310; Roman persecutions of Christians and, 1153, 1155, 1314; Spanish conversion or expulsion edict, 799; Spanish Inquisition and, 815, 816, 818; status in Roman Empire, 42, 1317; tiara origins and, 1489, 1490, 1492, *See also* anti-Semitism; Israel, State of; Old Testament

Judas (apostle), 90

judges delegate, **880–881**; appeal to the pope and, 85; canon law and, 224, 453; decretals and, 488

Judgment Day, 133

Jules. *See* Julius

Julian, emperor of Rome, 442, 946, 1317

Julian calendar, 209, 212, 213, 665

Julian of Cos, 917, 1060

Julian of Eclanum, 184, 700, 913, 1433

Julian of Norwich, 896

Julian of Toledo, St., 143, 153, 952

Julian the Apostate, 74–75, **881–882**, 1156

Julienne of Mont-Cornillon, 1554

Julius I, 32, 199, 432, 567, **882–884**, 970; arbitration by, 562; legate representation, 908; monasticism and, 1012; notaries and, 1054; primacy of Rome and, 34; tomb, 1391, 1496

Julius II, **884–886**; as Alexander VI adversary, 26, 27, 28, 884–885, 1102, 1621; appointment of bishops and, 93; architectural projects, 104–105, 255, 885, 886, 1116, 1117, 1127, 1340, 1382; arms, 114; banner, 689; brief office and, 464; cardinal protector limitations by, 247, 462; coins, 374; Colonna-Orsini rivalry and, 1048–1049; coronation of, 426; Council of Trent and, 429; Dominicans and, 509; ecclesiastical state consolidation, 1467, 1468; Fabric of St. Peter and, 558; film portrayal of, 322; Franciscans and, 595; French wars in Italy and, 1621, 1622, 1623; humanists and, 1295; indulgences and, 374; Innocent VIII and, 798, 799; Julius III and, 887; Lateran V and, 429, 898, 1425; Leo X as successor, 926; medallions, 982, 983; musical chapel of St. Peter's basilica and, 298; mustache and beard of, 143; nepotism and, 884, 1032; painting commissions, 1024, 1089, 1091, 1092, 1116, 1340; papal household, 740; papal primacy defense, 509; Paul III and, 1124; portrait of, 1093; reform resistance by, 1246; St. Peter's basilica reconstruction, 104, 549, 1382, 1502; simonical election nullification bull, 393, 1425; Sistine Chapel and, 1428–1429; Sixtus IV and, 1032, 1381, 1434, 1435, 1503; statuary collection, 1026; Swiss Guard and, 740, 1471; tiara, 1489; Tolfa alum and, 38; tomb of, 1386; Vatican gardens and, 1595; Vatican Palace and, 800

Julius III, 54, **886–888**, 1545; ancient marbles collection, 1024; Anglican ordinations and, 1073; arms, 114; arts projects and, 887; Council of Trent participation, 886, 887, 968, 1125, 1289, 1519, 1520; Fabric of St. Peter and, 558; Holy Year, 726; Jesuits and, 826; military orders, 990; nepotism and, 887; papal chapel musicians, 297; Urban VII and, 1559; villa and gardens of, 106, 107, 887, 1595

Juntes, 968

Jupiter Dolichenus, cult of, 443

jurisdictionalism, 358, 469, **888–889**, 1110, 1535; appeal to the pope and, 84–85; Clement XII problems with, 357, 469; Josephism and, 867, 868–869, 888–889; Pius VI and, 1180

jurisprudence. *See* Rota, tribunal of the

just war, 18, 98, 111; antiheresy measures as, 811; Benedict XV rejection of, 1625; John XXIII encyclical against, 856; World War II and, 1631, 1632, *See also* holy war

Justice and Peace, Pontifical Council for, 434

Justin I, emperor of Byzantium, 564, 737, 738, 831, 1318

Justin II, emperor of Byzantium, 13, 35, 141, 153, 198, 1378; election of bishops and, 91

Volume Key: Volume 1, pages 1–614; volume 2, pages 615–1266; volume 3, pages 1267–1637.

1721

Justin Martyr, St., 378–379, 696, 708, 1154, 1171, 1424

Justinian I, emperor of Byzantium: accomplishments of, 1318–1319; African Church and, 13; Agapitus I and, 14; Alexandrian Church and, 35, 36; apostolicity principle of Roman primacy and, 201, 207, 564; Byzantine popes and, 196; canon and, 221; Carthage and, 251; Church-State relationship and, 108, 1488; faith-defining edict by (533), 832, 833; Gregory II and, 642; Hormisdas and, 737, 738; Monophysites and, 699–700; Pelagius I and, 1145, 1146, 1147; suburbicarian Italy and, 1465; Three Chapters schism and, 1146, 1617; Vigilius and, 1497, 1616, 1617, 1618; Western Empire and, 14, 141, 198, 201, 575, 1047

Justinian II, emperor of Byzantium, 202, 412, 836; Constantine I and, 420; Quinisext synod and, 203, 428, 1412; Silverius and, 1418

Justus, archbishop of Canterbury, 188

Jutes, 140, 1318

Juvenal, 442–443

Kabbalism, 799, 1310

Kakowski, archbishop of Warsaw, 1200–1201

Kaljoanes, tsar of Bulgaria, 689

Kalo of Poitiers, 450

Kamil, Malik al-, sultan of Egypt, 439

Kandy pontifical seminary (Sri Lanka), 1373–1374

Kant, Immanuel, 603, 1007

Kantorowicz, Ernst H., 1284

Kanzler, Hermann, 1196, 1645, 1646

Kaspar, Cardinal, 1631

Kaunitz, Wenzel Anton von, 869

Kazakhstan, 522

Keane, John, 40, 41

Keble, John, 1086

Kempe, Margery, 1166

Kennedy, Rose Fitzgerald, 1051

Kennick, archbishop of St. Louis, 1567

Kepler, Johannes, 213, 518

Kerguenec, Henri Le Chauff de, 1644

Kerver, Jacqes, 995

kerygma, 1142

Ketteler, Wilhelm von, 892, 1396, 1448; subsidiarity concept, 1462

keys, 116, 138, 627, 689–694, **891**, 1168, 1385; crossed, 689–690, 693, 694; cursors, 475; ferula and, 575; Fisherman's Ring, 587; heraldic emblems, 689–692, 693, 1588; majordomo of household, 739; as papal gift, 598; pavilion, 1145; on pilgrims' clothing, 1168; symbolism of, 286, 287, 1483, 1488; on third party arms, 694–695

Khrushchev, Nikita, 855, 1085, 1140

Kiev, metropolitan of, 329

Kiliç Arslan, 1526

Kilwardby, Robert, 1038

King of the Romans. See Holy Roman Empire

Kirsch, Johannes-Peter, 101

kitchen. See food provision

Kjelt of Viborg, 331

Klein, Felix, 41

Kleindienst, Johann, 83

Klumper, Bernard, 365

Kneighton, Henry, 1221

Knightly Order of the Holy Sepulcher of Jerusalem. See Holy Sepulcher of Jerusalem, Knightly Order of the knights. See decorations; military orders

Knox, James Robert, 434

Knox, John, 1288

Koch, G., 1018

Kolbe, Father, 876

Kolbenheyer, E. G., 239

König Cardinal, 247, 863–864

Konrad. See Conrad

Koran. See Qur'an

Kostka, Stanislas, 827

Krämer, Heinrich, 799

Kraus, A., 1560

Krautheimer, Richard, 101

"Kristallnacht" (Germany), 875

Kubla Khan, 658

Kulturkampf, **891–894**, 934, 1009, 1110, 1207; educational reforms, 869; fundamentalism and, 614; infallibility dogma and, 779; interest in Canossa confrontation, 239; Ultramontanism and, 1530

Kuncewicz, Josaphat, 1531

Küng, Hans, 764, 1196

Kunigunde, St., 268

Kuschel, Karl Joseph, 283

Kuttner, Stephan, 227, 367

La Fontaine, Cardinal, 1201

La Haye Convention (1899), 98

La Mettrie, Julien, 362

La Pira, Giorgio, 540

La Roche, Alain de, 1275, 1346

La Roche, Androuin de, 796

La Sapienzia, Pontifical University of, 9, 413, 468

Labethonnière, Lucien, 1008, 1199

Labican Way, 258, 259

labor. See workers

Labor Employment Office (Apostolic See), 1594

Labor Office of the Apostolic See, 12

Laborem exercens (1981 encyclical), 1447, 1449, 1463

Laboureur, A.-M., 1373

Labre, Benoît-Joseph, 1181, 1260

Labrousse, Suzette, 1263

Lackland, John. See John (Lackland), king of England

Lacordaire, Henri-Dominique, 511, 512, 673, 674

Lacroix, Lucien, 1008, 1198

Lactantius, 75, 417, 1156

Lacunza, Manuel, 1260

Ladies' Peace (1529), 1624

Ladislao of Aquino, 667

Ladislas, king of Naples, 53–54, 660, 662, 797

Ladislas of Durazzo, 852

Lagier, Bertrand, 342

Lagrange, M. J., 512, 1008

Lailler, Jean, 814

laity, Middle Ages, **895–896**; election of bishops and, 89–92, 91, 93–94; Gentleman of His Holiness, 626–627; papal household positions, 739–740, 742; rosary and, 1346

Laity, Pontifical Council for the, 433–434

Lajeunie, E., 512

Volume Key: Volume 1, pages 1–614; volume 2, pages 615–1266; volume 3, pages 1267–1637.

1722

Lalande, J. J. Lefrançois, 1503–1507

Lallemand, Jean-Baptiste, 119

Lallemand, Leon, 1311

Lambert, Holy Roman emperor, 154, 838, 1460

Lambert of Ostia. *See* Honorius II

Lamberti, Nicola, 255

Lambertini, Prospero. *See* Benedict XIV

Lambeth Conference (1867), 56

Lambeth Conference (1920), 1075

Lambeth Conference (1930), 56

Lambeth Conference (1988), 56

Lambruschini, Cardinal, 673, 1191, 1192

Lamennais, Hughes de, 306, 511, 670, 673, 674, 778, 931, 933, 1191, 1448, 1566

Lamoricière, General de, 1643, 1645

Lamourette, Adrien, 78

Lampadius, 1045

Lamy, François, 77

Lancelotti, G. P., 228, 231

Landazuri Ricketts, 247

Landi, Stefano, 298–299

Landin, Taddeo, 1270

Lando, **896**

Lando of Sezze. *See* [Innocent III]

Landriano, Marsilio, 666

Lanfranc (prelate), 225, 649

Lanfranco, Giovanni, 1090–1091, 1270, 1372, 1383, 1385

Lang, Ossian, 608

Langenstein, Heinrich von. *See* Heinrich of Lagenstein

Langton, Stephen, 93, 451, 725, 785, 787, 897

Lanne, Emmanuel, 521

Lannoy, 1355, 1624

Lante, Alessandro, 1184

Lantoine, Albert, 608

Laocoön (statue), 886, 1024, 1025, 1026, 1595

lapsi controversy, 13, 43, 432, 543, 561, 698; Carthage and, 250–251; Cornelius/Novatian schism over, 250, 422, 1055, 1155, 1394; Marcellus I and, 967–968; Miltiades and, 1156; Stephen I and, 1455

Large Catechism (Luther), 262, 264

Larroca, J. M., 512

Las Casas, Bartholomé de, 99

lasagna, 302

Last Judgment, 64–67, 133, 1265; Lateran V on, 899

Last Judgment (Michelangelo), 1091, 1093, 1430–1431

Lateran. *See* St. John Lateran, basilica of; Lateran *listings below*

Lateran Council (1112), 900, 1113, 1281

Lateran I Council (1123), 1044, 1245, 1637; Callistus II and, 216, 428; investiture solution and, 1281; overview, 428, 900

Lateran II Council (1139), 533, 701, 785, 1044; canonical collections, 226; investiture solution and, 1281; nicolaism condemnation, 216, 429; overview, 429, 900–901; simony condemnation, 1425

Lateran III Council (1179), 897, 961, 1543; canonical collections, 226; on cardinalate election of pope, 241, 1356, 1405; on cathedral schools, 22, 1547; on clerical celibacy, 1044; on heresy, 701; on incardination, 766; national cleric post creation by, 1027; overview, 429, 901; purposes of, 22, 901; simony condemnation, 1425

Lateran IV Council (1215), 430, 734, **896–898**, 1028, 1044, 1521; Antichrist charges and, 66; canonical collections, 226, 227; on canonization, 233; Catholic reform and, 1274; crusade doctrine, 438, 439, 734, 787, 792, 897–898; election of bishops and, 92, 94; Franciscans and, 788; indulgences and, 774, 792; on infallibility, 777; Innocent III and, 787, 788, 789, 870, 896–897, 1379; Inquisition and, 811; on Jewish-Christian segregation, 870, 871; on laity obligations, 895; Maronites and, 998; monastic orders and, 507, 1015; overview, 429, 897–898; papal revenues after, 577; repressive measures, 1443; simony condemnation, 1425

Lateran V Council (1512–1517), 429, 886, **898–900**, 926; Antichrist charges and, 67, 899; calendar discussion, 213; cardinal protector limitations, 247; Curia reaction to, 1518; on exemptions, 1233; French wars in Italy and, 1622; on imprimatur, 763; Index and, 899, 1443; Julius II papal primacy doctrine and, 509; Leo X and, 429, 898, 899, 926, 927, 928, 1443; nepotism declaration, 1033; reforms of, 1354, 1443; simony declaration, 1425; works of, 899

Lateran church, 1301

Lateran councils, 428, **900–901**; papal power expansion from, 1246

Lateran pacts (1929), 397, 399, **901–905**, 1107, 1110, 1363, 1534, 1541; administrative offices and, 10; automobiles and traffic issues and, 126, 127; coin issuance and, 377; diplomatic corps and, 503–504; Holy See and, 719, 720, 1096, 1135; international organizations and, 687, 718, 1077; modifications (1967–1983), 904; national churches in Rome and, 317; 1984 accords, 904–905; Pacelli family and, 1210; papal finances and, 582–583; papal titles and, 1051; Paul VI prepapal position on, 1135–1136; Pius XI and, 1202, 1206, 1207, 1247; postage stamps issuance, 1229; provisions of, 1207; St. Peter's basilica alterations and, 1384; Vatican citizenship and, 323–324, 1115; Vatican City State creation, 389, 902, 1202, 1207, 1586, 1587, 1588–1589; Vatican Radio and, 1444, 1599–1600; World War II applications, 1628, 1629, 1630, 1632–1633

Lateran Palace, 644, 1045–1046, 1360, 1541, 1551; architecture, 1340, 1359; art iconography, 1284; artist commissions, 1091; Byzantine seizure of, 1354; as central to Papal States, 1097; decoration, 1117; Donation of Constantine and, 513, 514; as first papal residence, 1300; papal abandonment as residence, 1304, 1362, 1363, 1382; papal coronation and, 425, 426–427, 1228–1229; restoration and decoration, 1300–1301; as seat of bishop of Rome, 1304, 1363; Vatican City and, 1592

Lateran registers, 1293

Lateran synod (1059), 1036, 1037, 1043, 1282

Lateran University, Pontifical, 380

Latin America: appointment of bishops, 89, 94; bishops' conferences, 401; clerical suspensions, 1470; concordats with papacy, 397, 398, 399; Dominicans and, 509–510; Freemasonry and, 604; Holy See arbitrations in, 718, 719, 720; Inquisition in, 816; John XXIII and, 855; John Paul II tours of, 1510, 1511, 1513; Leo XII missions to, 932; Leo XIII council and, 1570; liberation theology and, 979; military chaplaincy, 991–992; missions, 348, 509–510, 530, 539, 999–1000, 1004, 1343–1344; papal arbitration in, 99; Paul VI travel to, 1515; Pius XII and, 1218; Roman Catholic

Volume Key: Volume 1, pages 1–614; volume 2, pages 615–1266; volume 3, pages 1267–1637.

1723

Church in, 541, 675; Vatican II representation, 1575, 1577, 1578, 1579–1580, *See also specific countries*

Latin America, Papal Commission for, 388

Latin Fathers of the Church. *See* Fathers of the Church, Latin

Latin Kingdom (Latin Empire of the East), 788, 1555

Latin language: Angelus text in, 50; apologetics in, 75–76; Christian inscriptions in, 100–101; encyclicals in, 524; Latinity, 905–906; liturgy in, 837; pontifical administrator requirements, 7; Renaissance humanism and, 1294–1295; Secretariat of Briefs to Princes and, 1401–1402, 1403; university teaching in, 1548; Vatican I and, 1567, 1568; Vulgate in, 1520

Latin Monetary Union, 377

Latin Way, 258, 260

Latini, Latino, 968

Latinity, **905–906**; Renaissance humanism and, 1294–1295; vernacular liturgy vs., 682, 837, 955–956, *See also* Latin language

latitudinarianism, 1472

Latium, 191, 1330, 1333, 1555; as early kernal of Papal States, 1097; Italian unity and, 1195, 1533, 1538, 1540; Napoleonic Empire and, 1104; Neopolitan invasion, 1434; nepotism, 1049; papal court and residences in, 1303, 1304; pillaging in, 535–536; Saracen incursions from, 645

Latvia, 175

Laud, W., 55

Lauer, Aloys, 597

Laurain-Portemer, M., 1560

Laurent of Odria, 622

Laurentian schism, 44

Laurentin, René, 1238

Laurentius, 446, 834

Lauri, Lorenzo, 575

Lausiac History, 1164

Lautrec, Aimery de, 694, 1623, 1624

Lavagna, Raffaello, 744

Laval, Gasbert de, 80, 81, 219, 578

Laval de Montigny, François de, 351

Lavalette, Father (Jesuit), 359, 1346

Lavenier, Jean, 1501

Lavigerie, Monsignor, 779, 934

law. *See* canon law; canonical collections; civil law; consistorial advocate; constitution, apostolic; judges delegate; Rota, tribunal of the

Law of Guarantees. *See* Guarantees, Law of

[Lawrence], 141, 181, **906–907**; Easter-date controversy, 517, 832; *Liber pontificalis* and, 942; schism over, 44, 70, 72, 502, 736, 831, 832, 1475–1476

Lawrence, St., 418, 1155, 1164, 1230, 1390, 1391, 1392, 1432, 1496

Lawrence of Milan. *See* Lorenzo of Milan

Lawrentian Fragment, 1475

laxism, 827, 1003, 1204

lay confraternities. *See* Roman confraternities

Lay Dependents of the Vatican, Association of. *See* Vatican labor union

lay investiture, 91, 1245, 1280, 1281; simony and, 1424, *See also* investiture controversy

Laynez, Diego, 1518

Lazarists, 1224, 1255, 1409, 1561

Lazzarini, Gregorio, 256

Le Blant, Edmund, 101

Le Bouluec, Alain, 697

Le Brun, Charles, 118, 1270–1271

Le Floch, Henri, 175, 1626

Le Goff, Jacques, 1220

Le Puy, Council of (987), 900

Le Roy, Edouard, 1008, 1199

Le Sillon movement. *See* Sillon

Le Vassor, Michel, 77

Le Viel, P., 1019

Lea, 1011–1012

League of Blois, 938

League of Cognac, 344, 345, 1624

League of Nations, 175, 712, 713, 1077–1078, 1206, 1630, 1632

League of San Marco, 26

Leahy, P. J., 512

Leander (Leandro) of Seville, 141, 639, 641

leap year, 213

Lebanon: Catholic missions, 1561; Maronites, 319, 370; synod of bishops, 1479

Lebret, J., 512

Leclercq, Father, 954

Lecto, Rainaldo di, 286

Lefebvre, Marcel, 388–389, 865, 1132, 1143; excommunication of, 1398, 1470; schism, 1397–1398; suspension of, 1470

legate, **907–913**; antiquity, **907–909**; Avignon, 128, 911; beatification/canonization ceremony and, 268; canon law and, 224, 909, 910; diplomatic corps and, 503–504; finances and, 580; function of, 1283; Middle Ages, 18, 240, **909–912**, 1283; modern and contemporary eras, **912–913**; monastery visits by, 1015; nunciature and, 911, 912, 1056, 1057, 1058; *pallium* bestowal on, 1608; Sicily and, 51, 52, 1053, 1054

Legations, 1104, 1183, 1184, 1185, 1188, 1189

Léger, St., 952

Legion of Decency, 320

Legislative Texts, Pontifical Council for the Interpretation of, 435, 474, 1150

Legna, Francesco, 364

Legnano, battle of (1176), 20, 217, 313

Legnano, Johannes de, 227

Legros, Pierre, 119, 1362

Lellis, Camille de, 666

Lemmens, Nicolas-Jacques, 954

Lemoine, Jean, 242, 281, 282

Lenin, V. I., 858, 977–978

Lennhoff, Eugen, 608

Lent, 210; Carnival and, 248; fasting, 1453; liturgy, 949, 950; papal chapel, 295, 296; stational processions, 1453, 1454

Leo I (the Great), 49, 639, 738, **913–919**, 931, 1165; "ad limina" visits and, 4; African Church relations, 13, 32–33, 34, 915, 917; Alexandrian see and, 32–33, 34, 35, 44; barbarian invasion and, 140, 1046, 1318, 1354; benefaction and, 179; Byzantium emperor and, 622; Celestine I and, 273; censorship by, 770; Christology, 428, 563, 572, 699, 916, 917, 1108, 1147; Council of Chalcedon and, 1318; Council of Ephesus and, 199, 200, 428, 432, 695–706, 1617; as Doctor of the Church, 568; Eastern Churches and, 14, 35, 199, 200,

Volume Key: Volume 1, pages 1–614; volume 2, pages 615–1266; volume 3, pages 1267–1637.

1724

201, 317–318, 563, 737, 915–918, 1060; election of bishops and, 91; as Father of the Church, 568; as former deacon, 484; Hilarus and, 705, 706; Latinity and, 905; legate mission and duties defined by, 908; as mosaics inspiration, 1020, 1365; papal office consolidation under, 1245; papal portraits series and, 1372; on Peter and Paul, 1160; *plenitudo potestatis* claim, 1108; pontifical titles, 1494, 1495; stational processions and, 1453; tiara, 1490; tomb of, 1391, 1496, 1497; *Tome* of, 916, 917, 1147; vicariate of Arles and, 1610

Leo I, emperor of Byzantium, 622, 917–918, 1318

Leo II, 143, 153, 900, **919**; Constantine I and, 420; Roman churches and, 1328

Leo II of Silesia, 998

Leo III, **919–921**; apostasy and, 79; bull use restrictions, 196; Charlemagne and, 254, 424, 437, 600, 920, 1108, 1320, 1331; coins, 372; finances of, 577; Lateran reconstruction by, 1300, 1360; long duration of papacy, 644–645; Paschal I and, 1111; St. Peter's basilica and, 1378; Stephen IV (V) and, 1458; Vatican Palace building by, 1301; violence against, 79, 122, 599, 920, 1320, 1458

Leo III (the Isaurian), emperor of Byzantium, 203–204, 644, 1639; iconoclast controversy, 203, 318, 372, 598, 642–643, 701

Leo IV, 154, **921–922**, 1367; Anastasius Bibliothecarius clash with, 46, 600; consistory meetings, 413; Franks and, 600; iconoclast controversy, 205; military role of, 109; St. Peter's basilica and, 254, 549, 1328; tomb of, 1497; Vatican walling by, 254, 645, 1301, 1373, 1393, *See also* Leonine City

Leo V, **922**; antipope Chrisopher's imprisonment of, 71, 312; deposition of, 495, 1413; iconoclasm and, 205

Leo V (the Armenian), emperor of Byzantium, 600

Leo VI, **922**

Leo VI, emperor of Byzantium, 45, 206, 839, 1414, 1459

Leo VII, 15, **922–923**

Leo VIII, 70, **923**; Benedict V deposition by, 155, 575; deposition of, 495, 841; as hypothetical antipope, 71, 841

Leo IX, **923–926**; bull design, 195, 925; Byzantium and, 206, 925; Carthage and, 251; death of the pope and, 487; Eastern Church schism and, 1245, 1280, 1395, 1461; election of bishops and, 91–92, 924; Golden Rose and, 1348; Gregory VII and, 449, 648; heresy condemnation, 701; legates and, 909; monasticism and, 1016, 1021; Norman conquests and, 109, 925, 1053; pontifical gloves, 620; reforms, 91–92, 448, 449, 924–925, 1031, 1043–1044, 1245, 1278, 1280, 1282; simony condemnation, 1424; Stephen IX (X) and, 1461; tiara, 1490; tomb of, 1498; travels of, 924, 1015; Tusculan opposition, 158; Victor II and, 1613; Victor III and, 1613, 1614

Leo X, 621, **926–929**; annona, 61; Apostolic Camera functions, 9; appointment of bishops and, 93; arms, 114, 693, 695; cardinal protector reforms, 247; Castel Sant'Angelo renovations, 255; censorship and, 1443; Clement VII and, 343, 344, 1032; coins, 374; conciliarism condemned by, 1518; Curia and, 462, 463, 464; cursors, 475; Dominicans and, 509; Ecclesiastical State formation, 1467; exemptions grants, 1233; extravagances of, 344, 374, 927; Franciscans and, 595; French wars in Italy and, 1623; Holy Places and, 722; Holy Sepulcher order and, 723; humanism and, 1295; hunting expeditions, 59, 927; imprimatur, 763, 770; indulgences abuse by, 374, 509, 775; Innocent VIII and, 799; Lateran V and, 429, 898,

899, 926, 927, 928, 1443; Latinity and, 906; Luther's doctrinal statement and, 1286, 1395; master of ceremonies, 284; menagerie, 58, 927; mendicant orders defense by, 509; Michelangelo paintings and, 272; musicians, 297, 299, 927; naval forces, 1029; nepotism and, 799, 1032; nunciature, 1057; painting commissions, 1089, 1091, 1116, 1340; papal chapel singers, 297; Paul III and, 1124; pet nightingale, 58; portrait of, 1093; Pragmatic Sanction and, 616; reform resistance by, 1123, 1246; Reformation and, 1285; St. Peter's basilica project, 104, 105, 549, 1382; secretariat, 1402; Service of the Cipher, 1464; simony and, 463, 927

Leo XI, 115, **929**, 1129

Leo XII, **929–933**; academies and, 2; Apostolic Camera functions, 9; Apostolic Palace management, 1093–1094; arms, 115; banner standardization, 138; beatifications and, 147; Catholic theological studies, 1544; Church-State powers and, 1536; congregations, 411; cursor reorganization, 475; encyclical list, 524; encyclicals, 931, 1544; Freemasonry condemnation, 605, 932; Gregory XVI and, 671, 672; Holy Year and, 727; master of the Sacred Palace and, 981; medallion table, 1652; Napoleonic wars and, 1186, 1189; Noble Guard and, 1051–1052; Papal States territorial redistributions and, 1538; pet cat of, 59; Pius VIII and, 1190, 1191; Pius IX and, 1192; St. Mary Major basilica restoration, 1364; St. Paul Outside the Walls restoration, 1016, 1190; sedan chair use, 1228; Swiss Guard and, 1471

Leo XIII, **933–936**; Americanism and, 41, 935; Anglican ordinations and, 55–56, 934, 1072–1073, 1074, 1075, 1076, 1395; Apostolic Camera functions, 9; arbitration by, 99; archives opening to researchers by, 935, 1603, 1604; arms, 116; beatifications and, 148; Benedict XV and, 1626; biblical commission, 388; biretta and, 180; bishops' conferences and, 401; blessing *urbi et orbi* and, 177, 1233; *bollatica* suppression by, 183; bull and, 195, 293; camauro reuse, 620; as cardinal, 245; Catholic University founding, 1546; chamberlains, 739–740; Christian Democracy and, 305, 306–307, 1023; cinema and, 321; *Civiltà Cattolica* and, 325; Code of Canons of Eastern Churches and, 370; on collegiality, 385; conclave bull, 395; conclave electing, 244, 396; courtly titles and, 627; Dante praised by, 482; datary reduction, 483; Dominicans and, 512; encyclical list, 525; encyclicals, 39, 305, 306, 385, 512, 518, 524, 539, 606–607, 934, 935, 943, 977, 983, 1023, 1515; exclusion right and, 550–551; filming of, 1163; financial management, 582, 583, 1210; Franciscan reunification, 596–597; Freemasonry anathema, 601, 605, 606–607, 874, 934; fundamentalist reaction to, 613, 614; German monarchy relations, 893, 1196; Holy Places and, 712; Holy Year and, 729; imprimatur, 763; Index revision, 770–771, 772; indigenous clergy and, 1004, 1374; Italian unity and, 175, 1023, 1541, 1570; Jesuits and, 828; Jewish policy, 873, 874; Latin American council and, 1570; letters to, 939; liberal leanings, 606; liberalism encyclical, 943; literary portrayals of, 758; medallion, 983, 1022; modernism and, 860, 1008, 1010, 1196, 1247; mosaic restorations, 1020; Movimento Cattolico and, 1023; nepotism and, 1033; Noble Guard and, 1052; Numismatic Cabinet of the Vatican, 983–984; *Osservatore romano* and, 1082–1083; papal apartments and, 72; papal protocol and, 125; papal remains and, 1500; papal titles and, 1051; photographic portraits of, 1163;

Volume Key: Volume 1, pages 1–614; volume 2, pages 615–1266; volume 3, pages 1267–1637.

1725

Pius X as successor, 679, 1198; pontifical patrimony administration, 10; Portugal and, 1195; *posesso* ceremony, 1228; press communication, 984; Propaganda Fide and, 1256; rosary devotion and, 512, 1347; Rota tribunals and, 1340; St. John Lateran restorations, 1363; St. Paul's Ouside the Walls restoration, 1372; sedan chair use, 1228; seminaries and, 1409; Signatura Apostolic and, 1525; social teachings, 983, 1077, 1110, 1311, 1443, 1444, 1447, 1448, 1449–1450, 1515 (*see also Rerum novarum*); socialism condemned by, 977; subsidiarity concept, 1462; Thomism encyclical, 512; tomb of, 1386, 1500; on unionism over ecumenism, 518, 539; Vatican I and, 1566; Vatican Library and, 1597, 1598; Vatican museum collection, 1026; Vatican Observatory and, 1062

Leo of Ostia, 1303

Leonard of Limoges, St., 952

Leonard of Port-Maurice, St., 168

Leonardo da Vinci, 928

Leoni, Leone, 982

Leonine City, 254, 921, 1107, 1301, 1306, 1328, 1373, 1393

Leonini, Angelo, 1057

Leontius, bishop of Arles, 707

Leontius, prefect of Milan, 945

leopards, 59

Leopold I, Holy Roman emperor, 31, 353, 375, 888

Leopold III of Habsburg, 340

Leopold IV of Austria, 734

Leovigild, king of the Visigoths, 141

Lepage, Marius, 609

Lepanto (1571), 194, 800, **936–939**, 1030, 1527; battle details, 937–938, 1177; consequences, 938, 1177, 1343; medallion commemorating, 983; origins of conflict, 936–937; Pius V and, 1176, 1179, 1369; rosary devotion and, 1347

Lepicier, Alexis, 364

Lepida, Domitia, 1594

Leti, Gregorio, 468

Leto, Pomponio, 2, 260, 1122, 1435

letters to the pope, **939–940**

Levi, Don Vergilio, 1239

Levillain, Philippe, 1238

Levitical miter, 1489, 1490, 1492

Leys (Lessius), Leonard, 68

Liber censuum, **940–941**; Celestine III and, 278; Census and, 219, 689, 733; Papal State administration and, 1098

Liber Extra (Raymond of Peñafort), 226, 663

Liber generationis (Hippolytus), 942

Liber pontificalis, **941–943**, 1563; Anacletus I misnamed in, 42; on benefactions, 178; on bishop of Rome, 180; on Clement I, 327; liturgy, 283–284; on Lombard pillages, 152, 153; on medieval Rome, 1327, 1328; papal death date and tomb site, 1495–1496; Ravenna and, 1274; on Silvester I, 1419–1420; on Symmachean schism, 141, *See also specific popes*

Liber septimus decretalium, 231, 363

liberalism, **943–945**; apologetics against, 78; Christian Democracy and, 304, 305; Church-State conflict and, 943, 1537–1538, 1539; Freemasonry and, 601–602, 604, 605, 606; fundamentalism as reaction to, 613–614; German *Kulturkampf* and, 891–892; Gregory XVI opposition to, 670, 672, 673–674; Leo XII battle against, 932; Leo XIII battle against, 934; myth of Pius IX and, 1193, 1323; papal con-demnations of, 605, 932, 979, 1009, 1109; Roman Republic of 1849 and, 1323–1326; Syllabus of Errors on, 1475

Liberati, Antonio, 256, 912

liberation theology, 819; John XXIII view of, 979; John Paul I view of, 858; John Paul II view of, 863, 979

Liberato (Pietro di Macerata), 281, 282

Liberatore, Matteo, 324, 325

Liberatus, 35

Liberius, 179, 199, 418, 477, 562, **945–947**, 1377, 1563; basilica construction, 144, 1327, 1364, 1366, 1368; Damasus I and, 477, 478; exile of, 199, 571, 881, 882; as former deacon, 484; Julian the Apostate and, 882; Marian legend and, 1367, 1368; monastic movement and, 1011, 1012; prefect arrest of, 1230; retraction and return to Rome by, 34, 571, 882; tomb of, 1391, 1392, 1496

libertas ecclesiae vs. *honor imperii. See* primacy, papal

libertinage movement (France), 76, 77

library, Vatican. *See* Vatican Library

Libri Carolini, 428, 681

Libro d'oro, 1049–1050

Libya, 399

Licinian of Cartagena, 568

Licinius, emperor of Rome, 417, 418, 1316

Liebana, Beatus de, 65

Liénart, Cardinal, 1578

Life and Action (Stockholm; 1925), 518

Life of Anthony (Athanasius), 1011

Life of Cola di Rienzo, 1327

Life of Saint Eloi, 598

Life of Saint Gregory, 748–749

Ligorio, Pirro, 1176, 1269, 1595

Liguori, Alphonsus, 78, 675, 1191

Liguria, 661, 1536, 1619

Limousin party, 339

Lincoln, Abraham, 1462

Linus, 327, **947–948**, 1244

lions, 58

List of Verona, 1464

literature. *See* Dante; image of Rome in literature

literature, forbidden. *See* Index

Lithuania: diplomatic relations restoration, 503; evangelization in, 522, 998; *ostpolitik*, 1084–1085; Uniates, 1531

Litta, Lorenzo, 1179

littera santi Petri. See bollatica

litterae (seal), 292

litterae apostolicae, 421

litterae encyclicae. See encyclical

Little Church (schism), 585

Liturgical Books, Congregation for, 470, 1002

liturgical calendar. *See* calendar

Liturgical Celebrations of the Supreme Pontiff, Office for the, 8, 11

liturgical chant, Roman, **948–949**; Gregorian, 298, 948, 950–951, 952, 954, 1198, 1619

liturgical movement, 955–956

liturgical objects, 980

liturgical vestments. *See* vestments, pope's liturgical

liturgical year, 194

liturgy, **951–957**; 7th to 15th centuries, **951–953**; since Council

Volume Key: Volume 1, pages 1–614; volume 2, pages 615–1266; volume 3, pages 1267–1637.

1726

of Trent, **953–957**; Anglican, 54, 55, 955; baptistry, 138–139; Benedict XIV and, 169; breviary reform, 193, 194, 953, 1109, 1178, 1277, 1289; French Church and, 1566; liturgical books and, 1002; missal revision, 995–996, 1109, 1178, 1277, 1289; non-Latin, 682, 837, 955–956, 997, 1459; papal ceremonials, 284–285; papal chapel, 295–300, 1282–1283; papal chaplain, 300; Pius V and, 1178; Pius X and, 1198; Pius XII and, 1217; Quinisext Council and, 202–203; Slavonic, 682, 837, 997, 1459; stational, 1454; subcinctorium, 1461; Vatican II renovation, 430, 955–956, 1142, 1143, 1583, *See also* liturgical chant, Roman; music

Liutprand, king of the Lombards, 108–109, 643, 644, 958, 1456; invasion of Rome by, 1331; Zacharias meeting with, 1639

Liutprand of Cremona, 188, 1332, 1414

Liutward of Vercelli, 1458–1459

Lives of the Popes (Platina), 830

Living Rosary, Association of the, 1347

Livonia, 989, 990, 997, 998

Livre des causes synodales, 231

local councils. *See* councils, particular or local

Locke, John, 603, 1182

Lodif, 1041

logic, 847

Loisy, Alfred, 176, 1007, 1008, 1199

Lollards, 703, 812, 1395

Lombard League (12th-13th centuries), 20, 21, 110, 217, 313, 315, 628, 715, 716, 910, 961

Lombard League (20th century), 311

Lombard Quarantotto, 1539

Lombards, **957–959**; as Agatho allies, 16; antipopes and, 71; Arian converts, 140, 142, 957; as Benedict VIII allies, 157; Boniface IV and, 186, 187; Byzantine popes and, 196, 197; Byzantium and, 1319; catacombs and, 261; Catholic conversions, 142–143; Exarchate of Ravenna and, 546–547, 599, 643, 644, 1273, 1274, 1319, 1331, 1639; Gregory I and, 141–142, 640, 1047, 1108; Gregory II and, 108–109, 643; Gregory III and, 109, 598, 644, 1331, 1639; Guelphs and, 627, 676; Hadrian I and, 679–680; heresy battles, 812; Holy Roman Empire and, 313; Honorius I and, 730; Italian invasion by, 1319, 1465; John VI and, 835; Leo III and, 920; Milan occupation by, 987; Nicholas II and, 1036; papal rivalry with, 1245; Papal States and, 1097; papal-Frankish alliance against, 598, 599, 1097; Patrimony of St. Peter and, 1115; Paul I and, 1120; Pelagius II and, 597, 1148–1149; [Philip] and, 1162; pilgrimages to Rome, 1166; pillaging by, 152, 153; Roman offensive by, 108–109, 203, 204, 833, 834, 1331, 1354; Roman Senate and, 1047; Saracens and, 645, 1393; Sicilian invasion by, 315; Stephen II (III) and, 1456–1457; Vitalian and, 1619; Zacharias confrontration with, 1456, 1639–1640

Lombardy: Benedict XIV concordat, 35; Church-State powers and, 23, 1535, 1536; jurisdictionalism and, 888; patron saint, 569; Pius XI roots in, 1200, 1201–1202; Risorgimiento, 1537, 1539; Urban II and, 1551; Urban VIII and, 1561

Lonck, Johannes, 260

Longhi, Giovanni, 745

Longinianus, 1046

Lopez Trujillo, Alfonso, 434

Lord's Prayer, 1346

Lorenzelli, Monsignor, 873

Lorenzo of Milan, 502, 987, 1475

Lorrain (Claude Gellée), 118, 1345, 1562

Lorraine (Lotharingia), 925

Loschi, Antonio, 851

Lotario "de Conti." *See* Innocent III

Lothair I, Holy Roman emperor, 154, 424, 532, 600, 645, 681, 714, 921, 1034; coronation by Paschal I, 1111; Papal States and, 1097; Sergius II and, 1413

Lothair II (or III), Holy Roman emperor, 42, 254, 276, 313, 732, 837; crowning of Innocent II by, 784, 900

Lothair III, Holy Roman emperor, 959, 1637

Lothair, constitution of (824), 154

Lotharingia. *See* Lorraine

Lothario, king of Italy, 237

Loubières, Jean de, 103

Louis, king of Hungary, 130, 337

Louis I (the Pious), Holy Roman emperor, 205, 314, 532, 645, 680; canonization and, 233; Church-State relations and, 1097, 1483; *Ludovicianum*, 513, 600; monasticism and, 1014; papal crowning of, 424, 600, 1458; Paschal I and, 600, 1111

Louis II, duke of Anjou, 25, 217, 341, 634, 660, 662, 852, 1393

Louis II, Holy Roman emperor, 109, 154, 424, 600, 681, 682, 835, 921, 1033, 1034; Anastasius Bibliothecarius support by, 46–47; Roman coronation of, 921

Louis II, king of Naples, 54

Louis II (the German), king of Germany, 645, 681, 837, 1033

Louis II (the Stammerer), king of France, 837

Louis III of Anjou-Provence, 54, 55

Louis III (the Blind), Holy Roman emperor, 154, 838

Louis IV, king of France, 15, 1460

Louis IV (the Bavarian), Holy Roman emperor, 72, 128, 131–132, 133, 316, 337, 415, 592, 628, 629, 716, 837, 850, 1039–1040, 1485; coronation of, 424, 1337; independence from papacy declaration (1338), 1109

Louis VI, king of France, 42, 625–626, 732, 784, 822; investiture controversy and, 1113

Louis VII, king of France, 20, 21, 276, 313, 533, 784, 990, 1291, 1616

Louis IX, St., king of France, 685, 1064, 1554, 1555; canonization of, 190, 657, 794, 973; Clement IV and, 332, 333; crusades and, 332, 440, 656, 657; *decima* (tax) and, 579; as French patron saint, 569; Holy Sepulcher order and, 722

Louis XI, king of France, 128, 884, 1122, 1172, 1434

Louis XII, king of France, 27, 885, 886, 898, 927; Italian wars of, 509, 1621–1622, 1623

Louis XIII, king of France, 55, 124, 510–511, 669, 1470, 1561

Louis XIV, king of France, 468, 529, 570, 617, 801, 838, 1267–1268; Alexander VII and, 30, 913; castrati of the papal chapel and, 257; Clement X and, 350–351, 352; Clement XI and, 353, 354; Dominican appointment, 510, 511; Innocent XI conflict with, 31, 118, 510, 528, 617, 805, 1267; Innocent XII rapprochement, 808; Inquisition suppression, 816; Jansenism and, 349, 704, 778, 803, 824; Jesuit disputes with, 827; John XXII conflict, 676; legates to, 912–913; missionizing and, 1003; poor relief, 1225; Urban VIII and, 912

Louis XV, king of France, 362, 711, 825, 827–828, 1346

Volume Key: Volume 1, pages 1–614; volume 2, pages 615–1266; volume 3, pages 1267–1637.

Louis XVI, king of France, 611, 612, 1181

Louis XVIII, king of France, 585, 586, 930, 1184, 1186, 1187, 1188, 1189

Louis Napoleon. *See* Napoleon III

Louis of Anjou, St., 340, 341, 848

Louis of Bavaria. *See* Louis IV (the Bavarian), Holy Roman emperor

Louis of Orleans, 634

Louis the German. *See* Louis II (the German), king of Germany

Louise de Marillac, St., 1204

Louise of Savoy, 344, 1337, 1623, 1624

Louis-Philippe, king of France, 674, 1191, 1194

Lourdes, grotto of, 1204, 1347, 1595

Louvain, Catholic University of, 177, 675, 686, 932, 1544, 1546; Index and, 770; infallibility thesis, 778; as Jansenist center, 808, 823

Louvel, Father, 955

Love and Responsibility (Wojtyla), 862

Loyola, Ignatius. *See* Ignatius of Loyola, St.

Lubac, Henri de, 828, 829, 861, 1005, 1358

Lublin, University of, 861, 862

Luca, Giuseppe di, 1135

Lucca, 662, 1538; as banking center, 137; collectors, 82; Lombards and, 958

Lucca, University of, 1558

Luchetti, Giuseppe, 1500

Luciani, Albino. *See* John Paul I

Lucifer of Cagliari, 945, 986

Luciferians (Satanists), 702

Lucinus crypts, 258

Lucius I, **959**, 1056, 1155, 1392

Lucius II, 532, **959–960**; Normans and, 1053; tomb of, 1499

Lucius III, **960–961**, 1054, 1553; decretals of, 897; exemptions and, 553; Inquisition and, 701, 811; monasticism and, 1015; tomb of, 1499

Ludendorff, Erich, 174

Ludovic, king of Italy, 1413

Ludovic the Moor, 26–27

Ludovicianum (Louis the Pious), 513, 600

Ludovisi, Alessandro. *See* Gregory XV

Ludovisi, Ippolita, 668

Ludovisi, Ludovico, 220, 668; painting collection, 1090, 1091, 1092

Ludovisi, Niccolò, 668, 1441

Ludovisi, Orazio, 668

Ludovisi family, 667, 668, 694, 1032

Ludwig of Bavaria. *See* Louis IV (the Bavarian), Holy Roman emperor

Luke, Gospel of, 49, 631, 697

Lull, Raymond, 76, 334

Lumen (Vatican information agency), 984

Lumière brothers, 320, 321

Luna, Pedro de. *See* [Benedict XIII]

Lupercalia (pagan festival), 248, 573, 624

Luther, Martin, 67, 68, 99, 344, 522, 686, 703, 816, 1342; Catholic refutations to, 429, 778; Catholic schism and, 1395; condemnation of indulgences. *See* Ninety-five theses; Council of Trent and, 429, 1517, 1520; as Curia reform impetus, 464; indulgences condemnation, 509, 726, 775, 926, 927–928, 1286, 1287, 1382, 1395; influence of, 1290; *Large* and *Small Catechism*, 262, 264; papism attack by, 1109, 1287–1288, 1354; on Peter in Rome, 1159; pilgrimage denunciation by, 1169; Schmalkalden Articles, 1289, *See also* Reformation

Lutheranism, 68, 663, 664; antipapism of, 1289, 1354; Catholic reform and, 1276; ecumenism, 518, 521; German conversions to, 1125, 1276–1287; Inquisition and, 816–817; Josephism and, 868, 869; pietism and, 704; Pope Joan story and, 830; sack of Rome (1527) and, 1354–1355; as schism with Church, 1395

Luzi, Luzio, 1362

Luzzati, Luigi, 1540–1541

Lvov synod (1946), 1532

LX patrician families, 1049, 1050

Ly Wei-kuang, Jean Baptiste, 1397

Lyon: Catholic Institute, 1544; Christian martyrs, 1315; Clement V crowning at, 334; liturgy, 952; papal court, 791–792, 1304; papal residence, 628; Propagation of the Faith inception, 1259; taurobolium (bull sacrifice) held in, 441; tiara and, 1492

Lyon I, Council of (1245), 92, 615, 655, 716; Clement IV and, 332; Frederick II deposed by, 439; Innocent IV and, 241, 315, 439, 655, 716, 791–792, 1603; overview, 429

Lyon II, Council of (1274), 92, 93, 428, 736, 1037, 1038; cardinalate and, 241; Church unity declaration, 319, 973, 1395; conclave insitutionalization, 241, 392; constitutions of, 440, 657; crusades and, 440; Eastern Churches and, 998; Greek Church delegation, 657–658; Gregory X and, 226, 657–658, 685, 794; Innocent V and, 794, 998; Jewish policy and, 871; mendicant orders and, 593; overview, 429; on regalia, 1291

Maastricht accords (1992), 1462

Mabillon, Jean, 528, 589, 954, 1182

Macao, 1003

Macarius, 711, 919

Maccagnani, E., 1373

Macedonia, 1611

Macedoninus, 44, 737

Macerata (Marches capital), 1342

Macerata, Pietro di (Fortunata), 281, 282

Machiavelli, Niccolò, 27, 1437, 1443

Macrian, 1155

Madalbert (legate bishop), 922

Maderno, Carlo, 106, 351, 1089, 1270, 1272, 1344, 1372, 1373, 1383, 1384, 1562

Maderno, Stefano, 1369

Madio, Emanuele de, 1335–1336

Madiran, Jean, 1397

Madonna of the Palafrenieri (Caravaggio), 1341

Madrid, treaty of (1526), 1624

Madruzzo, Cardinal, 912

Maffei, Bernardino, 968

Maffei, Marcantonio, 1177

Mafia, 311, 1232

Magalotti, Lorenzo, 1561

Maggee, John, 285

magic, 1274

magicians, 669

Volume Key: Volume 1, pages 1–614; volume 2, pages 615–1266; volume 3, pages 1267–1637.

1728

Maginulf. *See* [Silvester IV]

magisterium, **963–966**; anti-Jansenism, 824, 825; anti-Masonism, 601, 604; Chair of St. Peter and, 286; conference of bishops and, 403; Curia and, 450; degrees of adhesion to, 963–965; encyclical, 524, 965; Fathers of the Church and, 566; infallibility of, 776, 780, 963–966; modernism rejected by, 1005; offenses against ecclesiastical, 965–966; temporal moral judgments of, 965; Vatican I/Vatican II and, 1572

Maglione, Cardinal, 1136–1137, 1208, 1212, 1213, 1218, 1629, 1631–1632

Magna Carta (1215; England), 93, 787

Magnificenze di Roma (Vasi), 171

Mahomet (Voltaire), 170, 530

Mahomet II, Ottoman sultan, 1434

Mahon, Denis, 1090

Mai, Angelo, 1598

Maidalchini, Francesco, 801–802

Maidalchini, Olimpia, 801, 802, 803

Maine de Biran, 943

Maintenon, Mme de, 808, 1268

Mainz, University of, 1544

Maiolus, abbot of Cluny, 842

Mair, J., 616

Maistre, Joseph de, 78, 99, 586, 778, 1189, 1263

Maius cemetery, 259

majordomo, papal, 738–739, 740, 1094

Malabar rites. *See* Chinese rites

Malabranca, Giovanni Cencio, 1336

Malabranca, Latino Frangipane, 281, 284, 1038

Malachy. *See* Prophecies of Malachy

Malachy, St., 1261–1262

malaria epidemic, 1345, 1355

Malaspina family, 676–677

Malatesta, Carlo, 662

Malatesta, Galeotto, 110

Malatesta, Roberto, 1121, 1434

Malatesta, Sigismondo, 983, 1042, 1121, 1172

Malatesta family, 676–677, 976

Malaval, 1267

Mâle, Émile, 1020

Malebranche, Nicolas de, 77

Malines Conversations (1921–1925), 519, 1075

Malleus Maleficarum, 799

Mallinckrodt, Hermann von, 892

Malta: apostolic delegate, 1059; Jesuit expulsion from, 359; Ottoman seizure of, 1177; papal concordats, 399

Malta, Knights of, 488, 722

Mamiani, Terenzio, 1324, 1539

Mamluks, 440, 711

Mancinelli, Fabrzio, 1430–1431

Mancini, Giulio, 116, 1090, 1093

Mancini Palace, 118, 121

Manegold of Lautenbach, 1043

Manfred, king of Naples and Sicily, 23, 51, 628, 629, 685, 1554, 1555; crowning of, 315; crusade against, 332, 333, 440, 676, 685, 973

Manfredi, M., 1018

Mangnier, Marc, 1008

Mani, 697

Manica lunga (Quirinal), 1270–1271

Manicheism, 480, 697, 702, 737, 770, 914

Manini banks, 83

Mann, Thomas, 761

Manna, Paolo, 996

mannerism, 1430

Manning, Henry Edward, 934, 1074

Mansi, 231–232

Mansuerus of Milan, 16

Mantegna, Andrea, 800, 1594

Mantua, Council of (1536), 1289

Mantua, synod of (1064), 17, 731

Mantuan war of succession (1627–1631), 1561

Manuel I, emperor of Byzantium, 207, 533

Manuel I, king of Portugal, 816

Manuel II Palaeologus, emperor of Byzantium, 76

Manutius, Aldus, 1599

Manutius, Paolo, 263, 968, 995, 1176, 1296

Manzikert, battle of (1071), 437

Manzini, Raimondo, 1083, 1236

Manzoni, Alessandro, 1202, 1537

Manzoni Association, 1134

Manzu, Giacomo, 1083

Mao Tse-tung, 859, 1218

maps. *See* cartography

Maraini, Antonio, 1372

Marangoni, Giovanni, 70, 100

Marat, Jean-Paul, 612

Maratta, Carlo, 118, 1271

Marazzoli, Marco, 298–299

marbles, ancient, 1024, 1025

Marca, P. de, 617

Marcella, 1011, 1045

Marcellina (sister of Ambrose), 947, 1375

Marcellinus, **966–967**, 993; cemetery of, 259, 478, 1496; differentiated from Marcellus I, 967; elected bishop of Rome, 180; persecutions and, 1156; theft of relics of, 261

Marcellinus, Ammianus, 882, 1044, 1364, 1563

Marcello, Christopher, 284

Marcellus I, 444, 543, **967–968**, 1563–1564; elected bishop of Rome, 180; tomb of, 1496

Marcellus II, **968–969**, 1124, 1125, 1128; arms, 114; Council of Trent participation, 968, 1125, 1519; Jesuits and, 826; Vatican Library and, 887, 1597, 1598; virtues of, 969

Marcellus of Ancyra, 428, 479, 562, 883

Marche pontificale (Gounod), 299, 744

Marches, 23, 314, 582, 672, 675, 1561; Borgia conquest of, 27; Italian unification and, 1107, 1538, 1555; Napoléon's occupation of, 1103, 1187, 1188; in Papal States, 1098, 1100(map), 1101, 1102, 1104, 1105(map), 1342, *See also* Ancona

Marchetti, 932, 1212

Marchi, Giuseppe, 100, 260

Marcia (mistress of Commodus), 1154, 1612

Marcian, emperor of Byzantium, 34, 200, 916, 917, 1056, 1426

Marcian of Arles, 959, 1431, 1455

Marcinkus, Paul, 583

Marcion, 57, 697, 1171

Marcionism, 523–524, 697, 1394

Volume Key: Volume 1, pages 1–614; volume 2, pages 615–1266; volume 3, pages 1267–1637.

1729

Marconi, Guglielmo, 1205, 1444, 1600

Marcus Aurelius, emperor of Rome, 618, 1154, 1314–1315; statue of, 1359, 1362

Mardi Gras. *See* Carnival

Marefoschi, Cardinal, 1021

Marengo, battle of (1800), 1185

Marenzio, Luca, 298

Margaret, queen of Spain, 1470

Margaret of Austria, 345, 1124, 1622, 1624

Margaret of Durazzo, 192

Margaret of Provence, 51

Marguerite. *See* Margaret

Maria Laach, abbey of, 954–955

Maria Maddelena dei Pazzi, St., 349

Maria Theresa, empress of Austria, 169, 170, 869, 1535; Jansenism and, 867–868; neutrality on Jesuits, 358, 361

Maria-Carolina, queen of Naples, 361

Marian piety. *See* Virgin Mary

Mariani, Camillo, 1369

Mariano da Firenze, 1170

Marie de Medicis, queen of France, 929, 1470

Marie Louise, empress of France, 1187, 1272

Marie of Savoy, 349

Marie Thérèse, queen of France, 1347

Marignano, battle of (1515), 344, 926, 927, 1175, 1623

Marini, Leonard, 263

Marini, Piero, 285

Marinus I, also Martin II, 180, 426, 590, 682, **969–970**, 973, 1066, 1459

Marinus II, also Martin III, 15, **970**, 973, 1065

Marinus of Bomarzo, 15

Maris the Persian, 1146

Maritain, Jacques, 309, 310, 512, 1010, 1024, 1141, 1323

Marittima, 1538

Mark, **970–971**, 1159; emblem of, 693; *pallium*, 1608; tiara and, 1490; tomb of, 1496

Mark (St. Mark the Apostle), 32, 33, 569

Mark, Gospel of, 631, 1158

Markward of Anweiler, 439, 786, 789

Maron, Anton von, 119

Maronite College, 379, 404, 664, 1000

Maronites, 86, 319, 429; canon law, 370; Lateran IV and, 998; return to Roman Church, 1527

Marozia (senatrix), 254, 838, 839, 840, 922, 1097, 1332, 1460

marriage: Catholic/non-Catholic, 530, 674, 819, 1191, 1248–1250; Church authority on, 214, 407, 408, 429; *cicisbeo* companion, 1507; civil code in Germany and Austria, 892, 893; civil code in Italy, 1542; of clergy. *See* clerical marriage; Code of Canon Law (1917) on, 365; Decretum of Gratian on, 491–492, 1249; dispensations, 482, 483, 504, 505; encyclicals on (1930; 1968), 1141, 1143, 1204, 1584; as incompatible with perfection, 895, 896; Lateran pacts and, 902, 903; parental consent issue, 1522; Pauline privilege and, 1248–1249; Petrine privilege and, 1249–1250; Pontifical Council for the Family and, 434; Syllabus of Errors on, 1474–1475; theological debate on, 1544; Tridentine decree on, 1522

Marrou, Henri-Irénée, 101

Marseilles, plague epidemic, 1220, 1222

Marsilio of Padua, 98, 131–132, 316, 390, 513–514, 629, 849, 1109, 1485

Marsini, Antonio, 1026

Martì, Ramon, 872

Martial (Roman writer), 151

Martial of Emérita, 1455

Martial, St., 845

Martímont, Aimé-Georges, 955

Martin, king of Aragon, 165

Martin I, 6, 71, 74, 142, 196, 432, 531, **971–972**; condemned for high treason, 16, 972; deposition and exile of, 495, 972, 1305; evangelization by, 997; Franks and, 598; heresy charges and, 701, 971–972; martyrdom of, 122, 202, 971, 972, 1184, 1497; poor health of, 1416

Martin II. *See* Marinus I

Martin III. *See* Marinus II

Martin IV, 657, 735, **972–974**, 1554, 1555; Angevins and, 51, 736, 973; arms, 113; Boniface VIII and, 189; Clement IV and, 332; crusade against Eastern Church, 440, 973; Dante's consignment to purgatory, 481, 482; Jewish protection policy, 872; as Nicholas III successor, 1037; Nicholas IV and, 1038, 1039; non-Roman residence, 1302; tomb of, 1499, 1500

Martin V, 627, 798, **974–977**; Angevins and, 54, 55; annona, 60; archives and, 1604; arms, 114; arts patronage, 537, 976, 1380; [Benedict XIII] replacement by, 72, 165, 167, 637; benefice reserves reestablishment, 1298; camerlengo, 220; cardinal protector and, 247; ceremonial, 284; chef for, 302–303; Church unity and, 103, 111, 132, 242, 429, 974, 1101, 1246; Colosseum and, 388; conclave electing, 393; Curia and, 292, 461, 462, 464, 975; datary and, 482; Dominicans and, 508; Eugene IV and, 535; exemptions and, 1233; finances and, 580–581; first cardinal "in petto" and, 245; Franciscans and, 594; health and vitality of, 1416; Holy Year and, 725, 726; honorary protonotaries, 300; indulgences limitation, 774; infallibility and, 777; [John XXIII] submission to, 852; Lateran rebuilding and, 1360; medallions, 984; mendicant orders and, 593; military actions, 111; missions in New World and, 999; Naples and, 217; nepotism and, 975, 1032, 1048, 1049; papal authority restoration by, 1101, 1102; papal chapel and, 296; papal household and, 738; pet parrot, 58; plague and, 1222; St. Mary Major and, 1368; tax collection, 378; tomb of, 1361, 1500, 1502; Vatican Library and, 1597

Martin, Gregory, 1307

Martin, Jacques, 688

Martin de Braga, 231

Martin of Alpartil, 164

Martin of Tours, St., 6, 145, 1348

Martin of Troppau, 488, 1065

Martin of Zalba, 163

Martin the Pole, 830

Martinelli, Biaggio, 285

Martinez de Chiaves, Antonio, 1361, 1363

Martini, Angelo, 496

Martini, Raymond, 75

Martini, Simon, 1116

Martinian, St., 1497

Volume Key: Volume 1, pages 1–614; volume 2, pages 615–1266; volume 3, pages 1267–1637.

Martinists, 603

Marty, archbishop of Paris, 858, 864

Martyrdom of St. Petronilla (Le Guerchin), 971

martyrologies, 210, 232–233, 261

Martyrologium Romanum, 664–665, 1296

martyrs: antique monasticism and, 1011; basilica on grave of, 549; *beatus/beatissimus* terminology for, 145; canonization and, 232–233, 268; Catacomb tombs, 260, 261–262; celebration of cult of, 210; Colosseum as site for, 388; Damasus I cult promotion, 478–479, 1388; Diocletian's persecutions and, 1156, 1316; feasts of, 1453; papal altar and, 38; Peter and Paul as, 3, 548, 1119, 1153, 1158–1159; pilgrimages and, 1163, 1164, 1165; popes' tombs, 1495, 1496; Roman persecutions, 1315, 1316, 1432; Roman torture of Christians, 1153, 1432; veneration as saints, 1387, 1388–1389, 1392, *See also* relics, veneration of

Marucchi, Orazio, 101

Maruffi, Silvestro, 509

Marx, Karl. *See* Marxism and the papacy

Marxism and the papacy, **977–980**; Christian Democracy and, 309–310, 311; John Paul I and, 858; John Paul II and, 863; *ostpolitik* and, 1084–1086; Pius XI encyclical against, 110, 305, 978, 1110, 1209, 1447, 1449, 1462, 1629, 1631; Pius XII and, 1137, 1215–1216; Vatican II and, 1085; World War I events and, 1628; World War II and, 1629, 1631, 1632, *See also* cold war; Communist countries

Mary. *See* Virgin Mary

Mary I, queen of England, 54, 887, 913, 982, 1128, 1289

Mary II, queen of England, 55

Mary (Stuart), queen of Scots, 1177

Mary of Burgundy, 686

Marzi, Gian Battista, 1481

Masaccio, 1368, 1380

Mascherino, Ottaviano, 1025, 1269

Masella, Benedetto Aloisi, 221, 575, 935, 1574

Masolino, 1368

Masonic orders. *See* Freemasonry

masquerade, 249–250

Mass: bell ringing, 152; chants, 948, 949; medieval, 1275; novendials, 1056; Reformation suppression of, 1287; Slavonic, 837; Sunday hours, 1217; Tridentine dogma on, 1521; Tridentine missal and, 995–996, *See also* Eucharist; liturgy

Mass, papal. *See* chapel, papal

Mass, papal: liturgical objects, **980**, 1461

mass media. *See* media, communication, and the Vatican; social communications

Massarelli, Angelo, 968, 1519

Massimi, Massimo, 370

Massimo, Camillo, 350

Mastai-Ferretti, Giovanni Maria. *See* Pius IX

Master, Order of the, 1013

master of the Chapel, 296, 297, 300

master of the Sacred Palace, 457, 627, **980–981**, 1094; camera possession permission from, 1163; Dominicans as, 507, 508, 512, 981

masters of Ceremonies, 284–285, 294

Mater et magistra (1961 encyclical), 310, 526, 856, 1110, 1447, 1449; subsidiarity principle, 1463

Maternus, Julius Firmicus, 75

Mathias Corvino, king of Hungary, 798, 1122, 1172

Mathieu, Pierre, 363, 364

Matilda (of Canossa), countess of Tuscany, 102, 278, 330, 789, 1281, 1551, 1553; bequest to Roman Church by, 961; Canossa and, 238, 239; investiture controversy mediation by, 238, 239; monument in St. Peter's, 1383, 1386; Papal States and, 1098; tomb of, 1562; Victor III support by, 1614

Matilda (of England), 276, 533, 651, 784, 960

matrimonial law. *See* marriage

Mattei, Alessandro, 1184

Mattei collection, 1025

Mattei, Gaspare, 801

Matteo de Siena, 665

Matthew (St. Matthew the Apostle), 1244, 1499

Matthew, Gospel of, 534, 544, 631, 1157, 1160

Matthew, Pierre, 231

Matthew of Paris, 93, 653

Matthias of Janow, 67

Matthieu, P., 228

Mattioli, A., 1021, 1022

Mattuzzi, Pietro, 1338–1339

Maupertuis, Pierre-Louis, 170

Maur, St., 268

Mauri, Carlo, 1464

Mauri, Giles, 596

Mauri, Lorenzo, 221

Maurice (Byzantine *cartulary*), 1319, 1354

Maurice, Paul, 263

Maurice of Braga. *See* Gregory VIII

Maurice of Savoy, 243, 1560

Maurice of Saxony, 887, 1288

Maurists, 168, 169

Mauritus (Burdinus). *See* [Gregory VIII]

Maurras, Charles, 944, 1397

Maurus, archbishop of Ravenna, 1273

Maury, Cardinal, 1184, 1186, 1187, 1189

mausoleums, 259, 1377, 1378 (*see also* catacombs; tombs of the popes)

Maxentius, emperor of Rome, 417, 418, 543; defeat at Milvian Bridge, 993, 1156, 1316; *lapsi* controversy and, 967–968

Maxentius (Scythian monk), 738

Maximian, archbishop of Ravenna, 1273

Maximian, emperor of Rome, 1156, 1316

Maximilian I, Holy Roman emperor, 26–27, 424, 686, 716, 885, 886, 898, 927, 928, 1622, 1623

Maximilian II, Holy Roman emperor, 936

Maximilian of Austria. *See* Maximilian I, Holy Roman emperor

Maximilian of Bavaria, 669

Maximilla, 698

Maximin Daia, emperor of Rome, 417

Maximinus Thrax, emperor of Rome, 63, 1155, 1223

Maximus of Valencia, 184

Maximus the Confessor, St., 202, 204, 531, 1487

Maximus the Thracian, emperor of Rome, 557, 1317

May Laws (1873; Germany), 892

Mayeur, Jean-Marie, 306, 1631

Maymo of Faversham, 284

Mazarin, Jules, 510, 801, 802, 803, 1561; Alexander VII and, 28, 30; Jansenism and, 823–824

Mazio family (Giancomo, Francesco, and Giuseppe), 376

Volume Key: Volume 1, pages 1–614; volume 2, pages 615–1266; volume 3, pages 1267–1637.

1731

Mazzella, Cardinal, 1075

Mazzini, Giuseppe, 1536, 1537, 1539; monument to, 1018; Roman Republic and, 1324, 1325

Mazzochi, Giuseppe, 1362

McClosky, John, 1357

McQuaid, Bernard, 40

medallions, papal, 10, **981–984**, 1065; mosaic, 1022, 1492; Peter imagery, 1161

media, communication, and the Vatican, **984–985**; Curia and, 473; Paul VI and, 1139, 1142; photography and, 1163; Pius XI and, 1205; Pius XII use of, 1215; pontifical council and, 435–436; press office, 984, 985, 1049–1050, 1236–1240; private life of pope and, 1248; social communications, 1441–1447; travels of John Paul II and, 1512; Vatican II and, 1575; Vaticanists and, 1606–1607, *See also* cinema, popes and; Vatican Radio; Vatican Television

mediation. *See* arbitration, papal

Medici, Alessandro de', 345, 1624

Medici, Alessandro Ottoviano de'. *See* Leo XI

Medici, Catherine de'. *See* Catherine de Médicis

Medici, Charles de', 35

Medici, Cosimo I de', 888, 929, 1502

Medici family, 60, 105, 667; Alexander VI and, 26; arms, 695; arts patronage, 1089–1090; banking activity, 39, 82, 136, 137, 851, 884; career and, 247; Clement VII as last pope of, 343, 345, 1123; French wars in Italy and, 1621–1624; Leo X and, 926–927, 928, 1123; Leo XI and, 929; Pius IV and, 1175; Sixtus IV break with, 1434

Medici, Gian Angelo de'. *See* Pius IV

Medici, Giovanni de'. *See* Leo X

Medici, Giuliano de', 343, 884, 926, 928

Medici, Giulio de'. *See* Clement VII

Medici, Ippolito de', 345, 928

Medici, Laurent de', 344

Medici, Lorenzo de', 343, 799, 884, 926, 927, 928, 1434

Medici, Maddalena de', 799

Medici, Pietro de', 26, 1621

medicinal penalty, 1149–1151

medicine, 1547, 1548; Avignon papal doctors, 457; confraternity hospitals, 1309, 1310; John XXI studies and practice, 846, 847; papal embalming, 486; papal services, 1416–1417; plague treatment, 1221

medieval universities. *See* universities, medieval

Meersseman, G. A., 1312

Mehmet II, sultan, 1122, 1526

Meir, Golda, 877

Melanchthon, 686, 1125, 1287, 1288, 1355

Melchiades. *See* Miltiades

Melchisedech, 786

Melecea of Antioch, 69

Meletius, 419, 428

Melfi, 1552

Melfi, Constitutions of (1231), 315

Melfi, synod of (1089), 1282, 1552

Melior, Jacques and Agapitus, 1417

Melitian schism, 1427

Melkites, 86

Mellini, Paolo, 1362

Mellitus, 142, 187, 188

Mellor, A., 609

Melquart, cult of, 443

melusine (felt hat), 620

menageries, 58

Menander the Protector, 153

Menas, patriarch of Constantinople, 14, 15, 564, 1145, 1617, 1618

Mendelssohn, Felix, 257

mendicant orders: Alexander IV and, 23–24; Antichrist charges and, 66; banking activities, 136; Celestine V, 702; Church doctrine and, 133; exemptions and, 553, 702; Gregory XV bull, 510; Honorius IV and, 736; Innocent III and, 788; Jewish persecution by, 871–872; as missionaries, 998; missions to Far East, 348; movements against privileges of, 615; Nicholas III and, 702, 1038; Nicholas IV and, 1039; [Nicholas V] support by, 1040; papal allies, 280, 509, 593; reforms, 1275–1276; secular teachers' quarrel with (1253–1259), 792; Sixtus IV and, 1435; Sixtus V and, 1436, *See also* Dominicans; Franciscans

Ménestrier, Claude-François, 1261

Mengs, Anton Raphael, 117, 120, 1091, 1092, 1117

Menotti, Ciro, 672

Mentana action (1867), 1643–1644

Mercadier, Gérald, 58

mercantilism, 171

Mercati, Angelo, 5, 70

Mercati, Giovanni, 1598

Mercedarian Order, 989

mercenaries. *See* armies, papal

Mercurius. *See* John II

Merici, Angela, 360

Merocles of Milan, 986

Mérode, Xavier de, 1017, 1645

Merovingians, 91, 142, 597–598, 1319

Merry del Val, Raphael, 10, 364, 582, 1052, 1075, 1094; papal candidacy of, 1201; as Pius X secretary of state, 1197, 1211, 1464

Mesenguy (Jesuit), 359, 361

Messaggero (newspaper), 1238

messenger, papal. *See* cursor, apostolic

Messenger of Saint Anthony (Luciani), 857

Messmer, Sebastian, 40

Methodist churches, 904

Methodius, St., 541, 682, 837, 997, 1459

Metropolitan of the Province of Rome, 1495

Metternich, Klemens von, 672, 673, 674, 931, 1189, 1191

Metz, Diet of (1356), 796

Mexican Revolution, 977

Mexico: Catholic missions, 1343; diplomatic ties with Holy See, 503; Gregory XIII missions to, 664; Inquisition in, 816; John Paul II travel to, 10; papal arms composition, 692; Pius XI concerns and, 1208, 1209

Mexico, University of, 1544

Meyer de Schauense, Leopold, 1471

Mezzabarba, Ambrogio, 355, 1003

Mezzogiorno, 326, 1534

Michael, Archangel, 49, 65, 623; as Castel Sant'Angelo patron, 254

Michael, tsar of Russia, 1488

Volume Key: Volume 1, pages 1–614; volume 2, pages 615–1266; volume 3, pages 1267–1637.

1732

Michael I, emperor of Byzantium, 205

Michael II, emperor of Byzantium, 600

Michael III, emperor of Byzantium, 205, 206, 969, 1034

Michael VIII Palaeologus, emperor of Byzantium, 51, 208, 319, 440, 794, 1555; Eastern-Roman Church unification attempt, 657–658, 794; Martin IV excommunication of, 973

Michael Cerularius, patriarch of Constantinople, 925, 1043, 1280; Leo IX mutual excommunication, 206, 1245, 1395, 1461

Michael of Cesena, 133, 592, 849, 850

Michel Cerulaire, patriarch of Constantinople, 318

Michelangelo, 104, 549, 1029, 1116, 1378, 1506; Capitol design, 1116; Castel Sant'Angelo project, 255; Clement VII and, 928; in expatriate Roman confraternity, 1308–1309; film portrayal of, 322; Holy See commissions, 1089, 1092, 1093; Julius II and, 885, 886, 1091, 1092, 1340; Julius III and, 887; papal draping of *Last Judgment* by, 1093; Paul III and, 1127, 1382; Pius III commissions, 1174; Pius IV commissions, 1176; revenge against Martinelli, 285; St. Peter's dome design, 105–106, 107, 271, 273, 726, 1117, 1340, 1344, 1382; Sistine Chapel ceiling painting, 285, 886, 1091, 1117, 1340, 1429–1431

Michelezzo, Bernardo, 343, 1380, 1502

Michiel, Giovanni, 1121

Michonneau, Father, 1397

Mieszko of Poland, 843, 997

Migazzi, Cardinal, 867, 868, 869

Migliorati, Cosma de'. *See* Innocent VII

Mignard, Nicholas, 117

Migne, J. P., 228, 674

Mignot, Eudoxe-Irénée, 1007

Milan, **985–987**; Alexander II and, 17; Alexander VI and, 26; [Anacletus II] support in, 42; as banking center, 136, 137, 583; barbarians and, 987; Callistus III and, 218; Catholic University, 177; Church-State powers and, 1535; Constantine I and, 420–421; destruction and rebuilding of (12th-century), 20; first recorded bishop, 986; French domination of, 1103, 1621, 1623–1624; Great Schism and, 634; Inquisition abolishment, 819; Italian unity and, 1535, 1539; jurisdictionalism and, 888; Lombard occupation, 987; Nicholas II reforms and, 1036, 1044; Nicholas V and, 1041; Pataria movement, 17, 700, 1036; Paul VI as archbishop of, 1136–1137; Pius XI and, 1102, 1200, 1201; schism with Church, 1147, 1148; Sforza reestablishment in, 1623, 1624; vicar of (4th century), 1464–1466, *See also* Ambrose of Milan, St.

Milan Edict of Tolerance (313), 417, 844, 1003, 1316

Milanese rite, 948, 949, 951

military forces. *See* armies, papal; Zouaves, pontifical

military orders, **987–990**, 1016; Clement V and, 131, 333, 334, 429, 988, 989; Holy See recognition of, 488; list of, 988–990, *See also* specific orders

military ordinariates, **990–992**

Milites Sancti Sepulcri, 722

militia christi. *See* holy war

Militia of Jesus Christ, 987

Militia of the Glorious Virgin Mary. *See* Gaudenti

Militiades (or Melchiades), 251

millenarianism, 64, 65–66, 67; as heresy, 703, 704; Lateran V on, 899; prophecy and, 1260, 1261, *See also* Apocalypse; eschatology

millennium Holy Year, 729

Miller, Giovanni C. di, 1180

Miltiades (or Melchiades), 419, 432, **993–994**; Constantine's letter to, 993, 1156; successor Silvester I, 1418; tomb of, 1496

Milvian Bridge, battle of (312), 417, 418, 993, 1156, 1316

Milzetti-Machetti, Giacinta, 1192

Minardi, Tommaso, 1372–1373

Mincius, John. *See* [Benedict X]

Mindaugas of Lithuania, 998

Mindszenty, Cardinal, 1085–1086, 1215

Minghetti, Marco, 1018, 1537

miniaturization, mosaic, 1022

Mino da Fiesole, 1380, 1428, 1503

Mino del Reame, 1368

Minocchi, 1199

Minucius Felix, 75

minutante, **994–995**; in hierarchy, 7, 994–995

Mirabilia (guide to Rome), 1167

miracles: causes of canonization and, 268, 269, 270, 271, 283; Lateran V on fake, 899; prophecies and, 1260

Misensus, 572

Miserere (Allegri), 298

missal, 951, 952, 953, 954, 1275; Clement VIII and, 348; Roman stations, 1454; Urban VIII reform of, 1562, *See also* breviary, Roman

missal, Tridentine, 213, 954, **993–996**, 1109, 1175, 1178, 1277, 1289, 1522

Missing Persons Bureau (Vatican), 174

Mission Day of Priests, 1451

Mission Day of the Sick, 1451

Mission Exhibition (1925; Rome), 1205

Missionary Childhood. *See* Holy Childhood, Pontifical Society of the

missionary colleges, 378–379, 1001, 1002

Missionary Union, Pontifical, **996**, 1450

missions, **996–1005**; Middle Ages, **996–999**; modern era, 27, 668, **999–1004**; contemporary era, **1004–1005**; in Balkans and Near East, 1039; Benedict XIV and, 168, 169; Benedict XV and, 173, 176, 1110; Clement III and, 348; Clement V and, 335; Clement X and, 351; Clement XI and, 355; coin commemoratives, 375; Dominican, 506, 508, 509–510; in Eastern Europe, 522–523, 539, 542; Gregory I approach, 142, 641, 996–997; Gregory IX and, 655; Gregory XI and, 659; Gregory XIII and, 465, 664; Gregory XVI and, 675; Holy Childhood Society, 708–709; Innocent X and, 802; from Ireland and Britain, 518, 552; Israeli law against, 877; Jesuit, 169, 529, 664, 669, 827, 999, 1000, 1001, 1130, 1343; Jesuit expulsions, 1004; Jesuit local customs accomodations, 169, 355, 529, 1002–1004, 1345 (*see also* Chinese rites); John XVIII and, 845; native clergy, 1002, 1004, 1005, 1218, 1255, 1256, 1257, 1373–1374; to New World, 27, 509–510, 669, 999, 1002, 1255, 1343–1344; Paul V and, 1130; Petrine privilege and, 1249–1250; Pius XI and, 1205; Pontifical Mission Societies, 1450–1451; poor relief, 1224–1225; printing press and, 1444; Propaganda Fide creation and, 667, 668–669, 1254–1258, 1343; Propagation of the Faith and, 1259, 1343; of St. Paul the Apostle, 1118–1119; of St. Peter the Apostle, 1158; as separate from colonialism, 176, 1002; training colleges, 378–379, 1001, 1002; Urban VIII and, 1561, *See also*

Volume Key: Volume 1, pages 1–614; volume 2, pages 615–1266; volume 3, pages 1267–1637.

1733

evangelization; Evangelization of People, Congregation for the; Missionary Union, Pontifical; Propaganda Fide, Congregation of

Mit brennender Sorge (1937 encyclical), 305, 526, 828, 874, 978, 1110, 1203, 1209, 1212, 1447, 1449, 1629, 1631

miter, papal. *See* tiara

Mithra/Mithraism, 443

Mocenni, Imario, 582

modalism, 214, 699, 1640

Modena, 345, 1538; in Papal States, 17(map), 1342

modernism, **1005–1009**; antimodernist oath of 1910, 1251; apologetics against, 78, 79, 613; Benedict XV and, 172, 173, 1110; *Civiltà Cattolica* condemnation, 326; clerical effects of, 1535; Dominicans and, 512; as error in Pius IX *Syllabus*, 1195; fundamentalism vs., 613–614, 615; Gregory XVI opposition, 78, 670, 673, 1104, 1443, 1535; Lefebvre schismatic protest against, 1397–1398; Leo XIII view of, 860, 1196, 1247; liberalism and, 943, 944; Movimento Cattolico and, 1023; narrow vs. broad definitions of, 1005; papism vs., 1109, 1110; Pius IX condemnations, 860, 874, 1010, 1023, 1109, 1195, 1196, 1247, 1472–1475 (*see also* Syllabus of Errors); Pius X rejection, 79, 307, 1198–1199; Pius XI and, 1203; Pius XII positiion on, 1211; social communications and, 1443; Vatican I condemnation, 429

modernity, **1009–1011**; definition of western, 1005; John XXIII and, 853, 1247; John Paul II and, 1010–1011, 1247; Judaism and, 873, 874; liberalism and, 944, 979; modernism relationship, 1005; papal rejections of, 979–980, 1203, 1247; Paul VI and, 1010, 1247; prophetism and critics of, 1263; seminary changes, 1410

Moehler, Johann-Adam, 954

Mohammed. *See* Muhammad

Mohla Academy (Kiev), 1531

Mohyla, Piotr, 1531

Molchi, Francesco, 1383

Molina, Luis de, 348

Molinism, 348, 823, 825

Molinos, Miguel, 806, 1267, 1268

Mollat, M., 1223

Moluccas, 1561

Mommsen, Theodor, 5

Momo, Giuseppe, 1026

Monaco, 399

Monarchia Sicula, 1552

monarchianism, 698, 708

monastic schools, 379, 1543

monasticism, **1011–1016**; bell ringing, 151; Enlightenment critique, 528; Innocent X reforms, 802; missions, 998; papal evangelization and, 545–546; reforms, 1275–1276; Roman Curia ties, 450, *See also* religious orders; *specific orders*

monasticism, antiquity, **1011–1013**; Egyptian, 33, 34, 1011, 1012, 1013; Greek (in Italy), 638

monasticism, Middle Ages, 156, **1014–1016**; Benedict VII privileges and reforms, 156, 157; clerical education, 378, 379; Dominican, 506–507; exemptions, 551–554; military orders and, 987–988; north of Rome, 1329; reforms, 1280; simony and, 1424; vows of poverty, chastity, and obedience, 1011

Monçon, treaty of (1626), 1561

Mondeville, Henri de, 486

Mondy, Pierre, 322

money. *See* coins, papal; finances, papal; taxation

money changers. *See* banking and the papacy

Mongolia, 998

Mongols, 66, 440; Holy Russia and, 1488; Lyon II delegation, 658; missions and, 998; Nicholas IV and, 1039; Turks confused with, 1526

Monica, St., 976

Moñino, José, 361–362, 828

Monnot, Pierre, 1362

Monoenergism, 202

Monophysitism, 44, 564, 705, 1087; Agapitus I and, 14, 15; Antioch and, 69; Byzantium and, 198, 200, 201, 202; Chalcedon opposition by, 1318; Christology of, 35, 672, 699, 916, 1617; Egypt and, 36, 202; Ephesus and, 916; Gregory XIII reconciliatory moves, 664; *Henoticon* and, 200, 572, 1427; Hormisdas and, 737, 738, 1145; John II and, 833; Justinian and, 865; Leo I and, 915, 916, 917; Monotuelitism and, 701; orthodoxy compromise, 730; Simplicius and, 1425, 1426; Three Chapters schism and, 1146

Monosilo, Salvatore, 1372

monotheism, 444

Monothelitism, 16, 202, 204, 834, 919; Constantine I and, 420; Constantinople III and, 428; Martin I condemnation of, 971, 972; Roman council condemnations, 432; Vitalian opposition, 1619

Monotuelitism, 701

Montagnini affair, 1198

Montaigne, Michel, 76, 758, 1170

Montalembert, 673, 675, 1195

Montalto, Alessandro, 466

Montalto family, 667

Montanism, 48, 523, 698, 1550

Montanus, 698

Monte, Pietro da, 378, 911

Monte Cassino, 158, 276, 625, 732, 740, 741, 1640; Benedict and, 1013; as intellectual center, 379; Lucius II and, 959; St. Paul's Outside the Walls monastery, 1373; Saracen sack of, 1393; Stephen IX (X) and, 1461; Victor III as abbot of, 1613; as Victor III burial site, 1499

Monte Gargano, 623

Montecavallo, Pontifical Palace of. *See* Quirinal

Montecchi, Mattia, 1324

Montecitorio Palace, 9

Montefeltro, Federico da, 1042, 1172, 1434

Montefeltro, Guidantonio da, 111, 976

Montegaudio (Mons Gaudii) Order, 989

Montelongo, Gregorio da, 910

Montelupo, Raffaele de, 868, 869

Montepulciano, Francesco de, 67

Monteruc, Pierre de, 1558

Montesa (Our Lady) Order, 990

Montesquieu, Baron de Brède de la, 68, 170, 360

Montfort, Louis-Marie Grignion de, St., 1347

Monti, Vincenzo, 1183

Monticelli, Ottaviano de'. *See* [Victor IV (V)]

Montidi Pietà, 376

Montini, Giorgio, 1133

Montini, Giovanni Battista Cardinal. *See* Paul VI

Volume Key: Volume 1, pages 1–614; volume 2, pages 615–1266; volume 3, pages 1267–1637.

1734

Montini, Lodovico, 310
Montlauzun, Guillaume de, 227
Montmartre, vow of (1534), 826
Montone, Braccio da, 111, 975
Montpellier, Hospital of, 454, 1307
Montpellier, University of, 1544, 1548, 1549, 1556
Montrocher, Guy de, 1275
Montsegur massacre, 813, 814
monumentality and Roman urbanism (1848–1922), **1016–1018**, 1116
monuments, Roman, 107; Colosseum, 387–388; commemorative, 1018; medieval repair, 1329; Middle Ages, 1327; Pantheon, 1095–1096; papal patronage, 1116–1117, 1122, 1127; Paschal I and, 1112; post-Catholic reform, 1344; traveler's writings on, 1504, *See also* architecture, papal
Moors. *See* Saracens
Morales, Christobal de, 297, 298, 1002
Moralia on Job (Gregory I), 641
Moravia: Anabaptists, 704; Catholicism in, 1130; missions in, 682, 837, 997; Slavic liturgy dispute, 1459
Moravia, Alberto, 760, 761
Moravian Brothers, 669, 704
More, Jacques de, 703
Morelli, Cosimo, 1181
Moreschi, Alessandro, 257
Morichini, C. L., 1310–1311
Moriconi bank, 82
Morin, J., 954
Moriscos revolt (1569), 937
Moro, Aldo, 305, 310, 311, 859, 864, 1364
Morocco, 399, 938; John Paul II speech in, 1511
Morone, Aleandro, 1125
Morone, Giovanni, 818, 1124, 1276, 1519, 1520; Holy Office imprisonment and trial of, 1128
Moroni, Gaetano, 143, 294–295
Morosini, Tommaso, 207
Morra Benevento, Alberto de. *See* Gregory VIII
Morrone, Pietro del. *See* Celestine V
Morselli, Guido, 756–757, 761
Mortara, Edgardo, 873, 874
mosaics, **1018–1022**; excavations in St. Peter's, 547; Gregorian reform iconography, 1284; heraldic symbols on, 688; medallions, 1022, 1492; painting reproductions, 1090, 1385; Paschal I commissions, 1112; Renaissance and modern period, 1021–1022; restoration in St. Peter's apse, 786; St. John Lateran, 1019, 1021, 1116, 1360, 1361, 1363; St. Mary Major, 1020, 1364, 1365, 1366, 1367, 1368; St. Paul's Outside the Walls, 1370, 1372, 1373; St. Peter's, 1377, 1378, 1379, 1383, 1386
Mosca della Torre, Paganino di, 1336
Moscow: patriarchate of, 1531; Third Rome, 1487–1488
Moses: Peter portrayed as, 1161; subsidiarity concept and, 1462
mosetta (ermine cape), abolishment of, 267
motets, 296, 298
Mother of the Gods (pagan cult), 441–442
motion pictures. *See* cinema, popes and
Motta, Giuseppe, 175
motto, list of popes', 1262–1263
Mouton, Adrien, 117

Mouvement Républicain Populaire, 309
movies. *See* cinema, popes and
Movimento Cattolico, **1023–1024**, 1132, 1135
Movimento laureati, 1024, 1207
Moyes, 1075
Mozarabic Church, 18
Mozarabic liturgy, 952
mozzetta (cape), 620
Mozzi banks, 136, 452
MRP. *See* Mouvement Républicain Populaire
Mucante, Francesco, 285
Mucante, Gianpaolo, 285
Muezzinzâde Ali Pasha, 937
Muhammad, prophet, 76, 1319, 1393
Mühldorf, battle of (1322), 850
mule (shoe), 621
mules (animals), 58
Muller, Ignace, 868
Mun, Albert de, 306, 934, 935, 1448
Mun, Robert de, 935
Munich Accords (1938), 1206, 1213, 1630
Muñoz, Gil. *See* Clement VIII
Müntz, Eugène, 485, 1492
Müntzer, Thomas, 704
mural maps, 253–254
Murat, king of Naples, 1104, 1187, 1188, 1189
Muratori, Lodovico, 528, 1225
Murdac, Henry, 533
Muret, Marc-Antoine, 1296–1297
Murol, Jean de, 339
Murri, Romolo, 306, 307, 1008, 1023, 1197, 1198, 1199
Museo Capitolino, 1117
Museo Clementino, 1025
Museo Gregoriano Egizio, 1026
Museo Gregoriano Etrusco, 1026
Museo Gregoriano Profano, 1025, 1026, 1363
Museo Missionario Etnologico, 1026, 1363
Museo Pio-Clementino, 1025, 1091, 1092, 1117, 1180
Museo Pio-Cristiano, 1026, 1363
Museo Storico Vaticano, 1026, 1363
Museum of Christian Antiquities, 171
museums, Vatican, **1024–1026**; archeological collections, 100, 1117, 1180; Benedict XV and, 177; Clement XII and, 357, 1025, 1092; Clement XIII and, 359, 1025; entry fees, 10; Golden Rose specimens, 1347; painting commissions, 1091; papal patrons, 1117; St. John Lateran and, 1363; St. Peter's sarcophagus, 549; Vatican Library and, 1598
music, 295–300; Benedict XIV anti-baroque measures, 169; castrati of the papal chapel, 256–257, 297, 298; Catholic reform, 1340, 1341; Clement VI and, 457; Gregorian chant, 298, 948, 950–951, 952, 954, 1198, 1619; hymnal portrayals of Rome, 747; Julius III and, 887; Leo X sponsorship, 299, 927; liturgical, 954, 1198, 1412, 1619; liturgical chant, 948–949; Palestrina's Mass of Pope Marcellus, 968; Palestrina supporters, 298, 666; papal hymn, 194, 744–745, 949, 1562; Pius X modifications, 1198; polyphonic, 60, 298, 457, 1435; Roman liturgical songs, 948–951; traveler's view of, 1506
Musica Festiva (hymn), 744

Volume Key: Volume 1, pages 1–614; volume 2, pages 615–1266; volume 3, pages 1267–1637.

1735

Muslims. *See* Arabs; Islam; Saracens

Mussolini, Benito, 308, 322, 1136, 1541; Holy See diplomacy and, 1135; monumentality of, 1018; papal concordat with, 397, 901, 902 (*see also* Lateran pacts); Pius XI and, 1207; Pius XII and, 1213; view of Church by, 903; World War II and, 1629, 1630–1631, 1633, 1634

Mustafa, Domenico, 257

Muziano, Girolamo, 1021, 1090, 1092, 1383, 1385

Muzzarelli, Emanuele, 1324

Mylne, Robert, 120

mysticism, 603; Anabaptist and, 704; artists in Rome, 121; of Catherine of Siena, 265–266; Dominican, 506; laity and, 896; Quietist and, 1268

Nag Hammadi, 696, 697

"Nag's Head story" (Anglican ordination), 1073

name choices of popes. *See* onomastics, pontifical

Nanino, Giovanni Maria, 297–298, 1340

Nantes, Edict of (1598), 348

Napier, John, 68

Naples, kingdom of: Alexander VI and, 26, 27; Angevin dynasty, 50–54, 337, 676, 974; Anjou dynastic rights, 1621; Avignon and, 102; Benedict XIV dealings with, 169; Blessed Hat and Sword gift to, 182; Bourbons in, 357, 1623, 1624; chinea tribute, 303, 304, 1180; Eugene IV and, 537; French wars for, 1621–1624; Great Schism and, 340–341, 633, 634, 660, 661, 662; Greek monasteries, 638; Guelphism, 676–677, 716; Holy Places and, 722; Innocent VIII and, 798; Innocent XII and, 807; Inquisition abolishment, 819; Inquisition in, 817; Italian unity and, 1535, 1539, 1540; Jesuit expulsion from, 359, 362; jurisdictionalism and, 888, 889, 1180; Martin V and, 111; Napoléon and, 586, 1186; nepotism, 1032; Nicholas V and, 1041; in papal domain, 661, 1103; as papal feudal holding, 58, 1621; papal nunciature, 1059; Saracens in, 1393; Sixtus IV rout of, 1434; Urban VI refuge in, 1558, *See also* Normans of southern Italy and Sicily; Two Sicilies, kingdom of the

Naples, University of, 1544

Napoleon (film), 322

Napoléon I, emperor of France, 1272, 1544; arms of, 691; ban on castrati, 257; banner colors of, 138; Castel Sant'Angelo and, 255; French Church and, 1185, 1566; French Revolution and, 612–613; Holy Roman Empire and, 930; Hundred Days and, 1189; invasion of Italy, 670–671, 1183, 1263; Italian Jansenists and, 1536; military chaplaincy and, 990; papal coronation of, 423, 586, 1103, 1186; papal finances and, 377; Pius VII and, 99–100, 122–123, 398, 470, 496, 584–587, 618, 1103, 1182, 1183, 1185, 1186, 1598; Pius VIII and, 1190; Quirinal and, 1272; raids on Vatican museums, 1025; raids on Vatican treasures, 1378; regalia and, 1291; Roman monumentality and, 1016; Roman Republic and, 1320–1322; Vatican Archives damage, 1187, 1604, *See also* First French Empire and the papacy

Napoléon III, emperor of France, 671, 990, 1568, 1644, 1645; Italian unification and, 1107, 1195, 1539, 1540; Pius IX and, 1192; Roman Republic of 1849 and, 1326

Napoleonic Code, 228

Napoleonic Empire. *See* First French Empire and the papacy

Nardi, Lionello, 1134

Narses, 833, 1147, 1328

Nasir, Prince al-, 13

Natalius, 70

national cleric, **1027**

National Democratic League, 307

national determination, 174

National Guards, 1541

National Socialism. *See* Nazism

nationalism: Anglican schism and, 55; Italian unification and, 1533–1543; liberalism and, 943; papal abitration and, 99; Pius XI condemnation of, 309, 1201, 1206, 1208; socialism and, 978; Ultramontanism and, 1529, 1530; Uniates and, 1532; World War I and, 1628; World War II and, 1629

Native Americans, 1002

native clergy. *See* indigenous clergy

Nativity, 711

NATO (North Atlantic Treaty Organization), 1216

Natoire, Charles, 118

natural law, 1214, 1279, 1462, 1485; dispensation and, 504

natural rights, 99

naturalism, 1009, 1472

Naud, Gabriel, 1562

Navarre, 163, 340, 637

Navarro, Pedro, 1623

Navy, Congregation of the, 1438

navy, papal, **1027–1030**; banners, 138; crusades and, 218, 375, 653, 973, 1173; galley slaves, 1440–1441; Holy League and, 1177; Lepanto battle, 937–938, 1347; Saracen defeat by, 109; as Saracen defense, 1393; Sixtus IV and, 1434; Vatican City State and, 1588; Venetian fleet and, 938

Nazarenes, 1272

Nazism: Christian Democracy and, 308; invasion of and occupation of Poland, 860–861; Jewish persecutions, 853, 874 (*see also* Holocaust); John Paul II denuciation of, 876; papal concordat (1933), 397, 1110; papal status in Rome under, 1634–1636; persecution of Church by, 1629; Pius XI encyclical against, 305, 524, 526, 828, 874–875, 978, 1110, 1203, 1209, 1212, 1447, 1449, 1629, 1631; Pius XII and, 1212, 1214; rise of, 1207; Vatican Radio and, 1600, *See also* World War II

Nebbia, Cesare, 1090, 1091, 1362, 1383

Neckam, Alexander, 751

necropolis. *See* catacombs

Nectaire, Nicolas, 638

Negro, Silvio, 1236

Negroni, Andrea, 360

Neoclassicism, 1345, 1370

neo-Confucianism, 1003–1004

neo-Guelphism, 676, 1536, 1537, 1644

neo-Kantianism, 675

neo-Manicheaism, 897

neo-Platonism, 882

neo-Thomism, 828

neo-Ultramontanism, 618

nephew cardinal. *See* cardinal nephew; nepotism

nepotism, **1030–1033**; Alexander IV and, 22–23, 24, 685, 1031; Alexander VI and, 25–28, 1032; Alexander VII reforms, 30, 468; Alexander VIII and, 32, 468; Benedict VIII and, 156; Boniface VIII and, 1031, 1038, 1049; Boniface IX and, 192;

Volume Key: Volume 1, pages 1–614; volume 2, pages 615–1266; volume 3, pages 1267–1637.

1736

Callistus III and, 218, 1032; cardinal nephew, 245, 1402, 1469; cardinalate, 241, 242, 243, 1032–1033, 1356, 1357; Celestine III and, 277; Clement V and, 241, 335; Clement VI and, 129, 336, 658; Clement VII and, 345; Clement VIII and, 466; Clement XI condemnation draft, 352; conclave reform, 394; Curia, 466, 467, 468; Enlightenment reforms, 529; Eugene IV and, 534, 535, 536–537, 1032, 1048, 1121; Farnese family, 1032, 1049, 1102, 1103, 1123; Gregory XI and, 336, 658–659; Gregory XII and, 661, 662; Gregory XIV and, 666; Gregory XV and, 668, 1032; Hadrian V and, 685; Innocent IV and, 685, 793, 1031; Innocent VI and, 336, 795; Innocent VIII and, 799, 801, 1032; Innocent IX and, 243; Innocent X and, 801–802, 802; Innocent XI rejection of, 468, 806; Innocent XII bull against, 30, 394, 468, 807, 1033, 1402; John XXII and, 241, 848; Julius II and, 884, 1032; Julius III and, 887; legate and, 912; Leo X and, 799, 926; Martin V and, 975, 1032, 1048, 1049; Nicholas III and, 973, 1037–1038; papal temporal power and, 1102; patrimonies and, 1101–1103; Paul III and, 1032, 1102, 1124, 1126; Paul V and, 243, 1094, 1129–1130; Pius II and, 1032, 1173, 1174; Pius IV and, 1175; Pius V, 1469; Pius VI and, 1033, 1049, 1180, 1181; Sixtus IV and, 926, 1434–1435; Sixtus V and, 1437; Tridentine condemnation, 1469; Urban VIII, 912, 1560

Neri, Philip, St., 569, 669, 726, 801, 935; beatification and canonization of, 1130; Carnival Christianization by, 248; Clement VIII and, 346; confraternities and, 1309, 1310; Leo XI and, 929; Oratory congregation of, 664, 666; as Paul VI inspiration, 1133, 1134; pilgrim provisions, 1170, 1225; poor relief, 1225

Nerli, Francesco, 350

Nero, emperor of Rome, 64, 65, 387, 1119, 1374, 1383; persecutions by, 1153, 1159

Nerva, emperor of Rome, 1314

Nestorianism, 33, 141, 191, 536; Celestine I prosecution of, 274–275, 916; Fathers of the Church and, 563, 564, 566–567; as heresy, 699, 701, 832, 833; Justinian condemnation of, 1617; Leo I and, 913, 915, 916, 917; Rome/Byzantium conflict over, 199, 200; Theopaschite controversy and, 832, 833

Nestorius, patriarch of Constantinople, 34, 199, 274, 699, 706, 737; conflict with Cyril of Alexandria, 199, 274–275, 563, 567, 699, 1432, 1433, 1443; Council of Ephesus condemnation of, 428; Leo I and, 913

Netherlands: appointment of bishops, 87; Calvinism in, 1288; Church crisis in (1960s), 1143; Clement X and, 351; Great Schism and, 633, 636; Inquisition, 816–817; insurrection against Spain, 938; Jansenism, 354, 704, 808, 824, 825; revolt against Josephism, 869; Vatican II representation, 1579

Netter, Thomas, 777

Neuvenburg, Matthias von, 182

Nevsky, Alexander, 998

New Rome (Constantinople), 317, 428, 562–563

New Testament: anathema meanings, 47; Antichrist texts, 64, 65, 66; apologetics, 74, 75, 76; deacon reference, 484; election of bishops, 90; Gospels, 631–632, 1157–1158; humanist analysis of, 1294; modernism and, 1006, 1008; in papal coronation ceremony, 425, See also Acts of the Apostles

New World: Alexandrine bulls, 26, 27, 96; appointment of bishops and, 93; Benedict XIV policy, 530; gold shipments from, 28,

104; Jesuit expulsion, 1346; missions in, 27, 509–510, 669, 999, 1002, 1255, 1343–1344; papal abritration and, 98–99; Propaganda Fide and, 669, 1255; Spanish-Portuguese demarcation line, 27, 999–1000

Newbigin, N., 1308

Newman, John Henry, 55, 78, 675, 1074, 1086, 1087; Roman Catechism and, 265; Vatican I and, 1567

Nguyen Van Thuan, François Xavier, 434

Nicaea I, Council of (325), 198–199, 200, 427–428, 706, 917; Alexandrian Church and, 198; apologetic literature, 74; on bishops' election, 91; Church of Antioch and, 69, 198; Constantine the Great and, 198, 419, 427–428, 1316; consubstantiality definition, 33–34, 428, 699; Easter date, 213, 517, 562; ecclesiastical canons, 221; Fathers of the Church and, 561–562, 566; first historical censorship, 770; on Holy Spirit procession, 1394; incardination prohibition, 765; legates and, 907–908; papal primacy and, 1108; provincial councils and, 430; subirbicarian Italy and, 1465–1466; trinitarian creed, 897, 1419, See also Nicene Creed

Nicaea II, Council of (787), 91, 204; iconoclast controversy and, 428, 599, 600, 680, 681; overview, 428

Nicaea III, Council of (1208), 207

Nicaea VII, Council of (787), 47

Niccoló di Angelo, 1371

Nice, 1539

Nicea. See Nicaea

Nicene Creed, 206, 428, 479, 657, 699, 738, 836, 893, 897, 920, 945, 946, 986, 1419; Filioque addition, 206, 207, 208, 318, 657, 836, 920, 1394

Nicephorus, patriarch of Constantinople, 204

Nicetas of Byzantium, 76

Nicetas of Remesiana, 1164

Nicholas, St., 569

Nicholas I, 600, 601, 1033–1035; Anastasius Bibliotheque and, 46, 47; authority expansion by, 1245; Benedict III and, 154; Byzantium and, 46, 205–206, 318, 682; canonical collections, 224; as deacon prior to election, 180; Donation of Constantine reference, 513; evangelization and, 997; exemptions and, 552; Formosus and, 590; Latinity and, 905; Marinus I (Martin II) and, 969

Nicholas I, tsar of Russia, 674, 1532

Nicholas II, 72, 731, 1035–1037; antipope to, 329; on Berenger heresy, 701; burial site, 1499; cardinalate and, 240, 1356, 1483; Church-State conflicts, 17, 1036; conclave rules and, 42, 392, 649, 783, 1483; elected against Benedict X, 159, 160, 1035, 1036; Gregory VII and, 648, 1035, 1036; on investiture, 821; legates, 909; on Nicolaitan heresy, 1043, 1044; Norman allies, 1053; reform canons, 18, 1280; simony condemnation, 1424; Victor III and, 1613

Nicholas II, tsar of Russia, 174, 1532

Nicholas III, 440, 735, 1037–1038; Angevins and, 51, 972, 973, 1037, 1038; arms, 112, 113; canonical collections, 226; cardinal protector appointed by, 246; Castel Sant'Angelo as residence, 254; chaplaincy and, 454, 457; Clement IV and, 332; Curia and, 455–456; Dante's consignment to Hell, 481; Fisherman's Ring use, 587; Franciscans and, 592, 702, 1037, 1038, 1040; Jewish restrictions by, 872, 873; John XXI and, 846; liturgy and, 951; Martin IV and, 972, 973; nepotism and, 284, 1031, 1098; Nicholas IV and, 1038,

Volume Key: Volume 1, pages 1–614; volume 2, pages 615–1266; volume 3, pages 1267–1637.

1737

1039; regalia and, 1291; St. Peter's redecoration and, 1378; simony and, 481; sovereign claim to Rome by, 1336; tiara, 1491; tomb of, 1500; Vatican gardens and, 1038, 1302; Vatican Palace residence, 1302; Vatican-Castel Sant'Angelo corridor and, 254, 452

Nicholas IV, 281, 440, **1038–1039**, 1040; Angevins and, 52; arms, 112, 113; as first Franciscan pope, 593, 1038, 1039, 1040, 1366; mosaics commission by, 1019–1020, 1360; pontifical palace and gardens, 1594; residence, 1302; Rota member numbers, 1349; Sacred College and, 1356; St. John Lateran and, 1039, 1360, 1363; St. Mary Major and, 1366; tomb of, 1501; vacancy following death of, 189, 280

[Nicholas V], 66, 70, 72, 128, 131, 132, 133, **1039–1040**

Nicholas V, 72, 98, 537, 621, **1040–1042**; arms, 114, 693; army of, 111; art commissions, 509, 1089, 1091; Callistus III and, 217, 218; Carnival and, 248; Castel Sant'Angelo reinforcement by, 255; coins, 373; Ecclesiastical State formation, 1467; as [Felix V] replacement, 574, 1040; first papal medallion honoring, 982; Fisherman's Ring, 587; humanist interests, 1042, 1294, 1297, 1597; Inquisition and, 814; Latinity and, 906; missions in New World, 999; naval fleet, 1029; papal library, 1340, 1597; Paul II and, 1121; Pius II and, 1171; poor health of, 1416, 1417; St. Peter's basilica rebuilding and, 104, 549, 1042, 1382; tiara, 1492; tomb of, 1380, 1502; Vatican garden and, 1594

Nicholas de Clamanges, 193

Nicholas Mesarites, 207, 208

Nicholas of Beaufort, 659

Nicholas of Cusa, 76, 213, 242, 514, 911, 1041, 1172, 1173

Nicholas of Jerusalem, 1042, 1043, 1044

Nicholas the Mystic, patriarch of Constantinople, 839

Nicolai, Nicola, 1184

nicolaism, **1042–1044**; Clement II measures against, 328; [Clement III] measures against, 329; Gregorian reforms and, 1281; Gregory VII and, 649, 1278, 1483; as heresy, 700; Lateran II decree against, 216, 429; Leo IX and, 924; Nicholas II and, 1036; Urban II and, 1551

Nicolaitans. *See* nicolaism

Nicolas. *See* Nicholas

Nicole, Pierre, 76

Niem, Dietrich von, 25, 391

Nietzsche, Friedrich, 68

Nievo, 759

Niger, Ralph, 331

Nikodim, patriarch of Leningrad and Novgorod, 858

Nil de Rossano, 638

Nil Kabasilas, 207–208

Nile (statue), 1595

Nimègue, Peace of (1678), 805

Nina, Lorenzo, 10, 1094

Ninety-five Theses (Wittenberg; 1517), 726, 926, 927–928, 1286, 1382, 1395

Noailles, François de, 354–355, 938

nobility, Roman, **1044–1051**; up to Gregory the Great, **1044–1047**, 1317, 1411; Middle Ages, 601, **1047–1051**, 1331–1339; Adeodatus II and, 6; Alexander IV and, 23; Alexander VI and, 26–27; antipopes and, 1333; arms and emblems, 694–695; Boniface VII and, 189; Boniface IX and, 193; career and, 247–248; Celestine III and, 276–277; chari-

ties and, 448; Christian prefects, 1230; Curia and, 448, 449, 451; Eugene I and, 531; Eugene IV and, 536–537; feast day traditions, 570; financial drains on, 1340; First French Empire and, 1050, 1185; Gentlemen of His Holiness, 627; Ghibelline/Guelph conflicts, 627–631, 676–677; government and, 1331–1339; Gregory I and, 639; Gregory V and, 646; Gregory VI and, 647, 648; Gregory VII reforms and, 1035; [Gregory VIII] and, 652; Gregory XV and, 667, 668; Hadrian III and, 682; Honorius II and, 731–732; Honorius IV and, 735; Innocent X and, 801; Innocent XI and, 804; Innocent XII and, 807; John VII and, 836; John X conflict with, 838; John XV and, 842–843; John XV conflict with, 843; John XVIII and, 844; Julius II and, 884–885; Leo III assaulted by, 920; Lombards and, 957; Martin I and, 971; modern era, 1341, 1342; mosaic commissions, 1021; Nicholas IV and, 1038–1039; Nicholas V and, 1042; in Noble Guard, 1052; painting collections, 1091–1092; papal, 1050–1051; papal anarchy and, 1245; papal decorations, 488; papal domination by, 254, 416–417, 601; papal election conflicts, 240, 280, 329, 783; papal finances and, 577; papal household and, 740; ranking of, 1049–1050; real estate speculation, 1017; Senate and, 1044–1047, 1411; Sergius II and, 1413; Sergius III and, 1413, 1414; Stephen II (III), 1456; Stephen IV (V) and, 1458; Stephen V (VI) and, 1458; titles, 627, 1050; two types of, 1049; Vigilius and, 1047, 1616, 1617. *See also* nepotism; *zelanti* faction

Noble Ecclesiastics, Pontifical Academy for, 172, 1134

Noble Guard, 12, 138, 177, 582, 627, 740, **1051–1052**, 1095, 1185; brass band of, 299

Noè, Virgilio, 285

Noet, 1640

Noetus of Smyrna, 699

Nogaret, Guillaume (William) de, 131, 160, 191, 334, 1379, 1485

Nogari, Paris, 1362

Nogayrol, Bertrand, 796

Nolasco, Pedro, 989

nominalism, 508, 847

Non-Christian Religions, Declaration of (1965), 1140

Non-Christians, Secretariat for, 1405

Nonconformist Churches, 1289

Nonnotte, Claude-François, 77

Norbert, St., 42, 701, 732, 784

Normans of southern Italy and Sicily, **1052–1054**; Alexander II alliance, 17, 18, 111–112, 1053; Alexander III alliance, 19, 20, 21; [Anacletus II] support by, 42, 313, 784; Angevins and, 50–54; Byzantium conquest by (1071), 18, 206–207, 318, 684, 1036; Celestine III and, 277–278; Eugene III and, 533, 534; Ghibelline/Guelph conflict and, 628; Greek population and, 638; as Gregory VII allies, 239, 329, 650, 1329, 1354; [Gregory VIII] deposition by, 652; Hadrian IV and, 683–684; Hadrian V and, 685; Honorius II and, 732; Innocent III and, 786; legates and, 910; Leo IX war against, 109, 925, 1053; Lucius II and, 960; Lucius III and, 960, 961; mercenaries, 109, 157, 1052; Nicholas II grants, 1036; papal ecclesiastical influence in, 1036, 1052–1053; Papal States and, 1098; papal-Byzantium alliance against, 206; Paschal II and, 1112; sack of Rome by, 1329; Saracen threat to, 112, 1393; Stephen IX (X) and, 1461; Urban II support by, 684, 1551, 1552; Victor III and, 1613, 1614; [Victor IV] and, 1615

Volume Key: Volume 1, pages 1–614; volume 2, pages 615–1266; volume 3, pages 1267–1637.

1738

North Africa: Arab conquest of, 1319; Christian archaeology in, 101; slave market, 1439, 1440; Vandals and, 1318

North America: Catholic missionizing, 1255, 1343–1344; first bishopric, 351; Sacred College representation, 1357; Vatican I representation, 1566; Vatican II representation, 1578, 1580, 1581, *See also* Canada; United States

Norway: evangelization, 997; Hadrian IV in, 683; Reformation in, 1287

Nostra aetate (1965), 262

Nostradamus, 1261, 1262

notary, apostolic, 446, 1050, **1054–1055**; abbreviators and, 1; in administrative hierarchy, 7, 451, 459; Chancery and, 293, 446, 447, 449, 460; Fabric of St. Peter, 558; organization of, 289–290

Notre-Dame Cathedral, 1543

Nouvel, Arnaud, 160

Nouvelles ecclésiastiques (journal), 867

Novatian, 70, 71, 181, 561, 698, **1055–1056**; Celestine I opposition, 273; schism with Cornelius, 422, 959, 1155, 1394, 1455, *See also lapsi* controversy

Novatianism, 500, 698

Novelli, Angelo, 1201, 1202

novels. *See* image of Rome in literature

novena, 485, 486

Novendials, **1056**

Novissimae (Gregory X), 226

nuclear weapons, 856, 859

numbering of popes. *See* onomastics, pontifical

Numidian Church, 1394

Numismatic Cabinet of the Vatican, 983–984

numismatics. *See* postage stamps

nunciature, **1056–1058**, 1109, 1566; Counter Reformation and, 1177; Gregory XIII and, 465, 664, 1057; legate and, 911, 912; list of, 1057; nuncio, 1058–1060; Paul VI and, 1134–1135

nuncio, 911, 1057, **1058–1060**; as collectors, 80, 81–82, 580, 582; Pius XII as, 1211–1212

nuns, 507, 1343

Nuremberg, diet of (1356), 796

Nuremberg, diet of (1522–1523), 1287

oath of fidelity (text), 1252–1253

obelisks of Rome, 108, 803, **1061–1062**, 1362, 1374, 1383, 1384

Obici, Giuseppe, 1372

Observant Reforms (Franciscans), 594–595, 596

Observatory, Vatican, 177, **1062–1063**

occultism, 603

Oceania, 410, 675; John Paul II tours, 1510; Vatican II representation, 1575, 1576, 1577, 1578, 1580

Ochino, Barnardino d', 595, 1126

Ockhamism. *See* William of Ockham

O'Connell, Cardinal, 1201

O'Connell, Denis, 40, 675

O'Connor, J. M., 1237, 1445

O'Connor, John J., 1574

O'Connor, Martin, 1238–1239

Octave of Prayer for Christian Unity, 519

Octavian. *See* John XII

Octavius. *See* Augustus

Octogesima advensiens (1971 apostolic letter), 1447, 1449

Odescalchi, Benedetteo. *See* Innocent XI

Odescalchi family, 804

Odescalchi, Livio, 804

Odilon, abbot of Cluny, 157, 328, 845

Odo of Cluny, 15, 840, 922, 1043, 1460

Odo of Poli, 1098

Odoacer, first barbarian king of Italy, 140, 141, 621; deposition of Roman emperor by, 1318; Felix III and, 572; Milan and, 987; Ravenna and, 1273; Roman Senate and, 1046, 1411; Simplicius and, 1425, 1426

Odonis, Gerald, 592–593, 594

Odrowaz, Hyacinthe, 271

Offa, king of East Anglia, 421

offenses against the pope, **1063–1064**

Old Believers, 1488

Old Catholics, 1196, 1395–1396, 1577; schism, 778, 779, 1396, 1530, 1567, 1568

Old Testament: prophecies in, 1261; subsidiarity concept and, 1462; suspension origin in, 1470; tiara in, 1489, 1492

Oldest Daughter of the Church, **1064**, 1378

Olier, Jean-Jacques, 803, 1409

Olieu, Pierre de Jean, 66

Olin, Pierre (Peter John Olivi), 282

Olivier, Laurence, 322

Olivier, Seraphin, 213

Ollivier, Émile, 1568

Olmi, Ermanno, 323

Olympius, exarch of Ravenna, 972

Omar, caliph, 711

O'Margair, Malachy, 331

ombrellino. See pavilion

Omodeo, Adolfo, 1189, 1534

Onesti, Luigi and Romualdo, 1181

onomastics, pontifical, **1064–1068**; antipope and, 70; deposition of pope, 495; Great Schism and, 637; of John, 495, 846, 1066, 1068; Marinus/Martin confusion, 972–973; papal coronation and, 426; of Stephen, 1454–1455

Opera dei Congressi, 307, 1023, 1542

Oppizzoni, Cardinal, 672

Optatus of Mileva, 543, 571, 942, 993

Opus Dei, **1069–1072**, 1232, 1235, 1239

Orange, Council of (530), 185

Orange, University of, 1556

oratorio, 1341

Oratory, Congregation of the, 257, 665, 669, 806, 1130, 1276, 1310

Ordelaffi, Autario, 1042

Order of Christ, 488

Order of Conventual Friars Minor, 1546

Order of Pius IX, 487, 488

Order of Preachers. *See* Dominicans

Order of St. Gregory the Great, 487

Order of Saint Sylvester, 487

Order of the Golden Spur or Golden Host, 487, 488

orders, pontifical, **1072**

orders, religious: Alexander VI support for, 27; as bankers, 136; cardinal protectors for, 246, 247; Catholic reform and, 1275–1276; colleges, 1343; confraternal forms, 1309; exemptions and, 553, 1254; Gregory XIII support for, 664; In-

Volume Key: Volume 1, pages 1–614; volume 2, pages 615–1266; volume 3, pages 1267–1637.

nocent III support for, 788; liturgy and, 952; missionizing by, 1000–1001; Paul III reforms, 1126; Pius V and, 1177; poor relief by, 1224; Tridentine doctrine on, 1521, *See also* mendicant orders; monasticism; *specific orders*

ordination: Alexander VII standards, 30; of bishop of Rome, 181; diocese of Rome, 500; plague effects on, 1222; seminary training for, 1409; simony and, 1423–1425, *See also* investiture controversy

ordinations, Anglican, 55–56, 865, 934, **1072–1077**, 1395; of women, 56, 829, 1395

Ordines Romani, 284

Oreglia, Giuseppe, 324, 325

Orfeo (Rossi), 257

Orfini, Emiliano, 983

Organic Articles (1802; France), 585–586, 1186, 1566

Organization of American States, 1079

organizations, international, the Holy See and, 718, 719, 720, **1077–1081**; Helsinki Conference participation, 687–688; John Paul II travels and, 1511; Pius XI and, 1206; Pius XII and, 1214, 1216–1217; Secretariat of State and, 1403; Vatican City State and, 1588, 1589; Vatican communication and, 984, *See also* United Nations

Oriental Church, Congregation for the, 1257

Oriental Churches. *See* Eastern Churches

Oriental Institute, Pontifical, 176, 519

Origen, 3, 544, 561, 1222; Alexandria and, 33, 35; Anastasius condemnation of, 43, 770; on Clement I, 327; Gospel According to Peter reference, 631; heresies model, 696; Hippolytus and, 707; in Holy Land, 711; Pelagius I and, 1146; on Peter in Rome, 1158; Theotokis and, 428; trinitarianism, 699; Vigilius condemnation of, 1617

original sin, 251; Council of Trent definition, 429, 1289, 1520; Pelagianism and, 1641

Origines du culte chrétien (Duchesne), 954

Orioli, Cardinal, 1193

Orlando, V. E., 901

Orlandos, Anastasios K., 101

Orleans, Council of (511), 551

Orleans, Council of (549), 91, 597

Orleans, University of, 1548

Ormesson, Wladimir d', 1575, 1632–1633

Orsini, Bertoldo, 1038

Orsini family, 189, 656, 798, 1340; arms, 694; autonomous branches of, 1048; cardinals, 451; Castel Sant'Angelo seizure by, 254, 1302; Church-State conflict and, 131, 1048–1049; Colonna rivalry, 11, 280, 799, 976, 1048, 1049, 1434; Nicholas III and, 973, 1031, 1037–1038, 1098, 1336; Nicholas V and, 1042; papal chapel and, 740; papal tombs and, 1500; as Roman nobility, 1047, 1048, 1049; St. Peter's basilica and, 1302

Orsini, Giangaetano, 24

Orsini, Giordano, 1038

Orsini, Giovanni, 132

Orsini, Giovanni Gaetano. *See* Nicholas III

Orsini, Latino, 537, 1041

Orsini, Matteo, 1037

Orsini, Matteo Rosso, 279, 656, 1037, 1558; as Celestine V advisor, 280, 281, 282; as first cardinal protector, 246

Orsini, Napoleone, 280, 281, 850, 1039

Orsini, Niccolò, 885

Orsini, Orso, 735, 973, 1037

Orsini, Paolo, 111

Orsini, Pierfrancesco. *See* Benedict XIII

Orsini, Poncello, 192

Orsini, Rinaldo, 192

Orsini, Virginio, 26

Orthodox Church (Kiev), 522, 1533

Orvieto, 23, 1355

Osborne, Francis d'Arcy, 1631, 1632, 1633, 1634

Osius of Cordova, 945, 1419

Ospedale dei Mendicanti, 1308

Ossat, Arnaud d', 347

Osservatore romano, 1, 473, 584, **1081–1084**, 1095, 1588; administrative status of, 498; founding and purpose, 1444; on liberalism, 944; as official Vatican publication, 984; Pius XI and, 1205, 1207, 1630; Pius XI anti-Nazi statements in, 874; Pius XII denuciation of Jewish persecution in, 875; press service, 1236, 1237, 1239; Spanish-language edition, 984; on treaties of Rome, 540; on Vatican II, 1584; Vaticanists and, 1606

Ossius of Cordoba, 419

Osterreichische Historische Institut, 1603

Osterreichische Volkspartei, 309

Ostia, 159, 160, 1033; Clement VII and, 345; Gregory IV fortress, 1393; naval defenses, 645, 1027, 1028, 1029, 1030

ostpolitik, 540, **1084–1086**; absence of diplomatic relations, 503; John XXIII and, 855; John Paul II and, 312, 860, 862–863, 979; Paul VI and, 1137, 1140; Pius XII and, 1215–1216; Vatican II and, 862–863; Vatican Radio and, 984

Ostrogoths, 140, 141, 200, 573, 831, 1317; antisimony decree, 832; papal finances, 575, 576; as rulers of Italy, 1318, 1465, *See also* Goths

Oswy, Anglo-Saxon ruler, 518, 1619

O'Toole, Peter, 322

Otranto: iconoclast controversy, 638; Turkish capture of, 1434, 1526

Ottanianum (Otto I), 513

Ottaviani, Alfredo, 310, 855, 1135, 1141, 1203, 1218, 1236, 1571, 1572, 1574, 1615

Otto I (the Great), Holy Roman emperor, 15, 47, 122, 314, 426, 513, 547, 601, 648, 714, 840, 970, 1052, 1460; Benedict V and, 155; coronation of, 424; John XII legates to, 909; John XIII and, 841–842; Leo VIII and, 923; papal coronation by, 426; Papal States and, 157, 1097; Ravenna and, 1274; Rome and, 1332

Otto I of Bamberg, 331

Otto II, Holy Roman co-emperor, 71, 155, 157, 188, 189, 842, 843, 1386; Silvester II and, 1420

Otto III, Holy Roman emperor, 122, 155, 424, 842, 843, 844, 868; Church cooperation with, 714; cousin Gregory V, 645, 646–647; Donation of Constantine rejection, 513; John XV and, 842, 843; Papal States and, 1097; Roman nobility and, 1333; Silvester II relationship, 1414, 1421–1422

Otto IV (of Brunswick), Holy Roman emperor, 53, 314, 424, 513, 654, 715, 786–787, 789, 897

Otto of Brunswick, 341, 1098

Otto of Freising, 45

Ottoboni, Pietro. *See* Alexander VIII

Ottoboni family, 32, 694, 1032

Volume Key: Volume 1, pages 1–614; volume 2, pages 615–1266; volume 3, pages 1267–1637.

1740

Ottokar II Presysl, king of Bohemia, 333
Ottoman Empire. *See* Turks
Ottoni, Lorenzo, 1362
Ottonianum, 840
Oudinot, Nicolas-Charles, 1194, 1323, 1325, 1326
Ouen, St., 1166
Our Lady of the Germans of Jerusalem Hospital. *See* Teutonic Knights
Overseas Missions seminary, 1259
Oxford Movement, 55, 1074, **1086–1087**, 1566; liturgy and, 955
Oxford, University of, 133, 379, 1544, 1548, 1549; Franciscans and, 593; Great Schism and, 634

Paaulinus of Trevi, 945
Pacca, Bartolomeo, 930–931, 1187, 1188, 1189
Pacelli, Carlo, 1590
Pacelli, Ernesto, 582, 1210
Pacelli, Eugenio. *See* Pius XII
Pacelli family, 694
Pacelli, Francesco, 1210, 1590
Pacelli, Marcantonio, 1082
Pacem Dei munus (1920 encyclical), 175
Pacem in terris (1963 encyclical), 310, 516, 856, 877, 1078, 1085, 1110, 1240, 1447; subsidiarity principle, 1463
Pachomius, 33, 1013
padroado system, 1255, 1256
padronanza. See patronage, papal
Padroni, Mariano, 257
Padua, University of, 899, 1549
Paganelli, Bernardo. *See* Eugene III
pagans: barbarians as, 140; British temples converted to churches, 142; Carnival roots in feasts of, 248; eastern cults, 441–444; evangelization of, 544–546, 996–998; imagery in mosaics, 1020; Julian the Apostate and, 882; Paul as apostle to the, 1119; persecutions of Christians by. *See* persecutions; Peter's conversion of, 1158; prefects of Rome, 1230–1231; Roman Empire, 1313–1316, 1317; Roman festival celebrations, 624, 1389; Roman Pantheon temple, 1095; sacrifices by, 140
painting, **1089–1093**; academies, 118–121, 1092–1093, 1117; Catholic reform and, 1090, 1340–1341, 1431; Church censorship, 1341, 1342; foreign artists in Rome, 116–121, 1092, 1117, 1130; Gregorian reform and, 1284–1285; papal patronage, 27–28, 509, 1116, 1117, 1130, 1174, 1383–1384, 1435; papal portraiture, 1117, 1123, 1372, 1428, 1435; Peter portrayals, 1160–1161; post-Catholic reform, 1344–1345; St. Peter's basilica, 1383, 1385; Sistine Chapel, 1089, 1091, 1428–1431, 1435, *See also* frescoes; mosaics
Palace, Apostolic, **1093–1094**; cardinal residents, 462; death of the pope and, 10; enlargments and renovations, 1117; finances, 582; floreria (warehouse), 588; gardens, 1594–1596; library, 1597–1599; master of the Sacred Palace, 457, 627, 980–981, 1094; museum collections, 1025, 1026; Noble Guards, 1051; paintings, 1091, 1117; palatine designation, 1094–1095; papal chapel, 295–296; papal household, 738, 739; *portantina papale* used within, 1228; return from Avignon and, 104; Tridentine reforms, 465
Palace of Montecavallo at the Quirinal. *See* Quirinal
Palace of the Four Fountains, 245
Palais-Neuf (Avignon), 103

Palatine, **1094–1095**, 1127, 1300, 1327; excavations, 1345; Vatican II and, 741
Palatine Count of the Lateran, 1050–1051
Palatine Guard, 626, 740, 741, 1052, **1095**
Palazzeschi, A., 756
Palazzo Pio, 1600
Paleotti, Gabriele, 263
Palermo: Inquisition abolishment, 819; slave market, 1439
Palestine. *See* Holy Land; Holy Places; Jerusalem
Palestine Royal Commission, 712
Palestinians, 877
Palestrina, Giovanni Pierluigi da, 257, 297, 298, 666, 887, 1340; Mass of Pope Marcellus by, 968
palfrey. *See* chinea
Palinus of Nola, 43
Palladio, 1363
Palladius, bishop of the Scots, 273, 274
Palladus, 1012
Pallavicini, Uberto, 21
Pallavicino, P. Sforza, 29, 30
Pallavini, Cardinal, 361
pallium, 126, 181, 187, 688, 1283, 1284; overview, 1607–1608; in papal coronation ceremony, 425, 426; tiara and, 244, 1607
Pallotta, Cardinal, 932
Palm Sunday, 210, 952; penitentiaries, 1523
Palmieri, Gregorio, 285
Palmyrenian gods, 443
Palomar, John de, 535
Palombi, Domenico (Rodomonte), 257
Paluzzi, Gaspare, 350–351, 468
Paluzzi, Paluzzo degli Albertonio, 360
Pamfili family. *See* Pamphili family
Pammachius, 1013, 1377
Pamphili, Camillo, 257, 467, 801, 802, 803, 1469
Pamphili family, 694, 801, 803, 1032, 1090
Pamphili, Giovanni Battista. *See* Innocent X
Pamphili, Giuseppe Doria, 1187
Pamphili Palace, 1271
Pamphronius, 153
Panciroli, Romeo, 1239, 1469
Pandulf IV of Capua, 158
Pandulfus of Sabello, 152
Pane, Domenico dal, 257
Pane, Francesco Maria dal, 257
Panigarole (Franciscan), 666
Pannini, Paolo, 1363
Panormia (Yvo), 225
Panormitanus (Nicolas de Tudeschis), 777
Pantaleone (Amalfi merchant), 1370
Pantaleoni, Diomede, 1537
pantheism, 1096, 1268, 1472
Pantheon, 976, **1095–1096**, 1314, 1383; Alexander VII improvements, 30; Constans II pillage of, 1096, 1354, 1619; Eugene IV improvements, 537; literary images of, 753, 754; transformation into church, 187, 1096, 1328
Panvinio, Onofrio, 497, 830, 968
Paolucci, Fabrizio, 166
Papal Heraldry (Galbreath), 688
papal infallibility. *See* infallibility

Volume Key: Volume 1, pages 1–614; volume 2, pages 615–1266; volume 3, pages 1267–1637.

1741

papal nobility. *See under* nobility, Roman

papal primacy. *See* primacy, papal

papal residences. *See* residences, papal

Papal States, **1096–1107**; 8th to 13th centuries, **1096–1101**; 15th to 19th centuries, **1101–1107**; abolishment of, 582, 583, 1096, 1110, 1196; administrative reform, 672–673, 932; annona, 60–62; Apostolic Camera functions and, 8; armies, 108–112; bicameral constitution (1848), 1539; camerlengo's duties, 219–221; career, 247–248; Charles V assault on, 1624; coins, 374, 375–377; collapse of (1870), 39, 718; Congress of Vienna restitution of, 687, 1103, 1104, 1109, 1189, 1644; consolidation of, 1342, 1467; crusades as protector of, 439; Curia vs., 436; diocese of Rome, 500; diplomatic representation, 1056–1060; divisions of in restoration proclamation (1814), 1538; emblems and arms, 695; evolution as political entity, 1245; Exarchate of Ravenna integration into, 547, 599; final fall of, 1196; finances, 271, 375–377, 575–577, 578, 581, 1246; French Revolution and, 1109, 1181–1182; Great Schism of the West and, 163; Gregory XIV and problems of, 666; Gregory XVI and conflicts of, 670, 671–673; honorific titles, 627, 1050; Innocent III and, 789; Innocent VIII and, 799; Italian annexation of, 583, 901, 1195–1196, 1568, 1644; Italian military invasion of, 1646; Italian unification and, 39, 1105, 1107, 1539, 1540, 1541; Jewish expulsion from, 872, 873; Jewish restrictions in, 874; Julius II and, 884, 886, 1467; jurisdictionalism, 888–889; Leo XII restoration policies, 932; maps of, 1099, 1100, 1105, 1106; medallion portrayals, 982; military expenses, 110; Napoléon and, 122–123, 377, 470, 530, 585–587, 670, 1183, 1185–1187, 1349, 1598; nepotism. *See* nepotism; Nicholas V consolidation of, 1041–1042; Noble Guard, 1051–1052; Normans of Sicily and, 1052–1054; notaries, 1054; Otto I privileges for, 157, 1097; papal absolutism in, 1109; papal residences outside Rome, 1302–1303; Patrimony of St. Peter as core of, 1096, 1097, 1098, 1101, 1102, 1116, 1282; Paul II control of, 1121; Paul V public debt increases, 1130; Pius VI economic reforms, 1180; Pontifical Gendarmes, 626; revolts against (1840s), 675; Roman duchy as nucleus of, 1331; Roman nobility and, 535–536, 627, 1050–1051, 1052; Roman Republic (1798–1799) and, 1320–1322; Roman Republic (1849) and, 1323–1326; Signatura Apostolic, 1525; six principal districts, 1102; Sixtus IV policies, 1434; Sixtus V policies, 1437–1438; slavery in, 1439, 1440–1441; superintendent of, 1467–1470; Swiss Guard, 1471; Thirty Years War and, 1561; traveler's views of, 1504–1507; Urban IV and restoration of, 1554–1555; Viterbo and, 1620; War of the Austrian Succession and, 169–170; Zouaves defense of, 1107, 1643–1646

papal taxation. *See* taxation, papal

papal tombs. *See* tombs of the popes

Papareschi, Gregorio. *See* Innocent II

Paparo, John, 533

Paparone, Scoto and Giovanni, 1368

Papée, Casimir, 1632–1633

Papini, Giovanni, 283

papism, **1107–1111**; devotion to the pope and, 496–497; English antipathy to, 1289; Febronianism vs., 1345; Reformation characterization of, 1287–1288, 1289; sack of Rome (1527) and, 1354–1355; seen as Antichrist, 1287–1288; stereotypes, 1232–1233

Pappalardo, archbishop of Palermo, 864

papyrus, 289, 1293, 1603

Paraclete, 697

Paradise, popes consigned by Dante to, 481

Paraguay, 399, 1004, 1513; Jesuit expulsion, 1346; missionizing, 1130; Vatican II representation, 1579

pardoners. *See* indulgences

Paré, Ambroise, 256

Paredes, Joannes, 256

Parentucelli, Tommaso. *See* Nicholas V

Parercattil, Joseph, 370

Paris Academy, 1093

Paris, Congress of (1856), 1104

Paris, Council of (825), 600

Paris, Matthew, 1303

Paris Overseas Missions, 1255

Paris revolts of 17–30 July 1830, 1538

Paris, treaty of (1814), 1538

Paris, University of, 170, 379, 735, 850, 1543, 1544, 1547, 1548, 1549; Alexander IV and, 23–24; Averroist heresy and, 702; canonical law texts, 225–226, 227, 228; on Church-State relations, 1485; conciliarism defense by, 390; Curia career and, 451; Dominicans and, 507; Franciscans and, 593; Gallicanism and, 511, 616, 617, 778; Great Schism and, 24, 132, 193, 633, 634; Gregory IX support for, 655–656; Honorius III and, 654, 734; Index, 770; Jansenism and, 354, 823, 825; Leo X and, 927; logic and law, 133; Oriental languages study, 1039; on papal infallibility, 778; papal primacy questions, 509; pilgrimages and, 1168–1169; Talmud inquiry, 792; Tempier commission condemnation of (1277), 847

Parker, Matthew, 1073, 1074

Parliament of Religions, 40

Parma, 238, 328, 344, 887, 1049; Clement VII and, 345; Clement XII and, 357; Clement XIII and, 359; Leo X and, 928; papal dominace over, 17(map), 1102, 1103; Papal States and, 1342; Paul III and, 1124, 1125; Pius VII and, 1182

Parma, Gerardo di, 282

Parma, Luigi da, 596

parochial schools, 40

Parrocel, Pierre-Ignace, 304

parrots, 58, 59

pars Orientis. *See* Constantinople; Eastern Churches

Parsch, Pius, 955

particular councils. *See* councils, particular or local

Partita Populare. *See* Italian People's Party

Pascal (popes). *See* Paschal

Pascal, Blaise, 29, 76, 77, 529, 704, 806

Pascendi (1907 encyclical), 1005, 1006, 1008, 1199

[Paschal], 20, 70, 71, **1111**

Paschal I, 532, **1111–1112**, 1458; cross of, 437; documents, 289; iconoclast controversy and, 205; Louis the Pious coronation by, 424, 600, 1111; missions, 997; mosaics, 1020; tomb of, 1497; Valentine and, 1565

Paschal II, 215, 731–732, **1112–1114**; "ad limina" visits and, 4; [Albert] and, 17; Anastasius IV and, 45; antipopes to, 72, 330, 1112, 1113, 1423; Apostolic Camera and, 449; bull design, 195; Byzantium and, 207; consistory duties, 414, 415; funerary rites, 485; Gelasius II and, 625; Gregorian reforms, 1278, 1281; health and vitality of, 1416; Honorius II and, 731; in-

Volume Key: Volume 1, pages 1–614; volume 2, pages 615–1266; volume 3, pages 1267–1637.

1742

vestitures controversy, 109, 651–652, 821, 822, 900, 1112–1113, 1281, 1637; judges delegate and, 453; military orders and, 988; Normans and, 910; Saracen threat and, 1393; [Silvester IV] and, 1423; tomb of, 1499; [Victor IV] as critique of, 1615

[Paschal III], 70, 72, 217, 313, **1114–1115**; death of [Victor IV (V)] and, 1616; Viterbo residence, 1620

Paschal controvery. *See* Easter-date controversies

Paschal Tables, 517, 518

Paschasius, 1164

Pasolini, P. P., 761

Pasqualini, Marcantonio, 257

Passaglia, Carlo, 1537

Passarelli, Fausto, Lucio, and Vincenzo, 1026

Passarowitz, treaty of (1718), 1527

Passau, treaty of (1552), 1288

Passerin d'Entrèves, Ettore, 1538

Passignano, Domenico, 1385

Passion and Resurrection, 631, 728, 1158, 1275; relics of, 1359

Passion of Clement, 327

Passion Play, 1308

Passional Christi und Antichristi, 67

Passionei, Domenico, 170, 353, 1598

passport, Vatican, **1115**

Pastor Aeternus, 779

Pastor Angelicus (film documentary), 322

Pastor bonus (1335; Benedict XII reforms), 161

Pastor, L., 1560

Pastoral Care of Migrants and Itinerants, Pontifical Council of the, 434–435

Patarenes, 17, 648, 700, 1036, 1044, 1282

Pataria movement. *See* Patarenes

Patriarch of the West, 1495

patriarchates: cardinalitial dignity and, 244; election of bishops, 86; first five, 318; Nicaea I defining, 199; papal primacy and, 1245

patricians, Roman. *See* nobility, Roman

patriciate, 1049–1050, 1052

Patrick, St., 545

Patrimony of St. Peter, **1115–1116**; administration of, 10–11, 1126; cardinal nephew abuses and, 245; Celestine III and, 277; coins, 372; definition of, 1115; documents, 289; Donation of Constantine, 513; Exarchate of Ravenna and, 1064; finances, 578, 582, 583; food export prohibition, 60, 659; French Revolution and, 1109; Holy Roman Empire and, 715–717; Innocent III and, 1335; legates and, 909; Nicholas III and, 1037; Nicholas IV and, 1039; papal armies' defense of, 111; papal finances and, 576–577, 578, 582; as Papal States' nucleus, 1096–1098, 1101, 1102, 1116, 1282; Paul II and, 1121; Reformation effects on, 802; revenues report. *See Liber censum*; Theophylact and, 1332; Urban IV and, 1555; Victor II consolidation of, 1613

Patrimony of the Holy See, Administration of the, 1094

patriotism, nationalism vs., 1206

Patripassianism, 699, 708

patristic theology, 565, 566, 568

Patrizi, Agostino, 284, 1163

Patrizi, Francesco, 1296

Patrizi, Guido dei, 1338

Patroclus of Arles, 184, 185, 273, 1610, 1611, 1641

patron saints, 539, 540, 541, 569, 1378

patronage, papal, **1116–1117**; Alexander VI and, 27–28, 1340; Alexander VII and, 30; arms augmentation, 695–696; Benedict XIV and, 171; cardinal nephew and, 245; Clement VIII and, 1089, 1090, 1092; Clement XII and, 357; Clement XIII and, 359; Gregory XIII and, 665; Gregory XIV and, 666; humanists and, 1294–1295, 1296; Innocent VIII and, 799; Julius II and, 1024, 1089, 1091, 1092; Leo X and, 926, 927, 928; Martin V and, 537, 976; painting commissions, 1089–1093; Paul III and, 887, 1116, 1123, 1127; Paul V and, 1130; Pius III and, 1174; Pius IV and, 1176, 1177, 1296, 1431; Pius VI and, 1180; Pius IX and, 121, 1116; right to spoils and, 580; for Roman confraternities, 1308; Sergius I and, 1412; Sixtus IV and, 1435; Urban VIII and, 1091, 1560, 1562

Paucapalea (Rolland), 225

Paul (St. Paul the Apostle), 140, **1117–1120**; Antichrist concept and, 67; bishop of Rome ordination and, 181; cemetery of, 261; Christian conversion of, 1118; Clement I and, 327; evangelization by, 544, 1158; feast of, 303, 569; figure on banner, 138, 693; head on bull design, 195; heresies and, 696; Jewish segregation and Judaizing dictums, 870, 872, 873; liturgical calendar anniversary date, 1432; magaisterial authority and, 566; Peter and, 1157, 1158, 1159, 1160; pilgrimages to tomb of, 4, 1164, 1165; privileges and, 406, 1248–1249; relics of, 545, 1377; in Rome, 1119, 1153, 1160; as source of primacy of Rome, 199; "trophy" of, 548, *See also* St. Paul's Outside the Walls, basilica of

Paul I, 416, 679, **1120–1121**; death outside Rome, 1303; Pepin III and, 182, 1064, 1120, 1121; Ravenna and, 1274; relics and, 261, 1378; tomb of, 1497

Paul II, 104, **1121–1123**; annona, 60; architectural projects, 1121; arms, 114; army of, 111; bull design, 195; cardinal's biretta grant, 180; cardinals' red *cappa magna* and, 267; Carnival and, 248, 249, 1121; coins, 373–374; compassion for animals of, 59; Eugene IV and, 536, 537, 1032; humanist suppression by, 1294; medallions and, 982, 983; nepotism and, 537, 1032, 1121; Sacred College and, 242, 1121; tiara, 1121, 1489; Tolfa alum and, 38, 1121; tomb of, 1380, 1503

Paul III, 54, 143, **1123–1127**, 1129; architectural projects, 104, 105, 106, 255, 1116, 1117, 1123, 1170; arms, 114, 693; arts projects, 887, 1116, 1123, 1127, 1382; Calatrava Order and, 989; Capuchins and, 595; cardinal brotherhood and, 267; Chair of St. Peter and, 287; children of, 1102, 1123, 1124; Clement VII and, 344; coins, 374; confraternities and, 1308; congregation creation, 415, 416, 471; Constitution of 1546, 1027; Curia reform bull, 464, 1126; Dominicans and, 509, 510; Fabric of St. Peter and, 558; fanon, 1569; Farnese family and, 247, 1103, 1123, 1124, 1125–1126; French allies, 1624; heraldry, 692; heresies and, 709, 770; Holy Office (Inquisition) creation, 242, 416, 816, 1126, 1341, 1357; Holy Year and, 726; humanism and, 1296; hunting by, 59; Inquisition reestablishment, 1123, 1125, 1126, 1296, 1443; Jesuits founding bull, 195, 826, 1000, 1123, 1125, 1126; Julius III and, 886; Lateran palace and, 1362; legates and, 912; Marcellus II and, 968; medallions, 982; nepotism and, 1032, 1102, 1124, 1126; painting commissions, 1091, 1123; papal

Volume Key: Volume 1, pages 1–614; volume 2, pages 615–1266; volume 3, pages 1267–1637.

1743

legitimacy and, 1288; Papal States consolidation by, 1342; Paul IV and, 1128; pet dog and parrot, 58, 59; Petrine privilege and, 1250; pilgrim provisions, 1170; portraits of, 1123; Portuguese Inquisition and, 816; reform and, 1126–1127, 1276, 1289, 1425; Reformation and, 509, 1286, 1288, 1289; St. Peter's basilica rebuilding and, 1382; simony and, 1425; Sistine Chapel restoration and, 1430; slavery and, 510, 1439–1440; Swiss Guard and, 304; tomb of, 1126, 1383, 1386; Trent convocation by, 287, 429, 912, 1125, 1246, 1296, 1518, 1520; Vatican gardens and, 1595

Paul IV, **1127–1129**; Anglican ordinations and, 54, 1073, 1395; apostasy and, 79; arms, 693; breviary revision, 194; cardinal nephew, 245; Castel Sant'Angelo improvements, 255; coins, 375; conclave and, 393; confraternities and, 1308; congregations and, 415; Council of Trent and, 1128, 1519; Curia reforms and, 464–465, 471, 1128; French support by, 1624; Gregory XIII and, 663; heraldry, 691; Holy Office and, 465, 709, 1128, 1176; imprimatur, 763; Index, 770, 771–772, 1128, 1175; Inquisition and, 1126, 1128; Jesuits and, 826, 827; Jewish ghettoization by, 872–873, 1310; medallions, 982; Michelangelo's *Last Judgment* and, 1093; nepotism and, 466, 1148, 1469; Palestrina's expulsion from papal chapel by, 297; Paul III and, 1124; Pius V and, 1176, 1177; rigidity of, 1128; Spanish relations, 1102; Vatican gardens and, 1595

Paul V, 143, 351, **1129–1131**; administration, 220; Anglican schism and, 55; annona, 61, 62; architectural projects, 106, 1130, 1369; arms, 115, 693; arts patronage, 1092, 1116; beatifications and, 145; canonizations by, 235, 496, 1130, 1137; Capuchins and, 595, 1130; cardinal nephew brief, 245; cardinalitial titles and, 243; coins, 375; conclave electing, 394; Curia and, 467; datary and, 483; Gregory XV and, 667; Jansenist prohibitions, 823; Jesuits and, 827; nepotism and, 243, 1032, 1129–1130; painting commissions, 1090, 1091, 1130; papal chapel musicians, 298, 299; as Paul VI namesake, 1137; policies of, 1138–1139; Quirinal and, 483, 1269, 1270; St. Peter's basilica alterations, 1383; tomb of, 1130, 1369; Urban VIII and, 1560; Vatican Archives and, 1130, 1598, 1604; Vatican Library and, 1597; Venetian conflict with, 42–43, 1129

Paul VI, 69, 283, 1024, **1131–1145**, 1213, 1228, 1405; academies and, 2; "ad limina" visits and, 5; administrative offices, 10, 12, 221; allocution topics to Rota, 36–37; Angelus recitation, 50; Anglican relations and, 1076; Apostolic Camera functions, 9; apostolic constitution and, 421; arms, 115, 116, 693; assessment of pontificate, 1132, 1141–1144; automobiles, 127; background and earlier career, 310, 994, 1024, 1084, 1132–1137, 1213, 1481, 1583, 1584, 1629, 1632; beatifications and, 149, 271, 865; birth control enyclical, 1110, 1132, 1141–1142, 1143, 1247, 1584; bishops' conferences, 402, 1243; canonizations by, 236, 271; cardinal "in petto" and, 245; cardinal nephew, 245; Catholic universities and, 1544, 1546; causes of canonization, 269; celibacy encyclical, 1110; chamberlains, 288; Chancery abolishment, 294; chaplain elimination, 301; Christian Democracy and, 310; cinema and, 321, 323; *Civiltà Cattolica* and, 325; Code of Canon Law (1983) and, 229, 367, 369; Code of Canons of the Eastern Churches and, 370; on collegiality, 386, 1139; conclave electing, 1132, 1137; conclave rules and, 395; concordatory agreements, 397; Congregation for Bishops and,

409; Congregation for the Doctrine of the Faith and, 406, 763–764; congregations and, 404, 408, 409, 410, 411; coronation procedure and, 427; Curia reforms, 294, 472, 473, 710, 1141, 1258, 1401, 1404; daily life coverage, 1248; datary termination, 482; decorations and, 488; devotion to the pope and, 497; Doctors of the Church and, 265; dogmatic constitution and, 422; Dominicans and, 512; Eastern Churches and, 1245, 1357, 1395; ecclesiastical garb, 620, 621; ecumenism, 1141, 1404–1405, 1515; encyclical list, 527; encyclicals, 512, 609, 977, 1110, 1132, 1141, 1447, 1449; Europe/Church relationship and, 539, 540–541, 1079; Fabric of St. Peter and, 558; ferula replacement by, 575; finances, 583, 584; *flabellum* discontinuance, 588; fundamentalist reaction to, 614; gendarmes disbandment by, 626; Gentlemen of His Holiness and, 288, 626–627, 1052; Helsinki Conference message, 687; heraldry, 696; Holy Office reform, 171, 710, 772, 1443–1444; Holy Places and, 713; Holy Sepulcher order and, 723; Holy Year and, 728, 729; Index discontinuance, 710, 771, 772; International Theological Commission, 388; Jesuits and, 829; Jewish relations, 875, 876, 877; John Paul I and, 858; John Paul II and, 862, 863, 865, 1513; Josephist reforms and, 869; legates and, 1057; liturgical movement and, 956; Marxism condemnation by, 977, 978, 979; master of the Sacred Palace title change by, 981; medallion, 983; missal reform, 996, 1454; missions and, 1005; modernity outlook, 1010, 1247; Moro kidnapping and, 310; Noble Guard and, 1052, 1095; as nunciature to Poland, 1213; Opus Dei organization, 1071; *Osservatore Romano* press service and, 984; *ostpolitik*, 1085, 1086; papal apartments, 73; papal household, 738, 741; papal titles and, 1050; patriciate ending by, 1050; peacocks of, 59; Penitentiary modifications, 1152; personal qualities, 864; photographs of, 1163; pilgrimages and, 1170; Pius XII Holocaust controversy and, 496, 1214; pontifical councils, 434–435; popularity peak of, 1140; postage stamp issues, 1229; Prefecture of the Papal Household, 1231; prelatures and, 1234; press office, 1083, 1084, 1238–1239, 1240; protonotary measures, 1264; Roman Catechism and, 264; rosary devotion and, 1347; Rota tribunal and, 1351; Sacred College reforms, 245, 1357–1358, 1406; St. John Lateran and, 1363, 1364; St. Paul's Outside the Walls restoration, 1370, 1373; Secretariat of State, 1403; social teachings, 512, 1134, 1442, 1446, 1447, 1448, 1449; stational tradition, 1454; subsidiarity principle, 1463; Substitute of the Secretariat of State, 1464; Synod of Bishops and, 1477; tiara use suspension, 1139, 1489; travels, 126, 713, 1132, 1139, 1170, 1510, 1514–1517, 1569; United Nations and, 687, 1078–1079, 1132, 1140, 1510, 1514, 1515, 1584; on unity vs. ecumenism, 520–521, 539, 540–541; Vatican City State and, 1590, 1591; Vatican II and, 429–430, 609, 860, 864, 1110, 1132, 1137, 1138–1144, 1571, 1572, 1583–1585; on Virgin Mary, 1139; vocations of, 1133–1134

Paul Afiarta, 679, 680, 1458

Paul, exarch of Ravenna, 643

Paul of Samosate, 419, 561, 698, 702, 1156

Paul of Taba, 1145

Paul of the Cross, St., 168

Paul, patriarch of Constantinople, 202

Volume Key: Volume 1, pages 1–614; volume 2, pages 615–1266; volume 3, pages 1267–1637.

Paul the Deacon, 152, 1641

Paul, St. Vincent de. *See* Vincent de Paul

Paulin of Aquilea, 747–748

Pauline chapel (Quirinal), 1272

Pauline chapel (St. Mary Major), 1130, 1340–1341

Pauline privilege, 406, 1248–1249, 1250

Paulinus of Antioch, 69, 479, 570

Paulinus of Nola, 747, 1389–1390

Paulinus of York, 142

Paulinus, Sectus Anisius, 1045

Paulists, 41

pauperism. *See* poor relief

Pavia, 680; Church-State powers and, 343, 1536; Franks and, 1319, 1320; French siege of, 1623; Lombards and, 958

Pavia, Council of (1160), 20, 313, 715

Pavia, synod of (698), 143

Pavia, synod of (997), 646

Pavia, synod of (1022), 157, 646, 1043, 1279

pavilion, 692–693, 694, **1145**; keys and, 689, 691, 694–695; minor basilica display of, 144

Pawley, Bernard, 1577

pawnshops, 899, 1224

Pax Romana, 1049

Pázmány, Peter, 1561

Pazzi banks, 39, 137

Pazzi, Maria Maddelena di, 1562

Peace of God, 98, 216

Peace of the Church (313), 200–201, 566, 993, 1316; pontifical tombs and, 1496

Peace of the Church (1669), 824

Peace of Westphalia. *See* Westphalia, Peace of

peacocks, 59

Pecci, Giacchino. *See* Leo XIII

Pecci, Giuseppe, 1194

Pecorara, Giocomo, 451

pectoral cross, 619–620

Pedro. *See* Peter (for Iberian Peninsula kings)

Pedro of Alcantara, St., 349

Pègues, T., 512

Pelagianism, 13, 184, 185, 700, 738, 783; African bishops and, 251; Celestine I prosecution, 273, 274; doctrine, 251, 429, 1520; Gelasius and, 573, 624; Leo I and, 913, 914; Sixtus III and, 1432, 1433; Zosimus and, 1641

Pelagini of Brescia, 1268

Pelagius (deacon), 14–15, 1418, 1432; Agapitus representation, 74; condemnation of, 1641; rehabilitation of, 251, *See also* Pelagianism

Pelagius (Spanish cardinal), 439

Pelagius I, 15, 35, 108, **1145–1148**; Franks and, 597, 1147; legates to Byzantium, 909; tomb of, 1497; Vigilius and, 1145, 1146–1147, 1618

Pelagius II, 186, **1148–1149**; basilica renovations, 549, 1116, 1148–1149, 1388; death from plague, 1220; Franks and, 597; Gregory I and, 639

Pelegrua, Arnaldo, 246

Pellico, Francesco, 324

penal code, Italian, 1542

Penalosa, Francisco de, 297

penalties, ecclesiastical, **1149–1151**; expiatory, 1151; medicinal, 1149–1151; reserved cases and causes, 1297–1300, *See also* excommunication; interdict; suspension

penance, 1151; Holy Year pilgrimages, 727; indulgence vs., 773, 1286; Julius III reforms, 887; *lapsi* and, 250–251, 967–968, 1394; penitentiaries and, 1151; pilgrimage to Rome as, 1166–1167, 1168, 1169, 1170; reserved cases, 1298

Penitentiary, Apostolic, 130, 293, 454, 455, 471, **1151–1152**; bureaucracy of, 463; Curia reforms and, 464–465; Dominicans as, 507; Hadrian VI and, 464; overview, 1523–1524; papal funeral ritual, 485; Paul III reform commission, 1127; for pilgrims to Rome, 1169; Pius V reorganization of, 1178; Tridentine reforms, 465; usury rejection by, 1191

Penni, Francesco, 1373

Penni, Luca, 928

Pentapolis, 599, 643, 1098, 1274

pentarchy, Eastern orthodox, 200, 207

Pentecost, 194

Pentecostal Assemblies of God, 904

People's Action of Jacques Piou, 306

Pepe, Guglielmo, 1539

Pepin I, king of Aquitaine, 645, 680

Pepin II (the Younger), king of the Franks, 2, 598, 997

Pepin III (the Short), king of the Franks, 109, 204, 547, 577, 586, 597, 680, 1457; division of kingdom by, 1320 (*see also* Carloman; Charlemagne); Donation of, 513, 1097, 1319–1320; Donation of Constantine and, 447, 513, 1320; Gregorian chant and, 950, 952; missions and, 997; monasticism and, 1014; papal anointment, 1319; Paul I and, 182, 1064, 1120, 1121; Stephen II meeting with, 599, 1273, 1378, 1456–1457; Zacharias and, 1319, 1640

Pepoli, Count, 1342

peregrinatio (as monastic basis), 1011

Peregrinus of Misenus, 737

Peregrosso, Pietro, 280

Perennis (Roman prefect), 1154

Peres, Simon, 877

perestroika, 1086

Peretti, Alessandro, 1437

Peretti family, 1032, 1130

Peretti, Felice. *See* Sixtus V

Pericoli, Niccolò, 1595

Périer, Foulque, 82

Perigenes of Corinth, 184, 185, 1433

Perouse, republic of, 1105(map)

Perpetual Peace (1516), 1623

Perpignan, 165

Perrone, Giovanni, 78

persecutions, 63, 250, 251, 417, 422, 423, 544, 619, 966–967, 1055–1056, **1152–1156**, 1612; catacombs and, 257, 1152, 1496; by Decius, 501, 967, 1155, 1316, 1394, 1455; by Diocletian, 966, 967, 993, 1156, 1316, 1394, 1496; of early popes, 122, 214, 215, 422, 557, 831, 832, 1153, 1154, 1155, 1223, 1316; eschatology and, 1261; evangelization and, 544, 545; *lapsi* controversy, 43, 250–251, 543, 561, 698, 967–968, 1055, 1155, 1156, 1394; Marcellinus and, 966–967; martyrdoms of Peter and Paul, 1119, 1153, 1158–1159; Nero initiation of, 1153, 1314; Roman emperors and, 1313–1316; Roman prefect participation, 1230; Sixtus II as victim, 1431–1432

Volume Key: Volume 1, pages 1–614; volume 2, pages 615–1266; volume 3, pages 1267–1637.

1745

persecutions (non-Roman Empire): of early Christian heretics, 251, 545; ecumenical councils and, 427; of English Catholics, 802, 1130, 1177, 1561; by French Revolutionists, 57, 612–612; indulgences for apostasy, 773; *Kulturkampf* seen as, 892; of Montanists, 698; in Puritan England, 802; revolutionary France, 612, 613; by Vandals, 141

Persia: Arab conquest of, 1319; Byzantium and, 1318, 1319; cult of Mithra, 443; evangelization in, 544, 545, 1000, 1002; Nestorian Church, 699

personal prelature, 1234–1235

Peru: Catholic missions, 1343; Catholic University, 1544; concordat with papacy, 399; Gregory XIII missions to, 664; Inquisition in, 816

Perugia, 1342

Perugia, University of, 1544

Perugino, Pietro, 800, 1091, 1428, 1435

Peruzzi, Baldasarre, 105, 1382

Peruzzi banks, 82, 136, 137

Peruzzi, Sallustio, 1176

Pesaro, Francesco, 138, 690

Peter (St. Peter the Apostle), 140, **1156–1161**; *Acts of Peter*, 2–4, 1160; altar of confession, 38; Antioch and, 69; apolstolic blessings and, 177; Arles and, 1610; background of, 1157–1158; as basis of primacy of Rome, 32, 33, 199, 207–208, 913–914, 1107–1108, 1157, 1159, 1160, 1241–1243; beard of, 143; bishop of Rome ordination and, 181, 521, 631, 1107–1108; blessed sword and, 182; bronze statue of, 1379; Byzantine Church and, 197–198; cemetery of, 259, 261; as Church's true founder, 1119, 1159, 1160, 1161; collegiality and, 1242, 1243; election of bishops, 90; evangelization by, 544, 1158; family of, 1378, 1385–1386; feast of, 303, 569; figure on banner, 138, 693; film portrayal of, 321; Fisherman's Ring and, 587–588; Gospels and, 631–632, 1157–1158; head on bull design, 195; keys of, 138, 689–690, 692, 693, 891; Linus as successor, 947–948; liturgical calendar anniversary date, 1432; martyrdom account, 3, 548; Paul relationship, 1118–1120, 1157, 1160; pilgrimages and, 4, 548, 549, 1164, 1165, 1168; pope as title of successor, 1227; relics of, 261, 545, 1377, 1385–1386; Roman martyrdom of, 1153, 1158–1159, 1160; Simon Magus and, 1425; succession perpetuity, 1241; theft of relics of, 261; titles for sucessors, 1494–1495; tomb of, 4, 38, 478, 548, 1165, 1378, 1385, 1386, 1388; "trophy" of, 548, *See also* Chair of St. Peter; St. Peter's basilica

Peter, patriarch of Jerusalem, 14

Peter I, king of Aragon, 51, 52, 787

Peter I, king of Castille, 796

Peter I, king of Cyprus, 440

Peter II, king of Aragon, 989

Peter II, patriarch of Alexandria, 34

Peter III, king of Aragon, 440, 735, 973

Peter IV (the Cermonius), king of Aragon, 163, 659, 872

Peter Alphonse, 72, 75

Peter Capuanus, 788

Peter Chrysologus, 568, 914, 987

Peter de Bruys, 701

Peter Leopold I, ruler of Tuscany, 1535

Peter Lombard, 770, 897, 1249, 1543–1544

Peter of Ailly, 213, 238

Peter of Alexandria, 35, 44, 562, 567, 572, 573, 1426–1426

Peter of Altinum, 141, 907, 1476

Peter of Apamea, 1145

Peter of Bar, 451

Peter of Blois, 1553

Peter of Capua, 734

Peter of Cortona, 107

Peter of Cros, 459

Peter of Foulon, 737

Peter of Luxembourg, St., 340, 342

Peter of Mondovia, 192

Peter of Morrone. *See* Boniface VIII

Peter of Pavia. *See* John XIV

Peter of Pisa, 450

Peter of Ravenna, 1274

Peter of St. Chrysogone, 21

Peter of Spoleto, 838

Peter of Tarantaise, 593

Peter of Verona, 813

Peter of Villacreces, 594

Peter Os Porci. *See* Sergius IV

Peter the Chanter, 897

Peter the Fuller, 1426

Peter the Hermit, 437

Peter the Venerable, 76, 216, 276, 701, 959

Peter's Pence, 46, 372, 577, 582, 583, 584, 1644; Apostolic Palace maintenance and, 1094; devotion to the pope and, 497; first grant to John XIX, 846

Petersen, Olaf and Lawrence, 1287

petitions, 461, 462–463, 1152, **1161–1162**, 1266; datary, 461, 482, 483; registers of, 1293

Petitot, Edward, 304

Petrarch, 129, 161, 337, 906, 1221

Petriano Museum (Vatican City), 177

Petrine privilege, 1249–1250

Petrine succession. *See* papism; Peter

Petrobrusiani, 701

Petronilla, St., 549, 1064, 1121, 1378, 1386

Petrucci family, 928

Petrucci, Matteo, 31, 32, 806, 927, 1267

Petrus de Sampsone, 227

Petrus Mallinus, 188

pets. *See* animals

Pezzani, H. M., 228

Pfeiffer, Heinrich, 704

Pflug, Johann, 1125

Pharisees, 696

Philargès, Peter. *See* Alexander V

Philarghi, Pietro. *See* Alexander V

[Philip], 70, 71, **1162**

Philip, emperor of Rome, 1155

Philip I, king of France, 822, 909, 1113, 1551–1552; lay investiture renouncement, 1281

Philip II (Augustus), king of France, 278, 314, 663, 716, 787, 788; regalia and, 1291; Third Crusade and, 331, 438

Philip II, king of Spain, 317, 663, 664, 817, 887, 929, 1129, 1559; clerical marriage opposition by, 1176; conclave of 1590 and, 1608–1609; French treaty with, 1519; Lepanto and, 936, 938; marriage to Mary Tudor, 982, 1289; opposi-

Volume Key: Volume 1, pages 1–614; volume 2, pages 615–1266; volume 3, pages 1267–1637.

1746

tion to Dutch Calvinism by, 1288; papal domination by, 1102; papal elections and, 346, 394

Philip III, king of France, 440, 735, 973

Philip III, king of Spain, 667, 669, 1369, 1470

Philip IV (the Fair), king of France, 103, 127, 129, 131, 160, 615, 1622; Boniface VIII conflict, 190–191, 242, 282, 1291, 1379, 1481, 1485; Celestine V canonization campaign by, 283, 334; Clement V and, 333, 334, 335, 1604; conclave electing John XXII and, 847; *decima* and, 335, 579, 1481, 1485; Holy Roman Empire and, 316; military ordinariates, 991; papal dependency on, 1109; Templars arrest by, 988

Philip V, king of Spain, 353–354

Philip of Anjou, 353

Philip of Burgundy, 1172

Philip of Heinsberg, 313

Philip of Hesse, 1288

Philip of Swabia, 654, 715, 786

Philip the Evangelist, St., 1423

Philippe de Beaumanoir, 749

Philippe le Bel, 848

Philippines: Catholic missions in, 348, 664, 802, 1343; John Paul II travel to, 1510, 1513; plenary council (1991), 431; Vatican II representation, 1580

Philippians, Epistle to the, 327

Philomena, St., 262, 675

Philonomus the Galatian, 1164

Philosophes, 359, 360

Philosophumena (Hippolytus), 1640

Philoteus (monk), 1487

Phocas, emperor of Byzantium, 141, 1047, 1319; statue of, 186, 187

Photinus of Thessalonia, 44

Photius, patriarch of Constantinople, 202, 205–206, 207, 590, 1034; Anastasius Bibliothecarius and, 46; Constantinople IV and, 428, 682, 969, 1034; conversion of Bulgaria and, 318; forced resignation of, 1459; on Holy Spirit procession, 1394; John VIII and, 836–837, 969

photography, **1162–1163**; cinematic, 320–323, 435–436, 1164; of daily lives of popes, 1248

physicians. *See* medicine

Piacentini, P., 1018

Piacenza, 345, 928, 1031, 1102

Piacenza, Council of (1095), 1552

Piacenza, Dionigi di, 329

Piacenza, Umberto and Pietro da, 1360

Piacenza, University of, 1548

Pic de la Mirandole, 900 theses (1486), 799

Piccinino, Giacomo, 218

Piccirillo, Carlo, 324

Piccolomini, Agostino Patrizi, 284, 294, 485

Piccolomini, Enea Silvio. *See* Pius II

Piccolomini family, 692, 1032, 1173

Pichon, Charles, 1236

Pichon, Stephen, 174

Pico della Mirandola, Giovanni, 799, 898

Piedmont: French occupations, 1621, 1624; Guelphs and, 676; Italian unity and, 1017–1018, 1324, 1536, 1537, 1539, 1540, 1541, 1646; jurisdictionalism, 889; Napoléon's army in, 612

Piedmont-Sardinia, kingdom of, 1539, 1540

Pierbenedetti, Cardinal, 1129

Pierleoni family, 72, 451, 625, 731, 732, 733, 1035, 1048; [Anacetus II] and, 254, 900; Callistus II alliance, 216; Celestine II and, 275; Frangipani rivalry, 783; Paschal II and, 1114

Pierleoni, Giordano, 532, 960, 1334

Pierleoni, Piero. *See* [Anacletus II]

Piero of Taranto, 962

Pierozzi, Antonio, 508–509

Pierre. *For names not found below, see also* Peter; Petrus

Pierre, Jean-Baptiste, 250

Pierre d'Ailly. *See* Ailly, Pierre d'

Pierre de Besse, 457

Pierre de Capoue, 438

Pierre de Colmieu, 126, 1279

Pierre de Cros, 80, 219

Pierre de Cugnieres, 336

Pierre de la Vigne, 242

Pierre de Marca, 1466

Pierre de Monteruc, 460

Pierre de Mortemart, 336

Pierre de Tarentaise. *See* Innocent V

Pierre des Près, 460

Pierre Monge, 737

Pierre of Corbeil, 785

Pierro de Banhac, 460, 1556

Pietà dei Carcerati, 1309, 1311

Pietàs, 1033, 1275, 1385

Pietism, 704–705, 1272

Pietrasancta, Giscardo di, 1555

Pietri, Charles, 101, 1411

Pietro IV di Vico, 1555

Pietro da Ancharano, 635

Pietro da Cortona, 1089, 1091, 1092, 1271, 1344, 1560, 1562

Pietro di Oderisio, 1500

Pietro Leopoldo, grand duke of Tuscany, 1345

Pigalle, Jean-Baptiste, 118

Pignatelli, Antonio. *See* Innocent XII

Pignotte (almonry), 458

pilgrimage, **1163–1171**; antiquity, **1163–1165**; Middle Ages, **1165–1169**; modern and contemporary era, 173, 519, 520, **1169–1171**, 1345; "ad limina" visits, 4–5, 1167; Alexander VI and, 27; audiences with pope, 125; to Canterbury, 725, 1076; to catacombs, 260, 261, 1164, 1165; criticisms of, 1169; crusades linked with, 437; dispensations, 505; end of Avignon-Rome schism, 1041; Gregory II and, 643; guides to Rome, 1166, 1167, 1168, 1170, 1328; to Holy Land, 724, 1163, 1167; hospices for, 316–317, 448, 1165, 1168, 1169, 1170, 1225, 1301, 1310; indulgences and, 519, 724, 725, 774, 1165, 1168, 1169, 1170; Jansenist condemnation of, 867; John Paul II and, 865; liturgy and, 952; medallions and, 983; military orders assistance to, 987; national churches in Rome and, 316; papal fleet protection, 1029; Paul III and, 1170; Paul VI and, 1514, 1515, 1516; penitential, 1167, 1168; penitentiaries for, 1151, 1169, 1170, 1523; photographs of, 1163; religious life and, 1275; Roman architectural rebuilding and, 103, 104, 105, 106, 1116, 1328; Roman beautification and, 1340; Roman contraternities, 1307; to St. John Lateran basilica, 1362; to St. Peter's basilica, 4, 254, 548, 549, 1163, 1165, 1377, 1378, 1380; vicarious, 1168, *See also* Holy Year

Volume Key: Volume 1, pages 1–614; volume 2, pages 615–1266; volume 3, pages 1267–1637.

1747

pilgrimages, 1168, 1169

Pilippicus, emperor of Byzantium, 420

Pillet, A., 228, 364

Pinacoteca, 1117

Pinmei, Ignatius Gong, 245

Pinturicchio, 27–28, 800, 1174, 1428

Pio di Carpi, Rodolfo, 968

Pio di Savoia, 1117

Pipia, Augustin, 511

Pippinides, 957

Piranese, Giambattista, 171

Pironio, Edward, 434

Pirri, Pietro, 608

Pisa, 653, 1393

Pisa, Council of (1409), 162, 165, 594, 635–636, 637; cardinalate powers and, 242; conciliarism at, 390; Gregory XII and, 25, 72, 132, 137, 636, 661, 1305; [John XXIII] and, 852; Martin V and, 975; papal chaplain, 301; papal schism following, 1109, 1246

Pisa, Council of (1511), 391, 509; Lateran V as response to, 898

Pisanello, 537, 982, 983, 1361

Pisari, Pasquale, 298

Piscator, Edwin, 495, 496

piscina (baptistry pool), 139

Pistoia, synod of (1786), 505, 617, 670, 671, 825, 1180, 1345

Pitra, Cardinal, 1574

Pitti Palace, 1271

Pittochi, Francesco, 853

Pius I, 57, **1171**

Pius II, 25, 104, 471, 536, 1122, **1171–1174**; abbreviators for, 1; Alexander VI and, 25; animals and, 58; arms, 114; asssessment of, 1173; banner, 689; Callistus III and, 218; canonization of Catherine of Siena by, 265, 1173; cartography, 252; ceremonials, 284; children of, 26; conciliarism condemned by, 391, 1518; crusades, 38, 440, 1172–1173, 1417, 1526; as eyewitness to death of Eugene IV, 485; heraldry, 690; humanist works by, 1294; military orders and, 990; naval forces, 1030, 1173; nepotism and, 1032, 1173, 1174; painting commissions, 1089; on papal temporal authority, 1101; Paul II conflict with, 1121; pet parrot, 58; Pius III and, 1032; poor health of, 1416, 1417; slavery and, 1439, 1440; tomb of, 1384, 1503; writings by, 1173

Pius III, **1174–1175**; arms, 114; Discalced friars and, 595; humanism and, 1295; Julius II suceeding, 885; nepotism and, 1032; Pius II and, 1032, 1173, 1174

Pius IV, 669, 886, **1175–1176**; ancient marbles collection, 1024; Anglican schism and, 54–55; annona, 61; apostasy and, 79; arms, 693; art and architectural projects, 1176; cardinal nephew. *See* Borromeo, Charles; Castel Sant'Angelo improvements, 255; Church-State relations and, 1609; coins, 374; conclave regulatiopn, 393; Congregation of the Council founding, 415, 1357; council and, 242, 471; Curia reform, 465; Fabric of St. Peter and, 558; humanism and, 1296; Index revision, 763, 770, 772, 1175, 1296; Jesuits and, 827; Latinity and, 906; medallions, 982; Michelangelo's *Last Judgment* alteration and, 1093, 1431; mural map, 252, 253; nunciatures and, 664, 1059; palace, 1598; Pius V and, 1177; seminaries, 1408; slavery and, 1440; Tridentine reforms and, 416, 429, 471, 995, 1175–1176, 1277, 1408, 1518, 1519, 1522; Urban

VII and, 1559; Vatican Archives and, 1604; Vatican gardens and, 1595, 1596

Pius V, 346, 669, **1176–1178**; Anglican schism and, 55; arms, 114; beatification of, 145, 351; breviary text, 193, 194; canonical code, 363; canonization of, 496; cardinal nephew and, 245, 1469; Catechism of Council of Trent and, 263, 1522; Chancery changes, 293, 1590; chef for, 303; Congregation of the Index and, 465, 471, 770, 772, 1178, 1341, 1357; congregations and, 415; Counter Reformation and, 509, 1176, 1177–1178, 1246, 1342; Curia reforms, 465, 466, 471, 1467–1468; Dominicans and, 510, 1176, 1177; finances and, 374; Gregory XIII and, 663, 664; heraldry, 690; Holy League and, 938, 1177, 1179; humanism and, 1296; Inquisition and, 1176, 1177, 1179, 1199; Jesuits and, 827, 1000; Jewish expulsion by, 374, 873; Jewish ghettoization by, 1177; jurisdictional conflicts, 888; Lepanto and, 937, 1176, 1177, 1179, 1369; liturgical reform, 954, 995; Michelangelo's *Last Judgment* and, 1093; missions and, 1000, 1001, 1002; nepotism and, 1469; Papal States and, 1103; penitentiaries, 1152, 1523; Petrine privilege and, 1250; as Pius VI namesake, 1179; Reformation and, 1286; sedan chair use, 1228; Sixtus V and, 1436; slavery and, 1440; statuary removal by, 1024; superintendent of the Ecclesiastical State, 1469; Swiss Guard, 1471; tomb of, 1369

Pius VI, 170, 317, **1178–1182**; banner of, 138; beatifications and, 146; camauro disuse, 620; canonizations by, 235; cardinalate and, 244; chamberlains, 288; Clement XIII and, 359; Clement XIV and, 362; coins, 376–377; conclave procedure, 394; Counter Reformation and, 936; cursors, 475; death of, 1184, 1185; devotion to the pope and, 496; dispensations and, 505; Dominicans and, 511; encyclicals, 954, 977, 978, 1179; Enlightenment condemnation by, 528, 530, 671, 1178, 1179; exile of, 1181; French Revolution and, 122, 470, 530, 611–612, 613, 1010, 1103, 1178, 1181–1182; heraldry, 690, 693; Jesuits and, 470, 828; Jewish repression by, 1179; Leo XII and, 930; liturgy and, 954; as martyr pope, 1184; Marxism condemned by, 977, 978; mosaics commission, 1020; Napoleonic imprisonment of, 122, 298, 470, 613, 1103; nepotism, 1033, 1049, 1180, 1181; obelisks of Rome and, 1061; Pius VII and, 1182, 1183, 1184; printing press and, 1444; Prophecies of Malachy and, 1260, 1263; Ultramontism of, 617–618; Vatican museums and, 1025, 1092, 1117; Vatican Observatory and, 1062; witticism of, 743

Pius VII, 930, **1182–1190**; academies, 2; annona, 62; Apostolic Camera functions, 9; arms, 112, 115, 693; banner colors, 138; beatifications and, 147; bells, 152; camerlengo restrictions, 220–221; canonizations by, 235; chamberlains, 288; conclave electing, 244, 393, 1184, 1357; concordat with France, 398, 1185–1186; congregations and, 409; Congress of Vienna and, 687; datary reduction, 483; devotion to the pope and, 496; Dominicans and, 512; encyclicals, 1184; Fabric of St. Peter and, 558; film portrayal of, 322; finances and, 377; floreria (warehouse), 588; Freemasonry condemned by, 605, 1189; Gregory XVI and, 671; heraldry, 696; honorary private chaplains, 301; imprisonment of, 1187–1188; Jesuit reestablishment by, 362, 828, 1189, 1523; Leo XII and, 930, 931; medallion, 983, 1022; Napoléon's crowning by, 1186; Napoléon's relations with, 122–123, 584–587, 618, 1103, 1105, 1182, 1185–1188; Noble Guard

Volume Key: Volume 1, pages 1–614; volume 2, pages 615–1266; volume 3, pages 1267–1637.

creation, 740, 1051; obelisks of Rome and, 1061–1062; Palatine Guard, 1095; papal authority restoration by, 1103; papal chapel musicians and, 298; papal titles and, 1050; Pius VIII and, 1190; Pontifical Gendarmes, 626; Quirinal and, 1272; Roman monuments and, 1016; Roman Republic and, 1321; Rota decisions and, 1350; St. Paul's Outside the Walls fire and, 1371; secret societies denuciation, 605; Signatura Apostolic and, 1525; Substitute of the Secretariat of State creation, 1464; Swiss Guard and, 1471; tiara, 1489; Vatican Library and, 1598

Pius VIII, **1190–1191**; arms, 115; beatification, 147; Church-State powers and, 1536, 1538; encyclical list, 524; Gregory XVI and, 671, 672

Pius IX, 78, 679, 695, 932, **1191–1197**, 1198; administrators and, 8; antechamber rules and, 437; apostasy decretal, 79; Apostolic Camera functions, 9; Apostolic Palace management, 1094; arbitration proposal, 99; archeological interest, 100, 389; architectural projects, 1016, 1017, 1022; arms, 116; arts patronage, 121, 1116; assessment of pontificate, 1196; attacks on liberalism by, 306; beatification, 147; brief and, 195; camauro rare use, 620; camerlengo duties, 221; canonizations by, 235; cardinal "in petto," 245; cardinalate and, 244, 1357; Castel Sant'Angelo and, 255; chaplains, 301; chinea tribute, 303; Church-State conflicts and, 1110; *Civiltà Cattolica* and, 324, 325, 1194; Code of Canon Law (1917) and, 363, 395; Code of Canons of Eastern Churches and, 370; coins, 377; commission, 389; conclave electing, 1357; conclave secular nonintervention bull, 394–395; concordats, 397, 398, 1256; congregations and, 407; conservatism of, 605, 606; coronation anniversary, 299; daily life descriptions, 1248; datary powers, 483; decorations, 487, 488; devotion to the pope and, 497; Dominicans and, 511–512; encyclical list, 525; encyclicals, 525, 954, 977, 1109, 1192, 1195; Fabric of St. Peter and, 558; feast of Sacred Heart and, 211; finances, 582; free expression condemned by, 1443; Freemasonry condemned by, 601, 604–605, 606, 607; fundamentalism and, 613–614; heraldry, 696; Holy Childhood Society and, 709; Holy Sepulcher order and, 723; Holy Year and, 260, 728; Immaculate Conceptiion dogma proclamation, 1194; imprimatur, 763; infallibility proclamation, 512, 778, 1194, 1196; Italian unification and, 1023, 1107, 1191, 1193–1196, 1247, 1324, 1533, 1537, 1539, 1541, 1570; Jesuit relationship, 324, 828; Jewish policies, 864, 873; *Kulturkampf* reaction by, 892, 893; Leo XIII contrasted with, 933, 934; letters to, 939, 940; liberalism and, 944, 1109; liturgy, 954; Marxism denunciations by, 977; military chaplains and, 990; military mobilization, 1643, 1644, 1645; missions and, 176; modern society condemnation, 674, 860, 944, 1010, 1109, 1195, 1196, 1247, 1472–1475, 1565; Moroni's Church history and, 143; museum collection, 1026; Noble Guard and, 1052; official hymn, 744; Old Catholics schism and, 1395–1396; Order of, 487, 488; Palatine Guard founding, 740; papal apartments, 72; papal titles and, 1050, 1051; papal tombs and, 1386, 1499; Paul VI and, 1132, 1133; photography and, 1162, 1163; power and spiritual control by, 39; primacy doctrine, 1196; printing press and, 1444; Propaganda Fide and, 1256; protonotary measures, 1263; Quirinal and, 1272; reform and, 436, 1104, 1323, 1469; reserved cases reorganization, 1298; Roman nobility and, 1050; Roman Republic (1849) and,

1323, 1325, 1326; St. Paul's Outside the Walls rebuilding, 1031, 1372; Secretariat of State, 1402; sedan chair use, 1228; seminaries and, 1409; spiritual demands by, 1110; superintendent of the Ecclesiastical State and, 1469; Ultramontanism and, 1530; Vatican I convocation, 429, 778, 1195, 1196, 1565, 1567, 1568, 1572, 1574; Vatican I suspension, 1570; walks through Rome streets, 125; witticism of, 743, *See also* Syllabus of Errors

Pius X, 1133, **1197–1199**, 1384; abbreviator post elimination, 1; "ad limina" visits and, 4; administrative offices, 9; announcement of election, 679; Apostolic Camera functions, 9; apostolic constitution changes, 421–422, 1402; Apostolic Palace management, 1094; arms, 116, 693; automobile, 126; ban on castrati recruitment, 257; beatifications and, 148, 271, 322, 865; Benedict XV as successor, 173, 176; blessing *urbi et orbi* and, 177; breviary reform, 194; canonizations by, 234, 236, 271; catechism of, 1197, 1198; Catholic University founding, 1545, 1546; Chancery and, 293; Christian Democracy and, 306, 1197; Church-State conflict and, 175, 1110, 1541; Code of Canon Law (1917) and, 175, 228–229, 362–364, 366; Codes of Canons of Eastern Churches and, 370; conclave electing, 503, 551, 1197, 1609; conclave regulation bull, 395, 668, 1405; Congregation for Bishops and, 408–409; congregations and, 408, 409, 410, 411; consistorial advocates and, 413; Curia reform, 1, 7, 8, 10, 11, 12, 243, 472, 1197, 1257, 1349, 1357, 1403; datary reform, 483; decorations and, 487–488; Dominicans and, 512; encyclical list, 525; exclusion ban by, 551; Fabric of St. Peter and, 558; film biography of, 322; film viewing by, 320; financial management, 582, 583; Franciscans and, 597; Freemasonry opposition, 608; fundamentalism and, 613, 614; heraldry, 696; Holy Office and, 709, 710; Holy See missions, 718; Holy Sepulcher order and, 723; imprimatur, 763; Italian unity and, 1570; Jewish relations, 874; letters to, 939; liberalism and, 944; modernism encyclical, 79, 307, 1005, 1006, 1008, 1010, 1023, 1198–1199; Noble Guard and, 1052; Opera dei congressi suppression, 1023; papal apartments, 73; Penitentiary modifications, 1152, 1523; Propaganda Fide and, 1257; protonotary measures, 1, 1264; Rota tribunal and, 1350; Secretariat of Briefs, 1400; secretaries of state, 1197, 1211, 1464; seminaries and, 1407, 1409; Signatora Apostolic and, 1525; simonical election bull abrogation by, 393; social teachings, 1447; sociopolitical orientation, 1198; suburbicarian Italy and, 1466; temporal veto prohibition by, 1609; Vatican museum collection, 1026; Vatican Observatory and, 1063; Venice and, 863

Pius XI, 89, 177, 1132, **1199–1210** , 1464, 1598, 1628; academies and, 2; administrative offices, 10; Anglican reunion and, 1074; announcement of new pope simplification, 679; archaeology and, 101; arms, 116, 690, 693; assessment of pontificate, 1199–1200; *Auadragesimo anno* encyclical, 1447; automobile, 126–127; beatifications, 148, 271; bishops' conferences, 401; blessing *urbi et orbi* and, 177; bull design, 195; canon law and, 368; canon law of Eastern Churches and, 370; canonizations, 271, 1204; canonizations by, 236; cardinalate and, 243–244; Castel Gandolfo renovation, 73; Catholic university founding, 1546; causes of canonization and, 269; causes of saints and, 408; chamberlains, 288; Christian Democracy and, 308, 309, 1023; on Christ's

Volume Key: Volume 1, pages 1–614; volume 2, pages 615–1266; volume 3, pages 1267–1637.

1749

peace in Christ's kingdom, 1203–1204, 1206; cinema and, 320, 322, 1205; conciliarism and, 1571; conclave electing, 1201; conclave regulation, 395, 1405–1406; concordatory policy, 1206–1207, 1209; daily life descriptions, 1248; Dominicans and, 512; ecclesiastical faculties and, 1544; ecumenical council plans by, 1570–1571, 1572; encyclical list, 526; encyclicals, 305, 309, 320, 368, 518, 519, 524, 978, 1203, 1204, 1205, 1206, 1207, 1208, 1209, 1212, 1447, 1570; epitaph for, 1199; fascism and, 305, 308, 524, 874, 901, 903; Feast of Christ the King, 211; finances, 582, 583; fundamentalist reaction to, 614; heraldry, 696; on Holy Land status, 712, 723; on Holy Places, 712; Holy Year, 728, 729; Jesuits and, 828; Lateran pacts and, 317, 583, 901–904, 1202, 1247, 1541; League of Nations and, 1077–1078; legate of, 913; liberalism/socialism viewed by, 979; Marxism condemned by, 110, 305, 978, 1110, 1207–1209, 1447, 1449, 1462, 1629, 1631; Marxism-socialism distinction by, 977–978; media and information offices, 984; modernism viewed by, 1009, 1110, 1203; mountaineering, 1202, 1248; native clergy training and, 1004; Nazism condemned by, 305, 524, 874–875, 978, 979, 1110, 1203, 1209, 1212, 1447, 1449, 1629, 1631; *Osservatore Romano* support for, 1082; *ostpolitik*, 1084–1085; Paul VI relationship, 1136, 1141; Penitentiary, 1152; personality of, 864, 1201–1202; Petrine privilege and, 1250; Pius XII relationship, 1212–1213, 1630; *possesso* ceremony, 1228–1229; press coverage of death, 1236; protonotary measures, 1264; punning by, 743; Rota tribunal and, 1350; social teachings, 309, 674, 1447, 1449, 1462; statement against racism, 1209; subsidiarity definition, 1462, 1463; telephone, 1481; on unionism over ecumenism, 518, 519; Vatican citizenship and, 323–324; Vatican City State and, 1203, 1587, 1589, 1592; Vatican museum collection, 1026; Vatican Observatory and, 1063; Vatican Radio founding, 1205, 1444, 1600

Pius XII, 59, 70, **1210–1220**; academies and, 2; allocution topics to Rota, 36; announcement of election, 679; apostolic constitution use, 421; arms, 116, 692, 693; assessment of pontificate, 1247; Assumption of the Virgin Mary dogma, 124, 421; beatification of Innocent XI, 806; beatification process for, 1140; beatifications and, 149, 271, 865; Benedict XV and, 174, 175, 177; bishops' conferences, 401; camauro and, 620; as camerlengo, 221; canonizations by, 234, 236, 271; cardinal's *cappa magna* and, 267; Catholic Universities federation, 1544; chamberlains, 288; Chinese rites and, 529; Chinese schism encyclical, 1396–1397; Christian Democracy and, 305, 309, 310, 1136, 1215; Christmas message on democracy (1942), 305, 309; on Church neutrality, 1588; cinema and, 321, 322, 323, 436, 1444; Code of Canon Law (1917) and, 365; Code of Canons of Eastern Churches and, 370; conciliarism and, 1571, 1572; conclave vote reform, 22, 395, 1406; concordat with Franco Spain (1953), 397; congregations and, 406, 411; daily life descriptions, 1248; death photographs of, 1236, 1248; *Deputy* (Hochhuth) play about, 495–496, 1141, 1214; devotion to the pope renewal under, 497; Dominicans and, 512; ecumenical council plans by, 1570, 1571–1572; encyclical list, 526; encyclicals, 321, 519, 539, 955, 977, 1136, 1141, 1203, 1214, 1217, 1218, 1629; finances, 583; as former minutante, 994; on French Church "new theology," 1217; heraldry, 696; Holocaust and,

495–496, 875, 876, 877, 1214; Holy Places and, 713, 875; Holy Sepulcher order and, 723; Holy Year and, 728, 729; Index revision, 772, 1443; Jesuits and, 828; Jewish relations, 877, 1635 (*see also* Holocaust); John XXIII and, 853, 854; John Paul II and, 861; last years of pontificate, 1572; Latin America Commission, 388; as legate, 913; letters to, 940; liturgical movement support by, 955, 1217; Marxism denunciations and, 977, 1631; modernism encyclical, 1009; motto of, 1630; native clergy development and, 1005, 1218; Nazi condemnation by, 875, 876; nepotism, 1033; papal apartments, 73; Paul VI relationship, 1132, 1136–1137, 1140, 1141; personal qualities, 864; photographs of, 1163, 1248; Pius XI naming as successor, 1630; as Pius XI nuncio, 1203, 1207, 1208; as Pius XI secretary of state, 1212–1213; pontifical march, 299; *possesso* ceremony, 1229; press coverage, 1236, 1240, 1248; on public opinion, 1240; radio message on *Rerum novarum* anniversary, 1200, 1447, 1463; ransom paid for Roman Jewish population by, 1635; Roman nobility and, 1051; sedia gestatoria, 1405; social communications, 1444–1445, 1447, 1463; subsidiarity principle, 1463; telephone use, 1481; television use, 1444, 1445; Third World and, 1217–1218; tomb of, 1384; on Uniates, 1532; on unionism over ecumenism, 519, 520, 539–540; United Nations and, 1078, 1079; Vatican City State and, 1590, 1592; Vatican Radio and, 1444, 1600; World War I diplomacy by, 1627, 1630; World War II and, 174, 175, 305, 322, 583, 875, 978, 1085, 1212, 1213–1214, 1215, 1588, 1626, 1629–1636

Pius XII and the Second World War (Blet), 1214

Pizzardo, Cardinal, 1134, 1135, 1136, 1203, 1236, 1574, 1630

Placidia, Galla, 273

plague and the papacy, **1220–1222**; Cornelius and, 423, 1155; Dominicans and, 508; Flagellants and, 703; Frederick Barbarossa defeated by, 20; Great Schism and, 635; Gregory I and, 254, 1220; Gregory XIV measures, 666; [Paschal III] and, 1114; right of spoil and, 336; Roman epidemics, 1328, 1329; sack of Rome following, 1354, *See also* Black Death

Plantagenets, 21, 314, 881

Plantin, Christopher, 995

Platina (Barolomeo Sacchi), 830, 1065, 1122, 1434, 1435, 1597

Plato, 75, 1294, 1296

Pleart, Etienne, 1229

plenary congregation. *See* congregation, plenary

plenary council, 431, 1570

plenary indulgences. *See* indulgences

plenitudo potestatis, 786, 1031, 1032, 1484, 1485; cardinalate and, 242, 393, 1356; Innocent III claims, 786, 1246, 1484; Leo I claims, 1108

Plethon, George Gemist, 75

Pliny the Younger, 1153, 1154, 1314, 1594

Ploart, Etienne, 1229

Plüddemann, H., 239

Plutarch, 151

pluviale, 426

Pneumatomachians, 428

Podesti, Francesco, 1372–1373

Poggiani, Giulio, 263

Poggini, Domenico, 982

Poincaré, Henri, 174

Poirino, Giacomo da, 1195

Volume Key: Volume 1, pages 1–614; volume 2, pages 615–1266; volume 3, pages 1267–1637.

1750

Poland: Blessed Hat and Sword gifts to, 182; Calvinism in, 1288; Clement VIII and, 348; Clement X and, 351–352; Clement XI evangelization of, 355; concordat with (1993), 404; Council of Trent representation, 1518; Counter Reformation and, 1290; crusades, 333; diplomatic ties with Holy See, 503; feast days, 360; Great Schism and, 632, 636; Gregorian calendar and, 213; Gregory XIII and, 663–664; Gregory XVI and, 673; Holy Roman Empire and, 714; Innocent XII and, 808; Jesuit college, 379; Jesuits and, 371; Jewish persecution, 170, 371, 873, 876; John Paul II and, 859, 860–864, 876; John Paul II travel to, 10, 860, 1513; missions to, 997; Orthodox/Catholic confrontations, 522, 523; *ostpolitik*, 863, 1084–1085, 1086; in papal early 15th-century domain, 661; papal nunciature in, 1059, 1179; partitions of, 1532; Paul VI as nunciature attaché to, 1134–1135, 1223; Peter's Pence payment, 577; Pius XI as apostolic visitator, 1200–1201; Pius XII and, 1215, 1216; Protestantism in, 1128, 1288; Russian suppression of, 673; Turks in, 351; Uniates, 1531, 1532; Urban VI support by, 1558; Vatican I and, 1566; Vatican II representation, 1576, 1581, 1583; western European bishops and, 540; World War II and, 1631, 1632–1633

Polanski, Marco, 323

Polanski, Roman, 323

Pole, Reginald, 54, 56, 887, 913, 968, 1073, 1518, 1521; Paul III and, 1124, 1125; reform and, 1276; seminary proposal, 1407–1408

Poletti, L., 1016, 1372

Poli, Giovanni, 1335

police, Vatican. *See* Gendarmes, Pontifical

Polier, Jacques, 764

Polish College (Rome), 1408

Pollaiuolo, Antonio, 800, 1381, 1503

Pollak, Ludwig, 1026

Polo, Marco, 322, 658, 1526

polyandry, 1250

Polycarp of Smyrna, 57, 517, 560–561, 566, 620, 1612

Polycrates of Ephesus, 1031, 1612

polygamy, 1250

Polyglot Typology, 1198

polyphonic music, 298, 457, 954, 1435

Polyptique (Gelasius), 940

polyptych, 575–576

polytheism, 443

Pomarancio, Nicolo, 1090, 1383

Pompei, Emperor of Rome, 64

Pompeianus, 1046

Pomponazzi, Pietro, 899

Pons de Melgueil, 216

Pons of Cluny, 1113

Ponte Rotto, 665

Pontellil, Baccio, 106–107

Pontian, 63, 71, 181, 708, **1222–1223**, 1496; martyrdom of, 1155, 1223

pontifical academies. *See* academies, pontifical; *specific institutions by key words*

pontifical biographies. *See Liber pontificalis*

pontifical documents. *See* Chancery, papal

pontifical emblems. *See* heraldry

Pontifical Gregorian University. *See* Gregorian University

Pontifical Mission Societies. *See* Societies, Pontifical Mission

Pontifical Missionary Union. *See* Missionary Union, Pontifical

Pontifical Palace of Montecavallo. *See* Quirinal

Pontifical Salesian University. *See* Salesian Pontifical University

pontifical secret. *See* secret, pontifical

Pontifical Society of the Holy Childhood. *See* Holy Childhood, Pontifical Society of the

pontifical titles. *See* titles, pontifical

Pontine marshes drainage, 1180

Ponzio, Flaminio, 1270

Poor Clares, 13, 246, 591, 1038

poor relief, **1223–1227**; almonry, 37–38, 454, 458, 1225; Curia and, 448, 454, 458; *diaconia*, 497–498; Gregory I and, 1319; Innocent XII measures for, 809; John XXIII and, 855; John Paul I and, 857; papal subsidies, 580, 582, 583–584; Peter's Pence, 46, 577, 582, 583, 584; for pilgrimage beggars, 316, 1169; for plague victims, 1220, 1221; Roman confraternities, 1307–1313; Sixtus V public works program, 1437

pope, **1227**; "alternative," 283; appointment of bishops by, 93; beatification and canonization as prerogatives of, 268; as bishop of Rome, 180–181, 538; devotion to, 496–497, 1169, 1170; *Liber pontificalis* (biographies), 941–943; list of mottoes, 1262–1263; onomastics, 1064–1068; papism and, 1107–1111; private life, 1238; sex verification rite (supposed), 829, 830; as supreme judge, 84–85; veneration of, 1391–1392; vocation vs. career, 247–248, *See also* primacy, papal

popemobile, 127, 1405

"Popes' Prophecies." *See* prophecies (of Malarchy)

Popish Plot (1678; England), 55

Poppon (Poppo of Brixen). *See* Damasus II

Populars. *See* Italian People's Party

population policy. *See* birth control

Populorum progressio (1967 encyclical), 512, 1447, 1449

Porcari, Stefano, 1042

Pormarancio, Il, 665

Porphyry, 1157

Porsenna, 738

Porta Pia, 1272

Portal, Fernand, 56, 934, 1075, 1076, 1395

portantina papale, **1228**

Portogruaro, Bernardino da, 596

portraiture, papal, 1117, 1123, 1372; photographic, 1163; Sistine Chapel, 1428, 1435

Port-Royal circle, 29, 824

Portugal, 163; appointment of bishops, 89, 93, 94; artists in Rome, 119; Benedict XIV and Jesuits in, 169, 171, 530; Blessed Hat and Sword gifts to, 182; cardinalate and, 241; churches in Rome, 316–317; colonial policies, 1002–1003, 1343; concordat with (1857), 1194–1195, 1256; concordat with (1940), 397, 399, 1216; exclusion right, 550; Goa colony, 1193, 1194–1195, 1256; Great Schism, 340, 632, 633, 636; Gregorian calendar, 213; Gregory XVI and, 674; Inquisition in, 816, 817–820; Jesuit expulsion, 359, 828, 1004, 1346; John Paul II visit to, 1569; Lucius II and, 960; military orders, 989; missionizing by, 999–1000, 1002, 1255; New World conquests, 27, 98, 999–1000; papal nunciature in, 1059; Paul VI visit to, 1515, 1569; Pius VI and,

Volume Key: Volume 1, pages 1–614; volume 2, pages 615–1266; volume 3, pages 1267–1637.

1751

1179–1180; Urban VI support by, 1558; Vatican II representation, 1583

Portuguese Asia, 29, 999, 1000, 1002

Posi, Paolo, 304

positivism, 78, 1182

possesso, 425, 426–427, 475, **1228–1229**; route of, 1228, 1363–1364; tiara and, 1489

Possevins, Antonio, 1531

postage stamps, 10, **1229**

Postel, Guillaume, 968

Postel, Jean, 302

postmodernity, 1009

Potocki, Count, 893

Pottier, Antoine, 306

Poudres Conspiracy (1605), 55

Pouget, Bertrand du, 132

Pouilli, Jean de, 336

Pounjet, Betrand du, 911

Poupard, Paul, 435, 1237

Poussin, Nicolas, 118, 1090, 1092, 1345, 1383, 1562

poverty. *See* poor relief

poverty ideal, 133; Franciscans and. *See* Spirituals; as heresy, 574, 1096, 1121, 1122; of Jesus and apostles, 336, 415, 849; Lateran II silence on, 901; monastic vows and, 1011; Vercelli synod on, 1280

Pozzi, G., 982

Pozzo, Cassiano del, 1090, 1092, 1344, 1363

PPI. *See* Italian People's Party

Praeceptum (monastic rules), 1013

praecordia pontificis, 267

Praetextatus's catacombs, 258, 1496

Pragmatic Sanction (1438), 581, 926, 1623; abolishment of, 927, 928, 1122, 1172, 1623; benefices and, 1266, 1298; Eugene IV and, 536, 616; Lateran V and, 899, 926, 927, 928; Leo X and, 616; as negation of theocracy, 1486; Nicholas V and, 1041

Prague defenestration (1618), 1130

Prague, diocese of, 155

Prague, Soviet invasion (1968), 863

Prague, University of, 193, 703, 1544

Prata, Pileo da, 1558

Pravda (Soviet publication), 855

Praxeas, 699, 1640

preachers apostolic, 981

Preachers, Order of. *See* Dominicans

Preciado, Francisco, 119

predestination, 167, 704, 1288

predictions. *See* prophecies

prefect of the city, **1229–1231**; last, 1330; Roman nobles as, 1045, 1046

Prefecture for the Economic Affairs of the Holy See. *See* administrative offices, Roman

Prefecture of the Papal Household, 6–7, 221, 738, 739

Prefecture of the Praetorium, **1231**, 1610

prejudices, **1231–1233**; against Rome, 1354; confraternities and, 1311

prelatures, 992, **1233–1236**; Palatine, 1094–1095; personal, 1234–1235; territorial (list), 1233–1234

Prélot, Marcel, 944

Premonstratensians, 379, 655, 732

Pre-Raphaelites, 121

Presbyterian Church, 1288

presbyterium, 444, 445, 471, 941

Presentation of the Notre Dame, Congregation of, 553–554

press. *See* media, communication, and the Vatican; *specific publications*

Press and Entertainment, Secretariat for the, 1445

press freedom, 673, 1539; as error in Pius IX *Syllabus*, 1195, 1443; Holy Office control of, 1443–1444; as Holy See press office issue, 1239, 1240

press office of the Holy See, 984, 985, 1049–1050, **1236–1240**; daily life of pope and, 1248; social communications and, 1442

Pretaxtatus, 1046

Preussische Historische Institut, 1603

Prez, Josquin des, 297

Prierias, Silvester, 1286

priesthood training. *See* seminaries

Priests of the Mission. *See* Lazarists

Prignano, Bartolomeo. *See* Urban VI

Prígnano, Francesco, 53, 341

Prima Petri (First Letter of Peter), 197–198

primacy, papal, **1240–1248**; definition of, 1240–1241; over collegiality, 385, 1242–1243, 1244, 1247; legate as manifestation of, 907; Peter as basis. *See under* Peter; powers of, 1242; prophetism and, 1263; scriptural foundations, 631–632, 1241; Vatican I and, 56, 429, 1196, 1494, 1568, 1570, *See also* infallibility

primacy, papal, historical development of papal office, **1244–1248**; Agatho and, 16; Alexandria and, 32–33, 34, 915; Anglican communion and, 56; Byzantine Church and, 14, 199, 317–318, 480, 562–563, 564, 621–622, 657–658, 915, 1245, 1395, 1426; Carthage and, 250, 251; Clement V affirmation of, 796; Clement VI defense of, 336; consistorial allocution and, 37; council as challenge to, 1109; Curia functioning and, 464; Damasus I and, 479, 480; Dominican defense of, 509; Donation of Constantine bolstering, 513; ecumenical councils and, 427; ecumenism and, 521, 522; Felix I and, 571; Gallican resistance to, 615–618; Gelasius I and, 621–622; Gregorian reforms and, 1278, 1279; Gregory VII *Dictatus Papae* on, 650, 1108, 1280, 1281; Gregory XVI on, 671; Guelphs and, 676; heresies and, 700–701; Holy See and, 718; Innocent I and, 782, 783; Jansenism and decline of, 825; John XXII and, 850; John Paul II and, 865; Josphism and, 869; Julius II and, 34, 509; Lateran I and, 216; Leo I and, 913, 915, 917, 918; Luther's challenge to, 1286; Maronites and, 319; military orders and, 987; 19th-century movement, 1566; Pius VI and, 1179; Pius IX and, 1196; sack of Rome (1527) and, 1354; St. Peter's basilica as symbol of, 1377, 1384–1385, 1386; Stephen I and, 1108; Syllabus of Errors on, 1475; Symmachus and, 1108; theocratic arguments and, 1484–1485; Vatican I and, 429, 1196, 1494, 1568, 1570; Vatican I declaration of, 618, *See also* infallibility; Ultramontanism

Primate of Italy, 1495

Primina, 178

Prince, The (Machiavelli), 27, 1437

Princeton University, 1544, 1599

Volume Key: Volume 1, pages 1–614; volume 2, pages 615–1266; volume 3, pages 1267–1637.

1752

printing press: breviary and, 193; guidebooks to Rome, 1168; humanist works, 1296; imprimatur and, 763–764, 770; Index and, 770–771; Lateran V and, 899; Lutheranism disseminated by, 1290; master of the Sacred Palace and, 981; missionizing books, 1002, 1444; Paul II and, 1122; social communications and, 1442, 1443; Tridentine missal and, 995; Vatican, 1095

Prisca (canons collection), 201

Prisca (wife of Diocletian), 966

Priscilla, 698, 1153

Priscillan cemetery, 258, 260, 1391, 1392, 1419, 1496, 1497

Priscillianism, 700, 770, 782, 1427

prisoner relief, 1308–1309, 1310–1311

prisoners of war, 174

private lives, popes', **1248**

privilege, Pauline and Petrine, 406, **1248–1251**; Benedict VII grants, 156; Boniface IX and, 192; for crusaders, 438; Julius II selling of, 885, *See also* exemption

probabilism, 29, 809, 827, 1003

Probinus (Roman Senator), 907

Probus, emperor of Rome, 543

Probus, Petronius, 1046

processions: auditors' place in, 126; bell ringing, 152; brass band accompaniment, 299; canonizations, 570; caudatary in, 267; chaplaincy and, 454; chinea tribute, 303–304; Corpus Christi feast, 569; cross, 138, 437; *flabellum* use, 588; Gregory I organization of first, 1220; icon of the Virgin, 1367; papal coronation order, 426; papal coronation route, 829, 1363–1364; papal Mass prior to, 296; *possesso* ceremony, 1228–1229; sedia gestatoria, 1405; station and, 1453; Vatican II reforms, 741

Processus, St., 1497

Proclus of Constantinople, 1433, 1611

Proculus of Marseille, 273, 1610, 1641

procurators, 453, 507

Prodi, Paolo, 726, 1560

profession of faith and oath of fidelity, **1251–1253**

Profuturus of Braga, 1617

progressivism, 1009

Projectus of Poitiers, 1610

Prompsault, R., 228

Propaganda Fide, Congregation of, **1253–1259**; "ad limina" visits and, 4; Chinese rites and, 827, 1002–1003; Chinese schism and, 1397; Clement VIII and forerunner of, 348, 379, 407; Clement X and, 351; Clement XI and, 355; college of, 379, 380; composition and aims, 1001; Congregation of the Oriental Church and, 519; Freemasonry and, 609–610; Gregory XV creation of, 348, 409, 667, 668–669, 1001, 1253–1254, 1357, 1561; Gregory XVI as prefect, 671, 675; Holy Childhood Society and, 708–709; Innocent X and, 802; minutante and, 994; Missionary Union approval, 996; missionizing and, 409, 1001–1003, 1004, 1254–1258; name change (1967). *See* Evangelization of Peoples, Congregation for the; offenses reserved to, 1299; papal commissions and, 388; Penitentiary and, 1152; plenary councils and, 431; prefects list (1622–1990), 1258; Urban VIII and, 1561; Vatican II and, 1257–1258, 1574

Propagation of the Faith, 1258, **1259**; Benedict XV and, 176; missionizing and, 1004, 1205, 1343, 1374, 1451; Pius XII and, 1218; printing press, 1444; World Mission Day, 1451

Propagation of the Faith, Pontifical Society for the, 1450

prophecies, modern, **1259–1261**

Prophecies of Malachy, **1261–1263**; list of popes' mottoes, 1262–1263

Prosper of Aquitaine, 273, 913, 914, 1427, 1433; as Father of the Church, 567, 568

Protasius of Milan, 986

protection, apostolic, exemption vs., 553

Proterios of Alexandria, 917, 918

Protestantism: Anglican schism, 54–57, 1073–1077, 1087; Antichrist charges by, 67–68; apologetics against, 76; appointment of bishops and, 94; artists in Rome, 117, 120; Benedict XIV relations with, 170, 530; catechisms, 262, 263; Church imprimatur and, 770; Clement VIII counteractions, 348; Council of Trent and, 1518, 1519, 1520, 1521; cult of saints and, 234; ecumenism, 518, 519, 520–523, 541; effects on Catholic missionizing by, 1000; Enlightenment, 528; France and. *See* Wars of Religion; Germany and, 1125, 1518; Gregorian calendar opposition, 213; Gregory XIII counteractions, 663, 664; Holy Roman Empire and, 936, 1125, 1128; Inquisition and, 816–817, 818; Jesuit refutations, 827; John Paul II travels and, 1511; Josephist tolerance of, 868–869; *Kulturkampf* and, 891–893; Lateran pacts and, 904; Massacre of St. Bartholomew, 663; as Paul III threat, 1123; Paul IV and spread of, 1128; Paul V and, 1130; Propaganda Fide and, 1255; Thirty Years War and, 1561; Trent as response to, 93, 429, 1289–1290; Trent participants, 1289; two kingdoms concept, 99; Ultramontanism and, 1530; Vatican I and, 1566; Vatican II and, 1143, 1247, 1577, *See also* Calvinism; Luther, Martin; Reformation

protonotary, **1263–1264**; as abbreviator replacement, 1; Chancery and, 293; honorary apostolic, 300; major basilicas and, 144; nunciature and, 1057

Provence: Angevins and, 53; canonical collections, 226; Frankish occupation (538), 597, 598; Great Schism position, 635

province, ecclesiastical, **1264–1265**; ecclesiastical region and, 1292; particular councils and, 430, 431–432

provincial council. *See* council, particular or local

provisions, papal, **1265–1266**

proxies. *See* finances, papal

Prudentius, 747, 1045, 1120, 1164, 1230, 1496

Prussia: appointment of bishops, 87–88, 94; Benedict XIV relations with, 170; Church-State relations, 1191; concordats with papacy, 398, 1207; evangelization in, 997; Gregory XVI and, 674; Italian kingdom and, 1540; Jesuit support in, 361, 362, 1179; *Kulturkampf* and, 891–893; military orders, 987, 990, 998; Napoleonic wars and, 1186; Reformation in, 1287, *See also* Germany

psalmody, 193, 949, 950

psalter, 949, 1346–1347

pseudo-Clementines, 327

pseudo-Dionysius the Areopagite, 49

pseudo-Isidorian decretals, 589, 1283; canonical collection, 231; Donation of Constantine, 513, 514, *See also False Decretals*

pseudo-Malachi, 282

pseudo-Methodius, 282

Ptolemaic astronomy, 252, 253

public debt, papal, 30, 1130, 1340, 1345, 1437

Volume Key: Volume 1, pages 1–614; volume 2, pages 615–1266; volume 3, pages 1267–1637.

1753

public works, 1437

Publicani, 702

publications. *See* media, communciation, and the Vatican; *specific titles*

Pucci, Lorenzo, 927

Pufendorf, Samuel von, 99

Pulcheria, empress of Byzantium, 200, 705, 706, 1318

Pulleyn, Robert, 450, 960

purgatory, 429, 1125, 1289, 1521; popes consigned by Dante to, 481–482

Purists, 1272

Puritanism, 1289

Pusey, Edward Bouverie, 1074, 1086

putti, 693

Pyrrhus, patriarch of Constantinople, 834, 1487

Qesnelliana (Freising), 223

Quadragesimo anno (1931 encyclical), 309, 1447, 1449, 1462

Quadruple Alliance, 354

Quantum cura (1864 encyclical). *See* Syllabus of Errors

Quartodeciman rite, 517, 1612

Quebec, archbishopric of, 351, 1343–1344

Quellenforschung, 697

Querini, Querino, 170, 1311, 1598

Quesnel, Pasquier, 354–355, 529, 704, 825

Quesnelliana (canonical collection), 223, 224, 231

Quia nonnulli ([Boniface XIII]), 165

Quidort, Jean, 390

Quietism, 32, 805–806, 808, **1267–1269**

Quingue Compilations, 226, 227

Quinini, Angelo Maria, 357

Quinisext Council (692), 203, 222, 420, 428, 642, 1412

Quinn, Anthony, 322

Quiñones, Francisco, 193–194

Quirinal (Pontifical Palace of Montecavallo), 30, 666, 1016, 1093, **1269–1272**; architecture, 107, 1017, 1344; art, 694, 1091; ceremonials, 569; construction inception, 665; datary palace, 483; decoration, 1117; floreria (warehouse), 588; as King of Italy's residence, 1018; Leo VII imprisonment in, 1187; as literary image, 752; revolutionary occupation of, 1016; Sistine Chapel copy in, 295–296; Sixtus V creation of, 617, 619, 1437–1438; Swiss Guard, 1471

Quirini, Vincenzo, 898

Qumran manuscripts, 47, 64, 696

Qur'an, Latin translation of, 76, 1393

Rabanus Maurus, 941

rabbits, 58

Rabelais, François, 759–760, 1169

Raccomandati della Virgine, 1307

Radetzky, Joseph Graf, 1539

Radini-Tedeschi, G., 853

radio. *See* Vatican Radio

Raemond, Florimont de, 68

Raffaele, Vico, 1372

Raggi, Antonio, 1362

Raguzzin, Filippo, 1363

railroads, 1017, 1588

railway station, Vatican, **1273**, 1588

Raimon, Elie, 508

Rainald of Dassel, 715, 1114, 1616

Rainaldi, Carlo, 351, 1344, 1369

Rainalducci, Pietro. *See* [Nicholas V]

Rainerius of Perugia, 1054

Rainero. *See* Paschal II

Rainulf, Count of Aversa, 1053

Ramon of Cardona, 1623

Rampolla, Mariano, 172, 364, 550–551, 1211, 1626; Austrian imperial veto of, 1197, 1609

Ramsey, Michael, 56, 1076

Ranaldi family, 1598

Raoul, king of France, 839, 840

Raphael, 140, 886, 1025, 1117, 1340, 1344, 1345; banner design, 138; Holy See commissions, 1027, 1089, 1090; Lalande's impressions of frescoes of, 1506; Leo X and, 926, 928, 1340; mosaic copies of paintings, 1021, 1373; Pantheon burial site, 1096; papal portraiture, 1093; sack of Rome and, 1355; St. Peter's basilica works, 105, 1091, 1382; *Stanze*, 106; Vatican Palace works, 1117

Raphael, Archangel, 49

Rapondi, Dino, 137

Raspe, Hermann (Henry), 315, 716

Rastatt, treaty of (1714), 353

Rastislav, prince of Moravia, 997

Ratchis, king of the Lombards, 1457, 1639

rationalism, 1006, 1007–1008, 1009; dogmatic refutation of, 1567; Syllabus of Errors on, 1472

Ratti, Achille. *See* Pius XI

Ratti, Damiano, 1200

Ratti family, 693, 1200

Ratzinger, Joseph, 264, 265, 368, 610, 1398

Raulin, Jean, 1275

Rauscher, Joseph, 893, 1567

Ravenna, **1273–1274**; barbarian invasions and, 140, 141, 142, 196, 204, 1046, 1273, 1318; Boniface II and, 185; Byzantine popes and, 196, 197; Byzantium and. *See* Exarchate of Ravenna; [Clement III] residency, 329–330; Felix IV and, 573; Innocent I and, 781; John I in, 218; legation, 672; Martin I abduction by, 202; Napoleonic occupation, 1103; Nicholas I policy, 1034; papal confirmation by, 153; as papal territory, 109, 986; Pepin's return to papacy, 1319; as reform center, 1280; Roman popes and, 16; Zacharias and, 1642

Ravenna, synod of (419), 184

Ravenna, synod of (898), 590

Ravenna, synod of (967), 841–842

Ravenna, synod of (1014), 156–157, 1279

Ravennius of Arles, 915, 1611

Raymond IV, count of Toulouse, 438, 1552

Raymond of Capua, 266

Raymond of Peñafort, 226, 227, 507, 655, 871–872, 1281

Raymond of St. Giles, 897

Raymond of Turenne, 659

Raynal, Guillaume, 362

Reagan, Ronald, 504, 714

Real Presence, 1275, 1277; definition of, 887

rebaptism, 13, 214

Rebiol, Antoine, 284

Volume Key: Volume 1, pages 1–614; volume 2, pages 615–1266; volume 3, pages 1267–1637.

1754

Reccared, king of the Visigoths, 141, 639–640, 1318
recognitio, 97
Recollectio Villacreciana, 594
Recollects, 596, 597
Reconquista (Spain), 18, 787, 796, 1551, 1552
Reconstruction of Poland (MRP), 1216
rector-counts, 577
Red Brigade, 310, 1364
Red Cross, 1081, 1632
Red Shirts, 1540
Redemption, 728
Redemptor hominis (1979 encyclical), 1449
Reed, Carol, 322
referendarius, 460, 461
reform, Catholic, **1274–1278**; art and architecture and, 1090, 1270, 1340–1341, 1431; beatification and, 145, 1130; calendar, 213; canonizations, 234, 360, 669, 1130; Capuchins and, 595; catechism and, 262, 263, 264; Clement VIII and, 348; Clement XIII and, 359; confraternities and, 1307, 1309, 1310; Counter Reformation, 1275–1277, 1289, 1355; Curia as center, 465, 466; Dominicans and, 509; expenses of, 374–375; forgeries and, 589; Gregory XV and, 667, 668–669; Hadrian VI and, 686; Holy Year pilgrims and, 726–727; humanist controls of, 1296; Index and, 1443; Jansenism and, 704, 823–826, 867; Jesuit founding and, 1125, 1177, 1289; Josephism vs., 867, 868–869; Julius III and, 887; Lateran V and, 1354; Latinity and, 906; in medieval Church, 1274–1275; monuments and, 1270; nunciatures, 1059; papal primacy and, 1246–1247; Paul III and, 1123, 1125, 1126–1127; Paul IV and, 1128; Paul V and, 1129, 1130; pilgrimage renewal from, 1169–1170; Pius IV and, 1175–1176; Pius V and, 936, 1176, 1177–1178; as Pius XI influence, 1200, 1202; poor relief, 1224, 1225; Roman College and, 379; sack of Rome initiating, 1355; St. Peter's basilica rebuilding and, 1382–1383; seminaries and, 1277, 1342–1343, 1407–1409; of simony, 1425; Sixtus V and, 1246, 1342, 1436–1438; superintendent of the Ecclesiastical State, 1467–1470; Urban VIII and, 1561, 1562, *See also* Trent, Council of
reform, Gregorian, 91–92, 449, 648, 649–651, **1278–1285**; pre-Gregory VII (1046–1073), 1280; Gregorian period (1078–1085), 1280–1281; [Anacletus II] and, 42; anti-Roman satire and, 750; art and, 1284–1285; Callistus II and, 216, 731; canonical collection, 224–225, 231, 1283; canonization and, 233; cardinalate changes, 240, 241; Church-State relations and, 1483; conciliarism and, 390; consolidation of (1085–1124), 1281; Curia and, 449–450; custom and, 476; *Dictatus papae*, 499; dispensations, 504; ecumenical councils and, 428; fundamental achievements of, 1281–1284; heresies and, 701; Holy Roman Empire and, 714–715; indulgences and, 773–774; Innocent II and, 784, 785; interdict, 820; investiture controversy and, 820–822, 900; laity and, 895; Lateran councils and, 428, 429, 900–901; legates and, 909; Leo IX and, 924–925, 1245; *Liber censum* and, 940; liturgy and, 953; military orders and, 987; monasticism and, 1016; Norman military support for, 1054; nunciatures and, 1057; papal effects of, 1108; Papal States and, 1097–1098; Roman political framework and, 1333; signs presaging (1014–1046), 1279–1280; simony and, 1424, 1425; Tuscolani family power and, 1333

Reformation (1517–1565), **1285–1290**; allegorical map of papacy, 252; Antichrist charges and, 67–68; antipope debates and, 70; Avignon plagues linked with, 1222; as Catholic missionizing impetus, 1000; Catholic missionizing successes, 1343–1344; Catholic reforms in wake of, 1274, 1276, 1289, 1342–1343; Catholic restoration in England, 887, 1289; Catholic territorial losses, 802, 1176, 1177; charges against Boniface VII, 189; of Church of England, 54–57 (*see also* Anglicanism); Clement VII and, 1287; Dominican countermeasures, 509; ecumenism and, 518; heresies and, 703–704; Holy Year indulgences criticism, 726; Index as response, 770, 1443; Leo X excesses and, 927–928; Luther's Ninety-five Theses and, 509, 726, 926, 927–928, 1286, 1382, 1395; papal powers and, 1246; as papism attack, 1107, 1109; Peace of Westphalia and, 802; pilgrimage critics, 1169; poor relief philosophy, 1225; Propaganda Fide as response to, 669; prophetism and, 1263; sack of Rome (1527) and, 1354–1355; St. Peter's basilica reconstruction and, 1382; as schism, 1395; Trent doctrinal rebuttals, 1276–1277, 1289–1290, 1521; Trent origins and, 93, 429, 1289–1290, 1517–1518, *See also* Luther, Martin; Protestantism
refrigerium practice, 1389
Refutation of All Heresies (Hippolytus), 707–708
regalia, **1290–1292**; Blessed or Holy Hat and Sword, 182–183; Jansenism and, 824
Regalism, 313, 358, 361–362
Regensburg Book (1540), 1125
Reggio Emilia, 238, 344, 928, 1102
Reginald of Segni, 791
Reginon de Prüm, 231, 1035
region, ecclesiastical, **1292–1293**
Régis, John Francis, 827
registers, papal, 451, **1293**; *Dictatus papae*, 499; in Vatican Archives, 1603–1604, 1605
Registrum Commune, 294
Reichersberg, Gerhoh, 276
Reims, 15, 646–647, 840, 1000; papal coronation of Louis the Pious in, 424, 600, 1458
Reims, consistory of (1131), 450
Reims, Council of (1049), 701, 924
Reims, Council of (1148), 701
relics, veneration of, 204, 545; archeological searches and, 100; in baptistries, 139; catacombs as source, 260, 261–262, 351; Clement X regulations, 351; Congregation for the Causes of Saints and, 408; early martyrs and, 268; Gregory I and, 261; John IV and, 834; Lombard seizures, 1354; pilgrimages and, 1164, 1165–1166, 1168, 1170; pillaging of, 261–262; protection of, 1389, 1390; in St. John Lateran basilica, 1359, 1381; in St. Peter's basilica, 1376, 1378, 1385–1386; Tridentine decrees, 429, *See also* saints, veneration of
Religious, Congregation for, 247
religious orders. *See* orders, religious; *specific orders*
religious sciences, 1007
religious tolerance. *See* freedom of religion
Remi (Rémy), archbishop of Reims, 49, 597, 599, 924, 1120
Renaissance humanism and the papacy, **1293–1297**; Alexander VII and, 30; architecture and art, 104–107, 1089–1092, 1116, 1368–1369; [Benedict XIII] and, 164; Catholic uni-

Volume Key: Volume 1, pages 1–614; volume 2, pages 615–1266; volume 3, pages 1267–1637.

1755

versities and, 1544; ceremonials, 284–285; Ciceronianism, 906, 1295; Clement VI and, 337; coins, 374–376; Curia and, 464; Holy Year indulgences critique, 726; Julius III and, 887; Latinity and, 906, 1295; Leo X and, 926; Marcellus II and, 968; mosaics, 1021–1022; natural rights and, 99; nepotism, 1032–1033; Nicholas V and, 1042, 1294, 1597; painting commissions, 1089–1092; papal office diminishment and, 1246; Reformation misjudgments and, 1109; Rome as arts center, 1340; sacking of Rome (1527) ending, 1296; Sixtus IV and, 1294, 1295, 1435; Vatican Library collection, 1294, 1295, 1296, 1597

Renan, Joseph-Ernest, 443, 1008
René of Anjou, 54, 537, 1621
Renée of France, 1624
Reni, Guido, 668, 1022, 1090, 1091, 1092, 1270, 1341, 1345, 1369, 1385
Renzi, Bernardina, 1259
Reparatus, 14, 251, 514
Repond, Jules, 1471
representation, diplomatic. See nuncio
Rerum novarum (1891 encyclical), 524, 606, 614, 1077, 1133; Christian Democracy and, 306, 311; confraternities and, 1311; Dominicans and, 512; Jesuits and, 828; medallion commemorating, 983; Opera dei congressi and, 1023; Pius XI policy and, 1206, 1449; Pius XII commemoration of, 1200, 1447; as principal social teaching document, 1447; range and impact of, 935, 1515; as recognition of societal changes, 1110, 1447; significance of, 1449–1450; socialism and, 977; subsidiarity concept, 1462
Rerum orientalium (1925 encyclical), 1208
reserved cases and causes, **1297–1300**; definitions, 1297
residences, papal, **1300–1305**; apostolic palaces, 1093–1094; Avignon, 102–103, 128, 129; paintings, 1090, 1091; palatine as designation, 1094–1095; Quirinal, 107, 1269–1272; Rome as papal, 1339; suburban, 107; Swiss Guard, 1471; Symmachus and, 1476; Vatican gardens, 1594–1596; Vatican Radio link, 1600; Viterbo, 102, 1620, See also Lateran Palace; Vatican Palace
resignations, papal, **1305**; list of, 1305
Restitutus of Carthage, 946
Resurrection. See Passion and Resurrection
Rete (political party), 311
Reumano, Cardinal, 1177
Revelation, Book of, 1042, 1043, 1261
Revelation, Tridentine decrees on, 1277, 1289
revelations. See prophecies
Revelli, Salvatore, 1373
Reverend Fabric of St. Peter, Congregation of the. See Fabric of St. Peter
Revision and Correction of the Vulgate, Papal Commission for the, 388
Revision of the Roman Breviary, Congregation for the, 470
revolutions of 1830, 305, 670, 671, 672, 1104, 1191, 1192
revolutions of 1848, 305, 728, 1016, 1193–1194, 1537, 1539; Roman Republic of 1849 and, 1323–1326
Revue Internationale des Sociétés Secrètes, 608
Reynolds, Joshua, 120
Rezzonico, Carlo. See Clement XIII
Rezzonico family, 694, 1049

Rhapsodic Theater (anti-Nazi underground), 861
Rhine Flows into the Tiber, The (Witgen), 1143
Rhodes, 335, 928, 1527
Rhone River, 127
Rialian, Joseph, 1644
Riario, Cardinal, 899, 927
Riario, Girolamo, 884, 1434, 1435
Riario, Pietro, 111, 884, 1433, 1434, 1435
Riario, Raphael, 294, 1435
Ribbentrop, Joachim von, 1634
Riberi, Antonio, 1396
Riccardi, Andrea, 310, 1135, 1136
Ricci banks, 82
Ricci, G.-B., 1362
Ricci, Lorenzo, 530
Ricci, Matteo, 359, 362, 664, 828, 1343, 1345, 1403
Ricci, Scipione de', 889, 1180
Richard I, duke of Normandy, 842
Richard I (the Lionheart), king of England, 278, 314; military order and, 989; Third Crusade and, 331, 438
Richard II, king of England, 634–635
Richard Coeur de Lion. See Richard I (the Lionheart)
Richard d'Aversa, 1036, 1053
Richard of Capua, 1613
Richard of Cornwall, 315, 685, 716
Richard of Fournival, 655
Richelieu, Cardinal, 510, 912, 1000, 1561
Richer, Edmond, 778, 825
Righetti, Igino, 1024
right of asylum. See asylum, right of
right of exclusion. See exclusion
rigorism, 823
Rimini, 662, 675, 1121
Rimini, Council of (359), 882, 946
Rinaldo da Ienne. See Alexander IV
ring: episcopal insignia, 619, 620; as investiture symbol, 821, 1637
rioni, **1305–1307**
Ripert d'Alonzier family, 1050
Riquet, Michel, 609
Risorgimento, 308, 673, 1023, 1096, 1191, 1310, 1534–1536, 1645; Roman Republic of 1849 and, 1323, 1325, 1326
Rites and Ceremonies, Congregation of, 1438
ritual. See liturgy
Rivarola, Cardinal, 672, 932, 1188
roads, 108
Roads and Aqueducts, Congregation of, 1438
robbery. See banditry
Robert (son of Robert Guiscard), 1552
Robert (son of William I), 1551
Robert (the Wise), king of Naples, 316, 628, 676, 722, 850, 1337
Robert, archbishop of Trier, 15
Robert II, king of Sicily, 900
Robert II (the Pious), king of France, 224, 646, 844, 845, 1421
Robert de Courgon, 438–439
Robert Guiscard, 109, 1036, 1052, 1053, 1552; freeing of Gregory VII by, 254, 329, 650; as Monte Cassino benefactor, 1614; as papal vassal, 1613; sack of Rome by, 1329
Robert, Hubert, 119

Volume Key: Volume 1, pages 1–614; volume 2, pages 615–1266; volume 3, pages 1267–1637.

Robert, Léopold, 121Robert Le Bougre, 812
Robert of Anjou. *See* Robert (the Wise), king of Naples
Robert of Artois, 51
Robert of Capua, 683
Robert of Courson, 451, 788–789
Robert of Geneva. *See* [Clement VII]
Robert of Somercotes, 655
Robert of Tarento, 53
Robert of Torigny, 488–489
Roberti, Manfredo di, 1555
Rocasecca, battle of (1411), 662
Rocca, Nasalli, 59
Rocco, A., 902
Roch, St., 1168, 1222
Roche, Androin de la, 911; 1028, 1556
Roche, Guy de la, 82
Roderick Hudson (James), 759
Rodolphian Tables, 518
Rodomonte (Domenico Palombi), 257
Roes, Alexander von, 736
Rogation Days, 952
Roger, Guillaume, 337
Roger, Hugues, 336
Roger I Guiscard, count of Calabria and Sicily, 313, 1052, 1053, 1552
Roger II, king of Sicily, 50, 314, 533, 683, 732, 959, 1052, 1053, 1054; [Anacletus I] recognition by, 42, 43, 784, 890; Celestine II and, 276; Lucius II and, 960; [Victor IV] support by, 1615
Roger of Torrescuso, 655, 792
Roger of Worcester, 881
Roger, Pierre. *See* Clement VI
Roguet, Aimon-Marie, 955
Rolfe, F. (Baron Corvo), 758, 761
Rolland, Romain, 174
Roma (film), 323
Roma senza Papa (Morselli), 756–757
Romagna, 1561; Borgia conquest, 27; Italian unity and, 582, 1535, 1538, 1539, 1541; Martin V and, 975, 976; Napoleonic wars and, 1183, 1189; in Papal States, 1098, 1100(map), 1102, 1105(map), 1107, 1342; Pius IX and, 1192
Romaine, Françoise, St., 1130
Romains, Jules, 752
Roman Academy, 1294
Roman Atheneum of the Holy Cross, 1546
Roman Bullary, 232
Roman Catechism. *See* Catechism, Roman
Roman Circle, 1136
Roman College of the Society of Jesus, 664, 667, 827, 828; architecture, 1340; founding of, 379, 826, 1407, 1408; reopening of, 932; Thomastic philosophy, 1296, *See also* Gregorian University
Roman confraternities, 317, **1307–1313**; cursors and, 475; Eugene IV and, 537; historiography and debates over, 1310–1312; internationalization, 1309–1310; pilgrims and, 1169; poor relief, 1224, 1307–1308; rosary devotion and, 1346–1347; state control over, 1542
Roman congregations. *See* congregations, Roman
Roman Curia. *See* Curia

Roman Empire, **1313–1320**; pre-Constantine, **1313–1316**; Constantine to Charlemagne, **1316–1320**; Antichrist linked with, 64, 65; apologetics, 75, 1315; banking, 135; baptistry design, 139; barbarian invasions, 140–143, 563, 1046, 1315–1316, 1317; Castel Sant'Angelo and, 253–254; catacombs, 257–258; Christian archeological studies of, 100–102; Christian calendar, 210; Christian conversion of Constantine, 140, 417–418, 545, 1045; Christian nobility, 1045; Christian persecutions by. *See* persecutions; Christianity as established religion, 1317; Colosseum, 387–388; Constantine's donation. *See* Donation of Constantine; Constantinople as seat of, 197; division of (4th century), 417, 882; eastern cults and, 441–442; as ecclesiastical provinces model, 1264; ending in West (476), 563; evangelization in, 544–545; fall in West (5th century), 1317–1318; as Frankish, 1320; games, 618–619; gardens on banks of Tiber, 1594; Germanic. *See* Holy Roman Empire; as Holy Roman Empire antecedent, 715; Justinian's restoration efforts, 201; legate tradition, 908; Milan and, 985–987; Milan Edict of Tolerance (313), 417, 844, 1003; monument restorations, 1016; mosaics, 1018–1019; Pantheon, 1095–1096; papal office history, 1244–1245; Paul and, 1119–1120; Peter and, 1157; prefect of the city, 1229–1231; Ravenna and. *See* Exarchate of Ravenna; Ravenna; Renaissance humanism and, 1295; Senate, 1410–1411; Simplicius and last years of, 1425, 1526; structure reflected in early dioceses, 90–91, *See also* Byzantium and the papacy; Rome
Roman Inquisition. *See* Holy Office, Congregation of the
Roman law, 85, 98, 178, 229, 923, 1544, 1553; apostolic constitution derived from, 421; Boniface VIII-Philip IV conflict and, 615; canonical collections and, 223; heresies and, 701; Holy Roman Empire and, 715; Honorius III ban on study, 226, 734; Justinian's contributions, 1319; "legate" term from, 908; suspension of, 1470
Roman of Tusculum. *See* John XIX
Roman Pontifical (1596), 348
Roman Pontifical Academy of Archaeology, 2, 101
Roman Republic (c.500–31 B.C.), 1313, 1410, 1411
Roman Republic (1798–1799), 613, **1320–1323**, 1346; abolishment of noble titles, 1050; ending of, 1103; financial problems, 377; map of, 1106; papal chapel singers, 297, 298; Pius VII and, 1183
Roman Republic of 1849, **1323–1327**, 1539
Roman Seminary (Jesuit), 827, 1176, 1545
Roman Senate. *See* Senate, Roman, and the papacy
Roman stations. *See* stations, Roman
Roman Theological Pontifical Academy, 2
Romance of the Seven Sages, The, 748
Romani d'Osimo, Niccolò de, 459
Romania (Alba Iulia): canon law, 370; missionaries in, 998
Romano, Antonazzo, 1373
Romano, Giulio, 928
Romanov dynasty, 1488
Romanticism, 1538–1539
Romanus, **1327**
Romanus I, emperor of Byzantium, 840
Romanus, Aegidius. *See* Giles of Rome
Rome, **1327–1346**; Middle Ages, city and populations, **1327–1330**; Middle Ages: government, **1330–1339**; modern

Volume Key: Volume 1, pages 1–614; volume 2, pages 615–1266; volume 3, pages 1267–1637.

1757

era, **1339–1346**; "ad limina" visits to, 4–5; Allied bombings of (1943), 1635; Allied entrance into (1944), 1634; annona, 60–62, 1353; apostolic primacy of, 32–33, 34, 199, 200, 201, 202, 205, 207–208; aqueducts, 106, 108, 681, 1319, 1328, 1330, 1340, 1435; archeological studies, 100–102, 171; architecture, 102, 103–108, 1328, 1344; aristocratic nepotism, 1031; artists in, 116–121, 982, 1089–1093, 1340; banking, 137; barbarian invasion (5th century), 140, 986, 1318; bell ringing, 151, 152; Byzantine Empire and, 480, 1318, 1330, 1354, 1411; capitulation of (1870), 1646; captitulation of (1870), 901, 934, 1077, 1082, 1310, 1541, 1568, 1570; Carnival, 248–250; catacombs, 257–260; Catholic universities, 1545–1546; as Catholic world center, 1108, 1343; Charlemagne as protector of, 920; city planning, 1340; Clement III agreement with, 1334; Clement X projects, 351; Clement XII projects, 529; Clement XIII projects, 359; as clerical studies center, 664; coin mint, 372; colleges of, 378–379; Colosseum, 387–388; conclave sites, 392; confraternities, 1307–1312; Constantine the Great's projects, 418, 1419; Counter Reformation and, 1340; Damasus I building projects, 478; *diaconiae*, 497–498; diocese of, 499–500, 501, 1464–1467; Donation of Constantine, 513; earthquakes, 248, 387, 1329, 1388; first regulatory plan (1873), 1017–1018; Frederick I (Barbarossa) capture of (1167), 20; French occupation (1798), 122, 138, 394, 530, 586, 613, 671, 1103, 1104, 1181, 1187, 1272, 1321, 1346; French occupation (1849), 1194, 1323; German occupation (1943–1944), 1214, 1588, 1634–1635; Grand Tour to, 1345; Greek community, 638; Gregory I projects, 1319; Gregory XI return to, 103, 162, 1246; Gregory XIII projects, 665; Hadrian I rebuilding, 681; Hadrian IV interdict on, 683; Henry IV occupation of, 329, 650; Holy Roman Empire and, 1335; Innocent X projects, 802–803; as Italian capital, 901, 902, 1017–1018, 1107, 1195, 1198, 1533, 1535, 1540, 1644, 1645; Italian unification and, 10, 718, 1107, 1196, 1533, 1535, 1539, 1540, 1541, 1542, 1646; Jewish ghetto, 873, 874, 1188, 1310; John VII church projects, 836; John Paul II synagogue visit, 876–877; Julius II projects, 104–105, 885, 1127; Justinian novella IX (535) on primacy of, 201; Law of Guarantees and, 1077, 1541; Leo I as protector of, 914; literary images of, 747–762; Lombard invasion, 203, 204, 1331, 1354; malaria epidemic, 1345, 1355; Martin V construction renewal, 976; medallions commemorating, 982; minor basilicas, 144; monasticism, 1011–1013, 1016; monumentality and urbanism, 1016–1018; monuments, 107, 1112, 1116, 1270; mosaic workshops, 1021–1022; municipal statutes revision (1469), 1121; national churches in, 316–317; "national style" of, 1018; Nicholas III sovereignty claim, 1336; Nicholas V city planning, 1042, 1339–1340; nobility, 1044–1051, 1332–1333; Noble Guards and, 1052; obelisks, 108, 1061–1062; Otto I siege of (964), 155; Pantheon, 1095; papal armies' defense of, 109–110; papal control over (historical), 109, 1097; papal feasts, 568–570; papal rebuilding of, 103–108; papal residence at, 1339; papal return to (1367), 1556–1557; papal return to (1420), 975–976, 1339–1340; papal return to (1814), 1188; papal singers as tourist attraction, 298; Papal States and, 1096–1107, 1331; patrons of beautification, 245, 1329–1330, 1340; Paul III projects, 1127; Paul (Saint and Apostle) summons to, 1119, 1153; Paul V projects, 1130;

persecutions of Christians in. *See* persecutions; Peter (Saint and Apostle) in, 1158–1159; pilgrimages to. *See* Holy Year; pilgrimage; Pius IV projects, 1176; Pius VI public works, 1180; plague epidemics, 1220, 1328, 1329; pontifical blessing to, 177; poor relief, 1225–1226, 1308; popes from, 1210; Prefect of the City, 1229–1231; railroads, 1017; relics and, 261–262; Renaissance humanism and, 1294–1297; Renaissance rebuilding of, 1340; revolts against papacy, 155, 158, 254, 255, 797, 1042, 1128, 1332, 1333–1334, 1335, 1338–1339, 1422, 1458; rione (administrative divisions), 1305–1307; riots against Paul IV's rigorism, 1128; sacking of (410), 260, 781, 1046, 1318, 1327, 1353–1354, 1411; sacking of (452), 986; sacking of (546), 1146; sacking of (1084), 1329; sacking of (1413), 852; sacking of (1527). *See* sack of Rome; St. John Lateran as cathedral of, 1363, 1382; Saracen attacks on, 921, 1393; seminaries, 1342–1343; Senate. *See* Senate, Roman, and the papacy; Simplicius projects, 1425–1426; Sixtus III projects, 1433; Sixtus IV projects, 1340, 1435; Sixtus V urban development program, 1340, 1437–1438; slavery in, 1439, 1440; stations, 1452–1454; stereotypes of, 1232–1233, 1354; Symmachus projects, 1476; traveler's views of, 1503–1510; universities, 28, 30, 537, 583; Vandal control of (455), 1318, 1327; Vatacanistas in, 1606–1607; Vatican Archives and, 1603; Vatican City State status within, 1586; walled fortifications, 110, 254, 643, 644, 921, 1173, 1393; World War II and, 1633–1636, *See also* bishop of Rome; Papal States; Roman Republic; Roman Republic of 1849

Rome, Council of (1059), 1043, 1044
Rome, synod of (368–372), 479
Rome, synod of (377), 199
Rome, synod of (1014), 1279
Rome, treaties of (1957), 540
Rome, University of, 28, 30, 379, 411, 537, 887, 928, 1127, 1348; humanist professorships, 1295, 1296–1297; Sixtus IV and, 1435
Romulus Augustus, emperor of Rome, 1318, 1426
Roncaglia, Diet of (1158), 313, 1615
Roncalli, Angelo. *See* John XXIII
Roosevelt, Franklin D., 1213, 1214, 1588, 1631, 1633, 1634, 1635
Röpke, W., 1462
Rosa of Lima. *See* Rose of Lima, St.
rosary, **1346–1347**; feast of, 194; Leo XIII devotion, 512, 1347; medieval, 1275; Pius V and, 510, 1176
Rosary confraternity, 1309
Rose, Golden, 182, **1347–1348**; bestowed by Urban V, 1557; bestowed on Henry VIII of England, 928; chamberlain bearer of, 288; Noble Guard and, 1051; Vatican II and, 741
Rose of Lima, St., 145, 349, 351
Roselli, N., 1170
Rosemary's Baby (film), 323
Rosier, Bernard de, 689
Rosini, Girolamo, 256, 257
Rosminians, 1194
Rospigliosi, Camillo, 1052
Rospigliosi, Giacomo, 468
Rospigliosi, Giulio. *See* Clement IX
Rosselli, Cosimo, 1428

Volume Key: Volume 1, pages 1–614; volume 2, pages 615–1266; volume 3, pages 1267–1637.

Rossellino, Bernardo, 104, 549, 1173
Rossi, G. B. de, 258, 260, 1419
Rossi, Gian Antonio de, 982, 1362
Rossi, Luigi, 257
Rossi, Opilio, 434
Rossi, Pellegrino, 944, 1104, 1194, 1324, 1539
Rossini, Girolano, 256, 257
Rossini, Luigi, 1372
Rosso, Bertoldo, 1037
Rosso, Matteo, 973, 1554
Rota, tribunal of the, 130, 460, 471, 1094, **1348–1351**; allocution
    to, 36–37; Apostolic Signatura and, 1350, 1525; auditors,
    126, 130, 1349–1350; consistory advocates, 413; notaries,
    1054; overview, 1524–1525; papal allocution to, 36–37; Paul
    III reform commission, 1126–1127; Penitentiary and, 1152;
    Propaganda Fide and, 1257; Sixtus IV reorganization, 462;
    Tridentine reform, 465; Vatican City location, 1592
Rothad of Soissons, 1034
Rothari, king of the Lombards, 142, 958, 1619
Rousseau, Jean-Jacques, 77, 359, 1183
Rousseau, Olivier, 1574
Rousselot, P., 79
Rovere, Julian de la, 111
Roving Fathers for Christ, Society of, 508
Roy, Maurice, 434, 1447, 1449
Royal Academy of Paris, 118
Roye, Pierre, 1501
Rucellai banks, 39, 137
Rucellai, Bernardo, 1594
Rudolf I (of Habsburg), Holy Roman emperor, 51, 316, 716, 717,
    1037, 1038, 1039; Gregory X recognition of, 316, 658, 685;
    Honorius IV and, 735, 736; Martin IV and, 973–974; Papal
    States cessions by, 1098
Rudolf IV, duke of Austria, 717
Rudolf of Swabia, 650
Rudolf of Wied, 330, 961–962
Rudolph of Habsburg. *See* Rudolf I
Ruffini, Cardinal, 1143
Ruffo, Fabrizio, 1180, 1184
Ruffo, Tommaso, 1178
Rufinus, 93, 225, 327, 505, 700, 946, 1563
Rufinus, Aradius, 1230
Rufinus of Aquileia, 43, 1013
Rufus of Thessalonica, 184, 185, 783, 1611, 1642
Ruini, Camillo, 311
Rule of Eugippius, 1013
Rule of St. Augustine, 722, 987, 988, 989, 1013, 1015, 1044, 1280
Rule of St. Basil, 638, 1015
Rule of St. Benedict, 639, 1013, 1014, 1015, 1133; Benedict XII
    and, 161; Irish Church and, 142; Urban V observation of,
    1556
Rule of St. Francis, 591–593, 594, 595, 788
Rum, sultanate of, 1526
Runcie, Robert, 522, 1076
Rupert of Deutz, 75, 1043
Ruprecht of the Palatinate, 635, 636
Rusconi, Camillo, 1362
Rusconi, G. Enrico, 1534
Ruspoli family, 627

Russel, James, 120
Russia: Byzantine missions in, 997; Clement XI evangelization,
    355; Gregory XVI and, 673, 674; Holy Land rights, 711;
    Italian kingdom and, 1540; Jesuits in, 361, 362, 828, 1179;
    Jewish pogroms in, 874; John XV and, 843; Moscow as
    Third Rome, 1487–1488; Napoleonic wars and, 1186,
    1188; Paul II and, 1121; Paul V and, 1130; Pius VI and,
    1179; Pius IX concordat with, 1192; Pius XI interest in,
    1208; Roman Catholicism in, 522, 523; Uniates,
    1531–1533; World War I and, 1626, 1628, *See also* Soviet
    Union
Russian Orthodox Church, 522, 523, 1531, 1532–1533; Gregory
    XIII reconciliation moves, 664; Holy Land and, 711;
    Moscow as Third Rome and, 1487–1488; *ostpolitik* and,
    1085; Pius XI and, 1208
Russian Revolution (1917), 977
Rusuti, Filippo, 1116, 1367
Ruthenian Church. *See* Uniates
Ryswick, treaty of (1697), 808

Sabatier, Paul, 1008
Sabbah, patriarch of Jerusalem, 877
Sabbath day, 209
Sabellianism, 33, 479, 502, 561, 698
Sabellius, 214, 699
Sabina, 1538
Sabinian, 5, 196, 576, **1353**; Church use of bells, 151
Sacchetti, marquis of, 627
Sacchetti, Giulio, 801, 1117, 1591
Sacchi, Andrea, 1091, 1092
Sacchi, Bartolomeo (Platina), 1065, 1294
Sacconi, Giuseppe, 1018
Sacconi, Rainerio, 23
Sacerdotium/Imperium. *See* Church-State conflict
Sachsenhausen, appeal of (1324), 850
sack of Rome (1527), 255, 343, 345, 374, 464, 726, 886, 906,
    1124, 1225, 1287, 1296, 1340, 1353, **1353–1356**, 1388,
    1595, 1624; Michelangelo religious crisis and, 1430; St.
    Peter's basilica and, 1378; Swiss Guard and, 1471, *See also*
    subentries under Rome *for other instances*
sacraments: Luther critique of Church abuse of, 1286; suspension
    of censure and, 1149, 1151; Tridentine work on, 1277, 1289,
    1521, *See also* Eucharist
Sacred Archaeology, Pontifical Commission on, 100, 101, 260,
    389
Sacred College, **1356–1358**; administrative power, 241, 278, 462,
    1333; Alexander III prior career in, 19; Alexander IV and,
    24; Alexander VI prior career in, 25; Black Death victims,
    1221, 1222; cardinal camerlengo, 219, 221; cardinal orders,
    239; cardinals' ages and, 246; Ceremonial Congregation
    and, 12; Clement IV and, 1246; Clement VI conflict with,
    336–337; [Clement VII] appointments, 341; Clement VII
    appointments, 345; Clement XIV appointments, 361; con-
    clave, 239, 240, 392–395, 901, 1280, 1356, 1405–1406;
    conclavist, 396; consistory and, 413–415, 1356; crown car-
    dinal influence in, 393; cursors' duties, 475; death of the
    pope and, 9–10, 238; effort to end Great Schism, 660–661;
    election of pope and. *See* conclave; eminent canonical stand-
    ing of, 1280; extents of powers of, 1587; factional divisions,

Volume Key: Volume 1, pages 1–614; volume 2, pages 615–1266; volume 3, pages 1267–1637.

1759

280, 339, 667; [Felix V] appointments, 1041; French influence on, 1246; Great Schism's split in, 242, 339–340, 342, 1356; Gregorian reform and, 1282; Gregory IX appointments to, 655; Gregory XI appointments, 658–659; Gregory XII appointments, 661; Gregory XIII appointments, 929; Innocent III appointments, 788–789; Innocent VII appointments, 798; Innocent VIII appointments, 799; John XXIII appointments, 854, 1406; John Paul II appointments, 865; Leo IX development of, 1245; Leo X appointments, 927; Martin V approach to, 976; Napoléon and, 1187; national cleric representation, 1027, 1406; nepotism, 241, 242, 1356, 1357; nepotism reforms, 1357; Nicholas III appointments, 1038; Nicholas IV increased powers of, 1039; numerical limit, 245; origins, 239–240, 1356; in papal household, 740; Paul II appointments, 1121; Paul III appointments, 1124, 1128; Paul III renewal of, 1123, 1126; Paul VI changes in, 1357–1358; pavilion, 1145; Pius V appointments, 1177; Pius VI appointments, 1179; Pius VII and, 1185, 1186; Pius VII appointments, 931; Pius XI internationalization of, 1203; Pius XI naming of successor to, 1630; Pius XII and, 1218–1219, 1406; reform efforts, 242, 462, 1276; Roman influences, 731–732; Roman nobility members, 1048, 1050; Sixtus V limit on member numbers, 243, 465, 1357, 1437; Sixtus IV appointments, 1435; synod of bishops and, 1358; temporal veto and, 1608–1609; Tridentine reforms, 242, 243; 20th century, 1357–1358; Urban IV changes in, 1246, 1554; vacant Holy See and, 1406, 1407

Sacred College, Plenary Meeting of the, **1358–1359**

Sacred Congregation for the Eastern Church. *See* Eastern Churches, Congregation for the

Sacred Congregation for the Propagation of the Faith. *See* Propaganda Fide, Congregation of

Sacred Heart: confraternities of, 1310; cult of the, 360, 375, 1190, 1203; Leo XIII consecration to, 934

Sacred Liturgy, Constitution on the (1964), 1142

sacred music. *See* music

sacred ornaments, 12

sacred palace. *See* palace, apostolic

Sacred Sites. *See* Holy Places

Sacri caelibatus (1967 encyclical), 1110

sacristy, 12

Sadat, Anwar, 858

saddle. *See* chinea

Sadducees, 696

Sade, marquis de, 753, 755

Sadoleto, Jacopo, 968, 1124, 1276, 1295

Saffi, Aurelio, 1324, 1539

saint. *See* canonization; catacombs, saints' bodies in the; causes of canonization; relics, veneration of; saints, veneration of; *names of specific saints*

St. Agnes Outside the Walls, 1012, 1116, 1476

St. Albans abbey, 683, 684

St. Andrea della Valle church, 1562

St. Andrew monastery, 142

St. Anne, feast of, 194

St. Anselmo College (Rome), 379

St. Bartholomew Massacre (1572), 663

St. Bonaventure, Pontifical College of, 379, 1546

St. Clement College, 379

St. Clement's church (Rome), mosaics, 1019, 1020

St. Denis, congregation of, 554

St. Isidoro College, 379

St. Ivo alla Sapienza, 1344

St. James of the Sword Order, 989

St. John Latern, basilica of, 144, **1359–1364**, 1365, 1373, 1586; Middle Ages, 152, **1359–1362**; 16th to 20th centuries, **1362–1364**; Benediction loggia, 1362, 1363, 1364; blessing *urbi et orbi* from, 177; as cathedral of Rome, 1363, 1382; ceremonials, 569; Clement XII redecoration, 357; collapse of, 1460; conciliar assemblies, 900–901 (*see also specific Lateran councils*); Constantine the Great and, 418, 513, 514, 1362, 1375, 1419; death of the pope and, 10; Donation of Constantine and, 513, 514; facade reconstruction, 803, 1363; ferula receipt at, 575; frescoes, 537, 1363; Gregory XIII projects, 665; Hilarus oratories, 706; Holy Year ritual, 726, 729, 1361; Innocent X and, 1361–1362, 1383; John XXIII and, 854, 1363; large bell, 152; Martin V commissions, 1380; mosaics, 1019, 1021, 1116, 1360, 1361, 1363; Nicholas IV and, 1039, 1360, 1363; obelisk, 1062, 1362, 1383; painting commissions, 1090, 1362–1363; papal tombs, 1360, 1361, 1363, 1386, 1422, 1497, 1498, 1499, 1500, 1502; pavilion, 692; penitentiaries, 454, 1152, 1523; pilgrimage indulgences, 1170; pilgrimage medallions, 983; *possesso* ceremony, 1228; protonotaries, 1264; rebuilding of, 104, 976, 1116, 1117, 1359–1360, 1362–1363, 1367, 1413, 1460; relics theft, 1381; St. Peter's basilica resemblance, 1377; terrorist bomb damage, 1364

St. John of Jerusalem, Hospital of, 659, 722, 988

St. John of Rhodes, seal of, 692

St. Lawrence church (Perugia), 1499–1500

St. Lawrence's Outside the Walls, basilica of: cardinals and, 239; Constantine the Great and, 418; mosaic medallion, 1492; papal chapal, 1038, 1359; Simplicius building projects, 1426; Sixtus III and, 1433

St. Lazarus Order, 988

St. Louis des Françaiss (hospice), 1170

St. Marcellus's basilica, 418, 1497

St. Mark's cathedral, 320, 857

St. Mark's church (Rome), mosaics, 1019

St. Mary Major, basilica of, **1364–1370**, 1373, 1378, 1586; antiquity, **1364–1366**; Middle Ages, **1366–1367**; from 16th century, **1367–1370**; bells, 152; cardinals associated with, 239; Clement IX and, 349, 351; Clement XII and, 357; consecration feast day, 144; Dominican penitentiaries, 510; frescoes, 1340–1341, 1367, 1368, 1369; Gregory XIII and, 665; Holy Year ritual, 726, 729; liturgy, 283; mosaics, 1020, 1364, 1365, 1366, 1367, 1368; Nicholas IV and, 1039, 1366, 1501; obelisk, 1383; painting commissions, 1090, 1368; papal residence near, 1302, 1304; papal tombs, 349, 351, 1369, 1500, 1501; Pauline chapel, 1130, 1340–1341; penitentiaries, 454, 1152, 1523; pilgrimage indulgences, 1170; pilgrimage medallions, 983; pontifical blessing from, 177; protonotaries, 1264; Sangallo ceiling, 28; Sixtus III and, 179, 1327, 1364–1365, 1366, 1367, 1433; Symmachus oratory, 1476

St. Mary of Spain Order. *See* Star Order

St. Mary's Faculty of Theology (Baltimore, Md.), 1546

St. Matthew cathedral (Salerno), 1499

Volume Key: Volume 1, pages 1–614; volume 2, pages 615–1266; volume 3, pages 1267–1637.

1760

St. Maur, congregation of, 554

St. Paul the Apostle. *See* Paul

St. Paul's Outside the Walls, basilica of, **1370–1373**, 1375, 1586; Middle Ages, **1370–1371**; 16th to 20th centuries, **1371–1373**; Agapitus II and, 15; building of, 1120; cardinals associated with, 239; consecration feast day, 144; Constantine the Great and, 418, 513, 1419; Damasus I initiation of project, 478; fire destruction (1823), 1189–1190, 1370, 1371, 1372; Gregory XVI restoration, 1190; Holy Year ritual, 726, 729; Leo I restoration, 914; Leo VII and, 922; Leo XII restoration, 1016, 1190; medallions of popes, 983, 1022, 1065; monastery, 1373; Nazi pillaging of (1944), 1635; painting commissions, 1090, 1091, 1092, 1372; papal tombs in, 1497, 1498; pilgrimage medallions, 983; pilgrimages to, 1169, 1380; Pius IX restoration, 1031, 1372; rebuilding of, 1046, 1231, 1372; Saracen pillage of, 109, 921, 1354, 1373, 1393, 1413; Senate and, 1411; Sixtus III and, 1433; Symmachus projects, 1476; Vatican II ceremonies, 1141; wall enclosure, 836, 1373

St. Peter Institute, 1374

St. Peter, Patrimony of, 1538; blessing *urbi et orbi* from, 177; Nicholas III restoration, 1038

St. Peter the Apostle. *See* Peter

St. Peter the Apostle, Pontifical Society of, 1450

St. Peter the Apostle, Society of, **1373–1374**

St. Peter's basilica, 1016, 1328, 1365, 1373, **1374–1387**; antiquity, **1374–1378** ; Middle Ages, **1378–1382**; modern and contemporary era, **1382–1387**; altar, 38, 549, 1090; announcement of new pope from, 679; architectural reconstruction of, 104–106, 107, 108, 726, 885, 886, 887, 926, 976, 1116, 1117, 1130, 1339, 1340, 1344, 1375–1376, 1382–1384; baldachin, 1383, 1384; baptistry, 1377; bells, 152, 1378; Bernini's completion of, 1371, 1383–1384, 1562; bishop of Rome ordination in, 181; Cappella Giulia (musical chapel), 298; cardinals associated with, 239; ceremony, 283; Chair of St. Peter, 286–287, 1159, 1378–1379, 1382; chapel. *See* Sistine Chapel; consecration feast day, 144; consecration of new pope and, 425, 1377; Constantine the Great and, 418, 1374–1375, 1378, 1382, 1419; dome completion (1593), 1340; Donus paving of atrium, 514; emblem of back-to-back keys, 689, 692; excavations under, 547–549, 1375–1376; Fabric of, 558–559; feast of St. Peter and, 1159, 1160; Filarete decoration of doors, 537; funeral banquets, 259; Gregory XIII projects, 665; Gregory XIV and, 666; heraldry, 688; Holy Year ritual, 726, 729; as imperial coronation site, 424; indulgences and, 509, 775, 1395; Innocent III projects, 786, 1301; Innocent X projects, 803; Lateran competition with, 1302; Leo I restoration, 895; Leo IV building projects, 254, 549, 1328, 1373; literary images of, 751–757; liturgy, 951; Michelangelo dome design, 105–106, 107, 271, 273, 726, 1117, 1340; mosaic portrayals of, 1022; mosaics, 1020, 1021, 1090, 1378; necropolis under, 547–549; Nicholas V rebuilding plan, 104, 549, 1042, 1340; obelisk, 1374, 1383, 1384, 1438; painting commissions, 1090, 1117; Pantheon as architectural model, 1096; papal body viewing in, 1056; papal coronation and, 426; papal tombs in, 1344, 1345, 1377, 1379, 1380, 1381, 1383, 1384, 1385, 1386, 1391, 1434, 1496, 1497, 1498–1503; Pelagius II crypt design, 1148; penitentiaries, 454, 1152, 1523; pilgrimage medallions, 983; pilgrimages to, 1164, 1165, 1169, 1377; pillagings of, 1378;

protective neighborhood around, 254; protonotaries, 1264; Saracen plunder of, 109, 254, 921, 1328, 1354, 1373, 1378, 1393, 1413; Sistine Chapel damage, 1428; Sixtus III and, 1433; Sixtus IV ciborium, 1380–1381; Sixtus V and, 1382–1383, 1438; symbolism of, 1384–1387; Symmachus projects, 1377, 1476; as Vatican II site, 1569; Vatican Palace and, 1302; Visigoth sack of Rome and, 140; wall, 1328

St. Peter's church, 151, 1302

St. Peter's Square, 30, 108, 123, 1587; announcement of new pope in, 679; Bernini design, 1384; canonization procession, 570; fountain, 351; Italian jurisdiction over, 1384, 1586; papal installation and, 427; public papal audiences in, 125–126, 127

St. Peter's throne, 223

St. Peter's vestry, 498

St. Praxedes church (Rome), mosaics, 1020

St. Sebastian basilica, 260, 418

St. Stephen's cathedral (Vienna), 867

St. Suzanne, Jourdain, 960

St. Sylvester, Order of, 487

St. Thomas Aquinas, Pontifical University of, 380, 1544

St. Thomas of Acre Order, 989

Saint-Amour, Guillaume de, 66

Saint-Étienne, Bernard de, 1556

sainthood. *See* canonization

saints, veneration of, 204, **1387–1392**; blessed distinction, 145; bodies in catacombs, 250, 261–262, 557, 1121; causes of canonization, 268–272; Damaus I promotion of, 478–479; feast days, 211, 569, 1388–1389; Flagellant rejection of, 703; iconoclast controversy and, 643; list of, 234–237; non-Roman saints, 1390–1391; paintings of, 1090; papal tombs and, 1391–1392, 1496; pilgrimages and, 1163, 1164, 1165, 1166, 1169; Pius XI encyclicals on, 1204; popes, 1121; Tridentine defense of, 429, 1289, *See also* martyrs; relics, veneration

Saisset, Bernard, 191, 1485

Sal Salvatore (confraternity), 1307

Sala Leonina, 1598

Sala Regia (Quirinal), 1091, 1270, 1271

Saladin, 438, 711, 722, 1553

"Saladin tithe," 579, 1481

Salamanca, University of, 162, 379, 1544, 1548

Salazar, Antonio, 397, 1515

Saldanha, patriarch of Lisbon, 171

sale of duties. *See* simony

Salesian Pontifical University, 380, 1545–1546

Salian dynasty, 627, 732, 924, 1274

Salic Law, 912

Saliceti, Aurelio, 1324

Saliège, Cardinal, 875, 1199

Sallust, 1044, 1183

Salmeron, Alphonsus, 1518

Salone Sistino, 1598

Salotto Dipinto, 1091

salt war (1540–1541), 1049, 1342

Salus Populi Romani (Virgin Mary icon), 1367

Salvaggiani, Francesco Marchetti, 1136

salvation: crusaders and, 438; indulgences and, 1286; laity concerns in Middle Ages, 895–896; Lateran IV and, 1274; sus-

Volume Key: Volume 1, pages 1–614; volume 2, pages 615–1266; volume 3, pages 1267–1637.

1761

pension of censures and, 1149; works vs. grace dispute, 429, 438

Salvi, Nicola, 1363

Salviati, Bernardo, 1030, 1091, 1434

Samoré, Antonio, 1236

San Donnino, Gerardo de Borgo, 24, 66

San Germano, treaty of (1229), 315

San Giacomo degli Incurabili, 1310

San Lorenzo basilica, 706, 1116

San Luca, Academy of, 118, 119, 1269

San Marco convent, 509, 510

San Marco, University of, 1544

San Pellegrino, church and cemetery, 1472

Sancha of Mallorca, 722

Sanchez I Ramirez, king of Aragon, 18

Sancta Sanctorum (confraternity), 1307

Sancta Sanctorum (St. John Lateran), 1359, 1360, 1362, 1378

Sanders, Nicholas, 68

Sanfedist forces, 1179, 1181

Sangallo, Ambrogio di, 343

Sangallo, Antonio da (the Older), 255

Sangallo, Antonio da (the Younger), 28, 105, 106, 255, 926, 1029, 1127, 1382

Sangallo, Giuliano da, 104, 1368, 1382

Sangnier, Marc, 307, 1198

Sangro, Gentile di, 286

Sanholis, Jean de, 1501

"Sanpietrini" (artists), 1021

Sanseverino, Cardinal, 1126

Sanseverino, Robert, 111

Sanseverino, Tommaso di, 286

Sant'Alessio Falconieri, 1546

Sant'Anastasio, English (or Greek) College of, 664

Sant'Angelo. See Castel Sant'Angelo

Sant'Angelo bridge accident (1450), 725

Sant'Ignazio church, 668

Santa Casa of Loreto, 1170

Santa Maria alle Febere, 1374

Santa Maria del Fiore, 103, 104

Santa Maria dell'Anima (German church in Rome), 317

Santa Maria dell'Orazione e Morte (confraternity), 1309

Santa Maria di Galeria, 1600

Santa Maria, Guido de, 959

Santa Maria Novella, 509

Santa Maria Rotonda, 1096

Santiago (St. James of the Sword) Order, 989, 990

Santiago de Compostela, 1165, 1167

Santo Spirito de Maiella (hermitage), 280

Santo Spirito, Order of, 454, 1307, 1309

Santos, Juan, 256

Santucci, Carlo, 175, 1210

Sanuto, M., 926, 927

Sapaudus of Arles, 597, 1147, 1148

Sapienza. See Rome, University of

Sapiniere (Sodalitium pianum), 614

Saracens, **1392–1393**; attacks on papacy, 109, 254; Benedict VIII naval battle, 157, 1393; bishop expulsions by, 500–501; Byzantine Empire conquests by, 1319; crusades and, 440, 1393, 1552; Gregory IV defense, 645; in Holy Land, 318, 438, 711, 712, 722; invasion of Africa by, 218, 545; invasion of Sicily by, 638; invasion of Spain by, 143, 1319; John VIII campaign against, 836, 837, 1393; John X battle against, 839, 1027, 1393; Lateran III and, 901; Leo IV and, 921; military orders' offensives against, 987; naval defense against, 109, 1027–1028; Nicholas I defense, 1033; Norman war against, 112, 1393; St. Peter's and St. Paul's pillage by, 109, 254, 921, 1328, 1354, 1373, 1378, 1413; as slaves, 1439, 1440; as threat in *chansons de geste*, 749

Saragossa, cathedral of, 164

Sarcerdotium Imperium (1125–1356). See Church-State conflict

sarcophagus, 549, 1025

Sarda y Salvany, Felix, 943

Sardica, synod of (343–344), 199, 908, 909

Sardinia, kingdom of, 166, 169, 353–354; Hadrian IV claims to, 1098; Italian unity and, 1107, 1194, 1538, 1539, 1541; naval battle for, 1393

Sarpi, Paolo, 888, 1131

Sarto, Giuseppe Melchiorre. See Pius X

Sartori, Cardinal, 1001

Saso family, 451

Sassanites, 423

Satanists (Luciferians), 605, 702, 830, 943

satire, anti-Roman, 749–751

Satires (Juvenal), 442–443

Satolli, Francesco, 40, 364

Saturnalia, 248

Saul of Tarsus. See Paul

Sauli, Antonio Maria, 668, 927, 1129

Saumaise, Claude, 1466

Savelli, Cencio. See Honorius III

Savelli family, 280, 1047, 1048

Savelli, Giacomo. See Honorius IV

Savelli, Lucas, 735, 1335

Savelli, Pandulf, 735, 973

Savioni, Mario, 298–299

Savona, treaty of (1407), 635, 661

Savonarola, Giorlamo, 27, 67, 926, 928, 1276, 1342, 1621; apologetics, 76; Florentine leadership by, 509; Michelangelo religious crisis and, 1430

Savoy, 636, 1059, 1539; [Felix V] and, 574; French occupation, 1624

Saxo of Santo Stefano, 275, 732

Saxons, 1, 140, 141, 997, 1318; Charlemagne conquest of, 1320; pilgrimages to Rome, 1166

Saxony, 997, 1287

Scali banks, 136, 137

Scandinavia: Anastasius IV and, 46; artists in Rome, 121; ecumenism, 518; Eugene III and, 533, 683; evangelization of, 997; Great Schism and, 632, 636; Gregory XIII and, 663; Hadrian IV and, 46, 533, 683, 684; in papal early 15th-century domain, 661; Peter's Pence payment, 577; as Protestant, 1518; Urban VI support by, 1558, See also specific countries

Scannabecchi, Lamberto. See Honorius II

Scappi, Bartolomeo, 303

Scarampi, Ludovico, 58, 536

Scarlatti, Alessandro, 299

Scarpelli, Umberto, 322

Scarria, Giovanni, 192

Volume Key: Volume 1, pages 1–614; volume 2, pages 615–1266; volume 3, pages 1267–1637.

1762

Schauer, Angelo, 374

Scheler, Max, 861

Schelstrate (historian), 1598

Schepitski, Andrei, 1532

Schilbeeckx, Edward, 764

Schinner, Mathias, 1622

schism, **1393–1398**; antipopes and, 69–72; Chinese, 1396–1397; in early centuries, 1394 (*see also specific schisms*); Lefebvre, 1397–1398; Old Catholics, 778, 779, 1396, 1530, 1567, 1568; Uniate, 1531–1533, *See also* Great Schism of the West; heresies

Schmalkalden Articles, 1289

Schmalkaldic League, 1125, 1287

Schmemann, P. Alexander, 1577

Schmid, Conrad, 67

Schmidlin, J., 1311

Schneider, Burckhart, 496

Schola cantorum, 300, 379, 919, 949–950, 1412, 1413

Scholastica, St., 1613

scholasticism, 98, 336, 450, 846, 847, 1294, 1295, 1296

Schönborn, Christoph, 264–265

schools. *See* colleges of Rome; education; universities

Schuler, Dionysius, 597

Schulte, Johann von, 1396

Schuster, Ildefonse, 1135, 1372, 1373

Schutz, Roger, 520, 1577

science: Galileo trial, 467; Pius X mistrust of, 1197; Pius XI interest in, 1200, 1206; pontifical academy, 498, 1206, 1562; Silvester II (Gerbert) writings, 1422

Scientific Research, Bureau of, 1026

Sclafenatus, John, 695

Scolari, Paolo. *See* Clement III

Scoppolo, Pietro, 1538

Scotland: artists in Rome, 120; [Benedict XIII] and, 165; blessed hat and sword gifts to, 182; Calvinism in, 1519; Clement III and, 331; Eugene IV and, 536; evangelization by, 1108; Great Schism and, 340, 632; Hadrian IV and, 684; Jesuit college, 379; liturgy, 953; pilgrimages to Rome, 1167; Pius V's Catholic restoration attempts, 1177; Protestantism, 1288, 1519; Urban VIII and, 1560, 1561

Scotti bankers, 452

scribes of the Lateran. *See* scriptor

scriniarii sanctae Romanae, 289–290

scrinium, 289–290

scriptor, 449, 451–452, 455, 459, **1398**; kitchen, 458; simony and, 463

scriptore litterarum apostolicarum, 293

Scriptures. *See* Bible

scudo romano (coin), 376, 377

sculpture. *See* art; monumentality and Roman urbanism; monuments, Roman; museums, Vatican

Sea Beggars, 938

seal. *See* Fisherman's Ring

Sebond, Raymond de, 76

Sechaux, Aymon, 344

Second Coming, 64, 65

Second Crusade (1147–1149), 533, 534

Second International, 978

Second Vatican Council. *See* Vatican II (Ecumenical Council of)

secret, pontifical, **1398–1400**

secret chamberlains, 739–740

secret societies, 672, 605 (*see also* Freemasonry)

Secret Vatican Archive. *See* Vatican Secret Archives

Secretariat for Promoting Christian Unity, 520, 855, 856; Pontifical Council, 434, 474; Vatican II and, 1577

Secretariat of Briefs, 195, 461, 524, **1400–1401**

Secretariat of Briefs to Princes, 195, 1400, **1401–1402**, 1402, 1403

Secretariat of State, 125, **1402–1404**; "ad limina" visits and, 5; administrative services, 1403–1404; Alexander VII as, 28; *Annuario pontificio*, 63; Apostolic Palace management, 1093, 1094; Benedict XV and, 172–173; Clement VIII and, 347; on conferences of bishops, 402–403; Congregation of the Eastern Churches and, 407; contemporary divisions, 1403; Curia and, 463, 472, 473; decoration awards, 488; as dicastery, 498; election of bishops, 90; Enlightenment and, 529; financial management, 582; Holy See and, 717, 718, 720; Innocent IX changes, 800; John XXIII and, 854, 855; list of secretaries, 1404; minutante and, 994; *Osservatore* first-page column, 984, 1082; Palatine, 1094; in papal hierarchy, 1341; Paul VI as, 1135; Paul VI reforms of, 294; Pius IX succession of, 1191, 1193; Pius XII and, 1213, 1218–1219; Pius XII as, 1203; press office, 1236; Secretariat of Briefs to Princes and, 1401–1402; Statistical Office, 12; Substitute of, 1401, 1464; telephone network, 1482; Vatican Archives and, 1604; Vatican City State representation by, 1587; Vatican Radio and, 1601, 1602; World War I and, 1626

Secretariats of the Roman Curia, **1404–1405**, 1574–1575

secularism: of Austrian and German schools, 869, 893; Christian Democracy and, 304, 305, 311; in Eastern Europe, 542; in Europe, 539; French Revolution and, 1109; fundamentalism as reaction to, 614; Inquisition and, 815–816; in Italy, 1542; *Kulturkampf* effects, 891–893; modernism and, 1006, 1007; papal arbitration and, 98–99; Pius X efforts against, 173; prejudices of, 1232–1233; university, 1544, 1547, 1549

Secundus of Trent, 142

sedan chair. *See portantina papale*; sedia gestatoria

sedi vacante. See see, vacant and impeded

sedia gestatoria, 588, 1026, **1405**; filming of Leo XIII in, 1163; *flabellum* use with, 588; John Paul I as last user, 1229; John Paul II termination, 741; modern version of, 127

See, vacant and impeded, 486, **1405–1407**, 1479; deposition of pope and, 495

Sega, Filippo, 800

Segarelli, Gerardo, 702

Segneri, Paolo, 806

Segni. *See* Vitalian

Segni, Brunon de. *See* Bruno of Segni

Selim II, Ottoman sultan, 937

Seljuks. *See* Turks

sella, Quintino, 1018

seminaries, 378–385, 379, 411, **1407–1410**, 1547, 1548; antecedents, 1407–1408; Catholic reforms and, 1277, 1342–1343, 1407–1409; contemporary Church history, 1409–1410; indigenous clergy training, 1002, 1004, 1373–1374; Joseph II and, 868, 869; Pius X reorganization, 1197–1198; Pius XI curriculum development, 1206; Propaganda Fide and, 1254; Tridentine creation of, 429, 1175, 1176, 1407, 1408–1409, 1521–1522

Volume Key: Volume 1, pages 1–614; volume 2, pages 615–1266; volume 3, pages 1267–1637.

Seminaries and Teaching Institutions, Congregation of. *See* Catholic Education, Congregation for

semi-Pelagianism, 573, 700

Senarius, Senator, 831

Senate, Roman, and the papacy, 144, 1313, **1410–1412**; antisimony action, 832; Benedict XIV registry of, 1049–1050; coin minting and, 373; disappearance of (603), 1047, 1330, 1411–1412; Eugene III and, 532–534; King Theodoric conflict with, 831, 832; musical instruments, 299; Nicholas III and, 1037, 1038; Nicholas IV and, 1039; revival and status of, 1334–1335, 1336–1337; Roman nobility and, 1044–1047, 1411; status (mid–8th to mid–12th century), 1331, 1333–1334; Vigilius and, 1616, 1617

Seneca, 618, 1159

Sens, Council of (1140–1141), 450, 701

Sens, Council of (1528), 1521

Seper, Cardinal, 1085

Septimius Severus. *See* Severus, Lucius Septimius

Septizodium, 1329

Septuagint, 47

Serafini, Camillo, 1590

Serapion of Antioch, 631

Serapion the Simonite, 1164

Serapis, cult of, 442

Serbia, 522, 523, 542, 787

Sercambi, Giovanni, 138

Sergius (son of Christopher), 679, 1457, 1458

Sergius, exarch of Ravenna, 1120, 1274

Sergius, patriarch of Constantinople, 730, 834

Sergius I, 71, 598, 1111, 1359, **1412–1413**; coins, 372; missions and, 997; Quinisext Council and, 203, 428, 836, 1412

Sergius II, 71, 109, 600, 681, **1413**, 1458; antipope to, 831; Leo IV and, 921; tomb of, 1497

Sergius III, 45, 71, 839, **1413–1414**; [Christopher] imprisonment by, 312; coins, 372; Lateran rebuilding, 1359–1360, 1413; Stephen VI (VII) and, 1459, 1460

Sergius IV, **1414–1415**; Benedict VIII as successor, 157, 647; epitaph for Silvester II, 1422; tomb of, 1498, 1499

Sergius IV Severinus

Seripando, Girolamo, 263, 1126

Serlupi-Crescenzi families, 627

Serre, Michel, 117

Sertillanger, D., 512, 1628

Servant of the Servants of God, 1495

Service of the Cipher, 1464

Servites, 379, 1131, 1546

Seven Last Words, 1275

seven-day week, 209

Seventh Day Adventist Churches, Italian Union of, 904

Severinus, **1415**

Severoli, Cardinal, 931

Severus, Acilius, 1045, 1230

Severus Alexander, emperor of Rome, 63, 1550

Severus, Lucius Septimius, emperor of Rome, 1016, 1095, 1155, 1315, 1329

Severus of Antioch, 14, 1145

Severus, Sulpicius. *See* Sulpicius Severus

Sextus liber (1298), 226, 227

Sfondrato, Ercole, 666

Sfondrato family, 809

Sfondrato, Niccolò. *See* Gregory XIV

Sfondrato, Paolo, 666

Sforza, Ascanio, 26, 58, 1124

Sforza, Caterina, 1435

Sforza family, 667, 668

Sforza, Francesco, 26, 54, 111, 218, 535, 537, 928, 1041, 1122, 1124, 1172, 1623, 1624

Sforza, Galeazzo Maria, 1122

Sforza, Gian Galeazzo, 798, 1621

Sforza, Giovanni, 26, 27

Sforza, Ludovico (the Moor), 26, 885, 928, 1621

Sforza, Maximilian, 1623

Sforza, Muzio Attendolo, 975

Sforza, Riario, 363

Shamir, Y., 877

Shapuhr II, king of Perisa

sheep, blessing of, 59

shelters. *See* hospices

Shlomo, Goren, 714

Shoah. See Holocaust

shoes. *See* footwear

Shoes of the Fisherman (film), 322, 323

Shroud of Turin, carbon-dating of, 589

Sica, Vittorio de, 322

Sicco, count of Spoleto, 155, 156, 188

Sicco, John. *See* John XVII

Sicilian Church, 204

Sicilian Vespers (1282), 51, 280, 628; Byzantium and, 642; Charles of Anjou and, 315; Martin IV and, 440, 973

Sicily, 203, 1540, 1554, 1555; Alexander IV and, 23; Angevin-Aragonese conflict over, 51–52, 54, 160, 280, 628, 735–736, 973, 975, 1038, 1039; Angevins and, 50–54, 676, 716, 793; Benedict XIII and, 166; Boniface VIII and, 190; Byzantium and, 318, 644, 1318, 1319; Celestine III and, 277–278; Celestine V residence in, 1302; Charles of Anjou and, 656; Church suzerainty over, 277–278; Clement III and, 331; Clement IV and, 332; [Clement VII] and, 340; crusades and, 439; Ghibelline/Guelph conflict and, 628, 629, 676; Greeks in, 638; Gregory XI and, 659; Hadrian V and, 685; Holy Roman Empire and, 313, 314, 315, 331, 715, 716, 786–787, 961; Innocent IV and, 51, 315, 440; legates and, 51, 52, 1053, 1054; Lombard invasion of, 315; Lucius III and, 960; Normans in. *See* Normans of southern Italy and Sicily); as papal patrimony, 315, 331, 576, 577, 961, 1103; Saracen occupation of, 638, 645, 1392–1393; Vigilius in, 1617, *See also* Naples, kingdom of; Two Sicilies, kingdom of the

sicknesses of the pope, Middle Ages, **1415–1417**

Sicut iudaeis non doctrine, 872

Siena, 23; banking activity, 137; canonizations, 265–266; Lombards and, 958; papal war, 887; Pius II and, 1173

Siena, University of, 846

Sigebaut (deacon of Reims), 15

Sigebert of Gembloux, 623

Siger of Brabant, 702, 847

Sigismund, king of Hungary (and of the Romans), 165, 513, 535, 536, 636, 637, 662, 716, 1166; Hussites and, 775; [John XXIII] and, 852

Volume Key: Volume 1, pages 1–614; volume 2, pages 615–1266; volume 3, pages 1267–1637.

1764

Sigismond III Vasa, king of Sweden and Poland, 348

Sigismund of Tirol, 1172

Signatura Apostolica, Supreme Tribunal of, 292, 471, 1350, 1525–1526, 1592; list of cardinal prefects, 1525–1526

Signature of Graces, Congregation of the, 1438

Signorelli, Luca, 1091, 1428

Sigonio, Carlo, 1296

Silesia, 828

Sillon (youth movement), 307, 308, 1008, 1198, 1448

Silone, Angelo, 283

Silva Candida, Umberto. *See* Humbert da Silva Candida

Silvanus, 1158

silver coins, 372, 373, 374, 376, 377

"Silver Trumpets" (march), 745

Silverius, 141, 180, 196, **1417–1418**; death outside Rome, 1418, 1497; deposition of, 564, 1608, 1616

Silvester I, 500, 1045, **1418–1420**; Council of Nicaea representatives, 427–428, 1419; dioceses and, 500; Donation of Constantine to, 513, 514, 1294, 1300, 1320, 1374, 1419, 1420; Marcellus I tomb and, 968; mosaics depictions, 1020–1021; tiara, 1489, 1490, 1491, 1492; tomb of, 1121, 1391, 1392, 1419, 1496; veneration as saint, 1121, 1392

Silvester II, 156, 645, 646, 647, 842, 843, 844, **1420–1422**; as Boniface VII detractor, 189; Holy Roman Empire and, 714, 1414, 1421–1422; legends about, 1422; tomb of, 1414, 1422, 1497, 1498

Silvester III, 70, 71, 647, **1422–1423**; Benedict IX excommunication of, 158, 1422; deposition of, 328, 495, 1305, 1422, 1612

[Silvester IV], 70, 72, 1112, 1113, **1423**

Silvester of Ferrara, 509, 510

Silvester of Prierio, 778

Simeon of Bulgaria, 839

Simeon of Thessalonica, 208

Simeoni, Giovanni, 582, 1196, 1256

Simo, Francesco Jeronimo, 1267

Simon Cephas. *See* Peter

Simon de Bisignano, 21

Simon de Craud, 634

Simon de Montfort, 438, 897

Simon Magus, 65, 1043, 1044, 1160; *Acts of Peter* and, 3, 4; simony and, 1423, 1424, 1425

Simon of Bisignano, 225

Simon of Gitta, 1424

Simon of Langham, 659

Simon of Langres, 508, 795

Simon of Polirone, St., 232

Simone da Firenze, 977

Simonelli, Matteo, 298

Simonetta, Giacomo, 1124

Simonetti, Michelangelo, 1025

simony, **1423–1425**; Alexander II papacy and, 18, 731; Alexander VI election and, 393; anti-Roman satire on, 750; Benedict IX moves against, 158; [Benedict X] and, 159; bishops' elections and, 91; Clement II measures against, 328; [Clement III] measures against, 329; Clement III measures against, 331; conclave, 393, 1425; Curia duties and, 463, 468; Dante's *Inferno* and, 1038; Gregorian reforms and, 648, 649, 895, 1278, 1280, 1281, 1282, 1424, 1483; Gregory VI deposed for, 648; Henry III limiting, 1614; as heresy, 700; in-

dulgences and, 773; Innocent VIII and, 799; John XXII measures against, 848; Julius II limitations, 393, 885, 886; King Athalaric decree against, 832; Lateran Council decree against, 216, 900, 1036, 1037; lay investiture fostering, 91, 1280, 1281, 1424; Leo IX measures against, 924, 1245, 1280; Leo X activities, 463, 927; married clergy linked with, 1042, 1043, 1044; Nicholas III and, 481; Paschal II and, 1112; Pavia synod condemnation of, 646, 1279; Ravenna synod condemnation of, 156; Sixtus IV and, 463; Thomas Aquinas definition of, 1423; Urban II moves against, 1423, 1551, 1552, *See also* investiture controversy

Simor of Hungary, 893

Simplician of Milan, 43, 48–49, 986

Simplicius, 35, 572, 621, 1046, **1425–1427**; basilica projects, 1390; St. Peter's basilica alterations, 1377; tomb of, 1377, 1496

sin: of Adam, 429, 1520; indulgences and, 773–775; liberalism seen as, 943; penance and, 773; Penitentiary and, 1523–1524, *See also* original sin

Sincero, Luigi, 370

singers. *See* castrati of the papal chapel; music

Sion, Jean de, 284

Siri, Cardinal, 310, 858, 864, 1137, 1143

Siricius, 43, 444, 478, 1011, 1012, 1013, **1427–1428**; episcopal ordinations by, 500; as former deacon, 484; papal office and, 1244; saint veneration, 1390; Thessalonica and, 1611; tomb of, 1496; vicar of Milan and, 1466

Sirleto, Guglielmo, 213, 263, 665, 968; Pius IV support for, 1296; Tridentine missal and, 995; Vatican Library and, 1598

Sirmium, Council of (358), 881–882, 946

Sirmond, Jacques, 1466

Sisinnius, **1428**

Sistine Chapel, 1026, 1270, **1428–1431**; Apostolic Hospice and, 739; architecture, 104, 105, 107; caudatary, 267; Clement XIII cover for nude statuary, 359; as conclave site, 392; contemporary restoration, 1429, 1430–1431; filming in, 321, 1429; fresco restoration, 1026; Mass sung in, 294; Michelangelo ceiling painting, 285, 886, 1091, 1117, 1127, 1340, 1429–1431; painting commissions, 1089, 1091, 1428–1431, 1435; as papal chapel, 294, 295; Quirinal copy of, 295–296; Raphael tapestries in, 926; Sixtus IV and, 295, 392, 1435; white smoke signal for naming of new pope, 569, 679

Six Days' War (1967), 713

Sixtus I, **1431**, 1482

Sixtus II, **1431–1432**; African Church and, 13, 33, 251; execution of, 122, 1155, 1316, 1432; military forces, 111; tomb of, 1496, 1497; vicariate of Thessalonica and, 1611

Sixtus III, 35, **1432–1433**, 1641; benefaction by, 179; building program, 1433; Leo I and, 913; monasticism, 1013; mosaics commission, 1020; St. Mary Major basilica, 179, 1327, 1364–1365, 1366, 1367; St. Peter's basilica and, 1377; tomb of, 1391, 1496

Sixtus IV, 27, **1433–1436**; abbreviators for, 1; Alexander VI and, 26; annona, 60; appointment of bishops and, 93; architectural renovations, 104, 1340; archives, 1603; arms, 114; arts patronage, 1089, 1091, 1092, 1116; assessments of, 1434–1435; auditors, 126, 220; cardinal nephew office, 1402; cardinal protector abuse remedies, 247; censorship and, 1443; Chair of St. Peter covering, 1379; consistorial ad-

Volume Key: Volume 1, pages 1–614; volume 2, pages 615–1266; volume 3, pages 1267–1637.

1765

vocates, 413; Curia and, 463, 464, 471; humanism and, 1294, 1295, 1435; Inquisition bull, 816; Jewish policy, 872, 1435; Julius II and, 884, 1032; Leo X and, 926; nepotism and, 926, 1032, 1402; patronage by, 695, 799, 1434–1435, 1435; Paul II and, 1121; pet parrot, 58; rosary and, 1347; Rota tribunal reorganization, 462; St. Mary Major and, 1368; St. Peter's ciborium, 1380–1381; Signatura Apostolic and, 1525; simony and, 463; Sistine Chapel commission by, 295, 392, 1428; tomb, 1381, 1383, 1434, 1503; tribunal of Roman Rota and, 1524; Vatican library funding, 1294, 1435, 1597, 1598

Sixtus V, 143, 346, 359, 1092, 1177, 1362, 1367, **1436–1439**; "ad limina" visits and, 4; administrative offices, 11, 347; annona, 61; architectural projects, 106, 108, 1017, 1089, 1116, 1340, 1369, 1382; arms, 114; basilica decoration, 1090; breviary changes, 194; canonizations by, 235; canonizations proceedings and, 234, 268–269; cardinal protector limitations, 247; cardinalate limitation, 243, 1357; cardinalate nepotism and, 242, 1402; Carnival and, 248; Catholic reform and, 1246, 1342, 1436–1438; Catholic university founding, 1546; chamberlains, 288; coins, 374, 375; Colosseum and, 388, 1437; congregations created by, 406, 408, 410, 415, 995, 1438; congregations organization, 242, 411, 465, 666, 1437, 1443; Curia reform, 242, 247, 293, 465–466, 467, 471–473, 483, 1277, 1349, 1357; datary, 482, 483; Dominicans and, 510; Fabric of St. Peter and, 558; financial reforms, 374; Gregory XV and, 667, 669; Henry IV of France censured by, 929; Holy Office and, 709, 816; hospices, 1226; Huguenots and, 347; Index rules and, 770, 772, 1438, 1443; Jesuit modifications by, 826, 827; Lateran Palace and, 1359; medallions, 982; nepotism and, 1437; obelisks erected in Rome, 1061; Pantheon pillage by, 1096; papal chapel reorganization, 296; poor relief, 1226, 1308; *possesso* frescoe, 1229; protonotaries, 1263; provincial councils and, 430; Quirinal creation, 1269, 1271, 1437–1438; Recollects and, 596; reserved case, 1298; Roman city planning, 1340, 1437–1438; St. Mary Major renovation, 1367, 1369; St. Peter's basilica dome and, 1382–1383, 1438; Secretariat of Briefs, 1401; Signatura Apostolic and, 1525; state functionaries and, 1341; statuary removal by, 1024; tomb of, 1369; Urban VII and, 1559; Vatican gardens and, 1595; Vatican Library building, 1598; Vulgate revision, 1296

Skanderberg, George, 1122, 1172

skullcap. *See* calotte

slavery, **1439–1441**; Gregory XVI condemnation of, 675; missionary denouncement of, 510, 1002, 1343; Petrine privilege and, 1250; private, 1440–1441; state, 1440, 1441

Slavonic liturgy, 682, 837, 997, 1459

Slavs: Byzantium and, 202, 203, 205, 1319; first evangelization of, 541, 997

slippers, papal, 620

Slipyi, Cardinal (Uniate), 855, 1085, 1532–1533

Slodtz, Michel-Ange, 119

Slovakia, 523

Slovenia, 1215

Small Catechism for the Use of Less Educated Pastors (Luther), 262, 264

Smyrna, 440, 1434; crusade of (1342–48), 1526

Sobieski, Jan, 375

social Catholic movement. *See* Christian Democracy; social teaching

Social Communication, Pontifical Council for, 435–436, 984, 985, 1239, 1445–1446

social communications, **1441–1447**; cinema and, 321; conciliar decree on, 435–436, *See also* social teaching

Social Democratic party (Germany), 979

social documents, **1447**

social teaching, **1447–1450**; Benedict XV and, 174; Christian Democracy and, 305, 309, 310; confraternities and, 1311; documents, 1447; early evangelization and, 544–545; fundamentalism dissociated with, 614; international organizations and, 1077; John XXIII and, 853, 855, 856, 1110; John Paul I and, 857; labor unions and, 1596; Leo XIII and, 306, 935, 983, 1077, 1110, 1311, 1443, 1444, 1447, 1448, 1449–1450, 1515 (*see also Rerum novarum*); *Opera dei Congressi*, 307, 1023, 1542; Paul VI and, 512, 1134, 1442, 1446, 1447, 1448, 1449; *Quadragesimo anno* (1931) and, 309, 1447, 1449, 1462; subsidiarity principle, 1461, 1462–1463, *See also* poor relief

Social Weeks, 1008

socialism, 78, 904; Christian, 944, 1135; Leo XIII and, 935; liberalism and, 944; papal condemnation of, 977–978, 1109

Societies, Pontifical Mission, **1450–1451**

Society of Jesus. *See* Jesuits

Sodalicium pianum, 1199

Söderblom, Nathan, 518

Soderini family, 694

Sofronius, 1012

Soggifanti, Piero, 1029

Soglia, Cardinal, 1193

Soissons, Council of (1121), 701

Sokolov, N., 874, 875

Solemes, abbey of, 954

Soller, Philippe, 123

Sollicitudo rei socialis (1987 encyclical), 1447

Somaschi, 1126, 1276

Sophia, 704, 1378

Sophia of Bavaria, 1163

Sopraintendente dello Stato ecclesiastico, 1032–1033

Sorbonne. *See* Paris, University of

sorcery, 669, 813

Sorge, Father, 324, 325

Soter, 523, **1451–1452**, 1612

Soto de Langa, Francisco, 256, 297

Souabe dynasty, 51

Soubirous, Bernadette, St., 1204

soul/body distinction, 77

Sovereign Pontiff of the Universal Church, 1495

Soviet Union, 176; calendar, 213; Holy See relations, 540, 1216; John XXIII and, 855; papal *ostpolitik*, 1084–1086; Paul VI and, 1135, 1137, 1140; Pius XII contacts with, 1212; Roman Catholic evangelization in, 522, 523; Uniate communities, 1532–1533; World War II and, 1213, 1629, 1631, 1632, *See also* cold war; Marxism and the papacy; Russia

Spadolini, Giovanni, 325

Spagnoletto, Jacomo, 256

Spain: Alexander II and, 18; Alexander III and, 20; alum deposits, 38; ambassador to Holy See, 1057; apologetists, 78; appointment of bishops, 89, 91, 93, 94; artists in Rome, 116–117, 119; barbarians in, 140, 141, 142, 143, 1318;

Volume Key: Volume 1, pages 1–614; volume 2, pages 615–1266; volume 3, pages 1267–1637.

[Benedict XIII] and, 164, 165, 167; Benedict XIV concordat for, 169; bishops' conferences and, 404; Blessed Hat and Sword gifts to, 182; canonical collections, 223, 231; cardinalate and, 241; Celestine III and, 277; chinea tribute, 303; churches in Rome, 317; Clement X and, 352; Clement XI and, 353, 353–354; Clement XII and, 357; Clement XIII and, 360; Clement XIV and, 361; concordat with, 399–400, 483; Council of Trent and, 1518, 1519; crusade against Moors, 437; Discalced friars, 595; Dominicans, 508, 509; evangelization in, 544; exclusion right, 550; Franciscans, 594, 595; French wars in Italy and, 1622, 1623; fundamentalism, 614; Great Schism and, 164, 165, 340, 508, 632, 635, 637; Gregorian calendar, 213; Gregory VII and, 649; Gregory XI diplomacy and, 659; Gregory XIII and, 663; Gregory XVI and, 674; Holy Sepulcher order, 722, 723; Hormisdas and, 738; Innocent VIII and, 799; Inquisition in, 815–816, 817–820, 827, 1435; Islam in. *See subhead* Saracen invasion *below*; Jesuit expulsion, 359, 361, 362, 828, 1004, 1346; Jesuits and, 826–827; Jewish *conversos*, 799, 815, 816, 818, 870–871; Leo XII and, 932; Lepanto and, 937; liturgy, 948, 951, 953; military orders, 988, 989, 990; military ordinariates, 991; missionizing by, 509–510, 999–1000, 1255; monasticism, 1011; Moriscos revolt, 937; national cleric post, 1027; New World conquests, 27, 98, 509–510, 999–1000, 1002, 1343; Opus Dei organization, 1070–1071; papal domination by, 1102; papal nunciature in, 1058, 1059; papal titles in, 1051; patron saints, 569; Paul IV and, 1102, 1128; pilgrimages to Santiago de Compostela, 1165, 1167; Pius V and, 1176; Pius VI and, 1179–1180; Pius XI and, 1209; Pius XII and, 1216, 1218; Priscillianism, 782; provincial councils, 430; *Reconquista* in, 18, 787, 796, 1551, 1552; religious orders, 1343; sack of Rome (1527) and, 1355; Saracen invasion, 143, 1319; seminaries, 1342; Sixtus V and, 1437; temporal veto, 1608; treaty with Turks, 663; universities, 1544, 1548; Urban II and, 1551, 1552; Vandals and, 1318; Vatican II personnel, 1576; Vatican II representation, 1579, 1580, 1581, 1583; Vigilius and, 1617; Visigoth control of, 1318, *See also* Aragon; Castile; Léon

Spalding, John Lancaster, 40

Spanish Armada, 1437

Spanish Civil War, 978, 1070, 1209

Spanish Inquisition, 815–816, 817–820, 1435; anti-Jesuit moves, 827

Spanish Succession, War of the (1701–1713), 168, 469, 529; Clement XI and, 353, 1103; indigency from, 1225

Specchi, A., 1271

Spedalieri, Nicolà, 77, 78, 1018

Spellman, Francis, 713, 1213, 1515, 1634

Spener, Philippe-Jacob, 704

Speranza, Stefano, 239

Speronists, 701

Spifame bank, 137

Spina, Giuseppe, 1185

Spini banks, 452

Spinoza, Benedict, 77

Spiritans, 1255

Spirituals (Franciscans), 592, 594, 849–850; Catholic reform and, 1274; Celestine V and, 280, 281, 282; election of Boniface

VIII and, 282; as Inquisition target, 133, 813, 814; on true and false popes, 830

Spiritus Paraclitus (1920 encylical), 176

Split, 139, 839

spoil, 336, **1452**

Spoleto, 141, 192, 196, 643, 644, 1319; Gregory V retreat to, 646; Hadrian I and, 680; Lombards and, 954, 1120; Napoleonic annexation, 1104; in Papal States, 1098, 1100(map), 1101, 1102; Zacharias and, 1639

Sprenger, Jakob, 799, 1309

Staël, Mme. de, 751, 752, 753, 754, 756

Stafford, James Francis, 434

Staircase of the Ambassadors (Versailles), 1270

Stalin, Joseph, 859, 1209, 1216

Stanislaus, St., 569

Stapleton, Thomas, 778

Star Order, 990

stations, Roman, **1452–1454**

statuary. *See* art; monumentality and urban Romanism; monuments, Roman; museums, Vatican

Stefaneschi, Giacomo Caetani, 284, 1379–1380

Stefaneschi, Jacopo del fu Giovanni di Arlotto, 1337

Stefano, Giovanni, 1360, 1361

Steiger, Rod, 323

Stein, Edith, 874, 876

Stella, Tommaso, 1309, 1310

Stendhal, 569, 727, 752, 753–754, 755, 757, 759, 760, 761, 931, 1272, 1371

Stephani, 647

Stephanians, 158

Stephanus, 1617, 1618

Stephen, St., 69, 1118

Stephen (popes), **1454–1455**; numbering of, 1065–1066

Stephen (priest and assassin), 155, 188

Stephen, king of England, 533, 784

Stephen I, 561, 959, **1455–1456**; African Church and, 13, 1431, 1455; as bishop of Rome, 181, 1244; *lapsi* and, 250–251, 1455; Novatian and, 1056; Petrine succession and, 1108; successor Sixtus II, 1431; veneration as saint, 1121

Stephen I Bathory, king of Poland, 664

[Stephen II], 1454, 1455, **1456**

Stephen II (III), 109, 679, 837, 1367, 1454, **1456–1457**; bell tower of, 151, 1378; Byzantium and, 204; Exarchate of Ravenna and, 547, 1064, 1097, 1273, 1274, 1546–1547; exemptions, 552; Frankish support, 1319, 1331, 1378, 1456–1457, 1640; liturgy, 952; onomastics, 1454, 1455; Paul I as successor, 1120; Pepin III dynasty and, 599, 1319, 1378

Stephen III (IV), 679, 680, **1457–1458**; cardinal bishop and, 240; iconoclast controversy and, 204; suburbicarian dioceses, 501

Stephen IV (V), 424, 600, 681, 837, 1413, **1458**

Stephen V (VI), 590, 997, **1458–1459**

Stephen VI (VII), 487, 1327, **1459–1460**; exhuming of Formosus's body, 590, 1413, 1459, 1487; Sergius III and, 1413, 1459, 1460

Stephen VII (VIII), **1460**; murder of, 122

Stephen VIII (IX), 15, **1460–1461**; murder of, 122, 1461

Stephen IX (X), 648, 925, **1461**; [Benedict X] and, 159; Byzantium and, 206; onomastics, 1455; tomb of, 1498–1499; Victor III and, 1613

Volume Key: Volume 1, pages 1–614; volume 2, pages 615–1266; volume 3, pages 1267–1637.

1767

Stephen of Blois, 276

Stephen of Larissa, 14

Stephen of Orleans, 225

Stephen of St. Crisogno, 1036

Stephen of Tournai, 93

Stepinac, archbishop of Zagreb, 1215

Sterbini, Pietro, 1324

stereotypes. *See* prejudices

Stern, Raffaele, 1016, 1025, 1272

Stiernon, Daniel, 1573

Stilicho, 1318

Stoicism, 74, 1314

Stoppa, Paolo, 322

Strada Pia, 1270

Strambi, Vincenzo Maria, 931

Strato (deacon), 993–994

Strossmayer, Josip, 1396, 1567

Strozzi family, 343

Stuart dynasty, 55, 1130, 1177, 1386

Studies, Seminaries, and Universities, Congregation for. *See* Catholic Education, Congregation for

Studio del Vaticano, 1021, 1022

Studites, 1043

Studium Biblicum Franciscanum of Jerusalem, 1546

Studium Curiae (pontifical court), 379, 507, 792, 1548

studium generale, definition of, 1407, 1548

Studium Urbis. *See* Rome, University of

Stumpf, J., 239

Sturzo, Luigi, 175, 307, 308, 309, 310, 326, 902, 1023, 1134, 1198, 1207

Suarez, E., 512

Suarez, Francisco, 99

subcinctorium, **1461**

subdeacons, 484

Subiaco monastery, 22, 24, 1013

subordinationism, 214

subsidiarity, **1461–1464**; list of, 1464

Substitute of the Secretariat of State, 1401, **1464**; list of, 1464

suburbicarian dioceses. *See* dioceses, suburbicarian

suburbicarian Italy, 501, 942, **1464–1467**

Success of the Prince of Apostles (papal title), 1495

Suenens, Cardinal, 247, 1137, 1445, 1584

Suetonius, 544, 1153

Suger, abbot of Saint-Denis, 625–626, 784

Suhard, Cardinal, 613, 614

Suidger, bishop of Bamberg. *See* Clement II

Suleiman (the Magnificent), 711, 936

Sulpicians, 1210–1211, 1409

Sulpicius Severus, 945, 946

Summa Decreti (Stephen of Orleans), 225

Summi pontificatus (1939 encyclical), 1214, 1629

Summus Pontifex, 1495

Sunday, 209, 210

superintendent of the Ecclesiastical State, **1467–1470**; cardinal nephew as, 245, 1468, 1469

Supreme Order of Christ, 487

supreme pontiff. *See* titles, papal

Supreme Tribunal. *See* Signatura Apostolic, Supreme Tribunal of

surgeons. *See* medicine

suspension, **1470**; causes of, 1149–1150

Sutri, synod of (1046), 648

Suze, Ancher de, 1554

Suze, Henri de, 1554

swaddling clothes, consecrated, **1470**

Sweden, 140, 663; Clement VIII and, 348; evangelization of, 997; Hadrian IV in, 683; Reformation in, 1287

Swiss Cantons. *See* Switzerland

Swiss Guard, 138, 626, 627, 693, 1052, 1095, **1471–1472**, 1588; brass band, 299; chinea ceremonial procession and, 304; "national" church of, 316; papal court and, 436–437; papal household and, 739, 740

Swiss People's Party, 309

Switzerland: Christian Democracy in, 309; concordat with, 400; election of bishops, 88; French wars in Italy and, 1622, 1623; Gregory XVI and, 674–675; Latin Monetary Union, 377; Leo XII and, 932–933; Old Catholics, 1396; papal nunciature in, 1059; Paul VI visit to, 1515; Reformation, 1286–1287, 1288; Vatican II representation, 1579, 1583, *See also* Swiss Guard

sword. *See* Blessed or Holy Hat and Sword

Sword Bearers Order, 989, 990, 998

Syagius of Autun, 598

Sykes-Picot accords, 712

Syllabus of Errors, **1472–1475**; Americanism and, 41; Dominican support, 512; eighty propositions of, 1195; free expression control, 1195, 1443; Leo XIII commentary on, 934; liberalism and, 306, 944; list of, 1472–1475; modernity and, 674, 944, 1010, 1247; Old Catholics schism and, 1395–1396; as papism defense, 1109; Ultramontanism and, 1530; Vatican I and, 1565, 1566

Sylvester. *See* Silvester

symbolism, spiritual, 182–183; dove, 182, 693, 1020; Golden Rose, 1348; in images of Peter, 1161; mosaics, 1020–1021; of St. Peter's basilica, 1377, 1384–1387

Symeon, St., 158

Symmachus, 44, 49, 141, 622, 1046, 1374, **1475–1477**; antipope to, 71, 736, 906–907, 942; apostolicity principle and, 200; bishop of Rome ordination and, 181, 184; Chalcedonian bishops and, 564; Dioscorus support for, 502; Easter-date controversy, 517, 1475; finances, 135; Hilarus and, 707; Hormidas and, 736; John I and, 831; pilgrim lodgings and, 1165; *prima sedes a nemine iudicatur* claim, 1108; St. Peter's basilica alterations, 1377, 1476; saint veneration, 1388, 1390, 1391; schism with Lawrence, 7, 736, 1475–1476; Senate support for, 1411; Tiber valley home, 1594

Syndicate of the Vatican. *See* Vatican labor union

Synod of Bishops, **1477–1479**; Benedict XIV on, 168; conferences of bishops and, 402; contemporary Orthodox Churches and, 522; election of bishops and, 85–86; Sacred College and, 1358

Syria: Arab conquest of, 318; Byzantium loss of, 1319; canon law, 370; Catholic missions in, 1561; Church of, 86, 404, 998; Monophysite Church, 202; pagan cults, 442–443, *See also* Antioch

Taborites, 703–704

Tacchi-Venturi (Jesuit), 1629

Tacitus (historian), 1153

Volume Key: Volume 1, pages 1–614; volume 2, pages 615–1266; volume 3, pages 1267–1637.

1768

Tacitus, emperor of Rome, 543

Tagliacozzo, battle of (1268), 315, 440

Taine, Hippolyte, 755–756, 1534

Taiwan, 1218

Taizé community, 520, 521, 1577

Taja, Alessandro, 867

Talleyrand-Périgord, Charles-Maurice de, 63, 585, 586, 611, 796

Talmud, 792, 872

Tamburini, Cardinal, 171

Tanchelme, 66, 701

Tancred da Lecce, king of Sicily, 277–278, 314, 1052, 1054

Tanucci, Bernardo, 888

Tanzimet revolution, 1527

Taparelli, Massimo, 99

Taparelli d'Azeglio, Luigi, 324, 1462

Tapper, Ruard, 778

Tarasius, patriarch of Constantinople, 680

Tardieu, André, 1626

Tardini, Domenico, 325, 854, 855, 1218, 1629, 1630, 1631–1632; Paul VI and, 1132, 1135, 1136; on Pius XII, 1213; press office, 1236–1237; Vatican II and, 1572, 1573

Tarento family, 53

Tartars, 333, 451, 792, 998

Tassi, Agostino, 1270

Tau, Knights of, 987

taurobolium (bull sacrifice), 441–442

Tausen, Hans, 1287

taxation, papal: annataes, 59–60; anti-Roman satire on, 750; Apostalic Camera collectors, 80–84, 459; Avignon papacy and, 1246; Benedict XIV and, 169; Byzantium and, 644; camerlengo and, 219, 220; Clement III and, 331; Clement VI and, 335, 336; [Clement VII] and, 342; clerical exemption, 190; collectors, 378, 459, 466; of common and small services, 389; council of Basel abolishment (1435), 536; crusades. See tax/tithe crusade; of documents, 293; Gregory VII and, 1283; Luther's Ninety-five Theses and, 1286; medieval Church, 135–137; papal powers and, 1246, 1467; Pius VII reforms, 1184; for Roman construction projects, 1340; salt wars and, 1049, 1342; types of (13th to 15th centuries), 577–580, See also finances, papal; tax/tithe; tithes

Taxil, Léo, 601, 605, 607

tax/tithe, crusade, 136, 189, 579, 1246, **1481**, 1485; *decima* (10 percent), 82, 335, 438–440, 579, 580, 786, 787

Taylor, Myron, 1214, 1633–1634

Tedeschini Piccolomini, Francesco. See Pius III

Tedeschini Piccolomini, Laudomia, 1173, 1174

Teilhard de Chardin, Father, 326, 828, 829, 1008, 1009

telephone, **1481–1482**

Telesphorus, 327, 1154, 1244, **1482**

Television Center. See Vatican Television

Tellenbach, Gerd, 1278, 1279, 1284

Tellier, Jean, 1309

Tempier, Étienne, 702

Tempier, Stephen, 846–847

Templars, Knights, 362, 989, 990, 1016, 1028, 1554; banking activity, 136, 988; Clement V and, 131, 333, 334, 429, 988, 989; Holy Places defense by, 987; overview, 988

Temple of Jerusalem: crusaders and, 711; destruction of (70), 544; Knights Templars and, 987; St. Peter's basilica and, 1385

temporal regalia, 1290

Tencin, Cardinal de, 168, 170

Tentonico, rule of, 987

Teodoro de Cock, 354

Teresa, Mother, 1514

Teresa of Avila, St., 664, 669, 1510; beatification and canonization of, 1130

Teresa of Jesus, St., 1343

Terra Arnulforum, 1555

territorial prelature (list), 1233–1234

terrorism, 310, 311, 496, 859, 864, 1140; St. John Lateran and, 1364

Tertullian, 3, 64, 523, 544; apologetics, 75, 708, 1155, 1315; on dissolution of marriage, 1249; on excommunication and anathema, 48; on fasting, 1452; on Peter's martyrdom, 1153

Terza Loggia maps, 252, 253

tessera, 1018, 1020

Test Act of 1673 (England), 55

tetragamy crisis (906–920), 45, 206, 839, 1414

Tetzel, John, 509, 1382

Teutberga, queen of Lorraine, 1034

Teutonic Knights, 334, 488, 655, 987, 988, 1016; overview, 989; Reformation and, 1287; Sword Bearers combined with, 990, 998

Texier, Barthelemy, 508

Thalia (Arius), 770

Thanase of Alexandria, 428

theater: Carnival and, 248–249, 250; Leo X sponsorship, 927; traveler's writings on, 1506

Theatines, 351, 826, 1126, 1128, 1276, 1309

Theiner, Augustin, 1096

Theissling, L., 512

Theobald of Canterbury, 276

theocracy, papal, Middle Ages, 791, **1482–1486**; Boniface VIII and, 1109, 1485; devotion to the pope and, 496; Gregory VII beliefs, 1108–1109, 1278, 1280, 1284; Roman government and, 1333, See also investiture controversy

Theodahad, king of the Ostrogoths, 14, 141, 180, 1145, 1417, 1616

Theodelinda, queen of the Lombards, 142, 1166, 1389

[Theoderic], 70, 72, **1486**

Theodora, empress regent of Byzantium, 14, 35, 205, 600, 1318; Silverius and, 1417; Vigilius and, 1146, 1616, 1617

Theodora (mother of Paschal I), 1020

Theodora (wife of Theophylact), 1414

Theodore, archbishop of Canterbury, 16, 142, 997, 1619

Theodore, archbishop of Ravenna, 16, 1273

Theodore, duke of Bavaria, 643

Theodore, patriarch of Constantinople, 514–515

[Theodore], 71, **1486**

Theodore I, 202, **1486–1487**

Theodore II, 590, **1487**

Theodore Askidas, bishop of Caesarea, 1146, 1618

Theodore Balsamon, 207

Theodore of Mopsuestia, 201, 1146, 1617

Theodore of Tarsus. See Theodore, archbishop of Canterbury

Theodore Studites, 198, 204–205, 318, 920

Theodoret of Cyrrhus, 75, 201, 917, 1146, 1147, 1617, 1618

Theodoric I (the Great), king of the Ostrogoths, 44, 141, 564,

Volume Key: Volume 1, pages 1–614; volume 2, pages 615–1266; volume 3, pages 1267–1637.

1769

572, 621, 622, 623, 1046, 1165; Felix IV and, 573; Gelasius and, 200–201; John I persecution by, 831, 832, 1497; Milan and, 987; named king of Italy, 1318, 1465; papal finances and, 575, 576; Ravenna and, 1273; Roman Senate and, 1411; Symmachus support by, 502, 907, 1475, 1476

Theodosius I (the Great), emperor of Rome, 198, 199, 562, 563, 699, 908, 1317; Christian policies of, 480, 1317–1318; Code of, 223; Cybele worship ban, 442; fall of Rome and, 986, 1317–1318; Latinity and, 905; reign of, 1317–1318; St. Paul's basilica and, 1120; St. Peter's basilica and, 1378

Theodosius II, emperor of Byzantium, 184, 699, 705, 706, 915, 916; Alexandria and, 34–35; Christology and, 915; Ephesus convocation by, 199; Nestorius support by, 274, 275, 916; reign accomplishments, 1318; Thessalonica and, 1611

Theodosius, pope of Alexandria, 35

Theodosius of Cyr, 706

Theodotus of Byzantium, 1612

Theologican of the Papal Household (current title). *See* master of the Sacred Palace

theology faculties, 2, 1407, 1543

theology of liberation. *See* liberation theology

Theopaschite controversy, 14, 832

Theophano, empress of the Holy Roman empire, 842, 843

Theophilus, patriarch of Alexandria of Alexandria: Easter-date computation, 917; as Father of the Church, 563, 567; John Chrysostom rivalry, 782

Theophilus of Antioch, 43

Theophylact (Roman patrician), 1332, 1414

Theophylact Lecapene, patriarch of Constantinople, 206, 835, 840, 896, 1097

Theophylact of Tusculum. *See* Benedict VIII; Benedict IX

Theophylactus family, 447

Theosophists, 603

Theotokis, 274, 428, 699, 1365, 1366

Theresa of the Child Jesus, St., 270

Thérèse of Lisieu, St., 1202, 1204

Thessalonica, 184–185, 563, 783, 915, 1433, 1642; vicaraiate of, 1611

Thessalonica, edict of (380), 479–480, 699

Thiene, Gaetano, 1309

Thierry (antipope), 1112, 1423

Third Crusade (1189–1192), 278, 331, 438; tax/tithe financing of, 579, 1481

Third International, 977–978

Third Reich. *See* Nazism

Third Rome (Moscow), **1487–1488**

Third World, 1143, 1217–1218, 1239

Thirty Years War (1618–1648), 704, 1129; Gregory XV and, 667, 669; papal finances and, 30, 467; papal nuncios and, 1060; Paul V and, 1130; Urban VIII and, 801, 912, 1560, 1561, *See also* Westphalia, Peace of

Thirty-Nine Articles (1563; Anglican), 55, 1097, 1289

Thomas à Becket. *See* Becket, Thomas

Thomas Aquinas, St., 98, 379, 657, 1543, 1544; on apostasy, 79; canonization of, 508; on Church unity, 1394; on Church-State relations, 1484–1485; as *Civiltà Cattolica* doctrinal basis, 326; devotion to the pope and, 496, 497; on dispensation, 505; as Doctor of the Church, 510; Dominicans and, 508, 510, 511, 512, 569, 593; Jesuits and, 1296; on Jews, 871; John Paul II

theology and, 861–862; Leo XIII and, 512, 934–935; Leo XIII encyclical on, 306; Leonine edition of works, 512; on nepotism, 1031; papal rights defense by, 508; Pius XI encyclical on, 1204; relics of, 508; seminary philosophy of, 1409; simony definition, 1281, 1423; subsidiarity concept, 1461, 1462; Tempier commission attack on, 847; theology of, 133

Thomas of Carthage, 251

Thomas of Tournon, 1501

Thomassin, Louis, 954

Thomism. *See* Thomas Aquinas, St.

Thor (god), 140

Thorvaldsen, Albert, 1384

Thourotte, Robert de, 1554

Three Chapters, schism of, 13, 35, 141, 142–143, 187, 640, 700, 730, 834; African bishops and, 251; Gaul and, 597; inception of, 1146; Milan and, 987; Pelagius I and, 1146–1148; Pelagius II and, 1148; Vigilius and, 251, 1497, 1617, 1618

Thronstretregister (Innocent III), 786

Thuasne, Louis, 284

Thurian, Max, 1577

Thuringia, 997

tiara, 12, 116, 694, 941, 1145, 1284, **1488–1493**; banner, 138, 1588; camauro and, 620; Chair of St. Peter, 287; Eugene IV Ghiberti commission and, 537; Fisherman's Ring, 587; Gentlemen of His Holiness, 627; as heraldic emblem, 689, 690, 692, 693; keys and, 689, 690–691, 693, 694; *pallium* and, 244, 1607; papal coronation and, 425, 426, 1283; papal vs. bishop's miter, 1490; Paul II and, 1121, 1489; Paul VI relinquishment of, 1139, 1489

tiara-miter, 1492

Tiber (statue), 1595

Tiber River, 104, 107, 109, 547; Castel Sant'Angelo and, 253, 254, 255; Roman development near, 1329, 1340; Vatican Gardens and, 1594

Tiberius III, emperor of Byzantium, 203

Tici, Andrea di, 136, 137

Tiepoli, Pasqualino, 257

Timotheos Elure, 917–918

Timothy of Alexandria, 44, 563, 737, 1426

Timothy of Beirut, 479

Tincq, Henri, 523

Tiridatus, king of Armenia, 545

Tisserant, Cardinal, 1143, 1219, 1446, 1574, 1598

tithes: Boniface VIII and, 1485; collection of, 216, 335, 466; crusades financing. *See* tax/tithe, crusade; exemption from, 988; French Revolutionary abolishment of, 611; initiation of, 578, 579; protests against, 703

Titian, 138, 1092, 1123, 1271

titles, cardinals', **1493–1494**

titles, pontifical, 1109, **1494–1495**; administrative offices, 11–12; Church-State cooperation and, 21; 19th-century expansion of, 627, 1050; Roman nobility and, 1050–1051; Vatican II reforms, 741–742, *See also* decorations

Tito, Marshal, 1085, 1215

Titus, emperor of Rome, 387, 1016, 1314

Tivoli villa, 1269, 1345

Tivoli war (1142–1143), 1333

Toland, John, 77

Toledo: Domincans and, 506; metropolitans of, 143

Volume Key: Volume 1, pages 1–614; volume 2, pages 615–1266; volume 3, pages 1267–1637.

1770

Toledo, Council of (400), 782

Toledo III, Council of (589), 141

Toledo IV, Council of (633), 430

Toledo XII, Council of (681), 91

Tolentino, treaty of (1797), 470, 613, 1103, 1181, 1183, 1184, 1189

Tolerance, Edict of (1781), 868–869

Tolfa alum. *See* alum of Tolfa/Tolfa alum

Tolome of Lucca, 486, 791

Tolomeo da Lucca, 37

Tomacelli, Marino, 192

Tomacelli, Pietro. *See* Boniface IX

Tomano, Giulio, 1373

Tomasek, 1086

Tomb of the Unknown Soldier, 1018

Tombaldini, Domenico, 256

tombs of saints. *See* catacombs, saints' bodies in the

tombs of the popes, **1495–1503**; to year 1000, **1495–1498**; 11th to 15th centuries, **1498–1503**; Bernini sculpture, 1344; Canova sculptures, 1345; epitaphs for, 1380, 1422, 1497, 1498, 1500, 1502; papal altar, 38; worship of saints and, 478, 1391–1392, 1496, *See also* St. John Latern; St. Mary Major; St. Peter's basilica

Tome of Leo, 916, 917, 1147, 1426

Tome to Flavian, 567, 699, 706, 916, 917

Tomislav, king of Croatia, 839, 997

Tong Che-tche, 1396

Toniolo, Giuseppe, 306–307, 1023, 1024

Tonquédec, J. de, 79

tonsure, 1553

Torcello, Marino Sanudo, 440

Tordesillas, treaty of (1494), 999

Torelli, Luigi, 1536

Torlonia, Alessandro, 673, 1050

Torlonia family, 740

Torquemada, Juan de, 76, 509, 777

Torrigiani, Luigi, 359, 361, 470

Torriti, Giacomo, 1039, 1116

Torriti, Jacopo, 1019–1020, 1360, 1361, 1363, 1367, 1379

Tortelli, Giovanni, 1597

torture, 509, 703, 793, 811, 814, 817–818

Tossignano. *See* John X

totalitarianism: encyclicals against, 305, 1449, 1450, 1462, 1629, 1631; Holy See and, 903; liberalism compared with, 943

Totila, king of the Goths, 1146, 1328

Toubert, Pierre, 1332

Toulouse, 506; Inquisition in, 812, 814, 816

Toulouse, University of, 132, 635, 1544, 1548, 1549; College de Foix library, 1597; Innocent IV and, 792–793

tournaments, 901

Tournon, Millard de, 1003

Tours, battle of (732), 1319

Touzard, Jules, 176

Tract XC (Oxford Movement), 1087

Tractarians. *See* Oxford Movement

Tractatus Garsiae, 750

Tracts for the Times (Oxford Movement), 1086–1087

Traditio legis, imagery of, 1161

tradition, custom vs., 476

Traietto Palace, 1304

train-bearer. *See* caudatary

Trajan column, 108, 1329, 1381

Trajan, emperor of Rome, 443, 1153, 1314, 1315

tramontanism. *See* Ultramontanism

Transfiguration, feast of the, 218, 832

Transfiguration of Christ (Raphael), 1021, 1090

transubstantiation, 429, 887, 1277, 1521; Lutheran doctrinal rejection of, 1286

transumpta, 183

Trasimund, 644, 1639

Trasterverines, 1306

Trastevere, 571, 1328, 1329

Trautson, archbishop of Vienna, 867

traveler's views of Rome and the Vatican, **1503–1510**; list of travelers, 1507–1510; secular visitors, 1170, *See also* image of Rome in literature

travels of John Paul II, 10, 542, 860, 865, 1239, 1247, **1510–1514**, 1516, 1526, 1569; criticisms of, 1512; devotional significance of, 497; as Head of Church, 1110, 1589–1590; impact of, 1512–1513; impeded See provisions, 1407; to Israel, 877–878; Jewish issues and, 876; as pilgrimage model, 1170; pre-papal, 863

travels of Paul VI, 1139, 1143, **1514–1517**, 1569; automobiles and, 126; to Holy Land, 713, 1170; to United Nations, 687, 1078–1079, 1132, 1140, 1510, 1514, 1515, 1584

travels of popes, 536–1809, list of, **1517**

Traversi, Gaspare, 1373

"treasure of merits" doctrine, 438

treasurer, 80, 81, 83, 220, 452, 459, 483, 578, 580

Treasury of Charts, 1604

treasury, papal. *See* finances, papal

Treatise on Christian Freedom (Luther), 1286

Treatise on Lapsed Christians (Cyprian), 423

Trebeschi, Andrea, 1134

Trebonianus Gallus. *See* Gallus, Trebonianus

Tree of Life, 1020, 1429

Trent, Council of (1545–1563), 168, 469, 530, 867, **1517–1523**, 1562; Anglican schism and, 54; appointment of bishops and, 93; assessment of, 1522; background, 1517–1518; breviary reform, 193, 194, 954, 1130, 1175, 1178, 1522; calendar reform, 213; canon law, 227–228, 229; Capuchins and, 595; cardinalate reforms, 242, 243; Catechism, 262, 263, 264, 265, 1000, 1142, 1175, 1178, 1277, 1522; Catholic reform movement and, 530, 666, 667, 726–727, 1246–1247, 1276–1277, 1544; on church paintings and architecture, 1090, 1369; Church-State powers and, 1535; Clement VII and, 344; as Clement VIII influence, 347, 348; conciliarism vs. papism and, 1109; concilliarism and, 391, 1518; conclave reforms, 393, 394–395; confraternities and, 1309, 1310; Congregation of the Clergy implementation of, 410–411; congregations and, 394, 410, 471, 1522; Curia reforms, 465; devotion to the pope and, 496; dioceses *in partibus*, 500; disciplinary work at, 1521–1523; doctrinal work of, 1520–1521; dogma issues, 429; on Eucharist, 887; exemptions reforms, 553–554, 1233; Gallicanism and, 616; Gregory XIII and, 213, 663, 664; Gregory XIV and, 666; on incardination, 766; Index and, 763, 770, 771–772, 1296; on interdict, 820; Jansenism and, 824, 825; Jesuits and, 826; John XXIII references to, 1572; Julius

Volume Key: Volume 1, pages 1–614; volume 2, pages 615–1266; volume 3, pages 1267–1637.

1771

III and, 886, 887, 968, 1289, 1519, 1520; jurisdictionalism and, 888; Lateran IV teachings and, 897; legate representation, 912; Leo XI and, 929; liturgical reform, 953–954, 968, 1175; Marcellus II participation, 968, 1519; missal reform, 954, 995–996, 1175, 1178, 1522; move to Bologna, 429, 1125, 1519; nepotism restrictions, 1033, 1469; nunciatures and, 664, 1057, 1059; original sin definition, 429, 1520; overview of, 429, 1518–1522; papal primacy and, 1246–1247; Paul III and, 287, 1125–1126, 1246, 1296, 1520; Paul IV and, 826, 1128, 1519; Paul V decree applications, 1130, 1137; pilgrimage renewal from, 1169–1170; Pius IV and, 416, 1175–1176, 1519, 1522; Pius V and, 1177, 1468; poor relief and, 1224, 1225; printing press and, 1444; profession of faith, 1251; Protestant delegates, 1519; provincial councils and, 430; Reformation rebuttals, 1276–1277, 1289–1290; reopening of (1562), 1175; reserved cases right, 1298; Roman colleges and, 379; Roman renewal and, 1342–1343; sack of Rome and, 1355; seminaries inauguration, 1407, 1408–1409; simony reforms, 1425; superintendent of the Ecclesiastical State and, 1468; typhus outbreak, 1125; Urban VII and, 1559; Vatican I as first ecumenical council following, 1565, 1570

Trentino, 1540, 1630

Trento, John-Baptist, 252

treuga Dei. See Truce of God

Trevi Fountain, 359, 529, 1117, 1345

Treviso, University of, 868

tribunals, apostolic, **1523–1526**; consistorial advocates and, 413; as dicasteries, 498; Vatican City, 1591–1592, *See also* Rota, tribunal of the

Tribune of Honor, 1052

Tridentine Index, 770, 772

Tridentine reforms *See* Trent, Council of

Trier, University of, 1544

Trinità dei Pellegrini (confraternity), 1310

Trinitarian order, 664

Trinity. *See* Christology; Holy Spirit

Trionfo, Agostino, 242, 1494

Triple Alliance (1882), 934

triple crown. *See* tiara

Triton Fountain, 107, 1344, 1562

Triumph of Divine Providence, The (Pietro da Cortona), 1091

Triumph of the Holy See (Cappellari), 670–671, 1535

Troia, synod of (1093), 1552

trombones, 299

Troncio, Guglielmo, 375

Trophimus, St., 1610

Troyes, Jacques de. *See* Urban IV

Truce of God, 98, 109, 158; Alexander III and, 22; Benedict IX and, 158; Council of Clermont and, 900; Lateran I decree, 216, 900; Leo IX and, 924; Urban II and, 1053, 1551, 1552

Truman, Harry, 712–713

Tu es Pierre (film documentary), 322–323

Tucci, Roberto, 1239, 1240

Tudeschis, Nicolaus de (Panormitanus), 777

Tudor dynasty, 54–55, 799, 887, 982, 1288–1289

Tunisia, 400, 440

Turchi bank, 82

Turgot, A. R., 1225

Turin, 1059, 1539, 1540

Turin catalog (131), 1306

Turin, Council of (398), 1610

Turkey: anticlericalism, 176; Gregorian calendar delayed adoption, 213; Holy See relations, 1527; John Paul II visit to, 1511, 1526; Paul VI visit to, 1515; remains of Roman Empire in, 1319

Turks, **1526–1527**; Alexander VI and, 26, 27; Alexander VII and, 30; Alexander VIII and, 31; alum deposits, 38; as Antichrist, 66; Balkans occupation by, 638, 1526; Byzantine conquest with Normans (1071), 206–207; Callistus III and, 218; Church missionizing and, 1000, 1002; Clement VIII mobilization against, 347; Clement X and, 351–352; Clement XI and, 353; Constantinople's fall to (1453), 208, 218, 319, 440, 1041, 1526–1527, 1531; crusades against, 375, 440, 1122, 1124, 1172, 1177, 1526; defeat at Lepanto (1571), 936–939, 1177, 1179, 1343; defeat at Vienna (1683), 805, 1343; Eastern Churches and, 319; Gregory XIII and, 663; Gregory XV and, 669; Holy Land sovereignty, 711; Holy League defense against, 26–27, 528; Innocent VIII first diplomacy with, 799; Innocent XI defense against, 375, 540, 795, 1369; Leo X and, 928; papal naval defense, 1029, 1030; Paul III and, 1123, 1124–1125; Paul V and, 1130; Pius V and, 1177; Propaganda Fide and, 1255; Sixtus IV and, 1434; slavery and, 1439, 1440; as Venice threat, 353, 1124, 1125

Turmel, Joseph, 1007–1008

Turner, H. E. W., 696

Tuscany: banking agents, 136, 137, 581; Charles of Anjou and, 656; Church-State powers and, 23, 1535–1536, 1538, 1541; Enlightenment, 530; episcopalian and parochial reforms, 1180; French control of, 1182; Guelph/Ghibelline conflict and, 627, 628, 629, 676–677; Hundred Years War and, 1556; Italian unity and, 1535, 1540; jurisdictionalism, 888, 889; Nicholas II and, 1037–1038; papal relations, 1059, 1180; Papal States and, 1102

Tuscolani family, 647, 845, 1333

Tusculum, 158, 159; aristocratic families, 449, 647, 1048; Celestine III and, 277; Lucius III and, 960; Papal States and, 1097

Tutus (deacon), 572

Twelve Anathemas of Cyril, 34, 833

Two Laurels cemetery, 259

two powers, theory of, 108, 1108, 1482

Two Sicilies, kingdom of the, 1538, 1539, 1540; Jesuits and, 359, 828; Pius VII concordat with, 1189

typhus, 1125

Tyre, Council of (335), 883

Tyrrell, George, 1008, 1199

Tyrrhenian Sea, 645

Ubaldi, Baldo degli, 227, 505

Ubaldini, Ottaviano degli, 451, 656, 1554

Uberti, 676

Ubertin of Casale, 849

Ubi arcano Dei (1922 encyclical), 526, 1203

Ubi Periculum (1274), 486, 657; rescinded by John XXI, 846

Ubi primum (1824 encyclical), 931

Ubi primum (1840 encyclical), 169, 530

Uganda, 1515–1516

Ughelli, 30

Volume Key: Volume 1, pages 1–614; volume 2, pages 615–1266; volume 3, pages 1267–1637.

1772

Ugolino, Cardinal, 788, 910
Ugoni, Mattia, 391
Uguccione, Francesco, 163, 786
Uguccione da Pisa, 390
Ukraine: evangelization in, 522, 542, 998; *Ostpolitik*, 855, 1085, 1215; Uniates, 348, 674, 1085, 1130, 1531, 1532
Ulbaldi, Baldo degli, 227, 505
Ulbaldini, Ottaviano, 24, 1554
Uldaric of Constance, 268
Ulfila, 140, 699
Ulpien, 476
Ulrich of Augsburg, 233, 268, 842, 1043, 1280
Ultramontanism, **1529–1531**; American Church and, 40; anti-Jansenism and, 823; anti-Masonic encyclicals and, 605; devotion to Pius IX, 497; Franciscans and, 595; French clergy and, 1566; Gallican opposition to, 615, 616, 617; Great Schism historiography and, 637; infallibility and, 823, 825; Old Catholics schism and, 1396; papism linked with, 1107; Propaganda Fide and, 1256; Quietism and, 1267; *Rerum novarum* and, 935; titles issued by papacy and, 1050; Vatican I and, 1247
Uluç Ali, 937, 938, 1526
Umberto I, king of Italy, 1541
Umberto of Silva Candida. *See* Humbert of Silva Candida
Umbria, 582, 672, 1104, 1107, 1434, 1538
"Umiliati," 702, 788
Umur Pasha, emir of Aydin, 1526
UN. *See* United Nations
Unam sanctam (1302 bull), 1396, 1485
UNESCO (UN Economic and Social Council), 1020, 1080, 1240, 1589
Ungarelli, L., 1026
Uniates, 176, 208, 522–523, 1135, 1344, **1531–1533**; Antioch and, 69; canon law, 370; Clement VIII and, 348; clerical marriage of, 1043, 1531; conferences of bishops, 404; Gregory XVI and, 674; *ostpolitik* and, 855, 1085, 1215; Paul III and, 1130; Vatican II representation, 1581
uniforms. *See* clothing
Unigenitus (1714 bull), 511, 617, 824–825, 1246, 1345
Union of Freiburg, 935
Union of Jewish Italian Communities, 904
unionism: ecumenism vs., 518–523, 539–540; Oxford Movement and, 1074, 1086
Unità Catolica (Margotti), 1541
United Jewish Appeal, 875
United Nations, 521, 720, 983, 1077, 1078–1081, 1632; Holy Land status and, 713, 714, 877; John Paul II travels and, 1511, 1589; Paul VI and, 687, 1078–1079, 1132, 1140, 1510, 1514, 1515, 1584; Vatican City State status with, 1589
United Provinces, church of the, 825
United States: Americanism and, 39–41, 326, 935; bishops' conferences, 401; Catholic film code, 320; Church success in, 39–41; diplomatic ties with Holy See, 503, 504; election of bishops, 87, 94; first American cardinal, 244; first bishopric, 1344; Gregory XVI and, 675; Holy Land status and, 712–713; John Paul II visits to, 1512; Leo XIII relations, 934; military chaplaincy, 991; Paul V visit to, 1514–1515; Pius XII and, 1213, 1214, 1218; provincial councils, 431; subsidiarity concept, 1462; Vatican I and, 1566, 1567; Vati-

can II and, 1573, 1578; Vatican II representation, 1580, 1581; World War II and, 1214, 1588, 1631, 1633–1634
unity, Italian, **1533–1543**; anticlericalism, 308; Benedict XV and, 175–176; Castel Sant'Angelo and, 255; confraternity effects of, 1310, 1311; fundamentalist reaction, 614; Gregory XVI and, 670, 672, 674, 675; jurisdictionalism and, 889; Movimento Cattolico and, 1023–1024; papal resistance to, 1247; Papal States and, 1104, 1107, 1110, 1189; papism vs., 1109; Pius IX and, 1191, 1193–1196, 1247, 1324; Pius X and, 1198; Pontifical Zouave volunteers and, 1642, 1643–1646; Quirinial Palace and, 1272; Roman Republic of 1849 and, 1323, 1324–1326; Rome as capital, 1017–1018; Vatican I suspension and, 1247, 1568, 1570, 1645–1646, *See also* Risorgimento
Unity of Christians, Secretariat for the, 1404–1405
Universal Anti-Masonic Union, 607
Universal Evangelical Alliance, 518
Universal Postal Union, 1080, 1588
universities, Catholic, 129, **1543–1547**, 1556, 1558; Alexander III and, 22; Alexander VI and, 28; Alexander VII and, 30, 468; Americanism and, 40, 41; Avignon papacy and, 133; [Benedict XIII] and, 162; Benedict XV and, 176–177; Boniface VIII and, 128, 379, 1545; Boniface IX and, 152, 193; canon law code and, 364–365; colleges transformed into (list), 380–385; Congregation for Catholic Education and, 411–412, 1544, 1546; Congregation for the Evangelization of Peoples and, 410; Curia career and, 451; Decretum of Gratian as canon law text, 225–226; Dominicans and, 507, 593, 1549; Enlightenment and, 528; Franciscans and, 593, 1549; Great Schism debates, 633; Gregory IX and, 655–656, 1544, 1547, 1548; Gregory XIII and, 664, 1545; Gregory XVI and, 675; Honorius III and, 734; infallibility thesis, 778; Innocent VI and, 795; Jesuit, 826, 828; John Paul II and, 861, 862; Julius III and, 887; oriental languages chairs, 335; origins of, 1407; Pius XI and, 1201; Sixtus IV and, 1435; student union, 1024, *See also* colleges of Rome; seminaries; *specific institutions by key words*
universities, medieval, 379, **1547–1550**
University of. *See* key word, e.g. Rome, University of
University Federation of Italian Catholis, 310
University of Rome, Congregation of the, 1438
University of the Roman Curia, 1545
Unterberger, Christopher, 1117
Urban I, 1, 1496, **1550**; antipopes to, 1112; Pontian as successor, 1222
Urban II, 330, 731–732, 1303, **1550–1553**; bell ringing, 152; canonization and, 233, 268; cardinal priests and, 240; Chancery growth and, 1282; chaplains and, 449; consistory and, 240; consistory meetings, 413, 414; crusades and, 65, 112, 437, 711, 722, 774, 811, 1483–1484, 1551, 1552; Curia organization, 449, 1282, 1283, 1551; funerary rites, 485; Gelasius II and, 625; Golden Rose and, 1348; Gregorian reforms and, 1278, 1281; Gregory VII and, 1614; health and vitality of, 1416; indulgences and, 774; investitures interdiction, 821, 822, 1113; monasticism and, 1015, 1016; Norman alliance and, 684, 910, 1053; Paschal II and, 1112; satire against, 750; simony condemnation, 1423, 1424; theocracy and, 1483–1484; tomb of, 1499; travels by, 1015; Truce of God and, 900; Victor III and, 1614
Urban III, 143, 653, 1499, **1553–1554**

Volume Key: Volume 1, pages 1–614; volume 2, pages 615–1266; volume 3, pages 1267–1637.

1773

Urban IV, 110, 211, 1037, **1554–1555**; arms, 113, 693; Clement IV and, 332; Curia and, 452; Guelphs and, 629; Hadrian V and, 685; heresy and, 703; non-Roman residence, 1302; political alliances, 313–314, 628, 656, 716; Sacred College and, 1246, 1554; Sicilian kingdom and, 315; tomb of, 1499, 1500

Urban V, 58, 458, **1556–1557**; annates, 59; Apostolic Camera expansion, 8; appointment of bishops, 93; arms, 113, 690; Avignon papacy and, 129, 632; Blessed Hat and Sword offered by, 182; Castel Sant'Angelo possession by, 254; chaplains of the chapel, 300–301; coins, 373; cuisine, 302; Dominicans and, 508; fanon, 1607; Gregory XI and, 658, 659; Inquisition and, 814; Lateran rebuilding, 1360; military expenses, 110; return to Rome attempt, 103, 129, 132, 254; Roman government and, 1338; scriptor for, 459; tomb of, 1502

Urban VI, **1557–1559**; Angevins and, 53; Antichrist charges and, 67; Apostolic Camera expansion, 8, 220; arms, 113; [Benedict XIII] as antipope, 162, 163; Boniface IX as successor, 192; Byzantium and, 208; cardinal protector and, 247; Catherine of Siena support for, 266, 340, 508; ceremonial, 284; chamberlain of, 459; [Clement VII] as antipope, 339–341; crusade against Sicily and, 440; dissatisfactions with election of, 132, 162, 340; Dominicans and, 508; Great Schism inception and, 24, 25, 67, 72, 266, 339, 340–341, 342, 508, 632–633, 635, 637, 1557–1558; Holy Year and, 774; military forces, 111; Roman government and, 1338; tiara, 1492; tomb of, 1502

Urban VII, 114, 346, 666, **1559**

Urban VIII, 118, 667, 695, 801, **1560–1563**; Alexander VIII and, 31; Anglican schism and, 55; antislavery bull, 1002; arms, 115; arts patronage, 1092, 1093, 1116, 1117; beatifications and, 145, 1562; breviary reform, 194, 298; canonization procedure definition, 232, 234, 268, 270, 271; canonizations by, 235; cardinal "eminence" title and, 243; cardinal "in petto" and, 244; cardinalate and, 243, 1469; Castel Sant'Angelo improvements, 255; castrati of the papal chapel and, 256; Catholic University founding, 1545; Chair of St. Peter and, 287; chamberlains, 739; Clement XII and, 356; coins, 375; colleges, 379; Congregation for Bishops and, 408; congregations and, 409, 467; Curia and, 466; Dominicans and, 510; equivalent beatification and, 145, 1562; Farnese family and, 1342; French alliance with, 1000; Innocent XI and, 804; Jansenius and, 704; Jesuits and, 827; jurisdictionalism, 888; Latinity and, 906; legate and, 912; mendicant orders and, 510; missionizing and, 1000, 1001, 1002; nepotism and, 912, 1032, 1033; nunciatures, 1059; painting commissions, 1090, 1091; Pantheon pillage by, 1096; papal chapel musicians, 296, 298, 299; papal household, 738; plague and, 1222; portrait commission, 1117; Propaganda Fide and, 669; Quirinal, 1269, 1270; St. Peter's basilica redesigns, 38, 1383; slavery prohibitions, 1439; tomb of, 1344, 1383, 1386

Urban College for the Propagation of the Faith. *See* Collegio Urbaniano

urban topology, 101

Urbanian University, 380, 410, 1586

Urbanus, 1642

urbi et orbi (pontifical blessing), 177, 679, 1233; indulgences and, 775; as pilgrimage culmination, 1170; St. Peter's basilica and, 1384

Urbino, 30, 926, 928, 976, 1561; Italian unity and, 1538; in Papal States, 1103, 1105(map), 1342

[Ursinus], 70, 71, 181, 484, 1230, 1364, **1563–1564**; Damasus I antipope, 477, 478

Ursulines, 263, 360, 1126, 1343

Uruguay, 1580

usury: Benedict XIV encyclical on, 169; condemnation abolished, 1190, 1191; Jews linked with, 122, 332, 872; Lateran councils on, 899, 901

Ut unum sint (1995 encyclical), 1247

Utrecht, treaty of (1713), 1103

Uzès, Robert d', 282

vacant Holy See. *See* See, vacant and impeded

vacants. *See* benefices, vacant

Vaga, Perino del, 1091, 1096

Valadier, Giuseppe, 1372, 1384

Valadier, Paul, 265, 388, 1345

Valdes, Pierre, 901

Valdo, 21

Valence, Council of (855), 91

Valens, emperor of Byzantium, 479, 1317

Valenti Gonzaga, Silvio, 168–169, 236

Valentin (Gnostic), 57, 744

Valentin, August and Albert, 79

Valentine, **1565**

Valentinian I, emperor of Rome, 140, 478, 480, 914, 1230, 1317

Valentinian II, emperor of Rome, 122, 1046, 1231, 1411

Valentinian III, emperor of Rome, 387, 885, 914, 915, 916, 1610

Valentino, 1383

Valentinus, 1165, 1617

Valerga, José, 723, 1193

Valeri, Valerio, 853, 1574

Valeria (daughter of Diocletian), 966

Valerian, emperor of Rome, 502, 1155–1156, 1230, 1315, 1431, 1432, 1455

Valerius, St., 164

Valla, Lorenzo, 54, 218, 514, 589, 906, 1101, 1294, 1296, 1361

Valladolid, University of, 1544, 1548

Vallainc, Fausto, 1237–1238, 1239

Valls, Joachim Navarro, 1239

Valltellina affair (1624–1626), 1561

Valois, Noël, 1557

Valombrosians, 664

Valsecchi, Antonino, 77

Van Dyck, Anthony, 1562

Van Roey, Cardinal, 875

Van Ruysbroeck, Jan, 1229

Vandals, 140, 141, 545, 572, 573, 1317; African control by, 915, 1318; control of Rome (455), 1318, 1327, 1354; Leo I intercession with, 914, 915; papal finances and, 575

Vannutelli, Seraphin, 364

Vannutelli, Vincenzo, 364, 1210, 1211

Vanosino, 867

Vanvitelli, Luigi, 1363

Varisco, Giovanni, 995

Varna, battle of (1444), 440

Vasari, Giorgio, 106, 665, 982, 1091, 1127, 1308–1309, 1361, 1366, 1367; on Sistine Chapel paintings, 1429, 1430

Volume Key: Volume 1, pages 1–614; volume 2, pages 615–1266; volume 3, pages 1267–1637.

1774

Vasi, Guiseppe, 171, 304, 1229

Vassalletto, Pietro, 1371

Vatican: architectural renovation, 104–105, 666; archives. *See* Vatican Secret Artchives; artist commissions, 1089–1093; audience, 125–126; Colonnna destruction of, 1354; conclave site, 392; death of the pope and, 10; ecclesiastical garb within, 619–621; floreria (warehouse), 588; gardens. *See* Vatican gardens; heraldry, 688; library. *See* Vatican Library; media communications, 984–985; medieval construction, 1328; mosaic workshop, 1021, 1022; mural maps, 252–253; museum collections, 1025–1026; Noble Guard, 1052; Numismatic Cabinet, 983–984; observatory, 177, 1062–1063; papal apartments, 72; papal chapel. *See* Sistine Chapel; papal possession of, 1541; papal residency occasions, 296; photography, 1163; registers, 1293; stereotypes of, 1232; telephone service, 1481–1482; traveler's view of, 1503–1510; walls, 31, 254, 836, 1393; web site address, 985, *See also* Belvedere; St. Peter's basilica; Vatican City State; Vatican Palace

Vatican I (Ecumenical Council of; 1869–1870), **1565–1569**; "ad limina" visits and, 4; Anglican union and, 1074; apologetics and, 78; apostolic constitutions and, 422, 429; canon law code and, 228, 363; *Civiltà Cattolica* support, 326; Code of Canons of Eastern Churches and, 370; on collegiality, 385; critics of, 1110, 1567, 1568; dogmatic constitution, 422; Dominicans and, 512; exemptions and, 1233; Gallicanism defeat by, 618; Index revision, 772; infallibility dogma proclamation, 39, 429, 519, 618, 776, 777, 778–779, 855, 860, 892, 1110, 1196, 1247, 1541, 1568, 1570, 1645–1646; issues stemming from, 860; Italian unification and, 1247, 1568, 1570, 1645–1646; Jesuits and, 828; *Kulturkampf* as reaction to, 891, 892; Leo XIII attendance at, 933–934; Old Catholics schism and, 1395–1396; overview, 429; Pius IX convocation of, 1195, 1196, 1247; Pius XI and archives of, 1570; press relations, 1237; primacy of Rome and, 56, 429, 1196, 1494, 1568, 1570; profession of faith, 1251; Propaganda Fide and, 1256; Roman Catechism and, 263; suspension of, 1568, 1570; Syllabus and, 1247, 1565, 1566; Ultramontanism and, 1247; Vatican II in relation to, 1570, 1571–1572, 1573, 1574, 1575, 1576, 1578, 1584, 1585

Vatican II (Ecumenical Council of; 1962–1965), **1569–1586**; on Americanist position, 39, 41; Anglican observers, 56, 1075, 1076; apostolic constitutions and, 422; Apostolic See references, 717; appointment of bishops and, 89, 94; assessment of, 1143; background, 1570–1572; beatification and, 269; bishops' conferences and, 401–402; canon law and, 435; canonization and, 232, 269; cardinalate and, 244; catechism and, 264; Catholic education and, 1544; Christian Democracy and, 305, 310; cinema and, 321; closing cermonies, 1141; Code of Canon Law (1983) and, 229, 366; on collegiality, 385, 1139, 1242–1243, 1584, 1585; Communist/Holy See semi-détente, 540, 1532; concordats and, 396–397; consistories and, 416; critiques of, 1143; Curia changes, 472, 1142; documents promulgated (list), 1585–1586; Dominican participants, 512; Eastern Churches dialogue and, 370, 1395, 1584; ecclesiastical garb simplification, 619–620; ecclesiastical provinces and, 1264–1265; ecclesiastical region and, 1292; ecclesiology of, 1584–1585; on ecumenism, 56, 430, 520, 521, 1075, 1076, 1141, 1232, 1247, 1584; as ending apologetical hostility, 79; first session, 1575; Freemasonry and, 608, 609; Holy Office opposition, 710; Holy Year and, 728;

on incardination, 767–769; indulgences curtailment, 775; infallibility dogma and, 779–780, 1585; Jesuit participation, 829; John XXIII convocation of, 855, 856, 858, 1110, 1139, 1141, 1142, 1447, 1570, 1572–1585; John Paul I and, 858; John Paul II and, 859, 860, 862–863, 864, 865, 866, 1247, 1569; John Paul II travels and, 1510; Judaism and, 875–876; Lefebvre schism, 1397–1398; liberalism and, 943, 944; liturgy renovation, 430, 955–956, 1142, 1143; on magisterium submission criteria, 964–965; Marxism and, 978; media relations, 984–985, 1237–1239; military chaplaincy and, 992; minutante and, 994–995; missal reform, 996, 1454; missionizing policy, 1005, 1257–1258; modernity in relation to, 1010; nunciature and, 1057; *ostpolitik* and, 1085; overview, 429–430; papal ceremonials, 285; papal household and, 301, 740–742; papal liturgical vestments and, 1607; papal office contextualization, 1247, 1572; Paul VI and, 609, 860, 864, 1110, 1132, 1137, 1138–1144, 1514, 1583–1585; personnel of, 1575–1577; on pilgrimages, 1170; pontifical councils and, 433; Pontifical Mission Societies and, 1450, 1451; pontifical titles and, 1494–1495; as prejudice dispelling, 1232; prelatures and, 1233–1235; preparatory phases, 1572–1575; press office function, 1237–1239; on primacy of Peter, 1241; public reception of, 1142–1143; Secretariats of the Roman Curia and, 1404–1405, 1574–1575; seminaries, 1407, 1410; significance of, 1569; social communications and teachings, 1441, 1442–1447, 1449, 1463; subsidiarity principle, 1462, 1463; Synod of Bishops and, 1477–1479; tiara suspension and, 1489; vacant Holy See and, 1406; Vatican I in relation to, 1568, 1570, 1573, 1574, 1576, 1578, 1584, 1585; Vatican Radio and, 1602

Vatican Apostolic Library. *See* Vatican Library

Vatican Archives. *See* Vatican Secret Archives

Vatican Bookstore, 498

"Vatican caves," 549

Vatican City State, **1586–1594**; arms, 138; automobile registration, 127, 1588; citizenship, 323–324, 1587; creation of, 323–324, 583, 719, 902, 1202, 1203, 1207, 1247, 1363, 1541, 1586, 1587; financial management, 583, 1588; Gendarmes, 626; government, 389; Holy See relationship with, 503, 719–720, 1587; international organizations and, 720; labor organization, 1596–1597; map of, 1593; medallions, 983; neutrality of, 1588; *Osservatore romano* offices, 1083, 1588; papal household, 741–742; passport, 1115; as political refugee asylum, 1588, 1589, 1634–1635; postage stamps, 1229; radio station, 1600–1602; railway station, 1273, 1588; St. Peter's basilica safety measures, 1384; stereotypes of, 1232–1233; Swiss Guard, 1471–1472; telephone service, 1481–1482; World War II status, 1588, 1628–1629, 1633–1636

Vatican City State, Papal Commission on, 389

Vatican Commission for Religions Relations with the Jews, 877

Vatican Filmotheque, 436

Vatican gardens, 1127, **1594–1596**, 1598, 1604; chaplaincy revenue from, 454; Nicholas III founding, 1038, 1302

Vatican Grottoes, 1379, 1380, 1381, 1386

Vatican Hill, 1301, 1302, 1304, 1374, 1594, 1600

Vatican Information Service, 985

Vatican labor union, **1596–1597**

Volume Key: Volume 1, pages 1–614; volume 2, pages 615–1266; volume 3, pages 1267–1637.

1775

Vatican Library, 171, 1094, 1095, **1597–1599**; administrative status of, 498; Alexander VII and, 30, 467–468; antiquities collection, 1025, 1345; of [Benedict XIII], 164, 1597; Benedict XIV extension, 171; Clement XII development of, 357; Clement XII enlargement of, 529; collections, 1599; Curia and, 472, 473; Golden Rose representation, 1347; history, 1435, 1597–1599; letters to the pope collections, 939; *Liber censum* manuscript in, 941; Marcellus II and, 887, 1597, 1598; Napoleonic raid on, 1025; Nicholas V founding, 906, 1042, 1294, 1340; paintings commissions, 1091; Pius II and, 1173; Pius XI as prefect, 1200; prefects (list), 1599; Renaissance humanism and, 1294; sack of Rome (1527) losses, 1355; Sixtus IV formal founding, 1294, 1435, 1597; Sixtus V programs, 1437; telephone network, 1481, 1482; Urban VIII collection, 1562, *See also* Vatican Secret Archives

Vatican museums. *See* Museums, Vatican

Vatican Observatory. *See* Observatory, Vatican

Vatican Palace, 886, 1107, 1301–1302, 1362, 1382; architecture, 1340; artist commissions, 509, 1091, 1117; decoration, 1117; Leo III building of, 1298; as official papal residence, 1304; radio link, 1600; Scala Regia, 1384; significance of, 1354; Swiss Guard, 1471

Vatican Picture Gallery, 1025, 1026

Vatican Press, 1437, 1438

Vatican Press, Congregation of the, 1438

Vatican Press Room, 1095

Vatican Printing Press, 1095

Vatican Publishing House, 496, 1095

Vatican Radio, 10, 473, 584, 744, 875, 984, 1095, **1599–1602**; administrative status of, 498; founding (1931), 984, 1205, 1444, 1600; papal social messages, 1447; Pius XII death coverage, 1236, 1447; Pius XII messages, 1214, 1215, 1447; worker organization, 1596

Vatican School of Archives, 7

Vatican Secret Archives (Archivi Segreti del Vaticano—ASV), 30, 446, 447, 452, 1094, 1095, **1603–1605**; administrative status of, 498; Avignon Curia records, 456; Curia records, 467, 472, 473; Leo XIII opening to researchers, 935, 1603, 1604; Napoléon's attempts to move, 1187, 1255, 1293, 1604; Papal States documentation, 1096; Paul V installation, 1130, 1598, 1604; Progaganda Fides and, 1256; as research source on Pius XII's Holocaust position, 496, 1214; Secretariat of Briefs records, 1401; Secretariat of Briefs to Princes records, 1402; sources in, 1605, *See also* Museums, Vatican; Vatican Library

Vatican Television, 473, 498, 984, 1095, 1215, 1444, 1445, **1605–1606**

Vaticanist, **1606–1607**; press office of the Holy See and, 1236

Vauchez, André, 145, 1169

Vaughnan (Anglican cardinal), 1075

Vaussard, Maurice, 1023, 1536

Vega, Perin del, 255

Veláasquez, Diego, 1562

Velletri, 159, 1103, 1178, 1345

Venaissin, 1181, 1189

venality. *See* simony

veneration of images. *See* iconoclasm

veneration of saints and relics. *See* relics, veneration of; saints, veneration of

Venerius, 43, 251, 273

Venezia: Great Schism and, 632; Italian conquest of, 1533, 1539, 1540

Venezuela, 400, 1580

Venice, 1540; as banking center, 2; banner, 688–689; cardinalate and, 241; Carnival, 248, 249; Christian Democracy in, 311; Clement XI alliance, 353; crusades and, 438, 440, 1417; emblem of, 693; French wars in Italy and, 885, 1621, 1622, 1623, 1624; Great Schism and, 661; Greek migration to, 638; in Holy League, 26–27; Index and, 770; Inquisition abolishment, 819; Jesuit expulsion from, 1131; John Paul I as archbishop patriarch, 311, 857–858; Julius II and, 898; jurisdictionalism and, 888; Mark as patron saint, 569; mosaic workshops, 1021; in papal early 15th-century domain, 661; papal nunciature, 1056, 1058, 1059; Papal States and, 1102, 1342; Paul II and, 1122; Paul V conflict with, 1129, 1130–1131; Pius VII election in, 393, 394; Sixtus IV alliance, 1434; slave ownership, 1439; temporal independence of, 1131; treaty with Turks, 663; Turkish relations, 353, 375, 928, 936, 937, 938, 1124–1125, 1177, 1526

Venice, treaty of (1177), 785, 961

Venier, Sebastiano, 937, 938

Venini, Diego, 1201–1202

Ventura, Gioacchino, 78

Venturi, Tacchi, 903

Venturin of Bergamo, 508

Venuti, 1025

Verallo, Paolo Emilio, 1559

Vercelli, synod of (1050), 1280

Verdier, Cardinal, 875, 991, 1202

Verdun, treaty of (843), 600

Vergani, Paolo, 1180, 1184

Veritatis splendor (1993 encyclical), 524

vernacular: Bible in, 1354, 1522; liturgy in, 955–956; Luther's criticisms in, 1290

Vernazza, Battista, 1276

Vernet, Joseph, 117, 119

"Veronica," 1378

Veronica, St., 373; veil relic, 1168

Versailles conference and treaty (1919), 175, 1642

Verschaffelt, 868

Versus Romae, 749

Verucci, Guido, 305

Vespasian, emperor of Rome, 387, 442, 1314

Vespers, 295, 296, 298–299

Vespignani, Francesco, 1272, 1363

Vespignani, Virgilio, 1363, 1372

vestments, ecclesiastical, 267, 619–621

vestments, pope's liturgical, 621, **1607–1608**

veto, 1197, **1608–1609**

Vettori, 1025

Vetus Gallica, 231

Veuillot, Louis, 752, 753, 778, 1372

Vevilacqua, Father, 1133

vexillum. *See* banner

Via Appia. *See* Appian Way

Via Ardeatina, 1496

via crucis, rite of, 388

Volume Key: Volume 1, pages 1–614; volume 2, pages 615–1266; volume 3, pages 1267–1637.

1776

Via Gregoriana, 665
Via Labicana, 258, 259
Via Latina, 258, 259
Via Merulana, 665
Via Ostiensis, 1164, 1165
Vianney, John Marie, St., 1204
Vicar of Jesus Christ (*Vicarius Christi*), 1109, 1494–1495
vicariate, apostolic, 1233, 1363, **1610–1612**; Rome/Milan division, 1466
vice-camerlengo, 220, 221
Vicedomini Cardinal, 657, 658
Vichy France, 853
Vico, Giovanni di, 337
Victor I, 214, 1244, **1612**; Christian persecutions and, 1154, 1612; Easter-date controversy, 430, 517, 561, 1108, 1612
Victor II, 620, 648, 924, **1612–1613**; reforms of, 1245, 1280; tomb of, 1498
Victor III, 625, 1053, 1461, **1613–1615**; antipope to, 329, 1614; Gregorian reform and, 1281; Nicholas II and, 1036; Normans and, 18, 1613, 1614; tomb of, 1499
[Victor IV], 70, 72, 715, 1114, **1615**
[Victor IV (V)], 20, 43, 72, 217, 313, 534, 653, **1615–1616**
Victor Amadeus II, king of Sicily and Sardinia, 166
Victor Emmanuel II, king of Italy: death concurrent with Pius IX, 1196; excommunication of, 1541; Jewish policy, 874; monument to, 1018; Papal States demise and, 1644; unification and, 1533, 1539, 1540
Victor Emmanuel III, king of Italy, 1541
Victor of Carthage, 13
Victoria, Tomás Luis de, 298
Victorius of Aquitaine, 517
Victory (goddess), 1045, 1411
Victrice of Rouen, 782
Vieira, Antonio, 819
Vien, Joseph-Marie, 119
Vien, Marie-Thérèse, 120
Vienna: Pius VI journey to, 1179; Turks defeat at (1683), 805, 1343
Vienna, Congress of (1815), 99, 555, 1060, 1534, 1536, 1538; Holy See and, 718; nunciatures and, 1057; Papal States and, 672, 687, 1103, 1109, 1189; Vatican Archives returned to Rome following, 1604
Vienna, Congress of (1964), 1060
Vienna, Council of (1892), 909
Vienna, Peace of (1866), 1540
Vienne, Council of (1311–1312), 131, 226, 429, 452, 592, 616, 703, 1246; as birth of Catholic reform, 1274; dioceses *in partibus*, 500; John XXII and, 847, 848; Templars abolishment at, 988
Vienne, University of, 574, 1556
Vietnam, 1218
Vietnam War, 1140
Vigée-Lebrun, Elisabeth, 120
Viggiu, Silla da, 1369
Vigilance, Committees of, 176
Vigile, St., 882
Vigilius, 72, 141, **1616–1619**; as apocrisarius, 74; Byzantium and, 196, 201, 1418, 1616–1618; canonical collection, 231; Carthage and, 251; Constantinople II and, 428, 1618; encyclical, 1618; Franks and, 597; *Liber polntificalus* second

edition biographies up to, 942; Pelagius I and, 1145, 1146–1147, 1618; Roman nobility and, 1047, 1616, 1617; saint veneration, 1388, 1391; Three Chapters condemned by, 1146; tomb of, 1391, 1392, 1497
Vignier, Nicholas, 67
Vignola, Giacomo, 106, 107, 887, 1382
Villa Aldobrandini, 1091
Villa Barberini, 583
Villa Borghese, 1130
Villa de la Magliana, 800
Villa d'Este, 107
Villa Giulia, 106, 107, 887, 1595
Villa Medici, 107
Villa Pamfili, 803
Villafranca, Peace of (1859), 1539
Villalpando, J. B., 1385
Villani, Florentin, 334
Villani, Matteo, 337
villas, 570, 668; Medici arts patronage and, 1089–1090; painting collections, 1091–1092; Roman, 1017–1018, 1340, 1504; Vatican gardens, 1594, 1595
Villon, François, 555
Villot, Jean, 85, 434, 857, 1238, 1248
Vincent de Paul, 803, 1409
Vincent Ferrer, St., 67, 162, 165, 633; Callistus III and, 218; Great Schism and, 339, 340, 508
Vincent of Lérins, 567
Vincentius of Capua, 427–428, 946, 1419
Vinet, Alexandre, 1537
Virchow, Rudolf, 891
Viret, Pierre, 1169
Virgil, 747, 748
Virgin Mary, 32, 204; academy dedicated to, 2; Assumption dogma, 124, 421, 519, 1367; cult of, 1517; encyclicals on devotion to, 934; feasts, 211–212; Immaculate Conception dogma, 24, 27, 524, 675, 1520; medieval cult, 1275; miracles of 1796, 1181; miraculous images of, 1260; as Mother of God, 274, 428, 699, 832, 833, 1139, 1365, 1366; Nativity papal Mass, 295; Nestorian view of, 274, 699, 832; Our Lady of the Snows legend, 1367–1368; papal tomb dedications to, 1497; pilgrimages and, 1170; rosary devotion and, 1346–1348; St. Mary Major basilica, 1365–1370; Salus Populi Romani icon, 1367; Vatican II debate on, 1139, 1141
Virgin of Fátima, 1170, 1515, 1569
Virginio, Gentil, 1030
virginity, as perfect state, 895, 896
Visconti, Bernabò, 132, 659, 796, 1556
Visconti family, 659, 666, 676; as Ghibellines, 629, 677
Visconti, Felipe-Maria, 1041, 1042
Visconti, Filippo Aurelio, 1025
Visconti, Filippo Maria, 218, 535, 975–976, 1041
Visconti, Frederick, 655
Visconti, Galeas, 659
Visconti, Giambattista, 1025
Visconti, Gian Galeazzo, 24–25, 192, 339
Visconti, Giovanni, 337
Visconti, Matteo, 850
Visconti, Tebaldo (Tedaldo). *See* Gregory X
Visconti, Valentine, 1621

Volume Key: Volume 1, pages 1–614; volume 2, pages 615–1266; volume 3, pages 1267–1637.

1777

Visigothic liturgy, 952

Visigoths, 140, 141, 143, 781, 1317; Arab conquest in Spain, 1319; Arles occupation by, 1611; canonical collections, 223; Catholic Christian conversian, 1318; Jewish social separation by, 870; Odoacer as king of Italy, 1318; particular councils, 430; sack of Rome by, 260, 1318, 1327, 1353–1354, 1411; Spanish occupation by, 1318, *See also* Goths

visions. *See* prophecies

Visitandines, 1343, 1561

Visitation, feast of the, 1558

visits. *See* "ad limina" visits

Vitalian, 997, **1619**

Vitalini, Alberico, 744

Vitalis, Bishop, 572, 622

Vitelleschi, Giovanni, 54

Vitelli, Niccolò, 1434

Viterbo, **1620**; Alexander IV and, 23; Clement IV residence in, 333, 1500; Clement VII refuge in, 345; cross and keys, 689; Eugene III residence in, 532; first conclave, 392; Gregory X and, 102; Innocent IV and, 110; Innocent VII flight to, 797; papal court and residence, 1302–1304; papal tombs, 1500

Viterbo, conclave of (1271), 685

Vitiges, 254, 1327–1328

Vitori, Loreto, 256

Vitteleschi, Giovanni, 111, 536, 1101

Vittoria, Francisco da, 99

Vitus (legate), 427–428, 1419

Vivés, Juan Battista, 668–669, 1254

Vives, Juan Luis, 76, 1224, 1225

Vives y Tuto, Joseph, 364

Vix pervenit (1745 encyclical), 169

Vladier, G., 1016

Vladimir, prince of Kiev, 843

Volkmar, 330–331, 961, 962, 1553

Volonte, Gian Maria, 496

Volpini, Valerio, 1083

Voltaire, 77, 170, 360, 527, 530, 1345

Volterra, Daniele da, 1091, 1362, 1431

Vouet, Simon, 118

vow dispensations, 505–505

Vulgate, 194; first official edition (1592), 348; papal commission for revision of, 388; revision of, 1296; Sixtus V and, 1437; Tridentine authenticity declaration, 429, 1520

Wackenheim, Charles, 176

Wailing Wall (Jerusalem). *See* Western Wall

Wake, W. archbishop of Canterbury, 56

Waldensianism, 701, 702, 789, 904; Inquisition and, 813, 814

Waldheim, Kurt, 865, 876

Waldipert (priest), 1162

Waldrade, 1034

Waleys, Thomas, 508, 850

"War of Eight Saints," 132

War of Holland, 351

War of Independence (U.S.), 991

War of the Roses (England), 799

warehouse. *See* floreria

wars: John XXIII encyclical against, 856; military chaplaincy, 990–992; papal abritration, 98–99; papal armies, 108–112; papal navy, 1027–1030; papal objectives, 110, 111; Paul VI statement against, 1140; Pius XI doctrine on, 1206; Pius XII encyclical on, 1200; Pontifical Zouaves and, 1643–1646, *See also* holy war; just war; *key word for specific wars*

Wars of Italy, French (16th century), 1102, 1124–1125, **1621–1624**

Wars of Religion (France), 348, 663, 666, 807–808, 1288, 1342; Edict of Nantes (1598), 348

Warsaw ghetto, 876

Warsaw Pact. *See* Communist countries

Way of the Cross, 1275

Wazo of Liège, 1280

web site, Vatican, 985

Weber, Max, 1006

Weiss, A. M., 512

Weiszäcker, Ernst von, 1632, 1633, 1634

Welfs. *See* Guelphs

Wenceslas, Holy Roman emperor (and king of Bohemia), 193, 703–704; Great Schism and, 633, 634, 635

Wenceslas of Luxembourg, 1558

Wends, 997

Werner of Ancona, 1423

Werner of Obserwessel, 872

Wernz, Franz-Xavier, 364

West, Morris S., 322, 761

Western Wall (Jerusalem), 711, 713, 877

Westphalia, Peace of (1648), 170, 1057; weakening of papacy from, 28, 29, 30, 99, 467, 801, 802

Whitby, synod of (664), 142, 1619

white Guelphs, 481, 677

White Mountain, battle of (1620), 669, 1130, 1344

whore of Babylon, 830

Wibert, archbishop of Ravenna. *See* [Clement III]

Wiching, Bishop, 837

Wilfrid (monk of Lindisfarne), 16, 142, 153, 834, 835; pilgrimage to Rome, 1166

Wilhelm. *See* William

Willebrands, Johannes, 434, 1076

William I, emperor of Germany, 893

William I (the Bad), king of Sicily, 19, 683–684, 1053, 1615

William I (the Conqueror), king of England, 18, 111, 649, 822, 1551

William II, emperor of Germany, 1627

William II, king of England, 822, 1551

William II (the Good), king of Sicily, 21, 313, 314, 331, 961, 1053, 1054

William III (William of Orange), king of England, 55

William, archbishop of Mayence, 840

William & Mary College, 1544

William of Aquitaine, 552

William of Auxerre, 655

William of Champeaux, 1543, 1637

William of Furstenberg, 351

William of Holland, 315, 716, 1554

William of Mandagout, 848

William of Ockham (Occam), 98, 133, 229, 336, 390, 830, 850, 1109; accusations against John XXII by, 1492; on cardinalate powers, 242; Donation of Constantine doubts, 514

Volume Key: Volume 1, pages 1–614; volume 2, pages 615–1266; volume 3, pages 1267–1637.

1778

William of Orange (William III of England), 55
William of Rubruck, 998
William of Saint Bénigne, 845
William of St. Thierry, 701
William of Saint-Armour, 24, 792
William of Todi, 661
William of Tripoli, 658
William of Volpiano, 552, 924
Williams, Tennessee, 761
Willibrord, St., 598, 997, 1166, 1412
Wilpert, Joseph, 101
Wilson, Woodrow, 175, 1077, 1627, 1628
Winckelmann, Johann, 108, 117, 120, 171, 359, 1025, 1345
wind instrument, 299
wine, 457, 458
wine harvest feast, 570
Wisch, B., 1308
Wiseman, Nicholas, 55, 675
Wislicenus, H., 239
witchcraft, 799
Witelo, 1304
Witgen, R., 1143
Witiges, king of the Goths, 1417–1418
Wittenberg theses. *See* Ninety-five Theses
witticisms. *See* humor
Wizel, Georges, 68
Woden (war god), 140
Wojtyla, Karol. *See* John Paul XXII
Wolfgang of Ratisbonne, 924
Wolsey, Thomas, 344, 345, 927
women: banned from stage performance, 248–249, 1506; Counter Reformation religious orders, 1343; Dominican nuns, 507; as early Christian converts, 1045; exclusion from Church, 698; military orders and, 988; ordination of, 56, 829, 1076, 1395; Pope Joan legend, 829–830; Roman confraternity roles, 1307–1308; Roman etiquette for, 1507; in Roman nobility, 1044, 1045; as slaves, 1440
Words of a Believer (Lamennais), 674
Worker-priests, 512, 861, 1217
workers: Catholic association, 935; international organizations, 935, 1077, 1079, 1516; social teaching, 1448, 1449; unions, 1206, 1449, 1450, 1463; Vatican labor union, 1596–1597, *See also Rerum novarum*
workhouses. *See* poor relief
World Alliance of Christian Unions, 518
World Council of Churches, 519, 520, 521, 522
World Council of Churches, Paul VI visit to, 1515
World Health Organization, 1079
World Intellectual Property Organization, 1080
World Mission Day, 1451
World Reformed Alliance, 1577
World Synod of Bishops, 1247
World War I, **1624–1628**; Benedict XV and, 172, 173–175, 307, 512, 539, 540, 582, 1110, 1211–1212, 1624–1628, 1630, 1631; concordats following, 397; Holy Land status after, 712, 723; Holy See/Italian relations, 901, 1107; letters to the pope, 940; military chaplaincy, 990–991; *Osservatore romano* and, 1083; Pius X and, 1199; Pius XII and, 1211–1212; Versailles peace conference, 175, 1642

World War II, **1628–1636**; Catholic Church/modern Europe relationship and, 539, 542; Christian Democracy and, 305, 309–310; Holy Land status after, 712–713; Jewish victims, 853, 875, 887; John Paul II and, 860–861, 876; John XXIII and, 853; letters to the pope, 940; military chaplaincy, 991; *Osservatore romano* during, 1083, 1084; papal finances and, 583; papal relief effort, 1632; Pius XII and, 174, 175, 305, 322, 583, 875, 978, 1085, 1212, 1213–1214, 1215, 1588, 1626, 1629–1636; Vatican neutrality, 1588; Vatican Radio broadcasts, 984, 1600, *See also* Holocaust; Nazism
World Youth Day, 729
Worms, Concordat of (1122), **1636–1637**; art portraying, 1284; Callistus II and, 1281; canonical collections and, 225; cardinalate authority increased by, 349–450; as Church-State relations basis, 1278, 1281; Clement III and, 331; as first concordat, 397; Frederick I Barbarossa and, 19; Honorius II and, 731; investiture compromise, 92, 216, 239, 397, 650, 715, 783, 900, 1281, 1424, 1484; king of the Romans and, 313; Lateran I ratifiying, 428
Worms, Concordat of (1448), 1298
Worms, Diet of (1521), 1286
worship of saints. *See* saints, veneration of
Wulfila, 545
Wycliffe, John, 67, 133, 633, 703, 775, 814, 1395; infallibility challenges, 777
Wynfrith (Boniface), 598

Xystus. *See* Sixtus

Yad Vashem Holocaust memorial, 877
Yahballaha III, 998
Yale Colelge, 1544
Yale University Art Gallery, 138
York, archdiocese of, 16, 142, 153, 684, 730; dispute over, 46, 533, 835; founding of, 997
Young Catholic Workers (JOC), 861
Young Italy, 1324, 1536
Young Republic, 307
Yugoslavia, 542; concordat, 400; diplomatic relations with Holy See, 503; *ostpolitik*, 1084, 1085, 1215; Vatican II representation, 1577, 1579, 1581
Yves (Ivo) of Chartres, 231, 822, 871, 1113, 1281, 1283, 1284, 1637; canonical collection, 224, 225, 231, 489, 495; on dispensation, 504; on temporal vs. spiritual investitures, 900, 1637

Zabaglia, Niccola, 559
Zabarella, Francesco, 635, 852
Zaccaria, Antonio Maria, 1276
Zaccaria, Francantonio, 360, 1190
Zacconi, Ermete, 322
Zacharias, 681, 1097, **1639–1640**; "ad limina" visits and, 4; Byzantium and, 204, 420; cartography, 252; coins, 372; exemptions, 552; Frankish alliance, 598, 599, 1064, 1319, 1331; Lateran Palce reconstruction, 1300; Lombard confrontation, 1456, 1639–1640; Stephen V (VI) and, 1458; successor, 1456
Zaga, Domenico, 255
Zamometi, Andrea, 1434
Zanardelli code (1890), 1542

Volume Key: Volume 1, pages 1–614; volume 2, pages 615–1266; volume 3, pages 1267–1637.

Zanchini, Nicola, 1082

Zanussi, Krzysztof, 323

Zara, 438

zealots, 204–205, 206

zecchino romano (coin), 376

Zefirelli, Franco, 323

Zelada, Cardinal, 1598

zelanti faction, 358, 931, 932, 933; monasticism defense by, 1013; Pius VII and, 1188–1189; Pius VIII and, 1190

Zelus Fidei, 657

Zeno, emperor of Byzantium, 1318, 1426; *Henoticon* edict of union, 44, 200, 563, 564, 572, 622

Zeno, Battista, 1121

Zeno of Seville, 1425

Zentrum (German Catholic party), 305, 308, 891–893, 934

Zephyrinus, 63, 707, **1640**; antipope to, 70–71; Callistus I and, 214, 1640; Christian cemetery and, 258, 1640; tomb of, 1496

Ziani, Pietro, 1370

Zinzendorf, Cardinal, 170

Zionism, 874

Zoe Paleologus, 1434

Zoile (monk), 1145

Zoilo, Annibale, 297

Zola, Émile, 751, 752–753, 754, 755, 756, 758, 759

Zoroastrian dualism, 443

Zosimus, 184, 538, 908, 1046, 1432, **1640–1642**; African affairs, 13, 251; Celstine I and, 273, 327; monasticism and, 1013; primacy of Peter and, 1160; tomb of, 1391, 1496; vicariate of Arles and, 1610

Zouaves, Pontifical, 112, 497, 1107, **1642–1647**

Zuccari, Federico, 239, 665, 1092

Zuccarro, 1091

Zuria, Placido, 671

Zvonimir, king of Croatia and Dalmatia, 688

Zwingli, Huldrych, 1286–1287

Volume Key: Volume 1, pages 1–614; volume 2, pages 615–1266; volume 3, pages 1267–1637.

1780

For Reference

Not to be taken from this room